2

The Literary Filmography

The Literary Filmography

*6,200 Adaptations of Books, Short Stories
and Other Nondramatic Works*

Leonard Mustazza

Volume 2 : M–Z,
Bibliography, Index

McFarland & Company, Inc., Publishers
Jefferson, North Carolina, and London

2

LIBRARY OF CONGRESS CATALOGUING-IN-PUBLICATION DATA

Mustazza, Leonard, 1952–
The literary filmography : 6,200 adaptations of books, short stories
and other nondramatic works / Leonard Mustazza.
p.   cm.
Includes bibliographical references and index.

ISBN-13: 978-0-7864-2471-9
(2 volume set : softcover : 50# alkaline paper) ∞

1. Film adaptations— Bibliography.   2. Television adaptations— Bibliography.
3. Literature — Bibliography.   I. Title
Z5784.M9M87   2006   016.79143′6 — dc22   2006004472
[PN1997.85]

British Library cataloguing data are available

On the cover: Laurence Olivier as Heathcliff and Merle Oberon as Cathy
in the 1939 film *Wuthering Heights;* book image ©2006 Stockbyte

Manufactured in the United States of America

McFarland & Company, Inc., Publishers
Box 611, Jefferson, North Carolina 28640
www.mcfarlandpub.com

Contents

— Volume 1 —

— Volume 2 —

2700. *The Machine* (Rene Belletto, 1990). Translated in 1993, French novel originally titled *La Machine* about a psychiatrist who invents a machine that allows him to look into people's minds. An accident results in the exchange of his personality with that of a psychopathic killer. **Adaptation:** *The Machine* (Concorde/Castle Rock, 1994). Dir: Francois Dupeyron. Scr: Francois Dupeyron. Cast: Gerard Depardieu (Dr. Lacroix), Nathalie Baye (Marie), Didier Bourdon (Michel). VHS.

2701. *Mackenna's Gold* (Will Henry [pseudonym for Henry W. Allen], 1963). After a dying Indian gives him a map showing the way to a valuable gold vein, a marshal is forced by a brutal outlaw to take him there. **Adaptation:** *Mackenna's Gold* (Columbia, 1969). Dir: J. Lee Thompson. Scr: Carl Foreman. Cast: Gregory Peck (MacKenna), Omar Sharif (Colorado), Telly Savalas (Tibbs), Camilla Sparv (Inga), Keenan Wynn (Sanchez), Julie Newmar (Hesh-Ke), Edward G. Robinson (Adams), Eli Wallach (Ben). DVD, VHS.

The Mackintosh Man (see *The Freedom Trap*).

The Macomber Affair (*see* "The Short Happy Life of Francis Macomber").

2702. *Mad Cows* (Kathy Lette, 1997). An Australian woman in jail for shoplifting breaks out in order to stop her irresponsible upper-class lover from putting their child up for adoption. **Adaptation:** *Mad Cows* (Capitol, 1999). Dir: Sara Sugarman. Scr: Sasha Hails, Sara Sugarman. Cast: Anna Friel (Maddy), Joanna Lumley (Gillian), Greg Wise (Alex), Anna Massey (Edwina), Phyllida Law (Lady Drake). DVD, VHS.

Mad Little Island (see *Rocket's Galore!*)

Mad Love (see *The Hands of Orlac*).

2703. *Mad With Much Heart* (Gerald Butler, 1945). An urban cop is sent to a rural area to investigate the murder of a young girl and falls in love with blind woman whose brother is the murderer he is seeking. **Adaptation:** *On Dangerous Ground* (RKO, 1952). Dir: Nicholas Ray. Scr: A. I. Bezzerides, Nicholas Ray. Cast: Ida Lupino (Mary), Robert Ryan (Jim), Ward Bond (Walter), Ed Begley (Brawley). VHS.

2704. *Madame Bovary* (Gustave Flaubert. 1857). Tragic story of a passionate woman who, married to a provincial doctor and bored with her everyday existence, drifts into love affairs. **Adaptation 1:** *Unholy Love;* released in the UK as *Deceit* (Allied, 1932). Dir: Albert Ray. Scr: Frances Hyland. Cast: H. B. Warner (Dr. Gregory), Lila Lee (Jane), Beryl Mercer (Mrs. Cawley). Notes: A modern retelling of the story, set in Rye, New York, in the early 1930's. **Adaptation 2:** *Madame Bovary* (NSF/Tapernoux, 1933). Dir: Jean Renoir. Scr: Jean Renoir. Cast: Max Dearly (Homais), Valentine Tessier (Emma), Pierre Renoir (Charles). VHS. **Adaptation 3:** *Madame Bovary* (Casino, 1937). Dir: Gerhard Lamprecht. Scr: Erich Ebermayer, Hans Neumann. Cast: Pola Negri (Emma), Aribert Wascher (Charles), Ferdinand Marian (Rodolphe). **Adaptation 4:** *Madame Bovary* (MGM, 1949). Dir: Vincente Minnelli. Scr: Robert Ardrey. Cast: Jennifer Jones (Emma), James Mason (Flaubert), Van Heflin (Charles), Louis Jourdan (Rodolphe). VHS. **Adaptation 5:** *Madame Bovary* (BBC/PBS, 1975 TV Miniseries). Dir: Rodney Bennett. Scr: Giles Cooper. Cast: Francesca Annis (Emma), Tom Conti (Charles), Denis Lill (Rodolphe). DVD. **Adaptation 6:** *Madame Bovary* (Samuel Goldwyn, 1991). Dir: Claude Chabrol. Scr: Claude Chabrol. Cast: Isabelle Huppert (Emma), Jean-François Balmer (Charles), Christophe Malavoy (Rodolphe). Notes: Academy Award nomination for Best Costume Design; Golden Globe nomination for Best Film. DVD, VHS. **Adaptation 7:** *Madame Bovary* (BBC/PBS, 2000 TV Movie). Dir: Tim Fywell. Scr: Heidi Thomas. Cast: Frances O'Connor (Emma Bovary), Hugh Bonneville (Charles Bovary), Greg Wise (Rodolphe Boulanger).VHS.

2705. *Madame Curie: A Biography* (Eve Curie, 1937). A daughter's biography of Marie Sklodowska Curie (1867–1934), who discovered radium and who, along with her husband, Pierre, won the Nobel Prize in Physics in 1903. **Adaptation:** *Madame Curie* (MGM, 1943). Dir: Mervyn Le Roy. Scr: Paul Osborn, Paul H. Rameau. Cast: Greer Garson (Marie Curie), Walter Pidgeon (Pierre Curie), Henry Travers (Eugene Curie), Albert Bassermann (Jean Perot). Notes: Academy Award nominations for Best Picture, Actress (Garson), Actor (Pidgeon), Cinematography, Art Direction, Musical Score, and Sound. VHS.

2706. "Madame La Gimp" (Damon Runyon, 1929). A group of gangsters help a poor apple seller to pretend that she is a rich lady when her daughter comes to visit. **Adaptation 1:** *Lady for a Day* (Columbia, 1933). Cast: Frank Capra. Scr: Robert Riskin. Cast: Warren William (Dave), May Robson (Apple Annie), Guy Kibbee (Judge Blake). Notes: Academy Award nominations for Best Picture, Director, Screenplay, and Actress (Robson).

DVD, VHS. **Adaptation 2:** *Pocketful of Miracles* (United Artists, 1961). Dir: Frank Capra. Scr: Hal Kanter, Harry Tugend. Cast: Glenn Ford (Dave), Bette Davis (Apple Annie), Hope Lange (Queenie), Arthur O'Connell (Alfonso), Peter Falk (Joy Boy). Notes: Academy Award nominations for Best Supporting Actor (Falk), Costume Design, and Song (Sammy Cahn and Jimmy Van Heusen); Golden Globe Award for Best Actor (Ford). DVD, VHS.

Madame Pimpernel (see *Paris Underground*).

2707. *Madame Rosa* (Emile Ajar [pseudonym for Romain Gary], 1975, Goncourt Prize). French novel, originally titled *La Vie Devant Soi*, about an aging madam who runs a nursery for prostitutes' children. **Adaptation:** *Madame Rosa* (Atlantic, 1977). Dir: Moshe Mizrahi. Scr: Moshe Mizrahi. Cast: Simone Signoret (Rosa), Michal Bat-Adam (Nadine), Samy Ben-Youb (Momo). Notes: Academy Award for Best Foreign Film; Golden Globe nomination for Best Foreign-Language Film; Cesar Award (France) for Best Actress (Signoret) and nominations for Best Production Design and Sound. VHS.

The Maddening (see *Playmates*).

Made in U.S.A. (see *The Jugger*).

2708. *Madeline* (Ludwig Bemelmans, 1939). The first in the six-book children's series about the adventures of a young girl who lives in an orphanage run by a caring nun. **Adaptation:** *Madeline* (TriStar, 1998). Dir: Daisy Scherler Mayer. Scr: Mark Levin, Jennifer Flackett. Cast: Frances McDormand (Miss Clavel), Nigel Hawthorne (Lord Covington), Hatty Jones (Madeline), Ben Daniels (Leopold). DVD, VHS. Notes: The book was also the basis for a cartoon short in 1952, a 1990 television series (DVD, VHS), and a 1995 television series titled *The New Adventures of Madeline*.

2709. "Mademoiselle Fifi" (Guy De Maupassant, 1882). Set during the Franco-Prussian War, the short story concerns a poor and honest laundress traveling with aristocratic passengers on a stage coach. When she refuses the sexual advances of a military officer, the others try to pressure her into complying. The story, published anonymously in *Gil Blas* magazine in 1882, is a reworked version of another story by Maupassant, "Boule de Suif" (1880). **Adaptation:** *Mademoiselle Fifi* (RKO, 1944). Dir: Robert Wise. Scr: Josef Mischel, Peter Ruric. Cast: Simone Simon

(the Laundress), John Emery (Jean), Kurt Kreuger (von Eyrick), Alan Napier (the Count de Breville). Notes: The screenplay combines elements from "Boule de Suif" (1880) and "Mademoiselle Fifi" (1882). VHS.

Madhouse (see *Devilday*).

Madigan (see *The Commissioner*).

Madison Avenue (see *The Build Up Boys*).

2710. *Madness of the Heart* (Flora Sandstrom, 1947). A blind woman marries a French nobleman and must contend with a scheming jealous rival and hostile in-laws. **Adaptation:** *Madness of the Heart* (Universal International, 1949). Dir: Charles Bennett. Scr: Charles Bennett. Cast: Margaret Lockwood (Lydia), Maxwell Reed (Joseph), Kathleen Byron (Verite). VHS.

2711. *The Madonna of the Seven Moons* (Margery Lawrence, 1933). Years after being raped as a teenager, a respectable wife and mother experiences mental blackouts during which she becomes a wild dancing gypsy. **Adaptation:** *Madonna of the Seven Moons* (Universal, 1945). Dir: Arthur Crabtree. Scr: Roland Pertwee. Cast: Phyllis Calvert (Maddalena/Rosanna), Stewart Granger (Nino), Patricia Roc (Angela). VHS.

2712. *Madonna, Unauthorized* (Christopher Andersen, 1991). Celebrity biography of the singer and actress born Madonna Louise Veronica Ciccone in 1958. **Adaptation:** *Madonna: Innocence Lost* (Fox, 1994 TV Movie). Dir: Bradford May. Scr: Michael J. Murray. Cast: Terumi Matthews (Madonna), Wendie Malick (Camille), Jeff Yagher (Paul), Dean Stockwell (Tony). VHS.

2713. *Magic* (William Goldman, 1976). Horror novel about a ventriloquist whose dummy orders him to kill. **Adaptation:** *Magic* (20th Century–Fox, 1978). Dir: Richard Attenborough. Scr: William Goldman, Cast: Anthony Hopkins (Corky/voice of Fats the Dummy), Ann-Margret (Peggy Ann Snow), Burgess Meredith (Ben Greene), Ed Lauter (Duke). DVD, VHS.

2714. *The Magic Bow: A Romance of Paganini* (Manuel Kormoff, 1940). Historical fiction about the violin virtuoso Nicolo Paganini (1782–1840). **Adaptation:** *The Magic Bow* (Universal, 1946). Dir: Bernard Knowles. Scr: Roland Pertwee, Norman Ginsbury. Cast: Stewart Granger (Paganini), Phyllis Calvert (Jeanne), Jean Kent (Bianca), Dennis Price (Paul). VHS.

2715. *The Magic Christian* (Terry Southern, 1959). Satiric novel about the world's wealthiest man and his protégé, who devise schemes to prove that people are greedy enough to do anything for money. **Adaptation:** *The Magic Christian* (Commonwealth United, 1969). Dir: Joseph McGrath. Scr: Terry Southern, Joseph McGrath. Cast: Peter Sellers (Sir Guy Grand), Ringo Starr (Youngman Grand), Isabel Jeans (Dame Agnes), Wilfrid Hyde-White (Reginald), Laurence Harvey (Hamlet). DVD, VHS.

The Magic of Lassie (see *Lassie Come Home*).

2716. *The Magic Pudding* (Norman Lindsay, 1918). Australian children's classic about a man and his talking magic pudding, which replenishes itself as people eat it. **Adaptation:** *The Magic Pudding* (Australian Broadcasting Company, 2000). Dir: Karl Zwicky. Scr: Harry Cripps, Greg Haddrick, Simon Hopkinson. Cast: voices of John Cleese (Albert the Magic Pudding), Geoffrey Rush (Bunyip Bluegum), Sam Neill (Sam Sawnoff), Toni Collette (Meg Bluegum).

The Magic Sword (see *The King's Damosel*).

2717. *The Magic Toyshop* (Angela Carter, 1967). An orphaned girl is left in the care of her uncle, an imperious toy maker who can make his creations magically come to life. **Adaptation:** *The Magic Toyshop* (Granada/Roxie, 1987). Dir: David Wheatley. Scr: Angela Carter. Cast: Caroline Milmoe (Melanie), Tom Bell (Uncle Philip).

2718. *The Magician of Lublin* (Isaac Bashevis Singer, 1960). The 1978 Nobel laureate's picaresque novel set in Poland at the turn of the twentieth century and concerning a talented Jewish magician and his search for professional respect and personal identity. **Adaptation:** *The Magician of Lublin* (Cannon, 1979). Dir: Menahem Golan. Scr: Menahem Golan, Irving S. White. Cast: Alan Arkin (Yasha), Louise Fletcher (Emilia), Valerie Perrine (Zeftel), Shelley Winters (Elzbieta), Lou Jacobi (Wolsky). VHS.

2719. *The Magnificent Ambersons* (Booth Tarkington, 1918, Pulitzer Prize). Saga about a Midwest family at the turn of the twentieth century who lose their wealth and social standing as the mother and her son feud over her love affair with an old beau. **Silent Film:** 1925, titled *Pampered Youth*. **Adaptation 1:** *The Magnificent Ambersons* (RKO, 1942). Dir: Orson Welles. Scr: Orson Welles. Cast: Joseph Cotten (Eugene), Dolores Costello (Isabel), Anne Baxter (Lucy), Tim Holt (George), Agnes Moorehead (Fanny). Notes: Academy Award nominations for Best Picture, Supporting Actress (Moorehead), Cinematography, and Art Direction. VHS. **Adaptation 2:** *The Magnificent Ambersons* (A&E, 2002 TV Movie). Dir: Alfonso Arau. Scr: Orson Welles (1942 screenplay). Cast: Madeleine Stowe (Isabel), Bruce Greenwood (Eugene), Jonathan Rhys-Meyers (George), Gretchen Mol (Lucy), Jennifer Tilly (Fanny), Dina Merrill (Mrs. Johnson), James Cromwell (Major Amberson). DVD, VHS.

2720. *The Magnificent Bastards* (Lucy Herndon Crockett, 1954). During World War II in the Pacific, a widow falls in love with an American military officer. **Adaptation:** *The Proud and Profane* (Paramount, 1956). Dir: George Seaton. Scr: George Seaton. Cast: William Holden (Colonel Black), Deborah Kerr (Lee), Thelma Ritter (Kate), Dewey Martin (Eddie), William Redfield (Chaplain Holmes), Ross Bagdasarian (Louie).

2721. *Magnificent Obsession* (Lloyd C. Douglas, 1929). A drunken playboy kills a well-respected doctor and blinds his wife in an accident and later becomes a doctor himself just so that he can cure the woman. **Adaptation 1:** *Magnificent Obsession* (Universal, 1935). Dir: John M. Stahl. Scr: Sarah Y. Mason, Victor Heerman, George O'Neil. Cast: Irene Dunne (Helen), Robert Taylor (Dr. Merrick), Charles Butterworth (Tommy), Betty Furness (Hudson). **Adaptation 2:** *Magnificent Obsession* (Universal, 1954). Dir: Douglas Sirk. Scr: Sarah Y. Mason, Victor Heerman, George O'Neil (1935 screenplay), Robert Blees, Wells Root. Cast: Jane Wyman (Helen), Rock Hudson (Dr. Merrick), Barbara Rush (Joyce), Agnes Moorehead (Nancy), Otto Kruger (Edward). VHS.

A Magnum for Schnedier (see *A Red File for Callan*).

2722. *The Magus* (John Fowles, 1965). A British teacher visiting a Greek island falls under the influence of a local magician. **Adaptation:** *The Magus* (20th Century–Fox, 1968). Dir: Guy Green, Scr: John Fowles. Cast: Michael Caine (Nicholas), Anthony Quinn (Maurice), Candice Bergen (Lily), Anna Karina (Anne).

2723. *A Maiden's Grave* (Jeffrey Deaver, 1995). Three escaped prison convicts take a group of deaf students hostage, and an FBI negotiating team works for their release. **Adaptation:** *Dead Silence* (HBO, 1997 TV Movie). Dir: Daniel Petrie, Jr. Scr: Donald Stewart. Cast: James Garner (Cooper), Kim Coates (Theodora), Marlee Matlin (Melanie), Lolita Davidovich (Sharon), Charles Martin Smith (Roland), Kenneth Welsh (Sheriff Budd). VHS.

2724. Maigret (series) (Georges Simenon,

1931–1972). Between 1931 and 1972, Belgian writer Georges Simenon wrote seventy-five mystery novels and twenty-eight short stories featuring French police inspector Jules Maigret. **Adaptation 1:** *Maigret* (Columbia Television 1988 TV Movie). Dir: Paul Lynch. Scr: Arthur Weingarten. Cast: Richard Harris (Maigret), Patrick O'Neal (Portman), Victoria Tennant (Victoria), Ian Ogilvy (Daniel). Notes: This adaptation is not based on any particular Maigret title, but combines elements from the series. VHS. **Adaptation 2:** *Maigret* (Granada, 1992–93 TV Movie series). Dir: Stuart Burge, John Glenister, Nicholas Renton, John Strickland. Scr: Robin Chapman, William Humble, Douglas Livingstone. Cast: Michael Gambon (Maigret), Geoffrey Hutchings (Lucas), Jack Galloway (Janvier), James Larkin (La Pointe). Notes: The Maigret titles in the series are *Maigret and the Maid, Maigret on the Defensive, Maigret Goes to School, Maigret on Home Ground, The Patience of Maigret, Maigret Sets a Trap, Maigret and the Burglar's Wife, Maigret and the Mad Woman, Maigret and the Hotel Majestic, Maigret and the Minister, Maigret and the Night Club Dancer,* and *Maigret's Boyhood Friend.* DVD, VHS. See also *A Battle of Nerves, The Crossroads Murder,* and *Maigret Sets a Trap.*

2725. *Maigret Sets a Trap* (Georges Simeon, 1955). The Belgian writer produced seventy-five novels featuring French police inspector Jules Maigret (1931–1972). In this installment, originally titled *Maigret tend un piege,* the detective uses a policewoman as a decoy to lure a murderer. **Adaptation:** *Inspector Maigret;* released in the UK as *Maigret Sets a Trap;* reissued in the U.S. as *Woman-Bait* (Lopert, 1958). Dir: Jean Delannoy. Scr: Jean Delannoy, R. M. Arlaud, Michel Audiar. Cast: Jean Gabin (Maigret), Annie Girardot (Yvonne), Olivier Hussenot (Lagrume), Jeanne Boitel (Louise). Notes: Originally titled *Maigret tend un piege* and shown with subtitles. In addition, a French television adaptation was broadcast in 1996.

2726. *Main Street* (Sinclair Lewis, 1920). A sophisticated city woman, the wife of a doctor, clashes with her small-town neighbors as she pursues affairs in search of personal fulfillment. **Silent Film:** 1923. **Adaptation:** *I Married a Doctor* (Warner, 1936). Dir: Archie Mayo. Scr: Harriet Ford, Harvey J. O'Higgins, Casey Robinson. Cast: Pat O'Brien (Dr. Kennicott), Josephine Hutchinson (Carol), Ross Alexander (Erik), Guy Kibbee (Samuel).

2727. "The Majesty of the Law" (Frank O'-Connor [pseudonym for Michael O'Donovan], 1936). Irish short story about a man who has his day in court for illegally distilling whiskey. The short story appeared in O'Connor's 1936 collection *Bones of Contention and Other Stories.* **Adaptation:** *The Rising of the Moon* (Warner, 1957). Dir: John Ford. Scr: Frank S. Nugent. Cast: Tyrone Power (Narrator), Maureen Connell (May Ann), Edward Lexy (Quartermaster Sergeant), Denis O'Dea (the Police Sergeant), Noel Purcell (Dan). Notes: The film, which featured Dublin's Abbey Players, included an adaptation of this story as well as Lady Augusta Gregory's 1907 play *The Rising of the Moon* and Michael J. McHugh's 1914 play *A Minute's Wait.*

2728. *The Majorettes* (John A. Russo, 1979). Thriller about a hooded serial killer preying on a high-school majorettes team. **Adaptation:** *The Majorettes* (Vestron, 1986). Dir: Bill Hinzman. Scr: John A. Russo. Cast: Kevin Kindlin (Jeff), Terrie Godfrey (Vicky), Mark V. Jevicky (Sheriff Braden). DVD, VHS.

2729. *Make Haste to Live* (Mildred Gordon and Gordon Gordon [writing as The Gordons], 1950). The owner of a small-town newspaper is threatened by the appearance of her husband, a murderer whom she presumed was dead. **Adaptation:** *Make Haste to Live* (Republic, 1954). Dir: William A. Seiter. Scr: Warren Duff. Cast: Dorothy McGuire (Crystal), Stephen McNally (Steve), Mary Murphy (Randy), Edgar Buchanan (Sheriff Lafe). VHS.

Make Me a Star (see *Merton of the Movies*).

2730. *Make Me an Offer* (Wolf Mankowitz, 1952). Comic novel about antiques dealers vying for a famous vase. Mankowitz adapted his book as a 1959 stage musical, with music by David Heneker and Monty Norman. **Adaptation:** *Make Me an Offer* (Associated Artists/Dominant, 1955). Dir: Cyril Frankel. Scr: W. P. Lipscomb. Cast: Mark Baker (Mindel), Alfie Bass (Fred), Adrienne Corri (Nicky). VHS. Notes: A filmed version of the 1959 stage musical was broadcast on the BBC's Play of the Month series in 1966.

2731. *Make Room! Make Room!* (Harry Harrison, 1966). In 2022, the country is overcrowded, and people depend on government-manufactured food for survival. In the course of a murder investigation, a detective uncovers the government's dirty secret about the ingredients of the food. **Adaptation:** *Soylent Green* (MGM, 1973). Dir: Richard Fleischer. Scr: Stanley R. Greenberg. Cast: Charlton Heston (Detective Thorn), Leigh

Taylor-Young (Shirley), Chuck Connors (Tab), Joseph Cotten (Simonson), Brock Peters (Lieutenant Hatcher). DVD, VHS.

Make Way for Tomorrow (see *The Years Are So Long*).

Making Time (see *The Light Years*).

2732. "Malachi's Cove" (Anthony Trollope, 1864). In nineteenth century Cornwall, a poor young girl tries to survive by selling seaweed as fertilizer. The short story originally appeared in the December 1864 issue of *Good Words* magazine and was included in Trollope's 1867 collection *Lotta Schmidt and Other Stories*. **Adaptation:** *Malachi's Cove* (Penrith, 1974). Dir: Henry Herbert. Scr: Henry Herbert. Cast: Donald Pleasence (Malachi), Veronica Quilligan (Mally), John Barrett (Polwarth).

Malaga (see *The Scent of Danger*).

Malarek (see *Hey, Malarek!*).

Malcolm X (see *The Autobiography of Malcolm X*).

Malone (see *Shotgun*).

2733. *The Maltese Falcon* (Dashiell Hammett, 1930). Searching for the murderer of his partner, Sam Spade encounters a group of bizarre people, all of them looking for the statue of a bird that reportedly contains a fortune in jewels. **Adaptation 1:** *The Maltese Falcon;* broadcast on television under the title *Dangerous Female* (Warner, 1931). Dir: Roy Del Ruth. Scr: Maude Fulton, Brown Holmes. Cast: Bebe Daniels (Ruth), Ricardo Cortez (Spade), Dudley Digges (Casper), Una Merkel (Effie). VHS. **Adaptation 2:** *Satan Met a Lady* (Warner, 1936). Dir: William Dieterle. Scr: Brown Holmes. Cast: Bette Davis (Valerie), Warren William (Shayne), Alison Skipworth (Madame Barabbas), Arthur Treacher (Travers). VHS. **Adaptation 3:** *The Maltese Falcon* (Warner, 1941). Dir: John Huston. Scr: John Huston. Cast: Humphrey Bogart (Spade), Mary Astor (Bridget), Gladys George (Iva), Peter Lorre (Cairo), Sydney Greenstreet (Gutman). Notes: Academy Award nominations for Best Picture, Screenplay, and Supporting Actor (Greenstreet). DVD, VHS. Notes: In the 1975 spoof *Black Bird* (VHS), Sam Spade's son continues the quest for the Maltese Falcon.

2734. *Mama Flora's Family* (Alex Haley and David Stevens, 1999). Epic tale of a matriarch's indomitable spirit as she holds her family together through the historic upheavals of the twentieth century. Stevens completed the novel after Haley's death in 1992. **Adaptation:** *Mama Flora's Family* (CBS, 1998 TV Movie). Dir: Peter Werner. Scr: Carol Schreder, David Stevens. Cast: Cicely Tyson (Flora), Blair Underwood (Willie), Queen Latifah (Diana), Mario Van Peebles (Luke). DVD, VHS.

2735. *Mama's Bank Account* (Kathryn Forbes, 1943). The novelist's memoirs of growing up in a Norwegian-American family in San Francisco in the early twentieth century. John Van Druten adapted the book as a 1944 stage play titled *I Remember Mama*. **Adaptation:** *I Remember Mama* (RKO, 1948). Dir: George Stevens. Scr: De Witt Bodeen. Cast: Irene Dunne (Martha), Barbara Bel Geddes (Katrin), Oskar Homolka (Uncle Chris), Philip Dorn (Lars), Cedric Hardwicke (Jonathan), Edgar Bergen (Peter), Rudy Vallee (Dr. Johnson), Ellen Corby (Aunt Trina). Notes: Academy Award nominations for Best Actor (Homolka), Actress (Dunne), Supporting Actresses (Bel Geddes and Corby), and Cinematography; Golden Globe Award for Best Supporting Actress (Corby). DVD, VHS. Notes: The book was also the basis for a CBS television series (1949–1956).

2736. *The Mambo Kings Play Songs of Love* (Oscar Hijuelos, 1989, Pulitzer Prize). Two Cuban brothers leave home and go to New York in the hopes of starting a band. **Adaptation:** *The Mambo Kings* (Warner, 1992). Dir: Arne Glimcher. Scr: Cynthia Cidre. Cast: Armand Assante (Cesar), Antonio Banderas (Nestor), Cathy Moriarty (Lana), Maruschka Detmers (Dolores). DVD, VHS.

2737. *The Mammy* (Brendan O'Carroll, 1994). In 1960's Dublin, a woman with seven children suddenly finds herself widowed and struggling to survive. **Adaptation:** *Agnes Browne* (October/USA Films, 1999). Dir: Anjelica Huston. Scr: John Goldsmith, Brendan O'Carroll. Cast: Anjelica Huston (Agnes), Marion O'Dwyer (Marion), Niall O'Shea (Mark), Ciaran Owens (Frankie). DVD, VHS.

2738. *The Man* (Irving Wallace, 1964). After a freak accident kills the President and the Speaker of the House and the Vice President refuses the office, an unknown senator becomes the first black President of the United States. **Adaptation:** *The Man* (Paramount, 1972). Dir: Joseph Sargent. Scr: Rod Serling. Cast: James Earl Jones (Dilman), Martin Balsam (Jim), Burgess Meredith (Senator Watson), Lew Ayres (Noah), William Windom (Arthur), Barbara Rush (Kay).

2739. *A Man About the House* (Francis Brett

Young, 1942). Two British sisters inherit a villa in Italy, where they meet a handsome handyman. After one of the sisters marries him, their lives take a dark turn. The novel was adapted for the stage by John Perry in 1945. **Adaptation:** *A Man About the House* (20th Century–Fox, 1947). Dir: Leslie Arliss. Scr: Leslie Arliss. J. B. Williams. Cast: Margaret Johnston (Agnes), Dulcie Gray (Ellen), Kieron Moore (Salvatore), Guy Middleton (Sir Benjamin Dench). VHS.

A Man Alone (see "The Killers").

2740. *A Man Called Cervantes* (Bruno Frank, 1934). German historical novel about the author Miguel de Cervantes serving as a papal envoy sent to persuade Philip of Spain join the Holy League against the Moors in the sixteenth century. **Adaptation:** *Young Rebel* (American International, 1967). Dir: Vincent Sherman. Scr: Enrico Bomba, David Karp, Enrique Llovet. Cast: Horst Buchholz (Miguel de Cervantes), Gina Lollobrigida (Giulia), Jose Ferrer (Hassan Bey), Louis Jourdan (Cardinal Acquaviva). Originally released as *Cervantes* and dubbed in English.

A Man Called Gannon (see *Man Without a Star*).

2741. *The Man Called Noon* (Louis L'Amour, 1970). Western about a gunfighter who is shot and loses his memory. His life depends on recovering his identity and figuring out who shot him and why. **Adaptation:** *The Man Called Noon* (National General, 1973). Dir: Peter Collinson. Scr: Scott Finch, Antonio Recoder. Cast: Richard Crenna (Noon), Stephen Boyd (Rimes), Rosanna Schiaffino (Fan), Farley Granger (Judge Niland). VHS.

2742. *A Man Called Peter: The Story of Peter Marshall* (Catherine Marshall, 1951). Two years after his untimely death, his wife published this biography of Peter Marshall (1902–1949), a Scottish clergyman who became the chaplain to the United States Senate. **Adaptation:** *A Man Called Peter* (20th Century–Fox, 1955). Dir: Henry Koster. Scr: Eleanore Griffin. Cast: Richard Todd (Peter), Jean Peters (Catherine), Marjorie Rambeau (Laura). VHS.

A Man Could Get Killed (see *Diamonds for Danger*).

2743. *Man-Eaters of Kumaon* (Jim Corbett, 1946). Factual account of a hunter's quest for man-eating tigers in the Himalayas. **Adaptation:** *Man-Eater of Kumaon* (Universal, 1948). Dir: Byron Haskin. Scr: Jeanne Bartlett, Richard G. Hubler, Lewis Meltzer, Alden Nash. Cast: Sabu

(Narain), Wendell Corey (Dr. Collins), Joanne Page (Lali), Morris Carnovsky (Ganga Ram).

The Man from Dakota (see *Arouse and Beware*).

2744. "The Man from Snowy River" (A. B. "Banjo" Paterson, 1890). Nineteenth-century Australian poem about a young orphaned boy who goes to work for a cattleman and falls in love with the rancher's daughter and with the horses he tends. The long narrative poem was published in an Australian periodical titled *The Bulletin* on April 26, 1890. **Adaptation:** *The Man from Snowy River* (20th Century–Fox, 1982). Dir: George Miller. Scr: Cul Cullen, John Dixon. Cast: Tom Burlinson (Jim), Terence Donovan (Henry), Kirk Douglas (Harrison/Spur), David Bradshaw (Banjo), Sigrid Thornton (Jessica). Notes: Golden Globe nomination for Best Foreign Film. DVD, VHS. Notes: A sequel, *Return to Snowy Mountain*, was released in 1988 (DVD, VHS).

2745. "The Man From Texas" (William Gulick, 1952). Western about a man's attempts to keep his brother from becoming an outlaw and their ultimate conflict with each other. **Adaptation:** *The Road to Denver* (Republic, 1955). Dir: Joseph Kane. Scr: Horace McCoy, Allen Rivkin. Cast: John Payne (Bill), Mona Freeman (Elizabeth), Lee J. Cobb (Jim).

Man Hunt (see *Rogue Male*).

The Man I Married (see *Swastika*).

2746. *The Man in Grey* (Lady Eleanor Smith, 1942). During the early nineteenth century, an aristocratic young woman befriends a jealous and embittered poor girl, who, later in life, conspires to steal her friend's husband. **Adaptation:** *The Man in Grey* (Gainsborough/Universal, 1943). Dir: Leslie Arliss. Scr: Leslie Arliss, Margaret Kennedy, Doreen Montgomery. Cast: Margaret Lockwood (Hesther), Phyllis Calvert (Clarissa), James Mason (Lord Rohan), Stewart Granger (Rokeby). VHS.

Man in Hiding (see *Queen in Danger*).

Man in the Attic (see *The Lodger*).

The Man in the Attic (see *Sex and the Criminal Mind*).

2747. *The Man in the Brown Suit* (Agatha Christie, 1924). A woman unravels the clues to a diamond theft and a murder. **Adaptation:** *The Man in the Brown Suit* (Warner Brothers Television, 1989 TV Movie). Dir: Alan Grint. Scr: Carla

Jean Wagner. Cast: Rue McClanahan (Suzy), Tony Randall (Reverend Chichester), Edward Woodward (Sir Eustace), Stephanie Zimbalist (Anne), Ken Howard (Gordon).

2748. *The Man in the Gray Flannel Suit* (Sloan Wilson, 1955). A Madison Avenue executive suffers moral conflicts between his job and his family. **Adaptation:** *The Man in the Gray Flannel Suit* (20th Century–Fox, 1956). Dir: Nunnally Johnson. Scr: Nunnally Johnson. Cast: Gregory Peck (Tom), Jennifer Jones (Betsy), Fredric March (Ralph), Marisa Pavan (Maria), Lee J. Cobb (Judge Bernstein). VHS.

2749. *The Man in the Iron Mask* (Alexandre Dumas, pere, 1850). Fearing overthrow, Louis XIV of France keeps his twin bother Philippe imprisoned in an iron mask and away from the public until D'Artagnan and the Three Musketeers come to right the injustice. The novel, originally published as *Dix Ans Plus Tard Ou Le Vicomte De Bragelonne*, was serialized between 1848 and 1850 and was the third part of a saga that included *The Three Musketeers* (1844) and *Twenty Years Later* (1845). **Silent Film:** *The Iron Mask,* 1929, directed by Allan Dwan and starring Douglas Fairbanks (DVD, VHS). **Adaptation 1:** *The Man in the Iron Mask* (United Artists, 1939). Dir: James Whale. Scr: George Bruce. Cast: Louis Hayward (King Louis XIV/Philippe), Joan Bennett (Maria Theresa), Warren William (D'Artagnan), Joseph Schildkraut (Fouquet), Alan Hale (Porthos). VHS. **Adaptation 2:** *The Man in the Iron Mask* (NBC, 1977 TV Movie). Dir: Mike Newell. Scr: William Bast. Cast: Richard Chamberlain (King Louis XIV/Philippe), Patrick McGoohan (Fouquet), Louis Jourdan (D'Artagnan), Jenny Aguter (Louise), Ian Holm (Duval), Ralph Richardson (Colbert). Notes: Emmy nominations for Outstanding Screenplay and Costume Design. VHS. **Adaptation 3:** *The Fifth Musketeer;* also released as *Behind the Iron Mask* (Columbia, 1979). Dir: Ken Annakin. Scr: George Bruce (1939 screenplay), David Ambrose. Cast: Beau Bridges (King Louis XIV/Philippe), Cornel Wilde (D'Artagnan), Sylvia Kristel (Maria Theresa), Ursula Andress (Louise), Ian McShane (Fouquet), Alan Hale, Jr. (Porthos), Lloyd Bridges (Aramis), Jose Ferrer (Athos), Olivia de Havilland (Queen Anne), Rex Harrison (Colbert). DVD, VHS. **Adaptation 4:** *The Man in the Iron Mask* (United Artists/MGM, 1998). Dir: Randall Wallace. Scr: Randall Wallace. Cast: Leonardo Di Caprio (King Louis XIV/Philippe), Jeremy Irons (Father Aramis), John Malkovich (Athos), Gerard De-pardieu (Porthos), Gabriel Byrne (D'Artagnan). DVD, VHS. **Adaptation 5:** *The Man in the Iron Mask* (Invisible, 1998). Dir: William Richert. Scr: William Richert. Cast: Edward Albert (Athos), Dana Barron (Louise), Timothy Bottoms (Fouquet). VHS. See also *The Three Musketeers* and *Twenty Years Later.*

Man in the Middle (see *The Winston Affair*).

2750. "The Man in the Net" (Patrick Quentin [pseudonym for Hugh Wheeler], 1956). After his nagging wife disappears, an artist is falsely accused of killing her. He goes into hiding and is aided by the neighborhood children he has befriended. The short story appeared in the June 1956 issue of *Cosmopolitan* and was subsequently issued as a book. **Adaptation:** *The Man in the Net* (United Artists, 1959). Dir: Michael Curtiz. Scr: Reginald Rose. Cast: Alan Ladd (John), Carolyn Jones (Linda), Diane Brewster (Vicki).

2751. *Man in the Saddle* (Ernest Haycox, 1938). Western about a romantic triangle that leads to violence between two ranchers. **Adaptation:** *Man in the Saddle;* released in the UK as *The Outcast* (Columbia, 1951). Dir: Andre De Toth. Scr: Kenneth Gamet. Cast: Randolph Scott (Owen), Joan Leslie (Laurie), Ellen Drew (Nan), Alexander Knox (Will). VHS.

Man in the Vault (see *The Lock and the Key*).

2752. *The Man Inside* (M. E. Chaber [pseudonym for Kendell Foster Crossen], 1954). A jeweler's bookkeeper and his friends steal money from his employer and is pursued by a detective across Europe. The book, which was excerpted in the December 1953 issue of *Bluebook,* was also published as *Now It's My Turn.* **Adaptation:** *The Man Inside* (Columbia, 1958). Dir: John Gilling. Scr: John Gilling, Richard Maibaum, David Shaw. Cast: Jack Palance (Milo), Anita Ekberg (Trudie), Nigel Patrick (Sam), Anthony Newley (Ernesto). VHS.

Man of Evil (see *Fanny by Gaslight*).

Man of La Mancha (see *Don Quixote*).

2753. *Man of the Forest* (Zane Grey, 1917). Western about an outlaw who kidnaps a rancher's daughter in order to seize his land. The novel was serialized in *The Country Gentleman* beginning on October 20, 1917, and published as a novel in 1920. **Silent Films:** 1921 and 1926. **Adaptation:** *Man of the Forest* (Paramount, 1933). Dir: Henry Hathaway. Scr: Jack Cunningham, Harold Shumate. Cast: Randolph Scott (Brett), Verna Hillie

(Alice), Harry Carey (Jim), Noah Beery (Clint), Barton MacLane (Mulvey), Buster Crabbe (Yegg). VHS.

Man of the Hour (see *Colonel Effingham's Raid*).

2754. *Man of the West* (Philip Yordan, 1955). Western about a gunfighter who returns home and is rejected by his son and the community. He regains his honor when the town is threatened by vicious outlaws. **Adaptation:** *Gun Glory* (MGM, 1957), Dir: Roy Rowland. Scr: William Ludwig. Cast: Stewart Granger (Tom), Rhonda Fleming (Jo), Chill Wills (Preacher), Steve Rowland (Tom, Jr.), James Gregory (Grimsell). VHS.

Man of the West (1958) (see *The Border Jumpers*).

Man on a String (see *My Ten Years as a Counterspy*).

2755. *Man on Fire* (A. J. Quinnell, 1980). A former CIA agent hired to protect a family seeks revenge when a young girl in the family is kidnapped. **Adaptation 1:** *Man on Fire* (TriStar, 1987). Dir: Elie Chouraqui. Scr: Elie Chouraqui, Sergio Donati. Cast: Scott Glenn (Creasy), Jade Malle (Sam), Joe Pesci (David), Brooke Adams (Jane). VHS. **Adaptation 2:** *Man on Fire* (20th Century–Fox, 2004). Dir: Tony Scott. Scr: Brian Helgeland. Cast: Denzel Washington (Creasy), Dakota Fanning (Pita), Marc Anthony (Sam), Christopher Walken (Rayburn), Giancarlo Giannini (Manzano), Mickey Rourke (Jordan). DVD, VHS.

The Man on the Eiffel Tower (see *A Battle of Nerves*).

2756. "The Man on the Ledge" (Joel Sayre, 1949). Published in the April 16, 1949, issue of *The New Yorker,* this article chronicles a day in 1938 when a former mental patient walked onto the ledge of a tall building in New York and threatened to jump. **Adaptation:** *Fourteen Hours* (1951). Dir: Henry Hathaway. Scr: John Paxton. Cast: Paul Douglas (Officer Dunnigan), Richard Basehart (Cosick), Barbara Bel Geddes (Virginia), Debra Paget (Ruth), Agnes Moorehead (Christine), Jeffrey Hunter (Danny), Martin Gabel (Dr. Strauss), Grace Kelly (Louise). Notes: The article also inspired an episode of the 1955 CBS series *The 20th Century–Fox Hour.*

2757. *A Man on the Moon: The Voyages of the Apollo Astronauts* (Andrew L. Chaikin, 1994). A chronicle of the Apollo program (1961–1972), including interviews with astronauts and key NASA personnel involved. **Adaptation:** *From the Earth to the Moon* (HBO, 1998 TV Miniseries). Dir: Michael Grossman, David Carson, Sally Field, Gary Fleder, David Frankel, Tom Hanks, Frank Marshall, Jonathan Mostow, Jon Turteltaub, Graham Yost, Lili Fini Zanuck. Scr: Remi Aubuchon, Amy Baker, Erik Bork, Jonathan Marc Feldman, Jeffrey Alan Fiskin, Lawrence Gonzales, Tom Hanks, Laura Hubber, Karen Janszen, Steven Katz, Paul McCudden, Lisa Mohan, Peter Osterland, Al Reinert, Andy Wolk, Graham Yost. Cast: Timothy Daly (James Lovell), Cary Elwes (Michael Collins), Tony Goldwyn (Neil Armstrong), Mark Harmon (Walter Schirra), Chris Isaak (Edward White), Stephen Root (Chris Kraft), Lane Smith (Emmett Seaborn), Sally Field (Trudy Cooper). Notes: Emmy Awards for Outstanding Miniseries, Casting, and Hairstyling, and nominations for Outstanding Director, Teleplay (Part 1), Cinematography, Musical Score, Editing, Sounds, Costume Design, Visual Effects, and Makeup; Golden Globe Award for Best Television Miniseries. DVD, VHS.

Man-Proof (see *The Four Marys*).

2758. "Man Running" (Selwyn Jepson, 1947). A drama student flees a backstage murder, and he and his girlfriend set out to prove that the star of the show was responsible. The short story was published in *Collier's* on August 19, 1947. **Adaptation:** *Stage Fright* (Warner, 1950). Dir: Alfred Hitchcock. Scr: Whitfield Cook, Alma Reville. Cast: Jane Wyman (Eve), Marlene Dietrich (Charlotte), Michael Wilding (Detective Smith), Richard Todd (Jonathan), Alastair Sim (Commodore Gill), Sybil Thorndike (Mrs. Gill). DVD, VHS.

2759. "The Man That Corrupted Hadleyburg" (Mark Twain [pseudonym for Samuel Langhorne Clemens], 1899). A mysterious man gets his revenge on the sanctimonious citizens of a small town by corrupting them with a sack of gold. The short story was originally published in *Harper's Monthly* magazine in December 1899. **Adaptation:** *The Man That Corrupted Hadleyburg* (American Short Story, 1980 TV Movie). Dir: Ralph Rosenblum. Scr: Mark Harris. Cast: Robert Preston (the Stranger), Tom Aldredge (Edward), Fred Gwynne (Reverend Burgess), Frances Sternhagen (Mary Richards).

The Man Who Broke 1,000 Chains (see *I Am a Fugitive from a Georgia Chain Gang*).

The Man Who Captured Eichmann (see *Eichmann in My Hands*).

2760. "The Man Who Could Work Miracles" (H. G. Wells, 1898). Fantasy about a store clerk who discovers that he can perform miracles and soon realizes that his gift comes with a great deal of responsibility. The short story first appeared in the July 1898 issue of the *Illustrated London News* and was included in Wells' 1899 collection *Tales of Space and Time.* **Adaptation:** *The Man Who Could Work Miracles* (London/United Artists, 1936). Dir: Lothar Mendes. Scr: H. G. Wells. Cast: Roland Young (George), Ralph Richardson (Colonel Winstanley), Edward Chapman (Major Grigsby). VHS.

2761. *The Man Who Cried* (Catherine Cookson, 1979). A man takes his son and runs away from his cruel wife. He later unlawfully marries another woman, but is actually in love with her sister. Trouble finds him when his first wife discovers his new life. **Adaptation:** *The Man Who Cried* (Tyne Tees/World Wide, 1993 TV Movie). Dir: Michael Whyte. Scr: Stan Barstow. Cast: Ciaran Hinds (Abel), Kate Buffery (Florrie), Amanda Root (Hilda), Daniel Massey (Peter). DVD, VHS.

2762. *The Man Who Fell to Earth* (Walter Tevis, 1963). In this science-fiction novel, a visitor from another planet come to earth searching for water for his planet. To get enough money for his return, he becomes the head of an international corporation and in the process learns about the sweet and dark sides of human beings. **Adaptation 1:** *The Man Who Fell to Earth* (British Lion/Cinema 5, 1976). Dir: Nicolas Roeg. Scr: Paul Mayersberg. Cast: David Bowie (Thomas), Rip Torn (Nathan), Candy Clark (Mary-Lou), Buck Henry (Oliver), Bernie Casey (Peters). DVD, VHS. **Adaptation 2:** *The Man Who Fell to Earth* (MGM Television, 1987 TV Movie). Dir: Robert Roth. Scr: Richard Kletter. Cast: Lewis Smith (John), James Laurenson (Felix), Robert Picardo (Richard), Bruce McGill (Vernon), Wil Wheaton (Billy), Annie Potts (Louise), Beverly D'Angelo (Eva).

2763. *The Man Who Had Power Over Women* (Gordon Williams, 1967). Satiric novel about a successful British public-relations executive whose moral scruples force him to reexamine his work and personal life. **Adaptation:** *The Man Who Had Power Over Women* (AVCO Embassy, 1970). Dir: John Krish. Scr: Chris Bryant, Allan Scott. Cast: Rod Taylor (Peter), Carol White (Jody), James Booth (Val), Penelope Horner (Angela). VHS.

The Man Who Haunted Himself (see "The Case of Mr. Pelham").

2764. "The Man Who Knew Too Much" (Marie Brenner, 1996). Brenner's article, published on the May 1996 issue of *Vanity Fair,* is about a former scientist who worked for a large tobacco company. Persuaded by an aggressive producer for CBS-TV's *60 Minutes* to violate his nondisclosure agreement and reveal what the tobacco industry knew about the addictive nature of cigarettes, he finds himself caught between the punitive corporate giant and a cowardly TV program. **Adaptation:** *The Insider* (Buena Vista, 1999). Dir: Michael Mann. Scr: Eric Roth, Michael Mann. Cast: Al Pacino (Lowell), Russell Crowe (Dr. Wigand), Christopher Plummer (Mike Wallace), Diane Venora (Liane), Philip Baker Hall (Don Hewitt), Lindsay Crouse (Sharon), Debi Mazar (Debbie). Notes: National Board of Review Award for Best Picture and Actor (Crowe); Academy Award nominations for Best Picture, Director, Screenplay, Actor (Crowe), Cinematography, Editing, and Sound; Golden Globe nominations for Best Picture, Director, Screenplay, Actor (Crowe), and Musical Score. DVD, VHS.

2765. *The Man Who Lost Himself* (Henry de Vere Stacpoole, 1918). A poor American in England is asked to impersonate a wealthy British man he resembles. **Silent Film:** 1920. **Adaptation:** *The Man Who Lost Himself* (Universal, 1941). Dir: Edward Ludwig. Scr: Eddie Moran. Cast: Brian Aherne (John/Malcolm), Kay Francis (Adrienne), Henry Stephenson (Frederick).

2766. *The Man Who Loved Cat Dancing* (Marilyn Durham, 1972). Western about a woman who runs away from her abusive husband. While riding on a train, she is kidnapped by robbers and falls in love with one of her captors. **Adaptation:** *The Man Who Loved Cat Dancing* (MGM, 1973). Dir: Richard C. Sarafian. Scr: Eleanor Perry. Cast: Burt Reynolds (Jay), Sarah Miles (Catherine), Lee J. Cobb (Lapchance), Jack Warden (Dawes), George Hamilton (Crocker). VHS.

2767. *The Man Who Made Husbands Jealous* (Jilly Cooper, 1993). A young tennis pro who serves as a paid gigolo to wealthy married women falls in love with the wife of a famous musician. **Adaptation:** *The Man Who Made Husbands Jealous* (ITV, 1997 TV Miniseries), Dir: Robert Knights. Scr: Harvey Bamberg, Andrew MacLear.

Scr: Stephen Billington (Lysander), Hugh Bonneville (Ferdinand), Kate Byers (Kitty). VHS.

2768. *The Man Who Never Was: World War II's Boldest Counterintelligence Operation* (Ewen Montagu, 1953). First-hand account of the plot by the British secret service to drop a man with faked identification papers into the sea in order to confuse the Germans before the Allied invasion of Sicily. **Adaptation:** *The Man Who Never Was* (20th Century–Fox, 1956). Dir: Ronald Neame. Scr: Nigel Balchin. Cast: Clifton Webb (Montagu), Gloria Grahame (Lucy), Robert Flemyng (Acres), Josephine Griffin (Pam), Stephen Boyd (O'Reilly). Notes: BAFTA Award for Best Screenplay and nominations for Best British Film and Most Promising Newcomer (Boyd). VHS.

2769. *The Man Who Rocked the Boat* (William J. Keating, with Richard Carter, 1956). Memoir of a New York Assistant District Attorney and his battles with organized crime. **Adaptation:** *Slaughter on Tenth Avenue* (Universal, 1957). Dir: Arnold Laven. Scr: Lawrence Roman. Cast: Richard Egan (Keating), Jan Sterling (Madge), Dan Duryea (Masters), Julie Adams (Dee), Walter Matthau (Al).

The Man Who Understood Women (see *The Colors of the Day*).

2770. *The Man Who Watched the Trains Go By* (Georges Simenon, 1938). Belgian novel, originally titled *L'Homme Qui Regardait Passer Les Trains,* about a frustrated Dutch man who commits murder to get the money he needs to fulfill his dream of traveling the world. **Adaptation:** *The Man Who Watched the Trains Go By;* released in the U.S. as *Paris Express* (Schaefer/MacDonald, 1953). Cast: Harold French. Scr: Paul Jarrico, Harold French. Cast: Claude Rains (Kees), Marius Goring (Lucas), Herbert Lom (Julius). VHS.

2771. "The Man Who Would Be King" (Rudyard Kipling, 1888). In India during the late nineteenth century, two former British soldiers go to a remote village and pretend to be gods so that one of them could be made king. The short story was published in Kipling's 1888 collection *The Phantom Rickshaw.* **Adaptation:** *The Man Who Would Be King* (Columbia/Allied Artists, 1975). Dir: John Huston. Scr: Gladys Hill, John Huston. Cast: Sean Connery (Daniel Dravot), Michael Caine (Peachy Carnehan), Christopher Plummer (Rudyard Kipling), Saeed Jaffrey (Billy Fish). Notes: Academy Award nominations for Best Screenplay, Editing, Costume Design, and Art Direction; BAFTA nominations for Best Cin-

ematography and Costume Design; Golden Globe nomination for Best Musical Score. DVD, VHS.

The Man Who Wouldn't Die (see *No Coffin for the Corpse*).

Man with a Gun (see *The Shroud Society*).

The Man with a Hundred Faces (see *Crackerjack*).

Man with a Million (*see* "The Million Pound Banknote").

2772. *The Man with Bogart's Face* (Andrew J. Fenady, 1977). A private detective obsessed with Humphrey Bogart has plastic surgery so that he can look exactly like his hero and subsequently becomes involved in a case that resembles the Maltese Falcon. **Adaptation:** *The Man with Bogart's Face;* also released as *Sam Marlowe, Private Eye* (20th Century–Fox, 1980). Dir: Robert Day. Scr: Andrew J. Fenady. Cast: Robert Sacchi (Sam), Franco Nero (Hakim), Michelle Phillips (Gina), Olivia Hussey (Elsa), Victor Buono (Commodore Anastas), Herbert Lom (Zebra), George Raft (Petey), Yvonne De Carlo (Teresa). DVD, VHS.

2773. *The Man with My Face* (Samuel W. Taylor, 1948). A successful businessman returns home one day and finds another man there who looks just like him and has taken his place. With the help of friends, he soon discovers that his own wife is involved in an elaborate plot to frame him for a bank robbery. **Adaptation:** *Man with My Face* (United Artists, 1951). Dir: Edward Montagne. Scr: Vin Bogert, T. J. McGowan, Edward Montagne, Samuel W. Taylor. Cast: Barry Nelson (Charles/Albert), Carole Mathews (Mary), Lynn Ainley (Cora), Jack Warden (Walt).

The Man with the Deadly Lens (see *The Better Angels*).

2774. *The Man with the Golden Arm* (Nelson Algren, 1949, National Book Award). Algren's gritty portrait of a former drug addict who returns to his old Chicago neighborhood, where he faces the old temptations. **Adaptation:** *The Man with the Golden Arm* (United Artists, 1955). Dir: Otto Preminger. Scr: Walter Newman, Lewis Meltzer. Cast: Frank Sinatra (Frankie), Eleanor Parker (Zosch), Kim Novak (Molly), Arnold Stang (Sparrow), Darren McGavin (Louie). Notes: Academy Award nominations for Best Actor (Sinatra), Musical Score, and Art Direction; BAFTA nominations for Best Film and Actor (Sinatra). DVD, VHS.

2775. *The Man with the Golden Gun* (Ian

Fleming, 1965). James Bond is in the Far East matching wits with a formidable assassin named Scaramanga. This was Fleming's final Bond novel, published a year after his death in 1964. **Adaptation:** *The Man with the Golden Gun* (United Artists, 1974). Dir: Guy Hamilton. Scr: Richard Maibaum, Tom Mankiewicz. Cast: Roger Moore (James Bond), Christopher Lee (Scaramanga), Britt Ekland (Mary), Maud Adams (Andrea), Herve Villechaize (Nick Nack), Clifton James (Sheriff Pepper). Note: Roger Moore's debut as James Bond. DVD, VHS.

2776. *The Man Within* (Graham Greene, 1929). An orphaned boy discovers that his kind guardian is a smuggler and inadvertently betrays him. **Adaptation:** *The Man Within;* released in the U.S. as *The Smugglers* (Eagle-Lion, 1947). Dir: Bernard Knowles. Scr: Muriel Box, Sydney Box. Cast: Michael Redgrave (Richard), Jean Kent (Lucy), Joan Greenwood (Elizabeth), Richard Attenborough (Francis).

2777. *The Man Without a Face* (Isabelle Holland, 1972). A young fatherless boy dreams of entering a military academy, and he finds an unlikely mentor to help him — a disfigured ex-teacher who lives an isolated existence at the edge of town. **Adaptation:** *The Man Without a Face* (Warner, 1993). Dir: Mel Gibson. Scr: Malcolm MacRury. Cast: Mel Gibson (Justin), Nick Stahl (Chuck), Margaret Whitton (Catherine), Fay Masterson (Gloria), Gaby Hoffmann (Megan), Geoffrey Lewis (Wayne), Richard Masur (Carl). DVD, VHS.

2778. *Man Without a Star* (Dee Linford, 1952). Western about an itinerant cowboy who takes a job on a ranch owned by a beautiful woman. When she wants to put barbed wire up, he sides with those who oppose her even though he is in love with her. **Adaptation 1:** *Man Without a Star* (Universal International, 1955). Dir: King Vidor. Scr: Borden Chase, D. D. Beauchamp. Cast: Kirk Douglas (Dempsey), Jeanne Crain (Reed), Claire Trevor (Idonee), William Campbell (Jeff), Richard Boone (Steve), Jay C. Flippen (Strap). VHS. **Adaptation 2:** *A Man Called Gannon* (Universal, 1969). Dir: James Goldstone. Scr: D. D. Beauchamp, Borden Chase (1955 screenplay), Gene R. Kearney. Cast: Anthony Franciosa (Gannon), Michael Sarrazin (Jess), Judi West (Beth), Susan Oliver (Matty).

2779. *Man, Woman and Child* (Erich Segal, 1980). A happily married professor discovers that he has a son from an affair with a French doctor ten years earlier. When the child is left orphaned, the man creates family tension by suggesting to his wife that they take the boy in. **Adaptation:** *Man, Woman and Child* (Paramount, 1983). Dir: Dick Richards. Scr: Erich Segal, David Zelag Goodman. Cast: Martin Sheen (Robert), Blythe Danner (Sheila), Craig T. Nelson (Bernie), David Hemmings (Gavin). VHS.

2780. *The Manchurian Candidate* (Richard Condon, 1959). A brainwashed Korean War veteran is used as an unwitting political assassin. **Adaptation 1:** *The Manchurian Candidate* (United Artists, 1962). Dir: John Frankenheimer. Scr: George Axelrod. Cast: Frank Sinatra (Marco), Laurence Harvey (Shaw), Janet Leigh (Rosie), Angela Lansbury (Eleanor), Henry Silva (Chunjin), James Gregory (Senator Iselin). Notes: Golden Globe and National Board of Review Awards for Best Supporting Actress (Lansbury); Academy Award nominations for Best Supporting Actress (Lansbury) and Editing. DVD, VHS. **Adaptation 2:** *The Manchurian Candidate* (Paramount, 2004). Dir: Jonathan Demme. Scr: George Axelrod (1962 screenplay), Daniel Pyne, Dean Georgaris. Cast: Denzel Washington (Marco), Meryl Streep (Eleanor), Liev Schreiber (Shaw), Jeffrey Wright (Melvin), Kimberly Elise (Rosie), Jon Voight (Senator Jordan). Notes: This updated version takes place following America's involvement in the first Gulf War. Golden Globe nomination for Best Supporting Actress (Streep). DVD, VHS.

2781. *Mandingo* (Kyle Onstott, 1957). In Louisiana in the mid-nineteenth century, an arrogant plantation patriarch breeds slaves, but tries to keep his sexually obsessed wife and daughter away from them. The novel was adapted for the stage in 1961 by Jack Kirkland. **Adaptation:** *Mandingo* (Paramount, 1975). Dir: Richard Fleischer. Scr: Norman Wexler. Cast: James Mason (Maxwell), Susan George (Blanche), Perry King (Hammond), Richard Ward (Agamemnon). VHS. See also *Drum.*

Mandy (see *The Day Is Ours*).

Maneater (see *His Bones Are Coral*).

2782. "The Mangler" (Stephen King, 1973). An automatic speed iron and folder devours employees at a laundry. The story originally appeared in the July 1972 issue of *Cavalier* and was included in King's 1978 short-story collection *Night Shift.* **Adaptation:** *The Mangler* (New Line, 1995). Dir: Tobe Hooper. Scr: Stephen David Brooks, Tobe Hooper, Harry Alan Towers. Cast: Robert Englund (Bill), Ted Levine (John), Daniel Matmor

(Mark). DVD, VHS. Notes: A sequel, *The Mangler 2: Graduation Day,* was released in 2001 (DVD, VHS).

2783. *Manhattan Love Song* (Cornell Woolrich, 1932). A love story set in New York City. **Adaptation:** *Manhattan Love Song* (Monogram, 1934). Dir: Leonard Fields. Scr: David Silverstein, Leonard Fields. Cast: Robert Armstrong (Williams), Dixie Lee (Geraldine), Nydia Westman (Annette).

Manhunter (see *Red Dragon*).

The Manhunter (see *The Killer*).

Mania (see *The Body Snatcher*).

Maniac (*see* "The Black Cat").

2784. *The Manitou* (Graham Masterton, 1975). Horror novel about a fake psychic whose girlfriend becomes possessed by the spirit of a Native American bent on revenge against the white man. **Adaptation:** *The Manitou* (AVCO Embassy, 1978). Dir: William Girdler. Scr: Jon Cedar, William Girdler, Thomas Pope. Cast: Tony Curtis (Harry), Michael Ansara (John), Susan Strasberg (Karen), Stella Stevens (Amelia), Ann Sothern (Mrs. Karmann), Burgess Meredith (Dr. Snow). VHS.

2785. *Manon of the Spring* (Marcel Pagnol, 1963). In 1952, Pagnol wrote and directed a French film titled *Manon des Sources* (*Manon of the Spring*). Afterwards, he turned the story into two novels: *L'Eau des Collines* (*The Water of the Hills*) and *Manon des Sources.* The latter is a sequel in which a young shepherdess discovers the truth behind her father's mysterious death and exacts revenge against the peasants who murdered him. **Adaptation:** *Manon of the Spring* (Orion, 1986). Dir: Claude Berri. Scr: Claude Berri, Gerard Brach. Cast: Yves Montand (Cesar), Daniel Auteuil (Ugolin), Emmanuelle Beart (Manon). Notes: Originally released as *Manon des Sources* and shown with subtitles. National Board of Review Award for Best Foreign-Language Film; Cesar Award (France) for Best Supporting Actress (Beart); BAFTA nomination for Best Foreign-Language Film. DVD, VHS. See also *The Water of the Hills.*

2786. *Mansfield Park* (Jane Austen, 1814). A poor young woman is sent to live with wealthy relatives. Growing eventually into a beautiful and independent-minded woman, she falls in love with her cousin, but forces him to prove his worthiness. **Adaptation 1:** *Mansfield Park* (BBC, 1983

TV Miniseries). Dir: David Giles. Scr: Kenneth Taylor. Cast: Sylvestra Le Touzel (Fanny), Nicholas Farrell (Edmund), Liz Crowther (Julia), Anna Massey (Aunt Norris), Jonny Lee Miller (Charles). DVD, VHS. **Adaptation 2:** *Mansfield Park* (Miramax, 1999). Dir: Patricia Rozema. Scr: Patricia Rozema. Cast: Frances O'Connor (Fanny), Embeth Davidtz (Mary), James Purefoy (Tom), Jonny Lee Miller (Edmund), Hugh Bonneville (Mr. Rushworth). DVD, VHS.

The Mansion of Madness (*see* "The System of Doctor Tarr and Professor Fether").

Man-Trap (*see* "Taint of the Tiger").

Mantrap (see *Queen in Danger*).

2787. *Mantrap* (Sinclair Lewis, 1925). A woman pursues a professional man living in the Canadian wilderness. **Silent Film:** 1926. **Adaptation:** *Untamed* (Paramount, 1940). Dir: George Archainbaud. Scr: Frank Hazlitt Brennan, Frank Butler. Cast: Ray Milland (Dr. Crawford), Patricia Morison (Alverna), Akim Tamiroff (Joe), William Frawley (Les), Jane Darwell (Maggie).

2788. *Manuela* (William Woods, 1955). In a South American port, the captain of a steamer falls in love with a young stowaway. **Adaptation:** *Manuela;* released in the U.S. as *Stowaway Girl* (Paramount, 1957). Dir: Guy Hamilton. Scr: Ivan Foxwell, Guy Hamilton, William Woods. Cast: Trevor Howard (James), Elsa Martinelli (Manuela), Pedro Armendariz (Mario), Donald Pleasence (Evans).

2789. *A Map of the World* (Jane Hamilton, 1994). An accident on her property turns the townspeople against a farmer's wife, who is subsequently accused of child abuse. **Adaptation:** *A Map of the World* (USA Films, 1999). Dir: Scott Elliott. Scr: Peter Hedges, Polly Platt. Cast: Sigourney Weaver (Alice), Julianne Moore (Theresa), Dara Perlmutter (Emma), David Strathairn (Howard), Chloe Sevigny (Carole), Louise Fletcher (Nellie). Notes: National Board of Review Awards for Best Independent Film and Supporting Actress (Moore); Golden Globe nomination for Best Actress (Weaver). DVD, VHS.

2790. *Maracaibo* (Stirling Silliphant, 1953). An American firefighter goes to Venezuela to help put out an oil fire. **Adaptation:** *Maracaibo* (Paramount, 1958). Dir: Cornel Wilde. Scr: Ted Sherdeman. Cast: Cornel Wilde (Vic), Jean Wallace (Laura), Abbe Lane (Elena), Michael Landon (Lago), Joe E. Ross (Milt).

2791. *Marathon Man* (William Goldman,

1974). A graduate student and runner must confront an evil Nazi war criminal working as a New York dentist. **Adaptation:** *Marathon Man* (Paramount, 1976). Dir: John Schlesinger. Scr: William Goldman. Cast: Dustin Hoffman (Thomas), Laurence Olivier (Dr. Szell/Christopher Hess), Roy Scheider (Doc Levy), William Devane (Peter), Marthe Keller (Elsa), Fritz Weaver (Professor Biesenthal). Notes: Golden Globe Award for Best Supporting Actor (Olivier), and nominations for Best Director, Screenplay, Actor (Hoffman), and Supporting Actress (Keller); Academy Award nomination for Best Supporting Actor (Olivier). DVD, VHS.

2792. *Marching Along: Recollections of Men, Women, and Music* (John Philip Sousa, 1928). Autobiography of composer and bandmaster John Philip Sousa (1854–1932), popularly known as the "March King." **Adaptation:** *Stars and Stripes Forever;* released in the UK as *Marching Along* (20th Century–Fox, 1952). Dir: Henry Koster. Scr: Ernest Vajda, Lamar Trotti. Cast: Clifton Webb (Sousa), Debra Paget (Lily), Robert Wagner (Willie), Ruth Hussey (Jennie). Notes: Golden Globe nominations for Best Musical Picture, Actor (Webb), and Newcomer (Wagner). VHS.

Margaret's Museum (*see* "The Glace Bay Miners' Museum").

2793. *Marianne Dreams* (Catherine Storr, 1958). Children's book about a little girl who draws fantastic pictures and then dreams that she enters the dangerous world of her drawings. **Adaptation 1:** *Escape Into Night* (ITV, 1972 TV Miniseries). Dir: Richard Bramall. Scr: Ruth Boswell. Cast: Vicki Chambers (Marianne), Sonia Graham (Mrs. Austen), Steven Jones (Mark), Edmund Pegge (Dr. Burton). **Adaptation 2:** *Paperhouse* (Vestron, 1988). Dir: Bernard Rose. Scr: Matthew Jacobs. Cast: Charlotte Burke (Anna), Jane Bertish (Miss Vanstone), Samantha Cahill (Sharon), Glenne Headly (Kate). DVD, VHS.

2794. *Marie: A True Story* (Peter Maas, 1983). Factual account of a divorced mother who bravely exposed corporate corruption and later became the head of the Tennessee Board of Parole. **Adaptation:** *Marie* (MGM, 1985). Dir: Roger Donaldson. Scr: John Briley. Cast: Sissy Spacek (Marie), Jeff Daniels (Eddie), Keith Szarabajka (Kevin), Morgan Freeman (Charles). VHS.

2795. *Mariette in Ecstasy* (Ron Hansen, 1991). An emotionally fragile young postulant at a convent develops the stigmata of Christ and claims to divine possession. **Adaptation:** *Mariette in Ecstasy* (Savoy, 1996). Dir: John Bailey. Scr: Ron Hansen. Cast: Alex Appel (Sister Philomene), Rutger Hauer (the Chaplain), John Mahoney (Dr. Baptiste), Mary McDonnell (the Prioress).

2796. *Marilyn: A Biography* (Norman Mailer, 1973). A biography of Hollywood icon Marilyn Monroe (1926–1962) from her birth as Nora Jeane Baker through her untimely death. **Adaptation:** *Marilyn: The Untold Story* (ABC, 1980 TV Miniseries). Dir: Jack Arnold, John Flynn. Scr: Dalene Young. Cast: Catherine Hicks (Marilyn), Richard Basehart (Johnny), Frank Converse (Joe Di Maggio), John Ireland (John Huston), Viveca Lindfors (Natasha), Jason Miller (Arthur Miller).

2797. *Marion's Wall* (Jack Finney, 1973). A couple moves into a California apartment building where an aspiring 1920's starlet once lived. The actress takes over the body of the wife, hoping to have another chance at fame. **Adaptation:** *Maxie* (Orion, 1985). Dir: Paul Aaron. Scr: Patricia Resnick. Cast: Glenn Close (Jan/Maxie), Mandy Patinkin (Nick), Ruth Gordon (Mrs. Lavin), Barnard Hughes (Bishop Campbell), Valerie Curtin (Miss Sheffer). Notes: Golden Globe nomination for Best Actress (Close). DVD, VHS.

2798. *Marjorie Morningstar* (Herman Wouk, 1955). An ambitious Jewish girl from New York is disappointed when her romance with a theatrical writer fails. **Adaptation:** *Marjorie Morningstar* (Warner, 1958). Dir: Irving Rapper. Scr: Everett Freeman. Cast: Gene Kelly (Noel), Natalie Wood (Marjorie), Claire Trevor (Rose), Everett Sloane (Arnold), Martin Milner (Wally), Carolyn Jones (Marsha). DVD, VHS.

2799. "Mark of a Murderer" (Mike McAlary, 1997). McAlary's factual *Esquire* article concerns a loyal Manhattan homicide detective who is unwittingly investigating a murder committed by his own son. **Adaptation:** *City by the Sea* (Warner, 2002). Dir: Michael Caton-Jones. Scr: Ken Hixon. Cast: Robert De Niro (Vincent), Frances McDormand (Michelle), James Franco (Joey), Eliza Dushku (Gina), William Forsythe (Spyder), Patti Lu Pone (Maggie). DVD, VHS.

The Mark of Cain (see *Airing in a Closed Carriage*).

The Mark of the Whistler (*see* "Dormant Account").

The Mark of Zorro (see *The Curse of Capistrano*).

Mark Twain and Me (see *Enchantment*).

The Marked Man (*see* "Dormant Account").

Marlowe (see *The Little Sister*).

2800. *Marnie* (Winston Graham, 1964). A rich man marries a habitual thief and is determined to help her overcome her obsession. **Adaptation:** *Marnie* (Universal, 1964). Dir: Alfred Hitchcock. Scr: Jay Presson Allen. Cast: Tippi Hedren (Marnie), Sean Connery (Mark), Diane Baker (Lil), Martin Gabel (Sidney), Louise Latham (Bernice). DVD, VHS.

2801. *Marooned* (Martin Caidin, 1964). NASA launches a rescue mission when three astronauts become stranded in space. **Adaptation:** *Marooned;* reissued as *Space Travelers* (Columbia, 1969). Dir: John Sturges. Scr: Mayo Simon. Cast: Gregory Peck (Charles), Richard Crenna (Jim), David Janssen (Ted), James Franciscus (Clayton), Gene Hackman (Buzz), Lee Grant (Celia). Notes: Academy Award for Best Visual Effects and nominations for Best Cinematography and Sound. DVD, VHS.

2802. *The Marquise of O* (Heinrich von Kleist, 1808). Originally titled *La Marquise d'O,* the fanciful story of a widowed aristocrat living in northern Italy at the end of the eighteenth century. When the Russians invade the land, she is saved from rape by a young Russian soldier and later mysteriously finds herself pregnant, setting in motion a chain of events that will eventually lead to her finding love. **Silent Film:** 1920. **Adaptation:** *The Marquise of O* (New Line, 1976). Dir: Eric Rohmer. Scr: Eric Rohmer. Cast: Edith Clever (the Marquise), Bruno Ganz (the Count), Peter Luhr (the Marquise's Father), Edda Seippel (the Marquise's Mother). Notes: BAFTA Award for Best Costume Design; Cannes Film Festival Grand Prize for Best Director and nomination for the Golden Palm. DVD, VHS.

2803. *Marriage Is a Private Affair* (Judith Kelly, 1941). An immature woman wants to continue her wild social life even after she is married and becomes a mother. The novel was serialized in *The Ladies' Home Journal* (May–June 1941) and published as a book later that year. **Adaptation:** *Marriage Is a Private Affair* (MGM, 1944). Dir: Robert Z. Leonard. Scr: Lenore J. Coffee, David Hertz. Cast: Lana Turner (Thea), James Craig (Miles), John Hodiak (Tom), Frances Gifford (Sissy), Hugh Marlowe (Joseph), Natalie Schafer (Irene), Keenan Wynn (Bob).

2804. *The Marriage of a Young Stockbroker* (Charles Webb, 1970). Bored with his marriage and professional life, a successful stockbroker turns to voyeurism. **Adaptation:** *The Marriage of a Young Stockbroker* (20th Century–Fox, 1971). Dir: Lawrence Turman. Scr: Lorenzo Semple, Jr. Cast: Richard Benjamin (William), Joanna Shimkus (Lisa), Elizabeth Ashley (Nan), Adam West (Chester). VHS.

2805. *A Marriage of Convenience* (Georgia Bockoven, 1991). A successful businesswoman gives up her career to raise her late sister's son. For the sake of the child, she agrees to marry the boy's natural father, but the marriage of convenience soon leads to love. **Adaptation:** *A Marriage of Convenience* (CBS, 1998 TV Movie). Dir: James Keach. Scr: David J. Hill, Renee Longstreet. Cast: Jane Seymour (Chris), James Brolin (Manson), David Kaye (Kevin).

The Marriage Playground (see *The Children*).

2806. *Marry the Girl* (Edward Hope, 1935). Comic novel about an eccentric family struggling to run a newspaper empire. The novel appeared as a serial in the October and November 1935 issues of *The American Magazine.* **Adaptation:** *Marry the Girl* (Warner, 1937). Dir: William McGann. Scr: Pat C. Flick, Sig Herzig, Tom Reed. Cast: Mary Boland (Ollie), Frank McHugh (Party), Hugh Herbert (John), Carol Hughes (Virginia), Allen Jenkins (Specs).

2807. *Mars Project* (Wernher von Braun, 1953). The well-known rocket pioneer's speculation about future interplanetary space travel. **Adaptation:** *Conquest of Space* (Paramount, 1955). Dir: Byron Haskin. Scr: James O'Hanlon Cast: Walter Brooke (Samuel), Eric Fleming (Merritt), Mickey Shaughnessy (Mahoney), Phil Foster (Jackie). Notes: The screenplay is based on Willy Ley's *Conquest of Space* and Wernher von Braun's *Mars Project.* DVD, VHS. See also *Conquest of Space.*

2808. *Marshal of Medicine Bend* (Brad Ward [pseudonym for Samuel Peeples], 1954). Western about a disillusioned lawman who recalls his past romantic disappointments as he confronts a murderous gang. **Adaptation:** *A Lawless Street* (Columbia, 1955). Dir: Joseph H. Lewis. Scr: Kenneth Gamet. Cast: Randolph Scott (Marshal Ware), Angela Lansbury (Tally), Warner Anderson (Hamer), Jean Parker (Cora), Wallace Ford (Dr. Wynn). VHS.

2809. *Martians, Go Home* (Frederic Brown, 1955). Comic science-fiction tale about a songwriter who accidentally summons millions of wisecracking Martians to Earth and the struggle to find out how to get rid of the annoying little creatures. **Adaptation:** *Martians Go Home* (Taurus, 1990). Dir: David Odell. Scr: Charles Haas. Cast: Randy Quaid (Mark), Margaret Colin (Sara), Anita Morris (Dr. Buchanan), John Philbin (Donny), Ronny Cox (the President). VHS.

2810. *Martin Chuzzlewit* (Charles Dickens, 1843–44). When the news that a wealthy man is near death, the greed and hypocrisy of his family and colleagues begin to emerge. The novel was serialized under the title *The Life and Adventures of Martin Chuzzlewit, His Relatives, Friends, and Enemies* between January 1843 and July 1844. **Silent Film:** 1912. **Adaptation 1:** *Martin Chuzzlewit* (BBC, 1964 TV Miniseries). Dir: Joan Craft. Scr: Constance Cox. Cast: Gary Raymond (Martin), Barry Jones (Old Martin), Richard Pearson (Pecksniff). **Adaptation 2:** *Martin Chuzzlewit* (BBC, 1994 TV Miniseries). Dir: Pedr James. Scr: David Lodge. Cast: Pete Postlethwaite (Tigg), Paul Scofield (Old Martin/Anthony), Ben Walden (Martin), Tom Wilkinson (Pecksniff), Julian Fellowes (Dr. Jobling). Notes: BAFTA nominations for Best Television Actors (Postlethwaite, Scofield, and Wilkinson). VHS.

2811. *Martin Eden* (Jack London, 1909). Autobiographical novel about a sailor who battles a cruel captain while also trying to educate himself and get his fictional stories published. **Silent Films:** 1914 and 1918. **Adaptation:** *The Adventures of Martin Eden;* reissued as *The High Seas* (Columbia, 1942). Dir: Sidney Salkow. Scr: W. L. River. Cast: Glenn Ford (Martin), Claire Trevor (Connie), Evelyn Keyes (Ruth), Stuart Erwin (Joe), Dickie Moore (Johnny). Notes: The book was also adapted as an Italian/German television miniseries in 1979.

2812. *The Marvelous Land of Oz* (L. Frank Baum, 1904). A youngster goes to the Emerald City to warn the Scarecrow of a revolt against his rule, and the Scarecrow recruits the Tin Woodman and others to fight the assailants. **Adaptation 1:** *The Land of Oz: A Sequel to the Wizard of Oz* (United: 1932). Dir: Ethel Meglin. Scr: L. Frank Baum. Cast: Maryeruth Boone (Dorothy). Matt Flynn (Tip), Sissie Flynn (Mombi), Donald Henderson (the Scarecrow), Fred Osbourn (the Tin Woodman). **Adaptation 2:** *The Wonderful Land of Oz* (Childhood Productions, 1969). Dir: Barry Mahon. Scr: Barry Mahon. Cast: Channy Mahon (Tip), Al Joseph (the Tin Woodman), George Wadsworth (Pumpkinhead), Mike Thomas (the Scarecrow). DVD, VHS. **Adaptation 3:** *Journey Back to Oz* (Warner, 1974). Dir: Hal Sutherland. Scr: Fred Ladd, Norm Prescott,

Bernard Evslin. Cast: voices of Milton Berle (the Cowardly Lion), Herschel Bernardi (Woodenhead Pinto Stallion III), Paul Ford (Uncle Henry), Margaret Hamilton (Aunt Em), Paul Lynde (Pumpkinhead), Ethel Merman (Mombi), Liza Minnelli (Dorothy), Mickey Rooney (the Scarecrow). VHS. **Adaptation 4:** *Return to Oz* (Disney/Buena Vista, 1985). Dir: Walter Murch. Scr: Gill Dennis, Walter Murch. Cast: Fairuza Balk (Dorothy), Nicol Williamson (Dr. Worley/Gnome King), Jean Marsh (Nurse Wilson/Mombi), Piper Laurie (Aunt Em). Notes: The screenplay combines elements of *The Marvelous Land of Oz* (1904) and *Ozma of Oz* (1907). DVD, VHS. See also *Ozma of Oz* and *The Wonderful Wizard of Oz*.

2813. *Marvin and Tige* (Frankcina Glass, 1977). An alcoholic widower adopts an eleven-year-old black boy who had attempted suicide when his mother died. **Adaptation:** *Marvin and Tige;* broadcast on television in the U.S. as *Like Father, Like Son* (20th Century–Fox, 1983). Dir: Eric Weston. Scr: Wanda Dell, Eric Weston. Cast: John Cassavetes (Marvin), Billy Dee Williams (Richard), Gibran Brown (Tige). VHS.

Mary & Tim (see *Tim*).

2814. *Mary Ann* (Alex Karmel, 1958). French novel about a young rape victim who befriends a mechanic with lustful designs on her. **Adaptation:** *Something Wild* (United Artists, 1961). Dir: Jack Garfein. Scr: Jack Garfein, Alex Karmel. Cast: Carroll Baker (Mary Ann), Ralph Meeker (Mike), Mildred Dunnock (Mrs. Gates), Jean Stapleton (Shirley).

2815. *Mary Lavelle* (Kate O'Brien, 1936). A young Irish woman goes to Spain to get away from her boyfriend, a political activist. There she falls in love with a married Spaniard engaged in the political struggle against Franco. **Adaptation:** *Talk of Angels* (Miramax, 1998). Dir: Nick Hamm. Scr: Ann Guedes, Frank McGuinness. Cast: Polly Walker (Mary), Vincent Perez (Francisco), Franco Nero (Dr. Areavaga), Frances McDormand (Conlon). DVD, VHS.

2816. *Mary Poppins* (P. L. Travers, 1934). A perfect nanny brings about positive change in the lives of a London family. **Adaptation:** *Mary Poppins* (Disney/Buena Vista, 1964). Dir: Robert Stevenson. Scr: Bill Walsh, Don Da Gradi. Cast: Julie Andrews (Mary), Dick Van Dyke (Bert/Mr. Dawes), David Tomlinson (George), Glynis Johns (Winifred), Hermione Baddeley (Ellen). Notes: The screenplay for Disney's musical production is based on several Travers books featuring Mary

Poppins. Academy Awards for Best Actress (Andrews), Special Effects, Editing, Musical Score, and Song, and nominations for Best Picture, Director, Screenplay, Art Direction, Cinematography, Costume Design, and Sound; Golden Globe Award for Best Actress (Andrews), and nominations for Best Picture, Actor (Van Dyke), and Musical Score. DVD, VHS.

2817. *Mary Reilly* (Valerie Martin, 1990). A retelling of the Jekyll and Hyde story from the perspective of a chambermaid. **Adaptation:** *Mary Reilly* (TriStar, 1996). Dir: Stephen Frears. Scr: Christopher Hampton. Cast: Julia Roberts (Mary), John Malkovich (Dr. Jekyll/Mr. Hyde), George Cole (Mr. Poole), Michael Gambon (Mary's Father), Glenn Close (Mrs. Farraday). DVD, VHS. See also *The Strange Case of Dr. Jekyll and Mr. Hyde*.

Masada (see *The Antagonists*).

2818. *MASH* (Richard Hooker [psueudonym for Richard Hornberger], 1968). Black comedy about the 4077th Mobile Army Surgical Hospital during the Korean War. **Adaptation:** *MASH* (20th Century–Fox, 1970). Dir: Robert Altman. Scr: Ring Lardner, Jr. Cast: Donald Sutherland (Hawkeye), Elliott Gould (Trapper John), Tom Skerritt (Duke), Sally Kellerman (Hot Lips), Robert Duvall (Burns). Notes: Academy Award for Best Screenplay and nominations for Best Picture, Director, and Actress (Kellerman); Cannes Golden Palm Award for Best Director; Golden Globe Award for Best Film. DVD, VHS. The film and book also inspired a hit CBS TV series that ran from 1972 through 1983 (DVD, VHS).

2819. *The Mask of Dimitrios* (Eric Ambler, 1937). A mystery writer decides to research the life of a notorious criminal who was killed in Turkey and is drawn into an illicit scheme. The book was published in the U.S. as *A Coffin for Dimitrios*. **Adaptation:** *The Mask of Dimitrios* (Warner, 1944). Dir: Jean Negulesco. Scr: Frank Gruber. Cast: Sydney Greenstreet (Peters), Zachary Scott (Dimitrios), Faye Emerson (Irana), Peter Lorre (Cornelius). VHS.

2820. *The Mask of Fu Manchu* (Sax Rohmer [pseudonym for Arthur Sarsfield Ward], 1932). In this installment in Rohmer's series of books and stories featuring the evil Asian genius, Dr. Fu Manchu tries to get hold of the mask and sword of Genghis Khan with which he will be able to lead an attack against the Western world. **Adaptation 1:** *The Mask of Fu Manchu* (MGM, 1932). Dir: Charles Brabin. Scr: Irene Kuhn, Edgar Allan Woolf, John Willard. Cast: Boris Karloff (Dr. Fu Manchu), Lewis Stone (Nayland), Karen Morley (Sheila), Charles Starrett (Terrence), Myrna Loy (Fah Lo See), Jean Hersholt (Von Berg). VHS. **Adaptation 2:** *The Face of Fu Manchu* (Seven Arts, 1965). Dir: Don Sharp. Scr: Harry Alan Towers (writing as Peter Welbeck). Cast: Christopher Lee (Dr. Fu Manchu), Nigel Green (Nayland), Joachim Fuchsberger (Karl), Karin Dor (Maria). DVD, VHS. Several sequels followed: *The Brides of Fu Manchu* (1966) (DVD, VHS); *The Vengeance of Fu Manchu* (1967) (VHS); *The Castle of Fu Manchu* (1968) (DVD, VHS); and *The Blood of Fu Manchu* (1968) (DVD, VHS). See also *The Mysterious Dr. Fu Manchu*.

The Mask of Zorro (see *The Curse of Capistrano*).

2821. "The Masque of the Red Death" (Edgar Allan Poe, 1842). A European prince holds a ball for his aristocratic friends as the Black Plague rages outside his castle. The short story originally appeared in the April 30, 1842, issue of *Graham's Magazine*. **Silent Film:** 1919. **Adaptation 1:** *The Masque of the Red Death* (American International, 1964). Dir: Roger Corman. Scr: Charles Beaumont, R. Wright Campbell. Cast: Vincent Price (Prospero), Hazel Court (Juliana), Jane Asher (Francesca), David Weston (Gino). Notes: The screenplay combines elements of this story and Poe's "Hop Frog, Or the Eight Chained Ourang-Outangs" (1850). DVD, VHS. **Adaptation 2:** *Masque of the Red Death* (Concorde, 1989). Dir: Larry Brand. Scr: Daryl Haney, Larry Brand. Cast: Patrick Macnee (Machiavel), Adrian Paul (Prospero), Clare Hoak (Julietta). VHS. **Adaptation 3:** *Masque of the Red Death* (1990). Dir: Alan Birkinshaw. Scr: Michael J. Murray. Cast: Frank Stallone (Duke), Brenda Vaccaro (Elena), Herbert Lom (Ludwig). Notes: This is not an adaptation of Poe's tale, but a modern story about a photographer who wanders into a German castle, where a madman kills off his party guests. VHS.

Masquerade (see *Castle Minerva*).

2822. *The Masquerader* (Katherine Cecil Thurston, 1904). To save embarrassment, a drug-addicted Member of the British Parliament is replaced by his cousin, who looks exactly like him. The novel was adapted as a stage play in 1917 by John Hunter Booth. **Silent Film:** 1922. **Adaptation:** *The Masquerader* (United Artists, 1933). Dir: Richard Wallace. Scr: Howard Estabrook, Moss Hart. Cast: Ronald Colman (Chilcote),

Elissa Landi (Eve), Juliette Compton (Lady Joyce), David Torrence (Fraser). VHS.

2823. "Massacre" (James Warner Bellah, 1947). Western about a stubborn military officer who comes into conflict with his family, his men, and hostile Indians. **Adaptation:** *Fort Apache* (RKO, 1948). Dir: John Ford. Scr: Frank S. Nugent. Cast: John Wayne (Kirby), Henry Fonda (Owen), Shirley Temple (Philadelphia), Ward Bond (Michael), Victor McLaglen (Festus). DVD, VHS.

Massacre in Rome (see *Death in Rome*).

2824. *Master and Commander* (Patrick O'Brian, 1970). The first of O'Brian's twenty-novel series (1970–1999) about the friendship and adventures of nineteenth-century British navy captain James Aubrey and the ship's surgeon, Dr. Stephen Maturin. **Adaptation:** *Master and Commander: The Far Side of the World* (20th Century–Fox, 2003). Dir: Peter Weir. Scr: Peter Weir, John Collee. Cast: Russell Crowe (Aubrey), Paul Bettany (Maturin), James D'Arcy (Pullings), Edward Woodall (Mowett). Notes: Although the film is named for the first installment, the screenplay is based on elements from several novels in the series. Academy Awards for Best Cinematography and Sound Editing, and nominations for Best Picture, Director, Art Direction, Costume Design, Editing, Makeup, Sound, and Visual Effects; BAFTA Awards for Best Costume Design and Production Design and David Lean Award for Best Direction, and nominations for Best Picture, Supporting Actor (Bettany), Visual Effects, and Cinematography; Golden Globe nominations for Best Picture, Director, and Actor (Crowe). DVD, VHS.

The Master Blackmailer (see "The Adventure of Charles Augustus Milverton").

2825. *The Master of Ballantrae: A Winter's Tale* (Robert Louis Stevenson, 1889). The tale of two Scottish brothers and their role in the Jacobite rebellion of Bonnie Prince Charlie, who tried to reclaim the British throne in 1745. **Adaptation 1:** *The Master of Ballantrae* (Warner, 1953). Dir: William Keighley. Scr: Herb Meadow, Harold Medford. Cast: Errol Flynn (Jamie), Roger Livesey (Francis), Anthony Steel (Henry), Beatrice Campbell (Lady Alison). DVD, VHS. **Adaptation 2:** *The Master of Ballantrae* (CBS, 1984 TV). Dir: Douglas Hickox. Scr: William Bast. Cast: Michael York (James), Richard Thomas (Henry), John Gielgud (Lord Durrisdeer), Timothy Dalton (Francis), Ian Richardson (MacKellar).

Master of Bankdam (see *The Crowthers of Bankdam*).

2826. *Master of Dragonard Hill* (Rupert Gilchrist, 1976). A young eighteenth-century Scot imprisoned on a Caribbean island for rebelling against the British crown leads a slave revolt against their abusive jailers. **Adaptation:** *Master of Dragonard Hill* (Cannon, 1989). Dir: Gerard Kikoine. Scr: Rick Marx, Harry Alan Towers (writing as Peter Welbeck). Cast: Oliver Reed (Shanks), Eartha Kitt (Naomi), Herbert Lom (Le Farge).

2827. *Master of the Game* (Sidney Sheldon, 1982). On her ninetieth birthday, a wealthy woman is haunted by memories of her family's dark past. **Adaptation:** *Master of the Game* (CBS, 1984 TV Miniseries). Dir: Kevin Connor, Harvey Hart. Scr: Alvin Boretz, John Nation, Paul Yurick. Cast: Leslie Caron (Solange), David Birney (David), Dyan Cannon (Kate), Donald Pleasence (Salomon).

2828. *Master of the Hounds* (Algis Budrys, 1966). A couple in a troubled marriage move to an island off the coast of New England and are terrorized by a handicapped Vietnam veteran and his vicious dogs. **Adaptation:** *To Kill a Clown* (20th Century–Fox, 1972). Dir: George Bloomfield. Scr: George Bloomfield, I. C. Rapoport. Cast: Alan Alda (Evelyn), Blythe Danner (Lily), Heath Lamberts (Timothy), Eric Clavering (Stanley). VHS.

2829. *Master of the World* (Jules Verne, 1904). Originally titled *Maitre du Monde*, the sequel to Verne's 1886 novel *Robur, the Conqueror* concerns a scientist who invents a flying machine and uses it to advance world peace. **Adaptation:** *Master of the World* (American International, 1961). Dir: William Witney. Scr: Richard Matheson. Cast: Vincent Price (Robur), Charles Bronson (Strock), Henry Hull (Prudent), Mary Webster (Dorothy). Notes: The screenplay combines elements of Verne's *Robur, the Conqueror* and *Master of the World*. VHS.

2830. *Matchstick Men* (Eric Garcia, 2002). An obsessive-compulsive con artist gets a surprise when he meets the teenaged daughter he was unaware he had. **Adaptation:** *Matchstick Men* (Warner, 2003). Dir: Ridley Scott. Scr: Nicholas Griffin, Ted Griffin. Cast: Nicolas Cage (Roy), Sam Rockwell (Frank), Alison Lohman (Angela), Bruce Altman (Dr. Klein), Bruce McGill (Chuck). DVD, VHS.

2831. *Matilda* (Roald Dahl, 1988). Children's book about a precocious young girl who uses her telekinetic powers to escape a bad home life and to get revenge on a cruel school prinicipal. **Adaptation:** *Matilda* (TriStar, 1996). Dir: Danny De Vito. Scr: Nicholas Kazan, Robin Swicord. Cast: Mara Wilson (Matilda), Danny De Vito (Harry), Rhea Perlman (Zinnia), Embeth Davidtz (Jenny). DVD, VHS.

2832. *Matilda* (Paul Gallico, 1970), A small-time talent agent hopes to make it big with a boxing kangaroo. **Adaptation:** *Matilda* (American International, 1978). Dir: Daniel Mann. Scr: Timothy Galfas, Albert S. Ruddy. Cast: Elliott Gould (Bernie), Clive Revill (Billy), Harry Guardino (Uncle Nono), Roy Clark (Wild Bill). DVD, VHS.

The Mating Game (see *The Darling Buds of May*).

2833. *A Matter of Conviction* (Evan Hunter, 1959). A district attorney prosecuting the gang slaying of a blind youth begins to think that one of the accused may be innocent. **Adaptation:** *The Young Savages* (United Artists, 1961). Dir: John Frankenheimer. Scr: Edward Anhalt, J. P. Miller. Cast: Burt Lancaster (Hank), Dina Merrill (Karen), Edward Andrews (Dan), Shelley Winters (Mary), Telly Savalas (Gunderson). VHS.

A Matter of Time (see *The Film of Memory*).

2834. *Maurice* (E. M. Forster, 1971). Two young men discover their homosexuality when they meet at Cambridge and fall in love. The novel was written in 1914 but published posthumously a year after Forster's death in 1970. **Adaptation:** *Maurice* (Merchant-Ivory/Cinecom, 1987). Dir: James Ivory. Scr: Kit Hesketh-Harvey, James Ivory. Cast: James Wilby (Maurice), Hugh Grant (Clive), Rupert Graves (Alec), Denholm Elliott (Dr. Barry), Simon Callow (Mr. Ducie), Billie Whitelaw (Mrs. Hall). DVD, VHS.

2835. *Maurice Guest* (Henry Handel Richardson [pseudonym for Ethel Richardson Robertson], 1908). Disaster ensues when a wealthy Australian woman develops an infatuation for her music teacher. **Adaptation:** *Rhapsody* (MGM, 1954). Dir: Charles Vidor. Scr: Ruth Goetz, Augustus Goetz, Fay Kanin, Michael Kanin. Cast: Elizabeth Taylor (Louise), Vittorio Gassman (Paul), John Ericson (James), Louis Calhern (Nicholas). VHS.

2836. *The Maverick Queen* (Zane Grey, 1950). A female cattle rustler falls in love with the detective sent to arrest her and is prepared to go straight in order to win his affection. The book was published posthumously more than a decade after Grey's death in 1939. **Adaptation:** *The Mav-*

erick Queen (Republic, 1956). Dir: Joseph Kane. Scr: Kenneth Gamet, De Vallon Scott. Cast: Barbara Stanwyck (Kit), Barry Sullivan (Jeff), Scott Brady (Sundance), Mary Murphy (Lucy), Wallace Ford (Jamie), Howard Petrie (Butch Cassidy). VHS.

Maxie (see *Marion's Wall*).

Maximum Overdrive (*see* "Trucks").

Maybe Baby (see *Inconceivable*).

2837. *Mayerling: The Love and Tragedy of a Crown Prince* (Claude Anet [pseudonym for Jean Schopfer], 1930). A novel based on the true story of Austrian Crown Prince Rudolph, who fell in love with a commoner and later committed suicide with her in their country house. **Adaptation 1:** *Mayerling* (Pax, 1936). Dir: Anatole Litvak. Scr: Marcel Achard, Joseph Kessel, Irma von Cube. Cast: Charles Boyer (Rudolph), Danielle Darrieux (Marie), Marthe Regnier (Baroness Vetsera). VHS. **Adaptation 2:** *Mayerling* (MGM, 1968). Dir: Terence Young. Scr: Terence Young, Denis Cannan. Cast: Omar Sharif (Rudolph), Catherine Deneuve (Marie), James Mason (Emperor Franz Joseph), Ava Gardner (Empress Elizabeth), James Robertson Justice (Edward, Prince of Wales), Genevieve Page (Countess Larish). Notes: Golden Globe nominations for Best English-Language Foreign Film. VHS.

2838. *The Mayor of Casterbridge* (Thomas Hardy, 1886). Classic about a man who, in a drunken state, sells his wife at a fair. The novel first appeared as an illustrated weekly serial in *The Graphic* (London) and *Harper's Weekly* (New York). **Silent Film:** 1921. **Adaptation 1:** *The Mayor of Casterbridge* (BBC, 1978 TV Miniseries). Dir: David Giles. Scr: Dennis Potter. Cast: Alan Bates (Michael), Janet Maw (Elizabeth), Jack Galloway (Donald), Anne Stallybrass (Susan), Anna Massey (Lucetta). DVD, VHS. **Adaptation 2:** *The Mayor of Casterbridge* (A&E, 2003 TV Movie). Dir: David Thacker. Scr: Ted Whitehead. Cast: Ciaran Hinds (Michael), Juliet Aubrey (Susan), Jodhi May (Elizabeth), James Purefoy (Donald), Polly Walker (Lucetta). DVD, VHS. **Adaptation 3:** *The Claim* (United Artists, 2000). Dir: Michael Winterbottom. Scr: Frank Cottrell Boyce. Cast: Peter Mullan (Daniel), Milla Jovovich (Lucia), Wes Bentley (Dalglish), Nastassja Kinski (Elena), Sarah Polley (Hope). Notes: A modern retelling inspired by Hardy's novel. DVD, VHS.

2839. *McCabe* (Edmund Naughton, 1959). Western set at the turn of the twentieth century and involving a gambler who uses his winnings to set up brothels in a mining town. **Adaptation:** *McCabe & Mrs. Miller* (Warner, 1971). Dir: Robert Altman. Scr: Robert Altman, Brian McKay. Cast: Warren Beatty (McCabe), Julie Christie (Constance), Rene Auberjonois (Sheehan), William Devane (the Lawyer). DVD, VHS.

McGuire, Go Home! (see *The High Bright Sun*).

2840. "McLeod's Folly" (Louis Bromfield, 1939). After being jailed in a small town for vagrancy, a traveling journalist decides to stay around to help a struggling newspaper editor and to expose corrupt politicians. The short story appeared in Bromfield's 1939 collection *It Takes All Kinds.* **Adaptation:** *Johnny Come Lately* (United Artists, 1943). Dir: William K. Howard. Scr: John Van Druten. Cast: James Cagney (Tom), Grace George (Vinnie), Marjorie Lord (Jane), Hattie McDaniel (Aida). VHS.

Me and Him (see *Two: A Phallic Novel*).

2841. *Me and My Shadows: A Family Memoir* (Lorna Luft, 1998). A daughter's biography of entertainer Judy Garland (1922–1969) from the beginning of her career at age thirteen to her untimely death at the age of forty-seven. **Adaptation:** *Life with Judy Garland: Me and My Shadows* (ABC, 2001 TV Miniseries). Dir: Robert Allan Ackerman. Scr: Robert L. Freedman. Cast: Judy Davis (Judy Garland), Tammy Blanchard (Judy Garland as a child), Victor Garber (Sid Luft), Hugh Laurie (Vincente Minnelli), Alison Pill (Lorna Luft as a child). Notes: Emmy Awards for Outstanding Actress (Davis), Supporting Actress (Blanchard), Costume Design, Hairstyling, and Makeup, and nominations for Outstanding Miniseries, Director, Teleplay, Art Direction, Casting, Cinematography, and Editing; Golden Globe Awards for Best Television Actress (Davis), and nominations for Best Miniseries and Supporting Actress (Blanchard). DVD, VHS.

2842. *Me and the Arch Kook Petulia* (John Haase, 1966). A divorced physician is pursued by an eccentric, unhappily married woman. **Adaptation:** *Petulia* (Warner/Seven Arts, 1968). Dir: Richard Lester. Scr: Barbara Turner, Lawrence B. Marcus. Cast: Julie Christie (Petulia), George C. Scott (Archie), Richard Chamberlain (David), Arthur Hill (Barney), Shirley Knight (Polo), Pippa Scott (May). VHS.

2843. *Me Two* (Edwin Davis, 1983). Comedy about a crotchety old woman whose soul is accidentally transferred into the body of an idealis-

tic young lawyer. **Adaptation:** *All of Me* (Universal, 1984). Dir: Carl Reiner. Scr: Phil Alden Robinson, Henry Olek. Cast: Steve Martin (Roger), Lily Tomlin (Edwina), Victoria Tennant (Terry), Madolyn Smith (Peggy). DVD, VHS.

Mean Girls (see *Queen Bees and Wannabes*).

The Mean Season (see *In the Heat of the Summer*).

2844. *Medal for the General* (James Ronald, 1942). An old British general whose age prevents him from fighting in World War II helps some young evacuees and discovers new purpose in life. **Adaptation:** *Medal for the General* (British National/Four Continents, 1944). Dir: Maurice Elvey. Scr: Elizabeth Baron. Cast: Godfrey Tearle (General Church), Jeanne De Casalis (Lady Frome), Morland Graham (Bates).

2845. *The Medusa Touch* (Peter Van Greenaway, 1973). A novelist who can will disaster on others begins to fear his own powers. **Adaptation:** *The Medusa Touch* (Warner, 1978). Dir: Jack Gold. Scr: John Briley. Cast: Richard Burton (Morlar), Lino Ventura (Brunel), Lee Remick (Dr. Zonfeld), Michael Hordern (Atropos). VHS.

2846. *Meet Me in St. Louis* (Sally Benson, 1942). Autobiographical stories about the life of a close-knit family in St. Louis in 1904, the year of the World's Fair in that city. The book was serialized in *The New Yorker* in 1941 and 1942, beginning with the story "5135 Kensington, August 1903," published on August 23, 1941. The novel and 1944 film adaptation also inspired a 1989 Broadway musical. **Adaptation 1:** *Meet Me in St. Louis* (MGM, 1944). Dir: Vincente Minnelli. Scr: Irving Brecher, Fred F. Finklehoffe. Cast: Judy Garland (Esther), Margaret O'Brien (Tootie), Mary Astor (Anna), Lucille Bremer (Rose), Leon Ames (Alonzo). Notes: Academy Award nominations for Best Screenplay, Cinematography, Musical Score, and Song. DVD, VHS. **Adaptation 2:** *Meet Me in St. Louis* (MGM Television, 1959 TV Movie). Dir: George Schaefer. Scr: Irving Brecher, Fred F. Finklehoffe (1944 screenplay). Cast: Jane Powell (Esther), Patty Duke (Tootie), Jeanne Crain (Rose), Tab Hunter (John), Myrna Loy (Anna), Walter Pidgeon (Alonzo), Ed Wynn (Grandpa). Notes: A live television remake of the 1944 musical. **Adaptation 3:** *Meet Me in St. Louis* (MGM Television, 1966 TV Movie). Dir: Alan D. Courtney. Scr: Irving Brecher, Fred F. Finklehoffe (1944 screenplay). Cast: Shelley Fabares (Esther), Celeste Holm (Annie), Larry Merrill (Glenn), Judy Land (Faye), Reta Shaw (Katie). DVD.

Meet Mr. Callaghan (see *The Urgent Hangman*).

2847. *Meet the Tiger* (Leslie Charteris [pseudonym for Leslie Charles Bowyer Yin], 1928). In the first installment of Charteris' long-running series featuring Robin Hood-like sleuth Simon Templar, the Saint (as he is known) battles a criminal mastermind codenamed the Tiger, who is attempting to smuggle gold bullion out of England. **Adaptation:** *The Saint Meets the Tiger* (RKO, 1941). Dir: Paul Stein. Scr: Leslie Arliss, Wolfgang Wilhelm, James Seymour. Cast: Hugh Sinclair (Templar), Jean Gillie (Pat), Gordon McLeod (Inspector Teal), Clifford Evans (Tidemarsh/the Tiger), Wylie Watson (Horace). VHS.

2848. *The Megstone Plot* (Andrew Garve, 1956). Comic novel about a philandering British military official who disappears and hopes to be labeled a traitor by the press so that he can sue them for libel and make some money. **Adaptation:** *A Touch of Larceny* (Paramount, 1959). Dir: Guy Hamilton. Scr: Ivan Foxwell, Guy Hamilton, Roger MacDougall, Paul Winterton. Cast: James Mason (Commander Easton), George Sanders (Sir Charles), Vera Miles (Virginia), Robert Flemyng (Larkin).

2849. "The Melancholy Hussar of the German Legion" (Thomas Hardy, 1890). Based on a true story, the tale of a German cavalry officer's love for an English girl and his desertion, resulting in his capture and execution. The story story was written in 1888 and first published in two parts in the *Bristol Times and Mirror* in January 1890. The story was later included in the 1912 edition of Hardy's *Wessex Tales*. **Adaptation:** *The Scarlet Tunic* (Indy/Romance Classics, 1998). Dir: Stuart St. Paul. Scr: Colin Clements, Mark Jenkins, Stuart St. Paul. Cast: Jean-Marc Barr (Matthaus), Emma Fielding (Frances), Simon Callow (Captain Fairfax), Jack Shepherd (Dr. Grove). DVD, VHS.

Melissa (see *My Wife Melissa*).

2850. *The Melody Lingers On* (Lowell Brentano, 1934). During World War I, the poor mother of an illegitimate child gives him up to an orphanage but secretly watches him grow up. **Adaptation:** *The Melody Lingers On;* reissued in the U.S. as *The War Bride's Secret* (United Artists, 1935). Dir: David Burton. Scr: Ralph Block, Philip Dunne. Cast: Josephine Hutchinson (Ann), George Houston (Carlo), John Halliday (Marco), Mona Barrie (Sylvia).

2851. *Melville Goodwin, USA* (John P. Mar-quand, 1951). A female reporter tries to discredit a military official who is being considered for a top position with the Atomic Energy Commission and ends up falling in love with him. **Adaptation:** *Top Secret Affair;* released in the UK as *Their Secret Affair* (Warner, 1957). Dir: H. C. Potter. Scr: Roland Kibbee, Allan Scott. Cast: Susan Hayward (Dorothy), Kirk Douglas (General Goodwin), Paul Stewart (Phil), Jim Backus (Colonel Gooch).

2852. *The Member of the Wedding* (Carson McCullers, 1946). A precocious twelve-year-old tomboy begins to learn maturity as she prepares for her brother's marriage. McCullers also adapted her novel as a play in 1949. **Adaptation 1:** *The Member of the Wedding* (Columbia, 1952). Dir: Fred Zinnemann. Scr: Edna Anhalt, Edward Anhalt. Cast: Ethel Waters (Bernice), Julie Harris (Frankie), Brandon De Wilde (John Henry). Notes: Golden Globe Award for Best Juvenile Actor (DeWilde); Academy Award nomination for Best Actress (Harris). VHS. **Adaptation 2:** *The Member of the Wedding* (NBC, 1982 TV Movie). Dir: Delbert Mann. Scr: Carson McCullers (play). Cast: Pearl Bailey (Bernice), Dana Hill (Frankie), Howard E. Rollins, Jr. (Honey Brown), Lane Smith (Mr. Addams). Notes: An NBC Live Theater presentation. **Adaptation 3:** *The Member of the Wedding* (Hallmark, 1997 TV Movie). Dir: Fielder Cook. Scr: David W. Rintels. Cast: Anna Paquin (Frankie), Alfre Woodard (Bernice), Corey Dunn (John Henry), Enrico Colantoni (Mr. Addams). Notes: CableACE nomination for Best Supporting Actress (Woodard). VHS.

2853. *Memed, My Hawk* (Yasar Kemal, 1955). A Turkish novel set in 1923, it is the story of an incompetent village tyrant who drives young villagers to join the rebel forces opposing him. The novel was first translated into English in 1961. **Adaptation:** *Memed My Hawk* (Filmworld, 1984). Dir: Peter Ustinov. Scr: Peter Ustinov. Cast: Peter Ustinov (Abdi Aga), Herbert Lom (Ali Safa Bey), Denis Quilley (Rejeb), Michael Elphick (Jabbar).

2854. "Mememto Mori" (Jonathan Nolan, 2001). A Los Angeles insurance investigator who has lost his short-term memory uses clues to search for the man who raped and killed his wife. Although Jonathan Nolan's story idea inspired the film directed by his brother Christopher, it was not published until a year after the film appeared. The short story was published in the March 2001 issue of *Esquire*. **Adaptation:** *Memento* (Newmarket, 2000). Dir: Christopher Nolan. Scr: Christopher Nolan. Cast: Guy Pearce (Leonard), Carrie-Anne Moss (Natalie), Joe Pantoliano (Teddy), Jorja Fox (Catherine), Stephen Tobolowsky (Sammy). Notes: Independent Spirit Awards for Best Film, Director, Screenplay, and Actress (Moss), and nomination for Best Cinematography; Sundance Film Festival Award for Best Screenplay; Academy Award nominations for Best Film and Editing; Golden Globe nomination for Best Screenplay. DVD, VHS.

2855. *Memento Mori* (Muriel Spark, 1959). An elderly British woman facing the end of her life begins to receive strange phone calls while she is in the hospital. **Adaptation:** *Memento Mori* (BBC, 1992 TV Movie). Dir: Jack Clayton. Scr: Jack Clayton, Alan Kelley, Jeanie Sims. Cast: Maggie Smith (Mabel), Michael Hordern (Godfrey), Renee Asherson (Charmian), Stephanie Cole (Dame Lettie), Thora Hird (Jean), Maurice Denham (Guy).

2856. *Memoirs of a Survivor* (Doris Lessing, 1974). Futuristic tale set in a decaying city and involving a woman who is trying to survive in an old Victorian house. **Adaptation:** *Memoirs of a Survivor* (EMI, 1981). Dir: David Gladwell. Scr: Kerry Crabbe, David Gladwell. Cast: Julie Christie (Dee), Christopher Guard (Gerald), Leonie Mellinger (Emily), Debbie Hutchings (June). DVD, VHS.

2857. *Memoirs of an Invisible Man* (H. F. Saint, 1987). After an accident, a stock broker is rendered invisible, and a ruthless CIA agent pursues him in order to recruit him into the spy business. **Adaptation:** *Memoirs of an Invisible Man* (Warner, 1992). Dir: John Carpenter. Scr: Robert Collector, Dana Olsen, William Goldman. Cast: Chevy Chase (Nick), Daryl Hannah (Alice), Sam Neill (David), Michael McKean (George), Stephen Tobolowsky (Warren). DVD, VHS.

2858. *The Memoirs of Barry Lyndon, Esquire* (William Makepeace Thackeray, 1856). A charming eighteenth-century Irish rogue will stop at nothing to become a nobleman. The novel was serialized in 1844 under the title *The Luck of Barry Lyndon: A Romance of the Last Century* in *Fraser's Magazine* and was published under the revised title in 1856. **Adaptation:** *Barry Lyndon* (Warner, 1975). Dir: Stanley Kubrick. Scr: Stanley Kubrick. Cast: Ryan O'Neal (Barry), Marisa Berenson (Lady Lyndon), Patrick Magee (Chevalier de Balibari), Hardy Kruger (Captain Potzdorf). Notes: Academy Awards for Best Musical Score, Art Direction, Cinematography, and Costume Design, and nominations for Best Picture, Director, and

Screenplay; BAFTA Award for Best Cinematography and nominations for Best Film, Costume Design, and Art Direction; National Board of Review Awards for Best Picture and Director; Golden Globe nominations for Best Picture and Director. DVD, VHS.

2859. *Memories of Midnight* (Sidney Sheldon, 1990). In this sequel to Sheldon's 1974 novel *The Other Side of Midnight,* a French actress loses her memory, and her wealthy lover tries to make sure she does not recall information that may damage him. **Adaptation:** *Memories of Midnight* (CBS, 1991 TV Miniseries). Dir: Gary Nelson. Scr: Richard Hack, Michael Viner, Paul Wheeler. Cast: Jane Seymour (Catherine), Omar Sharif (Constantin), Theodore Bikel (Napoleon), Ken Howard (Kirk). VHS. See also *The Other Side of Midnight.*

2860. *Memory of Love* (Bessie Breuer, 1934). A wealthy man falls in love with a caring widow, but his manipulative wife will not give him a divorce. **Adaptation:** *In Name Only* (RKO, 1939). Dir: John Cromwell. Scr: Richard Sherman. Cast: Carole Lombard (Julie), Cary Grant (Alec), Kay Francis (Maida), Charles Coburn (Mr. Walker). VHS.

Memory Run (see *Season of the Witch*).

2861. *Men* (Margaret Diehl, 1988). A journey of self-discovery takes a young woman from New York to California, where she becomes involved with a married man and a photographer who is also a political radical. **Adaptation:** *Men* (Ardustry/Unapix, 1997). Dir: Zoe Clarke Williams. Scr: James Andronica, Karen Black, Zoe Clarke-William. Cast: Sean Young (Stella), Dylan Walsh (Teo), Robert Lujan (Zeke). DVD, VHS.

Men at Sea (see *Midshipman Easy*).

Men in War (see *Day Without End*).

2862. *Men of Iron* (Howard Pyle, 1892). Children's book about a young British man who sets out to restore his family's tarnished reputation by saving the life of King Henry IV. **Adaptation:** *The Black Shield of Falworth* (Universal International, 1954). Dir: Rudolph Maté. Scr: Oscar Brodney. Cast: Tony Curtis (Myles), Janet Leigh (Lady Anne), David Farrar (Gilbert), Barbara Rush (Meg). VHS.

2863. *Men Without Country* (Charles Nordhoff and James Norman Hall, 1942). During World War II, five French convicts escape from

Devil's Island, but on their way back to Marseille, they learn that France has surrendered to the Nazis. **Adaptation:** *Passage to Marseille* (Warner, 1944). Dir: Michael Curtiz. Scr: Casey Robinson, Jack Moffitt. Cast: Humphrey Bogart (Matrac), Claude Rains (Freycinet), Michele Morgan (Paula), Philip Dorn (Renault), Sydney Greenstreet (Duval), Peter Lorre (Marius). VHS.

2864. *Menace* (Philip MacDonald, 1933). Novella about a series of murders that follow the suicide of a mining engineer. The book was originally published in England under the title *R. I. P.* **Adaptation:** *Menace* (Paramount, 1934). Dir: Ralph Murphy. Scr: Chandler Sprague, Anthony Veiller. Cast: Gertrude Michael (Helen), Paul Cavanagh (Colonel Crecy), Henrietta Crosman (Sybil), Ray Milland (Freddie).

The Menace (see *The Feathered Serpent*).

2865. *The Men's Club* (Leonard Michaels, 1981). A group of male friends approaching middle age decides to form a discussion group. **Adaptation:** *The Men's Club* (Atlantic, 1986). Dir: Peter Medak. Scr: Leonard Michaels. Cast: David Dukes (Philip), Richard Jordan (Kramer), Harvey Keitel (Solly), Frank Langella (Harold), Roy Scheider (Cavanaugh), Craig Wasson (Paul), Treat Williams (Terry), Stockard Channing (Nancy). VHS.

2866. *The Men's Room* (Ann Oakley, 1988). A successful, married sociologist embarks on a passionate affair with the new head of her department. **Adaptation:** *The Men's Room* (BBC, 1991 Miniseries). Dir: Antonia Bird. Scr: Laura Lamson, Ann Oakley. Cast: Harriet Walter (Charity), Bill Nighy (Mark), James Aubrey (Steve), Charlotte Cornwell (Margaret).

Menu for Murder (see *Murder at the PTA Luncheon*).

2867. *Mephisto* (Klaus Mann, 1936). This novel by the son of German novelist Thomas Mann is the story of a poor actor whose fortunes improve when the Nazis make him the director of their new State Theater. **Adaptation:** *Mephisto* (Analysis, 1981). Dir: Istvan Szabo. Scr: Peter Dobai, Istvan Szabo. Cast: Klaus Maria Brandauer (Hendrik), Krystyna Janda (Barbara), Ildiko Bansagi (Nicoletta), Rolf Hoppe (Tabornagy). Notes: Academy Award for Best Foreign-Language Film; Cannes Awards for Best Screenplay and Director; National Board of Review Award for Best Foreign-Language Film. DVD, VHS.

2868. *The Mephisto Waltz* (Fred Mustard Stewart, 1969). A dying concert pianist who is also a Satanist wills his soul into the body of a journalist and talented pianist so that he can go on playing. **Adaptation:** *The Mephisto Waltz* (20th Century–Fox, 1971). Dir: Paul Wendkos. Scr: Ben Maddow. Cast: Alan Alda (Myles), Jacqueline Bisset (Paula), Barbara Parkins (Roxanne), Bradford Dillman (Bill), William Windom (Dr. West). VHS.

The Mercenaries (see *Dark of the Sun*).

Mercury Rising (see *Simple Simon*).

2869. *Mermaids* (Patty Dann, 1986). After a failed relationship, a single mother moves to a new town. There she runs into conflict with her teenaged daughter, who plans to become a nun but finds herself falling in love with a man her mother does not find entirely acceptable. **Adaptation:** *Mermaids* (Orion, 1990). Dir: Richard Benjamin. Scr: June Roberts. Cast: Cher (Rachel), Bob Hoskins (Lou), Winona Ryder (Charlotte), Christina Ricci (Kate), Caroline McWilliams (Carrie). Notes: National Board of Review Award for Best Supporting Actress (Ryder); Golden Globe nomination for Best Supporting Actress (Ryder). DVD, VHS.

2870. *Merrill's Marauders* (Charlton Ogburn, Jr., 1956). Factual account of the American military's battle with the Japanese in Burma during World War II. **Adaptation:** *Merrill's Marauders* (Warner, 1962). Dir: Samuel Fuller. Scr: Samuel Fuller, Milton Sperling, Charlton Ogburn Jr. Cast: Jeff Chandler (General Merrill), Ty Hardin (Stockton), Peter Brown (Bullseye), Andrew Duggan (Dr. Kolodny), Claude Akins (Kolowicz). VHS.

Merrily We Go to Hell (see *I, Jerry, Take Thee, Joan*).

Merry Christmas, Mr. Lawrence (see *The Seed and the Sower*).

A Merry War (see *Keep the Aspidistra Flying*).

2871. *Merton of the Movies* (Harry Leon Wilson, 1922). Comic novel about a young man obsessed with the movies who goes to Hollywood and becomes a major film star. The novel was adapted for the stage in 1922 by Marc Connelly and George S. Kaufman. **Silent Film:** 1924. **Adaptation 1:** *Make Me a Star* (Paramount, 1932). Dir: William Beaudine. Scr: Sam Mintz, Walter De Leon, Arthur Kober. Cast: Joan Blondell (Flips), Stuart Erwin (Merton), Zasu Pitts (Mrs.

Scudder), Ben Turpin (Ben). **Adaptation 2:** *Merton of the Movies* (MGM, 1947). Dir: Robert Alton. Scr: Lou Breslow, George Wells. Cast: Red Skelton (Merton), Virginia O'Brien (Phyllis), Gloria Grahame (Beulah). VHS.

2872. *Message from Nam* (Danielle Steel, 1990). When her boyfriend is killed during the Vietnam War, a grieving journalist has herself assigned to the front and becomes an acclaimed wartime correspondent. **Adaptation:** *Message from Nam* (NBC, 1993 TV Movie). Dir: Paul Wendkos. Scr: Suzanne Clauser. Cast: Jenny Robertson (Paxton), Nick Mancuso (Bill), Ed Flanders (Ed), Hope Lange (Marjorie), Vivian Wu (France), Billy Dee Williams (Felix), Esther Rolle (Queenie), Rue McClanahan (Beatrice). VHS.

2873. *Message in a Bottle* (Nicholas Sparks, 1998). Walking on a beach, a news reporter finds a bottle containing a love letter to a man's dead wife and tracks down the writer in North Carolina. Love and tragedy follow. **Adaptation:** *Message in a Bottle* (Warner, 1999). Dir: Luis Mandoki. Scr: Gerald Di Pego. Cast: Kevin Costner (Garrett), Robin Wright Penn (Theresa), Paul Newman (Dodge), John Savage (Johnny), Illeana Douglas (Lina), Robbie Coltrane (Charlie). DVD, VHS.

2874. "A Message to Garcia" (Elbert Hubbard, 1899). An essay about American military officer Andrew Rowan, who carried a message from President McKinley to the leader of the Cuban rebels during the Spanish-American War in 1898. **Silent Film:** 1916. **Adaptation:** *A Message to Garcia* (20th Century–Fox, 1936). Dir: George Marshall. Scr: Gene Fowler, Sam Hellman, Gladys Lehman, W. P. Lipscomb. Cast: Wallace Beery (Sergeant Dory), Barbara Stanwyck (Raphaelita), John Boles (Lieutenant Rowan), Alan Hale (Dr. Krug), Enrique Acosta (General Garcia). Notes: The screenplay was based on Hubbard's essay and on Andrew Rowan's 1923 book *How I Carried the Message to Garcia.* See also *How I Carried the Message to Garcia.*

Messenger of Death (see *Avenging Angel*).

2875. *Messiah* (Boris Starling, 1999). Police try to track down a psychopathic serial killer whose only clue is the removal of his victims' tongues and the placement of a silver spoon in their mouths. **Adaptation:** *Messiah* (BBC, 2001 TV Movie). Dir: Diarmuid Lawrence. Scr: Lizzie Mickery, Boris Starling. Cast: Ken Stott (Red), Neil Dudgeon (Duncan), Jamie Draven (Jez), Frances Grey (Kate), Michelle Forbes (Susan), Edward Woodward (Reverend Hedges), Art Malik (Emerson).

2876. *Methinks the Lady* (Guy Endore, 1945). A psychopathic terrorist hypnotizes a patient and has her do his dirty work. The book was also released under the title *Nightmare.* **Adaptation:** *Whirlpool* (20th Century–Fox, 1949). Dir: Otto Preminger. Scr: Ben Hecht, Andrew Solt. Cast: Gene Tierney (Ann), Richard Conte (Dr. Sutton), Jose Ferrer (David), Charles Bickford (Lieutenant Colton). DVD, VHS.

2877. *Metroland* (Julian Barnes, 1980). When an old friend visits a man, reminding him of their Bohemian days in Paris, he begins to question his marriage and comfortable suburban life. **Adaptation:** *Metroland* (Lions Gate/Pandora, 1997). Dir: Philip Saville. Scr: Adrian Hodges. Cast: Christian Bale (Chris), Emily Watson (Marion), Lee Ross (Toni), Elsa Zylberstein (Annick). DVD, VHS.

2878. "Metzengerstein" (Edgar Allan Poe, 1832). A feud between two Hungarian families over local superstitions. The short story originally appeared in the January 14, 1832, issue of *The Philadelphia Saturday Courier.* **Adaptation:** *Spirits of the Dead;* released in the UK as *Tales of Mystery and Imagination* (American International, 1968). Dir: Federico Fellini, Louis Malle, Roger Vadim. Scr: Roger Vadim, Pascal Cousin, Daniel Boulanger, Louis Malle, Clement Biddle Wood, Daniel Boulanger, Federico Fellini, Bernardino Zapponi. Cast: Jane Fonda (Contessa Frederica), James Robertson Justice (the Contessa's Advisor), Peter Fonda (Baron Wilhem), Georges Douking (Du Lissier). Notes: Originally released as *Histoires Extraordinaires.* The film contains adaptations of four separate horror stories. DVD, VHS. See also "William Wilson."

2879. "The Mexican" (Jack London, 1911). A Mexican boxer tries to earn money so that he can support a rebel group fighting the government forces who killed his family. The shory story was published in *The Saturday Evening Post* on August 19, 1911. **Adaptation:** *The Fighter* (United Artists, 1952). Dir: Herbert Kline. Scr: Aben Kandel, Herbert Kline. Cast: Richard Conte (Filipe), Vanessa Brown (Kathy), Lee J. Cobb (Durango), Frank Silvera (Paulino). DVD, VHS.

2880. *Mexican Village* (Josefina Niggli, 1945). A famous Mexican playwright's novel about lives and romantic relationships of three couples in a small village in northern Mexico. **Adaptation:** *Sombrero* (MGM, 1953). Dir: Norman Foster. Scr: Norman Foster, Josefina Niggli.

Cast: Ricardo Montalban (Pepe), Pier Angeli (Eufemia), Vittorio Gassman (Alejandro), Yvonne De Carlo (Maria), Cyd Charisse (Lola).

2881. *Miami Blues* (Charles Willeford, 1984). A psychopathic thief and murderer in Miami is pursued by the jaded policeman whose badge he stole and is using to pose as a cop. **Adaptation:** *Miami Blues* (Orion, 1990). Dir: George Armitage. Scr: George Armitage. Cast: Alec Baldwin (Frederick), Fred Ward (Hoke), Jennifer Jason Leigh (Susie), Charles Napier (Bill). DVD, VHS.

2882. *Miami Mayhem* (Marvin H. Albert, 1960). Miami private investigator Tony Rome is hired to guard a millionaire's daughter. **Adaptation:** *Tony Rome* (20th Century–Fox, 1967). Dir: Gordon Douglas. Scr: Richard L. Breen. Cast: Frank Sinatra (Tony), Jill St. John (Ann), Richard Conte (Santini), Gena Rowlands (Rita), Simon Oakland (Rudy). VHS.

Michael Jordan: An American Hero (see *Taking to the Air*).

Michael Shayne: Private Detective (see *Dividend on Death*).

2883. *Michel Strogoff, Courier of the Czar* (Jules Verne, 1876). During the Napoleonic Wars, a courier for the Russian czar carries critical military information to troops in Siberia. **Silent Films:** 1910, 1914, and 1926. **Adaptation 1:** *The Soldier and the Lady;* released in the UK as *Michael Strogoff* (RKO, 1937). Dir: George Nichols, Jr. Scr: Anne Morrison Chapin, Mortimer Offner, Anthony Veiller. Cast: Anton Walbrook (Strogoff), Elizabeth Allan (Nadia), Margot Grahame (Zangara), Akim Tamiroff (Ogareff). **Adaptation 2:** *Michel Strogoff* (Continental, 1956). Dir: Carmine Gallone, Scr: Marc-Gilbert Sauvajon. Cast: Curt Jurgens (Strogoff), Genevieve Page (Nadia), Jacques Dacqmine (the Grand Duke), Sylva Koscina (Sangarre). Notes: The book was also the basis for a miniseries on German television in 1975.

2884. "The Michigan Kid" (Rex Beach, 1925). Western about a principled couple who expose corrupt town politicians. The short story appeared in Beach's 1925 collection *The Goose Woman and Other Stories.* **Silent Film:** 1928. **Adaptation:** *The Michigan Kid* (Universal, 1947). Dir: Ray Taylor. Scr: Roy Chanslor, Robert Presnell Sr. Cast: Jon Hall (the Michigan Kid), Rita Johnson (Sue), Victor McLaglen (Curley), Andy Devine (Buster). VHS.

2885. *Midaq Alley* (Naguib Mahfouz, 1975). Egyptian novel by the winner of the 1988 Nobel Prize in literature about the interconnected lives of residents of a back alley in a poor Cairo neighborhood. **Adaptation:** *Miracle Alley* (Northern Arts, 1995). Dir: Jorge Fons. Scr: Vicente Lenero. Cast: Ernesto Gomez Cruz (Rutilio), María Rojo (Dona Cata), Salma Hayek (Alma), Margarita Sanz (Susanita), Luis Felipe Tovar (Guicho), Daniel Gimenez Cacho (Jose Luis), Oscar Yoldi (Ubaldo), Tiare Scanda (Maru). Notes: Originally released as *El Callejon de los Milagros* and shown with subtitles. The action is transposed to a poor Mexican neighborhood. Ariel Awards (Mexico) for Best Director, Screenplay, Actresses (Hayek and Sanz), Actor in a Minor Role (Tovar), Costume Design, Editing, Makeup, Musical Score and Song, and nominations for Best Actor (Cruz), Supporting Actor (Cacho), Supporting Actress (Scanda), Actor in a Minor Role (Yoldi), Actress in a Minor Role (Rojo), Cinematography, Set Design, and Sound. DVD, VHS.

2886. *Middlemarch* (George Eliot [pseudonym for Mary Ann Evans], 1871–72). Set at the beginning of the Industrial Revolution, the story of naïve, socially conscious small-town woman trapped in a loveless relationship with a boring intellectual. The novel was originally published in eight installments in *Blackwoods* magazine between December 1871 and December 1872. **Adaptation:** *Middlemarch* (BBC/PBS, 1994 TV Miniseries). Dir: Anthony Page. Scr: Andrew Davies. Cast: Juliet Aubrey (Dorothea), Patrick Malahide (Reverend Casaubon), Douglas Hodge (Dr. Lydgate), Trevyn McDowell (Rosamond). Notes: BAFTA Tewlevision Awards for Best Actress (Aubrey) and Musical Score, and nominations for Best Drama Serial, Costume Design, Photography and Lighting, and Sound. DVD, VHS.

2887. *Midnight* (John A. Russo, 1980). Thriller about a teenaged girl driven from her home by her lecherous stepfather. Hitchhiking to California, she becomes involved with a Satanic cult that sacrifices young women. **Adaptation:** *Midnight;* also released as *Backwoods Massacre* (Independent International, 1981). Dir: John A. Russo. Scr: John A. Russo. Cast: Lawrence Tierney (Bert), John Amplas (Abraham), Melanie Verlin (Nancy), Greg Besnak (Luke). VHS.

2888. *Midnight and Jeremiah* (Sterling North, 1943). A young boy is determined to enter his beloved black sheep in a competition at the state fair. **Adaptation:** *So Dear to My Heart* (Disney/RKO, 1949). Dir: Harold D. Schuster, Hamilton Luske (animated segments). Scr: John Tucker Battle, Ken Anderson, Marc Davis, Bill Peet, Maurice Rapf, Ted Sears. Cast: Bobby Driscoll (Jeremiah), Luana Patten (Tildy), Beulah Bondi (Grandma Kincaid). Notes: A musical adaptation combining live action and animation. DVD, VHS.

2889. *A Midnight Clear* (William Wharton, 1982). In the Ardennes Forest near the end of World War II, an American squad captures a German contingent. They decide to pass a peaceful Christmas together, but end up fighting each other. **Adaptation:** *A Midnight Clear* (Sovereign/ Interstar, 1992). Dir: Keith Gordon. Scr: Keith Gordon. Cast: Peter Berg (Bud), Kevin Dillon (Mel), Arye Gross (Stan), Ethan Hawke (Will), Gary Sinise (Vance). DVD, VHS.

2890. *Midnight Cowboy* (James Leo Herlihy, 1965). A young man from a small Southern town goes to New York to offer his services as a "stud" for lonely women and ends up befriending a crippled con man. **Adaptation:** *Midnight Cowboy* (United Artists, 1969). Dir: John Schlesinger. Scr: Waldo Salt. Cast: Dustin Hoffman (Rizzo), Jon Voight (Joe), Sylvia Miles (Cass), John McGiver (Mr. O'Daniel), Brenda Vaccaro (Shirley), Barnard Hughes (Towny). Notes: Academy Awards for Best Picture, Director, and Screenplay, and nominations for Best Actors (Hoffman and Voight), Supporting Actress (Miles), and Editing; Golden Globe Award for Most Promising Newcomer (Voight), and nominations for Best Picture, Director, Screenplay, Actors (Hoffman and Voight), and Supporting Actress (Vaccaro). DVD, VHS.

2891. *Midnight Express* (Billy Hayes and William Hoffer, 1977). Memoir of an American student who was brutalized in a Turkish prison when he tried to smuggle drugs out of the country. **Adaptation:** *Midnight Express* (Columbia, 1978). Dir: Alan Parker. Scr: Oliver Stone. Cast: Brad Davis (Billy), Irene Miracle (Susan), John Hurt (Max), Bo Hopkins (Tex), Randy Quaid (Jimmy). Notes: Academy Awards for Best Screenplay and Musical Score, and nominations for Best Picture, Director, Supporting Actor (Hurt), and Editing; Golden Globe Awards for Best Picture, Acting Debut (Miracle and Davis), Supporting Actress (Hurt), Screenplay, and Musical Score, and nominations for Best Director and Actor (Davis); Cannes Golden Palm nomination for Best Director. DVD, VHS.

2892. *Midnight in the Garden of Good and Evil: A Savannah Story* (John Berendt, 1994). True story set in Savannah, Georgia, where a journalist went to interview a rich man and ended up staying around to investigate the man's trial for killing his young homosexual lover. **Adaptation:** *Midnight in the Garden of Good and Evil* (Warner, 1997). Dir: Clint Eastwood. Scr: John Lee Hancock. Cast: John Cusack (John), Kevin Spacey (Jim), Jack Thompson (Sonny), Irma P. Hall (Minerva), Jude Law (Billy). DVD, VHS.

2893. *The Midnight Lady and the Mourning Man* (David Anthony [pseudonym for William Dale Smith], 1969). A college coed is murdered during a robbery, and a college security officer discovers the killer. **Adaptation:** *The Midnight Man* (Universal, 1974). Dir: Roland Kibbee, Burt Lancaster. Scr: Roland Kibbee, Burt Lancaster. Cast: Burt Lancaster (Slade), Susan Clark (Linda), Cameron Mitchell (Quartz).

Midnight Man (see *Eye of the Storm*).

The Midnight Man (see *The Midnight Lady and the Mourning Man*).

Midnight Sting (see *The Diggstown Ringers*).

2894. *Midshipman Easy* (Frederick Marryat, 1836). The nautical adventures of a young naval officer during the Napoleonic Wars. **Silent Film:** 1915. **Adaptation:** *Midshipman Easy;* released in the U.S. as *Men of the Sea* (ATP, 1935). Dir: Carol Reed. Scr: Anthony Kimmins. Cast: Hughie Green (Midshipman Easy), Roger Livesey (the Captain), Margaret Lockwood (Donna), Lewis Casson (Mr. Easy).

2895. *Midshipman Hornblower* (C. S. Forester, 1950). In 1807, a British naval vessel is sent to battle Napoleon's forces in Latin America. Forester wrote stories and novels featuring Horatio Hornblower from 1937 through 1967. **Adaptation:** *Captain Horatio Hornblower* (Warner, 1951). Dir: Raoul Walsh. Scr: Ivan Goff, Ben Roberts, Aeneas MacKenzie. Cast: Gregory Peck (Horatio), Virginia Mayo (Lady Barbara), Terence Morgan (Gerard), James Robertson Justice (Quist). Notes: The screenplay includes elements from this novel and other stories in the series. DVD, VHS. Notes: In addition, A&E television produced seven movies based on the books between 1998 and 2003 (DVD, VHS).

2896. *The Midwich Cuckoos* (John Wyndham, 1957). Children born at the same time in an English village turn out to be deadly creatures from another planet. **Adaptation 1:** *Village of the Damned* (1960). Dir: Wolf Rilla. Scr: Stirling Silliphant, Wolf Rilla, Ronald Kinnoch (writing as George Barclay). Cast: George Sanders (Gordon),

Barbara Shelley (Anthea), Martin Stephens (David), Laurence Naismith (Dr. Willers). DVD, VHS. Notes: Followed by a 1963 sequel, *Children of the Damned,* directed by Anton Leader (DVD, VHS). **Adaptation 2:** *Village of the Damned* (Universal, 1995). Dir: John Carpenter. Scr: Stirling Silliphant, Wolf Rilla, Ronald Kinnoch (1960 screenplay), David Himmelstein. Cast: Christopher Reeve (Dr. Chaffee), Kirstie Alley (Dr. Verner), Linda Kozlowski (Jill), Michael Pare (Frank), Meredith Salenger (Melanie), Mark Hamill (Reverend George). Notes: The action in this adaptation is moved to a California town. DVD, VHS.

2897. *The Midwife of Pont Clery* (Flora Sandstrom, 1958). The men of a small village are taken with an attractive midwife, causing the women to go on a sex strike. **Adaptation:** *Jessica* (United Artists, 1962). Dir: Jean Negulesco, Oreste Palella. Scr: Ennio De Concini, Edith R. Sommer. Cast: Maurice Chevalier (Father Antonio), Angie Dickinson (Jessica), Sylva Koscina (Nunzia), Agnes Moorehead (Maria). VHS.

2898. *Midwives* (Chris Bohjalian, 1997). A man whose wife died in childbirth unjustly blames a rural Vermont midwife, who is tried for manslaughter. **Adaptation:** *Midwives* (Lifetime, 2001 TV Movie). Dir: Glenn Jordan. Scr: Cynthia Saunders. Cast: Sissy Spacek (Sibyl), Peter Coyote (Stephen), Terry Kinney (Rand), Alison Pill (Connie).

The Mighty (see *Freak the Mighty*).

The Mighty Quinn (see *Finding Maubee*).

2899. *The Milagro Beanfield War* (John Treadwell Nichols, 1974). A novel based on a true story about poor New Mexico farmers who defy resort developers and the government to keep their land. **Adaptation:** *The Milagro Beanfield War* (Universal, 1988). Dir: Robert Redford. Scr: John Nichols, David Ward. Cast: Ruben Blades (Sheriff Montoya), Richard Bradford (Ladd), Sonia Braga (Ruby), Melanie Griffith (Flossie), John Heard (Charlie). DVD, VHS.

2900. *Mildred Pierce* (James M. Cain, 1941), After leaving her husband for another man, a woman opens a successful restaurant chain, but loses everything again as she battles her daughter for the love of the same man. **Adaptation:** *Mildred Pierce* (Warner, 1945). Dir: Michael Curtiz. Scr: Ranald MacDougall. Cast: Joan Crawford (Mildred), Jack Carson (Wally), Zachary Scott (Monte), Eve Arden (Ida), Ann Blyth (Veda). Notes: Academy Award for Best Actress (Crawford), and nominations for Best Picture, Screenplay, Supporting Actresses (Arden and Blyth), and Cinematography; National Board of Review Award for Best Actress (Crawford). DVD, VHS.

2901. *The Mill on the Floss* (George Eliot [pseudonym for Mary Ann Evans], 1860). When a Victorian mill owner loses his ancestral mill because of a local lawyer, a feud develops. Things become complicated, however, when the mill owner's daughter falls in love with the lawyer's son. **Silent Film:** 1915. **Adaptation 1:** *The Mill on the Floss* (Standard, 1937). Dir: Tim Whelan. Scr: John Drinkwater, Austin Melford, Garnett Weston, Tim Whelan. Cast: Frank Lawton (Philip), Victoria Hopper (Lucy), Fay Compton (Mrs. Tulliver), Geraldine Fitzgerald (Maggie), Griffith Jones (Stephen), Mary Clare (Mrs. Moss), James Mason (Tom). VHS. **Adaptation 2:** *The Mill On the Floss* (BBC, 1965 TV Movie). Dir: Rex Tucker. Scr: Rosemary Anne Sisson. Cast: Jane Asher (Maggie), Edward De Souza (Stephen), Betty Hardy (Mrs. Tulliver), Barry Justice (Tom). **Adaptation 3:** *The Mill On the Floss* (BBC, 1978 TV Miniseries). Dir: Ronald Wilson. Scr: James Andrew Hall. Cast: Pippa Guard (Maggie), Christopher Blake (Tom), Judy Cornwell (Bessy), Mona Durbridge (Lucy), Anton Lesser (Philip). **Adaptation 4:** *The Mill on the Floss* (PBS, 1997 TV Movie). Dir: Graham Theakston. Scr: Hugh Stoddart. Cast: Emily Watson (Maggie), Ifan Meredith (Tom), James Frain (Philip), Bernard Hill (Edward). VHS. Notes: A 1940 Mexican film titled *Odio* was also based on Eliot's novel.

Millennium (see "Air Raid").

Million Dollar Baby (see *Rope Burns*).

Million Dollar Ransom (see "Ransom, One Million Dollars").

2902. "The Million Pound Bank Note" (Mark Twain [pseudonym for Samuel Langhorne Clemens], 1893). A penniless man in London is given a one-million pound banknote and his attempt to spend it leads to a series of comic complications. The short story, sometimes bearing the title "The 1,000,000 Pound Bank Note," originally appeared in the January 1893 issue of *The Century* and was collected in Twain's *The Million Pound Note and Other New Stories* (1893). **Adaptation 1:** *The Million Pound Note;* released in the U.S. as *Man with a Million* (United Artists, 1953). Dir: Ronald Neame. Scr: Jill Craigie. Cast: Gregory Peck (Henry), Ronald Squire (Oliver), Joyce Grenfell (Duchess of Cromarty). VHS. **Adaptation 2:** *A Million to Juan* (Samuel Goldwyn, 1994). Dir: Paul Rodriguez. Scr: Robert Grasmere, Francisca Matos. Cast: Paul Rodriguez (Juan), Tony Plana (Jorge), Bert Rosario (Alvaro), Polly Draper (Olivia). Notes: This adaptation concerns a poor Mexican man in Los Angeles. VHS.

2903. "The Million Pound Day" (Leslie Charteris [pseudonym for Leslie Charles Bowyer Yin], 1932). In an installment of Charteris' long-running series featuring Robin Hood-like sleuth Simon Templar, the Saint (as he is known) exposes a gang of British counterfeiters with the help of a socially prominent woman. The short story appeared in Charteris' 1932 collection *The Holy Terror,* which was also published as *The Saint versus Scotland Yard.* **Adaptation:** *The Saint in London* (RKO, 1939). Dir: John Paddy Carstairs. Scr: Lynn Root, Frank Fenton. Cast: George Sanders (Templar), Sally Gray (Penny), David Burns (Dugan), Gordon McLeod (Inspector Teal). VHS.

A Million to Juan (*see* "The Million Pound Banknote").

The Millionaire (*see* "Idle Hands").

2904. *The Mills of God* (Ernst Lothar, 1947). A strict judge kills his terminally ill wife to end her suffering and then insists on being tried for the crime. **Adaptation:** *An Act of Murder;* also known as *Live Today for Tomorrow* (Universal, 1948). Dir: Michael Gordon. Scr: Michael Blankfort, Robert Thoereu. Cast: Frederic March (Judge Cooke), Edmond O'Brien (David), Florence Eldridge (Catherine), Geraldine Brooks (Ellie).

2905. *The Millstone* (Margaret Drabble, 1965). A pregnant British girl tries to get an abortion but then decides to keep her baby. **Adaptation:** *A Touch of Love;* released in the U.S. as *Thank You All Very Much* (Columbia, 1969). Dir: Waris Hussein. Scr: Margaret Drabble. Cast: Sandy Dennis (Rosamund), Ian McKellen (George), Eleanor Bron (Lydia), John Standing (Roger).

Mind Games (see *Agency*).

2906. *The Mind of Mr. J. G. Reeder* (Edgar Wallace, 1925). A shy, middle-aged government worker investigates a forgery and discovers a murderer. The book was released in the U.S. as *The Murder Book of Mr. J. G. Reeder.* **Adaptation:** *The Mind of Mr. Reeder* (Grand National, 1939). Dir:

Jack Raymond. Scr: Marjorie Gaffney, Michael Hogan, Bryan Edgar Wallace. Cast: Will Fyffe (Reeder), Kay Walsh (Peggy), George Curzon (Welford). Notes: Between 1969 and 1971, Thames Television in Great Britain broadcast a series titled *The Mind of Mr. J.G. Reeder* based on Wallace's stories featuring the amateur sleuth.

2907. *The Mind of Mr. Soames* (Charles Eric Maine [pseudonym for David McIlwain, 1961). Science fiction tale about a man in a coma since birth awakening after thirty years and beginning to learn about life. **Adaptation:** *The Mind of Mr. Soames* (Columbia, 1970). Dir: Alan Cooke. Scr: John Hale, Edward Simpson. Cast: Terence Stamp (Soames), Robert Vaughn (Dr. Bergen), Nigel Davenport (Dr. Maitland).

2908. *Mine Own Executioner* (Nigel Balchin, 1945). A psychiatrist tries unsuccessfully to treat a schizophrenic veteran who was tortured in a Japanese POW camp during World War II. **Adaptation:** *Mine Own Executioner* (London/20th Century–Fox, 1947). Dir: Anthony Kimmins. Scr: Nigel Balchin. Cast: Burgess Meredith (Felix), Dulcie Gray (Patricia), Michael Shepley (Peter), Christine Norden (Barbara), Kieron Moore (Adam). VHS.

2909. *The Ministry of Fear* (Graham Greene, 1943). In England during World War II, an emotionally disturbed man is released from a mental hospital and becomes unwittingly entangled in an espionage scheme. **Adaptation:** *Ministry of Fear* (Paramount, 1944). Dir: Fritz Lang. Scr: Seton I. Miller. Cast: Ray Milland (Stephen), Marjorie Reynolds (Carla), Carl Esmond (Willi/ Mr. Macklin). VHS.

Minne (see *L'Ingenue Libertine*).

2910. "The Minority Report" (Philip K. Dick, 1956). In the future, police are able to apprehend criminals even before they commit crimes. When one of the policemen is accused of future murder, however, he must find a way to prove his innocence. The short story was published in the January 1956 issue of *Fantastic Universe* magazine. **Adaptation:** *Minority Report* (20th Century–Fox, 2002). Dir: Steven Spielberg. Scr: Scott Frank, Jon Cohen. Cast: Tom Cruise (John), Colin Farrell (Danny), Samantha Morton (Agatha), Max von Sydow (Lamar). DVD, VHS.

2911. *Minotaur* (Benjamin Tammuz, 1981). Israeli novel about the tragic romance between a Mossad agent and a beautiful music student to whom he cannot reveal himself. **Adaptation:**

Minotaur (Columbia TriStar, 1997). Dir: Jonathan Tammuz. Scr: Dan Turgeman, Irving S. White. Cast: Mili Avital (Thea), Dan Turgeman (Alex), Georges Corraface (Nicos). DVD, VHS.

2912. *The Minus Man* (Lew McCreary, 1991). A psychotic serial killer who murders people who complain about their lives takes up residence in the home of a middle-aged suburban couple. **Adaptation:** *The Minus Man* (Artisan, 1999). Dir: Hampton Fancher. Scr: Hampton Fancher. Cast: Owen Wilson (Vann), Sheryl Crow (Laurie), Dwight Yoakam (Detective Blair), Dennis Haysbert (Detective Graves), Mercedes Ruehl (Jane). Notes: Sundance Film Festival nomination for Grand Jury Prize for Best Dramatic Film. DVD, VHS.

Miracle Alley (see *Midaq Alley*).

2913. *Miracle in the Rain* (Ben Hecht, 1943). Tragic love story about a lonely young woman who falls in love with a soldier in New York during World War II. **Adaptation:** *Miracle in the Rain* (Warner, 1956). Dir: Rudolph Mate. Scr: Ben Hecht. Cast: Jane Wyman (Ruth), Van Johnson (Arthur), Peggie Castle (Millie), Fred Clark (Steven), Eileen Heckart (Grace).

Miracle in the Sand (see *The Three Godfathers*).

2914. *The Miracle of the Bells* (Russell Janney, 1946). A young film star dies and is buried in her small hometown. When a seeming miracle occurs in the coal-mining town, a publicist exploits the story. **Adaptation:** *The Miracle of the Bells* (RKO, 1948). Dir: Irving Pichel. Scr: Ben Hecht, Quentin Reynolds. Cast: Fred MacMurray (Bill), Alida Valli (Olga), Frank Sinatra (Father Paul), Lee J. Cobb (Marcus). VHS.

2915. *Miracle on the 17th Green* (James Patterson and Peter De Jonge, 1996). After he loses his job, an advertising executive has an epiphany and announces to his family that he will try to qualify for the Senior Tour in golf. **Adaptation:** *Miracle on the 17th Green* (CBS, 1999 TV Movie). Dir: Michael Switzer. Scr: Wesley Bishop. Cast: Robert Urich (Mitch), Meredith Baxter (Susan), Donnelly Rhodes (Peter).

Miracles for Sale (see *Death from a Top Hat*).

Mirage (see *Fallen Angel* by Walter Ericson).

2916. *The Mirror Crack'd From Side to Side* (Agatha Christie, 1962). A Miss Marple mystery set in a small English village, where an American movie company is making a film. When a local woman is poisoned by a drink intended for one of the movie stars, Miss Marple investigates. The novel was published in the U.S. as *The Mirror Crack'd*. **Adaptation 1:** *The Mirror Crack'd* (EMI/Associated, 1980). Dir: Guy Hamilton. Scr: Jonathan Hales, Barry Sandler. Cast: Angela Lansbury (Miss Marple), Geraldine Chaplin (Ella), Tony Curtis (Martin), Edward Fox (Inspector Craddock), Rock Hudson (Jason), Kim Novak (Lola), Elizabeth Taylor (Marina). DVD, VHS. **Adaptation 2:** *The Mirror Crack'd* (BBC/A&E 1992 TV Movie series). Dir: Norman Stone. Scr: T. R. Bowen. Cast: Joan Hickson (Miss Marple), Claire Bloom (Marina), Barry Newman (Jason), Norman Rodway (Dr. Gilchrist). DVD, VHS.

The Misadventures of Margaret (see *Rameau's Niece*).

The Misadventures of Mr. Wilt (see *Wilt*).

2917. *Mischief* (Charlotte Armstrong[pseudonym for Charlotte Armstrong Lewi], 1950). An emotionally disturbed young woman takes a job as a babysitter at a hotel and threatens to kill her young charge. **Adaptation 1:** *Don't Bother to Knock* (20th Century–Fox, 1952). Dir: Roy Ward Baker. Scr: Daniel Taradash. Cast: Richard Widmark (Jed), Marilyn Monroe (Nell), Anne Bancroft (Lynn). DVD, VHS. **Adaptation 2:** *The Sitter* (FNM, 1991 TV Movie). Dir: Rick Berger. Scr: Rick Berger. Cast: Kim Myers (Nell), Brett Cullen (Jeff), Susan Barnes (Alice), Kimberly Cullum (Melissa).

2918. *Misery* (Stephen King, 1987). A popular writer is seriously injured in an automobile accident and taken in by a nurse, his Number One Fan, who forces him to re-write a manuscript with which she is not pleased. **Adaptation:** *Misery* (Columbia, 1990). Dir: Rob Reiner. Scr: William Goldman. Cast: James Caan (Paul), Kathy Bates (Annie), Richard Farnsworth (Sheriff McCain), Frances Sternhagen (Virginia), Lauren Bacall (Marcia). Notes: Academy Award and Golden Globe Award for Best Actress (Bates). DVD, VHS.

2919. *The Misfit Brigade* (Sven Hassel, 1977). A novel based on a true story about a group of German prisoners recruited by the Nazis, who were desperate for fighting men. **Adaptation:** *The Misfit Brigade;* also released as *Wheels of Terror* (TransWorld, 1987). Dir: Gordon Hessler. Scr: Nelson Gidding. Cast: Bruce Davison (Porta), David Patrick Kelly (the Legionnaire), D. W. Moffett (Von Barring), Oliver Reed (the General), David Carradine (Von Weisshagen). VHS.

2920. "The Misfits" (Arthur Miller, 1957). The story of a divorcee who becomes involved with modern-day cowboys in Nevada. The title refers to the cowboys, whose values no longer work in contemporary society. The short story was originally published in the October 1957 issue of *Esquire* and served as the basis for Miller's screenplay. In 1961, he released a novel based on the screenplay. **Adaptation:** *The Misfits* (United Artists, 1961). Dir: John Huston. Scr: Arthur Miller. Cast: Clark Gable (Gay), Marilyn Monroe (Roslyn), Montgomery Clift (Perce), Thelma Ritter (Isabelle), Eli Wallach (Guido). DVD, VHS.

2921. *Miss Bishop* (Bess Streeter Aldrich, 1933). The story of a dedicated teacher in a small town in the Midwest. **Adaptation:** *Cheers for Miss Bishop* (United Artists, 1941). Dir: Tay Garnett. Scr: Stephen Vincent Benét, Sheridan Gibney, Adelaide Heilbron. Cast: Martha Scott (Ella), William Gargan (Sam), Edmund Gwenn (James), Sterling Holloway (Chris). DVD, VHS.

2922. *Miss Lonelyhearts* (Nathanael West, 1933). The story of a disillusioned journalist who is assigned the advice column in his newspaper and becomes involved in the problems of his readers. The novel was adapted as a play in 1957 by Howard Teichmann. **Adaptation 1:** *Advice to the Lovelorn* (United Artists, 1933). Dir: Alfred L. Werker. Scr: Leonard Praskins. Cast: Lee Tracy (Toby), Sally Blane (Louise), Paul Harvey (Gaskell), Sterling Holloway (Benny). **Adaptation 2:** *Lonelyhearts* (United Artists, 1958). Dir: Vincent J. Donehue. Scr: Dore Schary. Cast: Montgomery Clift (Adam), Robert Ryan (William), Myrna Loy (Florence), Dolores Hart (Justy), Maureen Stapleton (Faye), Jackie Coogan (Ned). VHS. **Adaptation 3:** *Miss Lonelyhearts* (American Playhouse/PBS, 1983 TV Movie). Dir: Michael Dinner. Scr: Michael Dinner, Robert Bailey. Cast: Eric Roberts (Miss Lonelyhearts), Arthur Hill (Willy), Conchata Ferrell (Faye), John Ryan (Peter).

Miss Sadie Thompson (see "Miss Thompson").

2923. *Miss Shumway Waves a Wand* (James Hadley Chase [pseudonym for Rene Brabazon Raymond], 1944). A young apprentice magician learns ancient magic from a female shaman. **Adaptation:** *Rough Magic* (Goldwyn, 1995). Dir: Clare Peploe. Scr: Robert Mundi, William Brookfield, Clare Peploe. Cast: Bridget Fonda (Myra), Russell Crowe (Alex), Jim Broadbent (Doc Ansell), D. W. Moffett (Cliff), Kenneth Mars (the Magician), Paul Rodriguez (Diego). DVD, VHS.

2924. *Miss Susie Slagle's* (Augusta Tucker, 1939). The romantic affairs of doctors and nurses in a Baltimore boarding house in 1910. **Adaptation:** *Miss Susie Slagle's* (Paramount, 1946). Dir: John Berry. Scr: Hugo Butler, Anne Froelich, Adrian Scott, Theodore Strauss. Cast: Veronica Lake (Nan), Sonny Tufts (Pug), Joan Caulfield (Margaretta), Lillian Gish (Miss Slagle), Lloyd Bridges (Silas).

2925. "Miss Thompson" (W. Somerset Maugham, 1921). Stranded passengers on an island in the South Seas include an alluring woman, a military officer, and a self-righteous missionary. While publicly condemning the woman's promiscuity, the missionary's lust for her gets the better of him. The story originally appeared in the April 1921 issue of *The Smart Set* and was adapted by John Colton and Clemence Randolph in 1922 as a play titled *Rain*. **Silent Film:** 1928, titled *Sadie Thompson*, directed by Raoul Walsh and starring Lionel Barrymore and Gloria Swanson, who was nominated for an Academy Award as Best Actress (DVD, VHS). **Adaptation 1:** *Rain* (United Artists, 1932). Dir: Lewis Milestone. Scr: Maxwell Anderson. Cast: Joan Crawford (Sadie), Walter Huston (Alfred), Frederic Howard (Hodgson). DVD, VHS. **Adaptation 2:** *Dirty Gertie from Harlem U.S.A.* (Sack, 1946). Dir: Spencer Williams. Scr: True T. Thompson. Cast: Francine Everett (Gertie), Don Wilson (Diamond Joe), Katherine Moore (Stella). Notes: An adaptation with a black cast and set at a Caribbean island resort. VHS. **Adaptation 3:** *Miss Sadie Thompson* (Columbia, 1953). Dir: Curtis Bernhardt. Scr: Harry Kleiner. Cast: Rita Hayworth (Sadie), Jose Ferrer (Alfred), Aldo Ray (Phil). VHS. Notes: The short story was also adapted under the title *Rain* for a 1970 BBC television series based on Maugham's works.

Missing (see The Execution of Charles Horman).

The Missing (see The Last Ride).

2926. *Missing Joseph* (Elizabeth George, 1993). In the sixth installment in George's series of novels featuring Inspector Thomas Lynley of Scotland Yard, the detective is called in when a minister is poisoned and a couple's young son is placed in mortal jeopardy. **Adaptation:** *The Inspector Lynley Mysteries: Missing Joseph* (BBC/PBS, 2002 TV Movie series). Dir: Richard Laxton. Scr: Lizzie Mickery. Cast: Nathaniel Parker (Lynley), Sharon Small (Detective Havers), Pippa Haywood (Juliet), Charlotte Salt (Maggie). DVD, VHS.

2927. *Missing Men: The Story of the Missing Persons Bureau of the New York Police Department* (John H. Ayers and Carol Bird, 1932). A true account of some strange missing-persons cases in New York. **Adaptation:** *Bureau of Missing Persons* (Warner, 1933). Dir: Roy Del Ruth. Scr: Robert Presnell. Cast: Bette Davis (Norma), Lewis Stone (Captain Webb), Pat O'Brien (Butch). VHS.

The Missing Rembrandt (*see* "The Adventure of Charles Augustus Milverton").

Missing Ten Days (see *The Disappearance of Roger Tremayne*).

2928. *Mission to Moscow* (Joseph E. Davies, 1943). A memoir by the American ambassador to Russia (1936–1938) in the period before World War II. **Adaptation:** *Mission to Moscow* (Warner, 1943). Dir: Michael Curtiz. Scr: Howard Koch. Cast: Walter Huston (Ambassador Davies), Ann Harding (Marjorie), Oskar Homolka (Maxim), Gene Lockhart (Vyacheslav), Eleanor Parker (Emlen).

2929. "Mission With No Record" (James Warner Bellah, 1947). After the Civil War, a Union officer trains recruits to battle Apache Indians, and one of the new soldiers is his own estranged son. **Adaptation:** *Rio Grande* (Republic, 1950). Dir: John Ford. Scr: James Kevin McGuinness. Cast: John Wayne (Kirby), Maureen O'Hara (Kathleen), Ben Johnson (Travis), Claude Jarman Jr. (Jeff), Harry Carey Jr. (Sandy), Chill Wills (Dr. Wilkins), J. Carrol Naish (Philip), Victor McLaglen (Timothy). DVD, VHS.

Mississippi Mermaid (see *Waltz into Darkness*).

Mister ... (see under MR)

2930. *The Mists of Avalon* (Marion Zimmer Bradley, 1982). The Arthurian legend told from the perspective of the women in King Arthur's life. **Adaptation:** *The Mists of Avalon* (Turner, 2001 TV Miniseries). Dir: Uli Edel. Scr: Gavin Scott. Cast: Anjelica Huston (Viviane), Julianna Margulies (Morgaine), Joan Allen (Morgause), Samantha Mathis (Gwenwyfar), Caroline Goodall (Igraine), Edward Atterton (Arthur). Notes: Emmy Award for Best Makeup and nominations for Oustanding Miniseries, Supporting Actresses (Huston and Allen), Art Direction, Musical Score, Cinematography, Costume Design, and Hairstyling; Golden Globe nomination for Best Actress (Margulies). DVD, VHS.

2931. *Misunderstood* (Florence Montgomery, 1869). A busy man, distracted by the loss of his wife, ignores his emotionally needy son. **Adaptation:** *Misunderstood* (MGM-United Artists, 1984). Dir: Jerry Schatzberg. Scr: Barra Grant. Cast: Gene Hackman (Ned), Henry Thomas (Andrew), Rip Torn (Will), Susan Anspach (Lilly). VHS.

2932. *Mix Me a Person* (Jack Trevor Story, 1960). A lawyer's wife, a psychiatrist, treats one of her husband's clients who was convicted for murder and sentenced to death. **Adaptation:** *Mix Me a Person* (British Lion, 1962). Dir: Leslie Norman. Scr: Ian Dalrymple. Cast: Anne Baxter (Dr. Dyson), Donald Sinden (Philip), Adam Faith (Harry).

2933. *Mixed Blessings* (Danielle Steel, 1992). The story of three infertile couples and the extremes to which they will go to conceive a child. **Adaptation:** *Mixed Blessings* (NBC, 1995 TV Movie). Dir: Bethany Rooney. Scr: L. Virginia Browne, Rebecca Soladay. Cast: Gabrielle Carteris (Diana), Scott Baio (Charlie), Bruce Greenwood (Andy), James Naughton (Brad), Alexandra Paul (Beth). DVD, VHS.

2934. *M'Liss: An Idyl of Red Mountain* (Bret Harte, 1860). Western novella about an alcoholic former miner and his spirited young daughter, who falls in love with the town's new schoolteacher. **Silent Films:** 1915 and 1918. **Adaptation:** *M'Liss* (RKO, 1936). Dir: George Nichols Jr. Scr: Dorothy Yost. Cast: Anne Shirley (M'liss Smith), John Beal (Stephen), Guy Kibbee (Washoe).

2935. *Moby-Dick, or The Whale* (Herman Melville, 1851). Melville's classic about a sea captain's obsession with the great white whale that took his leg. **Silent Film:** 1926, titled *The Sea Beast,* and starring John Barrymore. **Adaptation 1:** *Moby Dick* (Warner, 1930). Dir: Lloyd Bacon. Scr: J. Grubb Alexander. Cast: John Barrymore (Ahab), Joan Bennett (Faith), Lloyd Hughes (Derek), Noble Johnson (Queequeg). **Adaptation 2:** *Moby Dick* (Warner, 1956). Dir: John Huston. Scr: Ray Bradbury, John Huston. Cast: Gregory Peck (Ahab), Richard Basehart (Ishmael), Leo Genn (Starbuck), James Robertson Justice (Boomer). Notes: National Board of Review Awards for Best Director and Supporting Actor (Basehart). DVD, VHS. **Adaptation 3:** *Moby Dick* (USA Networks/Hallmark, 1998 TV Miniseries). Dir: Franc Roddam. Scr: Anton Diether, Franc Roddam, Benedict Fitzgerald. Cast: Henry Thomas (Ishmael), Patrick Stewart (Ahab), Piripi Waretini (Queequeg), Ted Levine (Starbuck), Gregory Peck (Father Mapple). Notes: Golden Globe Award for Best Supporting Actor (Peck), and nomination for Best Actor (Stewart); Emmy nominations for Outstanding Miniseries, Actor (Stewart), Supporting Actor (Peck), Special Visual Effects, and Art Direction. DVD, VHS.

The Model Murder Case (see *The Nose on My Face*).

2936. *A Modern Hero* (Louis Bromfield, 1932). A young circus performer becomes wealthy as an automobile tycoon and munitions manufacturer, but his success takes a toll on his life and relationships. **Adaptation:** *A Modern Hero* (Warner, 1934). Dir: G. W. Pabst. Scr: Gene Markey, Kathryn Scola. Cast: Richard Barthelmess (Paul), Jean Muir (Joanna), Marjorie Rambeau (Madame Azais).

Moll Flanders (see *The Fortunes and Misfortunes of the Famous Moll Flanders*).

2937. *Molokai: The Story of Father Damien* (Hilde Eynikel, 1997). Originally titled *Damiaan, de Definitieve Biografie* and translated in 1999, the story of Father Damien (1840–1889), a Catholic missionary who volunteered to work at a leper colony in Hawaii and improved conditions for the patients. **Adaptation:** *Molokai: The Story of Father Damien* (Unapix, 1999). Dir: Paul Cox. Scr: John Briley. Cast: David Wenham (Father Damien), Kris Kristofferson (Rudolph), Peter O'-Toole (William), Derek Jacobi (Father Fouesnel). Notes: Australian Film Institiute Award nominations for Best Screenplay and Actor (Wenham). DVD, VHS.

Moment of Danger (see *The Scent of Danger*).

2938. *Mommie Dearest* (Christina Crawford, 1978). Factual account by the adopted daughter of actress Joan Crawford of the abuse suffered at the hands of the Hollywood icon. **Adaptation:** *Mommie Dearest* (Paramount, 1981). Dir: Frank Perry. Scr: Robert Getchell, Tracy Hotchner, Frank Perry, Frank Yablans. Cast: Faye Dunaway (Joan Crawford), Diana Scarwid (Christina Crawford), Steve Forrest (Greg Savitt), Howard Da Silva (Louis B. Mayer). DVD, VHS.

2939. *The Monarch of the Glen* (Compton Mackenzie, 1941). One of several books by Mackenzie about the adventures of an American millionaire, his new wife, and his unmarried sister in the Scottish Highlands. **Adaptation:** *Monarch of the Glen* (BBC, 2000–04 TV Series). Dir: Edward Bennett, A.J. Quinn, and others. Scr: Niall Leonard, and others. Cast: Alastair Mackenzie (Archibald), Dawn Steele (Lexie), Susan Hampshire (Molly), Julian Fellowes (Lord Angus).

Notes: The British television series is based in part on Mackenzie's Highland novels. DVD, VHS.

Money and the Woman (see "The Embezzler").

2940. "The Money Box" (W. W. Jacobs, 1902). Two drunken sailors contend over a box of money entrusted to them. The short story was first published in *The Strand* in July 1902 and included in Jacobs' 1903 collection *Odd Craft*. **Adaptation:** *Our Relations* (MGM, 1936). Dir: Harry Lachman. Scr: Felix Adler, Richard Connell, Jack Jevne, Charley Rogers. Cast: Stan Laurel (Stan/Alf), Oliver Hardy (Oliver/Bert), Alan Hale (Joe). Notes: Loosely based on Jacobs' short story, the film features comedians Laurel and Hardy, who are entrusted with a diamond ring and meet up with their long-lost twin brothers. VHS.

2941. *Money from Home* (Damon Runyon, 1935). A gambler and an assistant veterinarian must care for a racehorse owned by gangsters. **Adaptation:** *Money from Home* (Paramount, 1953). Dir: George Marshall. Scr: James Allardice, Hal Kanter. Cast: Dean Martin (Herman), Jerry Lewis (Virgil), Marjie Millar (Phyllis), Pat Crowley (Dr. Claypool).

2942. *Money Men* (Gerald Petievich, 1981). A treasury agent obsessively pursues the murderer of his partner. **Adaptation:** *Boiling Point* (1993). Dir: James B. Harris. Scr: James B. Harris. Cast: Wesley Snipes (Jimmy), Dennis Hopper (Red), Lolita Davidovich (Vikki), Viggo Mortensen (Ronnie). DVD, VHS.

2943. *The Money Movers* (Devon Minchin, 1972). Australian novel about armored-car employees who plan a large heist at their own company. **Adaptation:** *Money Movers* (Roadshow, 1979). Dir: Bruce Beresford. Scr: Bruce Beresford. Cast: Terence Donovan (Eric), Tony Bonner (Leo), Ed Devereaux (Dick), Charles Tingwell (Jack). VHS.

2944. *The Money Trap* (Lionel White, 1963). A police detective desperate for money goes on the take and becomes involved with killers. **Adaptation:** *The Money Trap* (MGM, 1965). Dir: Burt Kennedy. Scr: Walter Bernstein. Cast: Glenn Ford (Joe), Elke Sommer (Lisa), Rita Hayworth (Rosalie), Joseph Cotten (Dr. Van Tilden), Ricardo Montalban (Pete).

2945. *The Moneychangers* (Arthur Hailey, 1975). A bank president's announcement that he is stepping down sets off a battle among executives to succeed him. **Adaptation:** *The Moneychangers* (NBC, 1976 Miniseries). Dir: Boris Sagal. Scr: Dean Riesner, Stanford Whitmore. Cast: Kirk

Douglas (Alex), Christopher Plummer (Roscoe), Anne Baxter (Edwina), Ralph Bellamy (Jerome), Timothy Bottoms (Miles), Joan Collins (Avril), Susan Flannery (Margot), Robert Loggia (Tony). Notes: Emmy Award for Outstanding Actor (Plummer) and nominations for Outstanding Miniseries, Actress (Flannery), Cinematography, and Graphic Design.

2946. *The Monk* (Matthew Lewis, 1796). Gothic tale of a monk who, seduced by a woman wearing clerical garb, begins a life of debauchery and finally sells his soul to the devil. **Adaptation 1:** *The Monk* (Intercontinental, 1973). Dir: Adonis Kyrou. Scr: Luis Buñuel, Jean-Claude Carrière, Adonis Kyrou. Cast: Franco Nero (Ambrosio), Nathalie Delon (Mathilde), Nicol Williamson (the Duke of Talamur). **Adaptation 2:** *The Monk* (Celtic, 1990). Dir: Francisco Lara Polop. Scr: Francisco Lara Polop. Cast: Paul McGann (Father Rojas), Sophie Ward (Matilde), Isla Blair (Mother Agueda). VHS.

2947. *Monk Dawson* (Piers Paul Read, 1969). After leaving the priesthood and living a libertine life in London, a former monk begins to doubt his decision. **Adaptation:** *Monk Dawson* (Vision, 1998). Dir: Tom Waller. Scr: James Magrane. Cast: John Michie (Eddie), Benedict Taylor (Bobby), Paula Hamilton (Jenny), Martin Kemp (David). DVD, VHS.

2948. *Monkey Grip* (Helen Graham, 1977). Australian novel about a single mother who becomes romantically involved with a drug addict. **Adaptation:** *Monkey Grip* (Cinecom, 1982). Dir: Ken Cameron. Scr: Ken Cameron, Helen Garner. Cast: Noni Hazlehurst (Nora), Colin Friels (Javo), Alice Garner (Gracie). Notes: Australian Film Institute Awards for Best Actress (Hazlehurst) and nominations for Best Picture, Supporting Actress (Garner), Cinematography, and Editing. VHS.

2949. *Monkey Planet* (Pierre Boulle, 1963). Boulle's French novel *La Planete des Singes* concerns lost astronauts who land on a strange planet where apes are the dominant species and human beings uncivilized beasts. Before long, the astronauts discover that the strange planet is actually Earth in the distant future. The book was first translated into English in 1964 and was reissued under the title *Planet of the Apes* in 1968. **Adaptation 1:** *Planet of the Apes* (20th Century–Fox, 1968). Dir: Franklin J. Schaffner. Scr: Michael Wilson, Rod Serling. Cast: Charlton Heston (George), Roddy McDowall (Cornelius), Kim Hunter (Zira), Maurice Evans (Dr. Zaius), James

Whitmore (President of the Assembly). Notes: Academy Award for Best Makeup and nominations for Best Costume Design and Musical Score. DVD, VHS. Notes: Several sequels followed this film: *Beneath the Planet of the Apes* (1970) (DVD, VHS); *Escape from the Planet of the Apes* (1971) (DVD, VHS); *Conquest of the Planet of the Apes* (1972) (DVD, VHS); *Battle for the Planet of the Apes* (1973) (DVD, VHS). In addition, two television series also aired: *Planet of the Apes* (1974) and *Return to the Planet of the Apes* (1975–1976). **Adaptation 2:** *Planet of the Apes* (20th Century–Fox, 2001). Dir: Tim Burton. Scr: William Broyles Jr., Lawrence Konner, Mark Rosenthal. Cast: Mark Wahlberg (Leo), Tim Roth (General Thade), Helena Bonham Carter (Ari), Michael Clarke Duncan (Colonel Attar), Paul Giamatti (Limbo). DVD, VHS.

2950. *Monkey Shines* (Michael Stewart, 1983). Thriller about a paralyzed man who is assigned a genetically engineered monkey to assist him, but the monkey forms an emotional attachment that leads it to murder people whom the man does not like. **Adaptation:** *Monkey Shines* (Orion, 1988). Dir: George A. Romero. Scr: George A. Romero. Cast: Jason Beghe (Allan), John Pankow (Geoffrey), Kate McNeil (Melanie), Joyce Van Patten (Dorothy), Christine Forrest (Maryanne), Stephen Root (Dean), Stanley Tucci (Dr. Wiseman). DVD, VHS.

2951. *The Monkeys* (G. K. Wilkinson, 1962). An American inherits a French olive farm and uses four trained chimps to harvest his crop. **Adaptation:** *Monkeys, Go Home!* (Disney/Buena Vista, 1967). Dir: Andrew V. McLaglen. Scr: Maurice Tombragel. Cast: Maurice Chevalier (Sylvain), Dean Jones (Hank), Yvette Mimieux (Maria). DVD, VHS.

Monkeys, Go Home! (see The *Monkeys*).

2952. *The Monkey's Mask* (Dorothy Porter, 1994). Australian novel about a lesbian private investigator who forms a deadly sexual relationship with the teacher of a young woman whose murder she is investigating **Adaptation:** *The Monkey's Mask* (Strand, 2000). Dir: Samantha Lang. Scr: Anne Kennedy. Cast: Susie Porter (Jill), Kelly McGillis (Professor Maitland), Marton Csokas (Nick). DVD, VHS.

2953. *Monk's Hood* (Ellis Peters [pseudonym for Edith Pargeter], 1980, Silver Dagger, British Crime Writers Association). The third installment in Peters' twenty-volume series (1977–1994) featuring Brother Cadfael, a twelfth-century monk who, following service in the Crusades, tends to the herbarium at Shrewsbury Abbey and solves crimes. In this book, a wealthy landowner is poisoned by food that came from the abbey. Investigating the death, Brother Cadfael meets the man's widow and is shocked to discover that she is the woman he loved before he left for the Crusades. **Adaptation:** *Cadfael: Monk's Hood* (ITV/PBS, 1994 TV Movie series). Dir: Graham Theakston. Scr: Simon Burke. Cast: Derek Jacobi (Cadfael), Sean Pertwee (Hugh), Albie Woodington (Sergeant Warden). DVD, VHS.

2954. *Monsieur Beaucaire* (Booth Tarkington, 1901). A count pretends to be a hairdresser to win the affections of a bankrupt countess. Tarkington, along with Evelyn Greenleaf Tarkington, also adapted his novel as a 1901 play titled *Beaucaire*. **Silent Films:** 1905 (titled *Gentleman of France*) and 1924. **Adaptation 1:** *Monte Carlo* (Paramount, 1930). Dir: Ernst Lubitsch. Scr: Ernest Vajda. Cast: Jack Buchanan (Count Rudolph), Jeanette MacDonald (Countess Helene), Claud Allister (Prince Otto), Zasu Pitts (Bertha). Notes: The screenplay was also inspired by Hans Muller's play *The Blue Coast*. **Adaptation 2:** *Monsieur Beaucaire* (Paramount, 1946). Dir: George Marshall. Scr: Melvin Frank, Norman Panama. Cast: Bob Hope (Beaucaire), Joan Caulfield (Mimi), Patric Knowles (Duke le Chandre), Marjorie Reynolds (Princess Maria), Cecil Kellaway (Count D'Armand). DVD, VHS.

2955. *Monsignor* (Jack-Alain Leger, 1977). A cleric who manages Vatican finances commits adultery, theft, and other moral transgressions. **Adaptation:** *Monsignor* (20th Century–Fox, 1982). Dir: Frank Perry. Scr: Wendell Mayes, Abraham Polonsky. Cast: Christopher Reeve (Flaherty), Genevieve Bujold (Clara), Fernando Rey (Santoni), Jason Miller (Appolini). VHS.

2956. *The Monster Club* (R. Chetwynd-Hayes, 1975). A collection of vampire stories within an unusual frame narrative. An old vampire bites a horror writer, but when he realizes who the writer is, the vampire invites him to a club where ghouls and monsters tell scary stories. **Adaptation:** *The Monster Club* (ITC, 1980). Dir: Roy Ward Baker. Scr: Edward Abraham, Valerie Abraham. Cast: Vincent Price (Eramus), John Carradine (Chetwynd-Hayes), Anthony Steel (Lintom), Simon Ward (George), Donald Pleasence (Pickering), Stuart Whitman (Sam). DVD, VHS.

2957. *The Monster from the Earth's End* (Murray Leinster, 1959). Scientists bring back a specimen from Antarctica that proves to be a flesh-eating monster. **Adaptation:** *The Navy vs. the Night Monsters;* also released as *Monsters of the Night* and as *The Night Crawlers* (Realart, 1966). Dir: Michael A. Hoey. Scr: Michael A. Hoey. Cast: Mamie Van Doren (Nora), Anthony Eisley (Charles), Billy Gray (Fred), Bobby Van (Rutherford). VHS.

Monsters of the Night (see *The Monster from the Earth's End*).

Monte Carlo (see *Monsieur Beaucaire*).

2958. *Monte Walsh* (Jack Schaefer, 1963). Two aging cowboys find little to interest them on the shrinking American frontier. **Adaptation 1:** *Monte Walsh* (National General, 1970). Dir: William A. Fraker. Scr: David Zelag Goodman, Lukas Heller. Cast: Lee Marvin (Monte), Jeanne Moreau (Martine), Jack Palance (Chet). VHS. **Adaptation 2:** *Monte Walsh* (Turner, 2003 TV Movie). Dir: Simon Wincer. Scr: David Zelag Goodman, Lukas Heller (1970 screenplay), Michael Brandman, Robert B. Parker. Cast: Tom Selleck (Monte), Isabella Rossellini (Martine), Keith Carradine (Chet), Robert Carradine (Sunfish). Notes: Western Heritage Award for Outstanding Television Feature Film, DVD, VHS.

2959. "A Month by the Lake" (H. E. Bates, 1987). In 1937, a middle-aged British woman on vacation in Lake Como is attracted to a British military officer. The short story was published in Bates' 1987 collection *A Month by the Lake and Other Stories*. **Adaptation:** *A Month by the Lake* (Miramax, 1995). Dir: John Irvin. Scr: Trevor Bentham. Cast: Vanessa Redgrave (Miss Bentley), Edward Fox (Major Wilshaw), Uma Thurman (Miss Beaumont), Alida Valli (Signora Fascioli). DVD, VHS.

2960. *A Month in the Country* (J. L. Carr, 1980). A World War I veteran goes to an English country church where he works on restoring a medieval mural covered over by layers of white paint. **Adaptation:** *A Month in the Country* (Orion, 1987). Dir: Pat O'Connor. Scr: Simon Gray. Cast: Colin Firth (Tom), Jim Carter (Ellerbeck), Patrick Malahide (Reverend Keach), Kenneth Branagh (James). DVD, VHS.

Mood Swingers (see *Dead Babies*).

2961. *The Moon and Sixpence* (W. Somerset Maugham, 1919). Loosely based on the life of painter Paul Gauguin, the story of a married stockbroker who leaves his family and goes to Paris and then Tahiti to become a painter. **Adaptation 1: *The Moon and Sixpence* (United Artists, 1943). Dir: Albert Lewin. Scr: Albert Lewin. Cast: George Sanders (Charles), Herbert Marshall (Geoffrey), Doris Dudley (Blanche), Eric Blore (Captain Nichols). VHS. **Adaptation 2:** *The Moon and Sixpence* (NBC, 1959 TV Movie). Dir: Robert Mulligan. Scr: Robert Mulligan. Cast: Laurence Olivier (Charles), Judith Anderson (Tiare), Hume Cronyn (Dirk), Cyril Cusack (Dr. Coutras), Geraldine Fitzgerald (Amy), Jessica Tandy (Blanche). Notes: Emmy Awards for Outstanding Director and Actor (Olivier), and nomination for Outstanding Dramatic Program; Peabody Award for Best Drama.

2962. *The Moon in the Gutter* (David Goodis, 1953). A bitter dock worker searching for the man who raped his sister falls for a lonely rich woman. **Adaptation:** *The Moon in the Gutter* (Triumph, 1983). Dir: Jean-Jacques Beineix. Scr: Jean-Jacques Beineix, Olivier Mergault. Cast: Gerard Depardieu (Gerard), Nastassja Kinski (Loretta), Victoria Abril (Bella). VHS.

2963. *The Moon Is Down* (John Steinbeck, 1942). A village in Norway resists invasion by the Nazis during World War II. Steinbeck also adapted his novel as a 1942 Broadway play. **Adaptation:** *The Moon Is Down* (20th Century–Fox, 1943). Dir: Irving Pichel. Scr: Nunnally Johnson. Cast: Cedric Hardwicke (Colonel Lanser), Henry Travers (Mayor Orden), Lee J. Cobb (Dr. Winter).

2964. *The Moon-Spinners* (Mary Stewart, 1962). A young English woman and her aunt take a vacation in Greece, where they are drawn into a jewel-smuggling plot. **Adaptation:** *The Moon-Spinners* (Disney/Buena Vista, 1964). Dir: James Neilson. Scr: Michael Dyne. Cast: Hayley Mills (Nikki), Eli Wallach (Stratos), Peter McEnery (Mark), Joan Greenwood (Aunt Frances), Irene Papas (Sophia). DVD, VHS.

Moondance (see *The White Hare*).

2965. *Moonfleet* (J. Meade Falkner, 1898). In England, during the eighteenth century, a dying mother recommends a guardian for her son. The boy develops a relationship with the man, whom he soon discovers is actually a pirate. **Adaptation 1:** *Moonfleet* (MGM, 1955). Dir: Fritz Lang. Scr: Jan Lustig, Margaret Fitts. Cast: Stewart Granger (Jeremy), George Sanders (Lord Ashwood), Joan Greenwood (Lady Ashwood), Viveca Lindfors (Mrs. Minton). VHS. **Adaptation 2:** *Moonfleet* (BBC, 1984 TV Miniseries). Dir: Colin Cant. Scr: George Day. Cast: Victoria Blake (Grace), David Daker (Elzevir), Adam Godley (John), Hilary Mason (Jane).

2966. *Moonlight Becomes You* (Mary Higgins Clark, 1996). A woman goes to Newport, Rhode Island, to visit an old friend and discovers that her friend has been killed in a violent robbery. The only beneficiary to her wealthy friend's estate, the woman is soon targeted by a psychotic killer. **Adaptation:** *Moonlight Becomes You* (Family Channel, 1998 TV Movie). Dir: Bill Corcoran. Scr: David Kinghorn. Cast: Donna Mills (Maggie), Scott Hylands (Dr. Lane), Winston Rekert (Chet).

2967. *Moonraker* (Ian Fleming, 1955). James Bond has only four days to locate the Moonraker, a super-weapon capable of destroying the Earth. **Adaptation:** *Moonraker* (United Artists, 1979). Dir: Lewis Gilbert. Scr: Christopher Wood. Cast: Roger Moore (James Bond), Lois Chiles (Holly), Michael Lonsdale (Hugo), Richard Kiel (Jaws), Bernard Lee (M), Lois Maxwell (Miss Moneypenny). Notes: Despite the use of the title, the screenplay actually concerns a missing space shuttle. Screenwriter Christopher Wood "novelized" the screenplay and published it in 1979. DVD, VHS.

2968. *The Moon's Our Home* (Faith Baldwin, 1936). Comic misadventures of a stubborn movie actress who marries an equally stubborn New York novelist. **Adaptation:** *The Moon's Our Home* (Paramount, 1936). Dir: William A. Seiter. Scr: Alan Campbell, Isabel Dawn, Boyce De Gaw, Dorothy Parker. Cast: Margaret Sullavan (Cherry/Sarah), Henry Fonda (Anthony/John), Charles Butterworth (Horace), Beulah Bondi (Boyce). VHS.

2969. *The Moonshine War* (Elmore Leonard, 1969). Prohibition-era story about a corrupt revenue agent confiscating illegal whiskey in Kentucky. **Adaptation:** *The Moonshine War* (MGM, 1970). Dir: Richard Quine. Scr: Elmore Leonard. Cast: Patrick McGoohan (Frank), Richard Widmark (Dr. Taulbee), Alan Alda (John), Melodie Johnson (Lizann), Will Geer (Baylor).

2970. *The Moonstone* (Wilkie Collins, 1868). A London detective is on the trail of a stolen Indian jewel which purportedly brings bad luck to its owners. Collins adapted his own novel as a stage play in 1877. **Silent Film:** 1915. **Adaptation 1:** *The Moonstone* (Monogram, 1934). Dir: Reginald Barker. Scr: Adele S. Buffington. Cast: David Manners (Franklin), Phyllis Barry (Lady Verinder), Charles Irwin (Sergeant Cuff). **Adaptation 2:** *The Moonstone* (BBC, 1972 TV Miniseries). Dir: Paddy Russell. Scr: Hugh Leonard. Cast: Robin Ellis (Franklin), Kathleen Byron (Lady Verinder), John Welsh (Sergeant Cuff). **Adaptation 3:** *The Moonstone* (BBC/PBS, 1996 TV Miniseries). Dir: Robert Bierman. Scr: Kevin Elyot. Cast: Greg Wise (Franklin), Keeley Hawes (Lady Verinder), Antony Sher (Sergeant Cuff). VHS. Notes: In addition, the book served as the basis for a brief British television series in 1959.

2971. *Moontide* (Willard Robertson, 1940). A seaman falls in love with a beautiful young woman whom he prevented from committing suicide. **Adaptation:** *Moontide* (20th Century–Fox, 1942). Dir: Archie Mayo. Scr: John O'Hara. Cast: Jean Gabin (Bobo), Ida Lupino (Anna), Thomas Mitchell (Tiny), Claude Rains (Nutsy).

2972. *Moonwebs: A Journey into the Mind of a Cult* (Josh Freed, 1980). A journalist's account of how the cult of Sun Myung Moon persuaded a disaffected young man to join his group and the efforts of his friends and family to save him. **Adaptation:** *Ticket to Heaven* (United Artists, 1981). Dir: Ralph L. Thomas. Scr: Anne Cameron, Ralph L. Thomas. Cast: Nick Mancuso (David), Saul Rubinek (Larry), Meg Foster (Ingrid), Kim Cattrall (Ruthie), R. H. Thomson (Linc), Jennifer Dale (Lisa), Guy Boyd (Eric), Dixie Seatle (Sarah). Notes: Genie Awards (Canada) for Best Pictire, Actor (Mancuso), Supporting Actor (Rubinek), and Editing, and nominations for Best Director, Screenplay, Actor (Boyd), Actresses (Foster and Cattrall), Supporting Actor (Thomson), Supporting Actress (Seatle), Musical Score, Sound, and Sound Editing. DVD, VHS.

2973. *Morality Play* (Barry Unsworth, 1995). After breaking his vow of chastity, a medieval monk flees the church and a jealous husband by joining a group of traveling actors. Together they solve the murder of a boy in a small town by re-creating the crime in a play. **Adaptation:** *The Reckoning* (Paramount, 2003). Dir: Paul McGuigan. Scr: Mark Mills. Cast: Paul Bettany (Nicholas), Simon McBurney (Stephen), Tom Hardy (Straw), Brian Cox (Tobias), Willem Dafoe (Martin). DVD, VHS.

2974. *A Morbid Taste for Bones* (Ellis Peters [pseudonym for Edith Pargeter], 1977). The first installment in Peters' twenty-novel series (1977–1994) introduces Brother Cadfael, a twelfth-century monk who, following service in the Crusades, tends to the herbarium at Shrewsbury Abbey and solves murders. In this volume, the monks travel to Wales to excavate the holy relics of St. Winifred. When a man who objects to their taking the bones is murdered, the monks are held as suspects until Brother Cadfael solves the crime. **Adaptation:** *Cadfael: A Morbid Taste for Bones* (ITV/PBS, 1996 TV Movie series). Dir: Graham Theakston. Scr: Simon Burke. Cast: Derek Jacobi (Cadfael), Eoin McCarthy (Hugh), Albie Woodington (Sergeant Warden). DVD, VHS.

2975. "Morella" (Edgar Allan Poe, 1835). Embittered over the death of his wife during childbirth years earlier, a disturbed man cruelly exposes his estranged daughter to horror. The story was originally published in *The Southern Literary Messenger* in Aptil 1835 and was included in Poe's 1840 collection *Tales of the Grotesque and Arabesque*. **Adaptation 1:** *Tales of Terror* (American International, 1962). Dir: Roger Corman, Scr: Richard Matheson. Cast: Vincent Price (Locke), Maggie Pierce (Lenora), Leona Gage (Morella). Notes: The film features adaptations of four Poe stories: "Morella" (1835), "The Facts in the Case of M. Valdemar" (1844), and a segment that combines elements from "The Black Cat" (1843) and "The Cask of Amontillado" (1846). DVD, VHS. **Adaptation 2:** *The Haunting of Morella* (Concorde, 1990). Dir: Jim Wynorski. Scr: R. J. Robertson. Cast: David McCallum (Gideon), Nicole Eggert (Morella/Lenora), Christopher Halsted (Guy), Lana Clarkson (Coel). DVD, VHS. **Adaptation 3:** *Morella* (Taurus, 1997). Dir: James Dudelson. Scr: Ana Clavell. Cast: Angela Jones (Morella/Sarah), Nicholas Guest (Dr. Lynden), Khrystyne Haje (Inspector Farrow), Lou Rawls (Professor Larson). Notes: This adaptation is set in the future and involves genetic experiments that have gone terribly wrong. VHS.

2976. *Morning Glory* (La Vyrle Spencer, 1989). In 1941, an ex-convict is unjustly accused of murdering a small-town prostitute. **Adaptation:** *Morning Glory* (Academy, 1993). Dir: Steven Hilliard Stern. Scr: Charles Jarrott, Deborah Raffin. Cast: Christopher Reeve (Will), Deborah Raffin (Ellie), Lloyd Bochner (Bob), Nina Foch (Miss Beasly), Helen Shaver (Lula), J. T. Walsh (Sheriff Goodloe). VHS.

2977. *Morpho Eugenia* (A. S. Byatt, 1992). Set in Victorian England, the story of a poor naturalist who goes to live with a wealthy and eccentric old aristocrat and falls in love with one of his daughters. The novella, along with another one titled "Conjugal Angel," was published in a collection titled *Angels and Insects: Two Novellas* (1992). **Adaptation:** *Angels & Insects* (Samuel Goldwyn, 1995). Dir: Philip Haas. Scr: Belinda Haas, Philip Haas. Cast: Mark Rylance (William),

Kristin Scott Thomas (Matty), Patsy Kensit (Eugenia), Jeremy Kemp (Sir Harold). Notes: Academy Award nomination for Best Costume Design; Cannes Film Festival Golden Palm nomination for Best Director. DVD, VHS.

2978. *Mortal Fear* (Robin Cook, 1988). When healthy patients begin dying after routine physicals at a clinic , a doctor investigates and discovers a massive conspiracy. **Adaptation:** *Mortal Fear* (ACI, 1994 TV Movie). Dir: Larry Shaw. Scr: Rob Gilmer, Roger Young. Cast: Joanna Kerns (Dr. Kessler), Gregory Harrison (Philip), Max Gail (Detective Curran). DVD, VHS.

2979. *The Mortal Storm* (Phyllis Bottome, 1938). With the rise of Hitler and the Nazis in the early 1930's, a happy German family is torn apart by their political disagreements. **Adaptation:** *The Mortal Storm* (MGM, 1940). Dir: Frank Borzage. Scr: George Froeschel, Hans Rameau (writing as Andersen Ellis), Claudine West. Cast: Margaret Sullavan (Freya), James Stewart (Martin), Robert Young (Fritz), Frank Morgan (Viktor), Robert Stack (Otto). VHS.

2980. *Mortgage on Life* (Vicki Baum, 1946). An aspiring female singer being groomed for success turns on those who were trying to help her. **Adaptation:** *A Woman's Secret* (RKO, 1949). Dir: Nicholas Ray. Scr: Herman J. Mankiewicz. Cast: Maureen O'Hara (Marian), Melvyn Douglas (Luke), Gloria Grahame (Susan), Bill Williams (Lee). VHS.

2981. *Morvern Callar* (Alan Warner, 1995). After her boyfriend's suicide, an irresponsible Scottish supermarket worker passes off his unpublished novel as her own and uses the money she earns to leave her drab life behind. **Adaptation:** *Morvern Callar* (Cowboy, 2002). Dir: Lynne Ramsay. Scr: Liana Dognini, Lynne Ramsay. Cast: Samantha Morton (Morvern), Kathleen McDermott (Lana), Linda McGuire (Vanessa). Notes: British Independent Spirit Awards for Best Actress (Morton) and Cinematography, and nominations for Best Picture, Director, Screenplay, Production Design, and Most Promising Newcomer (McDermott); Cannes Film Festival Award of Youth for Best Director; BAFTA Scotland Award for Best Actress (McDermott). DVD, VHS.

Mosley (see *Beyond the Pale*).

2982. *The Mosquito Coast* (Paul Theroux, 1981). A visionary inventor and utopian dreamer moves his family to the jungles of Central America, where he builds his own village and gradually goes mad. **Adaptation:** *The Mosquito Coast*

(Warner, 1986). Dir: Peter Weir. Scr: Paul Schrader. Cast: Harrison Ford (Allie), Helen Mirren (Mrs. Fox), River Phoenix (Charlie), Martha Plimpton (Emily). DVD, VHS.

2983. "The Most Dangerous Game" (Richard Connell, 1924). A mad aristocrat lures people to his remote island, where he hunts them as big game. The short story was originally published in *Colliers* magazine on January 19, 1924. **Adaptation 1:** *The Most Dangerous Game;* released in the UK as *The Hounds of Zaroff* (RKO, 1932). Dir: Irving Pichel, Ernest B. Schoedsack. Scr: James Ashmore Creelman. Cast: Joel McCrea (Rainsford), Fay Wray (Eve), Leslie Banks (Count Zaroff), Robert Armstrong (Martin). DVD, VHS. **Adaptation 2:** *A Game of Death* (RKO, 1945). Dir: Robert Wise. Scr: Norman Houston. Cast: John Loder (Rainsford), Audrey Long (Ellen), Edgar Barrier (Kreiger), Russell Wade (Robert). **Adaptation 3:** *Run for the Sun* (United Artists, 1956). Dir: Roy Boulting. Scr: Roy Boulting, Dudley Nichols. Cast: Richard Widmark (Mike), Trevor Howard (Browne), Jane Greer (Katie), Peter van Eyck (Dr. Van Anders).

The Most Dangerous Man in the World (see *The Chairman*).

The Most Dangerous Sin (see *Crime and Punishment*).

A Most Deadly Family (see *The Mother, the Son and the Socialite*).

2984. *The Moth* (Catherine Cookson, 1986). In nineteenth-century England, a poor carpenter working for a wealthy family falls in love with the daughter, setting off family opposition based on their class differences. **Adaptation:** *The Moth* (Festival, 1997 TV Movie). Dir: Roy Battersby. Scr: Gordon Hann. Cast: Juliet Aubrey (Sarah), Alan Bird (the Solicitor), David Bradley (Dave), Jeremy Clyde (Reginald). VHS.

2985. *Mother Carey's Chickens* (Kate Douglas Wiggin, 1911). A New England widow struggles to bring up her children alone at the turn of the twentieth century. Wiggin and Rachel Crothers adapted the novel as a play in 1917. **Adaptation 1:** *Mother Carey's Chickens* (RKO, 1938). Dir: Rowland V. Lee. Scr: S. K. Lauren, Gertrude Purcell. Cast: Anne Shirley (Nancy), Ruby Keeler (Kitty), James Ellison (Ralph), Fay Bainter (Mrs. Carey), Walter Brennan (Ossian). **Adaptation 2:** *Summer Magic* (Disney/Buena Vista, 1963). Dir: James Neilson. Scr: Sally Benson. Cast: Hayley Mills (Nancy), Burl Ives (Osh), Dorothy McGuire (Mrs.

Carey), Deborah Walley (Julia), Eddie Hodges (Gilly). VHS.

Mother Didn't Tell Me (see *The Doctor Wears Three Faces*).

2986. *Mother Love* (Domini Taylor [pseudonym for Roger Erskine Longrigg], 1983). The unstable ex-wife of a concert musician takes savage revenge when she discovers that their adult son is secretly seeing his father. **Adaptation:** *Mother Love* (BBC, 1989 TV Miniseries). Dir: Simon Langton. Scr: Andrew Davies. Cast: Diana Rigg (Helena), David McCallum (Alex), James Wilby (Kit). Notes: BAFTA Television Awards for Best Drama Serial and Actress (Rigg).

2987. *Mother Night* (Kurt Vonnegut, 1961). Vonnegut's grimly satiric portrait of Howard W. Campbell, Jr., an American living in Germany during World War II and recruited to work as an agent for the Nazis and the Americans. The novel was published in 1961 as a paperback original. When it was released as a hardcover in 1966, the author added an introduction which stated the moral of the tale: "You are what you pretend to be, so be careful what you pretend to be." **Adaptation:** *Mother Night* (New Line, 1996). Dir: Keith Gordon. Scr: Robert B. Weide. Cast: Nick Nolte (Campbell), Sheryl Lee (Helga/Resi), Alan Arkin (Kraft), Bernard Behrens (Jones). DVD, VHS.

2988. *The Mother, the Son, and the Socialite: The True Story of a Mother-Son Crime Spree* (Adrian Havill, 1999). Factual account of an amoral mother who influences her son to commit various crimes. **Adaptation:** *Like Mother, Like Son: The Strange Story of Sante and Kenny Kimes;* released in Europe as *A Most Deadly Family* (CBS, 2001 TV Movie). Dir: Arthur Allan Seidelman. Scr: Paul Eric Myers. Cast: Mary Tyler Moore (Sante), Gabriel Olds (Kenny), Robert Forster (Ken), Jean Stapleton (Irene).

2989. *Mother Wore Tights* (Miriam Young, 1944). A memoir written for children about life in a family of vaudeville performers. **Adaptation:** *Mother Wore Tights* (20th Century–Fox, 1947). Dir: Walter Lang. Scr: Lamar Trotti. Cast: Betty Grable (Myrtle), Dan Dailey (Frank), Mona Freeman (Iris). Notes: Academy Award for Best Musical Score and nominations for Best Cinematography and Song. VHS.

2990. *Mother's Boys* (Bernard Taylor, 1988). Without much explanation, a woman leaves her husband and three children. When she returns three years later and wants to move back in, her husband refuses, and the family ends up in court.

Adaptation: *Mother's Boys* (Dimension, 1994). Dir: Yves Simoneau. Scr: Barry Schneider, Richard Hawley. Cast: Jamie Lee Curtis (Judith), Peter Gallagher (Robert), Joanne Whalley-Kilmer (Callie), Vanessa Redgrave (Lydia). DVD, VHS.

2991. *Mothertime* (Gillian White, 1993). On Christmas Eve, the children of an alcoholic mother lock her in a sauna to cure her. **Adaptation:** *Mothertime* (BBC, 1997 TV Movie). Dir: Matthew Jacobs. Scr: Matthew Jacobs. Cast: Sheila Allen (Eileen), Anthony Andrews (Robin), Felix Bell (Lot), Rosalind Bennett (Ruby).

2992. *The Mothman Prophecies* (John A. Keel, 1975). True story of a journalist who, several years after the death of his wife under mysterious circumstances, is involuntarily drawn to a small West Virginia town, where he investigates paranormal activity connected with his wife's death and other bizarre occurrences. **Adaptation:** *The Mothman Prophecies* (Screen Gems, 2002). Dir: Mark Pellington. Scr: Richard Hatem. Cast: Richard Gere (John), Laura Linney (Connie), Debra Messing (Mary), Will Patton (Gordon). DVD, VHS.

2993. *The Motorcycle Diaries: A Journey Around South America* (Che Geuvara, trans.lated by Ann Wright, 1995). As a young college student in the early 1950's, Cuban revolutionary Ernesto "Che" Guevara de la Serna (1928–1967) took a motorcycle trip across South America with his friend and classmate Dr. Alberto Granado. This book, translated by Ann Wright, is composed of his journal entries of the time. **Adaptation:** *The Motorcycle Diaries* (Focus, 2004). Dir: Walter Salles. Scr: Jose Rivera. Cast: Gael García Bernal (Ernesto), Rodrigo De la Serna (Alberto), Mía Maestro (Chichina). Notes: Originally titled *Diarios de Motocicleta* and shown with subtitles. The screenplay is also based on Dr. Alberto Grandado's book *Con el Che por America Latina* (*With Che Through Latin America*). Academy Award for Best Song and nomination for Best Screenplay; Cannes Film Festival Francois Chalais Award, Prize of the Ecumenical Jury, and Technical Grand Prize, and nomination for Golden Palm Award for Best Director; Independent Spirit Award nomination for Best Director. DVD, VHS.

2994. *The Mountain* (Henry Troyat, 1953). After a plane crashes in the mountains, a man wants to plunder the wreckage and his older brother tries to stop him. **Adaptation:** *The Mountain* (Paramount, 1956). Dir: Edward Dmytryk. Scr: Ranald MacDougall. Cast: Spencer Tracy (Zachary), Robert Wagner (Chris), Claire Trevor

(Marie), William Demarest (Father Belacchi). VHS.

2995. "Mountain Music" (MacKinlay Kantor, 1935). Fleeing from a shotgun marriage, a hillbilly takes a fall and loses his memory. The short story was published in the January 1935 issue of *Cosmopolitan*. **Adaptation:** *Mountain Music* (Paramount, 1937). Dir: Robert Florey. Scr: Duke Atteberry, Russel Crouse, Charles Lederer, John Moffitt. Cast: Bob Burns (Bob), Martha Raye (Mary), John Howard (Ardinger).

2996. *The Mountain Road* (Theodore H. White, 1958). Near the end of World War II, an American military officer helps to defend a peasant Chinese community against a Japanese invasion. **Adaptation:** *The Mountain Road* (Columbia, 1960). Dir: Daniel Mann. Scr: Alfred Hayes. Cast: James Stewart (Baldwin), Lisa Lu (Sue-Mei), Glenn Corbett (Collins), Harry Morgan (Michaelson), Frank Silvera (Kwan). VHS.

2997. *The Mountains Are My Kingdom* (Stuart Hardy, 1937). Western about a young man and his father who hide out in the mountains because the father is wanted for a murder he did not commit. **Adaptation 1:** *Forbidden Valley* (Universal, 1938). Dir: Wyndham Gittens, Scr: Wyndham Gittens. Cast: Noah Beery, Jr. (Ring), Frances Robinson (Wilda), Robert Barrat (Ramrod). **Adaptation 2:** *Sierra* (Universal, 1950). Dir: Alfred E. Green. Scr: Edna Anhalt, Milton Gunzburg. Cast: Wanda Hendrix (Riley), Audie Murphy (Ring), Burl Ives (Lonesome), Dean Jagger (Jeff).

Mountains of the Moon (see *Burton and Speke*).

2998. *The Mouse on the Moon* (Leonard Wibberley, 1962). In the sequel to Wibberley's 1955 novel *The Mouse That Roared,* the tiny duchy of Grand Fenwick discovers that its local wine makes an excellent rocket fuel. **Adaptation:** *The Mouse on the Moon* (1963). Dir: Richard Lester. Scr: Michael Pertwee. Cast: Margaret Rutherford (Grand Duchess Gloriana), Ron Moody (Prime Minister Mountjoy), Bernard Cribbins (Vincent Mountjoy), David Kossoff (Professor Kokintz), Terry-Thomas (Spender). DVD, VHS.

2999. *The Mouse That Roared* (Leonard Wibberley, 1955). The tiny duchy of Grand Fenwick decides to solves its financial problems by declaring war on the United States in order to collect aid when they lose. **Adaptation:** *The Mouse That Roared* (Columbia, 1959). Dir: Jack Arnold. Scr: Roger MacDougall, Stanley Mann. Cast: Peter Sellers (Gloriana/Rupert /Tully), Jean Seberg (Helen), William Hartnell (Will), David Kossoff (Professor Kokintz), Leo McKern (Benter). DVD, VHS.

3000. *The Mouse Who Wouldn't Play Ball* (Anthony Gilbert [pseudonym for Lucy Beatrice Malleson], 1943). Thriller about an heiress who goes to live in an old family mansion and is terrorized by a housekeeper. **Adaptation:** *Candles at Nine* (British National, 1944). Dir: John Harlow. Scr: John Harlow, Basil Mason. Cast: Eliot Makeham (Everard), Beatrix Lehmann (Julia), John Salew (Griggs), Jessie Matthews (Dorothea).

3001. *Move* (Joel Lieber, 1968). A frustrated New York playwright turns to writing pornography. He earns enough money to move to a larger apartment, where he begins to live his fictional fantasies. **Adaptation:** *Move* (20th Century–Fox, 1970). Dir: Stuart Rosenberg. Scr: Stanley Hart, Joel Lieber. Cast: Elliott Gould (Hiram), Paula Prentiss (Dolly), Graham Jarvis (Dr. Picker).

3002. *The Moving Finger* (Agatha Christie, 1942). Miss Marple is called in to investigate when residents of a small village begin to receive threatening letters. **Adaptation:** *The Moving Finger* (BBC/PSB/A&E, 1985 TV Movie series). Dir: Roy Boulting. Scr: Julia Jones. Cast: Joan Hickson (Miss Marple), Michael Culver (Symmington), Elizabeth Counsell (Angela), Deborah Appleby (Megan). DVD, VHS.

3003. *The Moving Target* (Ross Macdonald [pseudonym for Kenneth Millar], 1949). Los Angeles private detective Lew Archer is hired by a rich woman to find her missing husband. **Adaptation:** *Harper;* released in the UK as *The Moving Target* (Warner, 1966). Dir: Jack Smight. Scr: William Goldman. Cast: Paul Newman (Harper), Lauren Bacall (Elaine), Julie Harris (Betty), Arthur Hill (Graves), Janet Leigh (Susan), Pamela Tiffin (Miranda), Robert Wagner (Allan). VHS.

Mr. & Mrs. Bridge (see *Mr. Bridge* and *Mrs. Bridge*)

3004. *Mr. Arkadin* (Orson Welles, 1955). Claiming to have lost his memory, a shady millionaire hires a man to investigate his past. When all of the people he interviews are killed, the investigator enters a deadly struggle for his own life. **Adaptation:** *Mr. Arkadin;* released in the UK as *Confidential Report* (Cari, 1955). Dir: Orson Welles. Scr: Orson Welles. Cast: Orson Welles (Arkadin), Akim Tamiroff (Jakob), Gregoire Aslan (Bracco), Patricia Medina (Milly), Michael Redgrave (Burgomil). DVD, VHS.

3005. *Mr. Blandings Builds His Dream House* (Eric Hodgins, 1946). Comic story of the troubles encountered by an urban couple when they have a home built in the country. **Adaptation:** *Mr. Blandings Builds His Dream House* (RKO, 1948). Dir: H. C. Potter. Scr: Melvin Frank, Norman Panama. Cast: Cary Grant (Jim), Myrna Loy (Muriel), Melvyn Douglas (Bill), Reginald Denny (Simms). DVD, VHS.

3006. *Mr. Bridge* (Evan S. Connell, 1969). An aging Kansas City lawyer reflects back on his life in the 1930's and 1940's. **Adaptation:** *Mr. & Mrs. Bridge* (Miramax, 1990). Dir: James Ivory. Scr: Ruth Prawer Jhabvala. Cast: Paul Newman (Walter), Joanne Woodward (India), Blythe Danner (Grace), Simon Callow (Dr. Sauer), Kyra Sedgwick (Ruth). Notes: The screenplay is based on this novel and Connell's earlier book *Mrs. Bridge* (1959). Academy Award, Golden Globe, and Independent Spirit Award nominations for Best Actress (Woodward). DVD, VHS. See also *Mrs. Bridge.*

Mr. Buddwing (see *Buddwing*).

3007. *Mr. Bunting in Peace and War* (Robert Greenwood, 1941). The story of a patriotic Brtiish family during World War II. **Adaptation:** *Salute John Citizen* (Anglo-American, 1942). Dir: Maurice Elvey. Scr: Elizabeth Baron, Clemence Dane. Cast: Edward Rigby (Mr. Bunting), Mabel Constanduros (Mrs. Bunting), Jimmy Hanley (Ernest), Eric Micklewood (Chris).

Mr. Deeds (see "The Opera Hat").

Mr. Deeds Goes to Town (see "The Opera Hat").

3008. *Mr. Denning Drives North* (Alec Coppel, 1950). A wealthy businessman accidentally kills his daughter's unsavory boyfriend and hides the body. When the corpse disappears, he and his wife make inquiries. **Adaptation:** *Mr. Denning Drives North* (London/Carroll, 1952). Dir: Anthony Kimmins. Scr: Alec Coppel. Cast: John Mills (Tom), Phyllis Calvert (Kay), Eileen Moore (Liz), Sam Wanamaker (Chick), Herbert Lom (Mados).

Mr. Dodd Takes the Air (see *The Great Crooner*).

3009. *Mr. Emmanuel* (Louis Folding, 1939). An elderly Jewish man visits Nazi Germany just prior to World War II to search for the mother of an orphaned child and is shocked to see how his people are being treated there. **Adaptation:** *Mr. Emmanuel* (Two Cities/United Artists, 1944). Dir: Harold French. Scr: Louis Golding, Gordon Wellesley. Cast: Felix Aylmer (Mr. Emmanuel),

Greta Gynt (Elsie), Walter Rilla (Brockenburg), Peter Mullins (Bruno).

Mr. Forbush and the Penguins (see *Forbush and the Penguins*).

3010. *Mr. Hobbs' Vacation* (Edward Streeter, 1954). Comic tale of a harried man who wants to take a quiet vacation at the seashore with his family, but his wife wrecks his plans when she invites a large group of their relatives. **Adaptation:** *Mr. Hobbs Takes a Vacation* (20th Century–Fox, 1962). Dir: Henry Koster. Scr: Nunnally Johnson. Cast: James Stewart (Roger), Maureen O'Hara (Peggy), Fabian (Joe), John Saxon (Byron). VHS.

3011. *Mr. In-Between* (Neil Cross, 1998). A British hit man falls in love with a friend's wife, thereby compromising his loyalty to his secretive employer. **Adaptation:** *Mr. In-Between;* released on video in the U.S. as *The Killing Kind* (Verve, 2001). Dir: Paul Sarossy. Scr: Peter Waddington. Cast: Andrew Howard (Jon), Geraldine O'Rawe (Cathy), David Calder (the Tattooed Man), Andrew Tiernan (Andy). DVD, VHS.

3012. *Mister Johnson* (Joyce Cary, 1939). In West Afican in the 1920's, an educated and ambitious black man working for a British magistrate gets into trouble for the schemes he continually hatches. **Adaptation:** *Mister Johnson* (20th Century–Fox, 1990). Dir: Bruce Beresford. Scr: William Boyd. Cast: Maynard Eziashi (Johnson), Pierce Brosnan (Harry), Edward Woodward (Sargy), Beatie Edney (Celia). DVD, VHS.

3013. "Mr. Know-All" (W. Somerset Maugham, 1925). A talkative passenger on a luxury cruise annoys passengers until he becomes a hero. The story was first published in the January 1925 issue of *Cosmopolitan*. **Adaptation:** *Trio* (Gainsborough/Paramount, 1950). Dir: Ken Annakin, Harold French. Scr: W. Somerset Maugham, R. C. Sherriff, Noel Langley. Cast: Bill Travers (Fellowes), Naunton Wayne (Mr. Ramsey), Anne Crawford (Mrs. Ramsey), Wilfrid Hyde-White (Mr. Gray), Clive Morton (the Captain), Nigel Patrick (Kelada). Notes: This film was made following the success of the 1948 film *Quartet,* in which Maugham introduces four of his short stories. Here Maugham introduces three more stories: "Mr. Know-All," "The Sanitorium," and "The Verger." VHS.

3014. *Mr. Majestyk* (Elmore Leonard, 1974). A farmer takes violent action when brutal mobsters try to drive him off his land. **Adaptation:** *Mr. Majestyk* (United Artists, 1974). Dir: Richard Fleischer. Scr: Elmore Leonard. Cast: Charles

Bronson (Majestyk), Al Lettieri (Frank), Linda Cristal (Nancy). DVD, VHS.

3015. [*Mr.*] *Mister Moses* (Max Catto, 1961). A doctor in Africa warns a tribe about an impending flood and leads them to a new homeland. **Adaptation:** *Mister Moses* (United Artists, 1965). Dir: Ronald Neame. Scr: Charles Beaumont, Monja Danischewsky. Cast: Robert Mitchum (Moses), Carroll Baker (Julie), Ian Bannen (Robert), Alexander Knox (Reverend Anderson), Raymond St. Jacques (Ubi).

Mr. Moto in Danger Island (see *Murder in Trinidad*).

3016. *Mr. Murder* (Dean R. Koontz, 1993). Scientists produce a military assassin by cloning a mystery writer, who later discovers his murderous double. **Adaptation:** *Mr. Murder* (ABC, 1998 TV Miniseries). Dir: Dick Lowry. Scr: Stephen Tolkin. Cast: Stephen Baldwin (Marty/Alfie), Julie Warner (Paige), Bill Smitrovich (Lieutenant Lowbock), Thomas Haden Church (Drew, Jr.), James Coburn (Drew, Sr.). DVD, VHS.

Mr. North (see *Theophilus North*).

Mr. Peabody and the Mermaid (see *Peabody's Mermaid*).

3017. *Mr. Perrin and Mr. Traill* (Hugh Walpole, 1911). A popular young teacher with progressive ideas incurs the jealousy and vindictive wrath of an older colleague at a British boys' school. **Adaptation:** *Mr. Perrin and Mr. Traill* (Two Cities/Eagle-Lion, 1948). Dir: Lawrence Huntington. Scr: T. J. Morrison, L. A. G. Strong. Cast: David Farrar (David), Marius Goring (Vincent), Greta Gynt (Isabel).

3018. *Mr. Prohack* (Arnold Bennett, 1922). Comic story of an efficient treasury official who has problems managing his own finances. Bennett and Edward Knoblock adapted the novel as a play in 1927. **Adaptation:** *Dear Mr. Prohack* (1949). Dir: Thornton Freeland. Scr: Donald Bull, Ian Dalrymple. Cast: Cecil Parker (Arthur), Glynis Johns (Mimi), Hermione Baddeley (Eve), Dirk Bogarde (Charles). VHS.

3019. *Mr. Pye* (Mervyn Peake, 1953). Comic fantasy about an elderly man who goes to a mysterious island and sprouts angel's wings. Suspecting that the cause is his lifelong habit of being good, he tries to become evil. **Adaptation:** *Mr. Pye* (Lanseer, 1986 TV Miniseries). Dir: Michael Darlow. Scr: David Churchill. Cast: Derek Jacobi (Mr. Pye), Judy Parfitt (Miss Dredger), Patricia Hayes (Kaka), Betty Marsden (Miss George).

Mr. Quilp (see *The Old Curiosity Shop*).

Mr. Reeder in Room 13 (see *Room 13*).

3020. [*Mr.*] *Mister Roberts* (Thomas Heggen, 1946). The restless sailors aboard a cargo ship during World War II are eager to engage the enemy. The novel was adapted as a hit 1948 Broadway play by Heggen and Joshua Logan. **Adaptation 1:** *Mister Roberts* (Warner, 1955). Dir: John Ford, Mervyn Le Roy. Scr: Joshua Logan, Frank Nugent. Cast: Henry Fonda (Roberts), James Cagney (Captain Morton), William Powell (Doc), Jack Lemmon (Pulver), Betsy Palmer (Ann). Notes: Academy Award for Best Supporting Actor (Lemmon), and nominations for Best Picture and Sound. DVD, VHS. **Adaptation 2:** *Mister Roberts* (NBC, 1984 TV Movie). Dir: Melvin Bernhardt. Scr: Thomas Heggen, Joshua Logan (1948 play). Cast: Robert Hays (Roberts), Kevin Bacon (Pulver), Charles Durning (Captain Morton), Marilu Henner (Ann), Howard Hesseman (Doc). Notes: A sequel, *Ensign Pulver,* directed by Joshua Logan, was released in 1964 (VHS). In addition, the book and film also inspired a 1965 television series.

3021. *Mr. Skeffington* (Elizabeth Von Armin, 1940). After experiencing various hardships, a once beautiful woman is reunited with her estranged husband who is now blind. **Adaptation:** *Mr. Skeffington* (1944). Dir: Vincent Sherman. Scr: Julius J. Epstein, Philip G. Epstein. Cast: Bette Davis (Fanny), Claude Rains (Job), Walter Abel (George). Notes: Academy Award nominations for Best Actress (Davis) and Actor (Rains). VHS.

Mr. Skitch (*see* "Green Dice").

[*Mr.*] *Mister V* (see *The Scarlet Pimpernel*).

3022. *Mrs. 'arris Goes to Paris* (Paul Gallico, 1958). The comic adventures of a London charwoman who saves her money and travels to Paris to buy a designer dress. **Adaptation:** *Mrs. 'arris Goes to Paris* (Corymore, 1992 TV Movie). Dir: Anthony Shaw. Scr: John Hawkesworth. Cast: Angela Lansbury (Ada), Diana Rigg (Madame Colbert), Omar Sharif (Marquis Hippolite). VHS.

3023. *Mrs. Bridge* (Evan S. Connell, 1959). A story about a conservative Kansas City couple and the changes they've been through as they raised their five children in the 1930s and 1940s. **Adaptation:** *Mr. & Mrs. Bridge* (Miramax, 1990). Dir: James Ivory. Scr: Ruth Prawer Jhabvala. Cast:

Paul Newman (Walter), Joanne Woodward (India), Blythe Danner (Grace), Simon Callow (Dr. Sauer), Kyra Sedgwick (Ruth). Notes: The screenplay is based on this novel and Connell's later book *Mr. Bridge* (1969). Academy Award, Golden Globe, and Independent Spirit Award nominations for Best Actress (Woodward). DVD, VHS. See also *Mr. Bridge.*

3024. *Mrs. Caldicot's Cabbage War* (Vernon Coleman, 1993). A feisty widow leads her fellow residents in a nursing home in a protest against inhumane conditions. **Adaptation:** *Mrs. Caldicot's Cabbage War* (Evolution, 2000). Dir: Ian Sharp. Scr: Malcolm Stone. Cast: Pauline Collins (Thelma), Peter Capaldi (Derek), Anna Wilson-Jones (Veronica). DVD, VHS.

3025. *Mrs. Christopher* (Elizabeth Myers, 1946). The victims of a blackmailer are suspected of his murder. **Adaptation:** *Blackmailed* (Bell Pictures, 1950). Dir: Marc Allegret. Scr: Roger Vadim. Cast: Mai Zetterling (Carol), Dirk Bogarde (Stephen), Fay Compton (Mrs. Christopher).

3026. *Mrs. Dalloway* (Virginia Woolf, 1925). On a single day in 1923, Clarissa Dalloway reflects on her life and loves. Having chosen a safe and secure life, she wonders what might have been if she had chosen the passionate man she gave up in favor of her conservative husband. **Adaptation:** *Mrs. Dalloway* (BBC/First Look, 1997). Dir: Marleen Gorris. Scr: Eileen Atkins. Cast: Vanessa Redgrave (Clarissa), Natascha McElhone (Clarissa as a young woman), Michael Kitchen (Peter), Sarah Badel (Sally), John Standing (Richard). DVD, VHS. See also *The Hours.*

Mrs. Doubtfire (see *Alias Mrs. Doubtfire*).

3027. *Mrs. Frisby and the Rats of NIMH* (Robert C. O'Brien, 1971, Newbery Medal). Children's story about a widowed field mouse who, to save her sick son, seeks the aid of a wise owl and a society of intelligent rats. Together they thwart plans by land developers to tear down the mouse family's home. **Adaptation:** *The Secret of NIMH* (United Artists, 1982). Dir: Don Bluth. Scr: Don Bluth, Will Finn, Gary Goldman, John Pomeroy. Cast: Derek Jacobi (Nicodemus), Elizabeth Hartman (Mrs. Brisby), Arthur Malet (Mr. Ages), Dom De Luise (Jeremy), Hermione Baddeley (Auntie Shrew), Shannen Doherty (Teresa), Wil Wheaton (Martin). DVD, VHS. Notes: A video sequel, *The Secret of NIMH 2: Timmy to the Rescue,* was released in 1998 (DVD, VHS).

3028. *Mrs. McGinty's Dead* (Agatha Christie, 1952). After a man is convicted and sentenced to death for the murder of a London charwoman, Hercule Poirot looks into the case and concludes that someone else committed the murder. **Adaptation:** *Murder Most Foul* (MGM, 1964). Dir: George Pollock. Scr: David Pursall, Jack Seddon. Cast: Margaret Rutherford (Miss Marple), Ron Moody (Cosgood), Charles Tingwell (Inspector Craddock). Notes: In this adaptation, Christie's amateur sleuth Miss Jane Marple is substituted for Poirot. VHS.

3029. *Mrs. Miniver* (Jan Struther, 1940). The trials of a middle-class British family during World War II. **Adaptation 1:** *Mrs. Miniver* (MGM, 1942). Dir: William Wyler. Scr: George Froeschel, James Hilton, Claudine West, Arthur Wimperis. Cast: Greer Garson (Kay), Walter Pidgeon (Clem), Teresa Wright (Carol), May Whitty (Lady Beldon), Reginald Owen (Foley), Henry Travers (Ballard). Notes: Academy Awards for Best Picture, Director, Screenplay, Actress (Garson), Supporting Actress (Wright), and Cinematography, and nominations for Best Actor (Pidgeon), Supporting Actress (Whitty), Supporting Actor (Travers), Editing, Special Effects, and Sound. DVD, VHS. Notes: A sequel, *The Miniver Story,* was released in 1950 (VHS). **Adaptation 2:** *Mrs. Miniver* (CBS, 1960 TV Movie). Dir: Marc Daniels. Scr: Marc Daniels. Cast: Maureen O'Hara (Kay), Leo Genn (Clem), Kathleen Nesbitt (Lady Beldon), Juliet Mills (Carol).

3030. *Mrs. Munck* (Ella Leffland, 1985). Former lovers meet accidentally on a street and plot revenge on the woman's cruel handicapped husband. **Adaptation:** *Mrs. Munck* (Republic, 1995). Dir: Diane Ladd. Scr: Diane Ladd. Cast: Diane Ladd (Rose), Bruce Dern (Patrick), Kelly Preston (Rose as a young woman), Shelley Winters (Aunt Monica). VHS.

3031. *Mrs. Parkington* (Louis Bromfield, 1943). A wealthy society woman recalls her earlier life as a maid and the opportunities and challenges she faced along the way. **Adaptation:** *Mrs. Parkington* (MGM, 1944). Dir: Tay Garnett. Scr: Polly James, Robert Thoeren. Cast: Greer Garson (Susie), Walter Pidgeon (Gus), Edward Arnold (Amory), Agnes Moorehead (Aspasia), Cecil Kellaway (Edward, Prince of Wales). Notes: Academy Award nominations for Best Actress (Garson) and Supporting Actress (Moorehead); Golden Globe Award for Best Supporting Actress (Moorehead). VHS.

Mrs. Pollifax — Spy (see *The Unexpected Mrs. Pollifax*).

Mrs. Pym of Scotland Yard (see *Murder in Wardour Street*).

3032. *Mrs. White* (Margaret Tracy [pseudonym for Andrew Klavan and Laurence Klavan], 1983, Edgar Award). A husband and father in a small Arizona town is actually a serial killer of women. **Adaptation:** *White of the Eye* (Palisades, 1987). Dir: Donald Cammell. Scr: Donald Cammell, China Cammell. Cast: David Keith (Paul), Cathy Moriarty (Joan), Alan Rosenberg (Mike), Art Evans (Detective Mendoza). VHS.

3033. *Mrs. Wiggs of the Cabbage Patch* (Alice Hegan Rice, 1901). A woman in a poor section of Louisville tries to raise her brood of children and awaits the return of her missing husband. The novel was adapted as a 1904 Broadway play by Anne Crawford Flexner. **Silent Films:** 1914 and 1919. **Adaptation 1:** *Mrs. Wiggs of the Cabbage Patch* (Paramount, 1934). Dir: Norman Taurog. Scr: William Slavens McNutt, Jane Storm. Cast: Pauline Lord (Elvira), W. C. Fields (Mr. Stubbins), Zasu Pitts (Tabitha), Evelyn Venable (Lucy). **Adaptation 2:** *Mrs. Wiggs of the Cabbage Patch* (Paramount, 1942). Dir: Ralph Murphy. Scr: Doris Anderson. Cast: Fay Bainter (Elvira), Carolyn Lee (Europena), Hugh Herbert (Throckmorton).

Mrs. Winterbourne (see *I Married a Dead Man*).

3034. *Mud on the Stars* (William Bradford Huie, 1942). Autobiographical novel about the Depression-era South and its resistance to President Franklin Roosevelt's New Deal policies. **Adaptation:** *Wild River* (20th Century–Fox, 1960). Dir: Elia Kazan. Scr: Paul Osborn. Cast: Montgomery Clift (Chuck), Lee Remick (Carol), Jo Van Fleet (Ella), Albert Salmi (Hank). Notes: The screenplay combines elements from Borden Deal's *Dunbar's Cove* and William Bradford Huie's *Mud on the Stars*. See also *Dunbar's Cove*.

3035. *The Mudlark* (Theodore Bonnet, 1949). A young street dweller breaks into Windsor Castle to meet Queen Victoria and helps her break her seclusion following the death of her husband. **Adaptation:** *The Mudlark* (20th Century–Fox, 1950). Dir: Jean Negulesco. Scr: Nunnally Johnson. Cast: Irene Dunne (Queen Victoria), Alec Guinness (Benjamin Disraeli), Andrew Ray (Wheeler).

3036. *The Mugger* (Ed McBain [pseudonym for Evan Hunter], 1956. New York police search for a killer who mugs female victims at night, steals their purses, and leaves ritualistic slashings on their faces. **Adaptation:** *The Mugger* (United Artists, 1958). Dir: William Berke. Scr: Henry Kane. Cast: Kent Smith (Pete), Nan Martin (Claire), James Franciscus (Eddie), Stefan Schnabel (Fats).

Mulan (see *Fa Mulan*).

3037. *A Mule for Marquesa* (Frank O'Rourke, 1964). Western about a wealthy Texan who hires four men to rescue his wife who has been kidnapped by Mexican revolutionaries. **Adaptation:** *The Professionals* (Columbia, 1966). Dir: Richard Brooks. Scr: Richard Brooks. Cast: Burt Lancaster (Bill), Lee Marvin (Rico), Robert Ryan (Hans), Woody Strode (Jake), Jack Palance (Jesus), Claudia Cardinale (Maria), Ralph Bellamy (Joe), Marie Gomez (Chiquita). Notes: Academy Award nominations for Best Director, Screenplay, and Cinematography; Golden Globe nominations for Best Picture and Newcomer (Gomez). DVD, VHS.

3038. *The Mummy Market* (Nancy Brelis, 1966). Children's book about three youngsters who cast a magical spell and change mothers, discovering that the nagging one they already have is the best mother to them. **Adaptation:** *Trading Mom* (Trimark, 1994). Dir: Tia Brelis. Scr: Tia Brelis. Cast: Sissy Spacek (Mommy Martin), Anna Chlumsky (Elizabeth), Aaron Michael Metchik (Jeremy), Asher Metchik (Harry). Notes: Nearly thirty years after it was published, Tia Brelis adapted her mother's book for the screen, DVD, VHS.

Munchausen (see *The Adventures of Baron Munchausen*).

Murder! (see *Enter Sir John*).

Murder at the Baskervilles (*see* "Silver Blaze").

Murder at the Gallop (see *After the Funeral*).

3039. *Murder at the Mendel* (Gail Bowen, 1991). When an old friend is the prime suspect in the murder of her ex-husband, a former police detective turned college teacher investigates this crime and another murder involving her friend years earlier. The Canadian novel was published in the U.S. in 1993 under the title *Love and Murder*. **Adaptation:** *Love and Murder* (Carlton America, 2000 TV Movie). Dir: George Bloomfield. Scr: Rob Forsyth, R. B. Carney. Cast: Wendy Crewson (Joanne), Victor Garber (Inspector Millard), Caroline Goodall (Sally), Claire Bloom (Nina), Kenneth Welsh (Isaak).

3040. *Murder at the PTA Luncheon* (Valerie Wolzien, 1988). When the imperious head of a Connecticut PTA group is murdered at a luncheon, an idealistic housewife helps detectives find the killer. **Adaptation:** *Menu for Murder* (CBS, 1990 TV Movie). Dir: Larry Peerce. Scr: Duane Poole, Tom Swale. Cast: Julia Duffy (Susan), Morgan Fairchild (Paula), Ed Marinaro (Detective Russo), Cindy Williams (Connie), Joan Van Ark (Mrs. Alberts).

3041. *Murder by the Clock* (Rufus King, 1929). Suspicious of her relatives, a rich old woman builds a tomb from which she can escape if they bury her alive. The book was adapted as a play in 1929 by Charles Beachan. **Adaptation:** *Murder by the Clock* (Paramount, 1931). Dir: Edward Sloman. Scr: Charles Beahan, Rufus King, Henry Myers. Cast: William Boyd (Lieutenant Valcour), Lilyan Tashman (Laura), Irving Pichel (Philip), Regis Toomey (Officer Cassidy).

3042. *The Murder at the Vicarage* (Agatha Christie, 1930). In the first of Christie's novels featuring amateur sleuth Miss Jane Marple, a vicar and his wife are prime suspects in a man's murder. The novel was adapted as a stage play by Moie Charles and Barbara Toy in 1949. **Adaptation 1:** *The Murder at the Vicarage* (BBC/A&E, 1986 TV Movie series). Dir: Julian Amyes. Scr: T. R. Bowen. Cast: Joan Hickson (Miss Marple), Paul Eddington (Reverend Clement), Cheryl Campbell (Griselda), Robert Lang (Colonel Protheroe). Notes: BAFTA TV Award nomination for Best Actress (Hickson). DVD, VHS. **Adaptation 2:** *Marple: The Murder at the Vicarage* (ITV, 2004 TV Movie series). Dir: Charles Palmer. Scr: Stephen Churchett. Cast: Geraldine McEwan (Miss Marple), Tim McInnerny (Reverend Clement), Rachael Stirling (Griselda), Derek Jacobi (Colonel Protheroe). DVD, VHS.

3043. *Murder Goes to College* (Kurt Steel [pseudonym for Rudolf Kagey], 1936). A journalist on vacation helps to solve a murder on a college campus. **Adaptation:** *Murder Goes to College* (Paramount, 1937). Dir: Charles Reisner. Scr: Brian Marlow, Eddie Welch, Robert Wyler. Cast: Roscoe Karns (Perkins), Marsha Hunt (Nora), Lynne Overman (Hank).

3044. *Murder in Amityville* (Hans Holzer, 1979). True story that serves as the prequel to Jay Anson's 1977 book *The Amityville Horror*. A family moves into a Long Island home built over an ancient Indian burial group, and the father, possessed of evil spirits, murders his family. **Adaptation:** *Amityville II: The Possession* (Orion, 1982). Dir: Damiano Damiani. Scr: Tommy Lee Wallace. Cast: James Olson (Father Adamsky), Burt Young (Anthony), Rutanya Alda (Dolores), Jack Magner (Sonny), Andrew Prine (Father Tom). DVD, VHS. See also *The Amityville Curse, The Amityville Horror,* and *Amityville: The Evil Escapes.*

3045. *Murder in Greenwich: Who Killed Martha Moxley?* (Mark Fuhrman and Dominick Dunne, 1998). Furhman's investigation of the 1975 murder of Greenwich, Connecticut, teen Martha Moxley for which Kennedy cousin Michael Skakel was ultimately convicted. **Adaptation:** *Murder in Greenwich* (USA Networks, 2002 TV Movie). Dir: Tom McLoughlin. Scr: Dave Erickson. Cast: Christopher Meloni (Mark Fuhrman), Robert Forster (Steve), Maggie Grace (Martha Martha), Toby Moore (Tommy Skakel), Jon Foster (Michael Skakel). DVD, VHS.

3046. *Murder in Mesopotamia* (Agatha Christie, 1936). Hercule Poirot solves the murder of an archaeologist's wife in the Middle East. **Adaptation:** *Murder in Mesopotamia* (London Weekend?A&E, 2001 TV Movie series). Dir: Tom Clegg. Scr: Clive Exton. Cast: David Suchet (Poirot), Ron Berglas (Dr. Leidner), Dinah Stabb (Anne), Hugh Fraser (Hastings). DVD, VHS.

Murder in Three Acts (see *Three-Act Tragedy*).

3047. *Murder in Trinidad* (John W. Vandercook, 1933). Investigator Bertram Lynch looks into the disappearance of geologists in the Caribbean. **Adaptation 1:** *Murder In Trinidad* (Fox, 1934). Dir: Louis King. Scr: Seton I. Miller. Cast: Nigel Bruce (Lynch), Heather Angel (Joan), Victor Jory (Howard). **Adaptation 2:** *Mr. Moto in Danger Island;* also released as *Danger Island* (20th Century–Fox, 1939). Dir: Herbert I. Leeds. Scr: Peter Milne. Cast: Peter Lorre (Moto), Warren Hymer (Twister), Amanda Duff (Joan). Note: John Marquand's character Mr. Moto, a Chinese investigator, is substituted for Bertram Lynch in this screenplay. **Adaptation 3:** *The Caribbean Mystery* (20th Century–Fox, 1945). Dir: Robert Webb. Scr: Jack Andrews, Leonard Praskins. Cast: James Dunn (Mr. Smith), Sheila Ryan (Mrs. Gilbert), Edward Ryan (Gerald).

3048. *Murder in Wardour Street* (Nigel Morland, 1939). In the first in a series of mystery novels featuring a female Scotland Yard detective, Mrs. Pym is on the trail of a fake psychic. **Adaptation:** *Mrs. Pym of Scotland Yard* (Grand National, 1940). Dir: Fred Ellis. Scr: Peggy Barwell, Fred Ellis, Nigel Morland. Cast: Mary Clare (Mrs. Pym), Edward Lexy (Inspector Shott), Nigel Patrick (Richard).

3049. *A Murder Is Announced* (Agatha Christie, 1950). A newspaper in a small English town carries an ad announcing a forthcoming murder. People assume it is a party game, but when a real homicide occurs, Miss Jane Marple arrives to investigate. The novel was adapted as a stage play by Leslie Darbon in 1977. **Adaptation 1:** *A Murder Is Announced* (BBC/PBS, 1985 TV Movie series). Dir: David Giles. Scr: Alan Plater. Cast: Joan Hickson (Miss Marple), Ursula Howells (Lettie), Renee Asherson (Dora), Samantha Bond (Julia), Simon Shepherd (Patrick). DVD, VHS. **Adaptation 2:** *Marple: A Murder Is Announced* (ITV, 2005 TV Movie series). Dir: John Strickland. Scr: Stewart Harcourt. Cast: Geraldine McEwan (Miss Marple), Christian Coulson (Edmund), Cherie Lunghi (Sadie), Robert Pugh (Colonel Easterbrook), Keeley Hawes (Philippa), Zoe Wanamaker (Letitia). DVD, VHS.

3050. *Murder Is Easy* (Agatha Christie, 1939). A retired British policeman meets an old woman on a train who insists that people are being murdered in her village. He doubts the story until the old woman herself is killed, and then he goes to her town to investigate. The novel was released in the U.S. under the title *Easy to Kill*. **Adaptation:** *Murder Is Easy* (CBS, 1982 TV Movie). Dir: Claude Whatham. Scr: Carmen Culver. Cast: Bill Bixby (Luke), Lesley-Anne Down (Bridget), Olivia de Havilland (Honoria), Helen Hayes (Lavinia). Notes: The teleplay makes the investigator an American tourist in London rather than a retired detective. VHS.

Murder Is My Business (see *The Uncomplaining Corpse*).

Murder Most Foul (see *Mrs. McGinty's Dead*).

Murder, My Sweet (see *Farewell, My Lovely*).

3051. *The Murder of Bob Crane* (Robert Graysmith, 1993). Biography of Bob Crane (1928–1978), the popular television's *Hogan's Heroes*, focusing on his relationship with sex videographer John Carpenter and on his sexual addiction which led to his mysterious death in a Scottsdale, Arizona, motel room in 1978. **Adaptation:** *Auto Focus* (Sony, 2002). Dir: Paul Schrader. Scr: Michael Gerbosi. Cast: Greg Kinnear (Crane), Willem Dafoe (Carpenter), Rita Wilson (Anne), Maria Bello (Patricia/Sigrid), Ron Leibman (Lenny). DVD, VHS.

The Murder of Dr. Harrigan (see *From This Dark Stairway*).

3052. *Murder of Innocence: The Tragic Life and Final Rampage of Laurie Dann, "The Schoolhouse Killer"* (Joel Kaplan, George Papajohn and Eric Zorn, 1990). The true story of a shy Illinois woman whose psychosis caused her to go on a shooting spree at a suburban elementary school. **Adaptation:** *Murder of Innocence* (CBS, 1993 TV Movie). Dir: Tom McLoughlin. Scr: Philip Rosenberg. Cast: Valerie Bertinelli (Laurie Wade), Stephen Caffrey (Matthew Wade), Graham Beckel (Detective Frank Kendall).

3053. *The Murder of Roger Ackroyd* (Agatha Christie, 1926). Living in the countryside, Hercule Poirot investigates the murder of a wealthy industrialist. The novel was adapted by Michael Morton as the play *Alibi* in 1928, retitled *The Fatal Alibi* for its New York run. **Adaptation 1:** *Alibi* (Twickenham, 1931). Dir: Leslie Hiscott. Scr: H. Fowler Mear. Cast: Austin Trevor (Poirot), Franklin Dyall (Sir Roger Ackroyd). **Adaptation 2:** *The Murder of Roger Ackroyd* (BBC, 2000 TV Movie series). Dir: Andrew Grieve. Scr: Clive Exton. Cast: David Suchet (Poirot), Philip Jackson (Inspector Japp), Oliver Ford Davies (Dr. Sheppard), Selina Cadell (Caroline). DVD, VHS.

Murder on a Bridle Path (see *The Puzzle of the Red Stallion*).

Murder on a Honeymoon (see *The Puzzle of the Pepper Tree*).

Murder on Diamond Row (see *The Squeakers*).

Murder on the Bridge (see *The Judge and His Hangman*).

3054. *Murder on the Links* (Agatha Christie, 1923). A wealthy man is found stabbed to death on the golf course on his estate, and Hercule Poirot discovers that everyone in his family had a motive for killing him. **Adaptation:** *Murder on the Links* (London Weekend Television, 1995 TV Movie series). Dir: Andrew Grieve. Scr: Anthony Horowitz. Cast: David Suchet (Poirot), Hugh Fraser (Hastings), Diane Fletcher (Eloise), Damien Thomas (Paul). DVD, VHS.

3055. *Murder on the Orient Express* (Agatha Christie, 1934). Christie's Hercule Poirot investigates a murder that occurs on a snowbound train on which he is riding. **Adaptation 1:** *Murder on the Orient Express* (Paramount, 1974). Dir: Sidney Lumet. Scr: Paul Dehn. Cast: Albert Finney (Poirot), Lauren Bacall (Harriet), Martin Balsam (Signor Bianchi), Ingrid Bergman (Greta), Jacqueline Bisset (Countess Andrenyi), Jean-

Pierre Cassel (Pierre), Sean Connery (Colonel Arbuthnot), John Gielgud (Mr. Beddoes), Wendy Hiller (Princess Dragomiroff), Anthony Perkins (MacQueen), Vanessa Redgrave (Mary), Rachel Roberts (Hildegarde), Richard Widmark (Ratchett/Cassetti), Michael York (Count Andrenyi). Notes: BAFTA Awards for Best Supporting Actor (Gielgud), Supporting Actress (Bergman), and Musical Score, and nominations for Best Film, Director, Actor (Finney), Cinematography, Art Direction, Editing, and Costume Design; Academy Award nominations for Best Screenplay, Actor (Finney), Musical Score, Cinematography, and Costume Design. DVD, VHS. **Adaptation 2:** *Murder on the Orient Express* (MediaVest, 2001 TV Movie). Dir: Carl Schenkel. Scr: Stephen Harrigan. Cast: Alfred Molina (Poirot), Meredith Baxter (Caroline), Leslie Caron (Mrs. Alvarado), Peter Strauss (Mr. Ratchett).

Murder She Said (see *4.50 from Paddington*).

3056. *Murder Under Two Flags: The U.S., Puerto Rico, and the Cerro Maravilla Cover-Up* (Anne Nelson, 1986). Factual account of an American journalist looking into the FBI-assisted murder of two leftist radicals in Puerto Rico in 1978. **Adaptation:** *A Show of Force* (Paramount, 1990). Dir: Bruno Barreto. Scr: Evan Jones, John Strong. Cast: Amy Irving (Kate), Andy Garcia (Luis), Lou Diamond Phillips (Jesus), Robert Duvall (Howard), Kevin Spacey (Frank), Erik Estrada (Machado). DVD, VHS.

Murder with Mirrors (see *They Do It with Mirrors*).

3057. *Murderers' Row* (Donald Hamilton, 1962). In the fifth of Hamilton's twenty-six Matt Helm spy novels (1960–1993), the spy and assassin fakes his own death so that he can go undercover to find the kidnapped inventor of a powerful weapon. **Adaptation:** *Murderers' Row* (Columbia, 1966). Dir: Henry Levin. Scr: Herbert Baker. Cast: Dean Martin (Helm), Ann-Margret (Suzie), Karl Malden (Julian), Camilla Sparv (Coco), James Gregory (MacDonald), Beverly Adams (Lovey). VHS.

3058. *The Murders in Praed Street* (John Rhode, 1928). A prisoner escapes from prison and seeks vengeance on the jurors who convicted him. **Adaptation:** *Twelve Good Men* (Warner, 1936). Dir: Ralph Ince. Scr: Sidney Gilliat, Frank Launder. Cast: Henry Kendall (Charles), Nancy O'Neil (Ann), Joyce Kennedy (Lady Thora), Bernard Miles (Inspector Pine).

3059. "The Murders in the Rue Morgue" (Edgar Allan Poe, 1841). Widely considered the first detective story ever written, the short story concerns a French detective who discovers that a series of brutal murders is linked to a scientist's experiments on an ape. It was first published in *Graham's Magazine* in Philadelphia on April 1, 1841. **Silent Film:** 1914. **Adaptation 1:** *Murders in the Rue Morgue* (Universal, 1932). Dir: Robert Florey. Scr: Tom Reed, Dale Van Every, John Huston. Cast: Sidney Fox (Camille), Bela Lugosi (Dr. Mirakle), Leon Ames (Pierre Dupin). VHS. **Adaptation 2:** *Phantom of the Rue Morgue* (Warner, 1954). Dir: Roy Del Ruth. Scr: Harold Medford, James R. Webb. Cast: Karl Malden (Dr. Marais), Claude Dauphin (Bonnard), Patricia Medina (Jeanette), Steve Forrest (Dupin). VHS. **Adaptation 3:** *Murders in the Rue Morgue* (American International, 1971). Dir: Gordon Hessler. Scr: Christopher Wicking, Henry Slesar. Cast: Jason Robards (Charron), Herbert Lom (Marot), Christine Kaufmann (Madeleine), Adolfo Celi (Vidocq). DVD, VHS. **Adaptation 4:** *The Murders in the Rue Morgue* (Halmi/Vidmark, 1986 TV Movie). Dir: Jeannot Szwarc. Scr: David Epstein. Cast: George C. Scott (Dupin), Rebecca De Mornay (Claire), Ian McShane (Prefect of Police), Val Kilmer (Huron). VHS.

3060. *Murphy's War* (Max Catto, 1969). Near the end of World War II, the sole survivor of a German U-boat attack on a British ship plots revenge on the submarine. **Adaptation:** *Murphy's War* (Paramount, 1971). Dir: Peter Yates. Scr: Stirling Silliphant. Cast: Peter O'Toole (Murphy), Sian Phillips (Dr. Hayden), Philippe Noiret (Brezon). DVD, VHS.

3061. *Muscle Beach* (Ira Wallach, 1959). Comic novel about a man involved in an accident with a rich woman whose husband gives him a job as a swimming-pool salesman. **Adaptation:** *Don't Make Waves* (MGM, 1967). Dir: Alexander Mackendrick. Scr: George Kirgo, Maurice Richlin, Ira Wallach. Cast: Tony Curtis (Carlo), Claudia Cardinale (Laura), Robert Webber (Rod), Joanna Barnes (Diane), Sharon Tate (Malibu). VHS.

3062. "The Musgrave Ritual" (Arthur Conan Doyle, 1893). Sherlock Holmes investigates a series of murders at a home for retired military officers. The short story was published in England in *The Strand* (May 1893) and in the U.S. in *Harper's Weekly* (May 13, 1893) and included in Doyle's 1894 collection *The Memoirs of Sherlock Holmes*. **Adaptation:** *Sherlock Holmes Faces Death*

(Universal, 1943). Dir: Roy William Neill. Scr: Bertram Millhauser. Cast: Basil Rathbone (Holmes), Nigel Bruce (Watson), Dennis Hoey (Inspector Lestrade), Arthur Margetson (Dr. Sexton). Notes: The action us updated to World War II. DVD, VHS.

The Music Lovers (see *Beloved Friend*).

3063. *The Music of Chance* (Paul Auster, 1990). After losing at a card game to two old millionaires, two men agree to construct an elaborate wall on their estate. **Adaptation:** *The Music of Chance* (IRS Media, 1993). Dir: Philip Haas. Scr: Belinda Haas, Philip Haas. Cast: James Spader (Jack), Mandy Patinkin (Jim), M. Emmet Walsh (Calvin), Charles Durning (Flower), Joel Grey (Willy). DVD, VHS.

The Musketeer (see *The Three Musketeers*).

3064. *Mute Witness* (Robert L. Pike [pseudonym for Robert L. Fish], 1963). San Francisco detective Frank Bullitt searches for the mobsters who killed a witness under his protection. **Adaptation:** *Bullitt* (Warner-Seven Arts, 1968). Dir: Peter Yates. Scr: Alan Trustman, Harry Kleiner. Cast: Steve McQueen (Bullitt), Robert Vaughn (Chalmers), Jacqueline Bisset (Cathy), Don Gordon (Delgetti), Robert Duvall (Weissberg), Simon Oakland (Bennett), Norman Fell (Baker). DVD, VHS.

3065. *Mutiny* (Frank Tilsey, 1958). A mutinous crew takes over the British warship *Defiant* during the Napoleonic Wars of the eighteenth century. **Adaptation:** *H. M. S. Defiant;* released in the U.S. as *Damn the Defiant!* (Columbia, 1962). Dir: Lewis Gilbert. Scr: Nigel Kneale, Edmund H. North. Cast: Alec Guinness (Captain Crawford), Dirk Bogarde (Scott-Padget), Maurice Denham (Goss), Nigel Stock (Kilpatrick). DVD, VHS.

3066. *The Mutiny of the Elsinore* (Jack London, 1914). A journalist doing a story on a merchant ship finds himself in the middle of a mutiny. **Silent Film:** 1920. **Adaptation:** *The Mutiny of the Elsinore* (Associated British/Regal, 1937). Dir: Roy Lockwood. Scr: Walter Summers, Beaufoy Milton. Cast: Lyn Harding (Mr. Pike), Paul Lukas (Jack), Kathleen Kelly (Margaret).

3067. *Mutiny on the Bounty* (Charles Nordhoff and James Norman Hall, 1932). On a trip to Tahiti, a tyrannical sea captain's crew turns against him and casts him adrift. **Adaptation 1:** *Mutiny on the Bounty* (MGM, 1935). Dir: Frank Lloyd. Scr: Talbot Jennings, Jules Furthman, Carey Wilson. Cast: Charles Laughton (Captain Bligh), Clark Gable (Fletcher Christian), Franchot Tone (Byam), Herbert Mundin (Smith), Eddie Quillan (Ellison). Notes: Academy Award for Best Picture and nominations for Best Director, Screenplay, Actors (Laughton, Gable, and Tone), Musical Score, and Editing. DVD, VHS. **Adaptation 2:** *Mutiny on the Bounty* (MGM, 1962). Dir: Lewis Milestone. Scr: Charles Lederer. Cast: Marlon Brando (Fletcher Christian), Trevor Howard (Captain Bligh), Richard Harris (Mills), Hugh Griffith (Smith). Notes: Academy Award nominations for Best Picture, Musical Score, Song, Art Direction, Cinematography, Special Effects, and Editing; Golden Globe nomination for Best Film. VHS. See also *Captain Bligh and Mr. Christian.*

3068. *My Antonia* (Willa Cather, 1918). The struggles of a young immigrant girl in rural Nebraska in the late nineteenth century. **Adaptation:** *My Antonia* (USA Networks, 1995 TV Movie). Dir: Joseph Sargent. Scr: Victoria Riskin. Cast: Elina Lowensohn (Antonia), Neil Patrick Harris (Jimmy), Jason Robards (Grandfather), Eva Marie Saint (Grandmother). VHS.

3069. *My Autobiography* (Charles Chaplin, 1964). Autobiography of the comic genius from the time of his birth in London in 1889 through the early 1960's. **Adaptation:** *Chaplin* (TriStar, 1992). Dir: Richard Attenborough. Scr: William Boyd, Bryan Forbes, William Goldman. Cast: Robert Downey, Jr. (Chaplin), Geraldine Chaplin (Hannah), Paul Rhys (Sydney), Anthony Hopkins (Hayden), Dan Aykroyd (Mack Sennett), Marisa Tomei (Mabel Normand), Kevin Kline (Douglas Fairbanks). Notes: Academy Award nominations for Best Actor (Downey), Musical Score, and Art Direction; Golden Globe nominations for Best Actor (Downey), Supporting Actress (Chaplin), and Musical Score. Notes: The screenplay is based on Chaplin's autobiography and David Robinson's 1985 book *Chaplin: His Life and Art.* DVD, VHS. See also *Chaplin: His Life and Art.*

3070. *My Breast: One Woman's Cancer Story* (Joyce Wadler, 1992). Factual account of the radical changes that a New York writer underwent when she discovered that she had breast cancer. **Adaptation:** *My Breast* (CBS, 1994 TV Movie). Dir: Betty Thomas. Scr: Joyce Wadler. Cast: Meredith Baxter (Joyce), Jamey Sheridan (Nick), James Sutorius (Herb), Sara Botsford (Eve).

3071. *My Brilliant Career* (Miles Franklin, 1901). The story of a headstrong Australian girl who aspires to be a writer and is willing to endure hardship to realize her goal. **Adaptation:** *My Brilliant Career* (Analysis, 1979). Dir: Gillian Armstrong. Scr: Eleanor Witcombe. Cast: Judy Davis (Sybylla), Sam Neill (Harry), Wendy Hughes (Aunt Helen), Robert Grubb (Frank), Max Cullen (Mr. McSwatt), Aileen Britton (Grandma Bossier), Peter Whitford (Uncle Julius), Patricia Kennedy (Aunt Gussie). Notes: Australian Film Institute Awards for Best Film, Director, Screenplay, Cinematography, Production Design, and Costume Design, and nominations for Best Actress (Davis), Supporting Actor (Grubb), and Supporting Actresses (Britton, Hughes, and Kennedy); BAFTA Awards for Best Actress (Davis) and Newcomer (Davis); Academy Award nomination for Best Costume Design; Cannes Film Festival Golden Palm nomination for Best Director; Golden Globe nomination for Best Foreign Film. DVD, VHS.

3072. *My Brother Jonathan* (Francis Brett Young, 1928). A small-town doctor is disappointed that his dreams of becoming a great surgeon never came to be. **Adaptation 1:** *My Brother Jonathan* (Allied Artists, 1948). Dir: Harold French. Scr: Adrian Alington, Leslie Landau. Cast: Michael Denison (Jonathan), Dulcie Gray (Rachel), Stephen Murray (Dr. Craig). **Adaptation 2:** *My Brother Jonathan* (BBC, 1985 TV Movie). Dir: Anthony Garner. Scr: James Andrew Hall. Cast: Daniel Day-Lewis (Jonathan), Benedict Taylor (Harold), Barbara Kellerman (Rachel).

My Brother Talks to Horses (see *Joe the Wounded Tennis Player*).

3073. "My Brother Paul" (Theodore Dreiser, 1919). A biography and memoir about American composer Paul Dresser (1859–1906) by his younger brother. The article was published in Dreiser's 1919 book *Twelve Men*. **Adaptation:** *My Gal Sal* (20th Century–Fox, 1942). Dir: Irving Cummings. Scr: Seton I. Miller, Karl Tunberg, Darrell Ware. Cast: Rita Hayworth (Sally), Victor Mature (Paul), John Sutton (Fred), Carole Landis (Mae), James Gleason (Pat), Phil Silvers (Wiley).

3074. *My Cousin Rachel* (Daphne Du Maurier, 1951). After a British man marries in Italy and then dies suddenly, his cousin suspects that his new wife killed him. When he meets her, however, he, too, falls in love with her. **Adaptation 1:** *My Cousin Rachel* (20th Century–Fox, 1952). Dir: Henry Koster. Scr: Nunnally Johnson. Cast: Olivia de Havilland (Rachel), Richard Burton (Philip), Audrey Dalton (Louise), Ronald Squire

(Nick). **Adaptation 2:** *My Cousin Rachel* (BBC, 1983 TV Miniseries). Dir: Brian Farnham. Scr: Hugh Whitemore. Cast: Geraldine Chaplin (Rachel), Christopher Guard (Philip), Amanda Kirby (Louise), John Stratton (Nick).

My Darling Clementine (see *Wyatt Earp, Frontier Marshal*).

My Daughter Joy (see *David Golder*).

3075. *My Dog Skip* (Willie Morris, 1995). Memoir about the relationship in the 1940's between a young Mississippi boy and a special dog. **Adaptation:** *My Dog Skip* (Warner, 2000). Dir: Jay Russell. Scr: Gail Gilchriest. Cast: Frankie Muniz (Willie), Diane Lane (Ellen), Luke Wilson (Dink), Kevin Bacon (Jack). DVD, VHS.

3076. *My Early Life* (Winston Churchill, 1930). Autobiography by the British Prime Minister (1874–1965) covering the period from his birth through his election to Parliament in 1904. **Adaptation:** *Young Winston* (Columbia, 1972). Dir: Richard Attenborough. Scr: Carl Foreman. Cast: Robert Shaw (Lord Randolph Churchill), Anne Bancroft (Jenny Churchill), Simon Ward (Winston Churchill), Jack Hawkins (Welldon), Ian Holm (Buckle), Anthony Hopkins (David Lloyd George). Notes: Academy Award nominations for Best Screenplay, Art Direction, and Costume Design; BAFTA Award for Best Costume Design and nominations for Best Actor (Shaw), Actress (Bancroft), Newcomer (Ward), Art Direction, and Musical Score; Golden Globe Award for Best English-Language Foreign Film and nomination for Best Newcomer (Ward). VHS.

3077. *My Father's Glory* (Marcel Pagnol, 1957). In this book titled *La Gloire de Mon Pere*, French novelist and filmmaker Pagnol recalls his childhood trips to the Provence countryside, where he falls in love with nature. This is the first of a four-volume memoir published between 1957 and 1977. **Adaptation:** *My Father's Glory* (Orion, 1990). Dir: Yves Robert. Scr: Louis Nucera, Yves Robert, Jerome Tonnerre. Cast: Philippe Caubere (Joseph), Nathalie Roussel (Augustine), Didier Pain (Jules), Therese Liotard (Rose). DVD, VHS. Notes: Originally titled *La Gloire de mon pere* and shown with subtitles. The film was followed the same year by another installment in Pagnol's memoirs titled *My Mother's Castle*. See also *My Mother's Castle*.

My Foolish Heart (see "Uncle Wiggily in Connecticut").

My Forbidden Past (see *Carriage Entrance*).

3078. *My Friend Flicka* (Mary O'Hara, 1941). Beloved story of an aimless boy who is transformed by his love for a rebellious horse. The first installment in O' Hara's successful Flicka series, which included *Thunderhead — Son of Flicka* (1943) and *Green Grass of Wyoming* (1946). **Adaptation:** *My Friend Flicka* (20th Century–Fox, 1943). Dir: Harold Schuster. Scr: Francis Edward Faragoh, Lillie Hayward. Cast: Roddy McDowall (Ken), Preston Foster (Rob), Rita Johnson (Nell), James Bell (Gus). DVD, VHS. Notes: The book also inspired a television series (1956–1962). See also *Thunderhead — Son Of Flicka* and *Green Grass of Wyoming*.

3079. *My Friend Walter* (Michael Morpurgo, 1988). Children's book about a young girl who visits London and is befriended by the ghost of Sir Walter Raleigh. **Adaptation:** *My Friend Walter* (Thames/Portobello, 1991 TV Movie). Dir: Gavin Millar. Scr: Michael Morpurgo, Gavin Millar. Cast: Ronald Pickup (Sir Walter Raleigh), Polly Grant (Bess), Prunella Scales (Aunt Elle). VHS.

My Gal Sal (see "My Brother Paul").

3080. *My Gun Is Quick* (Mickey Spillane, 1950). Spillane's private detective Mike Hammer investigates the murder of a woman and comes upon a gang war between rival jewel thieves. **Adaptation:** *My Gun Is Quick* (United Artists, 1957). Dir: Phil Victor, George White. Scr: Richard Powell, Richard Collins. Cast: Robert Bray (Hammer), Whitney Blake (Nancy), Donald Randolph (Colonel Holloway).

3081. *My House in Umbria* (William Trevor, 1991). After a terrorist bomb is detonated at an Italian railway station, a kind English writer invites four people back to her villa, among them a young girl with whom she bonds. The novella was published in Trevor's 1991 collection *Two Lives.* **Adaptation:** *My House in Umbria* (HBO, 2003 TV Movie). Dir: Richard Loncraine. Scr: Hugh Whitemore. Cast: Maggie Smith (Emily), Emmy Clarke (Aimee), Ronnie Barker (the General), Chris Cooper (Tom), Giancarlo Giannini (Inspector Girotti). Notes: Emmy Award for Outstanding Actress (Smith), and nominations for Outstanding Movie, Director, Teleplay, Supporting Actor (Cooper), Art Direction, Casting, Costume Design, and Hairstyling; Golden Globe nominations for Best Television Movie and Actress (Smith). DVD, VHS.

3082. *My Husband* (Irene Castle, 1918). In her autobiographical book, Irene Castle recalls her life as a member of the famous early twentieth-century dance team until the time of her husband's death in World War I. **Adaptation:** *The Story of Vernon and Irene Castle* (RKO, 1939). Dir: H. C. Potter. Scr: Oscar Hammerstein II, Dorothy Yost, Richard Sherman. Cast: Fred Astaire (Vernon), Ginger Rogers (Irene), Edna May Oliver (Maggie), Walter Brennan (Walter). Notes: The screenplay also includes elements from Castle's book *My Memories of Vernon Castle.* VHS.

3083. *My Husband My Killer: The Murder of Megan Kalajzich* (Lindsay Simpson and Sandra Harvey, 1992). Factual account of an Australian hotel manager who murdered his wife in order to avoid paying her a divorce settlement. **Adaptation:** *My Husband My Killer* (Columbia TriStar, 2001 TV Movie). Dir: Peter Andrikidis. Scr: Greg Haddrick. Cast: Colin Friels (Bob), Martin Sacks (Andrew), Geoff Morrell (Richardson), Chris Haywood (George). Notes: Australian Film Institiute Awards for Best Director and Actor (Friels), and nominations for Best Television Movie and Musical Score.

3084. *My Laugh Comes Last* (James Hadley Chase [pseudonym for Rene Brabazon Raymond], 1977). An banker is blackmailed into robbing his own bank, whose security system is purportedly the best in the world. **Adaptation:** *The Set Up* (MGM, 1995). Dir: Strathford Hamilton. Scr: Michael Thoma. Cast: Billy Zane (Charles), Mia Sara (Gina), James Russo (Kliff), James Coburn (Jeremiah). VHS.

3085. *My Left Foot* (Christy Brown, 1954). Autobiography of the Irish writer and painter (1932–1981) who was born with cerebral palsy. **Adaptation:** *My Left Foot* (Miramax, 1989). Dir: Jim Sheridan. Scr: Shane Connaughton, Jim Sheridan. Cast: Daniel Day-Lewis (Christy), Brenda Fricker (Mrs. Brown), Alison Whelan (Sheila), Cyril Cusack (Lord Castlewelland), Fiona Shaw (Dr. Cole), Ray McAnally (Mr. Brown). Notes: Academy Awards for Best Actor (Day-Lewis) and Supporting Actress (Fricker), and nominations for Best Picture, Director, and Screenplay; BAFTA Awards for Best Actor (Day-Lewis) and Supporting Actor (McAnally), and nominations for Best Picture, Screenplay, and Makeup; Golden Globe nominations for Best Actor (Day-Lewis) and Supporting Actress (Fricker); Independent Spirit Award for Best Foreign Film. DVD, VHS.

3086. *My Life as a Dog* (Reidar Jonsson,

1983). The autobiographical Swedish novel, originally titled *Mitt Liv Som Hund*, is set in Sweden in the 1950's and concerns a spirited young boy who, after his mother's death, goes to live with relatives in a rural village. **Adaptation:** *My Life as a Dog* (Skouras, 1985). Dir: Lasse Hallstrom. Scr: Lasse Hallstrom, Reidar Jonsson, Brasse Brannstrom, Per Berglund. Cast: Anton Glanzelius (Ingemar), Tomas von Bromssen (Gunnar), Anki Liden (Ingemar's mother), Melinda Kinnaman (Saga). Notes: Originally titled *Mitt Liv Som Hund* and shown with subtitles. Academy Award nominations for Best Director and Screenplay; Golden Globe and Independent Spirit Awards for Best Foreign-Language Film. DVD, VHS. Notes: The book was also the basis for a Canadian television series in 1996 (VHS).

3087. *My Louisiana Sky* (Kimberly Willis Holt, 1998). Set in the early 1950's, the story of a Louisiana adolescent who must come to terms with her parents' mental handicaps. **Adaptation:** *My Louisiana Sky* (Showtime, 2001 TV Movie). Dir: Adam Arkin. Scr: Anna Sandor. Cast: Juliette Lewis (Dorie), Kelsey Keel (Tiger), Shirley Knight (Jewel), Amelia Campbell (Corrina). Notes: Daytime Emmy Awards for Outstanding Children's Special, Director, and Actress (Keel), and nominations for Outstanding Teleplay and Actress (Lewis). DVD, VHS.

3088. *My Man Godfrey* (Eric Hatch, 1935). Comic novel about a dizzy society woman who hires a vagabond as a butler and ends up learning lessons about life from him. **Adaptation 1:** *My Man Godfrey* (Universal, 1936). Dir: Gregory La Cava. Scr: Morrie Ryskind, Eric Hatch. Cast: William Powell (Godfrey), Carole Lombard (Irene), Alice Brady (Angelica), Mischa Auer (Carlo). Notes: Academy Award nominations for Best Director, Screenplay, Actor (Powell), Actress (Lombard), Supporting Actor (Auer), and Supporting Actress (Brady). DVD, VHS. **Adaptation 2:** *My Man Godfrey* (Universal International, 1957). Dir: Henry Koster. Scr: Peter Berneis, William Bowers, Everett Freeman. Cast: June Allyson (Irene), David Niven (Godfrey), Jessie Royce Landis (Angelica), Robert Keith (Mr. Bullock), Eva Gabor (Francesca). VHS.

3089. *My Mother's Castle* (Marcel Pagnol, 1958). Titled *Le Chauteau de Ma Mere,* the second installment in the childhood memoirs of French novelist and filmmaker Pagnol. In this book, he recalls his holiday trips to his mother's villa in the countryside. This is the second of a four-volume memoir published between 1957 and

1977. **Adaptation:** *My Mother's Castle* (Orion, 1990). Dir: Yves Robert. Scr: Yves Robert, Jerome Tonnerre. Cast: Philippe Caubere (Joseph), Nathalie Roussel (Augustine), Didier Pain (Jules), Therese Liotard (Rose), Julien Ciamaca (Marcel). DVD, VHS. Notes: Originally titled *Le Chauteau de Ma Mere* and shown with subtitles. Also released in 1990 was the first installment in Pagnol's memoirs, titled *My Father's Glory.* See also *My Father's Glory.*

My Mother's Ghost (see *Someone Else's Ghost*).

My Name Is Julia Ross (see *The Woman in Red*).

3090. "My Old Man" (Ernest Hemingway, 1923). A jockey who fails to throw a race is threatened by gangsters and escapes to Europe with his young son. The short story appeared in Hemingway's first book, a 1923 collection titled *Three Stories and Ten Poems* and was included in the 1925 short-story collection *In Our Time.* **Adaptation 1:** *Under My Skin* (20th Century–Fox, 1950). Dir: Jean Negulesco. Scr: Casey Robinson. Cast: John Garfield (Dan), Micheline Presle (Paule), Luther Adler (Louis). **Adaptation 2:** *My Old Man* (CBS, 1979 TV Movie). Dir: John Erman. Scr: Jerome Kass. Cast: Kristy McNichol (Jo), Warren Oates (Frank), Eileen Brennan (Marie).

3091. *My Philadelphia Father* (Cordelia Drexel Biddle, as told to Kyle Crichton, 1955). A Philadelphia socialite's memoir about her wealthy, prominent and eccentric father, Anthony J. Drexel Biddle (1874–1948), who was, among other things, and inventor and a boxing enthusiast. In 1956, the book was adapted by Kyle Crichton as a stage play titled *The Happiest Millionaire.* **Adaptation:** *The Happiest Millionaire* (Disney/Buena Vista, 1967). Dir: Norman Tokar. Scr: A. J. Carothers. Cast: Fred MacMurray (Anthony), Tommy Steele (Lawless), Greer Garson (Mrs. Biddle), Geraldine Page (Mrs. Duke), Gladys Cooper (Aunt Mary Drexel), Hermione Baddeley (Mrs. Worth), Lesley Ann Warren (Cordelia). DVD, VHS.

3092. *My Posse Don't Do Homework* (Louanne Johnson, 1992). Memoir by an ex-marine who became a teacher to students at a troubled inner-city high school. The book was reissued in 1995 under the title *Dangerous Minds.* **Adaptation:** *Dangerous Minds* (Buena Vista, 1995). Dir: John N. Smith. Scr: Ronald Bass. Cast: Michelle Pfeiffer (Louanne), George Dzundza (Hal), Courtney B. Vance (George). Notes: The book and film were also the basis for an ABC television series in 1996–97. DVD, VHS.

My Reputation (see *Instruct My Sorrows*).

3093. *My Sister Eileen* (Ruth McKinney, 1938). The adventures of two Ohio sisters who move to New York and take up residence in a Greenwich Village rooming house full of eccentric characters. The autobiographical stories that make up the 1938 book appeared that year in *The New Yorker*, and it was adapted as a Broadway play by Joseph Fields and Jerome Chodorov in 1940. The book was also the basis for the 1953 Broadway musical *Wonderful Town*. **Adaptation 1:** *My Sister Eileen* (Columbia, 1942). Dir: Alexander Hall. Scr: Joseph Fields, Jerome Chodorov (based on their 1940 play). Cast: Rosalind Russell (Ruth), Brian Aherne (Robert), Janet Blair (Eileen), George Tobias (Appopolous). VHS. **Adaptation 2:** *My Sister Eileen* (Columbia, 1955). Dir: Richard Quine. Scr: Blake Edwards, Richard Quine. Cast: Janet Leigh (Eileen), Jack Lemmon (Bob), Betty Garrett (Ruth), Bob Fosse (Frank). Notes: A musical adaptation. DVD, VHS. Notes: The book and films were also the basis for a CBS television series in 1960.

3094. *My Six Convicts: A Psychologist's Three Years in Fort Leavenworth* (Donald Powell Wilson, 1951). Memoir of a staff prison psychologist and his recollections of the inmates he befriended. **Adaptation:** *My Six Convicts* (1952). Dir: Hugo Fregonese. Scr: Michael Blankfort. Cast: Millard Mitchell (James), Gilbert Roland (Punch), John Beal (Doc).

3095. *My Son, My Son* (Howard Spring, 1938). A rich man regrets indulging his spoiled son. **Adaptation:** *My Son, My Son* (United Artists, 1940). Dir: Charles Vidor. Scr: Lenore J. Coffee. Cast: Brian Aherne (William), Madeleine Carroll (Livia), Louis Hayward (Oliver), Laraine Day (Maeve). VHS.

3096. "My Son the Fanatic" (Hanif Kureishi, 1994). A Pakistani cab driver in a small English village tries to assimilate to British life at the same time that his son becomes an Islamic fundamentalist. The short story appeared in the March 28, 1994, issue of *The New Yorker*. **Adaptation:** *My Son the Fanatic* (Miramax, 1997). Dir: Udayan Prasad. Scr: Hanif Kureishi. Cast: Om Puri (Parvez), Rachel Griffiths (Bettina), Stellan Skarsgard (Schitz), Akbar Kurtha (Farid). Notes: British Independent Film Awards nominations for Best Film and Actress (Griffiths); Independent Spirit Award nomination for Best Film. DVD, VHS.

3097. *My Summer of Love* (Helen Cross, 2001). Two eccentric young British women meet and fall in love during an eventful summer. **Adaptation:** *My Summer of Love* (Focus, 2004). Dir: Paul Pavlikovsky. Scr: Paul Pavlikovsky. Cast: Nathalie Press (Mona), Emily Blunt (Tamsin), Paddy Considine (Phil). Notes: BAFTA Alexander Korda Award for Best British Film. DVD, VHS.

My Summer Story (see *In God We Trust, All Others Pay Cash* and *Wanda Hickey's Night of Golden Memories and Other Disasters*).

3098. *My Ten Years as a Counterspy* (Boris Morros and Charles Samuels, 1959). Biography of Boris Morros, a Russian-born Hollywood filmmaker, who was asked by the Soviets to act as a spy during the Cold War and his decision to become a double agent. The book was also published under the title *Ten Years a Counterspy*. **Adaptation:** *Man on a String;* released in the UK as *Confessions of a Counterspy* (Columbia, 1960). Dir: Andre De Toth. Scr: John Kafka, Virginia Shaler. Cast: Ernest Borgnine (Boris), Kerwin Mathews (Bob), Colleen Dewhurst (Helen), Alexander Scourby (Vadja).

3099. *My Wife Melissa* (Francis Durbridge, 1967). A writer is the prime suspect in his wife's murder. **Adaptation 1:** *Melissa* (BBC/PBS, 1974 TV Movie). Dir: Peter Moffatt. Scr: Francis Durbridge. Cast: Moira Redmond (Melissa), Peter Barkworth (Guy), Philip Voss (Detective Carte). **Adaptation 2:** *Melissa* (Channel 4, 1997 TV Miniseries). Dir: Bill Anderson. Scr: Alan Bleasdale. Cast: Jennifer Ehle (Melissa), Tim Dutton (Guy), Adrian Dunbar (Graeme), Bill Paterson (Detective Cameron). Notes: In addition, the novel was adapted for television miniseries in Germany and Italy in 1966.

3100. *Myra Breckinridge* (Gore Vidal, 1968). A vindictive film critic has a sex change operation in Europe and returns to Hollywood as a sensual woman whose goal is to embarrass men. **Adaptation:** *Myra Breckinridge* (20th Century–Fox, 1970). Dir: Michael Sarne. Scr: David Giler, Michael Sarne. Cast: Mae West (Leticia), John Huston (Buck), Raquel Welch (Myra), Rex Reed (Myron), Farrah Fawcett (Mary Ann). DVD, VHS.

3101. "Myra Meets His Family" (F. Scott Fitzgerald, 1920). Romantic comedy about a young couple's insecurity about meeting his wealthy family. The short story was published in *The Saturday Evening Post* on March 20, 1920. **Silent Film:** 1920 (titled *The Husband Hunter*). **Adaptation:** *Under the Biltmore Clock* (PBS/

American Playhouse, 1986 TV Movie). Dir: Neal Miller. Scr: Ilene Cooper, Neal Miller. Cast: Sean Young (Myra), Barnard Hughes (Ludlow), Laura Hughes (Sally), Megan Mullally (Lilah). VHS.

3102. *The Mysterious Affair at Styles* (Agatha Christie, 1920). Set during World War I, Christie's first novel finds Lieutenant Arthur Hastings staying at the country estate of an old friend. When his friend's mother is killed that night, Hastings summons Belgian detective Hercule Poirot to solve the crime. **Adaptation:** *The Mysterious Affair at Styles* (London Weekend/A&E/PBS, 1990 TV Movie Series). Dir: Ross Devenish. Scr: Clive Exton. Cast: David Suchet (Poirot), Hugh Fraser (Hastings), Philip Jackson (Inspector Japp), Beatie Edney (Mary). DVD, VHS.

3103. *The Mysterious Dr. Fu Manchu* (Sax Rohmer [pseudonym for Arthur Sarsfield Ward], 1913). The first in Rohmer's series of novels and stories featuring the evil Asian genius pursued by a Scotland Yard inspector. **Adaptation:** *The Mysterious Dr. Fu Manchu* (Paramount, 1929). Dir: Rowland V. Lee. Scr: Lloyd Corrigan, Florence Ryerson. Cast: Warner Oland (Fu Manchu), Neil Hamilton (Dr. Petrie), Jean Arthur (Lia), O. P. Heggie (Nayland). VHS. Notes: Two sequels followed: *The Return of Dr. Fu Manchu* (1930) and *Drums of Fu Manchu* (1940). In 1980, a film combining elements from several of the novels was released, titled *The Fiendish Plot of Dr. Fu Manchu* and starring Peter Sellers in several roles (VHS). See also *The Mask of Fu Manchu*.

3104. *The Mysterious Island* (Jules Verne, 1874). *L'Ile Mysterieuse*, the two-part sequel to Verne's 1869 novel *20,000 Leagues Under the Sea*, is set at the end of the American Civil War and tells the story of a group of Confederate refugees who take a hot-air balloon and land on a strange island, where they must use their technological know-how to survive. **Adaptation 1:** *The Mysterious Island* (MGM, 1929). Dir: Lucien Hubbard. Scr: Lucien Hubbard. Cast: Lionel Barrymore (Andre), Lloyd Hughes (Nikolai), Montagu Love (Hubert). **Adaptation 2:** *Mysterious Island* (Columbia, 1951). Dir: Spencer Bennet. Scr: Lewis Clay, Royal K. Cole, George H. Plympton. Cast: Richard Crane (Cyrus), Marshall Reed (Jack), Ralph Hodges (Bert), Leonard Penn (Captain Nemo). **Adaptation 3:** *Mysterious Island* (Columbia, 1961). Dir: Cy Endfield. Scr: John Prebble, Daniel Ullman, Crane Wilbur. Cast: Michael Craig (Cyrus), Joan Greenwood (Lady Fairchild), Michael Callan (Bert), Gary Merrill (Gideon), Herbert Lom (Captain Nemo). DVD, VHS.

Adaptation 4: *The Mysterious Island of Captain Nemo* (Cinerama, 1973). Dir: Juan Antonio Bardem, Henri Colpi. Scr: Juan Antonio Bardem, Henri Colpi. Cast: Omar Sharif (Captain Nemo), Ambroise Bia (Nebuchadnezzar), Jess Hahn (Bonaventure), Philippe Nicaud (Gideon).

The Mysterious Magician (see *The Gaunt Stranger*).

3105. *The Mysterious Rider* (Zane Grey, 1919). Western about a rancher who seeks vengeance on a dishonest lawyer who cheated him out of his property. The novel was serialized in *The Country Gentleman* beginning on June 7, 1919, and published as a book in 1921. **Silent Films:** 1921 and 1927. **Adaptation 1:** *The Mysterious Rider* (Paramount, 1933). Dir: Fred Allen. Scr: Harvey Gates, Robert N. Lee. Cast: Kent Taylor (Wade), Lona Andre (Dorothy), Warren Hymer (Jitney), Irving Pichel (Cliff). **Adaptation 2:** *The Mysterious Rider* (Paramount, 1938). Dir: Lesley Selander. Scr: Maurice Geraghty. Cast: Douglass Dumbrille (Pecos Bill/Ben Wade), Sidney Toler (Frosty), Russell Hayden (Will).

3106. *The Mysterious Stranger* (Mark Twain [pseudonym for Samuel Langhorne Clemens], 1916). The story of a Satanic man who amuses boys and reveals the hypocrisy of adults in sixteenth-century Austria. The manuscript was discovered among Twain's papers after his death in 1910 and published in 1916. **Adaptation:** *The Mysterious Stranger* (PBS, 1982 TV Movie). Dir: Peter H. Hunt. Scr: Julian Mitchell. Cast: Chris Makepeace (August), Herbert Fux (Hans), Christoph Waltz (Ernst). VHS.

Mystery Liner (see "The Ghost of John Holling").

3107. *The Mystery of Edwin Drood* (Charles Dickens, 1870). Dickens' final novel is the tale of a drug-addicted choirmaster whose jealousy over his nephew's fiancée leads to murder. The novel was serialized from April through September of 1870, when Dickens died, having completed only six of twelve proposed chapters. The novel was the basis for a 1985 Broadway musical. **Silent Films:** 1909 and 1914. **Adaptation 1:** *The Mystery of Edwin Drood* (Universal, 1935). Dir: Stuart Walker. Scr: Leopold Atlas, John L. Balderston, Bradley King, Gladys Unger. Cast: Claude Rains (Jasper), Douglass Montgomery (Landless), Heather Angel (Rosa), Valerie Hobson (Helena), David Manners (Edwin). VHS. **Adaptation 2:** *The Mystery of Edwin Drood* (Standard Media, 1993). Dir: Timothy Forder. Scr: Timothy Forder. Cast: Robert Powell (Jasper), Gemma Craven

(Miss Twinkleton), Barry Evans (Bazzard), Rosemary Leach (Mrs. Tope), Nanette Newman (Mrs. Crisparkle), Jonathan Phillips (Edwin). VHS.

3108. "The Mystery of Marie Roget" (Edgar Allan Poe, 1842–1843). In this sequel to Poe's 1841 short story "The Murders in the Rue Morgue," a detective investigates grisly homicides in Paris. The short story was published serially in *Snowden's Ladies' Companion* (November-December 1842 and February 1843). **Adaptation:** *The Mystery of Marie Roget* (Universal, 1942). Dir: Phil Rosen. Scr: Michael Jacoby. Cast: Patric Knowles (Dr. Dupin), Lloyd Corrigan (Prefect Gobelin), Nell O'Day (Camille Roget).

3109. *The Mystery of Men* (Guy Bellamy, 1996). Black comedy about four friends at a local bar who agree to take out life insurance policies naming the others the beneficiaries. **Adaptation:** *The Mystery of Men* (BBC, 1999 TV Movie). Dir: Nick Vivian. Scr: Guy Bellamy. Cast: Warren Clarke (Vernon), Nick Berry (Colin), Neil Pearson (Julian), Robert Daws (Oscar).

The Mystery of Mr. X (see *X v. Rex*).

Mystery of the Thirteenth Guest (see *The Thirteenth Guest*).

3110. *Mystic Masseur* (V. S. Naipul, 1957). The first novel by the 2001 Nobel laureate is the semi-autobiographical story of an Indian writer growing up in Trinidad. To support himself, he becomes a masseur, like his father before him, and develops a reputation for mystical healing powers. **Adaptation:** *The Mystic Masseur* (2001). Dir: Ismail Merchant. Scr: Caryl Phillips. Cast: Om Puri (Ramlogan), Aasif Mandvi (Ganesh), Ayesha Dharker (Leela), Jimi Mistry (Partap). DVD, VHS.

3111. *Mystic River* (Dennis Lehane, 2001). Three childhood friends reunite as adults when the daughter of one of them is murdered, and one of the friends is the cop charged with investigating the crime. **Adaptation:** *Mystic River* (Warner, 2003). Dir: Clint Eastwood. Scr: Brian Helgeland. Cast: Sean Penn (Jimmy), Tim Robbins (Dave), Kevin Bacon (Sean), Laurence Fishburne (Whitey), Marcia Gay Harden (Celeste), Laura Linney (Annabeth). Notes: Academy Awards for Best Actor (Penn) and Supporting Actor (Robbins), and nominations for Best Picture, Director, Screenplay, and Supporting Actress (Harden); Golden Globe Awards for Best Actor (Penn) and Supporting Actor (Robbins), and nominations for Best Picture, Director, and Screenplay; National

Board of Review Awards for Best Picture and Actor (Penn); Cannes Film Festival Golden Coach Award for Best Director and Golden Palm nomination. DVD, VHS.

3112. *The Naked and the Dead* (Norman Mailer, 1948). Mailer's first novel is set on a South Pacific island during World War II and tells the stories of soldiers from vastly different backgrounds brought together by the war. **Adaptation:** *The Naked and the Dead* (Warner, 1958). Dir: Raoul Walsh. Scr: Denis Sanders, Terry Sanders. Cast: Aldo Ray (Sergeant Croft), Cliff Robertson (Lieutenant Hearn), Raymond Massey (General Cummings), Lili St. Cyr (Lily). VHS.

3113. *The Naked Country* (Morris L. West, 1960). An Australian rancher comes into conflict with Aborigines over lands they consider sacred. West originally published the novel under the pseudonym Michael East. **Adaptation:** *The Naked Country* (Hemdale, 1984). Dir: Tim Burstall. Scr: Tim Burstall, Ross Dimsey. Cast: John Stanton (Lance), Rebecca Gilling (Mary), Ivor Kantz (Sergeant Adams), Tommy Lewis (Mundaru). VHS.

The Naked Edge (see *First Train to Babylon*).

3114. *The Naked Face* (Sidney Sheldon, 1970). A New York psychiatrist is the prime suspect in the deaths of two of his patients. When he investigates the crimes in order to clear his name, he tangles with powerful Mafia bosses. **Adaptation:** *The Naked Face* (Cannon, 1984). Dir: Bryan Forbes. Scr: Bryan Forbes. Cast: Roger Moore (Dr. Stevens), Rod Steiger (McGreary), Elliott Gould (Angeli), Art Carney (Morgens), Anne Archer (Ann), David Hedison (Dr. Hadley). VHS.

The Naked Jungle (see "Leninger Versus the Ants").

3115. *Naked Lunch* (William S. Burroughs, 1959). A story about a heroin addict's odyssey from New York to Tangiers and from there to a strange drug-induced place called the Interzone, where he experiences nightmarish paranoid fantasies. The book was at the center of a landmark obscenity trial in 1962. **Adaptation:** *Naked Lunch* (20th Century–Fox, 1991). Dir: David Cronenberg. Scr: David Cronenberg. Cast: Peter Weller (Bill), Judy Davis (Joan), Ian Holm (Tom), Julian Sands (Yves), Roy Scheider (Dr. Benway), Monique Mercure (Fadela). Notes: Genie Awards (Canada) for Best Picture, Director, Supporting Actress (Mercure), Art Direction, Cinematography, and Sound, and nominations for Best Actor

(Weller), Musical Score, and Costume Design. DVD, VHS.

3116. *The Naked Runner* (Francis Clifford, 1966). A thriller about an American executive in England coerced into carrying out the assassination of a spy in East Germany. **Adaptation:** *The Naked Runner* (Warner, 1967). Dir: Sidney J. Furie. Scr: Stanley Mann. Cast: Frank Sinatra (Laker), Peter Vaughan (Slattery), Derren Nesbitt (Colonel Hartmann), Nadia Gray (Karen). VHS.

3117. *The Name of the Rose* (Umberto Eco, 1980). Eco's Italian novel *Il nome della rosa* is a medieval murder mystery set in an Italian Benedictine monastery during the fourteenth century. It is up to a traveling Franciscan and his young protégé to solve the crimes. The best-selling book was first translated into English in 1983. **Adaptation:** *The Name of the Rose* (20th Century–Fox, 1986). Dir: Jean-Jacques Annaud. Scr: Andrew Birkin, Gerard Brach, Howard Franklin, Alain Godard. Cast: Sean Connery (William of Baskerville), F. Murray Abraham (Bernardo), Christian Slater (Adso), Elya Baskin (Severinus), Michael Lonsdale (the Abbot). DVD, VHS.

3118. *The Name's Buchanan* (Jonas Ward, 1956). Western about an itinerant Texan who helps a Mexican accused of murder in a border town and his conflict with a corrupt local family. **Adaptation:** *Buchanan Rides Alone* (Columbia, 1958). Dir: Budd Boetticher. Scr: Charles Lang. Cast: Randolph Scott (Tom), Craig Stevens (Abe), Barry Kelley (Lew).

3119. *Nana* (Emile Zola, 1880). In late nineteenth-century Paris, a woman from the lower class aspires to social prominence and uses her beauty to climb in the world. **Silent Film:** 1926 (directed by Jean Renoir). **Adaptation 1:** *Nana*; released in the UK as *Lady of the Boulevards* (United Artists, 1934). Dir: Dorothy Arzner, George Fitzmaurice. Scr: Harry Wagstaff Gribble, Willard Mack. Cast: Anna Sten (Nana), Lionel Atwill (Muffat), Richard Bennett (Gaston), Mae Clarke (Satin). VHS. **Adaptation 2:** *Nana* (Times, 1955). Dir: Christian-Jaque. Scr: Christian-Jaque, Jean Ferry, Henri Jeanson, Albert Valentin. Cast: Charles Boyer (Muffat), Martine Carol (Nana), Walter Chiari (Fontan). **Adaptation 3:** *Nana* (BBC, 1968 TV Miniseries). Dir: John Davies. Scr: Robert Muller. Cast: Katherine Schofield (Nana), John Bryans (Steiner), Freddie Jones (Muffat). **Adaptation 4:** *Nana* (Cannon, 1982). Dir: Dan Wolman. Scr: Marc Behm. Cast: Katya Berger (Nana), Jean-Pierre Aumont (Muffat), Yehuda Efroni (Steiner).

Nancy Drew and the Hidden Staircase (see *The Hidden Staircase*).

Nancy Drew, Detective (see *The Password to Larkspur Lane*).

Nancy Steele Is Missing! (see *Ransom*).

3120. *The Nanny* (Evelyn Piper [pseudonym for Marryam Modell], 1964). Thriller about a psychologically disturbed woman who takes a job as a nanny and begins a battle of wills with the spirited ten-year-old boy for whom she cares. **Adaptation:** *The Nanny* (20th Century–Fox, 1965). Dir: Seth Holt. Scr: Jimmy Sangster. Cast: Bette Davis (Nanny), Wendy Craig (Virginia), William Dix (Joey), Jill Bennett (Aunt Pen), Pamela Franklin (Bobbie). VHS.

3121. *The Nanny* (Dan Greenburg, 1987). Horror thriller about a baby sitter who steals the children she cares for and sacrifices them to a mysterious tree. **Adaptation:** *The Guardian* (Universal, 1990). Dir: William Friedkin. Scr: Stephen Volk, Dan Greenburg, William Friedkin. Cast: Jenny Seagrove (Camilla), Dwier Brown (Phil), Carey Lowell (Kate), Brad Hall (Ned), Miguel Ferrer (Ralph). DVD, VHS.

3122. *The Narrow Corner* (W. Somerset Maugham, 1932). A fugitive from justice in England seeks refuge on an island in the South Seas. **Adaptation 1:** *The Narrow Corner* (Warner, 1933). Dir: Alfred E. Green. Scr: Robert Presnell. Cast: Douglas Fairbanks, Jr. (Fred), Patricia Ellis (Louise), Ralph Bellamy (Eric). **Adaptation 2:** *Isle of Fury* (Warner, 1936). Dir: Frank McDonald. Scr: Robert Andrews, William Jacobs. Cast: Humphrey Bogart (Valentine), Margaret Lindsay (Lucille), Donald Woods (Eric).

3123. *The Narrowing Circle* (Julian Symons, 1954). Two magazine staff writers compete for the love of the same woman. When one is found dead in the apartment of the other, a Scotland Yard inspector investigates the crime. **Adaptation:** *The Narrowing Circle* (Eros, 1956). Dir: Charles Saunders. Scr: Doreen Montgomery. Cast: Paul Carpenter (Dave), Hazel Court (Rosemary), Russell Napier (Sir Henry), Trevor Reid (Inspector Crambo).

Nasty Habits (see *The Abbess of Crewe*).

3124. *Natasha's Story* (Michael Nicholson, 1993). Factual account by a British journalist who covered the war in Bosnia in the 1990's and became involved with the plight of children in the ravaged nation. When he finally left the country, he smuggled out a young girl named Natasha and adopted her. **Adaptation:** *Welcome to Sarajevo* (Miramax, 1997). Dir: Michael Winterbottom. Scr: Frank Cottrell Boyce. Cast: Stephen Dillane (Michael), Woody Harrelson (Flynn), Marisa Tomei (Nina), Emira Nusevic (Emira), Kerry Fox (Jane), Goran Visnjic (Risto). Notes: Cannes Film Festival Golden Palm nomination for Best Director. DVD, VHS.

3125. *National Velvet* (Enid Bagnold, 1935). A young woman named Velvet has only one ambition: to train her horse to compete in the Grand National, Britain's most prestigious race. **Adaptation:** *National Velvet* (MGM, 1944). Dir: Clarence Brown. Scr: Helen Deutsch, Theodore Reeves. Cast: Mickey Rooney (Taylor), Donald Crisp (Mr. Brown), Elizabeth Taylor (Velvet), Anne Revere (Mrs. Brown), Angela Lansbury (Edwina). Notes: Academy Awards for Best Supporting Actress (Revere) and Editing, and nominations for Best Director, Art Direction, and Cinematography. DVD, VHS. Notes: In addition to a television series on NBC in 1960, the film also inspired a 1978 sequel, *International Velvet* (DVD, VHS).

3126. *Native Son* (Richard Wright, 1940). Bigger Thomas is a young black youth who moves to Chicago and believes that his future is secure. When he accidentally kills the daughter of his employer, however, life takes a nasty turn. **Adaptation 1:** *Native Son* (Classic, 1951). Scr: Pierre Chenal. Scr: Pierre Chenal. Cast: Richard Wright (Bigger), Gloria Madison (Bessie), Willa Pearl Curtis (Hannah), Nicholas Joy (Henry). VHS. **Adaptation 2:** *Native Son* (American Playhouse, 1986). Dir: Jerrold Freedman. Scr: Richard Wesley. Cast: Victor Love (Bigger), Carroll Baker (Mrs. Dalton), Matt Dillon (Jan), Elizabeth McGovern (Mary), Geraldine Page (Peggy), Ving Rhames (Jack), Lane Smith (Britton), Oprah Winfrey (Mrs. Thomas). Notes: Independent Spirit Award nomination for Best Male Lead (Love). VHS.

Nattlek (see *Night Games*).

3127. *The Natural* (Bernard Malamud, 1952). A talented middle-aged baseball player takes a losing team to the league championship with the aid of a magical bat. In the end, however, his dream of big-league stardom is cut short by a woman. **Adaptation:** *The Natural* (TriStar, 1984). Dir: Barry Levinson. Scr: Roger Towne, Phil Dusenberry. Cast: Robert Redford (Roy), Robert Duvall (Max), Glenn Close (Iris), Kim Basinger (Memo), Wilford Brimley (Pop Fisher),

Barbara Hershey (Harriet). Notes: Academy Award nominations for Best Supporting Actress (Close), Cinematography, Musical Score, and Art Direction; Golden Globe nomination for Best Supporting Actress (Basinger). DVD, VHS.

3128. *The Nature of the Beast* (Janni Howker, 1985). Children's book about a young boy and his friend who hunt a mysterious beast that is killing animals. **Adaptation:** *The Nature of the Beast* (British Screen, 1988). Dir: Franco Rosso. Scr: Janni Howker. Cast: Lynton Dearden (Bill), Paul Simpson (Mick), Tony Melody (Chunder).

Navigating the Heart (see *Fishing with John*).

The Navy vs. the Night Monsters (see *The Monster from the Earth's End*).

3129. *The Neat Little Corpse* (Max Murray, 1950). A hotel developer tries to seize a family's home by producing distant relatives who lay claim to the place. **Adaptation:** *Jamaica Run* (Paramount, 1953). Dir: Lewis R. Foster. Scr: Lewis R. Foster. Cast: Ray Milland (Patrick), Arlene Dahl (Ena), Wendell Corey (Todd).

3130. *Necessity* (Brian Garfield, 1984). After his wife runs away with their daughter and $2 million dollars of his money, a drug dealer dispatches hit men to deal with her. **Adaptation:** *Necessity* (CBS, 1988 TV Movie). Dir: Michael Miller. Scr: Michael Ahnemann. Cast: Loni Anderson (Lauren), Hank Baumert (Eddie), John Heard (Charlie).

3131. *The Necromancers* (Robert Hugh Benson, 1909). A medium raises the spirit of a young man's deceased fiancée. **Adaptation:** *Spellbound*; released in the U.S. as *The Spell of Amy Nugent* (Pyramid/PRC, 1940). Dir: John Harlow. Scr: Miles Malleson. Cast: Derek Farr (Laurie Baxter), Vera Lindsay (Diana Hilton), Diana King (Amy Nugent). VHS.

Ned Kelly (see *Our Sunshine*).

3132. *Needful Things* (Stephen King, 1991). In King's fictional Castle Rock, Maine, a mysterious man opens a shop where people can have whatever they desire as long as they are prepared to strike a Faustian bargain with the proprietor. **Adaptation:** *Needful Things* (Columbia, 1993). Dir: Fraser Clarke Heston. Scr: W. D. Richter. Cast: Max von Sydow (Gaunt), Ed Harris (Sheriff Pangborn), Bonnie Bedelia (Polly), Amanda Plummer (Nettie), J. T. Walsh (Buster). DVD, VHS.

3133. *Negatives* (Peter Everett, 1965). A married couple indulge in sexual fantasies by dressing up as infamous historical personages. **Adaptation:** *Negatives* (Continental, 1968). Dir: Peter Medak. Scr: Peter Everett, Roger Lowry. Cast: Peter McEnery (Theo), Diane Cilento (Reingard), Glenda Jackson (Vivien). VHS.

3134. *Neighbors* (Thomas Berger, 1980). Comic novel about the obnoxious couple who move in next door to a peaceful suburbanite and the havoc they bring to his quiet life. **Adaptation:** *Neighbors* (Columbia, 1981). Dir: John G. Avildsen. Scr: Larry Gelbart. Cast: John Belushi (Earl), Kathryn Walker (Enid), Cathy Moriarty (Ramona), Dan Aykroyd (Vic). VHS.

3135. *Neither the Sea Nor the Sand* (Gordon Honeycombe, 1969). Supernatural romance about a troubled married woman who takes a vacation on the Isle of Jersey and falls in love with a lighthouse keeper. Although he dies suddenly, their romance continues on. **Adaptation:** *Neither the Sea Nor the Sand* (International Amusements, 1972). Dir: Fred Burnley. Scr: Gordon Honeycombe. Cast: Susan Hampshire (Anna), Frank Finlay (George), Michael Petrovitch (Hugh).

3136. *Nemesis* (Agatha Christie, 1971). In Christie's final Miss Marple mystery, the amateur sleuth receives a letter from a dead friend asking her to investigate a crime but offering few details. **Adaptation:** *Nemesis* (BBC/PBS, 1987 TV Movie series). Dir: David Tucker. Scr: T. R. Bowen. Cast: Joan Hickson (Miss Marple), Peter Tilbury (Lionel), Valerie Lush (Lavinia), Margaret Tyzack (Clothilde). DVD, VHS.

3137. *The Neon Bible* (John Kennedy Toole, 1989). A boy growing up in Georgia in the 1940's leads a dreary life except for his flamboyant aunt, a singer with a zest for life. **Adaptation:** *The Neon Bible* (Strand, 1995). Dir: Terence Davies. Scr: Terence Davies. Cast: Jacob Tierney (David as a teenager), Drake Bell (David as a child), Gena Rowlands (Aunt Mae), Diana Scarwid (Sarah), Denis Leary (Frank). DVD, VHS.

Nero Wolfe (see *The Doorbell Rang*).

3138. *The Net* (John Pudney, 1952). Tension among British aviation researchers developing a secret supersonic jet leads to murder. **Adaptation:** *The Net*; released in the U.S. as *Project M7* (Universal International, 1953). Dir: Anthony Asquith. Scr: William Fairchild. Cast: Phyllis Calvert (Lydia), James Donald (Professor Heathley), Robert Beatty (Major Seagram), Herbert Lom (Dr. Leon).

The Neutralizer (see *A Red File for Callan*).

3139. *Nevada* (Zane Grey, 1926). Western about a gunfighter framed by the thieves who robbed his gambling winnings. The novel was serialized in *The American Magazine* beginning in November 1926 and published as a book in 1928. **Silent Film:** 1927. **Adaptation 1:** *Nevada* (Paramount, 1935). Dir: Charles Barton. Scr: Stuart Anthony, Garnett Weston. Cast: Buster Crabbe (Nevada), Kathleen Burke (Hettie), Monte Blue (Clem). **Adaptation 2:** *Nevada* (1944). Dir: Edward Killy. Scr: Norman Houston. Cast: Robert Mitchum (Nevada), Anne Jeffreys (Julie), Guinn Williams (Dusty).

Never a Dull Moment (1950) (see *Who Could Ask for Anything More?*).

Never a Dull Moment (1968) (see *The Reluctant Assassin*).

Never Back Losers (see *The Green Ribbon*).

3140. *Never Come Back* (John Mair, 1942). An American journalist in London accidentally kills a woman involved with a criminal organization and is pursued by the group because of the secrets he has learned. **Adaptation:** *Tiger by the Tail* (United Artists, 1955). Dir: John Gilling. Scr: John Gilling, Willis Goldbeck. Cast: Larry Parks (John), Constance Smith (Jane), Donald Stewart (Macauly).

3141. *Never Cry Wolf* (Farley Mowat, 1963). Memoir of a scientist who struggled to stay alive in the Arctic as he studied the behavior of wolves. **Adaptation:** *Never Cry Wolf* (Disney/Buena Vista, 1983). Dir: Carroll Ballard. Scr: Ralph Furmaniak, Sam Hamm, Richard Kletter. Cast: Charles Martin Smith (Farley), Brian Dennehy (Rosie), Zachary Ittimangnaq (Ootek), Samson Jorah (Mike). DVD, VHS.

3142. *Never Die Alone* (Donald Goines, 1974). An aspiring journalist wants to document the life of a ghetto drug dealer and gangster but ends up witnessing his murder, a crime that affects him profoundly. **Adaptation:** *Never Die Alone* (20th Century–Fox, 2004). Dir: Ernest Dickerson. Scr: James Gibson. Cast: DMX (King David), Michael Ealy (Michael), Drew Sidora (Ella), David Arquette (Paul). DVD, VHS.

Never Give an Inch (see *Sometime a Great Notion*).

Never Let Me Go (see *Came the Dawn*).

3143. *Never Love a Stranger* (Harold Robbins, 1948). A gangster helps his boyhood friend, now a prosecutor, entrap a vicious killer. **Adaptation:** *Never Love a Stranger* (Allied Artists, 1958). Dir: Robert Stevens. Scr: Richard Day, Harold Robbins. Cast: John Drew Barrymore (Frankie), Lita Milan (Julie), Robert Bray (Silk), Steve McQueen (Martin). VHS.

Never Say Never Again (see *Thunderball*).

3144. *Never So Few* (Tom T. Chamales, 1957). During World War II, American soldiers in the Pacific train Burmese guerillas to fight the Japanese. **Adaptation:** *Never So Few* (MGM, 1959). Dir: John Sturges. Scr: Millard Kaufman. Cast: Frank Sinatra (Tom), Gina Lollobrigida (Carla), Peter Lawford (Travis), Steve McQueen (Bill). VHS.

Never Take No for an Answer (see *The Small Miracle*).

3145. *Never Tell Me Never* (Janine Shepherd, 1994). Training for the Olympics as a cross-country skier, Shepherd had an accident from which she was not expected to recover. This memoir tells the story of her successful recovery and triumph over adversity. **Adaptation:** *Never Tell Me Never* (Lifetime, 1998 TV Movie). Dir: David Elfick. Scr: John Cundill. Cast: Claudia Karvan (Janine), Michael Caton (Max), Diane Craig (Shirley), John Howard (Uncle Darryl).

3146. *Never the Twain Shall Meet* (Peter B. Kyne, 1923). Romantic comedy about a San Francisco lawyer who falls in love with an girl from the South Seas and goes to her island paradise to live with her. **Silent Film:** 1925. **Adaptation:** *Never the Twain Shall Meet* (MGM, 1931). Dir: W. S. Van Dyke. Scr: Edwin Justus Mayer. Cast: Leslie Howard (Dan), Conchita Montenegro (Tamea), C. Aubrey Smith (Mr. Pritchard), Karen Morley (Maisie).

3147. *The NeverEnding Story* (Michael Ende, 1979). German children's book, originally titled *Die Unendliche Geschicte*, about a boy who uses a magical book to enter the mythical, doomed world of Fantastica, where he agrees to go undertake a dangerous mission to save the land and its fantastic inhabitants. **Adaptation:** *The NeverEnding Story* (Warner, 1984). Dir: Wolfgang Petersen. Scr: Wolfgang Petersen, Herman Weigel. Cast: Barret Oliver (Bastian), Gerald McRaney (Bastian's Father), Thomas Hill (Koreander), Moses Gunn (Cairon), Noah Hathaway (Atreyu). DVD, VHS. Notes: In addition to a 2001 television series titled *Tales from the NeverEnding Story*, the film also inspired two sequels: *The NeverEnding Story*

II: The Next Chapter (1990) (DVD, VHS), and *The NeverEnding Story III* (1994) (DVD, VHS).

The New Adventures of Pippi Longstocking (see *Pippi Longstocking*).

3148. *New Cardiff* (Charles Webb, 2001). After his girlfriend leaves him, a British artist goes to live in a Vermont hotel, where he meets and falls in love with another woman. Complications arise when this former lover wants to reunite. **Adaptation:** *Hope Springs* (Buena Vista, 2003). Dir: Mark Herman. Scr: Mark Herman. Cast: Colin Firth (Colin), Heather Graham (Mandy), Minnie Driver (Vera), Mary Steenburgen (Joanie). DVD, VHS.

3149. *The New Centurions* (Joseph Wambaugh, 1970). Wambaugh's dark look at rookie cops learning the ropes on the streets of Los Angeles. **Adaptation:** *The New Centurions*; released in the UK as *Precinct 45: Los Angeles Police* (Columbia, 1972). Dir: Richard Fleischer. Scr: Stirling Silliphant. Cast: George C. Scott (Kilvinski), Stacy Keach (Roy), Jane Alexander (Dorothy), Scott Wilson (Gus), Rosalind Cash (Lorrie), Erik Estrada (Sergio), Clifton James (Whitey). VHS.

The New Land (see *The Settlers*).

A New Leaf (*see* "The Green Heart").

The New Swiss Family Robinson (see *Swiss Family Robinson*).

Newly Rich (see *Let's Play King*).

3150. *The Newton Boys: Portrait of an Outlaw Gang* (Claude Stanush, 1994). Biography of four rural Texas brothers who became well-known bank and train robbers in the 1920's. **Adaptation:** *The Newton Boys* (20th Century–Fox, 1998). Dir: Richard Linklater. Scr: Richard Linklater, Claude Stanush, Clark Lee Walker. Cast: Matthew McConaughey (Willis), Skeet Ulrich (Joe), Ethan Hawke (Jess), Vincent D'Onofrio (Doc), Julianna Margulies (Louise). DVD, VHS.

3151. *The Next Corner* (Kate Jordan, 1921). An American businessman working in India leaves his wife in Paris, where she has a torrid affair with a Spanish gigolo. Jordan also adapted her novel as a play. **Adaptation:** *Transgression* (RKO, 1931). Dir: Herbert Brenon. Scr: Elizabeth Meehan. Cast: Kay Francis (Elsie), Paul Cavanagh (Robert), Ricardo Cortez (Don Arturo), Nance O'Neil (Nora).

3152. *The Next to Last Train Ride* (Charles

Dennis, 1974). Comic story about a con artist who crosses the United States by train with stolen money hidden in a coffin. **Adaptation:** *Finders Keepers* (Warner, 1984). Dir: Richard Lester. Scr: Charles Dennis, Ronny Graham, Terence Marsh. Cast: Michael O'Keefe (Rangeloff), Beverly D'Angelo (Standish), Louis Gossett, Jr. (Century), Pamela Stephenson (Georgiana), Ed Lauter (Joseph), David Wayne (Stapleton), Brian Dennehy (Frizzoli). DVD, VHS.

3153. *Nicholas Nickleby* (Charles Dickens, 1838–39). After the death of his father, young and penniless Nicholas goes to live with a cruel uncle, who tears his family apart. Nicholas joins a troupe of traveling entertainers and devises the means for reuniting his family. The serialized novel originally appeared under the title *The Life and Adventures of Nicholas Nickleby* in monthly installments between April 1838 and October 1939. **Silent Films:** 1903 and 1912. **Adaptation 1:** *Nicholas Nickleby* (Universal, 1947). Dir: Alberto Cavalcanti. Scr: John Dighton. Cast: Derek Bond (Nicholas), Cedric Hardwicke (Ralph), Stanley Holloway (Crummles), Bernard Miles (Noggs), Sally Ann Howes (Kate), Sybil Thorndike (Mrs. Squeers). VHS. **Adaptation 2:** *Nicholas Nickleby* (BBC, 1977 TV Miniseries). Dir: Christopher Barry. Scr: Hugh Leonard. Cast: Nigel Havers (Nicholas), Peter Bourke (Smike), Kate Nicholls (Kate), Derek Godfrey (Ralph). **Adaptation 3:** *The Life and Adventures of Nicholas Nickleby* (Channel 4/Mobil Showcase, 1982 TV Miniseries). Dir: John Caird, Jim Goddard, Trevor Nunn. Scr: David Edgar. Cast: Roger Rees (Nicholas), Emily Richard (Kate), David Threfall (Smike), Alun Armstrong (Squeers). Notes: This production was a stage play filmed for television. Emmy Award for Outstanding Miniseries and nominations for Outstanding Actor (Rees) and Supporting Actor (Threlfall). DVD, VHS. **Adaptation 4:** *The Life and Adventures of Nicholas Nickleby* (Company Television, 2001 TV Movie). Dir: Stephen Whittaker. Scr: Martyn Hesford. Cast: James D'Arcy (Nicholas), Sophia Myles (Kate), Diana Kent (Mrs. Nickleby), Charles Dance (Ralph). DVD, VHS. **Adaptation 5:** *Nicholas Nickleby* (MGM, 2002). Dir: Douglas McGrath. Scr: Douglas McGrath. Cast: Charlie Hunnam (Nicholas), Romola Garai (Kate), Tom Courtenay (Noggs), Christopher Plummer (Ralph), Anne Hathaway (Madeline), Jim Broadbent (Squeers). Notes: National Board of Review Award for Best Ensemble; Golden Globe nomination for Best Picture. DVD, VHS.

3154. *Nicholas and Alexandra* (Robert K. Massie, 1967). Factual account of the tragedy surrounding Russia's last czar and his family at the time of the Russian Revolution. **Adaptation:** *Nicholas and Alexandra* (Columbia, 1971). Dir: Franklin J. Schaffner. Scr: James Goldman. Cast: Michael Jayston (Tsar Nicholas II), Janet Suzman (Alexandra), Roderic Noble (Alexis), Fiona Fullerton (Anastasia), Harry Andrews (Grand Duke Nicholas), Irene Worth (Queen Mother Marie Fedorova), Tom Baker (Rasputin). Notes: Academy Awards for Best Art Direction and Costume Design, and nominations for Best Picture, Actress (Suzman), Cinematography, and Musical Score; Golden Globe nominations for Best Supporting Actor (Baker) and Most Promising Newcomers (Suzman and Baker). DVD, VHS.

3155. *The Nick Adams Stories* (Ernest Hemingway, 1972). A collection of Hemingway's early autobiographical short stories featuring a young man trying to make his way in the world in the early twentieth century. The earliest Nick Adams stories appeared in Hemingway's first collection, *In Our Time* (1925) and in *Men Without Women* (1927). Scribner's collected the stories in a single volume in 1972. **Adaptation:** *Hemingway's Adventures of a Young Man* (20th Century–Fox, 1962). Dir: Martin Ritt. Scr: A. E. Hotchner. Cast: Richard Beymer (Nick), Diane Baker (Carolyn), Dan Dailey (Billy), Arthur Kennedy (Doc Adams), Ricardo Montalban (Major Padula), Paul Newman (Ad), Susan Strasberg (Rosanna), Jessica Tandy (Mrs. Adams), Eli Wallach (John).

Night Ambush (see *Ill Met by Moonlight*).

3156. *Night and the City* (Gerald Kersh, 1938). A small-time hustler concocts a disastrous plan to promote a wrestling match and becomes involved with mobsters. **Adaptation 1:** *Night and the City* (20th Century–Fox, 1950). Dir: Jules Dassin. Scr: Jo Eisinger. Cast: Richard Widmark (Fabian), Gene Tierney (Mary), Googie Withers (Helen), Hugh Marlowe (Adam). **Adaptation 2:** *Night and the City* (20th Century–Fox, 1992). Dir: Irwin Winkler. Scr: Richard Price. Cast: Robert De Niro (Fabian), Jessica Lange (Helen), Cliff Gorman (Phil), Alan King (Ira), Jack Warden (Al), Eli Wallach (Peck). VHS.

Night After Night (see *Single Night*).

3157. "Night Bus" (Samuel Hopkins Adams, 1933). A runaway heiress falls in love with the journalist who is pursuing her for a story. The short story appeared in the August 1933 issue of

Cosmopolitan. **Adaptation 1:** *It Happened One Night* (1934). Dir: Frank Capra. Scr: Robert Riskin. Cast: Clark Gable (Peter), Claudette Colbert (Ellie), Walter Connolly (Alexander), Roscoe Karns (Oscar). Notes: Academy Awards for Best Picture, Director, Screenplay, Actor (Gable), and Actress (Colbert). DVD, VHS. **Adaptation 2:** *You Can't Run Away from It* (Columbia, 1956). Dir: Dick Powell. Scr: Claude Binyon, Robert Riskin. Cast: June Allyson (Ellie), Jack Lemmon (Peter), Charles Bickford (Alexander), Paul Gilbert (George). Notes: A musical remake of the earlier film. Although it does not credit Adams' story directly, the 1945 Columbia musical film *Eve Knew Her Apples* tells the same story except that the heiress is replaced by a radio star trying to escape her fame.

Night Caller from Outer Space (see *The Night Callers*).

3158. *The Night Callers* (Frank Crisp, 1960). Science-fiction thriller about aliens from an endangered planet who come to Earth and abduct women to repopulate their world. **Adaptation:** *The Night Caller*; released in the U.S. as *Blood Beast from Outer Space*; also released as *Night Caller from Outer Space* (1965). Dir: John Gilling. Scr: Jim O'Connolly. Cast: John Saxon (Dr. Costain), Alfred Burke (Detective Hartley), Patricia Haines (Ann), Maurice Denham (Dr. Morley). DVD, VHS.

Night Club Lady (see *About the Murder of the Night Club Lady*).

The Night Crawlers (see *The Monster from the Earth's End*).

Night Creature (see *Dr. Syn*).

3159. *Night Cry* (William L. Stuart, 1948). An unorthodox street cop accidentally kills a murder suspect and covers up the incident by pinning it on a gangster. **Adaptation:** *Where the Sidewalk Ends* (20th Century–Fox, 1950). Dir: Otto Preminger. Scr: Ben Hecht, Robert E. Kent, Frank P. Rosenberg, Victor Trivas. Cast: Dana Andrews (Mark), Gene Tierney (Morgan), Gary Merrill (Scalise). DVD, VHS.

3160. *Night Darkens the Streets* (Arthur La Bern, 1946). A young girl escapes from a group home and gets into trouble with the law. **Adaptation:** *Good Time Girl* (Rank/Eagle-Lion, 1948). Dir: David MacDonald. Scr: Muriel Box, Sydney Box, Ted Willis. Cast: Jean Kent (Gwen), Dennis Price (Red), Herbert Lom (Max).

Night Falls on Manhattan (see *Tainted Evidence*).

Night Fighters (see *A Terrible Beauty*).

3161. "The Night Flier" (Stephen King, 1988). Two investigative reporters look into gruesome murders at remote airfields, the work of a vampire who pilots a small plane. The short story first appeared in a 1988 collection titled *New Stories by the Masters of Modern Horror*, edited by Douglas E. Winter. It was subsequently included in King's 1993 short-story collection *Nightmares and Dreamscapes*. **Adaptation:** *Night Flier* (New Line, 1997). Dir: Mark Pavia. Scr: Mark Pavia, Jack O'Donnell. Cast: Miguel Ferrer (Richard), Julie Entwisle (Katherine), Dan Monahan (Merton), Michael H. Moss (Renfield). DVD, VHS.

3162. *Night Games* (Mai Zetterling, 1966). In this Swedish novel, originally titled *Nattlek*, a repressed middle-aged man recalls his mother's sexual perversions. **Adaptation:** *Night Games* (Mondial, 1966). Dir: Mai Zetterling. Scr: David Hughes, Mai Zetterling. Cast: Ingrid Thulin (Irene), Keve Hjelm (Jan), Lena Brundin (Mariana). Notes: Originally released as *Nattlek* and shown with subtitles.

3163. *Night Has a Thousand Eyes* (Cornell Woolrich, 1945). A stage mentalist is terrified when he discovers that he actually has the ability to predict the future but not to alter its course. Woolrich originally published the novel under the pseudonym George Hopley. **Adaptation:** *Night Has a Thousand Eyes* (Paramount, 1948). Dir: John Farrow. Scr: Barre Lyndon, Jonathan Latimer. Cast: Edward G. Robinson (John), Gail Russell (Jean), John Lund (Elliott), Virginia Bruce (Jenny), William Demarest (Lieutenant Shawn).

A Night in Paradise (see *Peacock's Feather*).

A Night in the Life of Jimmy Reardon (see *Aren't You Even Gonna Kiss Me Goodbye?*)

3164. *The Night Life of the Gods* (Thorne Smith, 1931). Comic fantasy about a scientist who invents a machine that turns flesh into stone and vice versa. Chaos ensues when he brings various Greek gods to life in modern-day New York City. **Adaptation:** *The Night Life of the Gods* (Universal, 1935). Dir: Lowell Sherman. Scr: Barry Trivers. Cast: Alan Mowbray (Hunter), Florine McKinney (Meg), Peggy Shannon (Daphne).

3165. *Night Nurse* (Dora Macy [pseudonym for Grace Perkins Oursler, 1930). A nurse working for a family enlists the help of a petty thief to foil a plot to murder two children in her charge.

Adaptation: *Night Nurse* (Warner, 1931). Dir: William A. Wellman. Scr: Oliver H. P. Garrett, Charles Kenyon. Cast: Barbara Stanwyck (Laura), Ben Lyon (Mortie), Joan Blondell (Mrs. Maloney), Clark Gable (Nick). VHS.

Night of Mystery (see *The Kennel Murder Case*).

3166. *Night of Reunion* (Michael Allegretto, 1990). An emotionally ill woman escapes from an mental institution and seeks vengeance on the man who adopted her baby years earlier. **Adaptation:** *Terror in the Shadows* (Hearst, 1995 TV Movie). Dir: William A. Graham. Scr: Matt Dorff. Cast: Genie Francis (Sarah), Leigh McCloskey (Alex), Victoria Wyndham (Kay), Mark D. Espinoza (Detective Alonso).

3167. *Night of the Big Heat* (John Lymington, 1959). In order to survive, space aliens take over a remote Scottish island and make it unbearably hot in the middle of winter. **Adaptation:** *Night of the Big Heat*; released in the U.S. as *Island of the Burning Damned* (Planet/Maron, 1967). Dir: Terence Fisher. Scr: Ronald Liles. Cast: Christopher Lee (Godfrey), Patrick Allen (Jeff), Peter Cushing (Dr. Stone), Jane Merrow (Angela), VHS.

Night of the Demon (see "Casting the Runes").

The Night of the Eagle (see *The Conjure Wife*).

The Night of the Following Day (see *The Snatchers*).

3168. *Night of the Fox* (Jack Higgins [pseudonym for Harry Patterson], 1986). When an American military officer carrying plans for the D-Day invasion is captured in Germany, the Allies send in a British agent disguised as a Nazi to rescue him. **Adaptation:** *Night of the Fox* (TF1/Vidmark, 1990 TV Movie). Dir: Charles Jarrott. Scr: Bennett Cohen. Cast: George Peppard (Colonel Martineau/Max Vogel), Michael York (Field Marshal Rommel/Berger), John Mills (General Munro), Deborah Raffin (Sarah), David Birney (Kelso). VHS.

3169. *The Night of the Generals* (Hans Hellmut Kirst, 1962). The German novel, originally titled *Die Nacht der Generale* and translated into English in 1964, concerns a German intelligence agent pursuing a psychopathic Nazi general who kills prostitutes in Warsaw during World Ear II. It takes the investigator twenty years to solve the crime. **Adaptation:** *The Night of the Generals* (Columbia, 1967). Dir: Anatole Litvak. Scr: Paul Dehn, Joseph Kessel. Cast: Peter O'Toole (General Tanz), Omar Sharif (Major Grau), Tom Courtenay (Hartmann/Lukener), Donald Pleasence (General Kahlenberg), Joanna Pettet (Ulrike), Philippe Noiret (Inspector Morand). DVD, VHS.

3170. *Night of the Hunter* (Davis Grubb, 1953). A psychotic thief posing as a preacher goes in search of an executed convict's hidden treasure, but only the dead man's orphaned children know where it is. **Adaptation 1:** *The Night of the Hunter* (United Artists, 1955). Dir: Charles Laughton. Scr: James Agee. Cast: Robert Mitchum (Harry), Shelley Winters (Willa), Lillian Gish (Rachel), James Gleason (Birdy), Evelyn Varden (Icy), Peter Graves (Ben). DVD, VHS. **Adaptation 2:** *Night of the Hunter* (NBC, 1991 TV Movie). Dir: David Greene. Scr: Edmond Stevens. Cast: Richard Chamberlain (Harry), Diana Scarwid (Willa), Amy Bebout (Pearl), Reid Binion (John), Ray McKinnon (Ben), Burgess Meredith (Birdy). DVD, VHS.

3171. *Night of the Juggler* (William P. McGivern, 1975). A former New York City policeman frantically searches for his daughter, who was kidnapped by a serial killer. **Adaptation:** *Night of the Juggler* (Columbia, 1980). Dir: Robert Butler. Scr: William P. McGivern, Rick Natkin, Bill Norton. Cast: James Brolin (Sean), Cliff Gorman (Gus), Richard S. Castellano (Lieutenant Tonelli). VHS.

Night of the Lepus (see *The Year of the Angry Rabbit*).

3172. *Night of the Running Man* (Lee Wells, 1981). After his passenger is murdered, a Las Vegas taxi driver finds a suitcase containing a million dollars and goes on the run with it, pursued by a ruthless mob hitman. **Adaptation:** *Night of the Running Man* (Trimark, 1994). Dir: Mark L. Lester. Scr: Lee Wells. Cast: Andrew McCarthy (Logan), Matthew Laurance (Eric), Carl Ciarfalio (the Hitman), Antony Ponzini (Ernie), Jeanna Michaels (Cynthia), Scott Glenn (David). VHS.

3173. *The Night of the Tiger* (Al Dewlen, 1956). Western about a buffalo hunter who seeks revenge after he is robbed and unjustly accused of cattle rustling. **Adaptation:** *Ride Beyond Vengeance* (Columbia, 1966). Dir: Bernard McEveety. Scr: Andrew J. Fenady. Cast: Chuck Connors (Trapp), Michael Rennie (Durham), Kathryn Hays (Jessie), Joan Blondell (Mrs. Lavender), Gloria Grahame (Bonnie).

3174. *The Night of Wenceslas* (Lionel Davidson, 1960). Spy spoof about a poor writer who goes to Czechoslovakia to work as a translator and is coaxed into doing espionage work. **Adap-**

tation: *Hot Enough for June*; released in the U.S. as *Agent 8 3/4* (Rank/Continental, 1964). Dir: Ralph Thomas. Scr: Lukas Heller. Cast: Dirk Bogarde (Nicholas), Sylva Koscina (Vlasta), Robert Morley (Cunliffe), Leo McKern (Simoneva).

3175. *Night Ride Home* (Barbara Esstman, 1997). After their son is killed in a riding accident on their horse ranch, a grieving couple's marriage crumbles. **Adaptation:** *Night Ride Home* (CBS/ Hallmark, 1999 TV Movie). Dir: Glenn Jordan. Scr: Ronald Parker, Darrah Cloud. Cast: Rebecca De Mornay (Nora), Keith Carradine (Neal), Thora Birch (Clea), Ellen Burstyn (Maggie), Lynne Thigpen (Fran). VHS.

3176. *Night Sins* (Tami Hoag, 1996). After the disappearance of a young boy in a small Minnesota town, a policeman and an investigator join forces to catch a serial killer who has reemerged after twenty years. **Adaptation:** *Night Sins* (CBS, 1997 TV Miniseries). Dir: Robert Allan Ackerman. Scr: John Leekley. Cast: Valerie Bertinelli (Megan), Harry Hamlin (Mitch), Karen Sillas (Dr. Garrison), Martin Donovan (Paul).

Night Sun (see *Father Sergius*).

3177. *The Night They Raided Minsky's* (Rowland Barber, 1960). An Amish girl goes to New York to become a dancer and ends up working in a burlesque hall, where she invents the art of striptease. **Adaptation:** *The Night They Raided Minsky's*; released in the UK as *The Night They Invented Striptease* (United Artists, 1968). Dir: William Friedkin. Scr: Norman Lear, Sidney Michaels, Arnold Schulman. Cast: Jason Robards (Raymond), Britt Ekland (Rachel), Norman Wisdom (Chick), Forrest Tucker (Trim), Harry Andrews (Jacob). VHS.

A Night to Remember (1943) (see *The Frightened Stiff*).

3178. *A Night to Remember* (Walter Lord, 1955). A minute-by-minute account of the 1912 sinking of the *Titanic*. **Adaptation:** *A Night to Remember* (Rank, 1958). Dir: Roy Ward Baker. Scr: Eric Ambler. Cast: Kenneth More (Lightoller), Ronald Allen (Clarke), Robert Ayres (Peuchen), Honor Blackman (Liz). Notes: Golden Globe Award for Best English-Language Foreign Film. DVD, VHS.

3179. *Night Unto Night* (Philip Wylie, 1944). Love story about the relationship between a dying scientist and an emotionally disturbed widow. **Adaptation:** *Night Unto Night* (1949). Dir: Don Siegel. Scr: Kathryn Scola. Cast: Ronald Reagan (John), Viveca Lindfors (Ann), Broderick Crawford (Shawn), Rosemary De Camp (Thalia).

3180. *Night Walker* (Donald Hamilton, 1954). As a wealthy rancher attempts to drive smaller ranches out of business, his wife begins an affair with his younger brother. The book was released in the UK as *Rough Company*. **Adaptation:** *The Violent Men*; released in the UK as *Rough Company* (Columbia, 1955). Dir: Rudolph Mate. Scr: Harry Kleiner. Cast: Glenn Ford (Parrish), Barbara Stanwyck (Martha), Edward G. Robinson (Lee), Dianne Foster (Judith), Brian Keith (Cole). VHS.

3181. *The Night Watch* (Thomas Walsh, 1952). A dishonest night watchman helps gangsters steal a fortune. **Adaptation:** *Pushover* (Columbia, 1954). Dir: Richard Quine. Scr: Roy Huggins. Cast: Fred MacMurray (Sheridan), Philip Carey (McAllister), Kim Novak (Lona), Dorothy Malone (Ann), E. G. Marshall (Lieutenant Eckstrom). Notes: The screenplay is based on Thomas Walsh's 1952 novel *The Night Watch* and on Bill S. Ballinger's 1953 novel *Rafferty*. VHS. See also *Rafferty*.

3182. *Night Without Stars* (Winston Graham, 1950). After World War II, a partially blind British lawyer investigates the death of a French resistance fighter and falls in love with his widow. **Adaptation:** *Night Without Stars* (Rank/RKO, 1951). Dir: Anthony Pelissier. Scr: Winston Graham. Cast: David Farrar (Giles), Nadia Gray (Alex), Maurice Teynac (Louis).

Nightbreed (see *Cabal*).

3183. *Nightfall* (David Goodis, 1947). After the murder of a bank robber, an innocent artist is sought by the police for killing the man and by the other robbers who think he knows where their loot is stashed. **Adaptation:** *Nightfall* (Columbia, 1957). Dir: Jacques Tourneur. Scr: Stirling Silliphant. Cast: Aldo Ray (James), Brian Keith (John), Anne Bancroft (Marie), Jocelyn Brando (Laura).

3184. *Nightflyers* (George R. R. Martin, 1985). Scientists journey into space to find a strange and beautiful creature but end up battling a murderous computer aboard their own spacecraft. The novella is the title work in Martin's 1985 collection of stories. **Adaptation:** *Nightflyers* (New Century Vista, 1987). Dir: T. C. Blake. Scr: Robert Jaffe. Cast: Catherine Mary Stewart (Miranda), Michael Praed (Royd), John Standing (Michael), Lisa Blount (Audrey). VHS.

Nightmare (1942) (see *Escape*).

3185. "Nightmare" (Cornell Woolrich, 1943). An unsuspecting musician is hypnotized and made to carry out a murder. When he begins to suspect that he has committed the crime, he reconstructs his life with the aid of a policeman. The short story, which was originally published under the pseudonym William Irish, appeared in Woolrich's 1943 collection *I Wouldn't Be in Your Shoes*. **Adaptation 1:** *Fear in the Night* (Paramount, 1947). Dir: Maxwell Shane. Scr: Maxwell Shane. Cast: Paul Kelly (Cliff), De Forest Kelley (Vince Grayson), Ann Doran (Lil). VHS. **Adaptation 2:** *Nightmare* (United Artists, 1956). Dir: Maxwell Shane. Scr: Maxwell Shane. Cast: Edward G. Robinson (Rene), Kevin McCarthy (Stan), Connie Russell (Gina).

3186. *Nightmare* (Anne Blaisdell [pseudonym for Elizabeth Linington], 1961). An American girl is taken prisoner in England by the psychotic mother of her dead fiancé. **Adaptation:** *Fanatic*; released in the U.S. as *Die! Die! My Darling* (Hammer/Columbia, 1965). Dir: Silvio Narizzano. Scr: Richard Matheson. Cast: Tallulah Bankhead (Mrs. Trefoile), Stefanie Powers (Pat), Peter Vaughan (Harry). VHS.

3187. *Nightmare Alley* (William Lindsay Gresham, 1946). A carnival barker discovers that he has a knack for conning people with his claims of supernatural powers. **Adaptation:** *Nightmare Alley* (20th Century–Fox, 1947). Dir: Edmund Goulding. Scr: Jules Furthman. Cast: Tyrone Power (Stanton), Coleen Gray (Molly), Joan Blondell (Zeena).

3188. *Nightmare in Manhattan* (Thomas Walsh, 1950, Edgar Award for Best First Novel). The kidnappers of a young blind woman try to use a crowded rail station as the collection point for their ransom. The novel was originally serialized in *The Saturday Evening Post* (July 9–August 13, 1949). **Adaptation:** *Union Station* (Paramount, 1950). Dir: Rudolph Mate. Scr: Sydney Boehm. Cast: William Holden (Lieutenant Calhoun), Nancy Olson (Joyce), Barry Fitzgerald (Inspector Donnelly), Lyle Bettger (Joe), Jan Sterling (Marge). VHS.

3189. *Nightmare of Ecstasy: The Life and Art of Edward D. Wood Jr.* (Rudolph Grey, 1992). Biography of director Ed Wood (1924–1978), focusing on his relationship with actor Bela Lugosi and on his strange films like *Glen or Glenda?* and *Plan Nine from Outer Space*. **Adaptation:** *Ed Wood* (Touchstone/Buena Vista, 1994). Dir: Tim Burton. Scr: Scott Alexander, Larry Karaszewski. Cast: Johnny Depp (Ed Wood), Martin Landau (Bela Lugosi), Sarah Jessica Parker (Dolores), Patricia Arquette (Kathy), Jeffrey Jones (Criswell). Notes: Academy Award for Best Supporting Actor (Landau) and Makeup; Golden Globe Award for Best Supporting Actor (Landau) and nominations for Best Picture and Actor (Depp); Cannes Golden Palm nomination for Best Director. DVD, VHS.

3190. *The Nightmare Rally* (Pierre Castex, 1964). Comedy about three youths pursued by thieves who have hidden stolen jewels in the old car that the young people have entered into a twenty-four hour race. The French novel was translated in 1965. **Adaptation:** *Diamonds on Wheels* (Disney/Buena Vista, 1974). Dir: Jerome Courtland. Scr: William R. Yates. Cast: Patrick Allen (Inspector Cook), George Sewell (Henry), Derek Newark (Mercer), VHS.

3191. *Nightwing* (Martin Cruz Smith, 1977). Mysterious deaths in the American Southwest are linked to supernatural vampire bats. **Adaptation:** *Nightwing* (Columbia, 1979). Dir: Arthur Hiller. Scr: Steve Shagan, Bud Shrake. Cast: Nick Mancuso (Youngman), David Warner (Philip), Kathryn Harrold (Anne), Stephen Macht (Walker), Strother Martin (Selwyn). VHS.

Nikki, the Wild Dog of the North (see *Nomads of the North*).

3192. *Nine and a Half Weeks: A Memoir of a Love Affair* (Elizabeth McNeill, 1978). A Wall Street executive and an art gallery manager enter into a brief and obsessive sexual affair. **Adaptation:** *Nine ½ Weeks* (MGM, 1986). Dir: Adrian Lyne. Scr: Sarah Kernochan, Zalman King, Patricia Louisianna Knop. Cast: Mickey Rourke (John), Kim Basinger (Elizabeth), Margaret Whitton (Molly), David Margulies (Harvey), Christine Baranski (Thea). DVD, VHS.

3193. *The Nine Days of Father Serra* (Isabelle Gibson Ziegler, 1951). Historical novel about the establishment of Spanish missions in by Father Junipero Serra (1713–1784) in California in the 1769. **Adaptation:** *Seven Cities of Gold* (20th Century–Fox, 1955). Dir: Robert D. Webb. Scr: Richard L. Breen, John C. Higgins. Cast: Richard Egan (Mendoza), Anthony Quinn (Gaspar), Michael Rennie (Father Serra), Jeffrey Hunter (Matuwir), Rita Moreno (Ula). VHS.

3194. *Nine Hours to Rama* (Stanley Wolpert, 1962). A fictionalized account of the events leading up to the assassination of Mahatma Gandhi (1869–1948). **Adaptation:** *Nine Hours to Rama*

(1963). Dir: Mark Robson. Scr: Nelson Gidding. Cast: Horst Buchholz (Godse), Jose Ferrer (Gopal Das), Valerie Gearon (Rani Mehta), Robert Morley (Mussadi), Diane Baker (Sheila), J. S. Casshyap (Mahatma Gandhi).

3195. *1984* (George Orwell, 1949). Classic futuristic dystopian vision of a repressive society where "Big Brother" is always watching and the clerk who defies the system to gain his freedom. **Adaptation 1:** *1984* (BBC, 1954 TV Movie). Dir: Rudolph Cartier. Scr: Nigel Kneale. Cast: Peter Cushing (Winston), Andre Morell (O'Brien), Yvonne Mitchell (Julia), Donald Pleasence (Syme). **Adaptation 2:** *1984* (Columbia, 1956). Dir: Michael Anderson. Scr: Ralph Gilbert Bettison, William Templeton. Cast: Edmond O'Brien (Winston), Jan Sterling (Julia), Michael Redgrave (O'Brien), Donald Pleasence (Parsons). VHS. **Adaptation 3:** *Nineteen Eighty Four* (BBC, 1965 TV Movie). Dir: Christopher Morahan. Scr: Christopher Morahan. Cast: David Buck (Winston), Joseph O'Conor (O'Brien), Jane Merrow (Julia), Cyril Shaps (Syme). **Adaptation 4:** *Nineteen Eighty-Four* (Atlantic Releasing, 1984). Dir: Michael Radford. Scr: Michael Radford. Cast: John Hurt (Winston), Richard Burton (O'Brien), Suzanna Hamilton (Julia), Cyril Cusack (Charrington). DVD, VHS.

3196. *Ninety-two in the Shade* (Thomas McGuane, 1973). Two fishing-boat captains in Key West compete with each other for supremacy. **Adaptation:** *92 in the Shade* (United Artists, 1975). Dir: Thomas McGuane. Scr: Thomas McGuane. Cast: Peter Fonda (Skelton), Warren Oates (Nichol), Margot Kidder (Miranda), Burgess Meredith (Goldsboro), Harry Dean Stanton (Carter), Elizabeth Ashley (Jeannie), Sylvia Miles (Bella). VHS.

The Ninth Configuration (see *Twinkle, Twinkle, Killer Kane*).

The Ninth Gate (see *The Club Dumas*).

The Ninth Guest (see *The Invisible Host*).

3197. *No Beast So Fierce* (Edward Bunker, 1973). In this novel written while Bunker himself was in jail, a parolee who tries to go straight is driven back into a life of crime by a vicious parole officer. **Adaptation:** *Straight Time* (Warner, 1978). Dir: Ulu Grosbard. Scr: Jeffrey Boam, Edward Bunker, Alvin Sargent. Cast: Dustin Hoffman (Max), Theresa Russell (Jenny), Gary Busey (Willy), Harry Dean Stanton (Jerry), M. Emmet Walsh (Earl), Rita Taggart (Carol), Kathy Bates (Selma). VHS.

No Big Deal (see *Would You Settle for Improbable?*)

No Blade of Grass (see *The Death of Grass*).

3198. *No Coffin for the Corpse* (Clayton Rawson, 1942). A former stage magician named the Great Merlini helps police solve the mystery of a dead man whose body disappeared from the cemetery. **Adaptation:** *The Man Who Wouldn't Die* (20th Century–Fox, 1942). Dir: Herbert I. Leeds. Scr: Arnaud d'Usseau. Cast: Lloyd Nolan (Shayne), Marjorie Weaver (Catherine), Helene Reynolds (Anna). Notes: The screenplay features Michael Shayne, a character featured in a series of mystery novels by Brett Halliday, and combines Halliday's characters with Rawson's plot.

3199. *No Difference to Me* (Phyllis Hambledon, 1947). A married couple preparing to divorce reconsider when their beloved daughter runs away in protest. **Adaptation:** *No Place for Jennifer* (Associated British/Stratford, 1950). Dir: Henry Cass. Scr: J. Lee Thompson. Cast: Leo Genn (William), Rosamund John (Rachel), Beatrice Campbell (Paula), Guy Middleton (Brian), Janette Scott (Jennifer).

No Escape (see *The Penal Colony*).

3200. *No Greater Love* (Danielle Steel, 1991). After her parents die on the *Titanic* in 1912, a young woman is left to raise her five younger siblings. **Adaptation:** *No Greater Love* (NBC, 1996 TV Movie). Dir: Richard T. Heffron. Scr: Carmen Culver. Cast: Kelly Rutherford (Edwina), Chris Sarandon (Sam), Nicholas Campbell (Malcolm), Daniel Hugh Kelly (Ben). DVD, VHS.

3201. *No Highway* (Nevil Shute [pseudonym for Nevil Shute Norway], 1948). An aeronautical engineer aboard a transatlantic flight calculates that the plane is likely to crash because of metal fatigue. **Adaptation:** *No Highway*; released in the U.S. as *No Highway in the Sky* (20th Century–Fox, 1951). Dir: Henry Koster. Scr: R. C. Sherriff, Oscar Millard, Alec Coppel. Cast: James Stewart (Theodore), Marlene Dietrich (Monica), Glynis Johns (Marjorie), Jack Hawkins (Dennis). VHS.

No Highway in the Sky (see *No Highway*).

3202. *No Love for Johnnie* (Wilfred Fienburgh, 1959). The personal and professional problems of a British politician running for reelection to Parliament. **Adaptation:** *No Love for Johnnie* (Rank/Embassy, 1961). Dir: Ralph Thomas. Scr: Nicholas Phipps, Mordecai Richler. Cast: Peter

Finch (Johnnie), Stanley Holloway (Fred), Mary Peach (Pauline). Notes: BAFTA Award for Best British Actor (Finch). VHS.

No Man of Her Own (see *I Married a Dead Man*).

No Mercy (see *Crime and Punishment*).

3203. *No More Gas* (Charles Nordhoff and James Norman Hall, 1940). Comic novel about a family living on an island in the South Seas and trying at all costs to avoid work. **Adaptation:** *The Tuttles of Tahiti* (RKO, 1942). Dir: Charles Vidor. Scr: Robert Carson, James Hilton, Lewis Meltzer. Cast: Charles Laughton (Jonas), Jon Hall (Chester), Peggy Drake (Tamara), Victor Francen (Mr. Blondin). VHS.

3204. *No Orchids for Miss Blandish* (James Hadley Chase [pseudonym for Rene Brabazon Raymond], 1939). In the late 1920's, a rich young woman is kidnapped for ransom and begins to develop romantic feelings for her vicious captor. **Adaptation 1:** *No Orchids for Miss Blandish* (RKO, 1948). Dir: St. John Legh Clowes. Scr: St. John Legh Clowes. Cast: Linden Travers (Miss Blandish), Jack La Rue (Slim), Walter Crisham (Eddie). **Adaptation 2:** *The Grissom Gang* (ABC, 1971). Dir: Robert Aldrich. Scr: Leon Griffiths. Cast: Kim Darby (Miss Blandish), Scott Wilson (Slim), Tony Musante (Eddie), Robert Lansing (Dave), Connie Stevens (Anna). DVD, VHS.

No Place for Jennifer (see *No Difference to Me*).

No Place Like Homicide (see *The Ghoul*).

3205. *No Place to Hide* (Ted Allbeury, 1984). Espionage thriller about a jaded British agent who wants to leave the service, but is not allowed to by his cruel superiors. **Adaptation:** *Hostage* (Columbia TriStar, 1993). Dir: Robert Young. Scr: Arthur Hopcraft. Cast: Sam Neill (John), Talisa Soto (Joanna), James Fox (Hugo), Michael Kitchen (Fredericks), Art Malik (Khalim). VHS.

3206. *No Resting Place* (Ian Niall [pseudonym for John McNeillie], 1948). An Irish drifter accidentally kills a man and is hounded by the police. **Adaptation:** *No Resting Place* (Associated British/Classic, 1950). Dir: Paul Rotha. Scr: Gerald Healy, Colin Lesslie, Michael Orrom, Paul Rotha. Cast: Michael Gough (Alec), Eithne Dunne (Meg), Noel Purcell (Mannigan). Notes: BAFTA nominations for Best British Film and Best Film from Any Source.

3207. *No Sad Songs for Me* (Ruth Southard, 1944). A woman puts her family's affairs in order when she discovers that she has only a short time to live. **Adaptation:** *No Sad Songs for Me* (Columbia, 1950). Dir: Rudolph Mate. Scr: Howard Koch. Cast: Margaret Sullavan (Mary), Wendell Corey (Brad), Viveca Lindfors (Chris), Natalie Wood (Polly), John McIntire (Dr. Frene).

3208. *No Time for Sergeants* (Mac Hyman, 1954). Comic novel about the misadventures of a country bumpkin who is drafted into the military. Ira Levin adapted the book for the Broadway stage in 1955. **Adaptation:** *No Time for Sergeants* (Warner, 1958). Dir: Mervyn Le Roy. Scr: Ira Levin (from his play), John Lee Mahin. Cast: Andy Griffith (Will), Myron McCormick (Sergeant King), Nick Adams (Whitledge), Murray Hamilton (Blanchard). VHS. Notes: The book was also the basis for an ABC television series in 1964.

No Way Out (see *The Big Clock*).

3209. *No Way to Treat a Lady* (William Goldman, 1964). An actor becomes a serial killer of women and eludes police with his many disguises. The book was adapted as an off–Broadway musical in 1996. **Adaptation:** *No Way to Treat a Lady* (Paramount, 1968). Dir: Jack Smight. Scr: John Gay. Cast: Rod Steiger (Christopher), Lee Remick (Kate), George Segal (Mr. Brummel), Eileen Heckart (Mrs. Brummel), Murray Hamilton (Inspector Haines). DVD, VHS.

Nobody Lives Forever (see *I Wasn't Born Yesterday*).

3210. *Nobody Loves a Drunken Indian* (Clair Huffaker, 1967). An outcast, alcoholic Native American living on a reservation leads a political demonstration. **Adaptation:** *Flap*; released in the UK as *The Last Warrior* (Warner, 1970). Dir: Carol Reed. Scr: Clair Huffaker. Cast: Anthony Quinn (Flapping Eagle), Claude Akins (Lobo), Tony Bill (Eleven Snowflake), Shelley Winters (Dorothy), Victor Jory (Wounded Bear).

Nobody Runs Forever (see *The High Commissioner*).

3211. *Nobody's Fool* (Richard Russo, 1993). An aging small-town handyman who has not had much luck in life gets a chance to redeem himself when his estranged adult son and grandson move back to town. **Adaptation:** *Nobody's Fool* (Paramount, 1994). Dir: Robert Benton. Scr: Robert Benton. Cast: Paul Newman (Sully), Jessica Tandy (Beryl), Bruce Willis (Carl), Melanie Griffith (Toby), Dylan Walsh (Peter). Notes: Academy Award nomination for Best

Screenplay and Actor (Newman); Golden Globe nomination for Best Actor (Newman). DVD, VHS.

Nobody's Perfect (see *The Crows of Edwina Hill*).

Noir et Blanc (*see* "Desire and the Black Masseur").

3212. *Nomads of the North* (James Oliver Curwood, 1919). The adventures of a Canadian trapper and his faithful wolf dog. **Silent Film:** 1920, starring Lon Chaney (DVD, VHS). **Adaptation:** *Nikki, Wild Dog of the North* (Disney/Buena Vista, 1961). Dir: Jack Couffer, Don Haldane. Scr: Dwight Hauser, Winston Hibler, Ralph Wright. Cast: Robert Rivard (Durante), Jean Coutu (Andre), Jacques Fauteux (Narrator). DVD, VHS.

Non-Stop New York (see *Sky Steward*).

3213. *None But the Lonely Heart* (Richard Llewellyn, 1943). When he learns that his beloved mother is dying, a London coachman reexamines his life and priorities. **Adaptation:** *None But the Lonely Heart* (RKO, 1944). Dir: Clifford Odets. Scr: Clifford Odets. Cast: Cary Grant (Ernie), Ethel Barrymore (Ma Mott), Barry Fitzgerald (Henry), June Duprez (Ada), Jane Wyatt (Aggie). Notes: Academy Award for Best Supporting Actress (Barrymore) and nominations for Best Actor (Grant), Editing, and Musical Score; National Board of Review Award for Best Picture. VHS.

3214. *None So Blind* (Mitchell Wilson, 1945). After World War II, a Coast Guard officer in California is attracted by a beautiful married woman he meets on a beach, but soon suspects that she and her blind husband are using him to play a devious game. **Adaptation:** *The Woman on the Beach* (RKO, 1947). Dir: Jean Renoir. Scr: Frank Davis, Michael Hogan, Jean Renoir. Cast: Joan Bennett (Peggy), Robert Ryan (Scott), Charles Bickford (Tod).

3215. *Nor the Moon by Night* (Joy Packer, 1957). An African game warden and his brother compete for the affections of a woman. **Adaptation:** *Nor the Moon by Night*; released in the U.S. as *Elephant Gun* (Rank/Lopert, 1958). Dir: Ken Annakin. Scr: Guy Elmes. Cast: Joan Brickhill (Harriet), Michael Craig (Rusty), Anna Gaylor (Thea), Ben Heydenrych (Sergeant Van Wyck).

3216. *Nora: The Real Life of Molly Bloom* (Brenda Maddox, 1988). Factual account of the relationship between a Dublin hotel maid and novelist James Joyce. **Adaptation:** *Nora* (Andora, 2000). Dir: Pat Murphy. Scr: Pat Murphy, Gerard Stembridge. Cast: Susan Lynch (Nora), Ewan McGregor (Joyce), Andrew Scott (Bodkin), Veronica Duffy (Annie). Notes: IFTA Award (Ireland) for Best Actress (Lynch) and nominations for Best Picture, Screenplay, Actor (McGregor), Cinematography, and Costume Design. DVD, VHS.

3217. "Norman and the Killer" (Joyce Carol Oates, 1965). A man tormented by guilt for a crime committed in the past has the opportunity to confront the real criminal. The short story was published in Oates' 1965 collection *Upon the Sweeping Flood and Other Stories*. **Adaptation:** *Norman and the Killer* (American Film Institute, 1991). Dir: Bob Graham. Scr: Lynn Thomas Pierce. Cast: John Durren (Cameron), Richard Hawkins (Norman), Jane Marla Robbins (Ellen). VHS.

3218. *Norman Vincent Peale: Minister to Millions* (Arthur Gordon, 1958). Biography of the influential minister (1898–1993), whose doctrine of the power of positive thinking inspired America. **Adaptation:** *One Man's Way* (United Artists, 1964). Dir: Denis Sanders. Scr: John W. Bloch, Eleanore Griffin. Cast: Gerald Gordon (Peale), David Bailey (Peale as a child), Sandra Gale Bettin (Alma), Veronica Cartwright (Mary), Virginia Christine (Hannah). VHS.

3219. *North* (Alan Zweibel, 1984). Believing that his parents do not appreciate him, an eleven-year-old boy successfully sues for the right to divorce them and then travels the world looking for the ideal parents. **Adaptation:** *North* (Columbia, 1994). Dir: Rob Reiner. Scr: Alan Zweibel, Andrew Scheinman. Cast: Elijah Wood (North), Jason Alexander (North's father), Julia Louis-Dreyfus (North's mother). VHS.

3220. *North and South* (Elizabeth Gaskell, 1855). During the Industrial Revolution of the nineteenth century, an innocent young British woman is forced to leave her idyllic country village and move to an industrial mill city in the north of England. **Adaptation:** *North and South* (BBC, 2004 TV Miniseries). Dir: Brian Percival. Scr: Sandy Welch. Cast: Daniela Denby-Ashe (Margaret), Richard Armitage (John), Tim Pigott-Smith (Richard), Pauline Quirke (Dixon), Sinead Cusack (Hannah).

3221. *North and South* (John Jakes, 1981). The first installment in Jakes' Civil War trilogy, which also includes *Love and War* (1984) and *Heaven and Hell* (1987), is the story of two friends who meet at West Point and end up on opposite sides of the national conflict. **Adaptation 1:** *North and South* (ABC, 1985 TV Miniseries). Dir:

Richard T. Heffron. Scr: Paul F. Edwards, Patricia Green, Douglas Heyes, Kathleen A. Shelley. Cast: Patrick Swayze (Orry), James Read (George), Lesley-Anne Down (Madeline), David Carradine (Justin), Wendy Kilbourne (Constance), Kirstie Alley (Virgilia), Jean Simmons (Clarissa). Notes: The teleplay combines elements from *North and South* and *Love and War*. Golden Globe nominations for Best Supporting Actor (Carradine) and Supporting Actress (Down). DVD, VHS. **Adaptation 2:** *North and South II* (ABC, 1986 TV Miniseries). Dir: Kevin Connor, Scr: Richard Fielder. Cast: Kirstie Alley (Virgilia), David Carradine (Justin), Philip Casnoff (Elkanah), Mary Crosby (Isabel), Lesley-Anne Down (Madeline). Notes: The teleplay for this sequel to the 1985 miniseries combines elements from *North and South* and *Love and War*. DVD, VHS. See also *Heaven and Hell*.

3222. *The North Avenue Irregulars: A Suburb Battles the Mafia* (Albert Fay Hill, 1968). True story of a Christian minister and his congregation battling to keep gangsters out of their suburban New York neighborhood. **Adaptation:** *The North Avenue Irregulars* (Disney/Buena Vista, 1979). Dir: Bruce Bilson. Scr: Don Tait. Cast: Edward Herrmann (Reverend Hill), Barbara Harris (Vicki), Susan Clark (Anne), Karen Valentine (Jane), Michael Constantine (Marvin), Cloris Leachman (Claire). DVD, VHS.

3223. *North Dallas Forty* (Peter Gent, 1973). Autobiographical novel about the difficult life of a professional football player. **Adaptation:** *North Dallas Forty* (Paramount, 1979). Dir: Ted Kotcheff. Scr: Peter Gent, Ted Kotcheff, Frank Yablans. Cast: Nick Nolte (Phillip), Mac Davis (Seth), Charles Durning (Coach Johnson), Dayle Haddon (Charlotte), Bo Svenson (Joe Bob). DVD, VHS.

North Sea Hijack (see *Esther, Ruth and Jennifer*)

3224. *North Shore* (Wallace Irwin, 1932). A female horse trainer marries a socially prominent man and endures the scorn of his friends and family. **Adaptation:** *The Woman in Red* (Warner, 1935). Dir: Robert Florey. Scr: Peter Milne, Mary C. McCall, Jr. Cast: Barbara Stanwyck (Shelby), Gene Raymond (Johnny), Genevieve Tobin (Mrs. Nicholas), John Eldredge (Fairchild).

3225. *The North Star* (Will Henry [pseudonym for Henry W. Allen], 1956). In Alaska in the late nineteenth century, a trapper battles a corrupt businessman over the use of sacred lands. **Adaptation:** *Tashunga*; released in the U.S. as *The North Star* (Regency, 1996). Dir: Nils Gaup. Scr:

Lorenzo Donati, Sergio Donati, Paul Ohl. Cast: James Caan (Sean), Christopher Lambert (Hudson), Catherine McCormack (Sarah), Burt Young (Reno). VHS.

3226. *Northanger Abbey* (Jane Austen, 1817). Posthumously published satiric novel about a naïve young woman obsessed with gothic romances who enters society in Bath and has difficulty distinguishing between fiction and reality. **Adaptation:** *Northanger Abbey* (BBC/A&E, 1986 TV Miniseries). Dir: Giles Foster. Scr: Maggie Wadey. Cast: Katharine Schlesinger (Catherine), Peter Firth (Henry), Robert Hardy (General Tilney), Googie Withers (Mrs. Allen), Geoffrey Chater (Mr. Allen). DVD, VHS.

3227. *Northwest Passage* (Kenneth Roberts, 1936). Colonial rangers battle hostile Native Americans and face other challenges to open up new territories in frontier America. **Adaptation:** *Northwest Passage* (MGM, 1940). Dir: King Vidor. Scr: Talbot Jennings, Laurence Stallings. Cast: Spencer Tracy (Rogers), Robert Young (Langdon), Walter Brennan (Marriner), Ruth Hussey (Elizabeth). Notes: The screenplay adapted only the first part of the novel, subtitled "Rogers' Rangers." A projected second film based on Part II was never made. VHS.

Northwest Stampede (see "Wild-Horse Roundup").

3228. *The Norwich Victims* (Francis Beeding [pseudonym for John Henry Palmer and Hilary St. George Sanders], 1935). A woman at a school for boys is murdered after winning a large sum in a lottery. **Adaptation:** *Dead Men Tell No Tales* (1939). Dir: David MacDonald. Scr: Stafford Dickens, Doreen Montgomery, Walter Summers. Cast: Emlyn Williams (Dr. Headlam), Sara Seegar (Marjorie), Hugh Williams (Detective Martin), Marius Goring (Greening).

3229. *The Nose on My Face* (Laurence Payne, 1961). In London, Scotland Yard detectives investigate the murder of a model. **Adaptation:** *Girl in the Headlines*; released in the U.S. as *The Model Murder Case* (British Lion/Cinema V, 1963). Dir: Michael Truman. Scr: Patrick Campbell, Vivienne Knight. Cast: Ian Hendry (Birkett), Ronald Fraser (Saunders), Margaret Johnston (Mrs. Gray).

Nosferatu (see *Dracula*).

3230. *Nostromo: A Tale of the Seaboard* (Joseph Conrad, 1904). A charismatic leader foments a revolution against an unjust South American country's government. **Silent Film:** 1926 (titled *The Silver Treasure*). **Adaptation:** *Nostromo* (BBC, 1996 TV Miniseries). Dir: Alastair Reid. Scr: John Hale. Cast: Claudio Amendola (Nostromo), Paul Brooke (Mitchell), Lothaire Bluteau (Martin), Claudia Cardinale (Teresa), Joaquim de Almeida (Sotillo), Brian Dennehy (Joshua), Albert Finney (Dr. Monygham), Colin Firth (Charles). VHS.

3231. *Not as a Stranger* (Morton Thompson, 1954). An arrogant doctor is supported by his wife and learns humility after a personal tragedy. **Adaptation:** *Not as a Stranger* (United Artists, 1955). Dir: Stanley Kramer. Scr: Edna Anhalt, Edward Anhalt. Cast: Olivia de Havilland (Christina), Robert Mitchum (Lucas), Frank Sinatra (Alfred), Gloria Grahame (Harriet), Broderick Crawford (Dr. Aarons), Charles Bickford (Dr. Runkleman). VHS.

3232. *Not Too Narrow, Not Too Deep* (Richard Sale, 1936). Allegorical novel about prisoners who escape from Devil's Island and are influenced by a Christ-like figure among them. **Adaptation:** *Strange Cargo* (MGM, 1940). Dir: Frank Borzage. Scr: Lawrence Hazard. Cast: Joan Crawford (Julie), Clark Gable (Andre), Ian Hunter (Cambreau), Peter Lorre (Cochon). VHS.

3233. *Not Without My Daughter* (Betty Mahmoody and William Hoffer, 1987). Memoir of an American woman whose Iranian husband persuaded her and their daughter to visit his family in Iran. Once there, he declared his intention to remain, and the wife had no rights under Islamic law. She decided to find a way to flee the country with her daughter. **Adaptation:** *Not Without My Daughter* (MGM, 1991). Dir: Brian Gilbert. Scr: David W. Rintels (writing as Pat Riddle). Cast: Sally Field (Betty), Alfred Molina (Moody), Sheila Rosenthal (Mahtob), Roshan Seth (Houssein). DVD, VHS.

3234. *The Notebook* (Nicholas Sparks, 1996). Teenaged lovers separate after World War II. After some fifty years, they are reunited as elderly people, and the man reads to her from the notebook he has kept. **Adaptation:** *The Notebook* (New Line, 2004). Dir: Nick Cassavetes. Scr: Jan Sardi, Jeremy Leven. Cast: Ryan Gosling (Noah), Rachel McAdams (Allie as a young woman), James Garner (Duke), Gena Rowlands (Allie), James Marsden (Lon), Sam Shepard (Frank). DVD, VHS.

3235. *Notes from Underground* (Fyodor Dostoyevsky, 1864). The story of a loner whose moral and intellectual superiority to those around him prevents him from living a fulfilling life. The novel was first published in *The Epoch* magazine in January and February 1864. **Adaptation:** *Notes From Underground* (Northern Arts/Olive, 1995). Dir: Gary Walkow. Scr: Gary Walkow. Cast: Henry Czerny (the Underground Man), Sheryl Lee (Liza), Jon Favreau (Zerkov). DVD, VHS.

Nothing But the Best (*see* "The Best of Everything")

Nothing But the Night (see *Children of the Night*).

3236. *Nothing But the Truth* (Frederic S. Isham, 1912). A stockbroker takes a bet that he can tell the truth for a full day. The novel was adapted as a 1916 Broadway play by James Montgomery. **Silent Film:** 1920. **Adaptation 1:** *Nothing But the Truth* (Paramount, 1929). Dir: Victor Schertzinger. Scr: William Collier Sr., John McGowan. Cast: Richard Dix (Robert), Berton Churchill (Burke), Louis John Bartels (Frank). **Adaptation 2:** *Nothing But the Truth* (Paramount, 1941). Dir: Elliott Nugent. Scr: Ken Englund, Don Hartman. Cast: Bob Hope (Steve), Paulette Goddard (Gwen), Edward Arnold (Ralston), Leif Erickson (Van).

3237. *Nothing Lasts Forever* (Roderick Thorp, 1979). A New York policeman battles terrorists in an office skyscraper where his wife is being held hostage. **Adaptation:** *Die Hard* (20th Century–Fox, 1988). Dir: John McTiernan. Scr: Jeb Stuart, Steven E. de Souza. Cast: Bruce Willis (McClane), Alan Rickman (Gruber), Bonnie Bedelia (Holly), Reginald Vel Johnson (Al), Alexander Godunov (Karl). DVD, VHS. Notes: Two sequels followed the original hit movie: *Die Hard 2* (1990) (DVD, VHS), and *Die Hard with a Vengeance* (1995) (DVD, VHS). See also *58 Minutes*.

3238. *Nothing Lasts Forever* (Sidney Sheldon, 1994). Three women from different backgrounds face personal and professional problems in their work as doctors at a San Francisco city hospital. **Adaptation:** *Nothing Lasts Forever* (CBS, 1995 TV Miniseries). Dir: Jack Bender. Scr: Gerald Di Pego. Cast: Gail O'Grady (Page), Brooke Shields (Beth), Vanessa L. Williams (Kathy), Gregory Harrison (Benjamin).

Nothing Personal (see *All Our Fault*).

3239. *Nothing to Lose* (R. J. Minney, 1946). A small English town's claim to having the highest employment rate in the land is threatened by an old Irish rebel who refuses to work and ends up exposing the town council's corruption. **Adaptation:** *Time, Gentlemen, Please!* (Group W/Mayer-Kinglsey, 1952). Dir: Lewis Gilbert. Scr: Peter

Blackmore. Cast: Eddie Byrne (Dan), Hermione Baddeley (Emma), Raymond Lovell (Sir Digby).

3240. *Nothing Too Good for a Cowboy* (Richmond P. Hobson, 1955). Memoirs of a twentieth-century cowboy and his eventful life on the ranch. **Adaptation:** *Nothing Too Good for a Cowboy* (Canadian Broadcasting, 1998 TV Movie). Dir: Kari Skogland. Scr: David Barlow. Cast: Chad Willett (Hobson), Ted Atherton (Pan), Sarah Chalke (Gloria). Notes: The movie served as the pilot for a 1998 Canadian television series.

Notre Dame de Paris (see *The Hunchback of Notre Dame*).

3241. *Now and Forever* (Danielle Steel, 1978). A woman helps her unfaithful husband, who has been falsely accused of rape. **Adaptation:** *Now and Forever* (Interplanetary, 1983). Dir: Adrian Carr. Scr: Richard Cassidy. Cast: Cheryl Ladd (Jessie), Robert Coleby (Ian), Carmen Duncan (Astrid). VHS.

3242. *Now, Voyager* (Olive Higgins Prouty, 1941). After psychological therapy, a frustrated spinster becomes more extroverted and becomes involved in a doomed love affair. **Adaptation:** *Now, Voyager* (Warner, 1942). Dir: Irving Rapper. Scr: Casey Robinson. Cast: Bette Davis (Charlotte), Paul Henreid (Jerry), Claude Rains (Dr. Jaquith), Gladys Cooper (Mrs. Vale), Bonita Granville (June). Notes: Academy Award for Best Musical Score and nominations for Best Actress (Davis) and Supporting Actress (Cooper). DVD, VHS.

3243. *Nowhere in Africa* (Stefanie Zweig, 1995). The autobiographical German novel, originally titled *Nirgendwo in Afrika*, is about a German-Jewish family who leave their native country and start a new life in Kenya. **Adaptation:** *Nowhere in Africa* (Zeitgeist, 2001). Dir: Caroline Link. Scr: Caroline Link. Cast: Juliane Kohler (Jettel), Merab Ninidze (Walter), Sidede Onyulo (Owuor), Matthias Habich (Susskind). Notes: Originally titled *Nirgendwo in Afrika* and shown with subtitles. Academy Award for Best Foreign Film; Golden Globe nomination for Best Foreign-Language Film; German Film Awards for Best Picture, Director, Actor (Habich), Cinematography, and Musical Score, and nomination for Best Actress (Kohler). DVD, VHS.

3244. *Nowhere to Go* (Donald MacKenzie, 1956). A thief escapes from a British prison and is taken in by a socially prominent woman, who falls in love with him. **Adaptation:** *Nowhere to Go* (Ealing/MGM, 1958). Dir: Basil Dearden, Seth Holt. Scr: Seth Holt, Kenneth Tynan. Cast: George Nader (Paul), Maggie Smith (Bridget), Bernard Lee (Victor), Geoffrey Keen (Inspector Scott).

Nuclear Terror (see *The Golden Rendezvous*).

3245. *The Nun and the Bandit* (E. L. Grant Watson, 1935). Australian novel about a thief and his brothers who take a nun hostage. **Adaptation:** *The Nun and the Bandit* (Victoria, 1992). Dir: Paul Cox. Scr: Paul Cox. Cast: Gosia Dobrowolska (Sister Lucy), Chris Haywood (Michael), Victoria Eagger (Maureen), Charlotte Haywood (Julie).

3246. *The Nun's Story* (Kathryn Hulme, 1956). A Belgian nun joins a strict order and is sent to the Congo. After serious philosophical disagreements with her superiors, she decides to leave the religious life. **Adaptation:** *The Nun's Story* (Warner, 1959). Dir: Fred Zinnemann. Scr: Robert Anderson. Cast: Audrey Hepburn (Sister Luke), Peter Finch (Dr. Fortunati), Edith Evans (Mother Emmanuel), Peggy Ashcroft (Mother Mathilde), Dean Jagger (Dr. Van Der Mal), Mildred Dunnock (Sister Margharita). Notes: Academy Award nominations for Best Picture, Director, Screenplay, Actress (Hepburn), Cinematography, Editing, Musical Score, and Sound; Golden Globe nominations for Best Film Promoting International Understanding, Film, Director, Actress (Hepburn), and Supporting Actress (Evans); National Board of Review Awards for Best Picture, Director, and Supporting Actress (Evans). VHS.

Nurse Edith Cavell (see *Dawn*).

3247. *The Nursemaid Who Disappeared* (Philip MacDonald, 1938). A babysitting agency is a front for a gang of kidnappers. **Adaptation:** *The Nursemaid Who Disappeared* (Warner, 1939). Dir: Arthur B. Woods. Scr: Connery Chappell, Paul Gangelin. Cast: Lesley Brook (Avis), Coral Browne (Mabel), Ian Fleming (Sir Egbert), Martita Hunt (Lady Ballister).

3248. *The Nutmeg Tree* (Margery Sharp, 1937). After many years apart, a dancehall performer and her estranged husband reunite as their daughter prepares to marry. **Adaptation:** *Julia Misbehaves* (MGM, 1948). Dir: Jack Conway. Scr: William Ludwig, Harry Ruskin, Arthur Wimperis. Cast: Greer Garson (Julia), Walter Pidgeon (William), Peter Lawford (Richie), Elizabeth Taylor (Susan), Cesar Romero (Fred). VHS.

O Brother, Where Art Thou? (see *The Odyssey*).

3249. *O Pioneers!* (Willa Cather, 1913). After her father's death, the eldest daughter of a Swedish immigrant family struggles to maintain their farm and support the family. **Adaptation 1:** *O Pioneers!* (PBS, 1991 TV Movie). Dir: Kirk Browning, Kevin Kuhlke. Scr: Darrah Cloud. Cast: Mary McDonnell (Alexandra), Randle Mell (Carl), Jennifer Bohn (Marie), John Carpenter (Ivar), Neil Maffin (Emil). VHS. **Adaptation 2:** *O Pioneers!* (Warner Brothers Television, 1992 TV Movie). Dir: Glenn Jordan. Scr: Robert W. Lenski. Cast: Jessica Lange (Alexandra), David Strathairn (Carl), Tom Aldredge (Ivar), Reed Diamond (Emil), Anne Heche (Marie). DVD, VHS.

3250. *O Que e Isso, Companheiro?* (Fernando Gabeira, 1979). A Brazilian journalist's account of his involvement during the late 1960's with a revolutionary group that kidnapped the American ambassador and offered him in exchange for political prisoners being held by the dictatorial government. **Adaptation:** *Four Days in September* (Miramax, 1997). Dir: Bruno Barreto. Scr: Leopoldo Serran. Cast: Alan Arkin (Charles), Fernanda Torres (Andrea/Maria), Pedro Cardoso (Gabeira/Paulo), Luiz Fernando Guimaraes (Marcao), Claudia Abreu (Renee). Notes: Originally released as *O Que e Isso, Companheiro?* and shown with subtitles. Academy Award nomination for Best Foreign-Language Film. DVD, VHS.

3251. *The Object of My Affection* (Stephen McCauley, 1987). A pregnant woman takes in a gay teacher as a roommate and falls in love with him. **Adaptation:** *The Object of My Affection* (20th Century–Fox, 1998). Dir: Nicholas Hytner. Scr: Wendy Wasserstein. Cast: Paul Rudd (George), Kali Rocha (Melissa), Jennifer Aniston (Nina). Alan Alda (Sidney), Allison Janney (Constance), Timothy Daly (Dr. Joley). DVD, VHS.

3252. "The Oblong Box" (Edgar Allan Poe, 1844). A sailor aboard a ship bound to New York from Charleston, South Carolina, befriends a bizarre man who insists on keeping secret the contents of an oblong box he keep near him. The short story was first published in *Godey's Lady's Book* in September 1844. **Adaptation:** *The Oblong Box* (American International, 1969). Dir: Gordon Hessler. Scr: Lawrence Huntington. Cast: Vincent Price (Sir Julian), Christopher Lee (Dr. Neuhart), Rupert Davies (Kemp), Alister Williamson (Sir Edward). Notes: Despite the title, the screenplay actually concerns a disfigured man's revenge on his brother for having him buried alive. DVD, VHS.

Obsessed (see *Hit and Run*).

3253. *Obsession* (Lionel White, 1962). An unhappily married man has a fling with a young babysitter. When he wakes up one morning, he finds himself the main suspect in a murder and goes on the run with his new girlfriend. **Adaptation:** *Pierrot le Fou* (Pathe, 1965). Dir: Jean-Luc Godard. Scr: Jean-Luc Godard. Cast: Jean-Paul Belmondo (Ferdinand), Anna Karina (Marianne), Graziella Galvani (Ferdinand's girlfriend). Notes: The novel is not credited in the film. Shown with subtitles. DVD, VHS.

3254. *An Occasional Hell* (Randall Silvis, 1993). When a married man is murdered and his mistress goes missing, the man's wife becomes the prime suspect. She turns to a disabled former policeman to help clear her name. **Adaptation:** *An Occasional Hell* (Greenlight, 1996). Dir: Salome Breziner. Scr: Anton Sanko, Randall Silvis. Cast: Tom Berenger (Ernest), Valeria Golino (Elizabeth), Kari Wuhrer (Jeri), Robert Davi (Abbott). DVD, VHS.

3255. "An Occurrence at Owl Creek Bridge" (Ambrose Bierce, 1891). During the Civil War, a man unjustly accused of blowing up a strategic bridge and about to be hanged by the Union Army imagines himself escaping his fate and returning home. The short story was included in Bierce's 1891 collection *Tales of Soldiers and Civilians*. **Adaptation:** *An Occurrence at Owl Creek Bridge*; released in the UK as *Incident at Owl Creek* (Showtime, 1962). Dir: Robert Enrico. Scr: Robert Enrico. Cast: Roger Jacquet (Peyton), Anne Cornaly (Mrs. Farquhar), Stephane Fey (Union Officer). DVD, VHS.

October Sky (see *Rocket Boys*).

3256. "Octopussy" (Ian Fleming, 1964). Years after killing a man and stealing the gold bars he was carrying, a former officer of the Royal Marines in hiding in Jamaica feels guilt for his crime. James Bond visits him to persuade the man to give himself up. The story was originally published in *Playboy* (March and April 1964) and served as the title story for a 1966 volume of short stories, which also included "The Living Daylights" and "Property of a Lady." **Adaptation:** *Octopussy* (United Artists, 1983). Dir: John Glen. Scr: George MacDonald Fraser, Richard Maibaum, Michael G. Wilson. Cast: Roger Moore (James Bond), Maud Adams (Octopussy), Louis Jourdan (Kamal Khan), Kristina Wayborn (Magda). Notes: The screenplay combines elements from the short stories "Octopussy" and "Property of a Lady." DVD, VHS. See also "Property of a Lady."

3257. *Odd Man Out* (F. L. Green, 1945). In Belfast, an IRA leader robs a bank to finance his revolutionary activities and is hunted by the police. **Adaptation 1:** *Odd Man Out*; also released as *Gang War* (Rank/Universal, 1947). Dir: Carol Reed. Scr: F. L. Green, R. C. Sherriff. Cast: James Mason (Johnny), Robert Newton (Lukey), Cyril Cusack (Pat). Notes: BAFTA Award for Best British Film. DVD, VHS. **Adaptation 2:** *The Lost Man* (Universal, 1969). Dir: Robert Alan Aurthur. Scr: Robert Alan Aurthur. Cast: Sidney Poitier (Jason), Joanna Shimkus (Cathy), Al Freeman, Jr. (Dennis), Michael Tolan (Inspector Hamilton). Notes: The story is recast, involving an African-American underground group robbing a bank to support their civil-rights activities. VHS.

3258. *Odds Against* (Dick Francis, 1965). A disabled jockey becomes an investigator looking into a scheme to bankrupt a racetrack so that the land can be sold to real-estate developers. **Adaptation:** *The Racing Game* (Yorkshire/PBS. 1979 TV Miniseries). Dir: Colin Bucksey, Lawrence Gordon Clark, Peter Duffell, John Mackenzie. Scr: Terence Feely, Leon Griffiths, Evan Jones, Trevor Preston. Cast: Mike Gwilym (Sid), Mick Ford (Chico), James Maxwell (Charles), Susan Wooldridge (Jenny). DVD, VHS.

3259. *Odds Against Tomorrow* (William P. McGivern, 1957). Three thieves plan to rob a bank, but the brutal racism of one of its members ruins their scheme. **Adaptation:** *Odds Against Tomorrow* (United Artists, 1959). Dir: Robert Wise. Scr: Abraham Polonsky (writing as John O. Killens), Nelson Gidding. Cast: Harry Belafonte (Johnny), Robert Ryan (Earl), Shelley Winters (Lorrie), Ed Begley (Dave), Gloria Grahame (Helen). DVD, VHS.

3260. *The Odessa File* (Frederick Forsyth, 1972). In 1963, a young journalist investigates a group of former Nazis living in Germany. **Adaptation:** *The Odessa File* (Columbia, 1974). Dir: Ronald Neame. Scr: Kenneth Ross, George Markstein. Cast: Jon Voight (Peter), Maximilian Schell (Roschmann), Maria Schell (Frau Miller), Mary Tamm (Sigi), Derek Jacobi (Wenzer). DVD, VHS.

3261. *Odette: The Story of a British Agent* (Jerrard Tickell, 1949). The true story of Odette Sansom-Hallowes (1912–1995), a heroic spy for the French resistance during World War II. Captured and tortured by the Nazis, she refused to identify those involved in her group. **Adaptation:** *Odette* (United Artists/Lopert, 1950). Dir: Herbert Wilcox. Scr: Warren Chetham Strode. Cast: Anna Neagle (Odette), Trevor Howard (Peter), Marius Goring (Colonel Henri), Bernard Lee (Jack), Peter Ustinov (Alex). VHS.

3262. *Odor of Violets* (Baynard Kendrick, 1940). A blind detective and his seeing-eye dog uncover a Nazi plot and prevent a young heiress from marrying a spy. **Adaptation:** *Eyes in the Night* (MGM, 1942). Dir: Fred Zinnemann. Scr: Howard Emmett Rogers, Guy Trosper. Cast: Edward Arnold (Duncan), Ann Harding (Norma), Donna Reed (Barbara), Katherine Emery (Cheli). DVD, VHS.

3263. *The Odyssey* (Homer, ca. 8th Century b.c.). In the second volume of Homer's epic about the Trojan War, Odysseus and his mariners must pass through many perils and adventures on their way home to Ithaca. **Adaptation 1:** *Ulysses* (Lux/Paramount, 1955). Dir: Mario Camerini. Scr: Franco Brusati, Mario Camerini, Ennio De Concini, Hugh Gray, Ben Hecht, Ivo Perilli, Irwin Shaw. Cast: Kirk Douglas (Ulysses), Silvana Mangano (Circe/Penelope), Anthony Quinn (Antinous). DVD, VHS. **Adaptation 2:** *The Odyssey*; also released as *The Adventures of Ulysses* (CBS, 1968 TV Miniseries). Dir: Franco Rossi, Piero Schivazappa, Mario Bava. Scr: Giampiero Bona, Vittorio Bonicelli, Fabio Carpi, Luciano Codignola, Mario Prosperi, Franco Rossi, Renzo Russo. Cast: Bekim Fehmiu (Odysseus), Irene Papas (Penelope), Michele Breton (Athena), Scilla Gabel (Helen), Fausto Tozzi (Menelaus). **Adaptation 3:** *The Odyssey* (NBC/Hallmark, 1997 TV Movie). Dir: Andrei Konchalovsky. Scr: Andrei Konchalovsky, Christopher Solimine. Cast: Armand Assante (Odysseus), Greta Scacchi (Penelope), Isabella Rossellini (Athena), Bernadette Peters (Circe), Eric Roberts (Eurymachus), Irene Papas (Anticlea). Notes: Emmy Awards for Outstanding Director and Special Effects, and nominations for Outstanding Film, Art Direction, and Hairstyling; Golden Globe nomination for Best Television Movie. DVD, VHS. **Adaptation 4:** *O Brother, Where Art Thou?* (Buena Vista, 2000). Dir: Joel Coen. Scr: Ethan Coen, Joel Coen. Cast: George Clooney (Everett), John Turturro (Pete), Tim Blake Nelson (Delmar), John Goodman (Big Dan), Holly Hunter (Penny), Charles Durning (Pappy O'Daniel). Notes: A retelling of the story set in Mississippi in the 1930's and involving escaped convicts trying to get home to recover their hidden loot. Academy Award nominations for

Best Screenplay and Cinematography; Cannes Film Festival Golden Palm nomination for Best Director; Golden Globe Award for Best Actor (Clooney) and nomination for Best Film. DVD, VHS. See also *The Iliad*.

3264. *O'Flynn* (Justin Huntly McCarthy, 1910). During the eighteenth century, a poor Irish youth thwarts Napoleon's plans to invade and conquer the island. The book served as the inspiration for a 1934 musical stage adaptation titled *The O'Flynn*, written by Brian Hooker and Russell Janney. **Adaptation:** *The Fighting O'Flynn* (Universal International, 1949). Dir: Arthur Pierson. Scr: Douglas Fairbanks, Jr., Robert Thoeren. Cast: Douglas Fairbanks, Jr. (O'Flynn), Helena Carter (Lady Benedetta), Richard Greene (Lord Philip).

3265. *Of Human Bondage* (W. Somerset Maugham, 1915). A handicapped medical student becomes the pawn of a low-class and abusive waitress with whom he is obsessed. **Adaptation 1:** *Of Human Bondage* (RKO, 1934). Dir: John Cromwell. Scr: Lester Cohen. Cast: Leslie Howard (Philip), Bette Davis (Mildred), Frances Dee (Sally), Kay Johnson (Nora), Reginald Denny (Harry), Alan Hale (Emil). DVD, VHS. **Adaptation 2:** *Of Human Bondage* (Warner, 1946). Dir: Edmund Goulding. Scr: Catherine Turney. Cast: Paul Henreid (Philip), Eleanor Parker (Mildred), Alexis Smith (Nora), Edmund Gwenn (Athelny). **Adaptation 3:** *Of Human Bondage* (MGM, 1964). Dir: Ken Hughes. Scr: Bryan Forbes. Cast: Kim Novak (Mildred), Laurence Harvey (Philip), Robert Morley (Dr. Jacobs), Siobhan McKenna (Nora), Roger Livesey (Athelny). VHS.

Of Human Hearts (*see* "Benefits Forgot").

3266. *Of Love and Shadows* (Isabel Allende, 1984). Chilean novel, originally titled *De amor y de sombra*, about the relationship between a fashion journalist and a photographer during the period of Chile's military dictatorship in 1973. When she learns that her lover is actually a revolutionary working against the military junta, the comfortably middle-class young woman joins in his underground activities. **Adaptation:** *Of Love and Shadows* (Miramax, 1994). Dir: Betty Kaplan. Scr: Donald Freed. Cast: Antonio Banderas (Francisco), Jennifer Connelly (Irene), Stefania Sandrelli (Beatriz), Diego Wallraff (Jose). DVD, VHS.

3267. *Of Mice and Men* (John Steinbeck, 1937). Set during the Depression, the story of a ranch hand and his best friend, a simple-minded giant, who dream of having their own ranch.

When the giant accidentally kills a woman, his friend is forced to make a terrible decision. **Adaptation 1:** *Of Mice and Men* (United Artists, 1939). Dir: Lewis Milestone. Scr: Eugene Solow. Cast: Burgess Meredith (George), Betty Field (Mae), Lon Chaney, Jr. (Lennie), Charles Bickford (Slim). Notes: Academy Award nominations for Best Film, Musical Score, and Sound. DVD, VHS. **Adaptation 2:** *Of Mice and Men* (Metromedia, 1981 TV Movie). Dir: Reza Badiyi. Scr: Eugene Solow (1939 screenplay), E. Nick Alexander. Cast: Robert Blake (George), Randy Quaid (Lennie), Lew Ayres (Candy), Mitch Ryan (Slim), Ted Neeley (Curley), Cassie Yates (Mae), Pat Hingle (Jackson). VHS. **Adaptation 3:** *Of Mice and Men* (MGM, 1992). Dir: Gary Sinise. Scr: Horton Foote. Cast: John Malkovich (Lennie), Gary Sinise (George), Ray Walston (Candy), Casey Siemaszko (Curley). Notes: Cannes Film Festival Golden Palm nomination for Best Director. DVD, VHS. Notes: In addition, an ABC television movie based on the novel was broadcast in 1970 and several European made-for-television adaptations have been produced.

Of Unknown Origin (see *The Visitor*).

3268. *The Off-Islanders* (Nathaniel Benchley, 1961). Comic novel about the panic that ensues when Soviet submarines surface along a New England beach. **Adaptation:** *The Russians Are Coming, the Russians Are Coming* (United Artists, 1966). Dir: Norman Jewison. Scr: William Rose. Cast: Carl Reiner (Walt), Eva Marie Saint (Elspeth), Alan Arkin (Rozanov), Brian Keith (Maddox), Jonathan Winters (Norman), Paul Ford (Hawkins), John Phillip Law (Alexei). Notes: Academy Award nominations for Best Picture, Screenplay, Actor (Arkin), and Editing; Golden Globe Awards for Best Picture and Actor (Arkin), and nominations for Best Screenplay and Newcomers (Arkin and Law). DVD, VHS.

3269. *Off Magazine Street* (Ronald Everett Capps, 2004). A young woman goes to a New Orleans rooming house to collect her late mother's personal effects and is befriended by the two misfits who live there. **Adaptation:** *A Love Song for Bobby Long* (Lions Gate, 2004). Dir: Shainee Gabel. Scr: Shainee Gabel. Cast: John Travolta (Bobby), Scarlett Johansson (Pursy), Gabriel Macht (Lawson), Deborah Kara Unger (Georgianna). Notes: Golden Globe nomination for Best Actress (Johansson). DVD, VHS.

3270. *Oh, God!* (Avery Corman, 1971). God comes to Earth and chooses a supermarket manager to be his messenger to let people know that life can be good if they try to help one another. **Adaptation:** *Oh, God!* (Warner, 1977). Dir: Carl Reiner. Scr: Larry Gelbart. Cast: John Denver (Jerry), George Burns (God), Teri Garr (Bobbie), Donald Pleasence (Dr. Harmon), Ralph Bellamy (Sam), William Daniels (George), Barnard Hughes (Judge Baker), Paul Sorvino (Reverend Williams).Notes: Academy Award nomination for Best Screenplay. DVD, VHS. Notes: Two sequels followed: *Oh God! Book II* (1980) (DVD, VHS) and *Oh God! You Devil* (1984) (DVD, VHS).

3271. *Oil for the Lamps of China* (Alice Tisdale Hobart, 1933). An American oil company executive working in China dedicates his life to the company, which shows little regard for him and his wife. **Adaptation:** *Oil for the Lamps of China* (Warner, 1935). Dir: Mervyn Le Roy. Scr: Laird Doyle. Cast: Pat O'Brien (Stephen), Josephine Hutchinson (Hester), Jean Muir (Alice).

3272. *The Old Curiosity Shop* (Charles Dickens, 1840–1841). The elderly owner of an antiques shop who cannot pay back a loan to his landlord, an evil and miserly dwarf, crosses England with his granddaughter and is pursued by the evil man. The story appeared in weekly installments in Dickens' own magazine *Master Humphrey's Clock* between April 1840 and February 1841. In 1841, the serial was separated and published as two books, *The Old Curiosity Shop* and *Barnaby Rudge*. **Silent Films:** 1911, 1912, 1913, and 1921. **Adaptation 1:** *The Old Curiosity Shop* (British International/First Division, 1934). Dir: Thomas Bentley. Scr: Margaret Kennedy, Ralph Neale. Cast: Elaine Benson (Nell), Ben Webster (Grandfather), Hay Petrie (Quilp), Gibb McLaughlin (Sampson). VHS. **Adaptation 2:** *The Old Curiosity Shop* (BBC, 1962 TV Miniseries). Dir: Joan Craft. Scr: Constance Cox. Cast: Michele Dotrice (Nell), Oliver Johnston (Grandfather), Patrick Troughton (Quilp), Bryan Pringle (Sampson). **Adaptation 3:** *The Old Curiosity Shop;* also released as *Mr. Quilp* (AVCO Embassy, 1975). Dir: Michael Tuchner. Scr: Irene Kamp, Louis Kamp. Cast: Anthony Newley (Quilp), David Hemmings (Richard), Jill Bennett (Sally), Sarah-Jane Varley (Nell), Michael Hordern (Grandfather), David Warner (Sampson). Notes: A musical adaptation. **Adaptation 4:** *The Old Curiosity Shop* (BBC, 1979 TV Miniseries). Dir: Julian Amyes. Scr: William Trevor. Cast: Natalie Ogle (Nell), Sebastian Shaw (Grandfather), Trevor Peacock (Quilp), Colin Jeavons (Sampson). **Adaptation 5:** *The Old Curiosity Shop*

(RHI/Disney, 1995 TV Miniseries). Dir: Kevin Connor. Scr: John Goldsmith. Cast: Sally Walsh (Nell), Peter Ustinov (Grandfather), Tom Courtenay (Quilp), Christopher Ettridge (Sampson), Anne White (Sally). VHS.

The Old Dark House (see *Benighted*).

3273. *The Old Gringo* (Carlos Fuentes, 1985). Fuentes' novel *El gringo viejo* is about a school teacher's relationship with the aging writer Ambrose Bierce in Mexico in 1913 during the time of Pancho Villa's revolutionary activities. **Adaptation:** *Old Gringo* (Columbia, 1989). Dir: Luis Puenzo. Scr: Aida Bortnik, Luis Puenzo. Cast: Jane Fonda (Harriet), Gregory Peck (Bierce), Jimmy Smits (Arroyo). DVD, VHS.

3274. *The Old Jest* (Jennifer Johnson, 1979, Whitbread Prize). Set amid the political turmoil in Ireland in the 1920's, the story of a teenaged girl who becomes involved with a mysterious young man involved in the struggle. **Adaptation:** *The Dawning* (TVS/Lawson/Vista, 1988). Dir: Robert Knights. Scr: Bernard MacLaverty, Moira Williams. Cast: Anthony Hopkins (Cassius), Rebecca Pidgeon (Nancy), Jean Simmons (Aunt Mary), Trevor Howard (Grandfather), Hugh Grant (Harry). DVD, VHS.

3275. *The Old Maid* (Edith Wharton, 1922). When her fiancé is killed in the Civil War, an unwed mother moves in with her married cousin and allows her to raise her daughter as her own. The novella was serialized in *The Red Book Magazine* between February and April 1922 and included in Wharton's 1924 novella collection, *Old New York*, which also included *False Dawn, The Spark,* and *New Year's Day. The Old Maid* was also adapted as a Pulitzer Prize–winning play in 1935 by Zoe Akins. **Adaptation:** *The Old Maid* (Warner, 1939). Dir: Edmund Goulding. Scr: Casey Robinson. Cast: Bette Davis (Charlotte), Miriam Hopkins (Delia), George Brent (Clem), Donald Crisp (Dr. Lanskell), Jane Bryan (Clementina). VHS.

Old Man (see *The Wild Palms*).

3276. *The Old Man and the Sea* (Ernest Hemingway, 1952, Pulitzer Prize). Hemingway's novella, originally published in *Life* magazine on September 1, 1952, is the story of an old Cuban fisherman's struggle with a gigantic fish and his momentary triumph over the forces of nature. **Adaptation 1:** *The Old Man and the Sea* (Warner, 1958). Dir: John Sturges. Scr: Peter Viertel. Cast: Spencer Tracy (Santiago), Felipe Pazos (the Boy),

Harry Bellaver (Martin). Notes: Academy Award for Best Musical Score and nominations for Best Actor (Tracy) and Cinematography; National Board of Review Awards for Best Picture and Actor (Tracy). DVD, VHS. **Adaptation 2:** *The Old Man and the Sea* (Yorkshire Television, 1990 TV Movie). Dir: Jud Taylor. Scr: Roger O. Hirson. Cast: Anthony Quinn (Santiago), Gary Cole (Tom), Patricia Clarkson (Mary), Joe Santos (Lopez). DVD, VHS.

3277. *Old Yeller* (Fred Gipson, 1956). In Texas in the 1860's, a young boy adopts an old yellow dog and develops a close relationship with it. **Adaptation:** *Old Yeller* (Disney/Buena Vista, 1957). Dir: Robert Stevenson. Scr: Fred Gipson, William Tunberg. Cast: Dorothy McGuire (Katie), Fess Parker (Jim), Chuck Connors (Burn), Tommy Kirk (Travis). DVD, VHS. See also *Savage Sam.*

3278. *The Oldest Confession* (Richard Condon, 1958). A gentleman thief and his accomplice plan to rob a museum but unwittingly become involved in a murder. **Adaptation:** *The Happy Thieves* (United Artists, 1962). Dir: George Marshall. Scr: John Gay. Cast: Rita Hayworth (Eve), Rex Harrison (Jimmy), Joseph Wiseman (Jean).

3279. *The Oldest Living Confederate Widow Tells All* (Allan Gurganus, 1989). A very old woman in a nursing home recalls her difficult life as the wife of a Confederate veteran of the Civil War. **Adaptation:** *The Oldest Living Confederate Widow Tells All* (CBS, 1994 TV Movie). Dir: Ken Cameron. Scr: Joyce Eliason. Cast: Diane Lane (Lucy), Anne Bancroft (Lucy, as an old woman), Donald Sutherland (William), Cicely Tyson (Castralia), Blythe Danner (Bianca), E. G. Marshall (Professor Taw), Gwen Verdon (Etta). Notes: Emmy Awards for Outstanding Supporting Actress (Tyson), Art Direction, and Hairstyling, and nominations for Outstanding Movie, Supporting Actress (Bancroft), Musical Score, and Sound. VHS.

3280. *Olimpia* (Burt Cole, 1959). An unsuccessful singing bullfighter agrees to a scheme to seduce a beautiful woman within three days in exchange for work. The novel was adapted as a play titled *The Bobo* by David R. Schwartz. **Adaptation:** *The Bobo* (Warner/Seven Arts, 1967). Dir: Robert Parrish. Scr: David R. Schwartz (based on his play). Cast: Peter Sellers (Juan), Britt Ekland (Olimpia), Rossano Brazzi (Carlos). VHS.

3281. *Oliver Twist* (Charles Dickens, 1837–1838). Dickens' classic novel, serialized in *Bentley's Miscellany* between January 1837 and January 1838, concerns an innocent young orphan who is pressed into service by a gang of thieves. The three-volume book was published in 1838 under the title *Oliver Twist, or the Parish Boy's Progress.* **Silent Films:** 1909, 1912, 1916, 1921, and 1922, directed by Frank Lloyd and starring Lon Chaney (DVD, VHS). **Adaptation 1:** *Oliver Twist* (Monogram, 1933). Dir: William J. Cowen. Scr: Elizabeth Meehan. Cast: Dickie Moore (Oliver), Irving Pichel (Fagin), William Boyd (Bill), Doris Lloyd (Nancy). VHS. **Adaptation 2:** *Oliver Twist* (Rank-/Eagle-Lion, 1948). Dir: David Lean. Scr: Stanley Haynes, David Lean. Cast: Robert Newton (Bill), Alec Guinness (Fagin), Kay Walsh (Nancy), Francis L. Sullivan (Mr. Bumble), John Howard Davies (Oliver). DVD, VHS. **Adaptation 3:** *Oliver Twist* (BBC, 1962 TV Miniseries). Dir: Constance Cox. Scr: Constance Cox. Cast: Max Adrian (Fagin), Melvyn Hayes (the Artful Dodger), Carmel McSharry (Nancy), Bruce Prochnik (Oliver), Peter Vaughan (Bill). VHS. **Adaptation 4:** *Oliver!* (Columbia, 1968). Dir: Carol Reed. Scr: Vernon Harris. Cast: Ron Moody (Fagin), Shani Wallis (Nancy), Oliver Reed (Bill), Harry Secombe (Mr. Bumble), Mark Lester (Oliver), Jack Wild (the Artful Dodger), Hugh Griffith (the Magistrate). Notes: This adaptation is a musical based on the hit play by Lionel Bart. Academy Awards for Best Picture, Director, Musical Score, Art Direction, and Sound, and nominations for Best Screenplay, Actor (Moody), Supporting Actor (Wild), Cinematography, Editing, and Costume Design; Golden Globe Awards for Best Picture and Actor (Moody), and nominations for Best Picture, Supporting Actor (Griffith), and Most Promising Newcomer (Wild); BAFTA nominations for Best Film, Director, Actor (Moody), Newcomer (Wild), Editing, Art Direction, Costume Design, and Soundtrack. DVD, VHS. **Adaptation 5:** *Oliver Twist* (Warner, 1974). Dir: Hal Sutherland. Scr: Ben Starr. Cast: voices of Davy Jones (the Artful Dodger), Billy Simpson (Oliver), Larry Storch (Fagin). Notes: An animated feature. DVD, VHS. **Adaptation 6:** *Oliver Twist* (CBS, 1982 TV Movie). Dir: Clive Donner. Scr: James Goldman. Cast: George C. Scott (Fagin), Tim Curry (Bill), Michael Hordern (Mr. Brownlow), Cherie Lunghi (Nancy), Richard Charles (Oliver). DVD, VHS. **Adaptation 7:** *Oliver Twist* (BBC, 1985 TV Miniseries). Dir: Gareth Davies. Scr: Alexander Baron. Cast: Ben Rodska (Oliver), Eric Porter (Fagin), Amanda Harris (Nancy), Michael Attwell (Bill). VHS **Adaptation 8:** *Oliver & Company* (Disney/Buena Vista, 1988). Dir: George Scribner. Scr: Jim Cox, Tim Disney, James

Mangold. Cast: voices of Joey Lawrence (Oliver), Billy Joel (Dodger), Cheech Marin (Ignacio), Richard Mulligan (Einstein), Roscoe Lee Browne (Francis), Dom De Luise (Fagin), Robert Loggia (Sykes). Notes: An animated feature set in New York and featuring dogs and cats as the Dickensian characters. DVD, VHS. **Adaptation 9:** *Oliver Twist* (Disney/Buena Vista Television, 1997 TV Movie). Dir: Tony Bill. Scr: Monte Merrick. Cast: Richard Dreyfuss (Fagin), Elijah Wood (the Artful Dodger), David O'Hara (Bill), Alex Trench (Oliver), Antoine Byrne (Nancy). DVD, VHS. **Adaptation 10:** *Oliver Twist* (PBS, 1999 TV Miniseries). Dir: Renny Rye. Scr: Alan Bleasdale. Cast: Sam Smith (Oliver), David Ross (Mr Bumble), Julie Walters (Mrs. Bumble), Michael Kitchen (Mr Brownlow), Keira Knightley (Rose), Robert Lindsay (Fagin), Alex Crowley (the Artful Dodger), Andy Serkis (Bill), Emily Woof (Nancy). DVD, VHS. Notes: The novel also inspired *Twist* (2003), an updated version about a gay man in Canada.

3282. *Oliver's Story* (Erich Segal, 1977). In this sequel to Segal's 1969 bestseller *Love Story*, a grieving Oliver Barrett finds love again when he meets a beautiful young heiress. **Adaptation:** *Oliver's Story* (Paramount, 1978). Dir: John Korty. Scr: John Korty, Erich Segal. Cast: Ryan O'Neal (Oliver), Candice Bergen (Marcie), Nicola Pagett (Joanna). DVD, VHS. See also *Love Story*.

The Omega Man (see *I Am Legend*).

3283. *Omoo* (Herman Melville, 1847). In the sequel to his 1846 novel *Typee*, Melville recounts his comic adventures dealing with natives during his residence on an island in the South Seas. **Adaptation:** *Omoo-Omoo the Shark God*; released in the UK as *The Shark God* (Lippert, 1949). Dir: Leon Leonard. Scr: George Green, Leon Leonard. Cast: Ron Randell (Jeff), Devera Burton (Julie), Richard Benedict (Richards), George Meeker (Dr. Long). VHS.

3284. *On Beulah Height* (Reginald Hill, 1998). In the seventeenth installment of Hill's popular series (1970–2004) featuring British policemen Andrew Dalziel and Peter Pascoe, the waters of a reservoir recede in a small English village, revealing the skeletons of missing of people who had disappeared years earlier. When a young girl from a neighboring town goes missing, the detectives must investigate both crimes. **Adaptation:** *Dalziel and Pascoe: On Beulah Height* (BBC/A&E, 1999 TV Movie series). Dir: Maurice Phillips. Scr: Michael Chaplin. Cast: War-

ren Clarke (Dalziel), Colin Buchanan (Pascoe), Susannah Corbett (Ellie), Abigail Fawcett (Lorraine), Jo-Anne Stockham (Shirley). Notes: Edgar Allan Poe Award for Best Television Feature Film.

3285. *On Borrowed Time* (Lawrence Edward Watkin, 1937). Fantasy about Death's agent coming to collect an elderly man. In order to get more time to settle the life of his beloved grandson, the man chases Death's minion up an old apple tree and keeps him there. The novel was adapted as a 1938 stage play by Paul Osborn. **Adaptation:** *On Borrowed Time* (MGM, 1939). Dir: Harold S. Bucquet. Scr: Alice D. G. Miller, Frank O'Neill, Claudine West. Cast: Lionel Barrymore (Grandfather Northrup), Cedric Hardwicke (Mr. Brink), Beulah Bondi (Grandmother Northrup), Una Merkel (Marcia), Bobs Watson (Pud). VHS.

On Dangerous Ground (1952) (see *Mad with Much Heart*).

3286. *On Dangerous Ground* (Jack Higgins, 1994). A secret government agreement on the legal status of Hong Kong sets off a fierce struggle for control among the Chinese and British governments, affluent Hong Kong business interests, and the mob. **Adaptation:** *On Dangerous Ground* (Showtime, 1996 TV Movie). Dir: Lawrence Gordon Clark. Scr: Christopher Wicking. Cast: Rob Lowe (Dillon), Kenneth Cranham (Ferguson), Deborah Moore (Hannah), Jurgen Prochnow (Morgan). DVD, VHS.

3287. *On Eagle's Wing* (A. E. Southon, 1939). Fictional retelling of the Biblical story of Moses and his selection by God to lead the Israelites out of their Egyptian captivity. **Adaptation:** *The Ten Commandments* (Paramount, 1956). Dir: Cecil B. De Mille. Scr: Aeneas MacKenzie, Jesse L. Lasky, Jr., Jack Gariss, Fredric M. Frank. Cast: Charlton Heston (Moses), Yul Brynner (Rameses), Anne Baxter (Nefretiri), Edward G. Robinson (Dathan), Yvonne De Carlo (Sephora), Debra Paget (Lilia), John Derek (Joshua), Cedric Hardwicke (Sethi). Notes: De Mille directed a silent film by the same title in 1923. For the 1956 screenplay, the writers used the original Biblical story and elements from three books: J. H. Ingraham's *The Pillar of Fire* (1859), A. E. Southon's *On Eagle's Wing*, (1939), and Dorothy Clarke Wilson's *Prince of Egypt* (1949). National Board of Review Award for Best Actor (Brynner); Academy Award for Best Special Effects, and nominations for Best Picture, Cinematography, Art Direction, Editing, Costume Design, and Sound. DVD, VHS. See also *Pillar of Fire* and *Prince of Egypt*.

On Friday at Eleven (see *The World in My Pocket*).

3288. *On Her Majesty's Secret Service* (Ian Fleming, 1963). James Bond saves a suicidal woman on a beach and is later introduced to her father, a powerful crime boss. Her father persuades Bond to marry his daughter in exchange for information about Bond's enemy and SPECTRE leader Ernst Blofield, who is in Switzerland planning to unleash a deadly virus on an unsuspecting world. **Adaptation:** *On Her Majesty's Secret Service* (United Artists, 1969). Dir: Peter R. Hunt. Scr: Richard Maibaum. Cast: George Lazenby (James Bond), Diana Rigg (Tracy), Telly Savalas (Blofeld), Gabriele Ferzetti (Draco), Lois Maxwell (Miss Moneypenny), Bernard Lee (M). DVD, VHS.

On Moonlight Bay (see *Penrod*).

3289. *On Our Selection* (Steele Rudd [pseudonym for Arthur Hoey Davis], 1899). The first in a series of books and stories about a large Queensland, Australia, family and their adventures on the family farm and in town. The book was first published in a an Australian newspaper called *The Bulletin* and was also adapted as a very successful play in 1916. **Silent Film:** 1920. **Adaptation:** *On Our Selection* (Cinesound, 1932). Dir: Ken G. Hall. Scr: Bert Bailey, Ken G. Hall. Cast: Bert Bailey (Dad Rudd), Fred MacDonald (Dave), Alfreda Bevan (Mom Rudd), John McGowan (Maloney). Notes: Two sequels, also directed by Ken G. Hall, followed: *Dad and Dave Come to Town* (1938), based on several stories by Steele Rudd, notably *Back at Our Selection* (1906), and *Dad Rudd, M.P.* (1940), based principally on Rudd's *Dad in Politics and Other Stories* (1908).

3290. *On the Beach* (Nevil Shute [pseudonym for Nevil Shute Norway], 1957). Set in Australia in the mid–1960's, two years after a devastating nuclear war, the novel shows how people in the Southern Hemisphere cope with impending doom. **Adaptation 1:** *On the Beach* (United Artists, 1959). Dir: Stanley Kramer. Scr: John Paxton. Cast: Gregory Peck (Dwight), Ava Gardner (Moira), Fred Astaire (Julian), Anthony Perkins (Peter). Notes: BAFTA UN Award for Best Director and nomination for Best Actress (Gardner); Golden Globe Award for Best Musical Score; Academy Award nominations for Best Musical Score and Editing. DVD, VHS. **Adaptation 2:** *On the Beach* (Showtime, 2000 TV Movie). Dir: Russell Mulcahy. Scr: John Paxton (1959 screenplay), David Williamson, Bill Kerby. Cast: Armand Assante (Dwight), Rachel Ward (Moira), Bryan Brown (Julian), Jacqueline McKenzie (Mary). Notes: Australian Film Institute Awards for Best Television Film and Set Design, and nomination for Best Cinematography; Golden Globe nominations for Best Television Movie and Actress (Ward). VHS.

3291. *On the Black Hill* (Bruce Chatwin, 1982). Generation-spanning novel about the lives of identical twin brothers on a farm on the English-Welsh border. **Adaptation:** *On the Black Hill* (British Screen, 1987). Dir: Andrew Grieve. Scr: Andrew Grieve. Cast: Mike Gwilym (Lewis), Robert Gwilym (Benjamin), Gemma Jones (Mary). VHS.

On the Fiddle (see *Stop at a Winner*).

3292. *On the Night of the Fire* (F. L. Green, 1939). A barber becomes involved in a petty crime and subsequently kills the man who is blackmailing his wife. **Adaptation:** *On the Night of the Fire*; released in the U.S. as *The Fugitive* (Universal, 1940). Dir: Brian Desmond Hurst. Scr: Brian Desmond Hurst, Patrick Kirwan, Terence Young. Cast: Ralph Richardson (Will), Diana Wynyard (Kit), Romney Brent (Jimsey), Mary Clare (Lizzie).

3293. *On the Run* (Nina Bawden [pseudonym for Nina Mabey Kark], 1964). Children's book about an African youth being held as a political prisoner in London and the two friends who help him escape. The book was also published under the title *Three on the Run*. **Adaptation:** *On the Run* (Children's Film Foundation, 1968). Dir: Pat Jackson. Scr: Pat Jackson. Cast: Dennis Conoley (Ben), Robert Kennedy (Thomas), Tracey Collins (Lil).

3294. *On the Trail: My Reminiscences as a Cowboy* (Frank Harris, 1930). The author's comic memoir about becoming a ranch hand to impress a young woman and his discontents with the hard work of tending to cattle. **Adaptation:** *Cowboy* (Columbia, 1958). Dir: Delmer Daves. Scr: Dalton Trumbo, Edmund H. North. Cast: Glenn Ford (Tom), Jack Lemmon (Frank), Anna Kashfi (Maria), Brian Donlevy (Doc Bender), Dick York (Charlie). DVD, VHS.

3295. *On the Trail of the Assassins* (Jim Garrison, 1988). The former New Orleans district attorney makes a case for a conspiracy in the assassination of President John Kennedy in 1963. **Adaptation:** *JFK* (Warner, 1991). Dir: Oliver Stone. Scr: Oliver Stone, Zachary Sklar. Cast: Kevin Costner (Jim Garrison), Tommy Lee Jones

(Clay Shaw), Gary Oldman (Lee Harvey Oswald), Sissy Spacek (Liz Garrison), Joe Pesci (David Ferrie). Notes: The screenplay is based on Jim Marrs' *Crossfire* and on Jim Garrison's *On the Trail of the Assassins*. Academy Awards for Best Cinematography and Editing and nominations for Best Picture, Director, Screenplay, Supporting Actor (Jones), Musical Score, and Sound; Golden Globe Award for Best Director and nominations for Best Picture, Screenplay, and Actor (Costner). DVD, VHS. See also *Crossfire*.

3296. *On the Yard* (Malcolm Braly, 1967). Written by a former convict, a novel about a tough prisoner whose authority is challenged when a murderer is placed on his cell block. **Adaptation:** *On the Yard* (Midwest, 1978). Dir: Raphael D. Silver. Scr: Malcolm Braly. Cast: John Heard (Juleson), Thomas G. Waites (Chilly), Mike Kellin (Red), Richard Bright (Nunn), Joe Grifasi (Morris), Lane Smith (Blake). VHS.

3297. *On Wings of Eagles* (Ken Follett, 1983). In Iran after the Islamic revolution, two American businessmen are taken hostage, and a retired American military officer is hired to rescue them. **Adaptation:** *On Wings of Eagles* (NBC, 1986 TV Miniseries). Dir: Andrew V. McLaglen. Scr: Sam H. Rolfe. Cast: Burt Lancaster (Simons), Richard Crenna (Perot), Paul Le Mat (Jay), Louis Giambalvo (Paul). Notes: Emmy Award nomination for Outstanding Miniseries. VHS.

3298. *The Once and Future King* (T. H. White, 1958). This omnibus volume collects White's four beloved novels about King Arthur, Guinevere, and the Knights of the Round Table, beginning with *The Sword in the Stone* (1938). **Adaptation 1:** *The Sword in the Stone* (Disney/Buena Vista, 1963). Dir: Wolfgang Reitherman. Scr: Bill Peet. Cast: voices of Karl Swenson (Merlin), Rickie Sorensen (Arthur/Wart), Sebastian Cabot (Sir Ector), Junius Matthews (Archimedes). Notes: This animated film combines elements from several novels in the series. DVD, VHS. **Adaptation 2:** *Camelot* (Warner/Seven Arts, 1967). Dir: Joshua Logan. Scr: Alan Jay Lerner. Cast: Richard Harris (King Arthur), Vanessa Redgrave (Guinevere), Franco Nero (Lancelot), David Hemmings (Mordred). Notes: The screenplay is based on White's book and on Lerner and Loewe's 1960 Broadway musical adaptation. Academy Awards for Best Art Direction, Costume Design, and Musical Score, and nominations for Best Cinematography and Sound; Golden Globe Awards for Best Actor (Harris) and Original Score, and nominations for Best Picture, Ac-

tress (Redgrave), and Newcomer (Nero). DVD, VHS.

3299. *Once in a Lifetime* (Danielle Steel, 1982). After her husband and daughter die in a fire, a famous novelist is left alone to raise her handicapped son. **Adaptation:** *Once in a Lifetime* (NBC, 1994 TV Movie). Dir: Michael Miller. Scr: Syrie Astrahan James. Cast: Lindsay Wagner (Daphne), Barry Bostwick (Dr. Dane), Amy Aquino (Barbara). DVD, VHS.

3300. *Once Is Not Enough* (Jacqueline Susann, 1973). The obsessive daughter of a movie producer spites him by having numerous Hollywood affairs. **Adaptation:** *Once Is Not Enough* (Paramount, 1975). Dir: Guy Green. Scr: Julius J. Epstein. Cast: Kirk Douglas (Mike), Alexis Smith (Deidre), David Janssen (Tom), George Hamilton (David), Melina Mercouri (Karla), Brenda Vaccaro (Linda), Deborah Raffin (January). Notes: Golden Globe Award for Best Supporting Actress (Vaccaro); Academy Award nomination for Best Supporting Actress (Vaccaro). VHS.

3301. *Once Off Guard* (J. H. Wallis, 1942). A professor becomes obsessed with a beautiful woman's portrait and soon has the opportunity to meet and accompany her home. When he accidentally kills her jealous boyfriend, he covers up the crime and must then contend with a blackmailer. **Adaptation:** *The Woman in the Window* (RKO, 1945). Dir: Fritz Lang. Scr: Nunnally Johnson. Cast: Edward G. Robinson (Richard), Joan Bennett (Alice), Raymond Massey (Frank), Edmund Breon (Dr. Barkstane), Dan Duryea (Heidt). VHS.

Once Upon a Time in America (see *The Hoods*).

3302. *Once Upon a Time When We Were Colored* (Clifton L. Taulbert, 1989). A prominent businessman's memoir of growing up in racially segregated Mississippi in the 1950's. **Adaptation:** *Once Upon a Time When We Were Colored* (BET, 1995). Dir: Tim Reid. Scr: Paul W. Cooper. Cast: Al Freeman, Jr. (Poppa), Phylicia Rashad (Ma Ponk), Paula Kelly (Pearl), Salli Richardson (Alice), Anna Maria Horsford (Annie), Bernie Casey (Mr. Walter), Isaac Hayes (Preacher Hurn). DVD, VHS.

3303. *Once Were Warriors* (Alan Duff, 1990). In Auckland, New Zealand, a troubled Maori woman comes to grips with her violent husband and her son's attraction to street gangs. **Adaptation:** *Once Were Warriors* (Fine Line, 1994). Dir: Lee Tamahori. Scr: Riwia Brown. Cast: Rena Owen (Beth), Temuera Morrison

(Jake), Mamaengaroa Kerr-Bell (Grace), Julian Arahanga (Nig), Taungaroa Emile (Boogie). Notes: New Zealand Film and TV Awards for Best Film, Director, Screenplay, Actor (Morrison), Juvenile Performance (Emile), Supporting Actress (Kerr-Bell), Editing, Musical Score, and Soundtrack; Australian Film Institute Award for Best Foreign Film. DVD, VHS. See also *What Becomes of the Broken Hearted?*

Once You Kiss a Stranger (see *Strangers on a Train*).

The One and Only Genuine Original Family Band (see *The Family Band*).

One Born Every Minute (see *The Ballad of the Flim-Flam Man*).

3304. *One Christmas* (Truman Capote, 1982). Depression-era Christmas story about a wealthy New Orleans socialite and her niece, who is attracted to a con artist. With the help of his own son, she helps to show the man the spirit of Christmas. **Adaptation:** *One Christmas* (Hallmark, 1994 TV Movie). Dir: Tony Bill. Scr: Duane Poole. Cast: Katharine Hepburn (Cornelia), Henry Winkler (Dad), Swoosie Kurtz (Emily), T. J. Lowther (Buddy), Julie Harris (Sook). DVD, VHS.

3305. *One Corpse Too Many* (Ellis Peters [pseudonym for Edith Pargeter], 1979). The second installment in Peters' twenty-volume series (1977–1994) featuring Brother Cadfael, a twelfth-century monk who, following service in the Crusades, tends to the herbarium at Shrewsbury Abbey and solves crimes. In this book, Brother Cadfael is asked to bury the bodies of ninety-four executed rebels who launched a civil war against King Stephen. When he counts the corpses, however, Cadfael finds one too many and investigates. **Adaptation:** *Cadfael: One Corpse Too Many* (ITV/PBS, 1994 TV Movie series). Dir: Graham Theakston. Scr: Simon Burke. Cast: Derek Jacobi (Cadfael), Sean Pertwee (Hugh), Albie Woodington (Will), Julian Firth (Brother Jerome). DVD, VHS.

3306. *One Day in the Life of Ivan Denisovich* (Aleksandr Solzhenitsyn, 1962). This autobiographical novel by the winner of the 1970 Nobel Prize for Literature is about a peasant who is sentenced to a Siberian labor camp in 1950. Originally titled *Odin den iz zhizni Ivana Denisovicha*, it first appeared in *Novy Mir*, a Russian literary magazine, in November 1962 and was translated into English and published in the West in 1963.

Adaptation: *One Day in the Life of Ivan Denisovich* (Group W/Cinerama, 1970). Dir: Caspar Wrede. Scr: Ronald Harwood. Cast: Tom Courtenay (Ivan), Espen Skjonberg (Tiurin), Alf Malland (Fetiukov). VHS.

3307. *One Deadly Summer* (Sebastien Japrisot [pseudonym for Jean-Baptiste Rossi], 1979). A young woman and her father move to a small village, where, as part of an elaborate revenge scheme, she marries a local fireman. Originally titled *L'ete Meurtrier*, the French novel was translated in 1980. **Adaptation:** *One Deadly Summer* (Universal, 1983). Dir: Jean Becker. Scr: Jean Becker, Sebastien Japrisot. Cast: Isabelle Adjani (Elle), Alain Souchon (Pin-Pon), Suzanne Flon (Cognata), François Cluzet (Mickey). Notes: Originally titled *L'ete Meurtrier* and shown with subtitles. Cesar Awards (France) for Best Screenplay, Actress (Adjani), Supporting Actress (Flon), and Editing, and nominations for Best Picture, Director, Actor (Souchon), Supporting Actor (Cluzet), and Musical Score; Cannes Film Festival Golden Palm nomination for Best Director. VHS.

One Desire (see *Tacey Cromwell*).

One-Eyed Jacks (see *The Authentic Death of Hendry Jones*).

3308. *One Flew Over the Cuckoo's Nest* (Ken Kesey, 1962). A new patient at a mental hospital tries to undermine the authority of a strict nurse and encourage the other patients to assert themselves. The 1962 novel was developed into a successful Broadway play by Dale Wasserman in 1963. **Adaptation:** *One Flew Over the Cuckoo's Nest* (United Artists, 1975). Dir: Milos Forman. Scr: Bo Goldman, Lawrence Hauben. Cast: Jack Nicholson (McMurphy), Louise Fletcher (Nurse Ratched), Scatman Crothers (Turkle), Danny De Vito (Martini), Christopher Lloyd (Taber), Brad Dourif (Billy). Notes: Academy Awards for Best Picture, Director, Screenplay, Actor (Nicholson), and Actress (Fletcher), and nominations for Best Supporting Actor (Dourif), Musical Score, Cinematography, and Editing; Golden Globe Awards for Best Picture, Director, Screenplay, Actor (Nicholson), Actress (Fletcher), and Acting Debut (Dourif). DVD, VHS.

3309. *One Foot in Heaven: The Life of a Practical Parson* (Hartzell Spence, 1940). Memoir by the son of a Methodist minister in small-town America, detailing the difficulties his father faced as faith clashed with modern American life.

Adaptation: *One Foot in Heaven* (Warner, 1941). Dir: Irving Rapper. Scr: Casey Robinson. Cast: Fredric March (William), Martha Scott (Hope), Beulah Bondi (Lydia), Gene Lockhart (Preston). Notes: Academy Award nomination for Best Picture.

3310. *One Gallant Rush: Robert Gold Shaw and His Brave Black Regiment* (Peter Burchard, 1965). True story of Robert Gould Shaw (1837–1863), who, born into a Boston abolitionist family, became a Civil War officer leading the first black regiment recruited to fight on the side of the Union. **Adaptation:** *Glory* (TriStar, 1989). Dir: Edward Zwick. Scr: Kevin Jarre. Cast: Matthew Broderick (Shaw), Denzel Washington (Trip), Cary Elwes (Forbes), Morgan Freeman (Rawlins), Andre Braugher (Searles). Notes: The screenplay is based on Burchard's book, along with Lincoln Kirstein's *Lay This Laurel* and the collected letters of Shaw, currently available in *Blue Eyed Child of Fortune: The Civil War Letters of Robert Gould Shaw*, edited by Russell Duncan (University of Georgia Press, 1992). Academy Awards for Best Cinematography, Supporting Actor (Washington), and Sound, and nominations for Best Art Direction and Film Editing; Golden Globe Award for Best Supporting Actor (Washington), and nominations for Best Picture, Director, Screenplay, and Musical Score (James Horner). DVD, VHS. See also *Lay This Laurel*.

One Horse Town (see *Small Town Girl*).

One Hundred and One Dalmatians (see *The Hundred and One Dalmatians*).

100 Rifles (see *The Californio*).

3311. *120 Days of Sodom* (Marquis de Sade, 1785). Wealthy men gather a group of children and adolescents for a prolonged experiment in deviant sexuality, pain, and murder. **Adaptation 1:** *Salo, or 120 Days of Sodom* (Zebra, 1976). Dir: Pier Paolo Pasolini. Scr: Sergio Citti, Pier Paolo Pasolini. Cast: Paolo Bonacelli (the Duke), Giorgio Cataldi (the Bishop), Umberto Paolo Quintavalle (the Magistrate), Aldo Valletti (the President). Notes: Originally titled *Salo o le 120 giornate di Sodoma* and shown with subtitles. Pasolini's adaptation for his final film is set in a Nazi-controlled northern Italian town in 1944. DVD, VHS. **Adaptation 2:** *Helter Skelter* (One Shot, 2000). Dir: Jesus Franco (as Clifford Brown, Jr.). Scr: Jesus Franco (as David J. Khunne). Cast: Mavi Tienda (Beatriz), Ezequiel Cohen (Herbie), Paul Lapidus (Don). Notes: The screenplay combines elements from this book and other writings by the Marquis de Sade. DVD, VHS.

3312. "One Man's Secret" (Rita Weiman, 1943). A psychologically unstable woman marries her wealthy employer but is actually in love with another man. When he rejects her advances, she kills him and finally ends up in a mental institution. The short story appeared in *Cosmopolitan* in March 1943. **Adaptation:** *Possessed* (Warner, 1947). Dir: Curtis Bernhardt. Scr: Ranald MacDougall, Lawrence Menkin, Silvia Richards. Cast: Joan Crawford (Louise), Van Heflin (David), Raymond Massey (Dean), Geraldine Brooks (Carol). Notes: Academy Award nomination for Best Actress (Crawford). VHS.

One Man's Way (see *Norman Vincent Peale*).

One Minute Before Death (*see* "The Oval Portrait").

3313. *One More River* (John Galsworthy, 1933). The final novel by the winner of the 1932 Nobel Prize for Literature is the tale of a wife who runs away from her ruthless husband and falls in love with a man on a river voyage. **Adaptation:** *One More River*; released in the UK as *Over the River* (Universal, 1934). Dir: James Whale. Scr: R. C. Sherriff. Cast: Diana Wynyard (Claire), Frank Lawton (Tony), Jane Wyatt (Dinny), Colin Clive (Sir Gerald), Reginald Denny (Dornford).

3314. *One More Spring* (Robert Nathan, 1933). During the Depression, three strangers in New York meet and decide to pool their meager resources in order to survive. **Adaptation:** *One More Spring* (Fox, 1935). Dir: Henry King. Scr: Edwin J. Burke. Cast: Janet Gaynor (Elizabeth), Warner Baxter (Jaret), Walter King (Morris), Jane Darwell (Mrs. Sweeney).

One Night in the Tropics (see *Love Insurance*).

One of Our Dinosaurs Is Missing (see *The Great Dinosaur Robbery*).

3315. *One Pair of Feet* (Monica Dickens, 1942). Autobiographical novel by the great-granddaughter of Charles Dickens about her experiences as a hospital nurse during World War II. **Adaptation:** *The Lamp Still Burns* (Rank, 1943). Dir: Maurice Elvey. Scr: Elizabeth Baron. Cast: Rosamund John (Hilary), Stewart Granger (Laurence), Godfrey Tearle (Sir Marshall).

3316. *One Point Safe* (Leslie Cockburn and Andrew Cockburn, 1997). Factual account of a West German terrorist group attempting to steal a nuclear weapon from an American facility. The book also underscores the danger posed by criminals who control the nuclear arsenal of the former Soviet Union and who would sell such devices to terrorists. **Adaptation:** *The Peacemaker* (DreamWorks, 1997). Dir: Mimi Leder. Scr: Michael Schiffer. Cast: George Clooney (Colonel Devoe), Nicole Kidman (Dr. Kelly), Marcel Iures (Gavrich). Notes: The screenplay, which is loosely based on magazine articles that the Cockburns wrote prior to the publication of the 1997 book, concerns Russian terrorists who steal a nuclear warhead and are pursued by American intelligence agents. DVD, VHS.

3317. *The One That Got Away* (Kendal Burt and James Leasor, 1956). Factual account of Luftwaffe pilot Franz von Werra, the only German taken as a prisoner of war in England during World War II, and his successful escape from various internment facilities and ultimate return to Germany. **Adaptation:** *The One That Got Away* (Rank, 1957). Dir: Roy Ward Baker. Scr: Howard Clewes. Cast: Hardy Kruger (von Werra), Michael Goodliffe (RAF officer), Alec McCowen (Hucknall). DVD, VHS.

3318. *One True Thing* (Anna Quindlen, 1994). A young career woman returns to her parents' home to care for her dying mother. There she gets a new perspective on herself and her parents. **Adaptation:** *One True Thing* (Universal, 1998). Dir: Carl Franklin. Scr: Karen Croner. Cast: Meryl Streep (Kate), Renee Zellweger (Ellen), William Hurt (George), Tom Everett Scott (Brian). Notes: Academy Award and Golden Globe nominations for Best Actress (Streep). DVD, VHS.

3319. *One-Upmanship* (Stephen Potter, 1952). A comic "advice" book promoting "one-upmanship," the art of seizing advantage in all social situations. **Adaptation:** *School for Scoundrels, or How to Win Without Actually Cheating!* (Associated British/Continental, 1960). Dir: Robert Hamer. Scr: Hal E. Chester, Patricia Moyes. Cast: Ian Carmichael (Henry), Terry-Thomas (Raymond), Alastair Sim (Mr. Potter), Janette Scott (April). Notes: This book and elements from two other volumes by Potter, *Gamesmanship* (1947) and *Lifemanship* (1950), served as the basis for the screenplay. The book also inspired a BBC television series in 1976. DVD, VHS.

3320. *One Who Walked Alone: Robert E. Howard, the Final Years* (Novalyne Price Ellis, 1986). The memoir of a Texas teacher and aspiring writer who, in the 1930's, met pulp-fiction writer Robert E. Howard, the author of stories

featuring Conan the Barbarian, and formed a life-long friendship **Adaptation:** *The Whole Wide World* (Sony, 1996). Dir: Dan Ireland. Scr: Michael Scott Myers. Cast: Vincent D'Onofrio (Howard), Renee Zellweger (Novalyne), Ann Wedgeworth (Mrs. Howard), Harve Presnell (Dr. Howard). Notes: Independent Spirit Award nominations for Best Screenplay and Female Lead (Zellweger). DVD, VHS.

Onegin (see *Eugene Onegin*).

3321. *The Onion Field* (Joseph Wambaugh, 1973). The true story of a policeman's loss of reputation among his colleagues and personal breakdown after witnessing the murder of his partner. **Adaptation:** *The Onion Field* (AVCO Embassy, 1979). Dir: Harold Becker. Scr: Joseph Wambaugh. Cast: John Savage (Karl), James Woods (Gregory), Franklyn Seales (Jimmy), Ted Danson (Ian), Ronny Cox (Pierce). DVD, VHS.

3322. *Onionhead* (Weldon Hill [pseudonym for William Ralph Scott], 1957). The comic misadventures of a Coast Guard cook in the days prior to World War II. **Adaptation:** *Onionhead* (Warner, 1958). Dir: Norman Taurog. Scr: Nelson Gidding. Cast: Andy Griffith (Al), Felicia Farr (Stella), Walter Matthau (Red), James Gregory (the Captain), Joey Bishop (Gutsell). VHS.

Only the Best (see *I Can Get It for You Wholesale*).

Only Two Can Play (see *That Uncertain Feeling*).

3323. *Only When I Larf* (Len Deighton, 1968). Comic novel about three con artists who try to sell an African revolutionary scrap metal as ammunition. **Adaptation:** *Only When I Larf* (Paramount, 1968). Dir: Basil Dearden. Scr: John Salmon. Cast: Richard Attenborough (Silas), David Hemmings (Bob), Alexandra Stewart (Liz), Nicholas Pennell (Spencer).

Open Range (see *The Open Range Men*).

3324. *The Open Range Men* (Lauran Paine, 1990). Western about a group of cowboys who graze their herds on the open range. When they choose a spot outside a town, they must battle the local cattle baron and a corrupt sheriff. **Adaptation:** *Open Range* (Touchstone/Buena Vista, 2003). Dir: Kevin Costner. Scr: Craig Storper. Cast: Robert Duvall (Boss Spearman), Kevin Costner (Charley), Annette Bening (Sue), Michael Gambon (Denton), Michael Jeter (Percy), Diego Luna (Button), James Russo (Sheriff Poole). Notes: Western Heritage Award for Outstanding Theatrical Film. DVD, VHS.

3325. "The Opera Hat" (Clarence Budington Kelland, 1935). A simple fellow inherits a fortune, is pursued by greedy people, and wins the day with his honesty and good heart. The short story first appeared in the July 1935 issue of *American Magazine*. **Adaptation 1:** *Mr. Deeds Goes to Town* (Columbia, 1936). Dir: Frank Capra. Scr: Robert Riskin. Cast: Gary Cooper (Longfellow), Jean Arthur (Louise), George Bancroft (MacWade), Lionel Stander (Cornelius). Notes: Academy Award for Best Director and nominations for Best Picture, Screenplay, Actor (Cooper), and Sound; National Board of Review Award for Best Picture. DVD, VHS. **Adaptation 2:** *Mr. Deeds* (Columbia, 2002). Dir: Steven Brill. Scr: Robert Riskin (1936 screenplay), Tim Herlihy. Cast: Adam Sandler (Longfellow), Winona Ryder (Babe), John Turturro (Emilio), Peter Gallagher (Chuck), Jared Harris (Mac). DVD, VHS.

Operation Amsterdam (see *Adventure in Diamonds*).

3326. *Operation Cicero: The Espionage Sensation of the War* (L. C. Moyazisch, 1950). Historical account describing how, during World War II, the valet to the British ambassador in Ankara, Turkey, passed Allied intelligence secrets to the Nazis. **Adaptation:** *Five Fingers* (20th Century–Fox, 1952). Dir: Joseph L. Mankiewicz. Scr: Joseph L. Mankiewicz, Michael Wilson. Cast: James Mason (Ulysses), Danielle Darrieux (Countess Anna), Michael Rennie (Travers), Walter Hampden (Sir Frederic). Notes: Golden Globe Award for Best Screenplay; Academy Award nominations for Best Director and Screenplay. VHS. Notes: The book was also the basis for an NBC television series in 1959.

Operation Daybreak (see *Seven Men at Daybreak*).

Operation Snafu (see *Stop at a Winner*).

3327. *Operation Terror* (Mildred Gordon and Gordon Gordon [writing as The Gordons], 1961). A bank robber terrorizes a female bank teller into helping him with his heist. **Adaptation:** *Experiment in Terror*; released in the UK as *The Grip of Fear* (Columbia, 1962). Dir: Blake Edwards. Scr: Mildred Gordon, Gordon Gordon. Cast: Glenn Ford (Ripley), Lee Remick (Kelly), Stefanie Powers (Toby), Roy Poole (Brad). DVD, VHS.

Operation Undercover (see *Report to the Commissioner*).

Operation War Head (see *Stop at a Winner*).

Operation X (see *David Golder*).

3328. *The Operator* (Budd Robinson and Rod Amateau, 1970). Satiric novel about a hospital administrator trying to make money through insurance fraud. **Adaptation:** *Where Does It Hurt?* (Cinerama, 1972). Dir: Rod Amateau. Scr: Budd Robinson, Rod Amateau. Cast: Peter Sellers (Dr. Hopfnagel), Jo Ann Pflug (Alice), Rick Lenz (Lester), Harold Gould (Dr. Zerny).

3329. *The Optimists of Nine Elms* (Anthony Simmons, 1964). A London street entertainer befriends two poor children. **Adaptation:** *The Optimists*; also released as *The Optimists of Nine Elms* (Paramount, 1973). Dir: Anthony Simmons. Dir: Tudor Gates, Anthony Simmons. Cast: Peter Sellers (Sam), Marjorie Yates (Chrissie), Donna Mullane (Liz), John Chaffey (Mark), David Daker (Bob). VHS.

3330. *Oranges Are Not the Only Fruit* (Jeanette Winterson, 1985). Autobiographical novel about a British girl raised by religious zealots. When she develops romantic feelings for another girl, she is brutally urged to repent of her "sin." **Adaptation:** *Oranges Are Not the Only Fruit* (BBC, 1990 TV Movie). Dir: Beeban Kidron. Scr: Jeanette Winterson. Cast: Charlotte Coleman (Jess), Geraldine McEwan (Mother), Emily Aston (Jess as a child). Notes: BAFTA Awards for Best Film, Actress (McEwan), and Sound, and nominations for Best Actresses (Aston and Coleman), Musical Score, and Costume Design. DVD, VHS.

3331. "The Orchard Walls" (Ruth Rendell, 1983). During World War II, a young British girl is sent to live at her aunt's house in the country and discovers some dark family secrets. The story was first published in the August 1983 issue of *Ms. Magazine* and was included in Rendell's 1985 collection *The New Girlfriend and Other Stories*. **Adaptation:** *The Orchard Walls* (Blue Heaven, 1998 TV Movie). Dir: Gwennan Sage. Scr: Jacqueline Holborough. Cast: Alexis Denisof (Dennis), Fiona Dolman (Ella), Marsha Fitzalan (Clara), Sylvia Syms (Mrs. Thorn), Honeysuckle Weeks (Jenny).

3332. *The Orchid House* (Phyllis Shand Allfrey, 1953). Three white Creole girls living abroad return to the Caribbean island where they were raised, and all three try to rekindle a love affair with a boy each of them knew years earlier. **Adaptation:** *The Orchid House* (Channel 4, 1991 TV Movie). Dir: Horace Ove. Scr: Jim Hawkins. Cast: Kate Buffery (Stella), Frances Barber (Joan),

Diana Quick (Madam), Nigel Quick (the Master), Madge Sinclair (Lally), Elizabeth Hurley (Natalie).

3333. *The Orchid Thief: A True Story of Beauty and Obsession* (Susan Orlean, 1998). Nonfiction book is about John Laroche, a plant dealer who sells rare orchids to collectors. **Adaptation:** *Adaptation* (Columbia, 2002). Dir: Spike Jonze. Scr: Charlie Kaufman, Donald Kaufman. Cast: Nicolas Cage (Charlie/Donald), Meryl Streep (Susan), Chris Cooper (Laroche), Cara Seymour (Amelia), Tilda Swinton (Valerie), Maggie Gyllenhaal (Caroline). Notes: The film concerns a screenwriter who is having difficulty adapting Susan Orlean's *The Orchid Thief* for a screenplay while his twin brother easily pens a murder mystery. In the course of the film, we see both Orlean's biographical story and the external fiction of the writer's struggle. Academy Award for Best Supporting Actor (Cooper), and nominations for Best Screenplay, Actor (Cage), and Supporting Actress (Streep); Golden Globe Awards for Best Supporting Actor (Cooper) and Supporting Actress (Streep), and nominations for Best Picture, Director, Screenplay, and Actor (Cage); National Board of Review Awards for Best Screenplay and Supporting Actor (Cooper). DVD, VHS.

3334. *Ordeal by Innocence* (Agatha Christie, 1958). A paleontologist goes to an English village in the 1950's and discovers that his friend has been convicted of murdering his wife and hanged. Convinced of his friend's innocence, he works to clear his name. **Adaptation:** *Ordeal by Innocence* (Cannon, 1984). Dir: Desmond Davis. Scr: Alexander Stuart. Cast: Donald Sutherland (Dr. Calgary), Faye Dunaway (Rachel), Christopher Plummer (Leo), Sarah Miles (Mary), Ian McShane (Philip). VHS.

Ordeal in the Arctic (see *Death and Deliverance*).

3335. *The Ordeal of Major Grigsby* (John Sherlock, 1964). After he is betrayed by his comrade in the Congo, a British mercenary seeks revenge. **Adaptation:** *The Last Grenade* (Cinerama, 1970). Dir: Gordon Flemyng. Scr: James Mitchell, John Sherlock, Kenneth Ware. Cast: Stanley Baker (Harry), Alex Cord (Kip), Honor Blackman (Katherine), Richard Attenborough (General Whiteley).

3336. *The Order of Death* (Hugh Fleetwood, 1976). A corrupt New York City policeman enters into a bizarre sadomasochistic relationship with a mysterious man as he hunts a cop killer. **Adaptation:** *Corrupt*; also released as *The Order*

of Death and as *Copkiller* (New Line, 1983). Dir: Roberto Faenza. Scr: Ennio De Concini, Roberto Faenza, Hugh Fleetwood. Cast: Harvey Keitel (Fred), John Lydon (Leo), Nicole Garcia (Lenore), Leonard Mann (Bob), Sylvia Sidney (Margaret). DVD, VHS.

3337. *Ordinary People* (Judith Guest, 1976). An affluent suburban family falls apart emotionally after the death of their eldest son. **Adaptation:** *Ordinary People* (Paramount, 1980). Dir: Robert Redford. Scr: Alvin Sargent. Cast: Donald Sutherland (Calvin), Mary Tyler Moore (Beth), Judd Hirsch (Dr. Berger), Timothy Hutton (Conrad), M. Emmet Walsh (Coach Salan), Elizabeth McGovern (Jeannine). Notes: Academy Awards for Best Film, Director, Screenplay, and Supporting Actor (Hutton), and nominations for Best Actress (Moore) and Supporting Actor (Hirsch); Golden Globe Awards for Best Picture, Director, Actress (Moore), and Supporting Actor (Hutton), and nominations for Best Screenplay, Actor (Sutherland), and Supporting Actor (Hirsch); National Board of Review Awards for Best Film and Director. DVD, VHS.

Orient Express (see *Stamboul Train*).

3338. *Original Sin* (P. D. James, 1995). Scotland Yard Inspector Adam Dalgliesh investigates a series of murders at a prestigious London publishing house. **Adaptation:** *Original Sin* (ITV/PBS, 1996 TV Miniseries). Dir: Andrew Grieve. Scr: Michael Chaplin. Cast: Roy Marsden (Dalgliesh), Ian Bannen (Dauntsey), Cathryn Harrison (Claudia), Amanda Root (Frances), Sylvia Syms (Esme). DVD, VHS.

Original Sin (2001) (see *Waltz into Darkness*)

3339. *Orlando* (Virginia Woolf, 1928). Over the course of a 400-year life, a male courtier in the court of Queen Elizabeth I later undergoes a sex-change operation and enjoys life as a twentieth-century woman. **Adaptation:** *Orlando* (Sony, 1992). Dir: Sally Potter. Scr: Sally Potter. Cast: Tilda Swinton (Orlando), Quentin Crisp (Queen Elizabeth I), Jimmy Somerville (Falsetto/Angel). DVD, VHS.

3340. *The Oscar* (Richard Sale, 1963). Five famous actors ruthlessly compete for Hollywood's highest honor. **Adaptation:** *The Oscar* (Embassy, 1966). Dir: Russell Rouse. Scr: Harlan Ellison, Clarence Greene, Russell Rouse. Cast: Stephen Boyd (Frankie), Elke Sommer (Kay), Milton Berle (Kappy), Eleanor Parker (Sophie), Joseph Cotten (Kenneth), Jill St. John (Laurel). VHS.

3341. *Oscar and Lucinda* (Peter Carey, 1988, Booker Prize). In the nineteenth century, a Victorian heiress and a misfit minister, both of them hard gamblers, transport a glass church to a remote location in the Australian outback. **Adaptation:** *Oscar and Lucinda* (Fox Searchlight, 1997). Dir: Gillian Armstrong. Scr: Laura Jones. Cast: Ralph Fiennes (Oscar), Cate Blanchett (Lucinda), Ciaran Hinds (Reverend Hasset), Tom Wilkinson (Hugh). Notes: Australian Film Institute Awards for Best Cinematography, Costume Design, Production Design, Sound, Musical Score, and nominations for Best Screenplay and Actress (Blanchette); Academy Award nomination for Best Costume Design. DVD, VHS.

3342. *Oscar Wilde* (Richard Ellman, 1987, Pulitzer Prize and National Book Critics Circle Award). Biography of the British writer and playwright (1854–1900), who was prosecuted in Victorian England for his homosexuality. **Adaptation:** *Wilde* (BBC/Dove/Sony, 1997). Dir: Brian Gilbert. Scr: Julian Mitchell. Cast: Stephen Fry (Wilde), Jude Law (Lord Douglas), Vanessa Redgrave (Lady Speranza), Jennifer Ehle (Constance), Gemma Jones (Lady Queensberry), Judy Parfitt (Lady Mount-Temple), Michael Sheen (Robbie), Zoe Wanamaker (Ada). Notes: BAFTA nominations for Best Supporting Actresses (Ehle and Wanamaker); Golden Globe nomination for Best Actor (Fry). DVD, VHS.

Ossessione (see *The Postman Always Rings Twice*).

3343. *The Osterman Weekend* (Robert Ludlum, 1972). A thriller in which a CIA bureau chief tries to convince a television journalist that some of his colleagues are spies for the Russians. **Adaptation:** *The Osterman Weekend* (20th Century–Fox, 1983). Dir: Sam Peckinpah. Scr: Ian Masters, Alan Sharp. Cast: Rutger Hauer (Tanner), John Hurt (Fassett), Craig T. Nelson (Osterman), Dennis Hopper (Tremayne), Chris Sarandon (Cardone), Meg Foster (Ali), Helen Shaver (Virginia). DVD, VHS.

3344. *The Other* (Thomas Tryon, 1971). In a Connecticut town in the 1930's, a twin insists that his evil brother is responsible for several unexplained murders. **Adaptation:** *The Other* (20th Century–Fox, 1972). Dir: Robert Mulligan. Scr: Thomas Tryon. Cast: Uta Hagen (Ada), Diana Muldaur (Alexandra), Chris Udvarnoky (Niles), Martin Udvarnoky (Holland). VHS.

3345. *Other Halves* (Sue McCauley, 1982, New Zealand Book Award). After the failure of her marriage, a middle-class New Zealand woman has a mental breakdown and is institutionalized. There she begins a romantic relationship with a teenaged Maori youth. **Adaptation:** *Other Halves* (Oringham/Galatea, 1984). Dir: John Laing. Scr: Sue McCauley. Cast: Lisa Harrow (Liz), Mark Pilisi (Tug), Paul Gittins (Ken), Clare Clifford (Aileen).

3346. *The Other Mother* (Seth J. Margolis, 1993). After a crack addict abandons her infant son in a trash can, a white Chicago social worker and her husband adopt the black child. When his mother is free of drugs a few years later, she goes to court to get her child back, an emotionally devastating experience for the adoptive family. **Adaptation:** *Losing Isaiah* (Paramount, 1995). Dir: Stephen Gyllenhaal. Scr: Naomi Foner. Cast: Jessica Lange (Margaret), Halle Berry (Khaila), David Strathairn (Charles), Cuba Gooding, Jr. (Eddie), Samuel L. Jackson (Kadar). DVD, VHS.

3347. *The Other One* (Catherine Turney, 1952). A newlywed woman is possessed by the spirit of her husband's first wife. **Adaptation:** *Back from the Dead* (20th Century–Fox, 1957). Dir: Charles Marquis Warren. Scr: Catherine Turney. Cast: Peggie Castle (Mandy), Arthur Franz (Dick), Marsha Hunt (Kate).

3348. *The Other Side of Dark* (Joan Lowery Nixon, 1986). A man returns home to find his wife dead and his daughter unconscious. When she emerges from a coma eighteen months later, she begins to recall the events of that night and fears that she will be the killer's target soon. **Adaptation:** *Awake to Danger* (NBC, 1995 TV Movie). Dir: Michael Tuchner. Scr: April Campbell Jones. Cast: Tori Spelling (Aimee), Michael Gross (Ben), John Getz (Steve).

The Other Side of Heaven (see *In the Eye of the Storm*).

3349. *The Other Side of Midnight* (Sidney Sheldon, 1974). Before World War II, a woman in Paris falls in love with an American pilot. As a famous actress, she meets him again after the war in Hollywood and rekindles their torrid romance under the nose of her jealous lover. **Adaptation:** *The Other Side of Midnight* (20th Century–Fox, 1977). Dir: Charles Jarrott. Scr: Herman Raucher, Daniel Taradash. Cast: Marie-France Pisier (Noelle), John Beck (Larry), Susan Sarandon (Catherine), Raf Vallone (Constantin), Clu Gulager (Bill). VHS. See also *Memories of Midnight*.

The Other Side of the Mountain (see *A Long Way Up*).

3350. *Other Voices, Other Rooms* (Truman Capote, 1948). Capote's first novel centers on a young boy who, after the death of his mother, goes searching for his long-lost father. When he locates him in a Gothic Southern mansion, he must first contend with a variety of eccentric relatives. **Adaptation:** *Other Voices, Other Rooms* (Golden Eye/Artistic License, 1995). Dir: David Rocksavage. Scr: Sara Flanigan, David Rocksavage. Cast: Lothaire Bluteau (Randolph), Anna Thomson (Amy), David Speck (Joel), April Turner (Zoo). DVD, VHS.

3351. *Otley* (Martin Waddell, 1966). Comic novel about a petty thief and a beautiful woman drawn into an espionage plot in London. **Adaptation:** *Otley* (Columbia, 1968). Dir: Dick Clement. Scr: Dick Clement, Ian La Frenais. Cast: Tom Courtenay (Otley), Romy Schneider (Imogen), Alan Badel (Sir Alex), James Villiers (Hendrickson).

3352. *Our Guys: The Glen Ridge Rape and the Secret Life of the Perfect Suburb* (Bernard Lefkowitz, 1997). A factual account of a 1989 incident involving a group of athletes at a New Jersey high school who gang raped a mentally retarded girl. When school and town officials conspired to cover up the crime to protect their star players, a police detective and a prosecutor exposed the truth. **Adaptation:** *Our Guys: Outrage at Glen Ridge* (Greenwald, 1999 TV Movie). Dir: Guy Ferland. Scr: Paul Brown. Cast: Ally Sheedy (Kelly), Eric Stoltz (Robert), Heather Matarazzo (Leslie).

3353. *Our Hearts Were Young and Gay* (Cornelia Otis Skinner and Emily Kimbrough, 1942). Memoir by two young women and their romantic misadventures on a trip to Europe in the early 1920's. **Adaptation:** *Our Hearts Were Young and Gay* (Paramount, 1944). Dir: Lewis Allen. Scr: Sheridan Gibney. Cast: Gail Russell (Cornelia), Diana Lynn (Emily), Charles Ruggles (Otis), Dorothy Gish (Mrs. Skinner), Beulah Bondi (Miss Horn). Notes: A sequel titled *Our Hearts Were Growing Up* and also starring Russell and Lynn was released in 1946.

3354. *Our Man in Havana* (Graham Greene, 1958). Spy spoof about a British vacuum-cleaner salesman who is recruited as a spy in Cuba. **Adaptation:** *Our Man in Havana* (Columbia, 1959). Dir: Carol Reed. Scr: Graham Greene. Cast: Alec Guinness (Wormold), Burl Ives (Dr. Hasselbacher), Maureen O'Hara (Beatrice), Ernie Kovacs (Segura), Noel Coward (Hawthorne).

3355. *Our Mother's House* (Julian Gloag,

1963). Fearing that they will be sent to an orphanage after their mother's death, seven siblings bury her in their garden and continue to live in the house. Their plan is complicated, however, when their long-absent father reappears. **Adaptation:** *Our Mother's House* (MGM, 1967). Dir: Jack Clayton. Scr: Jeremy Brooks, Haya Harareet. Cast: Dirk Bogarde (Charlie), Margaret Brooks (Elsa), Pamela Franklin (Diana), Louis Sheldon Williams (Hubert), John Gugolka (Dunstan), Mark Lester (Jiminee).

3356. *Our Mutual Friend* (Charles Dickens, 1864–1865). An heir to a British fortune is presumed drowned, and his estate is transferred to a poor family. The heir takes a job as secretary to the newly wealthy family to observe their behavior. Dickens' last completed novel appeared serially between May 1864 and November 1865. **Adaptation 1:** *Our Mutual Friend* (BBC, 1976 Miniseries). Dir: Peter Hammond. Scr: Donald Churchill, Julia Jones. Cast: Nicholas Jones (Eugene), Lesley Dunlop (Lizzie), Jane Seymour (Bella), Leo McKern (Boffin), Warren Clarke (Headstone). VHS. **Adaptation 2:** *Our Mutual Friend* (BBC, 1998 TV Miniseries). Dir: Julian Farino. Scr: Sandy Welch. Cast: Paul McGann (Eugene), Keeley Hawes (Lizzie), Steven Mackintosh (Rokesmith/Harmon), Anna Friel (Bella), David Morrissey (Headstone), Timothy Spall (Venus), Peter Vaughan (Boffin). Notes: BAFTA Awards for Best Drama, Production Design, Sound, and Makeup, and nominations for Best Actor (Spall), Costume Design, Musical Score, and Photography and Lighting. DVD, VHS.

Our Relations (see "The Money Box").

3357. *Our Sunshine* (Robert Drewe, 1991). Fictionalized account of notorious Australian outlaw Ned Kelly (1854–1880). **Adaptation:** *Ned Kelly* (Focus, 2003). Dir: Gregor Jordan. Scr: John M. McDonagh. Cast: Heath Ledger (Kelly), Orlando Bloom (Joe), Geoffrey Rush (Francis), Naomi Watts (Julia), Joel Edgerton (Aaron). Notes: Australian Film Institute Awards for Best Costume Design and Production Design, and nominations for Best Director, Screenplay, Actor (Ledger), Supporting Actor (Bloom), Cinematography, Editing, and Sound. DVD, VHS. Notes: Ned Kelly was also the subject of an Australian television series in 1960 and of a 1970 film, starring Mick Jagger as the legendary outlaw (DVD, VHS).

Our Vines Have Tender Grapes (see *For Our Vines Have Tender Grapes*).

3358. *Our Virgin Island: A Modern Crusoe and His Wife in the Tropics* (Robb White, 1953). Autobiographical book about a young couple who moved to a tropical island and experienced a variety of problems with the natives. **Adaptation:** *Virgin Island*; released in the U.S. as *Our Virgin Island* (British Lion, 1958). Dir: Pat Jackson. Scr: Pat Jackson, Ring Lardner, Jr. (writing as Philip Rush), Robb White. Cast: John Cassavetes (Evan), Virginia Maskell (Tina), Sidney Poitier (Marcus), Isabel Dean (Mrs. Lomax).

3359. *Out* (Ronald Sukenick, 1973). A New York guerilla fighter moves across the country carrying out assignments for a mysterious agency. **Adaptation:** *Out*; also released as *Deadly Drifter* (Cinema Group/Reel Media, 1982). Dir: Eli Hollander. Scr: Eli Hollander, Ronald Sukenick. Cast: Peter Coyote (Rex), O-Lan Jones (Nixie/Dinah), Jim Haynie (Carl/Tommy), Danny Glover (Jojo/Roland). DVD, VHS.

3360. *Out of Africa* (Isak Dinesen [pseudonym for Karen Blixen], 1938). Memoir of Dinesen's life in Africa from 1914 through 1931. Arriving on an African coffee plantation for a marriage of convenience to a German baron, Dinesen met and fell in love with renowned hunter Denys Finch Hatton, with whom she carried on a love affair for nearly twenty years before returning to her native Denmark. **Adaptation:** *Out of Africa* (Universal, 1985). Dir: Sydney Pollack. Scr: Kurt Luedtke. Cast: Meryl Streep (Dinesen), Robert Redford (Hatton), Klaus Maria Brandauer (Baron Blixen-Finecke), Michael Kitchen (Cole). Notes: The screenplay is based on Dinesen's memoirs and Errol Trzebinski's *Silence Will Speak: A Study of the Life of Denys Finch Hatton and His Relationship with Karen Blixen*. Academy Awards for Best Picture, Director, Screenplay, Musical Score, Cinematography, Art Direction, and Sound, and nominations for Best Actress (Streep), Supporting Actor (Brandauer), Editing, and Costume Design; BAFTA Awards for Best Screenplay, Cinematography, and Sound. And nominations for Best Actress (Streep), Supporting Actor (Brandauer), Musical Score, and Costume Design; Golden Globe Awards for Best Director, Screenplay, and Actress (Streep), and nominations for Best Picture, Supporting Actor (Brandauer), and Musical Score; National Board of Review nomination for Best Supporting Actor (Brandauer). DVD, VHS. See also *Silence Will Speak*.

3361. *Out of Sight* (Elmore Leonard, 1996). Despite their professional differences, a female U.S. marshal and the notorious bank robber and escaped prisoner she is pursuing are attracted to each other. **Adaptation:** *Out of Sight* (Universal, 1998). Dir: Steven Soderbergh. Scr: Scott Frank. Cast: George Clooney (Foley), Jennifer Lopez (Karen), Ving Rhames (Bragg), Don Cheadle (Maurice), Dennis Farina (Marshall Sisco), Albert Brooks (Ripley), Nancy Allen (Midge). Notes: Academy Award nominations for Best Screenplay and Editing. DVD, VHS.

Out of the Ashes (see *I Was a Doctor in Auschwitz*).

Out of the Clouds (see *The Springboard*).

3362. *Out of the Dark* (Ursula Reilly Curtiss, 1964). Two teenagers making prank calls lead a murderer to think that they witnessed his crime, and now he wants to kill them. The book was released in the UK as *Child's Play*. **Adaptation 1:** *I Saw What You Did*; released on DVD as *I Saw What You Did and I Know Who You Are* (Universal, 1965). Dir: William Castle. Scr: William P. McGivern. Cast: Joan Crawford (Amy), John Ireland (Steve), Leif Erickson (Dave). DVD, VHS. **Adaptation 2:** *I Saw What You Did … And I Know Who You Are* (CBS, 1988 TV Movie). Dir: Fred Walton. Scr: Cynthia Cidre. Cast: Shawnee Smith (Kim), Tammy Lauren (Lisa), Candace Cameron (Julia), Robert Carradine (Adrian), David Carradine (Stephen).

Out of the Past (see *Build My Gallows High*).

Outback (see *Wake in Fright*).

3363. *Outbreak* (Robin Cook, 1987). A rare African plague is released and spreading throughout the country, and a medical investigator discovers a conspiracy involving hospital personnel. **Adaptation:** *Virus*; also released as *Formula for Death* (NBC, 1995 TV Movie). Dir: Armand Mastroianni. Scr: Roger Young. Cast: Nicolette Sheridan (Marissa), William Devane (Dr. Harbuck), Stephen Caffrey (Tad), Dakin Matthews (Dr. Dubcheck), Kurt Fuller (Dr. Williams), Barry Corbin (Dr. Clayman), William Atherton (Dr. Holloway).

The Outcast (see *Man in the Saddle*).

Outcast Lady (see *The Green Hat*).

3364. *An Outcast of the Islands* (Joseph Conrad, 1896). A homeless young man uses his criminal wits to get by in the Dutch East Indies. **Adaptation:** *Outcast of the Islands* (London/Lopert, 1952). Dir: Carol Reed. Scr: William Fairchild. Cast: Ralph Richardson (Captain Lin-gard), Trevor Howard (Peter), Robert Morley (Mr. Almayer), Wendy Hiller (Mrs. Almayer). Notes: BAFTA nomination for Best British Film. VHS.

3365. "The Outcasts of Poker Flat" (Bret Harte, 1869). Western tale about four undesirables who are run out of a town and take refuge in the nearby mountains, where they are stranded in a snow storm. The short story was first published in *The Overland Monthly* magazine in January 1869. **Silent Film:** 1919. **Adaptation 1:** *The Outcasts of Poker Flat* (RKO, 1937). Dir: Christy Cabanne. Scr: John Twist, Harry Segall. Cast: Preston Foster (Oakhurst), Jean Muir (Helen), Van Heflin (Reverend Woods), Virginia Weidler (Luck). **Adaptation 2:** *The Outcasts of Poker Flat* (20th Century–Fox, 1952). Dir: Joseph M. Newman. Scr: Edmund H. North. Cast: Anne Baxter (Cal), Dale Robertson (Oakhurst), Miriam Hopkins (the Duchess), Cameron Mitchell (Ryker). **Adaptation 3:** *Four of the Apocalypse* (Coralta/Anchor Bay, 1975). Dir: Lucio Fulci. Scr: Ennio De Concini. Cast: Fabio Testi (Preston), Lynne Frederick (Bunny), Michael J. Pollard (Clem), Harry Baird (Bud), Tomas Milian (Chaco). Notes: The screenplay combines elements of several Harte stories, notably "The Outcasts of Poker Flat" and "The Luck of Roaring Camp" (1869). DVD, VHS.

3366. *The Outfit* (Donald E. Westlake, 1963). A bank robber is released from prison to find that his brother has been murdered by a crime syndicate and that they are now intent upon killing him too. Westlake originally published the novel under the pseudonym Richard Stark. **Adaptation:** *The Outfit* (MGM, 1973). Dir: John Flynn. Scr: John Flynn. Cast: Robert Duvall (Earl), Karen Black (Bett), Joe Don Baker (Cody), Robert Ryan (Mailer). VHS.

The Outlaw Josey Wales (see *Gone to Texas*).

3367. *Outlaw Marshal* (Ray Hogan, 1959). Western about a cowboy who, unjustly accused of murder, goes on the run from a posse led by a corrupt marshal. **Adaptation:** *Hell Bent for Leather* (Universal International, 1960). Dir: George Sherman. Scr: Christopher Knopf. Cast: Audie Murphy (Clay), Felicia Farr (Janet), Stephen McNally (Marshal Deckett), Robert Middleton (Ambrose).

3368. *Outlaw of Gor* (John Norman, 1967). The second installment in Norman's twenty-six-volume Chronicle of Counter-Earth series (1966–2002) finds a professor who had once been magically transported to the planet Gor returning to battle the evil queen and her priest-henchman. **Adaptation:** *Outlaw of Gor* (Breton/Cannon, 1989). Dir: John Cardos. Scr: Harry Alan Towers (writing as Peter Welbeck), Rick Marx. Cast: Urbano Barberini (Tarl Cabot), Rebecca Ferratti (Talena), Jack Palance (Xenos), Donna Denton (Queen Lara). VHS. Notes: See also *Tarnsman of Gor*.

Outlaw Territory (see *Wicked Water*).

3369. *Outlaws of Palouse* (Zane Grey, 1934). Western about two men who became friends at the Battle of San Juan Hill but find themselves on different sides of the law in civilian life. The novel was published as a three-part serial in *The Country Gentleman* magazine (May–July 1934). **Adaptation:** *End of the Trail* (Columbia, 1936). Dir: Erle C. Kenton. Scr: Harold Shumate. Cast: Jack Holt (Dale), Louise Henry (Belle), Douglass Dumbrille (Bill).

3370. *Outside Providence* (Peter Farrelly, 1988). After many encounters with the police, a tough New England teenager is sent to a fancy prep school by his frustrated father. Once there, he develops a new view of life and himself and falls in love for the first time. **Adaptation:** *Outside Providence* (Miramax, 1999). Dir: Michael Corrente. Scr: Peter Farrelly, Michael Corrente, Bobby Farrelly. Cast: Shawn Hatosy (Timothy), Tommy Bone (Jackie), Samantha Lavigne (Chaps), Jonathan Brandis (Mousy), Adam La Vorgna (Tommy), Alec Baldwin (Dunphy). DVD, VHS.

3371. *The Outsider* (Penelope Williamson, 1996). A Western love story about the unlikely relationship between a religious widow and the wounded gunfighter whom she takes into her home. **Adaptation:** *The Outsider* (Showtime/Hallmark, 2002 TV Movie). Dir: Randa Haines. Scr: Jenny Wingfield. Cast: Timothy Daly (Johnny), Naomi Watts (Rebecca), Keith Carradine (Noah), David Carradine (Dr. Henry). DVD, VHS.

3372. *The Outsiders* (A. E. Martin, 1945). A carnival worker investigates the murder of a female performer. **Adaptation:** *The Glass Cage*; released in the U.S. as *The Glass Tomb* (Hammer/Lippert, 1955). Dir: Montgomery Tully. Scr: Richard H. Landau. Cast: John Ireland (Pelham), Honor Blackman (Jenny), Geoffrey Keen (Harry). VHS.

3373. *The Outsiders* (S. E. Hinton, 1967). Turf wars between rival youth gangs in a small Oklahoma town in the 1960's. **Adaptation:** *The*

Outsiders (Warner, 1983). Dir: Francis Ford Coppola. Scr: Kathleen Rowell. Cast: Matt Dillon (Dallas), Ralph Macchio (Johnny), C. Thomas Howell (Ponyboy), Patrick Swayze (Darrel), Rob Lowe (Sodapop), Emilio Estevez (Keith), Tom Cruise (Steve), Glenn Withrow (Tim), Diane Lane (Sherri). DVD, VHS.

3374. *Outwitting the Gestapo* (Lucie Aubrac, 1984). Originally titled *Ils partiront dans l'ivresse* and translated into English in 1993, the story of a French resistance fighter's determination to free her husband and others from the Nazi Gestapo during World War II. **Adaptation:** *Lucie Aubrac* (USA Films, 1997). Dir: Claude Berri. Scr: Claude Berri. Cast: Carole Bouquet (Lucie), Daniel Auteuil (Raymond), Patrice Chereau (Max), Jean-Roger Milo (Maurice). VHS.

3375. "The Oval Portrait" (Edgar Allan Poe, 1842). An injured writer takes refuge at a chateau, where he reds the account of a painter whose beautiful wife died a moment after he completed an astonishing portrait of her. The short story was published under the title "Life in Death" in *Graham's Magazine* in April 1842. **Adaptation:** *One Minute Before Death* (Front Row, 1972). Dir: Rogelio A. Gonzalez, Jr. Scr: Enrique Torres Tudela. Cast: Wanda Hendrix (Genevieve), Barry Coe (Paul), Gisele MacKenzie (Agatha). VHS.

Over My Dead Body (see *As Good as Murdered*).

Over the Hill (see *Alone in the Australian Outback*).

Over the River (see *One More River*).

Owd Bob (see *Bob, Son of Battle*).

The Ox (see *The Emigrants* and *The Settlers*).

3376. *The Ox-Bow Incident* (Walter Van Tilburg Clark, 1940). An honest cowboy unsuccessfully attempts to prevent the mob lynching of three innocent men for cattle rustling. **Adaptation:** *The Ox-Bow Incident*; released in the UK as *Strange Incident* (20th Century–Fox, 1943). Dir: William A. Wellman. Scr: Lamar Trotti. Cast: Henry Fonda (Gil), Dana Andrews (Donald), Mary Beth Hughes (Rose), Anthony Quinn (Juan/Francisco). Notes: National Board of Review Award for Best Film; Academy Award nomination for Best Film. DVD, VHS.

3377. *Ozma of Oz* (L. Frank Baum, 1907). After being treated with electric shock treatments at a psychiatric facility, Dorothy and a pet chicken named Billina travel back to Oz, where an evil witch and the Nome King have captured the Scarecrow and laid waste to the Emerald City. **Adaptation:** *Return to Oz* (Disney/Buena Vista, 1985). Dir: Walter Murch. Scr: Gill Dennis, Walter Murch. Cast: Fairuza Balk (Dorothy), Nicol Williamson (Dr. Worley/Nome King), Jean Marsh (Nurse Wilson/Princess Mombi), Piper Laurie (Aunt Em). Notes: The screenplay combines elements of *The Marvelous Land of Oz* (1904) and *Ozma of Oz* (1907). DVD, VHS. See also *The Marvelous Land of Oz* and *The Wonderful Wizard of Oz*.

Pacific Destiny (see *A Pattern of Islands*).

3378. *The Pack* (John Rowan Wilson, 1955). Professional in-fighting at a local hospital. **Adaptation:** *Behind the Mask* (BL/GW Films, 1958). Dir: Brian Desmond Hurst. Scr: John Hunter. Cast: Michael Redgrave (Sir Arthur), Tony Britton (Philip), Carl Mohner (Dr. Romek), Niall MacGinnis (Isherwood).

3379. *The Pack* (Dave Fisher, 1975). Vacationers on a remote island are terrorized by a pack of vicious abandoned dogs. **Adaptation:** *The Pack*; also released as *The Long, Dark Night* (Warner, 1977). Dir: Robert Clouse. Scr: Robert Clouse. Cast: Joe Don Baker (Jerry), Hope Alexander-Willis (Millie), Richard B. Shull (Hardiman). VHS.

3380. *The Pact* (Jodi Picoult, 1998). After he does not go through with a suicide pact that he and his girlfriend made, a teenager is tried for her murder. **Adaptation:** *The Pact* (Lifetime, 2002 TV Movie). Dir: Peter Werner. Scr: Will Scheffer. Cast: Eric Lively (Christopher), Megan Mullally (Melanie), Jessica Steen (Detective Marrone).

3381. *Padre Padrone: The Education of a Shepherd* (Gavino Ledda, 1975). Memoir by a Sardinian writer recalling his brutal upbringing at the hands of his tyrannical father. The book was first translated into English in 1979. **Adaptation:** *Padre Padrone*; also released as *Father and Master* (Cinema 5, 1977). Dir: Paolo Taviani, Vittorio Taviani. Scr: Paolo Taviani, Vittorio Taviani. Cast: Omero Antonutti (Father), Saverio Marconi (Gavino), Marcella Michelangeli (Mother). Notes: Originally titled *Padre Padrone* and shown with subtitles. Cannes Film Festival Golden Palm Award for Best Directors. DVD, VHS.

3382. *A Painted House* (John Grisham, 2001). The story of a young boy's coming of age as he and the migrant workers who labor on his family's farm struggle to raise their crops and brings them to market. The novel was serialized in *The Oxford American* magazine in 2000 and published as a book the following year. **Adaptation:** *A Painted House* (CBS/Hallmark, 2003 TV Movie). Dir: Alfonso Arau. Scr: Patrick Sheane Duncan. Cast: Scott Glenn (Eli), Arija Bareikis (Kathleen), Robert Sean Leonard (Jesse), Melinda Dillon (Gran Chandler). DVD, VHS.

3383. *The Painted Veil* (W. Somerset Maugham, 1925). In China, an American scientist's wife begins an affair with a politician. When she accompanies her husband to treat a cholera epidemic, however, she grows closer to him and recaptures her self-respect. **Adaptation 1:** *The Painted Veil* (MGM, 1934). Dir: Richard Boleslawski. Scr: John Meehan, Salka Viertel, Edith Fitzgerald. Cast: Greta Garbo (Katrin), Herbert Marshall (Dr. Fane), George Brent (Jack), Warner Oland (General Yu), Jean Hersholt (Koerber). VHS. **Adaptation 2:** *The Seventh Sin* (MGM, 1957). Dir: Ronald Neame, Vincente Minnelli. Scr: Karl Tunberg. Cast: Eleanor Parker (Carol), Jean-Pierre Aumont (Paul), George Sanders (Tim), Bill Travers (Dr. Carwin).

The Pajama Game (see *Seven and a Half Cents*).

3384. *Pal Joey* (John O'Hara, 1940). A collection of short stories published in *The New Yorker* in 1938 about a Chicago nightclub singer who performs in dives and involves himself with gangsters and other low characters. In 1940, George Abbott adapted the collection as a hit Broadway musical with songs by Richard Rodgers and Lorenz Hart. **Adaptation:** *Pal Joey* (Columbia, 1957). Dir: George Sidney. Scr: Dorothy Kingsley. Cast: Rita Hayworth (Vera), Frank Sinatra (Joey), Kim Novak (Linda), Barbara Nichols (Gladys). Notes: Golden Globe Awards for Best Musical Actor (Sinatra) and nomination for Best Musical Picture; Academy Award nomination for Best Editing, Sound, Art Direction, and Costume Design. DVD, VHS.

3385. "The Palace Thief" (Ethan Canin, 1994). An idealistic classics teacher at a prep school meets a new student who challenges him, and the two develop a friendship that lasts for more than forty years. The story is the title piece in Canin's 1994 collection *The Palace Thief: Stories.* **Adaptation:** *The Emperor's Club* (Universal, 2002). Dir: Michael Hoffman. Scr: Neil Tolkin. Cast: Kevin Kline (William), Emile Hirsch (Sedgewick), Embeth Davidtz (Elizabeth), Rob Morrow (James), Edward Herrmann (Headmaster Woodbridge). DVD, VHS.

3386. *The Pale Horse* (Agatha Christie, 1961). A man is unjustly accused of killing a priest

at an inn and must try to clear his name. **Adaptation:** *The Pale Horse* (A&E, 1997 TV Movie). Dir: Charles Beeson. Scr: Alma Cullen. Cast: Colin Buchanan (Mark), Jayne Ashbourne (Kate), Hermione Norris (Hermia). DVD, VHS.

3387. "Palm Springs" (Leslie Charteris [pseudonym for Leslie Charles Bowyer Yin], 1942). In an installment of Charteris' long-running series featuring Robin Hood–like sleuth Simon Templar, the Saint (as he is known) delivers rare stamps to a collector and is accused of theft and murder. The short story appeared in Charteris' 1942 collection *The Saint Goes West.* **Adaptation 1:** *The Saint in Palm Springs* (RKO, 1941). Dir: Jack Hively. Scr: Jerome Cady. Cast: George Sanders (Templar), Wendy Barrie (Elna), Paul Guilfoyle (Clarence), Jonathan Hale (Inspector Fernack). Notes: The short story was published a year after the film appeared. VHS. **Adaptation 2:** *The Dance of Death* (Lux, 1960). Dir: Jacques Nahum. Scr: Albert Simonin, Jacques Nahum, Yvan Audouard. Cast: Felix Marten (Templar), Jean Desailly (Fred), Clement Harari (Archie).

Palmetto (see *Just Another Sucker*).

3388. *Palomino* (Danielle Steel, 1981). A photographer inherits a ranch in California and turns it into a riding school for paralyzed children. **Adaptation:** *Palomino* (NBC, 1991 TV Movie). Dir: Michael Miller. Scr: Karol Ann Hoeffner. Cast: Lindsay Frost (Samantha), Eva Marie Saint (Caroline), Rod Taylor (Bill). VHS.

Pampered Youth (see *The Magnificent Ambersons*).

3389. *Pandora's Clock* (John J. Nance, 1995). Thriller about a deadly virus spreading through a commercial airliner bound for New York. Fearing the spread of disease, the government will not allow the jumbo jet to land and secretly develops plans to shoot it down. **Adaptation:** *Pandora's Clock* (NBC, 1996 TV Movie). Dir: Eric Laneuville. Scr: David Israel. Cast: Richard Dean Anderson (Captain Holland), Daphne Zuniga (Dr. Sanders), Richard Lawson (Captain Robb), Jane Leeves (Rachel).

3390. *Panic in Needle Park* (James Mills, 1966). A stark portrait of heroin addiction, set in one of New York City's most notorious parks. **Adaptation:** *The Panic in Needle Park* (20th Century–Fox, 1971). Dir: Jerry Schatzberg. Scr: Joan Didion, John Gregory Dunne. Cast: Al Pacino (Bobby), Kitty Winn (Helen), Alan Vint (Detective Hotch), Richard Bright (Hank). Notes:

Cannes Film Festival Award for Best Actress (Winn), and Golden Palm nomination for Best Director. DVD, VHS.

3391. *Panther* (Melvin Van Peebles, 1995). A fictionalized account of the Black Panther Party and their struggles with the FBI in the 1960's. **Adaptation:** *Panther* (Gramercy, 1995). Dir: Mario Van Peebles. Scr: Melvin Van Peebles. Cast: Kadeem Hardison (Judge), Bokeem Woodbine (Tyrone), Joe Don Baker (Brimmer), Courtney B. Vance (Bobby Seale). DVD, VHS.

3392. *Papa Was a Preacher* (Alyene Porter, 1944). Biographical novel set in the 1950's about the lives of a Methodist pastor and his large family after he is transferred from Dallas to a small Texas town. **Adaptation:** *Papa Was a Preacher* (Rosie, 1985). Dir: Steve Feke. Scr: Steve Feke. Cast: Robert Pine (Reverend Porter), Georgia Engel (Mrs. Porter), Imogene Coca (Missy), Dean Stockwell (John).

3393. *The Paper Chase* (John Jay Osborn, Jr., 1971). A freshman law student at Harvard begins a relationship with a young woman only to discover that she is the daughter of his own tyrannical professor. **Adaptation:** *The Paper Chase* (20th Century–Fox, 1973). Dir: James Bridges. Scr: James Bridges. Cast: Timothy Bottoms (Hart), Lindsay Wagner (Susan), John Houseman (Professor Kingsfield), Graham Beckel (Ford), James Naughton (Brooks), Edward Herrmann (Anderson). Notes: Golden Globe and National Board of Review Award for Best Supporting Actor (Houseman); Academy Award for Best Supporting Actor (Houseman), and nominations for Best Screenplay and Sound. DVD, VHS. Notes: The book and film also inspired a successful CBS television series (1978–1986).

Paper Moon (see *Addie Pray*).

Paperhouse (see *Marianne Dreams*).

3394. *Papillon* (Henri Charriere, 1970). Autobiography of a French man unjustly convicted of murder and imprisoned on Devil's Island in French Guiana. After several attempts, he finally escaped to Venezuela in 1945. **Adaptation:** *Papillon* (Allied Artists, 1973). Dir: Franklin J. Schaffner. Scr: Dalton Trumbo, Lorenzo Semple, Jr. Cast: Steve McQueen (Papillon), Dustin Hoffman (Dega), Victor Jory (Indian Chief), Don Gordon (Julot). DVD, VHS.

3395. *The Paradine Case* (Robert Hichens, 1933). A beautiful woman accused of murdering her wealthy blind husband hires a prominent London attorney to defend her. The lawyer falls madly in love with her, jeopardizing his marriage and his career. **Adaptation 1:** *The Paradine Case* (United Artists, 1947). Dir: Alfred Hitchcock. Scr: Alma Reville, David O. Selznick, Ben Hecht, James Bridie. Cast: Gregory Peck (Anthony), Ann Todd (Gay), Charles Laughton (Judge Horfield), Charles Coburn (Sir Simon), Ethel Barrymore (Lady Sophie), Louis Jourdan (Andre), Alida Valli (Maddalena), Leo G. Carroll (Sir Joseph). DVD, VHS. **Adaptation 2:** *The Paradine Case* (ABC, 1962 TV Movie). Dir: Alex March. Scr: Alex March. Cast: Richard Basehart (Anthony), Viveca Lindfors (Maddalena), Boris Karloff (Judge Horfield), Robert Webber (Andre).

3396. *Paradise Postponed* (John Mortimer, 1985). Mystery about a cleric in a small British town who dies and leaves his fortune to a repugnant conservative politician rather than to his own family. **Adaptation:** *Paradise Postponed* (Thames Television, 1986 TV Miniseries). Dir: Alvin Rakoff. Scr: John Mortimer. Cast: Michael Hordern (Reverend Simcox), Annette Crosbie (Dorothy), Peter Egan (Henry), Paul Shelley (Fred), Colin Blakely (Dr. Salter).

Paradise Road (see *Song of Survival*).

3397. *The Parallax View* (Loren Singer, 1970). When witnesses to the assassination of a U.S. Senator are killed off, a persistent reporter goes undercover to investigate the conspiracy. **Adaptation:** *The Parallax View* (Paramount, 1974). Dir: Alan J. Pakula. Scr: David Giler, Lorenzo Semple, Jr. Cast: Warren Beatty (Joseph), Hume Cronyn (Bill), William Daniels (Austin). DVD, VHS.

Paratrooper (see *The Red Beret*).

The Parent Trap (see *Lottie and Lisa*).

3398. *Paris Blues* (Harold Flender, 1957). Novel about the romantic entanglements of jazz musicians living in Paris. **Adaptation:** *Paris Blues* (United Artists, 1961). Dir: Martin Ritt. Scr: Walter Bernstein, Irene Kamp, Lulla Rosenfeld, Jack Sher. Cast: Paul Newman (Ram), Joanne Woodward (Lillian), Sidney Poitier (Eddie), Louis Armstrong (Wild Man Moore), Diahann Carroll (Connie). VHS.

Paris Express (see *The Man Who Watched Trains Go By*).

3399. *Paris Trout* (Pete Dexter, 1988, National Book Award). In a small Georgia town in the 1940's, a brutal bigot kills a black girl and is astonished that he is being prosecuted for the shooting. **Adaptation:** *Paris Trout* (Palace/Fox, 1991 TV Movie). Dir: Stephen Gyllenhaal. Scr: Peter Dexter. Cast: Dennis Hopper (Trout), Barbara Hershey (Hanna), Ed Harris (Harry), Ray McKinnon (Carl). Notes: The film was made for theatrical release, but debuted on cable TV in the United States. Emmy nominations for Outstanding Drama, Screenplay, Actor (Hopper), Actress (Hershey), and Sound. VHS.

3400. *Paris Underground* (Etta Shriber, in collaboration with Anne and Paul Dupre, 1943). Memoir of an elderly American woman who, along with a British friend, were engaged in resistance activities against the Germans during World War II and were placed in a Nazi POW camp. **Adaptation:** *Paris Underground*; released in the UK as *Madame Pimpernel* (United Artists, 1945). Dir: Gregory Ratoff. Scr: Boris Ingster, Gertrude Purcell. Cast: Constance Bennett (Kitty), Gracie Fields (Emmeline), Georges Rigaud (Andre), Kurt Kreuger (Captain von Weber).

3401. *Parrish* (Mildred Savage, 1958). The romantic entanglements of a handsome young manager at a tobacco plantation. **Adaptation:** *Parrish* (Warner, 1961). Dir: Delmer Daves. Scr: Delmer Daves. Cast: Troy Donahue (Parrish), Claudette Colbert (Ellen), Karl Malden (Judd), Dean Jagger (Sala), Connie Stevens (Lucy). VHS.

3402. *The Partner* (Jenaro Prieto, 1928). An unemployed financial investor invents a fictitious partner and his life changes for the better professionally and the worse personally. The Chilean novel, originally titled *El Socio*, was translated as *The Partner* in 1931. **Adaptation 1:** *The Associate* (France 3/Quartet, 1979). Dir: Rene Gainville. Scr: Jean-Claude Carrière, Rene Gainville. Cast: Michel Serrault (Julien), Claudine Auger (Agnes), Catherine Alric (Alice). Notes: Originally released as *L'Associe* and shown with subtitles. VHS. **Adaptation 2:** *The Associate* (Hollywood/Buena Vista, 1996). Dir: Donald Petrie. Scr: Jean-Claude Carriere Rene Gainville (1979 screenplay), Nick Thiel. Cast: Whoopi Goldberg (Laurel), Dianne Wiest (Sally), Eli Wallach (Fallon), Timothy Daly (Frank), Bebe Neuwirth (Camille). Notes: In this remake, a black woman tries to make it in a white man's investment firm and invents a white male partner. DVD, VHS.

Partner (see *The Double*).

3403. *Pascali's Island* (Barry Unsworth, 1980). During the last year of the Ottoman Empire

in 1908, a Turkish spy and a British thief on a Greek island conspire to steal an archaeological treasure. **Adaptation:** *Pascali's Island* (Avenue, 1988). Dir: James Dearden. Scr: James Dearden. Cast: Ben Kingsley (Pascali), Charles Dance (Bowles), Kevork Malikyan (Mardosian), George Murcell (Gesing), Helen Mirren (Lydia). Notes: Cannes Film Festival Golden Palm nomination for Best Director. VHS.

3404. *Paso Por Aqui* (Eugene Manlove Rhodes, 1927). A young man swindles money from a bank to save his father's ranch and is pursued by a determined sheriff and a Mexican man who wants to claim the reward for the arrest of the bank robber. The novel was serialized in the February 1927 issues of *The Saturday Evening Post* and published later that year along with another Western by Rhodes, *Once in the Saddle*. **Adaptation:** *Four Faces West*; released in the UK as *They Passed This Way* (United Artists, 1948). Dir: Alfred E. Green. Scr: C. Graham Baker, Teddi Sherman. Cast: Joel McCrea (Ross), Frances Dee (Fay), Charles Bickford (Garrett), Joseph Calleia (Marquez), William Conrad (Sheriff Egan). DVD, VHS.

The Passage (see *Perilous Passage*).

Passage to Marseille (see *Men Without Country*).

3405. *A Passage to India* (E. M. Forster, 1924). Amid colonial tensions in British-occupied India in the late 1920's, a young Indian doctor is unjustly accused of and tried for raping an English tourist in the Marabar Caves. **Adaptation 1:** *A Passage to India* (BBC, 1965 TV Movie). Dir: Waris Hussein. Scr: John Maynard. Cast: Sybil Thorndike (Mrs. Moore), Virginia McKenna (Adela), Cyril Cusack (Fielding), Zia Mohyeddin (Dr. Aziz). **Adaptation 2:** *A Passage to India* (Columbia, 1984). Dir: David Lean. Scr: David Lean. Cast: Judy Davis (Adela), Victor Banerjee (Aziz), Peggy Ashcroft (Mrs. Moore), James Fox (Fielding), Alec Guinness (Godbole), Nigel Havers (Ronny). Notes: Academy Awards for Best Supporting Actress (Ashcroft) and Musical Score, and nominations for Best Film, Director, Screenplay, Actress (Davis), Cinematography, Art Direction, Editing, Costume Design, and Sound; BAFTA Award for Best Actress (Ashcroft), and nominations for Best Film, Screenplay, Actor (Banerjee), Supporting Actor (Fox), Cinematography, Production Design, Musical Score, and Costume Design; Golden Globe Awards for Best Film, Supporting Actress (Ashcroft), and Musical Score, nominations for Best Director and Screenplay. DVD, VHS.

3406. *The Passing of Evil* (Mark McShane, 1961). A beautiful young girl from a small Canadian town becomes a Las Vegas call girl. **Adaptation:** *The Grasshopper*; also released as *The Passing of Evil*; released on video as *Passions* (National General, 1970). Dir: Jerry Paris. Scr: Jerry Belson, Garry Marshall. Cast: Jacqueline Bisset (Christine), Jim Brown (Tommy), Joseph Cotten (Richard). VHS.

3407. *Passion Flower* (Kathleen Norris, 1929). Two rich girls marry working-class men and cause problems for their socially conscious families. **Adaptation:** *Passion Flower* (MGM, 1930). Dir: William C. de Mille. Scr: Martin Flavin, Laurence E. Johnson, Edith Fitzgerald. Cast: Kay Francis (Dulce), Kay Johnson (Cassy), Charles Bickford (Dan), Winter Hall (Leroy), Lewis Stone (Tony).

3408. *A Passion in the Desert* (Honoré de Balzac, 1830). During Napoleon's Egyptian campaign, a French officer escorting an artist to Cairo develops a strange relationship with a female leopard in the desert. Originally titled *Une Passion dans le Desert*, the novella was published in Balzac's 1830 collection *Scenes from the Military Life* and first translated into English and published in *The Strand* magazine in 1891. **Adaptation:** *Passion in the Desert* (Fine Line, 1997). Dir: Lavinia Currier. Scr: Lavinia Currier, Martin Edmunds. Cast: Ben Daniels (Augustin), Michel Piccoli (Jean-Michel), Paul Meston (Grognard). VHS.

3409. *The Passion of Ayn Rand* (Barbara Branden, 1986). A biography of Ayn Rand (1905–1982), the controversial author of *The Fountainhead* and *Atlas Shrugged*, by a former friend and artistic associate. **Adaptation:** *The Passion of Ayn Rand* (Showtime, 1999). Dir: Christopher Menaul. Scr: Howard Korder, Mary Gallagher. Cast: Helen Mirren (Rand), Eric Stoltz (Nathaniel), Julie Delpy (Barbara), Peter Fonda (Frank), Sybil Temchen (Caroline). Notes: Emmy Award for Outstanding Actress (Mirren) and nomination for Outstanding Supporting Actor (Fonda); Golden Globe Award for Best Television Supporting Actor (Fonda) and nomination for Best Actress (Mirren). DVD, VHS.

3410. *The Passionate Friends* (H. G. Wells, 1913). After marrying an older man for security, a woman meets her first lover, and the two have a final fling in the Swiss Alps. **Silent Film:** 1922. **Adaptation:** *The Passionate Friends*; originally released in the U.S. as *One Woman's Story* (Univer-

sal International, 1949). Dir: David Lean. Scr: Eric Ambler, Stanley Haynes, David Lean. Cast: Ann Todd (Mary), Claude Rains (Howard), Trevor Howard (Steven), Isabel Dean (Pat). DVD, VHS.

Passionate Summer (see *The Shadow and the Peak*).

3411. *The Passionate Witch* (Thorne Smith, with Norman Matson, 1941). Comic fantasy about a beautiful witch who comes back from the dead in Salem, Massachusetts, to haunt the descendant of the Puritan who had her burned at the stake. The novel was left unfinished at the time of Thorne Smith's death in 1934 and was subsequently completed by Norman Matson. **Adaptation:** *I Married a Witch* (United Artists, 1942). Dir: Rene Clair. Scr: Robert Pirosh, Marc Connelly. Cast: Fredric March (Jonathan), Veronica Lake (Jennifer), Robert Benchley (Dr. White), Susan Hayward (Estelle), Cecil Kellaway (Daniel). VHS.

Passions (see *The Passing of Evil*).

Passion's Way (see *The Reef*).

Passport to Fame (see *Jail Breaker*).

3412. *Passport to Oblivion* (James Leasor, 1964). Comic spy novel about a country doctor who is pressured into becoming a spy. **Adaptation:** *Where the Spies Are* (MGM, 1965). Dir: Val Guest. Scr: Wolf Mankowitz, Val Guest. Cast: David Niven (Dr. Love), Françoise Dorléac (Vikki), John Le Mesurier (MacGillivray), Cyril Cusack (Rosser).

3413. *The Password to Larkspur Lane* (Carolyn Keene [pseudonym for Mildred Wirt Benson], 1933). This installment in the enormously popular Nancy Drew mystery series finds Nancy and her brother investigating the disappearance of an old, wealthy woman. **Adaptation:** *Nancy Drew, Detective* (Warner, 1938). Dir: William Clemens. Scr: Kenneth Gamet. Cast: Bonita Granville (Nancy), John Litel (Carson), James Stephenson (Challon).

The Past of Mary Holmes (see "The Goose Woman").

Patch Adams (see *Gesundheit*).

A Patch of Blue (see *Be Ready with Bells and Drums*).

3414. *The Pathfinder* (James Fenimore Cooper, 1840). Cooper's Leather-Stocking Tale about a man raised by Mohican Indians and the vengeance he takes against the French for slaughtering his people. **Adaptation 1:** *The Pathfinder* (Columbia, 1952). Dir: Sidney Salkow. Scr: Robert E. Kent. Cast: George Montgomery (Hawkeye), Helena Carter (Alison), Jay Silverheels (Chingachgook), Walter Kingsford (Duncannon). **Adaptation 2:** *Hawkeye, the Pathfinder* (BBC, 1973 TV Miniseries). Dir: David Maloney. Scr: Alistair Bell, Allan Prior. Cast: Paul Massie (Hawkeye), CaJohn Abineri (Chingachgook), Windsor Davies (Dunham). **Adaptation 3:** *The Pathfinder* (Hallmark, 1996 TV Movie). Dir: Donald Shebib. Scr: Tommy Lynch, Bruce Reisman. Cast: Kevin Dillon (Hawkeye), Graham Greene (Chingachgook), Laurie Holden (Mabel), Stacy Keach (Compte du Leon). VHS.

3415. *Paths of Glory* (Humphrey Cobb, 1935). During World War I, a French commander tries to punish his troops for insubordination by sending them on a suicidal mission. When they refuse the assignment, he has them brought up on charges of cowardice. **Adaptation:** *Paths of Glory* (United Artists, 1957). Dir: Stanley Kubrick. Scr: Stanley Kubrick, Calder Willingham, Jim Thompson. Cast: Kirk Douglas (Colonel Dax), Ralph Meeker (Corporal Paris), Adolphe Menjou (General Broulard), George Macready (General Mireau). DVD, VHS.

The Patient Vanishes (see *They Called Him Death*).

3416. *Patriot Games* (Tom Clancy, 1987). CIA analyst Jack Ryan foils an IRA assassination attempt against the Prince and Princess of Wales and is targeted, along with his family, by the terrorists. **Adaptation:** *Patriot Games* (Paramount, 1992). Dir: Phillip Noyce. Scr: W. Peter Iliff, Donald Stewart. Cast: Harrison Ford (Ryan), Anne Archer (Catherine), Patrick Bergin (Kevin), Sean Bean (Sean), Thora Birch (Sally), James Fox (Lord Holmes), Samuel L. Jackson (Robby), James Earl Jones (Greer), Richard Harris (O'Neil). DVD, VHS.

3417. *Patrol* (Philip MacDonald, 1928). During World War I, a British army unit is lost and under attack by Arabs in the Mesopotamian desert. **Silent Film:** *Lost Patrol*, 1929. **Adaptation:** *Lost Patrol* (RKO, 1934). Dir: John Ford. Scr: Garrett Fort, Dudley Nichols. Cast: Victor McLaglen (the Sergeant), Boris Karloff (Sanders), Wallace Ford (Morelli), Reginald Denny (George Brown). VHS.

3418. *The Patron Saint of Liars* (Ann Patchett, 1992). A pregnant woman runs away from her husband and takes shelter at a Catholic girls'

school, where she meets and marries another man. Her stunned husband then begins a long search for his disturbed wife. **Adaptation:** *The Patron Saint of Liars* (Patchett-Kaufman, 1998 TV Movie). Dir: Stephen Gyllenhaal. Scr: Lynn Roth. Cast: Dana Delany (Rose), Sada Thompson (Sister Evangeline), Ellen Burstyn (June).

3419. *A Pattern of Islands* (Arthur Grimble, 1952). Memoir by a British government official who was assigned to the South Seas in 1912 and helped to quell native disputes there. **Adaptation:** *Pacific Destiny* (British Lion, 1956). Dir: Wolf Rilla. Scr: Richard Mason. Cast: Denholm Elliott (Grimble), Susan Stephen (Olivia), Michael Hordern (the Island Commissioner).

Patty Hearst (see *Every Secret Thing*).

3420. *Pavilion of Women* (Pearl S. Buck, 1946). In China in 1938, a wife informs her husband that she will no longer have sexual relations with him and encourages him to take a younger second wife. After he does, she meets and falls in love with a European missionary who is tutoring her son. **Adaptation:** *Pavilion of Women* (Universal, 2001). Dir: Ho Yim. Scr: Yan Luo, Paul Collins. Cast: Willem Dafoe (Father Andre), Yan Luo (Madame Wu), Shek Sau (Mr. Wu), John Cho (Fengmo). DVD, VHS.

3421. *The Pawnbroker* (Edward Lewis Wallant, 1961). A New York pawnbroker and concentration-camp survivor is haunted by memories of his experiences during the war. **Adaptation:** *The Pawnbroker* (Allied Artists, 1964). Dir: Sidney Lumet. Scr: Morton S. Fine, David Friedkin. Cast: Rod Steiger (Sol), Geraldine Fitzgerald (Marilyn), Brock Peters (Rodriguez), Jaime Sanchez (Jesus). Notes: Academy Award and Golden Globe nominations for Best Actor (Steiger). DVD, VHS.

3422. *Paxton Quigley's Had the Course* (Stephen H. Yafa, 1967). Comic story about a college student romancing three women. When they discover his deception, they lock him in a attic and force him to have sex until his desire is drained. **Adaptation:** *Three in the Attic* (American International, 1968). Dir: Richard Wilson. Scr: Stephen H. Yafa. Cast: Christopher Jones (Paxton), Yvette Mimieux (Toby), Judy Pace (Eulice), Maggie Thrett (Jan). VHS.

3423. *Pay It Forward* (Catherine Ryan Hyde, 1999). For a school assignment on improving the world, a boy devises a scheme whereby favors are paid forward to three complete strangers, and his idea catches on throughout the country. **Adapta-**

tion: *Pay It Forward* (Warner, 2000). Dir: Mimi Leder. Scr: Leslie Dixon. Cast: Kevin Spacey (Eugene), Helen Hunt (Arlene), Haley Joel Osment (Trevor), Jay Mohr (Chris), James Caviezel (Jerry), Jon Bon Jovi (Ricky), Angie Dickinson (Grace). DVD, VHS.

Payback (see *The Hunter*).

3424. "Paycheck" (Philip K. Dick, 1953). Science-fiction thriller about an electrical engineer who agrees to undertake a dangerous job, at the end of which his memory of the previous two years is erased. With objects he sent himself before the mission, he tries to recall his past and to prove his innocence for crimes he is accused of committing. The short story first appeared in *Imagination* magazine in June 1953. **Adaptation:** *Paycheck* (Paramount, 2003). Dir: John Woo. Scr: Dean Georgaris. Cast: Ben Affleck (Michael), Aaron Eckhart (James), Uma Thurman (Dr. Porter), Paul Giamatti (Shorty), Colm Feore (Wolfe). DVD, VHS.

3425. *Payment in Blood* (Elizabeth George, 1989). In the second installment in George's series of novels featuring Inspector Thomas Lynley of Scotland Yard, the detective investigates the murder of a playwright at a country inn where the members of a theatre company have assembled for a reading of a controversial new play. **Adaptation:** *Inspector Lynley Mysteries: Payment in Blood* (BBC/PBS, 2002 TV Movie). Dir: Kim Flitcroft, Scr: Lizzie Mickery. Cast: Nathaniel Parker (Lynley), Sharon Small (Detective Havers), James McAvoy (Ross), Naomi Frederick (Elizabeth). DVD, VHS.

3426. *Payroll* (Derek Bickerton, 1960). Petty crooks in England rob a large payroll, and the widow of the guard they killed in the heist tracks them down. **Adaptation:** *Payroll* (Allied Artists, 1961). Dir: Sidney Hayers. Scr: George Baxt. Cast: Michael Craig (Johnny), Francoise Prevost (Katie), Billie Whitelaw (Jackie), William Lucas (Dennis). VHS.

3427. *Peabody's Mermaid* (Guy Jones and Constance Jones, 1945). Comic fantasy about a middle-aged man who tells his psychiatrist that he met and fell in love with a mermaid while he was out fishing one day. **Adaptation:** *Mr. Peabody and the Mermaid* (Universal, 1948). Dir: Irving Pichel. Scr: Nunnally Johnson. Cast: William Powell (Arthur), Ann Blyth (Lenore), Irene Hervey (Polly). VHS.

3428. *Peace Marshal* (Frank Gruber, 1939). Western about a wandering gunman who becomes the marshal of a town and cleans up corruption and crime there. **Adaptation:** *The Kansan* (United Artists, 1943). Dir: George Archainbaud. Scr: Harold Shumate. Cast: Richard Dix (John), Jane Wyatt (Eleanor), Albert Dekker (Steve), Victor Jory (Jeff). DVD, VHS.

The Peacemaker (see *One Point Safe*).

3429. *The Peacock Feather* (Leslie Moore, 1913). A drifter befriends an orphaned girl and her grandfather. **Adaptation:** *Pennies from Heaven* (Columbia, 1936). Dir: Norman Z. McLeod. Scr: Jo Swerling. Cast: Bing Crosby (Larry), Madge Evans (Susan), Edith Fellows (Patsy), Louis Armstrong (Henry). DVD, VHS.

3430. *Peacock's Feather* (George S. Hellman, 1931). Fanciful story of ancient storyteller Aesop falling in love with a princess in the palace of King Croesus. **Adaptation:** *A Night in Paradise* (Universal, 1946). Dir: Arthur Lubin. Scr: Emmet Lavery, Ernest Pascal. Cast: Merle Oberon (Delarai), Turhan Bey (Aesop), Thomas Gomez (King Croesus), Gale Sondergaard (Attosa).

3431. *The Pearl* (John Steinbeck, 1947). Novella about a simple fisherman whose life is altered for the worse when he discovers a valuable pearl. **Adaptation 1:** *The Pearl* (RKO, 1947). Dir: Emilio Fernandez. Scr: John Steinbeck, Jack Wagner, Emilio Fernandez. Cast: Pedro Armendariz (Quino), Maria Elena Marques (Juana), Charles Rooner (the Doctor). Notes: Golden Globe Award for Best Cinematography; Ariel Awards (Mexico) for Best Actor (Armendariz) and Cinematography, and nominations for Best Screenplay, Actress (Marques), Editing, and Musical Score. VHS. **Adaptation 2:** *The Pearl* (Panorama, 2001). Dir: Alfredo Zacharias, Jr. Scr: Alfredo Zacharias, Jr. Cast: Richard Harris (Quino), Lukas Haas (Kino), Jorge Rivero (Professor Severin Costes).

The Pearl of Death (*see* "The Adventure of the Six Napoleons").

Peeper (see *Deadfall*).

3432. *The Pelican Brief* (John Grisham, 1992). When a law student speculates in a brief about the assassination of two Supreme Court justices, she becomes an assassination target herself and is forced to flee for her life with the help of an investigative reporter. **Adaptation:** *The Pelican Brief* (Warner, 1993). Dir: Alan J. Pakula. Scr: Alan J. Pakula. Cast: Julia Roberts (Darby), Denzel Washington (Grantham), Sam Shepard (Callahan), John Heard (Gavin). DVD, VHS.

3433. *Pelle the Conqueror* (Martin Andersen Nexo, 1906–1910). Four-volume Danish novel, originally titled *Pelle Erobreren*, about the struggles of a Swedish farmer and his young son, who emigrate to Denmark in the early twentieth century. The novel was first translated into English in 1930. **Adaptation:** *Pelle the Conqueror* (Miramax, 1987). Dir: Bille August. Scr: Bille August, Per Olov Enquist, Bjarne Reuter. Cast: Pelle Hvenegaard (Pelle), Max von Sydow (Lassefar), Erik Paaske (the Foreman), Bjorn Granath (Erik), Karen Wegener (Mrs. Olsen). Notes: Originally titled *Pelle Erobreren* and shown with subtitles. The screenplay is based only on the first part of the four-volume novel. Academy Award and Golden Globe Award for Best Foreign-Language Film; Cannes Film Festival Golden Palm Award for Best Director; Bodil Awards (Denmark) for Best Picture and Actor (von Sydow), and nominations for Best Supporting Actor (Granath) and Supporting Actress (Wegener). DVD, VHS.

3434. *The Penal Colony* (Richard Herley, 1987). In the year 2022, a man is sent to prison on an isolated island where only the strong rule and survive. **Adaptation:** *No Escape*; also released as *Escape from Absalom* (Allied/Columbia/Savoy, 1994). Dir: Martin Campbell. Scr: Michael Gaylin, Joel Gross. Cast: Ray Liotta (Robbins), Lance Henriksen (the Father), Stuart Wilson (Marek), Kevin Dillon (Casey), Ian McNeice (King), Ernie Hudson (Hawkins). DVD, VHS.

3435. *Penelope* (Howard Fast, 1965). Comic novel about a bored wife who disguises herself and robs her husband's bank of $60,000. When she later confesses to the crime, no one believes her. Fast published the novel under the pseudonym E. V. Cunningham. **Adaptation:** *Penelope* (MGM, 1966). Dir: Arthur Hiller. Scr: George Wells. Cast: Natalie Wood (Penelope), Ian Bannen (James), Dick Shawn (Dr. Mannix), Peter Falk (Lieutenant Bixbee), Jonathan Winters (Professor Klobb).

3436. *The Penguin Pool Murder* (Stuart Palmer, 1931). When a businessman is found floating in the penguin tank at an aquarium, schoolteacher and amateur detectibe Hildegard Withers helps a detective solve the crime. **Adaptation:** *Penguin Pool Murder* (RKO, 1932). Dir: George Archainbaud. Scr: Willis Goldbeck. Cast: Edna May Oliver (Hildegarde), Robert Armstrong (Barry), James Gleason (Inspector Piper), Mae Clarke (Gwen).

Penn of Pennsylvania (see *William Penn*).

Pennies from Heaven (see *The Peacock Feather*).

3437. *Penrod* (Booth Tarkington, 1914). The first of Tarkington's successful series of novels for young readers based on his own adventures as a boy and adolescent in Indiana. The other novels are *Penrod and Sam* (1916) and *Penrod Jashber* (1929). The novel was adapted as a play titled *Penrod: A Comedy in Four Acts* in 1918. **Silent Film:** 1922. **Adaptation 1:** *Penrod's Double Trouble* (Warner, 1938). Dir: Lewis Seiler. Scr: Ernest Booth, Crane Wilbur. Cast: Billy Mauch (Penrod), Bobby Mauch (Danny), Dick Purcell (Tex), Gene Lockhart (Mr. Schofield), Kathleen Lockhart (Mrs. Schofield). **Adaptation 2:** *Penrod and His Twin Brother* (Warner, 1938). Dir: William C. McGann. Scr: Hugh Cummings, William Jacobs. Cast: Billy Mauch (Penrod), Bobby Mauch (Danny), Frank Craven (Mr. Schofield), Spring Byington (Mrs. Schofield). **Adaptation 3:** *On Moonlight Bay* (Warner, 1951). Dir: Roy Del Ruth. Scr: Jack Rose, Melville Shavelson, Cast: Doris Day (Margie), Gordon MacRae (Bill), Billy Gray (Wesley), Rosemary De Camp (Alice), Mary Wickes (Stella). VHS. **Adaptation 4:** *By the Light of the Silvery Moon* (Warner, 1953). Dir: David Butler. Scr: Irving Elinson, Robert O'Brien. Cast: Doris Day (Margie), Gordon MacRae (Bill), Billy Gray (Wesley), Rosemary De Camp (Mrs. Winfield), Mary Wickes (Stella). VHS. Notes: The screenplays for both films combine elements from the Tarkington's three Penrod books. See also *Penrod and Sam*.

3438. *Penrod and Sam* (Booth Tarkington, 1916). In the sequel to Tarkington's 1914 children's novel, the junior sleuths pursue bank robbers. **Silent Film:** 1923. **Adaptation 1:** *Penrod and Sam* (Warner, 1931). Dir: William Beaudine. Scr: Waldemar Young. Cast: Leon Janney (Penrod), Junior Coghlan (Sam), Margaret Marquis (Margie). **Adaptation 2:** *Penrod and Sam* (Warner, 1937). Dir: William McGann. Scr: Lillie Hayward, Hugh Cummings. Cast: Billy Mauch (Penrod), Frank Craven (Mr. Schofield), Spring Byington (Mrs. Schofield), Craig Reynolds (Dude), Harry Watson (Sam). See also *Penrod*.

3439. *The Penthouse* (Elleston Trevor [pseudonym for Trevor Dudley Smith], 1983). A wealthy woman invites an old friend into her penthouse apartment, and the mentally deranged man takes her hostage. **Adaptation:** *The Penthouse* (Turner, 1989 TV Movie). Dir: David Greene. Scr: William Wood, Frank De Felitta. Cast: Robin Givens (Dinah), David Hewlett

(Joe), Donnelly Rhodes (Lieutenant Valeri), Robert Guillaume (Eugene). VHS.

3440. *Pentimento: A Book of Portraits* (Lillian Hellman, 1973). The second volume of autobiographical recollections by the famed writer and playwright (1905–1984). Among her subjects is Julia, a woman who drew Hellman into the European resistance movement in the 1930's and who was killed by the Nazis for her work. **Adaptation:** *Julia* (20th Century–Fox, 1977). Dir: Fred Zinnemann. Scr: Alvin Sargent. Cast: Jane Fonda (Hellman), Vanessa Redgrave (Julia), Jason Robards (Dashiell Hammett), Maximilian Schell (Johann), Hal Holbrook (Alan), Rosemary Murphy (Dorothy Parker), Meryl Streep (Anne Marie). Notes: Academy Award for Best Screenplay, Supporting Actress (Redgrave), and Supporting Actor (Robards), and nominations for Best Picture, Director, Actress (Fonda), Supporting Actor (Schell), Musical Score, Cinematography, Editing, and Costume Design; Golden Globe Awards for Best Actress (Fonda) and Supporting Actress (Redgrave), and nominations for Best Picture, Director, Screenplay, and Supporting Actors (Robards and Schell). VHS.

3441. *The People Against O'Hara* (Eleazar Lipsky, 1950). An alcoholic lawyer comes out of retirement to defend a man accused of murder. When the man is convicted because of the lawyer's incompetence, he works to clear the man's name. **Adaptation:** *The People Against O'Hara* (MGM, 1951). Dir: John Sturges. Scr: John Monks, Jr. Cast: Spencer Tracy (James), Pat O'Brien (Detective Ricks), Diana Lynn (Virginia), John Hodiak (Louis), Eduardo Ciannelli (Lanzetta), James Arness (Johnny).

3442. *The People That Time Forgot* (Edgar Rice Burroughs, 1918). In the sequel to *The Land That Time Forgot*, a group led by a military officer undertake a voyage to the Antarctic to look for a lost comrade and discover a dangerous prehistoric land. **Adaptation:** *The People That Time Forgot* (American International, 1977). Dir: Kevin Connor. Scr: Patrick Tilley. Cast: Patrick Wayne (Ben), Doug McClure (Bowen), Sarah Douglas (Lady Charlotte), Dana Gillespie (Ajor). DVD, VHS. See also *The Land That Time Forgot*.

3443. *Pepe le Moko* (Detective Ashelbe [pseudonym for Henri La Barthe], 1936). A thief operating in the Casbah section of Algiers romances a beautiful woman while trying to elude the policeman determined to catch him. **Adaptation 1:** *Pepe le Moko* (Paris Films, 1937). Dir: Julien Duvivier. Scr: Jacques Constant, Julien Duvivier, Henri Jeanson, Henri La Barthe. Cast: Jean Gabin (Pepe), Mireille Balin (Gisele), Line Noro (Inez), Lucas Gridoux (Slimane). Notes: National Board of Review Award for Best Foreign Film. DVD, VHS. **Adaptation 2:** *Algiers* (United Artists, 1938). Dir: John Cromwell. Scr: John Howard Lawson. Cast: Charles Boyer (Pepe), Sigrid Gurie (Inez), Hedy Lamarr (Gaby), Joseph Calleia (Slimane), Alan Hale (Grandfather), Gene Lockhart (Regis). Notes: Academy Award nominations for Best Actor (Boyer), Supporting Actor (Lockhart), Cinematography, and Art Direction. DVD, VHS. **Adaptation 3:** *Casbah* (Universal International, 1948). Dir: John Berry. Scr: Leslie Bush-Fekete, Arnold Manoff, Erik Charell. Cast: Yvonne De Carlo (Inez), Tony Martin (Pepe), Peter Lorre (Slimane). Notes: A musical remake, based on a musical screen story by Erik Charell. VHS.

3444. *The Peppermint Pig* (Nina Bawden [pseudonym for Nina Mabey Kark], 1975). Children's book about a brother and sister's joy over their new pet, a runt pig, and their attempts to save it from slaughter. **Adaptation:** *The Peppermint Pig* (BBC, 1977 TV Movie). Dir: Paul Stone. Scr: Julia Jones. Cast: Lucy Durham-Matthews (Poll), Ben Bethell (Theo), Tom Georgeson (James), Anne Stallybrass (Emily).

3445. *Percy* (Raymond Hitchcock, 1969). After an accident, a young man receives a penis transplant and then goes searching for the identity of the donor. **Adaptation:** *Percy* (MGM, 1971). Dir: Ralph Thomas. Scr: Terence Feely, Hugh Leonard. Cast: Hywel Bennett (Edwin), Denholm Elliott (Emmanuel), Elke Sommer (Helga), Britt Ekland (Dorothy). DVD, VHS. Notes: A sequel titled *Percy's Progress* was released in 1974, and Hitchcock published a tie-in novel based on the original screenplay the same year.

Perdita Durango (see *59 Degrees and Raining*).

3446. *The Perez Family* (Christine Bell, 1990). During the Mariel boat lift in 1981, a Cuban plantation owner imprisoned for twenty years is released and goes to Miami in search of his wife and daughter. On the way, he meets and bonds with a variety of Cubans also heading toward freedom in the United States. **Adaptation:** *The Perez Family* (Samuel Goldwyn, 1995). Dir: Mira Nair. Scr: Robin Swicord. Cast: Marisa Tomei (Dorita), Alfred Molina (Juan), Anjelica Huston (Carmela), Chazz Palminteri (Lieutenant Pirelli), Trini Alvarado (Teresa). DVD, VHS.

Perfect Alibi (see *Where's Mommy Now?*)

Perfect Crime (see *The Big Bow Mystery*).

3447. *The Perfect Murder* (H. R. F. Keating, 1964, Gold Dagger Award of the British Crime Writers Association). The first in a series of novels featuring Bombay detective Ganesh Ghote finds the policeman pursuing homicidal diamond smugglers. **Adaptation:** *The Perfect Murder* (Merchant-Ivory, 1988). Dir: Zafar Hai. Scr: H. R. F. Keating, Zafar Hai. Cast: Naseeruddin Shah (Ghote), Stellan Skarsgard (Axel), Amjad Khan (Lala), Madhur Jaffrey (Mrs. Lal). DVD, VHS.

3448. *Perfect Murder, Perfect Town: JonBenet and the City of Boulder* (Lawrence Schiller, 1999). An investigative history of the murder of six-year-old beauty queen JonBenet Ramsey on Christmas 1996. Schiller explores the possibilities that either her parents or an unknown intruder was involved in the crime. **Adaptation:** *Perfect Murder, Perfect Town: JonBenet and the City of Boulder* (CBS, 2000 TV Movie). Dir: Lawrence Schiller. Scr: Tom Topor. Cast: Marg Helgenberger (Patsy Ramsey), Kris Kristofferson (Lou Smit), Ronny Cox (John Ramsey), Dyanne Iandoli (JonBenet Ramsey), Ken Howard (Alex Hunter), John Heard (Larry Mason), Ann-Margret (Patsy's Mother). DVD, VHS.

3449. *A Perfect Spy* (John Le Carre [pseudonym for David Cornwell], 1986). Autobiographical novel about a British double agent in hiding who reflects on his remarkable life in a letter to his son. **Adaptation:** *A Perfect Spy* (BBC/PBS, 1987 TV Miniseries). Dir: Peter Smith. Scr: Arthur Hopcraft. Cast: Peter Egan (Pym), Ray McAnally (Rick), Peggy Ashcroft (Miss Dubber). Notes: BAFTA nomination for Best Actor (McAnally); Emmy Award nominations for Outstanding Miniseries and Actress (Ashcroft). VHS.

3450. *The Perfect Storm: A True Story of Men Against the Sea* (Sebastian Junger, 1997). Factual account of a fishing-boat crew from Gloucester, Massachusetts, heading out to fish in the North Atlantic in the fall of 1991. While there, they struggled to survive in and lost their lives to the "storm of the century," a ferocious convergence of three storm systems. **Adaptation:** *The Perfect Storm* (Warner, 2000). Dir: Wolfgang Petersen. Scr: Bill Wittliff. Cast: George Clooney (Captain Tyne), Mark Wahlberg (Bobby), Diane Lane (Christina), Karen Allen (Melissa), William Fichtner (Sullivan), John C. Reilly (Murphy), Mary Elizabeth Mastrantonio (Captain Greenlaw). DVD, VHS.

3451. *A Perfect Stranger* (Danielle Steel, 1983). A sheltered young woman married to a wealthy older man begins an affair with a hand-some attorney who lives in her neighborhood. **Adaptation:** *A Perfect Stranger* (NBC, 1994 TV Movie)Dir: Michael L. Miller. Scr: Jan Worthington. Cast: Robert Urich (Alex), Stacy Haiduk (Raphaella), Darren McGavin (John), Susan Sullivan (Kaye), Holly Marie Combs (Amanda), Marion Ross (Charlotte). DVD, VHS.

3452. *Peril at End House* (Agatha Christie, 1932). While on vacation on the British coast, Hercule Poirot finds himself protecting a pretty young women against various attempts on her life. The novel was adapted as a stage play by Arnold Ridley and Bernard Merrivale in 1940. **Adaptation:** *Peril at End House* (London Weekend Television, 1990 TV Movie series). Dir: Renny Rye. Scr: Clive Exton. Cast: David Suchet (Poirot), Hugh Fraser (Hastings), Philip Jackson (Inspector Japp), Pauline Moran (Miss Lemon). DVD, VHS.

3453. *Perilous Passage* (Bruce Nicolaysen, 1976). During World War II, a Basque shepherd helps a French scientist and his family cross the Pyrenees to escape the Nazis. **Adaptation:** *The Passage* (United Artists, 1979). Dir: J. Lee Thompson. Scr: Bruce Nicolaysen. Cast: Anthony Quinn (the Basque Shepherd), James Mason (Professor Bergson), Malcolm McDowell (Von Berkow), Patricia Neal (Ariel), Kay Lenz (Leah).

3454. *Permanent Midnight: A Memoir* (Jerry Stahl, 1995). Autobiographical account by a former television writer about his battle with heroin addiction and the loss of everything he held precious. **Adaptation:** *Permanent Midnight* (Artisan, 1998). Dir: David Veloz. Scr: David Veloz. Cast: Ben Stiller (Stahl), Maria Bello (Kitty), Owen Wilson (Nicky), Elizabeth Hurley (Sandra). DVD, VHS.

3455. *Perri* (Felix Salten, 1938). Children's book about the life of a squirrel in each of the four seasons. **Adaptation:** *Perri* (Disney/Buena Vista, 1957). Dir: Paul Kenworthy, Jr., Ralph Wright. Scr: Winston Hibler, Ralph Wright. Cast: Winston Hibler (Narrator).

3456. *Personal Velocity* (Rebecca Miller, 2001). A collection of stories about seven women who take to the road after disentangling themselves from unsatisfying relationships. **Adaptation:** *Personal Velocity: Three Portraits* (MGM, 2002). Dir: Rebecca Miller. Scr: Rebecca Miller. Cast: Kyra Sedgwick (Delia), Parker Posey (Greta), Fairuza Balk (Paula), David Warshofsky (Kurt). Notes: The screenplay focuses on three of the seven women featured in the book. Independent Spirit Award for Best Film and nominations for Best Female Lead (Posey) and Cinematography; Sundance Film Festival Award for Best Cinematography and Grand Jury Award for Best Dramatic Film. DVD, VHS.

3457. *Persons in Hiding* (J. Edgar Hoover, 1938). A book about wanted fugitives by the powerful director of the FBI. **Adaptation:** *Persons in Hiding* (Paramount, 1939). Dir: Louis King. Scr: William R. Lipman, Horace McCoy. Cast: Lynne Overman (Agent Griswold), Patricia Morison (Dorothy), J. Carrol Naish (Gunner Martin), William Henry (Agent Waldron). Notes: the screenplay focuses on the particular case of a bored and greedy young woman who joins a gang of thieves and becomes a public enemy.

3458. *Persuasion* (Jane Austen, 1818). In the early nineteenth century, a young woman is persuaded to break off her engagement with an impoverished sailor. When they meet again years later, he is rich, eligible, and pursued by other women, but the original lovers rediscover each other. The novel was published posthumously a year after Austen's death in 1817. **Adaptation 1:** *Persuasion* (BBC, 1960 TV Miniseries). Dir: Campbell Logan. Scr: Barbara Burnham , Michael Voysey. Cast: Daphne Slater (Anne), Paul Daneman (Frederick), George Curzon (Sir Walter), Jane Hardie (Elizabeth), Thea Holme (Mrs. Croft). **Adaptation 2:** *Persuasion* (Granada, 1971 TV Miniseries). Dir: Howard Baker. Scr: Julian Mitchell. Cast: Anne Firbank (Anne), Bryan Marshall (Frederick), Basil Dignam (Sir Walter), Valerie Gearon (Elizabeth), Marian Spencer (Lady Russell), Georgine Anderson (Mrs. Croft), Richard Vernon (Admiral Croft). DVD, VHS. **Adaptation 3:** *Persuasion* (BBC/Sony, 1995). Dir: Roger Michell. Scr: Nick Dear. Cast: Amanda Root (Anne), Ciaran Hinds (Frederick), Susan Fleetwood (Lady Russell), Corin Redgrave (Sir Walter), Fiona Shaw (Mrs. Croft), John Woodvine (Admiral Croft). Notes: BAFTA Awards for Best Film, Musical Score, Production Design, Costume Design, and Photography and Lighting. DVD, VHS.

Pete 'n' Tillie (see *Witch's Milk*).

3459. *Peter Ibbetson* (George Du Maurier, 1891). Fantasy-romance about two separated lovers who meet as adults. When he is unjustly imprisoned for a murder, they carry on their relationship in dreams. The novel, which first appeared in *Harper's New Monthly* in August 1891, was adapted as a play in 1917 by John N. Raphael. **Silent Film:** 1921, titled *Forever*. **Adaptation:** *Peter Ibbetson* (Paramount, 1935). Dir: Henry Hathaway. Scr: Constance Collier, Vincent Lawrence, Waldemar Young. Cast: Gary Cooper (Peter), Ann Harding (Mary), John Halliday (the Duke of Towers), Ida Lupino (Agnes), Douglass Dumbrille (Colonel Forsythe).

Peter Pan (see *The Little White Bird*).

3460. *Peter Pettinger* (William Riley, 1942). A factory laborer who becomes a strident union organizer is forced to reevaluate his position when he finds himself in a management position. **Adaptation:** *The Agitator* (Four Continents, 1944). Dir: John Harlow. Scr: Edward Dryhurst. Cast: Joss Ambler (Charles), William Hartnell (Peter), Mary Morris (Lettie), John Laurie (Tom).

3461. *Pet Sematary* (Stephen King, 1983). A physician and his family take up residence in a college town in Maine and discover the evil power of a pet cemetery that can restore life. **Adaptation:** *Pet Sematary* (Paramount, 1989). Dir: Mary Lambert. Scr: Stephen King. Cast: Dale Midkiff (Louis), Fred Gwynne (Jud), Denise Crosby (Rachel), Brad Greenquist (Pascow). DVD, VHS. Notes: Lambert also directed the 1992 sequel, *Pet Sematary II* (DVD, VHS).

Petulia (see *Me and the Arch Kook Petulia*).

3462. *Peyton Place* (Grace Metalious, 1956). Episodic tale of sex, violence, and assorted secrets in a small New England town. **Adaptation:** *Peyton Place* (20th Century–Fox, 1957). Dir: Mark Robson. Scr: John Michael Hayes. Cast: Lana Turner (Constance), Lee Philips (Michael), Diane Varsi (Alison), Lloyd Nolan (Dr. Swain), Arthur Kennedy (Lucas), Russ Tamblyn (Norman), Terry Moore (Betty), Mildred Dunnock (Mrs. Thornton), Hope Lange (Selena). Notes: Academy Award nominations for Best Picture, Director, Screenplay, Actor (Kennedy), Actress (Turner), Supporting Actor (Tamblyn), Supporting Actress (Varsi), and Cinematography, Golden Globe nominations for Best Supporting Actresses (Dunnock and Lange). DVD, VHS. Notes: The book also inspired a hit ABC television series (1964–69) and a variety of made-for-television movies, including *Peyton Place Revisited* (1973), *Murder in Peyton Place* (1977), and *Peyton Place: The Next Generation* (1985). See also *Return to Peyton Place.*

The Phantom Fiend (see *The Lodger*).

3463. *The Phantom Filly* (George Agnew Chamberlain, 1942). A young man is sent to live with relatives on a Kentucky horse farm and falls in love with the girl next door. **Adaptation 1:** *Home in Indiana* (20th Century–Fox, 1944). Dir: Henry Hathaway. Scr: Winston Miller. Cast: Walter Brennan (Bolt), Lon McCallister (Sparke), Jeanne Crain (Char). **Adaptation 2:** *April Love* (20th Century–Fox, 1957). Dir: Henry Levin. Scr: Winston Miller, Cast: Pat Boone (Nick), Shirley Jones (Liz), Dolores Michaels (Fran), Arthur O'-Connell (Jed). Notes: The title song by Sammy Fain and Paul Francis Webster was nominated for an Academy Award and became a hit single for Pat Boone.

3464. *Phantom Lady* (Cornell Woolrich, 1942). An unhappily married man is accused of killing his wife, and the only person who might be able to clear him is a mysterious woman he met in a bar on the day of the crime. Woolrich originally published the novel under the pseudonym William Irish. **Adaptation:** *Phantom Lady* (Universal, 1944). Dir: Robert Siodmak. Scr: Bernard C. Schoenfeld. Cast: Franchot Tone (Jack), Ella Raines (Carol), Alan Curtis (Scott), Aurora Miranda (Estela), Thomas Gomez (Inspector Burgess). VHS.

3465. *The Phantom of the Opera* (Gaston Leroux, 1911). Leroux's classic tale, originally titled *Le Fantome de l'Opera*, concerns a disfigured musician who haunts the Paris Opera House. He takes a beautiful young singer down into the catacombs where he resides and helps her with her career. The novel was the basis for Arthur Kopit's 1982 play and for Andrew Lloyd Webber's 1988 hit Broadway musical. **Silent Films:** 1916 and 1925, starring Lon Chaney (DVD, VHS). **Adaptation 1:** *Phantom of the Opera* (Universal, 1943). Dir: Arthur Lubin. Scr: Samuel Hoffenstein, Hans Jacoby, John Jacoby, Eric Taylor. Cast: Nelson Eddy (Garron), Susanna Foster (Christine), Claude Rains (Claudin), Edgar Barrier (Raoul), Leo Carrillo (Signor Ferretti). Notes: Academy Awards for Best Cinematography and Art Direction, and nomination for Best Musical Score. DVD, VHS. **Adaptation 2:** *The Phantom of the Opera* (Hammer/Universal, 1962). Dir: Terence Fisher. Scr: Anthony Hinds (writing as John Elder). Cast: Herbert Lom (the Phantom), Heather Sears (Christine), Thorley Walters (Lattimer), Michael Gough (Lord Ambrose), Edward de Souza (Harry). VHS. **Adaptation 3:** *The Phantom of the Opera* (ABC, 1983 TV Movie). Dir: Robert Markowitz. Scr: Sherman Yellen. Cast: Maximilian Schell (the Phantom), Jane Seymour (Maria/Elena), Michael York (Michael), Jeremy

Kemp (Baron Hunyadi), Diana Quick (Madame Bianchi). VHS. **Adaptation 4:** *The Phantom of the Opera* (21st Century, 1989). Dir: Dwight H. Little. Scr: Gerry O'Hara, Duke Sandefur. Cast: Robert Englund (the Phantom), Jill Schoelen (Christine), Alex Hyde-White (Dutton), Bill Nighy (Barton), Stephanie Lawrence (Carlotta), Terence Harvey (Inspector Hawkins). Notes: A modern variation on the original story. DVD, VHS. **Adaptation 5:** *The Phantom of the Opera* (ABC, 1990 TV Miniseries). Dir: Tony Richardson. Scr: Arthur Kopit (based on his 1982 play). Cast: Burt Lancaster (Carriere), Adam Storke (Count Philippe), Teri Polo (Christine), Charles Dance (the Phantom), Ian Richardson (Cholet). Notes: Emmy Award for Outstanding Art Direction; Golden Globe nominations for Best Television Movie and Actor (Lancaster). DVD, VHS. **Adaptation 6:** *The Phantom of the Opera* (1990 TV Movie). Dir: Darwin Knight. Scr: Bruce Falstein. Cast: David Staller (the Phantom), Elizabeth Walsh (Christine). Notes: A musical adaptation, though not Andrew Lloyd Webber's version, which appeared on Broadway at about the same time. DVD, VHS. **Adaptation 7:** *The Phantom of the Opera* (A-Pix, 1998). Dir: Dario Argento. Scr: Gerard Brach, Dario Argento, Giorgina Caspari. Cast: Julian Sands (the Phantom), Asia Argento (Christine), Andrea Di Stefano (Raoul), Nadia Rinaldi (Carlotta). DVD, VHS. **Adaptation 8:** *The Phantom of the Opera* (Warner, 2004). Dir: Joel Schumacher. Scr: Andrew Lloyd Webber (based on his 1988 Broadway musical), Joel Schumacher. Cast: Gerard Butler (the Phantom), Emmy Rossum (Christine), Patrick Wilson (Raoul), Miranda Richardson (Madame Giry), Minnie Driver (Carlotta), Ciaran Hinds (Firmin), Simon Callow (Andre). Notes: National Board of Review Award for Best Breakthrough Performance by an Actress (Rossum); Golden Globe nominations for Best Musical, Actress (Rossum), and Song. DVD, VHS.

The Phantom of the Rue Morgue (*see* "The Murders in the Rue Morgue").

The Phantom Strikes (see *The Gaunt Stranger*).

3466. *The Phantom Tollbooth* (Norton Juster, 1961). Children's book about a bored young boy who finds a mysterious tollbooth in his room one day. Entering it, he finds himself in a strange imaginary world where words are constantly at odds with numbers. **Adaptation:** *The Phantom Tollbooth* (MGM, 1970). Dir: Chuck

Jones, Abe Levitow, Dave Monahan. Scr: Chuck Jones. Sam Rosen. Cast: Butch Patrick (Milo), and voices of Mel Blanc (Officer Short Shrift/ Word Speller/Dodecahedron/Demon of Insincerity), Daws Butler (Whether Man), Candy Candido (Awful DYNN), Hans Conried (King Azaz/the MathemaGician). Notes: A feature film combining animation and live action. VHS.

3467. *Phantoms* (Dean R. Koontz, 1983). Horror story set in a peaceful California ski village, where all of the inhabitants seem to have disappeared. A group of people and the town's sheriff try to stop the supernatural creatures responsible. **Adaptation:** *Phantoms* (Dimension/ Miramax, 1998). Dir: Joe Chappelle. Scr: Dean R. Koontz. Cast: Ben Affleck (Sheriff Hammond), Peter O'Toole (Dr. Flyte), Rose McGowan (Lisa), Joanna Going (Dr. Pailey), Liev Schreiber (Deputy Wargle). DVD, VHS.

3468. *The Philadelphia Experiment* (William I. Moore and Charles Berlitz, 1979). An investigation into the purportedly true story that the U.S. Navy conducted an experiment in 1943 that made a destroyer and its crew disappear from the Philadelphia Navy Yard and reappear seconds later in Norfolk, Virginia. **Adaptation:** *The Philadelphia Experiment* (New World, 1984). Dir: Stewart Raffill. Scr: William Gray, Michael Janover. Cast: Michael Pare (David), Nancy Allen (Allison), Eric Christmas (Dr. Longstreet), Bobby Di Cicco (Jim), Louise Latham (Pamela). Notes: In the film, the crew disappears from Philadelphia in 1943 and finds itself in the same place in 1984. DVD, VHS.

3469. *The Philadelphian* (Richard Powell, 1956). An ambitious Philadelphia lawyer will do anything to enter the city's social elite. **Adaptation:** *The Young Philadelphians*; released in the UK as *The City Jungle* (Warner, 1959). Dir: Vincent Sherman. Scr: James Gunn. Cast: Paul Newman (Anthony), Barbara Rush (Joan), Alexis Smith (Carol), Brian Keith (Mike), Robert Vaughn (Chet). Notes: Academy Award nominations for Best Supporting Actor (Vaughn), Cinematography, and Costume Design; Golden Globe nomination for Best Supporting Actor (Vaughn). VHS.

3470. *Philly* (Dan Greenburg, 1969). A wealthy teenager is seduced by a beautiful maid, who is actually working with a dishonest chauffeur to blackmail the boy. **Adaptation:** *Private Lessons* (Jensen Farley, 1981). Dir: Alan Myerson. Scr: Dan Greenburg. Cast: Sylvia Kristel (Nicole), Howard Hesseman (Lester), Eric Brown

(Phillip), Meridith Baer (Miss Phipps). VHS. Notes: A sequel, *Private Lessons II*, was released in 1993.

3471. "Philomel Cottage" (Agatha Christie, 1924). After winning a lottery, a naïve young woman marries a charming man but soon has reason to suspect that he may be a killer. The short story originally appeared in the November 1924 issue of *The Grand Magazine* and was later included in Christie's 1933 collection *The Hound of Death and Other Stories*. It was adapted for the stage in 1936 by Frank Vosper under the title *Love from a Stranger*. **Adaptation 1:** *Love from a Stranger* (United Artists, 1937). Dir: Rowland V. Lee. Scr: Frances Marion, Cast: Ann Harding (Carol), Basil Rathbone (Gerald), Binnie Hale (Kate). VHS. **Adaptation 2:** *Love from a Stranger* (Eagle-Lion, 1947. Dir: Richard Whorf. Scr: Philip MacDonald, Cast: John Hodiak (Manuel), Sylvia Sidney (Cecily), Ann Richards (Mavia), John Howard (Nigel).

3472. *The Phoenix* (Lawrence Bachmann, 1955). After World War II, six German veterans reunite and form a bomb-disposal unit. The dangerous job and their competition for the same woman eventually takes a toll on their relationship. **Adaptation:** *Ten Seconds to Hell* (United Artists, 1959). Dir: Robert Aldrich. Scr: Robert Aldrich, Teddi Sherman. Cast: Jack Palance (Erik), Jeff Chandler (Karl), Martine Carol (Margot), Robert Cornthwaite (Franz).

3473. *The Phoenix and the Carpet* (Edith Nesbit, 1904). Children's story about five children who discover an old carpet and a golden egg in their late grandfather's cottage. When the egg is accidentally dropped into a fire, a Phoenix is born, and the mythic bird conducts the children on a series of adventures aboard the magic carpet. The book, along with Nesbit's *Five Children and It* (1902) and *The Story of the Amulet* (1906), make up a series known as the Psammead. **Adaptation 1:** *The Phoenix and the Carpet* (BBC, 1976 TV Miniseries). Dir: Clive Doig. Scr: John Tully. Cast: Jane Forster (Jane), Max Harris (Robert), Tamzin Neville (Anthea), Gary Russell (Cyril), Richard Warner (voice of the Phoenix). **Adaptation 2:** *The Phoenix and the Magic Carpet* (Smart Egg, 1995). Dir: Zoran Perisic. Scr: Florence Fox. Cast: Peter Ustinov (Grandfather/voice of the Phoenix), Dee Wallace-Stone (Mother), Timothy Hegemann (Chris), Laura Kamrath (Anthea). VHS. **Adaptation 3:** *The Phoenix and the Carpet* (BBC, 1997 TV Miniseries). Dir: Michael Kerrigan. Scr: Helen Cresswell. Cast: Miriam Margolyes (the Cook), Ivan Berry (Robert), David Suchet (the voice of the Phoenix), Lesley Dunlop (Eliza).

3474. *Photographing Fairies* (Steve Szilagyi, 1992). After the death of his young wife, a grieving photographer comes upon pictures of fairies taken by two young girls. He believes they are real and goes to a small village to investigate. **Adaptation:** *Photographing Fairies* (PolyGram, 1997). Dir: Nick Willing. Scr: Chris Harrald, Nick Willing. Cast: Toby Stephens (Charles), Emily Woof (Linda), Ben Kingsley (Reverend Templeton), Frances Barber (Beatrice). VHS.

3475. *The Pianist* (Wladyslaw Szpilman, 1946). Post-war memoir by a brilliant Polish Jewish musician who went into hiding in the Warsaw ghetto after his family was deported to the Nazi death camps. The book was first translated into English in 1999. **Adaptation:** *The Pianist* (Focus, 2002). Dir: Roman Polanski. Scr: Ronald Harwood. Cast: Adrien Brody (Szpilman), Thomas Kretschmann (Captain Hosenfeld), Frank Finlay (Father), Maureen Lipman (Mother), Emilia Fox (Dorota). Notes: Academy Awards for Best Director, Screenplay, and Actor (Brody), and nominations for Best Film, Cinematography, Editing, and Costume Design; BAFTA Awards for Best Film and Director, and nominations for Best Actor (Brody), Screenplay, Cinematography, and Sound; Cannes Film Festival Golden Palm Award for Best Director; Golden Globe nominations for Best Film and Actor (Brody). DVD, VHS.

3476. *The Piano Teacher* (Elfriede Jelinek, 1983). In this Austrian novel, originally titled *Die Klavierspielesin*, an inhibited middle-aged piano teacher begins an affair with one of her students and is introduced to a world of deviant sexuality. The novel was first translated into English in 1988, and Jelinek won the Nobel Prize for Literature in 2004. **Adaptation:** *The Piano Teacher* (Kino, 2001). Dir: Michael Haneke. Scr: Michael Haneke. Cast: Isabelle Huppert (Erika), Annie Girardot (Mother), Benoit Magimel (Walter), Susanne Lothar (Mrs. Schober). Notes: Originally titled *La Pianiste* and shown with subtitles. Cannes Film Festival Awards for Best Actor (Magimel) and Actress (Huppert) and Grand Jury Prize (Haneke), and nomination for Best Director; BAFTA nomination for Best Film; Independent Spirit Award nomination for Best Foreign Film. DVD, VHS.

3477. *Picasso: Creator and Destroyer* (Arianna Stassinopoulos Huffington, 1988). The story of the relationship between artist Pablo Picasso

and aspiring painter Francoise Gilet, who became his mistress and bore him two children. After decades of tolerating his many infidelities, Gilet finally left him. **Adaptation:** *Surviving Picasso* (Warner, 1996). Dir: James Ivory. Scr: Ruth Prawer Jhabvala. Cast: Anthony Hopkins (Picasso), Natascha McElhone (Francoise), Julianne Moore (Dora), Joss Ackland (Matisse). VHS.

3478. *Piccadilly Jim* (P. G. Wodehouse, 1917). An American cartoonist with a bad reputation in England tries to conceal his identity so that his father can marry a British woman. **Silent Film:** 1920. **Adaptation 1:** *Piccadilly Jim* (MGM, 1936). Dir: Robert Z. Leonard. Scr: Charles Brackett, Edwin Knopf. Cast: Robert Montgomery (Jim), Frank Morgan (James), Madge Evans (Ann), Eric Blore (Bayliss), Billie Burke (Eugenia). **Adaptation 2:** *Piccadilly Jim* (Universal International, 2004). Dir: John McKay. Scr: Julian Fellowes. Cast: Sam Rockwell (Jim), Lucy Brown (Connie), Nathan Osgood (the Reverend).

3479. *The Pickwick Papers* (Charles Dickens, 1836–1837). The adventures of the Pickwick Club as they travel England in search of interesting things. The work first appeared under the title *The Posthumous Papers of the Pickwick Club* in a serial that ran from April 1836 through November 1837. **Silent Films:** 1912, 1913, and 1921 (titled *The Adventures of Mr. Pickwick*). **Adaptation 1:** *The Pickwick Papers* (1952). Dir: Noel Langley. Scr: Noel Langley. Cast: James Hayter (Pickwick), James Donald (Winkle), Nigel Patrick (Jingle), Hermione Gingold (Miss Tompkins), Hermione Baddeley (Mrs. Bardell). VHS. **Adaptation 2:** *The Pickwick Papers* (BBC, 1985 TV Miniseries). Dir: Brian Lighthill. Scr: Jack Davies. Cast: Nigel Stock (Pickwick), Jeremy Nicholas (Winkle), Patrick Malahide (Jingle), Shirley Cain (Miss Witherfield).

3480. *Picnic at Hanging Rock* (Joan Lindsay, 1967). Three Australian students and a teacher disappear while on a school trip on Valentine's Day 1900. **Adaptation:** *Picnic at Hanging Rock* (Atlantic, 1975). Dir: Peter Weir. Scr: Cliff Green. Cast: Rachel Roberts (Mrs. Appleyard), Vivean Gray (Miss McCraw), Helen Morse (Miss de Poitiers), Kirsty Child (Miss Lumley). DVD, VHS.

3481. *The Picture of Dorian Gray* (Oscar Wilde, 1890). A corrupt young man contemplating a beautiful portrait of himself is granted his wish that the image in the picture age while he stays young and handsome. **Silent Films:** 1910, 1913, 1915, 1916, 1917, and 1918. **Adaptation 1:** *The*

Picture of Dorian Gray (MGM, 1945). Dir: Albert Lewin. Scr: Albert Lewin. Cast: George Sanders (Lord Henry), Hurd Hatfield (Dorian), Donna Reed (Gladys), Angela Lansbury (Sibyl), Peter Lawford (David). Notes: Academy Award for Best Cinematography and Award nominations for Best Supporting Actress (Lansbury) and Art Direction; Golden Globe Award for Best Supporting Actress (Lansbury). VHS. **Adaptation 2:** *Dorian Gray* (American International, 1970). Dir: Massimo Dallamano. Scr: Marcello Costa, Massimo Dallamano, Gunter Ebert. Cast: Helmut Berger (Dorian), Richard Todd (Basil), Herbert Lom (Lord Henry), Marie Liljedahl (Sybil), Margaret Lee (Gwendolyn). VHS. **Adaptation 3:** *The Picture of Dorian Gray* (ABC, 1973 TV Movie). Dir: Glenn Jordan. Scr: John Tomerlin. Cast: Shane Briant (Dorian), Nigel Davenport (Lord Henry), Charles Aidman (Basil), Fionnula Flanagan (Felicia), Linda Kelsey (Beatrice). DVD, VHS. **Adaptation 4:** *The Picture of Dorian Gray* (BBC, 1976 TV Movie). Dir: John Gorrie. Scr: John Osborne. Cast: John Gielgud (Lord Henry), Jeremy Brett (Basil), Peter Firth (Dorian), Mark Dignam (Lord Fermor). DVD, VHS. **Adaptation 5:** *The Sins of Dorian Gray* (ABC, 1983 TV Movie). Dir: Tony Maylam. Scr: Ken August, Peter Lawrence. Cast: Anthony Perkins (Henry), Belinda Bauer (Dorian), Joseph Bottoms (Stuart), Olga Karlatos (Sofia), Michael Ironside (Alan). Notes: A variant on the original story, with an actress whose image on film ages while she stays young. VHS. **Adaptation 6:** *The Picture of Dorian Gray* (American World, 2002). Dir: David Rosenbaum. Scr: David Rosenbaum. Cast: Josh Duhamel (Dorian), Branden Waugh (Lord Henry), Rainer Judd (Basil), Julie Amos (Laura).

3482. *The Pied Piper* (Nevil Shute [pseudonym for Nevil Shute Norway], 1942). An Englishman who is not very fond of children takes a vacation in France in 1940. When the Germans invade the country, he ends up smuggling several youngsters out of France and to safety in England. **Adaptation 1:** *The Pied Piper* (20th Century–Fox, 1942). Dir: Irving Pichel. Scr: Nunnally Johnson. Cast: Monty Woolley (Howard), Roddy McDowall (Ronnie), Anne Baxter (Nicole), Otto Preminger (Major Diessen), J. Carrol Naish (Aristide). Notes: Academy Award nominations for Best Picture, Actor (Woolley), and Cinematography. **Adaptation 2:** *Crossing to Freedom* (Proctor and Gamble, 1990 TV Movie). Dir: Norman Stone. Scr: Jerome Kass. Cast: Peter O'Toole (Howard), Mare Winningham (Nicole), Susan

Wooldridge (Mrs. Cavanaugh), Michael Kitchen (Major Diessen).

3483. *Pierre, or the Ambiguities* (Herman Melville, 1852). Autobiographical novel about a young writer who becomes romantically involved with a woman who claims to be his father's illegitimate daughter. **Adaptation:** *Pola X* (Arena/WinStar, 1999). Dir: Leos Carax. Scr: Leos Carax, Jean-Pol Fargeau, Lauren Sedofsky. Cast: Guillaume Depardieu (Pierre), Yekaterina Golubeva (Isabelle), Catherine Deneuve (Marie), Delphine Chuillot (Lucie). Notes: Cannes Film Festival Golden Palm nomination for Best Director. DVD, VHS.

Pierrot Le Fou (see *Obsession*).

3484. *Pigboats* (Edward Ellsberg, 1931). A decorated naval officer's fictional account of submarine warfare in the Mediterranean during World War I. **Adaptation:** *Hell Below* (MGM, 1933). Dir: Jack Conway. Scr: Laird Doyle, Raymond L. Schrock, John Lee Mahin, John Meehan. Cast: Robert Montgomery (Knowlton), Walter Huston (Toler), Madge Evans (Joan), Jimmy Durante (Ptomaine), Robert Young (Walters).

The Pigeon That Took Rome (see *The Easter Dinner*).

Pigeons (see *The Sidelong Glances of a Pigeon Kicker*).

3485. *The Pilgrim of Hate* (Ellis Peters [pseudonym for Edith Pargeter], 1984). The tenth installment in Peters' twenty-volume series (1977–1994) featuring Brother Cadfael, a twelfth-century monk who, following service in the Crusades, tends to the herbarium at Shrewsbury Abbey and solves crimes. In this book, Brother Cadfael suspects two pilgrims at the shrine of St Winifred of the murder of a knight. **Adaptation:** *Cadfael: The Pilgrim of Hate* (ITV/PBS, 1998 TV Movie series). Dir: Malcolm Mowbray, Herbert Wise, Scr: Russell Lewis, Paul Pender, Ben Rostul, Richard Stoneman. Cast: Derek Jacobi (Brother Cadfael), Michael Culver (Prior Robert), Anthony Green (Hugh), Julian Firth (Brother Jerome). DVD, VHS.

3486. *Pillar of Fire, or Israel in Bondage* (J. K. Ingraham, 1859). Fictional retelling of the Biblical story of Moses and his selection by God to lead the Israelites out of their Egyptian captivity. **Adaptation:** *The Ten Commandments* (Paramount, 1956). Dir: Cecil B. De Mille. Scr: Aeneas MacKenzie, Jesse L. Lasky, Jr., Jack Gariss, Fredric M. Frank. Cast: Charlton Heston (Moses), Yul Brynner (Rameses), Anne Baxter (Nefretiri), Edward G. Robinson (Dathan), Yvonne De Carlo (Sephora), Debra Paget (Lilia), John Derek (Joshua), Cedric Hardwicke (Sethi). Notes: De Mille directed a silent film by the same title in 1923. For the 1956 screenplay, the writers used the original Biblical story and elements from three books: J. H. Ingraham's *The Pillar of Fire* (1859), A. E. Southon's *On Eagle's Wing*, (1939), and Dorothy Clarke Wilson's *Prince of Egypt* (1949). National Board of Review Award for Best Actor (Brynner); Academy Award for Best Special Effects, and nominations for Best Picture, Cinematography, Art Direction, Editing, Costume Design, and Sound. DVD, VHS. See also *On Eagle's Wing* and *Prince of Egypt*.

3487. *The Pillars of Midnight* (Elleston Trevor [pseudonym for Trevor Dudley Smith], 1957). A doctor and his wife grow closer together as they battle a smallpox epidemic in an English town. **Adaptation:** *80,000 Suspects* (Rank/Continental, 1963). Dir: Val Guest. Scr: Val Guest. Cast: Claire Bloom (Julie), Richard Johnson (Steven), Cyril Cusack (Father Maguire).

Pillars of the Sky (see "Frontier Fury").

3488. *The Pilot* (Robert P. Davis, 1976). A commercial airline pilot with a sterling reputation is secretly an alcoholic. **Adaptation:** *The Pilot*; released on video as *Danger in the Skies* (Summit, 1981). Dir: Cliff Robertson. Scr: Robert P. Davis. Cast: Cliff Robertson (Mike), Diane Baker (Pat), Frank Converse (Jim), Milo O'Shea (Dr. O'Brien), Dana Andrews (Randolph), Gordon MacRae (Joe). VHS.

3489. *The Pilot's Wife* (Anita Shreve, 1998). The wife of a commercial airline pilot is devastated to learn of her husband's death in a catastrophic crash. When the fault for the crash is pinned on the pilot, she investigates the accident hoping to clear his name, but discovers that he had a secret life. **Adaptation:** *The Pilot's Wife* (CBS, 2002 TV Movie). Dir: Robert Markowitz. Scr: Anita Shreve, Christine Berardo. Cast: Christine Lahti (Kathryn), Campbell Scott (Robert), Alison Pill (Mattie), Kirsty Mitchell (Muire), John Heard (Jack). DVD, VHS.

"Pimpernel" Smith (see *The Scarlet Pimpernel*).

The Pink Jungle (see *Snake Water*).

Pinky (see *Quality*).

Pinocchio (see *The Adventures of Pinocchio*).

3490. *Pioneer, Go Home* (Richard Powell, 1959). Despite community protests, an itinerant family sets up a homestead on a Florida beach. **Adaptation:** *Follow That Dream* (United Artists, 1962). Dir: Gordon Douglas. Scr: Charles Lederer, Cast: Elvis Presley (Toby), Arthur O'Connell (Pop), Anne Helm (Holly), Joanna Moore (Alisha), Jack Kruschen (Carmine), Simon Oakland (Nick). DVD, VHS.

3491. *The Pioneers* (James Fenimore Cooper, 1823). The first in a series of frontier novels, which also included *The Pathfinder*, *The Deerslayer*, and *The Last of the Mohicans*, about the difficulties of life in the American West. **Adaptation:** *The Pioneers* (Monogram, 1941). Dir: Al Herman. Scr: Charles Anders. Cast: Tex Ritter (Tex), Red Foley (Red), Slim Andrews (Slim).

3492. *Pippi in the South Seas* (Astrid Lindgren, 1948). *Pippi Langstrump I Soderhavet*, the third and final installment in the Pippi Longstocking series of popular Swedish children's books about a feisty red-haired girl. In this book, Pippi travels to the South Seas to rescue her father, who has been captured by pirates. **Adaptation:** *Pippi in the South Seas* (G. G. Communications, 1970). Dir: Olle Hellbom. Scr: Olle Hellbom. Cast: Inger Nilsson (Pippi), Maria Persson (Annika), Par Sundberg (Tommy), Beppe Wolgers (Captain Longstocking). DVD, VHS. See also *Pippi Longstocking*.

3493. *Pippi Longstocking* (Astrid Lindgren, 1945). *Pippi Langstrump*, the first of three popular Swedish children's books about the adventures of a red-haired girl who is independent, strong, and free-spirited. **Adaptation 1:** *Pippi Longstocking* (G. G. Communications, 1969). Dir: Olle Hellbom. Scr: Olle Hellbom. Cast: Inger Nilsson (Pippi), Maria Persson (Annika), Par Sundberg (Tommy). **Adaptation 2:** *Pippi Longstocking* (ABC, 1985 TV Movie). Dir: Colin Chilvers. Scr: Cynthia Chenault. Cast: Carrie Kei Heim (Pippi), Eric Hebert (Tommy), Alyson Court (Annika). **Adaptation 3:** *The New Adventures of Pippi Longstocking* (Columbia, 1988). Dir: Ken Annakin. Scr: Ken Annakin. Cast: Tami Erin (Pippi), David Seaman (Tommy), Cory Crow (Annika), Eileen Brennan (Miss Bannister). Notes: The screenplay combines elements from all of the novels in the series. DVD, VHS. **Adaptation 4:** *Pippi Longstocking* (Legacy, 1997). Dir: Michael Schaack, Clive A. Smith, Bill Giggie. Scr: Frank Nissen, Ken Sobol. Cast: voices of Melissa Altro (Pippi), Catherine O'Hara (Mrs. Prysselius), Dave Thomas (Thunder-Karlsson). VHS. See also *Pippi in the South Seas*.

3494. *The Pirate* (Harold Robbins, 1974).

The oil empire of the world's wealthiest and most powerful Arab shiek is threatened by terrorists, dirty politics, and romance gone bad. **Adaptation:** *The Pirate* (CBS, 1978 TV Movie). Dir: Ken Annakin. Scr: Julius J. Epstein. Cast: Franco Nero (Baydr Al Fay), Anne Archer (Jordana), Olivia Hussey (Leila), Ian McShane (Rashid), Christopher Lee (Samir Al Fay), Michael Constantine (Yashir), James Franciscus (Dick), Armand Assante (Ahmed), Stuart Whitman (Sullivan).

3495. "The Pit and the Pendulum" (Edgar Allan Poe, 1842). A man judged guilty by the Spanish Inquisition is slowly tortured and is finally rescued by the invading French army. The short story originally appeared in an annual titled *The Gift: A Christmas and New Year's Present for 1843* (Philadelphia, 1842). **Silent Film:** 1913. **Adaptation 1:** *The Pit and the Pendulum* (American International, 1961). Dir: Roger Corman. Scr: Richard Matheson. Cast: Vincent Price (Sebastian), John Kerr (Francis), Barbara Steele (Elizabeth). DVD, VHS. **Adaptation 2:** *The Blood Demon*; also released as *The Torture Chamber of Dr. Sadism* (Hemisphere, 1967). Dir: Harald Reinl. Scr: Manfred R. Köhler. Cast: Lex Barker (Roger), Christopher Lee (Frederic), Karin Dor (Lillian). DVD, VHS. **Adaptation 3:** *The Pit and the Pendulum*; also released is *The Inquisitor* (Empire, 1990). Dir: Stuart Gordon. Scr: Dennis Paoli. Cast: Lance Henriksen (Torquemada), Stephen Lee (Gomez), William J. Norris (Dr. Heusos). DVD, VHS.

3496. *The Pitfall* (Jay Dratler, 1947). An unhappily married insurance investigator falls in love with the girlfriend of the felon he is investigating. **Adaptation:** *Pitfall* (United Artists, 1948). Dir: Andre De Toth. Scr: Karl Kamb. Cast: Dick Powell (John), Lizabeth Scott (Mona), Jane Wyatt (Sue), Raymond Burr (MacDonald). VHS.

3497. *Pity My Simplicity* (Chris Massie, 1944). A loving man helps a young woman who lost her memory during World War II recover. The book was reissued under the title *Love Letters* in 1946. **Adaptation:** *Love Letters* (Paramount, 1945). Dir: William Dieterle. Scr: Ayn Rand. Cast: Jennifer Jones (Victoria), Joseph Cotten (Allen), Ann Richards (Dilly), Cecil Kellaway (Mac). Notes: Academy Award nominations for Best Actress (Jones), Art Direction, Musical Score, and Song. VHS.

A Place in the Sun (see *An American Tragedy*).

3498. *A Place of One's Own* (Osbert Sitwell, 1941). An old couple and their young female companion move into an old mansion, and the young woman is possessed by the spirit of a girl who was murdered there. **Adaptation:** *A Place of One's Own* (Eagle-Lion, 1945). Dir: Bernard Knowles. Scr: Brock Williams. Cast: Margaret Lockwood (Annette), James Mason (Mr. Smedhurst), Barbara Mullen (Mrs. Smedhurst), Dennis Price (Dr. Selbie). VHS. Notes: A brief adaptation was produced in 1968 for the British television series *Mystery and Imagination*.

Plain of Battle (see *The Talented Mr. Ripley*).

3499. *Plain Truth* (Jodi Picoult, 2000). A Philadelphia lawyer defends a young Amish girl accused of murdering her infant. **Adaptation:** *Plain Truth* (Lifetime, 2004 TV Movie). Dir: Paul Shapiro. Scr: Matthew Tabak. Cast: Mariska Hargitay (Ellie), Alison Pill (Katie), Kate Trotter (Sarah), Alec McClure (Jacob). DVD, VHS.

3500. *The Plague* (Albert Camus, 1947). The French Nobel laureate's novel *La Peste* takes place in a South American city where people are dying from a deadly plague and an idealistic doctor stays behind to help the afflicted. **Adaptation:** *The Plague* (Republic, 1992). Dir: Luis Puenzo. Scr: Luis Puenzo, Norman Di Giovanni, Susan Ashe, Robert Katz. Cast: William Hurt (Dr. Rieux), Sandrine Bonnaire (Martine), Jean-Marc Barr (Jean), Robert Duvall (Joseph), Raul Julia (Cottard), Victoria Tennant (Alicia). VHS.

3501. *The Plague Dogs* (Richard Adams, 1977). Animal story about two dogs who escape from a research facility. As government officials, fearing that the animals may be carrying a deadly virus, hunt them down, the dogs try to survive on their own with the help of a wily fox. **Adaptation:** *The Plague Dogs* (Nepenthe/Trinity, 1982). Dir: Martin Rosen. Scr: Martin Rosen. Cast: voices of John Hurt (Snitter), Christopher Benjamin (Rowf), James Bolam (Tod), Nigel Hawthorne (Dr. Boycott), Warren Mitchell (Tyson/Wag). Notes: An animated feature intended for adults. VHS.

3502. *The Planet of Junior Brown* (Virginia Hamilton, 1971). Children's novel about an obese and immature young man whose eccentric friends offer escape from his oppressive environment dominated by his controlling mother. **Adaptation:** *The Planet of Junior Brown* (A-Pix/Evergreen, 1997). Dir: Clement Virgo. Scr: Cameron Bailey, Clement Virgo. Cast: Lynn Whitfield (Mrs. Brown), Martin Villafana (Junior), Rainbow Francks (Buddy), Clark Johnson (Mr. Pool), Sarah Polley (Butter), Margot Kidder (Miss Peebs). DVD, VHS.

Planet of the Apes (see *Monkey Planet*).

3503. *The Plastic Nightmare* (Richard Neely, 1969). After a serious car accident, a man with amnesia begins to suspect that his wife is manipulating him, and he hires a private detective to reconstruct his past. **Adaptation:** *Shattered* (MGM, 1991). Dir: Wolfgang Petersen. Scr: Wolfgang Petersen. Cast: Tom Berenger (Dan), Bob Hoskins (Gus), Greta Scacchi (Judith), Joanne Whalley-Kilmer (Jenny), Corbin Bernsen (Jeb). DVD, VHS.

3504. *Play It As It Lays* (Joan Didion, 1970). The neglected wife of a selfish film director reflects on her disappointing life. **Adaptation:** *Play It As It Lays* (Universal, 1972). Dir: Frank Perry. Scr: John Gregory Dunne. Cast: Tuesday Weld (Maria), Anthony Perkins (B. Z.), Tammy Grimes (Helene), Adam Roarke (Carter).

3505. *The Playboy and the Yellow Lady* (James Carney, 1986). Based on a true story, the novel is set in nineteenth-century Ireland and concerns a bored divorcee who becomes involved with a handsome land agent. After a dispute, he beats her severely and escapes to the United States to avoid imprisonment in Ireland. **Adaptation:** *Love and Rage* (New City, 1998). Dir: Cathal Black. Scr: Brian Lynch. Cast: Greta Scacchi (Agnes), Daniel Craig (James), Stephen Dillane (Dr. Croly), Valerie Edmond (Libby). DVD, VHS.

3506. *The Player* (Michael Tolkin, 1988). Black comedy about a Hollywood studio executive who murders a disappointed screenwriter in order to avoid being blackmailed. **Adaptation:** *The Player* (Fine Line, 1992). Dir: Robert Altman. Scr: Michael Tolkin. Cast: Tim Robbins (Griffin), Greta Scacchi (June), Fred Ward (Walter), Whoopi Goldberg (Detective Avery), Peter Gallagher (Larry). Notes: Cannes Film Festival Awards for Best Director and Actor (Robbins), and Golden Palm nomination for Best Director; Independent Spirit Awards for Best Film; Golden Globe Awards for Best Film and Actor (Robbins), and nominations for Best Director and Screenplay; Academy Award nominations for Best Director, Screenplay, and Editing. DVD, VHS.

3507. *Playing for the Ashes* (Elizabeth George, 1994). In the seventh installment in George's series of novels featuring Inspector Thomas Lynley of Scotland Yard, a star athlete is killed, and the detective finds that many people had a motive for murdering him. **Adaptation:** *Inspector Lynley Mysteries: Playing for the Ashes* (BBC/PBS, 2003 TV Movie series). Dir: Richard Spence. Scr: Kate Wood. Cast: Nathaniel Parker (Lynley), Sharon Small (Detective Havers), Clare Swinburne (Gabriella), Mark Brighton (Kenneth). DVD, VHS.

3508. *Playmates* (Andrew Neiderman, 1987). Horror novel about a deranged couple who pick up a woman and her young daughter after their car breaks down in the Florida backwoods and will not let them go. **Adaptation:** *The Maddening* (Trimark, 1995). Dir: Danny Huston. Scr: Henry Slesar, Leslie Greif. Cast: Burt Reynolds (Roy), Angie Dickinson (Georgina), Mia Sara (Cassie), Brian Wimmer (David), Josh Mostel (Chicky). VHS.

3509. *Please Don't Eat the Daisies* (Jean Kerr, 1957). Comic story about a New York drama critic who moves his family to the country. **Adaptation:** Please *Don't Eat the Daisies* (MGM, 1960). Dir: Charles Walters. Scr: Isobel Lennart. Cast: Doris Day (Kate), David Niven (Lawrence), Janis Paige (Deborah), Spring Byington (Suzie). VHS. Notes: The book was also the basis for a television series on NBC in 1965.

The Pleasure Seekers (see *Coins in the Fountain*).

3510. *The Pledge* (Friedrich Durrenmatt, 1957). The Swiss novel *Das Versprechen* is about a police inspector who promises the mother of a murdered girl that he will find the killer, a promise that turns into a personal obsession. **Adaptation 1:** *It Happened in Broad Daylight* (Continental, 1958). Dir: Ladislao Vajda. Scr: Hans Jacoby, Ladislao Vajda. Cast: Heinz Ruhmann (Matthai), Sigfrit Steiner (Feller), Siegfried Lowitz (Heinzi), Michel Simon (Jacquier), Gert Frobe (Schrott). **Adaptation 2:** *In the Cold Light of Day* (Meteor, 1994). Dir: Rudolf van den Berg. Scr: Doug Magee. Cast: Richard E. Grant (Viktor), Lynsey Baxter (Milena), Perdita Weeks (Anna), Simon Cadell (Vladimir). VHS. **Adaptation 3:** *The Pledge* (Warner, 2001). Dir: Sean Penn. Scr: Jerzy Kromolowski, Mary Olson-Kromolowski. Cast: Jack Nicholson (Jerry), Benicio Del Toro (Toby), Aaron Eckhart (Stan), Costas Mandylor (Monash), Robin Wright Penn (Lori), Vanessa Redgrave (Annalise), Mickey Rourke (Jim), Sam Shepard (Eric), Harry Dean Stanton (Floyd). Notes: Cannes Film Festival Golden Palm nomination for Best Director. DVD, VHS.

The Plot Thickens (see "The Riddle of the Dangling Pearl").

3511. *Plunder of the Sun* (David Dodge, 1949). An American insurance investigator searches for buried treasure in Mexico's Aztec ruins. **Adapta-**

tion: *Plunder of the Sun* (1953). Dir: John Farrow. Scr: Jonathan Latimer. Cast: Glenn Ford (Al), Diana Lynn (Julie), Patricia Medina (Anna).

3512. *The Plutocrat* (Booth Tarkington, 1927). Satire about a millionaire businessman who is tempted by a beautiful woman hired by his main competitor. The novel, which originally appeared in serial form in *The Ladies' Home Journal* (September 1926–January 1927), was also adapted as a stage play in 1930 by Arthur Goodrich. **Adaptation:** *Business and Pleasure* (Fox, 1931). Dir: David Butler. Scr: William M. Conselman, Gene Towne. Cast: Will Rogers (Earl), Jetta Goudal (Madame Momora), Joel McCrea (Lawrence), Dorothy Peterson (Mrs. Tinker).

3513. *Plymouth Adventure* (Ernest Gebler, 1950). Fictionalized account of the voyage of the Pilgrims and their difficult crossing to America on the *Mayflower*. **Adaptation:** *Plymouth Adventure* (MGM, 1952). Dir: Clarence Brown. Scr: Helen Deutsch. Cast: Spencer Tracy (Captain Jones), Gene Tierney (Dorothy), Van Johnson (John Alden), Leo Genn (William Bradford), Lloyd Bridges (Coppin). VHS.

3514. *A Pocket Full of Rye* (Agatha Christie, 1953). A wealthy man is poisoned, and Miss Jane Marple uses an old nursery rhyme to discover the murderer. **Adaptation:** *A Pocket Full of Rye* (BBC/PBS, 1985 TV Movie series). Dir: Guy Slater. Scr: T. R. Bowen. Cast: Joan Hickson (Miss Marple), Rachel Bell (Jennifer), Peter Davison (Lance), Timothy West (Rex), Tom Wilkinson (Detective Neele). DVD, VHS.

Pocket Money (see *Jim Kane*).

Pocketful of Miracles (*see* "Madame La Gimp").

The Poet (see *Little Girl Fly Away*).

3515. *Poet's Pub* (Eric Linklater, 1929). Romantic comedy about a man who takes over a Tudor pub in London and discovers a priceless artifact. **Adaptation:** *Poet's Pub* (General Film, 1949). Dir: Frederick Wilson. Scr: Diana Morgan. Cast: Derek Bond (Keith), Rona Anderson (Joanna), James Robertson Justice (Professor Benbow).

Point Blank (see *The Hunter*).

3516. *Point Counter Point* (Aldous Huxley, 1928). A satiric portrait of the passions and infidelities of intellectual England in the 1920's. **Adaptation:** *Point Counterpoint* (BBC, 1968 TV Miniseries). Dir: Rex Tucker. Scr: Simon Raven. Cast: Lyndon Brook (Philip), Patricia English (Eleanor), Valerie Gearon (Lucy).

The Point Men (see *The Heat of Ramadan*).

3517. *The Point of Honor: A Military Tale* (Joseph Conrad, 1908). In the early nineteenth century, two military officers carry on a longstanding feud through a series of duels. The novella appeared in *The Pall Mall Magazine* (January–May 1908) and was later retitled *The Duel*. **Adaptation:** *The Duellists* (Paramount, 1977). Dir: Ridley Scott. Scr: Gerald Vaughan-Hughes. Cast: Keith Carradine (D'Hubert), Harvey Keitel (Feraud), Albert Finney (Fouche), Edward Fox (Colonel), Cristina Raines (Adele). DVD, VHS.

3518. *The Point of Murder* (Margaret Yorke [pseudonym for Margaret Beda Nicholson], 1978). A killer stalks the only witness to his murder of a little girl. The novel was published in the U.S. as *The Come On*. **Adaptation:** *Kiss of a Killer* (ABC/Buena Vista, 1993 TV Movie). Dir: Larry Elikann. Scr: David Warfield. Cast: Annette O'Toole (Kate), Eva Marie Saint (Mrs. Wilson), Brian Wimmer (Gary), Gregg Henry (Richard). VHS.

Pola X (see *Pierre*).

3519. *The Polar Express* (Chris Van Allsburg, 1985, Caldecott Medal). Children's book about a boy who refuses to give up his belief in Santa Claus and the extraordinary journey that he and his doubting friends take to the North Pole on Christmas Eve. **Adaptation:** *The Polar Express* (Warner/Castle Rock, 2004). Dir: Robert Zemeckis. Scr: Robert Zemeckis, William Broyles, Jr. Cast: Tom Hanks (Hero Boy/Father/Conductor/ Hobo/Santa), Leslie Zemeckis (Sister Sarah/ Mother), Eddie Deezen (Know-It-All), Nona Gaye (Hero Girl), Peter Scolari (Lonely Boy). DVD, VHS.

Pollock (see *Jackson Pollock: An American Saga*).

Polly Fulton (see *B. F.'s Daughter*).

3520. *Pollyanna* (Eleanor H. Porter, 1913). An orphaned girl is sent to live with her grumpy aunt. The girl's boundless optimism and ability to look on the bright side of every situation eventually changes the outlook of her aunt and her entire town. **Silent Film:** 1920, starring Mary Pickford (VHS). **Adaptation 1:** *Pollyanna* (Disney/ Buena Vista, 1960). Dir: David Swift. Scr: David Swift. Cast: Hayley Mills (Pollyanna), Jane Wyman (Aunt Polly), Richard Egan (Dr. Chilton), Karl Malden (Reverend Ford), Nancy Olson (Nancy), Adolphe Menjou (Mr. Pendegast), Donald Crisp (Mayor Warren), Agnes Moorehead

(Mrs. Snow). Notes: Academy Award for Best Juvenile Performance (Mills); BAFTA nomination for Best British Actress (Mills). DVD, VHS. **Adaptation 2:** *Pollyanna* (BBC, 1973 TV Movie). Dir: June Wyndham-Davies. Scr: Joy Harington. Cast: Elizabeth Archard (Pollyanna), Elaine Stritch (Aunt Polly), Ray McAnally (John), Paul Maxwell (Dr. Chilton), Donald Bisset (Tom). VHS. **Adaptation 3:** *The Adventures of Pollyanna* (Disney/Buena Vista Television, 1982 TV Movie). Dir: Robert Day. Scr: Robert Day. Cast: Shirley Jones (Aunt Polly), Patsy Kensit (Pollyanna), Edward Winter (Dr. Chilton), Beverly Archer (Angelica), Lucille Benson (Mrs. Levelor), Nicholas Hammond (Reverend Tull), Gretchen Wyler (Mrs. Tarbell). **Adaptation 4:** *Polly*; also released as *Polly Comin' Home* (Disney/Buena Vista Television, 1989 TV Movie). Dir: Debbie Allen. Scr: William Blinn. Cast: Keshia Knight Pulliam (Polly), Phylicia Rashad (Aunt Polly), Dorian Harewood (Dr. Shannon), Barbara Montgomery (Mrs. Conley), Brock Peters (Mr. Pendergast), Celeste Holm (Miss Snow). Notes: A musical version about interracial harmony. **Adaptation 5:** *Pollyanna* (ITV, 2003 TV Movie). Dir: Sarah Harding. Scr: Eleanor H. Porter. Cast: Georgina Terry (Pollyanna), Amanda Burton (Aunt Polly), Kenneth Cranham (Mr. Pendleton), Aden Gillett (Dr. Chiltern), Pam Ferris (Mrs. Snow).

3521. *The Ponder Heart* (Eudora Welty, 1954). A rich man in a small Southern town marries a teenager, incurring the wrath of his greedy and manipulative niece. **Adaptation:** *The Ponder Heart* (2001) (TV). Dir: Martha Coolidge. Scr: Gail Gilchrist. Cast: Peter MacNicol (Uncle Daniel), JoBeth Williams (Edna), Angela Bettis (Bonnie), Boyce Holleman (Grandpa Ponder). VHS.

Pookie (see *The Sterile Cuckoo*).

Poopsie (*see* "Collared").

3522. *Poor Cow* (Nell Dunn, 1967). A young British woman marries an abusive thief and lives in squalor with him and their young son. When her husband is sent to prison, she takes up with his friend, another criminal, but she tries to improve her life when her young son is lost. **Adaptation:** *Poor Cow* (Anglo-Amalgamated/National General, 1967). Dir: Ken Loach. Scr: Nell Dunn, Ken Loach. Cast: Carol White (Joy), John Bindon (Tom), Queenie Watts (Aunt Em). Notes: Golden Globe nomination for Best English-Language Foreign Film. DVD, VHS.

3523. *Pop. 1280* (Jim Thompson, 1964). After suffering abuse from his wife and colleagues, a mild-mannered policeman decides to take violent revenge. **Adaptation:** *Coup de Torchon*; released in the UK as *Clean Slate* (Films A2/Moreno/Quartet, 1981). Dir: Bertrand Tavernier. Scr: Jean Aurenche, Bertrand Tavernier. Cast: Philippe Noiret (Lucien), Isabelle Huppert (Rose), Jean-Pierre Marielle (Le Peron), Stephane Audran (Huguette), Eddy Mitchell (Nono), Guy Marchand (Marcel). Notes: The screenplay sets the action in French West Africa in 1938. Academy Award nomination for Best Foreign-Language Film; Cesar Award (France) nominations for Best Film, Director, Screenplay, Actor (Noiret), Actress (Huppert), Supporting Actors (Mitchell and Marielle), Supporting Actress (Audran), and Editing. DVD, VHS.

3524. *The Pope of Greenwich Village* (Vincent Patrick, 1979). In New York's Little Italy, two small-time hustlers steal $150,000 from a safe and place a losing bet on a horserace. They soon discover that the money belonged to the mob and some corrupt cops, both of whom pursue them. **Adaptation:** *The Pope of Greenwich Village* (MGM-UA, 1984). Dir: Stuart Rosenberg. Scr: Vincent Patrick. Cast: Eric Roberts (Paulie), Mickey Rourke (Charlie), Daryl Hannah (Diane), Geraldine Page (Mrs. Ritter), Kenneth McMillan (Barney), Tony Musante (Pete), M. Emmet Walsh (Burns), Burt Young (Bedbug Eddie). DVD, VHS.

3525. *The Pork Butcher* (David Hughes, 1984). An elderly German man living in New York goes to France to visit his daughter and recalls his role in the Nazi massacre of French citizens during World War II. **Adaptation:** *Souvenir* (Paramount, 1989). Dir: Geoffrey Reeve. Scr: Paul Wheeler. Cast: Christopher Plummer (Ernst), Catherine Hicks (Tina), Michael Lonsdale (Xavier), Christopher Cazenove (William). DVD, VHS.

3526. *Pork Chop Hill: The American Fighting Man in Action, Korea, Spring 1953* (S. L. A. Marshall, 1956). Historical account of a ferocious battle to take and keep a hill during the Korean War. **Adaptation:** *Pork Chop Hill* (United Artists, 1959). Dir: Lewis Milestone. Scr: James R. Webb. Cast: Gregory Peck (Joe), Harry Guardino (Forstman), Rip Torn (Russel), George Peppard (Fedderson). DVD, VHS.

3527. *Port Afrique* (Bernard Victor Dryer, 1949). In Morocco, an American pilot investigates the secret adulterous life of his murdered wife. **Adaptation:** *Port Afrique* (Columbia, 1956). Dir:

Rudolph Mate. Scr: John Cresswell, Frank Partos. Cast: Pier Angeli (Inez), James Hayter (Nino), Richard Molinas (the Captain), Anthony Newley (Pedro), Christopher Lee (Franz Vermes).

3528. *Porterhouse Blue* (Tom Sharpe, 1974). Satiric novel about an all-male college in Cambridge, where a new master wants to introduce radical change while the old guard battles to preserve their traditional ways. **Adaptation:** *Porterhouse Blue* (Carnival/Channel 4, 1987 TV Miniseries). Dir: Robert Knights. Scr: Malcolm Bradbury. Cast: David Jason (Skullion), Ian Richardson (Evans), John Sessions (Lionel), Charles Gray (Sir Cathcart), Griff Rhys Jones (Cornelius). Notes: BAFTA Awards for Best Television Actor (Jason) and Musical Score, and nominations for Best Drama, Editing, Costume Design, Production Design, and Photography. DVD, VHS.

3529. "Portia on Trial" (Faith Baldwin, 1934). A female lawyer must use her formidable courtroom skills to clear her own name in a scandal. The short story was published in the *Ladies' Home Journal* in August 1934. **Adaptation:** *Portia on Trial* (Republic, 1937). Dir: George Nichols, Jr. Scr: Samuel Ornitz, Edward E. Paramore, Jr. Cast: Walter Abel (Dan), Frieda Inescort (Portia), Neil Hamilton (Earle), Heather Angel (Elizabeth).

3530. *Portnoy's Complaint* (Philip Roth, 1969). The story of a young Jewish man's bizarre relationship with his mother. **Adaptation:** *Portnoy's Complaint* (Warner, 1972). Dir: Ernest Lehman. Scr: Ernest Lehman. Cast: Richard Benjamin (Alexander), Karen Black (Mary Jane), Lee Grant (Sophie), Jack Somack (Jack), Renee Lippin (Hannah), Jill Clayburgh (Naomi). VHS.

3531. *The Portrait of a Lady* (Henry James, 1880–1881). A provincial and idealistic American heiress on a trip to England encounters jaded Europeans. An unhappy marriage leads to her disillusionment and determination to survive. The novel first appeared as a magazine serial in *Macmillan's Magazine* in England (October 1880 through November 1881) and in *The Atlantic Monthly* in the United States (November 1880 through December 1881). It appeared in book form in 1881. **Adaptation 1:** *The Portrait of a Lady* (BBC, 1968 TV Movie). Dir: James Cellan Jones. Scr: Jack Pulman. Cast: Richard Chamberlain (Ralph), Suzanne Neve (Isabel), Edward Fox (Lord Warburton), Beatrix Lehmann (Mrs. Touchett), Alan Gifford (Mr. Touchett), Edward Bishop (Caspar), James Maxwell (Gilbert). DVD, VHS. **Adaptation 2:** *The Portrait of a Lady*

(Gramercy, 1996). Dir: Jane Campion. Scr: Laura Jones. Cast: Nicole Kidman (Isabel), John Malkovich (Gilbert), Barbara Hershey (Serena), Mary-Louise Parker (Henrietta), Martin Donovan (Ralph), Shelley Winters (Mrs. Touchett), Richard E. Grant (Lord Warburton), Shelley Duvall (Countess Gemini), Christian Bale (Edward), Viggo Mortensen (Caspar). Notes: Academy Award nominations for Best Supporting Actress (Hershey) and Costume Design; Golden Globe nomination for Best Supporting Actress (Hershey). DVD, VHS.

3532. *Portrait of a Rebel* (Netta Syrett, 1929). During the British Victorian era, a woman campaigns for Women's Rights. **Adaptation:** *A Woman Rebels* (RKO, 1936). Dir: Mark Sandrich. Scr: Anthony Veiller, Ernest Vajda. Cast: Katharine Hepburn (Pamela), Herbert Marshall (Thomas), Elizabeth Allan (Flora), Donald Crisp (Judge Thistlewaite).

Portarit of a Sinner (see *The Rough and the Smooth*).

3533. *Portrait of a Young Man Drowning* (Charles M. Perry, 1962). A young Brooklyn man, sheltered by his overprotective invalid mother, shows a violent streak in a nightclub and is hired as an enforcer for the Jewish mobster. **Adaptation:** *Six Ways to Sunday* (Ardustry/Stratosphere, 1997). Dir: Adam Bernstein. Scr: Adam Bernstein, Marc Gerald. Cast: Norman Reedus (Harry), Deborah Harry (Kate), Adrien Brody (Arnie), Isaac Hayes (Bill). DVD, VHS.

3534. *Portrait of Clare* (Francis Brett Young, 1927). At the turn of the twentieth century, an elderly woman recalls her exciting romantic life. **Adaptation:** *Portrait of Clare* (Associated British/Stratford, 1950). Dir: Lance Comfort. Scr: Adrian Alington, Leslie Landau. Cast: Margaret Johnston (Clare), Richard Todd (Robert), Robin Bailey (Dudley), Ronald Howard (Ralph), Jeremy Spenser (Steven), Marjorie Fielding (Aunt Cathy).

3535. *Portrait of Jennie* (Robert Nathan, 1940). A poor New York artist is inspired by the spirit of a dead girl he meets in Central Park. **Adaptation:** *Portrait of Jennie* (Vanguard/Selznick, 1948). Dir: William Dieterle. Scr: Leonardo Bercovici, Paul Osborn, Peter Berneis. Cast: Jennifer Jones (Jennie), Joseph Cotten (Eben), Ethel Barrymore (Miss Spinney), Lillian Gish (Mother Mary), Cecil Kellaway (Matthews), David Wayne (Gus). DVD, VHS.

3536. *A Portrait of the Artist As a Young Man* (James Joyce, 1916). Joyce's first novel tells the story of Stephen Dedalus from his childhood in turn-of-the-century Ireland until his departure for the Continent as a disillusioned young man who questions his Catholic faith. **Adaptation:** *A Portrait of the Artist as a Young Man* (Howard Mahler, 1977). Dir: Joseph Strick. Scr: Judith Rascoe. Cast: Bosco Hogan (Stephen), T. P. McKenna (Simon), John Gielgud (the Preacher), Rosaleen Linehan (May). DVD, VHS.

3537. *The Poseidon Adventure* (Paul Gallico, 1969). On New Year's Eve, a group of passengers struggle to survive when their ocean liner is hit by a tidal wave and capsizes. **Adaptation:** *The Poseidon Adventure* (20th Century–Fox, 1972). Dir: Ronald Neame. Scr: Wendell Mayes, Stirling Silliphant. Cast: Gene Hackman (Frank), Ernest Borgnine (Mike), Red Buttons (James), Carol Lynley (Nonnie), Roddy McDowall (Acres), Stella Stevens (Linda), Shelley Winters (Belle), Jack Albertson (Manny), Pamela Sue Martin (Susan). Notes: Academy Award for Best Song and Special Award for Visual Effects, and nominations for Best Supporting Actress (Winters), Art Direction, Cinematography, Costume Design, Editing, Musical Score, and Sound; Golden Globe Award for Best Supporting Actress (Winters), and nominations for Best Picture, Musical Score, and Song. DVD, VHS. See also *Beyond the Poseidon Adventure*.

3538. *The Positronic Man* (Isaac Asimov and Robert Silverberg, 1992). A robot designed to do household chores develops human emotions and longs to become a real human being. The novel is based on Asimov's 1976 novelette *The Bicentennial Man*. **Adaptation:** *Bicentennial Man* (Buena Vista, 1999). Dir: Chris Columbus. Scr: Nicholas Kazan. Cast: Robin Williams (Andrew), Embeth Davidtz (Amanda), Sam Neill (Richard), Oliver Platt (Rupert). Notes: The screenplay is based on both Asimov's 1976 novelette *The Bicentennial Man* and Asimov and Robert Silverberg's 1992 novel *The Positronic Man*. DVD, VHS. See also *The Bicentennial Man*.

3539. *Posse from Hell* (Clair Huffaker, 1959). Western about a gunfighter and a small-town posse in pursuit of four escaped convicts who robbed their town and kidnapped a young woman. **Adaptation:** *Posse from Hell* (Universal International, 1961). Dir: Herbert Coleman. Scr: Clair Huffaker. Cast: Audie Murphy (Banner), John Saxon (Kern), Zohra Lampert (Helen), Vic Morrow (Crip), Robert Keith (Jeremiah).

Possessed (see *One Man's Secret*).

3540. *Possession* (A. S. Byatt, 1990, Booker Prize). Two academics set out to research the amorous exploits of a couple of Victorian poets and find themselves falling in love. **Adaptation:** *Possession* (2002). Dir: Neil La Bute. Scr: David Henry Hwang, Laura Jones, Neil La Bute. Cast: Gwyneth Paltrow (Maud Bailey), Aaron Eckhart (Roland), Jeremy Northam (Randolph), Jennifer Ehle (Christabel). DVD, VHS.

3541. *The Possession of Joel Delaney* (Ramona Stewart, 1970). A rich New York woman tries to protect her brother from a satanic group who believe that he is possessed and must be ritually murdered. **Adaptation:** *The Possession of Joel Delaney* (Paramount, 1972). Dir: Waris Hussein. Scr: Irene Kamp (writing as Grimes Grice), Matt Robinson. Cast: Shirley MacLaine (Norah), Perry King (Joel), Lisa Kohane (Carrie), David Elliott (Peter). VHS.

Postcards from America (see *Close to the Knives*).

3542. *Postcards from the Edge* (Carrie Fisher, 1987). Roman a clef about a drug-addicted woman trying to establish herself as an actress while dealing with her mother, a famous, aging film star. **Adaptation:** *Postcards from the Edge* (Columbia, 1990). Dir: Mike Nichols. Scr: Carrie Fisher. Cast: Meryl Streep (Suzanne), Shirley MacLaine (Doris), Dennis Quaid (Jack), Gene Hackman (Lowell), Richard Dreyfuss (Dr. Frankenthal), Rob Reiner (Joe), Annette Bening (Evelyn). Notes: Academy Award nominations for Best Actress (Streep) and Song; Golden Globe nominations for Best Actresses (Streep and MacLaine) and Song. DVD, VHS.

3543. *The Postman* (David Brin, 1985). After a devastating war in 2013, a wandering performer poses as a U.S. mail carrier and thereby unites a scattered community. **Adaptation:** *The Postman* (Warner, 1997). Dir: Kevin Costner. Scr: Eric Roth, Brian Helgeland. Cast: Kevin Costner (the Postman), Will Patton (General Bethlehem), Larenz Tate (Ford Lincoln Mercury), Olivia Williams (Abby), James Russo (Idaho). DVD, VHS.

3544. *The Postman* (Antonio Skarmeta, 1985). Skarmeta's Chilean novel *Ardiente Paciencia* is a romantic comedy about poet Pablo Neruda, who goes into exile on an Italian island. A local fisherman, hired as an additional postman to handle the large volume of mail that the poet receives, befriends the poet, who inspires the postman to woo a beautiful woman he loves. **Adaptation:** *The Postman* (Miramax, 1994). Dir: Michael Radford. Scr: Anna Pavignano, Michael

Radford, Furio Scarpelli, Giacomo Scarpelli, Massimo Troisi. Cast: Philippe Noiret (Neruda), Massimo Troisi (Mario), Maria Grazia Cucinotta (Beatrice), Linda Moretti (Donna Rosa). Notes: Originally released as *Il Postino* and shown with subtitles. BAFTA Awards for Best Foreign-Language Film and Musical Score, and nominations for Best Screenplay and Actor (Troisi); Academy Award nominations for Best Film, Director, Screenplay, and Actor (Troisi). DVD, VHS.

3545. *The Postman Always Rings Twice* (James M. Cain, 1934). Cain's first novel tells the story of a seductive woman at a roadside café who seduces a drifter and then persuades him to kill her husband. They do not live happily ever after. **Adaptation 1:** *Ossessione* (Ajay, 1943). Dir: Luchino Visconti. Scr: Luchino Visconti, Mario Alicata, Giuseppe De Santis, Gianni Puccini. Cast: Clara Calamai (Giovanna), Massimo Girotti (Gino), Juan de Landa (Giuseppe). Notes: An unofficial adaptation set in Fascist Italy during World War II (DVD, VHS). **Adaptation 2:** *The Postman Always Rings Twice* (1946). Dir: Tay Garnett. Scr: Harry Ruskin, Niven Busch. Cast: Lana Turner (Cora), John Garfield (Frank), Cecil Kellaway (Nick), Hume Cronyn (Arthur). DVD, VHS. **Adaptation 3:** *The Postman Always Rings Twice* (Paramount, 1981). Dir: Bob Rafelson. Scr: David Mamet. Cast: Jack Nicholson (Frank), Jessica Lange (Cora), John Colicos (Nick), Michael Lerner (Mr. Katz), John P. Ryan (Kennedy), Anjelica Huston (Madge). DVD, VHS.

3546. *The Potato Factory* (Bryce Courtenay, 1995). A young British maid engages in a sexual indiscretion and is forced into a life of prostitution at a brothel. She eventually goes to Australia, where her recipe for making whiskey from potatoes makes her rich. The novel is the first in Courtenay's Australian trilogy, which also includes *Tommo and Hawk* (1997) and *Solomon's Song* (1999). **Adaptation:** *The Potato Factory* (Screentime, 2000 TV Miniseries). Dir: Robert Marchand. Scr: Alan Seymour. Cast: Ben Cross (Ikey), Lisa McCune (Mary), Sonia Todd (Hannah), Robert Grubb (Emmett). Notes: Australian Film Institute nominations for Best Television Miniseries and Actresses (McCune and Todd).

3547. *The Potter's Field* (Ellis Peters [pseudonym for Edith Pargeter], 1989). The seventeenth installment in Peters' twenty-volume series (1977–1994) featuring Brother Cadfael, a twelfth-century monk who, following service in the Crusades, tends to the herbarium at Shrewsbury Abbey and solves crimes. In this book, a plow-

man unearths the body of a woman who went missing years earlier. Suspicion falls on one of the monks, a man who once owned the land and who was the husband of the missing woman. **Adaptation:** *Cadfael: The Potter's Field* (ITV/PBS, 1998 TV Movie series). Dir: Mary McMurray. Scr: Christopher Russell. Cast: Derek Jacobi (Brother Cadfael), Michael Culver (Prior Robert), Anthony Green (Hugh), Mel Martin (Lady Blount). DVD, VHS.

Power (see *Jew Suss*).

3548. *The Power and the Glory* (Graham Greene, 1940). A fugitive revolutionary priest in Mexico who opposes the communists is hunted by the authorities and betrayed by a man who offers him protection. **Adaptation 1:** *The Fugitive* (RKO, 1947). Dir: John Ford. Scr: Dudley Nichols. Cast: Henry Fonda (the Fugitive), Dolores del Rio (the Indian Woman), J. Carrol Naish (the Police Informer), Leo Carrillo (the Chief of Police). VHS. **Adaptation 2:** *The Power and the Glory* (National Telefilm, 1959 TV Movie). Dir: Carmen Capalbo. Scr: Pierre Bost, Denis Cannan. Cast: John Alderson (Miguel), Val Avery (the Chief of Police), Peter Falk (Mestizo). **Adaptation 3:** *The Power and the Glory* (CBS, 1961 TV Movie). Dir: Marc Daniels. Scr: Dale Wasserman. Cast: Laurence Olivier (the Priest), Julie Harris (Maria), George C. Scott (the Police Lieutenant), Martin Gabel (the Chief of Police), Roddy McDowall (Mestizo).

3549. *The Power and the Prize* (Howard Swigett, 1954). An ambitious American executive for a mining company begins to question his life and work when he falls in love with a beautiful Austrian refugee in London. **Adaptation:** *The Power and the Prize* (MGM, 1956). Dir: Henry Koster. Scr: Robert Ardrey. Cast: Robert Taylor (Cliff), Elisabeth Müller (Miriam), Burl Ives (George), Charles Coburn (Guy), Cedric Hardwicke (Mr. Carew), Mary Astor (Mrs. Salt).

3550. *The Power of One* (Bryce Courtenay, 1989). During World War II, a young British boy living in South Africa witnesses the brutality with which blacks are treated and vows to try to make life better for them and the country. **Adaptation:** *The Power of One* (Warner, 1992). Dir: John G. Avildsen. Scr: Robert Mark Kamen. Cast: Nigel Ivy (Newborn), Robbie Bulloch (Jaapie), Armin Mueller-Stahl (Doc), Clive Russell (Bormann), Morgan Freeman (Geel), John Gielgud (St. John). DVD, VHS.

3551. *The Powers Girls* (John Robert Powers, 1941). A description of the famous New York modeling school by its founder. **Adaptation:** *The Powers Girl*; released in the UK as *Hello, Beautiful* (United Artists, 1943). Dir: Norman Z. McLeod. Scr: Eddie Moran, Harry Segall. Cast: George Murphy (Jerry), Anne Shirley (Ellen), Carole Landis (Kay).

3552. *The Powwow Highway* (David Seals, 1979). An activist Native American leaves his reservation and journeys with a friend to rescue his sister, who has been unjustly imprisoned on drug charges. **Adaptation:** *Powwow Highway* (Handade/Warner, 1989). Dir: Jonathan Wacks. Scr: Janet Heaney, Jean Stawarz. Cast: A Martinez (Buddy), Gary Farmer (Philbert), Joannelle Nadine Romero (Bonnie), Amanda Wyss (Rabbit), Sam Vlahos (Chief Joseph). Notes: Sundance Film Festival Filmmakers Trophy for Best Director and nomination for Grand Jury Prize; Independent Spirit Award nominations for Best First Feature and Supporting Actor (Farmer). DVD, VHS.

3553. *Practical Magic* (Alice Hoffman, 1995). Two young women adept at magic have difficulty developing relationships because of an ancient family curse that dooms anyone with whom they fall in love. Together with their eccentric aunts, they must find a way to overcome the curse. **Adaptation:** *Practical Magic* (Warner, 1998). Dir: Griffin Dunne. Scr: Robin Swicord, Akiva Goldsman, Adam Brooks. Cast: Sandra Bullock (Sally), Nicole Kidman (Gillian), Stockard Channing (Frances), Dianne Wiest (Aunt Bridget), Goran Visnjic (Jimmy), Aidan Quinn (Gary), Evan Rachel Wood (Kylie). DVD, VHS.

3554. *A Prayer for Owen Meany* (John Irving, 1989). A boy whose growth is severely stunted accidentally kills his best friend's mother at a little-league baseball game. He comes to believe that it is God's will that he become a martyr for the betterment of the world. **Adaptation:** *Simon Birch* (Buena Vista, 1998). Dir: Mark Steven Johnson. Scr: Mark Steven Johnson. Cast: Ian Michael Smith (Simon), Joseph Mazzello (Joe), Ashley Judd (Rebecca), Oliver Platt (Ben), David Strathairn (Reverend Russell), Dana Ivey (Grandmother Wentworth). Notes: Irving was not pleased with the adaptation and insisted that the screenplay be described as merely "suggested by" his novel. DVD, VHS.

3555. *A Prayer for the Dying* (Jack Higgins, 1973). An IRA bomber accidentally blows up a school bus. He quits the organization and flees to London, where he goes to work as an assassin for a mobster. One of his jobs is witnessed by a Catholic priest, with whom he forms a relationship **Adaptation:** *A Prayer for the Dying* (Samuel Goldwyn, 1987). Dir: Mike Hodges. Scr: Edmund Ward, Martin Lynch. Cast: Mickey Rourke (Martin), Bob Hoskins (Father Da Costa), Alan Bates (Jack), Sammi Davis (Anna), Christopher Fulford (Billy), Liam Neeson (Liam). DVD, VHS.

A Prayer in the Dark (see *Stronghold*).

The Preacher's Wife (see *The Bishop's Wife*).

Precinct 45: Los Angeles Police (see *The New Centurions*).

3556. *Precious Bane* (Mary Webb, 1924). In a rural British town, a woman born with a harelip falls in love with an honest weaver, but her ambitious brother ruins her prospects for happiness. **Adaptation:** *Precious Bane* (BBC, 1989 TV Movie). Dir: Christopher Menaul. Scr: Maggie Wadey. Cast: Janet McTeer (Prue), John Bowe (Kester), Clive Owen (Gideon).

Prelude to Fame (*see* "Young Archimedes").

3557. *Prelude to Night* (Dayton Stoddart, 1945). A scheming tycoon abuses everyone around him to get to the top. **Adaptation:** *Ruthless* (Eagle-Lion, 1948). Dir: Edgar G. Ulmer. Scr: Alvah Bessie, S. K. Lauren, Gordon Kahn. Cast: Zachary Scott (Horace), Louis Hayward (Vic), Diana Lynn (Martha), Sydney Greenstreet (Buck). VHS.

3558. "The Premature Burial" (Edgar Allan Poe, 1844). Horror story about a medical student with an obsessive fear of being buried alive. The short story originally appeared in the July 31, 1844, issue of the *Philadelphia Dollar Newspaper*. **Adaptation 1:** *The Premature Burial* (American International, 1962). Dir: Roger Corman. Scr: Charles Beaumont, Ray Russell. Cast: Ray Milland (Guy), Hazel Court (Emily), Richard Ney (Miles), Heather Angel (Kate), Alan Napier (Dr. Gault). DVD, VHS. **Adaptation 2:** *Buried Alive* (21st Century Film, 1990). Dir: Gerard Kikoïne. Scr: Jake Chesi, Stuart Lee. Cast: John Carradine (Jacob), Robert Vaughn (Dr. Gary), Donald Pleasence (Dr. Schaeffer). Notes: The screenplay, which is not based directly on "The Premature Burial," combines elements from this story and others by Poe. VHS. Notes: The story also inspired *The Crime of Dr. Crespi*, a 1935 thriller about a mad scientist seeking vengeance on his enemies (VHS) and *Haunting Fear*, a 1991 horror film about a wife's revenge on her cheating husband (VHS).

Prescription for Murder (see *The Deeds of Dr. Deadcert*).

3559. *Presenting Lily Mars* (Booth Tarkington, 1933). A talented and determined country girl becomes a Broadway star. **Adaptation:** *Presenting Lily Mars* (MGM, 1943). Dir: Norman Taurog. Scr: Richard Connell, Gladys Lehman. Cast: Judy Garland (Lily), Van Heflin (John), Fay Bainter (Mrs. Thornway), Richard Carlson (Owen), Spring Byington (Flora). VHS.

3560. *The President's Lady* (Irving Stone, 1951). A fictionalized account of President Andrew Jackson's controversial marriage to divorcee Rachel Donaldson-Robards in 1794. **Adaptation:** *The President's Lady* (20th Century–Fox, 1953). Dir: Henry Levin. Scr: John Patrick. Cast: Susan Hayward (Rachel), Charlton Heston (President Jackson), John McIntire (John), Fay Bainter (Mrs. Donelson), Whitfield Connor (Lewis), Carl Betz (Charles). Notes: Charlton Heston played Andrew Jackson again in the 1958 film *The Buccaneer* (see *Lafitte the Pirate*).

Press for Time (see *Yea, Yea, Yea*).

3561. *Presumed Innocent* (Scott Turow, 1987, Silver Dagger Award of the British Crime Writers Association). A prosecutor is the prime suspect in his mistress's murder and must try to clear his name. **Adaptation:** *Presumed Innocent* (Warner, 1990). Dir: Alan J. Pakula. Scr: Frank Pierson, Alan J. Pakula. Cast: Harrison Ford (Rusty), Brian Dennehy (Raymond), Raul Julia (Sandy), Bonnie Bedelia (Barbara), Paul Winfield (Judge Lyttle), Greta Scacchi (Carolyn). DVD, VHS.

3562. *Pretend You Don't See Her* (Mary Higgins Clark, 1995). After she informs police about two murders, a New York real-estate agent is placed in the Witness Protection Program and conducts her own investigation into the homicides. **Adaptation:** *Pretend You Don't See Her* (PAX, 2002 TV Movie). Dir: Rene Bonnière. Scr: Donald Hounam. Cast: Emma Samms (Lacey), Hannes Jaenicke (Curtis), Beau Starr (Detective Sloan), Stewart Bick (Ken). DVD, VHS.

3563. *Pretty Maids All in a Row* (Francis Pollini, 1968). Black comedy about a high-school football coach and guidance counselor who kills off the pretty girls with whom he has had affairs in order to silence them. **Adaptation:** *Pretty Maids All in a Row* (MGM, 1971). Dir: Roger Vadim. Scr: Gene Roddenberry. Cast: Rock Hudson (Tiger), Angie Dickinson (Betty), Telly Savalas (Captain Surcher), John David Carson

(Harper), Roddy McDowall (Mr. Proffer), Keenan Wynn (Chief Poldaski). VHS.

Pretty Poison (see *She Let Him Continue*).

3564. "Prey" (Richard Matheson, 1969). An Afican tribal doll comes to life and terrorizes the woman who acquired it. The short story was published in *Playboy* in April 1969. **Adaptation 1:** *Trilogy of Terror* (ABC, 1975 TV Movie). Dir: Dan Curtis. Scr: Richard Matheson, William F. Nolan. Cast: Karen Black (Julie/Millicent/Therese/Amelia), Gregory Harrison (Arthur). DVD, VHS. **Adaptation 2:** *Trilogy of Terror II* (USA Networks, 1996 TV Movie). Dir: Dan Curtis. Dir: Dan Curtis, Richard Matheson, William F. Nolan. Cast: Lysette Anthony (Laura), Geraint Wyn Davies (Ben), Matt Clark (Ansford), Geoffrey Lewis (Stubbs). VHS. See also "The Graveyard Rats."

The Price of Freedom (see *Seven Men at Daybreak*).

The Price of Heaven (see *Blessed Assurance*).

3565. *Prick Up Your Ears: The Biography of Joe Orton* (John Lahr, 1978). The life of controversial British playwright Joe Orton (1933–1967) and his violent death at the hands of his homosexual lover, Kenneth Halliwell. **Adaptation:** *Prick Up Your Ears* (Samuel Goldwyn, 1987). Dir: Stephen Frears. Scr: Alan Bennett. Cast: Gary Oldman (Orton), Alfred Molina (Halliwell), Vanessa Redgrave (Peggy), Frances Barber (Leonie), Janet Dale (Mrs. Sugden), Julie Walters (Elsie). Notes: BAFTA nominations for Best Screenplay, Actor (Oldman), and Supporting Actress (Redgrave); Cannes Film Festival Award for Best Musical Score and Golden Palm nomination for Best Director; Golden Globe nomination for Best Supporting Actress (Redgrave). DVD, VHS.

3566. "Pride and Extreme Prejudice" (Frederick Forsyth, 1991). The CIA, KGB, and British intelligence all pursue a former spy who seems to have become psychologically unstable. The story was published in Forsyth's 1991 collection *The Deceiver*. **Adaptation:** *Pride and Extreme Prejudice* (London Weekend Television, 1990 TV Movie). Dir: Ian Sharp. Scr: Murray Smith. Cast: Brian Dennehy (Bruno), Simon Cadell (Wilson), Leonie Mellinger (Renate). Notes: Forsyth provided the story idea for the 1990 teleplay and published the short story the following year.

3567. *Pride and Prejudice* (Jane Austen, 1813). A couple with five daughters attempts to make socially favorable marriages for all of them. **Adaptation 1:** *Pride and Prejudice* (1940). Dir:

Robert Z. Leonard. Scr: Aldous Huxley, Helen Jerome, Jane Murfin. Cast: Greer Garson (Elizabeth), Laurence Olivier (Mr. Darcy), Mary Boland (Mrs. Bennet), Edna May Oliver (Lady Catherine), Maureen O'Sullivan (Jane), Ann Rutherford (Lydia), Frieda Inescort (Caroline), Edmund Gwenn (Mr. Bennet). VHS. **Adaptation 2:** *Pride and Prejudice* (BBC, 1952 TV Miniseries). Dir: Campbell Logan. Scr: Cedric Wallis. Cast: Ann Baskett (Jane), Peter Cushing (Mr. Darcy), Helen Haye (Lady Catherine), Richard Johnson (Mr. Wickham), Gillian Lind (Mrs. Bennet), David Markham (Mr. Bingley), Milton Rosmer (Mr. Bennet), Prunella Scales (Lydia), Daphne Slater (Elizabeth). **Adaptation 3:** *Pride and Prejudice* (BBC, 1967 TV Miniseries). Dir: Joan Craft. Scr: Nemone Lethbridge. Cast: Celia Bannerman (Elizabeth), Lewis Fiander (Mr. Darcy), Michael Gough (Mr. Bennet), Vivian Pickles (Mrs. Bennet), Polly Adams (Jane), Sylvia Coleridge (Lady Catherine), Julian Curry (Mr. Collins). **Adaptation 4:** *Pride and Prejudice* (BBC, 1980 TV Miniseries). Dir: Cyril Coke. Scr: Fay Weldon. Cast: Sabina Franklyn (Jane), Elizabeth Garvie (Elizabeth), Emma Jacobs (Georgiana), Priscilla Morgan (Mrs. Bennet), Natalie Ogle (Lydia), Judy Parfitt (Lady Catherine), Moray Watson (Mr. Bennet). DVD, VHS. **Adaptation 5:** *Pride and Prejudice* (BBC/A&E, 1995 TV Miniseries). Dir: Simon Langton. Scr: Andrew Davies. Cast: Colin Firth (Mr. Darcy), Jennifer Ehle (Elizabeth), David Bamber (Mr. Collins), Crispin Bonham-Carter (Charles), Anna Chancellor (Caroline), Susannah Harker (Jane), Barbara Leigh-Hunt (Lady Catherine). Notes: BAFTA Award for Best Actress (Ehle) and nominations for Best Miniseries, Actor (Firth), Costume Design and Makeup; Emmy Award for Outstanding Costume Design and nominations for Outstanding Miniseries, Teleplay, and Choreography. DVD, VHS. **Adaptation 6:** *Pride and Prejudice* (Excel, 2003). Dir: Andrew Black. Scr: Anne K. Black, Jason Faller, Katherine Swigert. Cast: Kam Heskin (Elizabeth), Orlando Seale (Darcy), Ben Gourley (Bingley), Lucila Sola (Jane), Kelly Stables (Lydia). Notes: A contemporary version of the novel. DVD, VHS. **Adaptation 7:** *Bride & Prejudice* (Miramax, 2004). Dir: Gurinder Chadha. Scr: Paul Mayeda Berges, Gurinder Chadha. Cast: Aishwarya Rai (Lalita), Martin Henderson (Will), Daniel Gillies (Mr. Wickham), Naveen Andrews (Balraj), Namrata Shirodkar (Jaya), Indira Varma (Kiran), Nadira Babbar (Mrs. Bakshi), Anupam Kher (Mr. Bakshi), Meghna Kothari (Maya).

Notes: Indian "Bollywood" update featuring an Indian family in modern-day England. DVD, VHS. **Adaptation 8:** *Pride & Prejudice* (Focus Features, 2005). Dir: Joe Wright. Scr: Deborah Moggach. Cast: Keira Knightley (Elizabeth), Matthew Macfadyen (Mr. Darcy), Talulah Riley (Mary), Rosamund Pike (Jane), Jena Malone (Lydia), Carey Mulligan (Kitty), Donald Sutherland (Mr. Bennet), Brenda Blethyn (Mrs. Bennet). Notes: Academy Award nominations for Best Actress (Knightley), Art Direction, Musical Score, and Costume Design; BAFTA Award for Most Promising Newcomer (Wright), and nominations for Best British Film, Screenplay, Supporting Actress (Blethyn), Costume Design, and Makeup and Hair Design. DVD, VHS.

The Pride and the Passion (see *The Gun*).

3568. *Priest of Love: A Life of D. H. Lawrence* (Harry T. Moore, 1954; revised edition 1974). A biography of the British writer (1885–1930). **Adaptation:** *Priest of Love* (Filmways, 1981). Dir: Christopher Miles. Scr: Alan Plater. Cast: Ian McKellen (D. H. Lawrence), Janet Suzman (Frieda Lawrence), Ava Gardner (Mabel Dodge Luhan), Penelope Keith (Dorothy Brett). DVD, VHS.

3569. *Primal Fear* (William Diehl, 1993). A high-powered attorney defends a mentally disturbed altar boy accused of murdering the popular archbishop who cared for him. **Adaptation:** *Primal Fear* (Paramount, 1996). Dir: Gregory Hoblit. Scr: Steve Shagan, Ann Biderman. Cast: Richard Gere (Martin), Laura Linney (Janet), Edward Norton (Aaron), John Mahoney (John), Frances McDormand (Dr. Arrington), Alfre Woodard (Judge Shoat), Terry O'Quinn (Bud Yancy), Andre Braugher (Tommy), Steven Bauer (Joey). Notes: Golden Globe and National Board of Review Awards for Best Supporting Actor (Norton); Academy Award nomination for Best Supporting Actor (Norton). DVD, VHS.

3570. *Primary Colors* (Joe Klein, 1996). Roman a clef about a womanizing Presidential candidate from a Southern state and his steadfast wife. The book was originally published anonymously. **Adaptation:** *Primary Colors* (MCA-Universal, 1998). Dir: Mike Nichols. Scr: Elaine May. Cast: John Travolta (Governor Stanton), Emma Thompson (Susan), Billy Bob Thornton (Richard), Kathy Bates (Libby), Adrian Lester (Henry), Maura Tierney (Daisy), Larry Hagman (Governor Picker), Diane Ladd (Mamma Stanton). Notes: Academy Award nominations for

Best Screenplay and Supporting Actress (Bates); Golden Globe nominations for Best Actor (Travolta) and Supporting Actress (Bates). DVD, VHS.

3571. *The Prime of Miss Jean Brodie* (Muriel Spark, 1961). An Edinburgh schoolteacher in the 1930's draws sharp criticism from school officials for inspiring a love of learning in her female students. The book was serialized in *The New Yorker* in 1961 and adapted as a 1968 play by Jay Presson Allen. **Adaptation:** *The Prime of Miss Jean Brodie* (20th Century–Fox, 1969). Dir: Ronald Neame. Scr: Jay Presson Allen (based on his 1968 play). Cast: Maggie Smith (Jean), Robert Stephens (Teddy), Pamela Franklin (Sandy), Gordon Jackson (Gordon), Celia Johnson (Miss Mackay). Notes: Academy Award for Best Actress (Smith) and nomination for Best Song; BAFTA Awards for Best Actress (Smith) and Supporting Actress (Johnson), and nomination for Best Supporting Actress (Franklin); Golden Globe Award for Best Song, and nominations for Best Picture and Actress (Smith); National Board of Review Award for Best Supporting Actress (Franklin); Cannes Film Festival Golden Palm nomination for Best Director. DVD, VHS. Notes: The book was also the basis for a Scottish television series in 1978.

Primrose Path (see *February Hill*).

3572. *The Prince and the Lily: The Story of Lillie Langtry* (James Brough, 1975). Biography of the beautiful British actress (1853–1929) and her affairs with the famous men of her day, including Oscar Wilde and the Prince of Wales. **Adaptation:** *Lillie* (ITV/PBS, 1978 TV Miniseries). Dir: John Gorrie, Christopher Hodson, Tony Wharmby. Scr: David Butler, John Gorrie. Cast: Francesca Annis (Lillie), Anton Rodgers (Edward), Denis Lill (the Prince of Wales/King Edward VII), Peter Egan (Oscar Wilde). Notes: BAFTA Award for Best Television Actress (Annis) and nominations for Best Costume Design and Sound. DVD, VHS.

3573. *The Prince and the Pauper* (Mark Twain [pseudonym for Samuel Langhorne Clemens], 1882). Classic tale of a prince and a look-alike street urchin who exchange places. **Silent Films:** 1909 and 1915. **Adaptation 1:** *The Prince and the Pauper* (Warner, 1937). Dir: William Keighley. Scr: Laird Doyle, Catherine Chisholm Cushing. Cast: Errol Flynn (Miles), Claude Rains (the Earl of Hertford), Henry Stephenson (the Duke of Norfolk), Barton MacLane (John), Billy Mauch (Tom). DVD,

VHS. **Adaptation 2:** *The Prince and the Pauper* (Disney, 1962 TV Movie). Dir: Don Chaffey. Scr: Jack Whittingham. Cast: Guy Williams (Miles Hendon), Sean Scully (Tom/Prince Edward), Jane Asher (Lady Jane). **Adaptation 3:** *The Adventures of the Prince and the Pauper* (Childhood, 1969). Dir: Elliot Geisinger. Scr: Elliot Geisinger, Alex Tartaglia. Cast: Kenny Morse (Prince Edward), Barry Pearl (Tom), Gene Bua (Miles), Barbara Huston (Lady Anne), Michael Brill (Lord Chamberlain), Tom Fleetwood (John). **Adaptation 4:** *The Prince and the Pauper* (BBC, 1976 TV Movie). Dir: Barry Letts. Scr: Richard Harris. Cast: Nicholas Lyndhurst (Tom/Prince Edward), June Brown (Mrs. Canty), Martin Friend (Lord Sudbroke), Martin Herdman (John), Barry Stokes (Miles). **Adaptation 5:** *Crossed Swords*; also released as *The Prince and the Pauper* (Warner, 1978). Dir: Richard Fleischer. Scr: Berta Domínguez, George MacDonald Fraser, Pierre Spengler. Cast: Oliver Reed (Miles), Raquel Welch (Edith), Mark Lester (Prince Edward/Tom), Ernest Borgnine (John), George C. Scott (the Ruffler), Rex Harrison (the Duke of Norfolk), David Hemmings (Hugh). DVD, VHS. **Adaptation 6:** *The Prince and the Pauper* (Disney/Buena Vista, 1990). Dir: George Scribner. Scr: Charles Fleischer, Gerrit Graham, Samuel Graham, Chris Hubbell, Jenny Tripp. Cast: voices of Wayne Allwine (Mickey Mouse/Prince Mickey), Bill Farmer (Goofy/Pluto), Arthur Burghardt (Captain Pete), Tony Anselmo (Donald Duck), Frank Welker (the Archbishop), Elvia Allman (Clarabelle), Roy Dotrice (Narrator). Notes: A Disney animated feature. DVD, VHS. **Adaptation 7:** *The Prince and the Pauper* (BBC, 1996 TV Movie). Dir: Andrew Morgan. Scr: Julian Fellowes. Cast: Philip Sarson (Tom/Prince Edward), John Bowe (the Earl of Hertford), Peter Jeffrey (the Duke of Norfolk), John Judd (John), Keith Michell (King Henry VIII), Sophia Myles (Lady Jane), James Purefoy (Miles). **Adaptation 8:** *The Prince and the Pauper* (HCC, 2000 TV Movie). Dir: Giles Foster. Scr: Duke Fenady, Dominic Minghella. Cast: Aidan Quinn (Miles), Alan Bates (King Henry VIII), Jonathan Hyde (Lord Hertford), Jonathan Timmins (Prince Edward), Robert Timmins (Tom). DVD, VHS.

3574. *Prince of Egypt* (Dorothy Clarke Wilson, 1949). Fictional retelling of the Biblical story of Moses and his selection by God to lead the Israelites out of their Egyptian captivity. **Adaptation:** *The Ten Commandments* (Paramount, 1956). Dir: Cecil B. De Mille. Scr: Aeneas MacKenzie, Jesse L. Lasky, Jr., Jack Gariss, Fredric M. Frank. Cast: Charlton Heston (Moses), Yul Brynner (Rameses), Anne Baxter (Nefretiri), Edward G. Robinson (Dathan), Yvonne De Carlo (Sephora), Debra Paget (Lilia), John Derek (Joshua), Cedric Hardwicke (Sethi). Notes: De Mille directed a silent film by the same title in 1923. For the 1956 screenplay, the writers used the original Biblical story and elements from three books: J. H. Ingraham's *The Pillar of Fire* (1859), A. E. Southon's *On Eagle's Wing*, (1939), and Dorothy Clarke Wilson's *Prince of Egypt* (1949). National Board of Review Award for Best Actor (Brynner); Academy Award for Best Special Effects, and nominations for Best Picture, Cinematography, Art Direction, Editing, Costume Design, and Sound. DVD, VHS. Notes: The 1998 Disney animated film by this title is not based directly on this book but recounts the same story. See also *Pillar of Fire* and *On Eagle's Wing*.

3575. *Prince of Foxes* (Samuel Shellabarger, 1947). A wandering adventurer in Renaissance Italy defies the powerful Borgias and must battle them to survive. **Adaptation:** *Prince of Foxes* (20th Century–Fox, 1949). Dir: Henry King. Scr: Milton Krims. Cast: Tyrone Power (Andrea), Orson Welles (Cesare), Wanda Hendrix (Camilla), Marina Berti (Angela), Everett Sloane (Mario).

3576. *Prince of Players: Edwin Booth* (Eleanor Ruggles, 1953). A biography of the renowned nineteenth-century actor Edwin Booth (1833–1893), the brother of John Wilkes Booth, who assassinated President Abraham Lincoln. **Adaptation:** *Prince of Players* (20th Century–Fox, 1955). Dir: Philip Dunne. Scr: Moss Hart. Cast: Richard Burton (Edwin Booth), Maggie McNamara (Mary Booth), John Derek (John Wilkes Booth), Raymond Massey (Junius Brutus Booth), Charles Bickford (Dave Prescott).

3577. *Prince of the City* (Robert Daley, 1978). True story of an honest New York policeman who is victimized by the corrupt colleagues against whom he testifies. **Adaptation:** *Prince of the City* (Warner/Orion, 1981). Dir: Sidney Lumet. Scr: Jay Presson Allen, Sidney Lumet. Cast: Treat Williams (Daniel), Jerry Orbach (Gus), Richard Foronjy (Joe), Don Billett (Bill), Kenny Marino (Dom). Notes: Academy Award nomination for Best Screenplay; Golden Globe nominations for Best Picture, Director, and Actor (Williams). VHS.

3578. *The Prince of Tides* (Pat Conroy, 1987). A troubled man talks to his suicidal sister's psychiatrist about their family's painful past, and

he and the married psychiatrist end up falling in love. **Adaptation:** *The Prince of Tides* (Columbia, 1991). Dir: Barbra Streisand. Scr: Pat Conroy, Becky Johnston. Cast: Barbra Streisand (Dr. Lowenstein), Nick Nolte (Tom), Blythe Danner (Sally), Kate Nelligan (Lila), Jeroen Krabbe (Herbert), Melinda Dillon (Savannah), George Carlin (Eddie). Notes: Golden Globe Award for Best Actor (Nolte) and nominations for Best Picture and Director; Academy Award nominations for Best Picture, Screenplay, Actor (Nolte), Supporting Actress (Nelligan), Musical Score, and Cinematography. DVD, VHS.

3579. "The Prince Who Was a Thief" (Theodore Dreiser, 1927). Short story about an Arabian prince who was lost as an infant and brought up by thieves. When he realizes who he is, he fights to regain his throne. **Adaptation:** *The Prince Who Was a Thief* (Universal International, 1951). Dir: Rudolph Mate. Scr: Gerald Drayson Adams, Aeneas MacKenzie. Cast: Tony Curtis (Julna), Piper Laurie (Tina), Everett Sloane (Yussef), Jeff Corey (Emir Mokar).

3580. *The Princess and the Goblin* (George MacDonald, 1872). Allegorical children's story about a young princess and a miner's son protecting their land against malicious goblins. **Adaptation:** *The Princess and the Goblin* (Hemdale, 1993). Dir: Jozsef Gemes. Scr: Robin Lyons. Cast: voices of Claire Bloom (the Fairy Godmother), Sally Ann Marsh (the Princess), Rik Mayall (Froglip), Mollie Sugden (Lotti). Notes: An animated feature. VHS.

3581. *The Princess Bride* (William Goldman, 1973). A grandfather reads his grandson a classic bedtime fairy tale about a beautiful princess kidnapped and forced into agreeing to marry an evil prince and the hero who comes to her rescue. **Adaptation:** *The Princess Bride* (20th Century–Fox, 1987). Dir: Rob Reiner. Scr: William Goldman. Cast: Cary Elwes (Westley), Mandy Patinkin (Inigo), Chris Sarandon (Prince Humperdinck), Christopher Guest (Count Rugen), Wallace Shawn (Vizzini), Andre the Giant (Fezzik), Fred Savage (the Grandson), Robin Wright (Buttercup/the Princess Bride), Peter Falk (the Grandfather). DVD, VHS.

3582. *The Princess Diaries* (Meg Cabot, 2000). Fanciful teen novel about the relationship between an awkward San Francisco teenager, the heir to the throne of a small European country, and her grandmother, the reigning queen, who must teach the girl the social skills necessary for her new role. **Adaptation:** *The Princess Diaries*

(Disney/Buena Vista, 2001). Dir: Garry Marshall. Scr: Gina Wendkos. Cast: Julie Andrews (Clarisse), Anne Hathaway (Mia), Hector Elizondo (Joe), Heather Matarazzo (Lilly), Mandy Moore (Lana), Caroline Goodall (Helen), Robert Schwartzman (Michael). DVD, VHS. Notes: A sequel, *The Princess Diaries 2: Royal Engagement*, was released in 2004 (DVD, VHS).

3583. "Princess O'Hara" (Damon Runyon, 1934). A New York hansom cab driver's horse dies, and his daughter finds him a new horse, not knowing that the animal she acquires is a stolen race horse. The short story was included in Runyon's 1938 collection *Furthermore*. **Adaptation 1:** *Princess O'Hara* (Universal, 1935). Dir: David Burton. Scr: Harry Clork, Doris Malloy. Cast: Jean Parker (Princess O'Hara), Chester Morris (Vic), Leon Errol (Last Card Louie), Ralph Remley (King O'Hara). **Adaptation 2:** *It Ain't Hay* (Universal, 1943). Dir: Erle C. Kenton. Scr: Allen Boretz, John Grant. Cast: Bud Abbott (Grover), Lou Costello (Wilbur), Grace McDonald (Kitty), Cecil Kellaway (King O'Hara), Patsy O'Connor (Princess O'Hara). VHS.

3584. "A Prisoner in the Caucasus" (Leo Tolstoy, 1862). A young Russian soldier is taken prisoner by Muslim revels in the Caucasus mountains. The short story was included in the 1872 book *Kavkazskij Plennik*. **Adaptation:** *Prisoner of the Mountains* (Orion, 1996). Dir: Sergei Bodrov. Scr: Arif Aliyev, Sergei Bodrov, Boris Giller. Cast: Oleg Menshikov (Sacha), Sergei Bodrov, Jr. (Vanya), Susanna Mekhraliyeva (Dina), Dzhemal Sikharulidze (Abdul-Murat). Notes: Originally released as *Kavkazskij Plennik* and shown with subtitles. Academy Award and Golden Globe nominations for Best Foreign-Language Film. DVD, VHS.

Prisoner of the Mountains (*see* "A Prisoner in the Caucasus").

3585. *The Prisoner of Zenda* (Anthony Hope [pseudonym for Anthony Hope Hawkins], 1894). A British man visiting his look-alike cousin, the crown prince of Ruritania, is forced to impersonate the kidnapped king at his coronation. The novel was adapted as a Broadway play by Edward Rose in 1895. **Silent Films:** 1913, 1915, and 1922. **Adaptation 1:** *The Prisoner of Zenda* (United Artists, 1937). Dir: John Cromwell. Scr: Wells Root, John L. Balderston, Donald Ogden Stewart. Cast: Ronald Colman (Rudolf Rassendyll/King Rudolf V), Madeleine Carroll (Princess Flavia), C. Aubrey Smith (Zapt), Raymond Massey

(Duke Michael), Mary Astor (Antoinette), David Niven (Fritz), Douglas Fairbanks, Jr. (Rupert). VHS. **Adaptation 2:** *The Prisoner of Zenda* (MGM, 1952). Dir: Richard Thorpe. Scr: Wells Root, John L. Balderston, Noel Langley, Donald Ogden Stewart. Cast: Stewart Granger (Rudolf Rassendyll/King Rudolf V), Deborah Kerr (Princess Flavia), Louis Calhern (Zapt), Jane Greer (Antoinette), Lewis Stone (the Cardinal), Robert Douglas (Duke Michael), James Mason (Rupert). VHS. **Adaptation 3:** *The Prisoner of Zenda* (Universal, 1979). Dir: Richard Quine. Scr: Dick Clement, Ian La Frenais. Cast: Peter Sellers (Rudolf IV/Rudolf V/Syd Frewin), Lynne Frederick (Princess Flavia), Lionel Jeffries (Sapt), Elke Sommer (the Countess), Gregory Sierra (the Count), Jeremy Kemp (Duke Michael), Catherine Schell (Antoinette). VHS. **Adaptation 4:** *The Prisoner of Zenda* (BBC, 1984 TV Miniseries). Dir: Leonard Lewis. Scr: James Andrew Hall. Cast: Malcolm Sinclair (Rudolf Rassendyll/King Rudolf V), George Irving (Duke Michael), Pauline Moran (Antoinette), Jonathon Morris (Rupert). **Adaptation 5:** *Prisoner of Zenda, Inc.* (Showtime/Hallmark, 1996 TV Movie). Dir: Stefan Scaini. Scr: Richard Clark, Rodman Gregg. Cast: Jonathan Jackson (Rudy/Oliver), Richard Lee Jackson (Douglas), William Shatner (Michael Gatewick), Jay Brazeau (Professor Wooley), Don S. Davis (Zapf), Katharine Isabelle (Fiona). Notes: A modern adaptation involving corporate intrigue. VHS.

The Private Affairs of Bel Ami (see *Bel Ami*).

3586. *Private Angelo* (Eric Linklater, 1946). Comic novel about an Italian soldier who hates war and does everything he can to avoid fighting in World War II. **Adaptation:** *Private Angelo* (Pilgrim/Associated British, 1949). Dir: Michael Anderson, Peter Ustinov. Scr: Michael Anderson, Peter Ustinov. Cast: Godfrey Tearle (Count Piccologrando), María Denis (Lucrezia), Peter Ustinov (Private Angelo), Marjorie Rhodes (the Countess), James Robertson Justice (Feste).

The Private History of a Campaign That Failed (see "The War Prayer").

Private Lessons (see *Philly*).

3587. *Private Life* (Alan Hackney, 1957). In this sequel to Hackney's 1954 comic novel *Private's Progress*, a naïve young man takes a job at a large company and becomes a pawn in the labor struggle between management and the employees' union. **Adaptation:** *I'm All Right, Jack* (British Lion, 1959). Dir: John Boulting. Scr: John Boulting, Alan Hackney, Frank Harvey. Cast: Ian Carmichael (Stanley), Terry-Thomas (Major Hitchcock), Peter Sellers (Fred/Sir John), Richard Attenborough (Sidney), Dennis Price (Bertram), Liz Fraser (Cynthia), Margaret Rutherford (Aunt Dolly). Notes: BAFTA Awards for Best Screenplay and Actor (Sellers), and nomination for Most Promising Newcomer (Fraser). DVD, VHS. See also *Private's Progress*.

3588. *Private Parts* (Howard Stern, 1993). Autobiography of the rebellious radio personality from his early days in the business in the 1970's through his meteoric rise to fame in New York. **Adaptation:** *Private Parts* (Paramount, 1997). Dir: Betty Thomas. Scr: Len Blum, Michael Kalesniko. Cast: Howard Stern (Howard Stern), Robin Quivers (Robin Quivers), Mary McCormack (Alison Stern), Fred Norris (Fred Norris), Paul Giamatti (Kenny "Pig Vomit" Rushton). DVD, VHS.

3589. *Private Worlds* (Phyllis Bottome [pseudonym for Phyllis Forbes-Dennis], 1934). The professional and romantic lives of doctors in a mental hospital. **Adaptation:** *Private Worlds* (Paramount, 1935). Dir: Gregory La Cava. Scr: Gregory La Cava, Lynn Starling. Cast: Claudette Colbert (Dr. Everest), Charles Boyer (Dr. Monet), Joan Bennett (Sally), Helen Vinson (Claire). Notes: Academy Award nomination for Best Actress (Colbert).

3590. *Private's Progress* (Alan Hackney, 1954). Comic story about a British university student drafted into the army during World War II. Although he's an inept officer, he teams up with a hustler who helps him navigate the military bureaucracy. **Adaptation:** *Private's Progress* (British Lion/DCA, 1956). Dir: John Boulting. Scr: John Boulting, Frank Harvey. Cast: Richard Attenborough (Percival), Dennis Price (Bertram), Henry Longhurst (Mr. Spottiswood), Terry-Thomas (Major Hitchcock), Ian Carmichael (Stanley). Notes: BAFTA nomination for Best Screenplay. DVD, VHS. Notes: A sequel, *I'm All Right Jack*, also directed by John Boulting, was released in 1959 (DVD, VHS). See also *Private Life*.

3591. *The Prize* (Irving Wallace, 1962). Cold War novel set at the Nobel Prize ceremony in Stockholm. The East Germans are particularly interested in one of the American laureates, a German-born physicist, and another American laureate investigates the physicist's strange behavior. **Adaptation:** *The Prize* (MGM, 1963). Dir: Mark Robson. Scr: Ernest Lehman. Cast: Paul Newman (Andrew), Elke Sommer (Inger), Edward G. Robinson (Max/Walter), Diane Baker (Emily). Notes: Golden Globe Award for Most Promising Newcomer (Sommer) and nomination for Supporting Actress (Baker). VHS.

3592. *The Prize: The Epic Quest for Oil, Money & Power* (Daniel Yergin, 1991, Pulitzer Prize). A history of the ways in which oil has shaped politics, war, and the global economy from the mid-nineteenth century to the present. **Adaptation:** *The Prize: The Epic Quest for Oil, Money & Power* (PBS, 1992 Documentary Miniseries). Series Producer: William Cran. Screenplay: Daniel Yergin. Cast: Donald Sutherland (Narrator). VHS.

3593. *A Prize of Gold* (Max Catto, 1953). During World War II, an American soldier in Berlin devises a plan to steal Nazi gold. **Adaptation:** *A Prize of Gold* (Columbia, 1955). Dir: Mark Robson. Scr: Robert Buckner, John Paxton. Cast: Richard Widmark (Sergeant Lawrence), Mai Zetterling (Maria), Nigel Patrick (Brian), George Cole (Sergeant Morris), Donald Wolfit (Stratton). VHS.

3594. *Prizzi's Honor* (Richard Condon, 1982). Black comedy about male and female Mafia assassins who fall in love. Complications arise, however, when they are ordered to kill each other. **Adaptation:** *Prizzi's Honor* (20th Century–Fox, 1985). Dir: John Huston. Scr: Richard Condon, Janet Roach. Cast: Jack Nicholson (Charley), Kathleen Turner (Irene), Robert Loggia (Eduardo), John Randolph (Angelo), William Hickey (Don Corrado), Anjelica Huston (Maerose). Notes: Golden Globe Awards for Best Picture, Director, Actor (Nicholson), and Actress (Turner), and nominations for Best Screenplay and Supporting Actress (Huston); National Board of Review Award for Best Director; Academy Award nominations for Best Picture, Director, Screenplay, Actor (Nicholson), Supporting Actor (Hickey), Editing, and Costume Design. DVD, VHS.

3595. *The Procane Chronicle* (Oliver Bleeck [pseudonym for Ross Thomas], 1971). An aspiring crime writer is hired by a wealthy thief to negotiate the return of stolen plans for a heist and becomes involved in a murder. **Adaptation:** *St. Ives* (Warner, 1976). Dir: J. Lee Thompson. Scr: Barry Beckerman. Cast: Charles Bronson (St. Ives), John Houseman (Procane), Jacqueline Bisset (Janet), Maximilian Schell (Dr. Constable), Harry Guardino (Detective Deal). VHS.

The Professional (see *Death of a Thin-Skinned Animal*).

The Professionals (see *A Mule for Marquesa*).

3596. *Professor Unrat* (Heinrich Mann, 1905). The older brother of German novelist Thomas Mann wrote this novel, whose title literally means "Professor Trash." It concerns a shy teacher whose life is ruined when he falls in love with a sensuous night-club entertainer. **Adaptation 1:** *The Blue Angel* (Universum/Paramount, 1930). Dir: Josef von Sternberg. Scr: Carl Zuckmayer, Karl Vollmoller, Robert Liebmann. Cast: Emil Jannings (Professor Rath), Marlene Dietrich (Lola Lola), Kurt Gerron (Klepert), Rosa Valetti (Guste), Hans Albers (Mazeppa). DVD, VHS. **Adaptation 2:** *The Blue Angel* (20th Century–Fox, 1959). Dir: Edward Dmytryk. Scr: Robert Liebmann, Karl Vollmoller, Carl Zuckmayer (1930 screenplay), Nigel Balchin. Cast: Curt Jurgens (Professor Rath), May Britt (Lola Lola), Theodore Bikel (Klepert), John Banner (Principal Harter).

Project M7 (see *The Net*).

Project X (see *The Artificial Man*).

Promise the Moon (see *The Four Arrows Fe-As-Ko*).

The Promoter (see *The Card*).

3597. *Pronto* (Elmore Leonard, 1993). When his mob boss tries to kill him for reasons unknown to him, a Miami Beach bookie flees the country, but is pursued nevertheless. **Adaptation:** *Pronto* (Showtime, 1997 TV Movie). Dir: Jim McBride. Scr: Michael Butler. Cast: Peter Falk (Harry), Glenne Headly (Joyce), James Le Gros (Raylan). VHS.

Proof of Life (*see* "Adventures in the Ransom Trade" and *The Long March to Freedom*).

3598. "*Property of a Lady* (Ian Fleming, 1964). James Bond and an art expert follow a female double agent to Sotheby's, where a rare emerald sphere is to be auctioned. The story was published in *Playboy* in January 1964 and was included in the 1966 volume *Octopussy*, along with the title story and "The Living Daylights." **Adaptation:** *Octopussy* (United Artists, 1983). Dir: John Glen. Scr: George MacDonald Fraser, Richard Maibaum, Michael G. Wilson. Cast: Roger Moore (James Bond), Maud Adams (Octopussy), Louis Jourdan (Khan), Kristina Wayborn (Magda). Notes: The screenplay combines elements from the short stories "Octopussy" and

"Property of a Lady." DVD, VHS. See also "Octopussy."

The Proud and the Profane (see *The Magnificent Bastards*).

3599. *Proved Innocent* (Gerry Conlon, 1990). Autobiography of a small-time thief in Belfast coerced into confessing to an IRA bombing and imprisoned along with his father for fourteen years until an idealistic British attorney proved their innocence. The book was subsequently retitled *In the Name of the Father*. **Adaptation:** *In the Name of the Father* (Universal, 1993). Dir: Jim Sheridan. Scr: Terry George, Jim Sheridan. Cast: Emma Thompson (Gareth), Daniel Day-Lewis (Gerry), Pete Postlethwaite (Giuseppe), Marie Jones (Sarah), Don Baker (Joe). Notes: Academy Award nominations for Best Picture, Director, Screenplay, Actor (Day-Lewis), Supporting Actor (Postlethwaite), Supporting Actress (Thompson), and Editing; BAFTA nominations for Best Screenplay and Actor (Day-Lewis); Golden Globe nominations for Best Picture, Actor (Day-Lewis), and Supporting Actress (Thompson). DVD, VHS.

3600. *Prozac Nation: Young and Depressed in America* (Elizabeth Wurtzel, 1994). Memoir of an emotionally disturbed woman who recalls her lifelong struggle with severe depression. **Adaptation:** *Prozac Nation* (Miramax, 2001). Dir: Erik Skjoldbjaerg. Scr: Galt Niederhoffer, Frank Deasy, Larry Gross. Cast: Christina Ricci (Elizabeth), Anne Heche (Dr. Sterling), Michelle Williams (Ruby), Jason Biggs (Rafe), Jonathan Rhys-Meyers (Noah). DVD.

3601. *P. S.* (Helen Schulman, 2001). Romantic story about a divorced woman who meets a younger man who appears the reincarnation of her dead high school boyfriend. **Adaptation:** *P. S.* (Newmarket, 2004). Dir: Dylan Kidd. Scr: Dylan Kidd. Cast: Laura Linney (Louise), Topher Grace (Scott), Gabriel Byrne (Peter), Marcia Gay Harden (Missy), Paul Rudd (Sammy). DVD, VHS.

3602. *Psyche '59* (Francoise des Ligneris, 1959). A woman suffering from psychosomatic blindness recovers her sight when she realizes that her husband and her sister are romantically involved. The 1959 French novel was translated and published in English the same year. **Adaptation:** *Psyche '59* (Royal Film International, 1964). Dir: Alexander Singer. Scr: Julian Zimet (writing as Julian Halevy). Cast: Curt Jurgens (Eric), Patricia Neal (Alison), Samantha Eggar (Robin), Ian Bannen (Paul).

3603. *Psycho* (Robert Bloch, 1959). Inspired by real events, the novel is about a deranged motel owner who assumes the personality (and retains the corpse of) his dead mother. **Adaptation 1:** *Psycho* (Paramount, 1960). Dir: Alfred Hitchcock. Scr: Joseph Stefano. Cast: Anthony Perkins (Bates), Janet Leigh (Marion), Vera Miles (Lila), John Gavin (Sam), Martin Balsam (Milton). Notes: Golden Globe Award for Best Supporting Actress (Leigh); Academy Award nominations for Best Director, Supporting Actress (Leigh), Cinematography, and Art Direction. DVD, VHS. **Adaptation 2:** *Psycho* (Universal, 1998). Dir: Gus Van Sant. Scr: Joseph Stefano (1960 screenplay). Cast: Vince Vaughn (Bates), Anne Heche (Marion), Julianne Moore (Lila), Viggo Mortensen (Samuel), William H. Macy (Milton), Robert Forster (Dr. Simon). DVD, VHS. Notes: Three sequels followed the 1960 film release, all of them starring Anthony Perkins in the role of Norman Bates: *Psycho II* (1983) (DVD, VHS); *Psycho III* (1986) (DVD, VHS); and *Psycho IV: The Beginning*, a 1990 television movie (VHS). In addition, the book and film also inspired the 1987 television movie *Bates Motel*.

3604. *Puberty Blues* (Gabrielle Carey and Kathy Lette, 1979). A novel by and about Australian teenaged surfer groupies and their carefree lifestyle made up mostly of beach parties and sex. **Adaptation:** *Puberty Blues* (Universal, 1981). Dir: Bruce Beresford. Scr: Margaret Kelly. Cast: Nell Schofield (Debbie), Jad Capelja (Sue), Geoff Rhoe (Gary), Tony Hughes (Danny), Sandy Paul (Tracy). VHS.

3605. *Puckoon* (Spike Milligan, 1963). Set in 1924, the story of a small Irish village through the middle of which runs the border between the Irish Republic and Northern Ireland, dividing families and their loyalties. **Adaptation:** *Puckoon* (United Artists, 2002). Dir: Terence Ryan. Scr: Terence Ryan. Cast: Sean Hughes (Dan), Elliott Gould (Dr. Goldstein), Daragh O'Malley (Father Rudden), John Lynch (O'Brien), Griff Rhys Jones (Stokes).

3606. *Pudd'nhead Wilson* (Mark Twain [pseudonym for Samuel Langhorne Clemens], 1894). A light-skinned slave child and the master's white child are switched at birth, and the young slave is raised as a white person. **Silent Film:** 1916. **Adaptation:** *Pudd'nhead Wilson* (PBS/American Playhouse, 1984 TV Movie). Dir: Alan Bridges. Scr: Philip H. Reisman, Jr. Cast: Lise Hilboldt (Roxy), Ken Howard (Pudd'nhead Wilson), James Pritchett (Traynor), Dick Latessa (Creech).

3607. *Puerto Vallarta Squeeze* (Robert James Waller, 1995). An American government hitman is forced to flee into the jungles of Mexico to save his own life. **Adaptation:** *Puerto Vallarta Squeeze* (Showcase, 2003). Dir: Arthur Allan Seidelman. Scr: Richard Alfieri. Cast: Scott Glenn (Clayton), Harvey Keitel (Walter), Craig Wasson (Danny), Giovanna Zacarias (Maria).

3608. *The Pumpkin Eater* (Penelope Mortimer, 1962). Portrait of a troubled woman, the mother of eight children, who has a breakdown when she discovers that her third husband is having an affair. **Adaptation:** *The Pumpkin Eater* (Romulus/Royal, 1964). Dir: Jack Clayton. Scr: Harold Pinter. Cast: Anne Bancroft (Jo), Peter Finch (Jake), James Mason (Bob), Janine Gray (Beth), Richard Johnson (Giles), Maggie Smith (Philpott). Notes: BAFTA Awards for Best Screenplay, Actress (Bancroft), and Costume Design, and nominations for Best Film and Art Direction; Cannes Film Festival Award for Best Actress (Bancroft); Academy Award nomination for Best Actress (Bancroft). VHS.

3609. *The Punk* (Gideon Sams, 1987). A London street youth falls in love with a wealthy American girl to the disapproval of their families and friends. When the youth kills a man in self-defense, they are forced to go on the run together. **Adaptation:** *The Punk*; also released as The *Punk and the Princess* (M2, 1993). Dir: Michael Sarne. Scr: Michael Sarne. Cast: Charlie Creed-Miles (David), Vanessa Hadaway (Rachel), David Shawyer (David's Father), Jess Conrad (Rachel's Father), Alex Mollo (Stray Cat), Peter Miles (Shakespeare). VHS.

3610. *The Puppet Masters* (Robert A. Heinlein, 1951). After alien slugs invade an Iowa time and take over people's minds, a government official goes there to fight them before they conquer the Earth. **Adaptation:** *The Puppet Masters* (Hollywood/Buena Vista, 1994). Dir: Stuart Orme. Scr: Ted Elliott, Terry Rossio, David S. Goyer. Cast: Donald Sutherland (Andrew), Eric Thal (Sam), Julie Warner (Mary), Keith David (Alex), Will Patton (Dr. Graves), Richard Belzer (Jarvis), Tom Mason (President Douglas), Yaphet Kotto (Ressler). DVD, VHS.

3611. *Puppet on a Chain* (Alistair MacLean, 1969). An American drug agent hunts down heroin smugglers in Amsterdam. **Adaptation:** *Puppet on a Chain* (Cinerama, 1970). Dir: Geoffrey Reeve. Scr: Alistair MacLean, Don Sharp, Paul Wheeler. Cast: Sven-Bertil Taube (Paul), Barbara Parkins (Maggie), Alexander Knox (Colonel De

Graaf), Patrick Allen (Inspector Van Gelder). VHS.

Purely Belter (see *The Season Ticket*).

Purple Noon (see *The Talented Mr. Ripley*).

3612. *The Purple Plain* (H. E. Bates, 1946). During World War II in the Pacific, a squadron leader who had a breakdown after losing his wife on their wedding night in London regains his control and saves his troops. **Adaptation:** *The Purple Plain* (Rank/United Artists, 1954). Dir: Robert Parrish. Scr: Eric Ambler. Cast: Gregory Peck (Bill), Win Min Than (Anna), Brenda De Banzie (Miss McNab), Bernard Lee (Dr. Harris), Maurice Denham (Blore). Notes: BAFTA nominations for Best Film, Screenplay, and Actor (Denham).

Pursuit (see *Binary*).

The Pursuit of D. B. Cooper (see *Free Fall*).

3613. *The Pusher* (Ed McBain [pseudonym for Evan Hunter], 1956). New York detectives suspect that the apparent suicide of a heroin addict was actually a homicide and pursue the killer. **Adaptation:** *The Pusher* (United Artists, 1960). Dir: Gene Milford. Scr: Harold Robbins. Cast: Kathy Carlyle (Laura), Robert Lansing (Detective Carella), Felice Orlandi (the Pusher), Douglas Rodgers (Detective Byrne).

Pushing Tin (*see* "Something's Got to Give").

Pushover (see *The Night Watch* and *Rafferty*).

3614. *The Puzzle of the Pepper Tree* (Stuart Palmer, 1933). When a fellow passenger on a plane is found dead upon arrival at Catalina Island, schoolteacher and amateur sleuth Hildegarde Withers suspects that he was murdered and investigates with the help of a police inspector. **Adaptation:** *Murder on a Honeymoon* (RKO, 1935). Dir: Lloyd Corrigan. Scr: Robert Benchley, Seton I. Miller. Cast: Edna May Oliver (Hildegarde), James Gleason (Inspector Piper), Lola Lane (Phyllis), George Meeker (Tom).

3615. *The Puzzle of the Red Stallion* (Stuart Palmer, 1935). Schoolteacher and amateur detective Hildegarde Withers investigates the murder of a woman found on a bridle path in Central Park. **Adaptation:** *Murder on a Bridle Path* (RKO, 1936). Dir: William Hamilton, Edward Killy. Scr: Dorothy Yost, Thomas Lennon, Edmund North, James Gow. Cast: James Gleason (Inspector Piper), Helen Broderick (Hildegarde), Louise Latimer (Barbara), Owen Davis, Jr. (Eddie).

3616. *Pylon* (William Faulkner, 1935). A newspaper reporter becomes fascinated with a family of a World War I veteran and hero, now a daredevil pilot working at an air circus. **Adaptation:** *The Tarnished Angels* (Universal International, 1958). Dir: Douglas Sirk. Scr: George Zuckerman. Cast: Rock Hudson (Burke), Robert Stack (Roger), Dorothy Malone (Laverne), Jack Carson (Jiggs). VHS.

3617. *Q & A* (Edwin Torres, 1976). A young and inexperienced prosecutor is assigned to investigate the killing of a Puerto Rican street thug by a detective and discovers high-level corruption within the police department. **Adaptation:** *Q & A* (TriStar, 1990). Dir: Sidney Lumet. Scr: Sidney Lumet. Cast: Nick Nolte (Brennan), Timothy Hutton (Reilly), Armand Assante (Texador), Patrick O'Neal (Quinn), Lee Richardson (Bloomenfeld), Luis Guzman (Valentin), Charles Dutton (Chapman). DVD, VHS.

3618. *QB VII* (Leon Uris, 1970). A distinguished British physician sues a journalist for libel when a newspaper story appears accusing the doctor of medical experimentation in the Nazi death camps during World War II. **Adaptation:** *QB VII* (ABC, 1974 Miniseries). Dir: Tom Gries. Scr: Edward Anhalt. Cast: Ben Gazzara (Abe), Anthony Hopkins (Dr. Kelno), Leslie Caron (Angela), Lee Remick (Lady Margaret), Juliet Mills (Samantha), Dan O'Herlihy (David), Robert Stephens (Robert), Anthony Quayle (Tom), Milo O'Shea (Dr. Lotaki), John Gielgud (Clinton-Meek), Edith Evans (Dr. Parmentier), Jack Hawkins (Justice Gilroy). Notes: Emmy Awards for Outstanding Supporting Actor (Quayle), Supporting Actress (Mills), Musical Score, and Editing, and nominations for Outstanding Miniseries, Telepay, Director, Actor (Hawkins), and Supporting Actress (Remick). DVD, VHS.

3619. *Quality* (Cid Ricketts Sumner, 1946). A light-skinned black woman who passes for white returns to her home in the South and encounters a variety of social and romantic problems. **Adaptation:** *Pinky* (20th Century–Fox, 1949). Dir: Elia Kazan. Scr: Philip Dunne, Dudley Nichols. Cast: Jeanne Crain (Pinky), Ethel Barrymore (Miss Em), Ethel Waters (Granny), William Lundigan (Dr. Adams). Notes: Academy Award nominations for Best Actress (Crain) and Supporting Actresses (Barrymore and Waters). DVD, VHS.

3620. *Quartet* (Jean Rhys [pseudonym for Ella Gwendoline Rees Williams], 1928). Autobiographical novel about a young woman whose husband is imprisoned and is taken in by a prominent writer and his wife. Before long, she becomes his mistress. The book is based on Rhys's own experiences with Ford Maddox Ford. **Adaptation:** *Quartet* (Merchant-Ivory/New World, 1981). Dir: James Ivory. Scr: Ruth Prawer Jhabvala. Cast: Alan Bates (Heidler), Maggie Smith (Lois), Isabelle Adjani (Marya), Anthony Higgins (Stephan), Pierre Clementi (Theo). Notes: Cannes Film Festival Award for Best Actress (Adjani) and Golden Palm nomination for Best Director; BAFTA nomination for Best Actress (Smith). DVD, VHS.

Quartet (1948) (*see* "The Alien Corn," "The Colonel's Lady," "The Facts of Life," and "The Kite").

3621. *Queen: The Story of an American Family* (Alex Haley and David Stevens, 1993). The story of Haley's father's family through three generations beginning with the emancipation of the slaves. Haley died in 1992, and Stevens completed the book and published it the following year. **Adaptation:** *Queen* (CBS, 1993 TV Miniseries). Dir: John Erman. Scr: David Stevens. Cast: Halle Berry (Queen), Danny Glover (Haley), Ann-Margret (Sally), Ossie Davis (Parson Dick), Jasmine Guy (Easter), Martin Sheen (James), Paul Winfield (Captain Jack). Notes: Emmy nominations for Outstanding Miniseries, Supporting Actress (Ann-Margret), Editing, Sound, Costume Design, and Makeup; Golden Globe nomination for Best Supporting Actress (Ann-Margret). VHS.

3622. *Queen Bee* (Edna Lee, 1949). A wealthy Southern woman cruelly dominates her family and ruins their lives. The novel was serialized in *The Woman's Home Companion* in June and July 1949 and published as a book the same year. **Adaptation:** *Queen Bee* (Columbia, 1955). Dir: Ranald MacDougall. Scr: Ranald MacDougall. Cast: Joan Crawford (Eva), Barry Sullivan (Avery), Betsy Palmer (Carol), John Ireland (Judson), Fay Wray (Sue). DVD, VHS.

3623. *Queen Bees and Wannabes: Helping Your Daughter Survive Cliques, Gossip, Boyfriends and Other Realities of Adolescence* (Rosalind Wiseman, 2002). An advice book for the parents of adolescent girls about the challenges young women face. **Adaptation:** *Mean Girls* (Paramount, 2004). Dir: Mark Waters. Scr: Tina Fey. Cast: Lindsay Lohan (Cady), Rachel McAdams (Regina), Tina Fey (Ms. Norbury), Tim Meadows (Mr. Duvall). Notes: The screenplay, inspired by the advice book, concerns a teenager who re-

turns to an American high school after spending years with her anthropologist parents in Africa. DVD, VHS.

3624. *Queen in Danger* (Trevor Dudley Smith, 1952). A man unjustly accused of murder escapes to search for the real murderer and discovers that his own wife is involved with the crime. Smith originally published the novel under the pseudonym Simon Rattray. **Adaptation:** *Mantrap*; released in the U.S. as *Man in Hiding* (Hammer, 1953). Dir: Terence Fisher. Scr: Terence Fisher, Paul Tabori. Cast: Paul Henreid (Hugo), Lois Maxwell (Thelma), Kieron Moore (Speight), Hugh Sinclair (Maurice).

3625. *Queen Margot* (Alexandre Dumas, pere, 1845). The elder Dumas's French novel *La Reine Margot* is set in August 1572 when the sister of Catholic French King Charles IX is forced by her mother, Catherine de Medici, to marry the Hugenot King Henri of Navarre. The marriage touches off the slaughter of Protestants known as the St. Bartholomew's Day Massacre. **Adaptation 1:** *A Woman of Evil* (Lux, 1954). Dir: Jean Dreville. Scr: Abel Gance. Cast: Jeanne Moreau (Queen Margot), Armando Francioli (the Duke of Mole), Robert Porte (Charles IX), Francoise Rosay (Catherine de Medici). **Adaptation 2:** *Queen Margot* (Miramax, 1994). Dir: Patrice Chereau. Scr: Daniele Thompson, Patrice Chereau. Cast: Isabelle Adjani (Queen Margot), Daniel Auteuil (Henri of Navarre), Jean-Hugues Anglade (Charles IX), Vincent Perez (the Duke of Mole), Virna Lisi (Catherine de Medici). Notes: Originally titled *La Reine Margot* and shown with subtitles. Cannes Film Festival Award for Best Actress (Lisi) and Jury Prize (Chereau), and Golden Palm nomination for Best Director; Academy Award nomination for Best Costume Design; BAFTA and Golden Globe nominations for Best Foreign-Language Film. DVD, VHS.

Queen of Crime (see *Kate Plus Ten*).

3626. *The Queen of Spades* (Aleksandr Pushkin, 1833). The story of a compulsive gambler who loses everything to cards. The novella, originally titled *Pikovaya Dama*, was the basis for an opera by Modest and Peter Tchaikovsky in 1890. **Silent Films:** 1910 and 1916. **Adaptation 1:** *Queen of Spades* (General/Rosner, 1937). Dir: Fyodor Otsep. Scr: Bernard Zimmer. Cast: Pierre Blanchar (Hermann), Andre Luguet (Iretski), Madeleine Ozeray (Lisa). Notes: Originally titled *La Dame de Pique* and shown with subtitles. **Adaptation 2:** *The Queen of Spades* (Associated

British/Monogram, 1949). Dir: Thorold Dickinson. Scr: Rodney Ackland, Arthur Boys. Cast: Anton Walbrook (Herman), Edith Evans (Countess Ranevskaya), Yvonne Mitchell (Lizaveta), Ronald Howard (Andrei). Notes: BAFTA nomination for Best British Film. **Adaptation 3:** *Queen of Spades* (Lenfilm/Artkino, 1960). Dir: Roman Tikhomirov. Scr: Roman Tikhomirov, Gennadi Vasilyev, P. Veisbrem, B. Yarustovsky. Cast: Oleg Strizhenov (Herman), Irina Gubanova (Polina), Olga Krasina (Lisa), Yelena Polevitskaya (Countess Ranevskaya). Notes: A musical film adaptation of the story and Tchaikovsky's opera. Originally titled *Pikovaya* Dam and shown with subtitles. VHS. Notes: In addition, a Metropolitan Opera production of Tchaikovsky's opera starring Placido Domingo, was broadcast on PBS in 1999. There are also two adaptations that were never released in English: a French-language adaptation, *La Dame de Pique*, in 1965, and a Russian television adaptation 1982.

3627. *Queen of the Damned: The Vampire Chronicles* (Anne Rice, 1988). The Vampire Lestat joins the rock scene, angering the Queen of the Vampires. **Adaptation:** *Queen of the Damned* (Warner, 2002). Dir: Michael Rymer. Scr: Scott Abbott, Michael Petroni. Cast: Aaliyah (Akasha), Stuart Townsend (Lestat), Marguerite Moreau (Jesse), Vincent Perez (Marius de Romanus), Paul McGann (David Talbot), Lena Olin (Maharet). DVD, VHS. See also *Interview with the Vampire*.

3628. *Quentin Durward* (Walter Scott, 1823). During the fifteenth century, an elderly Scottish nobleman sends his nephew to Paris to woo an aristocratic French woman on his behalf, and the young man falls in love with her. **Adaptation:** *Quentin Durward*; also released as *The Adventures of Quentin Durward* (MGM, 1955). Dir: Richard Thorpe. Scr: Robert Ardrey, George Froeschel. Cast: Robert Taylor (Quentin), Kay Kendall (Isabelle), Robert Morley (King Louis XI), George Cole (Hayraddin).

3629. *Querelle de Brest* (Jean Genet, 1947). A French sailor frequents a brothel and discovers his own homosexuality there. **Adaptation:** *Querelle* (Triumph, 1982). Dir: Rainer Werner Fassbinder. Scr: Burkhard Driest, Rainer Werner Fassbinder. Cast: Brad Davis (Querelle), Franco Nero (Seblon), Jeanne Moreau (Lysiane), Laurent Malet (Roger), Gunther Kaufmann (Nono). DVD, VHS.

Quest for Camelot (see *The King's Damosel*).

Quest for Love (*see* "Random Quest").

3630. *The Quick and the Dead* (Louis L'Amour, 1974). Western about a tough gunfighter who guides a family across the dangerous prairies to their new home. **Adaptation:** *The Quick and the Dead* (HBO, 1987 TV Movie), Dir: Robert Day. Scr: James Lee Barrett. Cast: Sam Elliott (Con), Tom Conti (Duncan), Kate Capshaw (Susanna), Kenny Morrison (Tom). DVD, VHS.

3631. *Quick, Before It Melts* (Philip Benjamin, 1964). Comic novel about a journalist who goes to Antarctica to do a story about naval operations there and becomes involved with a defecting Russian scientist and a scheme to supply women to the employees. **Adaptation:** *Quick, Before It Melts* (MGM, 1964). Dir: Delbert Mann. Scr: Dale Wasserman. Cast: George Maharis (Peter), Robert Morse (Oliver), Anjanette Comer (Tiara), James Gregory (the Admiral), Michael Constantine (Mikhail).

3632. *Quick Change* (Jay Cronley, 1981). Comic novel about three people who dress as clowns and successfully rob a bank but then have difficulty getting out of town with the loot. **Adaptation 1:** *Hold-Up* (Cinevideo, 1985). Dir: Alexandre Arcady. Scr: Alexandre Arcady, Daniel Saint-Hamont, Francis Veber. Cast: Jean-Paul Belmondo (Grimm), Kim Cattrall (Lise), Guy Marchand (George). **Adaptation 2:** *Quick Change* (Warner, 1990). Dir: Howard Franklin, Bill Murray. Scr: Howard Franklin. Cast: Bill Murray (Grimm), Geena Davis (Phyllis), Jason Robards (Chief Rotzinger), Randy Quaid (Loomis). VHS.

Quicksilver Highway (*see* "The Body Politic" and "Chattery Teeth").

3633. *The Quiet American* (Graham Greene, 1955). Set in Saigon in 1952, the story of a deadly love triangle involving a naïve American, an opium-addicted Briton, and a beautiful Vietnamese woman. **Adaptation 1:** *The Quiet American* (United Artists, 1958). Dir: Joseph L. Mankiewicz. Scr: Joseph L. Mankiewicz. Cast: Audie Murphy (Alden), Michael Redgrave (Thomas), Claude Dauphin (Inspector Vigot), Giorgia Moll (Phuong), Bruce Cabot (Bill). VHS. **Adaptation 2:** *The Quiet American* (Miramax/Buena Vista, 2002). Dir: Phillip Noyce. Scr: Christopher Hampton, Robert Schenkkan. Cast: Michael Caine (Thomas), Brendan Fraser (Alden), Do Thi Hai Yen (Phuong), Rade Serbedzija (Inspector Vigot). Notes: National Board of Review Award for Best Director; Academy Award, BAFTA, and Golden Globe nominations for Best Actor (Caine). DVD, VHS.

3634. *Quiet Days in Clichy* (Henry Miller, 1956). Autobiographical novel about an elderly writer recalling his friendships and sexual encounters in France in the 1930's. **Adaptation 1:** *Quiet Days in Clichy* (Grove/Sherpix, 1970). Dir: Jens Jorgen Thorsen. Scr: Jens Jorgen Thorsen. Cast: Paul Valjean (Joey), Wayne Rodda (Carl), Susanne Krage (Christine). DVD, VHS. **Adaptation 2:** *Quiet Days in Clichy* (WHAM, 1990). Dir: Claude Chabrol. Scr: Claude Chabrol, Ugo Leonzio. Cast: Andrew McCarthy (Miller), Nigel Havers (Alfred), Barbara De Rossi (Nys), Isolde Barth (Ania), Eva Grimaldi (Yvonne). VHS.

3635. *The Quiet Earth* (Craig Harrison, 1981). Science-fiction novel about a man who awakens to find himself alone in the world. He manages to locate a few other survivors, and together they discover that a failed government project was the cause of the catastrophe. **Adaptation:** *The Quiet Earth* (Skouras, 1985). Dir: Geoff Murphy. Scr: Bill Baer, Bruno Lawrence, Sam Pillsbury. Cast: Bruno Lawrence (Zack), Alison Routledge (Joanne), Pete Smith (Api). Notes: New Zealand Film and Television Awards for Best Film, Director, Screenplay, Actor (Lawrence), Supporting Actor (Smith), Cinematography, Editing, and Production Design. DVD, VHS.

3636. "The Quiet Man" (Maurice Walsh, 1933). An American boxer returns to Ireland and falls in love with a local woman. Before he can marry her, however, he must deal with her brother's objections and a variety of local customs. The story first appeared in the February 11, 1933, issue of *The Saturday Evening Post* and was included in Walsh's 1935 collection *Green Rushes*. **Adaptation:** *The Quiet Man* (Republic, 1952). Dir: John Ford. Scr: Frank S. Nugent. Cast: John Wayne (Sean), Maureen O'Hara (Mary Kate), Barry Fitzgerald (Michaleen), Ward Bond (Father Lonergan), Victor McLaglen (Red), Mildred Natwick (Sarah). Notes: Academy Awards for Best Director and Cinematography, and nominations for Best Picture, Screenplay, Supporting Actor (McLaglen), Sound, and Art Direction; National Board of Review Award for Best Film. DVD, VHS.

The Quiller Memorandum (see *The Berlin Memorandum*).

3637. "Quitters, Inc" (Stephen King, 1978). A clinic that helps people stop smoking provides deadly motivation to its clients. The story originally appeared in King's 1978 short-story collection *Night Shift*. **Adaptation:** *Cat's Eye* (MGM, 1985). Dir: Lewis Teague. Scr: Stephen King. Cast:

Drew Barrymore (Amanda), Kenneth McMillan (Cressner), Robert Hays (Johnny Norris), Charles Dutton (Dom). Notes: The screenplay includes three stories: "The Ledge," "Quitters, Inc," and "The General." DVD, VHS. See also "The Ledge."

Quiz Show (see *Remembering America*).

3638. *Quo Vadis?* (Henryk Sienkiewicz, 1895). After several years on military campaigns, a Roman general returns home and falls in love with a young Christian woman. As Nero's Rome disintegrates, he saves her and her family and is threatened with death by the wrathful emperor. **Silent Films:** 1902, 1912, and 1924. **Adaptation 1:** *Quo Vadis* (MGM, 1951). Dir: Mervyn Le Roy. Scr: S. N. Behrman, Sonya Levien, John Lee Mahin. Cast: Robert Taylor (Marcus Vinicius), Deborah Kerr (Lygia), Leo Genn (Petronius), Peter Ustinov (Nero). Notes: Golden Globe Awards for Best Supporting Actor (Ustinov) and Cinematography; Academy Award nominations for Best Picture, Actor (Ustinov), Supporting Actor (Genn), Cinematography, Editing, Musical Score, Art Direction, Costume Design, VHS. **Adaptation 2:** *Quo Vadis?* (Leone/Prism, 1985 TV Movie). Dir: Franco Rossi. Scr: Franco Rossi. Cast: Klaus Maria Brandauer (Nero), Frederic Forrest (Petronius), Francesco Quinn (Marcus Vinicius), Cristina Raines (Lygia), Max von Sydow (Peter). Notes: The adaptation was made for Italian television. VHS. **Adaptation 3:** *Quo Vadis?* (Chronos, 2001). Dir: Jerzy Kawalerowicz. Scr: Chuck Bush, Jerzy Kawalerowicz. Cast: Pawel Delag (Marcus Vinicius), Magdalena Mielcarz (Lygia), Boguslaw Linda (Petronius), Michal Bajor (Nero), Franciszek Pieczka (Peter). DVD, VHS.

Rabbit-Proof Fence (see *Follow the Rabbit-Proof Fence*).

3639. *Rabbit, Run* (John Updike, 1960). Updike's novel centers on Harold "Rabbit" Angstrom, a former high-school basketball star who becomes disillusioned with adult life and finally goes on the run to find himself. Updike subsequently published three more Rabbit novels, tracing Angstrom's life and ending in his death: *Rabbit Redux* (1971), *Rabbit Is Rich* (1981), and *Rabbit at Rest* (1990). **Adaptation:** *Rabbit, Run* (Warner, 1970). Dir: Jack Smight. Scr: Howard B. Kreitsek. Cast: James Caan (Rabbit), Carrie Snodgress (Janice), Anjanette Comer (Ruth), Jack Albertson (Marty), Melodie Johnson (Lucy), Henry Jones (Mr. Angstrom), Arthur Hill (Reverend Eccles).

3640. *The Racers* (Hans Ruesch, 1953). A female gambler finances a race-car driver in Monte Carlo. **Adaptation:** *The Racers*; released in the UK as *Such Men Are Dangerous* (20th Century–Fox, 1955). Dir: Henry Hathaway. Scr: Charles Kaufman. Cast: Kirk Douglas (Gino), Bella Darvi (Nicole), Gilbert Roland (Dell'Oro), Cesar Romero (Carlos), Lee J. Cobb (Maglio), Katy Jurado (Maria). VHS.

3641. "Rachel" (Howard Fast, 1941). A widowed farmer on the American frontier marries his indentured servant and eventually comes to love her. The short story was published in *The Saturday Evening Post* on June 14, 1941. **Adaptation:** *Rachel and the Stranger* (RKO, 1948). Dir: Norman Foster. Scr: Waldo Salt. Cast: Loretta Young (Rachel), William Holden (David), Robert Mitchum (Jim), Gary Gray (Davey), Tom Tully (Parson Jackson). Notes: The screenplay combines elements from this story and from Fast's short story "Neighbor Sam," published in the March 1942 issue of *American Magazine*. VHS.

Rachel and the Stranger (*see* "Rachel").

3642. *The Rachel Papers* (Martin Amis, 1973, Somerset Maugham Award). A British high-school student develops an obsessive fascination with an American girl living in London. **Adaptation:** *The Rachel Papers* (United Artists, 1989). Dir: Damian Harris. Scr: Damian Harris. Cast: Dexter Fletcher (Charles), Ione Skye (Rachel), Jonathan Pryce (Norman), James Spader (Deforest), Bill Paterson (Gordon), Michael Gambon (Dr. Knowd). DVD, VHS.

Rachel, Rachel (see *A Jest of God*).

The Racing Game (see *Odds Against*).

3643. *Rackety Rax* (Joel Sayre, 1932). Comic novel about gangsters who try to control the outcome of college football games. **Adaptation:** *Rackety Rax* (Fox, 1932). Dir: Alfred L. Werker. Scr: Lou Breslow, Ben Markson. Cast: Victor McLaglen (Knucks), Greta Nissen (Voine), Nell O'Day (Doris).

3644. *Rafferty* (Bill S. Ballinger, 1953). An honest cop falls for a gangster's girlfriend. **Adaptation:** *Pushover* (Columbia, 1954). Dir: Richard Quine. Scr: Roy Huggins. Cast: Fred MacMurray (Paul), Philip Carey (Rick), Kim Novak (Lona), Dorothy Malone (Ann), E. G. Marshall (Lieutenant Eckstrom). Notes: The screenplay is based on Thomas Walsh's 1952 novel *The Night Watch* and on Bill S. Ballinger's 1953 novel *Rafferty*. VHS. See also *The Night Watch*.

3645. *Raffles, the Amateur Cracksman* (E. W. Hornung, 1899). A socially prominent man is secretly a safe cracker and jewel thief. Hornung and Eugene Wiley Presbery also produced a Broadway play based on the novel in 1903. **Silent Films:** 1905, 1917, and 1925. **Adaptation 1:** *Raffles* (United Artists, 1930). Dir: George Fitzmaurice. Scr: Sidney Howard. Cast: Ronald Colman (Raffles), Kay Francis (Gwen), Bramwell Fletcher (Bunny). VHS. **Adaptation 2:** *Raffles* (United Artists, 1940). Dir: Sam Wood. Scr: Sidney Howard (1930 screenplay). Cast: David Niven (Raffles), Olivia de Havilland (Gwen), Dame May Whitty (Kitty). **Adaptation 3:** *Raffles* (Yorkshire, 1975 TV Movie). Dir: Christopher Hodson. Scr: Philip Mackie. Cast: Anthony Valentine (Raffles), Margot Lister (Lady Melrose), James Maxwell (Inspector MacKenzie), Christopher Strauli (Bunny). DVD, VHS. Notes: The book was also the basis of a 1958 Mexican film titled *Raffles Mexicano* and a 1977 British TV series (DVD, VHS).

3646. "The Raft" (Stephen King, 1982). Four teenagers on a rafting expedition are attacked by a monstrous blob that resides in a lake. The short story originally appeared in *Gallery* magazine in 1982 and a rewritten version was subsequently included in King's 1985 short story collection *Skeleton Crew*. **Adaptation:** *Creepshow 2* (Laurel/New World, 1987). Dir: Michael Gornick. Scr: Stephen King, George A. Romero. Cast: Domenick John (Billy), Tom Savini (the Creep), Paul Satterfield (Deke), Jeremy Green (Laverne), Daniel Beer (Randy), Page Hannah (Rachel). Notes: The film, the sequel to the 1982 Romero film *Creepshow* and yet another tribute to the E. C. Comics of the 1950's, includes three stories: "Old Chief Wood'nhead," "The Raft," and "The Hitchhiker." DVD, VHS.

3647. *The Rag Nymph* (Catherine Cookson, 1992). In nineteenth-century England, a beautiful young girl is preyed upon by a pimp who wants to sell her to the highest bidder. **Adaptation:** *The Rag Nymph* (Tyne Tees, 1997 TV Miniseries). Dir: David Wheatley. Scr: T. R. Bowen. Cast: Honeysuckle Weeks (Millie), Perdita Weeks (Millie as a young woman), Crispin Bonham-Carter (Bernard), Julia Dearden (Sister Cecilia). VHS.

3648. *A Rage in Harlem* (Chester Himes, 1958). A naïve working-class black man falls in love with a beautiful woman who is being pursued by gangsters. The novel — published in Paris under the title *The Five-Cornered Square* — introduced the detectives Grave Digger Jones and Coffin Ed Johnson, who would become featured characters in Himes's 1965 novel *Cotton Comes to Harlem*. **Adaptation:** *A Rage in Harlem* (Miramax, 1991). Dir: Bill Duke. Scr: John Toles-Bey, Bobby Crawford. Cast: Forest Whitaker (Jackson), Gregory Hines (Goldy), Robin Givens (Imabelle), Zakes Mokae (Big Kathy), Danny Glover (Easy Money). Notes: Cannes Film Festival Golden Palm nomination for Best Director. DVD, VHS.

3649. *Rage in Heaven* (James Hilton, 1932). Jealous of the attention a former friend pays to his attractive wife, a mentally unstable man devises a scheme to get rid of his rival. **Adaptation:** *Rage in Heaven* (MGM, 1941). Dir: W. S. Van Dyke. Scr: Christopher Isherwood, Robert Thoeren. Cast: Robert Montgomery (Philip), Ingrid Bergman (Stella), George Sanders (Ward), Lucile Watson (Mrs. Monrell).

3650. *Rage of Angels* (Sidney Sheldon, 1980). A successful attorney finds herself torn between two lovers— a politician and a mobster. **Adaptation:** *Rage of Angels* (NBC, 1983 TV Movie). Dir: Buzz Kulik. Scr: Robert L. Joseph. Cast: Jaclyn Smith (Jennifer), Ken Howard (Adam), Kevin Conway (Ken), Ron Hunter (Robert), Armand Assante (Michael). DVD, VHS. Notes: A made-for-television sequel, *Rage of Angels: The Story Continues*, was broadcast on NBC in 1986 (VHS).

3651. *The Rage of the Vulture* (Alan Moorehead, 1948). In rural India in 1947, an American arms dealer clashes with a local pacifist leader, but the men are forced to deal with each other when rebels threaten the town. **Adaptation:** *Thunder in the East* (Paramount, 1951). Dir: Charles Vidor. Scr: Frederick Hazlitt Brennan, Lewis Meltzer, Jo Swerling, George Tabori. Cast: Alan Ladd (Steve), Deborah Kerr (Joan), Charles Boyer (Singh), Corinne Calvet (Lizette), Cecil Kellaway (Dr. Willoughby).

3652. *A Rage to Live* (John O'Hara, 1949). A woman's compulsion to have sex with strange men threatens to destroy her otherwise happy marriage. **Adaptation:** *A Rage to Live* (United Artists, 1965). Dir: Walter Grauman. Scr: John T. Kelley. Cast: Suzanne Pleshette (Grace), Bradford Dillman (Sidney), Ben Gazzara (Roger), Peter Graves (Jack).

3653. *Raging Bull: My Story* (Jake La Motta, Joseph Carter, and Peter Savage, 1970). Autobiography of the middleweight boxing champion from his childhood in Bronx slums through his later self-destructive bouts with rage and paranoia. **Adaptation:** *Raging Bull* (United Artists, 1980). Dir: Martin Scorsese. Scr: Paul Schrader, Mardik Martin. Cast: Robert De Niro (La Motta), Cathy Moriarty (Vickie), Joe Pesci (Joey), Frank Vincent (Salvy), Nicholas Colasanto (Tommy), Theresa Saldana (Lenore). Notes: Academy Awards for Best Actor (De Niro) and Editing, and nominations for Best Picture, Director, Supporting Actor (Pesci), Supporting Actress (Moriarty), Cinematography, and Sound; Golden Globe Award for Best Actor (De Niro), and nominations for Best Picture, Director, Screenplay, Supporting Actor (Pesci), and Supporting Actress (Moriarty). DVD, VHS.

3654. *The Raging Moon* (Peter Marshall, 1966). Romance develops between two handicapped people in a hospital for the physically impaired. **Adaptation:** *The Raging Moon*; released in the U.S. as *Long Ago Tomorrow* (EMI/Cinema 5, 1971). Dir: Bryan Forbes. Scr: Bryan Forbes, Peter Marshall. Cast: Malcolm McDowell (Bruce), Nanette Newman (Jill), Georgia Brown (Sarah), Bernard Lee (Uncle Bob). Notes: BAFTA nominations for Best Actress (Newman) and Supporting Actress (Brown); Golden Globe nomination for Best English-Language Foreign Film. VHS.

The Raging Tide (see *Fiddler's Green*).

3655. "The Ragman's Daughter" (Alan Sillitoe, 1963). A young thief falls in love with a middle-class girl despite her parents' objections and other social pressures. The story was the title piece in Sillitoe's 1963 short-story collection. **Adaptation:** *The Ragman's Daughter* (Harpoon/Penelope, 1972). Dir: Harold Becker. Scr: Alan Sillitoe. Cast: Simon Rouse (Tony), Victoria Tennant (Doris), Leslie Sands (Doris's father), Rita Howard (Doris's mother).

3656. *Ragtime* (E. L. Doctorow, 1975, National Book Critics Circle Award). A semi-fictional account of prejudice and dirty politics in New York in the early years of the twentieth century. **Adaptation:** *Ragtime* (Paramount, 1981). Dir: Milos Forman. Scr: Michael Weller. Cast: James Cagney (Rheinlander), Brad Dourif (Younger Brother), Moses Gunn (Booker T. Washington), Elizabeth McGovern (Evelyn), Kenneth McMillan (Willie), Pat O'Brien (Delmas), Howard E. Rollins, Jr. (Coalhouse Walker), Mary Steenburgen (Mother). Notes: Cagney's final performance. Academy Award nominations for Best Screenplay, Supporting Actor (Rollins), Supporting Actress (McGovern), Musical Score, Song, Cinematography, Art Direction, and Costume Design; Golden Globe nominations for Best Picture, Director, Supporting Actress (Steenburgen), Supporting Actor (Rollins), New Stars (McGovern and Rollins), and Song. DVD, VHS.

3657. *Raiders of the Spanish Peaks* (Zane Grey, 1932). As he is about to be hanged for horse stealing, a man escapes and goes to work on a ranch, where he helps to stop cattle rustlers. The story was published in *The Country Gentleman* magazine in January 1932 and issued as a novel in 1938. **Adaptation:** *The Arizona Raiders* (Paramount, 1936). Dir: James P. Hogan. Scr: John W. Krafft, Robert Yost. Cast: Buster Crabbe (Laramie), Raymond Hatton (Tracks), Marsha Hunt (Harriet), Jane Rhodes (Lenta). VHS.

3658. *The Railway Children* (Edith Nesbit, 1906). At the turn of the twentieth children, three children and their mother move to Yorkshire while their father is falsely imprisoned for espionage. Living near a railway, the children wave to and get to know some of the commuters who use the train each day. **Adaptation 1:** *The Railway Children* (EMI/Universal, 1970). Dir: Lionel Jeffries. Scr: Lionel Jeffries. Cast: Dinah Sheridan (Mrs. Waterbury), Bernard Cribbins (Albert), Iain Cuthbertson (Charles), Jenny Agutter (Bobbie). DVD, VHS. **Adaptation 2:** *The Railway Children* (Carlton/PBS, 2000 TV Movie). Dir: Catherine Morshead. Scr: Simon Nye. Cast: Jack Blumenau (Peter), Clare Thomas (Phyllis), Jemima Rooper (Bobbie), Jenny Agutter (Mrs. Waterbury), Michael Kitchen (Mr. Waterbury). DVD, VHS. Notes: The book also inspired British TV series on the BBC in 1951, 1957, and 1968 (DVD, VHS).

Rain (1953) (*see* "Miss Thompson").

3659. *Rain* (Kirsty Gunn, 1994). During a summer vacation at a lakeside cottage in New Zealand in the 1920's, an adolescent girl watches her parents grow apart and her mother engage in a sexual affair. **Adaptation:** *Rain* (Fireworks, 2001). Dir: Christine Jeffs. Scr: Christine Jeffs. Cast: Alicia Fulford-Wierzbicki (Janey), Sarah Peirse (Kate), Marton Csokas (Cady), Alistair Browning (Ed), Aaron Murphy (Jim). Notes: New Zealand Film and Television Awards for Best Actress (Peirse), Supporting Actor (Browning), and Juvenile Performer (Fulford-Wierzbicki). DVD, VHS.

3660. *The Rainbird Pattern* (Victor Canning, 1972). Comic thriller about a fake medium who becomes involved in a plot to swindle an elderly woman by producing the heir she is seeking. **Adaptation:** *Family Plot* (Universal, 1976). Dir: Alfred Hitchcock. Scr: Ernest Lehman. Cast:

Karen Black (Fran), Bruce Dern (George), Barbara Harris (Blanche), William Devane (Arthur), Ed Lauter (Joe), Cathleen Nesbitt (Julia), Katherine Helmond (Mrs. Maloney). Notes: This was Alfred Hitchcock's final film. Golden Globe nomination for Best Actress (Harris). DVD, VHS.

3661. *The Rainbow* (D. H. Lawrence, 1915). Once suppressed as obscene, the novel tells interrelated stories about three generations of a Nottingham family, focusing on the sexual awakening of the youngest daughter. **Adaptation 1:** *The Rainbow* (BBC, 1988 TV Movie). Dir: Stuart Burge. Scr: Anne Devlin. Cast: Imogen Stubbs (Ursula), Martin Wenner (Anton), Sarah-Jane Holm (Dorothy), Jane Gurnett (Anna), Colin Tarrant (Will), Clare Holman (Gudrun). **Adaptation 2:** *The Rainbow* (Vestron, 1989). Dir: Ken Russell. Scr: Ken Russell, Vivian Russell. Cast: Sammi Davis (Ursula), Paul McGann (Anton), Amanda Donohoe (Winifred), Christopher Gable (Will), David Hemmings (Henry), Glenda Jackson (Anna). DVD, VHS.

Rainbow on the River (see *Toinette's Philip*).

3662. *The Rainbow Trail* (Zane Grey, 1912). In the sequel to the Grey's 1912 Western *Riders of the Purple Sage*, a cowboy makes a perilous journey into an isolated valley to rescue his uncle and a young girl who are lost there. The book was originally serialized in *Argosy* magazine in May 1915. **Silent Films:** 1918 and 1925, starring Tom Mix. **Adaptation:** *The Rainbow Trail* (Fox, 1932). Dir: David Howard. Scr: Barry Conners, Philip Klein. Cast: George O'Brien (Shefford), Cecilia Parker (Fay), Minna Gombell (Ruth), Roscoe Ates (Ike). See also *Riders of the Purple Sage*.

3663. *The Rainmaker* (John Grisham, 1995). A David and Goliath story about a young idealistic lawyer who takes on an insurance company that refuses to pay benefits to a dying man. **Adaptation:** *The Rainmaker* (Paramount, 1997). Dir: Francis Ford Coppola. Scr: Francis Ford Coppola. Cast: Matt Damon (Rudy), Danny De Vito (Deck), Claire Danes (Kelly), Jon Voight (Leo), Mary Kay Place (Dot), Dean Stockwell (Judge Hale), Teresa Wright (Miss Birdie), Virginia Madsen (Jackie), Mickey Rourke (Stone). DVD, VHS.

3664. *The Rains Came* (Louis Bromfield, 1937). During the British occupation of India, a married, upper-class woman falls in love with a Hindu doctor in a town threatened by an earthquake and a massive flood. **Adaptation 1:** *The Rains Came* (20th Century–Fox, 1939). Dir:

Clarence Brown. Scr: Philip Dunne, Julien Josephson. Cast: Myrna Loy (Lady Edwina), Tyrone Power (Dr. Safti), George Brent (Tom), Brenda Joyce (Fern), Nigel Bruce (Lord Albert). VHS. **Adaptation 2:** *The Rains of Ranchipur* (20th Century–Fox, 1955). Dir: Jean Negulesco. Scr: Merle Miller. Cast: Lana Turner (Lady Edwina), Richard Burton (Dr. Safti), Fred MacMurray (Tom), Joan Caulfield (Fern), Michael Rennie (Lord Albert).

The Rains of Ranchipur (see *The Rains Came*).

3665. *Raintree Country* (Ross Lockridge, 1948). During the Civil War, a New Orleans belle marries a schoolteacher but finds life with him too boring. Also dissatisfied with married life, her husband enlists as a soldier fighting on the side of the North. **Adaptation:** *Raintree County* (MGM, 1957). Dir: Edward Dmytryk. Scr: Millard Kaufman. Cast: Montgomery Clift (John), Elizabeth Taylor (Susanna), Eva Marie Saint (Nell), Nigel Patrick (Jerusalem), Lee Marvin (Orville), Rod Taylor (Garwood), Agnes Moorehead (Ellen). Notes: Academy Award nominations for Best Actress (Taylor), Musical Score, Art Direction, and Costume Design. VHS.

Raise the Red Lantern (see *Wives and Concubines*).

3666. *Raise the Titanic!* (Clive Cussler, 1976). In order to recover some rare minerals needed to power a laser, a team of adventurers concocts a plan to raise the famous ship, which sank in the North Atlantic in 1912. **Adaptation:** *Raise the Titanic* (ITC/Associated, 1980). Dir: Jerry Jameson. Scr: Adam Kennedy, Eric Hughes. Cast: Jason Robards (Admiral Sandecker), Richard Jordan (Dirk), David Selby (Dr. Seagram), Anne Archer (Dana), Alec Guinness (Bigalow), Bo Brundin (Captain Prevlov), M. Emmet Walsh (Giordino). DVD, VHS.

3667. *Raising a Riot* (Alfred Toombs, 1949). Comic novel about a British man who takes his three rambunctious children and cantankerous father on vacation while his wife is away from home. **Adaptation:** *Raising a Riot* (British Lion/Continental, 1955). Dir: Wendy Toye. Scr: Ian Dalrymple, James Matthews, Hugh Perceval. Cast: Kenneth More (Tony), Shelagh Fraser (Mary), Mandy Miller (Anne), Gary Billings (Peter), Fusty Bentine (Fusty).

3668. *Rally 'Round the Flag, Boys!* (Max Shulman, 1957). The residents of a small community protest the establishment of a military missile site. **Adaptation:** *Rally 'Round the Flag,*

Boys! (20th Century–Fox, 1958). Dir: Leo McCarey. Scr: Claude Binyon, Leo McCarey. Cast: Paul Newman (Harry), Joanne Woodward (Grace), Joan Collins (Angela), Jack Carson (Captain Hoxie), Dwayne Hickman (Grady), Tuesday Weld (Comfort), Gale Gordon (General Thorwold).

3669. *Rambling Rose* (Calder Willingham, 1972). An autobiographical novel set in Georgia during the 1930's about a young boy's fascination with a sensuous woman who comes to work as a domestic at his home. **Adaptation:** *Rambling Rose* (New Line, 1991). Dir: Martha Coolidge. Scr: Calder Willingham. Cast: Laura Dern (Rose), Robert Duvall (Buddy's Father), Diane Ladd (Buddy's Mother), Lukas Haas (Buddy), John Heard (Willcox), Kevin Conway (Dr. Martinson). Notes: Independent Spirit Awards for Best Picture, Director, and Supporting Actress (Ladd), and nominations for Best Actor (Duvall) and Cinematography; Academy Award nominations for Best Actress (Dern) and Supporting Actress (Ladd); Golden Globe nomination for Best Actress (Dern). DVD, VHS.

3670. *Rameau's Niece* (Cathleen Schine, 1993). While researching an erotic novel, a married American writer begins a dangerous flirtation in France. **Adaptation:** *The Misadventures of Margaret* (Granada, 1998). Dir: Brian Skeet. Scr: Brian Skeet. Cast: Parker Posey (Margaret), Jeremy Northam (Edward), Craig Chester (Richard), Elizabeth McGovern (Till), Brooke Shields (Lily), Corbin Bernsen (Art). VHS.

3671. *Ramona* (Helen Hunt Jackson, 1884). An aristocratic half–Indian girl and an Indian chief's son face fall in love and are shunned by white pioneer society. **Silent Films:** 1910 and 1916. **Adaptation 1:** *Ramona* (United Artists, 1928). Dir: Edwin Carewe. Scr: Finis Fox. Cast: Dolores del Rio (Ramona), Warner Baxter (Alessandro), Roland Drew (Felipe), Vera Lewis (Senora Moreno). **Adaptation 2:** *Ramona* (20th Century–Fox, 1936). Dir: Henry King. Scr: Lamar Trotti. Cast: Loretta Young (Ramona), Don Ameche (Alessandro), Kent Taylor (Felipe), Pauline Frederick (Senora Moreno), Jane Darwell (Aunt Ri Hyar), John Carradine (Jim), J. Carrol Naish (Juan).

3672. *Rampage* (Alan Caillou, 1961). Two white hunters in Malaysia compete brutally for the same seductive woman. **Adaptation:** *Rampage* (Warner, 1963). Dir: Phil Karlson. Scr: Robert I. Holt, Marguerite Roberts. Cast: Cely Carillo (Chep), Emile Genest (Schelling), Stefan

Schnabel (the Sakai Chief), David Cadiente (Baka). VHS.

3673. *Ramrod* (Luke Short [pseudonym for Frederick D. Glidden]. 1943). Western about a ruthless female ranch owner and her feud with her father, a rival rancher. The novel was serialized in *The Saturday Evening Post* in March 1943 and published as a book later that year. **Adaptation:** *Ramrod* (United Artists, 1947). Dir: Andre De Toth. Scr: Jack Moffitt, Graham Baker, Cecile Kramer. Cast: Joel McCrea (Dave), Veronica Lake (Connie), Don De Fore (Bill), Donald Crisp (Sheriff Crew), Preston Foster (Frank). VHS.

3674. *Rancid Aluminium* (James Hawes, 1997). When his friend inherits his father's business, a jealous accountant persuades him that they are broke and must seek help from Russian gangsters. **Adaptation:** *Rancid Aluminium* (Trimark, 2000). Dir: Edward Thomas. Scr: James Hawes. Cast: Rhys Ifans (Pete), Joseph Fiennes (Sean), Tara Fitzgerald (Masha), Sadie Frost (Sarah), Steven Berkoff (Mr Kant). DVD, VHS.

3675. *Random Harvest* (James Hilton, 1941). A World War I veteran suffering from amnesia is helped through his delusions by a supportive wife. **Adaptation:** *Random Harvest* (MGM, 1942). Dir: Mervyn Le Roy. Scr: Claudine West, George Froeschel, Arthur Wimperis. Cast: Ronald Colman (Charles Rainier/John Smith), Greer Garson (Paula Ridgeway/Margaret Hansen), Philip Dorn (Dr. Benet), Susan Peters (Kitty), Henry Travers (Dr. Sims), Reginald Owen (Biffer). Notes: Academy Award nominations for Best Picture, Director, Screenplay, Actor (Colman), Supporting Actress (Peters), Musical Score, and Art Direction. DVD, VHS.

3676. *Random Hearts* (Warren Adler, 1984). A dark love story about a policeman and a congresswoman who find each other after discovering that their respective spouses, who were both killed in a plane crash, were actually lovers. **Adaptation:** *Random Hearts* (Columbia, 1999). Dir: Sydney Pollack. Scr: Kurt Luedtke, Darryl Ponicsan. Cast: Harrison Ford (Dutch), Kristin Scott Thomas (Kay), Charles S. Dutton (Alcee), Bonnie Hunt (Wendy), Dennis Haysbert (George), Peter Coyote (Cullen), Sydney Pollack (Carl). DVD, VHS.

3677. "Random Quest" (John Wyndham, 1961). When an experiment goes wrong, a scientist finds himself trapped in another dimension, where he meets a woman he didn't like in his own world but falls in love with her here. When he returns to his own time, he goes searching for the woman and finds her just in time to save her life. The short story was included in Wyndham's 1961 collection *Consider Her Ways and Others.* **Adaptation:** *Quest for Love* (1971). Dir: Ralph Thomas. Scr: Terence Feely. Cast: Joan Collins (Ottilie/Tracy), Tom Bell (Colin), Denholm Elliott (Tom), Laurence Naismith (Sir Henry). Notes: The short story was also the basis for an episode in the 1969 BBC television series *Out of the Unknown.*

3678. *Ransom* (Charles Francis Coe, 1934). A former convict passes off a young girl as an heiress kidnapped years earlier. The novel appeared as a serial in *The Saturday Evening Post* (May 5–June 9, 1934). **Adaptation:** *Nancy Steele Is Missing!* (20th Century–Fox, 1937). Dir: George Marshall. Scr: Gene Fowler, Hal Long. Cast: Victor McLaglen (Danny), Walter Connolly (Michael), Peter Lorre (Sturm).

The Ransom (see *King's Ransom*).

3679. "The Ransom of Red Chief" (O. Henry [pseudonym for William Sydney Porter], 1907). Comic story about two men who kidnap a banker's son hoping to score a large ransom but not realizing what a trial it would be dealing with the hyperactive boy. The story originally appeared in the July 6, 1907, issue of *The Saturday Evening Post*, and was included in O. Henry's 1910 collection *Whirligigs.* **Adaptation 1:** *The Ransom of Red Chief* (Anchor Bay, 1975 TV Movie). Dir: Jeffrey Hayden. Scr: Jim Carlson, Terrence McDonnell. Cast: Strother Martin (Bill), Jack Elam (Sam), William Mims (Ebeneezer), Pat Petersen (Red Chief). VHS. **Adaptation 2:** *The Ransom of Red Chief* (Hallmark, 1998 TV Movie). Dir: Bob Clark. Scr: Ed Naha. Cast: Christopher Lloyd (Sam), Michael Jeter (Bill), Alan Ruck (Ambrose), Kaitlin Hopkins (Agnes), Richard Riehle (Sheriff Yankum).

3680. "Ransom, One Million Dollars" (Damon Runyon, 1933). To prevent his wealthy mother from marrying a man he despises, a son hires an ex-convict to fake his kidnapping. The short story was published in *Cosmopolitan* in October 1933. **Adaptation:** *Million Dollar Ransom* (Universal, 1934). Dir: Murray Roth. Scr: William R. Lipman, Ben Ryan. Cast: Henry Kolker (Dr. Davis), Edward Arnold (Vincent), Charles Coleman (Towers), Andy Devine (Careful).

3681. *The Rap* (Ernest Brawley, 1974). A corrupt prison guard takes bribes from a black revolutionary prisoner and from the people who want to kill him. **Adaptation:** *Fast-Walking* (Lorimar/Pickman, 1982). Dir: James B. Harris. Scr:

James B. Harris. Cast: James Woods (Fast-Walking), Tim McIntire (Wasco), Kay Lenz (Moke), Robert Hooks (William), Charles Weldon (Officer Jackson), M. Emmet Walsh (Sergeant Sanger). VHS.

The Rape of Malaya (see *A Town Like Alice*).

Rape Me (see *Baise-Moi*).

3682. "Rappaccini's Daughter" (Nathaniel Hawthorne, 1844). A deranged scientist inoculates his beautiful young daughter with poison to insure that she remains in her garden of poisonous plants. The story originally appeared in 1844 in *Democratic Review* and subsequently appeared in Hawthorne's 1846 collection *Mosses from an Old Manse.* **Adaptation 1:** *Twice-Told Tales* (United Artists, 1963). Dir: Sidney Salkow. Scr: Robert E. Kent. Cast: Vincent Price (Pyncheon), Beverly Garland (Alice), Jacqueline De Wit (Hannah). Notes: This film contains shortened versions of three Hawthorne works: "Rappaccini's Daughter," "Dr. Heidegger's Experiment" and *The House of the Seven Gables.* DVD, VHS. See also "Dr. Heidegger's Experiment" and *The House of the Seven Gables.* **Adaptation 2:** *Rappaccini's Daughter* (PBS/American Short Story, 1980 TV Movie). Dir: Dezso Magyar. Scr: Herbert Hartig. Cast: Kristoffer Tabori (Giovanni), Kathleen Beller (Beatrice), Michael Egan (Baglioni), Leonardo Cimino (Rappaccini). VHS.

Rapture (see *Rapture in My Rags*).

3683. *Rapture in My Rags* (Phyllis Hastings, 1954). A teenaged girl falls in love with a murderer on the run from justice. **Adaptation:** *Rapture* (Panoramic/International Classics, 1965). Dir: John Guillermin. Scr: Stanley Mann. Cast: Patricia Gozzi (Agnes), Melvyn Douglas (Frederick), Dean Stockwell (Joseph), Gunnel Lindblom (Karen).

3684. *Rascal: A Memoir of a Better Era* (Sterling North, 1963, Newbery Honor Book). Set in 1918, North's memoir of his experiences when he was eleven years old. His mother having died and his father away a great deal on business, the lonely boy adopted a young raccoon and named him Rascal. As the friendly raccoon aged, however, North had to make the painful decision to set it free. **Adaptation:** *Rascal* (Disney/Buena Vista, 1969). Dir: Norman Tokar. Scr: Harold Swanton. Cast: Steve Forrest (Willard), Bill Mumy (Sterling), Elsa Lanchester (Mrs. Satterfield), Henry Jones (Garth). DVD, VHS.

3685. "Rashomon" (Ryunosuke Akutagawa, 1915). Short story about four witness to a crime and their differing accounts of what they saw. **Adaptation:** *Rashomon*; also released as *In the Woods* (Daiei/RKO 1950). Dir: Akira Kurosawa. Scr: Akira Kurosawa, Shinobu Hashimoto. Cast: Toshiro Mifune (Tajomaru), Machiko Kyo (Masako), Masayuki Mori (Takehiro), Takashi Shimura (the Woodcutter). Notes: The screenplay combines elements from this story and Akutagawa's 1921 short story "In the Grove." Academy Award for Best Foreign-Language Film; National Board of Review Awards for Best Foreign-Language Film and Director; BAFTA nominations for Best Film from Any Source. DVD, VHS.

3686. *A Rather English Marriage* (Angela Lambert, 1992). After their wives die in the same hospital on the same night, two widowers put aside their class differences and move in together as they try to rebuild their lives. **Adaptation:** *A Rather English Marriage* (BBC, 1998 TV Movie). Dir: Paul Seed. Scr: Andrew Davies. Cast: Albert Finney (Reggie), Tom Courtenay (Roy), Joanna Lumley (Liz). Notes: BAFTA Awards for Best Television Drama, Actor (Courtenay), Music, and Editing, and nominations for Best Television Actor (Finney), Supporting Actress (Lumley), and Sound; Peabody Award for Best Television Drama. VHS.

3687. *Ratman's Notebooks* (Stephen Gilbert [pseudonym for Gilbert Ralston], 1968). A young social misfit trains a group of rats to take revenge on his tormentors. **Adaptation 1:** *Willard* (Cinerama, 1971). Dir: Daniel Mann. Scr: Gilbert Ralston. Cast: Bruce Davison (Willard), Elsa Lanchester (Henrietta), Ernest Borgnine (Al), Sondra Locke (Joan). VHS. **Adaptation 2:** *Willard* (New Line, 2003). Dir: Glen Morgan. Scr: Gilbert Ralston (1971 screenplay), Glen Morgan. Cast: Crispin Glover (Willard), R. Lee Ermey (Frank), Laura Elena Harring (Cathryn), Jackie Burroughs (Henrietta). DVD, VHS.

3688. *The Raven in the Foregate* (Ellis Peters [pseudonym for Edith Pargeter], 1986). The twelfth installment in Peters' twenty-volume series (1977–1994) featuring Brother Cadfael, a twelfth-century monk who, following service in the Crusades, tends to the herbarium at Shrewsbury Abbey and solves crimes. In this book, Brother Cadfael investigates the murder of a mean-spirited parish priest. **Adaptation:** *Cadfael: The Raven in the Foregate* (ITV/PBS, 1997 TV Movie series). Dir: Ken Grieve. Scr: Russell Lewis,

Paul Pender, Ben Rostul, Richard Stoneman. Cast: Derek Jacobi (Brother Cadfael), Michael Culver (Prior Robert), Anthony Green (Hugh), Julian Firth (Brother Jerome). DVD, VHS.

3689. *The Ravine* (Kendal Young, 1962). Someone is raping young girls in the woods near a school, and a teacher allows herself to be used as bait to lure him out. **Adaptation:** *Assault*; released in the U.S. as *In the Devil's Garden*; also known as *The Creepers; Satan's Playthings; Tower of Terror* (Rank, 1971). Dir: Sidney Hayers. Scr: John Kruse. Cast: Suzy Kendall (Julie), Frank Finlay (Detective Velyan), Freddie Jones (News Reporter). VHS.

3690. *The Rawhide Years* (Norman A. Fox, 1953). Western about an honest riverboat gambler who is unjustly accused of murder and must clear his name before he can settle down with the woman he loves. **Adaptation:** *The Rawhide Years* (Universal International, 1955). Dir: Rudolph Mate. Scr: Robert Presnell, Jr., D. D. Beauchamp, Earl Felton. Cast: Tony Curtis (Ben), Colleen Miller (Zoe), Arthur Kennedy (Rick), William Demarest (Brand), William Gargan (Marshal Sommers), Peter van Eyck (Andre).

3691. *Razorback* (Peter Brennan, 1981). Thriller about a vicious giant pig terrorizing people in Australia. **Adaptation:** *Razorback* (Warner, 1984). Dir: Russell Mulcahy. Scr: Everett De Roche. Cast: Gregory Harrison (Carl), Arkie Whiteley (Sarah), Bill Kerr (Jake), Chris Haywood (Benny). VHS.

3692. *The Razor's Edge* (W. Somerset Maugham, 1944). A disillusioned young man from Chicago returns from World War I and then travels to Paris and India to seek self-fulfillment. **Adaptation 1:** *The Razor's Edge* (20th Century–Fox, 1946). Dir: Edmund Goulding. Scr: Lamar Trotti. Cast: Tyrone Power (Larry), Gene Tierney (Isabel), John Payne (Gray), Anne Baxter (Sophie), Clifton Webb (Elliott). Notes: Academy Award for Best Supporting Actress (Baxter), and nominations for Best Picture, Supporting Actor (Webb), and Art Direction; Golden Globe Awards for Best Supporting Actress (Baxter) and Supporting Actor (Webb). VHS. **Adaptation 2:** *The Razor's Edge* (Columbia, 1984). Dir: John Byrum. Scr: John Byrum, Bill Murray. Cast: Bill Murray (Larry), Theresa Russell (Sophie), Catherine Hicks (Isabel), Denholm Elliott (Elliott), James Keach (Gray), Peter Vaughan (Mackenzie), Brian Doyle-Murray (Piedmont). DVD, VHS.

Re-Animator (*see* "Herbert West, Reanimator").

Reach for Glory (see *The Custard Boys*).

3693. *Reach for the Sky: The Story of Douglas Bader, Legless Ace of the Battle of Britain* (Paul Brickhill, 1954). Biography of a British flying ace who lost both legs in a 1931 accident and went on to become a heroic pilot during World War II. **Adaptation:** *Reach for the Sky* (Rank, 1956). Dir: Lewis Gilbert. Scr: Lewis Gilbert. Cast: Kenneth More (Bader), Muriel Pavlow (Thelma), Lyndon Brook (Johnny), Lee Patterson (Stan), Alexander Knox (Mr. Joyce), Dorothy Alison (Nurse Brace). Notes: BAFTA Award for Best British Film and nominations for Best Screenplay, Actor (More), and Actress (Alison). DVD, VHS.

Reaching for the Sun (see *F. O. B. Detroit*).

The Real McCoy (see *Bellman and True*).

3694. *Real Women* (Susan Oudot, 1995). Five women who were raised together in London reunite as adults and reflect on their unsatisfying lives. **Adaptation:** *Real Women* (BBC, 1998 TV Movie). Dir: Philip Davis. Scr: Susan Oudot. Cast: Pauline Quirke (Mandy), Frances Barber (Anna), Michelle Collins (Susie), Lesley Manville (Karen), Gwyneth Strong (Janet). VHS.

Real Women II (see *All That I Am*).

3695. *Reaper* (Ben Mezrich, 1998). Techothriller about a computer virus that leaves the machine and preys upon people. **Adaptation:** *Fatal Error* (TBS, 1999 TV Movie). Dir: Armand Mastroianni. Scr: Rockne O'Bannon, Vincent Monton, Matt Dorff. Cast: Antonio Sabato, Jr. (Nick), Janine Turner (Samantha), Robert Wagner (Albert), Jason Schombing (Charlie). DVD, VHS.

3696. *Rear Guard* (James Warner Bellah, 1951). An army doctor leads a wagon train to Wyoming, battling illness and hostile Indians along the way. **Adaptation:** *The Command* (Warner, 1954). Dir: David Butler. Scr: Russell Hughes, Samuel Fuller. Cast: Guy Madison (Robert), Joan Weldon (Martha), James Whitmore (Elliott).

Rear Window (see *It Had to Be Murder*).

3697. *Rebecca* (Daphne Du Maurier, 1938). A pretty young orphan marries an older aristocratic man obsessed with his first wife, Rebecca. **Adaptation 1:** *Rebecca* (United Artists, 1940). Dir: Alfred Hitchcock. Scr: Philip MacDonald, Michael Hogan, Robert E. Sherwood, Joan Harrison. Cast: Laurence Olivier (Maxim), Joan

Fontaine (Mrs. de Winter), George Sanders (Jack), Judith Anderson (Mrs. Danvers), Gladys Cooper (Beatrice), Nigel Bruce (Giles). Notes: Academy Awards for Best Picture and Cinematography, and nominations for Best Director, Screenplay, Actor (Olivier), Actress (Fontaine), Supporting Actress (Anderson), Musical Score, Editing, Art Direction, and Special Effects. DVD, VHS. **Adaptation 2:** *Rebecca* (BBC/PBS, 1979 TV Movie). Dir: Simon Langton. Scr: Hugh Whitemore. Cast: Jeremy Brett (Maxim), Joanna David (Mrs. de Winter), Elspeth March (Mrs. van Hopper), Anna Massey (Mrs. Danvers). **Adaptation 3:** *Rebecca* (ITV/PBS, 1997 TV Movie). Dir: Jim O'Brien. Scr: Arthur Hopcraft. Cast: Charles Dance (Maxim), Emilia Fox (Mrs. de Winter), Diana Rigg (Mrs. Danvers), Faye Dunaway (Mrs. Van Hopper). Notes: Emmy Award for Outstanding Supporting Actress (Rigg). DVD, VHS.

3698. *Rebecca of Sunnybrook Farm* (Kate Douglas Wiggin, 1903). A cheerful little girl is sent to live with her grumpy aunts and ends up cheering them up and finding ways to help the people of their small town. The novel was adapted as a Broadway play by Wiggin and Charlotte Thompson in 1910. **Silent Film:** 1917, directed by Marshall Neilan and starring Mary Pickford (VHS). **Adaptation 1:** *Rebecca of Sunnybrook Farm* (Fox, 1932). Dir: Alfred Santell. Scr: S. N. Behrman, Sonya Levien. Cast: Marian Nixon (Rebecca), Ralph Bellamy (Dr. Ladd), Mae Marsh (Aunt Jane), Alan Hale (Mr. Simpson). **Adaptation 2:** *Rebecca of Sunnybrook Farm* (20th Century–Fox, 1938). Dir: Allan Dwan. Scr: Don Ettlinger, Karl Tunberg. Cast: Shirley Temple (Rebecca), Randolph Scott (Tony), Jack Haley (Orville), Gloria Stuart (Gwen). VHS.

The Rebel Son (*see* "Taras Bulba").

3699. *Recalled to Life* (Reginald Hill, 1992). In the thirteenth installment of Hill's popular series (1970–2004) featuring British policemen Andrew Dalziel and Peter Pascoe, the detectives investigate three murders linked to the assassinations of a cabinet minister and an American diplomat three decades earlier. **Adaptation:** *Dalziel and Pascoe: Recalled to Life* (BBC/A&E, 1999 TV Movie). Dir: Suri Krishnamma. Scr: Timothy Prager. Cast: Warren Clarke (Dalziel), Colin Buchanan (Pascoe), Susannah Corbett (Ellie), David Royle (Edgar).

The Reckless Moment (see *The Blank Wall*).

3700. *The Reckoning* (Hugh Atkinson, 1965).

After a local man's wife is found murdered, people from a small town pursue their main suspect, an immigrant who has disappeared. **Adaptation:** *Weekend at Shadows* (Australian Film Commission, 1978). Dir: Tom Jeffrey. Scr: Peter Yeldham. Cast: John Waters (Rabbit), Wyn Roberts (Sergeant Caxton), Graham Rouse (Ab), Melissa Jaffer (Vi).

The Reckoning (1969) (see *The Harp That Once*).

The Reckoning (2003) (see *Morality Play*).

3701. *Recovery* (Steven L. Thompson, 1980). High-tech thriller about two American intelligence officers investigating a Russian missile base in East Germany during the Cold War. **Adaptation:** *Honor Bound* (Jadran/TCA, 1988). Dir: Jeannot Szwarc. Scr: Aiken Woodruff. Cast: Tom Skerritt (Cahill), George Dzundza (Wocjinski), John Philbin (Young), Gabrielle Lazure (Erika). VHS.

3702. *The Re-Creation of Brian Kent* (Harold Bell Wright, 1919). A polo player goes to Missouri, where he helps protect a woman and her niece from an unscrupulous businessman with designs on their ranch. **Adaptation:** *Wild Brian Kent* (20th Century–Fox, 1936). Dir: Howard Bretherton. Scr: James Gruen, Earle Snell. Cast: Ralph Bellamy (Brian), Mae Clarke (Betty), Helen Lowell (Aunt Sue).

3703. *The Rector's Wife* (Joanna Trollope, 1991). After a pastor is passed over for promotion, his wife takes a job at a supermarket so that she can give her children the things they want and meets with the disapproval of her husband and his congregation. **Adaptation:** *The Rector's Wife* (Channel 4/PBS, 1994 TV Movie). Dir: Giles Foster. Scr: Hugh Whitemore. Cast: Miles Anderson (Patrick), Thomas Bradford (Barnaby), Orla Brady (Sister Josephine), Jonathan Coy (Peter), Lucy Dawson (Flora). VHS.

3704. *Red Alert* (Peter George [pseudonym for Peter Bryant], 1958). Black comedy about an insane American general who launches nuclear missiles against Russia and the race by the President and the military to save the world from annihilation. The book was published in the UK under the title *Two Hours to Doom*. **Adaptation:** *Dr. Strangelove, or How I Learned to Stop Worrying and Love the Bomb* (Columbia, 1964). Dir: Stanley Kubrick. Scr: Stanley Kubrick, Terry Southern, Peter George. Cast: Peter Sellers (Captain Mandrake/President Muffley/Dr. Strangelove), George C. Scott (General Turgidson), Sterling

Hayden (General Ripper), Keenan Wynn (Colonel Guano), Slim Pickens (Major Kong), Peter Bull (Ambassador de Sadesky), James Earl Jones (Lieutenant Zogg). Notes: BAFTA Awards for Best British Film and Art Direction, and nominations for Best Screenplay, Actor (Sellers), and Foreign Actor (Hayden); Academy Award nomination for Best Picture, Director, Screenplay, and Actor (Sellers). DVD, VHS.

3705. *The Red and the Black* (Stendhal [pseudonym for Marie-Henri Beyle], 1830). In eighteenth-century France, a lower-class man is obsessed with entering high society. The French novel was originally titled *Le Rouge et le Noir*. **Adaptation:** *The Red and the Black*; released in the UK as *Scarlet and Black* (DCA, 1954). Dir: Claude Autant-Lara. Scr: Jean Aurenche, Claude Autant-Lara, Pierre Bost. Cast: Gerard Philipe (Julien), Danielle Darrieux (Madame de Renal), Antonella Lualdi (Mathilde), Jean Mercure (Marquis de La Mole). VHS. Notes: Television adaptations were also produced in France in 1961 and 1998.

3706. *The Red Badge of Courage: An Episode of the American Civil War* (Stephen Crane, 1895). During the Civil War, a young Union soldier contemplates desertion and discovers the consequences of cowardice and the meaning of courage. **Adaptation 1:** *The Red Badge of Courage* (MGM, 1951). Dir: John Huston. Scr: Albert Band, John Huston. Cast: Audie Murphy (Henry), Bill Mauldin (Tom), John Dierkes (Jim), Andy Devine (the Cheerful Soldier), Robert Easton Burke (Thompson), Douglas Dick (the Lieutenant), Tim Durant (the General), Arthur Hunnicutt (Bill), Royal Dano (the Tattered Soldier). DVD, VHS. **Adaptation 2:** *The Red Badge of Courage* (NBC, 1974 TV Movie). Dir: Lee Philips. Scr: John Gay. Cast: Richard Thomas (Henry), Michael Brandon (Jim), Wendell Burton (Tom), Charles Aidman (the Tattered Soldier).

3707. *The Red Beret: The Story of the Parachute Regiment at War, 1940–1945.* (Hilary St. George Saunders, 1950). A history of British paratroopers during World War II. **Adaptation:** *The Red Beret*; released in the U.S. as *Paratrooper* (Warwick/Columbia, 1953). Dir: Terence Young. Scr: Sy Bartlett, Richard Maibaum, Frank S. Nugent. Cast: Alan Ladd (Canada), Leo Genn (Major Snow), Susan Stephen (Penny), Harry Andrews (the Sergeant Major), Donald Houston (Taffy). Notes: The screenplay presents the fictional situation of an American soldier who joins the British paratroopers in 1940.

Red Canyon (see *Wildfire*).

The Red Circle (see *The Crimson Circle*).

The Red Danube (see *Vespers in Vienna*).

3708. *Red Dragon* (Thomas Harris, 1981). An FBI agent tracking a serial killer has to learn to think like the criminal in order to catch him. The book features the first appearance of Hannibal Lecter as a jailed criminal. Of course, this character would take center stage in Harris's subsequent books, *The Silence of the Lambs* and *Hannibal*. **Adaptation 1:** *Manhunter* (De Laurentiis/Anchor Bay, 1986). Dir: Michael Mann. Scr: Michael Mann. Cast: William Petersen (Will), Kim Greist (Molly), Joan Allen (Reba), Brian Cox (Dr. Hannibal Lecter), Dennis Farina (Jack). DVD, VHS. **Adaptation 2:** *Red Dragon* (De Laurentiis/MGM, 2002). Dir: Brett Ratner. Scr: Ted Tally. Cast: Anthony Hopkins (Dr. Hannibal Lecter), Edward Norton (Will), Ralph Fiennes (Francis), Harvey Keitel (Jack), Emily Watson (Reba), Mary-Louise Parker (Molly), Philip Seymour Hoffman (Freddy), Anthony Heald (Dr. Chilton). DVD, VHS. See also *The Silence of the Lambs* and *Hannibal*.

3709. *A Red File for Callan* (James Mitchell, 1969). Espionage tale about an aging British agent who is assigned to assassinate a German businessman. The book was published in the UK as *A Magnum for Schneider*. **Adaptation:** *Callan*; released on video as *The Neutralizer* and as *This Is Callan* (Cinema National, 1974). Dir: Don Sharp. Scr: James Mitchell. Cast: Edward Woodward (Callan), Eric Porter (Hunter), Carl Mohner (Schneider), Catherine Schell (Jenny). DVD, VHS.

3710. "Red for Danger" (Evadne Price [pseudonym for Helen Zenna Smith], 1936). A cab driver picks up a fare and becomes involved in a spy plot. The story originally appeared in August 22, 1936, issue of *The Thriller*. **Adaptation:** *Blondes for Danger* (British Lion, 1938). Dir: Jack Raymond. Scr: Gerald Elliott. Cast: Gordon Harker (Alf), Enid Stamp-Taylor (Valerie), Janet Johnson (Ann).

3711. *Red Harvest* (Dashiell Hammett, 1929). When his client is murdered, a detective pursues a criminal gang in a small town. **Adaptation:** *Roadhouse Nights* (Paramount, 1930). Dir: Hobart Henley. Scr: Garrett Fort, Ben Hecht, Cast: Helen Morgan (Lola), Charles Ruggles (Willie), Fred Kohler (Sam), Jimmy Durante (Daffy). Notes: In the film, a reporter exposes gangsters operating a night club. Although un-credited, the novel also inspired Joel and Ethan Coen's 1990 film *Miller's Crossing* (DVD, VHS).

3712. *Red-Headed Woman* (Katharine Brush, 1931). A gold-digging employee marries her wealthy boss but finds that she is not accepted in his social circles. The novel appeared as a seven part serial in *The Saturday Evening Post* (August 22–October 3, 1931). **Adaptation:** *Red-Headed Woman* (MGM, 1932). Dir: Jack Conway. Scr: Anita Loos. Cast: Jean Harlow (Lillian), Chester Morris (William), Lewis Stone (Mr. Legendre), Leila Hyams (Irene), Una Merkel (Sally), Henry Stephenson (Charles), May Robson (Aunt Jane), Charles Boyer (Albert). VHS.

3713. *The Red House* (George Agnew Chamberlain, 1945). A farmer is obsessed with a dark secret linked to a red house he refuses to approach. **Adaptation:** *The Red House* (United Artists, 1947). Dir: Delmer Daves. Scr: Delmer Daves. Cast: Edward G. Robinson (Pete), Lon McCallister (Nath), Judith Anderson (Ellen), Rory Calhoun (Teller), Allene Roberts (Meg), Julie London (Tibby). DVD, VHS.

3714. *Red Hugh, Prince of Donegal* (Robert T. Reilly, 1957). Children's book about Red Hugh O'Donnell, a spirited Irish teenager who, in 1587, tries to unite Ireland and is imprisoned in Dublin Castle by a treacherous nobleman. **Adaptation:** *The Fighting Prince of Donegal* (Disney/Buena Vista, 1966). Dir: Michael O'Herlihy. Scr: Robert Westerby. Cast: Peter McEnery (Hugh), Susan Hampshire (Kathleen), Tom Adams (Henry), Gordon Jackson (Captain Leeds). VHS.

3715. "The Red Pony" (John Steinbeck, 1938). A young boy receives a pony from his father, and when the pony dies accidentally, he loses faith in his family. The four-part story was originally published in magazine installments in 1933 (*North American Review*, November and December), 1936 (*Argosy*, August), and 1937 (*Harper's Magazine*, August) and brought together in Steinbeck's 1938 short-story collection *The Long Valley*. **Adaptation 1:** *The Red Pony* (Republic, 1949). Dir: Lewis Milestone. Scr: John Steinbeck. Cast: Myrna Loy (Alice), Robert Mitchum (Billy), Louis Calhern (Grandfather), Shepperd Strudwick (Fred), Peter Miles (Tom). DVD, VHS. **Adaptation 2:** *The Red Pony* (NBC, 1973 TV Movie). Dir: Robert Totten. Scr: Ron Bishop, Robert Totten. Cast: Henry Fonda (Carl), Maureen O'Hara (Ruth), Ben Johnson (Jess), Jack Elam (Grandfather), Clint Howard (Jody).

3716. *Red Sky at Morning* (Richard Bradford, 1968). During World War II, a military officer's adolescent children have difficulty adjusting to their new life in New Mexico. **Adaptation:** *Red Sky at Morning* (Universal, 1971). Dir: James Goldstone. Scr: Marguerite Roberts. Cast: Richard Thomas (Joshua), Catherine Burns (Marcia), Desi Arnaz, Jr. (William), Richard Crenna (Frank), Claire Bloom (Ann), John Colicos (Jimbob), Harry Guardino (Romeo), Strother Martin (John), Nehemiah Persoff (Amadeo).

3717. *Red Sorghum* (Mo Yan [pseudonym for Guan Moye], 1987). The Chinese novel *Hong gao liang jiatsu* concerns three generations of a single family spanning seven decades and focusing on the love affair between the narrator's grandparents in the 1920's. The book was translated into English in 1993. **Adaptation:** *Red Sorghum* (New Yorker, 1987). Dir: Yimou Zhang. Scr: Jianyu Chen, Wei Zhu. Cast: Li Gong (Grandma), Wen Jiang (Grandpa), Rujun Ten (Uncle Luohan). Notes: Originally released as *Hong gao liang* and shown with subtitles. Golden Rooster Award (China) for Best Film and nominations for Best Director, Actor (Jiang), and Art Direction. VHS.

3718. *Red Wagon* (Eleanor Smith, 1930). A tale of passion and jealousy among gypsies in a traveling circus. **Adaptation:** *Red Wagon* (British International/First Division, 1933). Dir: Paul L. Stein. Scr: Roger Burford, Edward Knoblock, Arthur B. Woods. Cast: Charles Bickford (Joe), Raquel Torres (Sheba/Starlina), Greta Nissen (Zara), Don Alvarado (Davey).

3719. *The Reef* (Edith Wharton, 1912). During the early twentieth century, an American widow in France resumes a romantic affair with a former lover only to discover that he is also involved with her children's nanny. **Adaptation:** *The Reef*; broadcast in the U.S. as *Passion's Way* (CBS, 1999 TV Movie). Dir: Robert Allan Ackerman. Scr: William Hanley. Cast: Sela Ward (Anna), Timothy Dalton (George), Alicia Witt (Sophie), Jamie Glover (Owen), Cynthia Harris (Adelaide), Leslie Caron (Regine). DVD, VHS.

A Reflection of Fear (see *Go to Thy Deathbed*).

3720. *Reflections in a Golden Eye* (Carson McCullers, 1941). The story of a homosexual officer at a military base in Georgia in the 1930's. **Adaptation:** *Reflections in a Golden Eye* (Warner/Seven Arts, 1967). Dir: John Huston. Scr: Gladys Hill, Chapman Mortimer. Cast: Elizabeth Taylor (Leonora), Marlon Brando (Weldon), Brian Keith (Morris), Julie Harris (Alison). VHS.

Reflections of Murder (see *The Woman Who Was*).

3721. *Regeneration* (Pat Barker, 1991). In 1917, poet Siegfried Sassoon is sent to an asylum because of his opposition to World War I. There he meets a like-minded soul, poet Wilfred Owen. **Adaptation:** *Regeneration*; released in the U.S. as *Behind the Lines* (BBC/Alliance, 1997). Dir: Gillies MacKinnon. Scr: Allan Scott. Cast: Jonathan Pryce (Rivers), James Wilby (Sassoon), Jonny Lee Miller (Prior), Stuart Bunce (Owen), Tanya Allen (Sarah). Notes: BAFTA nomination for Best British Film; British Independent Film Awards nominatons for Best Picture, Director, and Actor (Pryce); Genie Award nominations (Canada) for Best Picture, Director, Screenplay, Actor (Pryce), Art Direction, Cinematography, Costume Design, Editing, Musical Score, and Sound. DVD, VHS.

3722. *The Reincarnation of Peter Proud* (Max Ehrlich, 1974). A history professor is possessed by the spirit of a man murdered years earlier. **Adaptation:** *The Reincarnation of Peter Proud* (American International, 1975). Dir: J. Lee Thompson. Scr: Max Ehrlich. Cast: Michael Sarrazin (Peter), Jennifer O'Neill (Ann), Margot Kidder (Marcia), Cornelia Sharpe (Nora). VHS.

3723. *The Reivers* (William Faulkner, 1962, Pulitzer Prize). Set at the turn of the twentieth century, Faulkner's nostalgic last novel is about a young man who borrows a car and takes a road trip to Memphis with a white handyman and a black household servant. **Adaptation:** *The Reivers*; also released as *The Yellow Winton Flyer* (National General/Viacom, 1969). Dir: Mark Rydell. Scr: Irving Ravetch, Harriet Frank, Jr. Cast: Steve McQueen (Boon), Sharon Farrell (Corrie), Ruth White (Miss Reba), Michael Constantine (Mr. Binford), Rupert Crosse (Ned), Mitch Vogel (Lucius), Clifton James (Butch). Notes: Academy Award nominations for Best Supporting Actor (Crosse) and Musical Score; Golden Globe nominations for Best Actor (McQueen) and Supporting Actor (Vogel). DVD, VHS.

3724. *Relentless* (Brian Garfield, 1972). After his uncle is killed and a woman taken hostage by robbers, a Native American Arizona state trooper tracks the killers into the mountains. **Adaptation:** *Relentless* (CBS, 1977 TV Movie). Dir: Lee H. Katzin. Scr: Sam Rolfe. Cast: Will Sampson (Sam), Monte Markham (Paul), John Hillerman (Leo), Marianna Hill (Annie).

3725. *The Relic* (Douglas J. Preston and Lincoln Child, 1995). Thriller about American scientists who accidentally bring a murderous monster into the country from South America. **Adaptation:** *The Relic* (Paramount, 1997). Dir: Peter Hyams. Scr: Amy Holden Jones, John Raffo, Rick Jaffa, Amanda Silver. Cast: Penelope Ann Miller (Dr. Green), Tom Sizemore (Lieutenant D'Agosta), Linda Hunt (Dr. Cuthbert), James Whitmore (Dr. Frock). DVD, VHS.

3726. *The Religion* (Nicholas Conde, 1982). Thriller in which a widower and his son move to New York City and become involved with occult religion and child sacrifice. **Adaptation:** *The Believers* (Orion, 1987). Dir: John Schlesinger. Scr: Mark Frost. Cast: Martin Sheen (Cal), Helen Shaver (Jessica), Harley Cross (Chris), Robert Loggia (Lieutenant McTaggert). DVD, VHS.

3727. *The Reluctant Assassin* (John Godey [pseudonym for Morton Freedgood], 1966). Comic mystery about a struggling actor mistaken for a notorious gangster. **Adaptation:** *Never a Dull Moment* (Disney/Buena Vista, 1968). Dir: Jerry Paris. Scr: A. J. Carothers. Cast: Dick Van Dyke (Jack), Edward G. Robinson (Leo), Dorothy Provine (Sally), Henry Silva (Frank). DVD, VHS.

3728. *The Reluctant Landlord* (Scott Corbett, 1950). Autobiographical novel about a writer and his wife who invest in an apartment building after World War II and must contend with their eccentric tenants. **Adaptation:** *Love Nest* (20th Century–Fox, 1951). Dir: Joseph Newman. Scr: I. A. L. Diamond. Cast: June Haver (Connie), William Lundigan (Jim), Frank Fay (Charley), Marilyn Monroe (Roberta). DVD, VHS.

3729. *The Reluctant Widow* (Georgette Heyer, 1946). During the Napoleonic Wars of the eighteenth century, a French widow is coerced into becoming a spy. **Adaptation:** *The Reluctant Widow* (Two Cities/Fine Arts, 1951). Dir: Bernard Knowles. Scr: J. B. Boothroyd, Gordon Wellesley. Cast: Jean Kent (Helena), Guy Rolfe (Lord Carlyon), Paul Dupuis (Lord Nivelle), Lana Morris (Becky), Kathleen Byron (Annette).

3730. *The Remains of the Day* (Kazuo Ishiguro, 1989). A decorous butler in post World War II Britain discovers that his loyalty to his aristocratic master has been misplaced. **Adaptation:** *The Remains of the Day* (Columbia, 1993). Dir: James Ivory. Scr: Ruth Prawer Jhabvala. Cast: Christopher Reeve (Lewis), Anthony Hopkins (Stevens), Emma Thompson (Miss Kenton), James Fox (Lord Darlington). Notes: National Board of Review Award for Best Actor (Hopkins); Academy Award nominations for Best Picture, Director, Screenplay, Actor (Hopkins), Actress (Thompson), Musical Score, Art Direction, and

Costume Design; BAFTA nominations for Best Picture, Director, Screenplay, Actor (Hopkins), Actress (Thompson), and Cinematography; Golden Globe nominations for Best Picture, Director, Screenplay, Actor (Hopkins), and Actress (Thompson). DVD, VHS.

3731. *Remember* (Barbara Taylor Bradford, 1991). A woman travels throughout the world to investigate the suicide of her fiancé and discovers that he was leading a double life. **Adaptation:** *Remember* (Anchor Bay, 1993 TV Movie). Dir: John Herzfeld. Scr: Mart Crowley, Shelley List, Jonathan Estrin, John Herzfeld. Cast: Donna Mills (Nicki), Stephen Collins (Clee), Derek de Lint (Charles), Ian Richardson (Philip), Gail Strickland (Amanda). VHS.

Remember Last Night? (see *The Hangover Murders*).

3732. *Remembering America: A Voice from the Sixties* (Richard N. Goodwin, 1988). Goodwin's memoir of the 1960's includes his experiences as a young lawyer investigating and exposing the quiz-show scandal involving the program *Twenty-One*. **Adaptation:** *Quiz Show* (Buena Vista, 1994). Dir: Robert Redford. Scr: Paul Attanasio. Cast: John Turturro (Stempel), Rob Morrow (Goodwin), Ralph Fiennes (Charles Van Doren), Paul Scofield (Mark Van Doren), David Paymer (Enright), Hank Azaria (Freedman), Mira Sorvino (Sandra). Notes: Academy Award nominations for Best Picture, Director, Screenplay, and Supporting Actor (Scofield); Golden Globe nominations for Best Film, Director, Screenplay, and Supporting Actor (Turturro). DVD, VHS.

3733. *Remembrance* (Danielle Steel, 1981). During World War II, a beautiful Italian princess is left widowed in New York and struggling against his patrician family's hostility toward her. **Adaptation:** *Remembrance* (NBC, 1996 TV Movie). Dir: Bethany Rooney. Scr: David Ambrose. Cast: Eva La Rue Callahan (Princess Serena), Jeffrey Nordling (Brad), James Calvert (Teddy), Michael Lowry (Vasili). VHS.

Remo Williams: The Adventure Begins (see *Created*).

3734. *The Remorseful Day* (Colin Dexter, 2000). The final installment in Dexter's popular thirteen-novel series (1975–2000) featuring Chief Inspector Endeavour Morse of Oxford, England. In this book, Inspector Morse unofficially investigates the murder of a woman with whom he was once involved, but problems with his health lead to his own death. **Adaptation:** *Inspector Morse: The Remorseful Day* (Carlton/PBS, 2000 TV Movie series). Dir: Jack Gold. Scr: Stephen Churchett. Cast: John Thaw (Morse), Kevin Whately (Sergeant Lewis), James Grout (Superintendent Strange), Clare Holman (Dr. Hobson). Notes: BAFTA Lew Grade Award for Best Episode in a British TV Series. DVD, VHS.

Rendezvous (see *The American Black Chamber*).

3735. *The Renegade* (L. L. Foreman, 1949). A white boy raised by Indians of forced to choose sides when a battle breaks out. **Adaptation:** *The Savage* (Paramount, 1952). Dir: George Marshall. Scr: Sydney Boehm. Cast: Charlton Heston (War Bonnet/Jim), Susan Morrow (Tally), Peter Hansen (Weston), Joan Taylor (Luta).

3736. *Replacing Dad* (Shelley Fraser Mickle, 1993). A few days before their anniversary, a wife discovers that her husband is having an affair with their daughter's teacher. **Adaptation:** *Replacing Dad* (CBS, 1999 TV Movie). Dir: Joyce Chopra. Scr: David J. Hill. Cast: Mary McDonnell (Linda), William Russ (George), Jack Coleman (Dr. Chandler), Erik von Detten (Drew), Camilla Belle (Mandy).

3737. *Report to the Commissioner* (James Mills, 1972). A rookie police officer accidentally kills an undercover policewoman and becomes involved in a departmental cover-up of the incident. **Adaptation:** *Report to the Commissioner*; released in the UK as *Operation Undercover* (United Artists, 1975). Dir: Milton Katselas. Scr: Abby Mann, Ernest Tidyman. Cast: Michael Moriarty (Bo), Yaphet Kotto (Blackstone), Susan Blakely (Patty), Hector Elizondo (Captain D'Angelo), Bob Balaban (Joey), William Devane (Jackson), Richard Gere (Billy). VHS.

3738. *Reprieve: The Testament of John Resko* (John Resko, 1956). Autobiography by a nineteen-year inmate in Sing Sing whose death sentence was commuted just minutes before his execution. **Adaptation:** *Convicts 4*; also released as *Reprieve* (Allied Artists, 1962). Dir: Millard Kaufman. Scr: Millard Kaufman. Cast: Ben Gazzara (Resko), Stuart Whitman (Keeper), Ray Walston (Iggy), Vincent Price (Carl), Rod Steiger (Tiptoes), Broderick Crawford (the Warden). VHS.

3739. *Requiem for a Dream* (Hubert Selby, Jr., 1978). While her son and his friends grow more and more addicted to heroin, a Brooklyn woman becomes hooked on diet pills in this gritty portrait of four addicts. **Adaptation:** *Requiem for* *a Dream* (Artisan, 2000). Dir: Darren Aronofsky. Scr: Darren Aronofsky, Hubert Selby, Jr. Cast: Ellen Burstyn (Sara), Jared Leto (Harry), Jennifer Connelly (Marion), Marlon Wayans (Tyrone), Christopher McDonald (Tappy), Louise Lasser (Ada). Notes: Independent Spirit Awards for Best Actress (Burstyn) and Cinematography; and nominations for Best Picture, Director, and Supporting Actress (Connelly); Academy Award and Golden Globe nominations for Best Actress (Burstyn). DVD, VHS.

3740. *The Rescue: A Romance of the Shallows* (Joseph Conrad, 1920). Tale of the romantic affair between a seaman and a married woman. The novel was serialized in *Romance* magazine between November 1919 and May 1920 and published as a book in 1920. **Adaptation:** *The Rescue* (United Artists, 1929). Dir: Herbert Brenon. Scr: H .H. Caldwell, Katherine Hilliker, Elizabeth Meehan. Cast: Ronald Colman (Tom), Lili Damita (Lady Edith), Alfred Hickman (Mr. Travers).

3741. *The Rescuers* (Margery Sharp, 1959). The first in a series of children's books about the Mouse Rescue Society, a group of intrepid mice who rescue people and animals in trouble. **Adaptation:** *The Rescuers* (Disney/Buena Vista, 1977). Dir: John Lounsbery, Wolfgang Reitherman, Art Stevens. Scr: Ken Anderson, Ted Berman, Larry Clemmons, Vance Gerry, Fred Lucky, Burny Mattinson, David Michener, Dick Sebast, Frank Thomas. Cast: voices of Bob Newhart (Bernard), Eva Gabor (Miss Bianca), Geraldine Page (Madame Medusa), Joe Flynn (Mr. Snoops), Jeanette Nolan (Ellie Mae), Pat Buttram (Luke). Notes: The screenplay for this animated feature, which concerns the Society's rescue of a kidnapped girl, combines elements of *The Rescuers* and Sharp's 1962 book *Miss Bianca*. DVD, VHS. Notes: An animated sequel, *The Rescuers Down Under*, was released in 1990 (DVD, VHS).

3742. *Restoration* (Rose Tremain, 1989). In this historical novel, King Charles II asks an ambitious British physician to marry one of his mistresses as a front for the king's dalliances. When the physician falls in love with her, he earns the enmity of the monarch. **Adaptation:** *Restoration* (Miramax, 1995). Dir: Michael Hoffman. Scr: Rupert Walters. Cast: Robert Downey, Jr. (Robert), Sam Neill (King Charles II), David Thewlis (Pearce), Polly Walker (Celia), Meg Ryan (Katharine), Ian McKellen (Will), Hugh Grant (Elias). DVD, VHS.

3743. *Resurrection* (Leo Tolstoy, 1899). Orig-inally titled *Voskreseniye*, Tolstoy's last major novel concerns a Russian prince who suffers pangs of guilt over a young peasant girl he seduced and abandoned with their child years earlier. **Silent Films:** 1909, 1917, 1918, 1923, and 1927. **Adaptation 1:** *Resurrection* (Universal, 1931). Dir: Edwin Carewe. Scr: Finis Fox. Cast: John Boles (Prince Nekhludov), Lupe Velez (Katusha), Nance O'Neil (Princess Marya), William Keighley (Captain Schoenbock). **Adaptation 2:** *We Live Again* (United Artists, 1934). Dir: Rouben Mamoulian. Scr: Maxwell Anderson, Leonard Praskins, Preston Sturges. Cast: Anna Sten (Katusha), Fredric March (Prince Nekhludov), Jane Baxter (Missy), C. Aubrey Smith (Prince Kortchagin), Sam Jaffe (Gregory). DVD, VHS. **Adaptation 3:** *Resurrection* (Artkino, 1960). Dir: Mikhail Shvejtser. Scr: Yevgeni Gabrilovich, Mikhail Shvejtser. Cast: Tamara Syomina (Katusha), Yevgeni Matveyev (Prince Nekhludov), Pavel Massalsky (the Presiding Judge). Notes: Originally titled *Voskreseniye* and shown with subtitles. **Adaptation 4:** *Resurrection* (BBC, 1968 TV Miniseries). Dir: David Giles. Scr: Alexander Baron. Cast: Alan Dobie (Prince Nekhludov), Bridget Turner (Katusha), John Stratton (Maslennikov), Constance Lorne (Princess Sophia). Notes: In addition, an Italian-language adaptation was released in 1944, a German-language film in 1958, and an Italian-German television miniseries in 2001.

3744. *Resurrection* (William Valtos, 1988). Horror thriller about a psychology professor who is haunted by the spirit of her mother, who died many years earlier. **Adaptation:** *Almost Dead* (1994). Dir: Ruben Preuss. Scr: Miguel Tejada-Flores. Cast: Shannen Doherty (Katherine), Costas Mandylor (Dominic), John Diehl (Eddie), William R. Moses (Jim). VHS.

3745. *Resurrection Man* (Eoin McNamee, 1994). In Belfast in the 1970's, an emotionally disturbed Protestant man and his friends murder Catholics. **Adaptation:** *Resurrection Man* (Poly-Gram, 1998). Dir: Marc Evans. Scr: Eoin McNamee. Cast: Stuart Townsend (Victor), Brenda Fricker (Dorcas), George Shane (James). VHS.

The Resurrection Syndicate (see *Children of the Night*).

3746. *Return from the Ashes* (Hubert Monteilhet, 1963). A woman returns from a Nazi concentration camp to find her husband and stepdaughter are engaged in an affair and planning to murder her. **Adaptation:** *Return from the Ashes* (United Artists, 1965). Dir: J. Lee Thompson. Scr:

Julius J. Epstein. Cast: Maximilian Schell (Stanislaus), Samantha Eggar (Fabienne), Ingrid Thulin (Dr. Wolf), Herbert Lom (Dr. Bovard).

3747. *Return from the River Kwai* (Joan Blair and Clay Blair, Jr., 1979). Factual account of British and Australian prisoners of war forced to build the Burma-Thai railroad during World War II. On their way back to Japan, American subs sank the Japanese ships and rescued many of the prisoners. **Adaptation:** *Return from the River Kwai* (Universal, 1988). Dir: Andrew V. McLaglen. Scr: Sargon Tamimi, Paul Mayersberg. Cast: Nick Tate (Hunt), Timothy Bottoms (Miller), George Takei (Tanaka), Edward Fox (Benford). DVD, VHS.

3748. *Return from Witch Mountain* (Alexander Key, 1978). In this sequel to Key's 1968 children's book *Escape to Witch Mountain*, the children from outer space return to Earth and are kidnapped by thieves who want to abuse the children's special powers. **Adaptation:** *Return from Witch Mountain* (Disney/Buena Vista, 1978). Dir: John Hough. Scr: Malcolm Marmorstein. Cast: Bette Davis (Letha), Christopher Lee (Victor), Kim Richards (Tia), Ike Eisenmann (Tony), Jack Soo (Mr. Yokomoto). DVD, VHS. See also *Escape to Witch Mountain*.

3749. *Return Journey* (Abdullah Hussein, 1995). Hussein's novel *Wapsi Ka Safar* is set in the 1960's and tells the story of a young Pakistani who emigrates to England in search of a new and better life. **Adaptation:** *Brothers in Trouble* (Renegade/First Run, 1996). Dir: Udayan Prasad. Scr: Robert Buckler. Cast: Om Puri (Hussein), Pavan Malhotra (Amir), Angeline Ball (Mary), Ahsen Bhatti (Irshad). VHS.

3750. *The Return of Bulldog Drummond* (Sapper [pseudonym for Herman Cyril McNeile], 1932). British adventurer and detective Hugh "Bulldog" Drummond investigates the disappearance of dangerous explosives in Switzerland **Adaptation:** *Bulldog Drummond's Revenge* (Paramount, 1937). Dir: Louis King. Scr: Edward T. Lowe. Cast: John Barrymore (Colonel Nielson), John Howard (Drummond), Louise Campbell (Phyllis), Reginald Denny (Algy). Notes: Despite its title, this film is based on the novel *The Return of Bulldog Drummond*, whereas the 1934 film by that title is based on McNeile's 1922 novel *The Black Gang*. See also *The Black Gang*. DVD, VHS.

The Return of Bulldog Drummond (see *The Black Gang*).

The Return of Dr. X (*see* "The Doctor's Secret").

Return of the Frog (see *The India-Rubber Men*).

The Return of the Musketeers (see *Twenty Years Later*).

3751. *The Return of the Native* (Thomas Hardy, 1878). In this story of doomed romance, a man returns to his rural English home after living in Paris and is reunited with the beautiful, manipulative woman he once loved. The novel was first published serially in 1878 in *Belgravia* magazine in England and *Harper's New Monthly Magazine* in the United States. **Adaptation:** *The Return of the Native* (BBC, 1994 TV Movie). Dir: Jack Gold. Scr: Robert Lenski. Cast: Catherine Zeta-Jones (Eustacia), Clive Owen (Damon), Ray Stevenson (Clym), Steven Mackintosh (Diggory), Claire Skinner (Thomasin), Paul Rogers (Captain Vye), Joan Plowright (Mrs. Yeobright). DVD, VHS.

Return of the Scarlet Pimpernel (see *The Elusive Pimpernel*).

3752. *The Return of the Soldier* (Rebecca West, 1918). An emotionally disturbed, amnesiac soldier returns from World War I and can remember nothing about the recent past, only his childhood and adolescence. **Adaptation:** *The Return of the Soldier* (European Classics, 1982). Dir: Alan Bridges. Scr: Hugh Whitemore. Cast: Julie Christie (Kitty), Glenda Jackson (Margaret), Ann-Margret (Jenny), Alan Bates (Chris), Ian Holm (Dr. Anderson), Frank Finlay (William), Jeremy Kemp (Frank). VHS.

Return of the Texan (see *The Home Place*).

The Return of the Whistler (*see* "All at Once, No Alice").

Return to Oz (see *The Marvelous Land of Oz* and *Ozma of Oz*).

3753. *Return to Paradise* (James A. Michener, 1951). After abandoning his daughter following the death of his native wife, an American returns to an island in the South Pacific to seek the young woman. **Adaptation:** *Return to Paradise* (United Artists, 1953). Dir: Mark Robson. Scr: Charles Kaufman. Cast: Gary Cooper (Mr. Morgan), Barry Jones (Pastor Corbett), Roberta Haynes (Maeva), Moira MacDonald (Turia). VHS.

3754. *Return to Peyton Place* (Grace Metalious, 1959). In this sequel to Metalious' 1956 bestseller, *Peyton Place*, the town's most famous former resident writes a shocking novel about the secret lives of its citizens, touching off rifts among neighbors and within families. **Adaptation:** *Return to Peyton Place* (20th Century–Fox, 1961). Dir: Jose Ferrer. Scr: Ronald Alexander. Cast: Carol Lynley (Allison), Jeff Chandler (Lewis), Eleanor Parker (Connie), Mary Astor (Roberta Carter), Robert Sterling (Mike), Luciana Paluzzi (Raffaella), Brett Halsey (Ted). DVD, VHS. Notes: The book and film also inspired a television series on NBC in 1972. See also *Peyton Place*.

Return to the Blue Lagoon (see *The Garden of God*).

Returning Home (see *Glory for Me*).

3755. *Reuben, Reuben* (Peter De Vries, 1964). Comic novel about an alcoholic Scottish poet and his lecherous misadventures in a New England college town. The novel was adapted by Herman Shumlin as a Broadway play titled *Spofford* in 1967. **Adaptation:** *Reuben, Reuben* (20th Century–Fox, 1983). Dir: Robert Ellis Miller. Dir: Julius J. Epstein. Cast: Tom Conti (Gowan), Kelly McGillis (Geneva), Roberts Blossom (Frank), Cynthia Harris (Bobby), E. Katherine Kerr (Lucille), Joel Fabiani (Dr. Haxby). Notes: National Board of Review Award for Best Actor (Conti); Academy Award nominations for Best Screenplay and Actor (Conti); Golden Globe nominations for Best Picture, Screenplay, and Actor (Conti). DVD, VHS.

3756. *Reunion* (Fred Uhlman, 1971). After living in the United States since the 1930's, an elderly Jewish man returns to his hometown in Germany and recalls a boyhood friendship torn apart by the rise of the Nazis and anti–Semitism. He is surprised to meet his friend again after all this time. **Adaptation:** *Reunion* (Castle Hill, 1989). Dir: Jerry Schatzberg. Scr: Harold Pinter. Cast: Jason Robards (Henry), Samuel West (Count Konradin), Francoise Fabian (Countess von Lohenburg), Maureen Kerwin (Lisa). VHS.

3757. *Revenge* (Jim Harrison, 1979). A Navy veteran visits an old acquaintance in Mexico and falls in love with the powerful and possessive man's young and beautiful wife. The story was originally published in the May 8, 1979, issue of *Esquire*, and an expanded version appeared in Harrison's 1979 collection of three novellas titled *Legends of the Fall*. **Adaptation:** *Revenge* (Columbia, 1990). Dir: Tony Scott. Scr: Jim Harrison, Jeff Fiskin. Cast: Kevin Costner (Michael), Anthony Quinn (Tiburon), Madeleine Stowe (Mireya), Tomas Milian (Cesar). DVD, VHS.

Revenge in the House of Usher (see "The Fall of the House of Usher")

3758. *Reversal of Fortune: Inside the Von Bulow Case* (Alan M. Dershowitz, 1986). The true story of Claus Von Bulow, who was convicted of the attempted murder of his socialite wife, Sunny, and the appeal launched by Harvard law professor Alan Dershowitz. **Adaptation:** *Reversal of Fortune* (Warner, 1990). Dir: Barbet Schroeder. Scr: Nicholas Kazan. Cast: Glenn Close (Sunny), Jeremy Irons (Claus), Ron Silver (Dershowitz), Annabella Sciorra (Sarah), Uta Hagen (Maria), Fisher Stevens (David). Notes: Academy Award for Best Actor (Irons) and nominations for Best Director and Screenplay ; Golden Globe Award for Best Actor (Irons) and nominations for Best Picture, Director, and Screenplay. DVD, VHS.

3759. *The Revolt of Mamie Stover* (William Bradford Huie, 1951). A saloon singer goes to Hawaii, where she falls in love with a writer and tries to reform herself. **Adaptation:** *The Revolt of Mamie Stover* (20th Century–Fox, 1956). Dir: Raoul Walsh. Scr: Sydney Boehm. Cast: Jane Russell (Mamie), Richard Egan (Jim), Joan Leslie (Annalee), Agnes Moorehead (Bertha).

3760. *The Reward* (Michael Barrett, 1956). A group of people cross the desert to capture a murderer and claim the reward and then turn on each other to get a larger share of the money. **Adaptation:** *The Reward* (20th Century–Fox, 1965). Dir: Serge Bourguignon. Scr: Serge Bourguignon, Oscar Millard. Cast: Max von Sydow (Scott), Yvette Mimieux (Sylvia), Efrem Zimbalist, Jr. (Frank), Gilbert Roland (Captain Carbajal).

Rhapsody (see *Maurice Guest*).

3761. *The Rhinemann Exchange* (Robert Ludlum, 1974). Espionage novel set during World War II and involving American agents exchanging industrial diamonds with the Nazis in exchange for high-quality gyroscopes need for a rocket program. **Adaptation:** *The Rhinemann Exchange* (NBC, 1977 TV Miniseries). Dir: Burt Kennedy. Scr: Richard Collins. Cast: Stephen Collins (Spaulding), Lauren Hutton (Leslie), Claude Akins (Kendall), Vince Edwards (General Swanson), Jose Ferrer (Rhinemann), Larry Hagman (Colonel Pace), John Huston (Ambassador Granville), Roddy McDowall (Ballard).

3762. *Rhodes* (Sarah Millin, 1933). Biography of British businessman Cecil Rhodes (1853–1902), who opened British trading routes in Africa, allowed for the imperial takeover of the Transvaal, and became the first Prime Minister of Cape Colony, later renamed Rhodesia, in 1890. **Adaptation:** *Rhodes of Africa*; released in the U.S. as *Rhodes* (Gaumont, 1936). Dir: Berthold Viertel. Scr: Leslie Arliss, Michael Barringer, Miles Malleson, Sarah Millin. Cast: Walter Huston (Rhodes), Oskar Homolka (Kruger), Basil Sydney (Dr. Jameson), Frank Cellier (Barney), Peggy Ashcroft (Anna). VHS. Notes: In addition, an eight-part BBC miniseries titled *Rhodes* was broadcast in 1998 (VHS).

3763. *Rhubarb* (H. Allen Smith, 1946). Comic novel about an eccentric millionaire who leaves his fortune and a baseball team to his pet cat. **Adaptation:** *Rhubarb* (Paramount, 1951). Dir: Arthur Lubin. Scr: Francis M. Cockrell, Dorothy Davenport, David Stern. Cast: Ray Milland (Eric), Jan Sterling (Polly), Gene Lockhart (Thaddeus), William Frawley (Len).

3764. *Rich and Strange* (Dale Collins, 1931). After coming into a great deal of money, a bored young married couple take a trip around the world and have romantic flings with other people. **Adaptation:** *Rich and Strange*; released in the U.S. as *East of Shanghai* (British International/Powers, 1931). Dir: Alfred Hitchcock. Scr: Alfred Hitchcock, Alma Reville, Val Valentine. Cast: Henry Kendall (Fred), Joan Barry (Emily), Percy Marmont (Commander Gordon). DVD, VHS.

3765. *The Rich Are Always With Us* (E. Pettit, 1930). A wealthy society woman divorces her husband to pursue an affair with another man but, to her new lover's annoyance, continues to care for her former husband. **Adaptation:** *The Rich Are Always With Us* (Warner, 1932). Dir: Alfred E. Green. Scr: Austin Parker. Cast: Ruth Chatterton (Caroline), George Brent (Julian), Bette Davis (Malbro), John Miljan (Greg).

3766. *Rich in Love* (Josephine Humphreys, 1987). Living in an old Southern mansion, a teenaged girl tries to hold her family together after her mother leaves suddenly, her father falls apart emotionally, and her pregnant sister arrives home. **Adaptation:** *Rich in Love* (MGM, 1993). Dir: Bruce Beresford. Scr: Alfred Uhry. Cast: Albert Finney (Warren), Jill Clayburgh (Helen), Kathryn Erbe (Lucille), Kyle MacLachlan (Billy), Piper Laurie (Vera), Ethan Hawke (Wayne), Suzy Amis (Rae), Alfre Woodard (Rhody). VHS.

Rich Man's Folly (see *Dombey and Son*).

Ricochet (see *Angel of Terror*).

3767. *Ricochet River* (Robin Cody, 1992). Coming-of-age story set in a small Oregon logging town in the 1960's. Two adolescents feel constrained by small-town life until they meet a new friend, an Indian student, with whom they take a symbolic and inspiring journey down a river. **Adaptation:** *Ricochet River* (Dee Gee/Studio Home1998). Dir: Deborah Del Prete. Scr: Pat O'-Connor. Cast: John Cullum (Link), Eddie Thiel (Wade), Tyler Miller (Roy), Jason James Richter (Wade), Kate Hudson (Lorna). DVD, VHS.

3768. "The Riddle of the Dangling Pearl" (Stuart Palmer, 1933). Schoolteacher and amateur sleuth Hildegarde Withers helps police solve a murder linked to an art theft. The short story was published in *Mystery* magazine in November 1933. **Adaptation:** *The Plot Thickens* (RKO, 1936). Dir: Ben Holmes. Scr: Jack Townley, Clarence Upson Young. Cast: James Gleason (Oscar), Zasu Pitts (Hildegarde), Owen Davis, Jr. (Bob), Louise Latimer (Alice).

3769. *The Riddle of the Sands* (Erskine Childers, 1903). In 1901, a British yachtsman discovers that German military officers appear to be planning an invasion of England. **Adaptation:** *The Riddle of the Sands* (Rank/Satori, 1978). Dir: Tony Maylam. Scr: John Bailey, Tony Maylam. Cast: Michael York (Charles), Jenny Agutter (Clara), Simon MacCorkindale (Arthur), Alan Badel (Dollmann). VHS. Notes: The book was also adapted for a German television movie in 1987.

3770. *The Riddle of the Third Mile* (Colin Dexter, 1983). The sixth installment in Dexter's popular thirteen-novel series (1975–2000) featuring Chief Inspector Endeavour Morse of Oxford, England. In this book, Inspector Morse investigates the murder of an Oxford don, whose mutilated body is found in a canal. **Adaptation:** *Inspector Morse: The Last Enemy* (Carlton/PBS, 1989 TV Movie series). Dir: James Scott. Scr: Peter Buckman. Cast: John Thaw (Morse), Kevin Whately (Sergeant Lewis), James Grout (Superintendent Strange), Amanda Hillwood (Dr. Russell). DVD, VHS.

Ride a Wild Pony (see *A Sporting Proposition*).

Ride Beyond Vengeance (see *The Night of the Tiger*).

3771. *Ride the Man Down* (Luke Short [pseudonym for Frederick D. Glidden]. 1942). Western about the violent land dispute that follows the death of a rancher. The novel appeared as a serial in *The Saturday Evening Post* between April 4 and May 16, 1942, and was published as a book later that year. **Adaptation:** *Ride the Man Down* (Republic, 1952). Dir: Joseph Kane. Scr: Mary C. McCall, Jr. Cast: Brian Donlevy (Bide), Rod Cameron (Will), Ella Raines (Celia), Forrest Tucker (Sam), Barbara Britton (Lottie), Chill Wills (Ike), J. Carrol Naish (Sheriff Kneen), VHS.

3772. *Ride the Nightmare* (Richard Matheson, 1959). An American living in Paris is forced into drug smuggling when his wife is kidnapped by a gangster. **Adaptation:** *Cold Sweat* (Emerson, 1970). Dir: Terence Young. Scr: Albert Simonin, Shimon Wincelberg, Cast: Charles Bronson (Joe), Liv Ullmann (Fabienne), James Mason (Ross), Jill Ireland (Moira). DVD, VHS.

3773. *Ride the Pink Horse* (Dorotby B. Hughes, 1946). After World War II, a veteran goes to a small New Mexico to find the gangster who killed his friend and blackmail him. **Adaptation 1:** *Ride the Pink Horse* (Universal, 1947). Dir: Robert Montgomery. Scr: Ben Hecht, Charles Lederer. Cast: Robert Montgomery (Lucky), Wanda Hendrix (Pilar), Andrea King (Marjorie), Thomas Gomez (Pancho), Fred Clark (Frank). VHS. **Adaptation 2:** *The Hanged Man* (NBC, 1964 TV Movie). Dir: Don Siegel. Scr: Jack Laird, Stanford Whitmore. Cast: Robert Culp (Harry), Edmond O'Brien (Arnie), Vera Miles (Lois), Norman Fell (Gaylord), Gene Raymond (Whitey).

Ride with the Devil (see *Woe to Live On*).

3774. *Riders of the Purple Sage* (Zane Grey, 1912). Classic Western about a Texas Ranger pursuing the outlaw who kidnapped his sister. **Silent Films:** 1918 and 1925, starring Tom Mix (VHS). **Adaptation 1:** *Riders of the Purple Sage* (Fox, 1931). Dir: Hamilton MacFadden. Scr: Barry Conners, John Goodrich, Philip Klein. Cast: George O'Brien (Jim),Marguerite Churchill (Jane), Noah Beery (Judge Dyer), Yvonne Pelletier (Bess). VHS. **Adaptation 2:** *The Riders of the Purple Sage* (20th Century–Fox, 1941). Dir: James Tinling. Scr: William Bruckner, Robert F. Metzler. Cast: George Montgomery (Jim), Mary Howard (Jane), Robert Barrat (Judge Dyer), Lynne Roberts (Bess). **Adaptation 3:** *Riders of the Purple Sage* (Turner, 1996 TV Movie). Dir: Charles Haid. Scr: Gill Dennis. Cast: Ed Harris (Jim), Amy Madigan (Jane), Henry Thomas (Bern), Robin Tunney (Bess). VHS.

3775. *Riding in Cars with Boys: Confessions of a Bad Girl Who Makes Good* (Beverly Donofrio, 1990). Donofrio's memoir of a working-class adolescence and her dreams of becoming a writer derailed by pregnancy at 15 and marriage to a drug addict. **Adaptation:** *Riding in Cars with Boys* (Co-lumbia, 2001). Dir: Penny Marshall. Scr: Morgan Upton Ward. Cast: Drew Barrymore (Beverly), Steve Zahn (Raymond), Adam Garcia (Jason), Brittany Murphy (Fay), James Woods (Leonard), Lorraine Bracco (Teresa), Rosie Perez (Shirley), Sara Gilbert (Christina). DVD, VHS.

3776. *Riding the Bullet* (Stephen King, 2000). Novella about a hitchhiker picked up by a mysterious stranger with a deadly secret. **Adaptation:** *Riding the Bullet* (MPCA/Innovation, 2004). Dir: Mick Garris. Scr: Mick Garris. Cast: Jonathan Jackson (Alan), David Arquette (George), Cliff Robertson (Farmer), Barbara Hershey (Jean). DVD, VHS.

3777. *Riding the Bus with My Sister* (Rachel Simon, 2002). Memoir about the rocky relationship between the writer and her developmentally challenged sister. **Adaptation:** *Riding the Bus with My Sister* (CBS/Hallmark, 2005 TV Movie). Dir: Anjelica Huston. Scr: Joyce Eliason. Cast: Rosie O'Donnell (Beth), Andie MacDowell (Rachel), Richard T. Jones (Jesse), D. W. Moffett (Rick). DVD, VHS.

3778. *Rififi* (Auguste Le Breton, 1953). This French novel, originally titled *Du Rififi chez Les Hommes*, concerns four thieves who launch a successful burglary of a jewelry store but then have a bloody falling out among themselves. **Adaptation:** *Rififi* (UMPO, 1955). Dir: Jules Dassin. Scr: Jules Dassin, Rene Wheeler, Auguste Le Breton. Cast: Jean Servais (Tony), Carl Mohner (Joe), Robert Manuel (Mario), Jules Dassin (Cesar). Notes: Cannes Film Festival Award for Best Director. Notes: Originally released as *Du Rififi Chez les Hommes* and shown with subtitles. DVD, VHS.

The Rifle (see *The Tall Stranger*).

3779. *The Right Stuff* (Tom Wolfe, 1979, National Book Award). True account of daring test pilots who were recruited and trained to be America's first astronauts. **Adaptation:** *The Right Stuff* (Warner, 1983). Dir: Philip Kaufman. Scr: Philip Kaufman. Cast: Sam Shepard (Chuck Yeager), Scott Glenn (Alan Shepard), Ed Harris (John Glenn), Dennis Quaid (Gordon Cooper), Fred Ward (Gus Grissom), Barbara Hershey (Glennis Yeager). Notes: Academy Awards for Best Musical Score, Sound, Sound Effects Editing, and Editing, and nominations for Best Picture, Actor (Shepard), Cinematography, and Art Direction; Golden Globe nomination for Best Film. DVD, VHS.

The Right to Love (see *Brook Evans*).

3780. *The Ring* (Danielle Steel, 1980). After World War II, a concentration-camp survivor goes to America hoping to find her family. **Adaptation:** *The Ring* (NBC, 1996 TV Movie). Dir: Armand Mastroianni. Scr: Nancy Sackett, Carmen Culver. Cast: Nastassja Kinski (Ariana), Michael York (Walmar), Rupert Penry-Jones (Gerhard), Carsten Norgaard (Manfred), Linda Lavin (Ruth), Leslie Caron (Madame de Saint Marne). DVD, VHS.

3781. *The Ring* (Koji Suzuki, 1991). The Japanese horror novel, originally titled *Ringu*, concerns a reporter who investigates the deaths of teenagers after watching a video and receiving a mysterious telephone call. The novel was translated into English in 2002. **Adaptation 1:** *Ringu*; English version released as *The Ring* (Omega, 1998). Dir: Hideo Nakata. Scr: Hiroshi Takahashi. Cast: Nanako Matsushima (Reiko), Miki Nakatani (Mai), Hiroyuki Sanada (Ryuji), Yuko Takeuchi (Tomoko). DVD, VHS. Two Japanese sequels followed: *The Ring 2* (1999) and *Ring-O: Birthday* (2000). **Adaptation 2:** *The Ring* (DreamWorks, 2002). Dir: Gore Verbinski. Scr: Ehren Kruger. Cast: Naomi Watts (Rachel), Martin Henderson (Noah), David Dorfman (Aidan), Brian Cox (Richard), Jane Alexander (Dr. Grasnik), Lindsay Frost (Ruth). DVD, VHS. Notes: A sequel, *The Ring Two*, was released in 2005 (DVD, VHS).

3782. *Ring of Bright Water* (Gavin Maxwell, 1960). Nonfiction story about a Scottish man who moves to a small coastal village in the western Highlands with his pet Otter. **Adaptation:** *Ring of Bright Water* (Rank/Cinerama, 1969). Dir: Jack Couffer. Scr: Jack Couffer, Bill Travers. Cast: Bill Travers (Graham), Virginia McKenna (Mary), Peter Jeffrey (Colin), Helena Gloag (Flora). DVD, VHS.

The Ringer (see *The Gaunt Stranger*).

Ringu (see *The Ring* by Koji Suzuki).

Rio Conchos (see *Guns of Rio Conchos*).

Rio Grande (*see* "Mission with No Record").

3783. *The Riot* (Frank Elli, 1966). Fact-based novel about the violent uprising of convicts in a Minnesota prison. **Adaptation:** *Riot* (Paramount, 1969). Dir: Buzz Kulik. Scr: James Poe. Cast: Jim Brown (Cully), Gene Hackman (Red), Mike Kellin (Bugsy), Gerald S. O'Loughlin (Grossman). VHS.

3784. *Ripley's Game* (Patricia Highsmith, 1974). In this sequel to Highsmith's 1955 novel *The Talented Mr. Ripley*, the unscrupulous con man is pursued by mobsters and hires a terminally ill and naïve shopkeeper to kill them for him. **Adaptation 1:** *The American Friend* (New Yorker, 1977). Dir: Wim Wenders. Scr: Wim Wenders. Cast: Dennis Hopper (Ripley), Bruno Ganz (Jonathan), Lisa Kreuzer (Marianne), Gerard Blain (Raoul), Nicholas Ray (Derwatt). Notes: German Film Awards for Best Picture, Director, and Editing; Cannes Film Festival Golden Palm Award nomination for Best Director. DVD, VHS. **Adaptation 2:** *Ripley's Game* (Fine Line, 2002). Dir: Liliana Cavani. Scr: Liliana Cavani, Charles McKeown. Cast: Ray Winstone (Reeves), John Malkovich (Ripley), Uwe Mansshardt (Terry), Paolo Paoloni (Franco). DVD, VHS. See also *The Talented Mr. Ripley*.

The Rise of Helga (see *Susan Lenox, Her Fall and Rise*).

The Rising of the Moon (*see* "The Majesty of the Law").

3785. *Rising Sun* (Michael Crichton, 1992). When a young prostitute is murdered at the Los Angeles headquarters of a Japanese conglomerate, two detectives investigate the corrupt corporation's executives. **Adaptation:** *Rising Sun* (20th Century–Fox, 1993). Dir: Philip Kaufman. Scr: Philip Kaufman, Michael Crichton, Michael Backes. Cast: Sean Connery (John), Wesley Snipes (Web), Harvey Keitel (Graham), Cary-Hiroyuki Tagawa (Sakamura), Kevin Anderson (Bob). DVD, VHS.

3786. "Rita Hayworth and the Shawshank Redemption" (Stephen King, 1982). A banker is unjustly convicted for the murder of his wife and is sentenced to prison, where he earns the respect of fellow inmates by taking revenge on a brutal guard and devious warden. The novella appeared in King's 1982 collection *Different Seasons*. **Adaptation:** *The Shawshank Redemption* (Columbia, 1994). Dir: Frank Darabont. Scr: Frank Darabont. Cast: Tim Robbins (Andy), Morgan Freeman (Ellis), Bob Gunton (Warden Norton), William Sadler (Heywood), Clancy Brown (Hadley), James Whitmore (Brooks). Notes: Academy Award nominations for Best Picture, Actor (Freeman), Screenplay, Cinematography, Editing, Music, and Sound; Golden Globe nominations for Best Screenplay and Actor (Freeman). DVD, VHS.

Rivals (see *Elegant Edward*).

3787. *The River* (Rumer Godden, 1946). Autobiographical novel about British children living in a colony near the Ganges River in India during England's colonial period. **Adaptation:** *The River* (United Artists, 1951). Dir: Jean Renoir. Scr: Jean Renoir. Cast: Nora Swinburne (the Mother), Esmond Knight (the Father), Arthur Shields (John), Suprova Mukerjee (Nan), Thomas E. Breen (Captain John), Patricia Walters (Harriet). DVD, VHS.

3788. *River of Death* (Alistair MacLean, 1981). An adventurer assembles a crew to search for lost city in the Amazon Jungle. Instead of finding treasure, he comes upon a Nazi doctor carrying out gruesome human experiments. **Adaptation:** *River of Death* (Cannon, 1989). Dir: Steve Carver. Scr: Andrew Deutsch, Edward Simpson. Cast: Michael Dudikoff (Hamilton), Robert Vaughn (Manteuffel), Donald Pleasence (Spaatz), Herbert Lom (Colonel Diaz), L. Q. Jones (Hiller). DVD, VHS.

3789. *A River Ran Out of Eden* (James Vance Marshall, 1962). In an Aleutian Island community, a lonely boy befriends a rare golden seal and her pup and must protect them from greedy hunters, including his own father. **Adaptation:** *The Golden Seal* (Samuel Goldwyn, 1983). Dir: Frank Zuniga. Scr: John Groves. Cast: Steve Railsback (Jim), Michael Beck (Crawford), Penelope Milford (Tania), Torquil Campbell (Eric), Seth Sakai (Semeyon). VHS.

3790. "A River Runs Through It" (Norman Maclean, 1976). Although they are different and cannot agree on very much, the two sons of a Montana minister share a love of fly-fishing. The autobiographical novella is the title piece in Maclean's 1976 collection *A River Runs Through It and Other Stories.* **Adaptation:** *A River Runs Through It* (Columbia, 1992). Dir: Robert Redford. Scr: Richard Friedenberg. Cast: Craig Sheffer (Norman), Brad Pitt (Paul), Tom Skerritt (Reverend Maclean), Brenda Blethyn (Mrs. Maclean), Emily Lloyd (Jessie), Edie McClurg (Mrs. Burns). Notes: Academy Award for Best Cinematography and nominations for Best Screenplay and Musical Score; Golden Globe nomination for Best Director. DVD, VHS.

3791. *The Road Back* (Erich Maria Remarque, 1931). In the sequel to Remarque's 1929 book *All Quiet on the Western Front*, German soldiers return home from World War I and have difficulties adjusting to civilian life. **Adaptation:** *The Road Back* (Universal, 1937). Dir: James Whale. Scr: Charles Kenyon, R. C. Sherriff. Cast: John King (Ernst), Richard Cromwell (Ludwig), Slim Summerville (Tjaden), Andy Devine (Willy). See also *All Quiet on the Western Front.*

3792. *Road Rage* (Ruth Rendell, 1997). A police inspector tries to keep order as local protestors block the building of a road through a forest. When protesters begin to disappear mysteriously, including his own wife, the inspector takes a personal interest in the case. **Adaptation:** *Road Rage* (ITV, 1998 TV Movie). Dir: Bruce MacDonald. Scr: George Baker. Cast: George Baker (Inspector Wexford), Christopher Ravenscroft (Detective Burden), James Allen (Slesar), Christopher Connel (Jordan), Ian Bartholomew (Trotter). DVD, VHS.

3793. *Road Show* (Eric Hatch, 1934). Comic novel about a man who escapes from an insane asylum and joins a traveling carnival. **Adaptation:** *Road Show* (United Artists, 1941). Dir: Hal Roach. Scr: Arnold Belgard, Harry Langdon, Mickell Novack. Cast: Adolphe Menjou (Carleton), Carole Landis (Penguin), John Hubbard (Drogo), Charles Butterworth (Harry). DVD, VHS.

The Road to Avonlea (see *Anne of Avonlea*).

The Road to Denver (see "The Man from Texas").

The Road to Frisco (see *Long Haul*).

3794. *The Road to Perdition* (Max Allan Collins and Richard Piers Rayner, 1998). Graphic novel about a mob hitman's son who witnesses what his father secretly does for a living, thereby placing his entire family in peril. **Adaptation:** *The Road to Perdition* (DreamWorks, 2002). Dir: Sam Mendes. Scr: David Self. Cast: Tom Hanks (Michael), Paul Newman (Rooney), Tyler Hoechlin (Michael, Jr.), Liam Aiken (Peter), Jennifer Jason Leigh (Annie), Daniel Craig (Connor), Ciaran Hinds (Finn). Notes: Academy Award for Best Cinematography and nominations for Best Supporting Actor (Newman), Musical Score, Art Direction, and Sound. DVD, VHS.

3795. *The Road to Reno* (I. A. R. Wylie, 1937). Comic story of a rancher who refuses his wife's demand for a divorce because he is convinced they still love each other. The novel was originally published as a seven-part serial in *The Saturday Evening Post* (March 27–May 8, 1937). **Adaptation:** The *Road to Reno* (Universal, 1938). Dir: S. Sylvan Simon. Scr: F. Hugh Herbert, Charles Kenyon, Brian Marlow. Cast: Randolph Scott (Steve), Hope Hampton (Linda), Glenda Farrell (Sylvia), Helen Broderick (Aunt Minerva).

3796. *The Road to Wellville* (T. Coraghessan Boyle, 1993). In the early twentieth century, the eccentric inventor of corn flakes, Dr. John Harvey

Kellogg of Battle Creek, Michigan, runs a sanitarium for wealthy, health-conscious patrons. **Adaptation:** *The Road to Wellville* (Columbia, 1994). Dir: Alan Parker. Scr: Alan Parker. Cast: Anthony Hopkins (Dr. Kellogg), Bridget Fonda (Eleanor), Matthew Broderick (William), John Cusack (Charles), Dana Carvey (George), Michael Lerner (Goodloe), Colm Meaney (Dr. Badger), John Neville (Endymion), Lara Flynn Boyle (Ida). DVD, VHS.

Roadhouse Nights (see *Red Harvest*).

3797. *The Roar of the Crowd: The True Tale of the Rise and Fall of a Champion* (James J. Corbett, 1925). Autobiography of the heavyweight boxing champion Gentleman Jim Corbett (1866–1933). The book was serialized in *The Saturday Evening Post* in 1924 and appeared as a book in 1925. **Adaptation:** *Gentleman Jim* (Warner, 1942). Dir: Raoul Walsh. Scr: Vincent Lawrence, Horace McCoy. Cast: Errol Flynn (Gentleman Jim), Alexis Smith (Victoria), Jack Carson (Walter), Alan Hale (Pat). VHS.

Roaring Timber (see *Come and Get It*).

3798. *Rob Roy* (Walter Scott, 1817). In 1715, Scottish highlander Robert Roy MacGregor is forced to become an outlaw leader because his integrity will not allow him to follow unjust orders from the British. **Silent Films:** 1911, 1913, and 1922. **Adaptation 1:** *Rob Roy, the Highland Rogue* (Disney/RKO, 1954). Dir: Harold French. Scr: Lawrence Edward Watkin. Cast: Richard Todd (Rob Roy), Glynis Johns (Helen), Michael Gough (the Duke of Montrose), James Robertson Justice (the Duke of Argyll), Archie Duncan (Dugal). **Adaptation 2:** *Rob Roy* (United Artists, 1995). Dir: Michael Caton-Jones. Scr: Alan Sharp. Cast: Liam Neeson (Rob Roy), Jessica Lange (Mary), John Hurt (John), Tim Roth (Archibald), Eric Stoltz (Alan). Notes: BAFTA Award for Best Supporting Actor (Roth); Academy Award and Golden Globe nominations for Best Supporting Actor (Roth). DVD, VHS.

3799. *Robbers' Roost* (Zane Grey, 1932). Western about an honest cowboy who inadvertently becomes involved with cattle rustlers and a range war. **Adaptation 1:** *Robbers' Roost* (Fox, 1933). Dir: David Howard, Louis King. Scr: Dudley Nichols. Cast: George O'Brien (Jim), Maureen O'Sullivan (Helen), Walter McGrail (Brad), Maude Eburne (Aunt Ellen), Reginald Owen (Cecil). **Adaptation 2:** *Robbers' Roost* (United Artists, 1955). Dir: Sidney Salkow. Scr: John

O'Dea, Sidney Salkow, Maurice Geraghty. Cast: George Montgomery (Jim), Richard Boone (Hank), Sylvia Findley (Helen), Bruce Bennett (Bull), Peter Graves (Heesman).

3800. *Robbery Under Arms: A Story of Life and Adventure in the Bush and in the Goldfields of Australia* (Rolf Boldrewood [pseudonym for Thomas Alexander Browne], 1882–1883). The adventures of two Australian bushrangers who join the outlaw gang of gentleman-thief Captain Starlight. The novel originally appeared in serial form in *The Sydney Mail* between July 1882 and August 1883 and was published in book form in 1883. **Silent Films:** 1907 and 1920. **Adaptation 1:** *Robbery Under Arms* (Rank, 1957). Dir: Jack Lee. Scr: Alexander Baron, W. P. Lipscomb. Cast: David McCallum (Jim), Ronald Lewis (Dick), Peter Finch (Captain Starlight), Laurence Naismith (Ben), Jill Ireland (Jean). VHS. **Adaptation 2:** *Robbery Under Arms* (ITC, 1985 TV Movie). Dir: Donald Crombie, Ken Hannam. Scr: Michael Jenkins, Graeme Koetsveld, Tony Morphett. Cast: Sam Neill (Captain Starlight), Steven Vidler (Dick), Christopher Cummins (Jim), Liz Newman (Gracie), Jane Menelaus (Aileen). VHS.

3801. *The Robe* (Lloyd C. Douglas, 1942). A Roman soldier assigned to crucify Jesus Christ wins Jesus' robe in a dice game. Tormented by guilt and bad dreams, he sets out for Palestine to learn the identity of man he killed. **Adaptation:** *The Robe* (20th Century–Fox, 1953). Dir: Henry Koster. Scr: Gina Kaus, Albert Maltz, Philip Dunne. Cast: Richard Burton (Marcellus Gallio), Jean Simmons (Diana), Victor Mature (Demetrius), Michael Rennie (Peter), Jay Robinson (Caligula), Dean Jagger (Justus), Richard Boone (Pontius Pilate), Jeff Morrow (Paulus). Notes: Maltz was blacklisted at the time and was not originally credited. Academy Awards for Best Art Direction and Costume Design, and nominations for Best Picture, Actor (Burton), and Cinematography; Golden Globe Award for Best Picture; National Board of Review Award for Best Actress (Simmons). DVD, VHS. Notes: A sequel, *Demetrius and the Gladiators*, was released in 1954 (DVD, VHS).

Roberta (see *Gowns by Roberta*).

Robinson Crusoe (see *The Life and Adventures of Robinson Crusoe*).

Robo Man (see *Who?*).

3802. *Rocket Boys: A Memoir* (Homer H. Hickam, Jr., 1998). Memoir by a renowned NASA trainer of shuttle-mission astronauts of his childhood in West Virginia and his early interest in building rockets, kindled by the 1957 launch of the Russian satellite *Sputnik*. **Adaptation:** *October Sky* (Universal, 1999). Dir: Joe Johnston. Scr: Lewis Colick. Cast: Jake Gyllenhaal (Homer), Chris Cooper (John), Laura Dern (Frieda), Chris Owen (Quentin). DVD, VHS.

Rocket to the Moon (see *From the Earth to the Moon*).

3803. *The Rocketeer* (Dave Stevens, 1985, Jack Kirby Comic Book Award for Best Graphic Album). Graphic novel set in the 1930's about a pilot who discovers a jet-pack and becomes a flying hero battling Nazi spies. Stevens also produced a comic-book series (1985–1991) based on this character. **Adaptation:** *The Rocketeer* (Disney/Buena Vista, 1991). Dir: Joe Johnston. Scr: Danny Bilson, Paul De Meo. Cast: Bill Campbell (Cliff), Jennifer Connelly (Jenny), Alan Arkin (Peevy), Timothy Dalton (Neville), Paul Sorvino (Eddie). DVD, VHS.

3804. *Rockets Galore!* (Compton Mackenzie, 1957). The sequel to Mackenzie's 1948 novel *Whiskey Galore!* finds the same group of Scottish islanders opposing the construction of an RAF missile base on their territory. **Adaptation:** *Rockets Galore!*; released in the U.S. as *Mad Little Island* (Rank, 1957). Dir: Michael Relph. Scr: Monja Danischewsky. Cast: Jeannie Carson (Janet), Donald Sinden (Hugh), Roland Culver (Captain Waggett), Catherine Lacey (Mrs. Waggett), Noel Purcell (Father James). See also *Whiskey Galore!*

3805. "The Rocking Horse Winner" (D. H. Lawrence, 1926). A young boy discovers that he can predict racetrack winners when he rides an old rocking horse, but his mother's greed compromises the boy's life. The short story was originally published in *Harpers Bazaar* magazine in July 1926. **Adaptation 1:** *The Rocking Horse Winner* (Rank/Universal International, 1949). Dir: Anthony Pelissier. Scr: Anthony Pelissier. Cast: Valerie Hobson (Hester), John Howard Davies (Paul), Ronald Squire (Oscar), John Mills (Bassett), Hugh Sinclair (Richard). DVD, VHS. **Adaptation 2:** *The Rocking Horse Winner* (United International, 1983). Dir: Robert Bierman. Scr: Howard Schuman. Cast: Eleanor David (Hester), Charles Keating (Oscar), Charles Hathorn (Paul), Gabriel Byrne (Bassett). Notes: BAFTA nomination for Best Short Film.

3806. *Roemer: Man Against the Mob* (William F. Roemer, 1989). The memoirs of legendary FBI agent William Roemer (1926–1996) and the historic cases in which he was involved. **Adaptation:** *Sugartime* (HBO, 1995 TV Movie). Dir: John N. Smith. Scr: Martyn Burke. Cast: John Turturro (Sam Giancana), Mary-Louise Parker (Phyllis McGuire), Elias Koteas (Butch Blasi), Maury Chaykin (Tony Accardo). Notes: The teleplay, which focuses on the romance between singer Phyllis McGuire and mobster Sam Giancana, was merely suggested by Roemer's book. VHS.

3807. *Rogue Cop* (William P. McGivern, 1954). A corrupt detective is torn between the gangsters he serves and loyalty to his brother, whom the gangsters are threatening. **Adaptation:** *Rogue Cop* (MGM, 1954). Dir: Roy Rowland. Scr: Sydney Boehm. Cast: Robert Taylor (Christopher), Janet Leigh (Karen), George Raft (Dan), Steve Forrest (Eddie), Anne Francis (Nancy).

3808. *Rogue Male* (Geoffrey Household, 1939). Near the beginning of World War II, a British marksman in Germany takes aim at Hitler but misses his mark. After his return to England, he discovers that the Gestapo are pursuing him. **Adaptation 1:** *Man Hunt* (20th Century–Fox, 1941). Dir: Fritz Lang. Scr: Dudley Nichols. Cast: Walter Pidgeon (Thorndike), Joan Bennett (Gerri), George Sanders (Quive-Smith), John Carradine (Mr. Jones), Roddy McDowall (Vaner). **Adaptation 2:** *Rogue Male* (BBC, 1976 TV Movie). Dir: Clive Donner. Scr: Frederic Raphael. Cast: Peter O'Toole (Thorndike), John Standing (Quive-Smith), Alastair Sim (the Earl), Harold Pinter (Saul). DVD, VHS.

3809. *Rogue Trader: How I Brought Down Barings Bank and Shook the Financial World* (Nick Leeson and Edward Whitley, 1996). Autobiographical account of a British stockbroker in Singapore and his deceptive dealings that led to the collapse of his bank. **Adaptation:** *Rogue Trader* (Granada/Cinemax, 1999). Dir: James Dearden. Scr: James Dearden. Cast: Ewan McGregor (Leeson), Anna Friel (Lisa), Yves Beneyton (Beaumarchais), Betsy Brantley (Brenda), Caroline Langrishe (Ash). Notes: The film was released theatrically in Great Britain and on television in the United States. DVD, VHS.

Roll Along, Cowboy (see *The Dude Ranger*).

3810. *The Roman Spring of Mrs. Stone* (Tennessee Williams, 1950). After her husband dies suddenly on a trip to Italy, a middle-aged American actress has an impulsive affair with a gigolo in Rome. **Adaptation 1:** *The Roman Spring of Mrs. Stone* (Warner, 1961). Dir: Jose Quintero. Scr:

Gavin Lambert. Cast: Vivien Leigh (Karen), Warren Beatty (Paolo), Lotte Lenya (the Contessa), Coral Browne (Meg), Jill St. John (Barbara). VHS. **Adaptation 2:** *The Roman Spring of Mrs. Stone* (Showtime, 2003 TV Movie). Dir: Robert Allan Ackerman. Scr: Martin Sherman. Cast: Helen Mirren (Karen), Oliver Martinez (Paolo), Anne Bancroft (the Contessa), Brian Dennehy (Tom). Notes: Emmy nominations for Outstanding Director, Actress (Mirren), Supporting Actress (Bancroft), Musical Score, and Costume Design; Golden Globe nominations for Best Television Movie and Actress (Mirren). DVD, VHS.

3811. *The Romance of Rosy Ridge* (MacKinlay Kantor, 1937). Romantic comedy about a farmer in post–Civil War Missouri brought together with his feuding neighbor by the marriage of their children. **Adaptation:** *The Romance of Rosy Ridge* (MGM, 1947). Dir: Roy Rowland. Scr: Lester Cole. Cast: Van Johnson (Henry), Thomas Mitchell (Gill), Janet Leigh (Lissy), Marshall Thompson (Ben).

Romance of the Redwoods (*see* "The White Silence").

3812. *The Romantic Englishwoman* (Thomas Wiseman, 1972). After learning that his wife has had a brief fling with a man in Germany, a British novelist works the illicit romance into the book on which he is working. **Adaptation:** *The Romantic Englishwoman* (New World, 1975). Dir: Joseph Losey. Scr: Tom Stoppard, Thomas Wiseman. Cast: Glenda Jackson (Elizabeth), Michael Caine (Lewis), Helmut Berger (Thomas), Michael Lonsdale (Swan), Kate Nelligan (Isabel). VHS.

3813. *Rome Haul* (Walter D. Edmonds, 1929). In the early nineteenth century, an itinerant young woman happily settles down on a farm near the Erie Canal. The novel was adapted as a 1934 Broadway play titled *The Farmer Takes a Wife* by Frank Elser and Marc Connelly. **Adaptation 1:** *The Farmer Takes a Wife* (Fox, 1935). Dir: Victor Fleming. Scr: Edwin J. Burke. Cast: Janet Gaynor (Molly), Henry Fonda (Dan), Charles Bickford (Jotham), Jane Withers (Della), Andy Devine (Elmer). VHS. **Adaptation 2:** *The Farmer Takes a Wife* (20th Century–Fox, 1953). Dir: Henry Levin. Scr: Sally Benson, Walter Bullock, Joseph Fields. Cast: Betty Grable (Molly), Dale Robertson (Dan), Thelma Ritter (Lucy), John Carroll (Jotham). Notes: A musical adaptation based on Edmonds' novel and on Elser and Connelly's 1934 play. VHS.

3814. *Rommel* (Desmond Young, 1950). A biography of the famous World War II German field marshal General Erwin Rommel (1891–1944). **Adaptation:** *The Desert Fox: The Story of Rommel*; released in the UK as *Rommel, Desert Fox* (20th Century–Fox, 1951). Dir: Henry Hathaway. Scr: Nunnally Johnson. Cast: James Mason (Rommel), Cedric Hardwicke (Dr. Strolin), Jessica Tandy (Lucy), Luther Adler (Adolf Hitler), Everett Sloane (General Burgdorf), Leo G. Carroll (Field Marshal von Rundstedt). DVD, VHS. Notes: James Mason played Rommel again in the 1953 World War II film *The Desert Rats* (DVD, VHS).

3815. *Rookwood* (Harrison Ainsworth, 1834). A gothic romance featuring the legendary British thief and highwayman Dick Turpin, who is transformed in this narrative into a dashing rogue who helps the disadvantaged. **Adaptation:** *Dick Turpin* (Gaumont, 1933). Dir: Victor Hanbury, John Stafford. Scr: Victor Kendall. Cast: Victor McLaglen (Turpin), Jane Carr (Eleanor), Frank Vosper (Tom). VHS.

3816. *Room at the Top* (John Braine. 1957). A working-class British man gives up true love to marry into a wealthy family. **Adaptation:** *Room at the Top* (Continental, 1959). Dir: Jack Clayton. Scr: Neil Paterson. Cast: Simone Signoret (Alice), Laurence Harvey (Joe), Heather Sears (Susan), Donald Wolfit (Mr. Brown), Donald Houston (Charles), Hermione Baddeley (Elspeth), Mary Peach (June). Notes: Academy Awards for Best Screenplay and Actress (Signoret), and nominations for Best Picture, Director, Actor (Harvey), and Supporting Actress (Baddeley); BAFTA Awards for Best Picture and Foreign Actress (Signoret), and nominations for Best Actors (Harvey and Wolfit), Actress (Baddeley), and Newcomer (Peach); Cannes Film Festival and National Board of Review Awards for Best Actress (Signoret). DVD, VHS. Notes: Two sequels were also produced: *Life at the Top* (1965) (VHS), and *Man at the Top* (1975), based on a popular British TV series.

3817. *Room 13* (Edgar Wallace, 1924). The first of Wallace's series of mystery books and stories featuring J. G. Reeder, a mild-mannered, middle-aged government worker turned amateur detective. **Adaptation:** *Mr. Reeder in Room 13*; released in the U.S. as *The Mystery of Room 13* (Associated British, 1938). Dir: Norman Lee. Scr: Victor Kendall, Elizabeth Meehan, Doreen Montgomery. Cast: Gibb McLaughlin (Reeder), Peter Murray-Hill (Captain Gray), Sally Gray (Claire).

3818. *A Room With a View* (E. M. Forster,

1908). An innocent young woman falls in love during a trip to Italy but doesn't realize it until her return to England. **Adaptation:** *A Room with a View* (Merchant-Ivory/Cinecom, 1985). Dir: James Ivory. Scr: Ruth Prawer Jhabvala. Cast: Maggie Smith (Charlotte), Helena Bonham Carter (Lucy), Denholm Elliott (Mr. Emerson), Julian Sands (George), Simon Callow (Reverend Beebe), Rosemary Leach (Mrs. Honeychurch), Judi Dench (Eleanor), Daniel Day-Lewis (Cecil). Notes: Academy Awards for Best Screenplay, Art Direction, and Costume Design, and nominations for Best Picture, Director, Actor (Elliott), Actress (Smith), and Cinematography; BAFTA Awards for Best Film, Actress (Smith), Supporting Actress (Dench), and Production Design, and nominations for Best Director, Screenplay, Supporting Actress (Leach), Musical Score, Editing, Cinematography, and Sound; Golden Globe Award for Best Actress (Smith) and nominations for Best Picture and Director; National Board of Review Awards for Best Picture and Supporting Actor (Day-Lewis). DVD, VHS. Notes: The book was also adapted for the BBC television series Play of the Month in 1973.

3819. *Roommates: My Grandfather's Story* (Max Apple, 1994). Touching memoir of a Michigan man and his long relationship with his immigrant grandfather. His grandfather took him in when he was orphaned and later was his roommate when Apple was in graduate school. When Apple's wife died, the centenarian grandfather helped to raise their three children. **Adaptation:** *Roommates* (Buena Vista, 1995). Dir: Peter Yates. Scr: Max Apple, Stephen Metcalfe. Cast: Peter Falk (Rocky), D. B. Sweeney (Michael), Julianne Moore (Beth), Ellen Burstyn (Judith). DVD, VHS.

3820. *Rooney* (Catherine Cookson, 1957). Set in Dublin in the 1950's, the story of trash collectors and their amorous adventures. **Adaptation:** *Rooney* (Rank, 1958). Dir: George Pollock. Scr: Patrick Kirwan. Cast: John Gregson (Rooney), Muriel Pavlow (Maire), Barry Fitzgerald (Grandfather), June Thorburn (Doreen), Noel Purcell (Tim). VHS.

3821. *The Root of all Evil* (J. S. Fletcher, 1921). After her fiancé leaves her, a shrewd woman sets about to destroy his business by setting up a rival company. **Adaptation:** *Root of All Evil* (Gainsborough, 1947). Dir: Brock Williams. Scr: Brock Williams. Cast: Phyllis Calvert (Jeckie), Michael Rennie (Mortimer), John McCallum (Joe).

3822. *Roots: The Saga of an American Family* (Alex Haley, 1976, Pulitzer Prize and National Book Award). Haley's research into his own family's history was the basis for this epic story about an African man sold into slavery and taken to colonial America, where he and generations of his descendants struggled to survive. **Adaptation:** *Roots* (ABC, 1977 TV Miniseries). Dir: Marvin J. Chomsky, John Erman, David Greene, Gilbert Moses. Scr: William Blinn, M. Charles Cohen, Ernest Kinoy, James Lee. Cast: Maya Angelou (Nyo), Moses Gunn (Kintango), Le Var Burton (Kunta Kinte/Toby Reynolds), Edward Asner (Davies), O. J. Simpson (Kadi), Ralph Waite (Slater), Louis Gossett, Jr. (Fiddler), Sandy Duncan (Anne), Ben Vereen (Chicken George), Robert Reed (Dr. Reynolds), Cicely Tyson (Binta), John Amos (Toby), Olivia Cole (Mathilda), Leslie Uggams (Kizzy), Madge Sinclair (Belle), Lorne Greene (John). Notes: Emmy Awards for Outstanding Miniseries, Director (Greene), Teleplay, Actor (Gossett), Supporting Actor (Asner), Supporting Actress (Cole), Musical Score, and Editing, and nominations for Outstanding Directors, Actors (Amos, Burton, and Vereen), Actresses (Sinclair and Uggams), Supporting Actors (Gunn, Reed, and Waite), Supporting Actresses (Tyson and Duncan), Cinematography, Editing, Costume Design, Sound, and Art Direction; Golden Globe Award for Best Television Drama and nomination for Best TV Actress (Uggams); Peabody Award for Best Film. DVD, VHS. Notes: A television miniseries sequel, *Roots: The Next Generation* aired in 1977 (DVD, VHS).

3823. *The Roots of Heaven* (Romain Gary, 1956, Prix Goncourt). French novel, originally titled *Les Racines du Ciel*, about a white man in Africa and his work to prevent the wholesale slaughter of elephants. The novel was translated into English in 1958. **Adaptation:** *The Roots of Heaven* (20th Century–Fox, 1958). Dir: John Huston. Scr: Romain Gary, Patrick Leigh-Fermor. Cast: Errol Flynn (Forsythe), Juliette Greco (Minna), Trevor Howard (Morel), Eddie Albert (Abe), Orson Welles (Sedgewick), Paul Lukas (Saint Denis), Herbert Lom (Orsini).

3824. *Rope Burns: Stories from the Corner* (F. X. Toole, 2000). A collection of short stories about boxers, trainers, and others involved in the boxing game. **Adaptation:** *Million Dollar Baby* (Warner, 2004). Dir: Clint Eastwood. Scr: Paul Haggis. Cast: Clint Eastwood (Frankie), Hilary Swank (Maggie), Morgan Freeman (Scrap-Iron),

Jay Baruchel (Danger). Notes: The screenplay, which concerns a talented female boxer and the hardened trainer she persuades to work with her, is based on several stories in the collection. Academy Awards for Best Picture, Director, Actress (Swank), and Supporting Actor (Freeman), and nominations for Best Actor (Eastwood), Screenplay, and Editing; Golden Globe Awards for Best Director and Actress (Swank), and nominations for Best Picture, Supporting Actor (Freeman), and Musical Score; National Board of Review Special Achievement Award to Eastwood, who produced, directed, acted in, and composed the score for the film. DVD, VHS.

3825. *The Rosary Murders* (William X. Kienzle, 1979). An amateur-detective priest investigating the serial murder of priests and nuns becomes the confessor of the killer. **Adaptation:** *The Rosary Murders* (New Line, 1987). Dir: Fred Walton. Scr: Elmore Leonard, Fred Walton. Cast: Roger Angelini (Brainard), Anita Barone (Irene), B. Constance Barry (Sister Grace), Belinda Bauer (Pat). VHS.

3826. *The Rose and the Flame* (Jonreed Lauritzen, 1951). Historical romance set in 1680 about a Spanish princess who falls in love with the outlaw who is paid to escort her across hostile Mexican territory. **Adaptation:** *Kiss of Fire* (Universal International, 1955). Dir: Joseph M. Newman. Scr: Franklin Coen, Richard Collins. Cast: Jack Palance (El Tigre), Barbara Rush (Princess Lucia), Rex Reason (the Duke of Montera), Martha Hyer (Felicia).

3827. "A Rose for Emily" (William Faulkner, 1930). After her death, the people of a small town discover an elderly spinster's long-held romantic secret. The short story was published in *Forum* magazine on April 30, 1930. **Adaptation:** *A Rose for Emily* (Chubbuck, 1982). Dir: Lyndon Chubbuck. Scr: H. Kaye Dyal. Cast: John Houseman (Narrator), Anjelica Huston (Emily), John Randolph (Mr. Grierson), John Carradine (Colonel Sartoris), Jared Martin (Homer). VHS.

3828. *The Rose Rent* (Ellis Peters [pseudonym for Edith Pargeter], 1986). The thirteenth installment in Peters' twenty-volume series (1977–1994) featuring Brother Cadfael, a twelfth-century monk who, following service in the Crusades, tends to the herbarium at Shrewsbury Abbey and solves crimes. In this book, a widow donates her estate to the monks in exchange for a single white rose once a year. When a murdered man's body is found near the rose one year, Cadfael is called upon to solve the crime. **Adaptation:**

Cadfael: The Rose Rent (ITV/PBS, 1998 TV Movie series). Dir: Richard Stroud. Scr: Christopher Russell. Cast: Derek Jacobi (Brother Cadfael), Michael Culver (Prior Robert), Anthony Green (Hugh), Julian Firth (Brother Jerome). DVD, VHS.

3829. *Rosebud* (Joan Hemingway and Paul Bonnecarrere, 1974). Palestinian terrorists kidnap and hold five wealthy women hostage aboard a yacht. **Adaptation:** *Rosebud* (United Artists, 1975). Dir: Otto Preminger. Scr: Erik Lee Preminger. Cast: Peter O'Toole (Larry), Richard Attenborough (Edward), Cliff Gorman (Yafet), John V. Lindsay (Senator Donovan), Peter Lawford (Lord Carter), Raf Vallone (George). VHS.

3830. *Rosemary's Baby* (Ira Levin, 1967). Thriller about a young woman and her husband who move into a New York City apartment building, where the seemingly nice residents are actually a coven of Satanists. With her husband's cooperation, the woman gives birth to Satan's child. **Adaptation:** *Rosemary's Baby* (Paramount, 1968). Dir: Roman Polanski. Scr: Roman Polanski. Cast: Mia Farrow (Rosemary), John Cassavetes (Guy), Ruth Gordon (Minnie), Sidney Blackmer (Roman), Maurice Evans (Edward), Ralph Bellamy (Dr. Sapirstein). Notes: Academy Award for Best Supporting Actress (Gordon) and nomination for Best Screenplay; Golden Globe Award for Best Supporting Actress (Gordon) and nominations for Best Screenplay and Musical Score. DVD, VHS. Notes: A made-for-television sequel titled *Look What Happened to Rosemary's Baby* was broadcast in 1976.

Rosie Dixon, Night Nurse (see *Confessions of a Night Nurse*).

3831. *The Rough and the Smooth* (Robin Maugham, 1951). An archaeologist breaks his engagement to a wealthy woman to pursue an affair with a seductive siren. **Adaptation:** *The Rough and the Smooth*; released in the U.S. as *Portrait of a Sinner* (American International, 1959). Dir: Robert Siodmak. Scr: Audrey Erskine-Lindop. Cast: Nadja Tiller (Ila), Tony Britton (Mike), William Bendix (Reg), Natasha Parry (Margaret). VHS.

Rough Company (see *Night Walker*).

Rough Cut (see *Touch the Lion's Paw*).

Rough Magic (see *Miss Shumway Waves a Wand*).

3832. *A Rough Shoot* (Geoffrey Household, 1951). A retired American military officer living in

England believes that he has accidentally shot a poacher on his property and finds himself involved with international spies. **Adaptation:** *Rough Shoot*; released in the U.S. as *Shoot First* (United Artists, 1953). Dir: Robert Parrish. Scr: Eric Ambler. Cast: Joel McCrea (Robert), Evelyn Keyes (Cecily), Herbert Lom (Sandorski), Roland Culver (Randall), Marius Goring (Hiart).

3833. *Rough Sketch* (Robert Sylvester, 1948). An American adventurer helps Cuban rebels in their plot to assassinate a corrupt government leader. **Adaptation:** *We Were Strangers* (Columbia, 1949). Dir: John Huston. Scr: John Huston, Peter Viertel. Cast: Jennifer Jones (China), John Garfield (Tony), Pedro Armendariz (Armando), Gilbert Roland (Guillermo). DVD, VHS.

3834. *Roughing It* (Mark Twain [pseudonym for Samuel Langhorne Clemens], 1872). Autobiographical anecdotes about Twain's life as a gold prospector on the Western frontier. **Adaptation:** *Roughing It* (Hallmark, 2002 TV Movie). Dir: Charles Martin Smith. Scr: Steven H. Berman. Cast: James Garner (Samuel Clemens), Robin Dunne (Samuel Clemens as a young man), Adam Arkin (Henry), Eric Roberts (the Foreman), Ned Beatty (Slade). DVD, VHS.

3835. *Roughly Speaking* (Louise Randall Pierson, 1943). Autobiography of a businesswoman, her two marriages, and her eventful life through the first half of the twentieth century. **Adaptation:** *Roughly Speaking* (Warner, 1945). Dir: Michael Curtiz. Scr: Louise Randall Pierson, Catherine Turney. Cast: Rosalind Russell (Louise), Jack Carson (Harold), Donald Woods (Rodney), Alan Hale (Lew).

3836. *Roughshod* (Norman A. Fox, 1951). A cowboy hired by outlaws to kill a rancher befriends him instead and falls in love with the cattleman's spirited daughter. **Adaptation:** *Gunsmoke* (Universal International, 1953). Dir: Nathan Juran. Scr: D. D. Beauchamp. Cast: Audie Murphy (Kittridge), Susan Cabot (Rita), Paul Kelly (Saxon), Charles Drake (Lake). VHS.

3837. *Round the Moon* (Jules Verne, 1869). Originally titled *Autour de la Lune*, the sequel to Verne's 1865 science-fiction novel *From the Earth to the Moon* finds three explorers circling the moon and making discoveries. **Adaptation:** *From the Earth to the Moon* (Warner, 1958). Dir: Byron Haskin. Scr: Robert Blees, James Leicester. Cast: Joseph Cotten (Victor), George Sanders (Stuyvesant), Debra Paget (Virginia). Notes: The screenplay combines elements of this novel and

From the Earth to the Moon. VHS. See also *From the Earth to the Moon*.

3838. *The Round Tower* (Catherine Cookson, 1968). Romantic story about a wealthy woman and a working-class man unjustly accused of her pregnancy. **Adaptation:** *The Round Tower* (Festival, 1998 TV Movie). Dir: Alan Grint. Scr: T. R. Bowen. Cast: Emilia Fox (Vanessa), Isabelle Amyes (Irene), Keith Barron (Jonathan), Robert Cole (Michael), Christopher Connel (Smith). DVD, VHS.

3839. *The Rounders* (Max Evans, 1960). Western story about the adventures of two aging cowboys who are not yet willing to settle down and get married. **Adaptation:** *The Rounders* (MGM, 1965). Dir: Burt Kennedy. Scr: Burt Kennedy. Cast: Glenn Ford (Ben), Henry Fonda (Howdy), Sue Ane Langdon (Mary), Chill Wills (Jim), Edgar Buchanan (Vince). VHS. Notes: The book was also the basis for an ABC television series in 1966.

3840. *The Rover* (Joseph Conrad, 1923). A military officer's adventures during the Napoleonic Wars. **Adaptation:** *The Rover* (Cinerama, 1967). Dir: Terence Young. Scr: Jo Eisinger, Luciano Vincenzoni. Cast: Anthony Quinn (Peyrol), Rita Hayworth (Aunt Caterina), Richard Johnson (Real), Rosanna Schiaffino (Arlette). VHS.

Rowing Through (see *The Amateurs*).

3841. *Royal Flash* (George MacDonald Fraser, 1970). Comic adventures of a Victorian braggart who impersonates a Prussian nobleman in Ruritania. **Adaptation:** *Royal Flash* (20th Century–Fox, 1975). Dir: Richard Lester. Scr: George MacDonald Fraser. Cast: Malcolm McDowell (Captain Flashman), Alan Bates (Rudi), Florinda Bolkan (Lola), Oliver Reed (Otto von Bismarck), Tom Bell (De Gautet), Joss Ackland (Sapten). VHS.

The Ruby Ring (see *The Secret of the Ruby Ring*).

3842. *Rudy!: An Investigative Biography of Rudy Giuliani* (Wayne Barrett, 2000). A biography of the colorful New York City mayor. **Adaptation:** *Rudy: The Rudy Giuliani Story* (USA Networks, 2003 TV Movie). Dir: Robert Dornhelm. Scr: Stanley Weiser. Cast: James Woods (Rudolph Giuliani), Penelope Ann Miller (Donna Hanover), Michelle Nolden (Cristyne Lategano), John Bourgeois (Peter Powers). Notes: Emmy nominations for Outstanding Actor (Woods) and Makeup. DVD, VHS.

3843. *Ruggles of Red Gap* (Harry Leon Wilson, 1915). Comic story about a British butler who goes to work for an American family in the Old West. The novel originally appeared as a ten-part serial in *The Saturday Evening Post* (December 26, 1914–February 27, 1915). It was also adapted as a Broadway play by Harrison Rhodes in 1915. **Silent Films:** 1918 and 1923. **Adaptation 1:** *Ruggles of Red Gap* (Paramount, 1935). Dir: Leo McCarey. Scr: Walter De Leon, Humphrey Pearson, Harlan Thompson. Cast: Charles Laughton (Ruggles), Mary Boland (Effie), Charlie Ruggles (Egbert), Zasu Pitts (Prunella), Roland Young (the Earl of Burnstead/George). Notes: Academy Award nomination for Best Picture. VHS. **Adaptation 2:** *Fancy Pants* (Paramount, 1950). Dir: George Marshall. Scr: Edmund Hartmann, Robert O'Brien. Cast: Bob Hope (Humphrey/Arthur), Lucille Ball (Agatha), Bruce Cabot (Belknap), Jack Kirkwood (Mike), Lea Penman (Effie). DVD, VHS.

3844. "Ruidoso" (John McPhee, 1974). A Louisiana man and his sons living in New Mexico breed a champion race horse. The short story originally appeared in the April 29, 1974, issue of *The New Yorker* and was included in McPhee's 1975 collection *Pieces of the Frame*. **Adaptation:** *Casey's Shadow* (Columbia, 1978). Dir: Martin Ritt. Scr: Carol Sobieski. Cast: Walter Matthau (Lloyd), Alexis Smith (Sarah), Robert Webber (Mike), Murray Hamilton (Tom). Availability: DVD, VHS.

3845. *The Rules of Attraction* (Bret Easton Ellis, 1987). Set at a prestigious New England college in the mid–1980's, the story of student love affairs involving a drug dealer, a confirmed virgin, her promiscuous roommate, and a bisexual man. (Interestingly, the drug-dealing student is Sean Bateman, who is the brother of Patrick Bateman, the Wall Street trader and psychotic serial killer in Easton's *American Psycho*.) **Adaptation:** *The Rules of Attraction* (Kingsgate/Lions Gate, 2002). Dir: Roger Avary. Scr: Roger Avary. Cast: James Van Der Beek (Sean), Shannyn Sossamon (Lauren), Kip Pardue (Victor), Jessica Biel (Lara). DVD, VHS.

3846. *Ruling Passion* (Reginald Hill, 1973). In the third installment of Hill's popular series (1970–2004) featuring British policemen Andrew Dalziel and Peter Pascoe, three of Pascoe's friends die while they are together at a country home, and the local police ask him to help investigate. **Adaptation:** *Dalziel and Pascoe: Ruling Passion* (BBC/A&E, 1997 British TV Movie series). Dir: Gareth Davies. Scr: Malcolm Bradbury. Cast: Warren Clarke (Dalziel), Colin Buchanan (Pascoe), David Royle (Edgar).

3847. *Rumble Fish* (S. E. Hinton, 1975). A young gang member in Tulsa tries unsuccessfully to live up to the tough reputation of his absent older brother. **Adaptation:** *Rumble Fish* (Universal, 1983). Dir: Francis Ford Coppola. Scr: S. E. Hinton, Francis Ford Coppola. Cast: Matt Dillon (Rusty), Mickey Rourke (the Motorcycle Boy), Diane Lane (Patty), Dennis Hopper (Mr. James), Diana Scarwid (Cassandra), Vincent Spano (Steve), Nicolas Cage (Smokey), Christopher Penn (B. J.), Laurence Fishburne (Midget). DVD, VHS.

3848. *Rum Punch* (Elmore Leonard, 1992). A flight attendant transferring illegal money for her boyfriend finds herself caught between vicious gun runners and the FBI. **Adaptation:** *Jackie Brown* (Miramax, 1997). Dir: Quentin Tarantino. Scr: Quentin Tarantino. Cast: Pam Grier (Jackie), Samuel L. Jackson (Ordell), Robert Forster (Max), Bridget Fonda (Melanie), Michael Keaton (Ray), Robert De Niro (Louis). Notes: Academy Award nomination for Best Supporting Actor (Forster); Golden Globe nominations for Best Actor (Jackson) and Actress (Grier). DVD, VHS.

Run for the Sun (*see* "The Most Dangerous Game").

3849. *The Run of the Country* (Shane Connaughton, 1991). Set in a small Irish town, a story centering on the conflicts between a widowed policeman and his teenaged son. **Adaptation:** *The Run of the Country* (Columbia, 1995). Dir: Peter Yates. Scr: Shane Connaughton. Cast: Albert Finney (Danny's father), Matt Keeslar (Danny), Victoria Smurfit (Annagh), Anthony Brophy (Prunty). VHS.

Run Wild, Run Free (see *The White Colt*).

3850. *Runaway: Diary of a Street Kid* (Evelyn Lau, 1989). Memoir of a teenaged Asian girl who ran away from her strict mother and lived on the street, becoming a drug addict and prostitute. **Adaptation:** *The Diary of Evelyn Lau* (Canadian Broadcasting Company, 1993 TV Movie).Dir: Sturla Gunnarsson. Scr: Barry Stevens. Cast: Sandra Oh (Evelyn), Harrison Liu (Mr. Lau), Shirley Cui (Mrs. Lau).

3851. *Runaway Jury* (John Grisham, 1996). In a tobacco lawsuit, an insider on the jury and a mysterious woman outside manipulate the outcome of the trial. **Adaptation:** *Runaway Jury* (20th Century–Fox, 2003). Dir: Gary Fleder. Scr:

Brian Koppelman, David Levien, Rick Cleveland, Matthew Chapman. Cast: John Cusack (Nicholas), Gene Hackman (Rankin), Dustin Hoffman (Wendell), Rachel Weisz (Marlee), Bruce Davison (Durwood), Bruce McGill (Judge Harkin). Notes: For the film, the trial involves a gun manufacturer rather than a tobacco company. DVD, VHS.

3852. *The Runaway Summer* (Nina Bawden [pseudonym for Nina Mabey Kark], 1969). Children's book about a little girl who goes to live with her grandfather and aunt at their seaside cottage after her parents' divorce. She then runs away on a journey of self-discovery with an illegal immigrant one summer.**Adaptation:** *The Runaway Summer* (BBC, 1971 TV Miniseries). Dir: Mary Ridge. Scr: Rosemary Anne Sisson. Cast: Stephen Bone (Simon), Beryl Cooke (Aunt Alice), Carol Davis (Mary), Jeffrey Sirr (Krishna), John Welsh (Grandfather).

Running Away (see *Two Women*).

A Running Duck (see *Fair Game*).

The Running Man (1963) (see *The Ballad of the Running Man*).

3853. *The Running Man* (Stephen King, 1982). Originally published under the pseudonym Richard Bachman, this futuristic thriller is the tale of an innocent man framed for murder and made to compete on a game show whose object is to escape being killed by the forces of "justice." **Adaptation:** *The Running Man* (TriStar, 1987). Dir: Paul Michael Glaser. Scr: Steven E. de Souza. Cast: Arnold Schwarzenegger (Ben), Maria Conchita Alonso (Amber), Yaphet Kotto (William), Jim Brown (Fireball), Jesse Ventura (Captain Freedom). DVD, VHS.

3854. *Running Scared* (Gregory McDonald, 1964). A college student is blamed for the suicide death of a friend. **Adaptation:** *Running Scared* (Columbia, 1972). Dir: David Hemmings. Scr: Clive Exton, David Hemmings. Cast: Robert Powell (Tom), Maxine Audley (Mrs. Betancourt), Stephanie Bidmead (Mrs. Case), Georgia Brown (Sarah), Gayle Hunnicutt (Ellen). Barry Morse (Mr. Case), Edward Underdown (Mr. Betancourt).

3855. *Rush* (Kim Wozencraft, 1990). Two Texas cops go undercover to catch a drug dealer and end up becoming addicts themselves. **Adaptation:** *Rush* (MGM, 1991). Dir: Lili Fini Zanuck. Scr: Pete Dexter. Cast: Jason Patric (Jim), Jennifer Jason Leigh (Kristen), Sam Elliott (Dodd),

Max Perlich (Walker), Gregg Allman (Gaines). DVD, VHS.

3856. *The Russia House* (John Le Carre [pseudonym for David Cornwell], 1989). A British publisher in Soviet Russia is drawn into espionage by British Intelligence and a beautiful Russian woman. **Adaptation:** *The Russia House* (MGM, 1990). Dir: Fred Schepisi. Scr: Tom Stoppard. Cast: Sean Connery (Bartholomew), Michelle Pfeiffer (Katya), Roy Scheider (Russell), James Fox (Ned), John Mahoney (Brady), Michael Kitchen (Clive). DVD, VHS.

Russian Roulette (see *Kosygin Is Coming*).

The Russians Are Coming, The Russians Are Coming (see *The Off-Islanders*).

Ruthless (see *Prelude to Night*).

3857. *The Ruthless Ones* (Laurence Moody, 1969). A young man and his girlfriend try to kill off his elderly grandmother, but she unexpectedly turns the tables on them. **Adaptation:** *What Became of Jack and Jill?* (20th Century–Fox, 1972). Dir: Bill Bain. Scr: Roger Marshall. Cast: Vanessa Howard (Jill), Mona Washbourne (Alice), Paul Nicholas (Johnny), Peter Copley (Dickson).

RX for Murder (see *The Deeds of Dr. Deadcert*).

The Sacketts (see *The Day Breakers*).

Sabotage (see *The Secret Agent*).

3858. *Sad Cypress* (Agatha Christie, 1940). A beautiful young woman turns to Hercule Poirot when she is unjustly accused of killing her love rival. **Adaptation:** *Poirot: Sad Cypress* (London Weekend Television, 2003 TV Movie series). Dir: Dave Moore. Scr: Dave Moore. Cast: David Suchet (Poirot), Elisabeth Dermot-Walsh (Elinor), Rupert Penry-Jones (Roddy), Kelly Reilly (Mary). DVD, VHS.

Sadie Thompson (*see* "Miss Thompson").

3859. *The Safe House* (Nicci French [pseudonym for Nicci Gerrard and Sean French], 1998). After the brutal murder of her parents, a girl is sent to a safe house, where she works with a psychiatrist and uncovers the truth behind her parents' deaths. **Adaptation:** *The Safe House* (ITV, 2002 TV Movie). Dir: Simon Massey. Scr: David Pirie. Cast: Geraldine Somerville (Dr. Graham), Philip Davis (Inspector Baird), Robert Bathurst (Dr. Daley), Kelly Reilly (Fiona).

3860. *Safe Passage* (Ellyn Bache, 1988). The

unhappy single mother of seven grown sons is reunited with her estranged husband when it is feared that one of their sons, a soldier, may have been killed. **Adaptation:** *Safe Passage* (New Line, 1994). Dir: Robert Allan Ackerman. Scr: Deena Goldstone. Cast: Susan Sarandon (Margaret), Nick Stahl (Simon), Sam Shepard (Patrick), Marcia Gay Harden (Cynthia), Robert Sean Leonard (Alfred), Sean Astin (Izzy). DVD, VHS.

3861. *The Safety of Objects* (A. M. Homes, 1990). A collection of ten short stories centering around the personal problems of neighbors in a typical suburban community. **Adaptation:** *The Safety of Objects* (IFC/Killer, 2001). Dir: Rose Troche. Scr: Rose Troche. Cast: Glenn Close (Esther), Dermot Mulroney (Jim), Jessica Campbell (Julie), Patricia Clarkson (Annette), Moira Kelly (Susan), Robert Klein (Howard), Mary Kay Place (Helen). DVD, VHS.

3862. *The Saga of Erik the Viking* (Terry Jones, 1983). The Monty Python alumnus's comic novel about the fantastic adventures of a Viking who goes on a quest to find the meaning of life. **Adaptation:** *Erik the Viking* (Orion, 1989). Dir: Terry Jones. Scr: Terry Jones. Cast: Tim Robbins (Erik), Mickey Rooney (Erik's Grandfather), Eartha Kitt (Freya), Terry Jones (King Arnulf), Imogen Stubbs (Princess Aud), John Cleese (Halfdan the Black). DVD, VHS.

3863. *Sahara* (Clive Cussler, 1992). An American adventurer in search of a lost Civil War ship battles a powerful industrialist and a dictator who are conspiring to poison the environment. **Adaptation:** *Sahara* (Paramount, 2005). Dir: Breck Eisner. Scr: Thomas Dean Donnelly, Joshua Oppenheimer, John C. Richards, James V. Hart. Cast: Matthew McConaughey (Dirk), Steve Zahn (Al), Penelope Cruz (Eva), Delroy Lindo (Agent Carl), William H. Macy (Sandecker). DVD, VHS.

3864. *Sail a Crooked Ship* (Nathaniel Benchley, 1960). Comic novel about a young man and his fiancée held hostage on a ship by a group of incompetent thieves trying to make a getaway after a bank robbery. **Adaptation:** *Sail a Crooked Ship* (Columbia, 1961). Dir: Irving Brecher. Scr: Nathaniel Benchley, Ruth Brooks Flippen, Bruce Geller. Cast: Robert Wagner (Gilbert), Dolores Hart (Elinor), Carolyn Jones (Virginia), Ernie Kovacs (the Captain), Frankie Avalon (Rodney), Frank Gorshin (George), Jesse White (McDonald), Harvey Lembeck (Nickels). VHS.

3865. *The Sailor from Gibraltar* (Marguerite Duras [pseudonym for Marguerite Donnadieu],

1966). In the French novel originally titled *Le Marin de Gibraltar*, a mysterious woman searches the seas for her lost lover, who may have never existed. **Adaptation:** *The Sailor from Gibraltar* (Lopert, 1967). Dir: Tony Richardson. Scr: Christopher Isherwood, Don Magner, Tony Richardson. Cast: Jeanne Moreau (Anna), Ian Bannen (Alan), Vanessa Redgrave (Sheila), Orson Welles (Louis), Zia Mohyeddin (Noori), Hugh Griffith (Llewellyn).

Sailor of the King (see *Brown on Resolution*).

3866. *The Sailor Who Fell From Grace with the Sea* (Yukio Mishima [pseudonym for Kimitake Hiraoka], 1963). The Japanese novel, originally titled *Gogo no eiko*, concerns a disturbed young man who takes revenge on a sailor who is romantically involved with his mother. The book was first translated into English in 1965. **Adaptation:** *The Sailor Who Fell from Grace with the Sea* (AVCO Embassy, 1976). Dir: Lewis John Carlino. Scr: Lewis John Carlino. Cast: Sarah Miles (Anne), Kris Kristofferson (Jim), Jonathan Kahn (Jonathan), Margo Cunningham (Mrs. Palmer). DVD, VHS.

3867. *The Sailor's Return* (David Garnett, 1925). A British sailor during the later nineteenth century returns home with an African wife and opens a pub, causing controversy in his village. **Adaptation:** *The Sailor's Return* (Euston, 1978). Dir: Jack Gold. Scr: James Saunders. Cast: Tom Bell (William), Shope Shodeinde (Princess Tulip), Elton Charles (Billy/Olu), Denyse Alexander (Mrs. Cherret).

The Saint in London (see "The Million Pound Day").

3868. *The Saint in New York* (Leslie Charteris [pseudonym for Leslie Charles Bowyer Yin], 1935). In an installment of Charteris' long-running series featuring Robin Hood-like sleuth Simon Templar, the Saint (as he is known) helps New York police stop a crime ring led by a mysterious gangster known as the "Big Fellow." **Adaptation:** *The Saint in New York* (RKO, 1938). Dir: Ben Holmes. Scr: Charles Kaufman, Mortimer Offner. Cast: Louis Hayward (Templar), Kay Sutton (Fay), Sig Rumann (Hutch), Jonathan Hale (Inspector Fernack), Jack Carson (Red). VHS.

The Saint in Palm Springs (see "Palm Springs").

St. Ives (1976) (see *The Procane Chronicle*).

3869. *St. Ives: Being the Adventures of a French Prisoner in England* (Robert Louis Stevenson and Arthur Quiller Couch, 1897). During the Napoleonic Wars in 1812, a French prisoner plots his escape from Edinburgh Castle. Stevenson died in 1894 and the book was completed by Arthur Quller Couch. **Adaptation 1:** *The Secret of St. Ives* (Columbia, 1949). Dir: Philip Rosen. Scr: Eric Taylor. Cast: Richard Ney (Anatole), Vanessa Brown (Flora), Henry Daniell (Chevenish), Edgar Barrier (Carnac), Douglas Walton (St. Ives). **Adaptation 2:** *St. Ives* (BBC, 1955 TV Movie). Dir: Rex Tucker. Scr: Rex Tucker. Cast: William Russell (St. Ives), Noelle Middleton (Flora), Arthur Young (Romaine), Francis Matthews (Ronald), Gerald Lawson (Clausel). **Adaptation 3:** *St. Ives* (BBC, 1967 TV Movie). Dir: Christopher Barry. Dir: Rex Tucker. Cast: David Sumner (St. Ives), Gay Hamilton (Flora), Hamilton Dyce (Romaine), Mark Eden (Alain), Talfryn Thomas (Clausel). **Adaptation 4:** *St. Ives* (Buena Vista, 1999). Dir: Harry Hook. Scr: Allan Cubitt. Cast: Jean-Marc Barr (St. Ives), Miranda Richardson (Susan), Anna Friel (Flora), Richard E. Grant (Chevening), Tim Dutton (Francois). DVD, VHS.

3870. *Saint Jack* (Paul Theroux, 1973). A good-hearted American thrives as a pimp in Singapore in the early 1970's. **Adaptation:** *Saint Jack* (New World, 1979). Dir: Peter Bogdanovich. Scr: Peter Bogdanovich, Howard Sackler, Paul Theroux. Cast: Ben Gazzara (Jack), Denholm Elliott (William), Joss Ackland (Yardley). DVD, VHS.

3871. *Saint Johnson* (W. R. Burnett, 1930). Western about a cowboy who becomes a marshal and vows to clean up the town of Tombstone. **Adaptation 1:** *Law and Order* (Universal, 1932). Dir: Edward L. Cahn. Scr: John Huston, Tom Reed. Cast: Walter Huston (Frame), Harry Carey (Brandt), Russell Hopton (Luther), Raymond Hatton (Deadwood). **Adaptation 2:** *Wild West Days* (Universal, 1937). Dir: Ford Beebe, Clifford Smith. Scr: Wyndham Gittens, Norman S. Hall, Ray Trampe. Cast: Johnny Mack Brown (Wade), George Shelley (Hanford), Lynn Gilbert (Lucy). VHS. **Adaptation 3:** *Law and Order*; released in the UK as *Lucky Ralston* (Universal, 1940). Dir: Ray Taylor. Scr: Sherman Lowe, Victor McLeod. Cast: Johnny Mack Brown (Ralston), Fuzzy Knight (Deadwood), Nell O'Day (Sally). **Adaptation 4:** *Law and Order* (Universal International, 1953). Dir: Nathan Juran. Scr: John Bagni, Gwen Bagni, D. D. Beauchamp. Cast: Ronald Reagan (Johnson), Dorothy Malone (Jeannie), Preston Foster (Kurt), Alex Nicol (Lute). DVD, VHS.

3872. *Saint Maybe* (Anne Tyler, 1991). A lonely teenager feels compelled to tell his older married brother that his wife has been unfaithful, causing discord in his family. **Adaptation:** *Saint Maybe* (CBS/Hallmark, 1998 TV Movie). Dir: Michael Pressman. Scr: Robert W. Lenski. Cast: Thomas McCarthy (Ian), Mary-Louise Parker (Lucy), Blythe Danner (Bea), Edward Herrmann (Doug), Jeffrey Nordling (Danny Bedloe). VHS.

3873. *The Saint Meets His Match* (Leslie Charteris [pseudonym for Leslie Charles Bowyer Yin], 1931). In an installment of Charteris' long-running series featuring Robin Hood-like sleuth Simon Templar, the Saint (as he is known) goes to San Francisco to help a man being framed for murder. The book was published in the U.S. in 1932 as *Angels of Doom*. **Adaptation:** *The Saint Strikes Back* (RKO, 1939). Dir: John Farrow. Scr: John Twist. Cast: George Sanders (Templar), Wendy Barrie (Val), Jonathan Hale (Inspector Fernack), Jerome Cowan (Cullis), Barry Fitzgerald (Zipper). VHS.

The Saint Meets the Tiger (see *Meet the Tiger*).

3874. *St. Peter's Fair* (Ellis Peters [pseudonym for Edith Pargeter], 1981). The fourth installment in Peters' twenty-volume series (1977–1994) featuring Brother Cadfael, a twelfth-century monk who, following service in the Crusades, tends to the herbarium at Shrewsbury Abbey and solves crimes. In this book, a merchant is murdered during an argument between businessmen and the monks at the annual feast of St. Peter. Cadfael is called from his herbarium to investigate. **Adaptation:** Cadfael: St. Peter's Fair (ITV/PBS, 1997 TV Movie series). Dir: Herbert Wise. Scr: Russell Lewis, Paul Pender, Ben Rostul, Richard Stoneman. Cast: Derek Jacobi (Brother Cadfael), Michael Culver (Prior Robert), Anthony Green (Hugh), Julian Firth (Brother Jerome). DVD, VHS.

The Saint Strikes Back (see *Angels of Doom*).

The Saint's Vacation (see *Getaway*).

3875. *The Salamander* (Morris L. West, 1973). An Italian police official discovers a plot by fascists to take over Italy. **Adaptation:** *The Salamander* (ITC, 1981). Dir: Peter Zinner. Scr: Robert Katz. Cast: Franco Nero (Dante), Anthony Quinn (Bruno), Martin Balsam (Captain Steffanelli), Sybil Danning (Lili), Christopher Lee (General Magusari), Cleavon Little (Carl). DVD, VHS.

3876. *Salambo* (original French: *Salammbô*; Gustave Flaubert, 1862). Set during the conflict between ancient Rome and Carthage, the story of the love affair between the daughter of a Carthaginian general and a Roman military officer. **Silent Film:** 1924. **Adaptation:** *Salambo* (20th Century–Fox, 1960). Dir: Sergio Grieco. Scr: John Blamy, Barbara Sohmers, Andre Tabet. Cast: Jeanne Valerie (Salambo), Jacques Sernas (Mathos), Edmund Purdom (Narr Havas), Riccardo Garrone (Hamilcar).

3877. *'Salem's Lot* (Stephen King, 1975). A famous writer returns to his hometown in New England and finds that vampires are living there. He combats them with the help of an innocent young boy. **Adaptation 1:** *Salem's Lot* (CBS, 1979 TV Miniseries). Dir: Tobe Hooper. Scr: Paul Monash. Cast: David Soul (Ben), James Mason (Straker), Lance Kerwin (Mark), Bonnie Bedelia (Susan), Lew Ayres (Jason). Notes: A theatrical film cut from the miniseries was also released in 1979. DVD, VHS. **Adaptation 2:** *'Salem's Lot* (Turner, 2004 TV Movie). Dir: Mikael Salomon. Scr: Peter Filardi. Cast: Rob Lowe (Ben), Andre Braugher (Matt), Donald Sutherland (Straker), Samantha Mathis (Susan), Daniel Byrd (Mark), Rutger Hauer (Kurt), James Cromwell (Father Callahan). DVD, VHS. Notes: A sequel, *A Return to 'Salem's Lot* was released in 1987 (VHS).

3878. *Sally* (Howard Fast, 1967). A teacher who believes she is dying hires an assassin to kill her. When she discovers that she is not ill, she and a policeman must try to find the killer before he strikes. Fast originally published the novel under the pseudonym E. V. Cunningham. **Adaptation:** *The Face of Fear* (CBS, 1971 TV Movie). Dir: George McCowan. Scr: Edward Hume. Cast: Ricardo Montalban (Sergeant Ortega), Jack Warden (Lieutenant Coy), Elizabeth Ashley (Sally), Dane Clark (Tamworth).

Salo, or the 120 Days of Sodom (see *120 Days of Sodom*).

3879. *Salt on Our Skin* (Benoite Groult, 1988). The French novel, originally titled *Les Vaisseaux du Coeur*, is the romantic story of a young Scottish woman who returns from school in Paris to her country home and begins a torrid affair. Although class differences prevent the lovers from marrying, she continues the affair for years after her marriage. **Adaptation:** *Salt on Our Skin*; released in the U.S. as *Desire* (Warner, 1992). Dir: Andrew Birkin. Scr: Andrew Birkin, Bee Gilbert. Cast: Greta Scacchi (Georgia), Vincent D'Onofrio (Gavin), Anais Jeanneret (Frederique).

Salt to the Devil (see *Christ in Concrete*).

Salute John Citizen (see *Mr. Bunting in Peace and War*).

3880. *Salute to the Gods* (Malcolm Campbell, 1934). The story of a racecar driver's life and romantic relationships. The author, himself a racecar enthusiast, set a variety of world speed records on land and water between 1924 and 1935. **Adaptation:** *Burn 'Em Up O'Connor* (MGM, 1939). Dir: Edward Sedgwick. Scr: Milton Merlin, Byron Morgan. Cast: Dennis O'Keefe (Jerry), Cecilia Parker (Jane), Nat Pendleton (Buddy), Harry Carey (Pinky).

3881. *The Salzburg Connection* (Helen MacInnes, 1969). An American lawyer on vacation in Salzburg is accused of being a spy. **Adaptation:** *The Salzburg Connection* (20th Century–Fox, 1972). Dir: Lee H. Katzin. Scr: Edward Anhalt, Oscar Millard. Cast: Whit Bissell (Newhart), Klaus Maria Brandauer (Johann), Mischa Hausserman (Lev), Karen Jensen (Elissa), Anna Karina (Anna). VHS.

Sam Marlowe, Private Eye (see *The Man with Bogart's Face*).

The Same Skin (see *Household Ghosts*).

3882. *Sammy Going South* (W. H. Canaway, 1961). Orphaned in northern Africa, a ten-year-old boy travels thousands of miles on his own to find his aunt in Durban, South Africa. **Adaptation:** *Sammy Going South*; released in the U.S. as *A Boy Ten Feet Tall* (Seven Arts/Paramount, 1963). Dir: Alexander Mackendrick. Scr: Denis Cannan. Cast: Edward G. Robinson (Cocky), Fergus McClelland (Sammy), Constance Cummings (Gloria), Harry H. Corbett (Lem).

San Antone (see *The Golden Herd*).

3883. *The San Francisco Story* (Richard Summers, 1949). During the goldrush days of the nineteenth-century, a drifter goes to San Francisco, where he helps to eliminate crime and later enters politics. **Adaptation:** *The San Francisco Story* (Warner, 1952). Dir: Robert Parrish. Scr: D. D. Beauchamp. Cast: Joel McCrea (Rick), Yvonne De Carlo (Adelaide), Sidney Blackmer (Andrew), Richard Erdman (Shorty).

3884. *Sanctuary* (William Faulkner, 1931). Faulkner's novel is set in Mississippi during the 1920's and concerns Temple Drake, the beautiful but deranged daughter of a judge. After she is raped, she joins her abuser on a trail that leads to murder and betrayal. **Adaptation 1:** *The Story of Temple Drake* (Paramount, 1933). Dir: Stephen Roberts. Scr: Oliver H. P. Garrett. Cast: Miriam Hopkins (Temple), Jack La Rue (Trigger), William Gargan (Benbow), William Collier, Jr. (Toddy), Irving Pichel (Goodwin). **Adaptation 2:** *Sanctuary* (20th Century–Fox, 1961). Dir: Tony Richardson. Scr: Ruth Ford, James Poe. Cast: Lee Remick (Temple), Yves Montand (Candy), Bradford Dillman (Gowan), Harry Townes (Bobbitt).

3885. *Sanctuary* (Nora Roberts, 1997). Twenty years after the disappearance of her mother, a woman begins to receive anonymous messages and photographs of her mother's nude, dead body. She returns to the Georgia resort run by her estranged family to discover who killed her mother and is stalking her. **Adaptation:** *Sanctuary* (CBS, 2001 TV Movie). Dir: Katt Shea. Scr: Katt Shea, Vivienne Radkoff. Cast: Melissa Gilbert (Jo Ellen), Costas Mandylor (Nathan), Leslie Hope (Kirby), Kenneth Welsh (Sam), Kathy Baker (Aunt Kate).

3886. *The Sanctuary Sparrow* (Ellis Peters [pseudonym for Edith Pargeter], 1983). The seventh installment in Peters' twenty-volume series (1977–1994) featuring Brother Cadfael, a twelfth-century monk who, following service in the Crusades, tends to the herbarium at Shrewsbury Abbey and solves crimes. In this book, a young man accused of robbery and murder is pursued by a lynch mob and takes sanctuary in the abbey. Brother Cadfael is determined to prove his innocence. **Adaptation:** *Cadfael: The Sanctuary Sparrow* (ITV/PBS, 1994 TV Movie series). Dir: Graham Theakston. Scr: Simon Burke. Cast: Derek Jacobi (Brother Cadfael), Sean Pertwee (Hugh), Albie Woodington (Will). DVD, VHS.

3887. *The Sand Pebbles* (Richard McKenna, 1962). The sailors aboard an American gunboat assigned to rescue missionaries on the Yangtze River in China in 1926 clash with revolutionary warlords. **Adaptation:** *The Sand Pebbles* (20th Century–Fox, 1966). Dir: Robert Wise. Scr: Robert Anderson. Cast: Steve McQueen (Jake), Richard Attenborough (Frenchy), Richard Crenna (Captain Collins), Candice Bergen (Shirley), Mako (Pohan). Notes: Academy Award nominations for Best Picture, Actor (McQueen), Supporting Actor (Mako), Art Direction, Cinematography, Musical Score, Editing, and Sound; Golden Globe Award for Best Supporting Actor (Attenborough) and nominations for Best Picture, Director, Screenplay, Actor (McQueen), Musical Score, and Most Promising Newcomer (Bergen). DVD, VHS.

3888. *Sanders of the River* (Edgar Wallace, 1911). A series of stories about a British policeman in Africa and his encounters with the natives and with larcenous Westerners. Between 1911 and 1928, Wallace published several volumes featuring Sanders. **Adaptation 1:** *Sanders of the River* (United Artists, 1935). Dir: Zoltan Korda. Scr: Lajos Biro, Jeffrey Dell. Cast: Leslie Banks (Sanders), Paul Robeson (Bosambo), Nina Mae McKinney (Lilongo), Martin Walker (Ferguson). VHS. **Adaptation 2:** *Death Drums Along the River*, released in the U.S. as *Sanders* (Big Ben/Hallam/Planet, 1963). Dir: Lawrence Huntington. Scr: Lawrence Huntington, Kevin Kavanagh, Nicolas Roeg, Harry Alan Towers. Cast: Richard Todd (Sanders), Marianne Koch (Dr. Jung), Vivi Bach (Marlene), Albert Lieven (Dr. Weiss). DVD, VHS. Notes: *Coast of Skeletons*, a sequel, also written by Towers and starring Richard Todd as Harry Sanders, was released in 1964.

3889. *Sands of the Kalahari* (William Mulvihill, 1960). Survivors of a plane crash in the desert must battle savage baboons and one another to survive. **Adaptation:** *Sands of the Kalahari* (Paramount, 1965). Dir: Cy Endfield. Scr: Cy Endfield. Cast: Stuart Whitman (Brian), Stanley Baker (Mike), Susannah York (Grace), Harry Andrews (Grimmelman), Theodore Bikel (Dr. Bondrachai).

3890. *The Sands of Time* (Sidney Sheldon, 1988). Set in Spain in the post–Franco era, the story of four nuns who find themselves caught between Basque separatist guerillas and the Spanish government. **Adaptation:** *Sidney Sheldon's The Sands of Time* (Warner Bros. Television, 1992 TV Movie). Dir: Gary Nelson. Scr: Richard Hack, Michael Viner. Cast: Deborah Raffin (Sister Megan), Michael Nouri (Jaime), Amanda Plummer (Sister Graziella), Nina Foch (Ellen), Roddy McDowall (Alan), James Brolin (Colonel Acoca).

3891. *The Sandy Bottom Orchestra* (Garrison Keillor and Jenny Lind Nilsson, 1996). Young adult novel about a small-town family's love for classical music. Feeling unfulfilled and struggling to belong in their town, they decide to hold a classical concert that ends up improving their self-esteem and uniting them with their neighbors. **Adaptation:** *The Sandy Bottom Orchestra* (Showtime/Hallmark, 2000 TV Movie). Dir: Bradley Wigor. Scr: Joseph Maurer. Cast: Glenne Headly (Ingrid), Tom Irwin (Norman), Madeline Zima (Rachel), Jane Powell (Delia). Notes: Daytime Emmy nominations for Outstanding Children's Special, Director, and Sound. DVD, VHS.

3892. *Sangaree* (Frank G. Slaughter, 1948). An indentured servant is left in charge of a prosperous Southern plantation, and the late owner's family battle him for control. **Adaptation:** *Sangaree* (Paramount, 1953). Dir: Edward Ludwig. Scr: David Duncan, Frank L. Moss. Cast: Fernando Lamas (Dr. Morales), Arlene Dahl (Nancy), Patricia Medina (Martha), Francis L. Sullivan (Dr. Bristol).

3893. "The Sanitorium" (W. Somerset Maugham, 1938). A romance develops between two tuberculosis patients confined to a clinic. The story was first published in the December 1938 issue of *Cosmopolitan*. **Adaptation:** *Trio* (Gainsborough/Paramount, 1950). Dir: Ken Annakin, Harold French. Scr: Noel Langley, W. Somerset Maugham, R. C. Sherriff. Cast: Michael Rennie (Major Templeton), Jean Simmons (Evie), Roland Culver (Ashenden), Finlay Currie (McLeod), Betty Ann Davies (Mrs. Chester), Raymond Huntley (Mr. Chester), John Laurie (Mr. Campbell). Notes: This film was made following the success of the 1948 film *Quartet*, in which Maugham introduces four of his short stories. Here Maugham introduces three more stories: "Mr. Know-All," "The Sanitorium," and "The Verger." VHS.

3894. *Santa Fe Passage* (Henry W. Allen, 1952). Western about two Indian scouts who escort a wagon containing guns across the Southwestern territory controlled by hostile Indian tribes. Allen originally published the novel under the pseudonym Clay Fisher. **Adaptation:** *Santa Fe Passage* (Republic, 1955). Dir: William Witney. Scr: Lillie Hayward. Cast: John Payne (Kirby), Faith Domergue (Aurelie), Rod Cameron (Griswold), Slim Pickens (Sam).

3895. *Saraband for Dead Lovers* (Helen Simpson, 1935). Historical romance focusing on a young woman's arranged marriage to the future King George I of England and her love for a Swedish count. **Adaptation:** *Saraband for Dead Lovers*; released in the U.S. as *Saraband* (Ealing/Rank/Eagle Lion, 1948). Dir: Basil Dearden. Scr: John Dighton, Alexander Mackendrick. Cast: Stewart Granger (Count Philip), Joan Greenwood (Sophie), Flora Robson (Countess Clara). VHS.

3896. *The Saracen Blade* (Frank Yerby, 1952). During the thirteenth century, a young Italian nobleman avenges the murder of his father. **Adaptation:** *The Saracen Blade* (Columbia, 1954). Dir: William Castle. Scr: De Vallon Scott, George Worthing Yates. Cast: Ricardo Montalban (Pietro), Betta St. John (Iolanthe), Rick Jason (Enzio), Carolyn Jones (Elaine).

3897. *Sarah and Son* (Timothy Shea, 1929). Years after her former husband ran off with their child, a woman begins a search for her son. **Adaptation:** *Sarah and Son* (Paramount, 1930). Dir: Dorothy Arzner. Scr: Zoe Akins. Cast: Ruth Chatterton (Sarah), Fredric March (Howard), Fuller Mellish, Jr. (Jim), Gilbert Emery (John).

3898. *Sarah, Plain and Tall* (Patricia MacLachlan, 1985, Newbery Medal). Set at the turn of the century, children's book about a New England schoolteacher who responds to an advertisement by a Midwestern widower seeking a wife to help him raise his two children. The relationship turns out to be rewarding for all of the people involved. **Adaptation:** *Sarah, Plain and Tall* (Self/Trillium, 1991 TV Movie). Dir: Glenn Jordan. Scr: Patricia MacLachlan, Carol Sobieski. Cast: Glenn Close (Sarah), Christopher Walken (Jacob), Lexi Randall (Anna). Notes: Emmy Award for Outstanding Editing, and nominations for Outstanding Film, Director, Teleplay, Actress (Close), Actor (Walken), Art Direction, Costume Design, and Sound; Golden Globe nominations for Best Television Movie and Actress (Close). DVD, VHS. Notes: Two made-for-television sequels were also produced: *Skylark* (1993) (DVD, VHS) and *Sarah, Plain and Tall: Winter's End* (1999) (DVD, VHS).

3899. *Saratoga Trunk* (Edna Ferber, 1941). Western about a notorious woman who returns from Paris to her home in New Orleans, where she falls in love with a cowboy gambler. **Adaptation:** *Saratoga Trunk* (Warner, 1945). Dir: Sam Wood. Scr: Casey Robinson. Cast: Gary Cooper (Clint), Ingrid Bergman (Clio), Flora Robson (Angelique), Jerry Austin (Cupidon). VHS.

3900. *The Satan Bug* (Alistair MacLean, 1962). A madman steals a deadly virus from a government research lab, and agents try to stop him from unleashing it. **Adaptation:** *The Satan Bug* (United Artists, 1965). Dir: John Sturges. Scr: James Clavell, Edward Anhalt. Cast: George Maharis (Barrett), Richard Basehart (Dr. Hoffman), Anne Francis (Ann), Dana Andrews (General Williams). VHS.

Satan Met a Lady (see *The Maltese Falcon*).

3901. *Satan Never Sleeps* (Pearl S. Buck, 1961). A priest accompanies a young native girl to a missionary outpost in China. There she is raped by a Communist rebel leader, who subsequently joins her and the priest and flees from the Communists. **Adaptation:** *Satan Never Sleeps*; released in the UK as *The Devil Never Sleeps* (20th Century–Fox, 1962). Dir: Leo McCarey. Scr: Claude Binyon, Leo McCarey. Cast: William Holden (Father O'Banion), Clifton Webb (Father Bovard), France Nuyen (Siu Lan), Athene Seyler (Sister Agnes). DVD, VHS.

Satan's Playthings (see *The Ravine*).

3902. *Saturday Island* (Hugh Brooke, 1935). Romantic story centering on a nurse, an American soldier, and a wounded RAF pilot stranded on a deserted island in the South Seas during World War II. **Adaptation:** *Saturday Island*; released in the U.S. as *Island of Desire* (United Artists, 1952). Dir: Stuart Heisler. Scr: Stephanie Nordli. Cast: Linda Darnell (Elizabeth), Tab Hunter (Michael), John Laurie (Grimshaw). VHS.

3903. *Saturday Night and Sunday Morning* (Alan Sillitoe, 1958). Portrait of an angry and unfulfilled factory worker in a British industrial town. **Adaptation:** *Saturday Night and Sunday Morning* (Continental, 1960). Dir: Karel Reisz. Scr: Alan Sillitoe. Cast: Albert Finney (Arthur), Shirley Anne Field (Doreen), Rachel Roberts (Brenda), Hylda Baker (Aunt Ada). Notes: BAFTA Awards for Best British Film, Actress (Roberts), and Most Promising Newcomer (Finney), and nominations for Best Film, Screenplay, and Actor (Finney); National Board of Review Award for Best Actor (Finney). DVD, VHS.

Saturday Night Fever (*see* "Tribal Rites of the New Saturday Night").

Saturday's Hero (see *The Hero*).

The Savage (see *The Renegade*).

The Savage Innocents (see *Top of the World*).

3904. *Savage Messiah* (H. S. Ede, 1931). Biography of French sculptor Henri Gaudier-Brzeska (1891–1915), who carried on a Platonic love affair with Sophie Brzeska, a thirty-eight year old woman, and died in World War I at the age of twenty-four. **Adaptation:** *Savage Messiah* (1972). Dir: Ken Russell. Scr: Christopher Logue. Cast: Dorothy Tutin (Sophie), Scott Anthony (Henri), Helen Mirren (Gosh), Lindsay Kemp (Angus). VHS.

3905. *Savage Sam* (Fred Gipson, 1962). The sequel to Gipson's popular 1956 novel about a yellow dog, *Old Yeller*, is the story of Old Yeller's son, who is considered an uncontrollable problem until it tracks down Indians who are kidnapping children. **Adaptation:** *Savage Sam* (Disney/Buena Vista, 1963). Dir: Norman Tokar. Scr: Fred Gipson, William Tunberg. Cast: Brian Keith (Uncle Beck), Tommy Kirk (Travis), Kevin Corcoran (Arliss), Dewey Martin (Lester). DVD, VHS. See also *Old Yeller*.

Savage Wilderness (see *The Gilded Rooster*).

3906. *Saving Grace* (Celia Gittelson, 1981). A newly elected pope, bored with administrative work, sneaks out of the Vatican in disguise and goes to live in a poor village, where he learns important lessons. **Adaptation:** *Saving Grace* (Columbia/Embassy, 1985). Dir: Robert M. Young. Scr: Richard Kramer, Joaquin Montana. Cast: Tom Conti (Pope Leo XIV), Fernando Rey (Cardinal Biondi), Erland Josephson (Monsignor Ghezzi), Giancarlo Giannini (Abalardi), Edward James Olmos (Ciolino). VHS.

3907. *The Saxon Charm* (Frederic Wakeman, 1947). A ruthless Broadway producer ruins the lives of family and professional colleagues. **Adaptation:** *The Saxon Charm* (Universal, 1948). Dir: Claude Binyon. Scr: Claude Binyon. Cast: Robert Montgomery (Saxon), Susan Hayward (Janet), John Payne (Eric), Audrey Totter (Alma).

3908. *Sayonara* (James A. Michener, 1954). Set in Japan, the story of the doomed love affair between a young American four-star general and a Japanese entertainer. **Adaptation:** *Sayonara* (Warner, 1957). Dir: Joshua Logan. Scr: Paul Osborn. Cast: Marlon Brando (Lloyd), Patricia Owens (Eileen), James Garner (Mike), Martha Scott (Mrs. Webster), Miyoshi Umeki (Katsumi), Red Buttons (Joe). Notes: Academy Awards for Best Supporting Actor (Buttons), Supporting Actress (Umeki), Art Direction, and Sound, and nominations for Best Picture, Director, Screenplay, Actor (Brando), and Cinematography; Golden Globe Award for Best Supporting Actor (Buttons) and nominations for Best Picture, Director, Actor (Brando), and Supporting Actress (Umeki). DVD, VHS.

Scandal Sheet (see *The Dark Page*).

3909. *Scandalous John* (Richard Gardner, 1963). Comic Western about a cantankerous old rancher who refuses to sell his land to real estate developers. **Adaptation:** *Scandalous John* (Disney/Buena Vista, 1971). Dir: Robert Butler. Scr: Bill Walsh, Don Da Gradi. Cast: Brian Keith (John), Alfonso Arau (Paco), Michele Carey (Amanda), Rick Lenz (Jimmy), Harry Morgan (Sheriff Pippin), Simon Oakland (Barton). VHS.

Scandalous Me (see *Lovely Me*).

3910. *The Scapegoat* (Daphne Du Maurier, 1957). A French man murders his wife and then tries to convince a lookalike British man vacationing in France to impersonate him. **Adaptation:** *The Scapegoat* (MGM, 1959). Dir: Robert Hamer. Scr: Robert Hamer, Gore Vidal. Cast: Alec Guinness (John/Jacques), Bette Davis (the Countess), Nicole Maurey (Bela), Irene Worth (Francoise).

The Scar (see *Hollow Triumph*).

3911. *The Scarab Murder Case* (S. S. Van Dine [pseudonym for Willard Huntington Wright], 1930). In the fifth of Van Dine's twelve-twelve novel series featuring debonair Philo Vance, the detective investigates the murder of a man for a priceless jewel. **Adaptation:** *The Scarab Murder Case* (British Dominions, 1936). Dir: Michael Hankinson. Scr: Selwyn Jepson. Cast: Wilfrid Hyde-White (Philo), Graham Cheswright (Makeham), Henri De Vries (Dr. Bliss), Wally Patch (Inspector Moore).

3912. *Scaramouche* (Rafael Sabatini, 1921). In France in the late eighteenth century, a young man disguises himself as an actor to avenge the death of his friend by an evil nobleman. **Silent Film:** 1923. **Adaptation:** *Scaramouche* (MGM, 1952). Dir: George Sidney. Scr: Ronald Millar, George Froeschel. Cast: Stewart Granger (Moreau), Eleanor Parker (Lenore), Janet Leigh (Aline), Mel Ferrer (Noel), Henry Wilcoxon (Chevalier de Chabrillaine), Nina Foch (Marie Antoinette). DVD, VHS.

3913. *The Scarecrow* (Ronald Hugh Morrieson, 1963). Set in a small New Zealand town in the 1950's, the tragicomic story of a little girl's murder on the same day that six chickens disappear. When two teenagers search for their animals, they come across clues to the murder. **Adaptation:** *The Scarecrow*; released in the U.S. as *Klynham Summer* (New Zealand National Film/ Oasis, 1982). Dir: Sam Pillsbury. Scr: Michael Heath, Sam Pillsbury. Cast: Jonathan Smith (Ned), Tracey Mann (Prudence), Daniel McLaren (Les), John Carradine (Hubert). VHS.

The Scarecrow of Romney Marsh (see *Christopher Syn*).

3914. *Scarface* (Armitage Trail [pseudonym for Maurice Coons], 1930). The violent tale of the rise and fall of a Chicago gangster in the 1920's. **Adaptation 1:** *Scarface* (United Artists, 1932). Dir:

Howard Hawks, Richard Rosson. Scr: Ben Hecht, Seton I. Miller, John Lee Mahin, W. R. Burnett. Cast: Paul Muni (Tony), Ann Dvorak (Cesca), Karen Morley (Poppy), Osgood Perkins (Johnny), George Raft (Guino), Boris Karloff (Gaffney). DVD, VHS. **Adaptation 2:** *Scarface* (Universal, 1983). Dir: Brian De Palma. Scr: Oliver Stone. Cast: Al Pacino (Tony), Steven Bauer (Manny), Michelle Pfeiffer (Elvira), Mary Elizabeth Mastrantonio (Gina), Robert Loggia (Frank), F. Murray Abraham (Omar). Notes: An updated story set in Miami and involving Cuban drug dealers. The screenplay does not credit Trail's book or the 1932 screenplay. Golden Globe nominations for Best Actor (Pacino), Supporting Actor (Bauer), and Musical Score. DVD, VHS.

The Scarface Mob (see *The Untouchables*).

Scarlet and Black (see *The Red and the Black*).

3915. *The Scarlet Letter* (Nathaniel Hawthorne, 1850). Hawthorne's classic novel, set in Salem, Massachusetts, in 1642, centers on an unwed mother punished for refusing to reveal the name of her illegitimate child's father and a minister whose guilt finally consumes him. **Silent Films:** 1908, 1911, 1913, 1917, 1922, and 1926, directed by Victor Sjöström and starring Lillian Gish (VHS). **Adaptation 1:** *The Scarlet Letter* (Majestic, 1934). Dir: Robert G. Vignola. Scr: Leonard Fields, David Silverstein. Cast: Colleen Moore (Hester), Hardie Albright (Dimmesdale), Henry B. Walthall (Chillingworth), Cora Sue Collins (Pearl). DVD, VHS. **Adaptation 2:** *The Scarlet Letter* (Bauer, 1973). Dir: Wim Wenders. Scr: Tankred Dorst, Ursula Ehler, Bernardo Fernandez, Wim Wenders. Cast: Senta Berger (Hester), Hans Christian Blech (Chillingworth), Lou Castel (Dimmesdale). DVD, VHS. **Adaptation 3:** *The Scarlet Letter* (PBS, 1979 TV Miniseries). Dir: Rick Hauser. Scr: Allan Knee, Alvin Sapinsley. Cast: Josef Sommer (Nathaniel Hawthorne), Meg Foster (Hester), Elisa Erali (Pearl), John Heard (Dimmesdale), Kevin Conway (Chillingworth). DVD, VHS. **Adaptation 4:** *The Scarlet Letter* (Buena Vista, 1995). Dir: Roland Joffe. Scr: Douglas Day Stewart. Cast: Demi Moore (Hester), Gary Oldman (Dimmesdale), Robert Duvall (Chillingworth), Lisa Joliffe-Andoh (Mituba), Edward Hardwicke (Governor Bellingham), Robert Prosky (Horace), Roy Dotrice (Cheever), Joan Plowright (Harriet). DVD, VHS.

3916. *The Scarlet Pimpernel* (Baroness Emmuska Orczy, 1905). In the early days of the

French Revolution, an Englishman posing as a harmless fop rescues aristocrats from being executed on the guillotine. Orczy also adapted the novel as a London stage play in 1905. **Silent Film:** 1917. **Adaptation 1:** *The Scarlet Pimpernel* (London/United Artists, 1934). Dir: Harold Young. Scr: Lajos Biro, S. N. Behrman, Robert E. Sherwood. Arthur Wimperis. Cast: Leslie Howard (Sir Percy Blakeney/the Scarlet Pimpernel), Merle Oberon (Lady Marguerite), Raymond Massey (Chauvelin), Nigel Bruce (the Prince of Wales). DVD, VHS. **Adaptation 2:** *"Pimpernel" Smith*; also released as *The Fighting Pimpernel* and as *Mister V* (British National/United Artists, 1941). Dir: Leslie Howard. Scr: Ian Dalrymple, Anatole de Grunwald, Roland Pertwee. Cast: Leslie Howard (Professor Horatio Smith), Francis L. Sullivan (General von Graum), Mary Morris (Ludmilla), Hugh McDermott (Maxwell). Notes: A modern retelling involving an archaeology professor who rescues refugees in Europe during World War II. VHS. **Adaptation 3:** *The Scarlet Pimpernel* (London, 1982 TV Miniseries). Dir: Clive Donner. Scr: William Bast. Cast: Anthony Andrews (Sir Percy Blakeney/the Scarlet Pimpernel), Jane Seymour (Lady Marguerite), Ian McKellen (Chauvelin), James Villiers (Baron de Batz). Notes: The teleplay combines elements from Orczy's novels *The Scarlet Pimpernel* (1905), *The Elusive Pimpernel* (1908), and *Eldorado* (1913). DVD, VHS. **Adaptation 4:** *The Scarlet Pimpernel* (A&E/BBC, 1999 TV Miniseries). Dir: Simon Langton, Patrick Lau, Graham Theakston. Scr: Richard Carpenter. Cast: Richard E. Grant (Sir Percy Blakeney/the Scarlet Pimpernel), Elizabeth McGovern (Lady Marguerite), Martin Shaw (Chauvelin), Anthony Green (Sir Andrew), Ronan Vibert (Robespierre). DVD, VHS. See also *The Elusive Pimpernel*.

The Scarlet Tunic (*see* "The Melancholy Hussar of the German Legion").

3917. *Scarlett* (Alexandra Ripley, 1991). In this sequel to Margaret Mitchell's *Gone with the Wind*, set in 1873, Scarlett O'Hara is determined to win back Rhett Butler. **Adaptation:** *Scarlett* (RHI, 1994 TV Miniseries). Dir: John Erman. Scr: William Hanley. Cast: Joanne Whalley-Kilmer (Scarlett), Timothy Dalton (Rhett), Barbara Barrie (Pauline), Stephen Collins (Ashley), Annabeth Gish (Anne), George Grizzard (Henry), Julie Harris (Eleanor). DVD, VHS. See also *Gone with the Wind*.

3918. "Scattergood Baines—Invader" (Clar-

ence Budington Kelland, 1917). The first in a long series of comic stories featuring a crusty old Vermont businessman and the people he helps. The short story appeared in *The Saturday Evening Post* on June 30, 1917. **Adaptation:** *Scattergood Baines* (RKO, 1941). Dir: Christy Cabanne. Scr: Michael L. Simmons, Edward T. Lowe, Jr. Cast: Guy Kibbee (Baines), Carol Hughes (Helen), John Archer (Johnny), Dink Trout (Pickett). Notes: The screenplay combines elements from several stories in the series.

3919. *The Scent of Danger* (Donald MacKenzie, 1958). After a successful robbery, thieves have a violent falling out. **Adaptation:** *Moment of Danger*; released in the U.S. as *Malaga* (Warner, 1960). Dir: Laszlo Benedek. Scr: David Osborn, Donald Ogden Stewart. Cast: Trevor Howard (Bain), Dorothy Dandridge (Gianna), Edmund Purdom (Carran), Michael Hordern (Inspector Farrell).

Scent of Mystery (see *Ghost of a Chance*).

3920. *Schindler's List* (Thomas Keneally, 1982, Booker Prize). The story of a Polish factory owner during World War II who turns a profit by cooperating with the Nazis and then losing his fortune by hiding his Jewish workers, thus sparing them deportation to the death camps. **Adaptation:** *Schindler's List* (Universal, 1993). Dir: Steven Spielberg. Scr: Steven Zaillian. Cast: Liam Neeson (Schindler), Ben Kingsley (Itzhak), Ralph Fiennes (Amon), Caroline Goodall (Emily), Embeth Davidtz (Helen). Notes: Academy Awards for Best Picture, Director, Screenplay, Musical Score, Cinematography, Editing, and Art Direction, and nominations for Best Actor (Neeson), Supporting Actor (Fiennes), Costume Design, Makeup, and Sound; Golden Globe Awards for Best Picture, Director, and Screenplay, and nominations for Best Actor (Neeson), Supporting Actor (Fiennes), and Best Musical Score; National Board of Review Award for Best Picture. DVD, VHS.

School for Scoundrels (see *One-Upmanship*).

3921. *The Scold's Bridle* (Minette Walters, 1994, Golden Dagger Award of the British Crime Writers Association). Murder mystery about a detestable woman found dead wearing a scold's bridle, a medieval device designed to silence nagging wives. **Adaptation:** *The Scold's Bridle* (BBC, 1998 TV Movie). Dir: David Thacker. Scr: Tony Bicat. Cast: Miranda Richardson (Sarah), Bob Peck (Detective Cooper), Douglas Hodge (Jack), Sian Phillips (Mathilda). VHS.

3922. *Scoop* (Evelyn Waugh, 1938). Comic novel about a London newspaper and their frenzy to beat the competition. **Adaptation 1:** *Scoop* (BBC, 1972). Dir: Barry Took. Scr: Barry Took. Cast: Harry Worth (William), Sinead Cusack (Katchen), Meredith Edwards (Uncle Theodore), Gerald Flood (John), Hugh Latimer (Cuthbert), Brian Oulton (Salter), Kenneth J. Warren (Lord Copper). **Adaptation 2:** *Scoop* (London Weekend, 1987 TV Miniseries). Dir: Gavin Millar. Scr: William Boyd. Cast: Denholm Elliott (Mr. Salter), Michael Hordern (Uncle Theodore), Herbert Lom (Mr. Baldwin), Nicola Pagett (Julia), Donald Pleasence (Lord Copper). DVD, VHS.

Scotch on the Rocks (see *Laxdale Hall*).

Scream and Scream Again (see *The Disoriented Man*).

Screamers (*see* "Second Variety").

3923. *The Screaming Mimi* (Frederic Brown, 1949). After being sexually assaulted, a woman takes a job as an exotic dancer and commits murder at the suggestion of her manipulative therapist. **Adaptation:** *Screaming Mimi* (Columbia, 1958). Dir: Gerd Oswald. Scr: Robert Blees. Cast: Anita Ekberg (Virginia), Philip Carey (Bill), Gypsy Rose Lee (Joann), Harry Townes (Dr. Greenwood).

Scrooge (see *A Christmas Carol*).

3924. *Scudda Hoo! Scudda Hay!* (George Agnew Chamberlain, 1946). Comic novel about a young farmer and his two mules. **Adaptation:** *Scudda Hoo! Scudda Hay!*; released in the UK as *Summer Lightning* (20th Century–Fox, 1948). Dir: F. Hugh Herbert. Scr: F. Hugh Herbert. Cast: June Haver (Rad), Lon McCallister (Snug), Walter Brennan (Tony), Anne Revere (Judith), Natalie Wood (Bean). Notes: Marilyn Monroe made her screen debut as an uncredited bit player in the film.

3925. *The Sculptress* (Minette Walters, 1993, Edgar Allan Poe Award for Best Mystery Novel). A woman convicted of murdering her mother and sister writes a book about her experiences, and her co-author, convinced of her innocence, works to prove it. **Adaptation:** *The Sculptress* (BBC/PBS, 1996 TV Movie). Dir: Stuart Orme. Scr: Reg Gadney. Cast: Pauline Quirke (Olive), Caroline Goodall (Rosalind), Christopher Fulford (Hal). VHS.

3926. *The Sea Chase* (Andrew Geer, 1948). At the start of World War II, the captain of a Ger-

man freighter in Australia if forced to avoid Allied ships as he tries to get his boat back home. **Adaptation:** *The Sea Chase* (Warner, 1955). Dir: John Farrow. Scr: James Warner Bellah, John Twist. Cast: John Wayne (Ehrlich), Lana Turner (Elsa), David Farrar (Napier), Lyle Bettger (Kirchner), Tab Hunter (Wesser), James Arness (Schlieter). DVD, VHS.

3927. *The Sea of Grass* (Conrad Richter, 1937). A farmer and a cattle rancher feud over land in New Mexico. **Adaptation:** *The Sea of Grass* (MGM, 1947). Dir: Elia Kazan. Scr: Vincent Lawrence, Marguerite Roberts. Cast: Spencer Tracy (James), Katharine Hepburn (Lutie), Robert Walker (Brock), Melvyn Douglas (Brice). VHS.

Sea Wife (see *Sea-Wyf and Biscuit*).

3928. *The Sea Wolf* (Jack London, 1904). An affluent man survives a boating catastrophe in San Francisco Bay only to be held captive by an insane schooner captain, who forces him to work as a crewman. In the process, he is toughened and learns self-confidence. **Silent Films:** 1913, 1920, and 1926. **Adaptation 1:** *The Sea Wolf* (Fox, 1930). Dir: Alfred Santell. Scr: S. N. Behrman, Ralph Block. Cast: Milton Sills (Wolf Larsen), Jane Keithley (Lorna), Raymond Hackett (Allen), Mitchell Harris (Death), Nat Pendleton (Smoke). **Adaptation 2:** *The Sea Wolf* (Warner, 1941). Dir: Michael Curtiz. Scr: Robert Rossen. Cast: Edward G. Robinson (Wolf Larsen), Ida Lupino (Ruth), John Garfield (Leach), Alexander Knox (Humphrey), Gene Lockhart (Dr. Prescott), Barry Fitzgerald (Mugridge). VHS. **Adaptation 3:** *Barricade* (Warner, 1950). Dir: Peter Godfrey. Scr: William Sackheim. Cast: Dane Clark (Bob), Raymond Massey (Boss Kruger), Ruth Roman (Judith), Robert Douglas (Aubrey). Notes: A retelling of the story as a Western about a battle over a gold mine. **Adaptation 4:** *Wolf Larsen* (Allied Artists, 1958). Dir: Harmon Jones. Scr: Jack De Witt, Turnley Walker. Cast: Barry Sullivan (Wolf Larsen), Peter Graves (Humphrey), Gita Hall (Kristina), Thayer David (Mugridge). VHS. **Adaptation 5:** *Wolf Larsen*; also released as *The Legend of the Sea Wolf* and as *Larsen, Wolf of the Seven Seas* (Cougar, 1975). Dir: Giuseppe Vari (writing as Joseph Green). Scr: Marcello Ciorciolini. Cast: Chuck Connors (Wolf Larsen), Giuseppe Pambieri (Humphrey), Barbara Bach (Maude). DVD, VHS. **Adaptation 6:** *The Sea Wolf* (Turner, 1993 TV Movie). Dir: Michael Anderson. Scr: Andrew J. Fenady. Cast: Charles Bronson (Wolf Larsen), Catherine Mary Stewart (Flaxen), Marc Singer (Johnson), Len Cariou (Dr. Picard), Clive Revill (Mugridge), Christopher Reeve (Humphrey). VHS. **Adaptation 7:** *The Sea Wolf* (Concorde, 1997). Dir: Gary T. McDonald. Scr: Gary T. McDonald. Cast: Stacy Keach (Wolf Larsen), Alejandra Cruz (Maude), Rick Dean (Humphrey). VHS.

The Sea Wolves (see *The Boarding Party*).

3929. *Sea-Wyf and Biscuit* (J. M. Scott, 1995). After the survivors of a shipwreck near Singapore during World War II are rescued, a naval officer falls in love with the only female survivor unaware that she is actually a man. **Adaptation:** *Sea Wife* (20th Century–Fox, 1957). Dir: Bob McNaught. Scr: George K. Burke. Cast: Joan Collins (Sea Wife), Richard Burton (Biscuit), Basil Sydney (Bull Dog). VHS.

3930. *Seabiscuit: An American Legend* (Laura Hillenbrand, 2001). Depression-era history of the losing horse that was transformed into one of America's legendary racehorses. **Adaptation:** *Seabiscuit* (Universal, 2003). Dir: Gary Ross. Scr: Gary Ross. Cast: Jeff Bridges (Charles), Chris Cooper (Tom), Tobey Maguire (Red), William H. Macy (Tick Tock). Notes: Academy Award nominations for Best Picture, Screenplay, Cinematography, Editing, Art Direction, Costume Design and Sound; Golden Globe nomination for Best Picture and Supporting Actor (Macy). DVD, VHS.

3931. *A Seal Called Andre: The Two Worlds of a Marine Harbor Seal* (Harry Goodridge and Lew Dietz, 1975). Set in 1962, the true story of a young girl and her family who befriended a baby seal on the Maine coast and protected it from local townspeople who wanted to be rid of it. **Adaptation:** *Andre* (Paramount, 1994). Dir: George Miller. Scr: Dana Baratta. Cast: Keith Carradine (Harry), Chelsea Field (Thalice), Joshua Jackson (Mark), Tina Majorino (Toni). DVD, VHS.

Sealed Cargo (see *The Gaunt Woman*).

3932. *The Sealers* (Peter Tutein, 1929). Set in Oslo in the 1920's, Norwegian novel, originally titled *Larsen*, about a poet who goes to Greenland to become a trapper. When the brutal winter season arrives, he is forced to take shelter with a scientist and an old trapper with whom he comes into conflict. The novel was translated into English in 1938. **Adaptation:** *The Sealers* (Kino, 1995). Dir: Hans Petter Moland. Scr: Lars Bill Lundholm, Hans Petter Moland. Cast: Stellan Skars-

gard (Randbaek), Gard B. Eidsvold (Larsen), Bjorn Sundquist (Holm), Camilla Martens (Gertrude). DVD, VHS.

3933. *The Search for Bridey Murphy* (Morey Bernstein, 1956). Memoir of an amateur hypnotist who, in 1952, placed a neighbor into a trance, enabling her to recall a previous life as an Irish peasant woman. **Adaptation:** *The Search for Bridey Murphy* (1956). Dir: Noel Langley. Scr: Noel Langley. Cast: Teresa Wright (Ruth), Louis Hayward (Bernstein), Nancy Gates (Hazel), Kenneth Tobey (Rex). VHS.

3934. *The Searchers* (Alan Le May, 1954). A Civil War veteran in the late 1860's searches for his niece taken by Indians who killed her parents and siblings. **Adaptation:** *The Searchers* (Warner, 1956). Dir: John Ford. Scr: Frank S. Nugent. Cast: John Wayne (Ethan), Jeffrey Hunter (Martin), Vera Miles (Laurie), Ward Bond (Clayton), Natalie Wood (Debbie). DVD, VHS.

3935. *Searching for Bobby Fischer: The Father of a Prodigy Observes the World of Chess* (Fred Waitzkin, 1988). Memoir by the father of an ordinary six-year-old boy who proved to be a chess prodigy. Because of his father's persistent encouragement, the reluctant boy began by playing chess in a park and ended up going to the national chess championship. **Adaptation:** *Searching for Bobby Fischer*; released in the UK as *Innocent Moves* (Paramount, 1993). Dir: Steven Zaillian. Scr: Steven Zaillian. Cast: Max Pomeranc (Josh), Joe Mantegna (Fred), Joan Allen (Bonnie), Ben Kingsley (Bruce), Laurence Fishburne (Vinnie). DVD, VHS.

3936. *A Season for Miracles* (Marilyn Pappano, 1997). When a poor Boston woman's niece and nephew are about to be put into foster care because their drug-addicted mother cannot care for them, she and the children flee and end up in the small town of Bethlehem, New York, on Christmas Eve. Seemingly miraculous occurrences there conspire to keep the family together. **Adaptation:** *A Season for Miracles* (CBS/Hallmark, 1999 TV Movie). Dir: Michael Pressman. Scr: Maria Nation. Cast: Carla Gugino (Emily), Kathy Baker (Ruth), David Conrad (Nathan), Laura Dern (Berry), Patty Duke (Angel), Lynn Redgrave (Judge Jakes). VHS.

3937. *A Season in Purgatory* (Dominick Dunne, 1995). A young working-class man befriends a fellow student from a powerful and corrupt Irish-Catholic family in Boston. When his friend kills a girl who refuses to have sexual relations with him, the youth agrees to cover up the crime until, after many years, his conscience will not allow him to do so any longer. **Adaptation:** *A Season in Purgatory* (Spelling/Americana, 1996 TV Movie). Dir: David Greene. Scr: Robert W. Lenski. Cast: Patrick Dempsey (Harrison), Sherilyn Fenn (Kit), Craig Sheffer (Bradley), Edward Herrmann (Dr. Shugrue).

3938. *Season of the Witch* (Hank Stine, 1968). Science-fiction novel in which a man is transformed into a woman as punishment for rape and comes to enjoy his new role. **Adaptation:** *Memory Run*; also released as *Synapse* (Imperial, 1996). Dir: Allan A. Goldstein. Scr: Allan A. Goldstein, David N. Gottlieb, Dale Hildebrand. Cast: Karen Duffy (Celeste/Josette), Saul Rubinek (Dr. Munger), Matt McCoy (Gabriel), Lynne Cormack (Dr. Merain). DVD, VHS.

3939. *The Season Ticket* (Jonathan Tulloch, 2000, Betty Trask Prize for First Novel). Obsessed with their local soccer club, two British teenagers go to any extreme to get the money to buy season tickets. **Adaptation:** *Purely Belter* (FilmFour, 2000). Dir: Mark Herman. Scr: Mark Herman. Cast: Chris Beattie (Gerry), Greg McLane (Sewell), Kevin Whately (Caird). DVD, VHS.

3940. *Second Best* (David Cook, 1991). A shy Welsh postal worker adopts a troubled boy who has lived for years in an orphanage since his mother's suicide. **Adaptation:** *Second Best* (Warner, 1994). Dir: Chris Menges. Scr: David Cook. Cast: William Hurt (Graham), Nathan Yapp (Jimmy), Keith Allen (John), Chris Cleary Miles (James). VHS.

The Second Floor Mystery (see *The Agony Column*).

3941. *The Second Jungle Book* (Rudyard Kipling, 1895). The sequel to *The Jungle Book*, Kipling's successful 1894 book of stories about Mowgli and his jungle friends. **Adaptation:** *The Second Jungle Book: Mowgli & Baloo* (TriStar, 1997). Dir: Duncan McLachlan. Scr: Matthew Horton, Bayard Johnson. Cast: Gulshan Grover (Buldeo), Jamie Williams (Mowgli), Bill Campbell (Harrison), Roddy McDowall (King Murphy). DVD, VHS. See also *The Jungle Book*.

The Second Time Around (see *Star in the West*).

3942. "Second Variety" (Philip K. Dick, 1953). In the distant future, United Nations forces use killer robots to combat corrupt and authoritarian Soviet officials. The short story first appeared in the May 1953 issue of *Space Science Fiction*. **Adaptation:** *Screamers* (Columbia, 1995).

Dir: Christian Duguay. Scr: Dan O'Bannon, Miguel Tejada-Flores. Cast: Peter Weller (Hendricksson), Roy Dupuis (Becker), Jennifer Rubin (Jessica). DVD, VHS.

3943. *Seconds* (David Ely, 1964). Thriller about a secret organization that arranges faked deaths and new identities for rich people. **Adaptation:** *Seconds* (Paramount, 1966). Dir: John Frankenheimer. Scr: Lewis John Carlino. Cast: Rock Hudson (Tony), Salome Jens (Nora), John Randolph (Arthur), Jeff Corey (Mr. Ruby), Richard Anderson (Dr. Innes), Murray Hamilton (Charlie). Notes: Cannes Film Festival Golden Palm nomination for Best Director. DVD, VHS.

The Secret (see *The Harrogate Secret*).

3944. *The Secret Adversary* (Agatha Christie, 1922). After World War I, two friends hire themselves out as spies. A British government job to find a secret treaty soon has them protecting a mysterious young woman and places all of their lives in danger. **Silent Film:** 1928. **Adaptation:** *The Secret Adversary* (London Weekend/PBS, 1982 TV Movie). Dir: Tony Wharmby. Scr: Pat Sandys. Cast: James Warwick (Tommy), Francesca Annis (Tuppence), George Baker (Whittington), Honor Blackman (Rita). VHS.

3945. *A Secret Affair* (Barbara Taylor Bradford, 1996). An engaged American woman in Venice falls in love with an Irish television reporter. They plan to reunite in Ireland, but she later learns that he has been kidnapped while covering a war and is presumed dead. **Adaptation:** *A Secret Affair* (Adelson/Tracey Alexander, 1999 TV Movie). Dir: Bobby Roth. Scr: Carole Real. Cast: Janine Turner (Vanessa), Paudge Behan (Bill), Fionnula Flanagan (Drusilla), Robert Mailhouse (Stephen), Gia Carides (Mimi). DVD, VHS.

Secret Agent (see *Ashenden*).

3946. *The Secret Agent* (Joseph Conrad, 1907). A mild-mannered London theatre manager is actually a foreign spy and saboteur. The novel was adapted for the stage in 1921. **Adaptation 1:** *Sabotage* (Gaumont, 1936). Dir: Alfred Hitchcock. Scr: Charles Bennett, Ian Hay, Helen Simpson. Cast: Sylvia Sidney (Mrs. Verloc), Oskar Homolka (Verloc), John Loder (Detective Spencer). DVD, VHS. **Adaptation 2:** *The Secret Agent* (BBC, 1967 TV Miniseries). Dir: Gerald Blake. Scr: Alexander Baron. Cast: Nigel Green (Verloc), John Cater (the Professor), David Collings (Vladimir), George Pravda (Michaelis).

Adaptation 3: *The Secret Agent* (BBC, 1992 TV Miniseries). Dir: David Drury. Scr: Dusty Hughes. Cast: David Suchet (Verloc), Cheryl Campbell (Winnie), Peter Capaldi (Vladimir). **Adaptation 4:** *The Secret Agent* (Fox Searchlight, 1996). Dir: Christopher Hampton. Scr: Christopher Hampton. Cast: Bob Hoskins (Verloc), Patricia Arquette (Winnie), Gerard Depardieu (Ossipon), Jim Broadbent (Inspector Heat), Robin Williams (the Professor), Christian Bale (Stevie). VHS.

Secret Cutting (see *The Luckiest Girl in the World*).

Secret Friends (see *Ticket to Ride*).

The Secret Four (see *The Four Just Men*).

The Secret Game (see *Unknown Games*).

3947. *The Secret Garden* (Frances Hodgson Burnett, 1912). Children's book about an orphan girl who is sent to live with her glum uncle. When a robin leads her to a mysterious garden behind his Victorian estate, she cultivates it and brings happiness into the lives of her uncle and his neighbors. The novel was adapted as a Broadway musical in 1991. **Silent Film:** 1919. **Adaptation 1:** *The Secret Garden* (MGM, 1949). Dir: Fred M. Wilcox. Scr: Robert Ardrey. Cast: Margaret O'Brien (Mary), Herbert Marshall (Archibald), Dean Stockwell (Colin), Gladys Cooper (Mrs. Medlock), Elsa Lanchester (Martha), Reginald Owen (Ben). VHS. **Adaptation 2:** *The Secret Garden* (BBC, 1975 TV Movie). Dir: Katrina Murray. Scr: Dorothea Brooking. Cast: Sarah Hollis Andrews (Mary), John Woodnutt (Archibald), David Patterson (Colin), Jacqueline Hoyle (Martha), Hope Johnstone (Mrs. Medlock). VHS. **Adaptation 3:** *The Secret Garden* (Rosemont/Viacom, 1987 TV Movie). Dir: Alan Grint. Scr: Blanche Hanalis. Cast: Gennie James (Mary), Barret Oliver (Dickon), Jadrien Steele (Colin), Michael Hordern (Ben), Billie Whitelaw (Mrs. Medlock), Derek Jacobi (Archibald), Julian Glover (Colonel McGraw). Notes: Emmy Award for Outstanding Children's Program. DVD, VHS. **Adaptation 4:** *The Secret Garden* (Warner, 1993). Dir: Agnieszka Holland. Scr: Caroline Thompson. Cast: Kate Maberly (Mary), Heydon Prowse (Colin), Andrew Knott (Dickon), Maggie Smith (Mrs. Medlock). DVD, VHS. **Adaptation 5:** *The Secret Garden* (Greengrass, 1994 TV Movie). Dir: Dave Edwards. Scr: Libby Hinson. Cast: voices of Honor Blackman (Mrs. Medlock), Derek Jacobi (Archibald), Glynis Johns (Darjeeling),

Anndi McAfee (Mary), Joe Baker (Ben). Notes: An animated feature film. VHS. Notes: Two sequels were also produced—*Return to the Secret Garden* in 2000 and *Back to the Secret Garden* in 2001 (DVD, VHS).

3948. *The Secret House of Death* (Ruth Rendell, 1968). A woman finds the dead bodies of her neighbor and her lover. When she tries to help her neighbor's husband get over his grief and find his wife's killer, she puts her own life in danger. **Adaptation:** *The Secret House of Death* (ITV, 1996 TV Movie). Dir: Jim Goddard. Scr: John Harvey. Cast: Amanda Redman (Susan), Owen Teale (Bob), Nicola Redmond (Detective Janes), Trevor Sellers (Julian), Adam Welsh (Paul).

Secret Interlude (see *The View from Pompey's Head*).

3949. *The Secret Life of Algernon Pendleton* (Russell Greenan, 1973). An eccentric old man whose only companion is a talking Egyptian urn becomes involved with a young woman who is trying to get her hands on money that the old man's friend left him when he died suddenly. **Adaptation:** *The Secret Life of Algernon* (Marano, 1997). Dir: Charles Jarrott. Scr: John Cullum, John Gray, Charles Jarrott. Cast: John Cullum (Algernon), Carrie-Anne Moss (Madge), Charles Durning (Norbie), Kay Hawtrey (Mrs. Binney).

3950. "The Secret Life of Walter Mitty" (James Thurber, 1939). A henpecked man daydreams about a life of great adventures. The classic story was published in the March 18, 1939, issue of *The New Yorker*. **Adaptation:** *The Secret Life of Walter Mitty* (RKO, 1947). Dir: Norman Z. McLeod. Scr: Ken Englund, Everett Freeman. Cast: Danny Kaye (Walter), Virginia Mayo (Rosalind), Boris Karloff (Dr. Hollingshead), Fay Bainter (Mrs. Mitty), Ann Rutherford (Gertrude). DVD, VHS.

The Secret Lives of Dentists (see *The Age of Grief*).

The Secret of NIMH (see *Mrs. Frisby and the Rats of NIMH*).

The Secret of Roan Inish (see *The Secret of Ron Mor Skerry*).

3951. *The Secret of Ron Mor Skerry* (Rosalie K. Fry, 1957). Mythic story about a young Irish girl who goes to live with her grandmother on an island off the Donegal coast and tries to persuade her family to return to their ancestral home. **Adaptation:** *The Secret of Roan Inish* (Samuel Goldwyn, 1994). Dir: John Sayles. Scr: John

Sayles. Cast: Jeni Courtney (Fiona), Pat Slowey (the Priest), Dave Duffy (Jim). Notes: Independent Spirit Award nominations for Best Picture, Director, and Screenplay. DVD, VHS.

The Secret of St. Ives (see *St. Ives*).

3952. *The Secret of Santa Vittoria* (Robert Crichton, 1966). Comic World War II novel about an Italian village hiding its wine from Nazi occupiers. **Adaptation:** *The Secret of Santa Vittoria* (United Artists, 1969). Dir: Stanley Kramer. Scr: Ben Maddow, William Rose. Cast: Anthony Quinn (Italo), Anna Magnani (Rosa), Virna Lisi (Caterina), Hardy Kruger (Captain von Prum), Sergio Franchi (Tufa), Giancarlo Giannini (Fabio). Notes: Academy Award nominations for Best Editing and Musical Score; Golden Globe Award for Best Picture (Comedy) and nominations for Best Actor (Quinn), Actress (Magnani), Musical Score, and Song. VHS.

Secret of Stamboul (see *The Eunuch of Stamboul*).

3953. *The Secret of the Ruby Ring* (Yvonne MacGrory, 1994). Children's book about an Irish girl whose grandmother gives her a magical ring that grants two wishes to its wearer. When she wishes for a large home, she is transported to a castle in 1885, but loses the ring and must find it in order to get home. **Adaptation:** *The Ruby Ring* (Scottish Television/Showtime/Hallmark, 1997 TV Movie). Dir: Harley Cokeliss. Scr: Alan Moskowitz, Lin Oliver. Cast: Emily Hamilton (Lucy), Emma Cunniffe (Noreen/Nellie), Patricia Ross (Mrs. McLaughlin), Todd Boyce (Mr. McLaughlin).

3954. *Secret Places* (Janice Elliott, 1981). An English girl whose parents are German refugees befriends a schoolmate, and they find secret places where they talk about life. Their strong bond is shattered, however, with the start of World War II. **Adaptation:** *Secret Places* (Rank/20th Century–Fox, 1984). Dir: Zelda Barron. Scr: Zelda Barron. Cast: Marie-Theres Relin (Laura), Tara MacGowran (Patience), Claudine Auger (Sophie), Jenny Agutter (Miss Lowrie). VHS.

3955. *The Secret Ways* (Alistair MacLean, 1959). An American adventurer is hired to help a scholar escape from Soviet-controlled Hungary. **Adaptation:** *The Secret Ways* (Universal International, 1961). Dir: Phil Karlson. Scr: Jean Hazlewood. Cast: Richard Widmark (Michael), Sonja Ziemann (Julia), Charles Regnier (the Count), Walter Rilla (Jansci), Senta Berger (Elsa).

Secret Window (*see* "Secret Window, Secret Garden").

3956. "Secret Window, Secret Garden" (Stephen King, 1990). A writer is accused of plagiarism by a psychopathic stranger, who demands justice. The novella appeared in King's 1990 collection *Four Past Midnight*. **Adaptation:** *Secret Window* (2004). Dir: David Koepp. Scr: David Koepp. Cast: Johnny Depp (Mort), John Turturro (Shooter), Maria Bello (Amy), Timothy Hutton (Ted), Charles S. Dutton (Ken), Len Cariou (Sheriff Newsome). DVD, VHS.

3957. "Secretary" (Mary Gaitskill, 1988). After she is released from a mental institution, a masochistic secretary goes to work for an attorney with fetishes of his own. The short story appeared in Gaitskill's 1988 collection *Bad Behavior*. **Adaptation:** *Secretary* (Slough Pond, 2002). Dir: Steven Shainberg. Scr: Erin Cressida Wilson. Cast: James Spader (Grey), Maggie Gyllenhaal (Lee), Jeremy Davies (Peter), Lesley Ann Warren (Joan), Stephen McHattie (Burt). Notes: Independent Spirit Award for Best Screenplay, and nominations for Best Picture and Female Lead (Gyllenhaal); National Board of Review Award for Best Actress (Gyllenhaal); Sundance Film Festival Special Jury Prize (Shainberg); Golden Globe nomination for Best Actress (Gyllenhaal). DVD, VHS.

3958. *Secrets* (Danielle Steel, 1985). The cast of a prime-time soap opera have their own real-life secrets that can ruin their careers. **Adaptation:** *Secrets* (NBC, 1992 TV Movie). Dir: Peter H. Hunt. Scr: William Bast, Paul Huson. Cast: Christopher Plummer (Mel), Linda Purl (Jane), Gary Collins (Zack), Ben Browder (Bill). DVD, VHS.

3959. *See Here, Private Hargrove* (Marion Hargrove, 1942). Humorous anecdotes by a journalist who joined the military during World War II. **Adaptation:** *See Here, Private Hargrove* (MGM, 1944). Dir: Wesley Ruggles. Scr: Harry Kurnitz. Cast: Robert Walker (Hargrove), Donna Reed (Carol), Keenan Wynn (Private Mulvehill), Robert Benchley (Mr. Holliday). Notes: A sequel, *What's Next, Private Hargrove?*, was released in 1945.

See How They Fall (see *Triangle*).

3960. *Seed* (Charles G. Norris, 1930). After leaving his family ten years earlier to pursue his ambition to be a writer, a man returns to them. **Adaptation:** *Seed* (Universal, 1931). Dir: John M. Stahl. Scr: Gladys Lehman. Cast: John Boles

(Bart), Frances Dade (Nancy), Bette Davis (Margaret), Raymond Hackett (Junior), Zasu Pitts (Jennie).

3961. *The Seed and the Sower* (Laurens Van Der Post, 1963). Autobiographical novel about two British former prisoners of war in Japan in 1942. The men reunite on Christmas five years after the end of the war and recall their experiences under the POW camp's rigid commandant. **Adaptation:** *Merry Christmas, Mr. Lawrence* (Universal, 1983). Dir: Nagisa Oshima. Scr: Paul Mayersberg, Nagisa Oshima. Cast: David Bowie (Jack), Tom Conti (John), Ryuichi Sakamoto (Yonoi), Takeshi Kitano (Gengo). Notes: National Board of Review Award for Best Actor (Conti); BAFTA Award for Best Musical Score; Cannes Film Festival Golden Palm nomination for Best Director.

3962. *Seeing Red* (Coral Atkins, 1990). Autobiography by a well-known British television actress who left show business to open a home for disabled, neglected, and abused children, revolutionizing the foster-care system in Great Britain. **Adaptation:** *Seeing Red* (ITV, 2000 TV Movie). Dir: Graham Theakston. Scr: Christopher Monger. Cast: Sarah Lancashire (Coral), Ann Aris (Hillary), Joseph Aston (Marcus).

3963. *Seesaw* (Deborah Moggach, 1996). Jealous that a wealthy couple won a vacation in a raffle, a disturbed woman and her boyfriend kidnap the couple's daughter. **Adaptation:** *Seesaw* (Scottish Television, 1998 TV Movie). Dir: George Case. Scr: Deborah Moggach. Cast: David Suchet (Morris), Geraldine James (Val), Amanda Ooms (Eva), Neil Stuke (Jon).

See You in Hell, Darling (see *An American Dream*).

3964. *Seize the Day* (Saul Bellow, 1956). In the 1950's, a disillusioned salesman quits his job and leaves his family, erroneously believing that personal liberation will allow him to achieve success in life. **Adaptation:** *Seize the Day* (HBO/Cannon, 1986). Dir: Fielder Cook. Scr: Ronald Ribman. Cast: Robin Williams (Tommy), Richard B. Shull (Rojax), Glenne Headly (Olive). DVD, VHS.

3965. *Selma, Lord, Selma: Girlhood Memories of the Civil-Rights Days* (Sheyann Webb and Rachel West Nelson, as told to Frank Sikora, 1980). Memoir recalling the struggle for civil rights by two women who, as young girls in 1965, were inspired by hearing Dr. Martin Luther King, Jr. and joined the march from Selma to Birmingham. **Adaptation:** *Selma, Lord, Selma* (Disney/

Buena Vista, 1999 TV Movie). Dir: Charles Burnett. Scr: Cynthia Whitcomb. Cast: Mackenzie Astin (Jonathan), Jurnee Smollett (Sheyann), Clifton Powell (Martin Luther King, Jr.), Ella Joyce (Betty), Yolanda King (Miss Bright). DVD, VHS.

3966. *Semi-Tough* (Dan Jenkins, 1972). Comic novel about two professional football players in love with the same woman. **Adaptation:** *Semi-Tough* (United Artists, 1977). Dir: Michael Ritchie. Scr: Walter Bernstein. Cast: Burt Reynolds (Billy), Kris Kristofferson (Marvin), Jill Clayburgh (Barbara), Robert Preston (Big Ed), Bert Convy (Bismark). DVD, VHS. Notes: The book and film also inspired a 1980 television series on ABC.

3967. *Send Another Coffin* (F. G. Presnell, 1939). A corrupt politician tries to frame an honest attorney for murder. **Adaptation:** *Slightly Honorable* (United Artists, 1940). Dir: Tay Garnett. Scr: Ken Englund. Cast: Pat O'Brien (Webb), Edward Arnold (Cushing), Broderick Crawford (Sampson), Ruth Terry (Ann), Alan Dinehart (Commissioner Joyce). VHS.

3968. *Sense and Sensibility* (Jane Austen, 1811). In nineteenth-century Britain, two impoverished sisters—one who represents good sense and decorum, the other impulsivity and passion—try to find rich husbands. **Adaptation 1:** *Sense and Sensibility* (BBC, 1971 TV Movie). Dir: David Giles. Scr: Denis Constanduros. Cast: Joanna David (Elinor), Ciaran Madden (Marianne), Isabel Dean (Mrs. Dashwood), Michael Aldridge (Sir John). **Adaptation 2:** *Sense and Sensibility* (BBC, 1981 TV Movie). Dir: Rodney Bennett. Scr: Alexander Baron. Cast: Irene Richard (Elinor), Tracey Childs (Marianne), Diana Fairfax (Mrs. Dashwood), Peter Woodward (Willoughby), Donald Douglas (Sir John). DVD, VHS. **Adaptation 3:** *Sense and Sensibility* (Columbia, 1995). Dir: Ang Lee. Scr: Emma Thompson. Cast: Emma Thompson (Elinor), Kate Winslet (Marianne), Tom Wilkinson (Mr. Dashwood), Harriet Walter (Fanny), Gemma Jones (Mrs. Dashwood), Hugh Grant (Edward), Elizabeth Spriggs (Mrs. Jennings). Notes: Academy Award for Best Screenplay, and nominations for Best Film, Actress (Thompson), Supporting Actress (Winslet), Musical Score, Cinematography, and Costume Design; BAFTA Awards for Best Picture, Actress (Thompson), and Supporting Actress (Winslet), and nominations for Best Screenplay, Supporting Actor (Rickman), Supporting Actress (Spriggs), Musical Score, Cinematography, Costume Design, Makeup, and Production Design; Golden Globe Awards for Best Picture and Screenplay, and nominations for Best Director, Actress (Thompson), Supporting Actress (Winslet), and Musical Score; National Board of Review Awards for Best Picture, Director, and Actress (Thompson). DVD, VHS.

3969. "The Sensible Thing" (F. Scott Fitzgerald, 1924). Sad romantic tale about a young couple who choose practicality and social appearances over passion. The short story was published in *Liberty* magazine on July 15, 1924, and included in Fitzgerald's 1926 collection *All the Sad Young Men.* **Adaptation:** *The Sensible Thing* (PBS, 1996 TV Movie). Dir: Elise Robertson. Scr: Elise Robertson. Cast: Jason Cole (George), Kristina Robbins (Jonquil), Lee Michael Kopp (Mr. Cary), Barbara Van Dermeer (Mrs. Cary). VHS.

3970. *The Sentimentalist* (Dale Collins, 1929). A shipboard romance develops between a nurse and the captain of a freighter caring for a runaway girl and an abandoned baby. **Adaptation:** *His Woman* (Paramount, 1931). Dir: Edward Sloman. Scr: Melville Baker, Adelaide Heilbron. Cast: Gary Cooper (Sam), Claudette Colbert (Sally), Averell Harris (Gatson).

3971. "The Sentinel" (Arthur C. Clarke, 1951). After an alien artifact is found on Earth, astronauts go in search of life in space and discover that space beings have interacted with humans throughout history. The story first appeared in the Spring 1951 issue of *Ten Story Fantasy* and was also included in the 1953 collection *Expedition to Earth.* After the appearance of the film, the book was issued as a novella under the title *2001: A Space Odyssey.* **Adaptation:** *2001: A Space Odyssey* (MGM, 1968). Dir: Stanley Kubrick. Scr: Stanley Kubrick, Arthur C. Clarke. Cast: Keir Dullea (Dr. Bowman), Gary Lockwood (Dr. Poole), William Sylvester (Dr. Floyd), Leonard Rossiter (Dr. Smyslov). Notes: Academy Award for Best Special Effects, and nominations for Best Director, Screenplay, and Art Direction; BAFTA Awards for Best Cinematography, Production Design, and Soundtrack, and nominations for Best Film and Director. DVD, VHS. See also *2010: Odyssey Two.*

3972. *The Sentinel* (Jeffrey Konvitz, 1974). Thriller about a woman who moves into a New York City apartment haunted by the dead and discovers that her home is the gateway to Hell and that she is the designated sentinel **Adaptation:** *The Sentinel* (Universal, 1977). Dir: Michael Winner. Scr: Jeffrey Konvitz, Michael Winner. Cast: Chris Sarandon (Michael), Cristina Raines (Alison), Martin Balsam (Professor Ruzinsky), John Carradine (Father Halloran), Ava Gardner (Miss Logan), Arthur Kennedy (Monsignor Franchino), Burgess Meredith (Charles), Sylvia Miles (Gerde). DVD, VHS.

Separate Lives (see *A Way Through the Wood*).

3973. *The Separation* (Dan Franck, 1991). The French novel *La Separation* centers on a woman who tells her husband that she is in love with another man and his violent reaction to the disintegration of their relationship. **Adaptation:** *The Separation* (Phaedra, 1994). Dir: Christian Vincent. Scr: Christian Vincent. Cast: Isabelle Huppert (Anne), Daniel Auteuil (Pierre), Jerome Deschamps (Victor), Karin Viard (Claire). Notes: Originally titled *La Separation* and shown with subtitles. DVD, VHS.

3974. *Serenade* (James M. Cain, 1937). A laborer becomes a successful opera singer, but his life is dominated by his manipulative manager and two women in love with him. **Adaptation:** *Serenade* (Warner, 1956). Dir: Anthony Mann. Scr: Ivan Goff, Ben Roberts, John Twist. Cast: Mario Lanza (Damon), Joan Fontaine (Kendall), Sara Montiel (Juana), Vincent Price (Winthrop). VHS.

3975. *Serial: A Year in the Life of Marin County* (Cyra McFadden, 1977). In an affluent California neighborhood in the 1970's, a man tries to lead a normal life while his wife encourages them to experiment with the fads of the time including drugs, therapy, and free sex. **Adaptation:** *Serial* (Paramount, 1980). Dir: Bill Persky. Scr: Rich Eustis, Michael Elias. Cast: Martin Mull (Harvey), Tuesday Weld (Kate), Jennifer McAllister (Joanie), Sam Chew, Jr. (Bill), Sally Kellerman (Martha). VHS.

Serie Noire (see *A Hell of a Woman*).

3976. *A Series of Unfortunate Events* series (Lemony Snicket [pseudonym for Daniel Handler], 1999–2004). After the death of their parents, the Baudelaire children must use their wits to survive as grasping relatives try to get their hands on the children's family fortune. **Adaptation:** *Lemony Snicket's A Series of Unfortunate Events* (Paramount, 2004). Dir: Brad Silberling. Scr: Robert Gordon. Cast: Jim Carrey (Count Olaf), Meryl Streep (Aunt Josephine), Emily Browning (Violet), voice of Jude Law (Lemony Snicket). Notes: The screenplay uses elements from the first three books in the series—*The Bad*

Beginning, The Reptile Room, and *The Wide Window*— all of them published in 1999. DVD, VHS.

3977. *The Serpent and the Rainbow* (Wade Davis, 1985). A Harvard anthropologist's account of his trips to Haiti in search of the drug that black magicians used to turn people into zombies. **Adaptation:** *The Serpent and the Rainbow* (MCA-Universal, 1988). Dir: Wes Craven. Scr: Richard Maxwell, Adam Rodman. Cast: Bill Pullman (Dennis), Cathy Tyson (Marielle), Zakes Mokae (Dargent), Paul Winfield (Lucien), Brent Jennings (Louis). DVD, VHS.

3978. *Serpico* (Peter Maas, 1973). The true story of a New York undercover policeman who exposed corruption in the department in the early 1970's and became a target by his former colleagues. **Adaptation 1:** *Serpico* (Paramount, 1973). Dir: Sidney Lumet. Scr: Waldo Salt, Norman Wexler. Cast: Al Pacino (Frank Serpico), John Randolph (Chief Green), Jack Kehoe (Keough), Biff McGuire (Captain McClain), Barbara Eda-Young (Laurie). Notes: Academy Award nominations for Best Actor (Pacino) and Screenplay; Golden Globe Award for Best Actor (Pacino) and nomination for Best Picture; National Board of Review Award for Best Actor (Pacino). DVD, VHS. **Adaptation 2:** *Serpico: The Deadly Game* (NBC, 1976 TV Movie). Dir: Robert Collins. Scr: Robert Collins. Cast: David Birney (Frank Serpico), Allen Garfield (the Professor), Burt Young (Alec), Tom Atkins (Sullivan), Lane Bradbury (Carol). Notes: The movie served as the pilot for a television series in 1976.

3979. *The Servant* (Robin Maugham, 1948). A weak-willed man loses his authority to his abusive servant. The story was adapted as a stage play in 1958. **Adaptation:** *The Servant* (Landau, 1963). Dir: Joseph Losey. Scr: Harold Pinter. Cast: Dirk Bogarde (Hugo), Sarah Miles (Vera), Wendy Craig (Susan), James Fox (Tony). Notes: BAFTA Awards for Best Actor (Bogarde), Newcomer (Fox), and Cinematography, and nominations for Best Film, Screenplay, Actress (Miles), and Newcomer (Craig). DVD, VHS.

3980. *The Servants of Twilight* (Dean R. Koontz, 1984). A private detective is hired to protect a little boy targeted by religious cult members who believe he is the Biblical Antichrist. **Adaptation:** *The Servants of Twilight* (Trimark, 1991). Dir: Jeffrey Obrow. Scr: Stephen Carpenter, Jeffrey Obrow. Cast: Bruce Greenwood (Charlie), Jarrett Lennon (Joey), Belinda Bauer (Christine), Grace Zabriskie (Grace). DVD, VHS.

3981. *Service of All the Dead* (Colin Dexter, 1979). The fourth installment in Dexter's popular thirteen-novel series (1975–2000) featuring Chief Inspector Endeavour Morse of Oxford, England. In this book, Inspector Morse investigates the brutal murders of a suburban church warden and vicar. **Adaptation:** *Inspector Morse: Service of All the Dead* (ITV/PBS. 1987 TV Movie series). Dir: Peter Hammond. Scr: Julian Mitchell. Cast: John Thaw (Morse), Kevin Whately (Detective Lewis), James Grout (Superintendent Strange), Peter Woodthorpe (Max), Michael Hordern (Dr. Starkie). DVD, VHS.

3982. "The Set-Up" (Joseph Moncure March, 1928). Narrative poem about an aging boxer who, convinced that he can still win fights, refuses to take a dive and gets into trouble with gangsters who are betting against him. **Adaptation:** *The Set-Up* (RKO, 1949). Dir: Robert Wise. Scr: Art Cohn. Cast: Robert Ryan (Stoker), Audrey Totter (Julie), George Tobias (Tiny), Wallace Ford (Gus). VHS.

The Set Up (1995) (see *My Laugh Comes Last*).

3983. *The Settlers* (Vilhelm Moberg, 1956). Between 1949 and 1959, Swedish writer Vilhelm Moberg published four novels about the trials of a poor Swedish family in the nineteenth century and their emigration to the United States, where they settled in Minnesota: *The Emigrants* (1949), *Unto a Good Land* (1952), *The Settlers* (1956), and *Last Letter Home* (1959). This installment, originally titled *Nybyggarna*, concerns the family's life in Minnesota. **Adaptation:** *The New Land* (Svensk Filmindustri/Warner, 1972). Dir: Jan Troell. Scr: Bengt Forslund, Jan Troell. Cast: Max von Sydow (Karl), Liv Ullmann (Kristina), Eddie Axberg (Robert), Pierre Lindstedt (Arvid). Notes: This film and the 1971 installment *The Emigrants* were dubbed and edited for television into a single film titled *The Emigrant Saga*. Golden Globe Award for Best Foreign-Language Film; Academy Award nomination for Best Foreign-Language Film. VHS. Notes: The books and films also served as the basis for a 1974 ABC television series. In 1991, von Sydow and Ullman also starred in the Oscar-nominated Swedish film *The Ox*, directed by Sven Nykvist, which is based on a true story about a peasant farmer who kills his employer's ox and is condemned to hard labor. See also *The Emigrants*.

3984. *Seven and a Half Cents* (Richard Bissell, 1953). Comic novel about labor negotiations at a pajama factory. The book was adapted by Bissell and George Abbott in 1954 as the hit Broadway musical *The Pajama Game*. **Adaptation:** *The Pajama Game* (Warner, 1957). Dir: George Abbott, Stanley Donen. Scr: George Abbott, Richard Bissell. Cast: Doris Day (Babe), John Raitt (Sid), Carol Haney (Gladys), Eddie Foy, Jr. (Vernon), Reta Shaw (Mabel). DVD, VHS.

Seven Brides for Seven Brothers (*see* "The Sobbin' Women").

Seven Cities of Gold (see *The Nine Days of Father Serra*).

3985. *Seven Days in May* (Fletcher Knebel and Charles W. Bailey II, 1962). When the President of the United States signs a nuclear disarmament agreement with the Soviet Union, U.S. military leaders plot to overthrow the government. **Adaptation 1:** *Seven Days in May* (Paramount, 1964). Dir: John Frankenheimer. Scr: Rod Serling. Cast: Burt Lancaster (General Scott), Kirk Douglas (Colonel Casey), Fredric March (President Lyman), Ava Gardner (Eleanor), Edmond O'Brien (Senator Clark), Martin Balsam (Paul), Andrew Duggan (Colonel Henderson). Notes: Golden Globe Award for Best Supporting Actor (O'Brien), and nominations for Best Picture, Director, Actor (March), and Musical Score; Academy Award nominations for Best Supporting Actor (O'Brien) and Art Direction. DVD, VHS. **Adaptation 2:** *The Enemy Within* (HBO, 1994 TV Movie). Dir: Jonathan Darby. Scr: Rod Serling (1964 screenplay), Darryl Ponicsan, Ronald Bass. Cast: Forest Whitaker (Colonel Casey), Dana Delany (Betsy), George Dzundza (Jake), Jason Robards (General Lloyd), Sam Waterston (President Foster). DVD, VHS.

3986. *Seven Days to a Killing* (Clive Egleton, 1973). A secret agent searches for his kidnapped son. **Adaptation:** *The Black Windmill* (Universal, 1974). Dir: Don Siegel. Scr: Leigh Vance. Cast: Michael Caine (Tarrant), Donald Pleasence (Harper), Delphine Seyrig (Ceil), Clive Revill (Chestermann). VHS.

3987. *The Seven Dials Mystery* (Agatha Christie, 1929). A murder involving several alarm clocks leads a Scotland Yard detective to a nightclub which actually houses a secret society. **Adaptation:** *The Seven Dials Mystery* (London Weekend Television, 1982 TV Movie). Dir: Tony Wharmby. Scr: Pat Sandys. Cast: Terence Alexander (Lomax), Harry Andrews (Superintendent Battle), Hetty Baynes (Vera), Cheryl Campbell (Lady Bren). DVD, VHS.

3988. *711— Officer Needs Help* (Whit Masterson [pseudonym for Robert Wade], 1965). After he shoots an armed man in a robbery attempt and the gun disappears during the investigation, a policeman is charged with manslaughter. The book was also released as *Warning Shot*. **Adaptation:** *Warning Shot* (Paramount, 1967). Dir: Buzz Kulik. Scr: Mann Rubin. Cast: David Janssen (Valens), Ed Begley (Klodin), Keenan Wynn (Musso), Sam Wanamaker (Sanderman), Lillian Gish (Alice), Stefanie Powers (Liz).

Seven Faces of Dr. Lao (see *The Circus of Dr. Lao*).

3989. *Seven Keys to Baldpate* (Earl Derr Biggers, 1913). On a bet, an author agrees to move into a spooky mansion where he plans to write a Gothic novel in twenty-four hours. The novel was adapted for the Broadway stage in 1913 by George M. Cohan. **Silent Films:** 1917 and 1925. **Adaptation 1:** *Seven Keys to Baldpate* (RKO, 1929). Dir: Reginald Barker. Scr: Jane Murfin. Cast: Richard Dix (William), Miriam Seegar (Mary), Arthur Hoyt (Professor Boyle). **Adaptation 2:** *Seven Keys to Baldpate* (RKO, 1935). Dir: William Hamilton, Edward Killy. Scr: Anthony Veiller, Wallace Smith. Cast: Gene Raymond (William), Margaret Callahan (Mary), Eric Blore (Boulton), Grant Mitchell (Hayden). **Adaptation 3:** *Seven Keys to Baldpate* (RKO, 1947). Dir: Lew Landers. Scr: Lee Loeb. Cast: Phillip Terry (Kenneth), Jacqueline White (Mary), Eduardo Ciannelli (Cargan). **Adaptation 4:** *House of the Long Shadows* (Cannon, 1983). Dir: Pete Walker. Scr: Michael Armstrong. Cast: Vincent Price (Lionel), Christopher Lee (Corrigan/Roderick), Peter Cushing (Sebastian), Desi Arnaz, Jr. (Kenneth), John Carradine (Lord Grisbane). VHS.

3990. *Seven Men at Daybreak* (Alan Burgess, 1960). A novel based on the true World War II story of the assassination of the brutal Nazi overseer of Prague, Reinhard Heydrich, by Czech patriots. **Adaptation:** *Operation Daybreak*; reissued in the U.S. under the title *The Price of Freedom* (Warner, 1975). Dir: Lewis Gilbert. Scr: Ronald Harwood. Cast: Timothy Bottoms (Jan), Martin Shaw (Karel), Joss Ackland (Janak), Nicola Pagett (Anna), Anthony Andrews (Jozef), Anton Diffring (Heydrich). VHS.

3991. *The Seven Minutes* (Irving Wallace, 1969). A bookstore owner is prosecuted for selling a novel deemed obscene, and the mystery of the book's publication in the 1920's is unraveled at the trial. **Adaptation:** *The Seven Minutes* (20th Century–Fox, 1971). Dir: Russ Meyer. Scr: Richard Warren Lewis. Cast: Wayne Maunder

(Mike), Marianne McAndrew (Maggie), Philip Carey (Elmo), Jay C. Flippen (Luther), Edy Williams (Faye), Yvonne De Carlo (Constance). VHS.

3992. *The Seven Per-cent Solution* (Nicholas Meyer, 1974). In order to cure Sherlock Holmes of his psychological delusions and cocaine addiction, Dr. Watson introduces his colleague to Sigmund Freud. **Adaptation:** *The Seven Per-Cent Solution* (Universal, 1976). Dir: Herbert Ross. Scr: Nicholas Meyer. Cast: Alan Arkin (Freud), Vanessa Redgrave (Lola), Robert Duvall (Watson), Nicol Williamson (Holmes), Laurence Olivier (Professor Moriarty), Joel Grey (Lowenstein), Samantha Eggar (Mary), Jeremy Kemp (Baron von Leinsdorf). Notes: Academy Award nominations for Best Screenplay and Costume Design. DVD, VHS.

3993. *Seven Pillars of Widsom* (T. E. Lawrence, 1922). Autobiographical recollections of World War I British military officer T. E. Lawrence (1888–1935), who developed a close relationship with King Faisal and his Arab tribal army in North Africa. **Adaptation:** *Lawrence of Arabia* (Columbia, 1962). Dir: David Lean. Scr: Robert Bolt, Michael Wilson. Cast: Peter O'Toole (Lawrence), Alec Guinness (Prince Feisal), Anthony Quinn (Auda abu Tayi), Jack Hawkins (Lord Allenby), Omar Sharif (Sherif Kharish), Jose Ferrer (Turkish Bey), Anthony Quayle (Brighton), Claude Rains (Dryden), Arthur Kennedy (Bentley). Notes: Academy Awards for Best Picture, Director, Musical Score, Art Direction, Cinematography, Editing, and Sound, and nominations for Best Screenplay, Actor (O'Toole), and Supporting Actor (Sharif); BAFTA Awards for Best Film, Screenplay, and Actor (O'Toole), and nomination for Best Actor (Quinn); Golden Globe Awards for Best Picture, Director, Supporting Actor (Sharif), Cinematography, and Most Promising Newcomer (Sharif); National Board of Review Award for Best Director. DVD, VHS.

3994. *Seven Thunders* (Rupert Crofy-Cooke, 1955). In Marseilles during World War II, British prisoners of war escape and try to hide from the Nazis. **Adaptation:** *Seven Thunders*; released in the U.S. as *The Beasts of Marseilles* (Allied Artists/Lopert, 1957). Dir: Hugo Fregonese. Scr: John Baines. Cast: Stephen Boyd (Dave), James Robertson Justice (Dr. Martout), Kathleen Harrison (Madame Abou), Tony Wright (Jim).

3995. *Seven Years in Tibet* (Heinrich Harrer, 1953). Memoir of an Austrian mountain climber who escaped from a British prisoner-of-war camp in India during World War II and climbed the Himalayas in Tibet, where he entered the holy city of Lhasa and befriended the teenaged Dalai Lama. **Adaptation:** *Seven Years in Tibet* (TriStar, 1997). Dir: Jean-Jacques Annaud. Scr: Becky Johnston. Cast: Brad Pitt (Harrer), David Thewlis (Peter), B. D. Wong (Ngawang Jigme). DVD, VHS. Notes: There is also a 1956 British documentary based on the book.

3996. *Seventeen* (Booth Tarkington, 1915). A young man studying for college exams is distracted by a beautiful and sophisticated Chicago girl, and he goes to extreme lengths to impress her. The novel was adapted for the Broadway stage by Hugh Stanislaus Stange and Stannard Mears in 1918. **Silent Film:** 1916. **Adaptation:** *Seventeen* (Paramount, 1940). Dir: Louis King. Scr: Agnes Christine Johnston, Stuart Palmer, Hugh Stange, Stuart Walker. Cast: Jackie Cooper (William), Betty Field (Lola), Otto Kruger (Sylvanus), Ann Shoemaker (Mary).

3997. *The Seventh* (Donald E. Westlake, 1966). A group of daring thieves robs a Los Angeles stadium while a professional football game is in progress, but a falling out among them occurs when their loot disappears. Westlake originally published the novel under the pseudonym Richard Stark. **Adaptation:** *The Split* (MGM, 1968). Dir: Gordon Flemyng. Scr: Robert Sabaroff. Cast: Jim Brown (McClain), Diahann Carroll (Ellie), Ernest Borgnine (Clinger), Julie Harris (Gladys), Gene Hackman (Detective Brille), Jack Klugman (Harry).

3998. *The Seventh Cross* (Anna Seghers [pseudonym for Netty Reiling], 1939). In this German novel, originally titled *Das siebte Kreuz*, seven men escape from a concentration camp in Nazi Germany, and the camp commandant erects seven crosses on which the escapees will be executed. All but one of the inmates are caught, and the seventh cross remains unused as the man makes his way to freedom in Holland. The novel was first translated into English in 1942. **Adaptation:** *The Seventh Cross* (MGM, 1944). Dir: Fred Zinnemann. Scr: Helen Deutsch. Cast: Spencer Tracy (George), Signe Hasso (Toni), Hume Cronyn (Paul), Jessica Tandy (Liesel), Agnes Moorehead (Madame Marelli). VHS.

The Seventh Dawn (see *The Durian Tree*).

The Seventh Sin (see *The Painted Veil*).

3999. "The Seventh Victim" (Robert Sheckley, 1953). Futuristic science-fiction story about a society that legalizes hunting human beings as an outlet for violence. The short story was published in *Galaxy* in April 1953. **Adaptation:** *The Tenth Victim* (AVCO Embassy, 1965). Dir: Elio Petri. Scr: Ennio Flaiano, Tonino Guerra, Elio Petri, Giorgio Salvioni. Cast: Marcello Mastroianni (Marcello), Ursula Andress (Caroline), Elsa Martinelli (Olga). Notes: Originally released as *La Decima Vittima* and shown with English subtitles. DVD, VHS.

4000. *79 Park Avenue* (Harold Robbins, 1955). When New York City's most affluent madam is arrested and tried on prostiturion charges, her prosecutor is a man who once loved her and is torn between his ambition and his feelings. **Adaptation:** *Harold Robbins' 79 Park Avenue* (NBC, 1977 TV Miniseries). Dir: Paul Wendkos. Scr: Richard De Roy, Jack Guss, Lionel E. Siegel. Cast: Lesley Ann Warren (Marja/Marianne), Marc Singer (Ross), David Dukes (Mike), Barbara Barrie (Kaati), Polly Bergen (Vera), Raymond Burr (Armand). Notes: Golden Globe Award for Best Television Actress (Warren).

4001. *A Severed Head* (Iris Murdoch, 1961). A philandering wine merchant must tolerate his wife's affair with their best friend, a psychiatrist. The novel was adapted by Murdoch and J. B. Priestley in 1963. **Adaptation:** *A Severed Head* (Columbia, 1970). Dir: Dick Clement. Scr: Frederic Raphael. Cast: Lee Remick (Antonia), Richard Attenborough (Palmer), Ian Holm (Martin), Claire Bloom (Honor), Clive Revill (Alexander).

4002. *Sex and the Criminal Mind* (Norman Winski, 1965). A case history involving a young man who became the lover of his employer's wife and moved into the attic of their home in Miluakee in 1903. The man and his lover were subsequently charged with murdering her husband. **Adaptation:** *The Man in the Attic* (CBS, 1995 TV Movie). Dir: Graeme Campbell. Scr: Duane Poole, Tom Swale. Cast: Anne Archer (Krista), Len Cariou (Joseph), Neil Patrick Harris (Edward). VHS.

4003. *Sex and the Single Girl* (Helen Gurley Brown, 1962). A guide for single women, providing advice about dating, work, beauty, money, and sexuality. **Adaptation:** *Sex and the Single Girl* (Warner, 1964). Dir: Richard Quine. Scr: Joseph Heller, Joseph Hoffman, David R. Schwartz. Cast: Lauren Bacall (Sylvia), Tony Curtis (Bob), Mel Ferrer (Dr. DeMeyer), Henry Fonda (Frank), Edward Everett Horton (the Chief). Notes: The screenplay concerns a tabloid journalist who goes undercover to expose a feminist sex expert as a fraud. VHS.

Sex Pot (*see* "Collared").

4004. *SFW* (Andrew Wellman, 1990). A man held hostage in a convenience store for thirty-six days becomes famous worldwide for his indifference to the ordeal when television cameras capture his reactions to captivity. **Adaptation:** *SFW* (Gramercy, 1994). Dir: Jefery Levy. Scr: Danny Rubin, Jefery Levy. Cast: Stephen Dorff (Cliff), Reese Witherspoon (Wendy), Jake Busey (Morrow), Joey Lauren Adams (Monica). DVD, VHS.

4005. *The Shadow and the Peak* (Richard Mason, 1949). A divorced British teacher in Jamaica has affairs with three women. **Adaptation:** *Passionate Summer* (1958). Dir: Rudolph Cartier. Scr: Joan Henry. Cast: Virginia McKenna (Judy), Bill Travers (Douglas), Yvonne Mitchell (Mrs. Pawley), Alexander Knox (Leonard).

The Shadow Man (see *The Creaking Chair*).

4006. *Shadow of a Doubt* (William Couglin, 1991). Although he is not the skilled lawyer he once was, an alcoholic attorney returns to the courtroom to defend a former lover's stepdaughter, who is accused of murder. **Adaptation:** *Shadow of a Doubt* (Scripps-Howard, 1995 TV Movie). Dir: Brian Dennehy. Scr: Brian Dennehy, Bill Phillips. Cast: Brian Dennehy (Charlie), Bonnie Bedelia (Robin/Roberta), Fairuza Balk (Angel), Mike Nussbaum (Nate), Joe Grifasi (Sidney).

Shadow of the Wolf (see *Agaguk*).

4007. *The Shadow Over Innsmouth* (H. P. Lovecraft, 1936). Horror story set in a small town, where strange half-human, half-reptile creatures dwell. The book was privately published by Lovecraft in 1936. **Adaptation:** *Dagon: The Sect of the Sea* (Trimark, 2001). Dir: Stuart Gordon. Scr: Dennis Paoli. Cast: Ezra Godden (Paul), Francisco Rabal (Ezequiel), Raquel Merono (Barbara), Brendan Price (Howard). Notes: The screenplay combines elements of Lovecraft's short story "Dagon" and his book *The Shadow Over Innsmouth*. DVD, VHS. See also "Dagon."

4008. *The Shadow Riders* (Louis L'Amour, 1982). Western about two brothers who return from the Civil War to discover that their sister and the fiancée of one of them have been kdnapped by a gang of vicious raiders. **Adaptation:** *The Shadow Riders* (CBS, 1982 TV Movie). Dir:

Andrew V. McLaglen. Scr: Jim Byrnes. Cast: Tom Selleck (Mac), Sam Elliott (Dal), Ben Johnson (Black Jack), Geoffrey Lewis (Major Ashbury). DVD, VHS.

4009. *Shaft* (Ernest Tidyman, 1970). A black private eye is hired by a Harlem mobster to locate his missing teenaged daughter and tangles with gangsters who are trying to take back the Harlem heroin trade. **Adaptation 1:** *Shaft* (MGM, 1971). Dir: Gordon Parks. Scr: Ernest Tidyman, John D. F. Black. Cast: Richard Roundtree (Shaft), Moses Gunn (Bumpy), Charles Cioffi (Androzzi), Christopher St. John (Buford), Gwenn Mitchell (Ellie), Lawrence Pressman (Sergeant Hannon). Notes: Academy Award for Best Song and nomination for Best Musical Score; Golden Globe Award for Best Musical Score and nomination for Most Promising Newcomer (Roundtree). DVD, VHS. **Adaptation 2:** *Shaft* (Paramount, 2000). Dir: John Singleton. Scr: Richard Price, John Singleton, Shane Salerno. Cast: Samuel L. Jackson (Shaft), Vanessa Williams (Carmen), Jeffrey Wright (Hernandez), Christian Bale (Walter), Busta Rhymes (Rasaan), Dan Hedaya (Detective Roselli), Toni Collette (Diane), Richard Roundtree (Uncle John Shaft). Notes: Despite its title, the screenplay was only inspired by the original work and features John Shaft's nephew as the title character. DVD, VHS. Notes: The book and film inspired a brief CBS television series in 1973 and two movie sequels: *Shaft's Big Score* (1972), written by Tidyman and issued as a tie-in novel the same year (DVD, VHS), and 1973: *Shaft in Africa* (1973) (DVD, VHS).

The Shaggy Dog (see *The Hound of Florence*).

4010. *Shake Hands with the Devil* (Rearden Conner, 1933). In 1921, a young American is drawn into an Irish Republican Army unit led by a hardened professor, who regards fighting the British not as a means to an end but as an end in itself. **Adaptation:** *Shake Hands with the Devil* (United Artists, 1959). Dir: Michael Anderson. Scr: Marian Thompson, Ivan Goff, Ben Roberts. Cast: James Cagney (Sean), Don Murray (Kerry), Dana Wynter (Jennifer), Glynis Johns (Kitty), Michael Redgrave (the General), Sybil Thorndike (Lady Fitzhugh), Cyril Cusack (Chris). VHS.

4011. *Shalako* (Louis L'Amour, 1962). In New Mexico in the 1880's, a cowboy saves a group of aristocratic European hunters from an Indian uprising. **Adaptation:** *Shalako* (Cinerama, 1968). Dir: Edward Dmytryk. Scr: Scott Finch, J. J. Griffith, Hal Hopper. Cast: Sean Connery (Sha-

lako), Brigitte Bardot (Countess Irina), Stephen Boyd (Fulton), Jack Hawkins (Sir Charles), Peter van Eyck (Baron Von Hallstatt), Honor Blackman (Lady Julia). DVD, VHS.

Shame (see *The Intruder* by Charles Beaumont).

4012. *Shane* (Jack Schaefer, 1949). Set in 1889, Western about a retired gunfighter who becomes a farm hand on a ranch. When a rival rancher tries to intimidate his neighbors by hiring a gunfighter to assault them, Shane returns to the trade he knows best. **Adaptation:** *Shane* (Paramount, 1953). Dir: George Stevens. Scr: A. B. Guthrie, Jr. Cast: Alan Ladd (Shane), Jean Arthur (Marian), Van Heflin (Starrett), Brandon De Wilde (Joey Starrett), Jack Palance (Wilson), Ben Johnson (Chris), Edgar Buchanan (Fred). Notes: Academy Award for Best Cinematography, and nominations for Best Film, Director, Screenplay, and Supporting Actors (De Wilde and Palance); National Board of Review Award for Best Director. DVD, VHS.

Shanghai Surprise (see *Faraday's Flowers*).

4013. *The Shape of Things to Come* (H. G. Wells, 1933). Science-fiction novel about the future of humanity in the wake of devastating war. **Adaptation 1:** *Things to Come* (London/United Artists, 1936). Dir: William Cameron Menzies. Scr: H. G. Wells. Cast: Raymond Massey (Cabal), Edward Chapman (Pippa/Raymond), Ralph Richardson (the Boss), Margaretta Scott (Roxana/Rowena), Cedric Hardwicke (Theotocopulos). DVD, VHS. **Adaptation 2:** *The Shape of Things to Come* (Film Ventures, 1979). Dir: George McCowan. Scr: Mike Cheda, Joseph Glazner, Martin Lager. Cast: Jack Palance (Omus), Carol Lynley (Nikki), Barry Morse (Dr. Caball), John Ireland (Senator Smedley). DVD, VHS.

Shark! (see *His Bones Are Coral*).

The Shark God (see *Omoo*).

4014. *Sharky's Machine* (William Diehl, 1978). A detective with the Atlanta Vice Squad and his team go after an underworld capo, and in the process the detective falls in love with one of the mobster's high-priced call girls. **Adaptation:** *Sharky's Machine* (Warner/Orion, 1981). Dir: Burt Reynolds. Scr: Gerald Di Pego. Cast: Burt Reynolds (Sharky), Vittorio Gassman (Victor), Brian Keith (Papa), Charles Durning (Frisco), Earl Holliman (Hotchkins), Bernie

Casey (Arch), Henry Silva (Billy), Richard Libertini (Nosh). DVD, VHS.

4015. *Sharpe's Battle* (Bernard Cornwell [pseudonym for Bernard Wiggins], 1995). The thirteenth installment in the eighteen-novel series (1981–2002) about a British military officer battling the French during the Napoleonic era. In this novel, Sharpe is put in charge of a battalion to fight the French at the Battle of Fuentes De Onoro in Spain in 1811. **Adaptation: *Sharpe's Battle*** (Celtic/Picture Palace/PBS, 1995 TV Movie series). Dir: Tom Clegg. Scr: Russell Lewis, Cast: Sean Bean (Sharpe), Allie Byrne (Lady Kiely), Liam Carney (O'Rourke), Oliver Cotton (Loup). DVD, VHS.

4016. *Sharpe's Company* (Bernard Cornwell [pseudonym for Bernard Wiggins], 1982). The third installment in the eighteen-novel series (1981–2002) about a British military officer battling the French during the Napoleonic era. In this novel, Sharpe and his men are attacked by elite French troops as they take refuge in a crumbling Spanish fort in 1812. **Adaptation:** *Sharpe's Company* (Celtic/Picture Palace/PBS, 1994 TV Movie series). Dir: Tom Clegg. Scr: Charles Wood. Cast: Sean Bean (Sharpe), Daragh O'Malley (Harper), Hugh Fraser (Wellington), Michael Byrne (Nairn), Pete Postlethwaite (Obadiah), Assumpta Serna (Teresa). DVD, VHS.

4017. *Sharpe's Eagle* (Bernard Cornwell [pseudonym for Bernard Wiggins], 1981). The first installment in the eighteen-novel series (1981–2002) about a British military officer battling the French during the Napoleonic era. In this novel, Sharpe must lead an inexperienced battalion against the French in the Talavera Campaign in July 1809. **Adaptation:** *Sharpe's Eagle* (Celtic/Picture Palace/PBS, 1993 TV Movie series). Dir: Tom Clegg. Scr: Eoghan Harris. Cast: Sean Bean (Sharpe), Brian Cox (Hogan), Daragh O'Malley (Harper), Assumpta Serna (Teresa), Michael Cochrane (Simmerson), David Troughton (Wellesley). DVD, VHS.

4018. *Sharpe's Enemy* (Bernard Cornwell [pseudonym for Bernard Wiggins], 1983). The fifth installment in the eighteen-novel series (1981–2002) about a British military officer battling the French during the Napoleonic era. In this novel, Sharpe is assigned to rescue two kidnapped women being held for ransom in Portugal in 1813. **Adaptation:** *Sharpe's Enemy* (Celtic/Picture Palace/PBS, 1994 TV Movie series). Dir: Tom Clegg. Scr: Eoghan Harris. Cast: Sean Bean (Sharpe), Daragh O'Malley (Harper), Hugh Fraser

(the Duke of Wellington), Michael Byrne (Nairn), Pete Postlethwaite (Obediah), Assumpta Serna (Teresa), Jeremy Child (Sir Farthingale), Elizabeth Hurley (Lady Farthingdale). DVD, VHS.

4019. *Sharpe's Gold* (Bernard Cornwell [pseudonym for Bernard Wiggins], 1981). The second installment in the eighteen-novel series (1981–2002) about a British military officer battling the French during the Napoleonic era. In this novel, Sharpe contends with a beautiful Spanish spy in 1810. **Adaptation:** *Sharpe's Gold* (Celtic/Picture Palace/PBS, 1995 TV Movie series). Dir: Tom Clegg. Scr: Nigel Kneale. Cast: Sean Bean (Sharpe), Daragh O'Malley (Harper), Hugh Fraser (Wellington), Diana Perez (Ramona). DVD, VHS.

4020. *Sharpe's Honor* (Bernard Cornwell [pseudonym for Bernard Wiggins], 1985). The sixth installment in the eighteen-novel series (1981–2002) about a British military officer battling the French during the Napoleonic era. In this novel, Sharpe, wrongly accused of raping a Spanish woman and killing her husband, faces a court martial in 1813. **Adaptation:** *Sharpe's Honor* (Celtic/Picture Palace/PBS, 1994 TV Movie series). Dir: Tom Clegg. Scr: Colin MacDonald. Cast: Sean Bean (Sharpe), Daragh O'Malley (Harper), Hugh Fraser (Wellington), Michael Byrne (Nairn), Alice Krige (La Marquesa). DVD, VHS.

4021. *Sharpe's Regiment* (Bernard Cornwell [pseudonym for Bernard Wiggins], 1986). The seventh installment in the eighteen-novel series (1981–2002) about a British military officer battling the French during the Napoleonic era. In this novel, Sharpe investigates why the British army is losing recruits in 1813 and discovers that they are being auctioned off by unscrupulous officers. **Adaptation:** *Sharpe's Regiment* (Celtic/Picture Palace/PBS, 1996 TV Movie series). Dir: Tom Clegg. Scr: Colin MacDonald. Cast: Sean Bean (Sharpe), Daragh O'Malley (Harper), Michael Cochrane (Sir Henry), Julian Fellowes (the Prince Regent). DVD, VHS.

4022. *Sharpe's Rifles* (Bernard Cornwell [pseudonym for Bernard Wiggins], 1988). The ninth installment in the eighteen-novel series (1981–2002) about a British military officer battling the French during the Napoleonic era. In this novel, Sharpe's rifle company battles the French in the Invasion of Galicia in 1809. **Adaptation:** *Sharpe's Rifles* (Celtic/Picture Palace/PBS, 1993 TV Movie series). Dir: Tom Clegg. Scr: Eoghan Harris. Cast: Sean Bean (Sharpe), Daragh O'Malley (Harper), Assumpta Serna (Teresa), Brian Cox (Hogan). DVD, VHS.

4023. *Sharpe's Siege* (Bernard Cornwell [pseudonym for Bernard Wiggins], 1987). The eighth installment in the eighteen-novel series (1981–2002) about a British military officer battling the French during the Napoleonic era. In this novel, Sharpe leads a small group of riflemen as they try to protect an inept naval commander in the winter of 1814. **Adaptation:** *Sharpe's Siege* (Celtic/Picture Palace/PBS, 1996 TV Movie series). Dir: Tom Clegg. Scr: Eoghan Harris, Charles Wood. Cast: Sean Bean (Sharpe), Daragh O'Malley (Harper), Hugh Fraser (Wellington), Diana Perez (Ramona). DVD, VHS.

4024. *Sharpe's Sword* (Bernard Cornwell [pseudonym for Bernard Wiggins], 1983). The fourth installment in the eighteen-novel series (1981–2002) about a British military officer battling the French during the Napoleonic era. In this novel, Sharpe is seriously wounded in a fight with a French colonel. **Adaptation:** *Sharpe's Sword* (Celtic/Picture Palace/PBS, 1995 TV Movie series). Dir: Tom Clegg. Scr: Eoghan Harris, Charles Wood. Cast: Sean Bean (Sharpe), Daragh O'Malley (Harper), Michael Cochrane (Sir Henry), Diana Perez (Ramona). DVD, VHS.

Shattered (1972) (see *Something to Hide*).

4025. *Shattered* (Dean R. Koontz, 1973). A family driving cross country are terrorized by a man in a truck. Koontz originally published the novel under the pseudonym K. R. Dwyer. **Adaptation:** *The Intruder* (Trianon/VidAmerica, 1977). Dir: Serge Leroy. Scr: Christopher Frank. Cast: Jean-Louis Trintignant (Alex), Mireille Darc (Nicole), Bernard Fresson (Fabio), Richard Constantini (Marc). VHS.

Shattered (1991) (see *The Plastic Nightmare*).

4026. "Shattered Glass" (Buzz Bissinger, 1998). The true story of Stephen Glass, a young staff writer with *The New Republic* in the mid–1990's, who admitted that more than half of the articles he published in the magazine were fabricated. Bissinger's article appeared in the September 1998 issue of *Vanity Fair*. **Adaptation:** *Shattered Glass* (Lions Gate, 2003). Dir: Billy Ray. Scr: Billy Ray. Cast: Hayden Christensen (Glass), Peter Sarsgaard (Chuck), Chloe Sevigny (Caitlin), Rosario Dawson (Andy), Melanie Lynskey (Amy), Hank Azaria (Michael), Steve Zahn (Adam). DVD, VHS.

Shaughnessy (see *The Iron Marshal*).

The Shawshank Redemption (*see* "Rita Hayworth and the Shawshank Redemption").

4027. *She* (H. Rider Haggard, 1887). The adventure story centers on the exploits of an immortal female warrior and military leader in a lost city in Africa. **Silent Films:** 1908, 1911, 1916, 1917 and 1925. **Adaptation 1:** *She* (RKO, 1935). Dir: Lansing C. Holden, Irving Pichel. Scr: Ruth Rose, Dudley Nichols. Cast: Helen Gahagan (She), Randolph Scott (Leo), Helen Mack (Tanya), Nigel Bruce (Horace). DVD, VHS. **Adaptation 2:** *She* (Hammer/MGM, 1965). Dir: Robert Day. Scr: David T. Chantler. Cast: Ursula Andress (She), Peter Cushing (Major Holly), Bernard Cribbins (Job), Christopher Lee (Billali). DVD, VHS. **Adaptation 3:** *She* (Royal/American National, 1985). Dir: Avi Nesher. Scr: Avi Nesher. Cast: Sandahl Bergman (She), David Goss (Tom), Quin Kessler (Shandra), Harrison Muller, Jr. (Dick). VHS. **Adaptation 4:** *She* (Prophecy, 2001). Dir: Timothy Bond. Scr: Peter Jobin. Cast: Ophelie Winter (She), Martina Colombari (Ustane), Edward Hardwicke (Ludwig). Notes: A British sequel, *The Vengeance of She*, was released in 1968 (DVD, VHS).

She-Devil (see *The Life and Loves of a She-Devil*).

She Didn't Say No! (see *We Are Seven*).

4028. *She Let Him Continue* (Stephen Geller, 1966). A disturbed young arsonist meets a pretty adolescent girl who leads him into greater trouble and finally murder. **Adaptation 1:** *Pretty Poison* (20th Century–Fox, 1968). Dir: Noel Black. Scr: Lorenzo Semple, Jr. Cast: Anthony Perkins (Dennis), Tuesday Weld (Sue Ann), Beverly Garland (Mrs. Stepanek), John Randolph (Morton). VHS. **Adaptation 2:** *Pretty Poison* (20th Century–Fox Television, 1996 TV Movie). Dir: David Burton Morris. Scr: Lorenzo Semple, Jr. (1968 screenplay), Brian Ross. Cast: Grant Show (Dennis), Wendy Benson-Landes (Sue Ann), Michelle Phillips (Mrs. Stepanek).

4029. *She Loves Me Not* (Edward Hope, 1933). Comic novel about a female cabaret dancer who witnesses a murder and takes refuge at Princeton University disguised as a man. The book was adapted as a 1933 Broadway play by Howard Lindsay. **Adaptation 1:** *She Loves Me Not* (Paramount, 1934). Dir: Elliott Nugent. Scr: Benjamin Glazer. Cast: Bing Crosby (Paul), Miriam Hopkins (Curly), Kitty Carlisle (Midge), Edward

Nugent (Buzz). **Adaptation 2:** *True to the Army* (Paramount, 1942). Dir: Albert S. Rogell. Scr: Art Arthur, Val Burton, Edmund L. Hartmann, Bradford Ropes. Cast: Judy Canova (Daisy), Allan Jones (Stephen), Ann Miller (Vicki), Jerry Colonna (Pinky). **Adaptation 3:** *How to Be Very, Very Popular* (20th Century–Fox, 1955). Dir: Nunnally Johnson. Scr: Nunnally Johnson. Cast: Betty Grable (Stormy), Sheree North (Curly), Robert Cummings (Fillmore), Charles Coburn (Dr. Tweed).

She Played with Fire (see *Fortune Is a Woman*).

4030. *She Shall Have Murder* (Delano Ames, 1948). Comic mystery about a law clerk who is writing a novel based on stories she picks up in her office. When an elderly woman client dies in the same manner she describes in her book, she and her boyfriend investigate. **Adaptation:** *She Shall Have Murder* (Concanen/IFD, 1950). Dir: Daniel Birt. Cast: Rosamund John (Jane), Derrick De Marney (Dagobert), Beatrice Varley (Mrs. Hawthorne).

She Wore a Yellow Ribbon (see "War Party").

4031. *The Sheep Pig* (Dick King-Smith, 1983). An orphaned pig is adopted by a farmer and learns to herd sheep from a sheepdog and other friendly animals. **Adaptation:** *Babe* (Universal, 1995). Dir: Chris Noonan. Scr: George Miller, Chris Noonan. Cast: James Cromwell (Farmer Hoggett), Roscoe Lee Browne (Narrator), voices of Christine Cavanaugh (Babe), Miriam Margolyes (Fly), Danny Mann (Ferdinand), Hugo Weaving (Rex). Notes: Academy Award for Special Effects and nominations for Best Picture, Director, Screenplay, Supporting Actor (Cromwell), Editing, and Art Direction; Golden Globe Award for Best Picture. DVD, VHS. Notes: A sequel, *Babe: Pig in the City*, was released in 1998 (DVD, VHS).

4032. *The Sheltering Sky* (Paul Bowles, 1949). In the 1940's, an American couple wanders aimlessly around Africa trying to find enough excitement to rekindle their relationship. **Adaptation:** *The Sheltering Sky* (Warner, 1990). Dir: Bernardo Bertolucci. Scr: Mark Peploe, Bernardo Bertolucci. Cast: Debra Winger (Kit), John Malkovich (Port), Campbell Scott (George), Jill Bennett (Mrs. Lyle). Notes: BAFTA Award for Best Cinematography and nomination for Best Production Design; Golden Globe Award for Best Musical Score and nomination for Best Director. DVD, VHS.

4033. *The Shepherd of the Hills* (Harold Bell Wright, 1907). A moonshiner in the Ozark Mountains harbors a grudge against the man who abandoned his mother years earlier, and he has his suspicions about a mysterious stranger who appears in town one day. **Silent Films:** 1919 and 1927. **Adaptation 1:** *The Shepherd of the Hills* (Paramount, 1941). Dir: Henry Hathaway. Scr: Stuart Anthony, Grover Jones. Cast: John Wayne (Matt), Betty Field (Sammy), Harry Carey (Daniel), Beulah Bondi (Aunt Mollie). VHS. **Adaptation 2:** *The Shepherd of the Hills* (KYTV, 1960 TV Movie). Dir: Bob Irwin. Scr: Larry Dixon. Cast: Bob Nevins (Matt), Dee Petit (Sammy), Alfred Morrill (Uncle Ike). **Adaptation 3:** *The Shepherd of the Hills* (Howco, 1964). Dir: Ben Parker. Scr: Ben Parker. Cast: Richard Arlen (Matt), James Middleton (Daniel), Sherry Lynn (Sammy).

Sherlock Holmes and the House of Fear (see "The Five Orange Pips").

Sherlock Holmes and the Missing Rembrandt (see "The Adventure of Charles Augustus Milverton).

Sherlock Holmes and the Secret Weapon (see "The Adventure of the Dancing Men").

Sherlock Holmes and the Voice of Terror (see "His Last Bow").

Sherlock Holmes Faces Death (see "The Musgrave Ritual").

4034. *A Shilling for Candles* (Josephine Tey, 1936). An innocent man arrested for the murder of an actress escapes custody and goes on the run with the arresting officer's daughter to prove his innocence. **Adaptation:** *Young and Innocent* (Gaumont, 1937). Dir: Alfred Hitchcock. Scr: Charles Bennett, Edwin Greenwood, Anthony Armstrong, Gerald Savory, Alma Reville. Cast: Nova Pilbeam (Erica), Derrick De Marney (Robert), Percy Marmont (Burgoyne), Edward Rigby (Will), Mary Clare (Aunt Margaret). DVD, VHS.

4035. *Shiloh* (Phyllis Reynolds Naylor, 1991). Children's book about a young boy who befriends an abused beagle and takes it away from its owner, a mean-spirited hunter. **Adaptation:** *Shiloh* (Legacy/Warner, 1996). Dir: Dale Rosenbloom. Scr: Dale Rosenbloom. Cast: Michael Moriarty (Ray), Scott Wilson (Travers), Blake Heron (Marty), Rod Steiger (Doc Wallace). DVD, VHS.

4036. *Shiloh Season* (Phyllis Reynolds Naylor, 1996). In this sequel to Naylor's 1991 book

Shiloh, the young boy who adopted the beagle named Shiloh fears that its abusive owner wants it back because hunting season is about to begin, and the boy sets out to bring out the humanity in the mean-spirited man. **Adaptation:** *Shiloh 2: Shiloh Season* (Warner, 1999). Dir: Sandy Tung. Scr: Dale Rosenbloom. Cast: Zachary Browne (Marty), Scott Wilson (Travers), Michael Moriarty (Ray), Ann Dowd (Louise), Caitlin Wachs (Dara), Rachel David (Becky), Rod Steiger (Doc Wallace). DVD, VHS.

4037. *The Shining* (Stephen King, 1977). King's eerie tale about the evil influence of a haunted hotel over its winter caretaker and his family. **Adaptation 1:** *The Shining* (Warner, 1980). Dir: Stanley Kubrick. Scr: Stanley Kubrick, Diane Johnson. Cast: Jack Nicholson (Jack), Shelley Duvall (Wendy), Danny Lloyd (Danny), Scatman Crothers (Hallorann), Barry Nelson (Ullman). DVD, VHS. **Adaptation 2:** *The Shining* (Warner Bros. Television, 1997 TV Miniseries). Dir: Mick Garris. Scr: Stephen King. Cast: Steven Weber (Jack), Rebecca De Mornay (Wendy), Courtland Mead (Danny), Melvin Van Peebles (Hallorann). Notes: Emmy Awards for Outstanding Makeup and Sound and nomination for Outstanding Miniseries. DVD, VHS.

4038. *Shining Through* (Susan Isaacs, 1988). During World War II, a secretary falls in love with her boss, an American espionage agent, and he persuades her to take a job as a domestic in the home of a Nazi officer in order to spy on him. **Adaptation:** *Shining Through* (20th Century–Fox, 1992). Dir: David Seltzer. Scr: David Seltzer. Cast: Michael Douglas (Ed), Melanie Griffith (Linda), Liam Neeson (Franz), Joely Richardson (Margrete), John Gielgud (Konrad). DVD, VHS.

4039. *Ship of Fools* (Katherine Anne Porter, 1962). Conflicts arise among a group of passengers from different social classes and nationalities traveling on a German ship between Vera Cruz and Bremerhaven in 1931. **Adaptation:** *Ship of Fools* (Columbia, 1965). Dir: Stanley Kramer. Scr: Abby Mann. Cast: Vivien Leigh (Mary), Simone Signoret (the Contessa), Jose Ferrer (Siegfried), Lee Marvin (Bill), Oskar Werner (Dr. Schumann), Elizabeth Ashley (Jenny), George Segal (David), Michael Dunn (Carl). Notes: Academy Awards for Best Cinematography and Art Direction, and nominations for Best Picture, Screenplay, Actor (Werner), Actress (Signoret), Supporting Actor (Dunn), and Costume Design; National Board of Review Award for Best Actor (Marvin); BAFTA nominations for Best Actor (Werner) and Actress

(Signoret); Golden Globe nominations for Best Picture and Actor (Werner). DVD, VHS.

4040. "The Ship That Died of Shame" (Nicholas Monsarrat, 1944). After their naval service in World War II, three men buy their old military ship and use it for smuggling until the ship itself rebels. The short story first appeared in Monsarrat's 1944 collection of maritime memoirs and stories titled *Corvette Command* and was used as the title piece in the 1959 collection *The Ship That Died of Shame and Other Stories*. **Adaptation:** *The Ship That Died of Shame* (Ealing/Continental, 1955). Dir: Basil Dearden, Michael Relph. Scr: Basil Dearden, Michael Relph, John Whiting. Cast: Richard Attenborough (Hoskins), George Baker (Randall), Bill Owen (Birdie), Virginia McKenna (Helen). VHS.

4041. *The Shipping News* (E. Annie Proulx, 1993, Pulitzer Prize and National Book Award). An emotionally bruised man returns with his daughter to his home in Newfoundland, where he begins to regain his confidence. **Adaptation:** *The Shipping News* (Miramax, 2001). Dir: Lasse Hallstrom. Scr: Robert Nelson Jacobs. Cast: Kevin Spacey (Quoyle), Julianne Moore (Wavey), Judi Dench (Agnis), Cate Blanchett (Petal), Pete Postlethwaite (Tert), Scott Glenn (Jack), Rhys Ifans (Nutbeem). Notes: National Board of Review Award for Best Supporting Actress (Blanchett); BAFTA nominations for Best Actor (Spacey) and Supporting Actress (Dench); Golden Globe nominations for Best Actor (Spacey) and Musical Score. DVD, VHS.

4042. *The Shiralee* (D'Arcy Niland, 1955). An Australian drifter discovers his alcoholic wife with another man and takes his young daughter on the road with him. As they spend time together, he grows mature and responsible. **Adaptation 1:** *The Shiralee* (Ealing/MGM, 1957). Dir: Leslie Norman. Scr: Leslie Norman, Neil Paterson. Cast: Peter Finch (Macauley), Dana Wilson (Buster), Elizabeth Sellars (Marge), George Rose (Donny), Rosemary Harris (Lily). **Adaptation 2:** *The Shiralee* (Australian Film Commission, 1988 TV Miniseries). Dir: George Ogilvie. Scr: Tony Morphett. Cast: Bryan Brown (Macauley), Noni Hazlehurst (Lily), Rebecca Smart (Buster).

4043. *Shirley* (Howard Fast, 1964). A poor young woman who resembles a wealthy socialite is kidnapped and forced to impersonate the other woman. Fast published the novel under the pseudonym E. V. Cunningham. **Adaptation:** *What's a Nice Girl Like You ... ?* (ABC, 1971 TV Movie). Dir: Jerry Paris. Scr: Howard Fast. Cast: Brenda Vaccaro (Shirley), Jack Warden (Lieutenant Burton), Roddy McDowall (Albert), Jo Anne Worley (Cynthia), Edmond O'Brien (Morton), Vincent Price (William).

4044. *A Shock to the System* (Simon Brett, 1984). Black comedy about a disappointed executive who decides that his life will improve if he murders everyone in his life who has wronged him. **Adaptation:** *A Shock to the System* (Brigand/Corsair, 1990). Dir: Jan Egleson. Scr: Andrew Klavan. Cast: Michael Caine (Graham), Elizabeth McGovern (Stella), Peter Riegert (Robert), Swoosie Kurtz (Leslie), Will Patton (Laker). DVD, VHS.

4045. *Shoeless Joe* (W. P. Kinsella, 1982). Nostalgic tale about an Iowa corn farmer who hears voices directing him to build a baseball field on his farm. When he does, the ghosts of Shoeless Joe Jackson and other players involved in the Blacksox scandal in the 1919 World Series appear. **Adaptation:** *Field of Dreams* (Universal, 1989). Dir: Phil Alden Robinson. Scr: Phil Alden Robinson. Cast: Kevin Costner (Ray), Amy Madigan (Annie), Gaby Hoffmann (Karen), Ray Liotta (Shoeless Joe Jackson), Timothy Busfield (Mark), James Earl Jones (Terence), Burt Lancaster (Dr. Graham). Notes: Academy Award nominations for Best Picture, Screenplay, and Musical Score. DVD, VHS.

4046. *The Shoes of the Fisherman* (Morris L. West, 1963). After spending twenty years in a Siberian labor camp, a Russian priest goes to Rome, where the ailing pope makes him a cardinal. When the pope dies, he is elected pontiff, and, despite his own self-doubts, tries to improve the world. **Adaptation:** *The Shoes of the Fisherman* (MGM, 1968). Dir: Michael Anderson. Scr: James Kennaway, John Patrick. Cast: Anthony Quinn (Kiril), Laurence Olivier (Kamenev), John Gielgud (the Pope), Oskar Werner (Father Telemond), David Janssen (Faber), Vittorio De Sica (Cardinal Rinaldi), Leo McKern (Cardinal Leone). Notes: Golden Globe Award for Best Musical Score and nomination for Best Picture; National Board of Review Awards for Best Picture and Supporting Actor (McKern); Academy Award nominations for Best Musical Score and Art Direction. VHS.

4047. *Shogun* (James Clavell, 1975). In the early seventeenth century, an English ship captain goes to Japan and becomes involved with two powerful warring families struggling for the supreme title of Shogun. The book was the basis for a Broadway musical in 1990. **Adaptation:**

Shogun (NBC, 1980 TV Miniseries). Dir: Jerry London. Scr: Eric Bercovici. Cast: Richard Chamberlain (Blackthorne/Anjin-san), Toshiro Mifune (Toranaga), Yoko Shimada (Lady Toda), Frankie Sakai (Yabu), Alan Badel (Father Dell'Aqua), Damien Thomas (Father Alvito), Yuki Meguro (Omi), John Rhys-Davies (Rodriguez). Notes: Emmy Awards for Outstanding Miniseries, Costume Design, and Graphic Design, and nominations for Outstanding Teleplay, Director, Actors (Chamberlain and Mifune), Supporting Actors (Rhys-Davies and Meguro), Cinematography, Sound, Art Direction, and Editing; Golden Globe Awards for Best Miniseries, Actor (Chamberlain), and Actress (Shimada); Peabody Award for Best Miniseries. DVD, VHS.

Shoot First (see *A Rough Shoot*).

Shoot Out (see *Lone Cowboy*).

Shoot Out at Warlock (see *Warlock*).

Shoot the Piano Player (see *Down There*).

4048. *The Shooting Party* (Anton Chekhov, 1884–1885). Originally titled *Drama Na Okhote*, this novel by the famous Russian playwright concerns a group of people who assemble for a hunt at the country estate of a dissolute count. When an alluring woman is killed, it is discovered that most of the guests had a relationship with her and a motive for killing her. The novel was first translated in 1926. **Adaptation:** *Summer Storm* (United Artists, 1944). Dir: Douglas Sirk. Scr: Rowland Leigh, Michael O'Hara, Douglas Sirk. Cast: Linda Darnell (Olga), George Sanders (Fedor), Anna Lee (Nadena), Hugo Haas (Anton), Edward Everett Horton (Count Volsky).

4049. *The Shooting Party* (Isabel Colegate, 1980). On the eve of World War I in 1913, a group of wealthy people gather for a hunt at a gentleman's country estate, and their personal quarrels expose the hypocrisies of the British aristocracy. **Adaptation:** *The Shooting Party* (European Classics, 1985). Dir: Alan Bridges. Scr: Julian Bond. Cast: James Mason (Sir Randolph), Edward Fox (Lord Gilbert), Dorothy Tutin (Lady Minnie), John Gielgud (Cornelius). DVD, VHS.

4050. *The Shootist* (Glendon Swarthout, 1975). A dying gunfighter returns to his small town to put his affairs in order, but his presence causes problems that can only be settled by a return to his old profession. **Adaptation:** *The Shootist* (Paramount, 1976). Dir: Don Siegel. Scr: Scott Hale, Miles Hood Swarthout. Cast: John Wayne

(Books), Lauren Bacall (Bond), Ron Howard (Gillom), James Stewart (Dr. Hostetler), Richard Boone (Sweeney), Hugh O'Brian (Pulford). DVD, VHS.

4051. *Shopgirl* (Steve Martin, 2000). A disenchanted department-store salesgirl and aspiring artist must choose between two men. **Adaptation:** *Shopgirl* (20th Century–Fox/Buena Vista, 2005). Dir: Anand Tucker. Scr: Steve Martin. Cast: Steve Martin (Ray), Claire Danes (Mirabelle), Jason Schwartzman (Jeremy), Anne Marie Howard (Mandy). DVD, VHS.

4052. *Shore Leave* (Frederic Wakeman, 1944). The romantic misadventures of three World War II navy pilots on leave in San Francisco. Luther Davis adapted the novel for the 1945 Broadway play *Kiss Them for Me*. **Adaptation:** *Kiss Them for Me* (20th Century–Fox, 1957). Dir: Stanley Donen. Scr: Julius J. Epstein. Cast: Cary Grant (Andy), Jayne Mansfield (Alice), Leif Erickson (Eddie), Suzy Parker (Gwinneth), Ray Walston (McCann). DVD, VHS.

Short Cut to Hell (see *A Gun for Sale*).

4053. *Short Cuts* (Raymond Carver, 1993). A collection of previously published short stories about the lives of unhappy people living in contemporary Los Angeles. **Adaptation:** *Short Cuts* (Fine Line, 1993). Dir: Robert Altman. Scr: Robert Altman, Frank Barhydt. Cast: Andie MacDowell (Ann), Bruce Davison (Howard), Jack Lemmon (Paul), Julianne Moore (Marian), Matthew Modine (Dr. Wyman), Anne Archer (Claire), Fred Ward (Stuart), Jennifer Jason Leigh (Lois). Notes: The screenplay combines elements from nine of Carver's short stories and one poem. Academy Award nomination for Best Director; Golden Globe Special Award for Best Ensemble Cast and nomination for Best Screenplay. DVD, VHS.

4054. "The Short Happy Life of Francis Macomber" (Ernest Hemingway, 1936). A big-game hunter in Africa conducts a wealthy man and his domineering wife on a safari and has an affair with the woman. The short story originally appeared in the September 1936 issue of *Cosmopolitan* and was included in Hemingway's 1938 collection *The Fifth Column and the First Forty-Nine Stories*. **Adaptation:** *The Macomber Affair* (United Artists, 1947). Dir: Zoltan Korda. Scr: Seymour Bennett, Frank Arnold, Casey Robinson. Cast: Gregory Peck (Wilson), Joan Bennett (Margaret), Robert Preston (Francis).

4055. *The Short Timers* (Gustav Hasford,

1979). Autobiographical novel about a Marine war correspondent in Vietnam who recalls the dehumanization that occurs in basic training and its immoral effects as seen during the Tet offensive. **Adaptation:** *Full Metal Jacket* (Warner, 1987). Dir: Stanley Kubrick. Scr: Stanley Kubrick, Michael Herr, Gustav Hasford. Cast: Matthew Modine (Joker), Adam Baldwin (Animal Mother), Vincent D'Onofrio (Pyle), R. Lee Ermey (Hartman), Dorian Harewood (Eightball). Notes: The screenplay was based on Michael Herr's 1977 book *Dispatches* and on Hasford's novel. Academy Award nomination for Best Screenplay; Golden Globe nomination for Best Supporting Actor (Ermey). DVD, VHS. See also *Dispatches*.

4056. *Shot in the Dark* (Gerard Fairlie, 1932). A minister investigates the murder of an eccentric man who was loathed by his greedy relatives. **Adaptation:** *Shot in the Dark* (RKO, 1933). Dir: George Pearson. Scr: H. Fowler Mear. Cast: Dorothy Boyd (Alaris), O. B. Clarence (Reverend Makehan), Jack Hawkins (Norman), Russell Thorndike (Dr. Stuart).

4057. *Shot in the Heart: One Family's History in Murder* (Mikal Gilmore, 1994). A memoir by a writer for *Rolling Stone* magazine about his brother, Gary Gilmore, the convicted murderer who was executed in 1977, and his other brothers, who also died violently. **Adaptation:** *Shot in the Heart* (HBO, 2001 TV Movie). Dir: Agnieszka Holland. Scr: Frank Pugliese. Cast: Elias Koteas (Gary Gilmore), Amy Madigan (Bessie Gilmore), San Shepard (Frank Gilmore, Sr.), Lee Tergeson (Frank Gilmore, Jr.), Giovanni Ribisi (Mikal Gilmore). DVD, VHS.

4058. *Shotgun* (William Wingate, 1980). A former CIA hit man trying to forget his past uses his skill to liberate a small town from a megalomaniac millionaire with an eye toward national political office. **Adaptation:** *Malone* (Orion, 1987). Dir: Harley Cokeliss. Scr: Christopher Frank. Cast: Burt Reynolds (Malone), Cliff Robertson (Delaney), Kenneth McMillan (Hawkins), Cynthia Gibb (Jo). VHS.

4059. "The Shout" (Robert Graves, 1929). A drifter dominates the lives of a British country couple by convincing them that he knows a magical Aboriginal shout that can kill. The short story was originally published in *The Woburn Books*, Number 16, in 1929. **Adaptation:** *The Shout* (Rank/Films Incorporated, 1978). Dir: Jerzy Skolimowski. Scr: Michael Austin, Jerzy Skolimowski. Cast: Alan Bates (Crossley), Susannah York (Rachel), John Hurt (Anthony). Notes: Cannes

Film Festival Grand Prize of the Jury and nomination for Golden Palm for Best Director. VHS.

4060. *Shout at the Devil* (Wilbur Smith, 1968). At the start of World War I, an English poacher, an American adventurer, and his daughter conspire to destroy a German war ship near Zanzibar. **Adaptation:** *Shout at the Devil* (American International/Hemdale, 1976). Dir: Peter Hunt. Scr: Stanley Price, Alastair Reid, Wilbur Smith. Cast: Lee Marvin (Flynn), Roger Moore (Sebastian), Barbara Parkins (Rosa), Ian Holm (Mohammed). DVD, VHS.

4061. *The Shovel and the Loom* (Carl Friedman, 1993). The Dutch novel, originally titled *Twee Koffers Vol* and translated into English in 1996, tells the story of a liberal Jewish girl in Antwerp and her close relationship with the young Hasidic boy for whom she becomes a babysitter. **Adaptation:** *Left Luggage* (Castle Hill, 1998). Dir: Jeroen Krabbé. Scr: Edwin de Vries. Cast: Laura Fraser (Chaya), Adam Monty (Simcha), Isabella Rossellini (Mrs. Kalman), Jeroen Krabbé (Mr. Kalman), Chaim Topol (Mr. Apfelschnitt). DVD, VHS.

4062. *Show Boat* (Edna Ferber, 1926). The lives and loves of workers on a Mississippi show boat. The novel was adapted in 1927 as a Broadway musical by Oscar Hammerstein II and Jerome Kern. **Adaptation 1:** *Show Boat* (Universal, 1929). Dir: Harry A. Pollard, Arch Heath. Scr: Charles Kenyon, Harry Pollard, Tom Reed. Cast: Laura La Plante (Magnolia), Joseph Schildkraut (Gaylord), Otis Harlan (Captain Hawks). Notes: This film made early in the talkie era is part-silent, with songs and limited dialogue. **Adaptation 2:** *Show Boat* (Universal, 1936). Dir: James Whale. Scr: Oscar Hammerstein II (based on his 1927 play). Cast: Irene Dunne (Magnolia), Allan Jones (Gaylord), Charles Winninger (Captain Hawks), Paul Robeson (Joe), Helen Morgan (Julie). VHS. **Adaptation 3:** *Show Boat* (MGM, 1951). Dir: George Sidney. Scr: Oscar Hammerstein II (1927 play and 1936 screenplay), John Lee Mahin. Cast: Kathryn Grayson (Magnolia), Ava Gardner (Julie), Howard Keel (Gaylord), Joe E. Brown (Captain Hawks), Marge Champion (Ellie May), Gower Champion (Frank). Notes: Academy Award nominations for Best Musical Score and Cinematography. DVD, VHS.

Show Girl in Hollywood (see *Hollywood Girl*).

A Show of Force (see *Murder Under Two Flags*).

4063. *Shrek!* (William Steig, 1990). Children's book by the well-known *New Yorker* illustrator about an antisocial green monster and his sidekick, a loquacious donkey, who set out to save a beautiful princess. The monster also falls in love with her in the process. **Adaptation:** *Shrek* (DreamWorks, 2001). Dir: Andrew Adamson, Vicky Jenson. Scr: Ted Elliott, Terry Rossio, Joe Stillman, Roger S.H. Schulman. Cast: voices of Mike Myers (Shrek), Eddie Murphy (Donkey), Cameron Diaz (Princess Fiona), John Lithgow (Lord Farquaad). Notes: The computer-animated film was the winner of an Academy Award in a new category — Best Animated Feature — and nomination for Best Screenplay; Golden Globe nomination for Best Film. DVD, VHS. Notes: A sequel, *Shrek 2*, was released in 2004 (DVD, VHS).

4064. *The Shrinking Man* (Richard Matheson, 1956). After being caught in a radioactive mist, a man shrinks and views the world from a very different perspective. **Adaptation 1:** *The Incredible Shrinking Man* (Universal, 1957). Dir: Jack Arnold. Scr: Richard Matheson. Cast: Grant Williams (Scott), Randy Stuart (Louise), April Kent (Clarice), Paul Langton (Charles). DVD, VHS. **Adaptation 2:** *The Incredible Shrinking Woman* (Universal International, 1981). Dir: Joel Schumacher. Scr: Jane Wagner. Cast: Lily Tomlin (Pat/Judith), Charles Grodin (Vance), Ned Beatty (Dan), Henry Gibson (Dr. Nortz). Notes: A spoof of the original story. DVD, VHS.

4065. *Shroud for a Nightingale* (P. D. James, 1971). Scotland Yard detective Adam Dalgliesh investigates the mysterious murder of nurses at a London teaching hospital. **Adaptation:** *Shroud for a Nightingale* (ITV, 1984 TV Miniseries). Dir: John Gorrie. Scr: Robin Chapman. Cast: Roy Marsden (Dalgliesh), John Vine (Massingham), Joss Ackland (Dr. Courtney-Briggs), Sheila Allen (Mary). DVD, VHS.

4066. *The Shroud Society* (Hugh C. Rae, 1969). An assassin is hired to kill a loan shark's wife, who happens to be the hitman's own lover. **Adaptation:** *Man with a Gun* (October, 1995). Dir: David Wyles. Scr: Laurie Finstad-Knizhnik. Cast: Michael Madsen (John), Jennifer Tilly (Rena/Kathy), Gary Busey (Jack), Robert Loggia (Philip). VHS.

4067. "The Shuttered Room" (H. P. Lovecraft and August Derleth, 1959). Returning to their home on a remote island off the New England coast, a couple occupy an old house and are terrorized by an unseen creature. The short story was included in the 1959 collection *The Shuttered Room and Other Pieces*. **Adaptation:** *The Shuttered*

Room; also released as *Blood Island* (Warner/Seven Arts, 1967). Dir: David Greene. Scr: D. B. Ledrov, Nathaniel Tanchuck. Cast: Gig Young (Mike), Carol Lynley (Susannah/Sarah), Oliver Reed (Ethan), Flora Robson (Aunt Agatha). VHS.

4068. *The Sicilian* (Mario Puzo, 1984). A novel based on the true story of 1940's Sicilian brigand Salvatore Giuliano, who robbed from the rich to give to the poor and worked for the independence of Sicily from Italy. **Adaptation:** *The Sicilian* (20th Century–Fox, 1987). Dir: Michael Cimino. Scr: Steve Shagan. Cast: Christopher Lambert (Giuliano), Terence Stamp (Prince Borsa), Joss Ackland (Don Croce), John Turturro (Pisciotta). DVD, VHS. Notes: An Italian semi-documentary film on the same subject titled *Salavatore Giuliano*, directed by Francesco Rosi, was released in 1961.

4069. *Siddharta* (Hermann Hesse, 1922). A young upper-caste Indian leaves his privileged existence and joins a band of wandering holy men in a quest for a more spiritually fulfilling life. **Adaptation:** *Siddhartha* (Columbia, 1972). Dir: Conrad Rooks. Scr: Conrad Rooks, Paul Mayersberg, Natasha Ullman. Cast: Shashi Kapoor (Siddhartha), Simi Garewal (Kamala), Romesh Sharma (Govinda), Pincho Kapoor (Kamaswami). DVD, VHS.

4070. *The Sidelong Glances of a Pigeon Kicker* (David Boyer, 1968). A Princeton graduate who finds himself driving a taxicab in New York regards himself as superior to everyone he meets. **Adaptation:** *Pigeons*; also released as *The Sidelong Glances of a Pigeon Kicker* (MGM, 1971). Dir: John Dexter. Scr: Ron Whyte. Cast: Jordan Christopher (Jonathan), Jill O'Hara (Jennifer), Robert Walden (Winslow), Lois Nettleton (Mildred).

4071. *Sideways* (Rex Pickett, 1999). Before one of them is to be married, two middle-aged friends take a trip into California's wine country for a final bachelor fling. **Adaptation:** *Sideways* (20th Century–Fox, 2004). Dir: Alexander Payne. Scr: Alexander Payne, Jim Taylor. Cast: Paul Giamatti (Miles), Thomas Haden Church (Jack), Virginia Madsen (Maya), Sandra Oh (Stephanie). Notes: Academy Award for Best Screenplay and nominations for Best Picture, Director, Supporting Actor (Church), and Supporting Actress (Madsen); Golden Globe Awards for Best Picture and Screenplay, and nominations for Best Director, Actor (Giamatti), Supporting Actor (Church), Supporting Actress (Madsen), and Musical Score; National Board of Review Awards for Best Screenplay and Supporting Actor (Church); Independent Spirit Award nominations for Best Picture, Director, Screenplay, Actor (Giamatti), Supporting Actor (Church), and Supporting Actress (Giamatti). DVD, VHS.

4072. "The Siege" (James Lasdun, 1985). An African woman goes to work as a maid for a reclusive British musician in Rome. He falls in love with her and finally agrees to help liberate her husband, a political prisoner in Africa. The short story appears in the 1986 collection *Delirium Eclipse and Other Stories*. **Adaptation:** *Besieged* (Fine Line, 1998). Dir: Bernardo Bertolucci. Scr: Bernardo Bertolucci, Clare Peploe. Cast: Thandie Newton (Shandurai), David Thewlis (Jason), Claudio Santamaria (Agostino). DVD, VHS.

Siege at Ruby Ridge (see *Every Knee Shall Bow*).

4073. *The Siege of Battersea* (Robert Holles, 1962). Rebels attack a British regiment in Africa. **Adaptation:** *Guns at Batasi* (20th Century–Fox, 1964). Dir: John Guillermin. Scr: Leo Marks, C. M. Pennington-Richards, Marshall Pugh. Cast: Richard Attenborough (Lauderdale), Jack Hawkins (Deal), Flora Robson (Miss Wise), John Leyton (Wilkes), Mia Farrow (Karen). Notes: BAFTA Award for Best British Actor (Attenborough) and nominations for Best Cinematography and Art Direction. VHS.

4074. *The Siege of Trencher's Farm* (Gordon M. Williams, 1969). A mild-mannered American mathematician and his wife living in an isolated English village are harassed and assaulted by local people, and he is forced to take violent revenge. **Adaptation:** *Straw Dogs* (Cinerama, 1971). Dir: Sam Peckinpah. Scr: David Zelag Goodman, Sam Peckinpah. Cast: Dustin Hoffman (David), Susan George (Amy), Peter Vaughan (Tom), T. P. McKenna (Major Scott). DVD, VHS.

Sierra (see *The Mountains Are My Kingdom*).

4075. *Siesta* (Patrice Chaplin, 1986). A woman skydiver finds herself in Spain and suffering from amnesia. Because of blood on her clothing, she is suspected of having committed a murder, and it is only through flashbacks that she comes to remember what really happened. **Adaptation:** *Siesta* (Lorimar, 1987). Dir: Mary Lambert. Scr: Patricia Louisianna Knop. Cast: Ellen Barkin (Claire), Gabriel Byrne (Augustine), Julian Sands (Kit), Isabella Rossellini (Marie), Martin Sheen (Del), Grace Jones (Conchita), Jodie Foster (Nancy). VHS.

4076. *The Sign of Four* (Arthur Conan Doyle, 1890). Each year, an orphaned governess anonymously receives a perfect pearl in the mail, and she finally turns to Sherlock Holmes to investigate the mysterious source of the generous gifts. The novel first appeared in the February 1890 issue of *Lippincott's Monthly Magazine*. **Silent Films:** 1913 and 1923. **Adaptation 1:** *The Sign of Four* (Sono Art, 1932). Dir: Graham Cutts, Rowland V. Lee. Scr: W. P. Lipscomb. Cast: Arthur Wontner (Holmes), Isla Bevan (Mary), Ian Hunter (Watson), Graham Soutten (Jonathan). **Adaptation 2:** *The Sign of Four* (Mapleton, 1983 TV Movie). Dir: Desmond Davis. Scr: Charles Edward Pogue. Cast: Ian Richardson (Holmes), David Healy (Watson), Thorley Walters (Major Sholto), Cherie Lunghi (Mary). DVD, VHS. **Adaptation 3:** *The Sign of Four* (Granada, 1987 TV Movie). Dir: Peter Hammond. Scr: John Hawkesworth. Cast: Jeremy Brett (Holmes), Edward Hardwicke (Watson), Robin Hunter (Major Sholto), Alf Joint (McMurdo), John Thaw (Jonathan). DVD, VHS. **Adaptation 4:** *The Sign of Four* (Muse/Hallmark, 2001 TV Movie). Dir: Rodney Gibbons. Scr: Joe Wiesenfeld. Cast: Matt Frewer (Holmes), Kenneth Welsh (Watson), Sophie Lorain (Mary), Marcel Jeannin (Thaddeus), Michel Perron (Inspector Jones). DVD, VHS.

Sign of the Wolf (see *That Spot*).

4077. *Silas Marner: The Weaver of Raveloe* (George Eliot [pseudonym for Mary Ann Evans], 1861). A miserly weaver loses his money and then adopts an orphaned girl who changes his life for the better. **Silent Films:** 1909 (titled *A Fair Exchange* and directed by D. W. Griffith), 1911, 1913, 1916, and 1922 (titled *Are Children to Blame?*). **Adaptation 1:** *Silas Marner: The Weaver of Raveloe* (BBC/A&E, 1985 TV Miniseries). Dir: Giles Foster. Scr: Peerbux Ahmad, Giles Foster, Louis Marks. Cast: Ben Kingsley (Silas), Jenny Agutter (Nancy), Patrick Ryecart (Godfrey), Freddie Jones (Squire Cass), Jonathan Coy (Dunstan), Patsy Kensit (Eppie). DVD, VHS. **Adaptation 2:** *A Simple Twist of Fate* (Touchstone/Buena Vista, 1994). Dir: Gillies MacKinnon. Scr: Steve Martin. Cast: Steve Martin (Michael), Gabriel Byrne (John), Laura Linney (Nancy), Catherine O'Hara (Mrs. Simon). NOTE: A modern retelling of the story. DVD, VHS.

4078. *The Silence of the Lambs* (Thomas Harris, 1988). A young FBI agent turns to Hannibal "the Cannibal" Lecter, a brilliant psychiatrist and serial killer, to help catch a vicious killer. **Adaptation:** *The Silence of the Lambs* (Orion, 1991). Dir: Jonathan Demme. Scr: Ted Tally. Cast:

Jodie Foster (Clarice), Anthony Hopkins (Dr. Lecter), Scott Glenn (Crawford), Anthony Heald (Dr. Chilton), Ted Levine (Jamie), Frankie Faison (Barney). Notes: Academy Awards for Best Film, Director, Actor (Hopkins), Actress (Foster), and Screenplay, and nominations for Best Editing and Sound; Golden Globe Award for Best Actress (Foster), and nominations for Best Picture, Director, Screenplay, and Actor (Hopkins); National Board of Review Award for Best Film, Director, and Actor (Hopkins). DVD, VHS. See also *Hannibal* and *Red Dragon*.

4079. *The Silence of the North* (Olive Fredrickson and Ben East, 1972). Memoir of an independent-minded city girl who married a trapper and moved to the brutal Canadian north country in 1919. **Adaptation:** *Silence of the North* (Universal, 1981). Dir: Allan King. Scr: Patricia Louisianna Knop. Cast: Ellen Burstyn (Olive), Tom Skerritt (Walter), Gordon Pinsent (John), Donna Dobrijevic (Vala). Notes: Genie Award (Canada) for Best Cinematography and nominations for Best Director, Actor (Pinsent), Foreign Actor (Skerritt), Foreign Actress (Burstyn), Editing, Art Direction, Costume Design, and Song. VHS.

4080. *Silence Will Speak: A Study of the Life of Denys Finch Hatton and His Relationship With Karen Blixen* (Errol Trzebinski, 1977). A biography of the famous English hunter and adventurer who carried on a love affair with writer Isak Dinesen (Karen Blixen) from 1914 through 1931. **Adaptation:** *Out of Africa* (Universal, 1985). Dir: Sydney Pollack. Scr: Kurt Luedtke. Cast: Meryl Streep (Karen), Robert Redford (Denys), Klaus Maria Brandauer (Baron Blixen-Finecke), Michael Kitchen (Berkeley). Notes: The screenplay is based on Dinesen's memoirs and Trzebinski's book. Academy Awards for Best Picture, Director, Screenplay, Musical Score, Cinematography, Art Direction, and Sound, and nominations for Best Actress (Streep), Supporting Actor (Brandauer), Editing, and Costume Design; BAFTA Awards for Best Screenplay, Cinematography, and Sound, and nominations for Best Actress (Streep), Supporting Actor (Brandauer), Musical Score, and Costume Design; Golden Globe Awards for Best Director, Screenplay, and Actress (Streep), and nominations for Best Picture, Supporting Actor (Brandauer), and Musical Score; National Board of Review nomination for Best Supporting Actor (Brandauer). DVD, VHS. See also *Out of Africa*.

4081. *The Silencers* (Donald Hamilton, 1962). In the fourth of Hamilton's twenty-six

Matt Helm spy novels (1960–1993), the spy and assassin must stop an organization from detonating a nuclear device in New Mexico. **Adaptation:** *The Silencers* (Columbia, 1966). Dir: Phil Karlson. Scr: Oscar Saul. Cast: Dean Martin (Helm), Stella Stevens (Gail), Daliah Lavi (Tina), Victor Buono (Tung-Tze), Arthur O'Connell (Joe), Robert Webber (Sam). Notes: The screenplay combines elements from this novel and *Death of a Citizen* (1960), the first novel in the series, which introduced Matt Helm. DVD, VHS.

The Silent Enemy (see *Commander Crabb*).

The Silent Partner (see *Think of a Number*).

4082. *The Silent World of Nicholas Quinn* (Colin Dexter, 1977). The third installment in Dexter's popular thirteen-novel series (1975–2000) featuring Chief Inspector Endeavour Morse of Oxford, England. In this book, Inspector Morse investigates the murder of a deaf man appointed to the Foreign Examination Board at the university. **Adaptation:** *Inspector Morse: The Silent World of Nicholas Quinn* (ITV/PBS, 1987 TV Movie series). Dir: Brian Parker. Scr: Julian Mitchell. Cast: John Thaw (Morse), Kevin Whately (Sergeant Lewis), James Grout (Superintendent Strange), Peter Woodthorpe (Max). DVD, VHS.

4083. *Silk Hope, NC* (Lawrence Naumoff, 1994). After a long absence, an irresponsible woman returns to her family's farm to discover that her mother has died and her sister wants to sell the place. In order to get the money to buy her sister's half and keep the ancestral farm, she must learn to be mature and responsible very quickly. **Adaptation:** *Silk Hope* (CBS, 1999 TV Movie). Dir: Kevin Dowling. Scr: Dalene Young. Cast: Farrah Fawcett (Frannie), Brad Johnson (Ruben), Ashley Crow (Natalie), Scott Bryce (Jake), Herb Mitchell (Claude). DVD, VHS.

4084. *The Silver Bears* (Paul Erdman, 1974). A group of financial schemers manipulate the silver market to benefit their investments. **Adaptation:** *Silver Bears* (Columbia, 1977). Dir: Ivan Passer. Scr: Peter Stone. Cast: Michael Caine (Fletcher), Cybill Shepherd (Debbie), Louis Jourdan (Prince di Siracusa), David Warner (Firdausi), Tom Smothers (Luckman), Martin Balsam (Fiore). VHS.

4085. "Silver Blaze" (Arthur Conan Doyle, 1892). When a racehorse is suspected of having killed its trainer, Sherlock Holmes, who is visiting an old friend in the country, discovers the real murderer. The story originally appeared in *The Strand* in December 1892 and was included in Doyle's 1894 collection *The Memoirs of Sherlock Holmes*. **Silent Film:** 1923. **Adaptation:** *Silver Blaze*; released in the U.S. as *Murder at the Baskervilles* (Associated British/Astor, 1937). Dir: Thomas Bentley. Scr: Arthur Macrae, H. Fowler Mear. Cast: Arthur Wontner (Holmes), Ian Fleming (Watson), Lyn Harding (Professor Moriarty), John Turnbull (Inspector Lestrade). VHS.

4086. *The Silver Brumby* (Elyne Mitchell, 1958). The first in a series of thirteen Australian children's books about a stallion who becomes the leader of a herd of wild horses and the ruthless man who wants to tame the horse. **Adaptation:** *The Silver Brumby* (Skouras, 1993). Dir: John Tatoulis. Scr: Elyne Mitchell, Jon Stephens, John Tatoulis. Cast: Caroline Goodall (Elyne), Russell Crowe (the Man), Ami Daemion (Indi), Johnny Raaen (Jock), Buddy Tyson (Darcy). DVD, VHS. Notes: The book was also the basis for an Australian television series in 1998.

Silver Bullet (see *Cycle of the Werewolf*).

4087. *The Silver Chalice* (Thomas B. Costain, 1952). Biblical novel about a Greek artisan commissioned by the apostle Luke to create the chalice that Christ would use at the Last Supper. **Adaptation:** *The Silver Chalice* (Warner, 1954). Dir: Victor Saville. Scr: Lesser Samuels. Cast: Virginia Mayo (Helena), Pier Angeli (Debora), Jack Palance (Simon), Paul Newman (Basil), Alexander Scourby (Luke), Lorne Greene (Peter). VHS.

Silver City (see *Dead Freight for Piute*).

4088. *The Silver Darlings* (Neil M. Gunn, 1941). Poor Hebrides island natives try to avoid the need to emigrate abroad by becoming commercial herring fishermen. **Adaptation:** *Silver Darlings* (Hollywood, 1947). Dir: Clarence Elder, Clifford Evans. Scr: Clarence Elder. Cast: Clifford Evans (Roddy), Helen Shingler (Catrine), Carl Bernard (Angus).

4089. "The Silver Whip" (Jack Schaefer, 1953). Western about a stagecoach driver seeking violent revenge on a robber who wounded him and his conflict with his best friend, the deputy marshal, who wants the criminal legally prosecuted. The short story appeared in Schaefer's 1953 collection *The Big Range*. **Adaptation:** *The Silver Whip* (20th Century–Fox, 1953). Dir: Harmon Jones. Scr: Jack Schaefer, Jesse Lasky, Jr. Cast: Dale Robertson (Race), Rory Calhoun (Sheriff Davison), Robert Wagner (Jess), Kathleen Crowley (Kathy).

4090. *Silverado Squatters* (Robert Louis Stevenson, 1883). Noted for its evocative portrait of the American West in the late nineteenth century, an autobiographical memoir about Stevenson's trip to the California wine country in 1880. **Adaptation:** *Adventures in Silverado* (Columbia, 1948). Dir: Phil Karlson. Scr: Kenneth Gamet, Tom Kilpatrick, Jo Pagano. Cast: William Bishop (Bill), Gloria Henry (Jeannie), Edgar Buchanan (Dr. Henderson), Forrest Tucker (Zeke), Edgar Barrier (Stevenson).

4091. *Simisola* (Ruth Rendell, 1994). A black doctor in England turns to a detective to find his missing daughter. When the unidentified body of a black girl turns up, the detective fears that she may be the victim of a serial killer on the loose. **Adaptation:** *Simisola* (ITV. 1996 TV Movie). Dir: Jim Goddard. Scr: Alan Plater. Cast: George Baker (Detective Wexford), Christopher Ravenscroft (Detective Burden), Jane Lapotaire (Anouk), George Harris (Dr. Akande). DVD, VHS.

Simon Birch (see *A Prayer for Own Meany*).

4092. *A Simple Plan* (Scott Smith, 1993). Three men find more than $4 million in a wrecked aircraft and decide to keep the money. Their shared secret leads to tensions within the group and eventually to murder. **Adaptation:** *A Simple Plan* (Paramount, 1998). Dir: Sam Raimi. Scr: Scott B. Smith. Cast: Bill Paxton (Hank), Bridget Fonda (Sarah), Billy Bob Thornton (Jacob), Brent Briscoe (Lou), Jack Walsh (Tom). Notes: National Board of Review Award for Best Screenplay; Academy Award nominations for Best Screenplay and Supporting Actor (Thornton); Golden Globe nomination for Best Supporting Actor (Thornton). DVD, VHS.

4093. *Simple Simon* (Ryne Douglas Pearson, 1996). A nine-year-old autistic boy with a talent for math cracks a super government code, and agents decide to eliminate him for reasons of national security. It's up to a jaded FBI agent to save the boy's life. **Adaptation:** *Mercury Rising* (Universal/Imagine, 1998). Dir: Harold Becker. Scr: Lawrence Konner, Mark Rosenthal. Cast: Bruce Willis (Art), Alec Baldwin (Nicholas), Miko Hughes (Simon), Chi McBride (Thomas), Kim Dickens (Stacey). DVD, VHS.

A Simple Twist of Fate (see *Silas Marner*).

4094. *Simulacron-3* (Daniel F. Galouye, 1964). Before a computer scientist is murdered, he leaves clues for a friend in a computer-generated parallel world. **Adaptation:** *The Thirteenth Floor* (Columbia, 1999). Dir: Josef Rusnak.

Scr: Josef Rusnak, Ravel Centeno-Rodriguez. Cast: Armin Mueller-Stahl (Hannon/Grierson), Gretchen Mol (Jane/Natasha), Vincent D'Onofrio (Jason/Jerry), Dennis Haysbert (Detective McBain). DVD, VHS.

4095. *Sin City* (Frank Miller, 1992). Graphic-novel series about a life in a corrupt futuristic city. **Adaptation:** *Sin City* (Dimension, 2005). Dir: Frank Miller, Robert Rodriguez, Quentin Tarantino. Scr: Frank Miller, Robert Rodriguez. Cast: Jessica Alba (Nancy), Rosario Dawson (Gail), Elijah Wood (Kevin), Bruce Willis (John), Benicio Del Toro (Rafferty), Michael Clarke Duncan (Manute), Carla Gugino (Lucille), Josh Hartnett (the Salesman), Michael Madsen (Bob), Jaime King (Goldie/Wendy), Brittany Murphy (Shelly), Clive Owen (Dwight), Mickey Rourke (Marv). Notes: The screenplay combines elements from three graphic novels in the series—*The Hard Goodbye* (1992), *The Big Fat Kill* (1994) and *That Yellow Bastard* (1996). DVD, VHS.

Sin of Esther Waters (see *Esther Waters*).

The Sin of Father Amaro (see *The Crime of Father Amaro*).

4096. *The Sin of Susan Slade* (Doris Hume, 1954). To protect her child's reputation, a woman pretends to be the mother of her daughter's illegitimate child. **Adaptation:** *Susan Slade* (Warner, 1961). Dir: Delmer Daves. Scr: Delmer Daves. Cast: Troy Donahue (Hoyt), Connie Stevens (Susan), Dorothy McGuire (Leah), Lloyd Nolan (Roger).

4097. *The Sin Sniper* (Hugh Garner, 1970). A tough policeman investigates the serial murder of prostitutes and comes into conflict with mobsters. **Adaptation:** *Stone Cold Dead* (Dimension, 1979). Dir: George Mendeluk. Scr: George Mendeluk. Cast: Richard Crenna (Sergeant Boyd), Paul Williams (Kurtz), Linda Sorenson (Monica), Belinda J. Montgomery (Sandy). VHS.

4098. *Since You Went Away: Letters to a Soldier from His Wife* (Margaret Buell Wilder, 1943). Buell's poignant letters to her husband while he was fighting in World War II detail the difficulties that she and the family faced at home. **Adaptation:** *Since You Went Away* (United Artists, 1944). Dir: John Cromwell. Scr: David O. Selznick. Cast: Claudette Colbert (Anne), Jennifer Jones (Jane), Joseph Cotten (Tony), Shirley Temple (Bridget), Monty Woolley (Colonel Smollett), Robert Walker (William), Hattie McDaniel (Fidelia), Agnes Moorehead (Emily). Notes: Academy Award for

Best Musical Score and nominations for Best Picture, Actress (Colbert), Suporting Actor (Woolley), Supporting Actress (Jones), Art Direction, Cinematography, Editing, and Special Effects. DVD, VHS.

4099. *Sincerity* (John Erskine, 1929). Comic tale about a man whose wife leaves him after an argument. Believing that she has left permanently, he marries another woman. **Adaptation:** *A Lady Surrenders* (Universal, 1930). Dir: John M. Stahl. Scr: Gladys Lehman, Arthur Richman. Cast: Genevieve Tobin (Mary), Rose Hobart (Isabel), Conrad Nagel (Winthrop), Basil Rathbone (Carl).

4100. *The Singer Not the Song* (Audrey Erskine Lindop, 1953). A priest battles a bandit for control of a small Mexican town. **Adaptation:** *The Singer Not the Song* (Rank/Warner, 1961). Dir: Roy Ward Baker. Scr: Nigel Balchin. Cast: Dirk Bogarde (Anacleto), John Mills (Father Keogh), Mylene Demongeot (Locha). VHS.

The Singing Musketeer (see *The Three Musketeers*).

Single-Handed (see *Brown on Resolution*).

4101. *Single Lady* (John Monk Saunders, 1931). After World War I, four disillusioned American flyers remain in Paris and become members of the "Lost Generation." The novel was also adapted in 1931 as a Broadway musical titled *Nikki.* **Adaptation:** *The Last Flight* (Warner, 1931). Dir: William Dieterle. Scr: John Monk Saunders. Cast: Richard Barthelmess (Cary), David Manners (Shep), Johnny Mack Brown (Bill), Helen Chandler (Nikki).

4102. *Single Night* (Louis Bromfield, 1932). A former boxer opens a nightclub and falls in love with a society girl. The novella was published in *Cosmopolitan* in June 1932. **Adaptation:** *Night After Night* (Paramount, 1932). Dir: Archie Mayo. Scr: Vincent Lawrence, Kathryn Scola. Cast: George Raft (Joe), Constance Cummings (Jeri), Mae West (Maudie). VHS.

Single White Female (see *SWF Seeks Same*).

4103. *Sinister Errand* (Peter Cheyney, 1945). On a train from Trieste to Salzburg, an American diplomatic messenger battles a Russian spy to avenge the death of a friend. **Adaptation:** *Diplomatic Courier* (20th Century–Fox, 1952). Dir: Henry Hathaway. Scr: Liam O'Brien, Casey Robinson. Cast: Tyrone Power (Mike), Patricia Neal (Joan), Stephen McNally (Cagle), Hildegard Knef (Janine), Karl Malden (Ernie). VHS.

4104. *Sink the Bismarck* (C. S. Forester, 1959). Factual World War II account of the British Navy's campaign to find and destroy the German warship. The book was also released as *The Last Nine Days of the Bismarck* and as *Hunting the Bismarck.* **Adaptation:** *Sink the Bismarck!* (20th Century–Fox, 1960). Dir: Lewis Gilbert. Scr: Edmund H. North. Cast: Kenneth More (Captain Shepard), Dana Wynter (Officer Davis), Carl Mohner (Captain Lindemann). DVD, VHS.

Sinners in the Sun (see *Beachcomber*).

Sinners Need Company (see *The Sure Hand of God*).

The Sins of Dorian Gray (see *The Picture of Dorian Gray*).

4105. *The Sins of Rachel Cade* (Charles Mercer, 1956). During World War II, an American missionary nurse working in the Belgian Congo falls in love with a military pilot whose plane crashes there. **Adaptation:** *The Sins of Rachel Cade* (Warner, 1961). Dir: Gordon Douglas. Scr: Edward Anhalt, Cast: Angie Dickinson (Rachel), Peter Finch (Henry), Roger Moore (Paul), Errol John (Kulu), Woody Strode (Muwango).

4106. "The Sins of the Father" (Pamela Colloff, 2000). Historical article about the racially motivated bombing of an African-American church in Alabama in 1963 that took the lives of four young girls. Years later, the son of the man responsible turned in his own father. The article appeared in the April 2000 issue of *Texas Monthly.* **Adaptation:** *Sins of the Father* (Artisan/FX Networks, 2002 TV Movie). Dir: Robert Dornhelm. Scr: John Pielmeier. Cast: Tom Sizemore (Tom Cherry), Richard Jenkins (Bobby Frank Cherry), Ving Rhames (Garrick Jones), Colm Feore (Dalton Strong). DVD, VHS.

4107. *Sir Gawain and the Green Knight* (Anonymous, Late 14th Century). Medieval narrative poem about a legendary supernatural knight who challenges other warriors to kill him or be killed. **Adaptation 1:** *Gawain and the Green Knight* (United Artists, 1973). Dir: Stephen Weeks. Scr: Philip M. Breen, Stephen Weeks. Cast: Murray Head (Gawain), Ciaran Madden (Linet), Nigel Green (the Green Knight), Anthony Sharp (King Arthur). VHS. **Adaptation 2:** *Sword of the Valiant: The Legend of Sir Gawain and the Green Knight* (Cannon, 1982). Dir: Stephen Weeks. Scr: Philip M. Breen, Howard C. Penn, Stephen Weeks. Cast: Miles O'Keeffe (Gawain), Leigh Lawson (Humphrey), Trevor Howard (King Arthur), Sean Connery (the Green Knight), Emma Sutton (Morgan Le Fay). DVD, VHS.

Adaptation 3: *Gawain and the Green Knight* (Thames Television, 1991 TV Movie). Dir: John Michael Phillips. Scr: David Rudkin. Cast: Jason Durr (Gawain), Marie Francis (Guinevere), Malcolm Storry (the Green Knight/the Red Lord), Marc Warren (King Arthur).

4108. "The Sire de Maletroit's Door" (Robert Louis Stevenson, 1877). A young nobleman is lured to a mad squire's castle and held prisoner there. The short story originally appeared in *Cornhill* magazine. **Adaptation:** *The Strange Door* (Universal International, 1951). Dir: Joseph Pevney. Scr: Jerry Sackheim. Cast: Charles Laughton (Alain), Boris Karloff (Voltan), Sally Forrest (Blanche), William Cottrell (Corbeau). VHS.

Sirocco (see *Coup de Grace*).

4109. *Sister Act* (Fannie Hurst, 1937). The story of a small-town musician and his four daughters, whose romantic involvements complicate his life. The novel originally appeared in *Cosmopolitan* magazine. **Adaptation 1:** *Four Daughters* (Warner, 1938). Dir: Michael Curtiz. Scr: Lenore J. Coffee, Julius J. Epstein. Cast: Priscilla Lane (Ann), Rosemary Lane (Kay), Lola Lane (Thea), Gale Page (Emma), Claude Rains (Adam), John Garfield (Mickey). Notes: Academy Award nomination for Best Picture, Director. Screenplay, Actor (Garfield), and Sound. VHS. **Adaptation 2:** *Four Wives* (Warner, 1939). Dir: Michael Curtiz. Scr: Julius J. Epstein, Philip G. Epstein, Maurice Hanline, Cast: Priscilla Lane (Ann), Rosemary Lane (Kay), Lola Lane (Thea), Gale Page (Emma), Claude Rains (Adam). Notes: A sequel titled *Four Mothers* was released in 1941. **Adaptation 3:** *Young at Heart* (Warner, 1954). Dir: Gordon Douglas. Scr: Lenore Coffee, Julius J. Epstein, Liam O'Brien. Cast: Doris Day (Laurie), Frank Sinatra (Barney), Gig Young (Alex), Ethel Barrymore (Aunt Jessie), Dorothy Malone (Fran). DVD, VHS.

4110. *Sister Carrie* (Theodore Dreiser, 1900). A country girl goes to Chicago with big ambitions and ends up losing her innocence and ruining others in the bargain. **Adaptation:** *Carrie* (Paramount, 1952). Dir: William Wyler. Scr: Ruth Goetz, Augustus Goetz. Cast: Laurence Olivier (George), Jennifer Jones (Carrie), Miriam Hopkins (Julie), Eddie Albert (Charles). Notes: Academy Award nominations for Best Art Direction and Costume Design; BAFTA nominations for Best Film and Actor (Olivier). DVD, VHS.

4111. *The Sisterhood of the Traveling Pants*

(Ann Brashares, 2001). Young adult novel about four best girlfriends who spend their first summer apart and decide to share a pair of magical jeans which, despite their different shapes, fits each of them perfectly. **Adaptation:** *The Sisterhood of the Traveling Pants* (Warner, 2005). Dir: Ken Kwapis. Scr: Delia Ephron, Elizabeth Chandler. Cast: Amber Tamblyn (Tibby), Alexis Bledel (Lena), America Ferrera (Carmen), Blake Lively (Bridget), Jenna Boyd (Bailey). DVD, VHS.

4112. *The Sisters* (Myron Brinig, 1937). Three sisters from a small Montana town are married, and their experiences with wedded life turn out to be vastly different. **Adaptation:** *The Sisters* (Warner, 1938). Dir: Anatole Litvak. Scr: Milton Krims. Cast: Errol Flynn (Frank), Bette Davis (Louise), Anita Louise (Helen), Ian Hunter (William), Donald Crisp (Tim), Beulah Bondi (Rose), Jane Bryan (Grace), Alan Hale (Sam). VHS.

The Sitter (see *Mischief*).

Sitting Pretty (see *Belvedere*).

4113. *Sitting Target* (Laurence Henderson, 1970). A violent criminal escapes from jail and vows to take revenge on his cheating wife and her lover before fleeing the country. **Adaptation:** *Sitting Target* (MGM, 1972). Dir: Douglas Hickox. Scr: Alexander Jacobs. Cast: Oliver Reed (Harry), Jill St. John (Pat), Ian McShane (Birdy), Edward Woodward (Inspector Milton), Frank Finlay (Marty).

Situation Hopeless ... But Not Serious (see *The Hiding Place*).

4114. "A Situation of Gravity" (Samuel W. Taylor, 1959). A college professor invents a substance called "flubber," a kind of flying rubber that propels anything made of it into the air. An unscrupulous businessman wants to steal the substance, and the professor must keep him from doing so. **Adaptation 1:** *The Absent Minded Professor* (Disney/Buena Vista, 1961). Dir: Robert Stevenson. Scr: Bill Walsh. Cast: Fred MacMurray (Professor Brainard), Nancy Olson (Betsy), Keenan Wynn (Hawk), Tommy Kirk (Biff). Notes: Academy Award nominations for Best Art Direction, Cinematography, and Special Effects. DVD, VHS. **Adaptation 2:** *Son of Flubber* (Disney/Buena Vista, 1963). Dir: Robert Stevenson. Scr: Don Da Gradi, Bill Walsh. Cast: Fred MacMurray (Professor Brainard), Nancy Olson (Betsy), Keenan Wynn (Hawk), Tommy Kirk

(Biff). Notes: This film is the sequel to the 1961 Disney movie *The Absent-Minded Professor*. The screenplay is based on Samuel W. Taylor's short story "A Situation of Gravity" and several novels in the Danny Dunn series (1956–1967) by Jay Williams and Raymond Abrashkin. DVD, VHS. See also *Danny Dunn and the Weather Machine*. **Adaptation 3:** *The Absent-Minded Professor* (Echo Cove/Disney/Buena Vista, 1988 TV Movie). Dir: Robert Scheerer. Scr: Richard Chapman, Bill Dial. Cast: Harry Anderson (Professor Crawford), David Paymer (Oliphant), James Noble (Dr. Blount), Bibi Osterwald (Mrs. Nakamura). VHS. **Adaptation 4:** *Flubber* (Great Oaks/Disney/Buena Vista, 1997). Dir: Les Mayfield. Scr: John Hughes, Bill Walsh. Cast: Robin Williams (Professor Brainard), Marcia Gay Harden (Dr. Reynolds), Christopher McDonald (Wilson), Raymond Barry (Chester). DVD, VHS.

4115. *Six Days of the Condor* (James Grady, 1974). A CIA researcher returns from lunch one day to find all of his co-workers dead. He soon discovers that he is being targeted by another branch of his own outfit. **Adaptation:** *Three Days of the Condor* (Paramount, 1975). Dir: Sydney Pollack. Scr: Lorenzo Semple, Jr., David Rayfiel. Cast: Robert Redford (Turner), Faye Dunaway (Kathy), Cliff Robertson (Higgins), Max von Sydow (Joubert), John Houseman (Wabash). DVD, VHS.

The Six Million Dollar Man (see *Cyborg*).

4116. *633 Squadron* (Frederick E. Smith, 1956). In the first in a series of nine novels (1956–1996) about British RAF operations during World War II, the squadron is assigned to destroy a Nazi munitions factory in Norway. **Adaptation:** *633 Squadron* (United Artists, 1964). Dir: Walter E. Grauman. Scr: James Clavell, Howard Koch. Cast: Cliff Robertson (Roy), George Chakiris (Erik), Maria Perschy (Hilde), Harry Andrews (Davis), Donald Houston (Barrett). DVD, VHS.

Six Ways to Sunday (see *Portrait of a Young Man Drowning*).

4117. *Six Weeks* (Fred Mustard Stewart, 1976). A politician helps a female cosmetics tycoon care for her young daughter, who is dying of leukemia. **Adaptation:** *Six Weeks* (Universal, 1982). Dir: Tony Bill. Scr: David Seltzer. Cast: Dudley Moore (Patrick), Mary Tyler Moore (Charlotte), Katherine Healy (Nicole), Shannon Wilcox (Peg). VHS.

Sixth Happiness (see *Trying to Grow*).

4118. *The Sixteenth Round: From Number 1 Contender to #45472* (Rubin "Hurricane" Carter, 1974). Autobiography of a former middle-weight boxer who was wrongly convicted of a triple murder and his years in prison protesting his innocence. **Adaptation:** *The Hurricane* (Universal, 1999). Dir: Norman Jewison. Scr: Armyan Bernstein, Dan Gordon. Cast: Denzel Washington (Carter), Vicellous Reon Shannon (Lesra), Deborah Unger (Lisa), Liev Schreiber (Sam). Notes: The screenplay combines elements from Carter's autobiography, *The Sixteenth Round*, and Chaiton and Swinton's *Lazarus and the Hurricane*. Golden Globe Award for Best Actor (Washington) and nominations for Best Picture and Director; Academy Award nomination for Best Actor (Washington). DVD, VHS. See also *Lazarus and the Hurricane*.

4119. *The Sixth of June* (Lionel Shapiro, 1954). Two Allied military officers on their way to the Normandy invasion in 1944 recall their romantic involvements. **Adaptation:** *D-Day the Sixth of June* (20th Century–Fox, 1956). Dir: Henry Koster. Scr: Ivan Moffat, Harry Brown. Cast: Robert Taylor (Brad), Richard Todd (John), Dana Wynter (Valerie), Edmond O'Brien (Alex). DVD, VHS.

4120. *Skins* (Adrian C. Louis, 1995). The story of two Sioux Indian brothers on a reservation—one a policeman, the other the town drunk—and their close bond despite their differences. **Adaptation:** *Skins* (First Look, 2002). Dir: Chris Eyre. Scr: Jennifer D. Lyne. Cast: Eric Schweig (Rudy), Graham Greene (Mogie), Gary Farmer (Verdell), Noah Watts (Herbie). DVD, VHS.

4121. *Skipping Christmas* (John Grisham, 2001). A modern parable about the problems a husband and wife encounter when, fed up with the commercialism of Christmas, they decide not to celebrate the holiday. **Adaptation:** *Christmas with the Kranks* (Columbia, 2004). Dir: Joe Roth. Scr: Chris Columbus. Cast: Tim Allen (Luther), Jamie Lee Curtis (Nora), Julie Gonzalo (Blair). DVD, VHS.

The Skull (see "The Skull of the Marquis de Sade").

4122. "The Skull of the Marquis de Sade" (Robert Bloch, 1945). A collector of esoteric artifacts acquires the skull of the Marquis de Sade, which exercises an evil influence over him. The short story first appeared in *Weird Tales* in September 1945. **Adaptation:** *The Skull* (Paramount, 1965). Dir: Freddie Francis. Scr: Milton Subotsky. Cast: Peter Cushing (Dr. Maitland), Patrick Wymark (Anthony), Jill Bennett (Jane), Nigel Green (Inspector Wilson). VHS.

4123. *Sky Steward* (Ken Attiwill, 1936). Gangsters try to kill a key witness on a flight from London to New York. **Adaptation:** *Non-Stop New York* (Gaumont, 1937). Dir: Robert Stevenson. Scr: J. O. C. Orton, Roland Pertwee, Curt Siodmak. Cast: John Loder (Inspector Grant), Anna Lee (Jennie), Francis L. Sullivan (Hugo). DVD, VHS.

Sky Terror (see *Hijacked*).

Skyjacked (see *Hijacked*).

4124. *Skyscraper Souls* (Faith Baldwin, 1931). A ruthless New York businessman will stop at nothing to acquire an office building. **Adaptation:** *Skyscraper Souls* (MGM, 1932). Dir: Edgar Selwyn. Scr: C. Gardner Sullivan, Elmer Harris. Cast: Warren William (David), Maureen O'Sullivan (Lynn), Gregory Ratoff (Vinmont), Anita Page (Jenny), Jean Hersholt (Jake). VHS.

4125. *Slapstick, or Lonesome No More!* (Kurt Vonnegut, 1976). Grotesque twins, who together constitute the halves of a single genius, live happily in the blasted landscape of future America. **Adaptation:** *Slapstick (Of Another Kind)* (Entertainment Releasing, 1982). Dir: Steven Paul. Scr: Steven Paul. Cast: Jerry Lewis (Wilbur/Caleb), Madeline Kahn (Swain/Lutetia), Marty Feldman (Sylvester), John Abbott (Dr. Frankenstein), Jim Backus (the President). VHS.

4126. *Slattery's Hurricane* (Herman Wouk, 1956). A storm spotter for the U.S. weather bureau falls in love and decides to give up his dangerous work. Wouk co-wrote the script for the 1949 film and later expanded his screenplay into a novel. **Adaptation:** *Slattery's Hurricane* (20th Century–Fox, 1949). Dir: Andre De Toth. Scr: Herman Wouk, Richard Murphy. Cast: Richard Widmark (Slattery), Linda Darnell (Aggie), Veronica Lake (Dolores), John Russell (Hobson).

Slaughter on Tenth Avenue (see *The Man Who Rocked the Boat*).

4127. *Slaughterhouse-Five* (Kurt Vonnegut, 1969). Anti-war novel about Billy Pilgrim, a disturbed man who becomes "unstuck in time" and moves freely from horrid memories of his experiences in World War II to pleasant fantasies of life on an imaginary planet in outer space. **Adap-**

tation: *Slaughterhouse-Five* (Universal, 1972). Dir: George Roy Hill. Scr: Stephen Geller. Cast: Michael Sacks (Billy), Ron Leibman (Lazzaro), Eugene Roche (Edgar), Sharon Gans (Valencia), Valerie Perrine (Montana). DVD, VHS.

Slave Ship (see *The Last Slaver*).

4128. *Slaves of New York* (Tama Janowitz, 1986). A collection of satirical short stories about artists and other people living in the Soho section of New York City in the 1980's. **Adaptation:** *Slaves of New York* (TriStar, 1989). Dir: James Ivory. Scr: Tama Janowitz. Cast: Bernadette Peters (Eleanor), Chris Sarandon (Victor), Mary Beth Hurt (Ginger), Madeleine Potter (Daria). VHS.

4129. *Slayground* (Donald E. Westlake, 1971). A businessman hires a hit man to track down the robbers who accidentally killed his daughter. Westlake originally published the novel under the pseudonym Richard Stark. **Adaptation:** *Slayground* (Universal, 1983). Dir: Terry Bedford. Scr: Trevor Preston, Donald E. Westlake (writing as Richard Stark). Cast: Peter Coyote (Stone), Mel Smith (Terry Abbatt), Billie Whitelaw (Madge), Philip Sayer (Costello). DVD, VHS.

4130. *Sleep, My Love* (Leo Rosten, 1946). Suspense thriller about a woman who wakes up in the middle of the night on a train, not knowing how she got there. She eventually learns that her husband is giving her drugs to drive her insane. **Adaptation:** *Sleep, My Love* (United Artists, 1948). Dir: Douglas Sirk. Scr: St. Clair McKelway, Leo Rosten. Cast: Claudette Colbert (Alison), Robert Cummings (Bruce), Don Ameche (Richard), Rita Johnson (Barby).

The Sleep Room (see *In the Sleep Room*).

4131. *The Sleeper* (Gillian White, 1998). When a person from her past threatens to divulge her family secrets, a controlling woman resorts to murder in order to secure her ancestral farm. **Adaptation:** *The Sleeper* (BBC, 2000 TV Movie). Dir: Stuart Orme. Scr: Gwyneth Hughes. Cast: Eileen Atkins (Violet), Anna Massey (Lillian), Elizabeth Spriggs (Cath), George Cole (George), Ciaran Hinds (Fergus).

4132. *Sleepers* (Lorenzo Carcaterra, 1995). The true story of four boys from Hell's Kitchen in New York who are sent to a reform school, where they are brutalized by a sadistic guard. Ten years later, they take bitter revenge on him and the institution, and a priest helps to cover up their action. **Adaptation:** *Sleepers* (Warner, 1996). Dir: Barry Levinson. Scr: Barry Levinson. Cast: Kevin

Bacon (Sean), Billy Crudup (Tommy), Robert De Niro (Father Bobby), Ron Eldard (John), Minnie Driver (Carol), Vittorio Gassman (King Benny), Dustin Hoffman (Danny). DVD, VHS.

4133. *Sleepers East* (Frederick Nebel, 1933). A private detective is hired to protect a murder witness on a train on his way to court to testify. **Adaptation 1:** *Sleepers East* (Fox, 1934). Dir: Kenneth MacKenna. Scr: Lester Cole. Cast: Wynne Gibson (Lena), Preston Foster (Jason), Mona Barrie (Ada). **Adaptation 2:** *Sleepers West* (20th Century–Fox, 1941). Dir: Eugene Forde. Scr: Lou Breslow, Stanley Rauh. Cast: Lloyd Nolan (Shayne), Lynn Bari (Kay), Mary Beth Hughes (Helen), Louis Jean Heydt (Everett). Notes: The screenplay features Michael Shayne, a character in a series of mystery novels by Brett Halliday, and combines Halliday's characters with Nebel's plot.

4134. "Sleeping Beauty" (John Collier, 1938). In this variant on the well-known fairy tale, a man purchases a sleeping beauty at a California carnival and comes to regret his decision to wake her. The short story was published in *Harper's Bazaar* in May 1938. **Adaptation:** *Some Call It Loving* (Two World, 1973). Dir: James B. Harris. Scr: James B. Harris. Cast: Zalman King (Robert), Carol White (Scarlett), Tisa Farrow (Jennifer), Richard Pryor (Jeff). VHS.

4135. *The Sleeping Car Murders* (Sebastien Japrisot [pseudonym for Jean-Baptiste Rossi], 1962). In this French novel, originally titled *Compartment tueurs*, six people share a sleeping car on a train from Marseilles to Paris. When they arrive, a woman is found dead, and over the next couple of days three more are murdered. It is up to the remaining two to find out what is happening before they die, too. The book was translated into English in 1963. **Adaptation:** *The Sleeping Car Murders* (Seven Arts, 1965). Dir: Costa-Gavras. Scr: Costa-Gavras. Cast: Catherine Allegret (Bambi), Jacques Perrin (Daniel), Simone Signoret (Eliane), Michel Piccoli (Rene), Yves Montand (Inspector Grazzi). Notes: Originally released as *Compartment tueurs* and shown with subtitles. National Board of Review Award for Best Foreign-Language Film.

The Sleeping Cardinal (*see* "The Empty House").

Sleeping Dogs (*see* *Smith's Dream*).

4136. *Sleeping Murder* (Agatha Christie, 1976). A young married woman moves into a house in England and begins to have strange memories of a murder committed there years earlier. Before the killer can strike again, Miss Jane Marple, a family friend, arrives to solve the case. Although this was Christie's final Miss Marple mystery, it was actually written during World War II and left unpublished for more than thirty years. **Adaptation:** *Sleeping Murder* (BBC/PBS, 1987 TV Movie series). Dir: John Davies. Scr: Kenneth Taylor. Cast: Joan Hickson (Miss Marple), Geraldine Alexander (Gwenda), John Moulder-Brown (Giles), Frederick Treves (Dr. Kennedy). DVD, VHS.

4137. *Sleeping With the Devil: A True Story* (Suzanne Finstad, 1991). The true story of a Texas businessman's brutal attack on his former girlfriend, who was left paralyzed but determined to walk again with the help of a sympathetic doctor. **Adaptation:** *Sleeping with the Devil* (NBC, 1997 TV Movie). Dir: William A. Graham. Scr: Ellen Weston. Cast: Tim Matheson (Dick), Shannen Doherty (Rebecca), Bonnie Bartlett (Stasha), Steve Eastin (Wes), David Bowe (Dr. Petrofsky).

4138. *Sleeping With the Enemy* (Nancy Price, 1987). A brutalized woman fakes her own death to escape from her abusive husband. When he discovers that she is living in Iowa, he goes there, determined to kill her. **Adaptation:** *Sleeping with the Enemy* (20th Century–Fox, 1991). Dir: Joseph Ruben. Scr: Ronald Bass. Cast: Julia Roberts (Sara/Laura), Patrick Bergin (Martin), Kevin Anderson (Ben), Elizabeth Lawrence (Chloe), Kyle Secor (Fleishman). DVD, VHS.

Sleepy Hollow (see *The Legend of Sleepy Hollow*).

A Slight Case of Murder (see *A Travesty*).

Slightly Honorable (see *Send Another Coffin*).

Slightly Scarlet (see *Love's Lovely Counterfeit*).

Slip Slide Adventures (see *The Water Babies*).

4139. *A Slipping-Down Life* (Anne Tyler, 1970). After hearing a rock star on the radio, a shy young woman becomes obsessed with meeting him. **Adaptation:** *A Slipping-Down Life* (Lions Gate, 1999). Dir: Toni Kalem. Scr: Toni Kalem. Cast: Lili Taylor (Evie), Guy Pearce (Drumstrings Casey), Irma P. Hall (Clotelia), John Hawkes (David), Veronica Cartwright (Mrs. Casey), Marshall Bell (Mr. Casey), Shawnee Smith (Faye-Jean). DVD, VHS.

4140. *Sliver* (Ira Levin, 1991). When people begin to die mysteriously in her Manhattan apartment building, a young woman begins to suspect her voyeuristic landlord and a writer with whom she is romantically involved. **Adaptation:** *Sliver* (Paramount, 1993). Dir: Phillip Noyce. Scr: Joe Eszterhas. Cast: Sharon Stone (Carly), William Baldwin (Zeke), Tom Berenger (Jack), Polly Walker (Vida). DVD, VHS.

4141. *The Small Back Room* (Nigel Balchin, 1943). Psychological portrait of a physically disabled, alcoholic, and disillusioned bomb expert who defuses explosive devices in England during World War II. **Adaptation:** *The Small Back Room*; released in the U.S. as *Hour of Glory* (British Lion/Snader, 1949). Dir: Michael Powell, Emeric Pressburger. Scr: Michael Powell, Emeric Pressburger. Cast: David Farrar (Sammy), Kathleen Byron (Susan), Jack Hawkins (Waring), Milton Rosmer (Professor Mair), Cyril Cusack (Corporal Taylor). DVD, VHS.

4142. *The Small Miracle* (Paul Gallico, 1951). A young Italian boy travels to Rome to ask the Pope's permission to have his sick donkey blessed in church. **Adaptation:** *The Small Miracle*; also released as *Never Take No for an Answer* (Souvaine Selective, 1951). Dir: Maurice Cloche, Ralph Smart. Scr: Maurice Cloche, Pauline Gallico, Ralph Smart. Cast: Vittorio Manunta (Peppino), Denis O'Dea (Father Damico), Nerio Bernardi (Father Superior).

4143. *Small Sacrifices* (Ann Rule, 1987). True story about a young mother who murdered her three children. **Adaptation:** *Small Sacrifices* (ABC, 1989 TV Miniseries). Dir: David Greene. Scr: Joyce Eliason. Cast: Farrah Fawcett (Diane), Ryan O'Neal (Lew), Emily Perkins (Karen), Gary Chalk (Boyd), Gordon Clapp (Detective Welch). Notes: Emmy Award nominations for Outstanding Miniseries, Actress (Fawcett), and Editing; Golden Globe nominations for Best Television Miniseries and Actress (Fawcett); Peabody Award for Best Miniseries. VHS.

4144. *Small Town Girl* (Ben Ames Williams, 1935). A young woman meets a stranger who proposes to her while drunk. He regrets his decision in the morning, and she sets about making him fall in love with her and propose sober. **Adaptation:** *Small Town Girl*; broadcast on American television as *One Horse Town* (MGM, 1936). Dir: William A. Wellman. Scr: John Lee Mahin, Frances Goodrich, Albert Hackett, Edith Fitzgerald. Cast: Janet Gaynor (Kay), Robert Taylor (Bob), Binnie Barnes (Priscilla), Andy Devine (George).

4145. *The Small Voice* (Robert Westerby, 1940). A couple stops to help some men involved in a car accident. The men turn out to be crimi-

nals on the run from the police, and they take the man and his wife hostage at their country hideout. **Adaptation:** *The Small Voice*; released in the U.S. as *The Hideout* (British Lion/Snader, 1948). Dir: Fergus McDonell, Burgess McDonnell. Scr: George Barraud, Derek Neame, Julian Orde. Cast: Valerie Hobson (Eleanor), James Donald (Murray), Howard Keel (Boke), David Greene (Jim).

4146. *The Small Woman* (Alan Burgess, 1957). A biography of Gladys Aylward (1904–1970), a British maid who became a missionary to China. **Adaptation:** *The Inn of the Sixth Happiness* (20th Century–Fox, 1958). Dir: Mark Robson. Scr: Isobel Lennart. Cast: Ingrid Bergman (Gladys), Curt Jurgens (Lin Nan), Robert Donat (the Mandarin of Yang Cheng). Notes: Academy Award nomination for Best Director; Golden Globe Award for Best Film Promoting International Understanding and nominations for Best Actress (Bergman) and Actor (Donat). DVD, VHS.

Smash-Up on Interstate (see *Expressway*).

4147. *Smiley* (Moore Raymond, 1945). Comic tale about an Australian boy who, in his quest to acquire a bicycle, inadvertently becomes involved with drug smugglers. **Adaptation:** *Smiley* (London, 1956). Dir: Anthony Kimmins. Scr: Anthony Kimmins, Moore Raymond. Cast: Ralph Richardson (Reverend Lambeth), John McCallum (Rankin), Bruce Archer (Joey), Chips Rafferty (Sergeant Flaxman), Margaret Christensen (Mrs. Greevins). Notes: A sequel, *Smiley Gets a Gun*, was released in 1958.

4148. *Smiley's People* (John Le Carre [pseudonym for David Cornwell], 1979). Master spy George Smiley comes out of retirement to investigate the murder of a friend by Russian agents. **Adaptation:** *Smiley's People* (BBC, 1982 TV Miniseries). Dir: Simon Langton. Scr: John Hopkins, John Le Carre. Cast: Alec Guinness (Smiley), Patrick Stewart (Karla), Michael Lonsdale (Grigoriov), Beryl Reid (Connie). Notes: BAFTA Award for Best Actress (Reid) and nomination for Best Production Design; Emmy Award nomination for Outstanding Actor (Guinness). DVD, VHS.

4149. *Smilla's Sense of Snow* (Peter Hoeg, 1992). Danish novel, originally titled *Froken Smillas fornemmelse for sne*, about a woman who doubts that a local boy's death was accidental and finds her life in danger from conspiring government and corporate officials. The novel was translated into English in 1993. **Adaptation:** *Smilla's*

Sense of Snow (Fox Searchlight, 1997). Dir: Bille August. Scr: Ann Biderman. Cast: Ona Fletcher (Inuit), Julia Ormond (Smilla), Agga Olsen (Juliane). DVD, VHS.

4150. *Smith's Dream* (Christian K. Stead, 1971). A New Zealand man vainly tries to maintain his non-violence and neutrality as he is caught between warring government forces and revolutionary guerillas. **Adaptation:** *Sleeping Dogs* (Satori, 1977). Dir: Roger Donaldson. Scr: Arthur Baysting, Ian Mune. Cast: Sam Neill (Smith), Nevan Rowe (Gloria), Ian Mune (Bullen), Warren Oates (Colonel Willoughby). DVD, VHS.

Smoke Lightning (see *Canyon Walls*).

4151. *Smoky, the Cowhorse* (Will James, 1926), A wild and free-spirited horse is befriended by a cowboy, is stolen, and later turns up at a rodeo. **Adaptation 1:** *Smoky* (Fox, 1933). Dir: Eugene Forde. Scr: Stuart Anthony, Paul Perez. Cast: Victor Jory (Clint), Irene Bentley (Betty), Frank Campeau (Jeff), Hank Mann (Buck). **Adaptation 2:** *Smoky* (20th Century–Fox, 1946). Dir: Louis King. Scr: Dwight Cummins, Lillie Hayward, Dorothy Yost. Cast: Fred MacMurray (Clint), Anne Baxter (Julie), Burl Ives (Bill), Bruce Cabot (Frank), Esther Dale (Gram), Roy Roberts (Jeff). **Adaptation 3:** *Smoky* (20th Century–Fox, 1966). Dir: George Sherman. Scr: Dwight Cummins, Lillie Hayward, Dorothy Yost (1946 screenplay), Harold Medford. Cast: Fess Parker (Clint), Diana Hyland (Julie), Katy Jurado (Maria), Hoyt Axton (Fred), Robert J. Wilke (Jeff).

Smooth Talk (*see* "Where Are You Going, Where Have you Been?").

The Smugglers (see *The Man Within*).

4152. *Smuggler's Circuit* (Denys Roberts, 1954). After he is arrested, a confidence schemer decides to give up crime in order to spare his young son embarrassment. **Adaptation:** *Law and Disorder* (British Lion/Continental, 1958). Dir: Charles Crichton. Scr: T. E. B. Clarke, Patrick Campbell, Vivienne Knight. Cast: Michael Redgrave (Percy), Robert Morley (Judge Crichton), Joan Hickson (Aunt Florence), Lionel Jeffries (Major Proudfoot).

4153. *The Snake Pit* (Mary Jane Ward, 1946). Autobiographical novel about a woman's mental breakdown and her harrowing ordeal in an asylum. **Adaptation:** *The Snake Pit* (20th Century–Fox, 1948). Dir: Anatole Litvak. Scr: Millen Brand, Frank Partos. Cast: Olivia de Havilland (Virginia), Mark Stevens (Robert), Leo Genn (Dr. Kik), Celeste Holm (Grace). Notes: Academy Award for Best Sound and nominations for Best Picture, Director, Screenplay, Actress (de Havilland), and Musical Score; National Board of Review Award for Best Actress (de Havilland). DVD, VHS.

4154. *Snake Water* (Alan Williams, 1965). A Welsh architect mourning the death of his wife goes to a remote South American village, where he becomes involved with the hunt for diamonds that smugglers have stolen. **Adaptation:** *The Pink Jungle* (Universal, 1968). Dir: Delbert Mann. Scr: Charles Williams. Cast: James Garner (Ben), Eva Renzi (Alison), George Kennedy (Sammy), Michael Ansara (Raul). Notes: The film adaptation substitutes a fashion photographer and his model for the Welsh architect featured in the novel. VHS.

4155. *The Snapper* (Roddy Doyle, 1990). The second novel in Doyle's Barrytown Trilogy (along with *The Commitments* and *The Van*), *The Snapper* is concerned with a working-class Irish couple whose teenaged daughter becomes pregnant and refuses to identify the father. **Adaptation:** *The Snapper* (BBC, 1993 TV Movie). Dir: Stephen Frears. Scr: Roddy Doyle. Cast: Colm Meaney (Dessie), Tina Kellegher (Sharon), Ruth McCabe (Kay). Notes: BAFTA nominations for Best Drama, Editing, and Sound; Golden Globe nomination for Best Actor (Meaney). DVD, VHS. See also *The Commitments* and *the Van*.

4156. *The Snatchers* (Lionel White, 1953). A gang in Paris kidnaps a young heiress and holds her for ransom. **Adaptation:** *The Night of the Following Day* (Universal, 1968). Dir: Hubert Cornfield. Scr: Hubert Cornfield, Robert Phippeny, Lionel White. Cast: Marlon Brando (Bud), Richard Boone (Leer), Rita Moreno (Vi), Pamela Franklin (the Girl). DVD, VHS.

4157. *The Snow Birch* (John Mantley, 1958). A widow moves to the wilderness near the Canadian Rockies and marries a local man. **Adaptation:** *Woman Obsessed* (20th Century–Fox, 1959). Dir: Henry Hathaway. Scr: Sydney Boehm. Cast: Susan Hayward (Mary), Stephen Boyd (Fred), Barbara Nichols (Maime), Dennis Holmes (Robbie).

Snow Dogs (see *Winterdance*).

4158. *Snow Falling on Cedars* (David Guterson, 1994, PEN/Faulkner Prize). Set in an island community in the Pacific Northwest during the early 1950's, when anti–Japanese feeling from World War II still ran high, the story of a journalist who is torn between the desire to help a Japanese man unjustly accused of murder and his resentment over the man's having married a Japanese-American woman the journalist once loved **Adaptation:** *Snow Falling on Cedars* (Universal, 1999). Dir: Scott Hicks. Scr: Ronald Bass, Scott Hicks. Cast: Ethan Hawke (Ishmael), Youki Kudoh (Hatsue), Rick Yune (Kazuo), Max von Sydow (Nels), James Rebhorn (Alvin), James Cromwell (Judge Fielding). DVD, VHS.

4159. *Snow Treasure* (Marie McSwigan, 1958). Children's book based on a true World War II story about Norwegian youths who discover Nazi gold hidden in the snow and smuggle it out of the country. **Adaptation:** *Snow Treasure* (1968). Dir: Irving Jacoby. Scr: Irving Jacoby. Cast: Paul Austad (Peter), Wilfred Breistrand (Captain Kantzeler), James Franciscus (Lieutenant Kalasch).

The Snow Walker (*see* "Walk Well, My Brother").

Snowball Express (see *Chateau Bon Vivant*).

Snowbound (see *The Lonely Skier*).

4160. "The Snows of Kilimanjaro" (Ernest Hemingway, 1936). Seriously injured on the African mountain, a writer reflects on his professional disappointments and the failings of his personal life. The short story first appeared in *Esquire* in 1936 and was included in Hemingway's 1938 collection *The Fifth Column and the Forty-Nine Stories*. **Adaptation:** *The Snows of Kilimanjaro* (20th Century–Fox, 1952). Dir: Henry King. Scr: Casey Robinson. Cast: Gregory Peck (Harry), Susan Hayward (Helen), Ava Gardner (Cynthia), Hildegard Knef (Countess Liz), Leo G. Carroll (Uncle Bill). DVD, VHS.

4161. *So Big* (Edna Ferber, 1924). A young teacher settles in a small Dutch farming community in Illinois and struggles to raise her son to be independent. **Silent Film:** 1924. **Adaptation 1:** *So Big* (Warner, 1932). Dir: William A. Wellman. Scr: J. Grubb Alexander, Robert Lord. Cast: Barbara Stanwyck (Selina), George Brent (Rolf), Dickie Moore (Dirk), Bette Davis (Dallas). **Adaptation 2:** *So Big* (Warner, 1953). Dir: Robert Wise. Scr: John Twist. Cast: Jane Wyman (Selina), Sterling Hayden (Pervis), Nancy Olson (Dallas), Steve Forrest (Dirk), Elisabeth Fraser (Julie), Martha Hyer (Paula).

So Bright the Flame (see *Bowery to Bellevue*).

So Dear to My Heart (see *Midnight and Jeremiah*).

So Ends Our Night (see *Flotsam*).

4162. *So Evil My Love* (Joseph Shearing, 1947). A naïve widow comes under the spell of an attractive schemer and becomes involved in blackmail and other criminal activities. **Adaptation:** *So Evil My Love* (Paramount, 1948). Dir: Lewis Allen. Scr: Ronald Millar, Leonard Spigelgass. Cast: Ray Milland (Mark), Ann Todd (Olivia), Geraldine Fitzgerald (Susan), Leo G. Carroll (Jarvis).

4163. *So Red the Rose* (Stark Young, 1934). An aristocratic Southern family suffers hardship during the Civil War. **Adaptation:** *So Red the Rose* (Paramount, 1935). Dir: King Vidor. Scr: Maxwell Anderson, Edwin Justus Mayer, Laurence Stallings. Cast: Margaret Sullavan (Valette), Walter Connolly (Malcolm), Janet Beecher (Sally), Harry Ellerbe (Edward), Robert Cummings (George).

So This Is New York (see *The Big Town*).

4164. *So Well Remembered* (James Hilton, 1945). An honest newspaper editor and aspiring politician marries the daughter of a corrupt mill owner who nearly ruins his career. **Adaptation:** *So Well Remembered* (RKO, 1947). Dir: Edward Dmytryk. Scr: John Paxton. Cast: John Mills (George), Martha Scott (Olivia), Patricia Roc (Julie), Trevor Howard (Dr. Whiteside).

4165. "The Sobbin' Women" (Stephen Vincent Benét, 1926). Based on the ancient Roman story of the the rape of the Sabine women, a tale of seven lusty brothers in the American Northwest who forcibly take local women to be their wives. The short story originally appeared in *Country Gentleman* in May 1926. **Adaptation:** *Seven Brides for Seven Brothers* (MGM, 1954). Dir: Stanley Donen. Scr: Albert Hackett, Frances Goodrich, Dorothy Kingsley. Cast: Howard Keel (Adam), Jeff Richards (Benjamin), Russ Tamblyn (Gideon), Tommy Rall (Frankincense), Jane Powell (Millie). Notes: A musical adaptation, which was itself adapted as a Broadway play in 1982. Academy Award for Best Musical Score and nominations for Best Picture, Screenplay, Cinematography, and Editing. DVD, VHS.

Sol Madrid (see *Fruit of the Poppy*).

4166. *Solaris* (Stanislaw Lem, 1961). Science-fiction story about a psychologist who is sent to investigate strange occurrences over an ocean on a distant planet. There he meets his long-dead wife and realizes that the ocean allows those near it to live in an alternate dimension. **Adaptation 1:** *Solaris* (Magna, 1972). Dir: Andrei Tarkovsky. Scr: Fridrikh Gorenshtein, Andrei Tarkovsky. Cast: Natalya Bondarchuk (Hari), Donatas Banionis (Kris), Juri Järvet (Dr. Snaut).Notes: Originally released as *Solarys* and shown with subtitles. Cannes Film Festival Grand Jury Prize for Best Film and Golden Palm nomination for Best Director. DVD, VHS. **Adaptation 2:** *Solaris* (20th Century–Fox, 2002). Dir: Steven Soderbergh. Scr: Steven Soderbergh. Cast: George Clooney (Chris), Natascha McElhone (Rheya), Viola Davis (Gordon), Jeremy Davies (Snow), Ulrich Tukur (Gibarian). DVD, VHS.

The Soldier and the Lady (see *Michel Strogoff*).

Soldier Blue (see *Arrow in the Sun*).

4167. *Soldier in the Rain* (William Goldman, 1960). Comic novel about two army sergeants and their battles with military bureaucracy. **Adaptation:** *Soldier in the Rain* (Allied Artists, 1963). Dir: Ralph Nelson. Scr: Blake Edwards, Maurice Richlin. Cast: Jackie Gleason (Sergeant Slaughter), Steve McQueen (Sergeant Clay), Tuesday Weld (Bobby Jo), Tony Bill (Private Meltzer), Tom Poston (Lieutenant Magee). VHS.

4168. *Soldier of Fortune* (Ernest K. Gann, 1954). A woman whose husband was kidnapped in Hong Kong hires an American adventurer to find him. **Adaptation:** *Soldier of Fortune* (20th Century–Fox, 1955). Dir: Edward Dmytryk. Scr: Ernest K. Gann. Cast: Clark Gable (Hank), Susan Hayward (Jane), Michael Rennie (Inspector Merriweather), Gene Barry (Louis). VHS.

4169. *A Soldier's Daughter Never Cries* (Kaylie Jones, 1990). This autobiographical novel by the daughter of novelist James Jones tells the story of an eccentric expatriate family in Paris and their difficulties adjusting to life in America upon their return. **Adaptation:** *A Soldier's Daughter Never Cries* (Merchant-Ivory/October, 1998). Dir: James Ivory. Scr: James Ivory, Ruth Prawer Jhabvala. Cast: Kris Kristofferson (Bill), Barbara Hershey (Marcella), Leelee Sobieski (Charlotte), Jane Birkin (Mrs. Fortescue). DVD, VHS.

4170. "Soldier's Home" (Ernest Hemingway, 1925). A World War I veteran returns to his home town in Oklahoma and tries to convey the atrocities of war to people who insist on hearing tales of heroism and glory. The short story was included in Hemingway's 1925 collection *In Our Time*. **Adaptation:** *Soldier's Home* (PBS, 1977 TV Movie). Dir: Robert Young. Scr: Robert Geller.

Cast: Richard Backus (Harold), Lane Binkley (Roselle), Mark La Mura (Kenner), Nancy Marchand (Mrs. Krebs). VHS.

4171. *A Soldier's Tale* (M. K. Joseph, 1976). During World War II, a British military officer defends a young woman accused by French resistance fighters of being a German collaborator. **Adaptation:** *A Soldier's Tale* (Atlantic, 1988). Dir: Larry Parr. Scr: Grant Hinden Miller, Larry Parr. Cast: Gabriel Byrne (Saul), Marianne Basler (Belle), Paul Wyett (Charlie), Judge Reinhold (the Yank). DVD, VHS.

4172. *Soldiers Three* (Rudyard Kipling, 1892). Satiric tale set in India about three British soldiers whose friendship is ruined when one of them is promoted. **Adaptation:** *Soldiers Three* (MGM, 1951). Dir: Tay Garnett. Scr: Malcolm Stuart Boylan, Tom Reed, Marguerite Roberts. Cast: Stewart Granger (Ackroyd), Walter Pidgeon (Brunswick), David Niven (Pindenny), Robert Newton (Sykes), Cyril Cusack (Malloy).

4173. *Sole Survivor* (Dean R. Koontz, 1997). With the help of a survivor, a grieving reporter investigates the death of his wife and children in an air crash and discovers that a government agency was behind the disaster. **Adaptation:** *Sole Survivor* (Fox, 2000 TV Miniseries). Dir: Mikael Salomon. Scr: Richard Christian Matheson. Cast: Billy Zane (Joe), John C. McGinley (Yates), Isabella Hofmann (Barbara), Gloria Reuben (Rose).

4174. *The Solitary Child* (Nina Bawden [pseudonym for Nina Mabey Kark], 1956). A beautiful British woman marries a farmer who had been tried and acquitted of killing his first wife. Before long, she begins to wonder whether he was truly innocent. **Adaptation:** *The Solitary Child* (British Lion, 1958). Dir: Gerald Thomas. Scr: Robert Dunbar. Cast: Philip Friend (James), Barbara Shelley (Harriet), Sarah Lawson (Ann), Rona Anderson (Jean).

Solo (see *Weapon*).

Solo for Sparrow (see *The Gunner*).

Sombrero (see *Mexican Village*).

Some Call It Loving (*see* "Sleeping Beauty").

4175. *Some Came Running* (James Jones, 1957). A writer returns to his Indiana town from service in World War II and is torn between his friendships with a gambler and a prostitute and his attraction to a teacher, who encourages his writing ambitions. **Adaptation:** *Some Came Running* (MGM, 1958). Dir: Vincente Minnelli. Scr:

John Patrick, Arthur Sheekman. Cast: Frank Sinatra (Dave), Dean Martin (Bama), Shirley MacLaine (Ginny), Martha Hyer (Gwen), Arthur Kennedy (Frank). Notes: Academy Award nominations for Best Actress (MacLaine), Supporting Actor (Kennedy), Supporting Actress (Hyer), Costume Design, and Song. VHS.

4176. *Some Kind of Hero* (James Kirkwood, Jr., 1975). A prisoner of war in Vietnam returns to the United States as a hero but is soon forgotten and discovers that life at home will not be easy despite his former fame. **Adaptation:** *Some Kind of Hero* (Paramount, 1982). Dir: Michael Pressman. Scr: Robert Boris, James Kirkwood, Jr. Cast: Richard Pryor (Eddie/Ted), Margot Kidder (Toni), Ray Sharkey (Vinnie), Ronny Cox (Colonel Powers), Lynne Moody (Lisa). DVD, VHS.

4177. *Some Must Watch* (Ethel Lina White, 1933). In New England in 1906, a mute woman working as a domestic in a rich woman's home is in danger from a serial killer who resides in the same house. The novel was later reissued under the title *The Spiral Staircase*. **Adaptation 1:** *The Spiral Staircase* (RKO, 1946). Dir: Robert Siodmak. Scr: Mel Dinelli. Cast: Dorothy McGuire (Helen), George Brent (Professor Warren), Ethel Barrymore (Mrs. Warren), Kent Smith (Dr. Parry), Rhonda Fleming (Blanche). Notes: Academy Award nomination for Best Supporting Actress (Barrymore). DVD, VHS. **Adaptation 2:** *The Spiral Staircase* (Warner, 1975). Dir: Peter Collinson. Scr: Mel Dinelli (1946 screenplay), Chris Bryant, Andrew Meredith, Allan Scott. Cast: Jacqueline Bisset (Helen), Christopher Plummer (Dr. Sherman), John Phillip Law (Steven), Sam Wanamaker (Lieutenant Fields), Mildred Dunnock (Mrs. Sherman), Gayle Hunnicutt (Blanche). VHS. **Adaptation 3:** *The Spiral Staircase* (Fox Family, 2000 TV Movie). Dir: James Head. Scr: Mel Dinelli (1946 screenplay), Matt Dorff. Cast: Nicolette Sheridan (Helen), Judd Nelson (Philip), Alex McArthur (Steven), Debbe Dunning (Danielle), Holland Taylor (Emma).

4178. *Someone Else's Ghost* (Margaret Buffie, 1994). Children's book about a grieving family who move to a ranch after the death of one of the children. There the mother becomes convinced that the ghost of her son is trying to contact her. **Adaptation:** *My Mother's Ghost* (Fox Family, 1996 TV Movie). Dir: Elise Swerhone. Scr: Heather Conkie. Cast: Elisabeth Rosen (Jessie), Gabrielle Rose (Jeannie), Barry Flatman (Rick).

4179. *Someone Is Bleeding* (Richard Matheson, 1953). A man meets a beautiful woman and comes to suspect that she may the the serial killer of men. **Adaptation:** *Icy Breasts*; released in the UK as *Someone Is Bleeding* (Joseph Green, 1974). Dir: Georges Lautner. Scr: Georges Lautner. Cast: Alain Delon (Marc), Mireille Darc (Peggy), Claude Brasseur (Francois). Notes: Orginally titled *Les Seins de glace* and shown with subtitles. VHS.

4180. *Someone Is Killing the Great Chefs of Europe* (Nan Lyons and Ivan Lyons, 1976). Black comedy about a plot to kill the finest chefs in each of the European capitals. **Adaptation:** *Who Is Killing the Great Chefs of Europe?*; released in the UK as *Too Many Chefs* (Warner, 1978). Dir: Ted Kotcheff. Scr: Peter Stone. Cast: George Segal (Robby), Jacqueline Bisset (Natasha), Robert Morley (Max), Jean-Pierre Cassel (Kohner), Philippe Noiret (Moulineau). VHS.

4181. *Someone Like You* (Sarah Dessen, 1998). Young-adult novel about the relationship between teenaged friends in a suburban community. One is living in a home that causes her to doubt the possibility that true love exists, and the other facing pregnancy by her dead boyfriend. **Adaptation:** *How to Deal* (New Line, 2003). Dir: Clare Kilner. Scr: Neena Beber. Cast: Mandy Moore (Halley), Allison Janney (Lydia), Trent Ford (Macon), Alexandra Holden (Scarlett), Dylan Baker (Steve), Nina Foch (Grandma Halley). NOTE: The screenplay is based on this novel and Dessen's 1997 book *That Summer*. DVD, VHS. See also *That Summer*.

Someone Like You (1998) (see *Animal Husbandry*).

Something for Everyone (see *The Cook*).

4182. *Something of Value* (Robert Ruark, 1955). A young African joins with friends in the Mau-Mau uprising during the period of British colonial rule in Kenya. **Adaptation:** *Something of Value* (MGM, 1957). Dir: Richard Brooks. Scr: Richard Brooks. Cast: Rock Hudson (Peter), Dana Wynter (Holly), Sidney Poitier (Kimani), Wendy Hiller (Elizabeth), Juano Hernandez (Njogu). VHS.

4183. *Something to Hide* (Nicholas Monsarrat, 1965). After an abandoned pregnant girl manipulates a naïve man into taking her in, he kills his wife and hides her body. **Adaptation:** *Something to Hide*; reissued as *Shattered* (Atlantic, 1972). Dir: Alastair Reid. Scr: Alastair Reid. Cast: Peter Finch (Harry), Shelley Winters (Gabriella), Colin Blakely (Blagdon), John Stride (Sergeant Winnington), Linda Hayden (Lorelei). VHS.

4184. *Something Wicked This Way Comes* (Ray Bradbury, 1962). An evil carnival comes to a small Illinois town and seemingly makes all of its patrons' wishes come true. **Adaptation:** *Something Wicked This Way Comes* (Disney/Buena Vista, 1983). Dir: Jack Clayton. Scr: Ray Bradbury. Cast: Jason Robards (Charles), Jonathan Pryce (Mr. Dark), Diane Ladd (Mrs. Nightshade), Royal Dano (Tom). DVD, VHS.

Something Wild (see *Mary Ann*).

4185. "Something's Got to Give" (Darcy Frey, 1996). A profile of New York air-traffic controllers and the anxieties they face each day. The article appeared in *The New York Times Magazine* on March 24, 1996. **Adaptation:** *Pushing Tin* (20th Century–Fox, 1999). Dir: Mike Newell. Scr: Glen Charles, Les Charles. Cast: John Cusack (Nick), Billy Bob Thornton (Russell), Cate Blanchett (Connie), Angelina Jolie (Mary). Notes: The screenplay concerns a crack air-traffic controller and his rivalry with a newcomer to the job. DVD, VHS.

4186. *Sometimes a Great Notion* (Ken Kesey, 1964). A proud Oregon logging family struggles to maintain their business. **Adaptation:** *Sometimes a Great Notion*; broadcast on American television as *Never Give an Inch* (Universal, 1971). Dir: Paul Newman. Scr: John Gay. Cast: Paul Newman (Hank), Henry Fonda (Henry), Lee Remick (Viv), Michael Sarrazin (Leland), Richard Jaeckel (Joe Ben). VHS.

4187. "Sometimes They Come Back" (Stephen King, 1973). A high school teacher returns after many years to his hometown, where he must battle the ghosts of four teenagers who died in an accident along with his older brother. The story originally appeared in the January 1974 issue of *Cavalier* and was included in King's 1978 short-story collection *Night Shift*. **Adaptation:** *Sometimes They Come Back* (Paradise/Vidmark, 1991 TV Movie). Dir: Tom McLoughlin. Scr: Lawrence Konner, Mark Rosenthal. Cast: Tim Matheson (Jim), Brooke Adams (Sally), Robert Rusler (Richard), Chris Demetral (Wayne). DVD, VHS. Notes: Two sequels followed: *Sometimes They Come Back ... Again* (1996) (DVD, VHS), and *Sometimes They Come Back ... for More* (1999) (DVD, VHS).

Somewhere in Sonora (see *Somewhere South of Sonora*).

Somewhere in Time (see *Bid Time Return*).

4188. *Somewhere South of Sonora* (Will Lev-ington Comfort, 1925). Western about a cowboy who rescues a friend's missing son by joining the dangerous outlaw gang who kidnapped him. The novel was originally published as a short story in *The Saturday Evening Post*. **Silent Film:** 1927. **Adaptation:** *Somewhere in Sonora* (Warner, 1933). Dir: Mack V. Wright. Scr: Joe Roach. Cast: John Wayne (Bishop), Henry B. Walthall (Leadly), Shirley Palmer (Mary). VHS.

Son of Flubber (see "A Situation of Gravity" and *Danny Dunn and the Weather Machine*).

Son of Fury (see *Benjamin Blake*).

4189. *Son of Robin Hood* (Paul A. Castleton, 1941). Carrying on the tradition of his famous father, Robin Hood's son saves a boy king from the evil regent who plots to usurp the throne. **Adaptation:** *The Bandit of Sherwood Forest* (Columbia, 1946). Dir: Henry Levin, George Sherman. Scr: Melvin Levy. Cast: Cornel Wilde (Robert of Nottingham), Anita Louise (Lady Catherine), Jill Esmond (the Queen Mother), Edgar Buchanan (Friar Tuck).

4190. *The Son of the Wolf: Tales of the Far North* (Jack London, 1900). London's earliest stories center on a Malamute youth and his adventures in the Yukon. **Adaptation:** *The Cry of the Black Wolves* (Lisa/Rook, 1972). Dir: Harald Reinl. Scr: Kurt Nachmann. Cast: Ron Ely (Bill), Raimund Harmstorf (Jack), Angelica Ott (Taylor). Notes: The screenplay combines elements from several London stories. VHS.

4191. *The Song of Bernadette* (Franz Werfel, 1941). Fictionalized account of the appearance of the Virgin Mary to a French peasant girl at Lourdes during the nineteenth century. **Adaptation:** *The Song of Bernadette* (20th Century–Fox, 1943). Dir: Henry King. Scr: George Seaton. Cast: Jennifer Jones (Bernadette), William Eythe (Antoine), Charles Bickford (Peyramale), Vincent Price (Dutour), Lee J. Cobb (Dr. Dozous), Gladys Cooper (Sister Marie Therese), Anne Revere (Louise). Notes: Academy Awards for Best Actress (Jones), Cinematography, Art Direction, and Musical Score, and nominations for Best Picture, Director, Screenplay, Supporting Actor (Bickford), Supporting Actresses (Cooper and Revere), Editing, and Sound; Golden Globe Awards for Best Picture, Director, and Actress (Jones). DVD, VHS.

4192. *Song of Survival: Women Interned* (Helen Colijn, 1995). Autobiographical account of Colijn's experiences during World War II when she, along with a group of women, was imprisoned by the Japanese in Sumatra. To experience relief from their misery, they formed a musical chorus. **Adaptation:** *Paradise Road* (Fox Seachlight, 1997). Dir: Bruce Beresford. Scr: David Giles, Martin Meader, Bruce Beresford. Cast: Glenn Close (Adrienne), Frances McDormand (Dr. Verstak), Pauline Collins (Daisy), Cate Blanchett (Susan), Jennifer Ehle (Rosemary), Julianna Margulies (Topsy), Wendy Hughes (Mrs. Dickson). Notes: Although Colijn's book is not directly credited in the film, it served as one of the inspirations for the story. DVD, VHS.

4193. *Songs in Ordinary Time* (Mary McGarry Morris, 1995). A divorced mother of three takes in a con man as a boarder, and he soon ruins her financially and then threatens her life. **Adaptation:** *Songs in Ordinary Time* (CBS, 2000 TV Movie). Dir: Rod Holcomb. Scr: Malcolm MacRury. Cast: Sissy Spacek (Mary), Beau Bridges (Omar), Tom Guiry (Norm), Jordan Warkol (Ben), Careena Melia (Alice), Richard Yearwood (Earlie).

4194. *Sons and Lovers* (D. H. Lawrence, 1913). Lawrence's novel concerns a young man's sexually charged relationship with his doting mother, who tries to persuade him to leave their small coalmining town and make something of himself. **Adaptation 1:** *Sons and Lovers* (20th Century–Fox, 1960). Dir: Jack Cardiff. Scr: T. E. B. Clarke, Gavin Lambert. Cast: Trevor Howard (Walter), Dean Stockwell (Paul), Wendy Hiller (Gertrude), Mary Ure (Clara), Heather Sears (Miriam). Notes: Academy Award for Best Cinematography and nominations for Best Film, Director, Screenplay, Actor (Howard), Actress (Ure), and Art Direction; Golden Globe Award for Best Picture, and nomination for Best Supporting Actress (Ure); National Board of Review Awards for Best Picture and Director. **Adaptation 2:** *Sons and Lovers* (BBC, 1981 TV Miniseries). Dir: Stuart Burge. Scr: Trevor Griffiths. Cast: Eileen Atkins (Gertrude), Tom Bell (Walter), Geoffrey Burridge (William), Lynn Dearth (Clara), Leonie Mellinger (Miriam). **Adaptation 3:** *Sons and Lovers* (ITV, 2003 TV Movie). Dir: Stephen Whittaker. Scr: Simon Burke. Cast: Sarah Lancashire (Gertrude), Hugo Speer (Walter), James Murray (William), Rupert Evans (Paul), Esther Hall (Clara), Lyndsey Marshal (Miriam).

4195. *Sophie's Choice* (William Styron, 1979, National Book Award). A Polish survivor of a Nazi death camp moves to New York after the war but cannot escape memories of her dreadful experiences. **Adaptation:** *Sophie's Choice* (Universal, 1982). Dir: Alan J. Pakula. Dir: Alan J. Pakula. Cast: Meryl Streep (Sophie), Kevin Kline (Nathan), Peter MacNicol (Stingo), Rita Karin (Yetta), Stephen D. Newman (Larry), Greta Turken (Leslie), Josh Mostel (Morris). Notes: Academy Award for Best Actress (Streep), and nominations for Best Screenplay, Musical Score, Cinematography, and Costume Design; Golden Globe Award for Best Actress (Streep), and nomination for Newcomer of the Year (Kline); National Board of Review Award for Best Actress (Streep). DVD, VHS.

4196. *Sor Juana Inez de la Cruz* (Octavio Paz, 1982). Written by the Mexican poet and 1990 Nobel laureate, the biographical story of the seventeenth-century Mexican nun (1648–1695), whose sensual poetry brought about her condemnation by the Catholic Chuch. **Adaptation:** *I, Worst of All* (First Run, 1990). Dir: Maria Luisa Bemberg. Scr: Maria Luisa Bemberg, Antonio Larreta. Cast: Assumpta Serna (Juana), Dominique Sanda (La Virreina), Hector Alterio (the Viceroy), Lautaro Murua (the Archbishop). Notes: Originally released as *Yo, La Peor de Todas* and shown with subtitles. DVD, VHS.

Sorcerer (see *The Wages of Fear*).

4197. *Sorrell and Son* (Warwick Deeping, 1925). After his wife leaves him, a man sacrifices himself to raise their son. **Silent Film:** 1927. **Adaptation 1:** *Sorrell and Son* (United Artists, 1934). Dir: Jack Raymond. Scr: Lydia Hayward. Cast: H. B. Warner (Stephen), Hugh Williams (Kit), Margot Grahame (Dora), Peter Penrose (Kit as a child), Evelyn Roberts (Thomas), **Adaptation 2:** *Sorrell and Son* (Yorkshire/PBS, 1984 TV Miniseries). Dir: Derek Bennett. Scr: Jeremy Paul. Cast: Richard Pasco (Stephen), Peter Chelsom (Kit), Paul Critchley (Kit Sorrell as a child), John Shrapnel (Thomas).

Sorrowful Jones (see "Little Miss Marker").

4198. *A Sort of Traitor* (Nigel Balchin, 1949). An embittered research scientist investigating a cure for the plague betrays the British government. **Adaptation:** *Suspect* (British Lion/Kingsley, 1960). Dir: John Boulting, Roy Boulting. Scr: Nigel Balchin. Cast: Tony Britton (Dr. Marriott), Virginia Maskell (Dr. Byrne), Ian Bannen (Andrews), Kenneth Griffith (Dr. Shole), Peter Cushing (Professor Sewell). DVD, VHS.

4199. *The Sound and the Fury* (William Faulkner, 1929). The prominent Compson family of Jefferson, Mississippi, falls on hard times. The classic Faulkner novel is told subjectively from the points of view of various characters, who relate their memories of childhood. **Adaptation:** *The Sound and the Fury* (20th Century–Fox, 1959). Dir: Martin Ritt. Scr: Harriet Frank, Jr., Irving Ravetch. Cast: Yul Brynner (Jason), Joanne Woodward (Quentin), Margaret Leighton (Caddy), Stuart Whitman (Charlie), Ethel Waters (Dilsey), Jack Warden (Ben).

The Sound of Fury (see *The Condemned*).

The Sound of Music (see *The Story of the Trapp Family Singers*).

4200. *The Sound of One Hand Clapping* (Richard Flanagan, 1997, Victorian Premier's Prize For Best Novel, ABA Australian Book of the Year Prize). The daughter in a family that emigrated from Slovenia to Tasmania in Australia after World War II is abandoned by her mother and abused by her alcoholic father. She returns to her home as an adult many years later, and both she and her father confront their bad memories of the time. **Adaptation:** *The Sound of One Hand Clapping* (Australian Film/Palace, 1998). Dir: Richard Flanagan. Scr: Richard Flanagan. Cast: Kerry Fox (Sonja), Kristof Kaczmarek (Bojan), Rosie Flanagan (Sonja as a child), Evelyn Krape (Jenja), Melita Jurisic (Maria).

4201. *Sounder* (William A. Armstrong, 1969). Autobiographical book about a family of black sharecroppers in 1930's Louisiana and their struggle to survive after the father was imprisoned for a petty crime. **Adaptation 1:** *Sounder* (20th Century–Fox, 1972). Dir: Martin Ritt. Scr: Lonne Elder III. Cast: Cicely Tyson (Rebecca), Paul Winfield (Nathan), Kevin Hooks (David), Carmen Mathews (Mrs. Boatwright). Notes: National Board of Review Award for Best Actress (Tyson); Academy Award nominations for Best Film, Screenplay, Actor (Winfield), and Actress (Tyson); Golden Globe nominations for Best Actress (Tyson) and Newcomer (Hooks). DVD, VHS. **Adaptation 2:** *Sounder* (ABC, 2003) (TV). Dir: Kevin Hooks. Scr: Bill Cain. Cast: Carl Lumbly (Nathan), Suzzanne Douglass (Rebecca), Daniel Lee Robertson III (David), Peter MacNeill (the Sheriff), Paul Winfield (the Teacher). DVD, VHS. Notes: A sequel, *Sounder Part II*, was released in 1976.

South Central (see *Crips*).

South Pacific (see *Tales of the South Pacific*).

4202. *South Riding* (Winifred Holtby, 1936).

Completed just before Holtby's death in 1935, posthumously published novel about a Yorkshire teacher who exposes a crooked politician in a rural British town. **Adaptation 1:** *South Riding* (1937). Dir: Victor Saville. Scr: Donald Bull, Ian Dalrymple. Cast: Edna Best (Sarah), Ralph Richardson (Robert), Edmund Gwenn (Alfred), Ann Todd (Madge Carne). VHS. **Adaptation 2:** *South Riding* (Yorkshire Television, 1974 TV Miniseries). Dir: James Ormerod, Alastair Reid. Scr: Stan Barstow. Cast: Dorothy Tutin (Sarah), Nigel Davenport (Robert), Hermione Baddeley (Mrs. Beddows).

4203. *The Southern Blade* (Nelson Wolford and Shirley Wolford, 1963). Near the end of the Civil War, a Confederate prisoner escapes from a Union fort, and the jail's commander, whose fiancé the prisoner has taken hostage, goes in pursuit. **Adaptation:** *A Time for Killing*; released in the UK as *The Long Ride Home* (Columbia, 1967), Dir: Phil Karlson. Scr: Halsted Welles. Cast: Inger Stevens (Emily), Glenn Ford (Charles), Paul Petersen (Blue Lake), Timothy Carey (Billy Cat).

4204. *The Southern Star* (Jules Verne, 1884). Part of Verne's Voyages Extraordinaire series, the story of a French engineer in South Africa who creates a huge diamond for his girlfriend and is pursued by thieves for his treasure. Originally titled *L'Etoile du Sud*, the novel has also appeared in English as *The Vanished Diamond*. **Adaptation:** *The Southern Star* (Columbia, 1968). Dir: Sidney Hayers. Scr: David Pursall, Jack Seddon. Cast: George Segal (Dan), Ursula Andress (Erica), Orson Welles (Plankett), Ian Hendry (Karl).

The Southerner (see *Hold Autumn in Your Hand*).

Souvenir (see *The Pork Butcher*).

Soylent Green (see *Make Room! Make Room!*).

4205. *Space* (James A. Michener, 1982). A fictional account of the American space program from World War II through the 1970's. **Adaptation:** *Space* (CBS, 1985 TV Miniseries). Dir: Lee Philips, Joseph Sargent. Scr: Dick Berg, Stirling Silliphant. Cast: James Garner (Senator Grant), Susan Anspach (Elinor), Beau Bridges (Randy), Blair Brown (Penny), Bruce Dern (Stanley).

Space Travelers (see *Marooned*).

4206. *The Space Vampires* (Colin Wilson, 1976). Astronauts investigating Halley's Comet bring back alien vampires who turn the populace of London into obedient zombies. **Adaptation:** *Lifeforce* (Cannon/TriStar, 1985). Dir: Tobe Hooper.

Scr: Dan O'Bannon, Don Jakoby. Cast: Steve Railsback (Colonel Carlsen), Peter Firth (Colonel Caine), Frank Finlay (Dr. Fallada), Mathilda May (the Space Girl), Patrick Stewart (Dr. Armstrong). DVD, VHS.

A Spaceman in King Arthur's Court (see *A Connecticut Yankee in King Arthur's Court*).

The Spaniard's Curse (see *The Assize of the Dying*).

4207. *The Spanish Gardener* (A. J. Cronin, 1950). A British diplomat in Spain grows jealous when his young son develops a close friendship with the household gardener. **Adaptation:** *The Spanish Gardener* (Rank, 1956). Dir: Philip Leacock. Scr: John Bryan, Lesley Storm. Cast: Dirk Bogarde (Jose), Jon Whiteley (Nicholas), Michael Hordern (Harrington), Cyril Cusack (Garcia), Maureen Swanson (Maria).

4208. *Spare the Rod* (Michael Croft, 1957). A new teacher at a London high school develops a good relationship with his tough students. **Adaptation:** *Spare the Rod* (British Lion, 1961). Dir: Leslie Norman. Scr: John Cresswell. Cast: Max Bygraves (John), Geoffrey Keen (Arthur), Donald Pleasence (Jenkins), Betty McDowall (Ann).

4209. *Sparkling Cyanide* (Agatha Christie, 1944). Six people gather again for dinner at the very table where a friend died of poisoning a year earlier. One of them is concealing a secret. The book was published in the U.S. as *Remembered Death*. **Adaptation 1:** *Sparkling Cyanide* (CBS, 1983 TV Movie). Dir: Robert Lewis. Scr: Sue Grafton, Steve Humphrey, Robert Malcolm Young. Cast: Anthony Andrews (Tony), Deborah Raffin (Iris), Pamela Bellwood (Ruth), Nancy Marchand (Lucilla). VHS. **Adaptation 2:** *Sparkling Cyanide* (ITV, 2003 TV Movie). Dir: Tristram Powell. Scr: Laura Lamson. Cast: Kenneth Cranham (George), Rachel Shelley (Rosemary), Lia Williams (Ruth), Justin Pierre (Carl).

4210. *Spartacus* (Howard Fast, 1951). Trained to kill in the Roman arena, a slave leads a violent revolt against the corrupt emperor. **Adaptation 1:** *Spartacus* (Universal International, 1960). Dir: Stanley Kubrick. Scr: Dalton Trumbo. Cast: Kirk Douglas (Spartacus), Laurence Olivier (Marcus Licinius Crassus), Jean Simmons (Varinia), Charles Laughton (Sempronius Gracchus), Peter Ustinov (Lentulus Batiatus), Woody Strode (Draba), John Gavin (Julius Caesar), Nina Foch (Helena Glabrus), John Ireland (Crixus), Herbert Lom (Tigranes Levantus). Notes: Acad-

emy Awards for Best Supporting Actor (Ustinov), Art Direction, Cinematography, and Costume Design, and nominations for Best Musical Score and Editing; Golden Globe Award for Best Picture and nominations for Best Director, Actor (Olivier), and Supporting Actors (Strode and Ustinov). DVD, VHS. **Adaptation 2:** *Spartacus* (USA Network, 2004 TV Movie). Dir: Robert Dornhelm. Scr: Robert Schenkkan. Cast: Goran Visnjic (Spartacus), Alan Bates (Antonius Agrippa), Angus Macfadyen (Marcus Crassus), Rhona Mitra (Varinia), Ian McNeice (Lentulus Batiatus), James Frain (David). DVD, VHS.

Spasms (see *Death Bite*).

4211. *Speak* (Laurie Halse Anderson, 1999). Young adult book about a girl who becomes mute after a traumatic experience during the summer prior to entering high school. **Adaptation:** *Speak* (Showtime, 2004). Dir: Jessica Sharzer. Scr: Jessica Sharzer, Annie Young Frisbie. Cast: Kristen Stewart (Melinda), Hallee Hirsh (Rachel), Steve Zahn (Mr. Freeman), Grace Ameter (Emily), Michael Angarano (David).

Speak Easily (see *Footlights*).

4212. *The Speaker of Mandarin* (Ruth Rendell, 1983). Upon his return from a trip to China, a British police inspector investigates the murder of a fellow tourist on the trip. **Adaptation:** *The Speaker of Mandarin* (Blue Heaven/TVS, 1992 TV Movie). Dir: Herbert Wise. Scr: Trevor Preston. Cast: George Baker (Detective Wexford), Christopher Ravenscroft (Detective Burden), Virginia McKenna (Milborough), Helena Michell (Pandora).

The Speckled Band (see *The Adventure of the Speckled Band*).

4213. *Speedy Death* (Gladys Mitchell, 1929). At an engagement party for a relative, an aristocratic sleuth and her chauffeur solve a brutal murder. **Adaptation:** *The Mrs. Bradley Mysteries: Speedy Death* (BBC/PBS, 1998 TV Movie). Dir: Audrey Cooke. Scr: Simon Booker. Cast: Diana Rigg (Mrs. Bradley), Neil Dudgeon (George), John Alderton (Alastair), Lynda Baron (Mrs. MacNamara), Emma Fielding (Eleanor). DVD, VHS. Notes: The film served as the pilot for a 1999 British television series titled *The Mrs. Bradley Mysteries* (DVD, VHS).

The Spell of Amy Nugent (see *The Necromancers*).
　　Spellbound (1940) (see *The Necromancers*).

Spellbound (1945) (see *The House of Dr. Edwardes*).

4214. *Spencer's Mountain* (Earl Hamner, Jr., 1961). Autobiographical novel about rural life in Wyoming in the 1930's as a poor man builds a home for his family of nine. **Adaptation:** *Spencer's Mountain* (Warner, 1963). Dir: Delmer Daves. Scr: Delmer Daves. Cast: Henry Fonda (Clay), Maureen O'Hara (Olivia), James MacArthur (Clayboy), Donald Crisp (Grandpa Spencer), Wally Cox (Reverend Goodman). DVD, VHS. Notes: The book was the basis for the hit series *The Waltons*, which ran on CBS television from 1972 to 1981 (DVD, VHS).

4215. *Sphere* (Michael Crichton, 1987). Navy divers find a perfect golden sphere at the bottom of the ocean, and it turns out to be a three hundred-year-old space ship inhabited by a mysterious alien. **Adaptation:** *Sphere* (Warner, 1998). Dir: Barry Levinson. Scr: Stephen Hauser, Paul Attanasio, Kurt Wimmer. Cast: Dustin Hoffman (Dr. Goodman), Sharon Stone (Dr. Halperin), Samuel L. Jackson (Dr. Adams), Peter Coyote (Captain Barnes), Liev Schreiber (Dr. Fielding), Queen Latifah (Alice). DVD, VHS.

4216. *Sphinx* (Robin Cook, 1979). A beautiful Egyptologist locates clues to an ancient treasure and must battle human adversaries and a legendary mummy's curse. **Adaptation:** *Sphinx* (Orion/Warner, 1981). Dir: Franklin J. Schaffner. Scr: John Byrum. Cast: Lesley-Anne Down (Erica), Frank Langella (Ahmed), Maurice Ronet (Yeon), John Gielgud (Abdu-Hamdi), Vic Tablian (Khalifa), Martin Benson (Mohammed), John Rhys-Davies (Stephanos). VHS.

4217. *The Sphinx Has Spoken* (Maurice Dekobra, 1930). Originally titled *Le Sphinx a Parlé*, the story of British officers stationed in India who fall in love with a married socialite and are manipulated by her scheming husband. **Adaptation:** *Friends and Lovers* (RKO, 1931). Dir: Victor Schertzinger. Scr: Wallace Smith. Cast: Adolphe Menjou (Captain Roberts), Lili Damita (Alva), Laurence Olivier (Lieutenant Nichols), Erich von Stroheim (Colonel Sangrito).

4218. *Spider* (Patrick McGrath, 1990). Released from a mental institution after twenty years, a disturbed man goes to a halfway house, where he tries to reconnect the pieces of his life through memories, including recollections of abuse at the hands of his father. **Adaptation:** *Spider* (Sony, 2002). Dir: David Cronenberg. Scr: Patrick McGrath. Cast: Ralph Fiennes (Spider), Miranda Richardson (Yvonne), Gabriel Byrne (Bill), Lynn Redgrave (Mrs. Wilkinson), John Neville (Terence). Notes: Cannes Film Festival Golden Palm nomination for Best Director. DVD, VHS.

The Spider's Stratagem (*see* "The Theme of the Traitor and the Hero").

The Spikes Gang (see *The Bank Robber*).

4219. *Spinster* (Sylvia Ashton-Warner, 1958). Autobiographical novel about a New Zealand teacher of Maori children and her love affairs with two men. **Adaptation:** *Two Loves*; released in the UK as *The Spinster* (MGM, 1961). Dir: Charles Walters. Scr: Ben Maddow. Cast: Shirley MacLaine (Anna), Laurence Harvey (Paul), Jack Hawkins (Abercrombie), Nobu McCarthy (Whareparita).

4220. *The Spiral Road* (Jan De Hartog, 1947). In Java in 1936, an atheist doctor treats a leprosy epidemic and gradually becomes a Christian missionary. The Dutch novel, originally a trilogy of books titled *Gods Geuzen*, was translated in 1957. **Adaptation:** *The Spiral Road* (Universal International, 1962). Dir: Robert Mulligan. Scr: John Lee Mahin, Neil Paterson. Cast: Rock Hudson (Dr. Drager), Burl Ives (Dr. Jansen), Gena Rowlands (Els), Geoffrey Keen (Willem).

The Spiral Staircase (see *Some Must Watch*).

The Spirit Is Willing (see *The Visitors*).

4221. *Spirit Lost* (Nancy Thayer, 1988). A painter and his pregnant wife move from an apartment in Boston to an old house on Nantucket island, where the ghost of a beautiful woman tries to lure him from his wife. **Adaptation:** *Spirit Lost* (Live Entertainment, 1996). Dir: Neema Barnette. Scr: Joyce Renee Lewis. Cast: Regina Taylor (Willy), J. Michael Hunter (Harrison), Cynda Williams (Arabella). DVD, VHS.

4222. *The Spirit of St. Louis* (Charles A. Lindbergh, 1953, Pulitzer Prize). Autobiographical account of Lindbergh's historic nonstop flight from New York to Paris in 1927. **Adaptation:** *The Spirit of St. Louis* (Warner, 1957). Dir: Billy Wilder. Scr: Charles Lederer, Wendell Mayes, Billy Wilder. Cast: James Stewart (Lindbergh), Murray Hamilton (Gurney), Bartlett Robinson (Mahoney). VHS.

Spirits of the Dead (*see* "Metzengerstein" and "William Wilson").

4223. *The Splinter Fleet of the Otranto Bar-*

rage (Ray Milholland, 1936). Naval recruits at Annapolis are trained as submarine chasers, and their fleet escorts ships through the Mediterranean during World War I. **Adaptation:** *Submarine Patrol* (20th Century–Fox, 1938). Dir: John Ford. Scr: Rian James, Darrell Ware, Jack Yellen. Cast: Richard Greene (Townsend), Nancy Kelly (Susan), Preston Foster (Lieutenant Drake), George Bancroft (Captain Leeds), Slim Summerville (Fickett).

The Split (see *The Seventh*).

4224. *Split Images* (Elmore Leonard, 1981). No one believes a reporter when she says that a well-known millionaire committed a horrible murder. **Adaptation:** *Split Images* (Turner, 1992 TV Movie). Dir: Sheldon Larry. Scr: Pete Hamill, Vera Appleyard. Cast: Gregory Harrison (Robbie), Robert Collins (Gossage), Rebecca Jenkins (Angela).

4225. *The Spoilers* (Rex Beach, 1906). In Alaska during the gold rush, corrupt government officials try to cheat prospectors of their rightful claims. Beach and James MacArthur adapted the novel as a Broadway play in 1907. **Silent Films:** 1914 and 1923. **Adaptation 1:** *The Spoilers* (Paramount, 1930). Dir: Edward Carewe. Scr: Bartlett Cormack, Agnes Brand Leahy. Cast: Gary Cooper (Roy), Kay Johnson (Helen), Betty Compson (Cherry), William Boyd (Alexander). **Adaptation 2:** *The Spoilers* (Universal, 1942). Dir: Ray Enright. Scr: Lawrence Hazard, Tom Reed. Cast: Marlene Dietrich (Cherry), Randolph Scott (Alexander), John Wayne (Roy), Margaret Lindsay (Helen), Harry Carey (Dextry). DVD, VHS. **Adaptation 3:** *The Spoilers* (Universal International, 1955). Dir: Jesse Hibbs. Scr: Oscar Brodney, Charles Hoffman. Cast: Anne Baxter (Cherry), Jeff Chandler (Roy), Rory Calhoun (Alexander), Ray Danton (Bronco Blackie).

4226. *The Spoils of Poynton* (Henry James, 1897). Family members come into sharp conflict over inheriting a house and its valuable contents. **Adaptation:** *The Spoils of Poynton* (BBC, 1970 TV Miniseries). Dir: Peter Sasdy. Scr: Denis Constanduros, Lennox Phillips. Cast: June Ellis (Mrs. Brigstock), Diane Fletcher (Mona), Pauline Jameson (Mrs. Gereth), Gemma Jones (Fleda), Ian Ogilvy (Owen).

4227. *A Sporting Proposition* (James Aldridge, 1973). A poor boy and a crippled rich girl both lay claim to a pony and must decide on a way to determine the rightful owner. **Adaptation:** *Ride a Wild Pony* (Disney/Buena Vista, 1975). Dir: Don Chaffey. Scr: Rosemary Anne Sisson. Cast: Michael Craig (James), John Meillon (Charles), Robert Bettles (Scotty), Eva Griffith (Josie). VHS.

Spotted Horses (see *The Hamlet*).

4228. *The Springboard* (John Fores, 1956). An episodic look at the personal stories of various passengers and flight crew members at a fogged-in London airport. **Adaptation:** *Out of the Clouds* (Ealing/Rank, 1955). Dir: Basil Dearden. Scr: John Eldridge, Michael Relph, Cast: Anthony Steel (Gus), Robert Beatty (Nick), David Knight (Bill), Margo Lorenz (Leah), James Robertson Justice (Captain Brent).

4229. "Spurs" (Tod Robbins [pseudonym for Clarence Aaron Robbins], 1917). Lurid story about a traveling sideshow and the cruel trapeze artist who sets friends against each other. The story originally appeared in *Munsey's Magazine* in 1917 and was later collected in Robbins' book *Who Wants a Green Bottle and Other Uneasy Tales* (1926). **Adaptation:** *Freaks* (MGM, 1932). Dir: Tod Browning. Scr: Al Boasberg, Willis Goldbeck, Leon Gordon, Edgar Allan Woolf. Cast: Wallace Ford (Phroso), Leila Hyams (Venus), Olga Baclanova (Cleopatra). DVD, VHS.

4230. *The Spy in Black* (J. Storer Clouston, 1917). During World War I, a German U-boat is sent to Scotland on a spying mission, but one of the spies falls in love with the local school teacher. **Adaptation:** *The Spy in Black*; released in the U.S. as *U-Boat 29* (Columbia, 1939). Dir: Michael Powell. Scr: Emeric Pressburger, J. Storer Clouston. Cast: Conrad Veidt (Hardt), Sebastian Shaw (Ashington/Blacklock), Valerie Hobson (Frau Tiel/Jill), Marius Goring (Schuster). VHS.

The Spy in White (see *The Eunuch of Stamboul*).

4231. *A Spy of Napoleon* (Baroness Emmuska Orczy, 1934). A court dancer thwarts a plot to assassinate the Emperor Louis Napoleon. **Adaptation:** *Spy of Napoleon* (Grand National, 1936). Dir: Maurice Elvey. Scr: Fred V. Merrick, L. du Garde Peach, Harold Simpson. Cast: Richard Barthelmess (Gerard), Dolly Haas (Eloise), Frank Vosper (Napoleon III), Francis L. Sullivan (the Chief of Police).

4232. *A Spy Was Born* (Marthe McKenna, 1935). An English agent impersonates a German spy returning to Germany as a national hero. **Adaptation:** *Lancer Spy* (1937). Dir: Gregory Ratoff. Scr: Philip Dunne. Cast: Dolores del Rio (Dolores), George Sanders (Bruce), Peter Lorre (Sigfried), Virginia Field (Joan).

4233. *The Spy Who Came in From the Cold*
(John Le Carre [pseudonym for David Cornwell],
1963). A complex espionage tale about a British in-
telligence chief who, while posing as a defector to
East Germany, doubts his mission and his superiors. **Adaptation:** *The Spy Who Came In from
the Cold* (Paramount, 1965). Dir: Martin Ritt. Scr:
Paul Dehn, Guy Trosper. Cast: Richard Burton
(Leamas), Claire Bloom (Nan), Oskar Werner
(Fiedler), Sam Wanamaker (Peters), Rupert
Davies (Smiley), Cyril Cusack (Control), Peter
van Eyck (Mundt), Michael Hordern (Ashe),
Bernard Lee (Patmore). Notes: BAFTA Awards
for Best British Film, Actor (Burton), Art Direction, and Cinematography, and nominations
for Best Picture from Any Source and Actor
(Werner); Golden Globe Award for Best Supporting Actor (Werner); Academy Award nomina-
tions for Best Actor (Burton) and Art Direction.
DVD, VHS.

4234. *The Spy Who Loved Me* (Ian Fleming,
1962). Mobsters try to collect insurance money
by burning down a hotel owned by a woman
whom James Bond loves, and the spy shows up
just in time to save her. **Adaptation:** *The Spy Who
Loved Me* (United Artists, 1977). Dir: Lewis
Gilbert. Scr: Christopher Wood, Richard Maibaum.
Cast: Roger Moore (Bond), Barbara Bach (Anya),
Curt Jurgens (Stromberg), Richard Kiel (Jaws).
Notes: Despite the use of the title, the screenplay
has no connection with the novel. Rather, it concerns the collaboration of Bond and a female Soviet agent as they attempt to locate missing submarines carrying nuclear weapons. Screenwriter
Christopher Wood "novelized" the screenplay and
published it in 1977. DVD, VHS.

4235. *The Square Circle* (Daniel Carney,
1982). Mercenaries are hired to kidnap Nazi
Rudolf Hess from Berlin's Spandau prison. **Adap-
tation:** *Wild Geese II* (Universal, 1985). Dir: Peter
Hunt. Scr: Reginald Rose. Cast: Scott Glenn
(Haddad), Barbara Carrera (Kathy), Edward Fox
(Faulkner), Laurence Olivier (Hess), Robert Web-
ber (McCann). VHS. See also *The Wild Geese.*

4236. *Square Dance* (Alan Hines, 1984).
Coming-of-age novel about a thirteen-year-old
girl who leaves her severe grandfather's home in
rural Texas and visits with her estranged mother
in the city. **Adaptation:** *Square Dance*; broadcast
on U.S. television as *Home Is Where the Heart Is*
(Island, 1987). Dir: Daniel Petrie. Scr: Alan Hines.
Cast: Jason Robards (Grandpa Dillard), Jane
Alexander (Juanelle), Winona Ryder (Gemma),
Rob Lowe (Rory). DVD, VHS.

4237. *The Squeaker* (Edgar Wallace, 1927). A
disgraced policeman sets out to catch a dangerous
and notorious diamond fence known as "the
Squeaker." **Adaptation 1:** *The Squeaker* (British
Lion, 1930). Dir: Edgar Wallace. Scr: Edgar Wal-
lace. Cast: Percy Marmont (Captain Leslie), Anne
Grey (Beryl), Gordon Harker (Annerley), Trilby
Clark (Millie). **Adaptation 2:** *The Squeaker*; re-
leased in the U.S. as *Murder on Diamond Row*
(United Artists, 1937). Dir: William K. Howard.
Scr: Edward Berkman, Bryan Edgar Wallace.
Cast: Edmund Lowe (Inspector Barrabal), Sebas-
tian Shaw (Sutton), Ann Todd (Carol), Tamara
Desni (Tamara). VHS. **Adaptation 3:** *The
Squeaker* (UCC, 1963). Dir: Alfred Vohrer. Scr:
H. G. Petersson. Cast: Heinz Drache (Inspector
Elford), Barbara Rutting (Beryl), Gunter Pfitz-
mann (Sutton), Jan Hendriks (Leslie). VHS.

4238. *The Squeeze* (David Craig, 1974). In
London, an alcoholic former policeman rescues
the daughter of a friend from brutal kidnappers.
Adaptation: *The Squeeze* (Warner, 1977). Dir:
Michael Apted. Scr: Leon Griffiths. Cast: Stacy
Keach (Jim), David Hemmings (Keith), Edward
Fox (Foreman), Stephen Boyd (Vic). VHS.

Stage Fright (see "Man Running").

4239. *Stage Mother* (Bradford Ropes, 1932).
A widowed former vaudevillian will go to any
lengths to get her daughter into show business.
Adaptation: *Stage Mother* (MGM, 1933). Dir:
Charles R. Brabin. Scr: John Meehan, Bradford
Ropes. Cast: Alice Brady (Kitty), Maureen O'Sul-
livan (Shirley), Franchot Tone (Warren), Phillips
Holmes (Lord Aylesworth), Ted Healy (Ralph).

4240. "The Stage to Lordsburg" (Ernest
Haycox, 1937). Western about passengers aboard
a stagecoach attacked by warring Indians. The
short story originally appeared in the April 10,
1937, issue of *Colliers.* **Adaptation 1:** *Stagecoach*
(United Artists, 1939). Dir: John Ford. Scr: Dudley Nichols. Cast: Claire Trevor (Dallas), John
Wayne (the Ringo Kid), Andy Devine (Buck),
John Carradine (Hatfield), Thomas Mitchell (Doc
Boone). Notes: Academy Award for Best Supporting Actor (Mitchell) and Musical Score, and nominations for Best Picture, Director, Cinematography, Editing, and Art Direction. DVD, VHS.
Adaptation 2: *Stagecoach* (20th Century–Fox,
1966). Dir: Gordon Douglas. Scr: Dudley Nichols
(1939 screenplay), Joseph Landon. Cast: Ann-
Margret (Dallas), Red Buttons (Peacock), Mike
Connors (Hatfield), Alex Cord (the Ringo Kid),
Bing Crosby (Doc Boone), Bob Cummings

(Henry), Van Heflin (Marshal Wilcox), Slim Pickens (Buck), Stefanie Powers (Lucy), Keenan Wynn (Luke). **Adaptation 3:** *Stagecoach* (CBS, 1986 TV Movie). Dir: Ted Post. Scr: Dudley Nichols (1939 screenplay), James Lee Barrett. Cast: Willie Nelson (Doc Holliday), Kris Kristofferson (the Ringo Kid), Johnny Cash (Marshal Wilcox), Waylon Jennings (Hatfield), John Schneider (Buck), Elizabeth Ashley (Dallas), Anthony Newley (Peacock), Tony Franciosa (Gatewood), Mary Crosby (Lucy), June Carter Cash (Mrs. Pickett). VHS.

Stagecoach (*see* "Stage to Lordsburg").

4241. *Stairs of Sand* (Zane Grey, 1928). Western about a former stagecoach robber who helps a woman rancher when a cattle rustler raids her herd. The novel was serialized in *McCall's* in May and June 1928 and published as a book the same year. **Silent Film:**1929. **Adaptation:** *Arizona Mahoney* (Paramount, 1936). Dir: James P. Hogan. Scr: Stuart Anthony, Robert Yost. Cast: Joe Cook (Mahoney), Robert Cummings (Randall), Buster Crabbe (Talbot). VHS.

4242. *The Stalker* (Theodore Taylor, 1987). When his daughter's killer is released because he has diplomatic immunity from prosecution, an American military officer takes personal revenge. **Adaptation:** *Diplomatic Immunity* (Fries, 1991). Dir: Peter Maris. Scr: Randall Frakes, Jim Trombetta, Richard Donn. Cast: Bruce Boxleitner (Cole), Billy Drago (Cowboy), Tom Bresnahan (Klaus), Fabiana Udenio (Teresa), Christopher Neame (Stefan).

4243. *The Stalking Moon* (Theodore V. Olsen, 1965). Western about an aging army scout who helps a woman and her half-breed son escape from the Apache with whom she lived. The scout must protect the woman and the boy when his murderous father comes after them. **Adaptation:** *The Stalking Moon* (National General, 1969). Dir: Robert Mulligan. Scr: Wendell Mayes, Alvin Sargent. Cast: Gregory Peck (Sam), Eva Marie Saint (Sarah), Robert Forster (Nick), Noland Clay (the Boy). VHS.

4244. *Stalky & Co.* (Rudyard Kipling, 1899). Autobiographical novel about a group of spirited British schoolboys and the havoc they cause at school. **Adaptation:** *Stalky & Co.* (BBC, 1982 TV Miniseries). Dir: Rodney Bennett. Scr: Alexander Baron. Cast: Robert Addie (Stalky), David Parfitt (Beetle), Frederick Treves (the Headmaster), Paul Wilce (Tulke).

4245. *Stamboul Train* (Graham Greene, 1932). On board the famous Orient express from Turkey to England, a Jewish man and a chorus girl become involved in political intrigue and murder. The novel was released in the U.S. as *Orient Express*. **Adaptation:** *Orient Express* (Fox, 1934). Dir: Paul Martin. Scr: William M. Conselman, Carl Hovey. Cast: Heather Angel (Coral), Norman Foster (Carlton), Ralph Morgan (Dr. Czinner).

4246. *The Stand* (Stephen King, 1978). After the government accidentally unleashes a deadly plague decimating the population of the country, the survivors join the respective forces of good and evil, the former directed by an old woman who serves as God's agent, the latter led by a demonic figure. **Adaptation:** *The Stand* (ABC, 1994 TV Miniseries). Dir: Mick Garris. Scr: Stephen King. Cast: Gary Sinise (Stu), Molly Ringwald (Frannie), Jamey Sheridan (Flagg), Laura San Giacomo (Nadine), Ruby Dee (Mother Abigail), Ossie Davis (Judge Farris), Miguel Ferrer (Lloyd), Corin Nemec (Harold), Matt Frewer (Trashcan Man), Adam Storke (Larry), Ray Walston (Glen), Rob Lowe (Nick), Bill Fagerbakke (Tom). Notes: Emmy Awards for Outstanding Makeup and Sound, and nominations for Outstanding Miniseries, Art Direction, Cinematography, and Musical Score. DVD, VHS.

Stand by Me (see *The Body*).

4247. *Stand On It* (William Neely and Robert K. Ottum, 1973). A rebellious NASCAR driver clashes with his sponsor, the owner of a fast-food chain. **Adaptation:** *Stroker Ace* (Universal, 1983). Dir: Hal Needham. Scr: Hugh Wilson, Hal Needham. Cast: Burt Reynolds (Stroker), Ned Beatty (Clyde), Jim Nabors (Lugs), Parker Stevenson (Aubrey), Loni Anderson (Pembrook), John Byner (Doc Seegle). DVD, VHS.

4248. *Stand Up, Virgin Soldiers* (Leslie Thomas, 1975). The sequel to Thomas' comic 1966 book *The Virgin Soldiers* about raw British recruits in Singapore in 1950. **Adaptation:** *Stand Up, Virgin Soldiers* (Warner, 1977). Dir: Norman Cohen. Scr: Leslie Thomas. Cast: Robin Askwith (Brigg), Nigel Davenport (Driscoll), George Layton (Jacobs), John Le Mesurier (Colonel Bromley-Pickering). See also *The Virgin Soldiers*.

4249. *Standing in the Shadows of Motown: The Life and Music of Legendary Bassist James Jamerson* (Alan Slutsky, 1989). A musical history of bassist James Jamerson and the Funk Brothers, the anonymous back-up musicians who helped to shape the Motown Records sound beginning in the 1960's. **Adaptation:** *Standing in the Shadows of Motown* (Artisan, 2002). Dir: Paul Justman. Scr: Walter Dallas, Ntozake Shange. Cast: Andre Braugher (Narrator), Brian Marable (James Jamerson). Notes: The documentary includes interviews with Motown musicians and executives and archival footage of recording sessions. DVD, VHS.

Stanley and Iris (see *Union Street*).

4250. *Star* (Danielle Steel, 1989). In California after World War II, an aspiring actress and an older, socially prominent man meet and fall in love. **Adaptation:** *Star* (NBC, 1993 TV Movie). Dir: Michael Miller. Scr: Claire Labine. Cast: Jennie Garth (Crystal), Craig Bierko (Spencer), Terry Farrell (Elizabeth), Penny Fuller (Olivia), Mitch Ryan (Harrison). DVD, VHS.

Star in the Dust (see *Law Man*).

4251. *Star in the West* (Richard Emery Roberts, 1951). Comic Western about a widow who moves to Arizona and becomes a town's sheriff. **Adaptation:** *The Second Time Around* (20th Century–Fox, 1961). Dir: Vincent Sherman. Scr: Clair Huffaker (writing as Cecil Dan Hansen), Oscar Saul. Cast: Debbie Reynolds (Lucretia), Steve Forrest (Dan), Andy Griffith (Pat), Juliet Prowse (Rena), Thelma Ritter (Aggie).

Starlight Hotel (see *The Dream Monger*).

4252. *Stars and Bars* (William Boyd, 1984). Comedy about a British art expert who goes to Georgia to locate a lost Renoir and becomes involved with an eccentric rural family and mobsters. **Adaptation:** *Stars and Bars* (Columbia, 1988). Dir: Pat O'Connor. Scr: William Boyd. Cast: Daniel Day-Lewis (Henderson), Harry Dean Stanton (Loomis), Kent Broadhurst (Sereno), Maury Chaykin (Freeborn), Matthew Cowles (Beckman), Joan Cusack (Irene), Spalding Gray (Reverend Cardew), Glenne Headly (Cora). VHS.

Stars and Stripes Forever (see *Marching Along*).

4253. *Stars in My Crown* (Joe David Brown, 1949). After the Civil War, a feisty minister tames a rural Western town. **Adaptation:** *Stars in My Crown* (MGM, 1950). Dir: Jacques Tourneur. Scr: Margaret Fitts. Cast: Joel McCrea (Josiah), Ellen Drew (Harriet), Dean Stockwell (John), Alan Hale (Jed). VHS.

4254. *The Stars in Their Courses* (Harry Brown, 1960). Western about a gunfighter and an alcoholic sheriff who battle a vicious cattleman and avoid a range war. **Adaptation:** *El Dorado* (Paramount, 1966). Dir: Howard Hawks. Scr: Leigh Brackett. Cast: John Wayne (Cole), Robert Mitchum (Sheriff Harrah), James Caan (Mississippi), Charlene Holt (Maudie). DVD, VHS.

4255. *The Stars Look Down* (A. J. Cronin, 1935). The son of a Welsh coal miner aspires to public office to improve the harsh working conditions in the mines. **Adaptation 1:** *The Stars Look Down* (MGM, 1940). Dir: Carol Reed. Scr: A. Coppel, J. B. Williams. Cast: Michael Redgrave (David), Margaret Lockwood (Jenny), Emlyn Williams (Joe), Nancy Price (Martha). VHS. **Adaptation 2:** *The Stars Look Down* (Granada, 1974 TV Miniseries). Dir: Alan Grint, Roland Joffe. Scr: Alan Plater. Cast: Ian Hastings (David), Alun Armstrong (Joe), James Bate (Sammy), Avril Elgar (Martha). Notes: The novel was also adapted as a miniseries for Italian television in 1971.

4256. *Starship Troopers* (Robert A. Heinlein, 1959, Hugo Award). In the future, a group of high-school students try to become citizens by joining the military. When they do, however, they are sent to battle giant alien insects attempting to destroy humankind. **Adaptation:** *Starship Troopers* (TriStar, 1997). Dir: Paul Verhoeven. Scr: Ed Neumeier. Cast: Casper Van Dien (Johnny), Dina Meyer (Dizzy), Denise Richards (Carmen), Jake Busey (Ace), Neil Patrick Harris (Carl). DVD, VHS. Notes: A sequel, *Starship Troopers 2*, was released in 2004 (DVD, VHS). The book and film also inspired a 1999 television series titled *Roughnecks: The Starship Troopers* (DVD, VHS).

4257. *Starting Over* (Dan Wakefield, 1973). Comic novel about a divorced man who falls in love with a nursery-school teacher but still is not able to put aside his feelings for his ex-wife. **Adaptation:** *Starting Over* (Paramount, 1979). Dir: Alan J. Pakula. Scr: James L. Brooks. Cast: Burt Reynolds (Phil), Jill Clayburgh (Marilyn), Candice Bergen (Jessica), Charles Durning (Michael), Frances Sternhagen (Marva). Notes: Academy Award nominations for Best Actress (Clayburgh) and Supporting Actress (Bergen); Golden Globe nominations for Best Actor (Reynolds), Actress (Clayburgh), and Supporting Actress (Bergen). VHS.

4258. *State Fair* (Philip Stong, 1932). Comic tale of an Iowa pig farmer and his family enjoying a day at the state fair. A Broadway musical adaptation was staged in 1996. **Adaptation 1:** *State Fair* (1933). Dir: Henry King. Scr: Paul Green,

Sonya Levien. Cast: Janet Gaynor (Margie), Will Rogers (Abel), Lew Ayres (Pat), Sally Eilers (Emily). Notes: Academy Award nominations for Best Picture and Screenplay. VHS. **Adaptation 2:** *State Fair*, broadcast on American television as *It Happened One Summer* (20th Century–Fox, 1945). Dir: Walter Lang. Scr: Paul Green, Sonya Levien (1933 secreenplay), Oscar Hammerstein II. Cast: Jeanne Crain (Margie), Dana Andrews (Pat), Dick Haymes (Wayne), Vivian Blaine (Emily), Charles Winninger (Abel). Notes: A musical adaptation with the songs by Richard Rodgers and Oscar Hammerstein — the only music they wrote exclusively for a film score. Academy Award for Best Song and nomination for Best Musical Score. DVD, VHS. **Adaptation 3:** *State Fair* (20th Century–Fox, 1962). Dir: Jose Ferrer. Scr: Paul Green, Sonya Levien (1933 screenplay), Oscar Hammerstein II (1945 musical adaptation), Richard L. Breen. Cast: Pat Boone (Wayne), Bobby Darin (Jerry), Pamela Tiffin (Margie), Ann-Margret (Emily), Tom Ewell (Abel). VHS.

State Secret (*see* "Appointment with Fear").

4259. *The State Versus Elinor Norton* (Mary Roberts Rinehart, 1934). Torn between her lover and her jealous husband, a woman is suspected of committing murder and is tried for the crime. **Adaptation:** *Elinor Norton* (Fox, 1934). Dir: Hamilton MacFadden. Scr: Rose Franken, Philip Klein. Cast: Claire Trevor (Elinor), Gilbert Roland (Rene), Henrietta Crosman (Christine).

4260. *The Statement* (Brian Moore, 1995). An elderly man who was once a Nazi sympathizer responsible for the death of many Jews is discovered living in France, and the Catholic Church helps to conceal his real identity. **Adaptation:** *The Statement* (Sony, 2003). Dir: Norman Jewison. Scr: Ronald Harwood. Cast: Michael Caine (Brossard), Tilda Swinton (Annemarie), Jeremy Northam (Colonel Roux), Alan Bates (Bertier), Charlotte Rampling (Nicole), Ciaran Hinds (Pochon), Frank Finlay (Commissaire Vionnet). DVD, VHS.

4261. "The Statement of Randolph Carter" (H. P. Lovecraft, 1920). After the disappearance of his friend, a man tells the police that his friend descended a tunnel in an old cemetery and witnessed indescribable horrors which he communicated to him through a two-way phone they had concocted. The short story was written in 1919 and published in the May 1920 issue of *The Vagrant.* **Adaptation:** *Unnamable II: The Statement*

of Randolph Carter; also released as *The Unnamable Returns* (Prism, 1993). Dir: Jean-Paul Ouellette. Scr: Jean-Paul Ouellette. Cast: Mark Kinsey Stephenson (Carter), Charles Klausmeyer (Eliot), Maria Ford (Alyda), John Rhys-Davies (Professor Warren). Notes: The screenplay combines elements from this story and from Lovecraft's 1925 short story "The Unnamable." VHS. See also "The Unnamable."

4262. *Station West* (Luke Short [pseudonym for Frederick D. Glidden], 1946. Western about an undercover military intelligence officer who goes undercover to break up a gang of gold robbers. The novel was originally published as a seven-part serial in *The Saturday Evening Post* (October 19–November 30, 1946) and was published as a book in 1947. **Adaptation:** *Station West* (RKO, 1948). Dir: Sidney Lanfield. Scr: Frank Fenton, Winston Miller. Cast: Dick Powell (Haven), Jane Greer (Charlie), Agnes Moorehead (Mrs. Caslon), Tom Powers (Captain Isles). VHS.

4263. *Stay Away, Joe* (Dan Cushman, 1953). A Native American rodeo rider returns to his reservation in search of personal fulfillment. The book was adapted as a Broadway musical titled *Whoop Up* in 1958. **Adaptation:** *Stay Away, Joe* (MGM, 1968). Dir: Peter Tewksbury. Scr: Michael A. Hoey. Cast: Elvis Presley (Joe), Burgess Meredith (Charlie), Joan Blondell (Glenda), Katy Jurado (Annie), Thomas Gomez (Grandpa). VHS.

4264. *Stay Hungry* (Charles Gaines, 1972). The heir to a real-estate syndicate in Alabama incurs the wrath of his wealthy family by befriending people in a small body-building gym. **Adaptation:** *Stay Hungry* (United Artists, 1976). Dir: Bob Rafelson. Scr: Charles Gaines, Bob Rafelson. Cast: Jeff Bridges (Craig), Sally Field (Mary), Arnold Schwarzenegger (Joe), R. G. Armstrong (Thor), Robert Englund (Franklin). DVD, VHS.

4265. *Stealing Heaven: The Story of Heloise and Abelard* (Marion Meade, 1979). Fictionalized account of twelfth-century love affair between an aristocratic woman and her tutor. **Adaptation:** *Stealing Heaven* (Scotti, 1988). Dir: Clive Donner. Scr: Chris Bryant. Cast: Derek de Lint (Abelard), Kim Thomson (Heloise), Denholm Elliott (Fulbert), Kenneth Cranham (Suger). VHS.

4266. *Steamboat Round the Bend* (Ben Lucien Burman, 1933). A Mississippi steamboat captain helps to clear his nephew of murder charges. **Adaptation:** *Steamboat Round the Bend* (Fox, 1935). Dir: John Ford. Scr: Dudley Nichols, Lamar Trotti. Cast: Will Rogers (Dr. Pearly),

Anne Shirley (Fleety), Irvin S. Cobb (Captain Eli), Eugene Pallette (Sheriff Jeffers).

4267. *The Steel Mirror* (Donald Hamilton, 1948). A man whose car breaks down accepts a ride from a woman and becomes involved in a deadly scheme. The novel appeared as an eight-part serial in *The Saturday Evening Post* (April 21–October 9, 1948). **Adaptation:** *5 Steps to Danger* (United Artists, 1957). Dir: Henry S. Kesler. Scr: Henry S. Kesler. Cast: Ruth Roman (Ann), Sterling Hayden (John), Werner Klemperer (Dr. Simmons), Richard Gaines (Brant).

4268. *Steel Saraband* (Roger Dataller, 1938). After his promotion on the job, a steel worker's proud arrogance costs him his wife and friends. **Adaptation:** *Hard Steel*; also released as *What Shall It Profit?* (GHW, 1942). Dir: Norman Walker. Scr: Lydia Hayward. Cast: Wilfrid Lawson (Walter), Betty Stockfeld (Freda), John Stuart (Alan).

4269. *Stella* (Jan De Hartog, 1950). During World War II, a woman gives herself freely to seamen to ease their pain and anxiety. **Adaptation:** *The Key* (Columbia, 1958). Dir: Carol Reed. Scr: Carl Foreman. Cast: William Holden (David), Sophia Loren (Stella), Trevor Howard (Chris). VHS.

Stella (1990) (see *Stella Dallas*).

4270. *Stella Dallas* (Olive Higgins Prouty, 1923). An uncouth working-class woman sacrifices herself so that her daughter can have a better life than she did. **Silent Film:** 1925. **Adaptation 1:** *Stella Dallas* (Samuel Goldwyn/United Artists, 1937). Dir: King Vidor. Scr: Sarah Y. Mason, Victor Heerman. Cast: Barbara Stanwyck (Stella), John Boles (Stephen), Anne Shirley (Laurel), Barbara O'Neil (Helen), Alan Hale (Ed). Notes: Academy Award nominations for Best Actress (Stanwyck) and Supporting Actress (Shirley). DVD, VHS. **Adaptation 2:** *Stella* (Samuel Goldwyn/Buena Vista, 1990). Dir: John Erman. Scr: Robert Getchell. Cast: Bette Midler (Stella), John Goodman (Ed), Trini Alvarado (Jenny), Stephen Collins (Stephen), Marsha Mason (Janice), Eileen Brennan (Mrs. Wilkerson). DVD, VHS.

4271. *The Stepford Wives* (Ira Levin, 1972). A couple move to a suburban town, where all of the women, once feminists, are now robotic traditional housewives. **Adaptation 1:** *The Stepford Wives* (Columbia, 1975). Dir: Bryan Forbes. Scr: William Goldman. Cast: Katharine Ross (Joanna), Paula Prentiss (Bobbie), Peter Masterson (Walter), Nanette Newman (Carol), Tina Louise (Charmaine). DVD, VHS. **Adaptation 2:** *The Stepford Wives* (Paramount, 2004). Dir: Frank Oz. Scr: Paul Rudnick. Cast: Nicole Kidman (Joanna), Matthew Broderick (Walter), Bette Midler (Bobbie), Glenn Close (Claire), Christopher Walken (Mike), Roger Bart (Roger), David Marshall Grant (Jerry), Jon Lovitz (Dave), Faith Hill (Sarah). DVD, VHS. Notes Three made-for-television sequels followed the original film in 1975: *Revenge of the Stepford Wives* (1980) (VHS); *The Stepford Children* (1987) (VHS); and *The Stepford Husbands* (1996) (VHS).

4272. *Steppenwolf* (Hermann Hesse, 1927). This novel by the 1946 winner of the Nobel Prize for Literature is about a misanthropic writer who considers himself a social outsider and therefore disdains everyday life. He is changed when he meets a young woman who introduces him to a redemptive world of magic and illusion. **Adaptation:** *Steppenwolf* (DR Films, 1974). Dir: Fred Haines. Scr: Fred Haines. Cast: Max von Sydow (Harry), Dominique Sanda (Hermine), Pierre Clementi (Pablo), Carla Romanelli (Maria). VHS.

4273. *The Sterile Cuckoo* (John Nichols, 1965). A lonely college student forces herself on a naïve freshman and a strange romantic relationship develops. **Adaptation:** *The Sterile Cuckoo*; released in the UK as *Pookie* (Paramount, 1969). Dir: Alan J. Pakula. Scr: Alvin Sargent. Cast: Liza Minnelli (Pookie), Wendell Burton (Jerry), Tim McIntire (Charlie). Notes: Academy Awards nominations for Best Actress (Minnelli) and Song; BAFTA nomination for Most Promising Newcomer (Minnelli); Golden Globe nomination for Best Actress (Minnelli). VHS.

4274. *Stick* (Elmore Leonard, 1983). A former convict tries to avenge a close friend's death and becomes involved with drug dealers. **Adaptation:** *Stick* (Universal, 1985). Dir: Burt Reynolds. Scr: Elmore Leonard, Joseph Stinson. Cast: Burt Reynolds (Stickley), Candice Bergen (Kyle), George Segal (Barry), Charles Durning (Chucky). VHS.

4275. *Stiletto* (Harold Robbins, 1960). A wealthy playboy who works as a Mafia assassin wants to quit and is pursued by the mob. **Adaptation:** *Stiletto* (AVCO Embassy, 1969). Dir Bernard L. Kowalski. Scr: A. J. Russell. Cast: Alex Cord (Cesare), Britt Ekland (Illeano), Patrick O'Neal (Baker), Joseph Wiseman (Matteo), Barbara McNair (Ahn). VHS.

4276. *Still Missing* (Beth Richardson Gutcheon, 1981). The true story of a mother who tries to find her missing six-year-old son, alienating friends and government officials in the process. **Adaptation:** *Without a Trace* (20th Century–Fox, 1983). Dir: Stanley R. Jaffe. Scr: Beth Gutcheon. Cast: Kate Nelligan (Susan), Judd Hirsch (Al), David Dukes (Graham), Stockard Channing (Jocelyn), Jacqueline Brookes (Margaret). VHS.

4277. *Stillwatch* (Mary Higgins Clark, 1984). While investigating a politician, a television reporter tries to confront her horrible past by moving into the house in Washington where her father murdered her mother and tried to kill her. **Adaptation:** *Stillwatch* (CBS, 1987 TV Movie). Dir: Rod Holcomb. Scr: Laird Koenig, David E. Peckinpah. Cast: Lynda Carter (Patricia), Angie Dickinson (Abigail), Don Murray (Sam), Barry Primus (Toby), Louise Latham (Lila), Stuart Whitman (Luther).

4278. *Stir of Echoes* (Richard Matheson, 1958). A man hypnotized at a party is haunted by bizarre premonitions and terrifying visions of the ghost of a murdered child. **Adaptation:** *Stir of Echoes* (Artisan, 1999). Dir: David Koepp. Scr: David Koepp. Cast: Kevin Bacon (Tom), Kathryn Erbe (Maggie), Illeana Douglas (Lisa), Zachary David Cope (Jake), Kevin Dunn (Frank). DVD, VHS.

Stockade (see *Count a Lonely Cadence*).

4279. *The Stolen White Elephant* (Mark Twain [pseudonym for Samuel Langhorne Clemens], 1882). A young girl runs away with a circus elephant and is pursued by its owner. The novella was published in the 1882 collection *The Stolen White Elephant, Etc.* **Adaptation:** *Ava's Magical Adventure* (Prism, 1994). Dir: Patrick Dempsey, Rocky Parker. Cast: Skyler Shaye (Ava), Kandra Baker (Colleen), Priscilla Barnes (Sarah), Timothy Bottoms (Slayton), Patrick Dempsey (Jeffrey). VHS.

Stone Cold Dead (see *The Sin Sniper*).

4280. *A Stone for Danny Fisher* (Harold Robbins, 1952). A naïve young boxer is drawn into involvement with racketeers. **Adaptation:** *King Creole* (Paramount, 1958). Dir: Michael Curtiz. Scr: Herbert Baker, Michael V. Gazzo. Cast: Elvis Presley (Danny), Carolyn Jones (Ronnie), Walter Matthau (Maxie), Dolores Hart (Nellie), Dean Jagger (Mr. Fisher). Notes: The central character in the screenplay is a night-club singer rather than a boxer. DVD, VHS.

The Stone Killers (see *A Complete State of Death*).

4281. *Stonewall* (Martin Duberman, 1993). History of a police raid on a Greenwich Village gay club in 1969 and the subsequent riots that marked the beginning of the gay political movement in New York. **Adaptation:** *Stonewall* (BBC/Strand, 1995). Dir: Nigel Finch. Scr: Rikki Beadle Blair. Cast: Guillermo Díaz (La Miranda), Fred Weller (Matty), Brendan Corbalis (Ethan), Duane Boutte (Bostonia). DVD, VHS.

4282. *Stop at a Winner* (R. F. Delderfield, 1961). Comic novel about a British schemer and his partner who are drafted into the military during World War II and become heroes unintentionally. **Adaptation:** *On the Fiddle*; released in the U. S as *Operation Snafu* and reissued as *Operation War Head* (American International, 1961). Dir: Cyril Frankel. Scr: Harold Buchman. Cast: Alfred Lynch (Horace), Sean Connery (Pascoe), Cecil Parker (Captain Bascombe), Stanley Holloway (Mr. Cooksley), Alan King (Sergeant Buzzer). VHS.

Stop Me Before I Kill! (see *The Full Treatment*).

4283. *Stopover Tokyo* (John P. Marquand, 1957). An American spy is sent to Tokyo to capture a communist agent. The book, also published as *The Last of Mr. Moto*, is among the final installments in Marquand's series featuring Japanese-American detective Mr. Moto, who plays a minor role in this book. **Adaptation:** *Stopover Tokyo* (20th Century–Fox, 1957). Dir: Richard L. Breen. Scr: Richard L. Breen, Walter Reisch. Cast: Robert Wagner (Mark), Joan Collins (Tina), Edmond O'Brien (Underwood), Ken Scott (Tony). Notes: The character Mr. Moto does not appear in the screenplay. VHS.

4284. *Storm Boy* (Colin Thiele, 1963). Children's book about a lonely young boy who adopts a pet pelican. **Adaptation:** *Storm Boy* (South Australian Film/Roadshow, 1976). Dir: Henri Safran. Scr: Sonia Borg, Sidney L. Stebel. Cast: Greg Rowe (Mike), Peter Cummins (Tom), David Gulpilil (Fingerbone), Judy Dick (Miss Walker). Notes: Australian Film Institute Award for Best Picture and nomination for Best Director, Screenplay, Actor (Gulpilil), Costume Design, Production Design, and Sound.

4285. *Storm Fear* (Clinton Seeley, 1954). Three bank robbers on the run from the police hide in a mountain cabin during a fierce snow storm. **Adaptation:** *Storm Fear* (United Artists, 1955). Dir: Cornel Wilde. Scr: Horton Foote. Cast: Cornel Wilde (Charlie), Jean Wallace (Elizabeth), Dan Duryea (Fred), Lee Grant (Edna).

Storm Over the Nile (see *The Four Feathers*).

4286. *A Story Like the Wind* (Laurens Van Der Post, 1972). After his family is killed by ivory poachers, a teenaged boy escapes from the killers with the help of a young African bushman. **Adaptation:** *A Far Off Place* (Amblin/Disney/Buena Vista, 1993). Dir: Mikael Salomon. Scr: Robert Caswell, Jonathan Hensleigh, Sally Robinson. Cast: Reese Witherspoon (Nonnie), Ethan Randall (Harry), Jack Thompson (Ricketts), Maximilian Schell (Theron). Notes: The screenplay combines elements from this book and its 1974 sequel *A Far Off Place*. DVD, VHS. See also *A Far Off Place*.

Story of a Love Story (see *Impossible Object*).

4287. *The Story of an African Farm* (Olive Schreiner, 1883). Semi-autobiographical story about the life of an independent feminist on an ostrich farm in South Africa in the mid–nineteenth century. The book was controversial in its time because of its feminist and anti–Christian themes. **Adaptation:** *The Story of an African Farm* (Rodini, 2004). Dir: David Lister. Scr: Thandi Brewer, Bonnie Rodini. Cast: Luke Gallant (Waldo), Richard E. Grant (Bonaparte), Kasha Kropinski (Lyndall), Armin Mueller-Stahl (Otto).

4288. *The Story of Doctor Doolittle* (Hugh Lofting, 1920). The first of a series of novels and short stories about a British veterinarian who can talk with animals and understand their languages. **Adaptation 1:** *Doctor Dolittle* (20th Century–Fox, 1967). Dir: Richard Fleischer. Scr: Leslie Bricusse. Cast: Rex Harrison (Dr. Dolittle), Samantha Eggar (Emma), Anthony Newley (Matthew), Richard Attenborough (Albert), Peter Bull (General Bellowes). Notes: The screenplay for this musical adaptation includes elements from several of Lofting's Doolittle books and stories. Academy Awards for Best Special Effects and Song, and nominations for Best Picture, Musical Score, Cinematography, Editing, Art Direction, and Sound; Golden Globe Award for Best Supporting Actor (Attenborough) and nominations for Best Picture, Actor (Harrison), Musical Score, and Song. DVD, VHS. **Adaptation 2:** *Doctor Dolittle* (20th Century–Fox, 1998). Dir: Betty Thomas. Scr: Nat Mauldin, Larry Levin. Cast: Eddie Murphy (Dr. Dolittle), Ossie Davis (Archer), Oliver Platt (Dr. Weller), Peter Boyle (Calloway), Richard Schiff (Dr. Reiss), Kristen Wilson (Lisa), Jeffrey Tambor (Dr. Fish). Notes: In this screenplay, which combines elements from various Doolittle books and stories, the veterinarian is an American.

DVD, VHS. Notes: A sequel, *Dr. Doolittle 2*, was released in 2001 (DVD, VHS).

4289. *The Story of Dr. Wassell* (James Hilton, 1943). The true story of Dr. Corydon M. Wassell, a naval doctor who aided wounded soldiers in Java during World War II. **Adaptation:** *The Story of Dr. Wassell* (Paramount, 1944). Dir: Cecil B. DeMille. Scr: Charles Bennett, Alan Le May. Cast: Gary Cooper (Dr. Wassell), Laraine Day (Madeleine), Signe Hasso (Bettina), Dennis O'Keefe (Hopkins). VHS.

4290. *The Story of Esther Costello* (Nicholas Monsarrat, 1953). A young woman left deaf and blind after an accident is adopted by a wealthy woman, who establishes an international charitable foundation in the girl's name. **Adaptation:** *The Story of Esther Costello*; released in the U.S. as *The Golden Virgin* (Columbia, 1957). Dir: David Miller. Scr: Charles Kaufman. Cast: Joan Crawford (Margaret), Rossano Brazzi (Carlo), Heather Sears (Esther), Lee Patterson (Harry). Notes: BAFTA Award for Best British Actress (Sears) and nomination for Best Screenplay; Golden Globe nomination for Best Supporting Actress (Sears). VHS.

Story of G. I. Joe (see *Here Is Your War*).

4291. *The Story of Ivy* (Marie Belloc Lowndes, 1927). In Edwardian England, a beautiful woman poisons her husband and her lover in order to pursue a relationship with a wealthy older man. **Adaptation:** *Ivy* (Universal, 1947). Dir: Sam Wood. Scr: Charles Bennett. Cast: Joan Fontaine (Ivy), Patric Knowles (Roger), Herbert Marshall (Miles), Richard Ney (Jervis), Cedric Hardwicke (Inspector Orpington).

4292. *The Story of Mankind* (Hendrik Van Loon, 1921, Newbery Award). Children's book featuring highlights from human history. **Adaptation:** *The Story of Mankind* (Warner, 1957). Dir: Irwin Allen. Scr: Irwin Allen, Charles Bennett. Cast: Ronald Colman (the Spirit of Man), Hedy Lamarr (Joan of Arc), Groucho Marx (Peter Minuet), Harpo Marx (Sir Isaac Newton), Chico Marx (Monk), Virginia Mayo (Cleopatra), Agnes Moorehead (Queen Elizabeth), Vincent Price (the Devil), Peter Lorre (Nero). Notes: The adaptation features a comic heavenly debate over whether people should be allowed to endure given humankind's violent history.

4293. *The Story of O* (Pauline Reage [pseudonym for Anne Desclos], 1954). An erotic French novel, originally titled *L'histoire d'O*, about a Paris fashion photographer who agrees to participate in her lover's sadomasochistic fantasies. The book, which was translated in 1954 and again in 1957, is sometimes published under Desclos' other pseudonym, Dominique Aury. **Adaptation 1:** *The Story of O* (Allied Artists, 1975). Dir: Just Jaeckin. Scr: Sebastien Japrisot. Cast: Corinne Clery (O), Udo Kier (Rene), Anthony Steel (Sir Stephen). DVD, VHS. **Adaptation 2:** *The Story of O: Untold Pleasures* (Pathfinder, 2002). Dir: Phil Leirness. Scr: Phil Leirness, Ron Norman. Cast: Danielle Ciardi (O), Neil Dickson (Sir Stephen), Max Parrish (Rene).

The Story of Temple Drake (see *Sanctuary*).

4294. *The Story of the Trapp Family Singers* (Maria Agusta Von Trapp, 1949). Autobiography of an Austrian woman who left her convent as a novice nun to care for a widowed man's seven children. The man and his children fall in love with her, and he breaks his engagement to an aristocratic woman to marry her. When the Nazis demand that he return to service as a naval captain in 1938, she helps the family escape to America. The book was the basis for the hit 1959 Broadway musical *The Sound of Music* (book by Howard Lindsay and Russel Crouse and music by Richard Rodgers and Oscar Hammerstein). **Adaptation 1:** *The Trapp Family* (Divina/20th Century–Fox, 1956). Dir: Wolfgang Liebeneiner. Scr: George Hurdalek, Herbert Reinecker. Cast: Ruth Leuwerik (Maria), Hans Holt (Baron Trapp), Maria Holst (Graefin), Josef Meinrad (Wasne). Notes: A sequel, *The Trapp Family in America*, was released in 1958. **Adaptation 2:** *The Sound of Music* (20th Century–Fox, 1965). Dir: Robert Wise. Scr: Ernest Lehman (based on the 1959 musical play). Cast: Julie Andrews (Maria), Christopher Plummer (Captain Von Trapp), Richard Haydn (Max), Peggy Wood (Mother Abbess), Anna Lee (Sister Margaretta). Notes: Academy Awards for Best Picture, Director, Musical Score, Editing, and Sound, and nominations for Best Actress (Andrews), Supporting Actress (Wood), Art Direction, Cinematography, and Costume Design; Golden Globe Awards for Best Picture and Actress (Andrews), and nominations for Best Director and Supporting Actress (Wood); BAFTA nomination for Best British Actress (Andrews). DVD, VHS.

The Story of Vernon and Irene Castle (see *My Husband*).

Storyville (see *Juryman*).

Stowaway Girl (see *Manuela*).

Straight Time (see *No Beast So Fierce*).

Stranded (see *Swiss Family Robinson*).

4295. *The Strange Affair* (Bernard Toms, 1966). A young and idealistic London policeman exposes corruption in his department and pays the price. **Adaptation:** *The Strange Affair* (Paramount, 1968). Dir: David Greene. Scr: Eve Greene, Stanley Mann, Jerome Odlum, Oscar Saul. Cast: Michael York (Peter), Jeremy Kemp (Detective Pierce), Susan George (Freddie), Jack Watson (Quince).

Strange Boarders (see *The Strange Boarders of Palace Crescent*).

4296. *The Strange Boarders of Palace Crescent* (E. Phillips Oppenheim, 1934). A newlywed police detective postpones his honeymoon and goes undercover in a boarding house to catch a spy. The novel originally appeared as a seven-part serial in *The Saturday Evening Post* (April 7–May 19, 1934) and was published as a book in 1935. **Adaptation:** *Strange Boarders* (Gaumont, 1938). Dir: Herbert Mason. Scr: Sidney Gilliat, A. R. Rawlinson. Cast: Tom Walls (Tommy), Renee Saint-Cyr (Louise), Googie Withers (Elsie), Ronald Adam (Barstow).

Strange Cargo (see *Not Too Narrow, Not To Deep*).

4297. *The Strange Case of Dr. Jekyll and Mr. Hyde* (Robert Louis Stevenson, 1886). Stevenson's classic novel about a scientist who invents an uncontrollable drug that brings out his evil nature. **Silent Films:** 1908, 1910, 1912, 1913 and three productions in 1920, including the famous version directed by John S. Robertson and starring John Barrymore (DVD, VHS). **Adaptation 1:** *Dr. Jekyll and Mr. Hyde* (Paramount, 1931). Dir: Rouben Mamoulian. Scr: Samuel Hoffenstein, Percy Heath. Cast: Fredric March (Dr. Jekyll/Mr. Hyde), Miriam Hopkins (Ivy), Rose Hobart (Muriel). Notes: Academy Award for Best Actor (March) and nominations for Best Screenplay and Cinematography. DVD, VHS. **Adaptation 2:** *Dr. Jekyll and Mr. Hyde* (MGM, 1941). Dir: Victor Fleming. Scr: John Lee Mahin. Cast: Spencer Tracy (Dr. Jekyll/Mr. Hyde), Ingrid Bergman (Ivy), Lana Turner (Beatrix), Donald Crisp (Sir Charles). Notes: Academy Award nominations for Best Cinematography, Musical Score, and Editing. DVD, VHS. **Adaptation 3:** *The Two Faces of Dr. Jekyll*; released in the U.S. as *House of Fright* (Hammer/American International, 1960). Dir: Terence Fisher. Scr: Wolf Mankowitz. Cast: Paul

Massie (Dr. Jekyll/Mr. Hyde), Dawn Addams (Kitty), Christopher Lee (Paul). VHS. **Adaptation 4:** *Dr. Jekyll and Mr. Hyde* (ABC, 1968 TV Movie). Dir: Charles Jarrott. Scr: Ian McLellan Hunter. Cast: Jack Palance (Dr. Jekyll/Mr. Hyde), Denholm Elliott (Devlin), Tessie O'Shea (Tessie). DVD, VHS. **Adaptation 5:** *I, Monster* (Cannon, 1971). Dir: Stephen Weeks. Scr: Milton Subotsky. Cast: Christopher Lee (Dr. Marlowe/Mr. Blake), Peter Cushing (Utterson), Mike Raven (Enfield). Notes: The same story with different character names. VHS. **Adaptation 6:** *Dr. Jekyll and Mr. Hyde* (NBC, 1973 TV Movie). Dir: David Winters. Scr: Sherman Yellen. Cast: Kirk Douglas (Dr. Jekyll/Mr. Hyde), Susan George (Anne), Stanley Holloway (Poole), Michael Redgrave (Utterson), Donald Pleasence (Smudge). Notes: A musical adaptation. **Adaptation 7:** *Dr. Jekyll and Mr. Hyde* (PBS, 1981 TV Movie). Dir: Alastair Reid. Scr: Alastair Reid. Cast: David Hemmings (Dr. Jekyll/Mr. Hyde), Ian Bannen (Utterson), Lisa Harrow (Ann), Diana Dors (Kate). **Adaptation 8:** *The Strange Case of Dr. Jekyll and Mr. Hyde* (Cannon, 1989 TV Movie). Dir: Michael Lindsay-Hogg. Scr: J. Michael Straczynski. Cast: Anthony Andrews (Dr. Jekyll/Mr. Hyde), Nicholas Guest (Richard), Laura Dern (Rebecca). VHS. **Adaptation 9:** *Edge of Sanity* (Millimeter/Allied, 1989). Dir: Gerard Kikoïne. Scr: J. P. Felix, Ron Raley, Edward Simons. Cast: Anthony Perkins (Dr. Jekyll/Mr. Hyde), Glynis Barber (Elisabeth), Sarah Maur Thorp (Susannah). Notes: A variant on the original story, with Jekyll transforming himself into Jack the Ripper. DVD, VHS. **Adaptation 10:** *Jekyll & Hyde* (London Weekend Television/King Phoenix, 1990 TV Movie). Dir: David Wickes. Scr: David Wickes. Cast: Michael Caine (Dr. Jekyll/Mr. Hyde), Cheryl Ladd (Sara), Joss Ackland (Dr. Lanyon), Ronald Pickup (Utterson). Notes: Emmy and Golden Globe nominations for Best Actor (Caine). VHS. **Adaptation 11:** *Dr. Jekyll & Mr. Hyde* (Telescene, 1999 TV Movie). Dir: Colin Budds. Scr: Peter M. Lenkov. Cast: Adam Baldwin (Dr. Jekyll/Mr. Hyde), Steve Bastoni (McAfee/Newcomen), Anthony Wong (Barry). Notes: An updated version with the Jekyll/Hyde character as a martial-arts expert. DVD, VHS. **Adaptation 12:** *Dr. Jekyll and Mr. Hyde* (Redfield Arts, 2002). Dir: Mark Redfield. Scr: Mark Redfield, Stuart Voytilla. Cast: Mark Redfield (Dr. Jekyll/Mr. Hyde), Elena Torrez (Claire), Kosha Engler (Miriam), Carl Randolph (Utterson). DVD, VHS. **Adaptation 13:** *Jekyll & Hyde: The Musical* (Broadway Television, 2001 TV Movie).

Dir: Don Roy King. Scr: Leslie Bricusse, Frank Wildhorn. Cast: David Hasselhoff (Dr. Jekyll/Mr. Hyde), Coleen Sexton (Lucy), Andrea Rivette (Emma), George Merritt (Utterson), Barrie Ingham (Carew). Notes: Leslie Bricusse and Frank Wildhorn's Broadway musical taped at a live performance. DVD, VHS. **Adaptation 14:** *Dr. Jekyll and Mr. Hyde* (Clerkenwell/Working Title, 2002 TV Movie). Dir: Maurice Phillips. Scr: Martyn Hesford. Cast: John Hannah (Dr. Jekyll/Mr. Hyde), David Warner (Carew), Gerard Horan (Utterson). **Adaptation 15:** *The Dr. Jekyll & Mr. Hyde Rock 'n Roll Musical* (Omega, 2003). Dir: Andre Champagne. Scr: Alan Bernhoft, Robert Ricucci. Cast: Alan Bernhoft (Dr. Jekyll/Mr. Hyde), Susannah Devereux (Amanda), John Heffron (Utterson). Notes: As the title states, a musical adaptation. In addition to these film adaptations, Stevenson's famous story has also spawned a number of reworkings and spoofs, including *Extrano caso del hombre y la bestia* (*The Strange Case of the Man and Beast*), a Spanish-language film directed by Mario Soffici (1951); *Son of Dr. Jekyll* (1951); *Abbot and Costello Meet Dr. Jekyll and Mr. Hyde* (1953) (VHS); *La Testament du Docteur Cordelier* (1959), a French film directed by Jean Renoir; Jerry Lewis's *The Nutty Professor* (1963) (DVD, VHS); *Dr. Jekyll and Sister Hyde* (1971) (DVD, VHS); *The Man with Two Heads* (1972); *Jekyll and Hyde ... Together Again* (1982) VHS; *Dr. Jekyll and Ms. Hyde* (1995) (DVD, VHS); Eddie Murphy's *The Nutty Professor* (1996) (DVD, VHS) and *Nutty Professor II: The Klumps* (2000) (DVD, VHS); *Dr. Jekyll and Mistress Hyde* (2003) (DVD, VHS); *Jekyll* (2004). See also *Mary Reilly.*

The Strange Door (*see* "The Sire de Maletroit's Door").

Strange Incident (see *The Ox-Bow Incident*).

Strange Intruder (see *The Intruder*).

The Strange One (see *End as a Man*).

The Strange Ones (see *Les Enfants Terribles*).

Strange Wives (*see* "Bread Upon the Waters").

4298. *The Strange Woman* (Ben Ames Williams, 1941). In nineteenth-century Maine, a beautiful woman manipulates men to get her way. **Adaptation:** *The Strange Woman* (United Artists, 1946). Dir: Edgar Ulmer. Scr: Herb Meadow, Hunt Stromberg, Edgar Ulmer. Cast: Hedy Lamarr (Jenny), George Sanders (John), Louis

Hayward (Ephraim), Gene Lockhart (Isaiah). DVD, VHS.

4299. *The Strange World of Planet X* (Rene Ray, 1956). A mad scientist experimenting with magnetic fields accidentally allows insects to mutate into huge flesh eaters. **Adaptation:** *The Strange World of Planet X*; released in the U.S. as *The Cosmic Monster* (Eros/DCA, 1957). Dir: Gilbert Gunn. Scr: Paul Ryder. Cast: Forrest Tucker (Gil), Gaby Andre (Michele), Martin Benson (Smith), Alec Mango (Dr. Laird), Wyndham Goldie (General Cartwright). VHS. Notes: The book was the basis for a 1956 television series in England, and this film followed the program's success.

4300. *The Stranger* (Albert Camus, 1942). Camus' famous existential novel *L'Etranger* is about a Frenchman in Algiers who is accused and convicted of killing a young Arab man on a beach. The novel was first translated into English in 1946 and released as *The Stranger* in the United States and as *The Outsider* in Great Britain. **Adaptation:** *The Stranger* (Paramount, 1967). Dir: Luchino Visconti. Scr: Suso Cecchi D'Amico, Georges Conchon, Emmanuel Robles, Luchino Visconti. Cast: Marcello Mastroianni (Meursault), Anna Karina (Marie), Bernard Blier (the Defense Counsel), Georges Wilson (the Magistrate), Bruno Cremer (the Priest), Pierre Bertin (the Judge). Notes: Golden Globe nomination for Best Foreign-Language Film. VHS.

4301. *The Stranger* (Lillian Bos Ross, 1942). Western about a man who goes to live on the American frontier with his mail-order bride. **Adaptation:** *Zandy's Bride*; broadcast on American television as *For Better, For Worse* (Warner, 1974). Dir: Jan Troell. Scr: Marc Norman. Cast: Gene Hackman (Zandy), Liv Ullmann (Hannah), Eileen Heckart (Ma Allan), Susan Tyrrell (Maria), Harry Dean Stanton (Songer). VHS.

The Stranger (1961) (see *The Intruder* by Charles Beaumont).

4302. *Stranger at Home* (George Sanders [ghostwritten by Leigh Brackett], 1946). After being assaulted in Asia, an Englishman loses his memory. When he returns home three years later, he becomes involved in a murder plot. The novel was written by Leigh Brackett and published under the name of actor George Sanders. **Adaptation:** *A Stranger Came Home*; released in the U.S. as *The Unholy Four* (Hammer/Lippert, 1954). Dir: Terence Fisher. Scr: Michael Carreras. Cast: William Sylvester (Philip), Paulette Goddard (Angie), Patrick Holt (Crandall), Paul Carpenter (Bill). VHS.

4303. *The Stranger Beside Me* (Ann Rule, 1980). Autobiographical book about serial murderer Ted Bundy, with whom Ann Rule had worked years before his killing spree. **Adaptation:** *The Stranger Beside Me* (USA Network, 2003 TV Movie). Dir. Paul Shapiro. Scr: Matthew McDuffie, Matthew Tabak. Cast: Billy Campbell (Ted Bundy), Barbara Hershey (Ann Rule), Brenda James (Margo).

A Stranger Came Home (see *Stranger at Home*).

A Stranger in My Arms (see *And Ride a Tiger*).

4304. *A Stranger in the Kingdom* (Howard Frank Mosher, 1989). In Vermont in the 1950's, a new minister is chosen based on his sterling military record, but the townspeople are shocked to discover that he is black. When an abused young white woman to whom he is providing shelter is found murdered, he is accused of the crime. **Adaptation:** *Stranger in the Kingdom* (Ardustry, 1998). Dir: Jay Craven. Scr: Don Bredes, Jay Craven. Cast: David Lansbury (Charlie), Ernie Hudson (Reverend Andrews), Martin Sheen (Moulton), Bill Raymond (Resolved), Sean Nelson (Nathan). DVD, VHS.

4305. *A Stranger in the Mirror* (Sidney Sheldon, 1976). A famous comedian and a beautiful starlet with a mysterious past form a tempestuous relationship. **Adaptation:** *A Stranger in the Mirror* (CBS, 1993 TV Movie). Dir: Charles Jarrott. Scr: Stirling Silliphant. Cast: Perry King (Toby), Lori Loughlin (Jill), Geordie Johnson (David), Juliet Mills (Alice), Christopher Plummer (Clifton). VHS.

4306. *A Stranger Is Watching* (Mary Higgins Clark, 1977). A psychopathic killer who murdered a woman in front of her young son kidnaps the boy and a female news reporter and holds them in a bunker below Grand Central Station in New York. **Adaptation:** *A Stranger Is Watching* (MGM, 1982). Dir: Sean S. Cunningham. Scr: Earl Mac Rauch, Victor Miller. Cast: Kate Mulgrew (Sharon), Rip Torn (Artie), James Naughton (Steve), Shawn von Schreiber (Julie), Barbara Baxley (Lally), Stephen Joyce (Detective Taylor), James Russo (Ronald). VHS.

The Stranger Wore a Gun (see *Yankee Gold*).

4307. *Strangers May Kiss* (Ursula Parrott, 1930). A sophisticated woman ruins her life by spurning the affections of her faithful fiancée and fleeing to Europe with an urbane journalist who, unknown to her, is married and untrustworthy. **Adaptation:** *Strangers May Kiss* (MGM, 1931). Dir: George Fitzmaurice. Scr: John Meehan. Cast: Norma Shearer (Lisbeth), Robert Montgomery (Steve), Neil Hamilton (Alan), Marjorie Rambeau (Geneva).

4308. *Strangers on a Train* (Patricia Highsmith, 1950). On his way to ask his estranged wife for a divorce, a tennis player meets a psychotic man on a train, and they make a deadly bargain: the man will kill the tennis player's wife and the tennis pro will kill the man's father. **Adaptation:** *Strangers on a Train* (Warner, 1951). Dir: Alfred Hitchcock. Scr: Raymond Chandler, Whitfield Cook, Czenzi Ormonde. Cast: Farley Granger (Guy), Ruth Roman (Anne), Robert Walker (Bruno), Leo G. Carroll (Senator Morton), Patricia Hitchcock (Barbara). DVD, VHS. Notes: Although uncredited in the films, the book also served as the inspiration for the films *Once You Kiss a Stranger* (1969) and *Throw Momma From the Train* (1987). (DVD, VHS).

4309. *Strangers When We Meet* (Evan Hunter, 1958). A successful architect pursues a dangerous affair with his beautiful married neighbor. **Adaptation:** *Strangers When We Meet* (Columbia, 1960). Dir: Richard Quine. Scr: Evan Hunter. Cast: Kirk Douglas (Larry), Kim Novak (Maggie), Ernie Kovacs (Roger), Barbara Rush (Eve), Walter Matthau (Felix). DVD, VHS.

Straw Dogs (see *The Siege of Trencher's Farm*).

Strawberry and Chocolate (*see* "The Wolf, the Forest and the New Man").

4310. *The Strawberry Statement: Notes of a College Revolutionary* (James Kunen, 1969). Written in the form of journal entries, an account of student riots at Columbia University in 1968. **Adaptation:** *The Strawberry Statement* (MGM, 1970). Dir: Stuart Hagmann. Scr: Israel Horovitz. Cast: Bruce Davison (Simon), Kim Darby (Linda), Bud Cort (Elliot), Murray MacLeod (George). Notes: Cannes Film Festival Jury Prize for Best Film and nomination for Golden Palm for Best Director. VHS.

4311. *Stray Dogs* (John Ridley, 1997). A gambler is stranded in a small desert town, where a man hires him to kill his wife. The gambler falls in love with his target, however, and she asks him to kill her husband instead. **Adaptation:** *U-Turn* (TriStar, 1997). Dir: Oliver Stone. Scr: John Ridley. Cast: Sean Penn (Bobby), Nick Nolte (Jake),

Jennifer Lopez (Grace), Powers Boothe (Sheriff Potter), Claire Danes (Jenny), Joaquin Phoenix (TNT), Jon Voight (Blind Man), Billy Bob Thornton (Darrell). DVD, VHS.

Street of Chance (see *The Black Curtain*).

4312. *Street of No Return* (David Goodis, 1954). A singer helps police catch a drug dealer who hopes to incite race riots in order to drive down the price of real estate. **Adaptation:** *Street of No Return* (Jacques Bral, 1989). Dir: Samuel Fuller. Scr: Jacques Bral, Samuel Fuller. Cast: Keith Carradine (Michael), Valentina Vargas (Celia), Bill Duke (Lieutenant Borel), Andrea Ferreol (Rhoda). DVD, VHS.

Street of Shadows (see *The Creaking Chair*).

4313. *The Street of Women* (Polan Banks, 1931). A real-estate developer is forced to choose between his loving mistress and his shrewish wife. **Adaptation:** *Street of Women* (Warner, 1932). Dir: Archie Mayo. Scr: Mary McCall, Jr., Charles Kenyon, Brown Holmes. Cast: Kay Francis (Natalie), Roland Young (Linkhorne), Alan Dinehart (Lawrence), Gloria Stuart (Doris).

4314. *Streets of Laredo* (Larry McMurtry, 1993). In the sequel to McMurtry's Pulitzer Prize–winning 1985 novel *Lonesone Dove*, the former Texas Ranger is now a bounty hunter hired to track down a Mexican killer. **Adaptation:** *Streets of Laredo* (CBS, 1995 TV Miniseries). Dir: Joseph Sargent. Scr: Larry McMurtry, Diana Ossana. Cast: James Garner (Captain Call), Sissy Spacek (Lorena), Sam Shepard (Parker), Ned Beatty (Judge Roy Bean), Randy Quaid (Hardin). Notes: Western Heritage Award for Best Television Feature Film. DVD, VHS. See also *Lonesome Dove* and *Dead Man's Walk*.

Strike It Rich (see *Loser Takes All*).

4315. *Strip Tease* (Carl Hiaasen, 1993). A single mother loses custody of her son and goes to work as a stripper, becoming involved with the murder of a lecherous congressman. **Adaptation:** *Striptease* (Columbia, 1996). Dir: Andrew Bergman. Scr: Andrew Bergman. Cast: Demi Moore (Erin), Burt Reynolds (Congressman Dilbeck), Armand Assante (Al), Ving Rhames (Shad), Robert Patrick (Darrell). DVD, VHS.

Striptease Lady (see The *G-String Murders*).

Stroker Ace (see *Stand on It*).

4316. *Strong Medicine* (Arthur Hailey, 1984). An ethical female executive at an international pharmaceutrical company discovers the lengths to which the corporation will go to increase profits. **Adaptation:** *Strong Medicine* (syndicated for independent television, 1986 TV Miniseries). Dir: Guy Green. Scr: Rita Lakin. Cast: Pamela Sue Martin (Celia), Patrick Duffy (Dr. Jordan), Dick Van Dyke (Sam), Ben Cross (Martin), Sam Neill (Vince), Douglas Fairbanks, Jr. (Eli), Annette O'Toole (Jessica).

Stronger Than Desire (see *Evelyn Prentice*).

Stronger Than Fear (see *Edge of Doom*).

4317. *Stronghold* (Stanley Ellin, 1975). A family of peaceful Quakers is taken hostage and terrorized by bank robbers and try to resolve the situation without resorting to violence. **Adaptation:** *A Prayer in the Dark* (Paramount Television, 1997 TV Movie). Dir: Jerry Ciccoritti. Scr: Andrew Laskos. Cast: Lynda Carter (Emily), Teri Polo (Janet), Colin Ferguson (Jimmy), Phillip Jarrett (Digby). VHS.

4318. *Stuart Little* (E. B. White, 1945). Children's story about an adventurous mouse who sets out to find a bird that had once stayed in his human family's garden. **Adaptation:** *Stuart Little* (Columbia, 1999). Dir: Rob Minkoff. Scr: M. Night Shyamalan, Gregory J. Brooker. Cast: Geena Davis (Eleanor), Hugh Laurie (Fredrick), Jonathan Lipnicki (George), and voices of Michael J. Fox (Stuart), Nathan Lane (Snowbell), Chazz Palminteri (Smokey), Steve Zahn (Monty). Notes: The screenplay, which differs significantly from the book, concerns a mouse adopted by a human family, and his battle against a jealous house cat. DVD, VHS. Notes: A sequel, *Stuart Little 2*, was released in 2003 (DVD, VHS), and the story was also the basis for a 2003 television series on HBO.

Stuart Saves His Family (see *I'm Good Enough, I'm Smart Enough, and Doggone It, People Like Me!*).

4319. *The Stud* (Jackie Collins, 1969). A rich man's wife makes her lover the manager of her trendy disco, but soon the former waiter wants more out of life. **Adaptation:** *The Stud* (Trans American, 1978). Dir: Quentin Masters. Scr: Jackie Collins, Dave Humphries, Christopher Stagg. Cast: Joan Collins (Fontaine), Oliver Tobias (Tony), Sue Lloyd (Vanessa), Mark Burns (Leonard). VHS. Notes: Followed by a sequel titled *The Bitch*. See also *The Bitch*.

4320. *Studs Lonigan: A Trilogy* (James T. Farrell, 1932–35). In Chicago in the 1920's, an Irish-Catholic youth lives a wild life and dies young. Farrell's trilogy consists of the novels *Young Lonigan* (1932), *The Young Manhood of Studs Lonigan* (1934), and *Judgment Day* (1935). **Adaptation 1:** *Studs Lonigan* (United Artists, 1960). Dir: Irving Lerner. Scr: Philip Yordan. Cast: Christopher Knight (Studs), Frank Gorshin (Kenny), Venetia Stevenson (Lucy), Carolyn Craig (Catherine), Jack Nicholson (Weary). VHS. **Adaptation 2:** *Studs Lonigan* (NBC, 1979 TV Miniseries). Dir: James Goldstone. Scr: Reginald Rose. Cast: Harry Hamlin (Studs), Colleen Dewhurst (Mary), Brad Dourif (Danny), Charles Durning (Paddy), Lisa Pelikan (Lucy), Diana Scarwid (Catherine).

4321. *A Study in Scarlet* (Arthur Conan Doyle, 1887). In the first of the Sherlock Holmes stories (and one of only four full-length novels about Holmes and Watson), the deductive sleuth looks into the murders of two American Mormons and discovers a secret society of church elders operating in England. **Silent Film:** 1914. **Adaptation:** *A Study in Scarlet* (Fox, 1933). Dir: Edwin L. Marin. Scr: Robert Florey. Cast: Reginald Owen (Holmes), Anna May Wong (Madame Pyke), June Clyde (Eileen), Alan Dinehart (Thaddeus), John Warburton (Stanford), Alan Mowbray (Inspector Lestrade), Warburton Gamble (Watson). Notes: The film treatment departs considerably from its source. In the film, Holmes and Watson investigate the murder of a member of a British secret society. DVD, VHS.

4322. *The Stunt Man* (Paul Brodeur, 1970). A Vietnam veteran on the run from the police stumbles onto a movie set and is forced by a sinister director to work doing dangerous stunts. **Adaptation:** *The Stunt Man* (20th Century–Fox, 1980). Dir: Richard Rush. Scr: Lawrence B. Marcus, Richard Rush. Cast: Peter O'Toole (Eli), Steve Railsback (Cameron), Barbara Hershey (Nina), Alex Rocco (Jake). Notes: Golden Globe Award for Best Musical Score and nominations for Best Picture, Director, Screenplay, Actor (O'Toole), and New Star (Railsback); Academy Award nominations for Best Director, Screenplay, and Actor (O'Toole). DVD, VHS.

Submarine Patrol (see *The Splinter Fleet of the Otranto Barrage*).

4323. *The Subterraneans* (Jack Kerouac, 1958). The lives and loves of San Francisco beatniks in the 1950's. **Adaptation:** *The Subterraneans* (MGM, 1960). Dir: Ranald MacDougall. Scr: Robert Thom. Cast: Leslie Caron (Mardou),

George Peppard (Leo), Janice Rule (Roxanne), Roddy McDowall (Yuri), Anne Seymour (Charlotte), Jim Hutton (Adam).

4324. *Such a Gorgeous Kid Like Me* (Henry Farrell, 1967). Black comedy about a beautiful murderess who manipulates a young and gullible criminologist. **Adaptation:** *Such a Gorgeous Kid Like Me* (1972). Dir: François Truffaut. Scr: Jean-Loup Dabadie, François Truffaut. Cast: Bernadette Lafont (Camille), Claude Brasseur (Murene), Charles Denner (Arthur). Notes: Originally titled *Une Belle Fille Comme Moi* and shown with subtitles. VHS.

4325. *Such a Long Journey* (Rohinton Mistry, 1991). During the declared State of Emergency in India in 1975, a group of strangers endures hardships living together in a small apartment in Bombay. **Adaptation:** *Such a Long Journey* (Shooting Gallery, 1998). Dir: Sturla Gunnarsson. Scr: Sooni Taraporevala. Cast: Roshan Seth (Gustad), Soni Razdan (Noble), Om Puri (Ghulam), Naseeruddin Shah (Major Bilimoria), Sam Dastor (Dinshawji), Kurush Deboo (Tehmul). Notes: Genie Awards (Canada) for Best Actor (Seth), Editing, and Sound, and nominations for Best Picture, Director, Screenplay, Supporting Actor (Deboo), Cinematography, Art Direction, Musical Score, and Costume Design. DVD, VHS.

4326. *Such Good Friends* (Lois Gould, 1970). Black comedy about a man who goes into a coma following minor surgery. His wife then finds his little black book and discovers that he has had many love affairs over the years. **Adaptation:** *Such Good Friends* (Paramount, 1971). Dir: Otto Preminger. Scr: Elaine May (writing as Esther Dale), David Shaber. Cast: Dyan Cannon (Julie), James Coco (Dr. Spector), Jennifer O'Neill (Miranda), Ken Howard (Cal), Nina Foch (Mrs. Wallman), Laurence Luckinbill (Richard), Louise Lasser (Marcy), Burgess Meredith (Bernard).

Such Men Are Dangerous (see *The Racers*).

4327. *Such Sweet Thunder* (Peter Gilman, 1960). A domineering patriarch adversely affects the lives of his family. The book was subsequently released as *Diamond Head*. **Adaptation:** *Diamond Head* (Columbia, 1963). Dir: Guy Green. Scr: Marguerite Roberts. Cast: Charlton Heston (King Howland), Yvette Mimieux (Sloane), George Chakiris (Dr. Kahana), France Nuyen (Mai), James Darren (Paul). VHS.

4328. *Sudden Fury: A True Story of Adoption and Murder* (Leslie Walker, 1989). When a married couple is murdered in their home, their foster son becomes the chief suspect based on testimony by his siblings. **Adaptation:** *A Family Torn Apart* (NBC, 1993 TV Movie). Dir: Craig R. Baxley. Scr: Matthew Bombeck. Cast: Neil Patrick Harris (Brian), Johnny Galecki (Daniel), Linda Kelsey (Maureen), John M. Jackson (Joe), Lisa Banes (Barbara).

Sudden Terror (see *Eyewitness*).

Sugar Cane Alley (see *Black Shack Alley*).

4329. *Sugarfoot* (Clarence Budington Kelland, 1942). Western about a two former rivals who meet on a train bound for the same town in Arizona. **Adaptation:** *Sugarfoot*; reissued in the U.S. as *Swirl of Glory* (Warner, 1951). Dir: Edwin L. Marin. Scr: Russell Hughes. Cast: Randolph Scott (Sugarfoot), Adele Jergens (Reva), Raymond Massey (Jacob), S. Z. Sakall (Miguel), Robert Warwick (Crane).

Sugartime (see *Roemer*).

4330. "The Suicide Club" (Robert Louis Stevenson, 1878). A world-weary man joins an aristocratic British club for people tired of life and prepared to commit suicide, but changes his mind when he meets a beautiful woman there. The short story was published in installments in *London* magazine (June–October 1878) and was subsequently included in Stevenson's 1882 collection *New Arabian Nights*. **Silent Films:** 1909 (a short directed by D. W. Griffith) and 1913. **Adaptation 1:** *Trouble for Two*; released in the UK as *The Suicide Club* (MGM, 1936). Dir: J. Walter Ruben. Scr: Manuel Seff, Edward E. Paramore, Jr. Cast: Robert Montgomery (Florizel), Rosalind Russell (Miss Vandeleur), Frank Morgan (Colonel Geraldine), Reginald Owen (the President of the Club). **Adaptation 2:** *The Suicide Club* (Concorde-New Horizons, 2000). Dir: Rachel Samuels. Scr: Lev L. Spiro. Cast: Jonathan Pryce (Bourne), David Morrissey (Henry), Paul Bettany (Shaw), Neil Stuke (Captain May). DVD, VHS.

4331. *A Suitable Vengeance* (Elizabeth George, 1991). In the fourth installment in George's series of novels featuring Inspector Thomas Lynley of Scotland Yard, the detective takes his fiancée to his ancestral home and becomes involved in the brutal murder of a local journalist. **Adaptation:** *The Inspector Lynley Mysteries: A Suitable Vengeance* (BBC/PBS, 2003 TV Movie series). Dir: Edward Bennett. Scr: Valerie Windsor. Cast: Nathaniel Parker (Lynley), Sharon Small (Detective Havers), Lesley Vickerage (Helen). DVD, VHS.

4332. *The Sum of All Fears* (Tom Clancy, 1991). CIA analyst Jack Ryan must try to stop terrorists from detonating a nuclear device in the United States, an act that will threaten U.S.–Russian relations. **Adaptation:** *The Sum of All Fears* (Paramount, 2002). Dir: Phil Alden Robinson. Scr: Paul Attanasio, Daniel Pyne. Cast: Ben Affleck (Ryan), Morgan Freeman (William), James Cromwell (President Fowler), Ken Jenkins (Admiral Pollack), Liev Schreiber (Clark), Bruce McGill (Gene). DVD, VHS.

Summer Dreams (see *Heroes and Villains*).

Summer Fling (see *The Last of the High Kings*).

The Summer House (see *The Clothes in the Wardrobe*).

4333. *Summer Lightning* (Allene Corliss, 1936). A small-town woman resumes her relationship with a biology professor after her alcoholic husband dies. **Adaptation:** *I Met My Love Again* (United Artists, 1938). Dir: Joshua Logan, Arthur Ripley. Scr: David Hertz. Cast: Joan Bennett (Julie), Henry Fonda (Ives), Louise Platt (Brenda). VHS.

Summer Lightning (1948) (see *Scudda Hoo! Scudda Hay!*).

Summer Magic (see *Mother Carey's Chickens*).

4334. *The Summer of the Monkeys* (Wilson Rawls, 1976). Children's story set in nineteenth-century rural Canada, where a boy finds four circus chimps and decides to adopt them. **Adaptation:** *Summer of the Monkeys* (Edge/BWE, 1998). Dir: Michael Anderson. Scr: Greg Taylor, Jim Strain. Cast: Michael Ontkean (John), Leslie Hope (Sarah), Wilford Brimley (Grandpa Sam), Corey Sevier (Jay), Katie Stuart (Daisy). DVD, VHS.

4335. *A Summer Place* (Sloan Wilson, 1958). Teen romance and illicit adult affairs at a summer resort in Maine. **Adaptation:** *A Summer Place* (Warner, 1959). Dir: Delmer Daves. Scr: Delmer Daves. Cast: Richard Egan (Ken), Dorothy McGuire (Sylvia), Sandra Dee (Molly), Arthur Kennedy (Bart), Troy Donahue (Johnny), Constance Ford (Helen), Beulah Bondi (Mrs. Hamble). VHS.

Summer Storm (see *The Shooting Party*).

A Summer Story (*see* "The Apple Tree").

4336. *Summer's Lease* (John Mortimer, 1988). A mystery about a British woman and her family, who vacation at a beautiful Tuscan villa. When a neighbor dies suddenly, she begins to look into the affairs of the villa's mysterious absentee landlord. **Adaptation:** *Summer's Lease* (BBC, 1989 TV Miniseries). Dir: Martyn Friend. Scr: John Mortimer. Cast: Gabrielle Anwar (Chrissie), Feodor Chaliapin, Jr. (Prince Tosti-Castelnuovo), Annette Crosbie (Connie), Susan Fleetwood (Molly), John Gielgud (Haverford), Suzanne Hay (Samantha), Jeremy Kemp (Buck), Rosemary Leach (Nancy). Notes: Emmy Award for Outstanding Television Actor (Gielgud); BAFTA nominations for Best Television Drama, Actor (Gielgud), and Editing.

4337. *The Sun Also Rises* (Ernest Hemingway, 1926). Set in Paris after World War I, Hemingway's first novel is about an impotent man obsessed with a sexually liberated woman. **Adaptation 1:** *The Sun Also Rises* (20th Century–Fox, 1957). Dir: Henry King. Scr: Peter Viertel. Cast: Tyrone Power (Jake), Ava Gardner (Brett), Mel Ferrer (Robert), Errol Flynn (Mike), Eddie Albert (Bill). **Adaptation 2:** *The Sun Also Rises* (NBC, 1984 TV Miniseries). Dir: James Goldstone. Scr: Robert L. Joseph. Cast: Hart Bochner (Jake), Jane Seymour (Brett), Robert Carradine (Robert), Zeljko Ivanek (Bill), Leonard Nimoy (Count Mippipopolous).

4338. "The Sun Shines Bright" (Irwin S. Cobb, 1931). An installment in Cobb's long-running series of short stories featuring a Kentucky judge trying to mediate small-town disputes at the turn of the twentieth century. The short story appeared in *Cosmopolitan* in April 1931. **Adaptation 1:** *Judge Priest* (Fox, 1934), Dir: John Ford. Scr: Dudley Nichols, Lamar Trotti. Cast: Will Rogers (Judge Priest), Tom Brown (Jerome), Anita Louise (Ellie May), Henry B. Walthall (Reverend Brand). Notes: The screenplay combines elements from the several stories in the series. DVD, VHS. **Adaptation 2:** *The Sun Shines Bright* (Republic, 1953). Dir: John Ford. Scr: Laurence Stallings. Cast: Charles Winninger (Judge Priest), Stepin Fetchit (Jeff), John Russell (Ashby), Arleen Whelan (Lucy). Notes: Ford's remake of his 1934 film again combines elements from several of Cobb's Judge Priest stories, notably "The Sun Shines Bright," "The Mob from Massaq" (1912), and "The Lord Provides" (1915). VHS.

Sunburn (see *The Bind*).

Sunday (*see* "Ate/Menos, or The Miracle").

4339. *Sundown at Crazy Horse* (Howard Rigsby, 1957). Western about a battle of wills and wits between an outlaw and a determined sheriff during a cattle drive. **Adaptation:** *The Last Sunset* (Universal International, 1961). Dir: Robert Aldrich. Scr: Dalton Trumbo. Cast: Rock Hudson (Dana), Kirk Douglas (Brendan), Dorothy Malone (Belle), Joseph Cotten (John), Carol Lynley (Missy). VHS.

4340. *The Sundowners* (Jon Cleary, 1951). The adventures of a family of Australian sheepherders in the 1920's. **Adaptation:** *The Sundowners* (Warner, 1960). Dir: Fred Zinnemann. Scr: Isobel Lennart. Cast: Deborah Kerr (Ida), Robert Mitchum (Paddy), Peter Ustinov (Rupert), Glynis Johns (Mrs. Firth), Dina Merrill (Jean). Notes: Academy Award nominations for Best Picture, Director, Screenplay, Actress (Kerr), and Supporting Actress (Johns); BAFTA nominations for Best British Film, Film from Any Source, and British Actress (Kerr); Golden Globe Special Merit Award; National Board of Review Award for Best Actor (Mitchum). DVD, VHS.

The Sundowners (1950) (see *Thunder in the Dust*).

4341. *Sunset Pass* (Zane Grey, 1928). Western about a man unjustly accused of stealing money and the gang that is using him in order to stage a bank robbery. The novel originally appeared as a serial in *The American Magazine* (March–October 1928) and published as a novel in 1931. **Silent Film:** 1929. **Adaptation 1:** *Sunset Pass* (1933). Dir: Henry Hathaway. Scr: Jack Cunningham, Gerald Geraghty. Cast: Randolph Scott (Ash), Tom Keene (Jack/Jim), Kathleen Burke (Jane), Harry Carey (Hesbitt), Noah Beery (Marshal Blake). **Adaptation 2:** *Sunset Pass* (RKO, 1946). Dir: William Berke. Scr: Norman Houston. Cast: James Warren (Rocky), Nan Leslie (Jane), John Laurenz (Chito), Jane Greer (Helen), Robert Barrat (Curtis).

4342. *The Super Cops: The True Syory of the Cops Called Batman and Robin* (L. H. Whittemore, 1973). Factual account of two unorthodox New York policemen who battled the bureaucracy while trying to stop the drug trade in a tough Brooklyn neighborhood. **Adaptation:** *The Super Cops* (MGM, 1974). Dir: Gordon Parks. Scr: Lorenzo Semple, Jr. Cast: Ron Leibman (Greenberg), David Selby (Hantz), Sheila Frazier (Sara), Pat Hingle (Novick). DVD, VHS.

4343. "Supertoys Last All Summer Long" (Brian Aldiss, 1969). In the future, an advanced robotic child wants to become a real boy so that he can have the love of his human mother. The short story appeared in the December 1969 issue of *Harper's Bazaar*. **Adaptation:** *AI: Artificial Intelligence* (Warner, 2001). Dir: Steven Spielberg. Scr: Steven Spielberg. Cast: Haley Joel Osment (David), Frances O'Connor (Monica), Sam Robards (Henry), Jake Thomas (Martin), Jude Law (Gigolo Joe), William Hurt (Professor Hobby). Notes: Academy Award nominations for Best Special Effects and Musical Score; Golden Globe nominations for Best Director, Supporting Actor (Law), and Musical Score. DVD, VHS.

Supervivientes de los Andes (see *Survive*).

4344. *The Sure Hand of God* (Erskine Caldwell, 1947). A novel about a family victimized by scandal and petty hypocrisy in a small Southern town. **Adaptation:** *Sinners Need Company* (Lifetime, 2004 TV Movie). Dir: Michael Kolko. Scr: Horace Wilson. Cast: Gail O'Grady (Molly), Jennifer Morrison (Lily), Will Wallace (Claude), Daniel Roebuck (Marcus).

4345. *Surely You're Joking, Mr. Feynman!: Adventures of a Curious Character* (Richard P. Feynman, 1985). A 1965 Nobel-laureate physicist who worked on the Manhattan Project makes wry observations about science, technology, and life in our times. **Adaptation:** *Infinity* (First Look, 1996). Dir: Matthew Broderick. Scr: Patricia Broderick, Cast: Matthew Broderick (Feynman), Patricia Arquette (Arline), Peter Riegert (Mel). Notes: The screenplay combines elements from two of Feynman's books: *Surely You're Joking, Mr. Feynman* (1985) and *What Do You Care What Other People Think?* (1988). DVD, VHS. See also *What Do You Care What Other People Think?*

4346. *Surfacing* (Margaret Atwood, 1972). A young girl and her friends go into the wilderness to search for her missing father. **Adaptation:** *Surfacing* (Pan-Canadian, 1981). Dir: Claude Jutra. Scr: Bernard Gordon. Cast: Joseph Bottoms (Joe), Kathleen Beller (Kate), R. H. Thomson (David), Margaret Dragu (Anna), Michael Ironside (Wayne).

Surprise Package (see *A Gift from the Boys*).

4347. *Survive: The Most Shocking Episode in the History of Human Survival* (Clay Blair, Jr., 1973). True story of the Uruguayan rugby team traveling in South America and making a crash landing on a mountaintop in the Andes, where some were forced to eat their dead teammates to survive. **Adaptation:** *Survive!* (Avant/Paramount, 1976). Dir: Rene Cardona. Scr: Rene Cardona. Cast: Hugo Stiglitz (Francisco), Norma Lazareno (Silvia), Luz María Aguilar (Mrs. Madero), Fernando Larranaga (Madero). DVD, VHS. See also *Alive: The Story of the Andes Survivors.*

4348. *Survive the Savage Sea* (Dougal Robertson, 1973). The true story of how Robertson and his family survived for thirty-seven days on a raft in the ocean after the wreck of their yacht. **Adaptation:** *Survive the Savage Sea* (ABC, 1992 TV Movie). Dir: Kevin James Dobson. Scr: Fred Haines, Scott Swanton. Cast: Robert Urich (Jack), Ali MacGraw (Claire), Danielle von Zerneck (Susan), Mark Ballou (Gary). DVD, VHS.

Surviving Picasso (see *Picasso: Creator and Destroyer*).

4349. *Susan Lenox, Her Fall and Rise* (David Graham Phillips, 1917). A farm girl flees to the city to escape her brutal father. **Adaptation:** *Susan Lenox, Her Fall and Rise*; released in the UK as *The Rise of Helga* (MGM, 1931). Dir: Robert Z. Leonard. Scr: Leon Gordon, Zelda Sears, Wanda Tuchock. Cast: Greta Garbo (Susan), Clark Gable (Rodney), Jean Hersholt (Ohlin), Alan Hale (Mondstrum), VHS.

Susan Slade (see *The Sin of Susan Slade*).

Suspect (see *A Sort of Traitor*).

The Suspect (see *This Way Out*).

Suspicion (see *Before the Fact*).

4350. *Suspicious River* (Laura Kasischke, 1996). A married woman working at a small-town motel does business as a prostitute on the side. When she becomes involved with a dangerous client, she is forced to recall the murder of her mother years earlier. **Adaptation:** *Suspicious River* (Tartan, 2000). Dir: Lynne Stopkewich. Scr: Lynne Stopkewich. Cast: Molly Parker (Leila), Callum Keith Rennie (Gary), Joel Bissonnette (Rick). Notes: Leo Awards (Canada) for Best Picture, Actor (Rennie), and Cinematography and nominations for Best Director, Screenplay, Actress (Parker), Editing, Musical Score, and Sound. DVD, VHS.

4351. *Suzanne's Diary for Nicholas* (James Patterson, 2001). After her lover leaves her suddenly, a woman discovers a diary written by his wife containing letters to their child. **Adaptation:** *Suzanne's Diary for Nicholas* (CBS, 2005 TV Movie). Dir: Richard Friedenberg. Scr: Richard Friedenberg. Cast: Christina Applegate (Dr. Bedford), Jenna Friedenberg (Laurie), Trevor Hayes (Stephen), Kathleen Rose Perkins (Kate).

4352. *Suzy* (Herbert Gorman, 1934). An American dancer falls in love with a French World War I pilot, but their relationship is complicated when her husband, who was presumed dead, appears on the scene. **Adaptation:** *Suzy* (MGM, 1936). Dir: George Fitzmaurice. Scr: Dorothy Parker, Alan Campbell, Horace Jackson, Lenore Coffee. Cast: Jean Harlow (Suzy), Franchot Tone (Terry), Cary Grant (Andre), Lewis Stone (Baron Charville). VHS.

Svengali (see *Trilby*).

4353. *Swallows and Amazons* (Arthur Ransome, 1930). The first in a series of popular children's books about the adventures of children in Britain's Lake District in the late 1920's. **Adaptation:** *Swallows and Amazons* (Anglo-EMI, 1974). Dir: Claude Whatham. Scr: David Wood. Cast: Virginia McKenna (Mrs. Walker), Ronald Fraser (Uncle Jim), Simon West (John), Zanna Hamilton (Susan), Sophie Neville (Titty), Stephen Grendon (Roger). DVD, VHS. Notes: The books in the series also inspired a British television series in 1963 and two made-for television movies broadcast on the BBC in 1984: *Swallows and Amazons Forever!: Coot Club* and Swallows and *Amazons Forever!: The Big Six.*

4354. *Swann* (Carol Shields, 1987). An American author goes to a small Canadian town to research the life of a poet who was brutally murdered by her lover and competes with a local librarian to publish the poet's final manuscript. **Adaptation:** *Swann* (Norstar, 1996). Dir: Anna Benson Gyles. Scr: David Young. Cast: Brenda Fricker (Rose), Miranda Richardson (Sarah), Michael Ontkean (Stephen), David Cubitt (Brownie), Sean McCann (Homer). DVD, VHS.

4355. *Swann's Way* (Marcel Proust, 1913). *Au Cote de Chez Swann*, the first installment in Proust's sixteen-volume *A la Recherche du Temps Perdu* (1913–1927) focuses on the narrator's recollections of his childhood and adolescence and his relationship with a Parisian courtesan named Odette. The translated English title of the collection is *Remembrance of Things Past.* **Adaptation:** *Swann in Love* (Orion, 1984). Dir: Volker Schlondorff. Scr: Peter Brook, Jean-Claude Carrière, Marie-Helene Estienne, Volker Schlondorff. Cast: Jeremy Irons (Swann), Ornella Muti (Odette), Alain Delon (Baron de Charlus), Fanny Ardant (the Duchess of Guermantes). Notes: Originally released as *Un Amour de Swann* and shown with subtitles. DVD, VHS. See also *Time Regained.*

4356. *Swastika* (Oscar Schisgall, 1939). In the late 1930's, an American man travels with his wife to Germany to visit relatives, and the wife discovers that her husband is a Nazi sympathizer. **Adaptation:** *The Man I Married*; also released as *I Married a Nazi* (20th Century–Fox, 1940). Dir: Irving Pichel. Scr: Oliver H. P. Garrett. Cast: Joan Bennett (Carol), Francis Lederer (Eric), Lloyd Nolan (Kenneth), Anna Sten (Frieda), Otto Kruger (Heinrich).

4357. *Sweepings* (Lester Cohen, 1926). An ambitious Chicago man builds the city's largest department store but is unable to interest his four children in carrying on the business. **Adaptation 1:** *Sweepings* (RKO, 1933). Dir: John Cromwell. Scr: Lester Cohen. Cast: Lionel Barrymore (Daniel), Eric Linden (Freddie), William Gargan (Gene), Gloria Stuart (Phoebe). **Adaptation 2:** *Three Sons* (RKO, 1939). Dir: Jack Hively. Scr: John Twist. Cast: Edward Ellis (Daniel), William Gargan (Thane), Kent Taylor (Gene), J. Edward Bromberg (Abe), Katharine Alexander (Abigail), Virginia Vale (Phoebe).

4358. *The Sweet Hereafter* (Russell Banks, 1991). After a bus accident in a small Canadian town kills nearly all of the town's children, a lawyer, embittered by the drug addiction of his own daughter, goes there to persuade the parents to sue those responsible. **Adaptation:** *The Sweet Hereafter* (Fine Line, 1997). Dir: Atom Egoyan. Scr: Atom Egoyan. Cast: Ian Holm (Mitchell), Caerthan Banks (Zoe), Sarah Polley (Nicole), Tom McCamus (Sam), Gabrielle Rose (Dolores), Alberta Watson (Risa), Maury Chaykin (Wendell). Notes: Genie Awards (Canada) for Best Picture, Director, Actor (Holm), Cinematography, Musical Score, Editing, and Sound, and nominations for Best Screenplay, Actresses (Polley and Rose), Supporting Actor (McCamus), Art Direction, Costume Design, and Song; Cannes Film Festival Grand Jury Prize for Best Film and Golden Palm nomination for Best Director; Independent Spirit Award for Best Film; National Board of Review Award for Best Ensemble; Academy Award nominations for Best Director and Screenplay. DVD, VHS.

Sweet Kitty Bellairs (see *The Bath Comedy*).

4359. *The Sweet Ride* (William Murray, 1967). The romantic adventures of beach dwellers in southern California. **Adaptation:** *The Sweet Ride* (20th Century–Fox, 1968). Dir: Harvey Hart. Scr: Tom Mankiewicz. Cast: Anthony Franciosa (Collie), Michael Sarrazin (Denny), Jacqueline Bisset (Vickie), Bob Denver (Choo-Choo), Michael Wilding (Mr. Cartwright).

4360. *Sweet Thursday* (John Steinbeck, 1954). In this sequel to his 1945 novel *Cannery Row*, Steinbeck returns to Monterey's now defunct canning district and its lower-class denizens. **Adaptation:** *Cannery Row* (MGM, 1982). Dir: David S. Ward. Scr: David S. Ward. Cast: Nick Nolte (Doc), Debra Winger (Suzy), Audra Lindley (Fauna), M. Emmet Walsh (Mack). Notes: The screenplay combines elements from this work and Steinbeck's *Cannery Row*. VHS. See also *Cannery Row*.

4361. *Sweet William* (Beryl Bainbridge, 1973). A British woman is seduced by a handsome American and then discovers that she is merely one of his many romantic conquests. **Adaptation:** *Sweet William* (World Northal, 1980). Dir: Claude Whatham. Scr: Beryl Bainbridge. Cast: Sam Waterston (William), Jenny Agutter (Ann), Anna Massey (Edna), Geraldine James (Pamela). VHS.

4362. *A Swell-Looking Babe* (Jim Thompson, 1954). An ambitious bellhop at a hotel is drawn into a plot with a mysterious woman and her crooked associate. **Adaptation:** *Hit Me* (1996). Dir: Steven Shainberg. Scr: Denis Johnson. Cast: Elias Koteas (Sonny), Laure Marsac (Monique), Jay Leggett (Leroy), Bruce Ramsay (Del). DVD, VHS.

Swept From the Sea (see *Amy Foster*).

4363. *SWF Seeks Same* (John Lutz, 1990). A New York professional woman decides to share her apartment with a roommate and takes in a disturbed young woman who comes to dominate her life. **Adaptation:** *Single White Female* (Columbia, 1992). Dir: Barbet Schroeder. Scr: Don Roos. Cast: Bridget Fonda (Allie), Jennifer Jason Leigh (Hedy), Steven Weber (Sam), Peter Friedman (Graham), Stephen Tobolowsky (Mitch). DVD, VHS.

4364. *Swiftwater* (Paul Annixter, 1950). An eccentric Maine man and his family try to protect wild geese from hunters and unscrupulous land developers. **Adaptation:** *Those Calloways* (Disney/Buena Vista, 1965). Dir: Norman Tokar. Scr: Louis Pelletier. Cast: Brian Keith (Cam), Vera Miles (Lydia), Brandon De Wilde (Bucky), Walter Brennan (Alf), Ed Wynn (Ed), Linda Evans (Bridie). DVD, VHS.

4365. "The Swimmer" (John Cheever, 1964). A man in an affluent suburb decides to swim home from a party across the swimming pools of his rich friends. Each pool brings recollections of the past until he arrives at his empty home and realizes that his success is not real. The story first appeared in *The New Yorker* on July 18, 1964, and was collected in the 1978 volume *The Stories of John Cheever*, which won the Pulitzer Prize. **Adaptation:** *The Swimmer* (Columbia, 1968). Dir: Frank Perry. Scr: Eleanor Perry. Cast: Burt Lancaster (Ned), Janet Landgard (Julie), Janice Rule (Shirley), Tony Bickley (Donald). DVD, VHS.

4366. *Swimming Upstream* (Anthony Fingleton and Diane Fingleton, 2003). Autobiography by the 1950's Australian swimming champion and his sister focusing on their difficult family situation and his struggles to succeed nevertheless. **Adaptation:** *Swimming Upstream* (Crusader, 2003). Dir: Russell Mulcahy. Scr: Anthony Fingleton. Cast: Geoffrey Rush (Harold), Judy Davis (Dora), Jesse Spencer (Tony), Brittany Byrnes (Diane), Tim Draxl (John). Notes: The book was published the same year as the film was issued. Australian Film Institute Award nominations for Best Screenplay, Actor (Rush), Actress (Davis), Production Design, and Costume Design.

Swirl of Glory (see *Sugarfoot*).

4367. *Swiss Family Robinson* (Johann Wyss, 1812). A Swiss family on its way to a new life in Australia become shipwrecked on a deserted island and learn to live happily there despite the nearby presence of marauding pirates. **Adaptation 1:** *Swiss Family Robinson* (RKO, 1940). Dir: Edward Ludwig. Scr: C. Graham Baker, Walter Ferris, Gene Towne. Cast: Thomas Mitchell (William), Edna Best (Elizabeth), Freddie Bartholomew (Jack), Terry Kilburn (Ernst), Tim Holt (Fritz). VHS. **Adaptation 2:** *Swiss Family Robinson* (Disney/Buena Vista, 1960). Dir: Ken Annakin. Scr: Lowell S. Hawley. Cast: John Mills (William), Dorothy McGuire (Elizabeth), James MacArthur (Fritz), Janet Munro (Roberta), Sessue Hayakawa (Kuala), Tommy Kirk (Ernst). DVD, VHS. **Adaptation 3:** *The Swiss Family Robinson* (ABC, 1975 TV Movie). Dir: Harry Harris. Scr: Ken Trevey. Cast: George Di Cenzo (Suramin), Helen Hunt (Roberta), Martin Milner (Karl), Cameron Mitchell (Jeremiah), Eric Olson (Ernie), John Vernon (Charles). Notes: The film was the pilot for an ABC television series (1975–1976) (VHS). **Adaptation 4:** *The New Swiss Family Robinson* (Disney/Buena Vista, 1998 TV Movie). Dir: Stewart Raffill. Scr: Stewart Raffill. Cast: Jane Seymour (Anna), David Carradine (Sheldon), James Keach (Jack), John Asher (Shane), Blake Bashoff (Todd). DVD, VHS. **Adaptation 5:** *Stranded* (Hallmark, 2002 TV Movie). Dir: Charles Beeson. Scr: Greg Dinner, Dominic Minghella, Chris Harrald. Cast: Liam Cunningham (David), Brana Bajic (Lara), Roger Allam (Thomas), Jesse Spencer (Fritz), Neil Newbon (Ernst). DVD, VHS.

The Sword and the Rose (see *When Knighthood Was in Flower*).

The Sword in the Stone (see *The Once and Future King*).

4368. *Sword of Honor* Trilogy (Evelyn Waugh, 1952–1961). A trilogy of comic novels about the misadventures of a British gentleman as an officer during World War II. The series included three novels: *Men at Arms* (1952), *Officers and Gentlemen* (1955), and *Unconditional Surrender* (1961). An omnibus edition containing all three novels was published in 1965. **Adaptation 1:** *Sword of Honour* (BBC, 1967). Dir: Donald McWhinnie. Scr: Giles Cooper. Cast: Edward Woodward (Guy), James Villiers (Ian), Ronald Fraser (Apthorpe), Paul Hardwick (Ritchie-Hook), Freddie Jones (Ludovic), Vivian Pickles (Virginia). **Adaptation 2:** *Sword of Honour* (2001 TV Miniseries). Dir: Bill Anderson. Scr: William Boyd. Cast: Daniel Craig (Guy), Simon Chandler (Major Irvine), Richard Coyle (Trimmer), Megan Dodds (Virginia). DVD, VHS.

Sword of the Valiant: The Legend of Sir Gawain and the Green Knight (see *Sir Gawain and the Green Knight*).

4369. *Sybil* (Flora Rheta Schreiber, 1973). Factual account of a mentally disturbed woman whose terrible childhood caused her to develop sixteen distinct personalities. **Adaptation:** *Sybil* (NBC, 1976 TV Movie). Dir: Daniel Petrie. Scr: Stewart Stern. Cast: Sally Field (Sybil), Joanne Woodward (Dr. Wilbur), Brad Davis (Richard), Martine Bartlett (Hattie). Notes: Emmy Awards for Outstanding Movie, Teleplay, Actress (Field), and Musical Score, and nominations for Best Actress (Woodward) and Cinematography; Golden Globe nomination for Best Television Movie.

4370. *Sylvia* (Howard Fast, 1960). A wealthy man hires a detective to look into the shady past of his beautiful, mysterious fiancée. Fast originally published the novel under the pseudonym E. V. Cunningham. **Adaptation:** *Sylvia* (Paramount, 1965). Dir: Gordon Douglas. Scr: Sydney Boehm. Cast: Carroll Baker (Sylvia), George Maharis (Alan), Joanne Dru (Jane), Peter Lawford

(Frederic), Viveca Lindfors (Irma), Edmond O'Brien (Oscar), Aldo Ray (Jonas), Ann Sothern (Grace).

Sylvia (1985) (see *Teacher*).

Sylvia Scarlett (see *The Early Life and Adventure of Sylvia Scarlett*).

Synapse (see *Season of the Witch*).

4371. "The System of Doctor Tarr and Professor Fether" (Edgar Allan Poe, 1845). A traveler in France comes upon an insane asylum thsat boasts an innovative treatment for "soothing" the mentally ill. The short story was published in *Graham's Magazine* in November 1845. **Silent Film:** 1913. **Adaptation:** *The Mansion of Madness* (Group 1, 1972). Dir; Juan Lopez Moctezuma. Scr: Carlos Illescas, Juan Lopez Moctezuma, Gabriel Weiss. Cast: Claude Brook (Fragonard), Arthur Hansel (Gaston), Ellen Sherman (Eugenie), Martin La Salle (Julien). DVD, VHS.

4372. *Tacey Cromwell* (Conrad Richter, 1942). Western about the romantic relationship between an itinerant gambler and the proprietress of a honky-tonk saloon. **Adaptation:** *One Desire* (Universal International, 1955). Dir: Jerry Hopper. Scr: Lawrence Roman, Robert Blees. Cast: Anne Baxter (Tacey), Rock Hudson (Clint), Julie Adams (Judith), Natalie Wood (Seely).

4373. *Taggart* (Louis L'Amour, 1959). Western about a man who avenges the murder of his parents by killing a powerful rancher's son. When the rancher puts a bounty on his head, the man must flee to hostile Indian territory to avoid the bounty hunters out to kill him. **Adaptation:** *Taggart* (Universal, 1964). Dir: R. G. Springsteen. Scr: Robert Creighton Williams. Cast: Tony Young (Taggart), Dan Duryea (Jason), Dick Foran (Stark), Elsa Cardenas (Consuela).

4374. *Tai-Pan* (James Clavell, 1983). In 1841, a powerful businessman works to secure Hong Kong as a British financial territory. **Adaptation:** *Tai-Pan* (DeLaurentiis, 1986). Dir: Daryl Duke. Scr: John Briley. Cast: Bryan Brown (Dirk), Joan Chen (May–May), John Stanton (Tyler), Tim Guinee (Colum), Bill Leadbitter (Gorth), Russell Wong (Gordon). DVD, VHS.

4375. *The Tailor of Panama* (John Le Carre [pseudonym for David Cornwell], 1996). A disgraced British agent is sent to Panama, where he uses the political connections of a tailor to help restore his career. **Adaptation:** *The Tailor of Panama* (Columbia, 2001). Dir: John Boorman. Scr: Andrew Davies, John Le Carre, John Boorman. Cast: Pierce Brosnan (Andrew), Geoffrey

Rush (Harold), Jamie Lee Curtis (Louisa), Leonor Varela (Marta), Brendan Gleeson (Michelangelo), Harold Pinter (Uncle Benny), Catherine McCormack (Francesca), Daniel Radcliffe (Mark). DVD, VHS.

4376. "Taint of the Tiger" (John D. MacDonald, 1958). A former Marine is hired by an old military buddy to hijack a fortune in ransom money. The short story was published in the March 1958 issue of *Cosmopolitan*. **Adaptation:** *Man-Trap* (Paramount, 1961). Dir: Edmond O'Brien. Scr: Ed Waters. Cast: Jeffrey Hunter (Matt), David Janssen (Vince), Stella Stevens (Nina).

4377. *Tainted Evidence* (Robert Daley, 1993). An idealistic district attorney investigates the shooting of his father, a New York policeman, and discovers high-level corruption involving his father and his partner. **Adaptation:** *Night Falls on Manhattan* (Paramount, 1997). Dir: Sidney Lumet. Scr: Sidney Lumet. Cast: Andy Garcia (Sean), Ian Holm (Liam), James Gandolfini (Joey), Lena Olin (Peggy), Ron Leibman (Morgenstern), Richard Dreyfuss (Sam). DVD, VHS.

4378. *Take a Girl Like You* (Kingsley Amis, 1960). A virtuous young Englishwoman takes a job as a teacher in a small town and is pursued by the local boys. **Adaptation 1:** *Take a Girl Like You* (Columbia, 1970). Dir: Jonathan Miller. Scr: George Melly. Cast: Hayley Mills (Jenny), Oliver Reed (Patrick), Noel Harrison (Julian), John Bird (Dick), Sheila Hancock (Martha). VHS. **Adaptation 2:** *Take a Girl Like You* (BBC/PBS, 2001 TV Movie). Dir: Nick Hurran. Scr: Andrew Davies. Cast: Rupert Graves (Patrick), Hugh Bonneville (Julian), Robert Daws (Dick), Emma Chambers (Martha), Sienna Guillory (Jenny). VHS.

4379. *Take Me Home: An Autobiography* (John Denver and Arthur Tobier, 1994). Autobiography by the late country singer, focusing on his struggle to become famous, his failed marriage, and his commitment to the environment. **Adaptation:** *Take Me Home: The John Denver Story* (CBS, 2000 TV Movie). Dir: Jerry London. Scr: Stephen Harrigan. Cast: Chad Lowe (Denver), Kristin Davis (Annie), Gerald McRaney (Dutch), Brian Markinson (Hal), Susan Hogan (Irma). DVD, VHS.

Take Me Home Again (see *The Lies Boys Tell*).

4380. *Take Three Tenses: A Fugue in Time* (Rumer Godden, 1945). As he watches his adopted daughter and his nephew begin a romantic relationship, an elderly man reflects on his own tragic involvement with a woman many years earlier. **Adaptation:** *Enchantment* (RKO, 1948). Dir: Irving Reis. Scr: John Patrick. Cast: David Niven (Roland), Teresa Wright (Lark), Evelyn Keyes (Grizel), Farley Granger (Pax), Jayne Meadows (Selina), Leo G. Carroll (Proutie). VHS.

4381. *Taking Lives* (Michael Pye, 1999). An FBI profiler tracks a serial killer who assumes the identities of his victims. **Adaptation:** *Taking Lives* (Warner, 2004). Dir: D. J. Caruso. Scr: Jon Bokenkamp. Cast: Angelina Jolie (Illeana), Ethan Hawke (Costa), Kiefer Sutherland (Hart), Gena Rowlands (Mrs. Asher), Olivier Martinez (Paquette). DVD, VHS.

4382. *The Taking of Pelham One-Two-Three* (John Godey, 1973). Armed terrorists take the passengers of a New York City subway car hostage and demand their ransom in one hour. A transit policeman must negotiate with them while trying to discover how they will make their escape from the tunnel where the train in stalled. **Adaptation 1:** *The Taking of Pelham One Two Three* (United Artists, 1974). Dir: Joseph Sargent. Scr: Peter Stone. Cast: Walter Matthau (Detective Garber), Robert Shaw (Mr. Blue), Martin Balsam (Mr. Green), Hector Elizondo (Mr. Gray), Earl Hindman (Mr. Brown). DVD, VHS. **Adaptation 2:** *The Taking of Pelham One Two Three* (MGM Television, 1998 TV Movie). Dir: Felix Enriquez Alcala. Scr: Peter Stone (1974 screenplay), April Smith. Cast: Edward James Olmos (Detective Piscotti), Vincent D'Onofrio (Mr. Blue), Donnie Wahlberg (Mr. Gray), Richard Schiff (Mr. Green), Lisa Vidal (Babs), Tara Rosling (Mr. Brown), Lorraine Bracco (Detective Ray).

4383. *Taking to the Air: The Rise of Michael Jordan* (Jim Naughton, 1992). Biography of the basketball legend. **Adaptation:** *Michael Jordan: An American Hero* (Avalanche, 1999 TV Movie). Dir: Michael J. Murray. Scr: Michael J. Murray. Cast: Michael Jace (Jordan), Christopher Jacobs (Buzz), Debbie Allen (Deloris).

4384. *The Talented Mr. Ripley* (Patricia Highsmith, 1955). In the first of Highsmith's five novels featuring con man Tom Ripley, the young man is recruited by a millionaire to go to Europe and bring back his playboy son. Ripley locates the man but decides to kill him and assume his identity. **Adaptation 1:** *Purple Noon*; released in the UK as *Blazing Sun* (Times, 1960). Dir: Rene Clement. Scr: Rene Clement, Paul Gegauff. Cast: Alain Delon (Ripley), Maurice Ronet (Philippe), Marie Laforet (Marge), Erno Crisa (Riccordi). Notes: Originally released as *Plein soleil* and

shown with subtitles. DVD, VHS. **Adaptation 2:** *The Talented Mr. Ripley* (Paramount, 1999). Dir: Anthony Minghella. Scr: Anthony Minghella. Cast: Matt Damon (Ripley), Gwyneth Paltrow (Marge), Jude Law (Dickie), Cate Blanchett (Meredith), Philip Seymour Hoffman (Freddie). Notes: National Board of Review Awards for Best Director and Supporting Actor (Hoffman); Academy Award nominations for Best Screenplay, Supporting Actor (Law), Art Direction, Musical Score, and Costume Design; Golden Globe nominations for Best Picture, Director, Actor (Damon), Supporting Actor (Law), and Musical Score. DVD, VHS. See also *Ripley's Game.*

4385. *A Tale of Two Cities* (Charles Dickens, 1859). An irresponsible English lawyer sacrifices himself to save a French friend from the guillotine during the French revolution in the late eighteenth century. The novel was serialzed in *All Year Round* between July and December 1859. **Silent Films:** 1907, 1911, 1917, 1922, and 1925. **Adaptation 1:** *A Tale of Two Cities* (MGM, 1935). Dir: Jack Conway. Scr: W. P. Lipscomb, S. N. Behrman. Cast: Ronald Colman (Sydney), Elizabeth Allan (Lucie), Edna May Oliver (Miss Pross), Reginald Owen (Stryver), Basil Rathbone (Marquis St. Evremonde). Notes: Academy Award nominations for Best Film and Editing. VHS. **Adaptation 2:** *A Tale of Two Cities* (BBC, 1957 TV Miniseries). Dir: John Keir Cross. Scr: John Keir Cross. Cast: Peter Wyngarde (Sydney), Edward de Souza (Charles), Wendy Hutchinson (Lucie), Fred Fairclough (Dr. Manette), Margaretta Scott (Madame Defarge), Kenneth Thorne (Mr. Defarge). **Adaptation 3:** *A Tale of Two Cities* (Rank, 1958). Dir: Ralph Thomas. Scr: T. E. B. Clarke. Cast: Dirk Bogarde (Sydney), Dorothy Tutin (Lucie), Paul Guers (Charles), Marie Versini (Marie), Ian Bannen (Gabelle), Cecil Parker (Jarvis). DVD, VHS. **Adaptation 4:** *A Tale of Two Cities* (BBC, 1965 TV Miniseries). Dir: Joan Craft. Scr: Constance Cox. Cast: John Wood (Sydney), Nicholas Pennell (Charles), Patrick Troughton (Dr. Manette), Rosalie Crutchley (Madame Defarge), Kika Markham (Lucie), Ronnie Barker (Cruncher), Janet Henfrey (Mrs. Cruncher). **Adaptation 5:** *A Tale of Two Cities* (Hallmark/CBS, 1980 TV Miniseries). Dir: Jim Goddard. Scr: John Gay. Cast: Chris Sarandon (Sydney Carton), Peter Cushing (Dr. Manette), Kenneth More (Dr. Lorry), Barry Morse (St. Evremonde), Flora Robson (Miss Pross), Billie Whitelaw (Madame Defarge), Alice Krige (Lucie). Notes: Golden Globe nomination for Best Television Movie. VHS. **Adaptation 6:** *A Tale of Two Cities* (BBC, 1980 TV Miniseries). Dir: Michael E. Briant. Scr: Michael E. Briant, Peter Harding. Cast: Paul Shelley (Sydney), Sally Osborn (Lucie), Vivien Merchant (Miss. Pross), Ralph Michael (Dr. Manette), Judy Parfitt (Madame Defarge), Stephen Yardley (Mr. Defarge). **Adaptation 7:** *A Tale of Two Cities* (Granada, 1989 TV Miniseries). Dir: Philippe Monnier. Scr: Arthur Hopcraft. Cast: James Wilby (Sydney), Xavier Deluc (Charles), Serena Gordon (Lucie), John Mills (Jarvis), Jean-Pierre Aumont (Dr. Manette), Anna Massey (Miss Pross), Kathy Kriegel (Madame Defarge). DVD, VHS.

4386. *A Talent for Loving, or the Great Cowboy Race* (Richard Condon, 1964). Comic Western about a professional gambler who marries into a Mexican family whose women are under an Aztec curse to adore their husbands. **Adaptation:** *A Talent for Loving*; released on video as *Gun Crazy* (Paramount, 1969). Dir: Richard Quine. Scr: Richard Condon. Cast: Richard Widmark (the Cowboy), Cesar Romero (Dr. Vicuna), Caroline Munro (Maria). VHS.

Tales from the Darkside: The Movie (*see* "Cat from Hell" and "Lot No. 249").

Tales of Mystery and Imagination (*see* "Metzengerstein" and "William Wilson").

Tales of Ordinary Madness (see *Erections, Ejaculations, Exhibitions, and General Tales of Ordinary Madness*).

Tales of Terror (*see* "The Black Cat," "The Cask of Amontillado," "The Facts of the Case of M. Valdemar," and "Morella."

4387. *Tales of the South Pacific* (James A. Michener, 1947, Pulitzer Prize). Fictional vignettes set on an island in the South Pacific during World War II. In 1949, the book was adapted as the long-running Broadway musical *South Pacific* by Oscar Hammerstein II and Joshua Logan with music by Hammerstein and Richard Rodgers. **Adaptation 1:** *South Pacific* (20th Century–Fox, 1958). Dir: Joshua Logan. Scr: Oscar Hammerstein II and Joshua Logan (based on their 1949 play), Paul Osborn. Cast: Rossano Brazzi (Emile), Mitzi Gaynor (Nellie), John Kerr (Joseph), Ray Walston (Luther), Juanita Hall (Bloody Mary), France Nuyen (Liat). Notes: Academy Award for Best Sound and nomination for Best Musical Score; Golden Globe nominations for Best Musical Picture and Actress (Gaynor). DVD, VHS. **Adaptation 2:** *South Pacific* (ABC, 2001 TV Movie). Dir: Richard Pearce. Scr: Lawrence D. Cohen (based on Logan and Hammerstein's 1949 play). Cast: Glenn Close (Nellie), Harry Connick, Jr. (Joseph), Rade Sherbedgia (Emile), Jack Thompson (Captain Brackett), Lori Tan Chinn (Bloody Mary), Natalie Mendoza (Liat). DVD, VHS.

Talk About a Stranger (*see* "The Enemy").

Talk of Angels (see *Mary Lavelle*).

Talk Radio (see *Talked to Death*).

4388. *Talked to Death: The Life and Murder of Alan Berg* (Stephen Singular, 1987). Factual account of an abrasive radio talk-show host who was targeted by a neo–Nazi group and shot to death in front of his house in 1984. The book was adapted as the one-man play *Talk Radio* in 1985 by Eric Bogosian and Tad Savinar. **Adaptation:** *Talk Radio* (Universal, 1988). Dir: Oliver Stone. Scr: Eric Bogosian, Oliver Stone. Cast: Eric Bogosian (Barry), Ellen Greene (Ellen), Leslie Hope (Laura), John C. McGinley (Stu), Alec Baldwin (Dan), John Pankow (Dietz). Notes: Independent Spirit Award nominations for Best Director, Actor (Bogosian), and Cinematography. DVD, VHS.

4389. *Talking It Over* (Julian Barnes, 1991). Two friends compete for the love of the same woman. **Adaptation:** *Love, etc.* (Phaedra, 1996). Dir: Marion Vernoux. Scr: Dodine Herry, Marion Vernoux. Cast: Charlotte Gainsbourg (Marie), Yvan Attal (Benoit), Charles Berling (Pierre). DVD, VHS.

4390. *Talking to Strange Men* (Ruth Rendell, 1987). Separated from his wife and jealous of her relationship with another man, a husband frames him but discovers that her lover is a dangerous man. **Adaptation:** *Talking to Strange Men* (Blue Heaven/TVS, 1992 TV Movie). Dir: John Gorrie. Scr: Julian Bond. Cast: John Duttine (John), Mel Martin (Jennifer), Ralph Brown (Peter), Miles Anderson (Mark).

4391. *The Tall Headlines* (Audrey Erskine Lindop, 1950). A British family is torn apart when their son is tried for murder. **Adaptation:** *The Tall Headlines*; released in the U.S. as *The Frightened Bride* (Grand National/Beverly, 1952). Dir: Terence Young. Scr: Audrey Erskine Lindop, Dudley Leslie. Cast: Andre Morell (George), Flora Robson (Mary), Michael Denison (Philip), Jane Hylton (Frankie). DVD, VHS.

4392. *The Tall Men* (Henry W. Allen, 1954). Two bothers join a cattle drive from Texas to Montana, battling Indians and each other for the love of a woman. Allen originally published the novel under the pseudonym Clay Fisher. **Adaptation:** *The Tall Men* (20th Century–Fox, 1955). Dir: Raoul Walsh. Scr: Sydney Boehm, Frank Nugent. Cast: Clark Gable (Colonel Allison), Jane Russell (Nella), Robert Ryan (Nathan), Cameron Mitchell (Clint). VHS.

Tall Story (see *The Homecoming Game*).

4393. *The Tall Stranger* (Louis L'Amour, 1957). Western about a wounded rancher who is aided by people on a wagon train and who helps them find land to settle. **Adaptation:** *The Tall Stranger*; also released as *Walk Tall* and as *The Rifle* (Allied Artists, 1957). Dir: Thomas Carr. Scr: Christopher Knopf. Cast: Joel McCrea (Ned), Virginia Mayo (Ellen), Barry Kelley (Hardy), Michael Ansara (Zarata), Whit Bissell (Judson).

The Tall T. (see *The Captives*).

Tam Lin (*see* "The Ballad of Tam Lin").

4394. *Tamahine* (Thelma Nicklaus, 1957). Comic novel about the headmaster of a British boys' school whose beautiful and uninhibited Polynesian cousin comes to visit, causing a sensation among the students. **Adaptation:** *Tamahine* (Associated British/MGM, 1963). Dir: Philip Leacock. Scr: Denis Cannan. Cast: Nancy Kwan (Tamahine), John Fraser (Richard), Dennis Price (Charles), Coral Browne (Mrs. Becque).

4395. *The Tamarind Seed* (Evelyn Anthony [pseudonym for Evelyn Bridget P. Ward-Thomas], 1971). Vacationing in Barbados, a British widow falls in love with a Russian military officer. **Adaptation:** *The Tamarind Seed* (AVCO Embassy, 1974). Dir: Blake Edwards. Scr: Blake Edwards. Cast: Julie Andrews (Judith), Omar Sharif (Feodor), Anthony Quayle (Jack), Dan O'Herlihy (Fergus), Sylvia Syms (Margaret), Oskar Homolka (General Golitsyn). DVD, VHS.

Tammy and the Bachelor (see *Tammy Out of Time*).

4396. *Tammy Out of Time* (Cid Ricketts Sumner, 1948). A backwoods tomboy nurses a pilot who crashed near her property back to health and discovers love and romance in the process. **Adaptation:** *Tammy and the Bachelor*; released in the UK as *Tammy* (Universal International, 1957). Dir: Joseph Pevney. Scr: Oscar Brodney. Cast: Debbie Reynolds (Tammy), Leslie Nielsen (Peter), Walter Brennan (Grandpa), Mala Powers (Barbara), Sidney Blackmer (Professor Brent), Mildred Natwick (Aunt Renie). VHS. Notes: Two sequels followed the original film, *Tammy Tell Me True* in 1961, and *Tammy and the Doctor* in 1963 (VHS). The book

and films also inspired an ABC television series in 1965, and a film titled *Tammy and the Millionaire*, culled from episodes of the television series. See also *Tammy Tell Me True*.

4397. *Tammy Tell Me True* (Cid Ricketts Sumner, 1959). One of several books in Sumner's Tammy series, this one featuring the charming tomboy at college. **Adaptation:** *Tammy Tell Me True* (Universal International, 1961). Dir: Harry Keller. Scr: Oscar Brodney. Cast: Sandra Dee (Tammy), John Gavin (Tom), Charles Drake (Buford), Virginia Grey (Miss Jenks). See also *Tammy Out of Time*.

4398. *Tap Roots* (James Street, 1942). A Mississippi family tries to remain neutral during the Civil War as state officials threaten to withdraw from the Confederacy if the South secedes from the Union. **Adaptation:** *Tap Roots* (Universal, 1948). Dir: George Marshall. Scr: Alan Le May. Cast: Van Heflin (Keith), Susan Hayward (Morna), Boris Karloff (Tishomingo), Julie London (Aven).

Taps (see *Father Sky*).

4399. "Taras Bulba" (Nikolai Gogol, 1835). In the war between the Cossacks and the Poles, a Russian leader finds himself at odds with his headstrong son. The short story appeared in Gogol's 1835 collection *Mirgorod*. **Silent Films:** 1909 and 1924. **Adaptation 1:** *Taras Bulba* (GG, 1936). Dir: Alexis Granowsky. Scr: Pierre Benoit, Jacques Natanson, Carlo Rim. Cast: Harry Baur (Taras), Jean-Pierre Aumont (Andrei), Danielle Darrieux (Marina). **Adaptation 2:** *The Rebel Son*; also released as *Taras Bulba* and as *The Barbarian and the Lady* (London, 1938). Dir: Adrian Brunel, Albert de Courville, Alexis Granowsky. Scr: Adrian Brunel. Cast: Harry Baur (Taras), Anthony Bushell (Andrei), Roger Livesey (Peter), Patricia Roc (Marina). **Adaptation 3:** *Taras Bulba* (United Artists, 1962). Dir: J. Lee Thompson. Scr: Waldo Salt, Karl Tunberg. Cast: Tony Curtis (Andrei), Yul Brynner (Taras), Sam Wanamaker (Filipenko), Christine Kaufmann (Natalia). VHS. **Adaptation 4:** *Taras Bulba*; also released as *Plains of Battle* (Regionale, 1963). Dir: Ferdinando Baldi. Scr: Ennio De Concini. Cast: Vladimir Medar (Taras), Jean-Francois Poron (Andrei), Lorella De Luca (Natalia).

Tarnished Angels (see *Pylon*).

4400. *Tarnsman of Gor* (John Norman, 1966). The first installment in Norman's twenty-six-volume Gor or Chronicle of Counter-Earth series (1966–2002) concerns a man who is magically transported to the planet Gor, where he becomes a hero for taking arms against the ruling tyrants. **Adaptation:** *Gor* (Cannon, 1988). Dir: Fritz Kiersch. Scr: Rick Marx, Harry Alan Towers (writing as Peter Welbeck). Cast: Urbano Barberini (Tarl), Oliver Reed (Sarm), Paul L. Smith (Surbus), Rebecca Ferratti (Talena), Jack Palance (Xenos). VHS. See also *Outlaw of Gor*.

4401. *Tarzan of the Apes* (Edgar Rice Burroughs, 1914). The classic story of a baby orphaned in the jungles of Africa and raised by an ape to be a survivor in the harsh jungle environment. **Silent Film:** 1918, directed by Scott Sidney and starring Elmo Lincoln (VHS). **Adaptation 1:** *Tarzan the Ape Man* (MGM, 1932). Dir: W. S. Van Dyke. Scr: Cyril Hume, Ivor Novello. Cast: Johnny Weissmuller (Tarzan), Neil Hamilton (Harry), Maureen O'Sullivan (Jane), C. Aubrey Smith (Parker). VHS. **Adaptation 2:** *Tarzan the Ape Man* (MGM, 1959). Dir: Joseph Newman. Scr: Robert Hill. Cast: Denny Miller (Tarzan), Cesare Danova (Harry), Joanna Barnes (Jane), Robert Douglas (Parker) **Adaptation 3:** *Tarzan the Ape Man* (MGM, 1981). Dir: John Derek. Scr: Tom Rowe, Gary Goodard. Cast: Bo Derek (Jane), Richard Harris (Parker), John Phillip Law (Holt), Miles O'Keeffe (Tarzan). Notes: An updated adaptation told from Jane's point of view. VHS. **Adaptation 4:** *Greystoke: The Legend of Tarzan, Lord of the Apes* (Warner, 1984). Dir: Hugh Hudson. Scr: Robert Towne (writing as P. H. Vazak), Michael Austin. Cast: Ralph Richardson (the Sixth Earl of Greystoke), Ian Holm (Phillippe), James Fox (Lord Esker), Christopher Lambert (John/Tarzan), Andie MacDowell (Jane). Notes: Academy Award nominations for Best Screenplay, Supporting Actor (Richardson), and Makeup; BAFTA nominations for Best Supporting Actors (Holm and Richardson), Cinematography, Production Design, and Sound. VHS. **Adaptation 5:** *Tarzan* (Disney/Buena Vista, 1999). Dir: Chris Buck, Kevin Lima. Scr: Tab Murphy, Bob Tzudiker, Noni White, Henry Mayo, David Reynolds, Jeffrey Stepakoff, Ned Teitelbaum. Cast: voices of Tony Goldwyn (Tarzan), Minnie Driver (Jane), Glenn Close (Kala), Brian Blessed (Clayton), Nigel Hawthorne (Porter). Notes: An animated musical feature. DVD, VHS. Notes: In addition to these films, which were directly adapted from the book, Burroughs' story has inspired more than thirty-five films and several television series, including a 1966 program on NBC and a 2003 WB network series (DVD).

Tashunga (see *The North Star*).

4402. *A Taste for Death* (P. D. James, 1986, Diamond Dagger Award of the British Crime Writers Association). When a government minister and a homeless man are found dead together on a street, Inspector Adam Dagliesh investigates and discovers secrets in the minister's background. **Adaptation:** *A Taste for Death* (ITV, 1988 TV Miniseries). Dir: John Davies. Scr: Alick Rowe. Cast: Roy Marsden (Dalgliesh), Penny Downie (Inspector Miskin), Wendy Hiller (Lady Ursula), Bosco Hogan (Sir Paul), Fiona Fullerton (Lady Barbara), Simon Ward (Stephen). DVD, VHS.

Taste of Excitement (see *Waiting for a Tiger*).

4403. *A Taste of My Own Medicine: When the Doctor Is the Patient* (Edward Rosenbaum, M.D., 1988). True story about an arrogant surgeon who learned humility when he contracted cancer and was placed at the mercy of indifferent doctors and hospital staff. **Adaptation:** *The Doctor* (Buena Vista, 1991). Dir: Randa Haines. Scr: Robert Caswell. Cast: William Hurt (Dr. MacKee), Christine Lahti (Anne), Elizabeth Perkins (June), Mandy Patinkin (Dr. Kaplan), Adam Arkin (Dr. Blumfield). DVD, VHS.

Tea with Mussolini (see *Zeffirelli*).

4404. *Teacher* (Sylvia Ashton-Warner, 1963). Autobiographical account by the New Zealand teacher and writer (1905–1984) whose innovative methods for teaching Maori children to read in the 1940's provoked protests from the local government. **Adaptation:** *Sylvia* (MGM-UA, 1985). Dir: Michael Firth. Scr: Michael Firth, Michele Quill. Cast: Eleanor David (Sylvia), Nigel Terry (Aden), Tom Wilkinson (Keith), Mary Regan (Opal). Notes: The screenplay combines elements from this book and Ashton-Warner's autobiography *I Passed This Way* (1979). New Zealand Film and Television Award for Best Supporting Actress (Regan). VHS.

4405. *Tears Before Bedtime* (Barbara Skelton, 1987). The first volume of the novelist's memoirs, which include her reminiscences of her three marriages and numerous affairs, including one with King Farouk of Egypt. **Adaptation:** *A Business Affair* (Castle Hill, 1994). Dir: Charlotte Brandstrom. Scr: Charlotte Brandstrom, William Stadiem. Cast: Christopher Walken (Vanni), Carole Bouquet (Kate), Jonathan Pryce (Alec), Sheila Hancock (Judith). Notes: The screenplay, which concerns a failed writer's jealousy over his wife's success as a novelist and her affair with his agent, is based on this book and on the second installment of Skelton's memoirs, *Weep No More* (1989). DVD, VHS.

4406. *TekLab* (William Shatner, 1991). In the third installment of Shatner's popular science-fiction series featuring Jake Cardigan, the former policeman searches frantically for his missing son and his sworn enemy's young daughter in the ruins of London. **Adaptation:** *TekWar: TekLab* (Universal Television, 1994 TV Movie). Dir: Timothy Bond. Scr: Chris Haddock, Westbrook Claridge. Cast: Greg Evigan (Jake), Eugene Clark (Sid), William Shatner (Walter), Michael York (Richard).

4407. *TekLords* (William Shatner, 1991). In the second installment of Shatner's futuristic science-fiction thrillers featuring Jake Cardigan, the former policeman tries to stop the powerful Tek-Lords from spreading a deadly plague in San Francisco. **Adaptation:** *TekWar: TekLords* (Universal Television, 1994 TV Movie). Dir: George Bloomfield. Scr: Morgan Gendel, Westbrook Claridge, Alfonse Ruggiero, Cast: Greg Evigan (Jake), Eugene Clark (Sid), Torri Higginson (Beth), William Shatner (Walter).

4408. *TekWar* (William Shatner and Ron Goulart, 1989). In the first of Shatner's series of futuristic science-fiction thrillers featuring Jake Cardigan, the former policeman is released from prison and goes searching for those who framed him for drug dealing. **Adaptation:** *TekWar* (Universal Television, 1994 TV Movie). Dir: William Shatner. Scr: Westbrook Claridge, Alfonse Ruggiero. Cast: Greg Evigan (Jake), Eugene Clark (Sid), Torri Higginson (Beth), Ray Jewers (Bennett), Von Flores (Sonny). VHS. Notes: The film served as the pilot for a television series (1994–1996).

4409. *Telefon* (Walter Wager, 1975). A renegade KGB agent steals a notebook that contains the names of Russian sleeper agents in the United States and activates them to attack American targets. A Russian intelligence officer must eliminate him and stop the agents before a war is instigated. **Adaptation:** *Telefon* (MGM, 1977). Dir: Don Siegel. Scr: Peter Hyams, Stirling Silliphant. Cast: Charles Bronson (Grigori), Lee Remick (Barbara), Donald Pleasence (Nicolai), Tyne Daly (Dorothy). VHS.

4410. *Tell England: A Study in a Generation* (Ernest Raymond, 1922). A fictionalized account of the British battle in Gallipoli in Eastern Europe during World War I. **Adaptation:** *Tell England*; released in the U.S. as *The Battle of Gallipoli* (Capitol, 1931). Dir: Anthony Asquith. Scr: Anthony Asquith. Cast: Fay Compton (Mrs. Doe), Tony Bruce (Rupert), Carl Harbord (Edgar).

4411. *Tell Me a Lie* (Jung Il Jang, 1996). The Korean novel, originally titled *Gogitmal*, involves an eighteen-year-old girl who begins a deviant sexual affair with a middle-aged artist. The book was banned in Korea and the author jailed for obscenity. **Adaptation:** *Lies* (Cowboy Booking, 1999). Dir: Sun-Woo Jang. Scr: Sun-Woo Jang. Cast: Sang Hyun Lee (J), Tae Yeon Kim (Y), Hye Jin Jeon (Woori). Notes: Originally released as *Gojitmal* and shown with subtitles. DVD, VHS.

4412. *Tell Me a Riddle* (Tillie Olsen, 1961). Novella about an elderly woman who reconnects with her husband and relatives when she learns she is dying. **Adaptation:** *Tell Me a Riddle* (Filmways, 1980). Dir: Lee Grant. Scr: Joyce Eliason, Alev Lytle. Cast: Melvyn Douglas (David), Lila Kedrova (Eva), Brooke Adams (Jeannie), Dolores Dorn (Vivi). VHS.

4413. *Tell Me That You Love Me, Junie Moon* (Marjorie Kellogg, 1968). A disfigured young woman, a homosexual paraplegic man, and an introverted epileptic man take up residence together and find meaning in their lives. **Adaptation:** *Tell Me That You Love Me, Junie Moon* (Paramount, 1969). Dir: Otto Preminger. Scr: Marjorie Kellogg. Cast: Liza Minnelli (Junie), Ken Howard (Arthur), Robert Moore (Warren), James Coco (Mario).

4414. "The Tell-Tale Heart" (Edgar Allan Poe, 1843). A madman kills a former friend, but the sounds of the man's beating heart betray the killer. The short story was first published in *The Pioneer* in January 1843). **Adaptation 1:** *Bucket of Blood*; also released as *The Tell-Tale Heart* (DuWorld, 1934). Dir: Brian Desmond Hurst. Scr: David Plunkett Greene. Cast: Norman Dryden (the Boy), John Kelt (the Old Man), Yolande Terrell (the Girl). **Adaptation 2:** *The Tell-Tale Heart* (MGM, 1941). Dir: Jules Dassin. Scr: Doane Hoag. Cast: Joseph Schildkraut (the Young Man), Roman Bohnen (the Old Man). **Adaptation 3:** *The Tell-Tale Heart* (Columbia, 1953). Dir: Art Babbitt, Ted Parmelee. Scr: Fred Grable, Bill Scott. Cast: Stanley Baker (Poe), James Mason (Narrator). Notes: An animated feature. DVD, VHS. **Adaptation 4:** *The Tell-Tale Heart* (Brigadier, 1960). Dir: Ernest Morris. Scr: Brian Clemens, Eldon Howard. Cast: Laurence Payne (Edgar), Adrienne Corri (Betty), Dermot Walsh (Carl), Selma Vaz Díaz (Mrs. Vine). DVD, VHS. **Adaptation 5:** *The Tell-Tale Heart* (JM, 1986). Dir: Joseph Marzano. Scr: Joseph Marzano. Cast: Joseph Marzano (the Old Man). Notes: Marzano previously adapted the story for a short film in

1958. **Adaptation 6:** *The Tell Tale Heart* (Monterey, 1989). Dir: Steve Barry, Brenda Levert, Rohanna Mehta, Carl Ruscica. Scr: Rohanna Mehta, Carl Ruscica. Cast: Dennis St. John (the Old Man), Matt Holland (the Police Inspector). DVD, VHS. **Adaptation 7:** *The Tell-Tale Heart* (Bravo, 1991, TV Movie). Dir: John Carlaw. Scr: Steven Berkoff. Cast: Steven Berkoff (the Man), Peter Brennan (the Magistrate), Neil Caplan (the Doctor).

Tell Them Willie Boy Is Here (see *Willie Boy*).

Tempest (see *The Captain's Daughter*).

4415. *Temple Tower* (Sapper [pseudonym for Herman Cyril McNeile], 1929). As British detective Bulldog Drummond and his fiancée prepare to be married in an old mansion, he discovers that the place may house a hidden treasure. After several people are murdered in pursuit of the loot, Bulldog must delay his wedding to investigate. **Adaptation 1:** *Temple Tower* (Fox, 1930). Dir: Donald Gallaher. Scr: Llewellyn Hughes. Cast: Kenneth MacKenna (Drummond), Marceline Day (Patricia), Henry B. Walthall (Blackton), Cyril Chadwick (Peter). **Adaptation 2:** *Bulldog Drummond's Secret Police* (Paramount, 1939). Dir: James P. Hogan. Scr: Garnett Weston. Cast: John Howard (Drummond), Heather Angel (Phyllis), H. B. Warner (Colonel Nielson), Reginald Denny (Algy). DVD, VHS.

Temptation (see *Bella Donna*).

4416. *Ten Against Caesar* (K. R. G. Granger [pseudonym for Kathleen B. George and Robert A. Granger], 1952). Western about a man who pursues the outlaws who kidnapped his fiancée in a stagecoach robbery. **Adaptation:** *Gun Fury* (Columbia, 1953). Dir: Raoul Walsh. Scr: Irving Wallace, Roy Huggins. Cast: Rock Hudson (Ben), Donna Reed (Jennifer), Leo Gordon (Tom), Lee Marvin (Blinky), Neville Brand (Brazos). VHS.

The Ten Commandments (see *On Eagle's Wing*, *Pillar of Fire*, and *Prince of Egypt*).

Ten Days in Paris (see *The Disappearance of Roger Tremayne*).

Ten Little Indians (see *And Then There Were None*).

4417. *Ten North Frederick* (John O'Hara, 1955). At the funeral of a small-town politician, his family and friends reflect on his unhappy life with his abusive wife and discover that he once found happiness in an affair with a younger woman. **Adaptation:** *Ten North Frederick* (20th Century–Fox, 1958). Dir: Philip Dunne. Scr: Philip Dunne. Cast: Gary Cooper (Joe), Diane Varsi (Ann), Suzy Parker (Kate), Geraldine Fitzgerald (Edith). VHS.

4418. *Ten Plus One* (Ed McBain [pseudonym for Evan Hunter], 1963). Detectives work to catch a sniper terrorizing New York City. **Adaptation:** *Without Apparent Motive* (20th Century–Fox, 1971). Dir: Philippe Labro. Scr: Philippe Labro, Jacques Lanzmann. Cast: Jean-Louis Trintignant (Detective Carella), Dominique Sanda (Sandra), Sacha Distel (Julien). Notes: Originally released as *Sans Mobile Apparent* and shown with subtitles. The action is moved from New York to Nice on the French Riviera.

4419. *Ten Rillington Place* (Ludovic Kennedy, 1961). Factual account of the notorious John Christie, who, in London in the 1940's, was arrested for killing a pregnant woman and having sex with her corpse. **Adaptation:** *10 Rillington Place* (Columbia, 1971). Dir: Richard Fleischer. Scr: Clive Exton. Cast: Richard Attenborough (Christie), Judy Geeson (Beryl), John Hurt (Timothy), Pat Heywood (Ethel). VHS.

4420. *Ten Second Jailbreak* (Eliot Asinof, Warren Hinckle, and William Turner, 1973). A team of adventurers is hired to rescue an American businessman from a Mexican jail. **Adaptation:** *Breakout* (Columbia, 1975). Dir: Tom Gries. Scr: Elliott Baker, Howard B. Kreitsek, Marc Norman. Cast: Charles Bronson (Nick), Robert Duvall (Jay), Jill Ireland (Ann), Randy Quaid (Hawk), Sheree North (Myrna). DVD, VHS.

Ten Seconds to Hell (see *The Phoenix*).

4421. *Ten Thirty on a Summer Night* (Marguerite Duras [pseudonym for Marguerite Donnadieu], 1960). The French novel, originally titled *Dix Heures et Demie du Soir en Ete*, concerns the neurotic woman traveling in Spain with her husband and becoming obsessed with a fugitive murderer. The novel was first translated into English in 1962. **Adaptation:** *10:30 P.M. Summer* (Argos/Lopert, 1966). Dir: Jules Dassin. Scr: Marguerite Duras, Jules Dassin. Cast: Melina Mercouri (Maria), Romy Schneider (Claire), Peter Finch (Paul), Julian Mateos (Rodrigo).

4422. *The Tenant* (Roland Topor, 1964). French novel, originally titled *Le Locataire Chimerique*, about a boarder at a rooming house who is convinced his fellow lodgers are out to kill him. **Adaptation:** *The Tenant* (Paramount, 1976). Dir: Roman Polanski. Scr: Gerard Brach, Roman Polanski. Cast: Roman Polanski (Trelkovsky), Isabelle Adjani (Stella), Melvyn Douglas (Mr. Zy), Jo Van Fleet (Mrs. Dioz), Bernard Fresson (Scope), Lila Kedrova (Mrs. Gaderian). DVD, VHS.

4423. *The Tenant of Wildfell Hall* (Anne Bronte, 1848). A woman leaves her abusive husband and moves with her son to a small village, where they live under assumed names and keep to themselves to protect their shameful secret. **Adaptation 1:** *The Tenant of Wildfell Hall* (BBC, 1968 TV Miniseries). Dir: Peter Sasdy. Scr: Christopher Fry. Cast: Janet Munro (Helen), Jeremy Burring (Arthur), William Gaunt (Lawrence), Bryan Marshall (Gilbert), Corin Redgrave (Arthur). **Adaptation 2:** *The Tenant of Wildfell Hall* (BBC/PBS, 1996 TV Miniseries). Dir: Mike Barker. Scr: Janet Barron, David Nokes. Cast: Tara Fitzgerald (Helen), Cathy Murphy (Mrs. Myers), Jackson Leach (Arthur), Sarah Badel (Rachel), Toby Stephens (Gilbert), Rupert Graves (Arthur). VHS.

4424. *Tender Is the Night* (F. Scott Fitzgerald, 1934). An American psychiatrist in Europe begins a disastrous relationship with a schizophrenic patient. **Adaptation 1:** *Tender Is the Night* (20th Century–Fox, 1962). Dir: Henry King. Scr: Ivan Moffat. Cast: Jennifer Jones (Nicole), Jason Robards (Dr. Diver), Joan Fontaine (Baby), Tom Ewell (Abe), Cesare Danova (Tommy), Jill St. John (Rosemary). Notes: National Board of Review Award for Best Actor (Robards). **Adaptation 2:** *Tender Is the Night* (BBC/Showtime, 1985 TV Miniseries). Dir: Robert Knights. Scr: Dennis Potter. Cast: Peter Strauss (Dr. Diver), Mary Steenburgen (Nicole), John Heard (Abe), Sean Young (Rosemary), Edward Asner (Devereux).

4425. "Tennessee's Partner" (Bret Harte, 1869). Western based on a true story about a gambling man whose faithful partner helps him beat an unjust murder charge in a mining camp. The short story was published in *Overland Monthly* in October 1869 and included in Harte's 1870 collection *The Luck of Roaring Camp and Other Sketches.* **Adaptation:** *Tennessee's Partner* (RKO, 1955). Dir: Allan Dwan. Scr: C. Graham Baker, D. D. Beauchamp, Allan Dwan, Milton Krims, Teddi Sherman. Cast: John Payne (Tennessee), Ronald Reagan (Cowpoke), Rhonda Fleming (Elizabeth), Coleen Gray (Goldie). DVD, VHS.

Tension at Table Rock (see *Bitter Sage*).

The Tenth Victim (*see* "The Seventh Victim").

4426. *Term of Trial* (James Barlow, 1961). An emotionally unstable student falls in love with her teacher and has him arrested and tried for sexual assault when he rejects her advances. **Adaptation:** *Term of Trial* (Romulus/Warner, 1962). Dir: Peter Glenville. Scr: Peter Glenville. Cast: Laurence Olivier (Graham), Simone Signoret (Anna), Sarah Miles (Shirley), Terence Stamp (Mitchell).

4427. *Terminal* (Robin Cook, 1992). A medical student working at a hospital discovers dark secrets about the reasons for the hospital's unusually successful cancer treatments. **Adaptation:** *Terminal* (NBC, 1996 TV Movie). Dir: Larry Elikann. Scr: Nancy Isaak. Cast: Doug Savant (Dr. O'Grady), Nia Peeples (Janet), Michael Ironside (Sterling), Jenny O'Hara (Margaret). DVD, VHS.

4428. *The Terminal Man* (Michael Crichton, 1972). Science-fiction thriller about a scientist who, following an injury, has a computer implanted in his brain that makes him violent. **Adaptation:** *The Terminal Man* (Warner, 1974). Dir: Mike Hodges. Scr: Mike Hodges. Cast: George Segal (Harry), Joan Hackett (Dr. Ross), Richard A. Dysart (Dr. Ellis), Jill Clayburgh (Angela). VHS.

4429. *Terms of Endearment* (Larry McMurtry, 1975). An eccentric woman tries to ward off various suitors while battling with her willful daughter. When her daughter becomes seriously ill, however, their relationship takes a bittersweet turn. **Adaptation:** *Terms of Endearment* (Paramount, 1983). Dir: James L. Brooks. Scr: James L. Brooks. Cast: Shirley MacLaine (Aurora), Debra Winger (Emma), Jack Nicholson (Garrett), Danny De Vito (Vernon), Jeff Daniels (Flap), John Lithgow (Sam). Notes: Academy Awards for Best Picture, Director, Screenplay, Actress (MacLaine), and Supporting Actor (Nicholson); Golden Globe Awards for Best Picture, Screenplay, Actress (MacLaine), and Supporting Actor (Nicholson), and nominations for Best Director, Actress (Winger), Supporting Actress (Winger), Supporting Actor (Lithgow), Musical Score, Editing, Art Direction, and Sound; National Board of Review Awards for Best Picture, Director, Actress (MacLaine), and Supporting Actor (Nicholson). DVD, VHS. See also *The Evening Star*.

4430. *A Terrible Beauty* (Arthur Roth, 1958). In a village in Northern Ireland at the beginning of World War II, Irish Republicans plan to launch an attack on the British while they're busy fighting the Germans. **Adaptation:** *A Terrible Beauty*; released in the U.S. as *Night Fighters* (United Artists, 1960). Dir: Tay Garnett. Scr: Robert Wright Campbell. Cast: Robert Mitchum (Dermot), Richard Harris (Sean), Anne Heywood

(Neeve), Dan O'Herlihy (Don), Cyril Cusack (Jimmy). VHS.

4431. *The Terrible Game* (Dan Tyler Moore, 1957). An American gymnast competes to win an Asian military base for the United States by fighting in a game that combines gymnastics and martial arts. **Adaptation:** *Gymkata* (MGM, 1985). Dir: Robert Clouse. Scr: Charles Robert Carner. Cast: Kurt Thomas (Jonathan Cabot), Tetchie Agbayani (Princess Rubali), Richard Norton (Zamir), Edward Bell (Paley). VHS.

Terror in the Shadows (see *Night of Reunion*).

Terror in the Sky (see *Flight into Danger*).

4432. *Tess of the D'Urbervilles* (Thomas Hardy, 1891). A poor girl country goes out to locate her supposed aristocratic relatives and finds only a lifetime of pain and grief. Bearing the subtitle "A Poor Woman Faithfully Presented," the story was serialized in *The Graphic* between July 4 and December 26, 1891, and was published as a novel in December 1891. **Silent Films:** 1913 and 1924. **Adaptation 1:** *Tess* (Columbia, 1979). Dir: Roman Polanski. Scr: Gerard Brach, Roman Polanski, John Brownjohn. Cast: Nastassja Kinski (Tess), Peter Firth (Angel), Leigh Lawson (Alec), John Collin (Jack), Rosemary Martin (Joan). Notes: Academy Awards for Best Cinematography, Art Direction, and Costume Design, and nominations for Best Picture, Director, and Musical Score; BAFTA Award for Best Cinematography and nominations for Best Production Design and Costume Design; Golden Globe Awards for Best Foreign Film and New Star (Kinski), and nominations for Best Director and Actress (Kinski). VHS. **Adaptation 2:** *Tess of the D'Urbervilles* (London Weekend/A&E, 1998 TV Miniseries). Dir: Ian Sharp. Scr: Ted Whitehead. Cast: Justine Waddell (Tess), Jason Flemyng (Alec), Oliver Milburn (Angel), John McEnery (Jack), Lesley Dunlop (Joan). DVD, VHS.

4433. *Tess of the Storm Country* (Grace Miller White, 1909). Romantic tale about a poor Scottish woman who falls in love with the son of a wealthy landowner. The novel was adapted for the stage by Rupert Hughes in 1911. **Silent Films:** 1914 and 1922, starring Mary Pickford (DVD, VHS). **Adaptation 1:** *Tess of the Storm Country* (Fox, 1932). Dir: Alfred Santell. Scr: Rupert Hughes (based on his 1911 play), S. N. Behrman, Sonya Levien. Cast: Janet Gaynor (Tess), Charles Farrell (Frederick), Dudley Digges (Captain Howland), Jane Clyde (Teola). **Adaptation 2:** *Tess of*

the Storm Country (20th Century–Fox, 1960). Dir: Paul Guilfoyle. Scr: Charles Lang. Cast: Diane Baker (Tess), Jack Ging (Peter), Lee Philips (Eric), Archie Duncan (Hamish). Notes: An updated version set in Pennsylvania Dutch country in the 1960's and involving chemical pollution of a man's land.

4434. *Testament of Youth: An Autobiographical Study of the Years 1900–1925* (Vera Brittain, 1933). Memoir about life before World War I and the terrible toll the Great War took on the youth of her generation. **Adaptation:** *Testament of Youth* (BBC/PBS, 1979 TV Miniseries). Dir: Moira Armstrong. Scr: Elaine Morgan. Cast: Cheryl Campbell (Vera), Rosalie Crutchley (Miss Penrose), Hazel Douglas (Aunt Florence), Rupert Frazer (Edward). Notes: BAFTA Television Awards for Best Drama Serial and Actress (Campbell). VHS.

4435. *The Testimony of Taliesin Jones* (Rhidian Brook, 1996). A young boy whose mother left home meets an elderly piano teacher with magical healing abilities. **Adaptation:** *The Testimony of Taliesin Jones* (Impact, 2000). Dir: Martin Duffy. Scr: Maureen Tilyou. Cast: John-Paul Macleod (Taliesin), Jonathan Pryce (Tal's Father), Geraldine James (Tal's Mother), Matthew Rhys (Jonathan), Robert Pugh (Handycott).

4436. *Tex* (S. E. Hinton, 1979). Young-adult novel about two teenagers left to fend for themselves after their mother's death. **Adaptation:** *Tex* (Disney/Buena Vista, 1982). Dir: Tim Hunter. Scr: Charlie Haas, Tim Hunter. Cast: Matt Dillon (Tex), Jim Metzler (Mason), Meg Tilly (Jamie), Bill McKinney (Pop). DVD, VHS.

The Texan (see "The Double-Dyed Deceiver").

4437. *Texas* (James A. Michener, 1986). Fictional history of Texas from the time of the Mexican conquistadors through the war of independence and statehood. **Adaptation:** *Texas* (ABC, 1994 TV Movie). Dir: Richard Lang. Scr: Sean Meredith. Cast: Benjamin Bratt (Benito), Patrick Duffy (Austin), Chelsea Field (Mattie), Anthony Michael Hall (Yancey), Stacy Keach (Houston), David Keith (Bowie), John Schneider (Crockett). DVD, VHS.

4438. *Texasville* (Larry McMurtry, 1987). The sequel to McMurtry's 1966 novel *The Last Picture Show* features the same characters thirty years later, struggling with middle age and marital problems. **Adaptation:** *Texasville* (Columbia, 1990). Dir: Peter Bogdanovich. Scr: Peter Bogdanovich. Cast: Eileen Brennan (Genevieve),

Randy Quaid (Lester), Cloris Leachman (Ruth), Timothy Bottoms (Sonny), Annie Potts (Karla), Cybill Shepherd (Jacy), Jeff Bridges (Duane). DVD, VHS. See also *The Last Picture Show*.

Thank You All Very Much (see *The Millstone*).

4439. *Thank You, Jeeves* (P. G. Wodehouse, 1934). In this book in Wodehouse's series of comic short stories and novels about a naïve man and his wise butler, Jeeves keeps his employer from becoming involved with underworld types. **Adaptation:** *Thank You, Jeeves!* (20th Century–Fox, 1936). Dir: Arthur Greville Collins. Scr: Stephen Gross, Joseph Hoffman. Cast: Arthur Treacher (Jeeves), Virginia Field (Marjorie), David Niven (Bertram), Lester Matthews (Elliot). Notes: A sequel, *Step Lively, Jeeves!,* was released in 1937.

4440. *Thank You, Mr. Moto* (John P. Marquand, 1936). In this installment in Marquand's series of books and short stories featuring the Japanese-American detective, Mr. Moto prevents a gang of thieves from deciphering a code that will allow them to steal Genghis Khan's treasure. The novel was serialized in *The Saturday Evening Post* (February 8–March 14, 1936). **Adaptation:** *Thank You, Mr. Moto* (20th Century–Fox, 1937). Dir: Norman Foster. Scr: Willis Cooper, Norman Foster. Cast: Peter Lorre (Mr. Moto), Thomas Beck (Tom), Pauline Frederick (Madame Chung), Jayne Regan (Eleanor).

4441. *That Cold Day in the Park* (Richard Miles, 1965). A lonely and disturbed spinster invites a young drifter into her home, where she imprisons him. **Adaptation:** *That Cold Day in the Park* (Commonwealth United, 1969). Dir: Robert Altman. Scr: Gillian Freeman. Cast: Sandy Dennis (Frances), Michael Burns (the Boy), Susanne Benton (Nina), John Garfield, Jr. (Nick), Luana Anders (Sylvie). VHS.

That Darn Cat (see *Undercover Cat*).

4442. *That Eye, the Sky* (Tim Winton, 1986). Fantasy about a mysterious stranger who arrives at the home of a poor woman caring for her children and invalid relatives in the Australian outback. **Adaptation:** *That Eye, the Sky* (Working Title, 1994). Dir: John Ruane. Scr: Jim Barton, John Ruane. Cast: Jamie Croft (Morton), Mark Fairall (Sam), Lisa Harrow (Alice), Amanda Douge (Tegwyn), Peter Coyote (Henry). Notes: Australian Film Institute Award for Best Young Actor (Croft) and nominations for Best Film, Director, Screenplay, Actress (Harrow), Cine-

matography, Production Design, and Costume Design.

That Forsyte Woman (see *The Forsyte Saga*).

4443. *That Lady* (Kate O'Brien, 1946). Set in sixteenth-century Spain at the court of Philip II, a beautiful widow incurs the jealous wrath of the king when she falls in love with one of his ministers. The novel, which was released in the U.S. under the title *One Sweet Grape*, was adapted for the stage by O'Brien in 1949. **Adaptation:** *That Lady* (20th Century–Fox, 1955). Dir: Terence Young. Scr: Sy Bartlett, Anthony Veiller. Cast: Olivia de Havilland (Ana), Gilbert Roland (Antonio), Paul Scofield (King Philip II), Francoise Rosay (Bernardine).

4444. *That Night* (Alice McDermott, 1987). A little girl who idolizes a neighborhood teenager helps her run away with her disreputable boy friend. **Adaptation:** *That Night* (Warner, 1992). Dir: Craig Bolotin. Scr: Craig Bolotin. Cast: C. Thomas Howell (Rick), Juliette Lewis (Sheryl), Helen Shaver (Ann), Eliza Dushku (Alice). VHS.

4445. *That Spot* (Jack London, 1908). Thieves steal a dog from a trainer in Canada and teach it to raid fox farms. The novella was published in *The Early Sunset Magazine* in 1908. **Adaptation:** *Sign of the Wolf* (Monogram, 1941). Dir: Howard Bretherton. Scr: Elizabeth Hopkins, Edmond Kelso. Cast: Michael Whalen (Rod), Grace Bradley (Judy), Darryl Hickman (Billy).

4446. *That Summer* (Sarah Dessen, 1997, ALA Best Book for Young Adults). Young-adult novel about the coming of age of a teenaged girl who, over the course of a summer, watches her parents divorce and faces other personal crises that make her doubt the possibility of happiness in life. **Adaptation:** *How to Deal* (New Line, 2003). Dir: Clare Kilner. Scr: Neena Beber. Cast: Mandy Moore (Halley), Allison Janney (Lydia), Trent Ford (Macon), Alexandra Holden (Scarlett), Dylan Baker (Steve), Nina Foch (Grandma Halley). Notes: The screenplay is based on this novel and Dessen's 1998 book *Someone Like You.* DVD, VHS. See also *Someone Like You.*

4447. *That Uncertain Feeling* (Kingsley Amis, 1955). In a small Welsh town, a henpecked librarian begins an affair with a local politician's wife. **Adaptation:** *Only Two Can Play* (British Lion/Kingsley, 1962). Dir: Sidney Gilliat. Scr: Bryan Forbes. Cast: Peter Sellers (John), Mai Zetterling (Liz), Virginia Maskell (Jean), Richard Attenborough (Probert). Notes: BAFTA nominations for Best Picture, Screenplay, and Actor (Sellers). VHS.

4448. *That Was Then ... This Is Now* (S. E. Hinton, 1971). A delinquent teenager is upset when the older boy he idolizes finds a girlfriend. **Adaptation:** *That Was Then ... This Is Now* (Paramount, 1985). Dir: Christopher Cain. Scr: Emilio Estevez. Cast: Emilio Estevez (Mark), Craig Sheffer (Bryon), Larry B. Scott (Terry), Matthew Dudley (Curly), Jill Schoelen (Angela), Kim Delaney (Cathy), Barbara Babcock (Mrs. Douglas), Morgan Freeman (Charlie). DVD, VHS.

That Way with Women (*see* "Idle Hands").

That Woman Opposite (see *The Emperor's Snuff Box*).

4449. *The Theatre* (W. Somerset Maugham, 1937). A married middle-aged actress begins an affair with a younger man and takes vengeance on him when she realizes that he's using her. The novel was adapted for the stage by Maugham and Guy Bolton in 1941. **Adaptation 1:** *Adorable Julia* (See-Art, 1962). Dir: Alfred Weidenmann. Scr: Guy Bolton, Pascal Jardin, Eberhard Keindorff. Marc-Gilbert Sauvajon, Johanna Sibelius. Cast: Lili Palmer (Julia), Charles Boyer (Michael), Jean Sorel (Tom). VHS. **Adaptation 2:** *Being Julia* (Sony, 2004). Dir: Istvan Szabo. Scr: Ronald Harwood. Cast: Annette Bening (Julia), Catherine Charlton (Miss Phillips), Jeremy Irons (Michael), Michael Gambon (Jimmy), Bruce Greenwood (Lord Charles), Juliet Stevenson (Evie), Rosemary Harris (Mrs. Lambert). Notes: Golden Globe Award for Best Actress (Bening); Academy Award nomination for Best Actress (Bening). DVD, VHS.

4450. *Their Eyes Were Watching God* (Zora Neale Hurston, 1937). Set in an African-American community in Florida in the 1920's, an independent-minded young woman in search of fulfillment recalls her many marriages and the controversy they raised in her small town. **Adaptation:** *Their Eyes Were Watching God* (Harpo/ABC, 2005 TV Movie). Dir: Darnell Martin. Scr: Suzan-Lori Parks, Misan Sagay, Bobby Smith, Jr. Cast: Halle Berry (Janie), Ruben Santiago-Hudson (Joe), Michael Ealy (Tea Cake), Nicki Micheaux (Phoebe), Lorraine Toussaint (Pearl), Ruby Dee (Nanny). Notes: Emmy nominations for Best Actress (Berry) and Hairstyling; Golden Globe nomination for Best Actress (Berry). DVD, VHS.

Their Secret Affair (see *Melville Goodwin, USA*).

4451. "The Theme of the Traitor and the Hero" (Jorge Luis Borges, 1944). A man goes to his father's birthplace and learns unpleasant truths about the past. The short story appeared in Borges' 1944 collection *Ficciones*. **Adaptation:** *The Spider's Stratgem* (New Yorker, 1970). Dir: Bernardo Bertolucci. Scr: Bernardo Bertolucci. Eduardo de Gregorio, Marilu Parolini. Cast: Giulio Brogi (Athos, father and son), Alida Valli (Draifa), Pippo Campanini (Gaibazzi), Franco Giovanelli (Rasori). VHS.

4452. "Then We Were Three" (Irwin Shaw, 1955). Two American students vacationing in Europe become romantic rivals when they meet an English girl. The short story was published in *McCall's* in August 1955. **Adaptation:** *Three* (United Artists, 1969). Dir: James Salter. Scr: James Salter. Cast: Charlotte Rampling (Marty), Robie Porter (Bert), Sam Waterston (Taylor), Pascale Roberts (Claude).

4453. *Theophilus North* (Thornton Wilder, 1973). A stranger in a small New England town develops a reputation for special healing powers and aids an old man to rediscover the joys of life. **Adaptation:** *Mr. North* (Samuel Goldwyn, 1988). Dir: Danny Huston. Scr: Janet Roach, John Huston, James Costigan. Cast: Anthony Edwards (North), Robert Mitchum (James), Lauren Bacall (Amelia), Harry Dean Stanton (Henry), Anjelica Huston (Persis), Mary Stuart Masterson (Elspeth), Virginia Madsen (Sally), Tammy Grimes (Sarah), David Warner (Dr. McPherson). DVD, VHS.

4454. *Theorem* (Pier Paolo Pasolini, 1968). Italian novel, originally titled *Teorema*, about a mysterious stranger who visits and seduces a bored wealthy family, leaving them questioning the value of their lives. **Adaptation:** *Theorem* (Aetos/Continental, 1968). Dir: Pier Paolo Pasolini. Scr: Pier Paolo Pasolini. Cast: Silvana Mangano (Lucia), Terence Stamp (the Visitor), Massimo Girotti (Paolo), Anne Wiazemsky (Odetta). VHS.

4455. *There Ain't No Justice* (James Curtis, 1937). Although it means the ruin of his career, a young boxer refuses to throw a fight despite the urging of his dishonest promoter. **Adaptation:** *There Ain't No Justice* (Ealing, 1939). Dir: Penrose Tennyson. Scr: James Curtis, Sergei Nolbandov, Penrose Tennyson. Cast: Jimmy Hanley (Tommy), Edward Rigby (Pa Mutch), Mary Clare (Ma Mutch), Phyllis Stanley (Elsie).

4456. *There Are No Children Here: The Story of Two Boys Growing Up in the Other America* (Alex Kotlowitz, 1991). Factual account of two African-American teenaged brothers trying to survive the violence in their housing project on Chicago's West Side. **Adaptation:** *There Are No Children Here* (LOMO, 1993 TV Movie). Dir: Anita W. Addison. Scr: Bobby Smith, Jr. Cast:

Oprah Winfrey (LaJoe), Keith David (John Paul), Mark Lane (Lafayette), Norman D. Golden II (Pharoah), Maya Angelou (Lelia Mae). VHS.

4457. *There Was a Little Man* (Constance Jones and Guy Jones, 1948). An American journalist's life is complicated when he meets a leprechaun on a trip to Ireland. **Adaptation:** *The Luck of the Irish* (20th Century–Fox, 1948). Dir: Henry Koster. Scr: Philip Dunne. Cast: Tyrone Power (Stephen), Anne Baxter (Nora), Cecil Kellaway (Horace), Lee J. Cobb (Augur).

These Are the Damned (see *The Children of Light*).

4458. *These Our Strangers* (Adrian Alington, 1940). A British nobleman takes in poor London children evacuated from the city during World War II. **Adaptation:** *Those Kids from Town* (Anglo-American, 1942). Dir: Lance Comfort. Scr: Adrian Alington. Cast: Shirley Lenner (Liz), Jeanne De Casalis (Sheila), Percy Marmont (Earl).

These Things Happen (see *Intersection*).

4459. *These Thousand Hills* (A. B. Guthrie, Jr., 1956). Western about an ambitious cowboy who manages to earn the money to buy a ranch but soon realizes that his lifelong goal may cost him his friends **Adaptation:** *These Thousand Hills* (20th Century–Fox, 1959). Dir: Richard Fleischer. Scr: Alfred Hayes. Cast: Don Murray (Evans), Richard Egan (Jehu), Lee Remick (Callie), Patricia Owens (Joyce), Stuart Whitman (Tom), Albert Dekker (Marshal Conrad).

They All Died Laughing (see *Don Among the Dead Men*).

4460. *They Call It Sin* (Alberta Stedman Eagan, 1932). A Kansas girl falls for a slick New Yorker and is duped into following the deceiver to his city, where she discovers that he is not what he seems to be. **Adaptation:** *They Call It Sin*; released in *The Way of Life* (First National, 1932). Dir: Thornton Freeland. Scr: Lillie Hayward, Howard J. Green. Cast: Loretta Young (Marion), George Brent (Dr. Travers), Una Merkel (Dixie), David Manners (Jimmy). VHS.

4461. *They Called Him Death* (David Hume [pseudonym for John Victor Turner], 1934). A private investigator looks into a kidnapping and extortion attempt at a nursing home. **Adaptation:** *The Patient Vanishes*; also released as *This Man Is Dangerous* (Rialto/Film Classics, 1941). Dir: Lawrence Huntington. Scr: David Hume, John Argyle, Edward Dryhurst. Cast: James Mason (Mick), Mary Clare (the Matron), Margaret Vyner (Mollie), Gordon McLeod (Inspector Cardby).

They Came from Beyond Space (see *The Gods Hate Kansas*).

4462. *They Came to Cordura* (Glendon Swarthout, 1958). After the 1916 battle against Pancho Villa in Mexico, an officer cited for cowardice is assigned to conduct four military heroes back home. On the arduous journey, their roles reverse as he shows his heroism and they their cowardice. **Adaptation:** *They Came to Cordura* (Columbia, 1959). Dir: Robert Rossen. Scr: Ivan Moffat, Robert Rossen. Cast: Gary Cooper (Thorn), Rita Hayworth (Adelaide), Van Heflin (Chawk), Tab Hunter (Fowler), Richard Conte (Trubee), Michael Callan (Hetherington). DVD, VHS.

4463. *They Cracked Her Glass Slipper* (Gerald Butler, 1946). Two professional gamblers compete for the affections of a beautiful young woman. **Adaptation:** *Third Time Lucky* (Pentagon, 1948). Dir: Gordon Parry. Scr: Gerald Butler. Cast: Glynis Johns (Joan), Dermot Walsh (Lucky), Charles Goldner (Flash), Harcourt Williams (Doc).

4464. *They Do It with Mirrors* (Agatha Christie, 1952). Miss Jane Marple is invited to visit a friend's old Victorian mansion, which is also used as a home for juvenile delinquents. As people begin to die off, Miss Marple investigates the crimes. The book was released in the U.S. as *Murder with Mirrors*. **Adaptation 1:** *Murder with Mirrors* (CBS, 1985 TV Movie). Dir: Dick Lowry. Scr: George Eckstein. Cast: Helen Hayes (Miss Marple), Bette Davis (Carrie), John Mills (Lewis), Leo McKern (Inspector Curry). VHS. **Adaptation 2:** *They Do It with Mirrors* (BBC/A&E, 1991 TV Movie series). Dir: Norman Stone. Scr: T. R. Bowen. Cast: Joan Hickson (Miss Marple), Jean Simmons (Carrie), Joss Ackland (Lewis), Faith Brook (Ruth). DVD, VHS.

4465. *They Drive by Night* (James Curtis, 1937). A truck driver helps an ex-convict prove that he did not commit a crime for which he is under suspicion. **Adaptation:** *They Drive by Night* (Warner, 1938). Dir: Arthur B. Woods. Scr: James Curtis, Paul Gangelin, Derek N. Twist. Cast: Emlyn Williams (Shorty), Ernest Thesiger (Walter), Anna Konstam (Molly).

They Drive by Night (1940) (see *Long Haul*).

4466. *They Gave Him a Gun* (William Joyce Cowen, 1936). After World War I, a man tries unsuccessfully to stop his disturbed friend from becoming a gangster. **Adaptation:** *They Gave Him a Gun* (MGM, 1937). Dir: W. S. Van Dyke. Scr:

Cyril Hume, Richard Maibaum, Maurice Rapf. Cast: Spencer Tracy (Fred), Gladys George (Rose), Franchot Tone (Jimmy), Edgar Dearing (Sergeant Meadowlark).

4467. *They Knew Mr. Knight* (Dorothy Whipple, 1934). Comic novel about a poor British man and his family who take advice from a financial speculator and grow rich for a short while. **Adaptation:** *They Knew Mr. Knight* (General, 1946). Dir: Norman Walker. Scr: Victor MacLure, Norman Walker. Cast: Mervyn Johns (Tom), Nora Swinburne (Celia), Joyce Howard (Freda), Joan Greenwood (Ruth).

They Live (see "Eight O'Clock in the Morning").

They Live by Night (see *Thieves Like Us*).

They Made Me a Fugitive (see *A Convict Has Escaped*).

They Met in the Dark (see *The Vanishing Corpse*).

They Passed This Way (see *Paso Por Aqui*).

4468. *They Shoot Horses, Don't They?* (Horace McCoy, 1935). A man who killed his dance-marathon partner recalls the extraordinary circumstances behind his act as he is found guilty of the crime in court. **Adaptation:** *They Shoot Horses, Don't They?* (Cinerama, 1969). Dir: Sydney Pollack. Scr: James Poe, Robert E. Thompson. Cast: Jane Fonda (Gloria), Michael Sarrazin (Robert), Susannah York (Alice), Gig Young (Rocky), Red Buttons (Sailor), Bonnie Bedelia (Ruby), Michael Conrad (Rollo), Bruce Dern (James). Notes: Academy Award for Best Actor (Young) and nominations for Best Director, Screenplay, Actress (Fonda), Musical Score, Art Direction,, Editing, and Costume Design; National Board of Review Award for Best Picture; Golden Globe nominations for Best Picture, Director, Actress (Fonda), Supporting Actress (York), and Supporting Actor (Buttons). DVD, VHS.

4469. *They Were Expendable* (William L. White, 1942). Factual account of a PT boat squad during World War II facing danger in the Philippines as the crew conducted General Douglas MacArthur to Australia. **Adaptation:** *They Were Expendable* (MGM, 1945). Dir: John Ford. Scr: Frank Wead. Cast: Robert Montgomery (Lieutenant Brickley), John Wayne (Lieutenant Ryan), Donna Reed (Lieutenant Davies), Jack Holt (General Martin). DVD, VHS.

4470. *They Were Sisters* (Dorothy Whipple, 1943). Three sisters have vastly different lives because of the men they marry. **Adaptation:** *They Were Sisters* (Gainsborough/Universal, 1945). Dir: Arthur Crabtree. Scr: Roland Pertwee, Katherine Strueby. Cast: Phyllis Calvert (Lucy), James Mason (Geoffrey), Hugh Sinclair (Terry), Anne Crawford (Vera). VHS.

They Won't Forget (see *Death in the Deep South*).

4471. *They're a Weird Mob* (John O'Grady, 1957) Comic novel about the misadventures of an Italian immigrant to Australia. **Adaptation:** *They're a Weird Mob* (Roadshow, 1966). Dir: Michael Powell. Scr: Emeric Pressburger (writing as Richard Imrie). Cast: Walter Chiari (Nino), Clare Dunne (Kay), Chips Rafferty (Harry), Alida Chelli (Giuliana).

4472. *Thick as Thieves* (Patrick Quinn, 1995). A rivalry develops between two thieves—one a suave, low-key burglar, the other a flashy gangster. **Adaptation:** *Thick as Thieves* (October/Rogue, 1998). Dir: Scott Sanders. Scr: Scott Sanders, Arthur Krystal. Cast: Alec Baldwin (Mackin), Andre Braugher (Dink), Michael Jai White (Pointy), Rebecca De Mornay (Petrone), David Byrd (Sal Capetti), Bruce Greenwood (Bo). DVD, VHS.

Thief (see *The Home Invaders*).

4473. *A Thief of Time* (Tony Hillerman, 1988). A ceramics expert disappears from a Navajo reservation and tribal policemen must try to determine whether she is a missing person or a thief of valuable artifacts. **Adaptation:** *A Thief of Time* (Granada/PBS, 2004 TV Movie). Dir: Chris Eyre. Scr: Alice Arlen. Cast: Gary Farmer (Captain Largo), Adam Beach (Jim), Wes Studi (Joe). DVD, VHS.

4474. *The Thief Who Came to Dinner* (Terence Lore Smith, 1971). Comic novel about a Houston computer expert who becomes a jewel thief. **Adaptation:** *The Thief Who Came to Dinner* (Warner, 1973). Dir: Bud Yorkin. Scr: Walter Hill. Cast: Ryan O'Neal (Webster), Jacqueline Bisset (Laura), Warren Oates (Dave), Jill Clayburgh (Jackie), Charles Cioffi (Henderling), Ned Beatty (Deams), Austin Pendleton (Zukovsky), Gregory Sierra (Dynamite), Michael Murphy (Ted), John Hillerman (Lasker). VHS.

Thieves' Highway see (*Thieves' Market*).

4475. *Thieves Like Us* (Edward Anderson, 1937). A man falsely imprisoned for murder escapes from jail with other prisoners and tries to go straight when he meets a loving woman. However, his fellow escapees force him to take part in their crimes. **Adaptation 1:** *Thieves Like Us* (RKO, 1974). Dir: Robert Altman. Scr: Robert Altman, Joan Tewkesbury, Calder Willingham. Cast: Keith Carradine (Bowie), Shelley Duvall (Keechie), John Schuck (Chicamaw), Bert Remsen (T-Dub). VHS. **Adaptation 2:** *They Live by Night* (United Artists, 1949). Dir: Nicholas Ray. Scr: Nicholas Ray, Charles Schnee. Cast: Cathy O'Donnell (Keechie), Farley Granger (Bowie), Howard Da Silva (Chicamaw), Jay C. Flippen (T-Dub). VHS.

4476. *Thieves' Market* (A. I. Bezzerides, 1949). A World War II veteran returning to his home in California seeks to avenge the brutality done to his truck-driver father and brother by ruthless fruit dealers. **Adaptation:** *Thieves' Highway* (20th Century–Fox, 1949). Dir: Jules Dassin. Scr: A. I. Bezzerides. Cast: Richard Conte (Nico), Valentina Cortese (Rica), Lee J. Cobb (Mike), Barbara Lawrence (Polly). DVD, VHS.

4477. *The Thin Man* (Dashiell Hammett, 1934). A comic mystery featuring Nick and Nora Charles, retired private detectives who, on a visit to New York, investigate the murder of an eccentric inventor. **Adaptation:** *The Thin Man* (MGM, 1934). Dir: W. S. Van Dyke. Scr: Albert Hackett, Frances Goodrich. Cast: William Powell (Nick), Myrna Loy (Nora), Maureen O'Sullivan (Dorothy), Nat Pendleton (John). Notes: Academy Award nominations for Best Film, Director, Screenplay, and Actor (Powell). DVD, VHS. Notes: The book inspired a television series (1957–1959) and five film sequels: *After the Thin Man* (1936) (VHS), *Another Thin Man* (1939) (VHS), *Shadow of the Thin Man* (1941) (VHS), *The Thin Man Goes Home* (1944) (VHS), and *Song of the Thin Man* (1947) (VHS).

4478. *The Thin Red Line* (James Jones, 1962). Set in 1943, Jones's autobiographical novel concerns the bloody World War II battle of Guadalcanal in the Pacific. **Adaptation 1:** *The Thin Red Line* (Allied Artists, 1964). Dir: Andrew Marton. Scr: Bernard Gordon. Cast: Keir Dullea (Doll), Jack Warden (Welsh), James Philbrook (Tall), Robert Kanter (Fife), Ray Daley (Stone). DVD, VHS. **Adaptation 2:** *The Thin Red Line* (20th Century–Fox, 1998). Dir: Terrence Malick. Scr: Terrence Malick. Cast: Sean Penn (Welsh), Adrien Brody (Fife), James Caviezel (Witt), Ben Chaplin (Bell), George Clooney (Bosche), John Cusack (Gaff), Woody Harrelson (Keck), Elias Koteas (Staros), Jared Leto (Whyte). Notes: Academy Award nominations for Best Film, Director, Screenplay, Musical Score, Cinematography, Editing, and Sound. DVD, VHS.

The Thing (*see* "Who Goes There?").

The Thing from Another World (*see* "Who Goes There?").

The Things of Life (see *Intersection*).

Things to Come (see *The Shape of Things to Come*).

4479. *Think Fast, Mr. Moto* (John P. Marquand, 1936). This installment in Marquand's series of novel and stories featuring the Japanese-American detective finds Mr. Moto traveling from San Francisco to Shanghai in pursuit of diamond smugglers. The novel was serialized in *The Saturday Evening Post* (September 12–October 17, 1936). **Adaptation:** *Think Fast, Mr. Moto* (20th Century–Fox, 1937). Dir: Norman Foster. Scr: Norman Foster, Charles Kenyon, Howard Ellis Smith. Cast: Peter Lorre (Mr. Moto), Thomas Beck (Hitchings), Virginia Field (Gloria), Sig Ruman (Marloff).

4480. *Think of a Number* (Anders Bodelson, 1969). A bank teller fools a bank robber by transferring the bank's money into his own safety deposit box. He then decides to keep the money, but the frustrated thief pursues him. **Adaptation:** *The Silent Partner* (Carolco/EMC, 1978). Dir: Daryl Duke. Scr: Curtis Hanson. Cast: Elliott Gould (Miles), Christopher Plummer (Harry), Susannah York (Julie). VHS.

4481. *Thinner* (Stephen King, 1984). An overweight attorney accidentally kills a gypsy woman and is cursed with uncontrollable weight-loss by her grieving father. The novel was originally published under the pseudonym Richard Bachman. **Adaptation:** *Thinner* (Paramount, 1996). Dir: Tom Holland. Scr: Michael McDowell, Tom Holland. Cast: Robert John Burke (Billy), Joe Mantegna (Ginelli), Lucinda Jenney (Heidi), Michael Constantine (Tadzu), Kari Wuhrer (Gina). DVD, VHS.

4482. *The Third Day* (Joseph Hayes, 1964). A man suffering from amnesia discovers that he is wealthy and that he is wanted for murder. **Adaptation:** *The Third Day* (Warner, 1965). Dir: Jack Smight. Scr: Burton Wohl, Robert Presnell, Jr. Cast: George Peppard (Steve), Elizabeth Ashley (Alexandra), Roddy McDowall (Oliver), Arthur O'Connell (Dr. Wheeler). DVD, VHS.

4483. *The Third Man* (Graham Greene, 1950). An American writer arrives in Vienna after World War II and is told that his friend has died under mysterious circumstances. The stories about the death seem inconsistent to him, and he soon learns that his friend's involvement with the black market and his investigation by the international police may explain a great deal. Greene wrote the film treatment in 1949 and turned it into a novel the following year. **Adaptation:** *The Third Man* (British Lion/London/Selznick, 1949). Dir: Carol Reed. Scr: Graham Greene. Cast: Joseph Cotten (Holly), Alida Valli (Anna), Orson Welles (Harry), Trevor Howard (Major Calloway), Bernard Lee (Sergeant Paine). Notes: Academy Award for Best Cinematography and nominations for Best Director and Editing; BAFTA Award for Best Picture; Cannes Film Festival Grand Prize of the Festival (Carol Reed). DVD, VHS. Notes: The film also inspired a successful BBC television series (1959–1965).

Third Man on the Mountain (see *Banner in the Sky*).

4484. *The Third Miracle* (Richard Vetere, 1997). Seeking confirmation for a beatification process, the Vatican sends a priest suffering from a crisis of faith to investigate reports that the death of a simple woman has caused a statue of the Virgin Mary to bleed and has cured a young girl of a terminal illness. As he looks into the matter, he rediscovers the purpose of his life. **Adaptation:** *The Third Miracle* (Sony, 1999). Dir: Agnieszka Holland. Scr: John Romano, Richard Vetere. Cast: Sofia Polanska (Helena), Ed Harris (Frank), Pavol Simon (Helena's father), Ken James (Father Panak), Michael Rispoli (John). DVD, VHS.

4485. *The Third Round* (Sapper [pseudonym for Herman Cyril McNeile], 1924). British detective Hugh "Bulldog" Drummond investigates a series of murders linked to a shipment of synthetic diamonds. **Adaptation:** *Bulldog Drummond's Peril* (Paramount, 1938). Dir: James P. Hogan. Scr: Stuart Palmer. Cast: John Barrymore (Colonel Neilson), John Howard (Drummond), Louise Campbell (Phyllis), Reginald Denny (Algy). DVD, VHS.

Third Time Lucky (see *They Cracked Her Glass Slipper*).

4486. *The Third Twin* (Ken Follett, 1996). Thriller about a genetics researcher who stumbles upon a conspiracy as she studies twins separated at birth. **Adaptation:** *The Third Twin* (CBS, 1997 TV Movie). Dir: Tom McLoughlin. Scr: Cindy Myers. Cast: Kelly McGillis (Dr. Ferrami), Jason Gedrick (Steve), Larry Hagman (Berrington), Marion Ross (Lila).

The Third Voice (see *All the Way*).

Thirteen at Dinner (see *Lord Edgware Dies*).

The Thirteen Chairs (see *The Twelve Chairs*).

Thirteen Days (see *The Kennedy Tapes*).

4487. *Thirteen Women* (Tiffany Thayer, 1931). A woman with hypnotic powers seeks revenge on her sorority sisters who tormented her in school years earlier. **Adaptation:** *Thirteen Women* (RKO, 1932). Dir: George Archainbaud. Scr: Bartlett Cormack, Samuel Ornitz. Cast: Irene Dunne (Laura Stanhope), Ricardo Cortez (Sergeant Barry Clive), Jill Esmond (Jo Turner), Myrna Loy (Ursula Georgi).

The Thirteenth Floor (see *Simulacron-3*).

4488. *The Thirteenth Guest* (Armitage Trail [pseudonym for Maurice Coons], 1929). Thirteen years after a dinner party at which their host dropped dead and left his estate to a guest who did not attend, the host's guests are invited back to the mansion and are systematically killed. **Adaptation 1:** *The Thirteenth Guest* (Monogram, 1932). Dir: Albert Ray. Scr: Arthur Hoerl, Frances Hyland. Cast: Ginger Rogers (Marie), Lyle Talbot (Phil), J. Farrell MacDonald (Captain Ryan), James Eagles (Bud). VHS. **Adaptation 2:** *The Mystery of the Thirteenth Guest* (Monogram, 1943). Dir: William Beaudine. Scr: Arthur Hoerl, Charles Marion, Tim Ryan. Cast: Dick Purcell (Johnny), Helen Parrish (Marie), Tim Ryan (Burke), Frank Faylen (Speed).

4489. *The 13th Man* (Murray Teigh Bloom, 1977). When his wife is killed in a restaurant, a police investigator is convinced that he was the intended target and that he is being hunted, but his department will offer no assistance. **Adaptation:** *Last Embrace* (United Artists, 1979). Dir: Jonathan Demme. Scr: David Shaber. Cast: Roy Scheider (Harry), Janet Margolin (Ellie), John Glover (Richard), Charles Napier (Dave), Christopher Walken (Eckart). VHS.

The 13th Warrior (see *Eaters of the Dead*).

4490. *Thirty Day Princess* (Clarence Budington Kelland, 1933). Comic novel about an actress hired to impersonate a European princess who becomes ill while on tour in the United States to secure financing for her country. The novel was published as a six-part serial in *The Ladies' Home Journal* beginning in August 1933. **Adaptation:** *Thirty Day Princess* (Paramount, 1934). Dir: Marion Gering. Scr: Sam Hellman, Edwin Justus Mayer, Frank Partos, Preston Sturges. Cast: Sylvia

Sidney (Princess Catterina/Nancy), Cary Grant (Porter), Edward Arnold (Richard), Henry Stephenson (King Anatol).

4491. *The Thirty-Nine Steps* (John Buchan, 1915). Espionage tale about a Scottish man who is pursued by anarchists and drawn into a political conspiracy. **Adaptation 1:** Th*e 39 Steps* (Gaumont, 1935). Dir: Alfred Hitchcock. Scr: Charles Bennett, Ian Hay. Cast: Robert Donat (Hannay), Madeleine Carroll (Pamela), Lucie Mannheim (Annabella), Godfrey Tearle (Professor Jordan), Peggy Ashcroft (Margaret). DVD, VHS. **Adaptation 2:** *The 39 Steps* (Rank/20th Century–Fox, 1959). Dir: Ralph Thomas. Scr: Frank Harvey. Cast: Kenneth More (Hannay), Taina Elg (Fisher), Brenda De Banzie (Nellie), Barry Jones (Professor Logan), Reginald Beckwith (Lumsden). VHS. **Adaptation 3:** *The Thirty-Nine Steps* (Rank/International Picture Show, 1978). Dir: Don Sharp. Scr: Michael Robson. Cast: Robert Powell (Hannay), David Warner (Sir Edmund), Eric Porter (Lomas), Karen Dotrice (Mackenzie), John Mills (Scudder). VHS.

4492. *Thirty Seconds Over Tokyo* (Ted W. Lawson and Robert Considine, 1943). Memoir by Lawson, an officer involved in the first attack on Japan during World War II. **Adaptation:** *Thirty Seconds Over Tokyo* (MGM, 1944). Dir: Mervyn Le Roy. Scr: Dalton Trumbo. Cast: Van Johnson (Lawson), Robert Walker (Thatcher), Tim Murdock (Davenport), Scott McKay (Jones). Notes: Academy Award for Best Special Effects and nomination for Best Cinematography. VHS.

36 Hours to Kill (*see* "Across the Aisle").

4493. *This Above All* (Eric Knight, 1941). A servicewoman during World War II falls in love with an embittered deserter who ultimately proves to be a hero. **Adaptation:** *This Above All* (20th Century–Fox, 1942). Dir: Anatole Litvak. Scr: R. C. Sherriff. Cast: Tyrone Power (Clive), Joan Fontaine (Prudence), Thomas Mitchell (Monty), Henry Stephenson (General Cathaway).

4494. *This Boy's Life: A Memoir* (Tobias Wolff, 1989). Wolff's memoir about his difficult life with his mother and her abusive boyfriend in suburban Seattle and his determination to escape the town. **Adaptation:** *This Boy's Life* (Warner, 1993). Dir: Michael Caton-Jones. Scr: Robert Getchell. Cast: Robert De Niro (Dwight), Ellen Barkin (Caroline), Leonardo Di Caprio (Toby), Jonah Blechman (Arthur), Eliza Dushku (Pearl), Chris Cooper (Roy), Carla Gugino (Norma). DVD, VHS.

This Earth Is Mine (see *The Cup and the Sword*).

This Gun for Hire (see *A Gun for Sale*).

This Is Callan (see *A Red File for Callan*).

This Is My Affair (see *I Can Get It for You Wholesale*).

This Is My Life (see *This Is Your Life*).

4495. *This Is My Street* (Nan Maynard, 1962). A married British woman starts an affair with a man renting a room in her mother's house. **Adaptation:** *This Is My Street* (Warner, 1963). Dir: Sidney Hayers. Scr: Bill MacIlwraith. Cast: Ian Hendry (Harry), June Ritchie (Margery), Avice Landone (Lily), Meredith Edwards (Steve).

4496. *This Is Your Life* (Meg Wolitzer, 1988). A single mother realizes her dream of becoming a stand-up comedian, but her fame is causing her to neglect her young daughters. **Adaptation:** *This Is My Life* (20th Century–Fox, 1992). Dir: Nora Ephron. Scr: Nora Ephron, Delia Ephron. Cast: Julie Kavner (Dottie), Samantha Mathis (Erica), Gaby Hoffmann (Opal), Carrie Fisher (Claudia), Dan Aykroyd (Arnold). VHS.

4497. *This Island Earth* (Raymond F. Jones, 1952). Brilliant scientists are kidnapped by space aliens who need help defending their planet from hostile invaders. The novel was originally published in June 1949 as a short story titled "The Alien Machine" in *Thrilling Wonder Stories* magazine and expanded into a novel titled *This Island Earth* in 1952. **Adaptation:** *This Island Earth* (Universal International, 1955). Dir: Joseph Newman. Scr: Franklin Coen, Edward G. O'Callaghan. Cast: Jeff Morrow (Exeter), Faith Domergue (Dr. Adams), Rex Reason (Dr. Meacham), Lance Fuller (Brack), Russell Johnson (Steve). DVD, VHS.

This Man Is Dangerous (see *They Called Him Death*).

This Man Must Die (see *The Beast Must Die*).

4498. *This Sporting Life* (David Storey, 1960). Semi-autobiographical novel about a tough British miner who seizes the opportunity to become a champion rugby player but discovers that his success does not bring him contentment. **Adaptation:** *This Sporting Life* (Rank/Continental, 1963). Dir: Lindsay Anderson. Scr: David Storey. Cast: Richard Harris (Frank), Rachel Roberts (Mrs. Hammond), Alan Badel (Weaver), William Hartnell (Johnson), Colin Blakely (Maurice). Notes: Academy Award nominations for

Best Actor (Harris) and Actress (Roberts); BAFTA Award for Best British Actress (Roberts) and nominations for Best British Film, Screenplay, Actor (Harris), and Film from any Source; Cannes Film Festival Award for Best Actor (Harris); Golden Globe nominations for Best English-Language Foreign Film and Actress (Roberts). DVD, VHS.

4499. *This Way Out* (James Ronald, 1939). After he meets a lovely young woman, a man kills his abusive wife but soon finds himself blackmailed. **Adaptation:** *The Suspect* (Universal, 1944). Dir: Robert Siodmak. Scr: Arthur T. Horman, Bertram Millhauser. Cast: Charles Laughton (Philip), Ella Raines (Mary), Molly Lamont (Edith), C. Stanley Ridges (Inspector Huxley).

This Woman Is Mine (see *I, James Lewis*).

4500. "This World, Then the Fireworks" (Jim Thompson, 1988). A manipulative brother and sister attempt to swindle a shy policewoman. Thompson, who died in 1977, wrote the short story in 1955, and it was published in the 1988 collection *Fireworks: The Lost Writings of Jim Thompson*. **Adaptation:** *This World, Then the Fireworks* (Orion, 1997). Dir: Michael Oblowitz. Scr: Larry Gross. Cast: Billy Zane (Marty), Gina Gershon (Carol), Rue McClanahan (Mom Lakewood), Sheryl Lee (Lois), Seymour Cassel (Detective Harris), Will Patton (Lieutenant Morgan). VHS.

4501. *Thomasina: The Cat Who Thought She Was God* (Paul Gallico, 1957). In Scotland in 1812, a cruel veterinarian kills his daughter's beloved cat, and a mysterious and beautiful witch revives the animal to the girl's delight. **Adaptation:** *The Three Lives of Thomasina* (Disney/Buena Vista, 1964). Dir: Don Chaffey. Scr: Robert Westerby. Cast: Patrick McGoohan (Andrew), Susan Hampshire (Lori), Laurence Naismith (Reverend Peddie), Jean Anderson (Mrs. MacKenzie), Wilfrid Brambell (Willie). DVD, VHS.

4502. *Thor* (Wayne Smith, 1992). To protect its household members, a dog named Thor battles a family relative who is actually a werewolf. **Adaptation:** *Bad Moon* (Warner, 1996). Dir: Eric Red. Scr: Eric Red. Cast: Mariel Hemingway (Janet), Michael Pare (Uncle Ted), Mason Gamble (Brett), Ken Pogue (Sheriff Jenson). DVD, VHS.

Those Calloways (see *Swiftwater*).

Those Fantastic Flying Fools (see *From the Earth to the Moon*).

Those Kids from Town (see *These Our Strangers*).

4503. *A Thousand Acres* (Jane Smiley, 1991, Pulitzer Prize). Based on Shakespeare's *King Lear*, a dark tale of a family patriarch who divides his farm among his three daughters and the secrets that emerge as a result. **Adaptation:** *A Thousand Acres* (1997). Dir: Jocelyn Moorhouse. Scr: Laura Jones. Cast: Jessica Lange (Ginny), Michelle Pfeiffer (Rose), Jennifer Jason Leigh (Caroline), Jason Robards (Larry), Colin Firth (Jess), Keith Carradine (Ty), Kevin Anderson (Peter), Pat Hingle (Harold). DVD, VHS.

4504. "A Thousand Deaths" (Jack London, 1899). A mad scientist performs experiments on criminals aboard his private yacht. The short story was published in *The Black Cat* in May 1899. **Adaptation:** *Torture Ship* (PDC, 1939). Dir: Victor Halperin. Scr: Harvey Huntley, George Wallace Sayre. Cast: Lyle Talbot (Bennett), Irving Pichel (Dr. Stander), Sheila Bromley (Poison Mary), Anthony Averill (Dirk). DVD, VHS.

4505. *Thousand Pieces of Gold* (Ruthanne Lum McCunn, 1981). A novel based on the true story of a nineteenth-century Chinese woman who is sold into marriage by her poor father. She is sold to an American saloon owner, who wants to put her to work in a brothel. She finally escapes and makes her own way in the new land. **Adaptation:** *Thousand Pieces of Gold* (American Playhouse, 1991). Dir: Nancy Kelly. Scr: Anne Makepeace. Cast: Rosalind Chao (Lalu), Chris Cooper (Charlie), Michael Paul Chan (Hong), Dennis Dun (Jim). Notes: Western Heritage Award for Best Film. VHS.

4506. *The Thousand Plane Ride: The Story of the First Massive Air Raid — 1000 Bombers Against the City of Cologne* (Ralph Barker, 1966). A historical account of the massive Allied bombing of Hitler's Germany during World War II. **Adaptation:** *The Thousand Plane Raid* (United Artists, 1969). Dir: Boris Sagal. Scr: Donald S. Sanford, Robert Vincent Wright. Cast: Christopher George (Brandon), Laraine Stephens (Gabrielle), J. D. Cannon (Palmer), Gary Marshal (Howard).

Three (see "Then We Were Three").

4507. *Three-Act Tragedy* (Agatha Christie, 1934). Guests at a dinner party begin to die of acute poisoning, and Hercule Poirot tries to unveil the killer. The novel was released in the U.S. as *Murder in Three Acts*. **Adaptation:** *Murder in Three Acts* (CBS, 1986 TV Movie). Dir: Gary Nelson. Scr: Scott Swanton. Cast: Peter Ustinov (Poirot), Tony Curtis (Cartwright), Emma Samms (Jennifer), Jonathan Cecil (Hastings). Notes: The action is in this adaptation is moved from England to Acapulco, where Poirot has gone to work on his memoirs.

4508. *Three Blind Mice* (Ed McBain [pseudonym for Evan Hunter], 1990). A lawyer defends a Vietnam veteran unjustly accused of murdering three Vietnamese immigrants in New York. **Adaptation:** *Three Blind Mice* (Viacom, 2001 TV Movie), Dir: Christopher Leitch. Scr: Anne Gerard, Adam Greenman. Cast: Brian Dennehy (Mathew), Debrah Farentino (Leeds), John Doman (Stephen), Mary Stuart Masterson (Patricia). DVD, VHS.

4509. *Three Came Home* (Agnes Newton Keith, 1946). World War II memoir by an American woman married to a British man on Borneo and their brutal internment in a Japanese prison camp in 1941. **Adaptation:** *Three Came Home* (20th Century–Fox, 1950). Dir: Jean Negulesco. Scr: Nunnally Johnson. Cast: Claudette Colbert (Agnes), Patric Knowles (Harry), Florence Desmond (Betty), Sessue Hayakawa (Colonel Suga). DVD, VHS.

Three Coins in the Fountain (see *Coins in the Fountain*).

4510. *Three Comrades* (Erich Maria Remarque, 1937). A German novel, originally titled *Drei Kamarden*, about three disillusioned men returning home after World War I and falling in love with a woman dying of tuberculosis. The novel was translated in 1938. **Adaptation:** *Three Comrades* (MGM, 1938). Dir: Frank Borzage. Scr: F. Scott Fitzgerald, Edward E. Paramore, Jr. Cast: Robert Taylor (Erich), Margaret Sullavan (Patricia), Franchot Tone (Otto), Robert Young (Gottfried). VHS.

4511. *Three Cups of Coffee* (Ruth Feiner, 1940). The difficult life of a woman as seen in flashbacks during divorce proceedings in court. **Adaptation:** *The Woman's Angle* (Associated British/Stratford, 1952). Dir: Leslie Arliss. Scr: Leslie Arliss, Mabbie Poole. Cast: Lois Maxwell (Enid), Anthony Nicholls (Dr. Jarvis), Peter Reynolds (Brian), Isabel Dean (Isobel).

4512. "The Three-Day Blow" (Ernest Hemingway, 1925). Two lonely men drink and reminisce about their lives and loves. The short story appeared in Hemingway's 1925 collection *In Our Time*. **Adaptation:** *Best of Friends* (Halmi, 1987 TV Movie). Dir: Ron Satlof. Scr: Venable Hern-

don. Cast: Peter Graves (Nick Adams), Alex Cord (Bill), Carol Lynley (Marjorie).

Three Days of the Condor (see *Six Days of the Condor*).

4513. *Three Dollars* (Elliot Perlman, 1998). Australian novel about the trials of a professional man in his thirties who loses his job to downsizing. **Adaptation:** *Three Dollars* (Arenafilm, 2004). Dir: Robert Connolly. Scr: Elliot Perlman, Robert Connolly. Cast: David Wenham (Eddie), Robert Menzies (Nick).

4514. *The Three Faces of Eve* (Corbett Thigpen and Hervey M. Cleckley, 1954). A factual account by two psychiatrists about a woman who had three distinct personalities. **Adaptation:** *The Three Faces of Eve* (20th Century–Fox, 1957). Dir: Nunnally Johnson. Scr: Nunnally Johnson. Cast: Joanne Woodward (Eve White/Eve Black/Jane), David Wayne (Ralph), Lee J. Cobb (Dr. Luther), Edwin Jerome (Dr. Day). Notes: Academy Award, Golden Globe Award, and National Board of Review Award for Best Actress (Woodward). DVD, VHS.

4515. *Three Fevers* (Leo Walmsley, 1932). A feud between two families of fishermen ends in a marriage that unites them. **Adaptation:** *Turn of the Tide* (Gaumont, 1935). Dir: Norman Walker. Scr: J. O. C. Orton, L. Du Garde Peach. Cast: John Garrick (Marney), J. Fisher White (Isaac), Geraldine Fitzgerald (Ruth), Wilfrid Lawson (Luke). VHS.

4516. *Three for a Wedding* (Patte Wheat Mahan, 1965). Comic novel about a young pregnant woman and the three men who want to marry her. **Adaptation:** *Doctor, You've Got to Be Kidding* (MGM, 1967). Dir: Peter Tewksbury. Scr: Phillip Shuke. Cast: Sandra Dee (Heather), George Hamilton (Harlan), Celeste Holm (Louise), Bill Bixby (Dick).

4517. The *Three Godfathers* (Peter B. Kyne, 1913). During their flight from the law, three bank robbers in the Old West end up caring for a baby after the mother dies. **Silent Film:** 1916. **Adaptation 1:** *Hell's Heroes* (Universal, 1929). Dir: William Wyler. Scr: Tom Reed. Cast: Charles Bickford (Bob), Raymond Hatton (Tom), Fred Kohler (Wild Bill), Fritzi Ridgeway (the Mother). **Adaptation 2:** *Three Godfathers*; later reissued as *Miracle in the Sand* (MGM, 1936). Dir: Richard Boleslawski. Scr: Edward E. Paramore Jr., Manuel Seff. Cast: Chester Morris (Bob), Lewis Stone (Doc Underwood), Walter Brennan (Gus), Irene Hervey (Molly). **Adaptation 3:** *3 Godfathers*

(MGM, 1948). Dir: John Ford. Scr: Laurence Stallings, Frank S. Nugent. Cast: John Wayne (Bob), Harry Carey, Jr. (William), Ward Bond (Buck), Mae Marsh (Perley), Mildred Natwick (the Mother). DVD, VHS. **Adaptation 4:** *The Godchild* (ABC/MGM Television, 1974 TV Movie). Dir: John Badham. Scr: Ron Bishop. Cast: Jack Palance (Rourke), Jack Warden (Dobbs), Keith Carradine (Lewis), Ed Lauter (Crees), Fionnula Flanagan (Virginia).

Three in the Attic (see *Paxton Quigley's Had the Course*).

Three in the Cellar (see *The Late Boy Wonder*).

4518. *Three Into Two Won't Go* (Andrea Newman, 1967). A British executive's marriage is threatened when he begins an affair with a young hitchhiker he takes home. **Adaptation:** *Three Into Two Won't Go* (Universal, 1969). Dir: Peter Hall. Scr: Edna O'Brien. Cast: Rod Steiger (Steve), Claire Bloom (Frances), Judy Geeson (Ella), Peggy Ashcroft (Belle).

The Three Lives of Thomasina (see *Thomasina*).

4519. *Three Men in a Boat* (Jerome K. Jerome, 1889). The comic misadventures of three British men rowing down the Thames River in the late nineteenth century. **Silent Film:** 1920. **Adaptation 1:** *Three Men in a Boat* (Associated British, 1933). Dir: Graham Cutts. Scr: Reginald Purdell, D. B. Wyndham-Lewis. Cast: William Austin (Harris), Edmund Breon (George), Billy Milton (Jimmy), Davy Burnaby (Sir Henry). **Adaptation 2:** *Three Men in a Boat* (Romulus/Hal Roach, 1956). Dir: Ken Annakin. Scr: Hubert Gregg, Vernon Harris. Cast: Jimmy Edwards (Harris), David Tomlinson (Jay), Laurence Harvey (George), Adrienne Corri (Clara), Shirley Eaton (Sophie). VHS. **Adaptation 3:** *Three Men in a Boat* (BBC, 1975 TV Movie). Dir: Stephen Frears. Scr: Tom Stoppard. Cast: Tim Curry (Jerome), Michael Palin (Harris), Stephen Moore (George).

4520. *The Three Musketeers* (Alexandre Dumas, pere, 1844). Dumas' classic, *Les trois mousquetaires*, is set in seventeenth-century France in the age of Louis XIII and concerns young D'Artagnan, who goes to Paris to join the king's musketeers. It was the first in a series of popular novels that included *Twenty Years After* (1845) and *The Man in the Iron Mask* (1850). **Silent Films:** 1903, 1911, 1914, 1916, and 1921, directed by Fred Niblo and starring Douglas Fair-

banks (DVD, VHS). **Adaptation 1:** *The Three Musketeers* (RKO, 1935). Dir: Rowland V. Lee. Scr: Rowland V. Lee, Dudley Nichols. Cast: Walter Abel (D'Artagnan), Ian Keith (Count de Rochefort), Margot Grahame (Milady de Winter), Paul Lukas (Athos), Moroni Olsen (Porthos), Onslow Stevens (Aramis), Heather Angel (Constance). VHS. **Adaptation 2:** *The Three Musketeers*; released in the UK as *The Singing Musketeer* (20th Century–Fox, 1939). Dir: Allan Dwan. Scr: William A. Drake, Ray Golden, Sam Hellman, Sid Kuller, M. M. Musselman. Cast: Don Ameche (D'Artagnan), Binnie Barnes (Milady De Winter), Gloria Stuart (Queen Anne), Pauline Moore (Lady Constance), Joseph Schildkraut (King Louis XIII), John Carradine (Naveau). Notes: A musical version. VHS. **Adaptation 3:** *The Three Musketeers* (MGM, 1948). Dir: George Sidney. Scr: Robert Ardrey. Cast: Lana Turner (Milady de Winter), Gene Kelly (D'Artagnan), June Allyson (Constance Bonacieux), Van Heflin (Athos), Angela Lansbury (Queen Anne), Frank Morgan (King Louis XIII), Vincent Price (Cardinal Richelieu), Keenan Wynn (Planchet), John Sutton (the Duke of Buckingham), Gig Young (Porthos). VHS **Adaptation 4:** *The Three Musketeers* (Pathe, 1953). Dir: Andre Hunebelle. Scr: Michel Audiard. Cast: Louis Arbessier (King Louis XIII), Steve Barclay (the Duke of Buckingham), Gino Cervi (Porthos), Jacques Francois (Aramis). **Adaptation 5:** *The Three Musketeers* (Hal Roach, 1953 TV Movie). Dir: Budd Boetticher. Scr: Roy Hamilton. Cast: Robert Clarke (D'Artagnan), John Hubbard (Athos), Mel Archer (Portos), Keith Richards (Aramis), Marjorie Lord (Queen Anne), Kristine Miller (Milady De Winter), Paul Cavanagh (Cardinal Richelieu), Charles Lang (the Duke of Buckingham). **Adaptation 6:** *The Three Musketeers* (BBC, 1966 TV Miniseries). Dir: Peter Hammond. Scr: Anthony Steven. Cast: Brian Blessed (Porthos), Edward Brayshaw (Rochefort), Kathleen Breck (Constance), Jeremy Brett (D'Artagnan), John Carlin (King Louis XIII). **Adaptation 7:** *The Three Musketeers* (20th Century–Fox, 1973). Dir: Richard Lester. Scr: George MacDonald Fraser. Cast: Oliver Reed (Athos), Raquel Welch (Constance de Bonancieux), Richard Chamberlain (Aramis), Michael York (D'Artagnan), Frank Finlay (Porthos), Christopher Lee (Rochefort), Geraldine Chaplin (Anna of Austria). Notes: Golden Globe Award for Best Actress (Welch) and nomination for Best Picture. DVD, VHS. Notes: The following year, the same cast and crew reassembled for a sequel titled *The Four Musketeers: The Revenge of Milady* (DVD, VHS). **Adaptation 8:** *The Three Musketeers* (Disney/Buena Vista, 1993). Dir: Stephen Herek. Scr: David Loughery. Cast: Charlie Sheen (Aramis), Kiefer Sutherland (Athos), Chris O'Donnell (D'Artagnan), Oliver Platt (Porthos), Tim Curry (Cardinal Richelieu), Rebecca De Mornay (Milady De Winter). DVD, VHS. **Adaptation 9:** *The Musketeer* (Universal, 2001). Dir: Peter Hyams. Scr: Gene Quintano. Cast: Catherine Deneuve (Queen Anne), Mena Suvari (Francesca bon Ansau), Stephen Rea (Cardinal Richelieu), Tim Roth (Febre), Justin Chambers (D'Artagnan), Bill Treacher (Bonacieux), Daniel Mesguich (King Louis XIII). Notes: An updated version based on elements from all of the novels in the series and featuring martial artists instead of swordsmen. DVD, VHS. Notes: A sequel, released in the U.S. as *At Sword's Point* and in the UK as *Sons of the Musketeers*, was released in 1952 (VHS). See also *The Man in the Iron Mask* and *Twenty Years Later*.

Three on a Spree (see *Brewster's Millions*).

4521. *The Three Roads* (Ross Macdonald [pseudonym for Kenneth Millar], 1948). A photographer suffering from amnesia hunts for the murderer of his wife. **Adaptation:** *Double Negative*; also released as *Deadly Companion* (Quadrant, 1980). Dir: George Bloomfield. Scr: Janis Allen, Charles Dennis, Thomas Hedley, Jr. Cast: Michael Sarrazin (Michael), Susan Clark (Paula), Anthony Perkins (Lawrence), Howard Duff (Lester). VHS.

Three Sons (see *Sweepings*).

3-Way (see *Wild to Possess*).

The Three Weird Sisters (see *The Case of the Weird Sisters*).

The Three Worlds of Gulliver (see *Gulliver's Travels*).

4522. *The Three Worlds of Johnny Handsome* (John Godey, 1972). A criminal with a facial deformity is given a new face by a prison doctor. When he is released, he seeks vengeance on the man who killed his friend and sent him to prison. **Adaptation:** *Johnny Handsome* (Columbia TriStar, 1989). Dir: Walter Hill. Scr: Ken Friedman. Cast: Mickey Rourke (John), Ellen Barkin (Sunny), Elizabeth McGovern (Donna), Morgan Freeman (Drones), Forest Whitaker (Dr. Fisher). DVD, VHS.

Through the Looking Glass and What Alice Found There (see *Alice in Wonderland*).

Throw Momma From the Train (see *Strangers on a Train*).

4523. *Thumb Tripping* (Don Mitchell, 1970). During the late 1960's, a young man and woman team up as they hitchhike across the California. **Adaptation:** *Thumb Tripping* (AVCO Embassy, 1972). Dir: Quentin Masters. Scr: Don Mitchell. Cast: Michael Burns (Gary), Meg Foster (Shay), Marianna Hill (Lynn), Burke Byrnes (Jack), Michael Conrad (Diesel), Bruce Dern (Smitty). VHS.

4524. *Thumbsucker* (Walter Kirn, 1999). A neurotic, orally obsessed adult tries to give up his fixations. **Adaptation:** *Thumbsucker* (Sony, 2005). Dir: Mike Mills. Scr: Mike Mills. Cast: Lou Taylor Pucci (Justin), Tilda Swinton (Audrey), Vincent D'Onofrio (Mike), Kelli Garner (Rebecca), Keanu Reeves (Dr. Lyman), Vince Vaughn (Mr. Geary), Benjamin Bratt (Matt). Notes: Sundance Film Festival Special Jury Prize for Best Dramatic Actor (Pucci) and nomination for Grand Jury Prize (Mills). DVD. VHS.

4525. *Thunder Below* (Thomas Rourke, 1931). A woman falls in love with her husband's best friend but cannot bear to leave her spouse after he accidentally goes blind. **Adaptation:** *Thunder Below* (Paramount, 1932). Dir: Richard Wallace. Scr: Sidney Buchman, Josephine Lovett. Cast: Tallulah Bankhead (Susan), Charles Bickford (Walt), Paul Lukas (Ken), Eugene Pallette (Bill).

4526. *Thunder God's Gold* (Barry Storm [pseudonym for John Climenson], 1945). Western about a young German man who goes to Arizona in search of his grandfather's lost goldmine. **Adaptation:** *Lust for Gold* (Columbia, 1949). Dir: S. Sylvan Simon. Scr: Ted Sherdeman, Richard English. Cast: Ida Lupino (Julia), Glenn Ford (Jacob), Gig Young (Pete), Edgar Buchanan (Wiser), Will Geer (Deputy Covin), Paul Ford (Sheriff Early). VHS.

4527. *Thunder in the Dust* (Alan Le May, 1933). Western about feuding brothers who are rival ranchers. The novel was serialized in *Collier's* magazine (December 9 and 23, 1933) and published as a book in 1934. **Adaptation:** *The Sundowners* (Eagle-Lion, 1950). Dir: George Templeton. Scr: Alan Le May. Cast: Robert Preston (James), Robert Sterling (Tom), Chill Wills (Sam), Cathy Downs (Kathleen).

Thunder in the East (see *The Rape of the Vulture*).

Thunder in the Valley (see *Bob, Son of Battle*).

4528. *Thunder Mountain* (Zane Grey, 1932). Western about gold prospector who takes revenge when he is cheated out of a claim. The novel was serialized in *Collier's* beginning on October 22, 1932, and published as a book in 1935. **Adaptation 1:** *Thunder Mountain* (Fox, 1935). Dir: David Howard. Scr: Daniel Jarrett, Don Swift. Cast: George O'Brien (Kal), Frances Grant (Nugget), Barbara Fritchie (Sydney). **Adaptation 2:** *Thunder Mountain* (RKO, 1947). Dir: Lew Landers. Scr: Norman Houston. Cast: Tim Holt (Marvin), Martha Hyer (Ellie), Richard Martin (Chito). Notes: The screenplay combines elements from this book and Grey's 1921 novel *To the Last Man*. DVD, VHS.

4529. *Thunder Point* (Jack Higgins [pseudonym for Harry Patterson], 1993). Fifty years after World War II, a sunken U-Boat off the British coast contains a secret document that would embarrass the British government, and several people try to obtain it. **Adaptation:** *Thunder Point* (Showtime, 1998 TV Movie). Dir: George Mihalka. Scr: Morrie Ruvinsky. Cast: Kyle MacLachlan (Sean), Pascale Bussieres (Jenny), John Colicos (Heinzer), Alan Thicke (Hardy). DVD, VHS. Notes: In addition, a 1996 television movie titled *Windsor Protocol* uses characters from this book.

Thunder Trail (see *Arizona Ames*).

4530. *Thunderball* (Ian Fleming, 1961). James Bond is sent to stop a criminal agency that has hijacked two bombers with nuclear missiles aboard and is threatening to use the weapons unless NATO pays a large ransom. **Adaptation 1:** *Thunderball* (United Artists, 1965). Dir: Terence Young. Scr: Richard Maibaum, John Hopkins. Cast: Sean Connery (James Bond), Claudine Auger (Domino), Adolfo Celi (Emilio), Luciana Paluzzi (Fiona), Rik Van Nutter (Leiter). DVD, VHS **Adaptation 2:** *Never Say Never Again* (Warner, 1983). Dir: Irvin Kershner. Scr: Lorenzo Semple, Jr. Cast: Sean Connery (James Bond), Klaus Maria Brandauer (Largo), Max von Sydow (Blofeld), Barbara Carrera (Fatima), Kim Basinger (Domino), Bernie Casey (Leiter). Notes: An updating of the original story. Sean Connery returned to the role of James Bond after a twelve-year absence. DVD, VHS.

4531. *Thunderhead — Son of Flicka* (Mary O'Hara, 1943). The sequel to O'Hara's very successful *My Friend Flicka* (1941), continuing the story of a young boy's relationship with a beautiful stallion. This book was followed by a third in the series: *Green Grass of Wyoming* (1946). **Adaptation:** *Thunderhead — Son of Flicka* (20th Century–Fox, 1945). Dir: Louis King. Scr: Dwight Cummins, Dorothy Yost. Cast: Roddy McDowall (Ken), Preston Foster (Rob), Rita Johnson (Nelle), James Bell (Gus). DVD, VHS. See also *My Friend Flicka* and *Green Grass of Wyoming*.

4532. *The Thundering Herd* (Zane Grey, 1924). Western about outlaw buffalo hunters and their clash with Indians. The novel was serialized in *The Ladies' Home Journal* (February–May 1924) and published as a book in 1925. **Silent Film:** 1925. **Adaptation:** *The Thundering Herd* (Paramount, 1933). Dir: Henry Hathaway. Scr: Jack Cunningham. Cast: Randolph Scott (Tom), Judith Allen (Milly), Buster Crabbe (Bill), Noah Beery (Randall). VHS.

4533. *Thunderwith* (Libby Hathorn, 1989). After the death of her mother, a teenaged girl goes to live in the Australian outback with her father and his new family. **Adaptation:** *The Echo of Thunder* (Hallmark, 1998 TV Movie). Dir: Simon Wincer. Scr: H. Haden Yelin. Cast: Judy Davis (Gladwyn), Jamey Sheridan (Larry), Lauren Hewett (Lara), Ernie Dingo (Neil), Chelsea Yates (Pearl), Michael Caton (Bill). VHS.

4534. *Thursday's Child* (Donald Macardle, 1941). A young girl becomes a film star, but her success ruins her life and those of her family and friends. **Adaptation:** *Thursday's Child* (Associated British, 1943). Dir: Rodney Ackland. Scr: Rodney Ackland, Donald Macardle. Cast: Sally Ann Howes (Fennis), Wilfrid Lawson (Frank), Kathleen O'Regan (Ellen), Stewart Granger (David). VHS.

4535. *Thursday's Child* (Victoria Poole, 1980). A mother's autobiographical account of her teenaged son's heart transplant. **Adaptation:** *Thursday's Child* (CBS, 1983 TV Movie). Dir: David Lowell Rich. Scr: Gwen Bagni-Dubov. Cast: Gena Rowlands (Victoria), Don Murray (Parker), Jessica Walter (Roz), Rob Lowe (Sam), Tracey Gold (Alex).

4536. *Tiara Tahiti* (Geoffrey Cotterell, 1960). Two British army officers clash when they find themselves in Tahiti after World War II. **Adaptation:** *Tiara Tahiti* (Rank/Zenith, 1962). Dir: William T. Kotcheff. Scr: Geoffrey Cotterell, Ivan Foxwell, Mordecai Richler. Cast: James Mason (Brett), John Mills (Clifford), Claude Dauphin (Henri), Herbert Lom (Chong). VHS.

4537. *Ti-Coyo and His Shark: An Immoral Fable* (Clement Richer, 1941). A boy on an island in the South Seas befriends a baby shark, and they struggle together against the incursion of greedy fishermen. The French novel was translated into English in 1951. **Adaptation 1:** *Tiko and the Shark* (MGM, 1964). Dir: Folco Quilici. Scr: Ottavio Alessi, Augusto Frassinetti, Franco Prosperi, Giorgio Prosperi, Folco Quilici, Italo Calvino. Cast: Roau (Cocoyo), Al Kauwe (Ti-Koyo), Marlene Among (Diana). **Adaptation 2:** *Beyond the Reef* (Universal, 1981). Dir: Frank C. Clarke. Scr: James Carabatsos, Louis La Russo II. Cast: Dayton Ka'ne (Tikayo), Maren Jensen (Diana), Kathleen Swan (Milly), Keahi Farden (Jeff). DVD, VHS.

Ticket to Heaven (see *Moonwebs*).

4538. *Ticket to Ride* (Dennis Potter, 1986). On a train ride, an artist who is having marital problems alternates between reality and hallucination as he encounters an imaginary secret friend invented when he was a child. **Adaptation:** *Secret Friends* (Channel Four/Briarpatch, 1991). Dir: Dennis Potter. Scr: Dennis Potter. Cast: Alan Bates (John), Gina Bellman (Helen), Frances Barber (Angela), Tony Doyle (Martin). VHS.

4539. *The Tide of Life* (Catherine Cookson, 1976). Romantic story of a young woman who learns about life and love working on a farm. **Adaptation:** *The Tide of Life* (Festival, 1996 TV Miniseries). Dir: David Wheatley. Scr: Gordon Hann. Cast: Gillian Kearney (Emily), John Bowler (Sep), Susie Burton (Lucy), James Purefoy (Nick). DVD, VHS.

Tiger by the Tail (see *Never Come Back*).

4540. *The Tiger in the Smoke* (Marjorie Allingham, 1952). After World War II, former British commandos form a criminal organization and search London for hidden money. **Adaptation:** *Tiger in the Smoke* (Rank, 1956). Dir: Roy Baker. Scr: Anthony Pelissier. Cast: Donald Sinden (Geoffrey), Muriel Pavlow (Meg), Alec Clunes (Charles), Tony Wright (Jack), Bernard Miles (Doll).

4541. *A Tiger Walks* (Ian Niall, 1960). A young girl causes controversy in her small town when she tries to protect a tiger that has escaped from a traveling circus. **Adaptation:** *A Tiger Walks* (Disney/Buena Vista, 1963). Dir: Norman Tokar. Scr: Lowell S. Hawley. Cast: Brian Keith (Sheriff Williams), Vera Miles (Dorothy), Pamela Franklin (Julie), Sabu (Ram). VHS.

A Tiger's Tale (see *Love and Other Natural Disasters*).

Tight Little Island (see *Whiskey Galore*).

Tiko and the Shark (see *Ti-Coyo and His Shark*).

Til Death Do Us Part (*see* "Carmilla").

4542. *Till Death Us Do Part: A True Murder Mystery* (Vincent Bugliosi, with Ken Horwtiz, 1978, Edgar Award). True story by a Los Angeles proscutor about a couple of lovers who murder their respective spouses for the insurance money. **Adaptation:** *Till Death Us Do Part* (ABC, 1992 TV Miniseries). Dir: Yves Simoneau. Scr: Philip Rosenberg. Cast: Treat Williams (Alan), Arliss Howard (Bugliosi), Rebecca Jenkins (Sandra), J. E. Freeman (Detective Guy), Pruitt Taylor Vince (Michael), Embeth Davidtz (Katherine). VHS.

4543. *Tilly Trotter* (Catherine Cookson, 1980). In nineteenth century England, a working-class woman must overcome class prejudice to find true love. The is the first novel in a trilogy, which also includes *Tilly Trotter Wed* (1981) and *Tilly Trotter Widowed* (1982). **Adaptation:** *Tilly Trotter* (Festival, 1999 TV Movie). Dir: Alan Grint. Scr: Ray Marshall. Cast: Carli Norris (Tilly), Simon Shepherd (Mark), Gavin Abbott (Simon), Madelaine Newton (Biddy), Rosemary Leach (Forefoot). DVD, VHS.

4544. *Tim* (Colleen McCollough, 1974). McCollough's first novel is a romantic tale involving a successful middle-aged woman and a young, mentally handicapped man. **Adaptation 1:** *Tim* (Satori, 1979). Dir: Michael Pate. Scr: Michael Pate. Cast: Piper Laurie (Mary), Mel Gibson (Tim), Alwyn Kurts (Ron), Pat Evison (Em). Notes: Australian Film Institute Awards for Best Actor (Gibson), Supporting Actor (Kurts), and Supporting Actress (Evison). DVD, VHS. **Adaptation 2:** *Mary & Tim* (CBS/Hallmark, 1996 TV Movie). Dir: Glenn Jordan. Scr: Michael Pate (1979 screenplay), Ann Becket. Cast: Candice Bergen (Mary), Richard Kiley (Ron), Thomas McCarthy (Tim), Louise Latham (Forbsie).

4545. *Timberjack* (Dan Cushman, 1953). A young man returns to his father's lumber mill and finds that his father has been murdered and an unscrupulous rival is trying to get control of his business. **Adaptation:** *Timberjack* (Republic, 1955). Dir: Joseph Kane. Scr: Allen Rivkin. Cast: Sterling Hayden (Tim), Vera Ralston (Lynne), David Brian (Croft), Adolphe Menjou (Swifty).

4546. *Time at the Top* (Edward Ormondroyd, 1963). Children's story about a girl who uses the elevator in her apartment building to travel back in time to Philadelphia in 1881. There she meets a girl her own age, and they travel back and forth in time, altering the past and the future. **Adaptation:** *Time at the Top* (Showtime, 1999 TV Movie). Dir: Jimmy Kaufman. Scr: Linda Brookover, Alain Silver. Cast: Timothy Busfield (Frank), Elisha Cuthbert (Susan), Gabrielle Boni (Victoria), Matthew Harbour (Robert). VHS.

Time for Action (see *Tip on a Dead Jockey*).

A Time for Killing (see *The Southern Blade*).

Time, Gentlemen, Please! (see *Nothing to Lose*).

4547. *The Time Machine* (H. G. Wells, 1895). A scientist invents a machine that transports him far into the future to a world of warring humanity. **Adaptation 1:** *The Time Machine* (MGM, 1960). Dir: George Pal. Scr: David Duncan. Cast: Rod Taylor (Wells), Alan Young (David/James), Yvette Mimieux (Weena), Sebastian Cabot (Dr. Hillyer). Notes: Academy Award for Best Special Effects. DVD, VHS. **Adaptation 2:** *The Time Machine* (NBC, 1978 TV Movie). Dir: Henning Schellerup. Scr: Wallace C. Bennett. Cast: John Beck (Neil), Priscilla Barnes (Weena), Andrew Duggan (Bean), Rosemary De Camp (Agnes), Jack Kruschen (John). **Adaptation 3:** *The Time Machine* (Warner, 2002). Dir: Simon Wells. Scr: David Duncan (1960 screenplay), John Logan. Cast: Guy Pearce (Alexander), Mark Addy (David), Phyllida Law (Mrs. Watchett), Sienna Guillory (Emma), Orlando Jones (Vox), Jeremy Irons (Morlock). DVD, VHS.

4548. *The Time of the Hero* (Mario Vargas Llosa, 1962). The Peruvian novel, originally titled *La Cuidad y Los Perros*, concerns a cadet who exposes the brutality of life in a military academy. The novel was translated into English in 1966. **Adaptation:** *The City and the Dogs.* (Inca/Cinevista, 1985). Dir: Francisco J. Lombardi. Scr: Jose Watanabe. Cast: Pablo Serra (the Poet), Gustavo Bueno (Lieutenant Gamboa), Luis Alvarez (the Colonel), Juan Manuel Ochoa (the Jaguar). Notes: Originally titled *La Ciudad y Los Perros* and shown with subtitles.

4549. *Time Out of Mind* (Rachel Field, 1935). The unhappy son of a Maine shipbuilding family decides to pursue a musical career rather than the family business, and the housekeeper who is in love with him tries to help him. **Adaptation:** *Time Out of Mind* (Universal International, 1947). Dir: Robert Siodmak. Scr: Abem Finkel, Arnold Phillips. Cast: Phyllis Calvert (Kate), Robert Hutton (Chris), Ella Raines

(Rissa), Eddie Albert (Jake), Leo G. Carroll (Captain Fortune).

4550. *Time Regained* (Marcel Proust, 1927). *Le Temps Retrouve*, the posthumously published final installment in Proust's sixteen-volume *A la Recherche du Temps Perdu* (1913–1927), finds the narrator near death and imperfectly remembering his life and loves. The translated English title of the collection is *Remembrance of Things Past*. **Adaptation:** *Time Regained* (Kino, 1999). Dir: Raoul Ruiz. Scr: Raoul Ruiz, Gilles Taurand. Cast: Catherine Deneuve (Odette), Emmanuelle Beart (Gilberte), Vincent Perez (Morel), John Malkovich (Baron de Charlus). Notes: Originally released as *Le Temps Retrouve* and shown with subtitles. Cannes Film Festival Golden Palm nomination for Best Director. DVD, VHS. See also *Swann's Way*.

Time to Kill (see *The High Window*).

4551. *A Time to Kill* (John Grisham, 1989). In a small town in Mississippi, a black man kills two men who raped and murdered his young daughter. When an idealistic young lawyer takes his case, he must battle KKK members, who threaten the lawyer and his family. **Adaptation:** *A Time to Kill* (Warner, 1996). Dir: Joel Schumacher. Scr: Akiva Goldsman. Cast: Matthew McConaughey (Jake), Sandra Bullock (Ellen), Samuel L. Jackson (Carl), Kevin Spacey (Rufus), Oliver Platt (Harry), Charles Dutton (Sheriff Walls), Brenda Fricker (Ethel), Donald Sutherland (Lucien), Kiefer Sutherland (Freddie), Patrick McGoohan (Judge Noose), Ashley Judd (Carla). DVD, VHS.

4552. *A Time to Love and a Time to Die* (Erich Maria Remarque, 1954). The German novel, originally published as *Zeit Zu Leben und Zeit Zu Sterben*, concerns a World War II German officer who falls in love while on leave and is killed when he returns to the front. The novel was translated in 1954. **Adaptation:** *A Time to Love and a Time to Die* (Universal International, 1958). Dir: Douglas Sirk. Scr: Orin Jannings. Cast: John Gavin (Ernst), Lilo Pulver (Elizabeth), Jock Mahoney (Immerman), Don De Fore (Boettcher), Keenan Wynn (Reuter), Erich Maria Remarque (Professor Pohlmann). VHS.

4553. *Timeline* (Michael Crichton, 1999). Historical adventure about a group of archaeology students who use a time machine to travel back to France during the Middle Ages to rescue their professor. **Adaptation:** *Timeline* (Paramount, 2003). Dir: Richard Donner. Scr: Jeff

Maguire, George Nolfi. Cast: Paul Walker (Chris), Frances O'Connor (Kate), Gerard Butler (Andre), Billy Connolly (Professor Johnston), David Thewlis (Robert), Anna Friel (Lady Claire). DVD, VHS.

4554. *The Tin Drum* (Gunter Grass, 1959). Set in Germany during World War II, the novel, originally titled *Die Blechtrommel*, centers on a boy who grows disgusted with adults and resolves to stop growing and beat out his frustrations on a toy drum. **Adaptation:** *The Tin Drum* (New World, 1979). Dir: Volker Schlondorff. Scr: Jean-Claude Carrière, Gunter Grass, Volker Schlondorff, Franz Seitz. Cast: Mario Adorf (Alfred), Angela Winkler (Agnes), David Bennent (Oskar), Katharina Thalbach (Maria). Notes: Originally titled *Die Blechtrommel* and shown with subtitles. Academy Award and National Board of Review Award for Best Foreign-Language Film; Cannes Film Festival Golden Palm Award for Best Director. DVD, VHS.

4555. "The Tin Star" (John W. Cunningham, 1947). On the day he plans to retire, a marshal is informed that a gunman is seeking revenge on him. When none of the townspeople offers to help him, he decides to stay around and confront the outlaw. The story originally appeared in the December 6, 1947, issue of *Collier's*. **Adaptation 1:** *High Noon* (United Artists, 1952). Dir: Fred Zinnemann. Scr: Carl Foreman. Cast: Gary Cooper (Will), Thomas Mitchell (Jonas), Lloyd Bridges (Harvey), Katy Jurado (Helen), Grace Kelly (Amy), Otto Kruger (Judge Mettrick). Notes: Academy Awards for Best Actor (Cooper), Musical Score, Editing, and Song, and nominations for Best Picture, Director, and Screenplay; Golden Globe Awards for Best Film, Actor (Cooper), Supporting Actress (Jurado), and Cinematography. DVD, VHS. **Adaptation 2:** *High Noon* (TBS, 2000 TV Movie). Dir: Rod Hardy. Scr: Carl Foreman (1952 screenplay and teleplay), T. S. Cook. Cast: Tom Skerritt (Will), Randy Birch (Fellows), Susanna Thompson (Amy), Maria Conchita Alonso (Helen), Dennis Weaver (Mart), Michael Madsen (Frank). DVD, VHS. Notes: A sequel titled *High Noon, Part II: The Return of Will Kane* was produced as a made-for-television movie in 1980 (VHS).

4556. *Tinker, Tailor, Soldier, Spy* (John Le Carre [pseudonym for David Cornwell], 1974). Spy George Smiley is called out of retirement by the Prime Minister to find a high-ranking member of the British secret service who is actually a Russian agent. **Adaptation:** *Tinker, Tailor, Soldier, Spy* (BBC/PBS, 1979 TV Miniseries). Dir: Frances Alcock, John Irvin. Scr: Arthur Hopcraft. Cast: Alec Guinness (Smiley), Ian Richardson (Haydon), Ian Bannen (Prideaux), Beryl Reid (Connie), Joss Ackland (Westerby), Sian Phillips (Ann), Patrick Stewart (Karla). Notes: BAFTA Awards for Best Actor (Guinness) and Cameraman, and nominations for Best Actress (Reid) and Production Design; Emmy Award nomination for Outstanding Miniseries. DVD, VHS.

4557. *Tip on a Dead Jockey* (Irwin Shaw, 1957). Novella about a World War II pilot who becomes an international smuggler but eventually reforms his ways. **Adaptation:** *Tip on a Dead Jockey*; released in the UK as *Time for Action* (MGM, 1957). Dir: Richard Thorpe. Scr: Charles Lederer. Cast: Robert Taylor (Lloyd), Dorothy Malone (Phyllis), Marcel Dalio (Toto), Martin Gabel (Bert), Gia Scala (Paquita).

4558. *Tipping the Velvet* (Sarah Waters, 1998). In a London dance hall in the late nineteenth century, a lesbian love affair develops between a male impersonator and a young waitress. **Adaptation:** *Tipping the Velvet* (BBC, 2002 TV Miniseries). Dir: Geoffrey Sax. Scr: Andrew Davies. Cast: Rachael Stirling (Nan), Keeley Hawes (Kitty), Anna Chancellor (Diana), Jodhi May (Florence), Hugh Bonneville (Ralph). Notes: BAFTA nomination for Best Television Miniseries. DVD, VHS.

4559. *Titanic Town: Memories of a Belfast Girlhood* (Mary Costello, 1992). Autobiographical novel set in the 1970's about a young Belfast woman who, despite family opposition, organizes a group of women to end Irish Republican Army violence. **Adaptation:** *Titanic Town* (The Shooting Gallery, 1998). Dir: Roger Michell. Scr: Anne Devlin. Cast: Julie Walters (Bernie), Ciaran Hinds (Aidan), Nuala O'Neill (Annie), James Loughran (Thomas). VHS.

4560. *Titus Alone* (Mervyn Peake, 1959). In the final novel in the Peake's mythical Gormenghast trilogy (1946–1959), the young heir to the kingdom abdicates his throne and goes out to discover the world beyond the castle's walls. **Adaptation:** *Gormenghast* (BBC, 2000 TV Miniseries). Dir: Andy Wilson. Scr: Malcolm McKay. Cast: Jonathan Rhys-Meyers (Steerpike), Celia Imrie (Gertrude), Ian Richardson (Groan), Neve McIntosh (Fuchsia), Christopher Lee (Flay). DVD, VHS. See also *Titus Groan* and *Gormenghast*.

4561. *Titus Groan* (Mervyn Peake, 1946). In the first novel in the Peake's mythical Gormenghast trilogy (1946–1959), a young heir is born into a land of mysterious rituals and evil characters want to take over the land. **Adaptation:** *Gormenghast* (BBC, 2000 TV Miniseries). Dir: Andy Wilson. Scr: Malcolm McKay. Cast: Jonathan Rhys-Meyers (Steerpike), Celia Imrie (Gertrude), Ian Richardson (Groan), Neve McIntosh (Fuchsia), Christopher Lee (Flay). DVD, VHS. See also *Gormenghast* and *Titus Alone*.

4562. *To an Early Grave* (Wallace Markfield, 1964). Four Jewish intellectuals attend a friend's funeral and use the occasion to reflect on their lives and their futures. **Adaptation:** *Bye Bye, Braverman* (Warner/Seven Arts, 1968). Dir: Sidney Lumet. Scr: Herbert Sargent. Cast: George Segal (Morroe), Jack Warden (Barnet), Joseph Wiseman (Felix), Sorrell Booke (Holly), Jessica Walter (Inez), Phyllis Newman (Miss Mandelbaum).

4563. "To Build a Fire" (Jack London, 1902). A man traveling in the northern wilderness struggles to survive when he falls through the ice on a frozen pond. The classic short story was published in *The Youth's Companion* on May 29, 1902. **Silent Film:** 1929. **Adaptation:** *To Build a Fire* (Lupo, 2003). Dir: Luca Armenia. Scr: Luca Armenia. Cast: Olivier Pages (the Man). VHS.

4564. *To Catch a King* (Jack Higgins [pseudonym for Harry Patterson], 1979). During World War II, Hitler and his henchmen make plan to kidnap the Duke of Windsor and install a puppet government in England. The book was originally published under Patterson's own name and titled *The Judas Gate*. **Adaptation:** *To Catch a King* (HBO, 1984 TV Movie). Dir: Clive Donner. Scr: Roger O. Hirson. Cast: Robert Wagner (Joe), Teri Garr (Hannah), Horst Janson (General Schellenberg), John Standing (the Duke of Windsor), Barbara Parkins (the Duchess of Windsor).

To Catch a Spy (see *Catch Me a Spy*).

4565. *To Catch a Thief* (David Dodge, 1952). To clear his name, a retired jewel thief living on the French Riviera pursues a burglar using his own techniques. **Adaptation:** *To Catch a Thief* (Paramount, 1955). Dir: Alfred Hitchcock. Scr: John Michael Hayes. Cast: Cary Grant (John), Grace Kelly (Frances), Jessie Royce Landis (Jessie), John Williams (Hughson), Charles Vanel (Bertani). Notes: Academy Award for Best Cinematography and nominations for Best Art Direction and Costume Design. DVD, VHS.

4566. *To Dance with the White Dog* (Terry Kay, 1990). After the death of his wife, an elderly

widower finds a white dog with whom he takes a nostalgic journey to places that held special memories for the couple. **Adaptation:** *To Dance with the White Dog* (CBS/Hallmark, 1993 TV Movie). Dir: Glenn Jordan. Scr: Susan Cooper. Cast: Hume Cronyn (Robert), Jessica Tandy (Cora), Christine Baranski (Kate), Terry Beaver (Paul), Harley Cross (Bobby), Esther Rolle (Neelie). Notes: Emmy Award for Outstanding Actor (Cronyn) and nominations for Outstanding Movie, Director, Actress (Tandy), Editing, and Sound. DVD, VHS. Note: A Japanese-language adaptation was also produced in 2002.

4567. *To Die For* (Joyce Maynard, 1992). An aspiring television newswoman stops at nothing in the pursuit of her career plans, including the murder of her husband. **Adaptation:** *To Die For* (Columbia, 1995). Dir: Gus Van Sant. Scr: Buck Henry. Cast: Nicole Kidman (Suzanne), Matt Dillon (Larry), Joaquin Phoenix (Jimmy), Casey Affleck (Russell), Illeana Douglas (Janice), Dan Hedaya (Joe). Notes: Golden Globe Award for Best Actress (Kidman). DVD, VHS.

4568. *To Find a Man* (S. J. Wilson, 1970). Comic novel about a pregnant high school student and her boyfriend, who try to find an abortionist willing to secretly terminate her pregnancy. **Adaptation:** *To Find a Man* (Columbia, 1972). Dir: Buzz Kulik. Scr: Arnold Schulman. Cast: Pamela Sue Martin (Rosalind), Darren O'Connor (Andy), Phyllis Newman (Betty), Tom Bosley (Dr. Katchaturian), Tom Ewell (Dr. Hargrave).

4569. *To Have and Have Not* (Ernest Hemingway, 1937). A fishing boat owner in the Florida Keys turns to gun smuggling and murder. **Adaptation 1:** *To Have and Have Not* (Warner, 1944). Dir: Howard Hawks. Scr: Jules Furthman, William Faulkner. Cast: Humphrey Bogart (Morgan), Walter Brennan (Eddie), Lauren Bacall (Marie), Hoagy Carmichael (Cricket). DVD, VHS. **Adaptation 2:** *The Breaking Point* (Warner, 1950). Dir: Michael Curtiz. Scr: Ranald MacDougall. Cast: John Garfield (Morgan), Patricia Neal (Leona), Phyllis Thaxter (Lucy), Juano Hernandez (Wesley), Wallace Ford (Duncan). **Adaptation 3:** *The Gun Runners* (United Artists, 1958). Dir: Don Siegel. Scr: Daniel Mainwaring, Paul Monash. Cast: Audie Murphy (Sam), Everett Sloane (Harvey), Eddie Albert (Hanagan), Patricia Owens (Lucy).

4570. *To Hell and Back* (Audie Murphy, 1949). Autobiography of the Texas native who became World War II's most decorated veteran and later a well-known actor. **Adaptation:** *To Hell and*

Back (Universal International, 1955). Dir: Jesse Hibbs. Scr: Gil Doud. Cast: Audie Murphy (Murphy), Marshall Thompson (Johnson), Charles Drake (Brandon), Jack Kelly (Kerrigan), Gregg Palmer (Manning). DVD, VHS.

To Kill a Clown (see *Master of the Hounds*).

4571. *To Kill a Mockingbird* (Harper Lee, 1960, Pulitzer Prize). Set in a small Alabama town, the story a black man unjustly accused of raping a white woman, and the idealistic local lawyer who defends him. **Adaptation:** *To Kill a Mockingbird* (Universal International, 1962). Dir: Robert Mulligan. Scr: Horton Foote. Cast: Gregory Peck (Atticus), Mary Badham (Scout), Philip Alford (Jem), Robert Duvall (Boo), Brock Peters (Tom). Notes: Academy Awards for Best Actor (Peck), Screenplay, and Art Direction, and nominations for Best Picture, Director, Supporting Actress (Badham), Cinematography, and Musical Score; Gary Cooper Award at the Cannes Film Festival for Best Director; Golden Globe Awards for Best Film Promoting International Understanding, Actor (Peck), and Musical Score, and nomination for Best Film. Interestingly, too, in 2003 Gregory Peck's character, Atticus Finch, was voted the number one movie hero in the American Film Institute's list of top 100 film heroes and villains. DVD, VHS.

4572. *To Live and Die in L. A.* (Gerald Petievich, 1984). A Secret Service agent takes violent revenge on the counterfeiter who killed his partner. **Adaptation:** *To Live and Die in L. A.* (MGM-UA, 1985). Dir: William Friedkin. Scr: William Friedkin, Gerald Petievich. Cast: William L. Petersen (Chance), Willem Dafoe (Masters), John Pankow (Vukovich), Debra Feuer (Bianca), John Turturro (Cody), Dean Stockwell (Grimes). DVD, VHS.

4573. *To Play the King* (Michael Dobbs, 1992). In the second installment in Dobb's Urquhart trilogy (1989–1995), a conservative Member of Parliament becomes the Prime Minister and does battle with a liberal king while trying to keep his own dark secrets hidden from those around him. **Adaptation:** *To Play the King* (BBC/PBS, 1993 TV Movie). Dir: Paul Seed. Scr: Andrew Davies. Cast: Ian Richardson (Urquhart), Michael Kitchen (the King), Kitty Aldridge (Sarah), Colin Jeavons (Tim), Diane Fletcher (Elizabeth). Notes: BAFTA nominations for Best Television Actors (Richardson and Kitchen). DVD, VHS. See also *House of Cards* and *The Final Cut*.

4574. *To Save His Life* (Kelley Roos [pseu-donym for Audrey Kelley and William Roos], 1968). A photographer is mistaken for the target of professional killers. **Adaptation:** *Dead Men Tell No Tales* (CBS, 1971 TV Movie). Dir: Walter Grauman. Scr: Robert Dozier. Cast: Christopher George (Larry), Judy Carne (Midge), Patricia Barry (Lisa), Richard Anderson (Tom).

4575. "To See and Not See" (Oliver Sacks, 1995). The true story of a man who had an operation to correct his blindness and the problems he had adjusting to his new life. The story appeared in Dr. Sacks's 1995 collection *An Anthropologist on Mars: Paradoxical Tales.* **Adaptation:** *At First Sight* (MGM, 1999). Dir: Irwin Winkler. Scr: Steve Levitt. Cast: Val Kilmer (Virgil), Lee Rosen (Lee), Raisa Ivanic (Raisa), Mira Sorvino (Amy), Kelly McGillis (Jennie). DVD, VHS.

4576. *To Sir, with Love* (E. R. Braithwaite, 1959). Autobiographical novel about a black teacher who goes to work at a tough London school and comes to gain the respect of his unruly students. **Adaptation:** *To Sir, with Love* (Columbia, 1967). Dir: James Clavell. Scr: James Clavell. Cast: Sidney Poitier (Mark), Christian Roberts (Denham), Judy Geeson (Pamela), Suzy Kendall (Gillian), Lulu (Babs). DVD, VHS. Notes: A made-for-television sequel, *To Sir, with Love II,* was broadcast in 1996 (VHS).

4577. *To Smithereens* (Rosalyn Drexler, 1972). Autobiographical novel about a female wrestler who travels from town to town living in poverty and her unlikely relationship with an art critic. **Adaptation:** *Below the Belt* (Atlantic, 1980). Dir: Rob Fowler. Scr: Rob Fowler, Sherry Sonnet. Cast: Regina Baff (Rosa), Mildred Burke (Mildred), John C. Becher (the Promoter), James Ammon (Luke). VHS.

4578. *To the Devil a Daughter* (Dennis Wheatley, 1953). An occult novelist helps a young girl who is being pursued by a group of Satanists. **Adaptation:** *To the Devil a Daughter* (Hammer, 1976). Dir: Peter Sykes. Scr: John Peacock, Christopher Wicking. Cast: Richard Widmark (Verney), Christopher Lee (Father Rayner), Honor Blackman (Anna), Denholm Elliott (Beddows). DVD, VHS.

4579. *To the Last Man* (Zane Grey, 1921). Western about a family feud that leads to murder and revenge. The novel was serialized in *The Country Gentleman* magazine beginning on May 28, 1921, and published as a book the same year. **Silent Film:** 1923. **Adaptation:** *To the Last Man* (Paramount, 1933). Dir: Henry Hathaway. Scr: Jack Cunningham. Cast: Randolph Scott (Hayden), Esther Ralston (Colby), Jack La Rue (Daggs), Buster Crabbe (Bill). VHS.

4580. *To the Lighthouse* (Virginia Woolf, 1927). A teacher and his eccentric family spend a summer on an isolated British island. **Adaptation:** *To the Lighthouse* (BBC/PBS, 1983 TV Movie). Dir: Colin Gregg. Scr: Hugh Stoddart. Cast: Rosemary Harris (Mrs. Ramsay), Michael Gough (Mr. Ramsay), Suzanne Bertish (Lily), Lynsey Baxter (Nancy), Pippa Guard (Prue), Kenneth Branagh (Charles), T. P. McKenna (Augustus). DVD, VHS.

To the Victors (see *Bob, Son of Battle*).

4581. *Tobacco Road* (Erskine Caldwell, 1932). A portrait of a poor family in a backwoods Georgia community. The novel was adapted by Jack Kirkland as a Broadway play in 1933, and the show set theatrical records, running for eight years until 1941. **Adaptation:** *Tobacco Road* (20th Century–Fox, 1941). Dir: John Ford. Scr: Nunnally Johnson. Cast: Charley Grapewin (Jeeter), Marjorie Rambeau (Sister Bessie), Gene Tierney (Ellie May), William Tracy (Dude).

4582. *Toby Tyler, or Ten Weeks with a Circus* (James Otis Kaler, 1881). A young orphan in the American Midwest runs away from home and joins a traveling circus. **Adaptation:** *Toby Tyler, or Ten Weeks with a Circus* (Disney/Buena Vista, 1960). Dir: Charles Barton. Scr: Lillie Hayward, Bill Walsh. Cast: Kevin Corcoran (Toby), Henry Calvin (Ben), Gene Sheldon (Sam), Bob Sweeney (Harry). VHS.

Today We Live (see "Turn About").

4583. *Toinette's Philip* (C. V. Jamison, 1894). After the Civil War, an orphaned boy who is cared for by a kind black slave discovers that he has rich relations in New York. When he goes to live with them, he finds that he was happier before. **Adaptation:** *Rainbow on the River* (RKO, 1936). Dir: Kurt Neumann. Scr: Harry Chandlee, William Hurlbut, Clarence Marks, Earle Snell. Cast: Bobby Breen (Philip), May Robson (Harriet), Charles Butterworth (Barrett), Alan Mowbray (Ralph), Benita Hume (Julia), Henry O'Neill (Father Joseph), Louise Beavers (Toinette).

4584. *Tom Brown's Schooldays* (Thomas Hughes, 1857). A young boy attends a private boarding school, where he is subjected to a brutal hazing ritual and tormented by the school bully. **Silent Film:** 1916. **Adaptation 1:** *Tom Brown's School Days*; reissued in the U.S. as *Adventures at Rugby* (RKO, 1940). Dir: Robert Steven-

son. Scr: C. Graham Baker, Frank Cavett, Walter Ferris, Robert Stevenson, Gene Towne. Cast: Cedric Hardwicke (Dr. Arnold), Freddie Bartholomew (Ned), Jimmy Lydon (Tom), Josephine Hutchinson (Mrs. Arnold), Billy Halop (Flashman). VHS. **Adaptation 2:** *Tom Brown's Schooldays* (United Artists, 1951). Dir: Gordon Parry. Scr: Noel Langley. Cast: John Howard Davies (Tom), Robert Newton (Dr. Arnold), Diana Wynyard (Mrs. Arnold), Hermione Baddeley (Sally), Kathleen Byron (Mrs. Brown). **Adaptation 3:** *Tom Brown's Schooldays* (BBC, 1971 Miniseries). Dir: Gareth Davies. Scr: Anthony Stevens. Cast: Anthony Murphy (Tom), Iain Cuthbertson (Dr. Arnold), Simon Turner (Ned), Richard Morant (Flashman), Christine Pollon (Mrs. Brown). DVD, VHS. **Adaptation 4:** *Tom Brown's Schooldays* (ITV, 2005 TV Movie). Dir: Dave Moore. Scr: Ashley Pharoah. Cast: Julian Wadham (Squire Brown), Alex Pettyfer (Tom), Stephen Fry (Dr. Arnold), Jemma Redgrave (Mary), Harry Michell (Ned), Joseph Beattie (Flashman).

Tom Jones (see *The History of Tom Jones, a Foundling*).

Tom Sawyer (see *The Adventures of Tom Sawyer*).

4585. *Tom Sawyer, Detective* (Mark Twain [pseudonym for Samuel Langhorne Clemens], 1896). Twain's sequel to his enormously successful novels about Tom Sawyer and his friend Huckleberry Finn. In this episodic tale, originally serialized in *Harper's Monthly*, Tom and Huck become sleuths who solve an old murder case and other mysteries. This book, along with Twain's 1894 sequel, *Tom Sawyer Abroad*, were published together in a single volume in 1896. **Adaptation:** *Tom Sawyer, Detective* (Paramount, 1938). Dir: Louis King. Scr: Stuart Anthony, Lewis R. Foster, Robert Yost. Cast: Billy Cook (Tom), Donald O'-Connor (Huckleberry), Porter Hall (Uncle Silas), Phil Warren (Jeff), Janet Waldo (Ruth), Elisabeth Risdon (Aunt Sally). See also *The Adventures of Tom Sawyer* and *The Adventures of Huckleberry Finn*.

The Tomahawk and the Cross (see "Frontier Fury").

The Tomb of Ligeia (see "Ligeia").

4586. *The Tommyknockers* (Stephen King, 1987). Thriller about a buried alien spaceship that turns the people of a small town into the inventors of many ingenious devices. Only the town drunk sees through the aliens' murderous plans. **Adaptation:** *The Tommyknockers* (Vidmark, 1993

TV Movie). Dir: John Power. Scr: Lawrence D. Cohen. Cast: Jimmy Smits (Jim), Marg Helgenberger (Bobbi), John Ashton (Butch), Allyce Beasley (Becka), Robert Carradine (Bryant), Joanna Cassidy (Sheriff Ruth), Annie Corley (Marie), Cliff De Young (Joe), Traci Lords (Nancy), E. G. Marshall (Ev). DVD, VHS.

4587. *Tom's Midnight Garden* (Phillippa Pearce, 1958, Carnegie Medal). Children's book about a young boy sent to live with his kind aunt and uncle. He discovers a magical garden inside their grandfather clock, where he meets a young girl with whom he has a variety of adventures. **Adaptation 1:** *Tom's Midnight Garden* (BBC, 1989 TV Miniseries). Dir: Christine Secombe. Scr: Julia Jones. Cast: Jeremy Rampling (Tom), Shaughan Seymour (Uncle Alan), Isabelle Amyes (Aunt Gwen), Simon Fenton (Peter), Renee Asherson (Mrs. Bartholemew). **Adaptation 2:** *Tom's Midnight Garden* (Hyperion, 1999). Dir: Willard Carroll. Scr: Willard Carroll. Cast: Anthony Way (Tom), Greta Scacchi (Aunt Gwen), James Wilby (Uncle Alan), Joan Plowright (Mrs. Bartholomew). DVD, VHS.

Tonka (see *Comanche*).

Tony Rome (see *Miami Mayhem*).

Too Busy to Work (see "Jubilo").

Too Good to Be True (see *Leave Her to Heaven*).

4588. *Too Late for Tears* (Roy Huggins, 1947). After a couple finds money that belongs to a gangster, the wife insists on keeping it and uses her feminine charms when the mobster comes looking for his loot. **Adaptation:** *Too Late for Tears* (United Artists, 1949). Dir: Byron Haskin. Scr: Roy Huggins. Cast: Lizabeth Scott (Jane), Don De Fore (Don), Dan Duryea (Danny), Arthur Kennedy (Alan). DVD, VHS.

Too Many Chefs (see *Someone Is Killing the Great Chefs of Europe*).

4589. *Too Much, Too Soon* (Diana Barrymore with Gerold Frank, 1957). Autobiography of the daughter of noted actor John Barrymore and her problems with fame and alcoholism. **Adaptation:** *Too Much, Too Soon* (Warner, 1958). Dir: Art Napoleon. Scr: Art Napoleon, Jo Napoleon. Cast: Dorothy Malone (Diana Barrymore), Errol Flynn (John Barrymore), Efrem Zimbalist, Jr. (Bryant), Ray Danton (Howard).

4590. "Toomai of the Elephants" (Rudyard Kipling, 1894). A tale from Kipling's classic *The Jungle Book* about a native boy who has a special affinity with wild elephants. **Adaptation:** *Elephant Boy* (United Artists, 1937). Dir: Robert J. Flaherty, Zoltan Korda. Scr: John Collier, Marcia De Silva, Akos Tolnay. Cast: Sabu (Toomai), W. E. Holloway (Father), Walter Hudd (Petersen). VHS. See also *The Jungle Book*.

4591. *Top of the World* (Hans Ruesch, 1950). After accidentally killing a white man, an Eskimo and his wife flee the civil authorities into the frozen North. **Adaptation:** *The Savage Innocents* (Paramount, 1959). Dir: Nicholas Ray. Scr: Nicholas Ray, Hans Ruesch, Franco Solinas. Cast: Anthony Quinn (Inuk), Yoko Tani (Asiak), Peter O'Toole (the Trooper), Marie Yang (Powtee), Marco Guglielmi (the Missionary).

Top Secret Affair (see *Melville Goodwin, USA*).

4592. *Topaz* (Leon Uris, 1967). In 1962, a Russian defector to the United States reveals that a Frenchman is leaking NATO secrets to the Soviets. **Adaptation:** *Topaz* (Universal, 1969). Dir: Alfred Hitchcock. Scr: Samuel Taylor. Cast: Frederick Stafford (Andre), Dany Robin (Nicole), Claude Jade (Michele), Michel Subor (Francois), Karin Dor (Juanita), John Vernon (Rico), Michel Piccoli (Jacques), Philippe Noiret (Henri). Notes: National Board of Review Awards for Best Director and Supporting Actor (Noiret). DVD, VHS.

Topkapi (see *The Light of Day*).

4593. *Topper* (Thorne Smith, 1926). Comic novel about a shy banker who is befriended by a couple of high-toned ghosts. The novel was also published under the title *The Jovial Ghosts*. **Adaptation 1:** *Topper* (MGM, 1937). Dir: Norman Z. McLeod. Scr: Eric Hatch, Jack Jevne, Eddie Moran. Cast: Constance Bennett (Marion), Cary Grant (George), Roland Young (Cosmo), Billie Burke (Clara). DVD, VHS. **Adaptation 2:** *Topper* (ABC, 1979 TV Movie). Dir: Charles S. Dubin. Scr: Mary Ann Kasica, George Kirgo, Michael Scheff. Cast: Jack Warden (Cosmo), Rue McClanahan (Clara), Kate Jackson (Marion), Andrew Stevens (George). Notes: The 1937 film inspired two sequels, *Topper Takes a Trip* in 1939 (VHS) and *Topper Returns* in 1941 (DVD, VHS). The book was also adapted as a CBS television series in 1953. See also *Topper Takes a Trip*.

4594. *Topper Takes a Trip* (Thorne Smith, 1932). In this sequel to Smith's successful 1926 novel, *Topper*, the banker and the friendly ghosts pursue Mrs. Topper to Europe to stop her from divorcing him and taking up with an unscrupulous aristocrat. **Adaptation:** *Topper Takes a Trip* (United Artists, 1939). Dir: Norman Z. McLeod. Scr: Jack Jevne, Eddie Moran, Corey Ford. Cast: Constance Bennett (Marion), Roland Young (Cosmo), Billie Burke (Clara), Alan Mowbray (Wilkins), Verree Teasdale (Mrs. Parkhurst). VHS. See also *Topper*.

Tora! Tora! Tora! (see *The Broken Seal*).

Torch Song (see "Why Should I Cry?")

4595. *Torrents of Spring* (Ivan Turgenev, 1872). Russian novella, originally titled *Veshinye Vody*, about an aristocrat who is engaged to be married but pursues an affair with a beautiful married woman. The novel was translated into English in 1897. **Adaptation 1:** *The Torrents of Spring* (BBC, 1959 TV Movie). Dir: Anthony Pelissier. Scr: Anthony Pelissier. Cast: Charles Houston (James), Harry H. Corbett (Sonny), Sandra Dorne (the Princess), Penelope Horner (Tess), Wilfrid Brambell (Mr. Connor). DVD, VHS. **Adaptation 2:** *Torrents of Spring* (Millimeter, 1989). Dir: Jerzy Skolimowski. Scr: Jerzy Skolimowski, Arcangelo Bonaccorso. Cast: Timothy Hutton (Sanin), Nastassja Kinski (Maria), Valeria Golino (Gemma), William Forsythe (Polozov). VHS.

4596. *Torso: The Evelyn Dick Case* (Marjorie Freeman Campbell, 1974). The true story of a Canadian woman who, in 1946, was convicted of murdering her husband, but released on appeal. She was subsequently brought to trial again, this time for the murder years earlier of her infant son, whose remains were discovered in her home. **Adaptation:** *Torso: The Evelyn Dick Story* (Shaftesbury/Bedford, 2002 TV Movie). Dir: Alex Chapple. Scr: Dennis Foon. Cast: Kathleen Robertson (Evelyn), Brenda Fricker (Alexandra), Callum Keith Rennie (Inspector Wood), Victor Garber (Robinette), Ken James (Donald). Notes: Gemini Awards (Canada) for Best Television Movie and Sound, and nominations for Best Director, Actress (Robertson), Supporting Actress (Fricker), Musical Score, Costume Design, Production Design, and Photography. DVD, VHS.

4597. *Tortilla Flat* (John Steinbeck, 1935). Episodic tale about a group of California Mexican-Americans who pursue pleasure and avoid responsibility until they must pay the consequences when a fire sweeps through their town. **Adaptation:** *Tortilla Flat* (MGM, 1942). Dir: Victor Fleming. Scr: John Lee Mahin, Benjamin Glazer. Cast: Spencer Tracy (Pilon), Hedy Lamarr

(Dolores), John Garfield (Alvarez), Frank Morgan (the Pirate), Akim Tamiroff (Pablo), Sheldon Leonard (Tito). VHS.

The Torture Chamber of Dr. Sadism (*see* "The Pit and the Pendulum").

Torture Ship (*see* "A Thousand Deaths").

Total Recall (*see* "We Can Remember It for You Wholesale").

4598. *Touch* (Elmore Leonard, 1987). A simple man with miraculous healing powers is exploited by an unscrupulous evangelist and a conservative Catholic priest. **Adaptation:** *Touch* (United Artists, 1997). Dir: Paul Schrader. Scr: Paul Schrader. Cast: Skeet Ulrich (Juvenal/Charlie), Gina Gershon (Debra), Conchata Ferrell (Virginia), John Doe (Elwin), Christopher Walken (Bill).Notes: Independent Spirit Award nominations for Best Director and Screenplay. VHS.

Touch of Evil (see *Badge of Evil*).

A Touch of Larceny (see *The Megstone Plot*).

A Touch of Love (see *The Millstone*).

4599. *Touch the Lion's Paw* (Derek Lambert, 1975). Comedy about the romantic relationship that develops between a jewel thief and the female detective pursuing him. **Adaptation:** *Rough Cut* (Paramount, 1980). Dir: Don Siegel. Scr: Larry Gelbart (writing as Francis Burns). Cast: Burt Reynolds (Jack), Lesley-Anne Down (Gillian), David Niven (Inspector Willis), Timothy West (Nigel), Patrick Magee (Ernst). VHS.

4600. *Touching the Void* (Joe Simpson and Chris Bonington, 1988, Boardman Tasker Award). Dramatic autobiographical story about two climbers, Joe Simpson and Simon Yates, who scaled the Peruvian Andes in 1985. When Simpson fell, Yates assumed he was dead and cut him loose. Simpson survived, however, and was rescued three days later after he crawled down the mountain. **Adaptation:** *Touching the Void* (IFC, 2003). Dir: Kevin Macdonald. Scr: Kevin Macdonald. Cast: Nicholas Aaron (Simon), Brendan Mackey (Joe), Ollie Ryall (Richard), Richard Hawking (Richard Hawking), Joe Simpson (Joe Simpson), Simon Yates (Simon Yates). BAFTA Award for Best British Film; British Independent Spirit Awards for Best Documentary and Technical Achievement, and nominations for Best Film and Director. DVD, VHS.

4601. *Tough Guys Don't Dance* (Norman

Mailer, 1983). An alcoholic writer awakens in his blood-stained car and fears that he may have committed a murder, even though he has no recollection of the evening before. He then sets about trying to reconstruct the missing time period. **Adaptation:** *Tough Guys Don't Dance* (Cannon, 1987). Dir: Norman Mailer. Scr: Norman Mailer. Cast: Ryan O'Neal (Tim), Isabella Rossellini (Madeleine), Debra Sandlund (Patty), Wings Hauser (Alvin), Lawrence Tierney (Dougy), Frances Fisher (Jessica). Notes: Independent Spirit Award nominations for Best Film, Actress (Sandlund), Supporting Actor (Hauser), and Cinematography. DVD, VHS.

4602. *The Tower* (Richard Martin Stern, 1973). A high-rise office building catches fire, threatening the workers on the upper floors. **Adaptation:** *The Towering Inferno* (20th Century–Fox, 1974). Dir: Irwin Allen, John Guillermin. Scr: Stirling Silliphant. Cast: Steve McQueen (Chief O'Hallorhan), Paul Newman (Doug), William Holden (James), Faye Dunaway (Susan), Fred Astaire (Harlee), Susan Blakely (Patty), Richard Chamberlain (Roger), Jennifer Jones (Lisolette), Susan Flannery (Lorrie). Notes: The screenplay combines elements of Thomas Scortia and Frank M. Robinson's 1974 novel *The Glass Inferno* and Richard Martin Stern's 1973 novel *The Tower*. Academy Awards for Best Cinematography, Editing, and Song, and nominations for Best Picture, Supporting Actor (Astaire), Musical Score, Art Direction, and Sound; Golden Globe Awards for Best Supporting Actor (Astaire) and Newcomer (Flannery) and nominations for Best Screenplay, Supporting Actress (Jones), and Song. DVD, VHS. See also *The Glass Inferno*.

Tower of Terror (see *The Ravine*).

The Towering Inferno (see *The Tower* and *The Glass Inferno*).

4603. *A Town Like Alice* (Nevil Shute [pseudonym for Nevil Shute Norway], 1950). After enduring internment in a Japanese labor camp in Malaysia during World War II, a British woman leaves England and settles in Australia. **Adaptation 1:** *A Town Like Alice*; also released as *The Rape of Malaya* (Rank, 1956). Dir: Jack Lee. Scr: W. P. Lipscomb, Richard Mason. Cast: Virginia McKenna (Jean), Peter Finch (Joe), Kenji Takagi (the Japanese Sergeant). Notes: BAFTA Awards for Best Actor (Finch) and Actress (McKenna), and nominations for Best Picture and Screenplay. DVD, VHS. **Adaptation 2:** *A Town Like Alice*

(PBS, 1981 TV Miniseries). Dir: David Stevens. Scr: Tom Hegarty, Rosemary Anne Sisson. Cast: Helen Morse (Jean), Bryan Brown (Joe), Gordon Jackson (Noel), Dorothy Alison (Mrs. Frith). VHS.

Town Without Pity (see *The Verdict*).

4604. *Toy Soldiers* (William P. Kennedy, 1988). When South American terrorists take over a private boarding school, the rebellious rich boys in attendance fight back. **Adaptation:** *Toy Soldiers* (TriStar, 1991). Dir: Daniel Petrie, Jr. Scr: David Koepp, Daniel Petrie Jr. Cast: Sean Astin (Billy), Wil Wheaton (Joey), Keith Coogan (Snuffy), Andrew Divoff (Luis), R. Lee Ermey (General Kramer), Mason Adams (Otis), Denholm Elliott (the Headmaster), Louis Gossett, Jr. (Parker). DVD, VHS.

4605. *Track of the Cat* (Walter Van Tilburg Clark, 1949). A troubled family living in the California mountains in the nineteenth century are threatened by a savage cougar. **Adaptation:** *Track of the Cat* (Warner, 1954). Dir: William A. Wellman. Scr: A. I. Bezzerides. Cast: Robert Mitchum (Curt), Teresa Wright (Grace), Diana Lynn (Gwen), Tab Hunter (Harold), Beulah Bondi (Ma Bridges), Philip Tonge (Pa Bridges), William Hopper (Arthur), Carl "Alfalfa" Switzer (Joe). VHS.

4606. *Trader Horn: Being the Life and Works of Alfred Aloysius Horn* (Alfred Aloysius Horn and Ethelreda Lewis, 1927). Autobiography of the veteran white trader (1854–1927) and his encounters with hostile African tribes. **Adaptation 1:** *Trader Horn* (MGM, 1931). Dir: W. S. Van Dyke. Scr: Dale Van Every, John Thomas Neville, Richard Schayer, Cyril Hume. Cast: Harry Carey (Trader Horn), Edwina Booth (Nina), Duncan Renaldo (Peru), Mutia Omoolu (Rencharo). Notes: Academy Award nomination for Best Picture. VHS. **Adaptation 2:** *Trader Horn* (MGM, 1973). Dir: Reza Badiyi. Scr: Edward Harper, William W. Norton. Cast: Rod Taylor (Trader Horn), Anne Heywood (Nicole), Jean Sorel (Emil), Don Knight (Colonel Sinclair).

Trading Mom (see *The Mummy Market*).

4607. *The Tragedy of Korosko* (Arthur Conan Doyle, 1898). Adventure story about a group of British people on a Nile cruise and their harrowing ordeal in the desert. **Adaptation:** *Fires of Fate* (British International/Power, 1933). Dir: Norman Walker. Scr: Dion Titheradge. Cast: Lester Matthews (Lieutenant Egerton), Kathleen O'Regan (Nora), Dorothy Bartlam (Kay).

The Trail Beyond (see *The Wolf Hunters*).

4608. *The Trail of the Lonesome Pine* (John Fox, Jr., 1908). A deadly feud develops between rural families when a railroad is built on their land. The novel was adapted as a stage play in 1912 by Eugene Walter. **Silent Films:** 1914, 1916 (directed by Cecil B. De Mille), and 1923. **Adaptation:** *The Trail of the Lonesome Pine* (Paramount, 1936). Dir: Henry Hathaway. Scr: Grover Jones, Horace McCoy, Harvey F. Thew. Cast: Sylvia Sidney (June), Fred MacMurray (Jack), Henry Fonda (Dave), Fred Stone (Judd), Nigel Bruce (Thurber), Beulah Bondi (Melissa), Robert Barrat (Buck), George "Spanky" McFarland (Buddy). VHS.

Trail Street (see *Golden Horizons*).

4609. *Trainspotting* (Irvine Welsh, 1993). Young Scottish heroin users and their world of sex, theft, music, and violence. **Adaptation:** *Trainspotting* (Miramax, 1996). Dir: Danny Boyle. Scr: John Hodge. Cast: Ewan McGregor (Renton), Ewen Bremner (Spud), Jonny Lee Miller (Sick Boy), Kevin McKidd (Tommy), Robert Carlyle (Begbie), Kelly Macdonald (Diane). Notes: BAFTA Award for Best Screenplay and nomination for Best Picture; Academy Award nomination for Best Screenplay; Independent Spirit Award nomination for Best Picture. DVD, VHS.

4610. *Traitor's Gate* (Edgar Wallace, 1927). A British businessman and his friends attempt to steal the Crown Jewels in London. **Adaptation:** *Traitor's Gate* (Columbia, 1964). Dir: Freddie Francis. Scr: Jimmy Sangster (writing as John Sansom). Cast: Albert Lieven (Trayne), Gary Raymond (Graham/Dick), Margot Trooger (Dinah), Catherine Schell (Hope).

Transatlantic Tunnel (see *The Tunnel*).

Transgression (see *The Next Corner*).

The Trapp Family (see *The Story of the Trapp Family Singers*).

Trapped (see *24 Hours*).

Traps (see *Dreamhouse*).

4611. *Traumnovelle* (Arthur Schnitzer, 1926). After his wife describes her erotic fantasies, a Viennese doctor begins a sexual odyssey and eventually joins a secret sex club, where his life is threatened. The Austrian novel was translated into English in 1927 and originally published under the title *Rhapsody: A Dream Novel*. **Adap-**tation: *Eyes Wide Shut* (Warner, 1999). Dir: Stanley Kubrick. Scr: Stanley Kubrick, Frederic Raphael. Cast: Tom Cruise (Dr. Harford), Nicole Kidman (Alice), Madison Eginton (Helena), Jackie Sawiris (Roz), Sydney Pollack (Victor). Notes: Kubrick's final film. DVD, VHS.

4612. *Travels with My Aunt* (Graham Greene, 1969). The eccentric and vivacious aunt of a shy bank clerk takes him on a whirlwind adventure in her pursuit of shady schemes. **Adaptation:** *Travels with My Aunt* (MGM, 1972). Dir: George Cukor. Scr: Jay Presson Allen, Hugh Wheeler. Cast: Maggie Smith (Aunt Augusta), Alec McCowen (Henry), Lou Gossett (Wordsworth), Robert Stephens (Visconti), Cindy Williams (Tooley). Notes: Academy Award for Best Costume Design and nominations for Best Actress (Smith), Cinematography, and Art Direction; Golden Globe nominations for Best Comic Film, Actress (Smith), and Supporting Actor (McCowen). VHS.

4613. *A Travesty* (Donald E. Westlake, 1977). A film critic disguises his involvement in the accidental death of his lover by pretending to help a detective with screenwriting ambitions. The novella appeared in Westlake's 1977 collection *Enough!* **Adaptation:** *A Slight Case of Murder* (Turner, 1999 TV Movie). Dir: Steven Schachter. Scr: William H. Macy, Steven Schachter. Cast: William H. Macy (Terry), Adam Arkin (Detective Stapelli), Felicity Huffman (Kit), James Cromwell (Edgerson). Notes: Edgar Allan Poe Award for Best Television Film; Emmy Award nomination for Outstanding Actor (Macy). VHS.

Travis McGee (see *The Empty Copper Sea*).

4614. *Treasure Island* (Robert Louis Stevenson, 1883). A young man goes in search of a pirate's treasure and must contend with the murderous Long John Silver. In 1881, the story was serialized in seventeen installments under the title *The Sea Cook* in *Young Folks*, a children's magazine. It was edited, retitled, and published as a novel in 1883. **Silent Films:** 1912, 1918, and 1920. **Adaptation 1:** *Treasure Island* (MGM, 1934). Dir: Victor Fleming. Scr: John Lee Mahin. Cast: Wallace Beery (Long John), Jackie Cooper (Hawkins), Lionel Barrymore (Bones), Otto Kruger (Dr. Livesey), Lewis Stone (Captain Smollett), Nigel Bruce (Squire Trelawney). VHS. **Adaptation 2:** *Treasure Island* (RKO, 1950). Dir: Byron Haskin. Scr: Lawrence Edward Watkin. Cast: Bobby Driscoll (Hawkins), Robert Newton (Long John), Basil Sydney (Captain Smollett), Walter Fitzgerald (Squire Trelawney), Denis O'Dea (Dr. Livesey). DVD, VHS. **Adaptation 3:** *Treasure Island* (BBC, 1957 TV Movie). Dir: Joy Harington. Scr: Joy Harington. Cast: Richard Palmer (Hawkins), Derek Birch (Captain Smollett), Valentine Dyall (Dr. Livesay), Bernard Miles (Long John). **Adaptation 4:** *Treasure Island* (Trans-International, 1966 TV Miniseries). Dir: Wolfgang Liebeneiner. Scr: Walter Ulbrich. Cast: Michael Ande (Hawkins), Ivor Dean (Long John), Georges Riquier (Dr. Livesey), Jacques Dacqmine (Squire Trelawney), Jacques Monod (Captain Smollet). **Adaptation 5:** *Treasure Island* (National General, 1972). Dir: John Hough. Scr: Bautista de la Casa, Hubert Frank, Wolf Mankowitz, Antonio Margheriti, Gerard Vergez, Orson Welles (writing as O. W. Jeeves). Cast: Orson Welles (Long John), Kim Burfield (Hawkins), Walter Slezak (Squire Trelawney), Rik Battaglia (Captain Smollett), Lionel Stander (Bones). DVD, VHS. **Adaptation 6:** *Treasure Island* (BBC, 1977 TV Miniseries). Dir: Michael E. Briant. Scr: John Lucarotti. Cast: Alfred Burke (Long John), Anthony Bate (Dr. Livesey), Ashley Knight (Hawkins), Patrick Troughton (Israel), Jack Watson (Bones), Thorley Walters (Squire Trelawney). **Adaptation 7:** *Treasure Island* (Cannon, 1985). Dir: Raoul Ruiz. Scr: Raoul Ruiz. Cast: Melvil Poupaud (Hawkins), Martin Landau (Captain Smollett), Vic Tayback (Long John), Lou Castel (Dr. Livesey), Jeffrey Kime (Squire Trelawney). **Adaptation 8:** *Treasure Island* (Turner, 1990 TV Movie). Dir: Fraser Clarke Heston. Scr: Fraser Clarke Heston. Cast: Charlton Heston (Long John), Christian Bale (Hawkins), Oliver Reed (Bones), Christopher Lee (Blind Pew), Richard Johnson (Squire Trelawney), Julian Glover (Dr. Livesey). DVD, VHS. **Adaptation 9:** *Treasure Island* (Columbia TriStar, 1999). Dir: Peter Rowe. Scr: Peter Rowe. Cast: Jack Palance (Long John), Kevin Zegers (Hawkins), Patrick Bergin (Bones), Christopher Benjamin (Squire Trelawney), David Robb (Dr. Livesey). DVD, VHS. **Adaptation 10:** *Treasure Planet* (Disney/Buena Vista, 2002). Dir: Ron Clements, John Musker. Scr: Ron Clements, John Musker, Ted Elliott, Terry Rossio, Rob Edwards, Ken Harsha. Cast: voices of Roscoe Lee Browne (Mr. Arrow), Corey Burton (Onus), Patrick McGoohan (Bones), Brian Murray (Long John), David Hyde Pierce (Dr. Doppler), Martin Short (B.E.N.), Emma Thompson (Amelia). Notes: An animated feature set in outer space in the future and involving a boy who goes in search of a space pirate's loot. Academy Award nomina-

tion for Best Animated Feature. DVD, VHS. Notes: In addition, the book was adapted for animated features in 1973 (DVD, VHS) and 1997 and was spoofed in Disney's 1996 feature *Muppet Treasure Island* (DVD, VHS). It also inspired the film *Scalawag*, a 1973 musical set in the Old West.

4615. "The Treasure of Franchard" (Robert Louis Stevenson, 1883). A young man and his uncle discover a fortune in treasure and come to experience unhappiness as a result of their find. The short story was published in *Longman's Magazine* in April and May 1883 and included in Stevenson's 1887 collection *The Merry Men and Other Tales and Fables*. **Adaptation:** *The Treasure of Lost Canyon* (Universal International, 1952). Dir: Ted Tetzlaff. Scr: Emerson Crocker, Brainerd Duffield. Scr: William Powell (Doc Brown), Rosemary De Camp (Samuella), Julie Adams (Myra), Henry Hull (Cousin Lucius). VHS.

The Treasure of Lost Canyon (*see* "The Treasure of Franchard").

Treasure of the Golden Condor (see *Benjamin Blake*).

4616. *The Treasure of the Sierra Madre* (B. Traven, 1935). Set in Mexico, the story of three gold prospectors who make a fortune and then lose it because of their greed. **Adaptation:** *The Treasure of the Sierra Madre* (Warner, 1948). Dir: John Huston. Scr: John Huston. Cast: Humphrey Bogart (Dobbs), Walter Huston (Howard), Tim Holt (Curtin), Bruce Bennett (Cody), Barton MacLane (McCormick). Notes: Academy Awards for Best Director, Screenplay, and Supporting Actor (Huston), and nomination for Best Film; Golden Globe Awards for Best Picture, Director, and Supporting Actor (Huston); National Board of Review Awards for Best Screenplay and Actor (Huston). DVD, VHS.

Treasure Planet (see *Treasure Island*).

4617. *A Tree Grows in Brooklyn* (Betty Smith [pseudonym for Elisabeth Wehner], 1943). Set in the tenement slums of Williamsburg, Brooklyn, in 1912, the story of a poor Irish-American family's struggles to survive. **Adaptation 1:** *A Tree Grows in Brooklyn* (20th Century–Fox, 1945). Dir: Elia Kazan. Scr: Frank Davis, Tess Slesinger. Cast: Dorothy McGuire (Katie), Joan Blondell (Sissy), James Dunn (Johnny), Lloyd Nolan (Officer McShane), James Gleason (McGarrity), Ted Donaldson (Neeley), Peggy Ann Garner (Francie). Notes: Academy Award for Best Actor (Dunn) and Special Award for Best Juvenile Performance (Garner), and nomination for Best Screenplay. DVD, VHS. **Adaptation 2:** *A Tree Grows in Brooklyn* (NBC, 1974 TV Movie). Dir: Joseph Hardy. Scr: Frank Davis, Tess Slesinger (1945 screenplay), Blanche Hanalis. Cast: Cliff Robertson (Johnny), Diane Baker (Katie), James Olson (Officer McShane), Pamelyn Ferdin (Francie), Nancy Malone (Sissy).

4618. *The Tree of Hands* (Ruth Rendell, 1984). After the death of a writer's son, her disturbed mother kidnaps an abused boy to replace her grandson. **Adaptation:** *Tree of Hands*; released in the U.S. as *Innocent Victim* (British Screen/Catsle Hill, 1989). Dir: Giles Foster. Scr: Gordon Williams. Cast: Helen Shaver (Benet), Lauren Bacall (Marsha), Malcolm Stoddard (Dr. Raeburn), Peter Firth (Terence). VHS.

4619. *The Tree of Liberty* (Elizabeth Page, 1939). Historical novel about a Virginia family caught up in the American Revolutionary War. **Adaptation:** *The Howards of Virginia*; released in the UK as *The Tree of Liberty* (Columbia, 1940). Dir: Frank Lloyd. Scr: Sidney Buchman. Cast: Cary Grant (Matt), Martha Scott (Jane), Cedric Hardwicke (Fleetwood), Alan Marshal (Roger). DVD, VHS.

4620. *Trent's Last Case* (E. C. Bentley, 1913). After the sudden death of a millionaire businessman, a journalist suspects that he was murdered and investigates. **Silent Films:** 1920 and 1929. **Adaptation:** *Trent's Last Case* (Republic, 1952). Dir: Herbert Wilcox. Scr: Pamela Bower. Cast: Michael Wilding (Trent), Margaret Lockwood (Margaret), Orson Welles (Manderson), John McCallum (Marlowe). VHS.

4621. *Trial* (Don M. Mankiewicz, 1954). A lawyer defends a Mexican boy accused of rape and murder and is denounced as a communist by political conservatives. **Adaptation:** *Trial* (MGM, 1955). Dir: Mark Robson. Scr: Don M. Mankiewicz. Cast: Glenn Ford (David), Dorothy McGuire (Abbe), Arthur Kennedy (Barney), John Hodiak (Armstrong), Katy Jurado (Consuela). Notes: Golden Globe Award for Best Supporting Actor (Kennedy); Academy Award nomination for Best Supporting Actor (Kennedy).

4622. *The Trial* (Franz Kafka, 1925). The Czech writer's German-language novel *Der Prozess* is a classic existential work about a man lost in a bureaucratic maze as he is tried, convicted, and executed for an unspecified crime. The book was written in 1916 and published posthumously in 1925. **Adaptation 1:** *The Trial* (Astor, 1962). Dir: Orson Welles. Scr: Orson

Welles. Cast: Anthony Perkins (Josef K.), Arnoldo Foa (Inspector A), Jess Hahn (the Second Assistant Inspector), William Kearns (the First Assistant Inspector), Madeleine Robinson (Mrs. Grubach), Jeanne Moreau (Miss Burstner). DVD, VHS. **Adaptation 2:** *The Trial* BBC/Angelika, (1993). Dir: David Hugh Jones. Scr: Harold Pinter. Cast: Kyle MacLachlan (Josef K.), Anthony Hopkins (the Priest), Jason Robards (Dr. Huld), Juliet Stevenson (Fraulein Burstner), Polly Walker (Leni), Alfred Molina (Titorelli), David Thewlis (Franz), Michael Kitchen (Block). DVD, VHS.

4623. *Trial by Terror* (Paul Gallico, 1952). An American reporter in Europe goes to Yugoslavia and discovers a plot against the West by communist countries. **Adaptation:** *Assignment: Paris* (Columbia, 1952). Dir: Robert Parrish. Scr: Walter Goetz, Jack Palmer White. Cast: Dana Andrews (Jimmy), Marta Toren (Jeanne), Herbert Berghof (Prime Minister Ordy), George Sanders (Strang). Notes: Golden Globe nomination for Best Film Promoting Human Understanding.

4624. "The Trial of Johnny Nobody" (Albert Z. Carr, 1950). After an alcoholic Irish author challenges God to strike him dead, a mysterious man appears and kills him. A village priest investigates the crime and its religious implications. The short story appeared in the November 1950 issue of *Ellery Queen's Magazine*. **Adaptation:** *Johnny Nobody* (Columbia/Medallion, 1961). Dir: Nigel Patrick. Scr: Patrick Kirwan. Cast: Nigel Patrick (Father Carey), Yvonne Mitchell (Miss Floyd), William Bendix (Mulcahy), Aldo Ray (Johnny), Cyril Cusack (O'Brien). VHS.

The Trial of Portia Merriman (*see* "Portia on Trial").

4625. *The Trial of Vivienne Ware* (Kenneth M. Ellis, 1931). A woman set to testify at a murder trial is targeted for murder. The novel was adapted as a radio drama in 1931. **Adaptation:** *The Trial of Vivienne Ware* (Fox, 1932). Dir: William K. Howard. Scr: Barry Conners, Philip Klein. Cast: Joan Bennett (Vivienne), Donald Cook (Sutherland), Richard "Skeets" Gallagher (McNally), Zasu Pitts (Gladys).

4626. *Triangle* (Teri White, 1982, Edgar Allan PoeAward for Best Paperback Original). A physically handicapped con man takes on a young protégé, who ultimately betrays him. **Adaptation:** *See How They Fall* (MIHK, 1994). Dir: Jacques Audiard. Scr: Jacques Audiard, Alain Le Henry. Cast: Jean-Louis Trintignant (Marx), Jean Yanne (Simon), Mathieu Kassovitz (Johnny), Bulle Ogier (Louise). Notes: Cesar Awards (France) for

Best First Work (Audiard), Editing, and Most Promising Actor (Kassovitz), and nomination for Best Screenplay.

4627. "Tribal Rites of the New Saturday Night" (Nik Cohn, 1976). Article about Bay Ridge, Brooklyn, youths who escape their boring daily lives by going to the local disco on Saturday nights. The article appeared in the June 7, 1976, issue of *New York* magazine. **Adaptation:** *Saturday Night Fever* (Paramount, 1977). Dir: John Badham. Scr: Norman Wexler. Cast: John Travolta (Tony), Karen Lynn Gorney (Stephanie), Barry Miller (Bobby), Joseph Cali (Joey), Paul Pape (Double J.), Donna Pescow (Annette). Notes: National Board of Review Award for Best Actor (Travolta); Academy Award nomination for Best Actor (Travolta); Golden Globe nominations for Best Picture, Actor (Travolta), and Musical Score. DVD, VHS. Notes: The movie subsequently inspired a 1983 sequel, *Staying Alive*, directed by Sylvester Stallone (DVD, VHS) and a stage musical, which debuted in London in 1998 and on Broadway in 1999.

4628. "Tribute to a Bad Man" (Jack Schaefer, 1953). Western about a ruthless land owner who takes extreme measures to maintain his possessions from rustlers and robbers and the woman who tempers his possessiveness. The short story appeared in Schaefer's 1953 collection *The Big Range*. **Adaptation:** *Tribute to a Bad Man* (MGM, 1956). Dir: Robert Wise. Scr: Michael Blankfort. Cast: James Cagney (Jeremy), Don Dubbins (Steve), Stephen McNally (McNulty), Irene Papas (Jocasta), Vic Morrow (Lars). VHS.

4629. *Trilby* (George Du Maurier, 1894). In Paris in the late nineteenth century, a hypnotist places a beautiful young girl under his spell and makes her a great opera singer. The novel was adapted as a Broadway play by Paul M. Potter in 1895. **Silent Films:** 1914 and 1927. **Adaptation 1:** *Svengali* (Warner, 1931). Dir: Archie Mayo. Scr: J. Grubb Alexander. Cast: John Barrymore (Svengali), Marian Marsh (Trilby), Donald Crisp (the Laird), Bramwell Fletcher (Billee). DVD, VHS. **Adaptation 2:** *Svengali* (MGM, 1954). Dir: Noel Langley. Scr: Noel Langley. Cast: Hildegard Knef (Trilby), Donald Wolfit (Svengali), Terence Morgan (Billy), Derek Bond (the Laird). VHS.

Trilogy of Terror (see "Prey").

Trilogy of Terror II (see "The Graveyard Rats" and "Prey").

Trio (see "Mr. Know-All," "The Sanitorium," and "The Verger").

Triple Cross (see *The Eddie Chapman Story*).

4630. *The Triple Echo* (H. E. Bates, 1970). During World War II, a military deserter goes to the farm of a lonely married woman and, dressed as a woman, poses as her sister. **Adaptation:** *The Triple Echo* (Hemdale, 1972). Dir: Michael Apted. Scr: Robin Chapman. Cast: Glenda Jackson (Alice), Oliver Reed (the Sergeant), Brian Deacon (Barton). VHS.

The Triumph of Sherlock Holmes (see *The Valley of Fear*).

4631. *Triumph Over Pain* (Rene Fulop-Miller, 1938). A history of the invention and use of anesthesia in surgery. **Adaptation:** *The Great Moment* (Paramount, 1944). Dir: Preston Sturges. Scr: Preston Sturges. Cast: Joel McCrea (William), Betty Field (Elizabeth), Harry Carey (Professor Warren), William Demarest (Eben). VHS.

4632. "Trooper Hook" (Jack Schaefer, 1953). Western about a woman who, having been taken prisoner by Indians and bearing the chief's child, is returned to her community, where she and the boy face rejection and loneliness until a cavalry sergeant falls in love with her. The short story appeared in Schaefer's 1953 collection *The Big Range*. **Adaptation:** *Trooper Hook* (United Artists, 1957). Dir: Charles Marquis Warren. Scr: David Victor, Martin Berkeley, Herbert Little, Jr. Cast: Joel McCrea (Clovis), Barbara Stanwyck (Cora), Earl Holliman (Jeff), Edward Andrews (Charlie).

4633. *Tropic of Cancer* (Henry Miller, 1934). Banned for obscenity in the United States for many years, this novel is the autobiographical story of an expatriate, sexually obsessed writer (named Henry Miller, in fact) in Paris in the 1920's. **Adaptation:** *Tropic of Cancer* (Paramount, 1970). Dir: Joseph Strick. Scr: Betty Botley, Joseph Strick. Cast: Rip Torn (Miller), James T. Callahan (Fillmore), Ellen Burstyn (Mona), David Baur (Carl), Laurence Ligneres (Ginette). VHS.

4634. *Trottie True* (Caryl Brahms and S. J. Simon, 1946). The comic adventures of a showgirl who marries a British aristocrat. Brahms and Simon also adapted their novel as a stage play. **Adaptation:** *Trottie True*; released in the U.S. as *The Gay Lady* (Rank/Eagle-Lion, 1949). Dir: Brian Desmond Hurst. Scr: Denis Freeman. Cast: Jean Kent (Trottie), James Donald (Lord Landon), Hugh Sinclair (Maurice), Lana Morris (Bouncie). VHS.

Trouble for Two (see "The Suicide Club").

4635. *Trouble in the Glen* (Maurice Walsh, 1950). An American veteran returns to his native Scottish village, where he clashes with the locals over closing a private road that people have used for years. **Adaptation:** *Trouble in the Glen* (Republic, 1953). Dir: Herbert Wilcox. Scr: Frank S. Nugent, Maurice Walsh. Cast: Margaret Lockwood (Marissa), Orson Welles (Sanin), Forrest Tucker (Lansing), Victor McLaglen (Parlan), John McCallum (Malcolm). DVD, VHS.

The Trouble with Angels (see *Life with Mother Superior*).

The Trouble with Girls (see *The Chautaugua*).

4636. *The Trouble with Harry* (Jack Trevor Story, 1949). Comic mystery set in a small New England town, where a man's body is discovered in the woods and a variety of townspeople believe that they might be the cause of his death. **Adaptation:** *The Trouble with Harry* (Paramount, 1955). Dir: Alfred Hitchcock. Scr: John Michael Hayes. Cast: Edmund Gwenn (Albert), John Forsythe (Sam), Shirley MacLaine (Jennifer), Mildred Natwick (Ivy), Mildred Dunnock (Mrs. Wiggs), Jerry Mathers (Arnie), Royal Dano (Calvin). Notes: BAFTA nominations for Best Picture and Actress (MacLaine). DVD, VHS.

The Trouble with Spies (see *Apple Pie in the Sky*).

Troy (see *The Iliad*).

The Truce (see *If This Is a Man*).

4637. "Trucks" (Stephen King, 1973). Murderous tractor-trailers terrorize people at a truck stop. The story originally appeared in the June 1973 issue of *Cavalier* and was included in King's 1978 short-story collection *Night Shift*. **Adaptation 1:** *Maximum Overdrive* (DeLaurentiis, 1986). Dir: Stephen King. Scr: Stephen King. Cast: Emilio Estevez (Bill), Pat Hingle (Hendershot), Laura Harrington (Brett), Yeardley Smith (Connie), John Short (Curtis), Ellen McElduff (Wanda June). DVD, VHS. **Adaptation 2:** *Trucks* (Trimark, 1997 TV Movie). Dir: Chris Thomson. Scr: Brian Taggert. Cast: Timothy Busfield (Ray), Brenda Bakke (Hope), Aidan Devine (Bob), Roman Podhora (Thad), Jay Brazeau (Jack), Brendan Fletcher (Logan). DVD, VHS.

4638. *True Blue: The Oxford Boat Race Mutiny* (Daniel Topolski and Patrick Robinson, 1989). Factual account of a 1987 incident in which American students at Oxford University refused to participate in the annual boat race against Cambridge. **Adaptation:** *True Blue* (FilmFour, 1996). Dir: Ferdinand Fairfax. Scr: Rupert Walters. Cast: Johan Leysen (Topolski), Dominic West (MacDonald), Dylan Baker (Suarez), Geraldine Somerville (Ruth), Josh Lucas (Warren). DVD, VHS.

4639. *True Confessions* (John Gregory Dunne, 1977). A Los Angeles detective investigating the murder of a young prostitute discovers that his estranged brother, a well-regarded monsignor, is involved. The novel is loosely based on the unsolved Black Dahlia murder. **Adaptation:** *True Confessions* (United Artists, 1981). Dir: Ulu Grosbard. Scr: Joan Didion, John Gregory Dunne, Gary S. Hall. Cast: Robert De Niro (Des), Robert Duvall (Tom), Charles Durning (Jack), Kenneth McMillan (Frank), Ed Flanders (Dan), Cyril Cusack (Cardinal Danaher), Burgess Meredith (Seamus). VHS.

4640. *True Crime* (Andrew Klavan, 1995). A jaded journalist finds a renewed sense of purpose as he searches frantically for evidence to exonerate a death-row inmate from being executed the following day. **Adaptation:** *True Crime* (Warner, 1999). Dir: Clint Eastwood. Scr: Larry Gross, Paul Brickman, Stephen Schiff. Cast: Clint Eastwood (Steve), Isaiah Washington (Frank), Lisa Gay Hamilton (Bonnie), James Woods (Alan), Denis Leary (Bob), Bernard Hill (Warden Plunkitt), Diane Venora (Barbara), Michael McKean (Reverend Shillerman), Michael Jeter (Dale), Mary McCormack (Michelle). DVD, VHS.

4641. *True Grit* (Charles Portis, 1968). Set in the late nineteenth century, Western about a young woman out to revenge the murder of her father with the aid of one-eyed Marshal Rooster Cogburn. **Adaptation:** *True Grit* (Paramount, 1969). Dir: Henry Hathaway. Scr: Marguerite Roberts. Cast: John Wayne (Rooster), Glen Campbell (La Boeuf), Kim Darby (Mattie), Jeremy Slate (Emmett), Robert Duvall (Ned), Dennis Hopper (Moon). Notes: Academy Award for Best Actor (Wayne) and nomination for Best Song; Golden Globe Award for Best Actor (Wayne) and nominations for Best Newcomer (Campbell) and Song. DVD, VHS. Notes: Two sequels were produced: *Rooster Cogburn* (1975) (DVD, VHS), and *True Grit: A Further Adventure*, a made-for-television movie broadcast on ABC in 1978.

True to the Army (see *She Loves Me Not*).

4642. *True Women* (Janice Woods Windle, 1993). A young girl living happily with a friend in Georgia in 1853 is sent to live on her sister's farm in Texas after their father dies. **Adaptation:** *True Women* (Hallmark, 1997 TV Miniseries). Dir: Karen Arthur. Scr: Christopher Lofton. Cast: Dana Delany (Sarah), Annabeth Gish (Euphemia as an adult), Angelina Jolie (Georgia as an adult), Tina Majorino (Euphemia as a child), Rachael Leigh Cook (Georgia as a child), Michael York (Lewis). DVD, VHS.

4643. *Truman* (David McCollough, 1992, Pulitzer Prize). Biography of America's thirty-third President from his humble beginning in Missouri through his leading role in ending World War II and shaping the United States into a superpower. **Adaptation:** *Truman* (HBO, 1995 TV Movie). Dir: Frank Pierson. Scr: Tom Rickman. Cast: Gary Sinise (Harry Truman), Diana Scarwid (Bess Truman), Richard Dysart (Henry Stimson), Colm Feore (Charlie Ross), James Gammon (Sam Rayburn), Tony Goldwyn (Clark Clifford), Pat Hingle (Tom Pendergast). Notes: CableAce Award for Best Actor (Sinise); Golden Globe Award for Best Actor (Sinise) and nomination for Best TV Movie; Emmy Awards for Outstanding Movie and Casting, and nominations for Outstanding Teleplay, Actor (Sinise), Actress (Scarwid), Editing, Makeup, and Sound. DVD, VHS.

4644. *The Trumpet of the Swan* (E. B. White, 1970). Children's story about a silent swan who is ridiculed wherever he goes until he learns to communicate by means of a brass trumpet. **Adaptation:** *The Trumpet of the Swan* (TriStar, 2001). Dir: Terry L. Noss, Richard Rich. Scr: Judy Rothman Rofe. Cast: voices of Jason Alexander (Father), Mary Steenburgen (Mother), Reese Witherspoon (Serena), Seth Green (Boyd), Carol Burnett (Mrs. Hammerbotham), Joe Mantegna (Monty). Notes: An animated feature. DVD, VHS.

Try and Get Me! (see *The Condemned*).

4645. *Try This One for Size* (James Hadley Chase [pseudonym for Rene Brabazon Raymond], 1980). A private investigator pursues the thieves who stole a priceless Russian icon. **Adaptation:** *Try This One for Size* (Candice, 1989). Dir: Guy Hamilton. Scr: Sergio Gobbi, Alec Medieff. Cast: Michael Brandon (Tom), David Carradine (Bradley), Arielle Dombasle (Maggie), Guy Marchand (Ottavioni), Mario Adorf (Radnitz).

4646. *Trying to Grow* (Firdaus Kanga, 1994). Autobiographical novel about the adventures of a spirited Indian boy who is unable to grow because of a disease that makes his bones brittle. **Adaptation:** *Sixth Happiness* (BBC/Regent, 1997). Dir: Waris Hussein. Scr: Firdaus Kanga. Cast: Firdaus Kanga (Brit), Souad Faress (Sera), Khodus Wadia (Sam), Nina Wadia (Dolly).

4647. *Tuck Everlasting* (Natalie Babbitt, 1975). Children's book about a young girl who discovers a family living in the woods near her home. The family has drunk from a magical spring that has given them everlasting life. When she falls in love with one of the family's sons, she must decide whether everlasting life is preferable to mortality. **Adaptation 1:** *Tuck Everlasting* (One Pass, 1981). Dir: Frederick King Keller. Scr: Fred A. Keller, Frederick King Keller. Cast: Margaret Chamberlain (Winne), Paul Flessa (Jesse), Fred A. Keller (Angus), Sonia Raimi (Mae). VHS. **Adaptation 2:** *Tuck Everlasting* (Disney/Buena Vista, 2002). Dir: Jay Russell. Scr: Jeffrey Lieber, James V. Hart. Cast: Alexis Bledel (Winnie), William Hurt (Angus), Sissy Spacek (Mae), Jonathan Jackson (Jesse), Scott Bairstow (Miles), Ben Kingsley (the Man in the Yellow Suit), Amy Irving (Mrs. Foster). DVD, VHS.

4648. *Tucker's People* (Ira Wolfert, 1943). A lawyer is corrupted by greed when he is offered a great deal of money to represent gangsters. **Adaptation:** *Force of Evil* (MGM, 1948). Dir: Abraham Polonsky. Scr: Abraham Polonsky, Ira Wolfert. Cast: John Garfield (Joe), Thomas Gomez (Leo), Marie Windsor (Edna), Howland Chamberlain (Freddie), Roy Roberts (Ben). DVD, VHS.

4649. *Tuesdays with Morrie: An Old Man, a Young Man, and a Last Great Lesson* (Mitch Albom, 1997). The true account of a sports journalist who reunites with his dying college mentor and learns important lessons about what is important in life. **Adaptation:** *Tuesdays with Morrie* (ABC, 1999 TV Movie). Dir: Mick Jackson. Scr: Tom Rickman. Cast: Jack Lemmon (Morrie), Hank Azaria (Mitch), Wendy Moniz (Janine), Caroline Aaron (Connie), Bonnie Bartlett (Charlotte), Aaron Lustig (Rabbi Axelrod). Notes: Emmy Awards for Outstanding Television Movie, Actor (Lemmon), Supporting Actor (Azaria), and Editing, and nomination for Outstanding Sound; Golden Globe nomination for Best Television Actor (Lemmon). DVD, VHS.

4650. "Tugboat Annie" (Norman Reilly Raine, 1931). The first in a long series of short stories about the comic adventures on the waterfront of an elderly woman and her alcoholic husband. The story appeared in *The Saturday Evening Post* on July 11, 1931. **Adaptation:** *Tugboat Annie*

(MGM, 1933). Dir: Mervyn Le Roy. Scr: Zelda Sears, Eve Greene, Norman Reilly Raine. Cast: Marie Dressler (Annie), Wallace Beery (Terry), Robert Young (Alec), Maureen O'Sullivan (Pat). Notes: The screenplay combines elements from several stories in the series. Two sequels followed the 1933 film — *Tugboat Annie Sails Again* (1940) and *Captain Tugboat Annie* (1945). The stories also inspired a 1957 British television series.

Tune in Tomorrow (see *Aunt Julia and the Scriptwriter*).

4651. *Tunes of Glory* (James Kennaway, 1956). The strict new commander of the Scottish highland regiment clashes with his relaxed predecessor. **Adaptation:** *Tunes of Glory* (Lopert, 1960). Dir: Ronald Neame. Scr: James Kennaway. Cast: Alec Guinness (Jock), John Mills (Basil), Dennis Price (Charles), Kay Walsh (Mary), John Fraser (Ian), Susannah York (Morag). Notes: Academy Award nomination for Best Screenplay; BAFTA nominations for Best British Film, Film from Any Source, Screenplay, and Actors (Guinness and Mills). DVD, VHS.

4652. *The Tunnel* (Bernhard Kellermann, 1913). German novel, originally titled *Der Tunnel*, about the construction of a transatlantic tunnel connecting the United States and Europe. The novel was translated in 1915. **Adaptation:** *The Tunnel*; released in the U.S. as *Transatlantic Tunnel* (Gaumont, 1935). Dir: Maurice Elvey. Scr: Du Garde Peach, Kurt Siodmak. Cast: Richard Dix (Richard), Leslie Banks (Frederick), Madge Evans (Ruth), Helen Vinson (Varlia). VHS.

4653. *The Tunnel Escape* (Eric Williams, 1950). During World War II, British prisoners being held at a Nazi camp escape by tunneling below a vaulting horse. The book was also published as *The Tunnel*. **Adaptation:** *The Wooden Horse* (British Lion/Snader, 1950). Dir: Jack Lee. Scr: Eric Williams. Cast: Leo Genn (Peter), David Tomlinson (Phil), Anthony Steel (John), David Greene (Bennett), Peter Burton (Nigel). Notes: BAFTA nomination for Best British Film, VHS.

4654. "Turn About" (William Faulkner, 1932). During World War I, a beautiful English girl becomes a nurse and joins her fiancé, her lover, and her brother at the front. The story was published in *The Saturday Evening Post* on March 5, 1932. **Adaptation:** *Today We Live* (MGM, 1933). Dir: Howard Hawks, Richard Rosson. Scr: William Faulkner, Edith Fitzgerald, Dwight Taylor. Cast: Joan Crawford (Ann), Gary Cooper

(Richard), Robert Young (Claude), Franchot Tone (Ronnie). VHS.

4655. *The Turn of the Screw* (Henry James, 1898). Novella about a governess whose young charges are possessed by the spirits of dead household servants and her attempts to save the children from these evil beings. **Adaptation 1:** *The Turn of the Screw* (NBC, 1959 TV Movie). Dir: John Frankenheimer. Scr: James Costigan. Cast: Ingrid Bergman (the Governess), Isobel Elsom (Mrs. Grose), Laurinda Barrett (Miss Jessel), Hayward Morse (Miles), Paul Stevens (Peter), Alexandra Wager (Flora). Notes: Emmy Award for Outstanding Television Actress (Bergman) and nominations for Outstanding Movie, Director, and Teleplay. **Adaptation 2:** *The Innocents* (20th Century–Fox, 1961). Dir: Jack Clayton. Scr: William Archibald, Truman Capote, John Mortimer. Cast: Deborah Kerr (Miss Giddens), Peter Wyngarde (Peter), Megs Jenkins (Mrs. Grose), Michael Redgrave (the Uncle), Martin Stephens (Miles), Pamela Franklin (Flora), Clytie Jessop (Miss Jessel). Notes: National Board of Review Award for Best Director; BAFTA nomination for Best Picture. DVD, VHS. **Adaptation 3:** *The Turn of the Screw* (ABC, 1974 TV Movie). Dir: Dan Curtis. Scr: William F. Nolan. Cast: Lynn Redgrave (Jane), Jasper Jacob (Miles), Eva Griffith (Flora), Megs Jenkins (Mrs. Grose), John Barron (Mr. Fredricks), Anthony Langdon (Luke), Benedict Taylor (Timothy), James Laurenson (Peter), Kathryn Leigh Scott (Miss Jessel). DVD, VHS. **Adaptation 4:** *The Turn of the Screw* (Cannon, 1990 TV Movie). Dir: Graeme Clifford. Scr: Graeme Clifford. Cast: Amy Irving (the Governess), David Hemmings (Mr. Harley), Micole Mercurio (Mrs. Gross), Olaf Pooley (John), Cameron Milzer (Miss Jessel), Irina Cashen (Flora), Linda Hunt (the Voice), Bret Culpepper (Wyck). **Adaptation 5:** *The Turn of the Screw* (Electric, 1994). Dir: Rusty Lemorande. Scr: Rusty Lemorande. Cast: Patsy Kensit (Jenny), Stephane Audran (Mrs. Grose), Julian Sands (Mr. Cooper), Marianne Faithfull (Narrator), Olivier Debray (Peter), Bryony Brind (Miss Jessel). VHS. **Adaptation 6:** *The Haunting of Helen Walker* (CBS, 1995 TV Movie). Dir: Tom McLoughlin. Scr: Hugh Whitemore. Cast: Valerie Bertinelli (Helen), Florence Hoath (Flora), Aled Roberts (Miles), Michael Gough (Barnaby), Paul Rhys (Edward), Christopher Guard (Peter), Diana Rigg (Mrs. Grose), Elizabeth Morton (Miss Jessel). **Adaptation 7:** *The Turn of the Screw* (PBS, 1999 TV Movie). Dir: Ben Bolt. Scr: Nick Dear. Cast:

Jodhi May (the Governess), Pam Ferris (Mrs. Grose), Colin Firth (the Master), Joe Sowerbutts (Miles), Grace Robinson (Flora), Jason Salkey (Peter), Caroline Pegg (Miss Jessel). DVD, VHS. **Adaptation 8:** *Presence of Mind* (Cargo, 1999). Dir: Antonio Aloy. Scr: Antonio Aloy, Mitch Brian, Barbara Gogny. Cast: Sadie Frost (the Governess), Lauren Bacall (Mado), Ella Jones (Flora), Nilo Mur (Miles). DVD, VHS. **Adaptation 9:** *The Turn of the Screw* (Desperado/IRMI, 2003). Dir: Nick Millard. Scr: Nick Millard. Cast: Elaine Corral Kendall (Kathryn), Priscilla Alden (Mrs. Grose), Walter Dickhaut (Dr. Barrington), Cole Stratton (Miles), Remy Autumn Jagla (Flora).

Turn of the Tide (see *Three Fevers*).

4656. *Turn the Key Softly* (John Brophy, 1951). The difficult lives of three women after their release from prison. **Adaptation:** *Turn the Key Softly* (Rank/Astor, 1953). Dir: Jack Lee. Scr: Maurice Cowan, Jack Lee. Cast: Yvonne Mitchell (Monica), Terence Morgan (David), Joan Collins (Stella), Kathleen Harrison (Granny Quilliam).

4657. *Turnabout* (Thorne Smith, 1931). Comic novel about a bickering couple who are forced to inhabit each other's bodies when they speak to a statue of Buddha. **Adaptation:** *Turnabout* (United Artists, 1940). Dir: Hal Roach. Scr: Berne Giler, Rian James, John McClain, Mickell Novack. Cast: Adolphe Menjou (Phil), Mary Astor (Marion), Carole Landis (Sally), John Hubbard (Tim). Notes: The book also inspired a 1979 television series on NBC.

4658. *Turtle Beach* (Blanche D'Alpuget, 1981). Australian novel about a female reporter who leaves her husband and children in Sydney and travels to Malaysia to do a story on Vietnamese refugees. As the boat people land on the shore and are massacred, she writes an expose that places her own life in danger. **Adaptation:** *Turtle Beach* (Warner, 1992), Dir: Stephen Wallace. Scr: Ann Turner. Cast: Greta Scacchi (Judith), Joan Chen (Minou), Jack Thompson (Ralph), Art Malik (Kanan). VHS.

4659. *The Turtle Diary* (Russell Hoban, 1975). An eccentric British couple steals sea turtles from the London zoo and releases them in the ocean. **Adaptation:** *Turtle Diary* (Samuel Goldwyn, 1985). Dir: John Irvin. Scr: Harold Pinter. Cast: Glenda Jackson (Neaera), Ben Kingsley (William), Richard Johnson (Mr. Johnson), Michael Gambon (George), Rosemary Leach (Mrs. Inchcliff). VHS.

The Tuttles of Tahiti (see *No More Gas*).

4660. *The Twelve Chairs* (Ilya Ilf and Yevgeny Petrov, 1928). Russian comic novel, originally titled *Dvenadstat Stulyev*, about a bureaucrat who inherits family jewels hidden in twelve dining-room chairs that are missing. **Adaptation 1:** *Keep Your Seats, Please* (ATP, 1936). Dir: Monty Banks. Scr: Thomas J. Geraghty, Ian Hay, Anthony Kimmins. Cast: George Formby (George), Florence Desmond (Flo), Gus McNaughton (Max), Alastair Sim (Drayton). **Adaptation 2:** *It's in the Bag!;* released in the UK as *The Fifth Chair* (United Artists, 1945). Dir: Richard Wallace. Scr: Jay Dratler, Alma Reville, Morrie Ryskind. Cast: Fred Allen (Fred), Binnie Barnes (Eve), Robert Benchley (Parker), Jerry Colonna (Dr. Greengrass), John Carradine (Jefferson), and cameo appearances by Jack Benny, Don Ameche, William Bendix, Victor Moore, and Rudy Vallee. DVD, VHS. **Adaptation 3:** *The 13 Chairs;* released in the UK as *Twelve Plus One* (AVCO Embassy, 1969). Dir: Nicolas Gessner, Luciano Lucignani. Scr: Antonio Altoviti, Marc Behm, Lucia Drudi Demby, Nicolas Gessner, Luciano Lucignani, Denis Norden. Cast: Sharon Tate (Pat), Vittorio Gassman (Mario), Orson Welles (Markan), Vittorio De Sica (Di Seta). VHS. **Adaptation 4:** *The Twelve Chairs* (UMC, 1970). Dir: Mel Brooks. Scr: Mel Brooks. Cast: Ron Moody (Ippolit), Frank Langella (Bender), Dom De Luise (Fyodor), Andreas Voutsinas (Nikolai). Notes: National Board of Review Award for Best Supporting Actor (Langella). DVD, VHS.

Twelve Good Men (see *The Murders in Praed Street*).

Twelve Plus One (see *The Twelve Chairs*).

4661. *A Twelvemonth and a Day* (Christopher Rush, 1985). Autobiographical novel about a young boy growing up in a small Scottish fishing village in the 1950's. **Adaptation:** *Venus Peter* (BFI, 1989). Dir: Ian Sellar. Scr: Ian Sellar. Cast: George Anton (Billy), Louise Breslin (Leebie), Juliet Cadzow (Queen Paloma), Peter Caffrey (Father), Sinead Cusack (Miss Balsilbie).

4662. *Twenty Years Later* (Alexandre Dumas, pere, 1845). Dumas followed up his successful book *The Three Musketeers* with *Vingt Ans Apres*, which reunites the musketeers twenty years after the death of Milady de Winter. Their mission is to save Queen Anne from scheming Cardinal Mazarin. This book was the second installment in a series that included *The Three Musketeers*

(1844) and *The Man in the Iron Mask* (1850). **Adaptation:** *The Return of the Musketeers* (Universal, 1989). Dir: Richard Lester. Scr: George MacDonald Fraser. Cast: Michael York (D'Artagnan), Oliver Reed (Athos), Frank Finlay (Porthos), C. Thomas Howell (Raoul), Kim Cattrall (Justine), Geraldine Chaplin (Queen Anne), Roy Kinnear (Planchet), Christopher Lee (Rochefort), Philippe Noiret (Cardinal Mazarin), Richard Chamberlain (Aramis). VHS. See also *The Three Musketeers and The Man in the Iron Mask.*

4663. *24 Hours* (Louis Bromfield, 1930). A day in the life of an unhappily married couple. **Adaptation:** *24 Hours* (Paramount, 1931). Dir: Marion Gering. Scr: Will D. Lengle, Lew Levenson, Louis Weitzenkorn. Cast: Clive Brook (Jim), Kay Francis (Fanny), Miriam Hopkins (Rosie), Regis Toomey (Tony).

4664. *24 Hours* (Greg Iles, 2000). Two scheming criminals kidnap a wealthy couple's asthmatic daughter and hold her for ransom while also keeping the parents hostage, but before long the tables are turned on the kidnappers. **Adaptation:** *Trapped* (Columbia, 2002). Dir: Luis Mandoki. Scr: Greg Iles. Cast: Charlize Theron (Karen), Courtney Love (Cheryl), Stuart Townsend (William), Kevin Bacon (Joe), Pruitt Taylor Vince (Marvin), Dakota Fanning (Abigail). DVD, VHS.

4665. *24 Hours of a Woman's Life* (Stefan Zweig, 1931). Austrian novel, originally titled *24 Stunden aus dem Leben einer Frau*, about a rich widow who tries unsuccessfully to reform a hardened gambler. **Adaptation 1:** *24 Hours of a Woman's Life*; released in the U.S. as *Affair in Monte Carlo* (Allied Artists, 1952). Dir: Victor Saville. Scr: Warren Chetham Strode. Cast: Merle Oberon (Linda), Richard Todd (the Boy), Leo Genn (Robert), Stephen Murray (Father Benoit). **Adaptation 2:** *Twenty-Four Hours in a Woman's Life* (Rhino, 1961 TV Movie). Dir: Silvio Narizzano. Scr: John Mortimer. Cast: Ingrid Bergman (Clare), Rip Torn (Paul), Helena de Crespo (Helen), Jerry Orbach (Cristof). VHS. Notes: In addition, French-language adaptations were released in 1968 and 2002.

4666. *The 25th Hour* (David Benioff, 2001). A convicted drug dealer reflects on his past on the eve of beginning his prison term. **Adaptation:** *25th Hour* (Buena Vista, 2002). Dir: Spike Lee. Scr: David Benioff. Cast: Edward Norton (Monty), Philip Seymour Hoffman (Jacob), Barry Pepper (Frank), Rosario Dawson (Naturelle), Anna Paquin (Mary), Brian Cox (James). DVD, VHS.

4667. *The 27th Day* (John Mantley, 1956). Science fiction about five people from the earth's superpowers taken aboard an alien spacecraft and handed a weapon, giving each one the power of life and death over the enemy. **Adaptation:** *The 27th Day* (Columbia, 1957). Dir: William Asher. Scr: John Mantley. Cast: Gene Barry (Jonathan), Valerie French (Eve), George Voskovec (Klaus).

4668. *20,000 Leagues Under The Sea* (Jules Verne, 1869–1870). Verne's novel *Vingt Mille Lieues Sous les Mers* is about two castaway seamen who board an enormous submarine and begin a year-long adventure with a mysterious captain. The fantastic tale was originally serialized in *Magasin d'Education et de Recreation* between March 20, 1869, and June 20, 1870, and then released as a two-volume novel. **Silent Films:** 1907 and 1916 (DVD, VHS). **Adaptation 1:** *20,000 Leagues Under the Sea* (Disney/Buena Vista, 1954). Dir: Richard Fleischer. Scr: Earl Felton. Cast: Kirk Douglas (Ned), James Mason (Captain Nemo), Paul Lukas (Professor Arronax), Peter Lorre (Conseil). Notes: Academy Awards for Best Art Direction and Special Effects, and nomination for Best Editing. DVD, VHS. **Adaptation 2:** *20,000 Leagues Under the Sea* (Hallmark, 1997 TV Movie). Dir: Michael Anderson. Scr: Joe Wiesenfeld. Cast: Richard Crenna (Professor Arronax), Ben Cross (Captain Nemo), Julie Cox (Sophie/Charlie), Michael Jayston (Admiral Sellings), Paul Gross (Ned). VHS. **Adaptation 3:** *20,000 Leagues Under the Sea* (Pierce, 1997 TV Miniseries). Dir: Rod Hardy. Scr: Brian Nelson. Cast: Michael Caine (Captain Nemo), Patrick Dempsey (Professor Arronax), Mia Sara (Mara), Bryan Brown (Ned). Notes: Two sequels were also released: *Captain Nemo and the Underwater City* in 1968, and *The Return of Captain Nemo*, a made-for-television movie, broadcast in 1978.

4669. *20,000 Years in Sing Sing* (Lewis E. Lawes, 1932). A book on penal reform by the progressive warden of the Ossining Prison, popularly known as Sing Sing. **Adaptation 1:** *20,000 Years in Sing Sing* (First National, 1932). Dir: Michael Curtiz. Scr: Courtney Terrett, Robert Lord, Wilson Mizner, Brown Holmes. Cast: Spencer Tracy (Tommy), Bette Davis (Fay), Arthur Byron (Warden Long), Lyle Talbot (Bud). **Adaptation 2:** *Castle on the Hudson* (Warner, 1940). Dir: Anatole Litvak. Scr: Seton I. Miller, Brown Holmes, Courtney Terrett. Cast: John Garfield (Tommy), Ann Sheridan (Kay), Pat OBrien (Warden Long), Burgess Meredith (Steve).

23 Paces to Baker Street (see Warrant for X).

4670. *Twice Shy* (Dick Francis, 1981). Crimes from his past come back to haunt a retired jockey. **Adaptation:** *Dick Francis: Twice Shy* (Comedia, 1989 TV Movie). Dir: Deirdre Friel. Scr: Miles Henderson. Cast: Ian McShane (David), Kate McKenzie (Casssie), Karl Hayden (Derry). DVD, VHS.

Twice-Told Tales (see "Dr. Heidegger's Experiment," *The House of the Seven Gables*, and "Rappaccini's Daughter").

Twice Upon a Time (see Lottie and Lisa).

4671. *Twilight for the Gods* (Ernest K. Gann, 1956). The captain of an old ship takes it on a final, doomed trip from Tahiti to Mexico. **Adaptation:** *Twilight for the Gods* (Universal International, 1958). Dir: Joseph Pevney. Scr: Ernest K. Gann. Cast: Rock Hudson (Captain Bell), Cyd Charisse (Charlotte), Arthur Kennedy (Ramsay), Leif Erickson (Harry).

4672. *Twilight of Honor* (Al Dewlen, 1961). A young lawyer in a small town takes the case of a local tough charged with murder. **Adaptation:** *Twilight of Honor*; released in the UK as *The Charge Is Murder* (MGM, 1963). Dir: Boris Sagal. Scr: Henry Denker. Cast: Richard Chamberlain (David), Nick Adams (Ben), Claude Rains (Art), Joan Blackman (Susan), James Gregory (Norris), Joey Heatherton (Laura), Pat Buttram (Cole), Jeanette Nolan (Amy).

Twilight's Last Gleaming (see Viper 3).

4673. *Twin Sombreros* (Zane Grey, 1941). A retired gunfighter who has has vowed not to kill again is accused of murdering his best friend. **Adaptation:** *Gunfighters*; released in the UK as *The Assassin* (Columbia, 1947). Dir: George Waggner. Scr: Alan Le May. Cast: Randolph Scott (Kane), Barbara Britton (Bess), Bruce Cabot (Mackey).

4674. *Twinkle, Twinkle, Killer Kane* (William Peter Blatty, 1966). A military psychiatrist is sent to a remote castle to work with mentally disturbed soldiers and begins to terrorize the inmates. **Adaptation:** *The Ninth Configuration* (Warner, 1980). Dir: William Peter Blatty. Scr: William Peter Blatty. Cast: Stacy Keach (Kane), Scott Wilson (Cutshaw), Jason Miller (Reno), Ed Flanders (Fell), Neville Brand (Groper), George Di Cenzo (Fairbanks), Moses Gunn (Nammack), Robert Loggia (Bennish). Notes: Golden Globe Award for Best Screenplay and nominations for Best Picture and Supporting Actor (Wilson). DVD, VHS.

4675. *Twins* (Bari Wood and Jack Geasland, 1977). Twin gynecologists with a disturbing past share women between themselves, but trouble begins when one of them falls in love with a beautiful actress and refuses to share her. **Adaptation:** *Dead Ringers* (20th Century–Fox, 1988). Dir: David Cronenberg. Scr: David Cronenberg, Norman Snider. Cast: Jeremy Irons (Beverly/Elliot), Genevieve Bujold (Claire), Heidi von Palleske (Cary), Barbara Gordon (Danuta), Shirley Douglas (Laura). Notes: Genie Awards (Canada) for Best Picture, Director, Screenplay, Actor (Irons), Cinematography, Art Direction, Musical Score, Editing, Sound, and Sound Editing, and nominations for Best Actress (Bujold) and Costume Design. DVD, VHS.

4676. *A Twist of Sand* (Geoffrey Jenkins, 1959). A former Marine commander assembles a team to smuggle diamonds out of Africa, but the thieves fall out among themselves. **Adaptation:** *A Twist of Sand* (United Artists, 1968). Dir: Don Chaffey. Scr: Marvin H. Albert. Cast: Richard Johnson (Geoffrey), Honor Blackman (Julie), Jeremy Kemp (Harry), Peter Vaughan (Johann), Roy Dotrice (David).

4677. *Two: A Phallic Novel* (Alberto Moravia, 1971). In the Italian novel *Io e Lui*, a man's sex organs begin talking to him. **Adaptation:** *Me and Him* (Columbia, 1988). Dir: Doris Dorrie. Scr: Warren D. Leight. Cast: Griffin Dunne (Bert), Ellen Greene (Annette), Kelly Bishop (Eleanor). VHS.

4678. "Two Can Sing" (James M. Cain, 1938). Comic story about an aspiring singer who is upset when she learns that her boring husband has become a well-respected vocalist. The short story originally appeared in the April 1938 issue of *American Magazine*. **Adaptation 1:** *Wife, Husband and Friend* (20th Century–Fox, 1939). Dir: Gregory Ratoff. Scr: Nunnally Johnson. Cast: Loretta Young (Doris), Warner Baxter (Leonard), Binnie Barnes (Cecil), Cesar Romero (Hugo). **Adaptation 2:** *Everybody Does It* (20th Century–Fox, 1949). Dir: Edmund Goulding. Scr: Nunnally Johnson. Cast: Paul Douglas (Leonard), Linda Darnell (Cecil), Celeste Holm (Doris), Charles Coburn (Major Blair).

Two Deaths (see The Two Deaths of Senora Puccini).

4679. *The Two Deaths of Senora Puccini* (Stephen Dobyns, 1988). As a bloody revolution rages outside his home in Bucharest, a surgeon and his friends have a reunion dinner, and their conversation soon unearths dark secrets of the past, including admissions of sexual obsession and betrayal. **Adaptation:** *Two Deaths* (BBC/Castle Hill, 1995). Dir: Nicolas Roeg. Scr: Allan Scott. Cast: Sonia Braga (Ana), Patrick Malahide (George), Ion Caramitru (Carl), Sevilla Delofski (Ilena), Nickolas Grace (Marius), Michael Gambon (Daniel). DVD, VHS.

The Two Faces of Dr. Jekyll (see *The Strange Case of Dr. Jekyll and Mr. Hyde*).

4680. *Two for Texas* (James Lee Burke, 1982). In 1836, two brothers escape from a Louisiana chain gang, go to Texas, and join Sam Houston's army battling the Mexicans at the Alamo. **Adaptation:** *Two for Texas* (Turner, 1998 TV Movie). Dir: Rod Hardy. Scr: Larry Brothers. Cast: Kris Kristofferson (Hugh), Scott Bairstow (Son), Irene Bedard (Sana), Tom Skerritt (Sam Houston), Peter Coyote (Jim Bowie). VHS.

Two in the Dark (see *Two O'Clock Courage*).

Two Left Feet (see *In My Solitude*).

Two Loves (see *Spinster*).

Two Men Went to War (see *The Amateur Commandos*).

4681. *Two-Minute Warning* (George La Fountaine, Sr., 1975). A psychotic sniper terrorizes the spectators at a professional football game. **Adaptation:** *Two-Minute Warning* (Universal, 1976). Dir: Larry Peerce. Scr: Edward Hume. Cast: Charlton Heston (Peter), John Cassavetes (Button), Martin Balsam (Sam), Beau Bridges (Mike), Marilyn Hassett (Lucy), David Janssen (Steve), Jack Klugman (Sandman). DVD, VHS.

4682. *Two Much* (Donald E. Westlake, 1975). A scheming art dealer romancing a young woman invents a twin brother who becomes engaged to his girlfriend's sister. **Adaptation:** *Two Much* (Buena Vista, 1995). Dir: Fernando Trueba. Scr: Fernando Trueba, David Trueba. Cast: Antonio Banderas (Art), Melanie Griffith (Betty), Daryl Hannah (Liz), Danny Aiello (Gene), Joan Cusack (Gloria), Eli Wallach (Sheldon). DVD. VHS. Notes: In addition, a French-language adaptation titled *Le Jumeau* was released in 1984.

4683. *Two O'Clock Courage* (Gelett Burgess, 1934). A man suffering from amnesia tries to discover whether he murdered a theatrical producer. **Adaptation 1:** *Two in the Dark* (RKO, 1936). Dir:

Ben Stoloff. Scr: Seton I. Miller. Cast: Walter Abel (Ford), Margot Grahame (Marie), Wallace Ford (Hillyer), Gail Patrick (Irene), Alan Hale (Inspector Florio). **Adaptation 2:** *Two O'Clock Courage* (RKO, 1945). Dir: Anthony Mann. Scr: Robert E. Kent. Cast: Tom Conway (Ted), Ann Rutherford (Patty), Richard Lane (Al), Lester Matthews (Mark).

Two Rode Together (see *Comanche Captives*).

4684. "Two Soldiers" (William Faulkner, 1942). After his brother enlists in the army following the attack on Pearl Harbor, a youngster runs away from home to join him. The short story was published in *The Saturday Evening Post* on March 28, 1942. **Adaptation:** *Two Soldiers* (Shoe Clerk, 2003). Dir: Aaron Schneider. Scr: Aaron Schneider. Cast: Ben Allison (Pete), Jonathan Furr (Willie), Ron Perlman (Colonel McKellogg), Mike Pniewski (Sheriff Foote), Danny Vinson (Mr. Grier), Suellen Yates (Mrs. Grier). Notes: Academy Award for Best Live Action Short Film.

Two Times Lotte (see *Lottie and Lisa*).

4685. *Two Weeks in Another Town* (Irwin Shaw, 1960). In Rome, an unemployed filmmaker begins to work on a film and revives his career. **Adaptation:** *Two Weeks in Another Town* (MGM, 1962). Dir: Vincente Minnelli. Scr: Charles Schnee. Cast: Kirk Douglas (Jack), Edward G. Robinson (Maurice), Cyd Charisse (Carlotta), George Hamilton (Davy), Daliah Lavi (Veronica). VHS.

2001: A Space Odyssey (see "The Sentinel").

4686. *2010: Odyssey Two* (Arthur C. Clarke, 1982). Clarke's sequel to *2001* finds the Earth on the verge of war, and American and Russian scientists team up for a trip to Jupiter to decide on its fate and find out what happened to the original craft that had been sent there nine years earlier. **Adaptation:** *2010* (MGM, 1984). Dir: Peter Hyams. Scr: Peter Hyams. Cast: Roy Scheider (Dr. Floyd), John Lithgow (Dr. Curnow), Helen Mirren (Tanya), Bob Balaban (Dr. Chandra), Keir Dullea (Dave). DVD, VHS. See also "The Sentinel."

4687. *Two Women* (Alberto Moravia, 1957). Italian novel, originally titled *La Ciociara*, about a mother and daughter who are raped as they attempt to flee from Rome during the Allied invasion of Italy during World War II. The novel was translated in 1958. **Adaptation 1:** *Two Women* (1960). Dir: Vittorio De Sica. Scr: Vittorio De

Sica, Cesare Zavattini. Cast: Sophia Loren (Cesira), Jean-Paul Belmondo (Michele), Eleonora Brown (Rosetta). Notes: Originally released as *La Ciociara* and shown with subtitles. Academy Award for Best Actress (Loren); Cannes Film Festival Award for Best Actress (Loren) and Golden Palm nomination for Best Director; Golden Globe Award for Best Foreign-Language Film. DVD, VHS. **Adaptation 2:** *Running Away* (Paramount Television, 1988 TV Movie). Dir: Dino Risi. Scr: Diana Gould, Bernardino Zapponi, Lidia Ravera, Dino Risi. Cast: Sophia Loren (Cesira), Robert Loggia (Michele), Sydney Penny (Rosetta), Leonardo Ferrantini (Aurelio), Dario Ghirardi (Filippo). VHS.

4688. *Two Years Before the Mast: A Personal Narrative of Life at Sea* (Richard Henry Dana, Jr., 1840). The journal of a writer who signed on as a sailor in California in 1834 to document the mistreatment of seamen. **Adaptation:** *Two Years Before the Mast* (Paramount, 1946). Dir: John Farrow. Scr: Seton I. Miller, George Bruce. Cast: Alan Ladd (Charles), Brian Donlevy (Dana), William Bendix (Amazeen), Barry Fitzgerald (Dooley), Howard Da Silva (Captain Thompson). VHS.

4689. *Typee* (Herman Melville, 1846). Autobiographical novel about two sailors who jump ship on a South Pacific island, where they fall in love with a native girl and have to contend with the cannibals who live there. **Adaptation:** *Enchanted Island* (Warner, 1958). Dir: Allan Dwan. Scr: James Leicester, Harold Jacob Smith. Cast: Dana Andrews (Abner), Jane Powell (Fayaway), Don Dubbins (Tom), Arthur Shields (Jimmy). VHS.

U-Boat 29 (see *The Spy in Black*).

U-Turn (see *Stray Dogs*).

The UFO Incident (see *The Interrupted Journey*).

4690. *The Ugly American* (William J. Lederer and Eugene Burdick, 1958). A new American ambassador is appointed to a south Asian nation and clashes with pro–Communist elements in the government, showing the lengths to which America is willing to go to maintain power in the region. **Adaptation:** *The Ugly American* (Universal International, 1963). Dir: George Englund. Scr: Stewart Stern. Cast: Marlon Brando (Ambassador MacWhite), Eiji Okada (Deong), Sandra Church (Marion), Pat Hingle (Homer), Arthur Hill (Grainger), Jocelyn Brando (Emma). DVD, VHS.

4691. *The Ugly Dachshund* (G. B. Stern, 1938). Children's story about an adopted Great Dane puppy nursed by the family dog and entered into a dog show as an unusually large dachshund. **Adaptation:** *The Ugly Dachshund* (Disney/Buena Vista, 1966). Dir: Norman Tokar. Scr: Albert Aley. Cast: Dean Jones (Mark), Suzanne Pleshette (Fran), Charlie Ruggles (Dr. Pruitt), Kelly Thordsen (Officer Carmody). DVD, VHS.

4692. *Ulysses* (James Joyce, 1922). Joyce's famous novel is about a long day in the lives of three Dubliners—Leopold Bloom, his wife, Molly, and poet Stephen Dedalus. The book was originally published serially in *The Little Review* between March 1918 and December 1920. Revised and published as a book in 1922, it became the subject of many obscenity accusations and was banned in the United States and Europe. **Adaptation 1:** *Ulysses* (Continental, 1967). Dir: Joseph Strick. Scr: Fred Haines, Joseph Strick. Cast: Barbara Jefford (Molly), Milo O'Shea (Leopold), Maurice Roeves (Stephen), T. P. McKenna (Buck), Martin Dempsey (Simon). Notes: Academy Award nomination for Best Screenplay; BAFTA nominations for Best Actress (Jefford), Cinematography, and Most Promising Newcomer (O'Shea); Cannes Film Festival Golden Palm nomination for Best Director; Golden Globe nomination for Best English-Language Foreign Film. DVD, VHS **Adaptation 2:** *Bloom* (Odyssey, 2003). Dir: Sean Walsh. Scr: Sean Walsh. Cast: Stephen Rea (Leopold), Angeline Ball (Molly), Hugh O'Conor (Stephen), Neili Conroy (Driscoll), Eoin McCarthy (Blazes). Notes: IFTA Award (Ireland) for Best Actress (Ball) and nomination for Best Irish Film, New Talent (Sean Walsh), Cinematography, and Costume Design. DVD, VHS.

Ulysses (1955) (see *The Odyssey*).

4693. *The Unbearable Lightness of Being* (Milan Kundera, 1984). Set in Czechoslovakia in 1968, the novel concerns the many love affairs of a physician who cares nothing for politics until the Russian invasion that spring forces his attention to the political arena. **Adaptation:** *The Unbearable Lightness of Being* (Orion, 1988). Dir: Philip Kaufman. Scr: Jean-Claude Carrière, Philip Kaufman. Cast: Daniel Day-Lewis (Tomas), Juliette Binoche (Tereza), Lena Olin (Sabina), Derek de Lint (Franz). Notes: BAFTA Award for Best Screenplay; Independent Spirit Award for Best Cinematography; Academy Award nominations for Best Screenplay and Cinematography; Golden Globe nominations for Best Picture and Supporting Actress (Olin). DVD, VHS.

4694. *Uncharted Seas* (Dennis Wheatley, 1938). The passengers and crew of a steamer are stranded on a strange island in the Sargasso Sea, where the inhabitants are still practicing the Spanish Inquisition. **Adaptation:** *The Lost Continent* (Hammer/20th Century–Fox, 1968). Dir: Michael Carreras. Scr: Michael Carreras (writing as Michael Nash). Cast: Eric Porter (Captain Lansen), Hildegard Knef (Eva), Suzanna Leigh (Unity), Tony Beckley (Harry). DVD, VHS.

4695. *Uncle Silas* (Sheridan Le Fanu, 1864). Set in London, the tale of a Victorian heiress who is threatened by her vicious uncle and his diabolical housekeeper. **Adaptation:** *Uncle Silas*; released in the U.S. as *The Inheritance* (Two Cities/Fine Arts, 1947). Dir: Charles Frank. Scr: Ben Travers. Cast: Jean Simmons (Caroline), Katina Paxinou (Madame de la Rougierre), Derrick De Marney (Uncle Silas), Derek Bond (Lord Ilbury). DVD, VHS.

4696. *Uncle Tom's Cabin* (Harriet Beecher Stowe, 1852). The tragic story of abused slaves who are separated from their families prior to the Civil War. **Silent Films:** 1903, 1910, 1913, 1914, and 1918. **Adaptation 1**: *Uncle Tom's Cabin* (Universal, 1927). Dir: Harry Pollard. Scr: Walter Anthony, Harry Pollard, Harvey Thew, A. P. Younger. Cast: James B. Lowe (Uncle Tom), Virginia Grey (Eva), George Siegmann (Simon Legree), Margarita Fischer (Eliza). DVD, VHS. **Adaptation 2:** *Uncle Tom's Cabin* (KBA, 1965). Dir: Geza von Radvanyi. Scr: Fred Denger, Geza von Radvanyi. Cast: John Kitzmiller (Uncle Tom), Herbert Lom (Simon Legree), Olive Moorefield (Cassy), O. W. Fischer (Saint-Claire), Catana Cayetano (Eliza). VHS. **Adaptation 3:** *Uncle Tom's Cabin* (Republic, 1987 TV Movie). Dir: Stan Lathan. Scr: John Gay. Cast: Avery Brooks (Uncle Tom), Kate Burton (Ophelia), Bruce Dern (Augustine), Paula Kelly (Cassy), Phylicia Rashad (Eliza). VHS.

4697. "Uncle Wiggily in Connecticut" (J. D. Salinger, 1948). World War II romance between a happily married woman and the man she first loved. The short story was published in *The New Yorker* on March 20, 1948. **Adaptation:** *My Foolish Heart* (RKO, 1949). Dir: Mark Robson. Scr: Julius J. Epstein, Philip G. Epstein. Cast: Dana Andrews (Walt), Susan Hayward (Eloise), Kent Smith (Lew), Lois Wheeler (Mary Jane). VHS.

4698. *Uncle Willie and the Bicycle Shop* (Brock Williams, 1948). The comic misadventures of the alcoholic owner of a bicycle shop. **Adaptation:** *Isn't Life Wonderful!* (1953). Dir: Harold

French. Scr: Brock Williams. Cast: Cecil Parker (Father), Eileen Herlie (Mother), Donald Wolfit (Uncle Willie), Peter Asher (Charles).

4699. *Uncommon Danger* (Eric Ambler, 1937). Espionage thriller about an American in Turkey who foils a Nazi plot. **Adaptation:** *Background to Danger* (Warner, 1943). Dir: Raoul Walsh. Scr: W.R. Burnett. Cast: George Raft (Joe), Brenda Marshall (Tamara), Sydney Greenstreet (Colonel Robinson), Peter Lorre (Nikolai). VHS.

4700. *The Uncomplaining Corpse* (Brett Halliday, 1940). Private detective Michael Shayne, who is featured in several novels by Halliday, is hired to protect a woman from blackmailers. When she is murdered, he pursues the killers. **Adaptation:** *Murder Is My Business* (PRC, 1946). Dir: Sam Newfield. Scr: Fred Myton. Cast: Hugh Beaumont (Shayne), Cheryl Walker (Phyllis), Lyle Talbot (Renslow).

Uncensored (see *Underground News*).

4701. *Unconquered: A Novel of the Pontiac Conspiracy* (Neil H. Swanson, 1947). A female English prisoner is sent to the colonies and finds herself in Pittsburgh during Pontiac's War with white settlers in 1763. The novel was also released as *The Judas Tree*. **Adaptation:** *Unconquered* (Paramount, 1947). Dir: Cecil B. De Mille. Scr: Charles Bennett, Fredric M. Frank, Jesse Lasky, Jr. Cast: Gary Cooper (Holden), Paulette Goddard (Abby), Howard Da Silva (Garth), Boris Karloff (Chief Guyasuta), Cecil Kellaway (Jeremy). VHS.

4702. *Under Capricorn* (Helen Simpson, 1937). A British immigrant to Australia in the nineteenth century goes to stay with his cousin and finds that she has become an alcoholic because of her husband's cruelty. The novel was adapted as a stage play by John Colton and Margaret Linden. **Adaptation:** *Under Capricorn* (Warner, 1949). Dir: Alfred Hitchcock. Scr: Hume Cronyn, James Bridie. Cast: Ingrid Bergman (Lady Henrietta), Joseph Cotten (Sam), Michael Wilding (Charles), Margaret Leighton (Milly), Cecil Parker (the Governor). DVD, VHS. Notes: The novel was also adapted for a 1982 miniseries on Australian television.

Under Heaven (see *The Wings of the Dove*).

Under My Skin (*see* "My Old Man").

4703. *Under Satan's Sun* (Georges Bernanos, 1926). French novel, originally titled *Sous le Soleil de Satan*, about a rural French priest who believes that Satan is controlling humankind and tries to help a young woman who killed her lover. The novel was translated in 1940. **Adaptation:** *Under Satan's Sun* (Alive, 1987). Dir: Maurice Pialat. Scr: Sylvie Danton, Maurice Pialat. Cast: Gerard Depardieu (Donissan), Sandrine Bonnaire (Mouchette), Maurice Pialat (Menou-Segrais), Alain Artur (Cadignan). Notes: Originally released as *Sous le Soleil de Satan* and shown with subtitles. Cannes Film Festival Golden Palm Award for Best Direction; Cesar Awards nominations (France) for Best Picture, Director, Actor (Depardieu), Actress (Bonnaire), Cinematography, and Editing. VHS.

Under Suspicion (see *Brainwash*).

Under the Biltmore Clock (see "Myra Meets His Family").

4704. *Under the Red Robe* (Stanley J. Weyman, 1894). In 1630, Cardinal Richelieu asks a nobleman to fight the Huguenots, but he ends up opposing the powerful government. The novel was adapted as a stage play by Edward E. Rose. **Silent Films:** 1915 and 1923. **Adaptation:** *Under the Red Robe* (20th Century–Fox, 1937). Dir: Victor Seastrom. Scr: Lajos Biro, J. L. Hudson, Philip Lindsay, Arthur Wimperis. Cast: Conrad Veidt (Gil), Annabella (Lady Marguerite), Raymond Massey (Cardinal Richelieu), Romney Brent (Marius), Sophie Stewart (Elise). VHS.

4705. *Under the Tonto Rim* (Zane Grey, 1925). Western about a stage-coach owner who plots revenge against a gang that robbed one of his vehicles and killed the driver. The novel was serialized in *The Ladies' Home Journal* beginning in February 1925 and was published as a book in 1926. **Silent Film:** 1928. **Adaptation 1:** *Under the Tonto Rim* (Paramount, 1933). Dir: Henry Hathaway. Scr: Jack Cunningham, Gerald Geraghty. Cast: Stuart Erwin (Tonto), Fred Kohler (Munther), Raymond Hatton (Porky). **Adaptation 2:** *Under the Tonto* Rim (RKO, 1947). Dir: Lew Landers. Scr: Norman Houston. Cast: Tim Holt (Brad), Nan Leslie (Lucy), Richard Martin (Chito). DVD, VHS.

4706. *Under the Tuscan Sun: At Home in Italy* (Frances Mayes, 1996). Memoir of a San Francisco writer who, emotionally damaged by a painful divorce, took a trip to Tuscany, where she decided to buy and rehabilitate an old villa and in the process found personal fulfillment and love. **Adaptation:** *Under the Tuscan Sun* (Buena Vista, 2003). Dir: Audrey Wells. Scr: Audrey Wells.

Cast: Diane Lane (Frances), Sandra Oh (Patti), Lindsay Duncan (Katherine), Raoul Bova (Marcello). DVD, VHS.

4707. *Under the Volcano* (Malcolm Lowry, 1947). A novel about an alcoholic British official in Mexico and his failed career and personal relationships. **Adaptation:** *Under the Volcano* (Universal, 1984). Dir: John Huston. Scr: Guy Gallo. Cast: Albert Finney (Geoffrey), Jacqueline Bisset (Yvonne), Anthony Andrews (Hugh), Ignacio Lopez Tarso (Dr. Vigil), Katy Jurado (Senora Gregoria), James Villiers (Brit). Notes: Academy Award nominations for Best Actor (Finney) and Musical Score; Cannes Film Festival Golden Palm nomination for Best Director; Golden Globe nominations for Best Actor (Finney) and Supporting Actress (Bisset). VHS.

4708. *Under Two Flags* (Ouida [pseudonym for Marie Louise de la Ramee], 1867). Two women fall in love with a French Legionnaire, and his jealous commander sends him on a dangerous mission. **Silent Films:** 1912, 1916, and 1922). **Adaptation:** *Under Two Flags* (20th Century–Fox, 1936). Dir: Frank Lloyd. Scr: W. P. Lipscomb, Walter Ferris. Cast: Ronald Colman (Sergeant Victor), Claudette Colbert (Cigarette), Victor McLaglen (Doyle), Rosalind Russell (Lady Venetia), Gregory Ratoff (Ivan), Nigel Bruce (Captain Menzies).

4709. *Under World* (Reginald Hill, 1988). In the tenth installment of Hill's popular series (1970–2004) featuring British policemen Andrew Dalziel and Peter Pascoe, the detectives investigate the discovery of a young girl's skeleton in a deep mine shaft in a Yorkshire coalfield. **Adaptation:** *Dalziel and Pascoe: Under World* (BBC/A&E, 1998 TV Movie series). Dir: Edward Bennett. Scr: Michael Chaplin. Cast: Warren Clarke (Dalziel), Colin Buchanan (Pascoe), Susannah Corbett (Ellie), David Royle (Edgar), Joe Duttine (Colin).

4710. *Undercover Cat* (Gordon Gordon and Mildred Gordon[writing as The Gordons], 1963). Comic story about a cat that leads its owner and an FBI agent to a woman being held hostage by inept bank robbers. **Adaptation 1:** *That Darn Cat!* (Disney/Buena Vista, 1965). Dir: Robert Stevenson. Scr: Gordon Gordon and Mildred Gordon (writing as The Gordons), Bill Walsh. Cast: Hayley Mills (Patti), Dean Jones (Agent Kelso), Dorothy Provine (Ingrid), Roddy McDowall (Gregory), Neville Brand (Dan), Elsa Lanchester (Mrs. MacDougall), William Demarest (Mr. MacDougall), Frank Gorshin (Iggy). DVD, VHS.

Adaptation 2: *That Darn Cat* (Disney/Buena Vista, 1997). Dir: Bob Spiers. Scr: Gordon Gordon, Mildred Gordon, Bill Walsh (1965 screenplay), S. M. Alexander, Larry Karaszewski. Cast: Christina Ricci (Patti), Doug E. Doug (Agent Kelso), Dean Jones (Mr. Flint), George Dzundza (Agent Boetticher), Peter Boyle (Pa), Michael McKean (Mr. Randall), Bess Armstrong (Mrs. Randall), Dyan Cannon (Mrs. Flint), John Ratzenberger (Dusty). DVD, VHS.

4711. *The Underground Man* (Ross Macdonald [pseudonym for Kenneth Millar], 1971). Investigator Lew Archer searches for a missing child and stumbles upon the family's dark secret past. **Adaptation:** *The Underground Man* (NBC, 1974 TV Movie). Dir: Paul Wendkos. Scr: Douglas Heyes. Cast: Peter Graves (Archer), Celeste Holm (Beatrice), Sharon Farrell (Marty), Jim Hutton (Stanley), Kay Lenz (Sue).

4712. *Underground News: The Complete Story of the Secret Newspaper That Made War History* (Oscar E. Millard, 1938). Factual account of a secretly published newspaper in Brussels that led the patriotic opposition against German occupation during World War I. The book was published in the UK under the title *Uncensored*. **Adaptation:** *Uncensored* (Gainsborough/20th Century–Fox, 1942). Dir: Anthony Asquith. Scr: Rodney Ackland, Terence Rattigan, Wolfgang Wilhelm. Cast: Eric Portman (Andre), Phyllis Calvert (Julie), Griffith Jones (Father de Gruyte), Raymond Lovell (Von Koerner).

Underneath (see *Criss Cross*).

Underworld Informers (see *Death of a Snout*).

4713. *Undue Influence* (Steve Martini, 1994). A woman takes the blame for the murder of her ex-husband's new wife to protect her son. **Adaptation:** *Undue Influence* (Jaffe-Braunstein, 1996 TV Movie). Dir: Bruce Pittman. Scr: Philip Rosenberg. Cast: Brian Dennehy (Paul), Patricia Richardson (Laurel), Jean Smart (Dana), Alan Rosenberg (Harry), Joe Grifasi (Clem), Richard Masur (Jack).

4714. *The Undying Monster: A Tale of the Fifth Dimension* (Jessie Douglas Kerruish, 1922). As a result of a curse, a werewolf terrorizes members of a single family on a British estate. **Adaptation:** *The Undying Monster;* released in the UK as *The Hammond Mystery* (20th Century–Fox, 1942). Dir: John Brahm. Scr: Lillie Hayward, Michael Jacoby. Cast: James Ellison (Robert), Heather Angel (Helga), John Howard (Oliver), Bramwell Fletcher (Dr. Colbert). VHS.

4715. *Uneasy Freehold* (Dorothy Macardle, 1942). The new owners of an old house help a young woman who claims that she is being haunted by the ghost of her dead mother. **Adaptation:** *The Uninvited* (Paramount, 1944). Dir: Lewis Allen. Scr: Frank Partos, Dodie Smith. Cast: Ray Milland (Roderick), Ruth Hussey (Pamela), Donald Crisp (Commander Beech), Cornelia Otis Skinner (Miss Holloway). VHS.

4716. *Uneasy Terms* (Peter Cheyney, 1946). A British detective investigates a blackmail plot. **Adaptation:** *Uneasy Terms* (British National, 1948). Dir: Vernon Sewell. Scr: Peter Cheyney. Cast: Michael Rennie (Slim), Moira Lister (Corinne), Faith Brook (Viola), Joy Shelton (Effie).

4717. *The Unexpected Mrs Pollifax* (Dorothy Gilman, 1966). Comic espionage novel about a bored widow who volunteers to become a CIA spy. **Adaptation:** *Mrs. Pollifax — Spy* (United Artists, 1971). Dir: Leslie H. Martinson. Scr: Rosalind Russell (writing as C. A. McKnight). Cast: Rosalind Russell (Mrs. Pollifax), Darren McGavin (Farrell), Nehemiah Persoff (Berisha), Harold Gould (Nexdhet).

4718. *Unexpected Uncle* (Eric Hatch, 1940). Romantic comedy about a retired millionaire who plays Cupid to a feuding couple. The novel was serialized in *Liberty Magazine* beginning on October 5, 1940, and published as a book in 1941. **Adaptation:** *Unexpected Uncle* (RKO, 1941). Dir: Peter Godfrey. Scr: Delmer Daves, Noel Langley. Cast: Anne Shirley (Kathleen), James Craig (Johnny), Charles Coburn (Seton/Alfred), Ernest Truex (Wilkins).

4719. *The Unforgiven* (Alan Le May, 1957). A Western about the conflict brought about when a young girl living with her white adoptive parents is suspected of being an Indian. **Adaptation:** *The Unforgiven* (1960). Dir: John Huston. Scr: Ben Maddow. Cast: Burt Lancaster (Ben), Audrey Hepburn (Rachel), Audie Murphy (Cash), John Saxon (Johnny), Charles Bickford (Zeb), Lillian Gish (Matilda). DVD, VHS.

4720. *The Unholy Three* (Tod Robbins [pseudonym for Clarence Aaron Robbins], 1917). A carnival ventriloquist, strong man, and dwarf form a criminal gang. The novella originally appeared in *Munsey's Magazine*. **Silent Film:** 1925, directed by Tod Browning and starring Lon Chaney (VHS). **Adaptation:** *The Unholy Three* (MGM, 1930). Dir: Jack Conway. Scr: J. C. Nugent, Elliott Nugent. Cast: Lon Chaney (Professor Echo), Lila Lee (Rosie), Elliott Nugent (Hector), Harry Earles (Tweedledee), Ivan Linow (Hercules). VHS.

The Unholy Four (see *Stranger at Home*).

Unholy Love (see *Madame Bovary*).

Unidentified Flying Oddball (see *A Connecticut Yankee in King Arthur's Court*).

The Uninvited (see *Uneasy Freehold*).

Union City (*see* "The Corpse Next Door").

Union Station (see *Nightmare in Manhattan*).

4721. *Union Street* (Pat Barker, 1982, Fawcett Prize). Women struggle to survive in a poor working-class neighborhood in the north of England. **Adaptation:** *Stanley & Iris* (MGM, 1990). Dir: Martin Ritt. Scr: Irving Ravetch, Harriet Frank, Jr. Cast: Jane Fonda (Iris), Robert De Niro (Stanley), Swoosie Kurtz (Sharon), Martha Plimpton (Kelly), Harley Cross (Richard). Notes: Although the novel is credited in the film, the screenplay, which concerns the relationship between a young widow and an illiterate cook, is really not a direct adaptation. Only one character from the novel appears in the screenplay. DVD, VHS.

4722. *Unknown Games* (François Boyer, 1947). Set in 1940, the French novel, originally titled *Les Jeux Inconnus*, tells the story of a little orphaned girl who, after witnessing the murder of her parents and pet puppy, goes to live with a peasant family. **Adaptation:**; *Forbidden Games* (UK); released in the U.S. as *The Secret Game* (Silver/Times, 1952). Dir: Rene Clement. Scr: Jean Aurenche, Pierre Bost, Rene Clement. Cast: Georges Poujouly (Michel), Brigitte Fossey (Paulette), Laurence Badie (Berthe). Notes: Originally titled *Jeux Interdits* and shown with subtitles. Academy Award for Best Foreign-Language Film and nomination for Best Screenplay; BAFTA Award for Best Foreign-Language Film. VHS.

4723. *The Unknown Masterpiece* (Honoré de Balzac, 1831). Balzac's novella *Le chef-d'oeuvre inconnu* concerns a beautiful young model who inspires a famous artist who has not worked in ten years. **Adaptation:** *The Beautiful Troublemaker* (MK2 Diffusion, 1991). Dir: Jacques Rivette. Scr: Pascal Bonitzer, Christine Laurent, Jacques Rivette. Cast: Michel Piccoli (Edouard), Jane Birkin (Liz), Emmanuelle Beart (Marianne), Marianne Denicourt (Julienne). Notes: Originally titled *La Belle Noiseuse* and shown with subtitles. Cannes Film Festival Grand Prize of the Jury. DVD, VHS. Notes: A shorter, re-cut version was released the same year under the title *Divertimento* (DVD, VHS).

4724. "The Unnamable" (H. P. Lovecraft, 1925). Horror story about a couple who gives birth to a creature so monstrous that they refuse to name it. The evil offspring eventually kills the family and its demonic spirit lives on into the next century. The short story was written in 1923 and published in the July 1925 issue of *Weird Tales*. **Adaptation:** *The Unnamable* (Prism, 1988). Dir: Jean-Paul Ouellette. Scr: Jean-Paul Ouellette. Cast: Charles King (Howard), Mark Kinsey Stephenson (Randolph), Alexandra Durrell (Tanya), Laura Albert (Wendy). VHS. See also "The Statement of Randolph Carter."

The Unnamable II (*see* "The Statement of Randolph Cater")

The Unnamable Returns (*see* "The Statement of Randolph Cater")

4725. *Unstrung Heroes* (Franz Lidz, 1991). Memoir by a New York sports writer who went to live with his eccentric uncles after his mother's death in the 1960's. **Adaptation:** *Unstrung Heroes* (Buena Vista, 1995). Dir: Diane Keaton. Scr: Richard La Gravenese. Cast: Andie MacDowell (Selma), John Turturro (Sid), Michael Richards (Danny), Maury Chaykin (Arthur). DVD, VHS.

4726. *An Unsuitable Job for a Woman* (P. D. James, 1972). A young female detective investigates the suicide of a rich man's son and becomes obsessed with her subject. **Adaptation 1:** *An Unsuitable Job for a Woman* (Castle Hill, 1982). Dir: Christopher Petit. Scr: Elizabeth McKay, Christopher Petit, Brian Scobie. Cast: Billie Whitelaw (Elizabeth), Paul Freeman (James), Pippa Guard (Cordelia), Dominic Guard (Andrew). VHS. **Adaptation 2:** *An Unsuitable Job for a Woman* (Ecosse/PBS, 1997 TV Miniseries). Dir: Ben Bolt, David Evans, John Strickland. Scr: William Humble, Barbara Machin, Christopher Russell. Cast: Helen Baxendale (Cordelia), Annette Crosbie (Edith), Struan Rodger (Detective Ferguson). VHS.

4727. *The Unsuspected* (Charlotte Armstrong [pseudonym for Charlotte Armstrong Lewi], 1946). The star of a popular radio crime program commits murder and then uses his program to air clues to the unsolved crime. The novel was originally serialized in *The Saturday Evening Post* (August 11–September 29, 1945). **Adaptation:** *The Unsuspected* (Warner, 1947). Dir: Michael Curtiz. Scr: Bess Meredyth, Ranald MacDougall. Cast: Joan Caulfield (Matilda), Claude Rains (Victor), Audrey Totter (Althea), Constance Bennett (Jane).

Untamed (1940) (see *Mantrap*).

4728. *Untamed* (Helga Moray, 1950). A married Irish woman and her Boer lover traverse South Africa during a native uprising. **Adaptation:** *Untamed* (20th Century–Fox, 1955). Dir: Henry King. Scr: William A. Bacher, Michael Blankfort, Frank Fenton, Talbot Jennings. Cast: Tyrone Power (Paul), Susan Hayward (Katie), Richard Egan (Kurt), John Justin (Shawn), Agnes Moorehead (Aggie), Rita Moreno (Julia).

Unto a Good Land (see *The Emigrants*).

4729. *The Untouchables* (Eliot Ness and Oscar Fraley, 1957). Autobiography of the Federal Prohibition agent (1903–1957) whose work led to the arrest and conviction of infamous gangster Al Capone in Chicago in the 1920's. **Adaptation 1:** *The Scarface Mob* (Desilu, 1959 TV Movie). Dir: Phil Karlson. Scr: Paul Monash. Cast: Robert Stack (Ness), Keenan Wynn (Fuselli), Barbara Nichols (Brandy), Pat Crowley (Betty), Bill Williams (Flaherty), Joe Mantell (Ritchie), Bruce Gordon (Nitti), Neville Brand (Al Capone). Notes: The two-part television movie, which was also released theatrically as a single film, served as the pilot of the successful ABC series *The Untouchables* (1959–1963). VHS. **Adaptation 2:** *The Untouchables* (Paramount, 1987). Dir: Brian De Palma. Scr: David Mamet. Cast: Kevin Costner (Ness), Sean Connery (Malone), Charles Martin Smith (Oscar), Andy Garcia (George/Giuseppe), Robert De Niro (Al Capone), Billy Drago (Nitti). Notes: Academy Award for Best Supporting Actor (Connery) and nominations for Best Cinematography and Musical Score; Golden Globe Award for Best Supporting Actor (Connery) and nomination for Best Musical Score; National Board of Review Award for Best Supporting Actor (Connery). DVD, VHS. Notes: The book and films also inspired a short-lived television series in 1993.

4730. "An Unwanted Woman" (Ruth Rendell, 1990). A British detective refuses to believe that a conservative middle-class couple in a small town murdered their elderly mother. The story was originally published in the December 1990 issue of *Ellery Queen Mystery Magazine* and was included in Rendell's 1991 collection *The Copper Peacock and Other Stories*. **Adaptation:** *An Unwanted Woman* (TVS, 1992 TV Movie). Dir: Jenny Wilkes. Scr: Rosemary Anne Sisson. Cast: George Baker (Wexford), Christopher Ravenscroft (Burden), Louie Ramsay (Dora), Diane Keen (Jenny).

4731. *Up at the Villa* (W. Somerset Maugham, 1941). A poor English widow travels to Italy in 1938 and is romanced by a British aristocrat and an American playboy. **Adaptation:** *Up at the Villa* (October, 2000). Dir: Philip Haas. Scr: Belinda Haas. Cast: Kristin Scott Thomas (Mary), Sean Penn (Rowley), Anne Bancroft (Princess San Ferdinando), James Fox (Sir Edgar), Jeremy Davies (Karl), Derek Jacobi (Leadbetter). DVD, VHS. Notes: The book was also adapted as part of a 1968 BBC television series based on Maugham's works.

Up Close & Personal (see *Golden Girl*).

Up from the Beach (see *Epitaph for an Enemy*).

Up in the Cellar (see *The Late Boy Wonder*).

4732. *Up Periscope* (Robb White, 1956). During World War II, a submarine crew goes to a Pacific island to steal Japanese secrets. **Adaptation:** *Up Periscope* (Warner, 1959). Dir: Gordon Douglas. Scr: Richard H. Landau. Cast: James Garner (Kenneth), Edmond O'Brien (Paul), Andra Martin (Sally), Alan Hale, Jr. (Pat). VHS.

4733. *Up the Down Staircase* (Bel Kaufman, 1965). An inexperienced teacher goes to work at a tough New York City public school. **Adaptation:** *Up the Down Staircase* (Warner, 1967). Dir: Robert Mulligan. Scr: Tad Mosel. Cast: Sandy Dennis (Sylvia), Patrick Bedford (Paul), Eileen Heckart (Henrietta), Ruth White (Beatrice), Jean Stapleton (Sadie). VHS.

4734. *Up the Junction* (Nell Dunn, 1963). A group of working-class girls in London try to help a friend secure an abortion at a time when the procedure was illegal. **Adaptation 1:** *Up the Junction* (BBC, 1965 TV Movie). Dir: Ken Loach. Scr: Nell Dunn. Cast: Geraldine Sherman (Rube), Carol White (Sylvie), Vickery Turner (Eileen), Michael Standing (Terry). Notes: An installment in the BBC's Wednesday Play series. **Adaptation 2:** *Up the Junction* (Paramount, 1968). Dir: Peter Collinson. Scr: Roger Smith. Cast: Suzy Kendall (Polly), Dennis Waterman (Peter), Adrienne Posta (Rube), Maureen Lipman (Sylvie).

4735. *Up the Sandbox* (Anne Richardson Roiphe, 1970). Neglected by her husband, a pregnant woman escapes into a fantasy world. **Adaptation:** *Up the Sandbox* (National General, 1972). Dir: Irvin Kershner. Scr: Paul Zindel. Cast: Barbra Streisand (Margaret), David Selby (Paul), Ariane Heller (Elizabeth). DVD, VHS.

Up Tight! (see *The Informer*).

4736. *Upstairs and Downstairs* (Ronald Scott Thorn, 1957). Domestic comedy about man who marries his boss's daughter but is tempted by the sensuous maids in the household. **Adaptation:** *Upstairs and Downstairs* (Rank/20th Century–Fox, 1959). Dir: Ralph Thomas. Scr: Frank Harvey. Cast: Michael Craig (Richard), Anne Heywood (Kate), Mylene Demongeot (Ingrid), James Robertson Justice (Mansfield), Claudia Cardinale (Maria).

Urban Cowboy (*see* "The Ballad of the Urban Cowboy").

4737. *The Urgent Hangman* (Peter Cheyney, 1938). Slim Callaghan, a tough British investigator, discovers the killer of a wealthy man. The novel was adapted as a 1953 play titled *Meet Mr. Callaghan* by Gerald Verner. **Adaptation:** *Meet Mr. Callaghan* (Eros, 1954). Dir: Charles Saunders. Scr: Brock Williams. Cast: Derrick De Marney (Callaghan), Harriette Johns (Cynthia), Peter Neil (William).

4738. *Useless Cowboy* (Alan Le May, 1943). Comic western about a cowboy mistaken for a murderous gunfighter. The paperback edition of the book was released under the title *Hell for Breakfast*. **Adaptation:** *Along Came Jones* (RKO, 1945). Dir: Stuart Heisler. Scr: Nunnally Johnson. Cast: Gary Cooper (Melody), Loretta Young (Cherry), William Demarest (George), Dan Duryea (Monte). DVD, VHS.

4739. *Utah Blaine* (Louis L'Amour, 1954). Western about a gunfighter who battles greedy ranchers to save an honest man's land. **Adaptation:** *Utah Blaine* (Columbia, 1957). Dir: Fred F. Sears. Scr: James B. Gordon, Robert E. Kent. Cast: Rory Calhoun (Utah), Susan Cummings (Angie), Max Baer (Gus).

4740. *Utz* (Bruce Chatwin, 1989). An American art dealer tries to find an elderly man's priceless collection of figurines. **Adaptation:** *Utz* (Castle Hill, 1992). Dir: George Sluizer. Scr: Hugh Whitemore. Cast: Armin Mueller-Stahl (Baron von Utz), Brenda Fricker (Marta), Peter Riegert (Marius), Paul Scofield (Dr. Orlik). VHS.

V. I. Warshawski (see *Indemnity Only*).

4741. *The Vacillations of Poppy Carew* (Mary Wesley, 1986). After the death of her father, a young and independent woman goes in search of true love. **Adaptation:** *The Vacillations of Poppy Carew* (Meridian, 1995 TV Movie). Dir: James Cellan Jones. Scr: William Humble. Cast: Tara Fitzgerald (Poppy), Daniel Massey (Mr. Carew), Samuel West (Victor), Edward Atterton (Fergus). VHS.

4742. *The Valachi Papers* (Peter Maas, 1968). The true story of mobster Joe Valachi, a former member of New York's Genovese crime family, who testified against the mob and thus became the first member to break the Mafia's code of silence. **Adaptation:** *The Valachi Papers* (Columbia, 1972). Dir: Terence Young. Scr: Massimo De Rita, Stephen Geller, Arduino Maiuri. Cast: Charles Bronson (Valachi), Lino Ventura (Genovese), Jill Ireland (Maria), Walter Chiari (Gap). VHS.

4743. *The Valdez Horses* (Lee Hoffman, 1967, Golden Spur Award for Best Western). Western about a half–Indian horse breeder and loner who takes in a runaway boy and teaches him the business of ranching. **Adaptation:** *Chino*; also released as *The Valdez Horses* (Intercontinental, 1973). Dir: John Sturges. Scr: Clair Huffaker. Cast: Charles Bronson (Chino), Jill Ireland (Louise), Marcel Bozzuffi (Maral), Vincent Van Patten (Jamie). DVD, VHS.

4744. *Valdez Is Coming* (Elmore Leonard, 1970). Western about a Mexican-American deputy who clashes with a ruthless rancher and his henchmen. **Adaptation:** *Valdez Is Coming* (United Artists, 1971). Dir: Edwin Sherin. Scr: Roland Kibbee, David Rayfiel. Cast: Burt Lancaster (Valdez), Susan Clark (Gay), Frank Silvera (Diego), Jon Cypher (Tanner). DVD, VHS.

4745. *Valentine* (Tom Savage, 1996). Beautiful women are being systematically murdered, and the chief suspect is a man who was rejected and ridiculed by the girls years earlier when they were all in high school together. **Adaptation:** *Valentine* (Warner, 2001). Dir: Jamie Blanks. Scr: Donna Powers, Wayne Powers, Gretchen J. Berg, Aaron Harberts. Cast: Denise Richards (Paige), David Boreanaz (Adam), Marley Shelton (Kate), Jessica Capshaw (Dorothy). DVD, VHS.

4746. *Valentino: An Intimate and Shocking Expose* (Brad Steiger and Chaw Mank, 1966). A biography of Italian silent-film idol Rudolph Valentino (1895–1926). **Adaptation:** *Valentino* (United Artists, 1977). Dir: Ken Russell. Scr: Mardik Martin, Ken Russell. Cast: Rudolf Nureyev (Valentino), Leslie Caron (Alla), Michelle Phillips (Natasha), Felicity Kendal (June). DVD, VHS.

Valentino Returns (*see* "Christ Has Returned to Earth and Preaches Here Nightly").

4747. *Valiant Is the Word for Carrie* (Barry Benefield, 1935). A poor and selfless woman who runs an orphanage fights for the happiness of two of her young charges. **Adaptation:** *Valiant Is the Word for Carrie* (Paramount, 1936). Dir: Wesley Ruggles. Scr: Claude Binyon. Cast: Gladys George (Carrie), Arline Judge (Lady), John Howard (Paul), Dudley Digges (Dennis), Harry Carey (Phil).

4748. *The Valley of Decision* (Marcia Davenport, 1942). In Pittsburgh in 1870, a house maid defies her family and marries the son of a wealthy mine owner. **Adaptation:** *The Valley of Decision* (MGM, 1945). Dir: Tay Garnett. Scr: Sonya Levien, John Meehan. Cast: Greer Garson (Mary), Gregory Peck (Paul), Donald Crisp (William), Lionel Barrymore (Pat). VHS.

4749. *The Valley of Fear* (Arthur Conan Doyle, 1914–15). Sherlock Holmes investigates a series of murders tied to a secret society of miners. **Silent Film:** 1916. **Adaptation:** *The Triumph of Sherlock Holmes* (Gaumont, 1935). Dir: Leslie S. Hiscott. Scr: H. Fowler Mear, Cyril Twyford. Cast: Arthur Wontner (Holmes), Lyn Harding (Professor Moriarty), Leslie Perrins (Douglas), Ian Fleming (Watson), Charles Mortimer (Inspector Lestrade). DVD, VHS.

4750. *Valley of the Dolls* (Jacqueline Susann, 1966). Bestseller focusing on three women and their disastrous relationships with the entertainment industry. **Adaptation 1:** *Valley of the Dolls* (20th Century–Fox, 1967). Dir: Mark Robson. Scr: Jacqueline Susann, Helen Deutsch, Dorothy Kingsley. Cast: Barbara Parkins (Anne), Patty Duke (Neely), Paul Burke (Lyon), Sharon Tate (Jennifer). Notes: Academy Award nomination for Best Musical Score; Golden Globe nomination for Most Promising Newcomer (Tate). DVD, VHS. **Adaptation 2:** *Jacqueline Susann's Valley of the Dolls* (20th Century–Fox Television, 1981 TV Movie). Dir: Walter Grauman. Scr: Laurence Heath. Cast: Catherine Hicks (Ann), Lisa Hartman (Neely), Veronica Hamel (Jennifer), David Birney (Lyon), Jean Simmons (Helen), James Coburn (Henry), Gary Collins (Kevin), Bert Convy (Tony), Britt Ekland (Francoise). Notes: An updated version of the story.

4751. *The Valley of the Giants* (Peter B. Kyne, 1918). A lumberjack clashes with a greedy businessman who wants to cut down the giant California redwoods. **Silent Films:** 1919 and 1927. **Adaptation 1:** *Valley of the Giants* (Warner, 1938). Dir: William Keighley. Dir: Seton I. Miller, Michael Fessier. Cast: Wayne Morris (Bill), Claire Trevor (Lee), Frank McHugh (Fingers), Alan Hale (Ox). **Adaptation 2:** *The Big Trees* (Warner, 1952). Dir: Felix Feist. Scr: Kenneth Earl, John Twist,

James R. Webb. Cast: Kirk Douglas (Jim), Eve Miller (Alicia), Patrice Wymore (Daisy/Dora), Edgar Buchanan (Walter). DVD, VHS.

4752. *Valley of the Sun* (Clarence Budington Kelland, 1939–1940). Western about a government agent who battles dishonest Indian agents in Arizona, provoking a Native American uprising. The novel was serialized in *The Saturday Evening Post* (December 16, 1939–January 27, 1940). **Adaptation:** *Valley of the Sun* (RKO, 1942). Dir: George Marshall. Scr: Horace McCoy. Cast: Lucille Ball (Christine), James Craig (Johnny), Cedric Hardwicke (Lord Warrick), Dean Jagger (Sawyer). VHS.

Valmont (see *Dangerous Liaisons*).

The Vampire Lovers (see "Carmilla").

4753. *Vampire$* (John Steakley, 1990). The Vatican hires a group of commercial vampire hunters to kill the undead in the American Southwest before they can locate a magical black crucifix which will give them the ability to walk in the daylight. **Adaptation:** *Vampires* (1998). Dir: John Carpenter. Scr: Don Jakoby. Cast: James Woods (Jack), Daniel Baldwin (Montoya), Sheryl Lee (Katrina), Thomas Ian Griffith (Jan), Maximilian Schell (Cardinal Alba). DVD, VHS. Notes: A direct-to-video sequel, *John Carpenter's Vampires: Los Muertos*, was released in 2002 (DVD, VHS).

Vampyre (see "Carmilla").

4754. *The Van* (Roddy Doyle, 1991). The final installment in Doyle's Barrytown Trilogy (along with *The Commitments* and *The Snapper*). This one is about an Irish baker who buys a van and starts a mobile food business. **Adaptation:** *The Van* (BBC/Fox Searchlight, 1996). Dir: Stephen Frears. Scr: Roddy Doyle. Cast: Colm Meaney (Larry), Donal O'Kelly (Brendan), Ger Ryan (Maggie). Notes: Cannes Film Festival Golden Palm nomination for Best Director. VHS. See also *The Commitments* and *The Snapper*.

4755. *Vanessa* (Hugh Walpole, 1933). In the fourth and last installment in Walpole's Herries Chronicles (1930–1933), a woman falls in love with a gypsy after her husband loses his mind. **Adaptation:** *Vanessa: Her Love Story* (MGM, 1935). Dir: William K. Howard. Scr: Lenore Coffee, Hugh Walpole. Cast: Robert Montgomery (Benjamin), Helen Hayes (Vanessa), May Robson (Judith), Otto Kruger (Ellis).

4756. *Vanished* (Danielle Steel, 1993). In the

1930's, a young couple's child is kidnapped, and the wife's former lover is the prime suspect. **Adaptation:** *Vanished* (NBC, 1995 TV Movie). Dir: George Kaczender. Scr: Kathleen Rowell. Cast: George Hamilton (Malcolm), Lisa Rinna (Marielle), Robert Hays (John), Maurice Godin (Charles). DVD, VHS.

4757. *The Vanished Batallion* (Nigel McCrery, 1992). A true World War I mystery about King George V's Sandringham Batallion, who, entering battle in Gallipoli in 1915, seem to have vanished into a mysterious mist on the battlefield never to be seen again. Subsequent editions of the book were released as *All the King's Men.* **Adaptation:** *All the King's Men* (BBC/PBS, 1999 TV Movie). Dir: Julian Jarrold. Scr: Alma Cullen. Cast: David Jason (Captain Beck), Maggie Smith (Queen Alexandra), William Ash (Sergeant Grimes), Sonya Walger (Lady Frances). VHS.

The Vanishing (see *The Golden Egg*).

4758. *The Vanishing American* (Zane Grey, 1922–1923). Western about a brave Navajo Indian and his struggle against corrupt government forces seeking to dominate Native Americans. The novel was serialized in *The Ladies' Home Journal* (December 1922–March 1923) and published as a book in 1925. **Silent Film:** 1925, a classic directed by George B. Seitz and starring Richard Dix (DVD, VHS). **Adaptation:** *The Vanishing American* (Republic, 1955). Dir: Joseph Kane. Scr: Alan Le May. Cast: Scott Brady (Blandy), Audrey Totter (Marion), Forrest Tucker (Morgan), Gene Lockhart (Blucher).

4759. *The Vanishing Corpse* (Anthony Gilbert [pseudonym for Lucy Beatrice Malleson], 1941). A beautiful woman coaxes military secrets out of a British officer, and he seeks revenge when he realizes he was duped. The novel was published in the U.S. as *She Vanished in the Dawn.* **Adaptation:** *They Met in the Dark* (Rank, 1943). Dir: Karel Lamac. Scr: Anatole de Grunwald, Miles Malleson. Cast: James Mason (Heritage), Joyce Howard (Laura), Tom Walls (Christopher), Phyllis Stanley (Lily). VHS.

The Vanishing Train (see *Kate Plus Ten*).

4760. *The Vanishing Virginian* (Rebecca Yancey Williams, 1940). Biographical family tale about her father, a conservative local politician in Lynchburg, Virginia, and his relationship with his free-thinking daughters. **Adaptation:** *The Vanishing Virginian* (MGM, 1942). Dir: Frank Borzage. Scr: Jan Fortune. Cast: Frank Morgan (Robert), Kathryn Grayson (Rebecca), Spring Byington (Rosa), Natalie Thompson (Margaret).

4761. *Vanity Fair* (William Makepeace Thackeray, 1847–1848). Satiric work about a beautiful and devious young woman who befriends a rich merchant's daughter and together they set about the business of social climbing in Victorian England. The novel was published in serial installments from January 1847 through July 1848 and issued as a novel in 1848. **Silent Films:** 1911, 1915, 1922, and 1923. **Adaptation 1:** *Vanity Fair* (Allied, 1932). Dir: Chester M. Franklin. Scr: F. Hugh Herbert. Cast: Myrna Loy (Becky), Conway Tearle (Rawdon), Barbara Kent (Amelia). **Adaptation 2:** *Becky Sharp* (RKO, 1935). Dir: Rouben Mamoulian. Scr: Francis Edward Faragoh. Cast: Miriam Hopkins (Becky), Frances Dee (Amelia), Cedric Hardwicke (the Marquis of Steyne), Billie Burke (Lady Bareacres), Nigel Bruce (Joseph). Notes: The screenplay is based on the novel and the 1914 stage play *Becky Sharp* by Langdon Mitchell. Academy Award nomination for Best Actress (Hopkins). DVD, VHS. **Adaptation 3:** *Vanity Fair* (BBC, 1967 TV Miniseries). Dir: David Giles. Scr: Rex Tucker. Cast: Susan Hampshire (Becky), Roy Marsden (Osborne), John Moffatt (Joseph), Marilyn Taylerson (Amelia). VHS. **Adaptation 4:** *Vanity Fair* (BBC/A&E, 1987 TV Miniseries). Dir: Diarmuid Lawrence, Michael Owen Morris. Scr: Alexander Baron. Cast: Eve Matheson (Becky), Rebecca Saire (Amelia), James Saxon (Joseph). **Adaptation 5:** *Vanity Fair* (BBC/A&E, 1998 TV Miniseries). Dir: Marc Munden. Scr: Andrew Davies. Cast: Natasha Little (Becky), Nathaniel Parker (Rawdon), Frances Grey (Amelia). Notes: BAFTA nominations for Best Drama Serial, Actress (Little), Costume Design, Musical Score (Murray Gold), Editing, and Photography and Lighting. DVD, VHS. **Adaptation 6:** *Vanity Fair* (Gramercy/Focus, 2004). Dir: Mira Nair. Scr: Julian Fellowes, Matthew Faulk, Mark Skeet. Cast: Reese Witherspoon (Becky), Romola Garai (Amelia), Tony Maudsley (Joseph), Gabriel Byrne (the Marquess of Steyne). DVD, VHS.

4762. *Vanity Row* (W. R. Burnett, 1952). A police detective falls in love with a night-club singer and becomes involved with her gangster associates. **Adaptation:** *Accused of Murder* (Republic, 1956). Dir: Joe Kane. Scr: W. R. Burnett, Bob Williams. Cast: David Brian (Lieutenant Hargis), Claire Carleton (Marge), Vera Ralston (Ilona), Sidney Blackmer (Hobart).

4763. *The Velvet Fleece* (Lois Eby and John

Fleming, 1947). A grifter tries to swindle a young war widow out of funds to be used for her husband's memorial but ends up falling in love with her instead. **Adaptation:** *Larceny* (Universal International, 1948). Dir: George Sherman. Scr: William Bowers, Herbert H. Margolis, Louis Morheim. Cast: John Payne (Rick), Joan Caulfield (Deborah), Dan Duryea (Silky), Shelley Winters (Tory), Dorothy Hart (Madeline).

Vendetta (1950) (see *Columba*).

4764. *Vendetta: The True Story of a the Largest Lynching in American History* (Richard Gambino, 1977). Factual account of the lynching of Italian-Americans in New Orleans in the late nineteenth century following their trial for allegedly murdering the city's police chief. **Adaptation:** *Vendetta* (HBO, 1999 TV Movie). Dir: Nicholas Meyer. Scr: Timothy Prager. Cast: Christopher Walken (Houston), Luke Askew (Parkerson), Clancy Brown (Chief Hennessy), Louis Di Bianco (Polizzi), Richard Libertini (Giovanni), Gerry Mendicino (Mantranga), Stuart Stone (Tony), Giuseppe Tancredi (Scaffidi), Kenneth Welsh (Mayor Shakespeare). DVD, VHS.

4765. *Vendetta for the Saint* (Leslie Charteris [pseudonym for Leslie Charles Bowyer Yin], 1964). In a later installment of Charteris' long-running series featuring Robin Hood–like sleuth Simon Templar, the Saint (as he is known) witnesses a murder in Italy and becomes involved with the Mafia. **Adaptation:** *Vendetta for the Saint* (ITC, 1969 TV Movie). Dir: Jim O'Connolly. Scr: Harry W. Junkin, John Kruse. Cast: Roger Moore (Templar), Ian Hendry (Alessandro), Rosemary Dexter (Gina), Aimi MacDonald (Lily), George Pastell (Marco). DVD, VHS. Notes: Roger Moore also played the role in the British television series *The Saint*, which ran from 1962 through 1969. This television feature came at the end of that series. The character was also featured in a 1997 film titled *The Saint*, starring Val Kilmer in the title role (DVD, VHS).

4766. *The Venetian Affair* (Helen MacInnes, 1963). A former CIA agent is asked to investigate the apparent suicide of an American diplomat in Venice. **Adaptation:** *The Venetian Affair* (MGM, 1967). Dir: Jerry Thorpe. Scr: E. Jack Neuman. Cast: Robert Vaughn (Bill), Elke Sommer (Sandra), Felicia Farr (Claire), Karl Boehm (Robert), Luciana Paluzzi (Giulia), Boris Karloff (Dr. Vaugiroud), Roger C. Carmel (Ballard), Edward Asner (Rosenfeld).

4767. *Venetian Bird* (Victor Canning, 1951).

A private investigator goes to Venice to find a wartime patriot and discovers that he is now a notorious criminal. The novel was released in the U.S. as *Bird of Prey*. **Adaptation:** *Venetian Bird*; released in the U.S. as *The Assassin* (Rank/United Artists, 1952). Dir: Ralph Thomas. Scr: Victor Canning. Cast: Richard Todd (Edward), Eva Bartok (Adriana), John Gregson (Renzo), George Coulouris (Chief Spadoni).

4768. *Vengeance Valley* (Luke Short [pseudonym for Frederick D. Glidden], 1949–1950). Western about an honest rancher who feuds with his corrupt foster brother. The novel was serialized in *The Saturday Evening Post* (December 3, 1949–January 14, 1950). **Adaptation:** *Vengeance Valley* (MGM, 1951). Dir: Richard Thorpe. Scr: Irving Ravetch. Cast: Burt Lancaster (Owen), Robert Walker (Lee), Joanne Dru (Jen), Sally Forrest (Lily), John Ireland (Hub). DVD, VHS.

4769. *Venom* (Alan Scholefield, 1977). The plans of a terrorist group who kidnapped a wealthy couple's child go awry when a deadly snake gets loose in the house in which they are holding him and the criminals begin to die off. **Adaptation:** *Venom* (Paramount, 1982). Dir: Piers Haggard. Scr: Robert Carrington. Cast: Klaus Kinski (Jacques), Oliver Reed (Dave), Nicol Williamson (William), Sarah Miles (Dr. Stowe), Sterling Hayden (Howard). DVD, VHS.

4770. *Venus in Furs* (Leopold von Sacher-Masoch, 1869). Austrian novel, originally titled *Venus im Pelz*, about an artist's masochistic and voyeuristic fascination with a woman he meets on vacation. The term *masochism* derives from the author's name. **Adaptation 1:** *Venus in Furs* (Box Office International, 1967). Dir: Joseph Marzano. Scr: Barbara Ellen, Joseph Marzano. Cast: Shep Wild (Severin), Yolanda Signorelli (Wanda). DVD, VHS. **Adaptation 2:** *Devil in the Flesh* (Roxy, 1969). Dir: Massimo Dallamano (as Max Dillman). Scr: Inge Hilger, Fabio Massimo. Cast: Laura Antonelli (Wanda), Regis Vallee (Severin). Notes: Originally released as *Le Malizie di Venere* and shown with subtitles. **Adaptation 3:** *Venus in Furs* (K-Films, 1994). Dir: Victor Nieuwenhuijs, Maartje Seyferth. Scr: Victor Nieuwenhuijs, Maartje Seyferth. Cast: Andre Arend van de Noord (Severin), Anne van de Ven (Wanda). DVD, VHS.

Venus Peter (see *A Twelvemonth and a Day*).

The Verdict (1946) (see *The Big Bow Mystery*).

4771. *The Verdict* (Manfred Gregor, 1960). German novel, originally titled *Das Urteil*, about a girl who accuses four American servicemen of raping her and the defense attorney who must destroy the girl's credibility to save his clients in the prejudiced community where the trial takes place. **Adaptation:** *Town Without Pity* (United Artists, 1961). Dir: Gottfried Reinhardt. Scr: George Hurdalek, Jan Lustig, Silvia Reinhardt. Cast: Kirk Douglas (Steve), Barbara Rutting (Inge), Christine Kaufmann (Karin), E. G. Marshall (Jerome), Hans Nielsen (Karl), Ingrid van Bergen (Trude), Robert Blake (Jim). DVD, VHS.

4772. *The Verdict* (Barry Reed, 1980). An alcoholic lawyer regains his self-respect and professional reputation when he litigates a malpractice case. **Adaptation:** *The Verdict* (20th Century–Fox, 1982). Dir: Sidney Lumet. Scr: David Mamet. Cast: Paul Newman (Frank), Charlotte Rampling (Laura), Jack Warden (Mickey), James Mason (Concannon), Milo O'Shea (Judge Hoyle), Lindsay Crouse (Kaitlin). Notes: National Board of Review Award for Best Director; Academy Award and Golden Globe nominations for Best Picture, Director, Screenplay, Actor (Newman), and Supporting Actor (Mason). DVD, VHS.

4773. "The Verger" (W. Somerset Maugham, 1943). A church assistant loses his job because he cannot read or write. With the help of a sympathetic woman, he opens a successful business. The story was published in *Avon Modern Short Story Monthly* in 1943. **Adaptation:** *Trio* (Gainsborough/Paramount, 1950). Dir: Ken Annakin, Harold French. Scr: Noel Langley, W. Somerset Maugham, R. C. Sherriff. Cast: Michael Hordern (the Vicar), Henry Edwards (the Church Warden), James Hayter (Albert), Lana Morris (Gladys). Notes: This film was made following the success of the 1948 film *Quartet*, in which Maugham introduces four of his short stories. Here Maugham introduces three more stories: "Mr. Know-All," "The Sanitorium," and "The Verger." VHS.

4774. *The Veritas Project: Hangman's Curse* (Frank E. Peretti, 2001). Teen book about a group of Christian spiritual investigators who probe the mysterious illness afflicting school bullies who utter the name of a legendary ghost. **Adaptation:** *Hangman's Curse*; also released as *The Veritas Project: Hangman's Curse* (20th Century–Fox, 2003). Dir: Rafal Zielinski. Scr: Kathy Mackel, Stan Foster. Cast: David Keith (Nate), Mel Harris (Sarah), Leighton Meester (Elisha), Douglas Smith (Elijah). DVD, VHS.

Vertigo (see *The Living and the Dead*).

4775. *A Very Long Engagement* (Sebastien Japrisot [pseudonym for Jean-Baptiste Rossi], 1991, Prix Interallie). The French novel, originally titled *Un long dimanche de fiancailles*, concerns a crippled woman whose fiancé was sent, along with four other men, to the front during World War I as punishment for shooting themselves in order to avoid going to war. Years after the war, his girlfriend learns that three of the men may have survived, and she goes in search of him. The book was translated into English in 1993. **Adaptation:** *A Very Long Engagement* (Warner, 2004). Dir: Jean-Pierre Jeunet. Scr: Jean-Pierre Jeunet, Guillaume Laurant. Cast: Audrey Tautou (Mathilde), Gaspard Ulliel (Manech), Dominique Pinon (Sylvain), Clovis Cornillac (Benoit), Jerome Kircher (Bastoche). Notes: Originally released as *Un long dimanche de fiancailles* and shown with subtitles. DVD, VHS.

A Very Missing Person (see *Hildegarde Withers Makes the Scene*).

4776. *Vespers in Vienna* (Bruce Marshall, 1947). After World War II, a ballerina in Vienna hides in a convent from Soviet agents who are trying to repatriate her and other Russians living in the city. **Adaptation:** *The Red Danube* (MGM, 1949). Dir: George Sidney. Scr: Gina Kaus, Arthur Wimperis. Cast: Walter Pidgeon (Colonel Nicobar), Ethel Barrymore (the Mother Superior), Peter Lawford (Major McPhimister), Angela Lansbury (Audrey), Janet Leigh (Maria), Louis Calhern (Colonel Piniev).

4777. "Vessel of Wrath" (W. Somerset Maugham, 1931). A female missionary reforms an alcoholic beachcomber in the Dutch East Indies. The short story was originally published in the April 1931 issue of *Cosmopolitan*. **Adaptation 1:** *Vessel of Wrath* (Paramount, 1938). Dir: Erich Pommer. Scr: Bartlett Cormack. Cast: Charles Laughton (Ted), Elsa Lanchester (Martha), Tyrone Guthrie (Owen). VHS. **Adaptation 2:** *The Beachcomber* (United Artists, 1954). Dir: Muriel Box. Scr: Sydney Box. Cast: Glynis Johns (Martha), Robert Newton (Ted), Donald Sinden (Owen). VHS. Notes: The short story was also adapted for a BBC television series of the works of Maugham in 1970 and as an American television movie titled *Wilson's Reward*.

Vice Squad (see *Harness Bull*).

4778. *Vice Versa* (F. Anstey [pseudonym for Thomas Anstey Guthrie]. 1882). Fantasy about a father and his teenaged son who switch places after touching a mysterious Asian stone. **Silent Film:** 1916. **Adaptation 1:** *Vice Versa* (Rank, 1948). Dir: Peter Ustinov. Scr: Peter Ustinov. Cast: Roger Livesey (Paul), Kay Walsh (Fanny), Petula Clark (Dulcie), Anthony Newley (Dick). VHS. **Adaptation 2:** *Vice Versa* (Columbia, 1988). Dir: Brian Gilbert. Scr: Dick Clement, Ian La Frenais. Cast: Judge Reinhold (Marshall), Fred Savage (Charlie), Corinne Bohrer (Sam), Swoosie Kurtz (Tina), Jane Kaczmarek (Robyn). DVD, VHS. Notes: A similar idea was used in the 1987 film *Like Father Like Son* (DVD, VHS). Also, the same idea involving mother and daughter is the premise of Mary Rodgers' 1972 book *Freaky Friday*. See also *Freaky Friday*.

4779. *The Viceroy of Ouidah* (Bruce Chatwin, 1980). In the early nineteenth century, a poor Brazilian man sails to West Africa and makes his fortune as a master of the slave trade. **Adaptation:** *Cobra Verde* (Zweites Deutsches, 1987). Dir: Werner Herzog. Scr: Werner Herzog. Cast: Klaus Kinski (Francisco), Benito Stefanelli (Captain Vincente), Jose Lewgoy (Don Octavio). DVD, VHS.

Vicki (see *I Wake Up Screaming*).

The Victors (see *The Human Kind*).

4780. *Victory* (Joseph Conrad, 1915). A reclusive island dweller is menaced by three villains, who believe that he is hiding his wealth. **Silent Film:** 1919. **Adaptation 1:** *Dangerous Paradise* (Paramount, 1930). Dir: William A. Wellman. Scr: William Slavens McNutt, Grover Jones. Cast: Nancy Carroll (Alma), Richard Arlen (Heyst), Warner Oland (Schomberg), Gustav von Seyffertitz (Jones), Francis McDonald (Ricardo). **Adaptation 2:** *Victory* (Paramount, 1940). Dir: John Cromwell. Scr: John L. Balderston. Cast: Fredric March (Heyst), Betty Field (Alma), Cedric Hardwicke (Jones), Jerome Cowan (Ricardo). **Adaptation 3:** *Victory* (Miramax, 1995). Dir: Mark Peploe. Scr: Mark Peploe. Cast: Willem Dafoe (Heyst), Sam Neill (Jones), Irene Jacob (Alma), Rufus Sewell (Ricardo). DVD, VHS.

4781. *The View from Pompey's Head* (Hamilton Basso, 1954). A New York lawyer investigating a murder returns to his small home town and reconnects with a former lover. **Adaptation:** *The View from Pompey's Head*; released in the UK as *Secret Interlude* (20th Century–Fox, 1955). Dir: Philip Dunne. Scr: Philip Dunne. Cast: Richard Egan (Anson), Dana Wynter (Dinah), Cameron Mitchell (Mickey), Sidney Blackmer (Garvin), Marjorie Rambeau (Lucy).

A View to a Kill (see *For Your Eyes Only*).

4782. *Vigil in the Night* (A. J. Cronin, 1940). Two sisters who are nurses in a provincial British hospital help a doctor deal with a raging epidemic. The novel was serialized in *Good Housekeeping* (May–October 1939) and published as a book in 1940. **Adaptation:** *Vigil in the Night* (RKO, 1940). Dir: George Stevens. Scr: Fred Guiol, P. J. Wolfson, Rowland Leigh. Cast: Carole Lombard (Anne), Brian Aherne (Dr. Prescott), Anne Shirley (Lucy), Julien Mitchell (Matthew).

4783. *The Viking* (Edison Marshall, 1951). Viking half-brothers who have never met battle for the throne of Northumbria in Great Britain and for the love of a princess. **Adaptation:** *The Vikings* (United Artists, 1958). Dir: Richard Fleischer. Scr: Dale Wasserman, Calder Willingham. Cast: Kirk Douglas (Einar), Tony Curtis (Eric), Ernest Borgnine (Ragnar), Janet Leigh (Morgana), James Donald (Egbert). DVD, VHS.

4784. *Vile Bodies* (Evelyn Waugh, 1930). The story of a British writer and his circle of acquaintances in London in the 1920's. **Adaptation:** *Bright Young Things* (Icon, 2003). Dir: Stephen Fry. Scr: Stephen Fry. Cast: Emily Mortimer (Nina), Stephen Campbell Moore (Adam), James McAvoy (Simon), Michael Sheen (Miles). DVD, VHS.

4785. *Villa des Roses* (Willem Elsschot, 1913). Dutch novel about a French widow who goes to Paris to work in a boarding house and begins a relationship with a German artist. **Adaptation:** *Villa des Roses* (Moonstone, 2002). Dir: Frank Van Passel. Scr: Christophe Dirickx, Frank Van Passel. Cast: Julie Delpy (Louise), Shaun Dingwall (Richard), Shirley Henderson (Ella), Harriet Walter (Olive), Timothy West (Hugh). Notes: The book was also adapted for television miniseries in Holland and Belgium in 1968.

Village of the Damned (see *The Midwich Cuckoos*).

Village of the Giants (see *The Food of the Gods*).

4786. *Village Tale* (Philip Stong, 1934). The effects of prejudice and gossip in a small town, where two rural landowners clash. **Adaptation:** *Village Tale* (RKO, 1935). Dir: John Cromwell. Scr: Allan Scott. Cast: Randolph Scott (Somerville), Kay Johnson (Janet), Arthur Hohl (Elmer), Robert Barrat (Drury).

Villain (see *The Burden of Proof*).

4787. *Vinegar Hill* (Franklin Coen, 1950). A woman visiting her sister in a small town witnesses a murder and soon realizes that people close to her own family are involved. **Adaptation:** *Deadly Family Secrets* (Art & Anne, 1995 TV Movie). Dir: Richard T. Heffron. Scr: Brian Taggert. Cast: Loni Anderson (Martha), Gigi Rice (Linda), Greg Evigan (Eddie), Barry Corbin (Mr. Potter).

4788. *The Vintage* (Ursula Keir, 1953). Two criminal fugitives become grape pickers at a vineyard in France. **Adaptation:** *The Vintage* (MGM, 1957). Dir: Jeffrey Hayden. Scr: Michael Blankfort. Cast: Pier Angeli (Lucienne), Mel Ferrer (Giancarlo/Jean-Charles), John Kerr (Ernesto), Michele Morgan (Leonne), Theodore Bikel (Eduardo). VHS.

The Violent Enemy (see *A Candle for the Dead*).

The Violent Men (see *Night Walker*).

Violent Streets (see *The Home Invaders*).

4789. *Viper 3* (Walter Wager, 1971). A former military commander seizes an atomic missile base and threatens to launch the weapons if the President does not admit to secret plans concerning America's involvement in the Vietnam War. **Adaptation:** *Twilight's Last Gleaming* (Allied Artists, 1977). Dir: Robert Aldrich. Scr: Ronald M. Cohen, Edward Huebsch. Cast: Burt Lancaster (General Dell), Richard Widmark (General MacKenzie), Charles Durning (President Stevens), Paul Winfield (Powell). VHS.

4790. *Virgin* (James Patterson, 1980). Apocalyptic novel about a Catholic priest sent to investigate reports of two virgins expecting babies—one messianic, the other demonic—and to destroy the evil child. **Adaptation:** *Child of Darkness, Child of Light* (USA Networks, 1991 TV Movie). Dir: Marina Sargenti. Scr: Brian Taggert. Cast: Anthony John Denison (Father O'Carroll), Brad Davis (Dr. Phinney), Paxton Whitehead (Father Rosetti), Claudette Nevins (Lenore). VHS.

4791. *The Virgin and the Gypsy* (D. H. Lawrence, 1970). Posthumously published novella written in 1930 about a British clergyman's daughter who falls in love with a gypsy fortune teller. **Adaptation:** *The Virgin and the Gypsy* (Kenwood, 1970). Dir: Christopher Miles. Scr: Alan Plater. Cast: Joanna Shimkus (Yvette), Franco Nero (the Gypsy), Honor Blackman (Mrs. Fawcett), Mark Burns (Major Eastwood). VHS.

4792. *The Virgin in the Ice* (Ellis Peters [pseudonym for Edith Pargeter], 1982). The sixth installment in Peters' twenty-volume series (1977–1994) featuring Brother Cadfael, a twelfth-century monk who, following service in the Crusades, tends to the herbarium at Shrewsbury Abbey and solves crimes. In this book, three orphans and a nun are missing, and Cadfael leaves the abbey to find them. **Adaptation:** *Cadfael: The Virgin in the Ice* (ITV/PBS, 1995 TV Movie series). Dir: Malcolm Mowbray. Scr: Simon Burke. Cast: Derek Jacobi (Brother Cadfael), Eoin McCarthy (Hugh), Albie Woodington (Sergeant Warden), Julian Firth (Brother Jerome). DVD, VHS.

Virgin Island (see *Our Virgin Island*).

4793. *The Virgin Soldiers* (Leslie Thomas, 1966). Serio-comic novel about the exploits of a group of British Army recruits in Singapore in 1950. **Adaptation:** *The Virgin Soldiers* (Columbia, 1969). Dir: John Dexter. Scr: John Hopkins, Ian La Frenais, John McGrath. Cast: Lynn Redgrave (Phillipa), Hywel Bennett (Brigg), Nigel Davenport (Driscoll), Nigel Patrick (Raskin). VHS. See also *Stand Up, Virgin Soldiers*.

4794. *The Virgin Suicides* (Jeffrey Eugenides, 1993). A group of Michigan men obsessively look into the suicides years earlier of five teenaged sisters who lived in the same town. **Adaptation:** *The Virgin Suicides* (Paramount, 1999). Dir: Sofia Coppola. Scr: Sofia Coppola. Cast: James Woods (Mr. Lisbon), Kathleen Turner (Mrs. Lisbon), Kirsten Dunst (Lux), Josh Hartnett (Trip as a youth), Michael Pare (Trip as an adult), Scott Glenn (Father Moody), Danny De Vito (Dr. Horniker). DVD, VHS.

4795. *The Virginian: A Horseman of the Plains* (Owen Wister, 1902). Western about an enigmatic cowboy working as a ranch hand in Wyoming in the 1870's and contending with his friend, who joins with murderous rustlers. Wister and Kirke La Salle produced a stage version of the novel in 1904. **Silent Films:** 1914 (directed by Cecil B. De Mille) and 1923. **Adaptation 1:** *The Virginian* (Paramount, 1929). Dir: Victor Fleming. Scr: Howard Estabrook, Grover Jones, Edward E. Paramore, Jr. Scr: Gary Cooper (the Virginian), Walter Huston (Trampas), Richard Arlen (Steve), Mary Brian (Molly), Helen Ware (Ma Taylor). VHS. **Adaptation 2:** *The Virginian* (Paramount, 1946). Dir: Stuart Gilmore. Scr: Howard Estabrook, Frances Goodrich, Albert Hackett. Cast: Joel McCrea (the Virginian), Brian Donlevy (Trampas), Sonny Tufts (Steve), Barbara Britton (Molly), Fay Bainter (Mrs. Taylor). VHS. **Adap-**

tation **3**: *The Virginian* (Turner, 2000 TV Movie). Dir: Bill Pullman. Scr: Larry Gross. Cast: Bill Pullman (the Virginian), Diane Lane (Molly), John Savage (Steve), Harris Yulin (Judge Henry), Colm Feore (Trampas), James Drury (Rider). VHS. Notes: In addition, the book inspired a successful NBC television series (1962–1971).

Virtual Sexuality (see *Virtual Sexual Reality*).

4796. *Virtual Sexual Reality* (Chloe Rayban. 1994). A teenaged girl creates a computer-generated male counterpart of herself. When a freak accident brings her "dream man" to life, she falls in love with him. **Adaptation:** *Virtual Sexuality* (TriStar, 1999). Dir: Nick Hurran. Scr: Nick Fisher. Cast: Laura Fraser (Justine), Rupert Penry-Jones (Jake), Luke de Lacey (Chas), Kieran O'Brien (Alex). DVD, VHS.

Virtuous Sin (see *The General*).

Virus (see *Outbreak*).

4797. *Vision Quest: A Wrestling Story* (Terry Davis, 1979). A high school wrestler undergoes grueling discipline as he prepares to enter the state championships. At the same time, he falls in love with an older girl who is living at his parents' home. **Adaptation:** *Vision Quest* (Warner, 1985). Dir: Harold Becker. Scr: Darryl Ponicsan. Cast: Matthew Modine (Louden), Linda Fiorentino (Carla), Michael Schoeffling (Kuch), Ronny Cox (Louden's father), Harold Sylvester (Tanneran), Daphne Zuniga (Margie). DVD, VHS.

4798. *Visit to a Chief's Son: An American Boy's Adventure with an African Tribe* (Robert Halmi, 1963). Children's book about an anthropologist and his son who go to Africa to film the rituals of a native tribe and end up learning about themselves in the process. **Adaptation:** *Visit to a Chief's Son* (United Artists, 1974). Dir: Lamont Johnson. Scr: Albert Ruben. Cast: Jock Anderson (Jock), John Philip Hogdon (Kevin), Jesse Kinaru (Kondonyo), Chief Lomoiro (the Chief), Richard Mulligan (Robert), Johnny Sekka (Nemolok).

4799. *The Visitor* (Chauncey G. Parker, 1981). While his wife and son are away on vacation, a businessman battles a huge rat in his New York apartment. **Adaptation:** *Of Unknown Origin* (Warner, 1983). Dir: George P. Cosmatos. Scr: Brian Taggert. Cast: Peter Weller (Bart), Jennifer Dale (Lorrie), Lawrence Dane (Eliot), Kenneth Welsh (James). DVD, VHS.

4800. *The Visitors* (Nathaniel Benchley, 1965). Comic novel about a family who find that their vacation house is haunted by the ghosts of dead lovers. **Adaptation:** *The Spirit Is Willing* (Paramount, 1967). Dir: William Castle. Scr: Ben Starr. Cast: Sid Caesar (Ben), Vera Miles (Kate), Barry Gordon (Steve), John McGiver (Uncle George).

4801. *Viva Max!* (James Lehrer, 1966). Comic novel about an eccentric Mexican general who leads a band of men to Texas to take back the Alamo. **Adaptation:** *Viva Max!* (Commonwealth United, 1969). Dir: Jerry Paris. Scr: Elliott Baker. Cast: Peter Ustinov (General Rodrigues de Santos), Pamela Tiffin (Paula), Jonathan Winters (General Hallson), John Astin (Sergeant Valdez), Keenan Wynn (General Lacomber), Harry Morgan (Chief Sylvester), Alice Ghostley (Hattie), Kenneth Mars (Dr. Gillison). VHS.

4802. *The Vivero Letter* (Desmond Bagley, 1968). A man goes to the Yucatan in Mexico in search of the Mayans' lost gold and is pursued by the gangsters who killed his brother. **Adaptation:** *The Vivero Letter*, released on video as *The Forbidden City* (York, 1998). Dir: H. Gordon Boos. Scr: Denne Bart Pettitclerc, Arthur Sellers. Cast: Robert Patrick (James), Chiara Caselli (Caterina), Fred Ward (Andrew), John Verea (Raoul). DVD, VHS.

4803. *The Voice of Bugle Ann* (MacKinlay Kantor, 1935). On a Missouri farm, a fox hunter seeks vengeance on the sheepherder who killed his favorite dog. **Adaptation:** *The Voice of Bugle Ann* (MGM, 1936). Dir: Richard Thorpe. Scr: Harvey Gates, Samuel Hoffenstein. Cast: Lionel Barrymore (Springfield), Maureen O'Sullivan (Camden), Eric Linden (Benjy), Dudley Digges (Jacob), Spring Byington (Ma Davis).

4804. *Voices* (Dacia Maraini, 1994). Italian mystery novel, originally titled *Voci*, about a radio journalist doing a program on a series of crimes against women. Her subject hits home when she returns to her Rome apartment to discover that her own neighbor has been brutally murdered. The book was translated into English in 1997. **Adaptation:** *Voices* (Factory, 2000). Dir: Franco Giraldi. Scr: Serena Brugnolo, Alessio Cremonini, Franco Giraldi, Chiara Laudani. Cast: Sonia Bergamasco (Ludovica), Rossella Bergo (Sabrina), Erika Blanc (Augusta), Valeria Bruni Tedeschi (Michela), Gabriella Pession (Angela), Imma Piro (Adele). Notes: Originally released as *Voci* and shown with subtitles.

4805. *Von Ryan's Express* (David Westheimer, 1964). During World War II, an American captain leads a group of British and American prisoners of war in a daring escape from a freight train. **Adaptation:** *Von Ryan's Express* (20th Century–Fox, 1965). Dir: Mark Robson. Scr: Wendell Mayes, Joseph Landon. Cast: Frank Sinatra (Colonel Ryan), Trevor Howard (Major Fincham), Raffaella Carra (Gabriella), Brad Dexter (Sergeant Bostick), Sergio Fantoni (Captain Oriani), John Leyton (Orde), Edward Mulhare (Captain Costanzo). DVD, VHS.

4806. *The Voyage* (Luigi Pirandello, 1928). *Il Viaggio*, a novel by the famous Italian playwright, concerns the doomed affair between lovers who are forbidden by their families to marry. **Adaptation:** *The Voyage*; released in the UK as *The Journey* (United Artists, 1974). Dir: Vittorio De Sica. Scr: Diego Fabbri, Massimo Franciosa, Luisa Montagnana. Cast: Richard Burton (Cesare), Sophia Loren (Adriana), Ian Bannen (Antonio), Renato Pinciroli (Dr. Maccione).

4807. *Voyage of the Damned* (Gordon Thomas and Max Morgan Witts, 1974). Factual account of a ship carrying 937 Jews from Nazi Germany to Havana. When Cuba and the United States refused them entry, they were returned to Germany, where they faced the horrors of the Holocaust. **Adaptation:** *Voyage of the Damned* (AVCO Embassy, 1976). Dir: Stuart Rosenberg. Scr: David Butler, Steve Shagan. Cast: Faye Dunaway (Denise), Oskar Werner (Dr. Kreisler), Lee Grant (Lillian), Katharine Ross (Mira), Sam Wanamaker (Carl). Notes: Academy Award nominations for Best Screenplay, Supporting Actress (Grant), and Musical Score; Golden Globe Award for Best Supporting Actress (Ross) and nominations for Best Picture, Screenplay, Supporting Actor (Werner), Supporting Actress (Grant),and Musical Score. DVD, VHS.

Voyager (see *Homo Faber*).

4808. *W. C. Fields and Me* (Carlotta Monti, with Cy Rice, 1971). A biography of the comedian (1879–1946) by his last mistress. **Adaptation:** *W. C. Fields and Me* (Universal, 1976). Dir: Arthur Hiller. Scr: Bob Merrill. Cast: Rod Steiger (Fields), Valerie Perrine (Carlotta), John Marley (Bannerman), Jack Cassidy (John Barrymore), Bernadette Peters (Melody).

4809. *The W Plan* (Graham Seton [pseudonym for Graham Seton Hutchinson], 1929). Espionage novel about a British spy who destroys a secret German tunnel during World War I. **Adaptation:** *The W Plan* (British International/ RKO, 1930). Dir: Victor Saville. Scr: Frank Launder, Miles Malleson, Victor Saville. Cast: Brian Aherne (Duncan), Madeleine Carroll (Rosa), Gordon Harker (Waller), Gibb McLaughlin (McTavish).

Wag the Dog (see *American Hero*).

4810. *The Wages of Fear* (Georges Arnaud, 1950). The French novel, originally titled *Le Salaire de la Peur,* centers on oil workers in Central America volunteering for the perilous job of trucking nitroglycerine to put out an oil-well fire. **Adaptation 1:** *The Wages of Fear* (DCA, 1953). Dir: Henri-Georges Clouzot. Scr: Henri-Georges Clouzot, Jerome Geronimi. Cast: Yves Montand (Mario), Charles Vanel (Jo), Peter Van Eyck (Bimba). Notes: Originally released as *Le Salaire de la Peur* and shown with subtitles. BAFTA Award for Best Film; Cannes Grand Prize of the Festival (Clouzot). DVD, VHS. **Adaptation 2:** *Sorcerer*; released in the UK as *The Wages of Fear* (Paramount/Universal, 1977). Dir: William Friedkin. Scr: Walon Green. Cast: Roy Scheider (Jackie), Bruno Cremer (Victor), Francisco Rabal (Nilo). DVD, VHS.

Wagon Wheels (see *Fighting Caravans*).

The Wagons Roll at Night (see *Kid Galahad*).

Wait Till the Sun Shines, Nellie (see *I Heard Them Sing*).

4811. *Waiting for a Tiger* (Ben Healey, 1965). A young British woman vacationing on the Riviera has reason to believe that someone is trying to kill her. **Adaptation:** *Taste of Excitement* (Crispin, 1969). Dir: Don Sharp. Scr: Don Sharp. Cast: Eva Renzi (Jane), David Buck (Paul), Peter Vaughan (Inspector Malling).

4812. *Waiting to Exhale* (Terry McMillan, 1992). The story of four African-American women and their struggles with sexual relationships and careers. **Adaptation:** *Waiting to Exhale* (20th Century–Fox, 1995). Dir: Forest Whitaker. Scr: Terry McMillan, Ronald Bass. Cast: Whitney Houston (Vannah), Angela Bassett (Bernie), Loretta Devine (Gloria), Lela Rochon (Robin), Gregory Hines (Marvin), Dennis Haysbert (Kenneth), Mykelti Williamson (Troy). DVD, VHS.

4813. *Wake in Fright* (Kenneth Cook, 1961). Australian novel about a teacher who is brutalized by the primitive men of a small rural village. **Adaptation:** *Wake in Fright*; also released as *Outback* (Group W/United Artists, 1971). Dir: Ted Kotcheff. Scr: Evan Jones. Cast: Donald Pleasence (Doc Tydon), Gary Bond (Grant), Chips Rafferty (Crawford), Sylvia Kay (Janette). Notes: Cannes Film Festival Golden Palm nomination for Best Director.

4814. *Wake Me When It's Over* (Howard Singer, 1959). Comic World War II novel about a group of soldiers who build a luxury hotel out of army surplus materials on a Pacific island. **Adaptation:** *Wake Me When It's Over* (20th Century–Fox, 1960). Dir: Mervyn Le Roy. Scr: Richard L. Breen. Cast: Ernie Kovacs (Charlie), Dick Shawn (Gus), Margo Moore (Nora), Jack Warden (Doc Farrington).

4815. *Wake of the Red Witch* (Garland Roark, 1946). A ship's captain battles a Dutch shipping magnate for a fortune in gold and pearls and for the love of a woman. **Adaptation:** *Wake of the Red Witch* (Republic, 1948). Dir: Edward Ludwig. Scr: Harry Brown, Kenneth Gamet. Cast: John Wayne (Captain Ralls), Gail Russell (Angelique), Gig Young (Sam), Adele Mara (Teleia). DVD, VHS.

Wake Up and Dream (see *The Enchanted Voyage*).

4816. *Wake Up and Live!: A Formula for Success* (Dorothea Brande, 1936). A self-help book with inspirational advice about living life to the fullest. **Adaptation:** *Wake Up and Live* (20th Century–Fox, 1937). Dir: Sidney Lanfield. Scr: Curtis Kenyon, Harry Tugend, Jack Yellen. Cast: Walter Winchell (Walter Winchell), Ben Bernie (Ben Bernie), Alice Faye (Alice Huntley), Patsy Kelly (Patsy Kane). Notes: The film is a comedy about a feuding band leader and radio announcer.

4817. *Waking the Dead* (Scott Spencer, 1986). A man running for political office is haunted by visions of his former girlfriend, who died in Chile nine years earlier. **Adaptation:** *Waking the Dead* (USA, 2000). Dir: Keith Gordon. Scr: Robert Dillon. Cast: Billy Crudup (Fielding), Jennifer Connelly (Sarah), Molly Parker (Juliet), Janet McTeer (Caroline), Paul Hipp (Danny), Sandra Oh (Kim), Hal Holbrook (Isaac). Notes: Independent Spirit Awards nomination for Best Screenplay. DVD, VHS.

4818. *A Walk in the Spring Rain* (Rachel Maddux, 1969). A college professor and his wife move to the mountains, where she begins an affair with an attractive neighbor. **Adaptation:** *A Walk in the Spring Rain* (Columbia, 1970). Dir: Guy Green. Scr: Stirling Silliphant. Cast: Ingrid Bergman (Libby), Anthony Quinn (Will), Virginia Gregg (Ann), Fritz Weaver (Roger). VHS.

4819. *A Walk in the Sun* (Harry Brown, 1944). World War II novel about an American platoon landing in Italy in 1943 and attacking a Nazi position in a fortified farmhouse. **Adaptation:** *A Walk in the Sun* (20th Century–Fox,

1945). Dir: Lewis Milestone. Scr: Harry Brown, Robert Rossen. Cast: Dana Andrews (Bill), Richard Conte (Rivera), George Tyne (Friedman), John Ireland (Craven), Lloyd Bridges (Ward), Sterling Holloway (McWilliams). DVD, VHS.

4820. *Walk on the Wild Side* (Nelson Algren, 1956). In 1930's New Orleans, a poor farmer discovers the love of his life working in a bordello. **Adaptation:** *Walk on the Wild Side* (Columbia, 1962). Dir: Edward Dmytryk. Scr: John Fante, Edmund Morris. Cast: Laurence Harvey (Dove), Capucine (Hallie), Jane Fonda (Kitty), Anne Baxter (Teresina), Barbara Stanwyck (Jo). DVD, VHS.

4821. *A Walk to Remember* (Nicholas Sparks, 1999). Two North Carolina teenagers— he a brash member of the in-crowd, she a conservative minister's daughter — are forced together in a school play and find love. However, one of them harbors a tragic secret. **Adaptation:** *A Walk to Remember* (Warner, 2002). Dir: Adam Shankman. Scr: Karen Janszen. Cast: Shane West (Landon), Mandy Moore (Jamie), Peter Coyote (Reverend Sullivan), Daryl Hannah (Cynthia). DVD, VHS.

Walk Tall (see *The Tall Stranger*).

4822. "Walk Well, My Brother" (Farley Mowat, 1975). After crashing in the Arctic, a pilot and his passenger struggle to survive and are aided by Eskimos. The short story appeared in Mowat's 1975 collection *The Snow Walker*. **Adaptation:** *The Snow Walker* (First Look, 2003). Dir: Charles Martin Smith. Scr: Charles Martin Smith. Cast: Barry Pepper (Charlie), Annabella Piugattuk (Kanaalaq), James Cromwell (Shepherd), Kiersten Warren (Estelle). Notes: Leo Awards (Canada) for Best Actor (Pepper), Musical Score, Sound, Sound Editing, Visual Effects, and Costume Design, and nominations for Best Picture, Director, Screenplay, Editing, and Production Design; Genie Award nominations (Canada) for Best Picture, Director, Screenplay, Actor (Pepper), Actress (Piugattuk), Editing, Musical Score, Sound, and Sound Editing.

4823. *Walkabout* (James Vance Marshall, 1959). Two American children survive a plane crash in the Australian outback and are aided by an Aboriginal boy on "walkabout," a long journey of initiation into manhood. **Adaptation:** *Walkabout* (20th Century–Fox, 1971). Dir: Nicolas Roeg. Scr: Edward Bond. Cast: Jenny Agutter (the Girl), Lucien John (the White Boy), David

Gulpilil (the Black Boy), Pete Carver (No Hoper). Notes: Cannes Film Festival Golden Palm nomination for Best Director. DVD, VHS.

4824. *Walking Across Egypt* (Clyde Edgerton, 1987). An elderly woman in Florida helps to reform a teenaged delinquent. **Adaptation:** *Walking Across Egypt* (Keystone, 1999). Dir: Arthur Allan Seidelman. Scr: Paul Tamasy. Cast: Ellen Burstyn (Mattie), Jonathan Taylor Thomas (Wesley), Pat Corley (Sheriff Tillman), Mark Hamill (Lamar), Edward Herrmann (Reverend Vernon), Dana Ivey (Beatrice), Harve Presnell (Finner), Gwen Verdon (Alora). DVD, VHS.

4825. *The Walking Stick* (Winston Graham, 1967). A beautiful polio victim falls in love with an attractive stranger, who eventually involves her in his criminal activities. **Adaptation:** *The Walking Stick* (MGM, 1970). Dir: Eric Till. Scr: George Bluestone. Cast: David Hemmings (Leigh), Samantha Eggar (Deborah), Emlyn Williams (Jack), Phyllis Calvert (Erica).

4826. *Walking Through the Fire: A Hospital Journal* (Laurel Lee, 1977). Memoir of a woman diagnosed with Hodgkin's Disease. Unable to cope with her illness, her husband left her and their children for another woman, and the sick wife, determined to survive, moved in with her parents. **Adaptation:** *Walking Through the Fire* (CBS, 1979 TV Movie). Dir: Robert Day. Scr: Sue Grafton. Cast: Bess Armstrong (Laurel), Tom Mason (Richard), Richard Masur (Dr. Maitland), Swoosie Kurtz (Caria), Ken Kercheval (Dr. Freeman), June Lockhart (Ruth), J. D. Cannon (Dr. Goodwin), Bonnie Bedelia (Dr. Rand).

4827. *The Wall* (John Hersey, 1950). A novel about the Jewish uprising against the Nazis in Warsaw in April 1943. The book was adapted as a Broadway play by Millard Lampell in 1960. **Adaptation:** *The Wall* (CBS, 1982 TV Movie). Dir: Robert Markowitz. Scr: Millard Lampell (based on his 1960 play). Cast: Tom Conti (Dolek), Lisa Eichhorn (Rachel), Gerald Hiken (Fischel), Rachel Roberts (Regina). DVD, VHS.

4828. *A Wall for San Sebastian* (William Barby Flaherty, 1965). In the mid eighteenth century, a Mexican bandit becomes a hero by defending a village against an Indian attack. **Adaptation:** *Guns for San Sebastian* (MGM, 1967). Dir: Henri Verneuil. Scr: Serge Ganz, Miguel Morayta, Ennio De Concini, James R. Webb. Cast: Anthony Quinn (Leon), Anjanette Comer (Kinita), Charles Bronson (Teclo), Sam Jaffe (Father Joseph).

4829. *The Walls Came Tumbling Down* (Jo Eisinger, 1943). A New York investigator searches

for the murderer of a parish priest. **Adaptation:** *The Walls Came Tumbling Down* (Columbia, 1946). Dir: Lothar Mendes. Scr: Wilfred H. Petitt. Cast: Lee Bowman (Gilbert), Marguerite Chapman (Patricia), Edgar Buchanan (George), George Macready (Matthew).

4830. *The Walls of Jericho* (Paul I. Wellman, 1947). A politically ambitious small-town lawyer is thwarted by his vindictive, alcoholic wife. **Adaptation:** *The Walls of Jericho* (20th Century–Fox, 1948). Dir: John M. Stahl. Scr: Lamar Trotti. Cast: Cornel Wilde (Dave), Linda Darnell (Algeria), Anne Baxter (Julia), Kirk Douglas (Tucker), Ann Dvorak (Belle).

4831. *The Walton Experience* (Travis Walton, 1978). The true story of Travis Walton, who claims to have been taken aboard an alien spacecraft for five days. A revised edition of the book titled *Fire in the Sky: The Walton Experience* was released in 1996. **Adaptation:** *Fire in the Sky* (Paramount, 1993). Dir: Robert Lieberman. Scr: Tracy Torme. Cast: D. B. Sweeney (Walton), Robert Patrick (Rogers), Craig Sheffer (Allan), Peter Berg (Whitlock), Henry Thomas (Greg). VHS.

4832. *Waltz into Darkness* (Cornell Woolrich, 1947). A tobacco farmer sends for a mail-order bride. The woman who arrives is far more beautiful than the one in the picture he had been sent, and he falls in love with her. When she disappears with the money in his bank account, he realizes his mistake and pursues her relentlessly. Woolrich originally published the novel under the pseudonym William Irish. **Adaptation 1:** *Mississippi Mermaid* (United Artists, 1969). Dir: François Truffaut. Scr: François Truffaut. Cast: Jean-Paul Belmondo (Louis), Catherine Deneuve (Julie/Marion), Nelly Borgeaud (Berthe). DVD, VHS. **Adaptation 2:** *Original Sin* (MGM, 2001). Dir: Michael Cristofer. Scr: Michael Cristofer. Cast: Antonio Banderas (Luis), Angelina Jolie (Julia), Thomas Jane (Walter), Jack Thompson (Alan). DVD, VHS.

4833. *Wanda Hickey's Night of Golden Memories and Other Disasters* (Jean Shepherd, 1971). Shepherd's comic autobiographical stories about growing up in Indiana in the 1940's. **Adaptation:** *My Summer Story*; also released as *It Runs in My Family* (MGM, 1994). Dir: Bob Clark. Scr: Jean Shepherd, Leigh Brown, Bob Clark. Cast: Charles Grodin (Mr. Parker), Kieran Culkin (Ralphie), Christian Culkin (Randy). Notes: The screenplay combines elements from two of Shepherd's works: *In God We Trust, All Others Pay Cash* (1966) and

Wanda Hickey's Night of Golden Memories and Other Disasters (1971). VHS. See also *In God We Trust, All Others Pay Cash.*

4834. *Wanderer of the Wasteland* (Zane Grey, 1920). Western about a young cowboy framed for the murder of the man who killed his father years earlier. The novel was serialized in *McClure's* magazine beginning in May 1920 and published as a book in 1923. **Silent Film:** 1924. **Adaptation 1:** *Wanderer of the Wasteland* (Paramount, 1935). Dir: Otho Lovering. Scr: Stuart Anthony. Cast: Dean Jagger (Adam), Gail Patrick (Ruth), Edward Ellis (Dismukes). **Adaptation 2:** *Wanderer of the Wasteland* (RKO, 1945). Dir: Wallace Grissell, Edward Killy. Scr: Norman Houston. Cast: James Warren (Adam), Richard Martin (Chito), Audrey Long (Jeannie), Robert Barrat (Uncle Jim). DVD, VHS.

4835. *The Wanderers* (Richard Price, 1974). Portrait of a street gang in the Bronx in 1963. **Adaptation:** *The Wanderers* (Orion, 1979). Dir: Philip Kaufman. Scr: Rose Kaufman, Philip Kaufman. Cast: Ken Wahl (Richie), John Friedrich (Joey), Karen Allen (Nina), Toni Kalem (Despie). DVD, VHS.

4836. *War and Peace* (Leo Tolstoy, 1865–1869). Epic Russian novel, originally titled *Voyna i Mir*, about a Russian family at time time of Napoleon's invasion in 1812. **Silent Film:** 1915. **Adaptation 1:** *War and Peace* (Paramount, 1956). Dir: King Vidor. Scr: Bridget Boland, Mario Camerini, Ennio De Concini, Ivo Perilli, King Vidor, Robert Westerby. Cast: Audrey Hepburn (Natasha), Henry Fonda (Pierre), Mel Ferrer (Prince Bolkonsky), Vittorio Gassman (Anatole), Herbert Lom (Napoleon), Oscar Homolka (General Kutuzov), Anita Ekberg (Helene). Notes: Academy Award nominations for Best Director, Cinematography, and Costume Design; Golden Globe Award for Best Foreign-Language Film and nominations for Best Picture, Director, Actress (Hepburn), and Supporting Actor (Homolka). DVD, VHS. **Adaptation 2:** *War and Peace* (Mosfilm/Continental, 1968). Dir: Sergei Bondarchuk. Scr: Sergei Bondarchuk, Vasili Solovyov. Cast: Lyudmila Savelyeva (Natasha), Vyacheslav Tikhonov (Prince Bolkonsky), Irina Gubanova (Soniya), Antonina Shuranova (Princess Mariya), Sergei Bondarchuk (Pierre). Notes: Academy Award, Golden Globe Award, and National Board of Review Award for Best Foreign-Language Film. DVD, VHS. **Adaptation 3:** *War and Peace* (PBS, 1972 TV Miniseries). Dir: John Davies. Scr: Jack Pulman. Cast: Morag Hood (Natasha), Anthony Hopkins (Pierre), Faith Brook (Countess Rostova), Rupert Davies (Count Rostov). Notes: BAFTA Award for Best Actor (Hopkins). VHS.

4837. *War and Remembrance* (Herman Wouk, 1978). In this sequel to Wouk's 1971 novel *The Winds of War*, several families are affected when the United States enters World War II after the Japanese attack on Pearl Harbor. **Adaptation:** *War and Remembrance* (ABC, 1988 TV Miniseries). Dir: Dan Curtis. Scr: Earl W. Wallace, Dan Curtis, Herman Wouk. Cast: Robert Mitchum (Captain Henry), Jane Seymour (Natalie), Hart Bochner (Byron), Victoria Tennant (Pamela), Polly Bergen (Rhoda), Barry Bostwick (Lady), E. G. Marshall (Dwight D. Eisenhower), Ralph Bellamy (President Franklin Delano Roosevelt), John Gielgud (Aaron). Notes: Emmy Awards for Oustanding Miniseries, Visual Effects, and Editing, and nominations for Outstanding Director, Actor (Gielgud), Actress (Seymour), Supporting Actress (Bergen), Cinematography, Art Direction, Musical Score, Costume Design, Hairstyling, Makeup, and Sound Editing; Golden Globe Awards for Best Miniseries and Supporting Actor (Bostwick), and nomninations for Best Actor (Gielgud) and Actress (Seymour). DVD, VHS. See also *The Winds of War.*

The War Bride's Secret (see *The Melody Lingers On*).

4838. *The War Lover* (John Hersey, 1959). The professional and romantic experiences of two American pilots in England during World War II. **Adaptation:** *The War Lover* (Columbia, 1962). Dir: Philip Leacock. Scr: Howard Koch. Cast: Steve McQueen (Buzz), Robert Wagner (Ed), Shirley Anne Field (Daphne), Gary Cockrell (Marty), Michael Crawford (Junior). DVD, VHS.

4839. *The War of the Buttons* (Louis Pergaud, 1912). Comic novel about children from neighboring villages and their bloodless gang warfare. The French novel, originally titled *La Guerre des Boutons*, was translated into English in 1968. **Adaptation 1:** *The War of the Buttons* (Comet, 1962). Dir: Yves Robert. Scr: François Boyer, Yves Robert. Cast: Pierre Tchernia (Bedouin), Claude Confortes (Nestor), Paul Crauchet (Touegueule). Notes: Originally released as *La Guerre des Boutons* and shown with subtitles. **Adaptation 2:** *War of the Buttons* (Warner, 1994). Dir: John Roberts. Scr: Colin Welland. Cast: Gregg Fitzgerald (Fergus), Gerard Kearney (Big Con), Darragh Naughton (Boffin), Brendan McNamara (Tim). Notes: The action is set in neighboring Irish villages. VHS.

4840. *The War of the Roses* (Warren Adler, 1981). Black comedy about the divorce of a suburban couple and their vicious battle over possession of their house. **Adaptation:** *The War of the Roses* (20th Century–Fox, 1989). Dir: Danny De Vito. Scr: Michael Leeson. Cast: Michael Douglas (Oliver), Kathleen Turner (Barbara), Danny De Vito (Gavin), Marianne Sägebrecht (Susan). Notes: Golden Globe nominations for Best Picture, Actor (Douglas), and Actress (Turner). DVD, VHS.

4841. *The War of the Worlds* (H. G. Wells, 1898). Wells' science-fiction classic about a Martian takeover of Earth. The story was the basis of Orson Welles' infamous Mercury Theater radio broadcast on October 30, 1938, when many listeners were convinced that the nation was really under Martian attack. **Adaptation 1:** *The War of the Worlds* (Paramount, 1953). Dir: Byron Haskin. Scr: Barre Lyndon. Cast: Gene Barry (Dr. Forrester), Ann Robinson (Sylvia), Les Tremayne (General Mann), Bob Cornthwaite (Dr. Pryor). DVD, VHS. **Adaptation 2:** *War of the Worlds* (Paramount, 2005). Dir; Steven Spielberg. Scr: David Koepp. Cast: Tom Cruise (Ray), Justin Chatwin (Robbie), Dakota Fanning (Rachel), Tim Robbins (Ogilvy), Miranda Otto (Mary Ann). DVD, VHS. Notes: The book also inspired a television series in 1988.

4842. "War Party" (James Warner Bellah, 1948). Western about a cavalry officer about to retire who leads his troops into battle against Indian raiders. The short story appeared in *The Saturday Evening Post* on June 19, 1948. **Adaptation:** *She Wore a Yellow Ribbon* (RKO, 1949). Dir: John Ford. Scr: Frank Nugent, Laurence Stallings. Cast: John Wayne (Brittles), Joanne Dru (Olivia), John Agar (Cohill), Ben Johnson (Sergeant Tyree), Harry Carey, Jr. (Penell), Victor McLaglen (Sergeant Quincannon), Mildred Natwick (Abby). Notes: The screenplay also includes elements from "The Big Hunt," a 1947 Bellah short story published in *The Saturday Evening Post.*

4843. "The War Prayer" (Mark Twain [pseudonym for Samuel Langhorne Clemens], 1916). A short story about frightened soldiers praying in church one Sunday before leaving for battle. The anti-war story was written in 1905 and rejected by a magazine as too "radical." In November 1916, six years after Twain's death, it was posthumously published in *Harper's Monthly.* **Adaptation:** *The Private History of a Campaign That Failed* (PBS, 1981 TV Movie). Dir: Peter H. Hunt. Scr: Peter H. Hunt. Cast: Joseph Adams (Captain Lyman), Roy Cockrum (Sergeant Bowers), Harry Crosby (Corporal Stevens). VHS.

The War Wagon (see *Badman*).

4844. *The War Zone* (Alexander Stuart, 1989). When his family moves from London to a country home, a fifteen-year-old boy discovers his sister's incestuous relationship with their father. **Adaptation:** *The War Zone* (Channel Four/ Lot 47, 1999). Dir: Tim Roth. Scr: Alexander Stuart. Cast: Kate Ashfield (Lucy), Lara Belmont (Jessie), Freddie Cunliffe (Tom), Colin Farrell (Nick). Notes: Independent Spirit Award nomination for Best Picture. DVD, VHS.

4845. *Warlock* (Oakley Hall, 1958). Western about a town whose cowardly citizens hire a gunman to act as their unofficial sheriff and his conflict with the duly sworn marshal. **Adaptation:** *Warlock*; reissued as *Shoot Out at Warlock* (20th Century–Fox, 1959). Dir: Edward Dmytryk. Scr: Robert Alan Aurthur. Cast: Richard Widmark (Gannon), Henry Fonda (Clay), Anthony Quinn (Morgan), Dorothy Malone (Lily), Dolores Michaels (Jessie), Wallace Ford (Judge Holloway). VHS.

Warning Shot (see *711— Officer Needs Help*).

4846. *A Warning to Wantons* (Mary Mitchell, 1934). Romantic comedy about an alluring young woman who schemes to improve her fortunes by marrying a British nobleman. **Adaptation:** *Warning to Wantons* (General, 1948). Dir: Donald B. Wilson. Scr: James Laver, Donald B. Wilson. Cast: Harold Warrender (Count Kardak), Anne Vernon (Renee), David Tomlinson (Max).

4847. *Warrant for X* (Philip MacDonald, 1938). A blind playwright in a London pub overhears a murder plot and decides to follow the conspirators at great risk to his own safety. The book was published in the UK as *The Nursemaid Who Disappeared.* **Adaptation:** *23 Paces to Baker Street* (20th Century–Fox, 1956). Dir: Henry Hathaway. Dir: Nigel Balchin. Cast: Van Johnson (Phillip), Vera Miles (Jean), Cecil Parker (Bob), Patricia Laffan (Alice). VHS.

4848. *The Warriors* (Sol Yurick, 1965). After a deadly meeting in the Bronx, a New York street gang must fight their way across various enemy turfs to get back to their home in Brooklyn. **Adaptation:** *The Warriors* (Paramount, 1979). Dir: Walter Hill. Scr: David Shaber, Walter Hill. Cast: Michael Beck (Swan), James Remar (Ajax), Dorsey Wright (Cleon), Brian Tyler (Snow), David Harris (Cochise). DVD, VHS.

4849. *Washington Square* (Henry James, 1880). In nineteenth-century New York City, a domineering father opposes his awkward daughter's plans to marry a handsome fortune hunter. The novel was originally serialized in *Cornhill Magazine* in England (June through November 1880) and in *Harper's New Monthly* in the United States (July through December 1880). The novel was the basis for *The Heiress*, a 1947 Broadway play, written by Ruth and Augustus Goetz. **Adaptation 1:** *The Heiress* (Paramount, 1949). Dir: William Wyler. Scr: Augustus Goetz, Ruth Goetz (based on their play). Cast: Olivia de Havilland (Catherine), Montgomery Clift (Morris), Ralph Richardson (Dr. Sloper), Miriam Hopkins (Lavinia), Vanessa Brown (Maria). Notes: Academy Awards for Best Actress (de Havilland), Musical Score, Art Direction, and Costume Design, and nominations for Best Picture, Director, Supporting Actor (Richardson), and Cinematography; Golden Globe Award for Best Actress (de Havilland); National Board of Review Award for Best Actor (Richardson). VHS. **Adaptation 2:** *The Heiress* (CBS, 1961 TV Movie). Dir: Marc Daniels. Scr: Jacqueline Babbin, Audrey Gellen (based on the 1947 play by Augustus Goetz, and Ruth Goetz). Cast: Julie Harris (Catherine), Farley Granger (Morris), Barry Morse (Dr. Sloper), Muriel Kirkland (Lavinia). **Adaptation 3:** *Washington Square* (Buena Vista, 1997). Dir: Agnieszka Holland. Scr: Carol Doyle. Cast: Jennifer Jason Leigh (Catherine), Albert Finney (Dr. Sloper), Maggie Smith (Lavinia), Ben Chaplin (Morris), Judith Ivey (Elizabeth). DVD, VHS.

4850. "Wasn't She Great?" (Michael Korda, 1995). An article about the life of best-selling author Jacqueline Susann (1918–1974) and her relationship with her manager-husband Irving Mansfield. The article appeared in the August 14, 1995, issue of *The New Yorker*. **Adaptation:** *Isn't She Great?* (Universal, 2000). Dir: Andrew Bergman. Scr: Paul Rudnick. Cast: Bette Midler (Susann), Nathan Lane (Mansfield), Stockard Channing (Florence), David Hyde Pierce (Michael), John Cleese (Henry), John Larroquette (Maury), Amanda Peet (Debbie). DVD, VHS.

4851. *The Watcher in the Woods* (Florence Engel Randall, 1976). Two adolescent sisters and their family move into an English country house, where the spirit of a teenaged girl who disappeared there years earlier makes contact with them. **Adaptation:** *The Watcher in the Woods* (Disney/Buena Vista, 1980). Dir: John Hough. Scr: Brian Clemens, Rosemary Anne Sisson,

Harry Spalding. Cast: Bette Davis (Mrs. Aylwood), Lynn-Holly Johnson (Jan), Kyle Richards (Ellie), Carroll Baker (Helen), David McCallum (Paul). DVD, VHS.

4852. *Watchers* (Dean R. Koontz, 1987). A boy takes in a stray dog that was the subject of genetic experiments at a research lab, rendering it highly intelligent. Now a monstrous creature from the same lab is stalking the dog and the boy. **Adaptation:** *Watchers* (Universal, 1988). Dir: Jon Hess. Scr: Bill Freed, Damian Lee. Cast: Michael Ironside (Lem), Corey Haim (Travis), Dale Wilson (Bill), Colleen Winton (Deputy Porter), Duncan Fraser (Sheriff Gaines). DVD, VHS. Notes: Three sequels followed: *Watchers II* (1990) (DVD, VHS); *Watchers III* (1994) (VHS); and *Watchers Reborn* (1998) (VHS).

4853. *The Water Babies: A Fairy Tale for a Baby Land* (Charles Kingsley, 1863). In the mid-nineteenth century, a chimney sweep falls into a river and discovers a magical underwater world. The children's book was originally serialized in *Macmillan's Magazine*. **Adaptation:** *The Water Babies*; also released as *Slip Slide Adventures* (Pethurst, 1978). Dir: Lionel Jeffries. Scr: Michael Robson. Cast: James Mason (Mr. Grimes/voice of Killer Shark), Bernard Cribbins (Masterman/voice of Eel), Billie Whitelaw (Mrs. Doasy-ouwouldbedoneby/the Old Crone/Mrs. Tripp/the Woman in Black/the Water Babies' Gate Keeper), Joan Greenwood (Lady Harriet). Notes: The film combines live action and animation. DVD, VHS.

4854. *The Water Gypsies* (A. P. Herbert, 1930). The comic adventures of two British girls who live on a boat on the Thames River. Herbert and Vivian Ellis adapted the novel as a London stage musical in 1954. **Adaptation:** *The Water Gypsies* (Radio Pictures, 1932). Dir: Maurice Elvey. Scr: John Paddy Carstairs, Basil Dean, Miles Malleson, Alma Reville. Cast: Ann Todd (Jane), Sari Maritza (Lily), Ian Hunter (Fred).

4855. *The Water Is Wide* (Pat Conroy, 1972). Autobiographical account of Conroy's experiences as an idealistic white teacher who goes to work in a poor black school on an island off the coast of South Carolina. **Adaptation:** *Conrack* (20th Century–Fox, 1974). Dir: Martin Ritt. Scr: Irving Ravetch, Harriet Frank, Jr. Cast: Jon Voight (Conroy), Paul Winfield (Billy), Madge Sinclair (Mrs. Scott), Tina Andrews (Mary), Antonio Fargas (Quickfellow). VHS.

4856. *The Water of the Hills* (Marcel Pagnol, 1963). In 1952, Pagnol wrote and directed a French film titled *Manon des Sources* (*Manon of the*

Spring). Afterwards, he turned the story into two novels: *L'Eau des Collines* (*The Water of the Hills*) and *Manon des Sources*. The former tells the tale of peasants in a small village who concoct a murderous scheme to get their hands on some farmland containing a natural spring. **Adaptation:** *Jean de Florette* (Orion, 1986). Dir: Claude Berri. Scr: Claude Berri, Gerard Brach. Cast: Yves Montand (Cesar), Gerard Depardieu (Jean), Daniel Auteuil (Ugolin), Elisabeth Depardieu (Aimee), Margarita Lozano (Baptistine). Notes: BAFTA Awards for Best Picture, Screenplay, Supporting Actor (Auteuil), and Cinematography, and nominations for Best Foreign-Language Film, Actors (Montand and Depardieu), Makeup, and Production Design; National Board of Review Award for Best Foreign-Language Film; Golden Globe nomination for Best Foreign Language Film. DVD, VHS. See also *Manon of the Spring*.

4857. *Waterfront* (John Brophy, 1934). After abandoning his family in Liverpool years earlier, a sailor returns, but his wife and grown daughter are not happy to see him. **Adaptation:** *Waterfront*; released in the U.S. as *Waterfront Women* (Rank, 1950). Dir: Michael Anderson. Scr: John Brophy, Paul Soskin. Cast: Robert Newton (McCabe), Kathleen Harrison (Mrs. McCabe), Avis Scott (Nora), Susan Shaw (Connie). VHS.

Waterfront Women (see *Waterfront*).

4858. *Waterland* (Graham Swift, 1983). A stressed middle-aged history teacher about to lose his job and to have his wife committed to a mental hospital reflects on his difficult life growing up in England's Fen district. **Adaptation:** *Waterland* (Fine Line, 1992). Dir: Stephen Gyllenhaal. Scr: Peter Prince. Cast: Jeremy Irons (Tom), Sinead Cusack (Mary), Callum Dixon (Freddie). VHS.

4859. *Watermelon* (Marian Keyes, 1995). Irish novel about a young woman who gives birth and is left by her husband on the same day. She leaves London and goes to live with her parents and younger sisters in Dublin, where she struggles to raise her child and to become emotionally independent. **Adaptation:** *Watermelon* (ITV, 2003 TV Movie). Dir: Kieron J. Walsh. Scr: Colin Bateman. Cast: Anna Friel (Claire), Brenda Fricker (Teresa), Ciaran McMenamin (Adam), Sean McGinley (Joe).

4860. *Watership Down* (Richard Adams, 1972). Fable about a family of rabbits who, after the destruction of their warren, find a new home protected from human and animal predators.

Adaptation: *Watership Down* (AVCO Embassy, 1978). Dir: Martin Rosen. Scr: Martin Rosen. Cast: voices of John Hurt (Hazel), Richard Briers (Fiver), Michael Graham Cox (Bigwig), John Bennett (Holly), Ralph Richardson (Chief Rabbit), Simon Cadell (Blackberry), Roy Kinnear (Pipkin), Denholm Elliott (Cowslip). Notes: An animated feature film for adults. DVD, VHS. Notes: The book also inspired a Canadian TV series in 1999 (DVD, VHS).

4861. *Way for a Sailor* (Albert Richard Wetjen, 1928). A British sailor tries to court a working-class London woman, but she mistrusts sailors and rejects his advances. **Adaptation:** *Way for a Sailor* (MGM, 1930). Dir: Sam Wood. Scr: W. L. River, Laurence Stallings. Cast: John Gilbert (Jack), Wallace Beery (Tripod), Jim Tully (Ginger), Leila Hyams (Joan).

4862. *Way of a Gaucho* (Herbert Childs, 1948). In the nineteenth century, an cowboy in Argentina struggles to survive in a savage land. **Adaptation:** *Way of a Gaucho* (20th Century–Fox, 1952). Dir: Jacques Tourneur. Scr: Philip Dunne. Cast: Rory Calhoun (Martin), Gene Tierney (Teresa), Richard Boone (Salinas), Hugh Marlowe (Miguel), Everett Sloane (Falcon).

The Way of Life (see *They Call It Sin*).

4863. *A Way Through the Wood* (Nigel Balchin, 1951). When his young wife begins an affair, a man tolerates the infidelity, hoping that she will eventually get over her infatuation. The novel was adapted by Ronald Millar as a 1954 stage play titled *Waiting for Gillian*. **Adaptation:** *Separate Lives* (Celador, 2004). Dir: Julian Fellowes. Scr: Julian Fellowes. Cast: Linda Bassett (Maggie), Rupert Everett (William), John Neville (Rawston), Hermione Norris (Priscilla), Emily Watson (Anne Manning), Tom Wilkinson (James).

4864. *The Way Through the Woods* (Colin Dexter, 1992, Golden Dagger Award of the British Crime Writers Association). The tenth installment in Dexter's popular thirteen-novel series (1975–2000) featuring Chief Inspector Endeavour Morse of Oxford, England. On vacation at a seaside hotel, Morse becomes involved in the kidnapping of an exchange student. **Adaptation:** *Inspector Morse: The Way Through the Woods* (ITV/PBS, 1995 TV Movie series). Dir: John Madden. Scr: Russell Lewis. Cast: John Thaw (Morse), Kevin Whately (Sergeant Lewis), James Grout (Superintendent Strange), Clare Holman (Dr. Hobson). DVD, VHS.

4865. *The Way to Dusty Death* (Alistair MacLean, 1973). A race-car driver puts his life in danger when he investigates a series of mysterious accidents at the track. **Adaptation:** *The Way to Dusty Death* (CBS, 1995 TV Movie). Dir: Geoffrey Reeve. Scr: Paul Wheeler, Christopher Wicking. Cast: Linda Hamilton (Beth), Simon MacCorkindale (Johnny), Uwe Ochsenknecht (Gerhard), Anthony Valentine (James).

4866. *The Way to the Gold* (Wilbur Steele, 1955). A former convict searches for his hidden gold and is pursued by other thieves who are also after the loot. **Adaptation:** *The Way to the Gold* (20th Century–Fox, 1957). Dir: Robert D. Webb. Scr: Wendell Mayes. Cast: Jeffrey Hunter (Joe), Sheree North (Hank), Barry Sullivan (Marshal Hannibal), Walter Brennan (Uncle George), Neville Brand (Williams).

The Way to the Stars (see "For Johnny").

4867. *The Way We Were* (Arthur Laurents, 1972). Romantic story about the marriage of an upper-class writer and a Jewish political activist spanning three decades. **Adaptation:** *The Way We Were* (Columbia, 1973). Dir: Sydney Pollack. Scr: Arthur Laurents. Cast: Barbra Streisand (Katie), Robert Redford (Hubbell), Bradford Dillman (J .J.), Lois Chiles (Carol Ann), Patrick O'Neal (George Bissinger), Viveca Lindfors (Paula Reisner). Notes: Academy Awards for Best Musical Score and Song, and nominations for Best Actress (Steisand), Cinematography, Art Direction, and Costume Design; Golden Globe Award for Best Song and nomination for Best Actress (Steisand). DVD, VHS.

4868. *The Way West* (A. B. Guthrie, Jr., 1949, Pulitzer Prize). In Missouri in 1843, a former senator and a scout lead a group of settlers across hostile Indian territory. **Adaptation:** *The Way West* (United Artists, 1967). Dir: Andrew V. McLaglen. Scr: Mitch Lindemann, Ben Maddow. Cast: Kirk Douglas (Senator Tadlock), Robert Mitchum (Summers), Richard Widmark (Evans), Lola Albright (Becky), Sally Field (Mercy). VHS.

4869. *The Wayward Bus* (John Steinbeck, 1947). Assorted passengers on a bus are stranded on a farm after a landslide. **Adaptation:** *The Wayward Bus* (20th Century–Fox, 1957). Dir: Victor Vicas. Scr: Ivan Moffat. Cast: Joan Collins (Alice), Jayne Mansfield (Camille), Dan Dailey (Ernest), Rick Jason (Johnny).

We Are in the Navy Now (see *We Joined the Navy*).

4870. *We Are Not Alone* (James Hilton, 1937). Symbolic anti-war novel about a rural doctor who takes in a troubled young woman as a governess and is later accused of adultery and murder when his shrewish wife is killed. **Adaptation:** *We Are Not Alone* (Warner, 1939). Dir: Edmund Goulding. Scr: James Hilton, Milton Krims. Cast: Paul Muni (Dr. Newcome), Jane Bryan (Leni), Flora Robson (Jessica), Raymond Severn (Gerald). VHS.

4871. *We Are Seven* (Una Troy, 1955). Comic novel about a poor Irish dressmaker with six illegitimate children, each with a different father. **Adaptation:** *She Didn't Say No!* (Seven Arts, 1958). Dir: Cyril Frankel. Scr: T. J. Morrison. Cast: Eileen Herlie (Bridget), Perlita Neilson (Mary), Wilfred Downing (Tommy), Anne Dickins (Poppy).

4872. "We Can Remember It For You Wholesale" (Philip K. Dick, 1966). Science-fiction story about a man whose virtual memories cause him to have disturbing dreams. He eventually discovers that he is actually an agent whose job it is to battle a powerful madman on Mars. The short story was first published in *Fantasy and Science Fiction* magazine in April 1966. **Adaptation:** *Total Recall* (TriStar, 1990). Dir: Paul Verhoeven. Scr: Ronald Shusett, Dan O'Bannon, Gary Goldman. Cast: Arnold Schwarzenegger (Quaid/Hauser), Rachel Ticotin (Melina), Sharon Stone (Lori), Ronny Cox (Vilos), Michael Ironside (Richter). DVD, VHS. Notes The story and film also inspired a 1999 television series on Showtime (DVD, VHS).

4873. *We Joined the Navy* (John Winton, 1959). The comic adventures of a naval commander and three cadets in the Mediterranean. **Adaptation:** *We Joined the Navy*; broadcast on American television as *We Are in the Navy Now* (Warner, 1962). Dir: Wendy Toye. Scr: Howard Dimsdale (writing as Arthur Dales). Cast: Kenneth More (Commander Badger), Lloyd Nolan (Ryan), Joan O'Brien (Carol), Mischa Auer (the Colonel).

We Live Again (see *Resurrection* by Leo Tolstoy).

4874. *We of the Never Never* (Jeannie Gunn [writing as Mrs. Aeneas Gunn], 1908). Memoir of a courageous woman who became a pioneer for operating an isolated cattle ranch in Australia's North Territory in 1900. **Adaptation:** *We of the Never Never* (Triumph, 1982). Dir: Igor Auzins. Scr: Peter Schreck. Cast: Angela Punch McGregor (Jeannie), Arthur Dignam (Aeneas), Martin Vaughan (Dan), Lewis Fitz-Gerald (Jack), John

Jarratt (Dandy). Notes: Australian Film Institiute Award for Best Cinematography and nominations for Best Picture, Screenplay, Actress (McGregor), Musical Score, and Costume Design. VHS.

4875. *We Only Kill Each Other: The Life and Bad Times of Bugsy Siegel* (Dean Jennings, 1967). Biography of Benjamin "Bugsy" Siegel (1906–1947) from street hoodlum to inventor of Las Vegas. **Adaptation:** *Bugsy* (TriStar, 1991). Dir: Barry Levinson. Scr: James Toback. Cast: Warren Beatty (Siegel), Annette Bening (Virginia), Harvey Keitel (Cohen), Ben Kingsley (Lansky), Elliott Gould (Greenberg), Joe Mantegna (George Raft). Notes: Harvey Keitel, who plays mobster Mickey Cohen in the film, played Bugsy Siegel in the 1994 television movie *The Virginia Hill Story*, about Siegel's girlfriend in the 1940's. Academy Awards for Best Art Direction and Costume Design, and nominations for Best Picture, Director, Screenplay, Actor (Beatty), Supporting Actors (Keitel and Kingsley), Musical Score, and Cinematography; Golden Globe Award for Best Picture and nominations for Best Director, Screenplay, Actor (Beatty), Actress (Bening), Supporting Actors (Kingsley and Keitel), and Musical Score; National Board of Review Award for Best Actor (Beatty). DVD, VHS.

4876. "We So Seldom Look on Love" (Barbara Gowdy, 1992). A young woman with a long-time sexual attraction to the dead gets a job at a funeral home, where she meets a man who shares her obsession. The story was the title piece in Gowdy's 1992 short-story collection. **Adaptation:** *Kissed* (Goldwyn, 1996). Dir: Lynne Stopkewich. Scr: Angus Fraser, Lynne Stopkewich. Cast: Molly Parker (Sandra), Peter Outerbridge (Matt), Jay Brazeau (Mr. Wallis). Notes: Genie Award (Canada) for Best Actress (Parker) and nominations for Best Picture, Director, Screenplay, Actor (Outerbridge), Cinematography, and Musical Score. VHS.

4877. *We the Living* (Ayn Rand [pseudonym for Alyssa Rosenbaum], 1936). Rand's first novel is set in Soviet Russia in the 1920's and concerns an anticommunist woman who has an affair with a party official in order to save the life of her fugitive lover. **Adaptation:** *We the Living* (1942; re-released 1986). Dir: Goffredo Alessandrini. Scr: Corrado Alvaro, Anton Giulio Majano, Orio Vergani. Cast: Alida Valli (Kira), Fosco Giachetti (Andrei), Rossano Brazzi (Leo), Emilio Cigoli (Pavel), Giovanni Grasso (Stephan). Notes: Originally produced as two Italian films, *Addio, Kira* and *Noi Vivi*, in 1942, the films were banned in

Mussolini's Italy for their anti-fascist theme. The current release, which brings the two earlier movies together as a single film, was issued in 1986. DVD, VHS.

4878. *We Think the World of You* (J. R. Ackerley, 1960). Set in London in the 1950's, an autobiographical novel about a middle-aged British homosexual who binds with his former lover's dog. **Adaptation:** *We Think the World of You* (Cinecom, 1988). Dir: Colin Gregg. Scr: Hugh Stoddart. Cast: Alan Bates (Frank), Max Wall (Tom), Liz Smith (Millie), Frances Barber (Megan). VHS.

4879. *We Were Soldiers Once ... and Young* (Harold G. Moore and Joseph L. Galloway, 1992). The true story of Lieutenant Hal Moore, who led his men in the America's first bloody engagement in Vietnam in 1965. **Adaptation:** *We Were Soldiers* (Paramount, 2002). Dir: Randall Wallace. Scr: Randall Wallace. Cast: Mel Gibson (Hal), Madeleine Stowe (Julie), Greg Kinnear (Bruce), Sam Elliott (Basil), Chris Klein (Jack), Keri Russell (Barbara), Barry Pepper (Joe). DVD, VHS.

We Were Strangers (see *Rough Sketch*).

4880. *We Were the Mulvaneys* (Joyce Carol Oates, 1996). The portrait of a happy family torn apart by the rape of their daughter, setting in motion a chain of tragic events. **Adaptation:** *We Were the Mulvaneys* (Lifetime, 2002 TV Movie). Dir: Peter Werner. Scr: Joyce Eliason, Peter Silverman, Nancy Dalton Silverman. Cast: Beau Bridges (Michael), Blythe Danner (Corinne), Tammy Blanchard (Marianne), Thomas Guiry (Judd), Jacob Pitts (Patrick), Mark Famiglietti (Mike, Jr.). Notes: Emmy nominations for Outstanding Actor (Bridges), Actress (Danner), and Musical Score. DVD, VHS.

The Weak and the Wicked (see *Who Lie in Goal*).

4881. *Weapon* (Robert Mason, 1989). Science-fiction novel about an android solider who refuses to murder innocent people and is targeted for destruction by the military. **Adaptation:** *Solo* (Triumph, 1996). Dir: Norberto Barba. Scr: David Corley. Cast: Mario Van Peebles (Solo), Barry Corbin (General Haynes), William Sadler (Colonel Madden), Jaime Gomez (Sergeant Lorenzo). DVD, VHS.

4882. *The Weather in the Streets* (Rosamond Lehmann, 1936). In the sequel to Lehmann's 1932 novel *Invitation to the Waltz*, a woman's marriage breaks down, and she soon finds herself involved in an illicit secret love affair with a man she knew years earlier. **Adaptation:** *The Weather in the Streets* (BBC, 1983 TV Movie). Dir: Gavin Millar. Scr: Julian Mitchell. Cast: Michael York (Rollo), Lisa Eichhorn (Olivia), Joanna Lumley (Kate), Rosalind Ayres (Etty). DVD, VHS.

Web of Evidence (see *Beyond This Place*).

4883. *The Wedding* (Dorothy West, 1995). In an upscale African-American community on Martha's Vineyard in 1953, a young woman from a prominent family causes an uproar when she decides to marry a white jazz musician from New York. The novel was written by the last surviving writer of the Harlem Renaissance. **Adaptation:** *The Wedding* (Harpo, 1998 TV Movie). Dir: Charles Burnett. Scr: Lisa Jones. Cast: Halle Berry (Shelby), Eric Thal (Meade), Lynn Whitfield (Corinne), Carl Lumbly (Lute).

The Wedding Date (see *Asking for Trouble*).

The Wedding Gift (see *Diana's Story*).

Wee Geordie (see *Geordie*).

4884. "Wee Willie Winkie" (Rudyard Kipling, 1888). A child wins the heart of hardened British soliders serving in India in the nineteenth century. The short story was included in Kipling's 1888 collection *Wee Willie Winkie and Other Stories.* **Adaptation:** *Wee Willie Winkie* (20th Century–Fox, 1937). Dir: John Ford. Scr: Julien Josephson, Ernest Pascal. Cast: Shirley Temple (Priscilla), Victor McLaglen (Sergeant MacDuff), C. Aubrey Smith (Colonel Williams), June Lang (Joyce). DVD, VHS.

4885. "Weeds" (Stephen King, 1976). A lonely farmer discovers a meteorite that turns anything it touches into plants. The short story originally appeared in *Cavalier* magazine in May 1979 and was subsequently included under the title "The Lonesome Death of Jordy Verrill" in King's 1982 paperback comic strip *Creepshow*, a tie-in to the film, which was released the same year. **Adaptation:** *Creepshow* (Warner, 1982). Dir: George A. Romero. Scr: Stephen King. Cast: Bingo O'Malley (Jordy's father), Viveca Lindfors (Bedelia), Leslie Nielsen (Vickers), E. G. Marshall (Upson). Notes: The film, a tribute to the E. C. Comics of the 1950's, includes five stories: ""Father's Day," "The Lonesome Death of Jordy Verrill," "Something to Tide You Over," "The Crate," and "They're Creeping Up on You." DVD, VHS. See also "The Crate."

Weekend at the Waldorf (see *Grand Hotel*).

4886. *Week-end Marriage* (Faith Baldwin, 1932). Comic story about a married couple who bicker over money. **Adaptation:** *Week-end Marriage* (Warner, 1932). Dir: Thornton Freeland. Scr: Sheridan Gibney. Cast: Loretta Young (Lola), Norman Foster (Ken), Aline MacMahon (Agnes), George Brent (Peter).

Weekend at Shadows (see *The Reckoning*).

Weep No More (see *Tears Before Bedtime*).

4887. *Weep No More, My Lady* (Mary Higgins Clark, 1987). A woman whose sister died mysteriously confronts a group of people who had motive to kill her, thereby placing herself in danger. **Adaptation:** *Weep No More, My Lady* (CBS, 1992 TV Movie). Dir: Michel Andrieu. Scr: Michel Andrieu, Leila Basen, Robert Levine. Cast: Kristin Scott Thomas (Elisabeth), Daniel J. Travanti (Ted), Francesca Annis (Leila). VHS.

4888. *The Weight of Water* (Anita Shreve, 1997). A photojournalist researching the ax murder of two women in 1873 returns to the scene of the crime, an island near New Hampshire. There her poet-husband becomes involved with his brother's girlfriend. **Adaptation:** *The Weight of Water* (Manifest/Palomar, 2000). Dir: Kathryn Bigelow. Scr: Alice Arlen, Christopher Kyle. Cast: Catherine McCormack (Jean), Sarah Polley (Maren), Sean Penn (Thomas), Josh Lucas (Rich), Elizabeth Hurley (Adaline), Ciaran Hinds (Louis). DVD, VHS.

Weird Woman (see *Conjure Wife*).

4889. *Welcome to Hard Times* (E. L. Doctorow, 1960). Doctorow's first novel, a Western about a mysterious outlaw who brutalizes a small town and the people who take revenge on him. **Adaptation:** *Welcome to Hard Times*; released in the UK as *Killer on a Horse* (MGM, 1967). Dir: Burt Kennedy. Scr: Burt Kennedy. Cast: Henry Fonda (Mayor Blue), Janice Rule (Molly), Keenan Wynn (Zar), Janis Paige (Ada).

Welcome to Sarajevo (see *Natasha's Story*).

4890. *Welcome to the Club* (Clement Biddle Wood, 1966). Comic World War II tale about a military morale officer who battles his superiors over their show of prejudice in denying an African-American singing group living quarters on their USO tour. **Adaptation:** *Welcome to the Club* (Columbia, 1970). Dir: Walter Shenson. Scr: Clement Biddle Wood. Cast: Brian Foley (Andrew), Jack Warden (General Strapp), Andy Jarrell (Fairfax), Kevin O'Connor (Harrison).

4891. *Welcome to the Monkey House* (Kurt Vonnegut, 1968). A collection of previously published short stories by the author of *Slaughterhouse-Five*. **Adaptation:** *Kurt Vonnegut's Monkey House* (Showtime, 1991–92 TV series). Dir: Allan King, Paul Shapiro, Brad Turner, Wayne Towell. Scr: Stan Daniels, Jeremy Hole, Chris Haddock. Cast: Frank Langella (Demarest), Madeline Kahn (Anne), Stuart Margolin (Alan), David Lereaney (Congressman White). Notes: The series featured Vonnegut introducing adaptations of seven of his short stories: "Next Door," "The Euphio Question," "All the King's Horses," "EPICAC," "Fortitude," "More Stately Mansions," and "The Foster Portfolio." CableACE Awards for Best Drama Special ("All the King's Horses") and Actor (Langella in "Fortitude"). VHS. See also "DP," "Harrison Bergeron," and "Who Am I This Time?"

Welcome to Woop Wop (see *The Dead Heart*).

4892. *The Well* (Elizabeth Jolley, 1986, Miles Franklin Award, Australia). The story of the sexual awakening of two women who live together on an isolated farm in western Australia. **Adaptation:** *The Well* (Cowboy, 1997). Dir: Samantha Lang. Scr: Laura Jones. Cast: Pamela Rabe (Hester), Miranda Otto (Katherine), Paul Chubb (Harry), Frank Wilson (Francis), Steve Jacobs (Rod). Notes: Australian Film Institute Awards for Best Screenplay, Actress (Rabe), and Production Design, and nominations for Best Picture, Director, Cinematography, Musical Score, Editing, Costume Design, and Sound; Cannes Film Festival Golden Palm nomination for Best Director. DVD, VHS.

4893. *Well Schooled in Murder* (Elizabeth George, 1990). In the third installment in George's series of novels featuring Inspector Thomas Lynley of Scotland Yard, the British policeman investigates the murder of a young student at a public school. **Adaptation:** *The Inspector Lynley Mysteries: Well Schooled in Murder* (BBC/PBS, 2002 TV Movie series). Dir: Robert Young. Scr: Simon Block. Cast: Nathaniel Parker (Inspector Lynley), Sharon Small (Detective Havers), John Sessions (Corntel), Lise Stevenson (Patsy). DVD, VHS.

4894. *The Wench Is Dead* (Colin Dexter, 1989, Golden Dagger Award of the British Crime Writers Association). The eighth installment in Dexter's popular thirteen-novel series (1975–2000) featuring Chief Inspector Endeavour Morse of Oxford, England. In this book, Morse becomes convinced that the men executed for the murder of a woman were innocent, and he launches a new

investigation. **Adaptation:** *Inspector Morse The Wench Is Dead* (ITV/PBS, 1998 TV Movie series). Dir: Robert Knights. Scr: Malcolm Bradbury. Cast: John Thaw (Morse), Kevin Whately (Sergeant Lewis), James Grout (Superintendent Strange), Clare Holman (Dr. Hobson). DVD, VHS.

Went the Day Well? (see "The Lieutenant Died Last").

4895. *The Werewolf of Paris* (Guy Endore, 1933). Set amind historical events in nineteenth-century Paris, this classic early werewolf novel concerns a beggar who rapes a household servant and the werewolf child born of their union. **Adaptation:** *The Curse of the Werewolf* (Hammer/Universal International, 1961). Dir: Terence Fisher. Scr: John Elder. Cast: Clifford Evans (Don Corledo), Oliver Reed (Leon), Catherine Feller (Cristina). VHS.

West 11 (see *The Furnished Room*).

4896. *West of the Pecos* (Zane Grey, 1931). In Texas after the Civil War, a man and his daughter are aided by an outlaw and become involved in his problems. The novel was serialized in *American Magazine* beginning in August 1931 and published as a novel in 1937. **Adaptation 1:** *West of the Pecos* (RKO, 1935). Dir: Phil Rosen. Scr: Milton Krims, John Twist. Cast: Richard Dix (Pecos Smith), Martha Sleeper (Rill), Samuel S. Hinds (Colonel Lambeth), Fred Kohler (Sawtelle). **Adaptation 2:** *West of the Pecos* (RKO, 1945). Dir: Edward Killy. Scr: Norman Houston. Cast: Robert Mitchum (Pecos Smith), Barbara Hale (Rill), Richard Martin (Chito), Thurston Hall (Colonel Lambeth). DVD, VHS.

4897. *Western Union* (Zane Grey, 1939). Western about an outlaw's attempts to stop the construction of the company's cross-country communications cables. **Adaptation:** *Western Union* (20th Century–Fox, 1941). Dir: Fritz Lang. Scr: Robert Carson. Cast: Robert Young (Blake), Randolph Scott (Shaw), Dean Jagger (Creighton), Virginia Gilmore (Sue), John Carradine (Doc Murdoch).

The Westland Case (see *Headed for a Hearse*).

4898. *Westward Passage* (Margaret Ayer Barnes, 1931). Years after divorcing his wife, who remarried in the meantime, a writer meets her in Europe and tries to rekindle their romance. **Adaptation:** *Westward Passage* (RKO, 1932). Dir: Robert Milton. Scr: Bradley King, Humphrey

Pearson. Cast: Ann Harding (Olivia), Laurence Olivier (Nick), Zasu Pitts (Mrs. Truesdale), Irving Pichel (Harry).

4899. *The Wet Parade* (Upton Sinclair, 1931). Set during Prohibition, a story about how alcohol abuse affects two families. **Adaptation:** *The Wet Parade* (MGM, 1932). Dir: Victor Fleming. Scr: John L. Mahin. Cast: Dorothy Jordan (Maggie), Robert Young (Kip), Lewis Stone (Roger), Walter Huston (Pow), Jimmy Durante (Abe), Myrna Loy (Eileen).

4900. *Whale Music* (Paul Quarrington, 1989, Canadian Governor General's Literary Award). Canadian novel about a girl who arrives at an aging and disillusioned rock musician's coastal home and inspires him to make music again. **Adaptation:** *Whale Music* (Alliance/Seventh Art, 1994). Dir: Richard J. Lewis. Scr: Paul Quarrington, Richard J. Lewis. Cast: Maury Chaykin (Desmond), Cynthia Preston (Claire), Paul Gross (Daniel), Jennifer Dale (Fay). Notes: Genie Awards (Canada) for Best Actor (Chaykin), Song, Sound, and Sound Editing, and nominations for Best Picture, Director, Screenplay, and Musical Score.

4901. *Whale Rider* (Witi Ihimaera, 1987). In a native New Zealand community, a young Maori girl has to prove to her grandfather that she has the fortitude to become a tribal chief even though that role has always been reserved for men. **Adaptation:** *Whale Rider* (Newmarket, 2002). Dir: Niki Caro. Scr: Niki Caro. Cast: Keisha Castle-Hughes (Paikea), Rawiri Paratene (Koro), Vicky Haughton (Nanny), Cliff Curtis (Porourangi), Grant Roa (Uncle Rawiri), Mana Taumaunu (Hemi). Notes: New Zealand Film and Television Awards for Best Picture, Director, Screenplay, Actress (Castle-Hughes), Supporting Actor (Curtis), Supporting Actress (Haughton), Juvenile Performance (Taumauna), Musical Score, and Costume Design, and nominations for Best Actor (Paratene), Supporting Actor (Roa), Production Design, Cinematography, Editing, and Makeup; Academy Award nomination for Best Actress (Castle-Hughes); Australian Film Institute and Independent Spirit Award nominations for Best Picture. DVD, VHS.

What a Carve Up (see *The Ghoul*).

What Became of Jack and Jill? (see *The Ruthless Ones*).

4902. "What Beckoning Ghost" (Harold Lawlor, 1948). A concert pianist begins to fear that her husband is trying to kill her. After her death, she returns to haunt him. The short story was published in the July 1948 issue of *Weird Tales*. **Adaptation:** *Dominique*; also released as *Dominique Is Dead* and as *Avenging Spirit* (Viacom, 1978). Dir: Michael Anderson. Scr: Edward Abraham, Valerie Abraham. Cast: Cliff Robertson (David), Jean Simmons (Dominique), Jenny Agutter (Ann), Simon Ward (Tony), Ron Moody (Dr. Rogers), Judy Geeson (Marjorie). DVD, VHS.

4903. *What Becomes of the Broken Hearted?* (Alan Duff, 1996, Montana New Zealand Book Award for Fiction). The sequel to Duff's 1990 novel *Once Were Warriors* features a Maori family in Auckland, New Zealand, whose son is killed in a gang fight. The family tragedy forces the abusive father to reexamine his troubled relationship with his wife and children. **Adaptation:** *What Becomes of the Broken Hearted?* (New Zealand Film Commission, 1999). Dir: Ian Mune. Scr: Alan Duff. Cast: Nancy Brunning (Tania), Temuera Morrison (Jake), Taungaroa Emile (Boogie), Clint Eruera (Sonny), Joseph Kairau (Huata Heke), Rena Owen (Beth), Hope Thompsons (Polly). Notes: New Zealand Film and TV Awards for Best Director, Screenplay, Actor (Morrison), Actress (Brunning), Supporting Actor (Eruera), Musical Score, Cinematography, Costume Design, and Special Effects. DVD, VHS. See also *Once Were Warriors*.

4904. *What Changed Charley Farthing* (John Harris [pseudonym for Mark Hebden], 1965). Comic tale of a philandering Irish sailor trying to escape from a small tropical island to avoid a jealous husband. **Adaptation:** *What Changed Charley Farthing*; released in the U.S. as *The Bananas Boat* (Stirling Gold, 1974). Dir: Sidney Hayers. Scr: John Harris, Jack Seddon. Cast: Hayley Mills (Jenny), Doug McClure (Charley), Lionel Jeffries (Houlihan), Warren Mitchell (MacGregor). VHS.

4905. *What? ... Dead Again* (Neil B. Schulman, 1979). On the way to a new job in Hollywood, a plastic surgeon has an accident in a small South Carolina town and is sentenced to deliver needed medical attention to the citizens of the town. After carrying out his sentence, his original plans change. The novel was subsequently reissued under the title *Doc Hollywood*. **Adaptation:** *Doc Hollywood* (Warner, 1991). Dir: Michael Caton-Jones. Scr: Laurian Leggett, Jeffrey Price, Peter S. Seaman, Daniel Pyne. Cast: Michael J. Fox (Dr. Stone), Julie Warner (Vialula), Barnard

Hughes (Dr. Hogue), Woody Harrelson (Hank), David Ogden Stiers (Mayor Nicholson), Frances Sternhagen (Lillian), George Hamilton (Dr. Halberstrom), Bridget Fonda (Nancy). DVD, VHS.

4906. *What Do You Care What Other People Think?: Further Adventures of a Curious Character* (Richard Feynman, 1988). The follow-up volume to the Nobel laureate's 1985 book, *Surely You're Joking, Mr. Feynman*, offers more observations on science in our time and describes his relationship with his first wife, Arlene, whom he married even though she had a terminal illness. **Adaptation:** *Infinity* (First Look, 1996). Dir: Matthew Broderick. Scr: Patricia Broderick, Cast: Matthew Broderick (Feynman), Patricia Arquette (Arlene), Peter Riegert (Mel). Notes: The screenplay combines elements from two of Feynman's books: *Surely You're Joking, Mr. Feynman* (1985) and *What Do You Care What Other People Think?* (1988). DVD, VHS. See also *Surely You're Joking, Mr. Feynman!*

4907. *What Dreams May Come* (Richard Matheson, 1978). A man is killed in a car crash and goes to heaven, a wonderful place where he meets his children, who had died earlier. When his despairing wife commits suicide, however, she does not join them in heaven, and he must make the journey to hell to find her. **Adaptation:** *What Dreams May Come* (PolyGram, 1998). Dir: Vincent Ward. Scr: Ron Bass. Cast: Robin Williams (Chris), Cuba Gooding, Jr. (Albert), Annabella Sciorra (Annie), Max von Sydow (the Tracker). DVD, VHS.

Whatever Happened to Aunt Alice? (see *The Forbidden Garden*).

4908. *What Ever Happened to Baby Jane?* (Henry Farrell, 1960). A demented former child star torments her crippled sister, a Hollywood star and well-known adult actress, who lives with her. The novel was the basis for a musical play in 2002. **Adaptation 1:** *What Ever Happened to Baby Jane?* (Warner, 1962). Dir: Robert Aldrich. Scr: Lukas Heller. Cast: Bette Davis (Jane), Joan Crawford (Blanche), Victor Buono (Edwin), Wesley Addy (Marty). Notes: Academy Award for Best Costume Design and nominations for Best Actress (Davis), Supporting Actor (Buono), Cinematography, and Sound; Golden Globe nominations for Best Actress (Davis) and Supporting Actor (Buono). DVD, VHS. **Adaptation 2:** *What Ever Happened to Baby Jane?* (ABC, 1991 TV Movie). Dir: David Greene. Scr: Brian Taggert. Cast: Vanessa Redgrave (Blanche Hudson), Lynn Redgrave (Jane), Bruce A. Young (Dominick), Amy Steel (Connie). VHS.

What Lola Wants (see *The Year the Yankees Lost the Pennant*).

4909. *What Love Sees* (Susan Vreeland, 1988). A novel based on a true story about a blind couple from different social classes who fall in love and marry during World War II and go on to establish a successful ranch. **Adaptation:** *What Love Sees* (Rosemont, 1996 TV Movie). Dir: Michael Switzer. Scr: Robert L. Freedman. Cast: Richard Thomas (Gordon), Annabeth Gish (Jean), August Schellenberg (Earl), Kathleen Noone (Sarah). DVD, VHS.

What Shall It Profit? (see *Steel Saraband*).

4910. *What the Deaf-Mute Heard* (G. D. Gearino, 1996). In 1945, a young boy watches as his mother is abducted and murdered in a Georgia bus station. Refusing to speak or acknowledge those speaking to him, the boy is mistakenly diagnosed as deaf and mute. **Adaptation:** *What the Deaf Man Heard* (Hallmark, 1997 TV Movie). Dir: John Kent Harrison. Scr: Robert W. Lenski. Cast: Matthew Modine (Sammy), Claire Bloom (Mrs. Tynan), Judith Ivey (Lucille), James Earl Jones (Archibald), Jerry O'Connell (Reverend Pruitt), Bernadette Peters (Helen), Tom Skerritt (Norm). Notes: Emmy Award for Outstanding Cinematography and nominations for Outstanding Movie and Supporting Actress (Ivey); Golden Globe nomination for Best Actor in a Television Movie (Modine). DVD, VHS.

What's a Nice Girl Like You...? (see *Shirley*).

4911. *What's Eating Gilbert Grape?* (Peter Hedges, 1991). A depressed young man caring for his retarded brother, obese mother, and troubled sisters falls in love with a woman but has difficulty finding the time to see her. **Adaptation:** *What's Eating Gilbert Grape* (1993). Dir: Lasse Hallstrom. Scr: Peter Hedges. Cast: Johnny Depp (Gilbert), Leonardo Di Caprio (Arnie), Juliette Lewis (Becky), Mary Steenburgen (Betty). Notes: National Board of Review Award for Best Supporting Actor (Di Caprio); Academy Award and Golden Globe nominations for Best Supporting Actor (Di Caprio). DVD, VHS.

What's Love Got to Do With It? (see *I, Tina*).

4912. *What's the Worst That Could Happen?* (Donald E. Westlake, 1996). A rich man catches a thief in his home and takes his lucky ring. The thief and his friends plot an elaborate scheme for revenge. **Adaptation:** *What's the Worst That Could Happen?* (MGM, 2001). Dir: Sam Weisman. Scr: Matthew Chapman. Cast: Martin Lawrence (Kevin), Danny De Vito (Max), John Leguizamo (Berger), Glenne Headly (Gloria), Bernie Mac (Uncle Jack), Nora Dunn (Lutetia). DVD, VHS.

4913. *The Wheel Spins* (Ethel Lina White, 1933). A young couple investigates when an elderly woman disappears on a train between Switzerland and England. **Adaptation 1:** *The Lady Vanishes* (Gaumont, 1938). Dir: Alfred Hitchcock. Scr: Sidney Gilliat, Frank Launder. Cast: Margaret Lockwood (Iris), Michael Redgrave (Gilbert), Cecil Parker (Eric), Linden Travers (Margaret). DVD, VHS. **Adaptation 2:** *The Lady Vanishes* (Hammer, 1979). Dir: Anthony Page. Scr: George Axelrod (based on the 1938 screenplay by Sidney Gilliat and Frank Launder. Cast: Elliott Gould (Robert), Cybill Shepherd (Amanda), Angela Lansbury (Miss Froy), Herbert Lom (Dr. Hartz), Ian Carmichael (Caldicott), Gerald Harper (Mr. Todhunter), Jenny Runacre (Mrs. Todhunter). DVD, VHS.

4914. *Wheels* (Arthur Hailey, 1971). The lives and romantic relationships of Detroit auto-industry executives. **Adaptation:** *Wheels* (NBC, 1978 TV Miniseries). Dir: Jerry London. Scr: Robert Hamilton, Millard Lampell, Nancy Lynn Schwartz, Hank Searls. Cast: Rock Hudson (Adam), Lee Remick (Erica), Blair Brown (Barbara), John Beck (Peter), Ralph Bellamy (Lowell).

Wheels of Terror (see *The Misfit Brigade*).

4915. *When Eight Bells Toll* (Alistair Mac-Lean, 1966). British secret service agents investigate the theft of gold from ships in the Irish Sea. **Adaptation:** *When Eight Bells Toll* (Rank, 1971). Dir: Etienne Perier. Scr: Alistair MacLean. Cast: Anthony Hopkins (Philip), Robert Morley (Uncle Arthur), Nathalie Delon (Charlotte), Jack Hawkins (Sir Anthony). DVD, VHS.

4916. *When Heaven and Earth Changed Place* (Le Ly Hayslip and Jay Wurts, 1989). True account of a Vietnamese woman's painful displacement from her small village and the hardships she had to endure both in Vietnam and in the United States after the war. **Adaptation:** *Heaven & Earth* (Warner, 1993). Dir: Oliver Stone. Scr: Oliver Stone. Cast: Haing S. Ngor (Papa), Bussaro Sanruck (Le Ly as a child), Supak Pititam (the Buddhist Monk), Joan Chen (Mama).

Notes: Stone's screenplay is based Le Ly and James Hayslip's *Child of War, Woman and Peace* and on Le Ly Hayslip and Jay Wurts' *When Heaven and Earth Changed Place*. DVD, VHS. See also *Child of War, Woman of Peace*.

When I Fall in Love (see *Everybody's All-American*).

4917. *When Knighthood Was in Flower* (Charles Major, 1898). Fictionalized account of the young Mary Tudor (1496–1533) and Henry VIII's opposition to her marriage to Captain of the Guard Charles Brandon in 1515. The novel was adapted for the Broadway stage in 1901 by Paul Lester. **Silent Films:** 1908 and 1922. **Adaptation:** *The Sword and the Rose*; broadcast on television as *When Knighthood Was in Flower* (Disney/RKO, 1953). Dir: Ken Annakin. Scr: Lawrence Edward Watkin. Cast: Richard Todd (Brandon), Glynis Johns (Mary), James Robertson Justice (King Henry VIII), Michael Gough (the Duke of Buckingham). VHS.

4918. *When the Bough Breaks* (Jonathan Kellerman, 1985). In the first of Kellerman's novels featuring child psychologist Alex Delaware, the doctor works with a withdrawn young girl who may have witnessed a double murder. **Adaptation:** *When the Bough Breaks* (NBC, 1986 TV Movie). Dir: Waris Hussein. Scr: Phil Penningroth. Cast: Ted Danson (Alex), Richard Masur (Milo), Rachel Ticotin (Lisa), James Noble (Dr. Towle). VHS.

When the Devil Commands (see *The Edge of Running Water*).

When the Door Opened (see *Escape*).

4919. *When the Legends Die* (Hal Borland, 1963). An aging and disillusioned rodeo star befriends a young Native American and teaches him the trade. **Adaptation:** *When the Legends Die* (20th Century–Fox, 1972). Dir: Stuart Millar. Scr: Robert Dozier. Cast: Richard Widmark (Red), Frederic Forrest (Tom), Luana Anders (Mary), Vito Scotti (Meo). VHS.

When the Whales Came (see *Why the Whales Came*).

4920. *When the Wind Blows* (Raymond Briggs, 1982). Children's illustrated book about an elderly couple and their preparations for what they believe is imminent nuclear war. **Adaptation:** *When the Wind Blows* (King's Road, 1986). Dir: Jimmy T. Murakami. Scr: Raymond Briggs.

Cast: voices of Peggy Ashcroft (Hilda), John Mills (Jim). Notes: An animated feature film. VHS.

When Time Ran Out (see *The Day The World Ended*).

4921. *When Worlds Collide* (Philip Wylie and Edwin Balmer, 1933). When he realizes that a planet is on a collision course with Earth, an astronomer builds a space ship with which to escape. **Adaptation:** *When Worlds Collide* (Paramount, 1951). Dir: Rudolph Mate. Scr: Sydney Boehm. Cast: Richard Derr (David), Barbara Rush (Joyce), Peter Hansen (Dr. Drake), John Hoyt (Sydney). Notes: Academy Award for Best Special Effects and nomination for Best Cinematography. DVD, VHS.

4922. *Where Angels Fear to Tread* (E. M. Forster, 1905). A young middle-class British woman marries a poor Italian on a trip to Italy. When she dies in childbirth, her parents go to Italy to claim the child. **Adaptation:** *Where Angels Fear to Tread* (Fine Line, 1991). Dir: Charles Sturridge. Scr: Tim Sullivan, Derek Granger, Charles Sturridge. Cast: Rupert Graves (Philip), Helen Mirren (Lilia), Helena Bonham Carter (Caroline), Barbara Jefford (Mrs. Herriton), Judy Davis (Harriet). DVD, VHS.

4923. *Where Are the Children?* (Mary Higgins Clark, 1975). Two children vanish, and their father soon begins to suspect his wife, whose children from a previous marriage disappeared in a similar manner nine years earlier. **Adaptation:** *Where Are the Children?* (Columbia, 1986). Dir: Bruce Malmuth. Scr: Jack Sholder. Cast: Jill Clayburgh (Nancy), Max Gail (Clay), Harley Cross (Michael), Elisabeth Harnois (Missy), Elizabeth Wilson (Dorothy), Barnard Hughes (Jonathan), Frederic Forrest (Courtney), Clifton James (Chief Coffin). VHS.

4924. "Where Are You Going, Where Have You Been?" (Joyce Carol Oates, 1966). A confused teenager becomes involved with a dangerous psychopath. The short story was originally published in the journal *Epoch* in 1966 and included in Oates' 1970 collection *The Wheel of Love*. **Adaptation:** *Smooth Talk* (American Playhouse, 1985). Dir: Joyce Chopra. Scr: Tom Cole. Cast: Treat Williams (Arnold), Laura Dern (Connie), Mary Kay Place (Katherine), Margaret Welsh (Laura). Notes: Sundance Film Festival Grand Prize of the Jury for Best Dramatic Film; Independent Spirit Award nominations for Best Picture, Director, Screenplay, Actress (Dern), and Actor (Williams). DVD, VHS.

Where Does It Hurt? (see *The Operator*).

4925. *Where Eagles Dare* (Alistair MacLean, 1967). During World War II, British Special Forces raid a mountaintop castle, where Nazis are holding an Allied general who has information about the imminent D-Day invasion. **Adaptation:** *Where Eagles Dare* (MGM, 1968). Dir: Brian G. Hutton. Scr: Alistair MacLean. Cast: Richard Burton (Major Smith), Clint Eastwood (Lieutenant Schaffer), Mary Ure (Mary), Patrick Wymark (Colonel Turner), Michael Hordern (Admiral Rolland). DVD, VHS.

4926. *Where Love Has Gone* (Harold Robbins, 1962). The teenaged daughter of a divorced couple is arrested and tried for killing her mother's latest lover. **Adaptation:** *Where Love Has Gone* (Paramount, 1964). Dir: Edward Dmytryk. Scr: John Michael Hayes. Cast: Susan Hayward (Valerie), Bette Davis (Mrs. Hayden), Mike Connors (Major Miller), Joey Heatherton (Danielle), Jane Greer (Marian). VHS.

4927. *Where the Boys Are* (Glendon Swarthout, 1960). On spring break, college coeds head to Florida looking for boys. **Adaptation 1:** *Where the Boys Are* (MGM, 1960). Dir: Henry Levin. Scr: George Wells. Cast: Dolores Hart (Merritt), George Hamilton (Ryder), Yvette Mimieux (Melanie), Jim Hutton (TV Thompson), Barbara Nichols (Lola), Paula Prentiss (Tuggle). DVD, VHS. **Adaptation 2:** *Where the Boys Are '84* (Columbia TriStar, 1984). Dir: Hy Averback. Scr: George Wells (1960 screenplay), Stu Krieger, Jeff Burkhart. Cast: Lisa Hartman (Jennie), Lorna Luft (Carole), Wendy Schaal (Sandra), Lynn-Holly Johnson (Laurie). VHS.

4928. *Where the Heart Is* (Billie Letts, 1995). After being abandoned by her boyfriend at an Oklahoma Wal-Mart, a pregnant teenaged girl without a home or money hides out in the store for six weeks until her baby is born. **Adaptation:** *Where the Heart Is* (20th Century–Fox, 2000). Dir: Matt Williams. Scr: Lowell Ganz, Babaloo Mandel. Cast: Natalie Portman (Novalee), Ashley Judd (Lexie), Stockard Channing (Thelma), Sally Field (Lil), Joan Cusack (Ruth). DVD, VHS.

Where the Heart Is (1998) (see *If Beale Street Could Talk*).

4929. *Where the Lilies Bloom* (Vera Cleaver and Bill Cleaver, 1969). Children's book about a group of poor Appalachian children who conceal the death of their father and fend for themselves in order to avoid being sent to an orphanage.

Adaptation: *Where the Lilies Bloom* (United Artists, 1974). Dir: William A. Graham. Scr: Earl Hamner, Jr. Cast: Julie Gholson (Mary), Jan Smithers (Devola), Matthew Burrill (Romey), Helen Harmon (Ima). VHS.

Where the River Bends (see *Bend of the Snake*).

Where the River Runs Black (see *Lazaro*).

4930. "Where the Rivers Flow North" (Howard Frank Mosher, 1978). In Vermont in 1927, a lumberjack comes into conflict with a construction company and the local government when he refuses to let them build a dam on his land. The novella is the title piece in Mosher's 1978 collection of short stories, all of them set in the same Vermont location. **Adaptation:** *Where the Rivers Flow North* (Ardustry, 1993). Dir: Jay Craven. Scr: Don Bredes, Jay Craven. Cast: Rip Torn (Noel), Tantoo Cardinal (Bangor), Bill Raymond (Wayne), Mark Margolis (New York Money), Michael J. Fox (Clayton). DVD, VHS.

Where the Sidewalk Ends (see *Night Cry*).

Where the Spies Are (see *Passport to Oblivion*).

4931. *Where There's Smoke* (Simon Beckett, 1997). Thriller about a professional woman who seeks a man to donate sperm for artificial insemination and finds herself in danger from the elegant madman who volunteers his services. **Adaptation:** *Where There's Smoke* (Carlton, 2000 TV Movie). Dir: Richard Signy. Scr: Mark Burt. Cast: Zara Turner (Kate), Nick Reding (Timothy/Dr. Turner), Rosie Rowell (Lucy), Rob Spendlove (Jack).

Where Time Began (see *Journey to the Center of the Earth*).

4932. *Where's Mommy Now?* (Rochelle Majer Krich, 1990). A wealthy doctor's wife hires a French au pair to look after their children and discovers that the young woman is her husband's lover with plans to become more. **Adaptation:** *Perfect Alibi* (Rysher, 1995). Dir: Kevin Meyer. Scr: Kevin Meyer. Cast: Teri Garr (Laney), Hector Elizondo (Detective Ryker), Alex McArthur (Keith), Lydie Denier (Janine), Kathleen Quinlan (Melanie). VHS.

4933. *Where's Poppa?* (Robert Klane, 1970). A lawyer dominated by his senile mother falls in love and tries to avoid the elderly woman's interference in his romantic affairs. **Adaptation:** *Where's Poppa?* (United Artists, 1970). Dir: Carl Reiner. Scr: Robert Klane. Cast: George Segal (Gordon), Ruth Gordon (Mrs. Hocheiser), Trish Van Devere (Louise), Ron Leibman (Sidney), Rae Allen (Gladys), Vincent Gardenia (Coach Williams). DVD, VHS.

4934. *While I Was Gone* (Sue Miller, 1999). When a man with whom she had been involved three decades earlier moves to her town, a veterinarian jeopardizes her happy family life and confronts dark secrets from her past. **Adaptation:** *While I Was Gone* (CBS, 2004 TV Movie). Dir: Mike Robe. Scr: Alan Sharp. Cast: Kirstie Alley (Jo), Peter Horton (Eli), Kim Poirier (Dana), Bill Smitrovich (Daniel).

4935. *While My Pretty One Sleeps* (Mary Higgins Clark, 1989). A boutique owner is implicated in the disappearance of a nasty gossip columnist. **Adaptation:** *While My Pretty One Sleeps* (Hallmark/Family Channel, 1997 TV Movie). Dir: Jorge Montesi. Scr: David Kinghorn, Marilyn Kinghorn. Cast: Connie Sellecca (Neeve), Beau Starr (Myles), Frankie Pellegrino (Nick).

While the City Sleeps (see *The Bloody Spur*).

4936. *While the Patient Slept* (Mignon G. Eberhart, 1930). A nurse tending to a rich man helps police catch the killer of the man's son. **Adaptation:** *While the Patient Slept* (Warner, 1935). Dir: Ray Enright. Scr: Robert N. Lee, Eugene Solow. Cast: Aline MacMahon (Sarah), Guy Kibbee (Detective O'Leary), Lyle Talbot (Ross).

4937. *The Whipping Boy* (Sid Fleischman, 1986, Newbery Medal). Children's book about the relationship that develops between a spoiled prince and an orphan boy who resembles him and who agrees to take the corporal punishments meted out for the prince's bad behavior. **Adaptation:** *The Whipping Boy* (Disney Channel, 1995 TV Movie). Dir: Sydney Macartney. Dir: Sid Fleischman (writing as Max Brindle). Cast: George C. Scott (Blind George), Kevin Conway (Hold-Your-Nose-Billy), Vincent Schiavelli (Cutwater), Nicolas Amer (Lord Chancellor), Jane Hazlegrove (Mrs. Chestney). Notes: CableACE Award for Best Children's Special. VHS.

Whirlpool (1949) (see *Methinks the Lady*).

Whirlpool (1959) (see *The Lorelei*).

4938. *Whiskey Galore!* (Compton MacKenzie, 1947). A novel based on a true story about a cargo ship that founders near an island in the Scottish Hebrides. When thousands of bottles of Scotch whiskey go down with the ship, the islanders devise ways to recover the loot. **Adaptation:** *Whisky Galore!*; released in the U.S. as *Tight Little Island* (Ealing/Universal International, 1949). Dir: Alexander Mackendrick. Scr: Compton MacKenzie, Angus MacPhail. Cast: Basil Radford (Captain Waggett), Catherine Lacey (Mrs. Waggett), Bruce Seton (Sergeant Odd), Joan Greenwood (Peggy). Notes: BAFTA nomination for Best British Film. VHS. See also *Rockets Galore!*

4939. *The Whisperers* (Robert Nicolson, 1965). A lonely old woman who lives in a fantasy world hears voices and believes that she is being watched by people with bad intentions toward her. **Adaptation:** *The Whisperers* (United Artists, 1967). Dir: Bryan Forbes. Scr: Bryan Forbes. Cast: Edith Evans (Mrs. Ross), Eric Portman (Archie), Nanette Newman (the Girl Upstairs), Gerald Sim (Conrad). Notes: BAFTA and National Board of Review Awards for Best Actress (Evans); Academy Award nomination for Best Actress (Evans); Golden Globe Award for Best Actress (Evans) and nomination for Best Picture. VHS.

4940. *Whispering Smith* (Frank. H. Spearman, 1906). Western about a railroad investigator who discovers that his friend is behind a series of robberies. **Silent Films:** 1916 and 1926. **Adaptation:** *Whispering Smith* (Paramount, 1948). Dir: Leslie Fenton. Scr: Frank Butler, Karl Kamb. Cast: Alan Ladd (Smith), Robert Preston (Sinclair), Brenda Marshall (Marian), Donald Crisp (Rebstock), William Demarest (Dansing). DVD, VHS. Notes: The book also inspired a 1961 television series on NBC and two theatrical sequels—*Whispering Smith Speaks* (1935) and *Whispering Smith Hits London* (1951).

4941. *Whispers* (Dean R. Koontz, 1980). A serial murderer who hears voices ordering him to commit homicides is killed by one of his intended victims, but apparently returns from the dead to finish his deadly work. **Adaptation:** *Whispers* (ITC, 1989). Dir: Douglas Jackson. Scr: Anita Doohan. Cast: Victoria Tennant (Hilary), Jean Le Clerc (Bruno), Chris Sarandon (Tony), Peter MacNeill (Frank). VHS.

4942. *The Whistle Blower* (John Hale, 1984). The brilliant son of a former British spy is murdered, and his father's investigation leads to a cover-up at the highest levels of government. **Adaptation:** *The Whistle Blower* (Hemdale, 1986). Dir: Simon Langton. Scr: Julian Bond. Cast: Michael Caine (Frank), James Fox (Lord), Nigel Havers (Jones), John Gielgud (Sir Adrian), Felicity Dean (Cynthia), Barry Foster (Charles). DVD, VHS.

4943. *Whistle Down the Wind* (Mary Hayley Bell, 1957). Three innocent British children think that the escaped criminal hiding in their barn is Jesus Christ. **Adaptation:** *Whistle Down the Wind* (Rank, 1961). Dir: Bryan Forbes. Scr: Keith Waterhouse, Willis Hall. Cast: Hayley Mills (Kathy), Bernard Lee (Mr. Bostock), Alan Bates (the Man), Norman Bird (Eddie). Notes: The author is actress Hayley Mills' mother. BAFTA nominations for Best British Film, Screenplay, Actress (Mills), and Film from Any Source. DVD, VHS.

4944. *Whistle Stop* (Maritta M. Wolff, 1941). A woman tries to get her lazy boyfriend to make something of himself while also pursuing a relationship with a club owner. **Adaptation:** *Whistle Stop* (United Artists, 1946). Dir: Leonide Moguy. Scr: Philip Yordan. Cast: George Raft (Kenny), Ava Gardner (Mary), Victor McLaglen (Gillo), Tom Conway (Lew). VHS.

4945. *White Banners* (Lloyd C. Douglas, 1936). A mysterious woman takes a job with an Indiana family in 1919 so that she can observe the son she gave up for adoption years earlier. **Adaptation:** *White Banners* (Warner, 1938). Dir: Edmund Goulding. Scr: Lenore J. Coffee, Abem Finkel, Cameron Rogers. Cast: Claude Rains (Paul), Fay Bainter (Hannah), Jackie Cooper (Peter), Bonita Granville (Sally).

4946. *The White Buffalo* (Richard Sale, 1975). Western about Wild Bill Hickok, who dreams of a rampaging white buffalo and teams up with Chief Crazy Horse to hunt the beast. **Adaptation:** *The White Buffalo*; broadcast on U.S. television as *Hunt to Kill* (United Artists, 1977). Dir: J. Lee Thompson. Scr: Richard Sale. Cast: Charles Bronson (Hickok), Jack Warden (Charlie), Will Sampson (Crazy Horse), Clint Walker (Whistling Jack), Slim Pickens (Pickney), Stuart Whitman (Winifred), Kim Novak (Poker Jenny), John Carradine (Amos). DVD, VHS.

White Cargo (see *Hell's Playground*).

4947. *White Cliffs* (Alice Duer Miller, 1940). Long narrative poem about an American woman who married an Englishman and the personal sacrifices she made during World War I. **Adaptation:** *The White Cliffs of Dover* (MGM, 1944). Dir: Clarence Brown. Scr: George Froeschel, Jan Lustig, Claudine West. Cast: Irene Dunne (Susan), Alan Marshal (Sir John Ashwood), Roddy McDowall (John Ashwood II), Frank Morgan (Hiram), Van Johnson (Sam). VHS.

The White Cliffs of Dover (see *White Cliffs*).

4948. *The White Cockatoo* (Mignon G. Eberhart, 1933). A brother and sister who stand to inherit a large fortune are menaced by others who want the money. **Adaptation:** *The White Cockatoo* (Warner, 1935). Dir: Alan Crosland. Scr: Lillie Hayward, Ben Markson. Cast: Jean Muir (Sue), Ricardo Cortez (Jim), Ruth Donnelly (Felicia).

4949. *The White Colt* (David Rook, 1967). A mute boy is inspired by his love for a white horse. **Adaptation:** *Run Wild, Run Free* (Columbia, 1969). Dir: Richard C. Sarafian. Scr: David Rook. Cast: Mark Lester (Philip), Fiona Fullerton (Diana), Gordon Jackson (Mr. Ransome), Bernard Miles (Reg), John Mills (the Moorman), Sylvia Syms (Mrs. Ransome). VHS.

White Corridors (see *Yeoman's Hospital*).

4950. *White Dog* (Romain Gary, 1970). Originally titled *Chien Blanc*, an autobiographical French novel about a couple who purchase a guard dog unaware that it was trained by racists to attack black people. The novel was translated in 1972. **Adaptation:** *White Dog* (Paramount, 1982). Dir: Samuel Fuller. Scr: Samuel Fuller, Curtis Hanson. Cast: Kristy McNichol (Julie), Jameson Parker (Roland), Lynne Moody (Molly), Paul Winfield (Keys), Burl Ives (Carruthers). Notes: Because it sparked controversy for its racist theme, the film was not released theatrically in the United States.

4951. *White Fang* (Jack London, 1906). The classic story of the close relationship between a Yukon gold trader and his wolf-dog, told from the perspective of the dog. The novel was originally serialized in *The Outing Magazine* between May and October 1906. **Silent Film:** 1925. **Adaptation 1:** *White Fang* (20th Century–Fox, 1936). Dir: David Butler. Scr: S. G. Duncan, Gene Fowler, Hal Long. Cast: Michael Whalen (Weedon), Jean Muir (Sylvia), Slim Summerville (Slats), Charles Winninger (Doc McFane), Jane Darwell (Maud), John Carradine (Smith). **Adaptation 2:** *White Fang* (American Cinema, 1973). Dir: Lucio Fulci. Scr: Guy Elmes, Roberto Gianviti, Thom Keyes, Piero Regnoli, Guillaume Roux, Harry Alan Towers (writing as Peter Welbeck). Cast: Franco Nero (Scott), Virna Lisi (Sister Evangelina), Fernando Rey (Father Oatley), John Steiner (Smith). VHS. Notes: *The Return of White Fang*, a sequel also featuring Franco Nero as Scott, was released in 1974. **Adaptation 3:** *White Fang* (Disney/Buena Vista, 1991). Dir: Randal Kleiser. Scr: Jeanne Rosenberg, Nick Thiel, David Fallon. Cast: Klaus Maria Brandauer (Larson), Ethan Hawke (Conroy), Seymour Cassel (Skunker), Susan Hogan (Belinda). Notes: Gemini Award (Canada) for Best Family Feature Film. DVD, VHS. Notes: A sequel, *White Fang 2: Myth of the White Wolf*, was released in 1994 (DVD, VHS). In addition to being the basis for a Russian-language film in 1946 and a Canadian television series in 1993, the novel also inspired a number of loose adaptations and sequels, including *Wolf Call* (1939), *White Fang to the Rescue* (1974) (DVD, VHS), *White Fang and the Gold Diggers* (1974), and *White Fang and the Hunter* (1975) (VHS).

4952. *The White Hare* (Francis Stuart, 1936). Two happy Irish brothers fall out over a beautiful young girl who arrives in their village. **Adaptation:** *Moondance* (Little Bird, 1995). Dir: Dagmar Hirtz. Scr: Mark Watters, Burt Weinshanker. Cast: Ruaidhri Conroy (Dominic), Ian Shaw (Patrick), Julia Brendler (Anya), Marianne Faithfull (Mother). DVD, VHS.

White Hot (see *Hot Toddy*).

4953. *White Hunter, Black Heart* (Peter Viertel, 1953). Fact-based novel about a film director who goes to Africa to make a movie but is more interested in hunting an elephant instead. The story is based on Viertel's experiences as he observed John Huston during the making of *The African Queen*. **Adaptation:** *White Hunter Black Heart* (Warner, 1990). Dir: Clint Eastwood. Scr: Peter Viertel, James Bridges, Burt Kennedy. Cast: Clint Eastwood (John), Jeff Fahey (Pete), Charlotte Cornwell (Miss Wilding), Norman Lumsden (Butler), George Dzundza (Paul). Notes: Cannes Film Festival Golden Palm nomination for Best Director. DVD, VHS.

4954. *White Mischief: The Murder of Lord Errol* (James Fox, 1982). An officer is found shot to death in the decadent British community known as Happy Valley in Kenya in 1941. **Adaptation:** *White Mischief* (Warner, 1987). Dir: Michael Radford. Scr: Michael Radford, Jonathan Gems. Cast: Greta Scacchi (Lady Diana), Charles Dance (Josslyn), Joss Ackland (Sir Jock), Sarah Miles (Alice), Geraldine Chaplin (Nina), John Hurt (Gilbert), Trevor Howard (Jack), Hugh Grant (Hugh). VHS.

White of the Eye (see *Mrs. White*).

4955. *White Oleander* (Janet Fitch, 1999). After her mother goes to prison for murdering her lover, a teenager drifts from one foster home to another, learning about herself and life in the process. **Adaptation:** *White Oleander* (Warner,

2002). Dir: Peter Kosminsky. Scr: Mary Agnes Donoghue. Cast: Alison Lohman (Astrid), Michelle Pfeiffer (Ingrid), Renee Zellweger (Claire), Robin Wright Penn (Starr), Billy Connolly (Barry), Noah Wyle (Mark). DVD, VHS.

4956. *White Palace* (Glenn Savan, 1987). After the death of his wife, a young executive meets an eccentric middle-aged waitress in a diner. Despite the obstacles presented by differences in age and social class, they fall in love. **Adaptation:** *White Palace* (Universal, 1990). Dir: Luis Mandoki. Scr: Ted Tally, Alvin Sargent. Cast: Susan Sarandon (Nora), James Spader (Max), Jason Alexander (Neil), Kathy Bates (Rosemary), Eileen Brennan (Judy), Steven Hill (Sol). DVD, VHS.

The White River Kid (see *The Little Brothers of Sr. Mortimer*).

4957. *White Shadows in the South Seas* (Frederick O'Brien, 1919). Factual account of O'Brien's experiences on the island of Marquesa in the early twentieth century. **Adaptation:** *White Shadows in the South Seas* (MGM, 1928). Dir: W. S. Van Dyke. Scr: Ray Doyle, Jack Cunningham, John Colton. Cast: Monte Blue (Dr. Lloyd), Raquel Torres (Fayaway). Notes: The film is about a white doctor in love with a native girl and his clashes with white imperialists in Tahiti. Academy Award for Best Cinematography.

4958. "The White Silence" (Jack London, 1899). A logger unjustly accused of murdering a romantic rival is exonerated in time to rescue a group of men from a ferocious forest fire. The story was published in *The Overland Monnthly* in February 1899. **Adaptation:** *Romance of the Redwoods* (Columbia, 1939). Dir: Charles Vidor. Scr: Michael L. Simmons. Cast: Charles Bickford (Steve), Jean Parker (June), Alan Bridge (Boss Whittaker), Gordon Oliver (Jed).

4959. *The White Sister* (F. Marion Crawford, 1909). After her husband's reported death in war, an aristocratic woman becomes a nun, but her husband eventually returns. The novel was adapted as a Broadway play in 1909 by Crawford and Walter C. Hackett. **Silent Films:** 1915 and 1923, directed by Henry King and starring Lillian Gish and Ronald Colman (VHS). **Adaptation:** *The White Sister* (MGM, 1933). Dir: Victor Fleming. Scr: Donald Ogden Stewart. Cast: Helen Hayes (Angela), Clark Gable (Giovanni), Lewis Stone (Prince Chiaromonte), Louise Closser Hale (Mina), May Robson (Mother Superior), Edward Arnold (Father Saracinesca). VHS. Notes: A Spanish-language adaptation titled *La Hermana Blanca* was released in Mexico in 1960 (DVD, VHS).

4960. *The White South* (Hammond Innes, 1949). A seaman agrees to accompany the daughter of a whaling captain to the Antarctic to find her father's killer. The book was released in the U.S. as *The Survivors*. **Adaptation:** *Hell Below Zero* (Columbia, 1954). Dir: Mark Robson. Scr: Alec Coppel, Richard Maibaum, Max Trell. Cast: Alan Ladd (Duncan), Joan Tetzel (Judy), Basil Sydney (John), Stanley Baker (Erik).

4961. *White Teeth* (Zadie Smith, 2000, Whitbread First Novel Award). Beginning in the 1960's and extending through the present, the story of three multicultural London families and their ambivalence about Western culture. **Adaptation:** *White Teeth* (Channel Four/PBS, 2002 TV Movie). Dir: Julian Jarrold. Scr: Simon Burke. Cast: Om Puri (Samad), Phil Davis (Archie), Geraldine James (Joyce), Robert Bathurst (Marcus).

4962. *The White Tower* (James Ramsay Ullman, 1945). People from various nationalities come together to climb a high peak in the Swiss Alps. **Adaptation:** *The White Tower* (RKO, 1950). Dir: Ted Tetzlaff. Scr: Paul Jarrico. Cast: Glenn Ford (Martin), Alida Valli (Carla), Claude Rains (Paul), Oscar Homolka (Andreas), Cedric Hardwicke (Dr. Radcliffe), Lloyd Bridges (Hein). VHS.

4963. *The White Unicorn* (Flora Sandstrom, 1946). An inmate in a home for delinquent girls reflects back on her troubled life. **Adaptation:** *The White Unicorn*; released in the U.S. as *Bad Sister* (Universal, 1947). Dir: Bernard Knowles. Scr: Moie Charles, A. R. Rawlinson, Robert Westerby. Cast: Margaret Lockwood (Lucy), Dennis Price (Richard), Ian Hunter (Philip).

4964. *White Witch Doctor* (Louise A. Stinetorf, 1950). A nurse goes to the Congo to bring modern medicine to the natives and clashes with white adventurers in search of gold. **Adaptation:** *White Witch Doctor* (20th Century–Fox, 1953). Dir: Henry Hathaway. Scr: Ivan Goff, Ben Roberts. Cast: Susan Hayward (Ellen), Robert Mitchum (Lonni), Walter Slezak (Huysman).

4965. *Who?* (Algis Budrys, 1958). Science-fiction novel about an American who disappears after a car crash in Russia. When he returns months later, he has been transformed into a killing machine. **Adaptation:** *Who?*; released on video as *Robo Man* (Allied Artists, 1973). Dir: Jack Gold. Scr: John Gould. Cast: Elliott Gould (Sean), Trevor Howard (Colonel Azarin), Joseph Bova (Lucas), Ed Grover (Finchley). VHS.

4966. "Who Am I This Time?" (Kurt Vonnegut, 1961). A shy man transforms himself into a raging tough guy when he joins a theatrical group and takes the part of Stanley in *A Streetcar Named Desire.* The short story was published in *The Saturday Evening Post* on December 16, 1961, and included in Vonnegut's 1968 collection *Welcome to the Monkey House.* **Adaptation:** *Who Am I This Time?* (PBS, 1982 TV Movie). Dir: Jonathan Demme. Scr: Morton Neal Miller. Cast: Susan Sarandon (Helene), Christopher Walken (Harry), Robert Ridgely (George). VHS. See also *Welcome to the Monkey House.*

4967. *Who Censored Roger Rabbit?* (Gary K. Wolf, 1981). A cartoon rabbit hires a human detective who detests "toons" to follow his wife and later to clear him of charges that he murdered a studio executive. **Adaptation:** *Who Framed Roger Rabbit?* (Buena Vista, 1988). Dir: Robert Zemeckis. Scr: Jeffrey Price, Peter S. Seaman. Cast: Bob Hoskins (Eddie), Christopher Lloyd (Judge Doom), Joanna Cassidy (Dolores), Stubby Kaye (Marvin), and the voices of Kathleen Turner (Jessica), Charles Fleischer (Roger/Benny/Greasy/Psycho). Notes: Academy Awards for Best Sound Effects, Visual Effects, and Editing, and nominations for Best Art Direction, Cinematography, and Sound. DVD, VHS.

4968. *Who Could Ask for Anything More?* (Kay Swift, 1943). A music critic marries a rodeo cowboy and must face the challenges of living on a Wyoming ranch. **Adaptation:** *Never a Dull Moment* (RKO, 1950). Dir: George Marshall. Scr: Doris Anderson, Lou Breslow. Cast: Irene Dunne (Kay), Fred MacMurray (Chris), William Demarest (Mears), Andy Devine (Orvie), Natalie Wood (Nancy). VHS.

Who Framed Roger Rabbit? (see *Who Censored Roger Rabbit?*)

4969. "Who Goes There?" (Don A. Stuart [pseudonym for John W. Campbell, Jr.], 1938). An Arctic scientific expedition turns deadly when researchers accidentally thaw a ferocious alien creature frozen in a space ship. The short story was published in *Astounding Stories* magazine in August 1938. **Adaptation 1:** *The Thing From Another World* (RKO, 1951). Dir: Christian Nyby. Scr: Charles Lederer. Cast: Margaret Sheridan (Nikki), Kenneth Tobey (Captain Hendry), Robert Cornthwaite (Dr. Carrington), Douglas Spencer (Scotty). DVD, VHS. **Adaptation 2:** *The Thing* (Universal, 1982). Dir: John Carpenter. Scr: Bill Lancaster. Cast: Kurt Russell (MacReady),

Wilford Brimley (Dr. Blair), T. K. Carter (Nauls), David Clennon (Palmer), Keith David (Childs), Richard Dysart (Dr. Copper). DVD, VHS.

Who Is Killing the Great Chefs of Europe? (see *Someone Is Killing the Great Chefs of Europe*).

4970. *Who Killed Sir Harry Oakes?* (Marshall Houts, 1976). Factual account of a wealthy Briton who struck gold in Canada. In 1943, when he was living in the Bahamas, his bludgeoned body was discovered, a crime thought to be linked to American gangsters. **Adaptation:** *Eureka* (MGM/United Artists, 1984). Dir: Nicolas Roeg. Scr: Paul Mayersberg. Cast: Gene Hackman (Jack), Theresa Russell (Tracy), Rutger Hauer (Claude), Jane Lapotaire (Helen), Mickey Rourke (Aurelio), Ed Lauter (Charles), Joe Pesci (Mayakofsky). DVD, VHS.

4971. *Who Lie in Gaol* (Joan Henry, 1952). The lives of various imprisoned women, detailing their crimes, their experiences in prison, and their rehabilitation and return to society. **Adaptation:** *The Weak and the Wicked* (Allied Artists, 1953). Dir: J. Lee Thompson. Scr: J. Lee Thompson, Anne Burnaby, Joan Henry. Cast: Glynis Johns (Jean), Diana Dors (Betty), John Gregson (Dr. Hale), Olive Sloane (Nellie), Rachel Roberts (Pat).

4972. *Who Rides with Wyatt?* (Will Henry [pseudonym for Henry W. "Heck" Allen], 1955). Western set in a small frontier town, where Marshal Wyatt Earp trains a young lawman seeking revenge for the murder of his son. **Adaptation:** *Young Billy Young* (United Artists, 1969). Dir: Burt Kennedy. Scr: Burt Kennedy. Cast: Robert Mitchum (Deputy Kane), Angie Dickinson (Lily), Robert Walker, Jr. (Billy), David Carradine (Jesse). VHS.

The Whole Town's Talking (see *Jail Breaker*).

The Whole Wide World (see *The One Who Walked Alone*).

Who'll Stop the Rain? (see *Dog Soldiers*).

Who's Got the Action? (see *Four Horse Players Are Missing*).

Why Bother to Knock? (see *Don't Bother to Knock*).

4973. *Why Didn't They Ask Evans?* (Agatha Christie, 1934). A man retrieving a golf ball comes upon a dying man and decides to look into his cryptic dying words. The novel was released in the U.S. as *The Boomerang Case.* **Adaptation:** *Why Didn't They Ask Evans?* (London Weekend

Television, 1980 TV Movie). Dir: John Davies, Tony Wharmby. Scr: Pat Sandys. Cast: Francesca Annis (Lady Frances), John Gielgud (Reverend Jones), Bernard Miles (Dr. Thomas), Eric Porter (Dr. Nicholson). DVD, VHS.

4974. *Why Me?* (Leola Mae Harmon, 1982). Autobiography of an Air Force nurse who suffered a disfiguring automobile accident in which she also lost her unborn child. After more than forty surgeries, her face was reconstructed, and she subsequently married her plastic surgeon. **Adaptation:** *Why Me?* (Lorimar, 1984 TV Movie). Dir: Fielder Cook. Scr: Dalene Young. Cast: Glynnis O'Connor (Leola), Armand Assante (Dr. Stallings), Craig Wasson (Brian), Annie Potts (Daria).

4975. *Why Me?* (Donald E. Westlake, 1983). Two Los Angeles thieves steal a priceless ruby and are pursued by the CIA, terrorists, and the Turkish government. **Adaptation:** *Why Me?* (1990). Dir: Gene Quintano. Scr: Donald E. Westlake, Leonard Maas, Jr. Cast: Christopher Lambert (Gus), Kim Greist (June), Christopher Lloyd (Bruno), J. T. Walsh (Francis). VHS.

4976. *Why Shoot the Teacher?* (Max Braithwaite, 1965). Canadian novel about a teacher who goes to work in an isolated farming community in Saskatchewan during the Depression. **Adaptation:** *Why Shoot the Teacher?* (Quartet, 1977). Dir: Silvio Narizzano. Scr: James Defelice. Cast: Bud Cort (Max), Samantha Eggar (Alice), Chris Wiggins (Lyle), Gary Reineke (Harris). VHS.

4977. "Why Should I Cry?" (I. A. R. Wylie, 1949). A domineering theatrical star falls in love with a blind pianist who refuses to put up with her abuse. The short story was published in *The Saturday Evening Post* on December 24, 1949. **Adaptation:** *Torch Song* (MGM, 1953). Dir: Charles Walters. Scr: John Michael Hayes, Jan Lustig. Cast: Joan Crawford (Jenny), Michael Wilding (Tye), Gig Young (Cliff), Marjorie Rambeau (Mrs. Stewart), Harry Morgan (Joe). VHS.

4978. *Why the Whales Came* (Michael Morpurgo, 1985). Set during World War I, a children's book about two children who befriend an eccentric old man on a remote island and the secret he shares with them. **Adaptation:** *When the Whales Came* (20th Century–Fox, 1989). Dir: Clive Rees. Scr: Michael Morpurgo. Cast: Paul Scofield (the Birdman), David Threlfall (Jack), Helen Mirren (Clemmie), David Suchet (Will), Helen Pearce (Gracie), Max Rennie (Daniel). VHS.

The Wicked Lady (see *The Life and Death of the Wicked Lady Skelton*).

4979. *Wicked Water* (MacKinlay Kantor, 1949). Western about a marshal who investigates the murder of land squatters by killers hired by greedy cattlemen. **Adaptation:** *Hannah Lee*; reissued as *Outlaw Territory* (Realart, 1953). Dir: Lee Garmes, John Ireland. Scr: Rip Van Ronkel. Cast: Macdonald Carey (Bus), Joanne Dru (Hannah), John Ireland (Marshal Rochelle), Stuart Randall (Montgomery).

4980. *A Wicked Woman* (Anne Austin, 1933). A woman stands trial and is exonerated for killing her abusive husband to protect her children. The novel was published in *Household Magazine* in November 1933. **Adaptation:** *A Wicked Woman* (MGM, 1934). Dir: Charles Brabin. Scr: Florence Ryerson, Zelda Sears. Cast: Mady Christians (Naomi), Jean Parker (Rosanne), Charles Bickford (Pat), Betty Furness (Yancey).

Wide-Eyed and Legless (see *Diana's Story*).

4981. *Wide Sargasso Sea* (Jean Rhys [pseudonym for Ella Gwendoline Rees Williams], 1966). Set in Jamaica in the nineteenth century, the novel is a prequel to Charlotte Bronte's *Jane Eyre*, involving the Creole woman who marries Rochester and eventually becomes his "madwoman in the attic." **Adaptation:** *Wide Sargasso Sea* (New Line, 1993). Dir: John Duigan. Scr: Carole Angier, John Duigan, Jan Sharp. Cast: Karina Lombard (Antoinette), Nathaniel Parker (Rochester), Rachel Ward (Annette), Michael York (Paul), Martine Beswick (Aunt Cora). DVD, VHS.

4982. *A Widow for One Year* (John Irving, 1998). The marriage of a famous children's book author and his wife disintegrates after the death of their two sons in a car accident. **Adaptation:** *The Door in the Floor* (Focus, 2004). Dir: Tod Williams. Scr: Tod Williams. Cast: Elle Fanning (Ruth), Jeff Bridges (Ted), Kim Basinger (Marion), Jon Foster (Eddie). DVD, VHS.

Wife, Husband and Friend (see "Two Can Sing").

4983. *Wife Versus Secretary* (Faith Baldwin, 1934). Romantic comedy about a publisher's wife who begins to wonder about the real nature of her husband's relationship with his efficient and beautiful secretary. **Adaptation:** *Wife vs. Secretary* (MGM, 1936). Dir: Clarence Brown. Scr: Norman Krasna, John Lee Mahin, Alice Duer Miller. Cast: Clark Gable (Van), Jean Harlow (Helen), Myrna Loy (Linda), May Robson (Mimi). VHS.

4984. *The Wilby Conspiracy* (Peter Driscoll, 1972). A British engineer helps a black anti-apartheid revolutionary escape corrupt South African officials. **Adaptation:** *The Wilby Conspiracy* (United Artists, 1975). Dir: Ralph Nelson. Scr: Rodney Amateau, Harold Nebenzal. Cast: Sidney Poitier (Shack), Michael Caine (Jim), Nicol Williamson (Major Horn), Prunella Gee (Rina). DVD, VHS.

The Wild Affair (see *The Last Hours of Sandra Lee*).

4985. *Wild at Heart: The Story of Sailor and Lula* (Barry Gifford, 1990). After his release from prison, a young man and his girlfriend flee from her mother, who has hired a detective to find her and a hit man to kill him. **Adaptation:** *Wild at Heart* (1990). Dir: David Lynch. Scr: David Lynch. Cast: Nicolas Cage (Sailor), Laura Dern (Lula), Willem Dafoe (Bobby), J. E. Freeman (Santos), Crispin Glover (Dell), Diane Ladd (Marietta), Calvin Lockhart (Reggie), Isabella Rossellini (Perdita), Harry Dean Stanton (Johnnie). Notes: Cannes Film Festival Golden Palm Award for Best Director; Independent Spirit Award for Best Cinematography and nomination for Best Supporting Actor (Dafoe); Academy Award and Golden Globe nominations for Best Supporting Actress (Ladd). DVD, VHS.

Wild Bill (see *Deadwood*).

Wild Brian Kent (see *The Re-Creation of Brian Kent*).

4986. *Wild Calendar* (Libbie Block, 1946). A young wife tries to escape from her oppressive husband, an emotionally disturbed millionaire. **Adaptation:** *Caught* (MGM, 1949). Dir: Max Ophuls. Scr: Arthur Laurents. Cast: James Mason (Larry), Barbara Bel Geddes (Leonora), Robert Ryan (Smith), Frank Ferguson (Dr. Hoffman). VHS.

The Wild Country (see *Little Britches*).

Wild Drifter (see *Cockfighter*).

4987. *The Wild Geese* (Daniel Carney, 1977). Mercenaries battle a vicious dictator in central Africa and free an honest rebel leader. **Adaptation:** *The Wild Geese* (Allied Artists, 1978). Dir: Andrew V. McLaglen. Scr: Reginald Rose. Cast: Richard Burton (Allen), Roger Moore (Shawn), Richard Harris (Rafer), Hardy Kruger (Pieter), Stewart Granger (Sir Edward). DVD, VHS.

4988. *Wild Geese Calling* (Stewart Edward White, 1940). A young lumberjack in Oregon marries a dancehall girl and leaves to seek his for-

tune in Alaska. **Adaptation:** *Wild Geese Calling* (20th Century–Fox, 1941). Dir: John Brahm. Scr: Horace McCoy. Cast: Henry Fonda (John), Joan Bennett (Sally), Warren William (Blackie).

Wild Geese II (see *The Square Circle*).

The Wild Heart (see *Gone to Earth*).

4989. *Wild Horse Mesa* (Zane Grey, 1924). Western about a rancher who tries to make money by corralling wild horses and selling them. The novel was originally published as a serial in *Country Gentleman* magazine beginning in April 1924 and published as a novel in 1928. **Silent Film:** 1925. **Adaptation 1:** *Wild Horse Mesa* (Paramount, 1932). Dir: Henry Hathaway. Scr: Frank Howard Clark, Harold Shumate. Cast: Randolph Scott (Chane), Sally Blane (Sandy), Fred Kohler (Rand). **Adaptation 2:** *Wild Horse Mesa* (RKO, 1947). Dir: Wallace A. Grissell. Scr: Norman Houston. Cast: Tim Holt (Dave), Nan Leslie (Sue), Richard Martin (Chito).

4990. "Wild-Horse Roundup" (Jean Muir, 1946). A feature story about Texas cowboys who capture and tame wild horses. The article appeared in *The Saturday Evening Post* on September 28, 1946. **Adaptation:** *Northwest Stampede* (Eagle-Lion, 1948). Dir: Albert S. Rogell. Scr: Art Arthur, Lillie Hayward. Cast: Joan Leslie (Honey), James Craig (Dan), Jack Oakie (Mike), Chill Wills (Mileaway).

Wild in the Country (see *The Lost Country*).

The Wild One (*see* "The Cyclists' Raid").

4991. *The Wild Palms* (William Faulkner, 1939). Novella about a Mississippi convict and young woman and her child caught in a small boat during a flood. The novella was also published under the title *If I Forget Thee, Jerusalem*. **Adaptation:** *Old Man* (Hallmark, 1997 TV Movie). Dir: John Kent Harrison. Scr: Horton Foote. Cast: Jeanne Tripplehorn (Addie), Arliss Howard (Taylor), Jerry Leggio (the Warden). Notes: Emmy Award for Outstanding Teleplay. VHS.

4992. "The Wild Party" (Joseph Moncure March, 1928). A narrative poem by the editor of *The New Yorker* about a vaudeville dancer's wild party at which someone is killed. The controversial poem, which was banned in several cities for obscenity, was published in a limited edition. **Adaptation:** *The Wild Party* (American International, 1975). Dir: James Ivory. Scr: Walter Marks. Cast: James Coco (Jolly), Raquel Welch (Queenie), Perry King (Dale), Tiffany Bolling (Kate), Royal Dano (Tex). Notes: Loosely based on the life of Fatty Arbuckle, the film concerns a fading silent-film star throwing a party in an attempt to save his failing career. DVD, VHS.

Wild River (see *Dunbar's Cove* and *Mud on the Stars*).

4993. *Wild Times* (Brian Garfield, 1978). Set in the period between the Civil War and the turn of the twentieth century, Western about the life and adventures of Colonel Hugh Cardiff, sharpshooter and creator of the original Wild West Show. **Adaptation:** *Wild Times* (Metromedia, 1980 TV Miniseries). Dir: Richard Compton. Scr: Don Balluck. Cast: Sam Elliott (Cardiff), Ben Johnson (Doc Bogardus), Bruce Boxleitner (Vern), Penny Peyser (Libby).

4994. *Wild to Possess* (Gil Brewer, 1959). Overhearing a couple planning a lucrative kidnapping, a small-time hustler decides to kidnap the victim himself and then blackmail the original schemers. **Adaptation:** *3-Way* (Hyperion, 2004). Dir: Scott Ziehl. Scr: Russell P. Marleau. Cast: Dominic Purcell (Lew), Joy Bryant (Rita), Ali Larter (Isabel), Desmond Harrington (Ralph), Dwight Yoakam (Herbert), Gina Gershon (Florence), Roxana Zal (Janice). DVD, VHS.

Wild West Days (see *Saint Johnson*).

Wilde (see *Oscar Wilde*).

4995. *Wildfire* (Zane Grey, 1917). Western about a cowboy and a lady who tame a wild stallion. **Adaptation:** *Red Canyon* (Universal, 1949). Dir: George Sherman. Scr: Maurice Geraghty. Cast: Ann Blyth (Lucy), Howard Duff (Lin), George Brent (Matthew), Edgar Buchanan (Jonah), John McIntire (Floyd), Chill Wills (Brackton), Jane Darwell (Aunt Jane).

4996. *Wilhelm Meister's Apprenticeship* (Johann Wolfgang von Goethe, 1795). *Wilhelm Meisters Lehrjahre* is Goethe's tale of a young German man's journey from naïve youth to mature and self-aware adult. **Adaptation:** *False Movement*; released in the UK as *The Wrong Move*; released on video as *The Wrong Movement* (Bauer, 1975). Dir: Wim Wenders. Scr: Peter Handke. Cast: Rudiger Vogler (Wilhelm), Hans Christian Blech (Laertes), Hanna Schygulla (Therese).Notes: Originally released as *Falsche Bewegung* and shown with subtitles. VHS.

Willard (see *Ratman's Notebooks*).

4997. *William Penn* (C. E. Vulliamy, 1934).

Biography of William Penn (1644–1718), the English Quaker who founded the American colony of Pennsylvania in 1681. **Adaptation:** *Penn of Pennsylvania*; released in the U.S. as *Courageous Mr. Penn* (British National/Hoffberg, 1942). Dir: Lance Comfort. Scr: Anatole de Grunwald. Cast: Clifford Evans (Penn), Deborah Kerr (Guglielma), Dennis Arundell (Charles II). VHS.

4998. "William Wilson" (Edgar Allan Poe, 1839). A man meets his mirror image on the street, setting off a lifelong crisis of conscience. The short story originally appeared in *The Gift: A Christmas and New Year's Present for 1840*. **Silent Film:** 1913. **Adaptation:** *Spirits of the Dead*; released in the UK as *Tales of Mystery and Imagination* (American International, 1968). Dir: Federico Fellini, Louis Malle, Roger Vadim. Scr: Roger Vadim, Pascal Cousin, Daniel Boulanger, Louis Malle, Clement Biddle Wood, Federico Fellini, Bernardino Zapponi. Cast: Brigitte Bardot (Giuseppina), Alain Delon (Wilson), Umberto D'Orsi (Hans). Notes: Originally released as *Histoires Extraordinaires*. The film contains adaptations of four separate horror stories. DVD, VHS. See also "Metzengerstein."

Willie and Phil (see *Jules et Jim*).

4999. *Willie Boy: A Desert Manhunt* (Harry Lawton, 1960). Fact-based story about a Native American who kills his girlfriend's father in self-defense and is hunted by a posse. **Adaptation:** *Tell Them Willie Boy Is Here* (Universal, 1969). Dir: Abraham Polonsky. Scr: Abraham Polonsky. Cast: Robert Redford (Sheriff Cooper), Katharine Ross (Lola), Robert Blake (Willie Boy), Susan Clark (Dr. Arnold). VHS.

5000. *The Willing Flesh* (Willi Heinrich, 1955). German novel, originally titled *Das Geduldige Fleisch,* about the bitter defeat of the Nazis at the hands of the Russians on the eastern front during World War II. **Adaptation:** *Cross of Iron* (AVCO Embassy, 1977). Dir: Sam Peckinpah. Scr: Julius Epstein, James Hamilton, Walter Kelley. Cast: James Coburn (Steiner), Maximilian Schell (Stransky), James Mason (Brandt), David Warner (Kiesel). DVD, VHS.

5001. *The Willows in Winter* (William Horwood, 1994). In this literary sequel to Kenneth Grahame's 1908 children's classic *The Wind in the Willows,* Mole is missing, and his friends search for him. **Adaptation:** *The Willows in Winter* (ITV, 1996 TV Movie). Dir: Dave Unwin. Scr: Ted Walker. Cast: voices of Alan Bennett (Mole), Vanessa Redgrave (Narrator), Michael Gambon

(Badger), Rik Mayall (Toad), Michael Palin (Rat). Notes: Emmy nomination for Outstanding Animated Program. DVD, VHS. See also *The Wind in the Willows*.

Willy Wonka and the Chocolate Factory (see *Charlie and the Chocolate Factory*).

5002. *Wilt* (Tom Sharpe, 1976). In the first in Sharpe's series about the comical misadventures Henry Wilt, a college lecturer who fantasizes about killing his uncaring wife, the wife disappears, and Wilt becomes an inept policeman's prime suspect. **Adaptation:** *Wilt*; released in the U.S. as *The Misadventures of Mr. Wilt* (Samuel Goldwyn, 1989). Dir: Michael Tuchner. Scr: Andrew Marshall, David Renwick. Cast: Griff Rhys Jones (Henry), Mel Smith (Inspector Flint), Alison Steadman (Eva), Diana Quick (Sally). DVD, VHS.

5003. *The Wimbledon Poisoner* (Nigel Williams, 1990). A meek British lawyer's attempts to murder his domineering wife go horribly wrong. **Adaptation:** *The Wimbledon Poisoner* (BBC, 1994 TV Miniseries). Dir: Robert W. Young. Scr: Nigel Williams. Cast: Robert Lindsay (Henry), Alison Steadman (Elinor), Philip Jackson (Detective Rush).

5004. *The Wind Cannot Read* (Richard Mason, 1947). During World War II, a British soldier held prisoner in a Japanese camp falls in love with a Japanese-language expert. **Adaptation:** *The Wind Cannot Read* (Rank/20th Century–Fox, 1958). Dir: Ralph Thomas. Scr: Richard Mason. Cast: Dirk Bogarde (Quinn), Yoko Tani (Sabbi), Ronald Lewis (Fenwick), John Fraser (Munroe). VHS.

5005. *The Wind in the Willows* (Kenneth Grahame, 1908). Children's story about Mr. Toad, a landowner whose preserve is invaded by the Weasels. With the help of his friends, Mole and Rat, he regains his ancestral lands. **Adaptation 1:** *The Adventures of Ichabod and Mr. Toad* (RKO/Disney, 1949). Dir: James Algar, Clyde Geronimi, Jack Kinney. Scr: Homer Brightman, Winston Hibler, Erdman Penner, Harry Reeves, Joe Rinaldi, Ted Sears. Cast: voices of Bing Crosby (Narrator), J. Pat O'Malley (Cyril Proudbottom), Campbell Grant (Angus MacBadger). Notes: A Disney animated musical that combines narrations of Irving's "The Legend of Sleepy Hollow" and Kenneth Grahame's *The Wind in the Willows*. DVD, VHS. **Adaptation 2:** *The Wind in the Willows* (Thames Television, 1983 TV Movie). Dir: Mark Hall, Chris Taylor. Scr: Rosemary Anne Sisson.

Cast: voices of Richard Pearson (Mole), Ian Carmichael (Rat), David Jason (Toad), Michael Hordern (Badger), Beryl Reid (the Magistrate). Notes: BAFTA Award for Best Children's Program. DVD, VHS. **Adaptation 3:** *The Wind in the Willows* (Television Theatre Company, 1983 TV Movie). Dir: John Driver. Scr: Sharon Holland. Cast: Julee Cruise (Elspeth Grahame/voice of Mr. Otter), John Allen (Miles Grahame/voice of Portly), George Muschamp (Kenneth Grahame/voice of Mr. Mole), Gary Briggle (Pritchard/voice of Mr. Toad). Notes: A play for television. VHS. **Adaptation 4:** *The Wind in the Willows* (Rankin-Bass, 1987 TV Movie). Dir: Jules Bass, Arthur Rankin Jr. Scr: Romeo Muller. Cast: voices of Eddie Bracken (Mole), Jose Ferrer (Badger), Roddy McDowall (Rat), Charles Nelson Reilly (Mr. Toad). VHS. **Adaptation 5:** *The Wind in the Willows* (Goodtimes, 1995 TV Movie). Dir: Dave Unwin. Scr: Ted Walker. Cast: voices of Vanessa Redgrave (Narrator/Grandmother), Alan Bennett (Mole), Michael Palin (Rat), Michael Gambon (Badger), Rik Mayall (Toad). DVD, VHS. **Adaptation 6:** *The Wind in the Willows* (1996). Dir: Terry Jones. Scr: Terry Jones. Cast: Steve Coogan (Mole), Eric Idle (Rat), Terry Jones (Toad), Antony Sher (Chief Weasel), Nicol Williamson (Badger), John Cleese (Mr. Toad's Lawyer). DVD, VHS. Notes: The book was also the basis of an animated British television series (1984–1988). See also *The Willows in Winter*.

5006. *Windmills of the Gods* (Sidney Sheldon, 1987). An American ambassador to Romania and her family are threatened by communists. **Adaptation:** *Windmills of the Gods* (CBS, 1988 TV Movie). Dir: Lee Philips. Scr: Sidney Sheldon. Cast: Jaclyn Smith (Mary), Robert Wagner (Mike), Ian McKellen (the Chairman), Michael Moriarty (Ellison). VHS.

5007. *Windom's Way* (James Ramsey Ullman, 1952). A British doctor working in a remote Asian village tries to stop a takeover by communist insurgents. **Adaptation:** *Windom's Way* (Rank, 1957). Dir: Ronald Neame. Scr: Jill Craigie. Cast: Peter Finch (Alec), Mary Ure (Lee), Natasha Parry (Anna), Robert Flemyng (George). Notes: BAFTA nominations for Best British Film, Actor, Screenplay, and Film from Any Source.

The Window (see "Fire Escape").

A Window to the Sky (see *A Long Way Up*).

5008. *The Winds of War* (Herman Wouk, 1971). Fictionalized account of the events leading up to World War II. **Adaptation:** *The Winds of War* (ABC, 1983 TV Miniseries). Dir: Dan Curtis. Scr: Herman Wouk. Cast: Robert Mitchum (Victor), Ali MacGraw (Natalie), Jan-Michael Vincent (Byron), John Houseman (Aaron), Ralph Bellamy (President Franklin Delano Roosevelt), Victoria Tennant (Pamela), Polly Bergen (Rhoda). Notes: Emmy Award nominations for Outstanding Miniseries, Director, Supporting Actor (Bellamy) and Supporting Actress (Bergen); Golden Globe Award nominations for Best Television Miniseries, Supporting Actors (Houseman and Vincent), and Supporting Actress (Tennant). DVD, VHS. See also *War and Remembrance*.

5009. *Windwalker* (Blaine Yorgason, 1979). A very old Indian chief dies and then returns to life to save his tribe from a raiding Indian group led his by his own son, a twin stolen at birth. **Adaptation:** *Windwalker* (Pacific International, 1980). Dir: Kieth Merrill. Scr: Ray Goldrup, Blaine Yorgason. Cast: Trevor Howard (Windwalker), Nick Ramus (Smiling Wolf/Crow Brother), Serene Hedin (Tashina), Dusty McCrea (Dancing Moon). DVD, VHS.

Wine, Women and Horses (see *Dark Command*).

5010. *The Wingless Bird* (Catherine Cookson, 1990). Just prior to World War I, a strong-willed businesswoman must choose between a gentleman and his brother, a soldier, over her parents' opposition. **Adaptation:** *The Wingless Bird* (Festival/Tyne Tees/PBS, 1997 TV Movie). Dir: David Wheatley. Scr: Alan Seymour. Cast: Claire Skinner (Agnes), Dale Meeks (Mike), Edward Atterton (Charles), Shaun Mechen (Jimmy), Julian Wadham (Reginald). DVD, VHS.

5011. *The Wings of the Dove* (Henry James, 1902). In the early twentieth century, a poor orphaned woman under the control of her imperious wealthy aunt devises a plan to escape with the help of her boyfriend and a terminally ill American woman. **Adaptation 1:** *The Wings of the Dove* (Miramax, 1997). Dir: Iain Softley. Scr: Hossein Amini. Cast: Helena Bonham Carter (Kate), Linus Roache (Merton), Charlotte Rampling (Aunt Maude), Michael Gambon (Lionel), Elizabeth McGovern (Susie). Notes: BAFTA Awards for Best Cinematography and Makeup, and nominations for Best Screenplay, Actress (Carter), and Costume Design; National Board of Review Award for Best Actress (Carter); Academy Award nominations for Best Screenplay, Actress (Carter), Cinematography, and Costume Design; Golden Globe nomination for Best Actress (Carter).

DVD, VHS. **Adaptation 2:** *Under Heaven*; broadcast on U.S. television as *In a Private Garden*; released on video as *In the Shadows* (Banner/Ardustry, 1998). Dir: Meg Richman. Scr: Meg Richman. Cast: Joely Richardson (Eleanor), Aden Young (Buck), Molly Parker (Cynthia), Kevin Phillip (John). Notes: An updated adaptation. DVD, VHS. Notes: In addition, a French-language adaptation was produced in 1981.

Winstanley (see *Comrade Jacob*).

5012. *The Winston Affair* (Howard Fast, 1959). In India during World War II, an American military officer is court-martialed for killing a British soldier, and his military defense attorney resists pressure from his superiors to lose the case. **Adaptation:** *Man in the Middle* (20th Century–Fox, 1964). Dir: Guy Hamilton. Scr: Willis Hall, Keith Waterhouse. Cast: Robert Mitchum (Barney), France Nuyen (Kate), Barry Sullivan (General Kempton), Trevor Howard (John), Keenan Wynn (Charles), Sam Wanamaker (Leon).

5013. "Winter Cruise" (W. Somerset Maugham, 1947). A talkative older woman on a cruise annoys the other passengers, who conspire to arrange a romance between her and a porter. The story was included in Maugham's 1947 collection *Creatures of Circumstance*. **Adaptation:** *Encore* (Paramount, 1952). Dir: Harold French, Pat Jackson. Scr: Eric Ambler, T. E. B. Clarke, Arthur Macrae. Cast: Nigel Patrick (Tom), Roland Culver (George), Kay Walsh (Molly), Glynis Johns (Stella), Terence Morgan (Syd). Note: Following *Quartet* (1948) and *Trio* (1952), the third installment in a series of films featuring Maugham introducing adaptations of his own short stories. This film includes three stories: "The Ant and the Grasshopper," "Gigolo and Gigolette," and "Winter Cruise." VHS.

5014. *Winter Kills* (Richard Condon, 1974). Nearly two decades after the assassination of an American President, his younger brother tries to track down the killer, but dark forces — including his own wealthy father — try to stop him. **Adaptation:** *Winter Kills* (AVCO Embassy, 1979). Dir: William Richert. Scr: William Richert. Cast: Jeff Bridges (Nick), John Huston (Pa Kegan), Anthony Perkins (John), Eli Wallach (Joe), Sterling Hayden (Dawson), Dorothy Malone (Emma). DVD, VHS.

5015. *Winter Meeting* (Ethel Vance [pseudonym for Grace Zaring Stone], 1946). A disillusioned poet falls for a Naval pilot but soon realizes that his ambition is to become a priest.

Adaptation: *Winter Meeting* (Warner, 1948). Dir: Bretaigne Windust. Scr: Catherine Turney. Cast: Bette Davis (Susan), Janis Paige (Peggy), James Davis (Slick), John Hoyt (Stacy). VHS.

5016. *The Winter of Our Discontent* (John Steinbeck, 1961). An honest man battles immorality and unbridled materialism in a suburban town. **Adaptation:** *The Winter of Our Discontent* (CBS, 1983 TV Movie). Dir: Waris Hussein. Scr: Michael De Guzman. Cast: Donald Sutherland (Ethan), Teri Garr (Mary), Tuesday Weld (Margie), Michael V. Gazzo (Marullo), Richard Masur (Danny), E. G. Marshall (Baker).

5017. *Winter People* (John Ehle, 1982). In 1934, a young widower moves with his daughter to a small North Carolina town, where he becomes involved in the family feud between a woman with an illegitimate child and the child's father, who wants custody. **Adaptation:** *Winter People* (Columbia, 1989). Dir: Ted Kotcheff. Scr: Carol Sobieski. Cast: Lloyd Bridges (William), Kelly McGillis (Collie), Kurt Russell (Wayland). DVD, VHS.

5018. *Winter Solstice* (Rosamunde Pilcher, 2000). A British woman's life is altered profoundly when some of her neighbors are killed in a car accident. **Adaptation:** *Winter Solstice* (BBC, 2003 TV Movie). Dir: Martyn Friend. Scr: William Corlett. Cast: Jan Niklas (Oscar), Geraldine Chaplin (Gloria), Sinead Cusack (Elfrida), Jean Simmons (Lucinda), Peter Ustinov (Hughie).

5019. *Winterdance: The Fine Madness of Running the Iditarod* (Gary Paulsen, 1994). Memoir of Paulsen's experiences in a grueling seventeen-day dog-sled race from Anchorage to Nome, Alaska. **Adaptation:** *Snow Dogs* (Disney/Buena Vista, 2002). Dir: Brian Levant. Scr: Jim Kouf, Tommy Swerdlow, Michael Goldberg, Mark Gibson, Philip Halprin. Cast: Cuba Gooding, Jr. (Ted), James Coburn (Thunder Jack), Sisqo (Dr. Brooks), Nichelle Nichols (Amelia), M. Emmet Walsh (George), Graham Greene (Yellowbear), Brian Doyle-Murray (Ernie). **Notes:** The screenplay, whose premise is only suggested by Paulsen's book, concerns a Miami dentist who goes to Alaska to learn about his family and enters the race. DVD, VHS.

5020. *Wired: The Short Life and Fast Times of John Belushi* (Bob Woodward, 1984). Cautionary biography of the comic actor (1949–1984), who died of a massive drug overdose. **Adaptation:** *Wired* (Taurus, 1989). Dir: Larry Peerce. Scr: Earl Mac Rauch. Cast: Michael Chiklis (Belushi), Ray Sharkey (Angel), J. T. Walsh (Woodward), Patti D'Arbanville (Cathy). VHS.

5021. *Wise Blood* (Flannery O'Connor, 1952). An Army veteran becomes a traveling atheist preacher and founder of the "Church of Truth Without Jesus Christ Crucified." **Adaptation:** *Wise Blood* (New Line, 1979). Dir: John Huston. Scr: Benedict Fitzgerald, Michael Fitzgerald. Cast: Brad Dourif (Hazel), John Huston (Grandfather), Dan Shor (Enoch), Harry Dean Stanton (Asa). VHS.

5022. *Wiseguy: Life in a Mafia Family* (Nicholas Pileggi, 1985). Factual account of Henry Hill, a young Brooklyn man involved with New York's Luchese crime family beginning in the 1950's. After he and his friends robbed Lufthansa Airlines of six million dollars, their relationship soured, and he was forced into the Federal Witness Protection program. **Adaptation:** *Goodfellas* (Warner, 1990). Dir: Martin Scorsese. Scr: Nicholas Pileggi, Martin Scorsese. Cast: Robert De Niro (Jimmy), Ray Liotta (Henry), Joe Pesci (Tommy), Lorraine Bracco (Karen), Paul Sorvino (Paul). **Notes:** Academy Award for Best Supporting Actor (Pesci) and nominations for Best Picture, Director, Screenplay, Supporting Actress (Bracco), and Editing; National Board of Review Award for Best Supporting Actor (Pesci); Golden Globe nominations for Best Picture, Director, Screenplay, Supporting Actor (Pesci), and Supporting Actress (Bracco). DVD, VHS.

5023. *The Witches* (Roald Dahl, 1983). A young boy is transformed into a mouse by a group of witches who are planning to kill all of the children in England. With the help of his grandmother, he sets out to thwart their plan. **Adaptation:** *The Witches* (Warner, 1990). Dir: Nicolas Roeg. Scr: Allan Scott. Cast: Anjelica Huston (Eva), Mai Zetterling (Helga), Jasen Fisher (Luke), Jane Horrocks (Miss Irvine). **Notes:** The witches and the mouse were created by Jim Henson's Creature Shop. It was the late Henson's final film project. DVD, VHS.

The Witches (1966) (see *The Devil's Own*).

Witches' Brew (see *Conjure Wife*).

5024. *The Witches of Eastwick* (John Updike, 1984). Three bored women in a New England village discover their supernatural powers and conjure up a flamboyant and mysterious man, who turns out to be the devil himself. **Adaptation:** *The Witches of Eastwick* (Warner, 1987). Dir: George Miller. Scr: Michael Cristofer. Cast:

Jack Nicholson (Daryl), Cher (Alexandra), Susan Sarandon (Jane), Michelle Pfeiffer (Sukie), Veronica Cartwright (Felicia). DVD, VHS.

5025. *Witchfinder General* (Ronald Bassett, 1966). Historical novel about a seventeenth century English lawyer who profits by accusing people of being witches. **Adaptation:** *Witchfinder General*; released in the U.S. as *The Conqueror Worm* (American International, 1968). Dir: Michael Reeves. Scr: Tom Baker. Michael Reeves. Cast: Vincent Price (Matthew), Ian Ogilvy (Richard), Rupert Davies (John), Hilary Dwyer (Sarah). Notes: The screenplay also contains elements from Edgar Allan Poe's 1843 poem "The Conqueror Worm." VHS.

5026. *The Witch's Daughter* (Nina Bawden [pseudonym for Nina Mabey Kark], 1966). Children's novel about an orphaned girl who is shunned in her Scottish coastal town because the locals believe that her dead mother was a witch. **Adaptation:** *The Witch's Daughter* (Scottish Television/Hallmark, 1996 TV Movie). Dir: Alan Macmillan. Scr: Simon Booker. Cast: Sammy Glenn (Perdita), Simone Lahbib (Zelda), Patrick Bergin (Mr. Smith).

5027. *Witch's Milk* (Peter De Vries, 1968). After the death of their son, a feuding married couple decides to divorce. **Adaptation:** *Pete 'n' Tillie* (Universal, 1972). Dir: Martin Ritt. Scr: Julius J. Epstein. Cast: Walter Matthau (Pete), Carol Burnett (Tillie), Geraldine Page (Gertrude), Barry Nelson (Burt). Notes: Academy Award nominations for Best Screenplay and Supporting Actress (Page); Golden Globe nominations for Best Actor (Matthau), Actress (Burnett), and Supporting Actress (Page). VHS.

Without a Trace (see *Still Missing*).

Without Apparent Motive (see *Ten Plus One*).

5028. "Witness for the Prosecution" (Agatha Christie, 1925). A lawyer take on the difficult case of a man accused of killing a middle-aged widow who had given him financial support. The short story was published in *Flynn's* magazine on January 31, 1925, and included in Christie's 1933 short-story collection *The Hound of Death and Other Stories*. It was later adapted by Christie as a successful stage play, which ran in London in 1953 and on Broadway in 1954. **Adaptation 1:** *Witness for the Prosecution* (United Artists, 1957). Dir: Billy Wilder. Scr: Lawrence B. Marcus, Billy Wilder, Harry Kurnitz. Cast: Tyrone Power (Leonard), Marlene Dietrich (Christine), Charles

Laughton (Sir Wilfrid), Elsa Lanchester (Miss Plimsoll), John Williams (Mr. Brogan-Moore). Notes: Academy Award nominations for Best Picture, Director, Actor (Laughton), Supporting Actress (Lanchester), Editing, and Sound; Golden Globe Award for Best Supporting Actress (Lanchester), and nominations for Best Picture, Director, Actor (Laughton), and Actress (Dietrich). DVD, VHS. **Adaptation 2:** *Witness for the Prosecution* (CBS, 1982 TV Movie). Dir: Alan Gibson. Scr: Billy Wilder, Harry Kurnitz, Lawrence B. Marcus (1957 screenplay), John Gay. Cast: Ralph Richardson (Sir Wilfred), Deborah Kerr (Miss Plimsoll), Beau Bridges (Leonard), Donald Pleasence (Mr. Myers), Wendy Hiller (Janet), Diana Rigg (Christine).

5029. *The Witnesses* (Anne Holden, 1971). After his lover witnesses a sexual attack on a woman from his bedroom window, a man having an affair with his boss's wife protects her by claiming to be the witness and immediately becomes the prime suspect in the crime. Now he must try to find the real rapist in order to clear his name. **Adaptation:** *The Bedroom Window* (De Laurentiis, 1987). Dir: Curtis Hanson. Scr: Curtis Hanson. Cast: Steve Guttenberg (Terry), Elizabeth McGovern (Denise), Isabelle Huppert (Sylvia), Carl Lumbly (Quirke). DVD, VHS.

5030. *Wives and Concubines* (Su Tong, 1990). The Chinese novella is set in the 1920's and centers on a young woman who becomes the fourth wife of rich old merchant, finding herself in competition with his other three wives for his attention. The novella appeared in the collection *Raise the Red Lantern: Three Novellas*, which was translated into English in 1991. **Adaptation:** *Raise the Red Lantern* (Orion, 1991). Dir: Yimou Zhang. Scr: Ni Zhen. Cast: Li Gong (Songlian), Caifei He (the Third Concubine), Jingwu Ma (the Master), Cuifen Cao (the Second Concubine). Notes: Originally released as *Da Hong Deng Long Gao Gao Gua* and shown with subtitles. BAFTA Award for Best Foreign-Language Film; Academy Award and Independent Spirit Award nominations for Best Foreign-Language Film. DVD, VHS.

5031. *Wives and Daughters* (Elizabeth Cleghorn Gaskell, 1866). After the death of his wife, a doctor with a young daughter marries a widow who also has a daughter, The two young women eventually fall in love with a pair of aristocratic brothers, whose father opposes the matches. The novel was published posthumously a year after Gaskell's sudden death in 1865. **Adaptation 1:** *Wives and Daughters* (BBC, 1971 TV

Miniseries). Dir: Hugh David. Scr: Michael Voysey. Cast: Zhivila Roche (Molly), Alan MacNaughtan (Dr. Gibson), Helen Christie (Clare), Rosalind Lloyd (Cynthia), Stephan Chase (Osborne). **Adaptation 2:** *Wives and Daughters* (BBC/PBS, 1999 TV Miniseries). Dir: Nicholas Renton. Scr: Andrew Davies. Cast: Justine Waddell (Molly), Bill Paterson (Dr. Gibson), Francesca Annis (Claire), Keeley Hawes (Cynthia), Tom Hollander (Osborne), Anthony Howell (Roger), Michael Gambon (Squire Hamley). Notes: BAFTA Awards for Best Television Actor (Gambon), Production Design, Makeup and Hairstyling, and Photography and Lighting, and nominations for Best Miniseries, Actress (Annis), and Sound. DVD, VHS.

5032. *Wives of Bath* (Susan E. Swan, 1993). A coming-of-age novel about a teenaged girl who is sent to an exclusive girls' boarding school, where she discovers that her roommates are involved in a lesbian affair. **Adaptation:** *Lost and Delirious* (Lions Gate, 2001). Dir: Lea Pool. Scr: Judith Thompson. Cast: Piper Perabo (Pauline), Jessica Pare (Victoria), Mischa Barton (Mary), Jackie Burroughs (Fay). DVD,VHS.

The Wiz (see *The Wonderful Wizard of Oz*).

The Wizard (see *The Gaunt Stranger*).

5033. *The Wizard of Loneliness* (John Treadwell Nichols, 1966). After his mother's death and his father's departure for World War II, a mean-spirited adolescent moves in with his grandparents in Vermont in the 1940's. When he witnesses the abuse of his aunt by her boyfriend, a disturbed ex-convict, the boy gradually matures. **Adaptation:** *The Wizard of Loneliness* (American Plahouse/Skouras, 1988). Dir: H. Anne Riley. Scr: Nancy Larson, H. Anne Riley. Cast: Alan Wright (Conductor), Lukas Haas (Wendall), Steve Hendrickson (Fred), Dylan Baker (Duffy). VHS.

The Wizard of Oz (see *The Wonderful Wizard of Oz*).

5034. *Woe to Live On* (Daniel Woodrell, 1987). Two friends in Missouri during the Civil War join the Bushwhackers, irregular soldiers fighting on the side of the South, and take part in a massacre of the people in a small Kansas town. The book was subsequently reissued under the title *Ride with the Devil*. **Adaptation:** *Ride with the Devil* (Universal, 1999). Dir: Ang Lee. Scr: James Schamus. Cast: Skeet Ulrich (Jack), Tobey Maguire (Jake), Jewel Kilcher (Sue), Jeffrey

Wright (Daniel), Simon Baker (George), Jonathan Rhys-Meyers (Pitt), James Caviezel (Black John). DVD, VHS.

5035. *The Wolf Hunters* (James Oliver Curwood, 1908). Western about a cowboy who travels to Canada to locate a missing miner and his young daughter. **Adaptation:** *The Trail Beyond* (Monogram, 1934). Dir: Robert Bradbury. Scr: Lindsley Parsons. Cast: John Wayne (Rod), Verna Hillie (Felice), Noah Beery (George), Noah Beery, Jr. (Wabi), Robert Frazer (Jules). DVD, VHS.

Wolf Larsen (see *The Sea Wolf*).

5036. "The Wolf, the Forest and the New Man" (Senel Paz, 1991). The Cuban short story, originally titled *El lobo, el bosque y el hombre nuevo*, is about the relationship that develops between a naïve communist student and a cultured homosexual subversive. The story was translated and published in the Fall 1996 issue of *Conjunctions*. **Adaptation:** *Strawberry and Chocolate* (Miramax, 1994). Dir: Tomas Gutierrez Alea, Juan Carlos Tabio. Scr: Senel Paz. Cast: Jorge Perugorria (Diego), Vladimir Cruz (David), Mirta Ibarra (Nancy), Francisco Gattorno (Miguel). Notes: Originally released as *Fresa y Chocolate* and shown with subtitles. Academy Award nomination for Best Foreign-Language Film. DVD, VHS.

5037. *Wolfen* (Whitley Strieber, 1978). A New York detective investigates a series of mutilation murders carried out by the spirits of savage beasts which, according to Native American legend, have emerged from the supernatural underground. **Adaptation:** *Wolfen* (Orion/Warner, 1981). Dir: Michael Wadleigh. Scr: David Eyre, Michael Wadleigh. Cast: Albert Finney (Dewey), Diane Venora (Rebecca), Edward James Olmos (Eddie), Gregory Hines (Whittington). DVD, VHS.

The Wolvercote Tongue (see *The Jewel That Was Ours*).

5038. *The Wolves of Willoughby Chase* (Joan Aiken, 1962). Two young sisters discover that their governess is plotting to steal their family's home and fortune. **Adaptation:** *The Wolves of Willoughby* Chase (Atlantic, 1988). Dir: Stuart Orme. Scr: William M. Akers. Cast: Stephanie Beacham (Letitia), Mel Smith (Mr. Grimshaw), Emily Hudson (Bonnie), Aleks Darowska (Sylvia). VHS.

A Woman Alone (see *The Secret Agent*).

Woman-Bait (see *Maigret Sets a Trap*).

The Woman in Red (1935) (see *North Shore*).

5039. *The Woman in Red* (Anthony Gilbert [pseudonym for Lucy Beatrice Malleson], 1941). A young woman employed by a wealthy family is kidnapped and forced to impersonate an heiress. **Adaptation 1:** *My Name Is Julia Ross* (Columbia, 1945). Dir: Joseph H. Lewis. Scr: Muriel Roy Bolton. Cast: Nina Foch (Julia), Dame May Whitty (Mrs. Hughes), George Macready (Ralph). **Adaptation 2:** *Dead of Winter* (MGM, 1987). Dir: Arthur Penn. Scr: Marc Shmuger, Mark Malone. Cast: Mary Steenburgen (Julie /Katie/Evelyn), Roddy McDowall (Mr. Murray), Jan Rubes (Dr. Lewis). DVD, VHS.

5040. *Woman in the Dark* (Dashiell Hammett, 1933). A couple living in an isolated house take in a frightened girl and are threatened by the men pursuing her. The novella was published in three installments in *Liberty* magazine in April 1933. **Adaptation:** *Woman in the Dark* (RKO, 1934). Dir: Phil Rosen. Scr: Sada Cowan. Cast: Fay Wray (Louise), Ralph Bellamy (John), Melvyn Douglas (Tony), Roscoe Ates (Tommy). VHS.

5041. *The Woman in the Hall* (G. B. Stern, 1939). A poor woman becomes a professional beggar in order to get a good edication for her daughters. **Adaptation:** *The Woman in the Hall* (Eagle-Lion, 1947). Dir: Jack Lee. Scr: Ian Dalrymple, Jack Lee, G. B. Stern. Cast: Ursula Jeans (Lorna), Jean Simmons (Joy), Cecil Parker (Sir Halmar), Joan Miller (Susan).

5042. "The Woman in the Room"(Stephen King, 1978). A fatally ill woman asks her son to help her die, a request he carries out but comes to regret. The story was originally published in King's 1978 short-story collection *Nightshift*. **Adaptation:** *The Woman in the Room*; released on video as *Stephen King's Night Shift Collection* (Granite/Interglobal, 1983). Dir: Frank Darabont. Scr: Frank Darabont. Cast: Michael Cornelison (John), Dee Croxton (John's Mother). VHS.

The Woman in the Window (see *Once Off Guard*).

5043. *The Woman in White* (Wilkie Collins, 1860). A mad aristocrat drugs and imprisons his sister so that he can inherit her estate. **Silent Films:** 1912, 1917, and 1929. **Adaptation 1:** *Crimes at the Dark House* (British Lion/Exploitation, 1940). Dir: George King. Scr: Edward Dryhurst, Frederick Hayward, H. F. Maltby. Cast: Tod Slaughter (Percival), Sylvia Marriott (Laurie), Hilary Eaves (Marion), Geoffrey Wardwell (Paul).

VHS. **Adaptation 2:** *The Woman in White* (Warner, 1948). Dir: Peter Godfrey. Scr: Stephen Morehouse Avery. Cast: Alexis Smith (Marian), Eleanor Parker (Laura/Ann), Sydney Greenstreet (Count Fosco), Gig Young (Walter), Agnes Moorehead (Countess Fosco). **Adaptation 3:** *The Woman in White* (BBC/PBS, 1982 TV Miniseries). Dir: John Bruce. Scr: Ray Jenkins. Cast: Deirdra Morris (Ann), Daniel Gerroll (Walter), Milo Sperber (Pesca), Ann Queensberry (Mrs. Hartright). **Adaptation 4:** *The Woman in White* (BBC/PBS, 1997 TV Miniseries). Dir: Tim Fywell. Scr: David Pirie. Cast: Tara Fitzgerald (Marian), Justine Waddell (Laura), Andrew Lincoln (Walter), Susan Vidler (Anne). Notes: BAFTA Awards for Best Production Design and Photography and Lighting, and nominations for Best Drama Serial and Costume Design. VHS.

Woman Obsessed (see *The Snow Birch*).

A Woman of Evil (see *Queen Margot*).

5044. *A Woman of Independent Means* (Elizabeth Forsythe Hailey, 1978). After the death of her husband, a prominent Dallas woman suffers through an unhappy second marriage and the death of her oldest son, but ultimately emerges strong and independent. **Adaptation:** *A Woman of Independent Means* (NBC, 1995 TV Miniseries). Dir: Robert Greenwald. Scr: Cindy Myers. Cast: Sally Field (Bess), Ron Silver (Arthur), Tony Goldwyn (Robert), Jack Thompson (Sam). Notes: Emmy Award for Outstanding Costume Design and nominations for Outstanding Miniseries, Lead Actress (Field), and Casting; Golden Globe Award for Best Television Actress (Field).

5045. *Woman of Straw* (Catherine Arley, 1957). The nurse to a wealthy old man schemes to murder him with the help of his nephew. **Adaptation:** *Woman of Straw* (United Artists, 1964). Dir: Basil Dearden. Scr: Stanley Mann, Robert Muller, Michael Relph. Cast: Gina Lollobrigida (Maria), Sean Connery (Anthony), Ralph Richardson (Charles). DVD, VHS.

A Woman of the World (see *The Green Hat*).

The Woman on the Beach (see *None So Blind*).

A Woman Rebels (see *Portrait of a Rebel*).

5046. *Woman, Thou Art Loosed!: Healing the Wounds of the Past* (T. D. Jakes, 1993). Inspirational Christian book aimed at helping women who have suffered various kinds of abuse. The book was adapted as a 1999 stage play. **Adapta-**

tion: *Woman, Thou Art Loosed* (Magnolia, 2004). Dir: Michael Schultz. Scr: Stan Foster. Cast: Kimberly Elise (Michelle), Loretta Devine (Cassie), Debbi Morgan (Twana), Michael Boatman (Todd), Clifton Powell (Reggie). DVD, VHS.

5047. *The Woman Who Was* (Pierre Boileau and Thomas Narcejac, 1952). The French novel, originally titled *Celle qui n'etait plus*, concerns a sadistic school headmaster and the plot by his wife and mistress to kill him. Although they are successful, he comes back to haunt them. **Adaptation 1:** *Diabolique*; released in the UK as *The Fiends* (UMPO, 1955). Dir: Henri-Georges Clouzot. Scr: Henri-Georges Clouzot, Jerome Geronimi, Frederic Grendel, Rene Masson. Cast: Simone Signoret (Nicole), Vera Clouzot (Christina), Paul Meurisse (Michel), Charles Vanel (Alfred). Notes: Originally released as *Les Diaboliques* and shown with subtitles. DVD, VHS. **Adaptation 2:** *Reflections of Murder* (ABC, 1974 TV Movie). Dir: John Badham. Scr: Carol Sobieski. Cast: Tuesday Weld (Vicky), Joan Hackett (Claire), Sam Waterston (Michael), Lucille Benson (Mrs. Turner). **Adaptation 3:** *House of Secrets* (NBC, 1993 TV Movie). Dir: Mimi Leder. Scr: Andrew Laskos. Cast: Melissa Gilbert (Marion), Bruce Boxleitner (Dr. Ravinel), Kate Vernon (Laura), Michael Boatman (Sergeant DuBois), Cicely Tyson (Evangeline). **Adaptation 4:** *Diabolique* (Warner, 1996). Dir: Jeremiah Chechik. Scr: Henri-Georges Clouzot (1955 screenplay), Don Roos. Cast: Sharon Stone (Nicole), Isabelle Adjani (Mia), Chazz Palminteri (Guy), Kathy Bates (Shirley), Spalding Gray (Simon). DVD, VHS.

The Woman with No Name (see *Happy Now I Go*).

Woman Without a Face (see *Buddwing*).

The Woman's Angle (see *Three Cups of Coffee*).

A Woman's Secret (see *Mortgage on Life*).

A Woman's Vengeance (see "The Gioconda Smile").

Women in Film (see *I'm Losing You*).

5048. *Women in Love* (D. H. Lawrence, 1920). The sequel to Lawrence's 1915 novel *The Rainbow* concerns two sisters who travel from their small coalmining town to Switzerland, where they explore their sexuality. **Adaptation:** *Women in Love* (United Artists, 1969). Dir: Ken Russell. Scr: Larry Kramer. Cast: Alan Bates (Rupert), Oliver Reed (Gerald), Glenda Jackson (Gudrun), Jennie Linden (Ursula). Notes: Academy Award for Best Actress (Jackson) and nomina-

tions for Best Director, Screenplay, and Cinematography; National Board of Review Award for Best Actress (Jackson); Golden Globe Award for Best Foreign Film and nominations for Best Director and Actress (Jackson); BAFTA nominations for Best Film, Director, Screenplay, Actor (Bates), Actress (Jackson), Newcomer (Linden), Cinematography, Art Direction, Costume Design, and Soundtrack. DVD, VHS.

5049. *Women in the Wind* (Francis Walton, 1935). A woman enters an air show to earn money for a family member's medical needs. **Adaptation:** *Women in the Wind* (Warner, 1939). Dir: John Farrow. Scr: Lee Katz, Albert De Mond. Cast: Kay Francis (Janet), William Gargan (Ace), Victor Jory (Dr. Wilson).

5050. *The Women of Brewster Place* (Gloria Naylor, 1982, National Book Award). A look at the lives of seven black women living in a walled-off tenement and struggling to survive amid the poverty and violence in their neighborhood. **Adaptation:** *The Women of Brewster Place* (ABC 1989 TV Miniseries). Dir: Donna Deitch. Scr: Karen Hall. Cast: Oprah Winfrey (Mattie), Mary Alice (Fannie), Olivia Cole (Sophie), Robin Givens (Kiswana), Moses Gunn (Ben), Paula Kelly (Theresa). Notes: Emmy nominations for Outstanding Miniseries and Supporting Actress (Kelly). DVD, VHS. Notes: In addition, the book was also the basis for a short-lived television series in 1990 titled *Brewster Place* (VHS).

5051. *Women Talking Dirty* (Isla Dewar, 1996). Scottish novel about a young pregnant woman and a female graphic artist who become friends based on their bad experiences with men. **Adaptation:** *Women Talking Dirty* (Petunia/Doumanian, 1999). Dir: Coky Giedroyc. Scr: Isla Dewar. Cast: Helena Bonham Carter (Cora), Gina McKee (Ellen), Eileen Atkins (Emily), Kenneth Cranham (George), James Nesbitt (Stanley), James Purefoy (Daniel). DVD, VHS.

5052. *The Women's Room* (Marilyn French, 1977). After her divorce in the late 1960's, a submissive suburban housewife goes back to college and discovers a liberating new world. **Adaptation:** *The Women's Room* (ABC, 1980 TV Movie). Dir: Glenn Jordan. Scr: Carol Sobieski. Cast: Lee Remick (Mira), Colleen Dewhurst (Val), Patty Duke (Lily), Kathryn Harrold (Bliss), Tovah Feldshuh (Iso), Tyne Daly (Adele). Notes: Emmy Award nominations for Outstanding Dramatic Special, Supporting Actresses (Dewhurst and Duke), and Editing.

5053. *Wonder Boys* (Michael Chabon, 1995).

An English professor who once published a well-regarded novel is experiencing writer's block and tries to contend with his nagging agent, his pregnant married lover, and other personal problems. **Adaptation:** *Wonder Boys* (Paramount, 2000). Dir: Curtis Hanson. Scr: Steve Kloves. Cast: Michael Douglas (Grady), Tobey Maguire (James), Frances McDormand (Sara), Robert Downey, Jr. (Terry). Notes: Academy Award for Best Song and nominations for Best Screenplay and Editing; Golden Globe nominations for Best Screenplay and Actor (Douglas). DVD, VHS.

5054. *The Wonderful Country* (Tom Lea, 1952). Western about a gunrunner who is persuaded to go straight and join the Texas Rangers. **Adaptation:** *The Wonderful Country* (United Artists, 1959). Dir: Robert Parrish. Scr: Robert Ardrey. Cast: Robert Mitchum (Martin), Julie London (Helen), Gary Merrill (Major Colton), Albert Dekker (Captain Rucker).

The Wonderful Land of Oz (see *The Marvelous Land of Oz*)

5055. *The Wonderful Wizard of Oz* (L. Frank Baum, 1900). Baum's classic children's story tells of young Dorothy's "trip" from a farm in Kansas to the land of Oz, where she encounters many dangers, makes close friends, and learns about herself in the process. The book was adapted for the stage in 1902 and made its Broadway debut in 1903. **Silent Films:** 1910, 1914, written and directed by Baum and titled *His Majesty, the Scarecrow of Oz*, combining elements from this book and *The Scarecrow of Oz*, which was published in 1915 (DVD, VHS), and 1925, directed by Larry Semon and co-written by L. Frank Baum, Jr. (DVD, VHS). **Adaptation 1:** *The Wizard of Oz* (MGM, 1939). Dir: Victor Fleming. Scr: Noel Langley, Florence Ryerson, Edgar Allan Woolf. Cast: Judy Garland (Dorothy), Frank Morgan (the Wizard/Professor Marvel), Ray Bolger (Huck/ the Scarecrow), Bert Lahr (Zeke/the Cowardly Lion), Jack Haley (Hickory/the Tin Man), Billie Burke (Glinda), Margaret Hamilton (Miss Gulch/ the Wicked Witches). Notes: Academy Awards for Best Musical Score and Song, Special Academy Award for Juvenile Performer (Garland), and nominations for Best Picture, Cinematography, Art Direction, and Special Effects; Cannes Film Festival Golden Palm nomination for Best Director. DVD, VHS. **Adaptation 2:** *The Wiz* (1978). Dir: Sidney Lumet. Scr: Joel Schumacher. Cast: Diana Ross (Dorothy), Michael Jackson (the Scarecrow), Nipsey Russell (the Tinman), Ted

Ross (the Cowardly Lion), Lena Horne (Glinda), Richard Pryor (the Wiz). Notes: A modern black musical adaptation, originally a 1975 Broadway play written by Charlie Smalls and William Brown. DVD, VHS. **Adaptation 3:** *The Wonderful Wizard of Oz* (Cinar, 1987). Dir: Gerald Potterton, Tim Reid. Scr: Don Arioli, Tim Reid. Cast: voices of Margot Kidder (Narrator), Morgan Hallet (Dorothy), George Morris (the Tinman), Neil Shee (the Cowardly Lion), Richard Dumont (the Scarecrow). Notes: An animated feature film. DVD, VHS. See also *The Marvelous Land of Oz* and *Ozma of Oz*.

5056. *The Wood Beyond* (Reginald Hill, 1995). In the sixteenth installment of Hill's popular series (1970–2004) featuring British policemen Andrew Dalziel and Peter Pascoe, Pascoe attends his grandmother's funeral and tries to reconnect with his past while Dalziel becomes romantically involved with an animal-rights activist who may be a murderer. **Adaptation:** *Dalziel and Pascoe: The Wood Beyond* (BBC/A&E, 1998 TV Movie series). Dir: Edward Bennett. Scr: Ed Whitmore. Cast: Warren Clarke (Dalziel), Colin Buchanan (Pascoe), Susannah Corbett (Ellie), David Royle (Edgar), Frances Barber (Amanda).

The Wooden Horse (see *The Tunnel Escape*).

5057. *The Woodlanders* (Thomas Hardy, 1887). The daughter of a rural British merchant returns from finishing school and prepares to marry her childhood sweetheart. However, her father insists that she do better, and she marries a doctor with whom she is unhappy. The novel was originally serialized in *Macmillan's Magazine* in England and *Harper's* in the United States. **Adaptation:** *The Woodlanders* (Miramax, 1997). Dir: Phil Agland. Scr: David Rudkin. Cast: Emily Woof (Grace), Rufus Sewell (Giles), Cal Macaninch (Dr. FitzPiers), Tony Haygarth (Mr. Melbury), Jodhi May (Marty). DVD, VHS.

5058. *The Word* (Irving Wallace, 1972). An archaeologist discovers a lost gospel that calls into question the foundations of Christianity and various interested parties try to obtain it. **Adaptation:** *The Word* (CBS, 1978 TV Miniseries). Dir: Richard Lang. Scr: Richard Berg, Richard Fielder, Robert L. Joseph, S. S. Schweitzer. Cast: David Janssen (Steve), James Whitmore (George), Florinda Bolkan (Angela), Eddie Albert (Ogden), Geraldine Chaplin (Naomi). VHS.

5059. *Word of Honor* (Nelson De Mille, 1985). A recently published book accuses a former military officer of leading a massacre in a small village during the Vietnam War, and he is brought up on murder charges as the military tries to cover up its involvement. **Adaptation:** *Word of Honor* (Turner, 2003 TV Movie). Dir: Robert Markowitz. Scr: Jacob Epstein, Leslie Greif, Jean-Yves Pitoun, Tom Topor. Cast: Don Johnson (Benjamin), Jeanne Tripplehorn (Major Harper), Sharon Lawrence (Marcy), John Heard (Dr. Brandt), Arliss Howard (Runnells).

The Working Man (see *The Adopted Father*).

5060. *The World According to Garp* (John Irving, 1978, National Book Award). The episodic tale of a serious writer's determination to succeed and his mother's fame as the author of a feminist tract. **Adaptation:** *The World According to Garp* (Warner, 1982). Dir: George Roy Hill. Scr: Steve Tesich. Cast: Robin Williams (Garp), Mary Beth Hurt (Helen), Glenn Close (Jenny), John Lithgow (Muldoon), Hume Cronyn (Mr. Fields), Jessica Tandy (Mrs. Fields). Notes: National Board of Review Award for Best Supporting Actress (Close); Academy Award nominations for Best Supporting Actress (Close) and Supporting Actor (Lithgow);. DVD, VHS.

5061. *The World in His Arms* (Rex Beach, 1946). In San Francisco in the mid–nineteenth century, a tough seaman falls in love with a Russian aristocrat. **Adaptation:** *The World in His Arms* (Universal International, 1952). Dir: Raoul Walsh. Scr: Borden Chase. Cast: Gregory Peck (Jonathan), Ann Blyth (Countess Marina), Anthony Quinn (Portugee), John McIntire (Greathouse). VHS.

5062. *The World in My Pocket* (James Hadley Chase [pseudonym for Rene Brabazon Raymond], 1959. A British gang plans to rob an American army supply truck. **Adaptation:** *On Friday at Eleven*; released in the U.S. as *The World in My Pocket* (MGM, 1961). Dir: Alvin Rakoff. Scr: Frank Harvey. Cast: Nadja Tiller (Ginny), Rod Steiger (Morgan), Peter van Eyck (Bleck), Ian Bannen (Kitson).

5063. *The World Is Full of Married Men* (Jackie Collins, 1968). The wife of a philandering advertising executive has affairs of her own. **Adaptation:** *The World Is Full of Married Men* (New Line, 1979). Dir: Robert William Young. Scr: Jackie Collins. Cast: Anthony Franciosa (David), Carroll Baker (Linda), Sherrie Lee Cronn (Claudia), Paul Nicholas (Gem). VHS.

5064. *The World of Henry Orient* (Nora Johnson, 1958). Satiric comedy about two teen-aged girls who follow their idol, an eccentric concert pianist, around Manhattan as he pursues a young woman. **Adaptation:** *The World of Henry Orient* (United Artists, 1964). Dir: George Roy Hill. Scr: Nora Johnson, Nunnally Johnson. Cast: Peter Sellers (Henry), Paula Prentiss (Stella), Angela Lansbury (Isabel), Tom Bosley (Frank), Phyllis Thaxter (Mrs. Gilbert), Bibi Osterwald (Erica), Merrie Spaeth (Marian), Tippy Walker (Val). DVD, VHS.

5065. *The World of Suzie Wong* (Richard Mason, 1957). An American artist in Hong King falls in love with an affable prostitute. The novel was adapted as a Broadway play by Paul Osborn in 1958. **Adaptation:** *The World of Suzie Wong* (Paramount, 1960). Dir: Richard Quine. Scr: John Patrick. Cast: William Holden (Robert), Nancy Kwan (Suzie), Sylvia Syms (Kay), Michael Wilding (Ben). DVD, VHS.

5066. *The World Owes Me a Living* (John Llewellyn-Rhys, 1939). After a crash, a pilot suffers from amnesia and tries to recall his past. **Adaptation:** *The World Owes Me a Living* (British National, 1944). Dir: Vernon Sewell. Scr: Irwin Reine, Vernon Sewell. Cast: David Farrar (Paul), Judy Campbell (Moira), Sonia Dresdel (Eve).

5067. *Worth Winning* (Dan Lewandowski, 1985). On a bet with his friends, a womanizing man proposes to three women. **Adaptation:** *Worth Winning* (20th Century–Fox, 1989). Dir: Will Mackenzie. Scr: Josann McGibbon, Sara Parriott. Cast: Mark Harmon (Taylor), Madeleine Stowe (Veronica), Lesley Ann Warren (Eleanor), Maria Holvoe (Erin), Mark Blum (Ned), Andrea Martin (Clair). VHS.

5068. *Would You Settle for Improbable?* (P. J. Petersen, 1981). Children's book about a troubled teen from a juvenile-detention facility who tries to fit in with his high-school peers. **Adaptation:** *No Big Deal* (Cinetudes, 1983). Dir: Robert Charlton. Scr: Robert Charlton. Cast: Kevin Dillon (Arnold), Christopher Gartin (Michael), Tammy Grimes (Arnold's Mother), Stacy Lauren (Jennifer), Sylvia Miles (the Principal). VHS.

5069. *The Wounded and the Slain* (David Goodis, 1955). An alcoholic writer and his troubled wife visit Haiti, where he kills a black man who was trying to rob him. **Adaptation:** *Descent into Hall* (Images, 1986). Dir: Francis Girod. Scr: Jean-Loup Dabadie, Francis Girod. Cast: Claude Brasseur (Alan Kolber), Sophie Marceau (Lola Kolber), Betsy Blair (Mrs. Burns).

5070. *The Wrath of God* (Jack Higgins [pseudonym for Harry Patterson], 1971). During the 1920's a bootlegger and a defrocked priest become involved in a political revolution in Mexico.

The novel was originally published under the pseudonym James Graham and later issued under Patterson's more famous pen name, Jack Higgins. **Adaptation:** *The Wrath of God* (MGM, 1972). Dir: Ralph Nelson. Scr: Jack Higgins (writing as James Graham), Ralph Nelson. Cast: Robert Mitchum (Van Horne), Frank Langella (De La Plata), Rita Hayworth (Senora De La Plata), John Colicos (Colonel Santilla), Victor Buono (Jennings). VHS.

5071. *The Wreck of the Mary Deare* (Hammond Innes, 1956). A salvage-boat captain is unjustly accused of negligence when his ship is wrecked on the high seas. The book was published in the UK as *The Mary Deare*. **Adaptation:** *The Wreck of the Mary Deare* (MGM, 1959). Dir: Michael Anderson. Scr: Eric Ambler. Cast: Gary Cooper (Gideon), Charlton Heston (Sands), Michael Redgrave (Nyland), Emlyn Williams (Sir Wilfred). VHS.

5072. *The Wrecking Crew* (Donald Hamilton, 1960). In the second of Hamilton's twenty-six Matt Helm spy novels (1960–1993), the spy and assassin is sent to stop a criminal who has stolen a cache of gold and plans to use it to cause a financial crisis. **Adaptation:** *The Wrecking Crew* (Columbia, 1969). Dir: Phil Karlson. Scr: William P. McGivern. Cast: Dean Martin (Helm), Elke Sommer (Linka), Sharon Tate (Freya), Nancy Kwan (Wen), Nigel Green (Count Contini), Tina Louise (Lola). VHS.

5073. *Written in Blood* (Caroline Graham, 1994). The fourth of Graham's six novels (1987–1999) featuring British Inspector Tom Barnaby finds the policeman investigating the murder of an amateur writer. **Adaptation:** *Midsomer Murders: Written in Blood* (BBC/A&E, 1997–2004 TV Movie Series). Dir: Jeremy Silberston. Scr: Anthony Horowitz. Cast: John Nettles (Barnaby), Daniel Casey (Gavin), Jane Wymark (Joyce), Laura Howard (Cully), Barry Jackson (Dr. Bullard). DVD, VHS.

5074. *Written on the Wind* (Robert Wilder, 1946). A secretary marries her boss, an oil tycoon, and clashes with his dysfunctional family. **Adaptation:** *Written on the Wind* (Universal International, 1956). Dir: Douglas Sirk. Scr: George Zuckerman. Cast: Rock Hudson (Mitch), Lauren Bacall (Lucy), Robert Stack (Kyle), Dorothy Malone (Marylee). Notes: Academy Award for Best Supporting Actress (Malone) and nominations for Best Supporting Actor (Stack) and Musical Score; Golden Globe Award nomination for Best Supporting Actress (Malone). DVD, VHS.

5075. *The Wrong Box* (Robert Louis Stevenson and Lloyd Osbourne, 1889). Two elderly Victorian brothers, the last survivors in a lottery game in which the prize goes to the final man left alive, try to kill each other. Stevenson wrote the book with his stepson, Lloyd Osbourne. **Adaptation:** *The Wrong Box* (Columbia, 1966). Dir: Bryan Forbes. Scr: Larry Gelbart, Burt Shevelove. Cast: Jeremy Lloyd (Brian), John Mills (Masterman), Ralph Richardson (Joseph), Michael Caine (Michael), James Villiers (Sydney). Notes: BAFTA Award for Best Costume Design and nominations for Best British Actor (Richardson) and Art Direction. VHS.

Wrong Is Right (see *The Better Angels*).

Wrong Move (see *Wilhelm Meister's Apprenticeship*).

5076. *The Wrong Venus* (Charles Williams, 1966). Comic novel about a timid man hired to finish the sex novel begun by a well-known writer who has disappeared. **Adaptation:** *Don't Just Stand There!* (Universal, 1968). Dir: Ron Winston. Scr: Charles Williams. Cast: Robert Wagner (Lawrence), Mary Tyler Moore (Martine), Glynis Johns (Sabine), Harvey Korman (Merriman).

WUSA (see *A Hall of Mirrors*).

5077. *Wuthering Heights* (Emily Bronte, 1847). The classic British novel centers on the doomed love affair between an unhappy middle-class woman and her foster brother, a gypsy who was raised in her household. **Silent Film:** 1920. **Adaptation 1:** *Wuthering Heights* (United Artists, 1939). Dir: William Wyler. Scr: Charles MacArthur, Ben Hecht. Cast: Merle Oberon (Cathy), Laurence Olivier (Heathcliff), David Niven (Edgar), Flora Robson (Ellen), Donald Crisp (Dr. Kenneth), Geraldine Fitzgerald (Isabella). Notes: Academy Award for Best Cinematography and nominations for Best Picture, Director, Screenplay, Actor (Olivier), Supporting Actress (Fitzgerald), and Musical Score. DVD, VHS. **Adaptation 2:** *Wuthering Heights* (BBC, 1967 TV Miniseries). Dir: Peter Sasdy. Scr: Hugh Leonard. Cast: Ian McShane (Heathcliff), Angela Scoular (Cathy), Drewe Henley (Edgar), Angela Douglas (Isabella). **Adaptation 3:** *Wuthering Heights* (American International, 1970). Dir: Robert Fuest. Scr: Patrick Tilley. Cast: Anna Calder-Marshall (Cathy), Timothy Dalton (Heathcliff), Harry Andrews (Mr. Earnshaw), Pamela Brown (Mrs. Linton), Judy Cornwell

(Nellie), James Cossins (Mr. Linton). DVD, VHS. **Adaptation 4:** *Wuthering Heights* (BBC, 1978 TV Miniseries). Dir: Peter Hammond. Scr: Hugh Leonard, David Snodin. Cast: Kay Adshead (Cathy), Ken Hutchison (Heathcliff), David Robb (Edgar), Dennis Burgess (Mr. Linton), John Duttine (Earnshaw). **Adaptation 5:** *Wuthering Heights* (Paramount, 1992). Dir: Peter Kosminsky. Scr: Anne Devlin. Cast: Juliette Binoche (Cathy), Ralph Fiennes (Heathcliff), Janet McTeer (Ellen), Sophie Ward (Isabella), Simon Shepherd (Edgar), Jeremy Northam (Earnshaw). DVD, VHS. **Adaptation 6:** *Wuthering Heights* (London Weekend/ PBS, 1998 TV Miniseries). Dir: David Skynner. Scr: Neil McKay. Cast: Sarah Smart (Cathy), Robert Cavanah (Heathcliff), Peter Davison (Lockwood), Matthew MacFadyen (Earnshaw). DVD, VHS. Notes: The novel also inspired a 1954 Mexican film titled *Abismos de Pasion*, directed by Luis Buñuel (VHS) and a 1985 French film titled *Hurlevent* and released in English as *Wuthering Heights*, although it is only partially based on the novel (DVD, VHS). Also a contemporary teen love story titled *Wuthering Heights* and directed by Suri Krishnamma, was released as a made-for-television movie in 2003 (DVD, VHS).

5078. *Wyatt Earp: Frontier Marshal* (Stuart N. Lake, 1931). Marshal Wyatt Earp of Tombstone takes on the notorious Doc Holliday and his gang at the OK Corral. **Adaptation 1:** *Frontier Marshal* (Fox, 1934). Dir: Lew Seiler. Scr: Stuart Anthony, William Conselman. Cast: George O'Brien (Michael), Irene Bentley (Mary), George E. Stone (Abe), Alan Edwards (Doc Warren), Ruth Gillette (Queenie). Notes: In this version, the marshal is named Michael Wyatt. **Adaptation 2:** *Frontier Marshal* (20th Century–Fox, 1939). Dir: Allan Dwan. Scr: Sam Hellman. Cast: Randolph Scott (Earp), Nancy Kelly (Sarah), Cesar Romero (Doc Holliday), Binnie Barnes (Jerry), John Carradine (Ben). **Adaptation 3:** *My Darling Clementine* (20th Century–Fox, 1946). Dir: John Ford. Scr: Samuel G. Engel, Winston Miller. Cast: Henry Fonda (Earp), Linda Darnell (Chihuahua), Victor Mature (Doc Holliday), Cathy Downs (Clementine), Walter Brennan (Clanton). DVD, VHS. Notes: In addition, a film titled *Wyatt Earp* was released in 1994, directed by Lawrence Kasdan, written by Kasdan and Dan Gordon, and starring Kevin Costner. In this version, which is not based on Lake's novel, the legend of Earp is explored, and the character comes across as more cynical and vindictive than he does in earlier treatments (DVD, VHS).

5079. *X v. Rex* (Philip MacDonald, 1933). A jewel thief tries to clear his name when Scotland Yard makes him their prime suspect in a string of London murders. **Adaptation:** *The Mystery of Mr. X* (MGM, 1934). Dir: Edgar Selwyn. Scr: Howard Emmett Rogers, Monckton Hoffe. Cast: Robert Montgomery (Nick), Elizabeth Allan (Jane Frensham), Lewis Stone (Superintendent Connor).

5080. *Yangtse Incident: The Story of HMS Amethyst* (Lawrence Earl, 1950). Historical account involving a British warship attacked by Chinese communists on the Yangtse River in 1949. **Adaptation:** *Yangtse Incident: The Story of HMS Amethyst*; released in the U.S. as *Battle Hell* (British Lion/DCA, 1957). Dir: Michael Anderson. Scr: Eric Ambler. Cast: Richard Todd (Commander Kerans), William Hartnell (Seaman Frank), Akim Tamiroff (Colonel Peng), Donald Houston (Lieutenant Weston). VHS.

5081. *Yankee Gold* (John W. Cunningham, 1946). Western about an honest man who unwittingly becomes involved with stagecoach robbers. **Adaptation:** *The Stranger Wore a Gun* (Columbia, 1953). Dir: Andre De Toth. Scr: Kenneth Gamet. Cast: Randolph Scott (Travis), Claire Trevor (Josie), Joan Weldon (Shelby), George Macready (Jules), Alfonso Bedoya (Degas), Lee Marvin (Kurth), Ernest Borgnine (Bull). VHS.

A Yankee in King Arthur's Court (see *A Connecticut Yankee in King Arthur's Court*).

5082. *Yankee Pasha: The Adventures of Jason Starbuck* (Edison Marshall, 1947). In the nineteenth century, an American fur trader travels to Morocco to rescue the woman he loves from pirates. **Adaptation:** *Yankee Pasha* (Universal International, 1954). Dir: Joseph Pevney. Scr: Joseph Hoffman. Cast: Jeff Chandler (Jason), Rhonda Fleming (Roxana), Mamie Van Doren (Lilith), Lee J. Cobb (the Sultan).

5083. *Yea, Yea, Yea* (Angus McGill, 1963). Comic story about the grandson of England's prime minister and the havoc he causes working as a journalist in a small seaside village. **Adaptation:** *Press for Time* (Rank, 1966). Dir: Robert Asher. Scr: Eddie Leslie, Norman Wisdom. Cast: Norman Wisdom (Norman), Derek Bond (Major Bartlett), Angela Browne (Eleanor). DVD, VHS.

5084. *A Year in Provence* (Peter Mayle, 1989). Autobiographical book about a British couple who quit their jobs and moved to the south of France to live the good life. Once there, however, their idyllic lifestyle was often disturbed by conflicts with the locals. **Adaptation:** *A Year in Provence* (BBC, 1993 TV Miniseries). Dir: David Tucker. Scr: Michael Sadler. Cast: John Thaw (Peter), Lindsay Duncan (Annie), Jean-Pierre Delage (Colombani), Jo Doumerg (Amedee), Marcel Champel (Antoine). DVD, VHS.

5085. *The Year of Living Dangerously* (C. J. Koch, 1978). The story of an Australian journalist's adventures in love and politics in Jakarta, Indonesia, in 1965 as President Sukarno's rule was coming to an end. **Adaptation:** *The Year of Living Dangerously* (MGM, 1982). Dir: Peter Weir. Scr: C. J. Koch, Peter Weir, David Williamson. Cast: Mel Gibson (Guy), Sigourney Weaver (Jill), Linda Hunt (Billy), Michael Murphy (Pete). Notes: Academy Award and National Board of Review Award for Best Supporting Actress (Hunt); Australian Film Institute Award for Best Supporting Actress (Hunt) and nominations for Best Picture, Director, Screenplay, Actor (Gibson), Musical Score, Cinematography, Costume Design, Editing, Production Design, and Sound; Cannes Film Festival Golden Palm nomination for Best Director; Golden Globe nomination for Best Supporting Actress (Hunt). DVD, VHS.

5086. *The Year of the Angry Rabbit* (Russell Braddon, 1964). A scientist trying to develop a drug to control the rabbit population accidentally turns them into monstrous four-foot beasts. **Adaptation:** *Night of the Lepus* (MGM, 1972). Dir: William F. Claxton. Scr: Don Holliday, Gene R. Kearney. Cast: Stuart Whitman (Roy), Janet Leigh (Gerry), Rory Calhoun (Cole), De Forest Kelley (Elgin).

5087. *The Year of the Dragon* (Robert Daley, 1981). A tough New York detective battles murderous youth gangs in the city's Chinatown district. **Adaptation:** *Year of the Dragon* (MGM, 1985). Dir: Michael Cimino. Scr: Oliver Stone, Michael Cimino. Cast: Mickey Rourke (Stanley), John Lone (Joey), Ariane (Tracy), Victor Wong (Harry), Leonard Termo (Angelo). DVD, VHS.

5088. *Year of the Gun* (Michael Mewshaw, 1984). In the 1970's, an American writer in Italy becomes a target of the communist Red Brigades when he discovers their plot to kidnap the Italian president. **Adaptation:** *Year of the Gun* (Triumph, 1991). Dir: John Frankenheimer. Scr: David Ambrose. Cast: Andrew McCarthy (David), Sharon Stone (Alison), Valeria Golino (Lia), John Pankow (Italo). DVD, VHS.

5089. *The Year of the Horse* (Eric Hatch, 1965). Juvenile novel about an advertising man who buys a horse for his teenaged daughter and also uses the horse in a successful ad campaign. **Adaptation:** *The Horse in the Gray Flannel Suit* (Disney/Buena Vista, 1968). Dir: Norman Tokar. Scr: Louis Pelletier. Cast: Dean Jones (Fredrick), Diane Baker (Suzie), Lloyd Bochner (Archer), Fred Clark (Tom), Ellen Janov (Helen), Morey Amsterdam (Charlie), Kurt Russell (Ronnie). DVD, VHS.

5090. *The Year the Yankees Lost the Pennant* (Douglas Wallop, 1954). Faustian fantasy about an obsessive baseball fan who makes a pact with the devil to allow his hometown team to win the World Series. In 1955, George Abbott adapted the novel for his hit Broadway musical *Damn Yankees!* **Adaptation:** *Damn Yankees!*; released in the UK as *What Lola Wants* (Warner, 1958). Dir: George Abbott, Stanley Donen. Scr: George Abbott. Cast: Tab Hunter (Joe), Gwen Verdon (Lola), Ray Walston (Mr. Applegate), Russ Brown (Benny). Notes: Academy Award nomination for Best Musical Score; Golden Globe nomination for Best Musical Film. DVD, VHS.

5091. *The Yearling* (Marjorie Kinnan Rawlings, 1938, Pulitzer Prize). Set in rural Florida after the Civil War, the coming-of-age story of a young boy who is emotionally drawn to a stray deer and convinces his parents to let him adopt it. **Adaptation 1:** *The Yearling* (MGM, 1946). Dir: Clarence Brown. Scr: Paul Osborn. Cast: Gregory Peck (Penny), Jane Wyman (Ma Baxter), Claude Jarman, Jr. (Jody), Chill Wills (Buck). Notes: Academy Awards for Best Cinematography and Art Direction, and nominations for Best Picture, Director, Actor (Peck), Actress (Wyman), and Editing; Golden Globe Award for Best Actor (Peck). DVD, VHS. **Adaptation 2:** *The Yearling* (Turner, 1994 TV Movie). Dir: Rod Hardy. Scr: Joe Wiesenfeld. Cast: Peter Strauss (Penny), Jean Smart (Ora), Wil Horneff (Jody), Philip Seymour Hoffman (Buck). VHS.

5092. *The Years Are So Long* (Josephine Lawrence, 1934). Grim portrait of a poor elderly couple pushed aside by their children and society. The novel was adapted as a stage play titled *Make Way for Tomorrow* by Henry and Noah Leary. **Adaptation:** *Make Way for Tomorrow* (Paramount, 1937). Dir: Leo McCarey. Scr: Vina Delmar. Cast: Victor Moore (Pa Cooper), Beulah Bondi (Ma Cooper), Fay Bainter (Anita), Thomas Mitchell (George).

5093. *Yekl: A Tale of the New York Ghetto* (Abraham Cahan, 1896). Old and New World traditions clash as Jewish immigrants ib New York in the late nineteenth century try to adjust to their new home. **Adaptation:** *Hester Street* (Midwest, 1975). Dir: Joan Micklin Silver. Scr: Joan Micklin Silver. Cast: Carol Kane (Gitl), Steven Keats (Jake), Mel Howard (Bernstein). DVD, VHS.

The Yellow Canary (see *Evil Come, Evil Go*).

The Yellow Winton Flyer (see *The Reivers*).

5094. *Yellowstone Kelly* (Henry W. Allen, 1957). Western about a reclusive mountain man who falls in love with a Sioux woman and helps to avert an Indian uprising. Allen originally published the novel under the pseudonym Clay Fisher. **Adaptation:** *Yellowstone Kelly* (Warner, 1959). Dir: Gordon Douglas. Scr: Burt Kennedy. Cast: Clint Walker (Kelly), Edd Byrnes (Harper), John Russell (Chief Gall), Ray Danton (Sayapi).

5095. "Yentl, the Yeshiva Boy" (Isaac Bashevis Singer, 1962). Set in Lublin, Poland, in 1873, a Yiddish short story about a young girl who disguises herself as a boy in order to pursue an education. The story, which was adapted as a 1975 Broadway play by Singer and Leah Napolin, was translated in 1983. **Adaptation:** *Yentl* (MGM, 1983). Dir: Barbra Streisand. Scr: Jack Rosenthal, Barbra Streisand. Cast: Barbra Streisand (Yentl), Mandy Patinkin (Avigdor), Amy Irving (Hadass), Nehemiah Persoff (Mendel). Notes: Academy Award for Best Musical Score and nominations for Best Supporting Actress (Irving), Art Direction, and Song; Golden Globe Awards for Best Picture and Director (Steisand), and nominations for Best Actor (Patinkin), Actress (Steisand), Musical Score, and Song. VHS.

5096. *Yeoman's Hospital* (Helen Ashton, 1944). At a hospital in the British Midlands, a female surgeon is torn between her love for a doctor and an opportunity to advance herself in London. **Adaptation:** *White Corridors* (Universal, 1951). Dir: Pat Jackson. Scr: David E. Jackson, Pat Jackson, Jan Read. Cast: Googie Withers (Dr. Dean), James Donald (Neil), Godfrey Tearle (Mr. Groom), Petula Clark (Joan). Notes: BAFTA Award nominations for Best British Film and Best Film from Any Source.

5097. *Yes, Giorgio* (Anne Piper, 1961). A famous opera singer on tour in the United States develops laryngitis and falls in love with the doctor who treats him. **Adaptation:** *Yes, Giorgio* (MGM, 1982). Dir: Franklin J. Schaffner. Scr: Norman Steinberg. Cast: Luciano Pavarotti (Giorgio), Kathryn Harrold (Pamela), Eddie Albert (Henry), Paolo Baroni (Sister Theresa), James Hong (Kwan). VHS.

5098. *Yes, Madam?* (K. R. G. Browne, 1932). Comic novel about the heirs to a fortune forced to work as servants for three months. The novel was adapted as a musical play in 1934. **Adaptation 1:** *Yes, Madam?* (British Lion/Fox, 1933). Dir: Leslie S. Hiscott. Scr: Michael Barringer. Cast: Frank Pettingell (Albert), Kay Hammond (Pansy), Harold French (Bill). **Adaptation 2:** *Yes, Madam?* (Associated British, 1939). Dir: Norman Lee. Scr: William Freshman, Clifford Grey, Bert Lee. Cast: Bobby Howes (Bill), Diana Churchill (Sally), Wylie Watson (Albert). Notes: A musical adaptation.

5099. *Yield to the Night* (Joan Henry, 1954). A novel based on a true story of an abused woman convicted of killing her boyfriend's mistress and sentenced to death. **Adaptation:** *Yield to the Night*; released in the U.S. as *Blonde Sinner* (Allied Artists, 1956). Dir: J. Lee Thompson. Scr: John Cresswell, Joan Henry. Cast: Diana Dors (Mary), Yvonne Mitchell (Matron MacFarlane), Michael Craig (Jim). Notes: BAFTA Award nominations for Best British Film, Film from Any Source, and Screenplay.

5100. *You Belong to Me* (Mary Higgins Clark, 1998). A radio reporter doing a story on missing women uncovers a scheme by a man who lures his victims aboard luxury cruise ships. **Adaptation:** *You Belong to Me* (PAX, 2001) (TV). Dir: Paolo Barzman. Scr: Irina Diether. Cast: Lesley-Anne Down (Susan), Barclay Hope (Aidan), Megan Fahlenbock (Tiffany). DVD, VHS.

5101. *You Can't Go Home Again* (Thomas Wolfe, 1940). Autobiographical novel about the relationships of a young Southern writer trying to establish himself in New York in the 1920's. **Adaptation:** *You Can't Go Home Again* (CBS, 1979 TV Movie). Dir: Ralph Nelson. Scr: Ian McLellan Hunter. Cast: Lee Grant (Esther), Chris Sarandon (George), Hurd Hatfield (Foxhall), Tammy Grimes (Amy).

You Can't Run Away from It (see "Night Bus").

5102. *You Only Live Twice* (Ian Fleming, 1964). After the death of his wife, James Bond is sent to Japan to destroy the estate of a mad doctor who encourages people to commit suicide. **Adaptation:** *You Only Live Twice* (United Artists, 1967). Dir: Lewis Gilbert. Scr: Roald Dahl. Cast: Sean Connery (Bond), Akiko Wakabayashi (Aki), Mie Hama (Kissy), Tetsuro Tamba (Tiger). Notes: Although the film also places Bond in Japan, its plot centers around the disappearance of American and Russian spacecraft and Bond's role in preventing war between the superpowers. DVD, VHS.

5103. *You Pay Your Money* (Michael Cronin, 1954). A couple uncovers a plot by Arabs to take over the world. **Adaptation:** *You Pay Your Money* (Butcher's Film, 1957). Dir: Maclean Rogers. Scr: Maclean Rogers. Cast: Hugh McDermott (Bob), Jane Hylton (Mrs. Delgado), Honor Blackman (Susie).

5104. *You'll Like My Mother* (Naomi A. Hintze, 1969). Thriller about a pregnant widow who visits her mother-in-law's remote mountain home during a snow storm and discovers the family's deadly secrets. **Adaptation:** *You'll Like My Mother* (Universal, 1972). Dir: Lamont Johnson. Scr: Jo Heims. Cast: Patty Duke (Francesca), Rosemary Murphy (Mrs. Kinsolving), Richard Thomas (Kenny), Sian Barbara Allen (Kathleen). DVD, VHS.

5105. "You'll Never See Me Again" (Cornell Woolrich, 1939). After a couple argues, the wife vanishes suddenly, and her husband soon realizes that he is being framed for her disappearance. The short story was published in *Detective Story Weekly* in November 1939. **Adaptation:** *You'll Never See Me Again* (ABC, 1973 TV Movie). Dir: Jeannot Szwarc. Scr: Gerald Di Pego, William Wood. Cast: David Hartman (Ned), Jane Wyatt (Mary), Ralph Meeker (Will).

5106. *Young Adam* (Alexander Trocchi, 1954). Scottish novel about a young drifter who gets a job on a barge run by an unhappily married couple and begins an affair with the wife. When a dead body is discovered in the water near their barge, she finds out that her lover had a romantic relationship with the dead woman. **Adaptation:** *Young Adam* (Sony, 2003). Dir: David Mackenzie. Scr: David Mackenzie. Cast: Ewan McGregor (Joe), Tilda Swinton (Ella), Peter Mullan (Les), Emily Mortimer (Cathie). Notes: British Independent Spirit Award nominations for Best Picture, Director, Actor (McGregor), and Actress (Swinton). DVD, VHS.

Young and Eager (see *Claudelle Inglish*).

Young and Innocent (*A Shilling for Candles*).

5107. "Young Archimedes" (Aldous Huxley, 1924). A British couple vacationing in Italy discover a young math prodigy and decide to share his abilities with the world to the young child's detriment. The short story was the lead piece in Huxley's 1924 collection *Young Archimedes and Other Stories* (published in the UK as *The Little Mexican and Other Stories*). **Adaptation:** *Prelude to Fame* (Rank/Universal International, 1950). Dir: Fergus McDonnell. Scr: Robert Westerby, Bridget Boland. Cast: Guy Rolfe (John), Kathleen Byron (Signora Bondini), Kathleen Ryan (Catherine), Jeremy Spenser (Guido). Notes: In the screenplay, the boy is a musical prodigy. An Italian-language film based on the story, *Il Piccolo Archimede*, was released in 1979.

Young at Heart (see *Sister Act*).

5108. *Young Bess* (Margaret Irwin, 1945). Historical novel about the early life of Britain's Queen Elizabeth I and her romantic relationship with Thomas Seymour. **Adaptation:** *Young Bess* (MGM, 1953). Dir: George Sidney. Scr: Jan Lustig, Arthur Wimperis. Cast: Jean Simmons (Queen Elizabeth I), Stewart Granger (Seymour), Deborah Kerr (Catherine), Charles Laughton (King Henry VIII). Notes: National Board of Review Award for Best Actress (Simmons); Academy Award nominations for Best Art Direction and Costume Design. VHS.

Young Billy Young (see *Who Rides with Wyatt?*)

5109. *The Young Black Stallion* (Walter Farley and Steve Farley, 1989). The prequel to Farley's beloved Black Stallion novels, this one tells the story of Black before the stallion is shipwrecked. Born in the mountaintop home of an Arabian sheik, the horse is stolen by robbers but escapes and learns to live on its own and survive in the rugged mountains. Walter Farley, who died the same year the novel was published, wrote this installment with his son, Steve. **Adaptation:** *The Young Black Stallion* (Disney/Buena Vista, 2003). Dir: Simon Wincer. Scr: Jeanne Rosenberg. Cast: Richard Romanus (Ben), Biana Tamimi (Neera), Patrick Elyas (Aden), Gerard Rudolf (Rhamon). DVD, VHS. See also *The Black Stallion* and *The Black Stallion Returns*.

A Young Connecticut Yankee in King Arthur's Court (see *A Connecticut Yankee In King Arthur's Court*).

The Young Doctors (see *The Final Diagnosis*).

The Young in Heart (see *The Gay Banditti*).

Young Lady Chatterley (see *Lady Chatterley's Lover*).

5110. *The Young Lions* (Irwin Shaw, 1948). During World War II, a German officer meets two American soldiers and comes to doubt his role in the war. **Adaptation:** *The Young Lions* (20th Century–Fox, 1958). Dir: Edward Dmytryk. Scr: Edward Anhalt. Cast: Marlon Brando (Lieutenant Diestl), Montgomery Clift (Noah), Dean Martin (Michael), Hope Lange (Hope), Barbara Rush (Margaret), May Britt (Gretchen), Maximilian Schell (Captain Hardenberg). Notes: Academy Award nominations for Best Musical Score, Cinematography, and Sound; BAFTA nominations for Best Picture and Actor (Brando). DVD, VHS.

Young Man of Music (see *Young Man with a Horn*).

5111. *Young Man with a Horn* (Dorothy Baker, 1938). Based on a true story, a novel about a trumpeter who becomes obsessed with his music to the exclusion of all else. **Adaptation:** *Young Man with a Horn*; released in the UK as *Young Man of Music* (Warner, 1950). Dir: Michael Curtiz. Scr: Carl Foreman, Edmund H. North. Cast: Kirk Douglas (Rick), Lauren Bacall (Amy), Doris Day (Jo), Hoagy Carmichael (Smoke). DVD, VHS.

The Young Philadelphians (see *The Philadelphian*).

Young Rebel (see *A Man Called Cervantes*).

The Young Savages (see *A Matter of Conviction*).

Young Scarface (see *Brighton Rock*).

The Young Warriors (see *The Beardless Warriors*).

5112. *Young Widow* (Clarissa Fairchild Cushman, 1941). The inconsolable widow of a dead soldier returns to the Virginia farm where they spent their happiest days. The novel was serialized in *Good Housekeeping* magazine in March 1941 and published as a book in 1942. **Adaptation:** *Young Widow* (United Artists, 1946). Dir: Edwin L. Marin. Scr: Richard Macaulay, Margaret Buell Wilder. Cast: Jane Russell (Joan), Louis Hayward (Jim), Faith Domergue (Gerry).

Young Winston (see *My Early Life*).

5113. *Youngblood Hawke* (Herman Wouk, 1961). A naïve Southerner becomes a famous novelist and soon enters the high life in New York. **Adaptation:** *Youngblood Hawke* (Warner, 1964). Dir: Delmer Daves. Scr: Delmer Daves, Herman Wouk. Cast: James Franciscus (Hawke), Genevieve Page (Frieda), Suzanne Pleshette (Jeanne), Eva Gabor (Fannie), Mary Astor (Irene).

5114. *The Youngest Profession* (Lillian Day, 1941). Factual account of young autograph hounds pursuing stars. **Adaptation:** *The Youngest Profession* (MGM, 1943). Dir: Edward Buzzell. Scr: George Oppenheimer, Charles Lederer, Leonard Spigelgass. Cast: Virginia Weidler (Joan), Edward Arnold (Burton), John Carroll (Dr. Hercules).

5115. *You're a Big Boy Now* (David Benedictus, 1964). A young librarian who has been sheltered by his protective parents falls for an aggressive young actress. **Adaptation:** *You're a Big Boy Now* (Seven Arts, 1966). Dir: Francis Ford Coppola. Scr: Francis Ford Coppola. Cast: Elizabeth Hartman (Barbara), Geraldine Page (Margery), Peter Kastner (Bernard), Rip Torn (I. H.), Michael Dunn (Richard), Tony Bill (Rafe), Julie Harris (Nora), Karen Black (Amy), Dolph Sweet (Officer Graf). Notes: Academy Award nomination for Best Supporting Actress (Page); Cannes Film Festival Golden Palm nomination for Best Director; Golden Globe nominations for Best Picture, Actress (Hartman), and Supporting Actress (Page). VHS.

5116. *Z* (Vassili Vassilikos, 1966). Based on a true story, a Greek novel about a political candidate murdered at a rally and the prosecutor investigating the case who discovers a high-level government conspiracy. **Adaptation:** *Z* (Cinema V, 1969). Dir: Costa-Gavras. Scr: Jorge Semprun. Cast: Yves Montand (the Deputy), Irene Papas (Helene), Jean-Louis Trintignant (the Examining Magistrate). Notes: The English adaptation is shown with subtitles. Academy Award for Best Foreign-Language Film and Editing, and nominations for Best Picture, Director, and Screenplay; Cannes Film Festival Award for Best Actor (Trintignant) and Jury Prize (Costa-Gavras), and Golden Palm nomination for Best Director; Golden Globe Award for Best Foreign-Language Film. DVD, VHS.

Zandy's Bride (see *The Stranger* by Lillian Bos Ross).

5117. *Zazie in the Subway* (Raymond Queneau, 1959). While her mother is carrying on a love affair, her daughter is sent to live with an uncle in Paris. The little girl sneaks out of his apartment and rides the metro, creating havoc and exploring the city on her own. The French novel was translated in 1960. **Adaptation::** *Zazie in the Subway*; released in the UK as *Zazie in the Underground* (Astor, 1960). Dir: Louis Malle. Scr: Louis Malle, Jean-Paul Rappeneau. Cast: Catherine Demongeot (Zazie), Philippe Noiret (Uncle Gabriel), Hubert Deschamps (Turandot), Carla Marlier (Albertine). Notes: Originally released as

---

Zazie Dans Le Metro and shown with subtitles. VHS.

5118. *Zeffrelli: An Autobiography* (Franco Zeffirelli, 1986). The famous Italian director's autobiographical recollections, including his youth in Florence, where the orphaned boy was cared for by British and American expatriate women. **Adaptation:** *Tea with Mussolini* (G2, 1999). Dir: Franco Zeffirelli. Scr: John Mortimer. Cast: Cher (Elsa), Judi Dench (Arabella), Joan Plowright (Mary), Maggie Smith (Lady Hester), Lily Tomlin (Georgie), Baird Wallace (Luca). Notes: BAFTA Award for Best Supporting Actress (Smith). DVD, VHS.

Zero Kelvin (see *The Sealers*).

5119. *ZigZag* (Landon J. Napoleon, 1999). A mildly autistic teenaged boy gets into trouble for stealing money from his employer so that his abusive father can pay the rent. **Adaptation:** *ZigZag* (Silver Nitrate, 2002). Dir: David S. Goyer. Scr: David Goyer. Cast: John Leguizamo (Singer), Wesley Snipes (Fletcher), Oliver Platt (Toad), Natasha Lyonne (Jenna), Luke Goss (Cadillac Tom), Sam Jones III (ZigZag). DVD, VHS.

5120. *Zorba the Greek* (Nikos Kazantzakis, 1946). On Crete, a conservative and inhibited British writer meets a passionate, larger-than-life Greek peasant who comes to dominate the writer's life until he changes it completely. The Greek novel, originally titled *Vios kai politeia tou Alexi Zorba*, was the basis for a 1968 Broadway musical titled *Zorba*. **Adaptation:** *Zorba the Greek* (20th Century–Fox, 1964). Dir: Michael Cacoyannis. Scr: Michael Cacoyannis. Cast: Anthony Quinn (Zorba), Alan Bates (Basil), Irene Papas (the Widow), Lila Kedrova (Madame Hortense). Notes: Academy Award for Best Supporting Actress (Kedrova), Cinematography, and Art Direction, and nominations for Best Picture, Director, Screenplay, and Actor (Quinn); National Board of Review Award for Best Actor (Quinn); Golden Globe nominations for Best Picture, Director, Actor (Quinn), Actress (Kedrova), and Musical Score. DVD, VHS.

Zorro (see *The Curse of Capistrano*).

5121. *Zoya* (Danielle Steel, 1989). During the Russian Revolution in 1917, a beautiful aristocratic woman flees the country and make her way to a new life in America. **Adaptation:** *Zoya* (NBC, 1995 TV Miniseries). Dir: Richard A. Colla. Scr: L. Virginia Browne. Cast: Melissa Gilbert (Zoya), Bruce Boxleitner (Clayton), Denise Alexander (Axelle), Don Henderson (Feodor). DVD, VHS.

Selected Bibliography

Based on the Book. Mid-Continent Public Library (Missouri). http://www.mcpl.lib.mo.us/readers/movies/movie.cfm.

Baskin, Ellen, ed. *Enser's Filmed Books and Plays: A List of Books and Plays from Which Films Have Been Made 1928–2001.* Burlington, VT: Ashgate, 2003.

Bleiler, David, ed. *TLA Video and DVD Guide 2005.* New York: St. Martin's Press, 2005.

Books into Film and Television. Christchuch City Library (New Zealand). http://library.christchurch.org.nz/Guides/BooksIntoFilm.

Costello, Tom, ed. *International Guide to Literature on Film.* London: Bowker-Saur, 1994.

Craddock, Jim, ed. *Videohound's Golden Movie Retriever 2005.* Farmington Hills, MI: Thomson Gale, 2004.

Ebert, Roger, ed. *Roger Ebert's Movie Yearbook 2005.* Kansas City, MO: Andrews McMeel, 2004.

Elliott, Kamilla. *Rethinking the Novel/Film Debate.* Cambridge: Cambridge University Press, 2003.

Goble, Alan, ed. *The Complete Index to Literary Sources in Film.* London: Bowker-Saur, 1999.

The Internet Movie Database. http://www.imdb.com.

Katz, Ephraim, ed. *The Film Encyclopedia,* 4th ed. Revised by Fred Klein and Ronald Dean Nolen. New York: HarperResource, 2001.

Larson, Randall D. *Films into Books: An Analytical Bibliography of Film, Novelizations, Movie, and TV Tie-ins.* Lanham, MD: Scarecrow, 1995.

Maltin, Leonard, ed. *Leonard Maltin's 2005 Movie Guide.* New York: Signet, 2004.

Martin, Mick, and Marsha Porter, eds. *DVD and Video Guide 2005.* New York: Ballantine, 2004.

Moses, Robert, ed. *American Movie Classics Classic Movie Companion.* New York: Hyperion, 1999.

Moss, Joyce. *From Page to Screen: Children's and Young Adult Books on Film and Video.* Farmington Hills, MI: Gale Research, 1992.

Pym, John, ed. *Time Out Film Guide.* 13th ed. London: Time Out, 2004.

Readers Read: Books to Film. http://www.readersread.com/bookstofilm.

Smiley, Robin H. *Books into Film: The Stuff That Dreams Are Made Of.* Santa Barbara, CA: Capra, 2003.

Tibbetts, John C., and James M. Welsh. *The Encyclopedia of Novels into Film.* 2nd ed. New York: Facts on File, 2005.

_____, and _____. *Novels into Film: The Encyclopedia of Movies Adapted from Books.* New York: Checkmark, 1999.

Walker, John, ed. *Halliwell's Film Guide.* 20th ed. New York: HarperCollins, 2005.

Index of Persons

Aaliyah 3627
Aaron, Caroline 4649
Aaron, Nicholas 4600
Aaron, Paul 2175, 2797
Aaron, Sidney 106
Aaronson, David 2034
Abagnale, Frank W. 705
Abate, Bobby 719
Abbey, Edward 519
Abbot, Anthony 6, 7
Abbott, Bruce 1965
Abbott, Bud 2672, 3583
Abbott, Gavin 4543
Abbott, George 89, 3384, 3984, 5090
Abbott, John 1266, 4125
Abbott, Scott 3627
Abdullah, Achmed 2598
Abel, Walter 1160, 2243, 3021, 3529, 4520, 4683
Abgayani, Tetchie 4431
Abineri, John 2461, 3414
Abraham, Edward 2956, 4902
Abraham, F. Murray 1045, 1376, 2304, 3117, 3914
Abraham, Valerie 2956, 4902
Abrahams, Doris Caroline 1295
Abrahams, Peter 1432
Abrashkin, Raymond 998, 4114
Abreu, Claudia 3250
Abril, Victoria 2962
Achard, Marcel 2837
Acker, Sharon 2690
Ackerman, Robert Allan 234, 2841, 3176, 3719, 3810, 3860
Ackland, Joss 130, 200, 538, 585, 892, 1018, 1333, 1823, 2059, 2099, 2370, 2589, 3477, 3841, 3870, 3990, 4065, 4068, 4297, 4464, 4556, 4954
Ackland, Rodney 1918, 3626, 4534, 4712
Acklerley, J. R. 4878
Ackroyd, David 1915
Acosta, Enrique 2077, 2874
Acton-Bond, Brandon 2650
Adair, Deborah 2559
Adair, Gilbert 2020, 2667

Adam, Ronald 4296
Adams, Amy 203
Adams, Beverly 114, 1879, 3057
Adams, Brooke 482, 1050, 1200, 1204, 2209, 2626, 2755, 4187, 4412
Adams, Douglas 2008
Adams, Edie 1371
Adams, Gerald Drayson 3579
Adams, Hunter Doherty "Patch" 1691
Adams, Ian 242
Adams, Jeb Stuart 1542
Adams, Joey Lauren 984, 4004
Adams, John L. 1050
Adams, Joseph 4843
Adams, Julie 228, 336, 2552, 2769, 4372, 4615
Adams, Mason 4603
Adams, Maud 2045, 2775, 3256, 3598
Adams, Nick 2216, 3208, 4672
Adams, Polly 3567
Adams, Richard (actor) 2425
Adams, Richard (writer) 1725, 3501, 4860
Adams, Samuel Hopkins 1800, 3157
Adams, Simon 2565
Adams, Tom 3714
Adamson, Andrew 2565, 4063
Adamson, Ewart 371
Adamson, Joy 495
Adamson, Raymond 1307, 2054
Aday, Meat Loaf 930, 1489, 1606
Addams, Dawn 451, 863, 4297
Addie, Robert 4244
Addison, Anita W. 4456
Addy, Mark 4547
Addy, Wesley 1355, 4908
Adjani, Isabelle 1219, 3307, 3620, 3625, 4422, 5047
Adleman, Robert H. 1128
Adler, Felix 2940
Adler, Luther 3090, 3814

Adler, Warren 3676, 4840
Adolfi, John G. 25, 2142
Adorf, Mario 2656, 4554, 4645
Adrian, Max 332, 3281
Adshead, Kay 5077
Aesop 3430
Affleck, Ben 972, 1760, 3424, 3467, 4332
Affleck, Casey 4567
Agar, John 2485, 4842
Agee, James 46, 1069, 3170
Aghdashloo, Shohreh 2067
Agland, Phil 5057
Aguar, Daniel 2354, 2355
Aguilar, Luz María 4347
Agutter, Jenny 1254, 2124, 2387, 2607, 2749, 3658, 3769, 3954, 4077, 4361, 4823, 4902
Aherne, Brian 353, 896, 1257, 1627, 2765, 3093, 3095, 4782, 4809
Aherne, Michael 866
Ahlberg, Mac 1434
Ahmad, Peerbux 4077
Ahn, Philip 2302
Ahnemann, Michael 3130
Ahrens, Lynn 780
Ahwesh, Peggy 719
Aidman, Charles 2416, 3481, 3706
Aiello, Danny 1979, 2034, 2452, 4682
Aiken, Joan 5038
Aiken, Liam 2114, 3794
Aimee, Anouk 2342
Ainley, Lynn 2773
Ainley, Richard 1472
Ainsworth, Harrison 3815
Aird, Holly 2004
Aitken, Alexandra 1328
Aitken, Will 111
Ajar, Emile 2707
Akers, Andra 1107
Akers, William M. 5038
Akins, Claude 592, 1817, 1994, 2374, 2870, 3210, 3761
Akins, Rhett 42
Akins, Zoe 559, 621, 785, 1844, 3275, 3897
Akutagawa, Ryunoske 3685

Alba, Jessica 4095
Albee, Edward 257
Albee, Josh 42
Albers, Hans 38, 3596
Albert, Eddie 397, 497, 578, 642, 1255, 1347, 1496, 1587, 2153, 2300, 2360, 2632, 3823, 4110, 4337, 4549, 4569, 5058, 5097
Albert, Edward 413, 1031, 1191, 2749
Albert, Laura 4724
Albert, Marvin H. 1193, 2431, 2482, 2882, 4676
Albertson, Frank 892, 1791
Albertson, Jack 734, 1597, 3537, 3639
Albom, Mitch 1522, 4649
Albrand, Martha 49, 1115
Albright, Hardie 25, 260, 2228, 3915
Albright, Lola 839, 2313, 2360, 2643, 4868
Alcala, Felix Enriquez 4382
Alcazar, Damian 936
Alcock, Frances 4556
Alcott, Louisa May 2206, 2584, 2594
Alda, Alan 136, 713, 2828, 2868, 2969, 3251
Alda, Robert 2161
Alda, Rutanya 3044
Alden, Debra 830
Alden, Priscilla 4655
Alderman, Tom 2007
Alderson, John 3548
Alderton, John 2252, 4213
Aldiss, Brian 1605, 4343
Aldredge, Tom 2759, 3249
Aldrich, Bess Streeter 2921
Aldrich, Robert 148, 558, 772, 1147, 2400, 3204, 3472, 4339, 4789, 4908
Aldridge, James 647, 4227
Aldridge, Kitty 2137, 4573
Aldridge, Michael 3968
Aldruch, Robert 1536
Alea, Tomas Gutierrez 5036
Alessandrini, Goffredo 4877
Alessi, Ottavio 4537
Alexander, Caroline 1327
Alexander, Denise 5121
Alexander, Denyse 3867

Lacey, Catherine 1339, 3804, 4938
Lacey, Ronald 2054
Lachman, Harry 2940
LacLachlan, Kyle 4622
Laclos, Pierre Ambrose Choderlos de 994
Ladd, Alan 49, 134, 205, 501, 509, 574, 664, 1012, 1095, 1740, 1824, 1867, 1874, 2238, 2750, 3651, 3707, 4012, 4688, 4940, 4960
Ladd, Cheryl 64, 729, 950, 1184, 3241, 4297
Ladd, David 1184
Ladd, Diane 662, 2398, 2635, 3030, 3570, 3669, 4184, 4985
Ladd, Fred 2812
Lady, Steph 1604
Laffan, Patricia 4847
Lafitte, Jean 2437
La Fleur, Jean 2663
Lafont, Bernadette 4324
Laforet, Marie 4384
La Fountaine, George 1529
La Fountaine, George, Sr. 4681
La Frenais, Ian 585, 704, 866, 3351, 3585, 4778, 4793
La Freniere, Celine 1568
La Garde, Jocelyne 1923
Lager, Martin 4013
Lagrange, Veronique 843
La Gravenese Richard 331, 544, 2039, 2590, 4725
Lahbib, Simone 5026
Lahr, Bert 5055
Lahr, John 3565
Lahti, Christine 1380, 1583, 1980, 2074, 2130, 3489, 4403
Laing, John 359, 3345
Laird, Jack 3773
Lait, Jack 748
Lake, Diane 1616
Lake, Ricki 2119
Lake, Stuart N. 5078
Lake, Veronica 1740, 1867, 2055, 2924, 3411, 3673, 4126
Lakin, Rita 4316
Lakso, Edward J. 1681
Lam, Nora 761
Lama, Dalai 3995
Lamac, Karel 4759
Lamarr, Hedy 895, 1389, 1959, 2009, 3443, 4292, 4298, 4597
Lamas, Fernando 610, 1609, 2663, 3892
Lamb, Harold 2437
Lambert, Angela 3686
Lambert, Christopher 343, 1942, 3225, 4068, 4401, 4975
Lambert, Derek 4599
Lambert, Gavin 2121, 2210, 3810, 4194
Lambert, Madeleine 994
Lambert, Mary 226, 3461, 4075
Lambert, Peter 529

Lamberts, Heath 458, 2828
Lamburn, Richmal Crompton 2339, 2340
La Mond, Bill 950
La Mond, Jo 950
Lamont, Molly 4499
La Motta, Jake 3653
Lamour, Dorothy 1156, 2104, 2691
L'Amour, Louis 556, 592, 708, 875, 948, 1021, 1214, 1715, 1874, 1958, 2036, 2237, 2361, 2365, 2469, 2471, 3630, 4008, 4011, 4373, 4393, 4739
Lampell, Millard 447, 1970, 4827, 4914
Lampert, Zohra 1732, 3539
Lampin, Georges 935, 2141
Lamprecht, Gerhard 1306, 2704
Lamprecht, Gunter 345
Lamson, Laura 70, 2866, 4209
La Mura, Mark 4170
Lancashire, Sarah 3962, 4194
Lancaster, Bill 4969
Lancaster, Burt 67, 398, 558, 694, 709, 941, 1108, 1301, 1632, 1653, 1875, 1877, 2002, 2195, 2245, 2374, 2402, 2515, 2833, 2893, 3037, 3297, 3465, 3985, 4045, 4365, 4719, 4744, 4768, 4789
Lanchester, Elsa 341, 1116, 2447, 3684, 3687, 3947, 4710, 4777, 5028
Lanctot, Micheline 180
Land, Judy 2846
Landau, David 1969, 2488
Landau, Leslie 3072, 3534
Landau, Martin 41, 1417, 1877, 2218, 3189, 4614
Landau, Richard H. 1526, 1604, 3372, 4732
Lander, Eric 798
Landers, Lew 1097, 3989, 4528, 4705
Landfield, Timothy 746
Landgard, Janet 4365
Landham, Sonny 1460
Landi, Elissa 913, 2822
Landis, Carole 1710, 2128, 3073, 3551, 3793, 4657
Landis, Jessie Royce 1724, 3088, 4565
Landon, Christopher B. 161
Landon, Joseph 1873, 2392, 4240, 4683
Landon, Laurene 2126
Landon, Margaret 155
Landon, Michael 2790
Landone, Avice 4495
Landor, Rosalyn 1707
Landry, Aude 457
Lane, Abbe 2790
Lane, Colin 456
Lane, Diane 189, 709, 1057, 1898, 2621, 3075, 3279, 3373, 3450, 3847, 4706, 4795
Lane, John Francis 164
Lane, Lola 3614, 4109

Lane, Mark 4456
Lane, Nathan 4318, 4850
Lane, Priscilla 4109
Lane, Richard 81, 401, 4683
Lane, Rosemary 1179, 4109
Laneuville, Eric 3389
Lanfield, Sidney 2054, 2413, 2586, 4262, 4816
Lang, Andre 2519
Lang, Barbara 2066
Lang, Charles 1110, 1579, 3118, 4433, 4520
Lang, Charley 2354, 2355
Lang, Daniel 696
Lang, Fritz 119, 378, 463, 1700, 2057, 2087, 2909, 2965, 3301, 3808, 4897
Lang, June 4884
lang, k. d. 1394
Lang, Matheson 2578
Lang, Richard 4437, 5058
Lang, Robert 3042
Lang, Samantha 2952, 4892
Lang, Stephen 52, 1755, 2369, 2453
Lang, Walter 155, 334, 745, 2590, 2989, 4258
Langdon, Anthony 4655
Langdon, Harry 3793
Langdon, Sue Ane 1861, 3839
Lange, Carl 468, 2461
Lange, David 2110
Lange, Hellmut 1571
Lange, Hope 353, 387, 1085, 1419, 1808, 2110, 2653, 2706, 2872, 3462, 5110
Lange, Jessica 375, 919, 1366, 1379, 3156, 3249, 3346, 3545, 3798, 4503
Lange, John 394
Langelaan, George 1545
Langella, Frank 752, 818, 964, 1140, 1219, 2158, 2608, 2865, 4216, 4660, 4891, 5070
Langley, Andria Locke 2564
Langley, Noel 780, 899, 1353, 2255, 3013, 3479, 3585, 3893, 3933, 4584, 4629, 4718, 4773, 5055
Langlois, Lisa 457
Langmann, Arlette 1690
Langrishe, Caroline 3809
Langton, Paul 4064
Langton, Simon 53, 156, 793, 2015, 2656, 2986, 3567, 3697, 3916, 4148, 4942
Langtry, Lillie 3572
Lanier, Kate 2127
Lanovoy, Vasili 156
Lansbury, Angela 4, 310, 323, 570, 869, 901, 1082, 1578, 1878, 2149, 2180, 2475, 2780, 2808, 2916, 3022, 3125, 3481, 4520, 4776, 4913, 5064
Lansbury, Bruce 2156
Lansbury, David 4304
Lansing, Robert 1312, 2541, 3204, 3613
Lanza, Mario 3974
Lanzmann, Jacques 4418
La Paglia, Anthony 409, 813, 2065, 2636

Lapidus, Paul 3311
Lapierre, Dominique 801, 2240
Lapine, James 1258
La Plante, Laura 4062
La Plante, Lynda 327
Lapotaire, Jane 4091, 4970
Lara, Alexandra Maria 1178
Larbey, Bob 1014
Lardner, Ring 74, 385, 724
Lardner, Ring, Jr. 553, 792, 1224, 1570, 1832, 2818, 3358
Larkin, Bryan 496
Larkin, James 2724
Laroche, John 3333
Laroche, Pierre 1716, 2423
Larranga, Fernando 4347
Larreta, Antonio 4196
Larroquette, John 1847, 4850
Larry, Sheldon 2290, 4224
Larsen, Keith 194
Larsen, Trygve 939, 1002, 1472, 2202
Larson, Charles 716
Larson, Nancy 5033
Larteguy, Jean 718
Larter, Ali 4994
Lartigau, Gerard 2218
La Rue, Eva 1225, 3204, 3884, 4579
La Russo, Louis, II 4537
La Salle, Kirke 4795
La Salle, Martin 4371
Lasdun, James 216, 4072
Laser, Dieter 2656
Lash, Joseph 1290
Lasker, Alex 1508
Laski, Marghanita 2571
Laskin, Larissa 1774
Laskos, Andrew 4317, 5047
Lasky, Jesse L. Jr. 2497, 2650, 3287, 3486, 3574, 4089, 4701
Lasser, Louise 1367, 3739, 4326
Latessa, Dick 3606
Latham, Aaron 258
Latham, Louise 1902, 2800, 3468, 4277, 4544
Lathan, Sanaa 1152
Lathan, Stan 4696
Latifah, Queen 484, 2734, 4215
Latimer, Hugh 3922
Latimer, Jonathan 373, 501, 1040, 1740, 1928, 2434, 3163, 3511
Latimer, Louise 583, 3615, 3768
Lattuada, Alberto 644
Lau, Evelyn 3850
Lau, Patrick 1133, 3916
Lau, Siu-Ming 1264
Laudani, Chiara 4804
Laughton, Charles 43, 184, 284, 339, 373, 629, 2094, 2245, 2268, 2519, 3067, 3170, 3203, 3395, 3843, 4108, 4210, 4499, 4777, 5028, 5108
Laumer, Keith 1052
Launder, Frank 470, 535, 1577, 1687, 2397, 3058, 4809, 4913